Quantitative Psychological Research: The Complete Student's Companion expertly guides the reader through all the stages involved in undertaking quantitative psychological research: designing a study, choosing a sample of people, undertaking the study, analysing the data, and reporting the research.

Accessibly written and clearly presented, the book is designed for anyone learning to conduct quantitative psychological research. It covers the full research process, from the original idea to reporting the completed study, emphasising the importance of looking beyond statistical significance in evaluating data. The book provides step-by-step guidance on choosing, interpreting and reporting the appropriate analysis, featuring worked examples and extended calculations as appendices for advanced readers.

This edition features new chapters on exploratory factor analysis, logistic regression and Bayesian statistics, and has been thoroughly updated throughout to reflect the latest research practices. Care has been taken to avoid tying the book to any specific statistical software, providing readers with a thorough grounding in the basics no matter which package they go on to use.

Whether you're at the beginning of your undergraduate degree or working towards your masters or doctorate, this book will be invaluable for anyone looking to understand how to conduct quantitative psychological research.

David Clark-Carter is Professor of Psychological Research Methods at Staffordshire University and Consultant Editor of the *British Journal of Mathematical and Statistical Psychology*. In 2016 he was awarded the lifetime achievement award by the Education and Public Engagement Board of the British Psychological Society.

Quantitative Psychological Research

The Complete Student's Companion

4th Edition

David Clark-Carter

 Routledge
Taylor & Francis Group

LONDON AND NEW YORK

Fourth edition published 2019
by Routledge
2 Park Square, Milton Park, Abingdon, Oxon OX14 4RN

and by Routledge
52 Vanderbilt Avenue, New York, NY 10017

Routledge is an imprint of the Taylor & Francis Group, an informa business

© 2019 David Clark-Carter

First edition published by Psychology Press 1997
Third edition published by Psychology Press 2010

British Library Cataloguing-in-Publication Data
A catalogue record for this book is available from the British Library

Library of Congress Cataloging-in-Publication Data
Names: Clark-Carter, David, author.   10 08034195
Title: Quantitative psychological research : the complete student's companion / David Clark-Carter.
Description: 4th Edition. | New York : Routledge, 2019. | Series: Revised edition of the author's
   Quantitative psychological research, 2009. | Includes bibliographical references and index.
Identifiers: LCCN 2018029146 (print) | LCCN 2018030791 (ebook) | ISBN 9781315398129 (ePub) |
   ISBN 9781315398136 (Web PDF) | ISBN 9781315398112 (Mobipocket) | ISBN 9781138226173
   (hardback) | ISBN 9781138226180 (pbk.) | ISBN 9781315398143 (ebook)
Subjects: LCSH: Psychology—Research—Methodology—Textbooks.
Classification: LCC BF76.5 (ebook) | LCC BF76.5 .C53 2019 (print) | DDC 150.72—dc23
LC record available at https://lccn.loc.gov/2018029146

ISBN: 978-1-138-22617-3 (hbk)
ISBN: 978-1-138-22618-0 (pbk)
ISBN: 978-1-315-39814-3 (ebk)

Typeset in Minion
by Apex CoVantage, LLC

Visit the eResources: www.routledge.com/9781138226180

To Anne, Tim and Rebecca

Brief contents

APPENDICES   401

Detailed contents of chapters

This book is designed to take the reader through all the stages of research: from choosing the method to be employed, through the aspects of design, conduct and analysis, to reporting the results of the research. The book provides an overview of the methods which psychologists employ in their research but concentrates on the practice of quantitative methods.

However, such an emphasis does not mean that the text is brimming with mathematical equations. The aim of the book is to explain how to do research, not how to calculate statistical techniques by hand or by simple calculator. The assumption is that the reader will have access to a computer and appropriate statistical software to perform the necessary calculations. Accordingly, the equations in the body of the text are there to enhance understanding of the technique being described. Nonetheless, the equations and worked examples for given techniques are contained in appendices for more numerate readers who wish to try out the calculations themselves and for those occasions when no computer is available to carry out the analysis. In addition, some more complex ideas are only dealt with in the appendices.

The structure of the book

A book on research methods has to perform a number of functions. Initially, it introduces researchers to basic concepts and techniques. Once they are mastered, it introduces more complex concepts and techniques. Finally, it acts as a reference work. The experienced researcher often is aware that a method exists or that there is a restriction on the use of a statistical technique but needs to be reminded of the exact details.

This book is structured in such a way that the person new to the subject can read selected parts of selected chapters. Thus, first-level undergraduates will need an overview of the methods used in psychology, a rationale for their use and ethical aspects of such research. They will then look at the stages of research, followed by a discussion of variables and an overview of research designs and their internal validity. Then, depending on the methods they are to conduct, they will read selected parts of the chapters on specific research methods. In order to analyse data they will need to be aware of the issues to do with scales of measurement and how to explore and summarise data. Next they will move on to trying to draw inferences from their data – how likely their results are to have occurred by chance. They should be aware of how samples can be chosen to take part in a study and how to compare the results from a sample with those from a population.

It is important that, as well as finding out about how likely their results are to have occurred by chance, they know how to state the size of any effect they have detected and how likely they were to detect a real effect if it exists. They need to know the limitations on the type of data which certain statistical tests can handle and of alternative tests which are available and which do not have the same limitations. They may restrict analysis to situations involving looking at differences between two conditions and simple analysis of the relationships between two measures. Finally, they will need to know how to report their research as a laboratory report. Therefore, a first-level course could involve the following chapters and parts of chapters:

1　The methods used in psychological research.
2　The preliminary stages of research.
3　Variables and the validity of research designs.

The sections on types of designs and on terminology in:

4   Research designs and their internal validity.

One or more of:

5   Asking questions I: interviews and surveys.
6   Asking questions II: measuring attitudes and meaning.
7   Observation and content analysis.

Then:

8   Scales of measurement.
9   Summarising and describing data.
10   Going beyond description.

The sections on statistics, parameters and choosing a sample from:

11   Samples and populations.

The sections on *z*-tests and *t*-tests in:

12   Analysis of differences between a single sample and a population.
13   Effect size and power.
14   Parametric and non-parametric tests.
15   Analysis of differences between two levels of an independent variable.

The first section in:

19   Analysis of relationships I: correlation.

Possibly the section on simple regression in:

20   Analysis of relationships II: regression.

The sections on non-sexist language and on the written report in:

25   Reporting research.

Students in their second level should be dealing with more complex designs. Accordingly, they will need to look at more on the methods, on the designs and on their analysis. They may look at further analysis of relationships and be aware of other forms of reporting research. Therefore they are likely to look at:

The section on specific examples of research designs in:

4   Research designs and their internal validity.

Anything not already read in:

5   Asking questions I: Interviews and surveys.
6   Asking questions II: Measuring attitudes and meaning.
7   Observation and content analysis.

The section on confidence intervals in:

11   Samples and populations.
16   Preliminary analysis of designs with one independent variable with more than two levels.
17   Analysis of designs with more than one independent variable.

At least the section on contrasts in:

18   Subsequent analysis after ANOVA or χ^2.

The remaining material in:

19   Analysis of relationships I: correlation.

At subsequent levels, I would hope that students would learn about other ways of analysing data once they have conducted an analysis of variance, that they would learn about multiple regression, analysis of covariance, factor analysis and meta-analysis, and that they would be aware of the range of multivariate analyses. At each stage researchers need to be aware of data screening and so it is important that they look at the material in Chapter 23. Nonetheless, this chapter contains some complex ideas and methods, and so it is likely that until later chapters in the book have been covered, greater guidance from tutors will be necessary over the material in this chapter.

As psychologists we have to treat methods as tools which help us carry out our research, not as ends in themselves. However, we must be aware of the correct use of the methods and be aware of their limitations. The debate about failure to replicate findings discussed in Chapter 1 should make this clear. Above all the things that I hope readers gain from conducting and analysing research is the excitement of taking an idea, designing a way to test it empirically and seeing whether the evidence is consistent with your original idea.

A note to tutors

Tutors will notice that I have tried to place greater emphasis on statistical power, effect size and confidence intervals than is often the case in statistical texts which are aimed at psychologists. Without these tools psychologists are in danger of producing findings which lack generalisability because they are overly dependent on what have become conventional inferential statistics.

I have not given specific examples of how to perform particular analyses in any particular computer package because of lack of space, because I do not want the book to be tied to any one package and because the different generations of the packages involve different ways of achieving the same analysis. The growth in the use and development of the open source language R confirms me in my decision not to select one statistical package to illustrate how to implement the analyses. Nonetheless, I make reference to what you can expect from the IBM Statistical Package for the Social Sciences (SPSS). There are many 'how to' books for computer packages and I recommend Gray and Kinnear (2012) for SPSS. However, it does need updating to take account of more recent developments. Kabacoff (2015) would be a useful starting point if your students want to learn about R.

The new edition

When people have heard that I was writing another edition they have often said that they didn't think the topic changed that much. They clearly don't read the statistics and methodology journals, which are constantly exploring new aspects of the subject. Apart from anything else, the development of more powerful computers has meant that the limits of statistical techniques can be tested, using simulations. In addition, my own thinking changes as I read about, use or teach a technique.

Most chapters and appendices have been altered to a certain extent. I have introduced three new chapters: one on logistic regression, one on exploratory factor analysis and one on Bayesian statistics. Details of the first two were briefly covered in the chapter on multivariate analysis in previous editions.

The decision over what other new material to put in has again partly been guided by wanting to explain to psychologists terms and procedures which are used within disciplines with which psychologists are likely to work, in particular those in the medical professions and epidemiologists. I have included sections on using intraclass correlations to measure interrater agreement, interaction contrasts as a way of examining interactions, power analysis for individual predictors in multiple regression, bootstrapping and focused comparison and forest plots in meta-analysis. I have expanded the power tables to include logistic regression. To accommodate new material in the second edition, and given the main focus of the book, I reluctantly took out the section on specific qualitative methods which had been in the first edition. In its place are details of books on the topic.

Acknowledgements

I would like to thank those people who started me off on my career as a researcher and in particular John Valentine, Ray Meddis and John Wilding, who introduced me to research design and statistics. I have learned a lot from many others in the intervening years, not least from all the colleagues and students who have asked questions which have forced me to clarify my own thoughts. I would also like to thank Marian Pitts, who encouraged me when I first contemplated writing this book and has continued to be supportive.

First edition

Ian Watts and Julie Adams, from Staffordshire University's Information Technology Services, often gave me advice on how to use the numerous generations of my word-processing package to achieve what I wanted. Rachel Windwood, Rohays Perry, Paul Dukes, Kathryn Russell and Kirsten Buchanan from Psychology Press all gave me help and advice as the book went from original idea to camera ready copy.

Paul Kinnear, Sandy Lovie and John Valentine all made helpful comments on an earlier draft of the book. Tess and Steve Moore initiated me into some of the mysteries of colour printing. Anne Clark-Carter acted as my person on the Stoke-on-Trent omnibus and pointed out where I was making the explanation particularly complicated. This effort was especially heroic given her aversion to statistics. In addition, she, Tim and Rebecca all tolerated, with various levels of equanimity, my being frequently superglued to a computer.

Second edition

Peter Harris, Darren Van Laar and John Towse all made helpful comments on the proposals I put forward about the second edition. Chris Dracup, Astrid Schepman, Mark Shevlin and A. H. Wallymahmed made helpful comments on the first draft of that edition. A number of people at Psychology Press and Taylor & Francis (some of whom have moved on) had a hand in the way that edition developed. In fact, there were so many that I apologise if I've left anyone out of the following list: Alison Dixon, Caroline Osborne, Sue Rudkin and Vivien Ward. I would also like to thank all the students and colleagues at Staffordshire University who commented on the first edition or asked questions which suggested ways in which the first edition could be amended or added to. Finally, although I have already thanked them in the preface to the first edition, I want again to thank Anne, Tim and Rebecca for their forbearance and for dragging me from the study when I was in danger, rather like Flann O'Brien's cycling policeman, of exchanging atoms with the chair and computer keyboard.

Third edition

The following helped me with the third edition. Sarah Gibson, Sharla Plant, Tara Stebnicky and Rebekah Edmondson, all of Taylor & Francis, helped at various points from the initial invitation to write the third edition to seeing it through to publication. Charlotte Brownlow, Pat Dugard and Mark Shevlin made helpful comments on the changes I proposed to make to the third edition. Charlotte Brownlow and Pat Dugard made further useful comments on the first draft of the third edition. Once again, Anne, Tim and Rebecca have supported me throughout.

Despite all the efforts of others, any mistakes which are still contained in the book are my own.

Fourth edition

The following helped me with the fourth edition. Ceri McLardy, Sophie Crowe, Jenny Guildford, Elizabeth Rankin and Michael Strang helped by, among other things, commissioning the new edition, seeking reviews of my proposals for this edition and checking the manuscript. Zaheer Hussain and Nathalie Noret provided useful comments on my proposed changes. Tina Cottone and the team from ApexCoVantage have, among other things, thoroughly checked and copyedited the manuscript and kept me up to date with when the next task would be arriving. Once again, Anne helped me to complete what has been an enormous undertaking. As time went on and deadlines approached she absorbed ever more tasks to give me the time to get on with writing. Nonetheless, we continued to take the final dog walk of the day together.

PART 1

Introduction

1 The methods used in psychological research

Introduction

This chapter deals with the purposes of psychological research. It explains why psychologists employ a method in their research and describes the range of quantitative methods employed by psychologists. It addresses the question of whether psychology is a science. Finally it deals with ethical issues to do with psychological research.

What is the purpose of research?

Psychological research is conducted in order to increase our knowledge of humans. Research is generally seen as having one of four aims, which can also be seen as stages: the first is to describe, the second to understand, leading to the third, which is to predict, and then finally to control. In the case of research in psychology the final stage is better seen as trying to intervene to improve human life. As an example, take the case of non-verbal communication (NVC). Firstly, psychologists might describe the various forms of NVC, such as eye contact, body posture and gesture. Next they will try to understand the functions of the different forms and then predict what will happen when people display abnormal forms of NVC, such as making too little eye contact or standing too close to others. Finally they might devise a means of training such people in ways of improving their NVC. This last stage will also include some evaluation of the success of the training.

What is a method?

A method is a systematic approach to a piece of research. Psychologists use a wide range of methods. There are a number of ways in which the methods adopted by psychologists are classified. One common distinction which is made is between quantitative and qualitative methods. As their names suggest, quantitative methods involve some form of numerical measurement while qualitative methods involve verbal description.

Why have a method?

The simple answer to this question is that without a method the research of a psychologist is no better than the speculations of a layperson, for, without a method, there is little protection against our hunches overly guiding what information is available to us and how we interpret it. In addition, without method our research is not open to the scrutiny of other psychologists. As an example of the dangers of not employing a method, I will explore the idea that the consumption of coffee in the evening causes people to have a poor night's sleep.

I have plenty of evidence to support this idea. Firstly, I have my own experience of the link between coffee consumption and poor sleep. Secondly, when I have discussed it with others they confirm that they have the same experience. Thirdly, I know that caffeine is a stimulant and so it seems a perfectly reasonable assumption that it will keep me awake.

However, there are a number of flaws in my argument. In the first place I know my prediction. Therefore the effect may actually be a consequence of that knowledge. To control for this possibility I should study people who are unaware of the prediction. Alternatively, I should give some people who are aware of the prediction what is called a placebo – a substance which will be indistinguishable from the substance being tested but which does not have the same physical effect – in this case a drink which they think contains caffeine. Secondly, because of my prediction I normally tend to avoid drinking coffee in the evening; I only drink it on special occasions and it may be that other aspects of these occasions are contributing to my poor sleep.

The occasions when I do drink coffee in the evenings are when I have gone out for a meal at a restaurant or at a friend's house or when friends come to my house. It is likely that I will eat differently on these occasions: I will have a larger meal or a richer meal and I will eat later than usual. In addition, I may drink alcohol on these occasions and the occasions may be more stimulating in that we will talk about more interesting things than usual and I may disrupt my sleeping pattern by staying up later than usual. Finally, I have not checked on the nature of my sleep when I do not drink coffee; I have no baseline for comparison.

Thus, there are a number of factors which may contribute to my poor sleep, which I need to control for if am going to properly study the relationship between coffee consumption and poor sleep. Applying a method to my research allows me to test my ideas more systematically and more completely.

Tensions between control and ecological validity

Throughout science there is a tension between two approaches. One is to investigate a phenomenon in isolation or, at least, with a minimum of other factors, which could affect it, being present. For example, I may isolate the consumption of caffeine as the factor which contributes to poor sleep. The alternative approach is to investigate the phenomenon in its natural setting. For example, I may investigate the effect of coffee consumption on my sleep in its usual context. There are good reasons for adopting each of these approaches.

By minimising the number of factors present, researchers can exercise control over the situation. Thus, by varying one aspect at a time and observing any changes, they can try to identify relationships between factors. Thus, I may be able to show that caffeine alone is not the cause of my poor sleep. In order to minimise the variation which is experienced by the different people they are studying, psychologists often conduct research in a laboratory.

However, a phenomenon often changes when it is taken out of its natural setting. It may have been the result of a large number of factors working together or it may be that, by conducting my research in a laboratory, I have made it so artificial that it bears no relation to the real world. The term *ecological validity* is used to refer to research which *does* relate to real-world events. Thus, the researcher has to adopt an approach which maximises control while at the same time being aware of the problem of artificiality. Another approach is to have a research strategy which has two strands: one maximising control and the other maximising ecological validity. Then an attempt will be made to reconcile the results from the two strands; this is called triangulation. For example, researchers could test the effects of caffeine on sleep in two ways. In one they could conduct the study in a laboratory. They allocate participants to either a caffeine or a placebo condition, give them drinks appropriate for the group they have been put in and observe them at night. In the second approach they could ask participants to keep diaries of their consumption of drinks such as coffee and tea and other events in the day. In addition, they would record their sleep patterns.

Distinctions between quantitative and qualitative methods

The distinction between quantitative and qualitative methods can be a false one, in that they may be two approaches to studying the same phenomena. Or they may be two stages in the same piece of research, with a qualitative approach yielding ideas which can then be investigated via a quantitative approach. Not surprisingly, this combination is sometimes called mixed methods. The problem arises when they provide different answers. Nonetheless, the distinction can be a convenient fiction for classifying methods.

Quantitative methods

One way to classify quantitative methods is under the headings of experimenting, asking questions and observing. The main distinction between the three is that in the experimental method researchers manipulate certain aspects of the situation and measure the presumed effects of those manipulations. Questioning and observational methods generally involve measurement in the absence of manipulation. Questioning involves asking people about details such as their behaviour and their beliefs and attitudes. Observational methods, not surprisingly, involve watching people's behaviour.

Thus, in an experiment to investigate the relationship between coffee drinking and sleep patterns I might give one group of people no coffee, another group one cup of normal coffee and a third group decaffeinated coffee and then measure how much sleep members of each group had. Alternatively, I might question a group of people about their patterns of sleep and about their coffee consumption, while in an observational study I might stay with a group of people for a week, note each person's coffee consumption and then, using a closed circuit television system, watch how well they sleep each night.

The distinction between the three methods is, once again, artificial, for the measures used in an experiment could involve asking questions or making observations. Before I deal with the methods referred to above I want to mention one which is often left out of consideration and gives the most control to the researcher – modelling.

Modelling and artificial intelligence

Modelling

Modelling refers to the development of theory through the construction of models to account for the results of research and to explore more fully the consequences of the theory. The consequences can then be subjected to empirical research to test how well the model represents reality. Models can take many forms. They have often been based on metaphors borrowed from other disciplines. For example, the information-processing model of human cognition can be seen to be based on the computer. As Gregg (1986) points out, Plato viewed human memory as being like a wax tablet, with forgetting being due to the trace being worn away or effaced; see also Randall (2007) for a discussion of metaphors of memory.

Modelling can be in the form of the equivalent of flow diagrams as per Atkinson and Shiffrin's (1971) model of human memory, where memory is seen as being in three parts: immediate, short-term and long-term. Alternatively, it can be in the form of mathematical formulae, as were Hull's models of animal and human learning (see Estes, 1993). Friston (2005) discusses models of how the brain functions, including statistical models.

With the advent of the computer, models can now be explored through computer programs. For example, Newell and Simon (1972) explored human reasoning through the use of computers. This approach to modelling is called computer simulation. Miller (1985) has a good account of the nature of computer simulation, while Brattico (2008) and Fodor (2000) discuss the limitations of current approaches.

Artificial intelligence

A distinction needs to be made between computer simulation and artificial intelligence. The goal of computer simulation is to mimic human behaviour on a computer in as close a way as possible to the way humans perform that behaviour. The goal of artificial intelligence is to use computers to perform tasks in the most efficient way that they can and not necessarily in the way that humans perform the tasks. Nonetheless, the results of computer simulation and of artificial intelligence can feed back into each other, so that the results of one may suggest ways to improve the other. See Boden (1987, 2016) and Bostrom (2014) for accounts of artificial intelligence.

The experiment

Another common classification of methods is into experimental, quasi-experimental and non-experimental methods. According to this classification an experiment involves a researcher manipulating variables and allocating participants to different conditions randomly. In the preceding example of an experiment into the effects of consuming caffeine, participants would be allocated to the three different groups on a random basis.[1] According to the classification, a quasi-experiment also involves the researcher manipulating variables but the allocation to conditions is not random (see Shadish & Luellen, 2005), while a non-experiment does not involve manipulation, as in observation and asking questions.

Experiments can take many forms, as you will see when you read Chapter 4 on designs of research. For the moment I simply want to re-emphasise that the experimenter manipulates an aspect of the situation and measures what are presumed to be the consequences of those manipulations. I use the term *presumed* because an important issue in research is attempting to identify causal relationships between phenomena. As explained earlier, I may have poorer sleep when I drink coffee but it might not be the cause of my poor sleep; rather, it might take place when other aspects of the situation, which do impair my sleep, are also present. It is felt that the properly designed experiment is the best way to identify causal relationships.

By a properly designed experiment I mean one in which all those aspects of the situation which may be relevant are being controlled for in some way. Chapter 4 discusses the various means of control which can be exercised by researchers.

The quasi-experiment

The quasi-experiment can be seen as a less rigorous version of the experiment. According to some definitions it involves manipulation by the researchers but with less rigorous means of allocating participants to different conditions. For example, researchers might wish to evaluate a method to increase children's eating of a healthy diet. They would want some children to be exposed to the new method and some to be exposed to existing methods of persuading children to eat more healthily. If they found two local schools and arbitrarily chose one to be where children were treated with the new method and the other to act as a control then this would be an example of a quasi-experiment. However, although the distinction between experiment, quasi-experiment and non-experiment seems straightforward, Pedhazur and Schmelkin (1991) state that 'there is no consensus regarding the definition of quasi-experiment' (p. 278) and note that some naturally occurring events are sometimes seen as a treatment even though there was no manipulation. Because the quasi-experiment is less well controlled than an experiment, identifying causal relationships can be more problematic. Nonetheless, this method can be used for at least two good reasons: firstly, when it is not possible to manipulate the situation; secondly, when it can have better ecological validity than the experimental equivalent.

---

1   Chapter 4 explains the randomisation process more thoroughly.

Asking questions

There are at least three formats for asking questions and at least three ways in which questions can be presented and responded to. The formats are unstructured (or free) interviews, semi-structured interviews and structured questionnaires. The presentation modes are face-to-face, by telephone or through written questionnaire. Surveys of people usually employ some method for asking questions.

Unstructured interviews

An unstructured interview is likely to involve a particular topic or topics to be discussed but the interviewer has no fixed wording in mind and is happy to let the conversation deviate from the original topic if potentially interesting material is touched upon. Such a technique could be used when a researcher is initially exploring an area with a view to designing a more structured format for subsequent use. In addition, this technique can be used to produce the data for a content analysis (see below) or for a qualitative method such as discourse analysis or interpretative phenomenological analysis (IPA; see Potter & Wetherall, 1995; Smith, Flowers, & Larkin, 2009; Tileagă & Stokoe, 2016).

Semi-structured interviews

Semi-structured interviews are used when the researcher has a clearer idea about the questions which are to be asked but is not necessarily concerned about the exact wording, or the order in which they are to be asked. It is likely that the interviewer will have a list of questions to be asked in the course of the interview. The interviewer will allow the conversation to flow comparatively freely but will tend to steer it in such a way that he or she can introduce specific questions when the opportunity arises. An example of the semi-structured interview is the typical job interview.

The structured questionnaire

The structured questionnaire will be used when researchers have a clear idea about the range of possible answers they wish to elicit. It will involve precise wording of questions, which are asked in a fixed order and each one of which is likely to require respondents to answer one of a number of alternatives which are presented to them. For example:

People should not be allowed to keep animals as pets:

strongly agree   agree   no opinion   disagree   strongly disagree

There are a number of advantages of this approach to asking questions. Firstly, respondents could fill in the questionnaire themselves, which means that it could save the researcher's time both in interviewing and in travelling to where the respondent lives. Secondly, a standard format can minimise the effect of the way in which a question is asked on the respondent and on his or her response. Without this check any differences which are found between people's responses could be due to the way the question was asked rather than any inherent differences between the respondents. A third advantage of this technique is that the responses are more immediately quantifiable. In the preceding example, respondents can be said to have scored 1 if they said that they strongly agreed with the statement and 5 if they strongly disagreed.

Structured questionnaires are mainly used in health and social psychology, by market researchers and by those conducting opinion polls. Interviews and questionnaires can be used with focus groups.

Focus groups

Focus groups can be used to assess the opinions and attitudes of a group of people. They allow discussion to take place during or prior to the completion of a questionnaire and the discussion itself can be recorded. They can be particularly useful in the early stages of a piece of research when the researchers are trying to get a feel for a new area. Interviews and surveys are discussed further in Chapters 5 and 6.

Observational methods

There is often an assumption that observation is not really a method as a researcher can simply watch a person or group of people and note down what happened. However, if an observation did start with this approach it would soon be evident to the observer that, unless there was little behaviour taking place, it was difficult to note everything down.

There are at least three possible ways to cope with this problem. The first is to rely on memory and write up what was observed subsequently. This approach has the obvious problem of the selectivity and poor retention of memory. A second approach is to use some permanent recording device, such as audio or video, which would allow repeated listening or viewing. If this is not possible, the third possibility is to decide beforehand what aspects of the situation to concentrate on. This can be helped by devising a coding system for behaviour and preparing a checklist beforehand.

You may argue that this would prejudge what you were going to observe. However, you must realise that even when you do not prepare for an observation, whatever *is* noted down is at the expense of other things which were not noted. You are being selective and that selectivity is guided by some implicit notion, on your part, as to what is relevant. As a preliminary stage you can observe without a checklist and then devise your checklist as a result of that initial observation but you cannot escape from the selective process, even during the initial stage, unless you are using a means of permanently recording the proceedings. Remember, however, that even a video camera will be pointed in a particular direction and so may miss things.

Methods involving asking questions and observational methods span the qualitative–quantitative divide.

Structured observation

Structured observation involves a set of classifications for behaviour and the use of a checklist to record the behaviour. An early version, which is still used for observing small groups, is the interaction process analysis (IPA) devised by Bales (1950) (see Hewstone & Stroebe, 2001).

Using this technique, verbal behaviour can be classified according to certain categories, such as 'Gives suggestion and direction, implying autonomy for others'. Observers have a checklist on which they record the nature of the behaviour and to whom it was addressed. The recording is done simply by making a mark in the appropriate box on the checklist every time an utterance is made. The IPA loses a lot of the original information but that is because it has developed out of a particular theory about group behaviour. In this case, the theory is that groups develop leaders, that leaders can be of two types, that these two can co-exist in the same group and that interactions with the leaders will be of a particular type. A more complicated system could involve symbols for particular types of behaviour, including non-verbal behaviour.

Structured observation does not only have to be used when present at the original event. It is also often used to summarise the information on a video or audio recording. It has the advantage that it prepares the information for quantitative statistical analysis.

A critical point about structured observation, as with any measure which involves a subjective judgement, is that the observer, and preferably observers, should be clear about the classificatory system before implementing it. In Chapter 2, I return to this theme under the heading of the reliability of measures. For the moment, it is important to stress that an observer should classify the same piece of behaviour in the same way from one occasion to another. Otherwise, any attempt to quantify the behaviour is subject to error, which in turn will affect the results of the research. Observers should undergo a training phase until they can classify behaviour with a high degree of accuracy. It is preferable to have more than one observer because if they disagree over a classification this will show that the classification is unclear and needs to be refined further. Structured observation is dealt with in Chapter 7.

Content analysis

Content analysis is a technique used to quantify aspects of written or spoken text or of some form of visual representation. The role of the analyst is to decide on the unit of measurement and then apply that measure to the text or other form of representation. For example, Pitts and Jackson (1989) looked at the presence of articles on the subject of AIDS in Zimbabwean newspapers, to see whether there was a change with a government campaign designed to raise awareness and whether any change was sustained. In a separate study, Manstead and McCulloch (1981) looked at the ways in which males and females were represented in television adverts. C. O'Connor (2017) looked at 'appeals to nature' in newspaper and Twitter prior to the 2015 referendum in the Republic of Ireland over same sex marriage. Content analysis is dealt with in Chapter 7.

Meta-analysis

Meta-analysis is a means of reviewing quantitatively the results of the research in a given area from a number of researchers. It allows the reviewer to capitalise on the fact that while individual researchers may have used small samples in their research, an overview is based on a number of such small samples. Thus, if different pieces of research come to different conclusions, the overview will show the direction of the general trend of relevant research points. Techniques have been devised which allow the reviewer to overcome the fact that individual pieces of research may have used different statistical procedures in producing the summary. A fuller discussion can be found in Chapter 26.

Case studies

Case studies are in-depth analyses of one individual or, possibly, one institution/organisation at a time. They are not strictly a distinct method but employ other methods to investigate the individual. Thus, a case study may involve both interviews and experiments. They are generally used when an individual is unusual: for example, when an individual has a particular skill such as a phenomenal memory (see Luria, 1975a). Alternatively, they are used when an individual has a particular deficit such as a form of aphasia – an impairment of memory (see Luria, 1975b). Cognitive neuropsychologists frequently use case studies with impaired people to help understand how normal cognition might work (see Humphreys & Riddoch, 1987). For more detail see Chapter 4.

Qualitative methods

Two misunderstandings which exist about the qualitative approach to research are, firstly, that it does not involve method and, secondly, that it is easier than quantitative research. While this may be true of bad research, good qualitative research will be just as rigorous as good quantitative research. Many forms of qualitative research start from the point of view that measuring people's behaviour and their views fails to get at the essence of what it is to be human. To reduce aspects of human psychology to numbers is, according to this view, to adopt a reductionist and positivist approach to understanding people.

Reductionism refers to reducing the object of study to a simpler form. Critics of reductionism would argue, for example, that you cannot understand human memory by giving participants lists of unrelated words, measuring recall and looking at an average performance. Rather, you have to understand the nature of memories for individuals in the wider context of their experience, including their interaction with other people. Positivism refers to a mechanistic view of humans which seeks understanding in terms of cause and effect relationships rather than the meanings which individuals have. The point is made that the same piece of behaviour can mean different things to different people and even to the same person in different contexts. Thus, a handshake can be a greeting, a farewell, the conclusion of a contest or the sealing of a bargain. In addition, the intentions of the participants will be important. Thus a handshake as a greeting could be seen by one or both participants as a chance to show how strong they are. To understand the significance of a given piece of behaviour, the researcher needs to be aware of the meaning which it has for the participants. Probably the most extreme form of positivism which has been applied in psychology is the approach adopted by behaviourism.

In the first edition of this book I briefly described some qualitative methods. In subsequent editions I have had a dilemma in that I wanted to expand that section to cover some more methods while at the same time I needed to include other new material elsewhere and yet keep the book to roughly the same size. Given the title of the book I decided to remove that section. Instead I would recommend that interested readers look at Banister et al. (2011), Hayes (1997), Smith (2015) and Willig (2013). These provide an introduction to a number of such methods and references for those wishing to pursue them further.

Is psychology a science?

The classic view of science is that it is conducted in a number of set stages. Firstly, the researcher identifies a hypothesis which he or she wishes to test. The term *hypothesis* is derived from the Greek prefix *hypo*, meaning less than or below or not quite, and *thesis*, meaning theory. Thus, a hypothesis is a tentative statement which does not yet have the status of a theory. For example, I think that when people consume coffee in the evening they have poorer sleep. Usually the hypothesis will have been derived from previous work in the area or from some observations of the researcher. Popper (1972) makes the point that, as far as the process of science is concerned, the source of the hypothesis is immaterial. While this is true, anyone assessing your research would not look favourably upon it if it appeared to have originated without any justification.

The next stage is to choose an appropriate method. Once the method is chosen, the researcher designs a particular way of conducting the method and applies it. The results of the research are then analysed, and the hypothesis is either supported by the evidence, abandoned in the light of the evidence or modified to take account of any counter-evidence. This approach is described as the *hypothetico-deductive* approach and has been derived from the way that the natural sciences – such as physics – are considered to conduct research.

The assertion that psychology is a science has been discussed at great length. Interested readers can pursue this more fully by referring to Valentine (1992). The case usually presented for its being a science is that it practises the hypothetico-deductive method and that this renders it a science. Popper (1974) argues that for a subject to be a science the hypotheses which it generates should be capable of being falsified by the evidence. In other words, if my hypothesis will remain intact regardless of the outcome of any piece of research designed to evaluate it, then I am not practising science. Popper has attacked both psychoanalysis and Marxism on these grounds as not being scientific. Rather than explain the counter-arguments to Popper, I want to question whether use of the hypothetico-deductive approach defines a discipline as a science. I will return to the Popperian approach in Chapter 10 when I explain how we test hypotheses statistically.

Putnam (1979) points out that even in physics there are at least two other ways in which the science is conducted. The first is where the existing theory cannot explain a given phenomenon. Rather than scrap the theory, researchers look for the special conditions which could explain the phenomenon. Putnam uses the example of the orbit of Uranus not conforming to Newton's theory of gravity. The special condition was the existence of another planet – Neptune – which was distorting the orbit of Uranus. Researchers, having arrived at the hypothesis that another planet existed, proceeded to look for it. The second approach which is not hypothetico-deductive is where a theory exists but the predictions which can be derived from it have not been fully explored. At this point mathematics has to be employed to elucidate the predictions and only once this has been achieved can hypotheses be tested. Recent research has explored predictions made in physics developed from theories proposed by Albert Einstein in 1900. For example, in 2013 the Higgs particle was finally discovered (Rovelli, 2017).

The moral which psychologists can draw from Putnam's argument is that there is more than one approach which is accepted as scientific and that in its attempts to be scientific, psychology need not simply follow one approach. Modelling is an example of how psychology also conducts research in the absence of the hypothetico-deductive approach. Cognitive neuropsychologists build models of human cognition from the results of their experiments with humans and posit areas of the brain which might account for particular phenomena: for example, when an individual is found to have a specific deficit in memory or recognition, such as prosopagnosia – the inability to recognise faces. Computer simulation is the extension of exploring a theory mathematically to generate and test hypotheses. Conroy-Beam and Buss (2016) used agent-based models to simulate different ideas of mate selection. Such models are programmed to follow certain rules, but the researchers can manipulate aspects of the input to the programs. The authors then compared the results from their simulations with actual behaviour in human couples. Seitz, Templeton, Drury, Köster, and Philippedes (2017) emphasise the need to include knowledge gained from research on actual behaviour when creating computer simulations of crowd behaviour.

One measure of whether an academic discipline is a science is whether the findings which have been found by one researcher can be replicated or reproduced by another. There has been recent interest in this.

Reproducibility

When I was an undergraduate we were told that there were famous studies in psychology which it was known others had tried to replicate but not found the same results. At that time, Ray Meddis suggested that it would be useful if there was a journal devoted to attempted replications. The topic has been raised a few times since then, but a wider debate started in 2015 when a paper was published which suggested that the results of a large proportion of published studies in psychology could not be replicated (Open Science Collaboration, 2015). This has produced a number of responses, including criticism of the paper itself (Gilbert, King, Pettigrew, & Wilson, 2016).

The debate sparked by the paper has led to many suggestions for possible cures and, at the same time, highlighted some interesting acronyms, including QRPs (questionable research practices). Among the suggestions to deal with the problem(s) is that researchers should pre-register their research designs and hypotheses. This should prevent HARKing (deciding the hypotheses after results are known); distinguishing between specific hypothesis testing and exploratory analysis of data, as the latter increases the likelihood that a result will be found which appears to be genuine but may just be due to chance; choosing more appropriate sample sizes for the type of statistical testing which will be used (see Chapter 13); setting a more stringent threshold for what is considered a genuine finding; better reporting of results, including those that do not support hypotheses (see recommendations for reporting in each chapter describing a type of analysis); making multiple attempts at replication by different researchers rather than just one or no attempt to replicate; using a different approach to analysis (for example, Bayesian statistics, see Chapter 27) and journals being willing to publish studies which fail to support hypotheses.

When you've read further on some of the topics and are more familiar with some of the issues, see Shrout and Rodgers (2018), Grice et al. (2017), Johnson, Payne, Wang, Asher, and Mandal (2017), Anderson and Maxwell (2016), Benjamin et al. (2018), Etz and Vandekerckhove (2016), Anderson et al. (2016) and Munafò et al. (2017).

Ethical issues in psychological research

Whatever the research method you have chosen, there are certain principles which should guide how you treat the people you approach to take part in your research, and in particular the participants who do take part in your research. Also, there are principles which should govern how you behave towards fellow psychologists.

Both the BPS (British Psychological Society, 2014) and the APA (American Psychological Association, 2017) have written guidelines on how to conduct ethical research, and both are available via their websites. In May 2018, the European Union introduced the General Data Protection Regulation (GDPR). This will lead to changes in ethical guidelines, including about gaining consent from participants.

To emphasise the point that behaving ethically can have benefits as well as obligations, I have summarised the issues under the headings of *Obligations* and then *Benefits*. I have further subdivided the obligations into the stages of planning, conduct and reporting of the research. Many of the topics covered are a matter of judgement so that a given decision about what is and what is not ethical behaviour will depend on the context.

Obligations

Planning

As researchers, we should assess the risk/benefit ratio. In other words, we should look to see whether any psychological risks, to which we are proposing to expose participants, are outweighed by the benefits which the research could show. Thus, if we were investigating a possible means of alleviating psychological suffering we might be willing to put our participants at more risk than if we were trying to satisfy intellectual curiosity over a matter that has no obvious benefit to people.

Linked to this is the notion of what constitutes a risk. The term 'minimal risk' is used to describe the level of risk which a given participant might have in his or her normal life. Thus, if the research involved no more than this minimum of risk it would be more likely to be considered ethically acceptable than research which went beyond this minimum.

It is always good practice to be aware of what other researchers have done in an area, before conducting a piece of research. This will prevent research being conducted which is an unnecessary replication of previous research. In addition, it may reveal alternative techniques which would be less ethically questionable. It is also a good idea, particularly as a novice researcher, to seek advice from more experienced researchers. This will be even more important if you are proposing to conduct research with people from a special group, such as those with a sensory impairment. This will alert you to ethical issues which are particular to such a group. In addition, it will prevent you from making basic errors which would give your research a less professional feel and which could possibly make the participants less co-operative.

What constitutes a risk worth taking will also depend on the researcher. An experienced researcher with a good track record is likely to show a greater benefit than a novice.

If risks are entailed which go beyond the minimum, then the researchers should put safeguards in place, such as having counselling available.

Conduct

Work within your own level of competence. That is, if you are not clinically trained and you are trying to do research in such an area, then have a clinically trained person on your team.

Approach potential participants with the recognition that they have a perfect right to refuse; approach them politely and accept rejection gracefully. Secondly, always treat your participants with respect. They have put themselves out to take part in your research and you owe them the common courtesy of not treating them as research-fodder, to be rushed in when you need them and out when you have finished with them. You may be bored stiff by going through the same procedure many times but think how *you* feel when you are treated as though you are an object on a conveyor belt.

Participants may be anxious about their performance and see themselves as being tested. If it is appropriate, reassure them that you will not be looking at individual performances but at the performance of people in general.

Resist the temptation to comment on their performance while they are taking part in the study; this can be a particular danger when there is more than one researcher. I remember, with dismay, working with a colleague who had high investment in a particular outcome from the experiments on which we were working and who would loudly comment on participants who were not performing in line with the hypothesis.

Obtain informed consent. In other words, where possible, obtain the agreement from each participant to taking part, with the full knowledge of the greatest possible risk that the research could entail. In some cases, the consent may need to be obtained from a parent or guardian, or even someone who is acting *in loco parentis* – acting in the role of parent – such as a teacher.

Obviously, there are situations in which it will be difficult, and counterproductive, to obtain such consent. For example, you may be doing an observation in a natural setting. If the behaviour is taking place in a public place, then the research would be less ethically questionable than if you were having to utilise specialist equipment to obtain the data.

Although you should ideally obtain informed consent, do not reveal your hypotheses beforehand to your participants: neither explicitly by telling them directly at the beginning nor implicitly by your behaviour during the experiment. This may affect their behaviour in one of two ways. On the one hand, they may try to be kind to you and give you the results you predict. On the other hand, they may be determined not to behave in the way you predict; this can be particularly true if you are investigating an aspect of human behaviour such as conformity.

If you are not using a cover story, it is enough to give a general description of the area of the research, such as that it is an experiment on memory. Be careful that your own behaviour does not inadvertently signal the behaviour you are expecting. Remember the story of the horse Clever Hans, who appeared to be able to calculate mathematically, counting out the answer by pawing with his hoof. It was discovered that he was reacting to the unconscious signals which were being sent by his trainer (Pfungst, 1911/1965). One way around such a danger is to have the research conducted by someone who is unaware of the hypotheses or of the particular treatment a given group has received and in this case is unaware of the expected response – a blind condition.

Do not apply undue pressure on people to take part. This could be a particular problem if the people you are studying are in some form of institution, such as a prison or mental hospital. They should not get the impression that they will in some way be penalised if they do not take part in the research. On the other hand, neither should you offer unnecessarily large inducements, such as disproportionate amounts of money. I have seen participants who were clearly only interested in the money on offer, who completed a task in a totally artificial way just to get it over with and to obtain the reward.

Assure participants of confidentiality, that you will not reveal to others what you learn about your individual participants. If you need to follow up people at a later date, you may need to identify who provided you with what data. If this is the case, then you can use a code to identify people and then, in a separate place from the data, have your own way to translate from the code to find who provided the particular data. In this way, if someone came across, say, a sensitive questionnaire, they would not be able to identify the person whose responses were shown.

If you do not need to follow up your participants, then they can remain anonymous. For example, if you are conducting an opinion poll and are collecting your information from participants you gather from outside a supermarket, then they can remain anonymous.

Make clear to participants that they have a right to withdraw at any time during the research. In addition, they have the right to say that you cannot use any information that you have collected up to that point.

If you learn of something about a participant during the research which could be important for them to know, then you are obliged to inform them. For example, if while conducting research you found that a person appeared to suffer from colour blindness, then they should be told. Obviously you should break such news gently. In addition, keep within your level of competence. In the previous example, recommend that they see an eye specialist. Do not make diagnoses in an area for which you are not trained.

There can be a particular issue over psychometric tests, such as personality tests. Only a fully trained person should utilise these for diagnostic purposes. However, a researcher can use such tests as long as he or she does not tell others about the results of individual cases.

In research which involves more than one researcher there is collective responsibility to ensure that the research is being conducted within ethical guidelines. Thus, if you suspect that someone on the team may not be behaving ethically, it is your responsibility to bring him or her into line.

You should debrief participants. In other words, after they have taken part you should discuss the research with them. You may not want to do this, in full, immediately, as you may not want others to learn about your full intentions. However, under these circumstances you can offer to talk more fully once the data have been collected from all participants or even offer a summary of the research and its findings.

Reporting

Be honest about what you found. If you do make alterations to the data, such as removing some participants' scores, then explain what you have done and why.

Maintain confidentiality. If you are reporting only summary statistics, such as averages for a group, rather than individual details, then this will help to prevent individuals being identified. However, if you are working with special groups, such as those in a unique school or those with prodigious memories, or even with individual case studies, then confidentiality may be more difficult. Where feasible, false names or initials can improve confidentiality. However, in some cases participants may need to be aware of the possibility of their being identified and at this point given the opportunity to veto publication. This can be an issue when you wish to use quotes from your participants. Clearly you would not be maintaining confidentiality and so your participants need to be aware of this before they take part. However, you need to do as much as possible to maintain anonymity. Saunders, Kitzinger, and Kitzinger (2015) raise interesting issues when research is conducted with families of those with rare conditions, where it may not be possible for participants to remain anonymous. In such cases the participants need to be aware of the issues and decide whether they want the possibility of having their identities revealed.

Many obligations are to fellow psychologists.

If, after reporting the results of the research, you find that you have made important errors you should make those who have access to the research aware of your mistake. In the case of an article published in a journal you will need to write to the editor.

Do not use other people's work as though it were your own. In other words, avoid plagiarism. Similarly, if you have learned about another researcher's results before they have been published anywhere, report them only if you have received permission from the researcher. Once published, they are in the public domain and can be freely discussed but must be credited accordingly. You should also give due credit to all those who have worked with you on the research. This may entail joint authorship if the contribution has been sufficiently large. Alternatively, an acknowledgement may be more appropriate. It is a good idea at an early stage in the research to agree on who will be in the list of authors of any publications and the order of the names, as, in psychology, the first named author is seen as the senior author.

Once you have published your research and are not expecting to analyse the data further, you should be willing to share those data with other psychologists. They may wish to analyse them from another perspective.

Benefits

In addition to all the obligations, acting ethically can produce benefits for the research.

If you treat participants as fellow human beings whose opinions are important, then you are likely to receive greater co-operation. In addition, if you are as open as you can be, within the constraints of not divulging your expectations before participants have taken part in the research, then the research may have more meaning to them and this may prevent them from searching for some hidden motive behind it. In this way, their behaviour will be less affected by a suspicion about what the research might be about, and the results will be more valid.

If you have employed a cover story you can use the debriefing as an opportunity to disclose the true intentions behind the research, to find out how convincing the cover story was and to discuss how participants feel. This is particularly important if you have required them to behave in a way that they may feel worried about. For example, in Milgram's experiments where participants thought that they were delivering electric shocks to another person, participants were given a long debriefing (Milgram, 1974). See Nicholson (2011) for a critique of Milgram's work.

Another useful aspect of debriefing is that participants may reveal strategies which they employed to perform tasks, such as using a particular mnemonic technique in research into memory. Such information may help to explain variation between participants in their results, as well as giving further insight into human behaviour in the area you are studying.

Keeping data secure

There has always been a need to store data safely so that information about participants cannot be revealed to people who should not have access to it. There are some simple rules about retaining such information safely, but the use of computers and the Internet has meant that we have to be more vigilant. Whatever the storage medium two main rules apply: do not keep information which could identify a participant with the rest of that person's data; keep the data locked away. To deal with the first rule it is a good idea to give participants a code or pseudonym which is kept with the data and then separately keep a record of which code or pseudonym goes with which participant. This could be needed if a participant asks to have his or her data withdrawn from the study. To deal with the second rule you need to be able to lock a drawer or cabinet that only you or the research team has access to. I don't think it is sufficient to have a facility which is shared with others not connected to the research.

Computer storage

As a minimum the computer should need to have a password to be used. Ideally files should be encrypted. If the data are on a portable device such as a laptop, a tablet or a memory system such as a USB pen or a CD then they should not be left unattended and when not in use should be locked away. It is a good idea to keep a second copy as files can become corrupted. One way to make it less likely that data can be stolen when a computer is connected to the Internet is not to store such files on the computer but to keep them on removable media such as a separate hard drive.

There is an increasing tendency to store information on remote devices such as the cloud. Lustgarten (2015) warns that such material can be accessed by others and that if using such forms of storage we need to be particularly careful about maintaining anonymity of clients. He argues that the guidelines from professional bodies about record keeping need to keep pace with such technological developments.

How long to keep material

There are competing demands over this. On the one hand, it might seem to make sense to delete data as soon as their purpose is completed, such as when a degree is awarded or when a journal article has been published. However, institutions have processes for auditing how research has been conducted and being able to inspect data may be part of it. In addition, many academic journals require authors to keep data for a specified time. This could be for their auditing processes or for occasions when an error has been found in the article. Therefore you need to check with your institution, and where appropriate, a journal to which you are submitting an article, what their policy is over the retention of data.

Summary

The purpose of psychological research is to advance knowledge about humans by describing, predicting and eventually allowing intervention to help people. Psychology can legitimately be seen as a science because it employs rigorous methods in its research in order to avoid mere conjecture and to allow fellow psychologists to evaluate the research. However, in common with the natural sciences, such as physics, psychologists employ a range of methods in their research. These vary in the amount of control the researcher has over the situation and the degree to which the context relates to people's daily lives. Such research is often classified as being either quantitative – involving the collection of numerical data – or qualitative – to do with the qualities of the situation.

Throughout the research process psychologists should bear in mind that they should behave ethically not only to their participants but also to their fellow psychologists.

The next chapter outlines the preliminary stages of research.

PART 2

Choice of topic, measures and research design

2 The preliminary stages of research

Introduction

This chapter describes the preliminary stages through which researchers have to go before they actually conduct their research with participants. In addition, it highlights the choices which researchers have to make at each stage. The need to check, through a trial run – a pilot study – that the research is well designed is emphasised.

There are a number of stages which have to be undertaken prior to collecting data. You need to choose a topic, read about the topic, focus on a particular aspect of the topic and choose a method. Where appropriate, you need to decide on your hypotheses. You will also need to choose a design, and choose your measure(s) and how you are going to analyse the results. In addition, you need to choose the people you are going to study.

Choice of topic

The first thing that should guide your choice of a topic to study is your interest. If you are not interested in the subject, then you are unlikely to enjoy the experience of research. A second contribution to your choice should be the ethics of conducting the research. Research with humans or animals should follow a careful cost–benefit analysis. That is, you should be clear that if the participants are paying some cost, such as being deceived or undertaking an unpleasant experience, then the benefits derived from the research should outweigh those costs. Using these criteria means that research which is not designed to increase human knowledge, including most student projects, should show the maximum consideration for the participants. See Chapter 1 for a fuller discussion of ethical issues.

A third point should be the practicalities of researching in your chosen area. There are some areas where the difficulties of conducting empirical research, as a student, are evident before you read further. For example, your particular interest may be in the profiling of criminals by forensic psychologists but it is unlikely, unless you have special contacts, that you are going to be able to carry out more than library research in that area. However, before you can decide how practical it would be to conduct research in a given area you will usually need to read other people's research and then focus on a specific aspect of the area which interests you.

Reviewing the literature

Before conducting any research you need to be aware of what other people have done in the area. Even if you are trying to replicate a piece of research in order to check its results, you will need to know how that research has been conducted in the past. In addition, you may have thought of what you consider to be an original approach to an area, in which case it would be wise to check that it *is* original.

There are two quick ways to find out about what research has been conducted in the area. The first is to ask an expert in the field. The second is to use some form of database of previous research.

Asking an expert

First you have to identify who the experts are in your chosen field. This can be achieved by asking more experienced researchers in your department for advice, by interrogating the databases referred to in a later section or by searching on the Internet. Once you have identified the expert, you have to think what to ask him or her. Too often I have received letters or emails which tell me that the writer wants to conduct research in the area of blindness and then go on to ask me to give them any information which might be useful to them. This is far too open-ended a request. I have no idea what aspect of blindness they wish to investigate and so the only thing I can offer is for them to email, visit or phone me to discuss the matter. Researchers are far more likely to respond if you can give them a clear idea of your research interest. Unless you can be sufficiently specific, I recommend that you explore the literature through a database of research.

Places where research is reported

Psychologists have four main ways of reporting their research – at conferences, in journal articles, in books and on the Internet. A conference is the place where research which is yet to be published in other forms is reported, so it will tend to be the most up-to-date source of research. However, when research-ers become more eminent they are invited to present reviews of their work at conferences as what are often called keynote speakers.

Conferences are of two types. Firstly, there are general conferences, such as the annual conferences of the British Psychological Society or the American Psychological Association, in which psychologists of many types present papers. Secondly, there are specialist conferences, which are devoted to a more specific area of psychology such as cognitive psychology or developmental psychology. However, even in the more general conferences there are usually symposia which contain a number of papers on the same theme.

There are problems with using conferences as your source of information. Firstly, they tend to be annual and so they may not coincide with when you need the information. A bigger problem is that they may not have any papers on the area of your interest. However, abstracts of the proceedings of previous conferences can be useful to identify who the active researchers are in a given area. A third problem can be that research reported at a conference often has not been fully assessed by other psychologists who are experts in the area, and so it should be treated with greater caution.

Accordingly, you are more likely to find out about previous research from academic journal arti-cles or books. Psychologists tend to follow other sciences and publish their research first in journal articles. The articles will generally have been reviewed by other researchers and only those which are considered to be well conducted and of interest will be published.

Once they have become sufficiently well known, researchers may be invited to contribute a chap-ter to a book on their topic. When they have conducted sufficient research they may produce a book devoted to their own research – what is sometimes called a research monograph. Alternatively, they may write a general book which reports their research and that of others in their area of interest. The most general source will be a textbook devoted to a wider area of psychology, such as social psychology, or even a general textbook on all areas of psychology.

Most books take a while to get published and so they tend to report slightly older research. Although there is a time lag between an article being submitted to a journal and its publication, journals are the best source for the most up-to-date research.

Journals, like conferences, can be either general, such as the *British Journal of Psychology* or *Psy-chological Bulletin*, or more specific, such as *Cognition* or *Memory and Language*. Many journal arti-cles are available on the Internet and this is likely to be a growing phenomenon once problems over copyright have been resolved. Publishers have a number of arrangements which will allow you access to an Internet-based version of their journals. In some cases your institution will have subscribed to a particular package which will include access to electronic versions of certain journals. Under other schemes an electronic version will be available if your institution already subscribes to the paper version.

Beyond the electronic versions of journals, and the research databases which are mentioned later, the Internet can be a mixed blessing. On the one hand, it can be a very quick way to find out about research which has been conducted in the area you are interested in. On the other hand, there is no quality control at all and so you could be reading complete drivel which is masquerading as science. Accordingly, you have to treat what you find on the Internet with more caution than any of the other sources. Nonetheless, if you can find the web pages of a known researcher in a field, they can often tell you what papers that person has published on the topic and they may have copies of some of those papers available to download.

While it is possible to identify relevant research by looking through copies of journals, a more efficient search strategy is to use some form of database of research.

Databases of previous research

There are a number of ways to find out what research has already been conducted in the area you are interested in. The most efficient is to search a database. What databases you have access to will depend on what your institution's library subscribes to. As a minimum they give you details of the published research, including the journal in which it was published, details of the author(s) and the abstract. An abstract is a summary of the research. This gives you an opportunity to decide whether the article is sufficiently relevant for you to want to read the full article. Examples of these types of database are PsycINFO, the Web of Science and Scopus.

Doing the search

The databases have a vast number of articles and so it is very easy to be overwhelmed by the numbers which are identified if you search in an indiscriminate way. As an example I put *depression* as a search term in the Web of Science and it identified 411,323 articles. To narrow the search one can use what are called Boolean operators. These include: AND, OR, NOT. Be careful how you use them as OR will mean you get different sets of articles added together. Searching for *depression* OR *anxiety* produced 533,364 articles, while *depression* AND *anxiety* produced 93,127; *depression* AND *anxiety* AND *pain* reduced the results to 10,540, while *depression* AND *anxiety* AND *pelvic* AND *pain* reduced the number to a more manageable 226.

Web of Science, which now contains the Social Science Citation Index (SSCI), and Scopus also allow you to do citation searches.

Citation searches

If you have found an article which reports research which is relevant but which was published a while ago, you can find more recent relevant articles by getting a list of which articles cited (i.e. referred to) the earlier article and so bring you more up to date.

Access to the articles

In the databases described previously, to get a copy of an article your search has identified you may have to contact the author described as the *corresponding author* and ask for an offprint. However, the database may indicate that you have access to the full version of the article by clicking on the appropriate button. What level of access you have will depend on what your library subscribes to, the policy of the journal the article was published in, how the research or publication was paid for, whether the author(s) have made the publication available and, for some journals, whether you are a member of a learned society which publishes those journals.

Open access

The full version of an article or an entire journal may be available as soon as it is published.

Open archive

Articles from a journal will be available after a prearranged period after publication.

Repository

An author places a version of an article on a website, usually of a university. However, this version will often not be the same as the one which finally gets published, in either format or sometimes exact content. Some articles may be in the final version which the author(s) sent to the publisher and so will not be in the format of the journal but that for submitted manuscripts. Some may even still show what are called *author queries*, where the copy editor of the journal has asked the authors to clarify something in the manuscript. If you are trying to quote from the article I would recommend obtaining a copy of the version which was published so that you can refer to the appropriate page numbers from the journal.

Learned societies

If you are a member of the British Psychological Society then you have access to all the journals which it publishes.

Full text databases

These allow you to identify articles and then open the complete article. An example of this type of database is PsycARTICLES.

Email alerts

Many publishers have a facility whereby you can request that you are sent an email when research is published in particular journals. You can receive such emails when an article is first published online and when a complete part of the journal is published.

Inter-library loans

Sometimes you will identify an article or a book which your library does not have and, in the case of articles, you are not been able to get a copy from the author(s). It is possible in some libraries to borrow a copy of such a book or journal article through what is termed an inter-library loan. You will need to talk to your librarians about whether this facility is available and what the restrictions are at your institution with regard to the number you can have, whether you have to pay for them and, if so, how much they will cost you.

Focusing on a specific area of research

It is likely that in the process of finding out about previous research you will have expanded your understanding of an area, not only of the subject matter but also of the types of methods and designs which have been employed. This should help you narrow your focus to a specific aspect of the area which interests you particularly and which you think needs investigating. In addition, you are now in a better position to consider the practicalities of doing research in the area. You will have seen various aspects of the research which may constrain you: the possible need for specialised equipment, such as an eye-movement recorder, and the number of participants which are considered necessary for a particular piece of research. In addition, you will have an idea of the time it would take to conduct the research.

An additional consideration which should motivate you to narrow your focus is that if you try to include too many aspects of an area into one piece of research you will be making a common mistake of novice researchers. By trying to be too all-encompassing you will make the results of the research difficult to interpret. Generally, a large-scale research project involves a number of smaller-scale pieces of research which, when put together, address a larger area. Accordingly, I advise you not to be too ambitious – better a well-conducted, simple piece of research which is easy to interpret than an over-ambitious one which yields no clear-cut results; scientific knowledge mainly increases in small increments.

Choice of method

See Chapter 1 for a description of the range of quantitative methods which are employed by psychologists.

In choosing a method, you have to take account of a number of factors. The first criterion must be the expectations you have of the research. The point has already been made, in Chapter 1, that you need to balance the advantages of greater control against the concomitant loss of ecological validity. Thus, if your aim is to refine understanding in an area which has already been researched quite thoroughly, then you may use a tightly controlled experimental design. However, if you are entering a new area you may use a more exploratory method such as one of the qualitative methods. Similarly, if you are interested in people's behaviour but not in their beliefs and intentions, then an experiment may be appropriate. But if you want to know the meaning that that behaviour has for the participants, then you may use a qualitative method.

It is worth making the point that if a number of methods are used to focus on the same area of research – usually termed *triangulation* – and they indicate a similar result to each other, then the standing of those findings is enhanced. In other words, do not feel totally constrained to employ the same method as those whose research you have read. By taking a fresh method to an area you can add something to our understanding of that area.

Once again, not least to be considered are the practicalities of the situation. You may desire to have the control of an experiment but be forced to use a different method because an experiment would be impractical. For example, you may wish to compare two ways of teaching children to read. However, if your time is limited you may be forced to compare children in different schools where the two techniques are already being used rather than train the children yourself. Nonetheless, you should be aware of the problems that can exist for interpreting such a design (see Chapter 4).

Choice of hypotheses

A sign of a clearly focused piece of research can be that you are making specific predictions as to the outcomes – you are stating a hypothesis. Stating a hypothesis can help to direct your attention to particular aspects of the research and help you to choose the design and measures. The phrasing of hypotheses is inextricably linked with how they are tested, and it is dealt with in Chapter 10.

Choice of research design

Chapter 4 describes the research designs which are most frequently employed by psychologists.

Once you have chosen a method, you need to consider whether you are seeking a finding which might be generalisable to other settings, in which case you ought to choose an appropriate design which has good *external validity* (see Chapter 3). Similarly, if you are investigating cause and effect relationships within your research, then you need to choose a design which is not just appropriate to the area of research but one which has high *internal validity* (see Chapters 3 and 4). Once again, there are likely to be certain constraints on the type of design which you can employ. For example, if you have less than a year to conduct the research and you want to conduct longitudinal research, then you can only do so with a phenomenon which has a cycle of less than a year.

An aspect of your design will be the measure(s) which you take in the research. The next section considers the types of measures which are available to psychologists and factors which you have to take into account when choosing a measure.

Measurement in psychology

The phenomena which psychologists measure can be seen as falling under three main headings: overt non-verbal behaviour, verbal behaviour and covert non-verbal behaviour.

Overt non-verbal behaviour

By this term I mean behaviour which can be observed directly. This can take at least two forms. Firstly, an observer can note down behaviour at a distance: for example, that involved in non-verbal communication, such as gestures and facial expressions. Alternatively, more proximal measures can be taken, such as the speed with which a participant makes an overt judgement about recognising a face (reaction times).

Verbal behaviour

Verbal behaviour can be of a number of forms. Researchers can record naturally occurring language. Alternatively, they can elicit it either in spoken form through an interview or in written form through a questionnaire or a personality test.

Covert behaviour

By covert behaviour I mean behaviour which cannot be observed directly – for example, physiological responses, such as heart rate.

As psychologists we are interested in the range of human experience: behaviour, thought and emotion. However, all the measures I have outlined are at one remove from thought and emotion. We can only *infer* the existence and nature of such things from our measures. For example, we may use heart rate as a measure of how psychologically stressed our participants are. However, we cannot be certain that we have really measured the entities in which we are interested, for there is no perfect one-to-one relationship between such measures and emotions or thoughts. For example, heart rate can also indicate the level of a person's physical exertion.

It might be thought that by measuring verbal behaviour we are getting nearer to thought and emotion. However, verbal behaviour has to be treated with caution. Even if people are trying to be honest, there are at least two types of verbal behaviour which are suspect. Firstly, if we are asking participants to rely on their memories, then the information they give us may be misremembered. Secondly, there are forms of knowledge, sometimes called procedural knowledge, to which we do not have direct access.

For example, as a cyclist, I could not tell you how to cycle. When I wanted to teach my children how to cycle I did not give them an illustrated talk and then expect them to climb on their bicycles and know how to ride. The only way they learned was through my running alongside them and letting go for a brief moment and allowing them to try to maintain their balance. As the moments grew longer their bodies began to learn how to cycle. Accordingly, to be an acceptable measure verbal behaviour usually has to be about the present and be about knowledge to which participants do have access (see Ericsson & Simon, 1980; Nisbett & Wilson, 1977).

The choice of measures

The measures you choose will obviously be guided by the type of study you are conducting. If you are interested in the speed with which people can recognise a face, then you are likely to use reaction times which are measured using a standard piece of apparatus. On the other hand, if you want to measure aspects of people's personalities, then you may use an available test of personality. Alternatively, you may wish to measure something which has not been measured before or has not been measured in the way you intend, in which case you will need to devise your own measure.

Whatever the measures you are contemplating using, there are two points which you must consider: whether the measures are reliable and whether they are valid. To answer these questions more fully involves a level of statistical detail which I have yet to give. Accordingly, at this stage, I am going to give a brief account of the two concepts and postpone the fuller account until Chapter 19.

Reliability

Reliability refers to the degree to which a measure would produce the same result from one occasion to another: its consistency. There are at least two forms of reliability. Firstly, if a measure is taken from a participant on two occasions, a measure with good reliability will produce a very similar result. Thus, a participant who on two occasions takes an IQ test which has high reliability should achieve the same score, within certain limits. No psychological measure is 100% reliable and therefore you need to know just how reliable the measure is in order to allow for the degree of error which is inherent in it. If the person achieves a slightly higher IQ on the second occasion he or she takes the test, you want to know whether this is a real improvement or one that could have been due to the lack of reliability of the test.

If you are developing a measure, then you should check its reliability, using one of the methods described in Chapter 19. If you are using an existing psychometric measure, such as an IQ test or a test of personality, then the manual to the test should report its reliability.

A second form of reliability has to do with measures which involve a certain amount of judgement on the part of the researchers. For example, if you were interested in classifying the non-verbal behaviour of participants, you would want to be sure that you and your fellow researchers are being consistent in applying your classification. This form of reliability can be termed *intrarater* reliability if you are checking how consistent one person is in classifying the same behaviour on two occasions. It is termed *interrater* reliability when the check is that two or more raters are classifying the same behaviour in the same way.

If you are using such a subjective measure, then you should check the intra- and interrater reliability before employing the measure. It is usual for raters to need to be trained and for the classificatory system to need refining in the light of unresolvable disagreements. This has the advantage of making any classification explicit rather than relying on 'a feeling'.

Obviously, there are measures which are designed to pick up changes and so you do not want a consistent score from occasion to occasion. For example, in the area of anxiety, it is recognised that there are two forms: state-specific anxiety and trait anxiety. The former should change depending on the state the person is in. Thus, the measure should produce a similar score when the person is in the same state but should be sensitive enough to identify changes in anxiety across states. On the other hand, trait anxiety should be relatively constant.

Validity

The validity of a test refers to the degree to which what is being measured is what the researchers intended. There are a number of aspects of the validity of a measure which should be checked.

Face validity

Face validity refers to the perception which the people being measured, or the people administering the measures, have of the measure. If participants in your research misperceive the nature of the measure, then they may behave in such a way as to make the measure invalid. For example, if children are given a test of intelligence but perceive the occasion as one for having a chat with an adult, then their performance may be poorer than if they had correctly perceived the nature of the test. Similarly, if the person administering the test does not understand what it is designed to test, or does not believe that it is an effective measure, then the way he or she administers it may affect the results.

The problem of face validity has to be weighed against the dangers of the participants being aware of the hypothesis being tested by the researchers. Participants may try to help you get the effect you are predicting. Alternatively, they may deliberately work against your hypothesis. However, it is naive to assume that because you have disguised the true purpose of a measure, participants will not arrive at their own conclusions and behave accordingly. Orne (1962) described the clues which participants pick up about a researcher's expectations as the *demand characteristics* of the research. He pointed out that these will help to determine participants' behaviour. He noted that in some situations it was enough to engineer different demand characteristics for participants for them to alter their behaviour even though there had been no other experimental manipulation. Therefore, if you do not want the people you are studying to know your real intentions you have to present them with a cover story which convinces them. Milgram (1974) would not have obtained the results he did in his studies of obedience if he had told participants that he was studying obedience. Before you do give participants a cover story you must weigh the costs of lying to your participants against the benefits of the knowledge to be gained.

Bear in mind the fact that you can give a vague explanation of what you are researching if this does not give the game away. For example, you can say that you are researching memory rather than the effect of delay on recall.

Construct validity

If a measure has high construct validity, then it is assessing some theoretical construct well. In fact, many measures which psychologists use are assessing theoretical entities, such as intelligence or extroversion. In order to check the construct validity of a measure it is necessary to make the construct explicit. This can often be the point at which a psychological definition starts to differ from a lay definition of the same term, because the usage made by non-psychologists is too imprecise. That is not to say that psychologists will agree about the definition. For example, some psychologists argue that IQ tests test intelligence while others have simply said that IQ tests test what IQ tests test.

Further evidence of construct validity can be provided if the measure shows links with tests of related constructs – it converges with them (convergent construct validity) – and shows a difference from measures of unrelated constructs – it diverges from them (divergent construct validity).

Convergence

For example, if we believe that intelligence is a general ability and if we have devised a measure of numerical intelligence, then our measure should produce a similar pattern to that of tests of verbal intelligence.

Divergence

If we had devised a measure of reading ability we would not want it producing too similar a pattern to that produced by an intelligence test. For if the patterns were too similar it would suggest that our new test was merely one of intelligence.

Content validity

Content validity refers to the degree to which a measure covers the full range of behaviour of the ability being measured. For example, if I had devised a measure of mathematical ability, it would have low content validity if it only included measures of the ability to add numbers. One way of checking the content validity of a measure is to ask experts in the field whether it covers the range that they would expect. Nonetheless, it is worth checking whether certain aspects of a measure are redundant and can be omitted because they are measuring the same thing. Staying with the mathematical example, if it could be shown that the ability to perform addition went with the ability to perform higher forms of mathematics successfully, then there is no need to include the full content of mathematics in a measure of mathematical ability. Thus, a shorter and quicker measure could be devised.

Criterion-related validity

Criterion-related validity addresses the question of whether a measure fulfils certain criteria. In general this means that it should produce a similar pattern to another existing measure. There are two forms of criteria which can be taken into account: concurrent and predictive.

Concurrent validity

A measure has concurrent validity if it produces a similar result to that of an existing measure which is taken around the same time. Thus, if I devise a test of intelligence I can check its concurrent validity by administering an established test of intelligence at the same time.

This procedure obviously depends on having a pre-existing and valid measure against which to check the validity of the new measure. This raises the question of why one would want another test of the same thing. There are a number of situations in which a different test might be required. A common reason is the desire to produce a measure which takes less time to administer and is less onerous for the participants; people are more likely to allow themselves to be measured if the task is quicker.

Another reason for devising a new measure when one already exists is that it is to be administered in a different way from the original. For example, suppose that the pre-existing measure was for use in a face-to-face interview, such as by a psychiatrist, and it was now meant to be used when the researcher was not present (such as a questionnaire). Alternatively, a common need is for a measure which can be administered to a group at the same time, rather than individually.

Predictive validity

A measure has predictive validity if it correctly predicts some future state of affairs. Thus, if a measure of academic aptitude has been devised it could be used to select students for entry to university. The measure would have good predictive validity if the scores it provided predicted the class of degree achieved by the students.

With both forms of criterion validity one needs to check that *criterion contamination* does not exist. This means that those providing the criteria should be unaware of the results of the measure. If a psychiatrist or a teacher knows the results of the measure it may affect the way they treat the person when they are taking their own measures. Such an effect would suggest that the measure has better criterion validity than it really has.

Floor and ceiling effects

There are two phenomena which you should avoid when choosing a measure, both of which entail restricting the range of possible scores which participants can achieve. A floor effect in a measure means that participants cannot achieve a score below a certain point. An example would be a measure of reading age which did not go below a reading age of 7 years. A ceiling effect in a measure occurs when people cannot score higher than a particular level. An example would be when an IQ test is given to high achievers. Floor and ceiling effects hide differences between individuals and can prevent changes from being detected. Thus a child's reading might have improved but if it is still below the level for a 7-year-old, then the test will not detect the change.

The accuracy of measures

Those wishing to classify people – for example, as to whether someone has a condition such as depression – use *sensitivity* and *specificity* when evaluating the accuracy of a measure. Sensitivity is the likelihood that a person who does have the condition will be classified as having the condition, while specificity is the likelihood that someone who doesn't have the condition will be correctly shown as not having the condition. Appendix XIV deals with how these and related indexes are calculated.

The appropriateness of a measure for a given situation

In Chapter 5, I discuss the various settings in which questions could be asked, such as face-to-face or on the telephone, and their relative merits. An additional issue which researchers have to be aware of is whether a scale created for one setting is appropriate in another setting. As researchers increasingly use measures on the Internet which were originally created to be paper-and-pencil tests, while they can relatively straightforwardly examine the internal consistency of the test, the validity of the test for the sample they have used should not be taken for granted (see Buchanan & Smith, 1999).

The appropriateness of measures for particular participants

Measures should be tailored for the population with whom they are to be used. There are many participants who may need standard measures to be altered for them. These include people with sensory impairments, such as partial sight, blindness or deafness; people with cognitive deficits, such as those who have dementia or a form of learning impairment; and people with language difficulties, either in understanding, such as Wernicke's aphasia, or in production, such as someone who has had a stroke which affects speech production but not the understanding of speech. In addition, there may be participants who are not fluent in the language in which the original material is written. As stated previously, we shouldn't assume that a measure can be employed across different platforms without any change in its psychometric properties. In the same way, we shouldn't assume that changes made to take account of different participants' needs will leave psychometric properties unchanged. If we translate material into Braille, simplify it for those with a cognitive impairment or translate it into another language we need to check that its psychometric properties are those we require. Back translation is considered to be a gold standard when translating material into another language. This entails translating it from the original language to the target language and then having someone else translate it back to the original language. If the starting version and the final version in the same language are the same then this can reassure us that the translation is accurate. Nonetheless, we should check the validity and reliability of the new version with the new population as nuances of meaning can differ across cultures.

We must also be aware of the need to check the integrity of a measure when a third person is administering it, such as reading out questions or translating them, or helping the participant to complete the answers, as may be the case for someone with impaired speech. Relying on family members to translate between a participant and researcher can be problematic as they may decide to alter the message. See Patel, Peacock, McKinley, Clark-Carter, and Watson (2009).

In every case we need to think of what is called *participant burden*. This refers to where we could be asking the participant to do more than is reasonable. During the design stage it is tempting to include as many measures as possible, but we need to think of how large a task we are setting the participants and trim back where necessary. In some cases we may need to make a certain sacrifice of a quality of measure in order not to overburden participants. For example, in a battery of tests we may want measures of depression and anxiety. The General Health Questionnaire (GHQ, Goldberg & Williams, 1991) has a 60-item, a 30-item, a 28-item and even a 12-item version. However, you need to check that a particular version is designed to measure what you want measured.

Once the area of research, the method, the design, the hypotheses and the measures to be used in a study have been chosen, you need to decide the method of analysis you are going to employ.

Choice of analysis

Chapters 9 to 27 describe various forms of analysis. Particular forms will be appropriate for particular types of measure and for particular designs. It is good practice to decide what form of analysis you are going to employ prior to collecting the data. This may stop you from collecting data which cannot be analysed in ways that would address your hypotheses and would stop you from collecting data that you will not be analysing. There is a temptation, particularly among students, to take a range of measures, only to drop a number of them when arriving at the analysis stage. An additional advantage of planning the analysis will become clearer in Chapter 18, where it will be shown that your hypotheses can be given a fairer chance of being supported if the analysis is planned than when it is unplanned.

Chapter 13 shows that knowing the form of analysis you will employ can provide you with a means of choosing an appropriate sample size.

Choice of participants – the sample

Next you need to choose whom you are going to study. There are two aspects to the choice of participants: firstly, what characteristics they should have; secondly, the number of participants. The answer to the first question will depend on the aims of your research. If you are investigating a particular population because you want to relate the results of your study to the population from which your sample came, then you will need to select a representative sample. For example, you might want to investigate the effect of different types of slot machines on the gambling behaviour of adolescents who are regular gamblers. In this case you would have to define what you meant by a regular gambler (devise an operational definition) and then sample a range of people who conformed to your definition, in such a way that you had a representative sample of the age range and levels of gambling behaviour and any other variables which you considered to be relevant. See Chapter 11 for methods of sampling from a population.

Often researchers who are employing an experimental method are interested in the wider population of all people and wish to make generalisations which refer to people in general rather than some particular subpopulation. This can be a naive approach as it can lead to the sample merely comprising those who were most available to the researchers, which generally means undergraduate psychologists. This may in turn mean that the findings do not generalise beyond undergraduate psychologists. However, even within this restricted sample there is generally some attempt to make sure that males and females are equally represented.

The number of participants you use in a study depends on the design you are employing for at least three reasons. The first guide is likely to be the practical one of the nature of your participants. If you are studying a special population, such as people with a particular form of brain damage, then the size of your sample will be restricted by their availability. A second practical point is the willingness of participants to take part in your research; the more onerous the task, the fewer participants you will get. A third guide should be the statistics you will be employing to analyse your research. As you will see in Chapter 13, it is possible to work out how many participants you need for a given design, in order to give the research the chance of supporting your hypothesis if it is correct. There is no point in reducing the likelihood of supporting a correct hypothesis by using too few participants. Similarly, it is possible to use an unnecessarily large sample if you do not calculate how many participants your design requires.

The procedure

The procedure is the way that the study is conducted: how the design decisions are carried out. This includes what the participants are told, what they do, in what order they do it and whether they are debriefed (see Chapter 1).

When there is more than one researcher or when the person carrying out the study is not the person who designed it, each person dealing with the participants needs to be clear about the design and needs to run it in the same way. This can be helped by having standardised instructions for the researchers and for the participants.

New researchers are often concerned that having a number of researchers on a project can invalidate the results: firstly, because there were different researchers, and, secondly, because each researcher may have tested participants in a different place. As long as such variations do not vary systematically with aspects of the design this will not be a problem; if anything it can be a strength. Examples of systematic variation would be if one researcher only tested people in one condition of the study or only tested one type of person, such as only the males. Under these circumstances, any results could be a consequence of such limitations. However, if such potential problems have been eradicated, then the results will be more generalisable to other situations than research conducted by one researcher in one place.

Finally, regardless of the method you are employing in your research, it is important that a pilot study be conducted.

Pilot studies

A pilot study is a trial run of the study and should be conducted on a smaller sample than that which will be used in the final version of the study. Regardless of the method you adopt, it is essential that you carry out a pilot study first. The purpose of a pilot study is to check that the basic aspects of the design and procedure work. Accordingly, you want to know whether participants understand the instructions they are given and whether your measures have face validity or, if you are using a cover story, whether it is seen as plausible. In an experiment you will be checking that any apparatus works as intended and that participants are able to use the apparatus. Finally, you can get an idea of how long the procedure takes with each participant so that you can give people an indication of how long they will be required, when you ask them to take part, and you can allow enough time between participants. It is particularly useful to debrief the people who take part in your pilot study as their thoughts on the study will help to reveal any flaws, including possible demand characteristics.

Without the information gained from a pilot study you may be presented with a dilemma if you discover flaws during the study: you can either alter the design midway through the study or you can plough on regardless with a poor design. Changing the design during the study obviously means that participants in the same condition are likely not to have been treated similarly. This will mean that you are adding an extra source of variation in the results, which can be a problem for their interpretation. On the other hand, to continue with a design which you know is flawed is simply a waste of both your time and that of your participants. Save yourself from confronting this dilemma by conducting a pilot study.

It is particularly important to conduct a pilot study when you are using measures which you have devised, such as in a questionnaire or in designs where training is needed in taking the measures. In the chapters devoted to asking questions and observations (Chapters 5–7) I will describe how to conduct the necessary pilot studies for those methods.

The pilot study should be conducted on a small number of people from your target population. There is not much point in checking whether the design works with people from a population other than the one from which you will be sampling. As, in most cases, you should not use these people again in your main study, the number you use can be dictated by the availability of participants from your population. Thus, if the population is small or you have limited access to members of the population, such as people born totally blind, then you may choose only to use two or three in the pilot study. Nonetheless, it is preferable if you can try out every condition that is involved in the study.

Chapter 13 also describes a further advantage of using a pilot study as it can help to decide on the appropriate sample size for your main study.

Once you have completed the pilot study you can make any alterations to the design which are revealed as being necessary and then conduct the final version of the study.

Summary

Prior to conducting a piece of research you have to narrow your focus to a specific aspect of your chosen area. This can be helped by reading previous research which has been conducted in the area and possibly through talking to experts in the field. You have to choose a method from those described in Chapter 1. You have to choose a design from those described in Chapter 4. You have to choose the measure(s) you are going to take during your research and you will need to check that they are both reliable and valid. You have to choose whom you are going to study and this will depend partly on the particular method you are employing. Finally, you must conduct a pilot study of your design. Once these decisions have been made and the pilot study has been completed, you are ready to conduct the final version of your research.

The next two chapters consider aspects of the variables which are involved in psychological research and the most common research designs which psychologists employ. In addition, they explain the importance of checking whether any findings from a piece of research which employs a given design can be generalised to people and settings other than those used in the research and whether given designs can be said to identify the cause and effect relationships within that research.

3

Variables and the validity of research designs

Introduction

This chapter describes the different types of variables which are involved in research. It then explains why psychologists need to consider the factors in their research which determine whether their findings are generalisable to situations beyond the scope of their original research. It goes on to explore the aspects of research which have to be considered if researchers are investigating the causes of human behaviour. Finally, it discusses the ways in which hypotheses are formulated.

Variables

Variables are entities which can have more than one value. The values do not necessarily have to be numerical. For example, the variable gender can have the value male or the value female.

Independent variables

An independent variable is a variable which could affect another variable. For example, if I consider that income affects happiness, then I will treat income as an independent variable which is affecting the variable happiness.

In experiments, an independent variable is a variable which the researchers have manipulated to see what effect it has on another variable. For example, in a study comparing three methods of teaching reading, children are taught to recognise words by sight – the whole-word method – or to learn to recognise the sound of parts of words which are common across words – the phonetic method – or by a combination of the whole-word and phonetic methods. In this case the researchers have manipulated the independent variable – teaching method – which has three possible values in this study: whole-word, phonetic or combined. The researchers are interested in whether teaching method has an effect on the variable reading ability. In other words, they are interested in whether different teaching methods produce different performances on reading.

The term *level* is used to describe one of the values which an independent variable has in a given study. Thus, in the preceding study, the independent variable – teaching method – has three levels: whole-word, phonetic or combined.

The term *condition* is also used to describe a level of an independent variable. The preceding study of teaching methods has a whole-word condition, a phonetic condition and a combined condition.

Independent variables can be of two basic types – fixed and random – depending on how the levels of that variable were selected.

Fixed variables

A fixed variable is one where the researcher has chosen the specific levels to be used in the study. Thus, in the experiment on reading, the variable – teaching method – is a fixed variable.

Random variables

A random variable is one where the researcher has randomly selected the levels of that variable from a larger set of possible levels. Thus, if I had a complete list of all the possible methods for teaching reading and had picked three randomly from the list to include in my study, teaching method would now be a random variable.

It is unlikely that I would want to pick teaching methods randomly; the following is a more realistic example. Assume that I am interested in seeing what effect listening to relaxation tapes of different length has on stress levels. In this study, duration of tape is the independent variable. I could choose the levels of the independent variable in two ways. Firstly, I could decide to have durations of 5, 10, 15 and 30 minutes. Duration of tape would then be a fixed independent variable. Alternatively, I could randomly choose four durations from the range 1 to 30 minutes. This would give a random independent variable. Participants are usually treated as a random variable in statistical analysis.

The decision as to whether to use fixed or random variables has two consequences. Firstly, the use of a fixed variable prevents researchers from trying to generalise to other possible levels of the independent variable, while the use of a random variable allows more generalisation. Secondly, the statistical analysis can be affected by whether a fixed or a random variable was used.

Dependent variables

A dependent variable is a variable on which an independent variable could have an effect. In other words, the value which the dependent variable has is dependent on the level of the independent variable. Thus, in the study of reading, a measure of reading ability would be the dependent variable, while in the study of relaxation tapes, a measure of stress would be the dependent variable. Notice that in each of these examples of an experiment the dependent variable is the measure provided by the participants in the study: a reading score or a stress score.

Variables in non-experimental research

The description of variables given previously is appropriate when the design is experimental or quasi-experimental and the researcher has manipulated a variable (the independent variable) to find out what effect the manipulation could have on another variable (the dependent variable). However, there are situations when no manipulation has occurred but such terminology is being used as shorthand. In non-experimental research the equivalent of the independent variable could be gender or smoking status or some other pre-existing grouping. In research where relationships between variables, such as age and IQ, are being investigated, using the techniques described in Chapter 19, neither term is necessary. However, when the values of one variable are being used to predict the values of another, using the techniques described in Chapters 20 and 21, then the often preferred terms are *predictor variable* and *criterion variable*. This usage emphasises the point that no manipulation has occurred.

Other forms of variable

In any study there are numerous possible variables. Some of these will be part of the study as independent or dependent variables. However, others will exist which the researchers need to consider.

Mediators

In some situations there will be variables which intervene between an independent and a dependent variable, and we need to be aware of their role in the relationship between the other two variables. A common example in health psychology is where people's intentions to perform a behaviour, for example, quitting smoking, are acting as a mediator between their desire to give up smoking and their attempts to quit smoking.

Confounding variables

Some variables could potentially affect the relationship between the independent and dependent variables which are being sought. Such variables are termed *confounding variables*. For example, in the teaching methods study, different teachers may have taken the different groups. If the teachers have different levels of skill in teaching reading, then any differences in reading ability between the children in the three teaching methods may be due to the teachers' abilities and not the teaching methods. Thus, teachers' skill is a confounding variable. Alternatively, in the relaxation study it could be that the people who receive the longest duration tape are inherently less relaxed than those who receive the shortest tape, and this may mask any improvements which might be a consequence of listening to a longer tape. In this case, the participant's initial stress level is a confounding variable.

There are ways of trying to minimise the effects of confounding variables, and many of the designs described in the next chapter have been developed for this purpose.

Irrelevant variables

Fortunately, many of the variables which are present in a study are not going to affect the dependent variable and are thus not relevant to the study and do not have to be controlled for. For example, it is unlikely that what the teacher was wearing had an effect on the children's reading ability. However, researchers must consider which variables are and which are not relevant. In another study, say, on obedience, what the experimenter wore might well affect obedience.

Researchers have been criticised for assuming that certain variables are irrelevant. As Sears (1986) noted, frequently psychology undergraduates are used as participants in research. There are dangers in generalising findings of such research to people in general, to non-students of the same age or even to students who are not studying psychology.

In addition, it has been suggested that the experimenter should not be treated as an irrelevant variable (Bonge, Schuldt, & Harper, 1992). It is highly likely, particularly in social psychology experiments, that aspects of the experimenter are going to affect the results of the study.

The validity of research designs

The ultimate aim of a piece of research may be to establish a connection between one or more independent variables and a dependent variable. In addition, it may be to generalise the results found with the particular participants used in the study to other groups of people. No design will achieve these goals perfectly. Researchers have to be aware of how valid their design is for the particular goals of the research. The threats to validity of designs are of two main types: threats to what are called external validity and internal validity.

External validity

External validity refers to the generalisability of the findings of a piece of research. Similarities can be seen between this form of validity and ecological validity. There are two main areas where the generalisability of the research could be in question. Firstly, there may be an issue over the degree to which the particular conditions pertaining in the study can allow the results of the study to be generalised to other conditions – the tasks required of the participants, the setting in which the study took place or the time when the study was conducted. Secondly, we can question whether aspects of the participants can allow the results of a study to be generalised to other people – whether they are representative of the group from whom they come and whether they are representative of a wider range of people.

Threats to external validity

Particular conditions of the study

Task

Researchers will have made choices about aspects of their research, and these may limit the generalisability of the findings. For example, in an experiment on face recognition, the researchers will have presented the pictures for a particular length of time. The findings of their research may only be valid for that particular duration of exposure to the pictures. A further criticism could be that presenting people with two-dimensional pictures, which are static, does not mimic what is involved in recognising a person in the street: Is the task ecologically valid?

Setting

Many experiments are conducted in a laboratory and so generalisability to other settings may be in question. However, it is not only laboratory research which may have limited generalisability with respect to the setting in which it is conducted. For example, a clinical psychologist may have devised a way to lessen people's fear of spiders through listening to audio tapes of a soothing voice talking about spiders. The fact that it has been found to work in the psychologist's consulting room does not necessarily mean that it will elsewhere; see the section on efficacy and effectiveness later in this chapter.

Time

Some phenomena may be affected by the time of day, such as just after lunch, in which case, if a study was conducted at that time only, the results might not generalise to other times. Alternatively, a study carried out at one historical time might produce results which are valid then but later cease to be generalisable due to subsequent events. For example, early research in which people were subjected to sensory deprivation found that they were extremely distressed. However, with the advent of people exploring mystical experiences, participants started to enjoy the experience and it has even been used for therapeutic purposes (see Suedfeld, 1980).

Aspects of the participants

Researchers may wish to generalise from the particular participants they have used in their study – their sample – to the group from which those participants come – the population. For example, a study of student life may have been conducted with a sample selected from people studying a particular subject, at a particular university. Unless the sample is a fair representation of the group from which they were selected, there are limitations on generalising any findings to the wider group.

Generalising to other groups

As mentioned earlier, even if the research can legitimately be generalised to other students studying that subject at that university, this does not mean that they can be generalised to other students studying the same subject at another institution, never mind to those studying other subjects or even to non-students.

Many aspects of the participants may be relevant to the findings of a particular piece of research: for example, their ages, gender, educational levels and occupations.

Laboratory experiments are particularly open to criticism about their external validity because they often treat their participants as though they were representative of people in general. However, the aim of the researchers may not be to generalise but simply to establish that a particular phenomenon exists. For example, they may investigate whether people take longer to recognise faces when they are presented upside down than when presented the right way up. Nonetheless, they should be aware of the possible limitations of generalising from the people they have studied to other people.

Improving external validity

The two main ways to improve external validity are replication and the careful selection of participants.

Replication

Replication is the term used to describe repeating a piece of research. Replications can be conducted under as many of the original conditions as possible. While such studies will help to see whether the original findings were unique and merely a result of chance happenings, they do little to improve external validity. This can be helped by replications which vary an aspect of the original study: for example, by including participants of a different age or using a new setting. If similar results are obtained then this can increase their generalisability.

Selection of participants

There are a number of ways of selecting participants and these are dealt with in greater detail in Chapter 11. For the moment, I simply want to note that randomly selecting participants from the wider group which they represent gives researchers the best case for generalising from their participants to that wider group. In this way researchers are less likely to have a biased sample of people because each person from the wider group has an equal likelihood of being chosen. I will define 'random' more thoroughly in Chapter 11, but it is worth saying here what is not random. If I select the first 20 people whom I meet in the university refectory, I have not achieved a random sample but an opportunity sample – my sample may only be representative of people who go to the refectory at that particular time and on that particular day.

Internal validity

Internal validity is the degree to which a design successfully demonstrates that changes in a dependent variable are caused by changes in an independent variable. For example, you may find a relationship between television viewing and violent behaviour, such that those who watch more television are more violent, and you may wish to find out whether watching violent TV programmes causes people to be violent. Internal validity tends to be more of a problem in quasi-experimental and non-experimental research, where researchers have less control over the allocation of participants to different conditions and so cannot assign them on a random basis, or in research where the researchers have simply observed how two variables – such as TV watching and violent behaviour – are related.

Threats to internal validity

Selection

The presence of participants in different levels of an independent variable may be confounded with other variables which affect performance on the dependent variable. A study of television and violence may investigate a naturally occurring relationship between television watching and violent behaviour. In other words, people are in the different levels of the independent variable, television watching, on the basis of their existing watching habits, rather than because a researcher has randomly assigned them to different levels. There is a danger that additional variables may influence violent behaviour: for example, if those with poorer social skills watched more television. Thus, poor social skills may lead to both increased television watching and more violent behaviour but the researchers may only note the television and violence connection.

Maturation

In studies which look for a change in a dependent variable, over time, in the same participants, there is a danger that some other change has occurred for those participants which also influences the dependent variable. Imagine that researchers have established that there is a link between television watching and violence. They devise a training programme to reduce the violence, implement the training and then assess levels of violence among their participants. They find that violence has reduced over time. However, they have failed to note that other changes have also occurred which have possibly caused the reduction. For example, a number of the participants have found partners and, although they now watch as much television as before, they do not put themselves into as many situations where they might be violent. Thus, the possible continued effects of television have been masked and the training programme is falsely held to have been successful.

Recovery

Researchers and therapists need to be aware that changes in a participant's behaviour over time may be due to recovery rather than any intervention which is being employed. This can be a particular issue for case studies involving a single participant. An example of this would be where a therapist is testing a technique to improve the memory of someone who has suffered a stroke. The therapist needs to be careful about attributing improvements in the patient's memory to the intervention when they could be due to spontaneous recovery.

History

An event which is out of the researchers' control may have produced a change in the dependent variable. Television executives may have decided, as a consequence of public concern over the link between television and violence, to alter the schedule and censor violent programmes. Once again, any changes in violent behaviour may be a consequence of these alterations rather than any manipulations by researchers. Duncan (2001) found an example of the effects of history when he was called in by an organisation to reduce the number of staff who were leaving. He devised a programme which he then implemented and found that staff turnover was reduced. However, during the same time the unemployment rate had increased and this is likely also to have affected people's willingness to leave a job, or their ability to find alternative employment.

Instrumentation

If researchers measure variables on more than one occasion, changes in results between the occasions could be a consequence of changes in the measures rather than in the phenomenon that is being measured. This is a particular danger if a different measure is used; for example, a different measure of violence might be employed because it is considered to be an improvement over an older one.

Testing

Participants' responses to the same measure may change with time. For example, with practice participants may become more expert at performing a task. Alternatively, they may change their attitude to the measure. For example, they may become more honest about the levels of violence in which they participate. Thus, changes which are noted between two occasions when a measure is taken may not be due to any manipulations of researchers but due to the way the participants have reacted to the measure used.

Attrition

This refers to loss of participants from the study; an alternative which is sometimes used is *mortality*. In a study, some of the original participants might not take part in later stages of the research. There may be a characteristic which those who dropped out of the research share and which is relevant to the study. In this case, an impression of the relationship between independent and dependent variables may be falsely created or a real one masked. For example, if the more violent members of a sample dropped out of the research, then a false impression would be created of a reduction in violence among the sample. Accordingly, we should always examine aspects of those who drop out of a study to see whether they share any characteristics which are relevant to the study. See the entry on Intention to Treat in Chapter 23 as one way to take account of attrition in the analysis stage.

Selection by maturation

Two of the preceding threats to internal validity may work together and affect the results of research. Imagine that you have two groups – high television watchers and low television watchers. You have tried to control for selection by matching participants on the basis of the amount of violence in which they indulge. It is possible that changes which affect levels of violence occur to one of the groups and not the other and that this is confounded with the amount of television watched: for example, if those who watch more television also have more siblings and learn violent behaviour from them. Thus, your basis of selection may introduce a confounding variable, whereby the members of one group will change in some relevant way relative to the members of the other group, regardless of the way they are treated in the research.

The next four threats to internal validity refer to designs in which there is more than one condition and where those in one group are affected by the existence of another group – there is contamination across the groups.

Imitation (diffusion of treatments)

Participants who are in one group may learn from those in another group aspects of the study which affect their responses. For example, in a study of the relative effects of different training films to improve awareness of AIDS, those watching one film may tell those in other groups about its content.

Compensation

Research can be undermined by those who are dealing with the participants, particularly if they are not the researchers, in the ways they treat participants in different groups. For example, researchers may be trying to compare a group which is receiving some training with a group which is not. Teachers who are working with the group not receiving the training programme may treat that group, because it is not being given the programme, in a way that improves that group's performance, anyway. This would have the tendency of reducing any differences between the groups which were a consequence of the training. Weiss and Koepsell (2014) give an example which illustrates the problem. Researchers investigated the detrimental effects of the then standard procedure of giving high concentrations of oxygen to premature babies. They were studying whether this practice was a possible cause of a form of blindness known as *retrolental fibroplasia* (RLF, now known as *retinopathy of prematurity*). One group of premature children were to be given a lower concentration of oxygen than was usual and then only if there were signs that it was necessary. However, some nurses treating the children did not think this was safe and they raised the concentration at night for babies in that group. Clearly this made interpreting the results harder.

Compensatory rivalry

This can occur if people in one group make an extra effort in order to be better than those in another group, for example, in a study comparing the effects of different working conditions on productivity.

Demoralisation

The reverse to compensatory rivalry would be if those in one group felt that they were missing out and decided to make less effort than they would normally. This would have the effect of artificially lowering the results for that group.

Regression to the mean

As I explained in Chapter 2, most measures are imperfect in some way and will be subject to a certain amount of error and are thus not 100% reliable. In other words, they are unlikely to produce exactly the same result from one occasion to the next; for example, if a person's IQ is measured on two occasions and the IQ test is not perfectly reliable, then the person is likely to produce a slightly different score on the two occasions. There is a statistical phenomenon called the regression to the mean. This refers to the fact that, people who score above the average, for their population, on one occasion, when measured the next time are likely to score nearer the average, while those who scored below average on the first occasion will also tend to score nearer the average on a second occasion. Thus, those scoring above the average will tend to show a drop in score between the two occasions, while those scoring below the average will tend to show a rise in score.

If participants are selected to go into different levels of an independent variable on the basis of their score on some measure, then the results of the study may be affected by regression to the mean. For example, imagine a study into the effects of giving extra tuition to people who have a low IQ. In this study participants are selected from a population with a normal range of IQ scores and from a population with a low range of IQ scores. A sample from each population is given an IQ test and, on the basis of the results, two groups are formed with similar IQs, one comprising people with low IQs from the normal-IQ population and one of people with the higher IQs in the low-IQ population. The samples have been matched for IQ so that those in the normal-IQ group can act as a control group which receives no treatment, while those from the low-IQ population are given extra tuition. The participants in the two groups then have their IQs measured again. Regression to the mean will have the consequence that the average IQ for the sample from the normal-IQ population will appear to have risen towards the mean for that population, while the average IQ for the sample from the low-IQ population will appear to have lowered towards its population mean. Thus, even if the extra tuition had a beneficial effect, the average scores of the two groups may remain close and suggest to the unwary researcher that the tuition was not beneficial.

Improving internal validity

Many of the threats to internal validity can be lessened by the use of a control group which does not receive any treatment. In this way, if the independent variable is affecting the dependent variable, any changes in a dependent variable over time will only occur in a treatment group. The threats which involve some form of contamination between groups require more careful briefing of participants and those conducting the study – such as teachers implementing a training package. Whenever possible, participants should be allocated to different conditions on a random basis. This will lessen the dangers of selection and selection by maturation being a threat to internal validity. In addition, it conforms to one of the underlying assumptions of most statistical techniques.

Efficacy and effectiveness

When looking at therapeutic interventions, for example to reduce anxiety, a distinction is sometimes made between the *efficacy* and the *effectiveness* of the intervention. Efficacy refers to whether the therapy works. Effectiveness, on the other hand, refers to whether the therapy works in the usual therapeutic conditions rather than only as part of a highly controlled experiment. As Chambless and Ollendick (2001) point out, this distinction is similar to the one made between internal and external validity: an efficacious treatment may be shown to work in controlled conditions but may not generalise to a clinical setting.

The choice of hypotheses

An explicit hypothesis or set of hypotheses is usually tested in experiments and often in studies which employ other research methods. When hypotheses are to be evaluated statistically, there is a formal way in which they are expressed and in the way they are tested. The procedure is to form what are termed a *Null Hypothesis* and an *Alternative Hypothesis*. In experiments the Null Hypothesis is generally stated in the form that the manipulation of the independent variable will not have an effect upon the dependent variable. For example, imagine that researchers are comparing the effects of two therapeutic techniques on participants' level of stress – listening to a relaxation tape and doing exercise. The Null Hypothesis, often symbolised as H_0, is likely to be of the form: *There is no difference, after therapy, in the stress levels of participants who listen to a relaxation tape and those who take exercise.* The Alternative Hypothesis (H_A), which is the outcome predicted by the researchers, is also known as the research hypothesis or the experimental hypothesis (in an experiment) or even H_1, if there is more than one prediction.

Researchers will only propose one Alternative Hypothesis for each Null Hypothesis, but that alternative hypothesis can be chosen from three possible versions. The basic distinction between Alternative Hypotheses is whether they are non-directional or directional. A non-directional (or bidirectional) hypothesis is one that does not predict the direction of the outcome. In the preceding example the non-directional Alternative Hypothesis would take the form: *There is a difference between the stress levels of participants who experience the two different therapeutic regimes.* Thus, this hypothesis predicts a difference between the two therapies but it does not predict which will be more beneficial.

A directional (or unidirectional) hypothesis, in this example, can be of two types. On the one hand, it could state that *participants who receive relaxation therapy are less stressed than those who take exercise.* On the other hand, it could state that *participants who take exercise are less stressed than those who receive relaxation therapy.* In other words, a directional hypothesis not only states that there will be a difference between the levels of the independent variable but it also predicts which direction the difference will take.

It may seem odd that in order to test a prediction researchers have not only to state that prediction but also to state a Null Hypothesis which goes against their prediction. The reason follows from the point that it is logically impossible to *prove* that something is true while it *is* possible to prove that something is false. For example, if my hypothesis is that I like *all* flavours of whisky, then, however many whiskies I might have tried, even if I have liked them all to date, there is always the possibility that the next whisky I try I will dislike, and that one example will be enough to disprove my hypothesis. Accordingly, if the evidence does not support the Null Hypothesis, it is taken as support for our Alternative Hypothesis; not as *proof* of the Alternative Hypothesis, because that can never be obtained, but as support for it.

Chapter 10 will show the main way that statistics are used to decide whether the Null Hypothesis or its Alternative Hypothesis is the more likely to be true. Once we have met a number of statistical concepts in the subsequent chapters, in Chapter 27 I will introduce a different approach – Bayesian statistics – which is gaining popularity.

Summary

Researchers often manipulate *independent variables* in their research and observe the consequences of such manipulations on *dependent variables*. In so doing, they have to take account of other aspects of the research which could interfere with the results that they have obtained. In addition, if they wish their findings to be generalisable, they have to consider the *external validity* of their research designs. If researchers want to investigate the causal relationship between the independent and dependent variables in their research they have to consider the *internal validity* of their research designs. Researchers who are testing an explicit hypothesis, statistically, have to formulate it as an *Alternative Hypothesis* and propose a *Null Hypothesis* to match it. The research will then provide evidence which will allow the researchers to choose between the hypotheses.

The next chapter introduces a number of research designs which can be employed and points out the ways in which each design might fail to fulfil the requirements of internal validity. Remember, however, that internal validity is only a problem if you are trying to establish a causal link between independent and dependent variables.

4 Research designs and their internal validity

Introduction

This chapter describes a range of designs which are employed in psychological research. It introduces and defines a number of terms which are used to distinguish designs. In addition, it describes particular versions of designs and evaluates the problems which can prevent each design from being used to answer the question of whether a dependent variable (DV) can be shown to be affected by independent variables (IVs).

The three sections of this chapter need to be treated differently. The initial overview of the types of designs and the terminology which is used to distinguish designs should be read before moving on to other chapters. However, the remainder of the chapter, which gives specific examples of the designs, could be treated more for reference or when you have more experience in research.

Types of designs

Designs can be classified in a number of ways. One consideration which should guide your choice of design and measures should be the statistical analysis you are going to employ on your data. It is better to be clear about this before you conduct your study rather than find afterwards that you are having to do the best you can with a poor design and measures which do not allow you to test your hypotheses.

Accordingly, I am choosing to classify the designs according to the possible aims of the research and the type of analysis which could be conducted on the data derived from them. In this way, there will be a link between the types of designs and the chapters devoted to their analysis. The designs are of seven basic types:

1   Measures of a single variable are taken from an individual or a group. For example, the IQ of an individual or those of members of a group are measured. Such designs could be used for descriptive purposes; descriptive statistics are dealt with in Chapter 9. Alternatively, these designs could be used to compare an individual or a group with others, such as a population, to see whether the individual or group is unusual. This form of analysis is dealt with in Chapter 12.

2   A single IV is employed with two levels and a single DV. Such designs are used to look for differences in the DV between the levels of the IV. An example would be if researchers compared the reading abilities of children taught using two techniques. The analysis of such designs is dealt with in Chapter 15.

3   A single IV is employed with more than two levels and a single DV. This is an extension of the previous type of design, which could include the comparison of the reading abilities of children taught by three different techniques. The analysis of such designs is dealt with in Chapter 16.

4   More than one IV is involved and a single DV. An example of such a design would be where one IV is type of reasoning problem with three levels – verbal, numerical and spatial – and a second IV is gender, with number of problems solved as the DV. As with designs 2 and 3, researchers would be

looking for differences in the DV between the levels of the IVs. In addition, they can explore any ways in which the two IVs interact – an example of an interaction in this case would be if females were better than males at verbal tasks but there was no difference between the genders on the other tasks. The analysis of such designs is covered in Chapter 17. A variant of this design is where one IV is time and the same variable is measured on more than one occasion, say, before a treatment and after a treatment. Analysis of such designs is dealt with in Chapter 22.

5   An alternative version of designs with one DV and one or more IVs would be where researchers were interested in how well they could use measures (treated as IVs or predictor variables), such as students' school performance and motivation, to predict what level of university degree (treated as a DV or criterion variable) students would achieve. The analysis of this version of such designs is dealt with in the latter half of Chapter 20; Chapter 21 deals with the analysis when the outcome variable is categorical such as pass or fail.

The first five types of design are usually described as *univariate* because they contain a single DV.

6   Designs used to assess a relationship between two variables.

   6a   This design is described as *bivariate* because it involves two variables but neither can necessarily be classified as an IV or a DV – for example, where researchers are looking at the relationship between performance at school and performance at university. The analysis of such designs is dealt with in Chapter 19.

   6b   This is fundamentally the same design (and a simpler version of design 5), but one of the variables is treated as an IV (or predictor variable) and is used to predict the other, treated as a DV (or criterion variable) – for example, if admissions tutors to a university wanted to be able to predict from school performance what performance at university would be. The analysis is dealt with in the first part of Chapter 20.

7   Finally, there are designs with more than one DV – for example, where children have been trained according to more than one reading method and researchers have measured a range of abilities, such as fluency in reading, spelling ability and ability to complete sentences. Such designs are described as *multivariate* because there is more than one DV. Brief descriptions of such designs and the techniques used to analyse them are contained in Chapter 25.

Further description of designs of types 5, 6 and 7 will be left until the chapters which deal with their analysis.

All the designs which are described in the rest of this chapter are used to see whether an individual differs from a group or whether groups differ. Typically the designs look to see whether a group which is treated in one way differs from a group which is treated in another way. Usually, the members of a group are providing a single summary statistic – often an average for the group – which is used for comparison with other groups. This approach treats variation by individuals within the same group as a form of error.[1] There are a number of factors which contribute to individuals *in the same group* giving different scores:

1   Individual differences, such as differences in ability or motivation.
2   The reliability of the measure being used.
3   Differences in the way individuals have been treated in the research.

The more variation in scores which is present within groups, the less likely it is that any differences between groups will be detected. Therefore, where possible, such sources of variation are minimised

---

1   See Danziger (1990) for an account of how psychologists came to adopt this approach. Designs 5 and 6b take a different approach and are interested in individual differences.

in designs. An *efficient* design is one which can detect genuine differences between groups. However, researchers wish to avoid introducing any confounding variables which could produce spurious differences between different treatments or mask genuine difference between treatments. Some attempts to counter confounding variables in designs can increase individual differences within groups and thus can produce less efficient designs.

Terminology

As with many areas of research methods, there is a proliferation of terms which are used to describe designs. What makes it more complex for the newcomer is that similar designs are described in different ways in some instances, and the same designs are referred to in different ways by different writers. I will describe the most common terms and then try to stick to one consistent set.

Replication

'Replication' is used in at least two senses in research. In Chapter 3, I mentioned that replication can mean rerunning a piece of research. However, the term is also used to describe designs in which more than one participant is treated in the same way. Thus, a study of different approaches to teaching is likely to have more than one child in each teaching group. Otherwise, the results of the research would be overly dependent on the particular characteristics of the very limited sample used.

Most studies involve some form of replication, for this has the advantage that the average score across participants for that condition can be used in an analysis. This will tend to lessen the effect of the variation in scores which is due to differences between people in the same condition. Nonetheless, there may be situations where replication is kept to a minimum because the task for participants is onerous or time-consuming or because there are too few participants available – for example, in a study of patients with a rare form of brain damage.

The allocation of participants

The biggest variation in terminology is over descriptions of the way in which participants have been employed in a piece of research. As a starting point I will use as an example a design which has one IV with two levels.

Between-subjects designs

One of the simplest designs would involve selecting a sample of people and assigning each person to one of the two levels of the IV – for example, when two ways of teaching children to read are being compared.

Such designs have a large number of names: *unrelated, between-subjects, between-groups, unpaired* (in the case of an IV with two levels), *factorial* or even *independent groups*. I will use the term *between-subjects*. These designs are relatively inefficient because the overall variation in scores (both within and between groups) is likely to be relatively large, as the people in each group differ and there is more scope for individual differences.

Such designs have the additional disadvantage that the participants in the different levels of the IV may differ in some relevant way such that those in one group have an advantage which will enhance their performance on the DV. For example, if the children in one group were predominantly from middle-class families which encourage reading, this could mean that that group may perform better on a reading test regardless of the teaching method employed.

There are a number of ways around the danger of confounding some aspect of the participants with the condition to which they are allocated. One is to use a random basis to allocate them to the conditions. Many statistical techniques are based on the assumption that participants have been randomly assigned to the different conditions. This approach would be preferable if researchers were not aware of the existing abilities of the participants, as it would save testing them before allocating them to groups. An alternative which is frequently used, when more obvious characteristics of the participants are known, is to control for the factor in some way.

A method of control which is not recommended is to select only people with one background – for example, only middle-class children – to take part in the research. Such a study would clearly have limited generalisability to other groups; it would lack external validity.

A more useful approach comes under the heading of 'blocking'.

Blocks

Blocking involves identifying participants who are similar in some relevant way and forming them into a subgroup or block. You then ensure that the members of a block are randomly assigned to each of the levels of the IV being studied. In this way, researchers could guarantee that the same number of children from each socio-economic group experienced each of the reading methods.

One example of blocking is where specific individuals are *matched* within a block for a characteristic – for example, if existing reading age scores were being used to form blocks of children. Matching can be of at least two forms. *Precision matching* would involve having blocks of children with the same reading ages, within a block, while *range matching* would entail the children in each block having similar reading ages. Block designs are more efficient than simple between-subjects designs because they attempt to remove the variability which is due to the blocking factor. However, they involve a slightly more complex analysis as they have introduced a second IV: the block.

One problem with matching is that many factors may be relevant to the study so that perfect matching becomes difficult. In addition, matching can introduce an extra stage in the research: we have to assess the participants on the relevant variables, if the information is not already available. A way around these problems is to have the ultimate match, where the same person acts as his or her own match. It is then a *within-subjects* design.

Within-subjects designs

If every participant takes part in both levels of the IV, then the design can be described as *related, paired, repeated measures, within-subjects, dependent* or even *non-independent*. If an IV with more than two levels is used, then *within-subjects* or *repeated measures* tend to be the preferred terms. I am going to use *within-subjects* to describe such designs.

This type of design can introduce its own problems. Two such problems are order effects and carry-over effects.

Order effects

If the order in which participants complete the levels of the IV is constant, then it is possible that they may become more practised and so they will perform better with later tasks – a practice effect – or they may suffer from fatigue or boredom as the study progresses and so perform less well with the later tasks – a fatigue effect. In this way, any differences between levels of an IV could be due to an order effect, or alternatively a genuine difference between treatments could be masked by an order effect.

One way to counter possible order effects would be to randomise the order for each participant. A second way would be to alternate the order in which the tasks are performed by each participant: to *counterbalance* the order. Some of the participants would do the levels in one order while others would complete them in another order. A negative effect of random orders and counterbalancing is that they are likely to introduce more variation in the scores, because people in the same condition have been treated differently; the design is less efficient. However, this can be dealt with by one of two systematic methods which can be seen as forms of blocking: complete counterbalancing or Latin squares.

Complete counterbalancing

An example would be where researchers wished to compare the number of words recalled from a list after two different durations of delay: 5 seconds and 30 seconds. They could form the participants into two equally sized groups (blocks) and give those in one block a list of words to recall after a 5-second delay followed by another list to recall after a 30-second delay. The second group would receive the delay conditions in the order 30 seconds and then 5 seconds. This design has introduced a second IV – order. Thus we have a within-subjects IV – delay before recall – and a between-subjects IV – order. Designs which contain both within- and between-subjects IVs are called *mixed* or *split-plot*. However, some writers and some computer programs refer to them as *repeated measures* because they have at least one IV which entails repeated measures.

Latin squares

I will deal here, briefly, with Latin squares. Without replication of an order, they require as many participants as there are levels of the IV for each Latin square. Thus, for three levels of an IV there will need to be three participants – for example, if the effects of three different delay conditions (5, 10 and 20 seconds) on recall are being compared. Notice that each participant has been in each treatment and that each treatment has been in each order once.

TABLE 4.1   A Latin square for a design with three treatments

	Order of treatment		
	First	*Second*	*Third*
Participant 1	Treatment 1	Treatment 2	Treatment 3
Participant 2	Treatment 2	Treatment 3	Treatment 1
Participant 3	Treatment 3	Treatment 1	Treatment 2

There are 12 different possible Latin squares for such a 3 by 3 table; I will let sceptics work them out for themselves. If further replication is required, extra participants can be allocated an order for completing the levels of the IV by drawing up a fresh Latin square for every three participants. In this way, when there are three treatments, more than 36 participants would be involved before any Latin square need be reused. Those wishing to read more on Latin squares can refer to Myers and Well (2003), which has an entire chapter devoted to the subject.

Carry-over effects

If taking part in one level of an IV leaves a residue of that participation, this is called a carry-over effect. One example would be if participants were to be tested on two occasions, using the same version of a test. They are likely to remember, for a while after taking the test for the first time, some of the items in the test and some of the answers. A second example would be where a drug such as alcohol has been administered and its effects will be present for a while after any measurement has been taken.

One way around carry-over effects is to use a longer delay between the different levels of the IV. However, this may not always be possible as the residue may be permanent; for example, once a child has learned to read by one method the ability cannot be erased so that the child can be trained by another method.

Another way around carry-over effects (and another solution for order effects) is to use different participants for the different levels of the IV. This brings us full circle, back either to a between-subjects design or some form of blocking (matching) with more than one participant in each block.

In quasi-experiments, researchers may have limited control over the allocation of participants to treatments, in which case there are potential threats to the internal validity of the design.

A further aspect of designs is whether every level of one IV is combined with every level of all other IVs. If they are, then the design is described as *crossed*; if they are not, the design is called *nested*.

Crossed designs

Crossed designs are those in which every level of one IV is combined with every level of another IV. For example, in an experiment on speed of face recognition the design would be crossed if it included all possible combinations of the levels of the IVs, orientation and familiarity: upside-down familiar faces, upside-down unfamiliar faces, correctly oriented familiar faces and correctly oriented unfamiliar faces.[2] Such designs allow researchers to investigate *interactions* between the IVs, that is, how the two variables combine to affect the DV. (Interactions are discussed in Chapter 17.)

One example of a crossed design is the standard within-subjects design – participants are crossed with the IV(s), and every participant takes part in every condition.

Nested designs

A disadvantage of crossed designs can be that they necessitate exhaustively testing each possible combination of the levels of the IVs, which means that the task will take longer for participants in a within-subjects design or the study will require more participants in a between-subjects design. An alternative approach is to nest one variable within another – in other words, to refrain from crossing every level of one IV with every level of another. In fact, between-subjects designs have participants nested within the levels of the IV(s).

Some studies may be forced to use nested designs. For example, if researchers wished to compare two approaches to teaching mathematics – formal and 'new' mathematics – they might have to test children in schools which have already adopted one of these approaches. Thus, the schools would be nested in the approaches. Designs which involve the nesting of one variable within another in this way are termed *hierarchical* designs. A disadvantage of this design, using more conventional analysis, is that it is not possible to assess the interaction between IVs: in this case, school and teaching approach. However, it is likely that it would be possible to conduct the analysis by using multi-level modelling. This is briefly described in Chapter 25. Hence, hierarchical nesting should only be adopted when the researcher is forced to, where no interaction is suspected or where specialist software is available to conduct multi-level modelling and a sufficiently large sample is being studied.

Balanced designs

Whenever using between-subjects or mixed designs it is advisable to have equal numbers of participants in each level of each IV. This produces what is termed a 'balanced design' and is much more easily analysed and interpreted than a poorly balanced design.

---

2 By unfamiliar I mean faces which were not familiar to the participants before the study but have been shown during the study prior to the testing phase.

The remainder of the chapter describes specific versions of the first four designs which were identified at the beginning of the chapter. As mentioned in the Introduction, this part of the chapter could be treated more for reference purposes than for reading at one sitting.

Specific examples of research designs

Designs which have one variable with one level

Design 1: the one-shot case study

This type of design can take a number of forms; each involves deriving one measure on one occasion either from an individual or from a group (Figures 4.1 and 4.2). It allows researchers to compare the measure taken from the individual or group with that of a wider group. In this way, I could compare the performance of an individual who has brain damage with the performance of people who do not have brain damage to see whether he or she has impaired abilities on specific tasks.

Design 1.1: a single score from an individual

An example of this design would be measuring the IQ (intelligence quotient) of a stroke patient.

Design 1.2a: an average score from an individual

An example would be setting an individual a number of similar logic puzzles, timing how long he or she took to solve them and then noting the average time taken.

Design 1.2b: a one-shot case study with a summary statistic from a group

This can be a replicated version either of design 1.1, where the average IQ of a group is noted, or of design 1.2a, where the average time taken to solve the logic puzzles is noted for a group.

FIGURE 4.1   A one-shot case study involving a single measure from one person

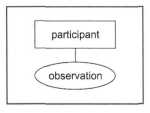

FIGURE 4.2   A one-shot case study with a summary statistic from one person

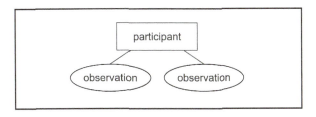

Such designs are mainly useful for describing an individual or a group (Figure 4.3). For example, in a survey of students, participants are asked whether they smoke and the percentages who do and do not smoke are noted. Alternatively, such designs can be used to see whether an individual or a particular group differs from the general population. For example, researchers could compare the IQs of a group of mature students with the scores which other researchers have found for the general population to see whether the mature students have unusually high or low IQs.

FIGURE 4.3   A one-shot case study with a summary statistic from a group

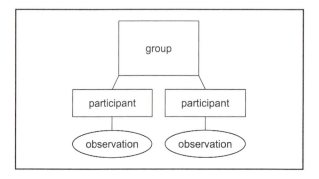

Design 1.2c: post-test only, with one group

This type of design could involve an intervention or manipulation by researchers – for example, if a group of criminals were given a programme which is designed to prevent them from reoffending (Figure 4.4).

There are no problems of internal validity with this type of design, which is sometimes described as pre-experimental, because it is pointless to use it to try to establish causal relationships. For, even in the example of the programme for criminals, as a study on its own, there is no basis for assessing the efficacy of the programme. Even if we find that the group offends less than criminals in general, we do not know whether the group would have reoffended less without the intervention. To answer such questions, researchers would have to compare the results of the programme with other programmes and with a control group. In so doing they would be employing another type of design.

FIGURE 4.4   A post-test-only design, with one group

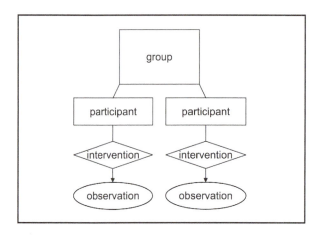

Designs which have one IV with two levels

Between-subjects designs

Design 2.1a: cross-sectional design, two groups

Two groups are treated as levels of an IV and the members of each are measured on a single variable. It is likely that the two groups will differ in some inherent way – such as gender – in which case the design can be described as a *static* group or *non-equivalent* group comparison and another example of a pre-experimental design. Examples of such a design would be if researchers asked a sample of males and a sample of females whether they smoked or tested their mathematical abilities.

  This design may include time as an assumed variable by taking different participants at different stages in a process, but measured at the same time (Figure 4.5). For example, if researchers wanted to study differences in IQ with age, they might test the IQs of two different age groups – at 20 years and at 50 years. This design suffers from the problems of history: if educational standards had changed with time, differences in IQ between the age groups could be a consequence of this rather than a change for the individuals. A way around this problem is to use a longitudinal design in which the same people are measured at the different ages, which would be an example of the panel design given later in the chapter.

FIGURE 4.5 A cross-sectional design with two groups

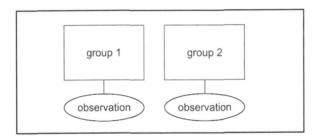

Design 2.1b: case-control design

This is a design which is often used in epidemiology, the study of causes of diseases, but can be used by psychologists to investigate possible causes of a condition. Instead of forming or identifying groups on the basis of an IV, participants are identified on the basis of an assumed DV. For example, researchers investigating possible causes of anxiety could form two groups of participants: one group of people already diagnosed with anxiety and another of those without anxiety. The researchers would then look at aspects of the participants' pasts for possible sources of differences between the two groups. For example they might find that those with anxiety had been bullied at school. This design is particularly useful if the phenomenon being studied is relatively rare as, instead of sampling a large number of people in the hope of including a sufficient number with the rare condition, those with the condition are already identified. However, as this is a retrospective design, it would be better for there to be well-documented evidence rather than reliance on participants' memories.

Design 2.1c: two-group, post-test only

Two groups are formed, each is treated in a different way and then a measure is taken (Figure 4.6). An example of a study which utilised this design would be one in which two training methods for radiographers to recognise tumours on X-rays were being compared. However, preferably, one of the groups

FIGURE 4.6   A two-group, post-test-only design

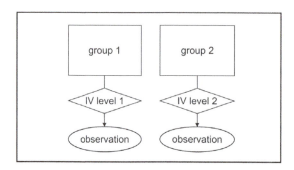

would be a control group. The advantage of a control group is that it helps to set a baseline against which to compare the training method(s). For, if we found no difference between groups who had been trained, without a control group we could not say whether either training was beneficial; it may be that both are equally beneficial or that neither is. However, if those in training groups were no better than the controls we have failed to show any benefit of training. Thus, if we wish to compare two interventions we are better using a different design.

When naturally occurring groups are used, rather than randomly assigned participants, design 2.1c can also be described as *static* or *non-equivalent group comparison* designs. They can be subject to selection as a threat to internal validity.

Design 2.1d: quasi-panel

One purpose of this design can be to measure participants prior to an event and then attempt to assess the effect of the event. For example, we could take a sample of drama students prior to their attendance on a drama course and measure how extrovert they are. After the first year of the course, we could take another sample from the same population of students, which may or may not include some of those we originally tested, and measure their extroversion. In addition to selection, maturation and selection by maturation are potential threats to internal validity, as could be instrumentation (Figure 4.7).

FIGURE 4.7   The quasi-panel design

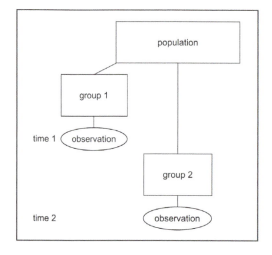

Matched participants

Design 2.2: two matched groups, post-test only

This design could compare two levels of an IV or one treatment with a control group (Figure 4.8).

FIGURE 4.8   A post-test-only design with two matched groups

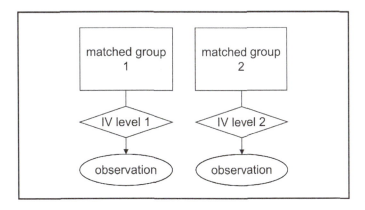

Within-subjects designs

Design 2.3a: within-subjects, post-test only, two conditions

For example, participants are given two types of logic puzzle to solve and the time taken to solve each type is noted. Here type of logic puzzle is the IV with two levels and time taken is the DV (Figure 4.9).

In this design, if an intervention is being tested, it would be better to have one condition as a control condition. Where possible the order of conditions should be varied between participants so that order effects can be controlled for.

FIGURE 4.9   A within-subjects, post-test-only design

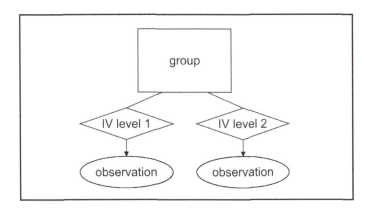

Design 2.3b: one-group, pre-test, post-test

The measures could be taken before and after training in some skill. There are a number of variants of this design; for example, a single treatment could occur – such as being required to learn a list – after which participants are tested following an initial duration and again following a longer duration (Figure 4.10).

FIGURE 4.10   A one-group, pre-test, post-test design

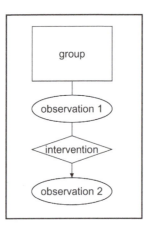

This design, another sometimes described as pre-experimental or quasi-experimental, could be subject to a number of criticisms. Firstly, because no control group is included, we have no protection against maturation and history, particularly if there is an appreciable delay between the times when the two measures are taken; we do not know whether any differences between the two occasions could have come about even without any training. Secondly, we have to be careful that any differences which are detected are not due to instrumentation, attrition, order or carry-over effects.

In the context of surveys, where the intervention could be some event which has not been under the control of the researchers, the design is described as a *simple panel* design. An example would be of a sample of the electorate whose voting intentions are sought before and after a speech made by a prominent politician.

Another variant of this design would be where time is introduced as a variable, retrospectively, by measuring participants after an event and then having them recall how they were prior to the event – a *retrospective panel* design. For example, we might ask students to rate their attitude to computers after they had attended a computing course and then ask them to rate what they thought their attitudes had been prior to the course. An additional problem with retrospective designs is that they rely on people's memories, which can be fallible.

Designs which have one IV with more than two levels

The following designs are simple extensions of the designs described in the previous section. However, they are worth describing separately as the way they are analysed is different. I am mainly going to give examples with three levels of the IV, but the principle is the same regardless of the number of levels. Needless to say, each design suffers from the same problems as its equivalent with only two levels of an IV, except that two treatments can be compared *and* a control condition can be included.

Between-subjects designs

Design 3.1a: multi-group cross-sectional (static or non-equivalent)

This can be a quasi-experimental or non-experimental design in which participants are in three groups (as three levels of an IV) and are measured on a DV (Figure 4.11). For example, children in three age groups have their understanding of the parts of the body assessed.

FIGURE 4.11   A multi-group cross-sectional design

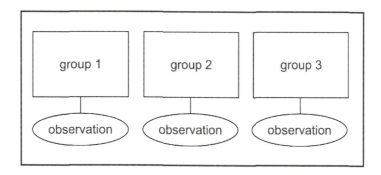

Design 3.1b: multi-group, post-test only

Each group is given a different treatment and then a measure is taken (Figure 4.12). For example, children are placed in three groups. Their task is to select a piece of clay which is as large as a chocolate bar which they have been shown. Prior to making the judgement, one group is prevented from eating for 6 hours. A second group is prevented from eating for 3 hours while the final group is given food just prior to being tested. Here time without food is the IV, with three levels, and the judgement about the weight of the clay is the DV. The advantage of this design over the equivalent with only two levels of an IV is that one of the levels of the IV could be a control group. In this way, two treatments can be compared with each other and with a control group.

FIGURE 4.12   A multi-group, post-test-only design

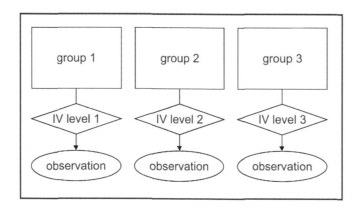

Design 3.1c: the multi-group quasi-panel

This is an extension of the two-group quasi-panel (2.1c). Here, three samples are taken from a population at different times to measure whether changes have occurred (Figure 4.13). Imagine that a third sample of drama students had their extroversion levels measured after the second year of their course.

FIGURE 4.13   The multi-group, quasi-panel design

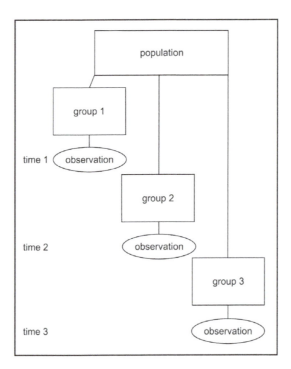

Matched participants

Design 3.2: multi-group, matched, post-test only

This design is the equivalent of design 3.1b, but three matched groups are each treated in a different way and then a measure is taken (Figure 4.14). Once again, one group could be a control group.

FIGURE 4.14   A multi-group, matched, post-test-only design

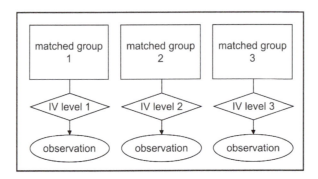

Within-subjects designs

Design 3.3a: within-subjects, post-test only, more than two conditions

Participants each provide a measure for three different conditions (Figure 4.15). For example, each participant in a group is asked to rate physics, sociology and psychology on a scale which ranges from 'very scientific' to 'not very scientific'.

As with other within-subjects designs, the order in which the observations from the different levels of the IV are taken should be varied between participants to control for order effects.

FIGURE 4.15   A within-subjects, post-test-only design with more than two conditions

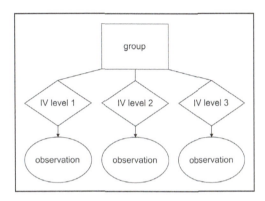

Design 3.3b: interrupted time series

This is an extension of the one-group, pre-test, post-test design which can help to protect against instrumentation and, to a certain extent, maturation and history. It is frequently described as a quasi-experimental design. An interrupted time series is a design in which measures are taken at a number of points (Figure 4.16). For example, a study could be made of training designed to help sufferers from

FIGURE 4.16   An interrupted time series design

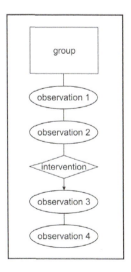

Alzheimer's disease to be better at doing basic tasks. Once again, in the context of a survey this can be called a *panel* design.

Gradual effects of history and maturation should show up as a trend, while any effects of the intervention should show up as a change in the trend. An additional advantage of taking measures on a number of occasions after the intervention is that it will help to monitor the longer-term effects of the intervention. This design can be carried out retrospectively when appropriate records are kept. However, when the intervention is not under the control of the researchers and where records are not normally kept, the researchers obviously have to know about the impending change well in advance in order to start taking the measures.

A problem with this design is that sometimes it can be difficult to identify the effects of an intervention when there is a general trend. For example, if I had devised a method for improving the language ability of stroke patients I would obviously need to demonstrate that any change in language ability after the intervention of my training technique was not simply part of a general trend to improve. The analysis of such designs can involve time series analysis to ascertain whether there is a trend which needs to be allowed for. Such analysis is beyond the scope of this book. For details on time series analysis see McCain and McCleary (1979) or Tabachnick and Fidell (2013).

This design can be used for single-case designs such as with an individual sufferer of Alzheimer's disease. There is an additional complication with such designs in that we clearly cannot randomly assign a participant to a condition. However, we can circumvent this problem to a certain extent by starting the intervention at a random point in the sequence of observations which we take. This will allow analysis to be conducted which can try to distinguish the results from chance effects. See Dugard, File, and Todman (2011) for details on the randomisation process and analysis of such designs when single cases or small samples are being used. Borckardt et al. (2008) propose a method for dealing with the possible trend with time in single-case designs, where the number of observations is smaller than that recommended for standard time series analysis.

Designs which have more than one IV and only one DV

The following examples will be of designs which have a maximum of two IVs. Designs with more than two IVs are simple extensions of these examples. In addition, most of the examples given here show only two or three levels of an IV. This is for simplicity in the diagrams and not because there is such a limit on the designs.

Between-subjects designs

Design 4.1a: fully factorial

In this design each participant is placed in only one condition, that is, one combination of the levels of the two IVs. For example, one IV is photographs of faces with the levels *familiar* and *unfamiliar* and the other IV is the orientation in which the photographs are presented, with the levels *upside down* and *normal way up*. Speed of naming the person would be the DV. The number of IVs in a design is usually indicated: a one-way design has one IV, a two-way design has two IVs and so on (Figure 4.17).

Design 4.1b: two-way with blocking on one IV

For example, in a study of the effects of memory techniques, level of education might be considered to be a factor which needs to be controlled. Participants are placed in three blocks depending on the highest level of education they achieved. Participants in each education group are formed into two subgroups, with one subgroup being told simply to repeat a list of pairs of numbers while the other subgroup is

FIGURE 4.17 A two-way, fully factorial design

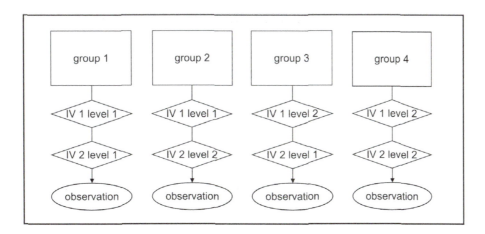

told to form an image of a date which is related to each pair of numbers; for example, 45 produces an image of the end of the Second World War. Thus, the IVs are education (with three levels) and memory technique (with two levels). The DV is number of pairs correctly recalled.

Quasi-experiments and surveys or experiments which entail a number of levels of the IVs but have a limited number of participants may force the researchers to use a less exhaustive design. A hierarchical design with one variable nested within another is one form of such designs.

Design 4.2: nesting

In the example given earlier in which mathematics teaching method was nested within school, imagine there are two methods being compared: formal and topic-based. Imagine also that four schools are involved: two adopting one approach and two adopting the other. This design involves two IVs: the school and the teaching method, with schools (and children) nested within teaching methods (Figure 4.18).

FIGURE 4.18 A design with one IV nested within another

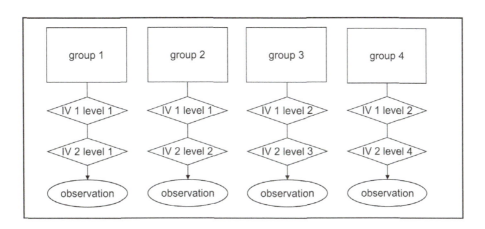

Mixed (split-plot) designs

Design 4.3a: the classic experiment or two-group, pre-test, post-test

In this design two groups are formed, and, as the name suggests, each is tested prior to an intervention. Each is then treated differently and then tested again. One group could be a control group. For example, participants are randomly assigned to two groups. Their stress levels are measured. Members of one group are given relaxation training at a clinic. Members of a second group are given no treatment. After 2 months each participant's stress level is measured again. Here the first IV, which is between-subjects, is a type of treatment (control or relaxation), while the second IV, which is within-subjects, is stage (pre- or post-) (Figure 4.19).

FIGURE 4.19   The two-group, pre-test, post-test design

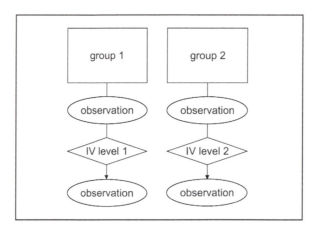

Design 4.3b: the Regression Discontinuity Design (RDD)

This is a variant of the previous design and is often described as quasi-experimental. In the RDD, participants are allocated to control and treatment groups on the basis of their pre-treatment score, using a threshold or *cutting point* as the criterion for allocating to groups. An example would be giving children a test of scholastic ability and then allocating those below a certain score on the test to the treatment group where they receive extra tuition, while those above that cutting point are placed in the control group. After the intervention scholastic scores would be measured again. This particular variant has additional problems, compared with random allocation, which are discussed when the method of analysis is presented in Appendix XIII.

Design 4.3c: two-way mixed

A variant of design 4.3a could entail two different IVs but with one of them being a within-subjects variable and the other a between-subjects variable (Figure 4.20): for example, if, in the face recognition study, some participants are measured on photographs (both familiar and unfamiliar) in an upside-down orientation while others are measured only on faces which are presented the normal way up.

Another example of the preceding would be where one IV is block, where the blocks have been formed in order to counter order effects. For example, if, in a memory experiment, one IV was length of delay before recall, with two levels – after 5 seconds and after 20 seconds – then one block of participants

FIGURE 4.20   A mixed design involving two IVs

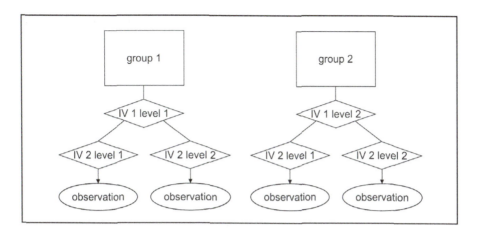

would do the levels in the order 5 seconds and then 20 seconds, while another block would do them in the order 20 seconds and then 5 seconds.

Yet another variant would be a Latin squares design with the order of treatments varying between participants.

Time can be built into the design in the same way as for designs with a single IV, retrospectively or as part of a time series; again the inclusion of a control group should improve internal validity. However, once again, if participants are not randomly assigned to the groups – non-equivalent groups – there could be problems of selection.

Design 4.4: Solomon four group

One design which attempts to control for various threats to internal validity is the Solomon four group. It combines two previously mentioned designs. As with design 2.1b, it is used in situations where two levels of an IV are being compared or where a control group and an experimental group are being employed. However, as with design 4.3a, some of the groups are given pre- and post-tests. This allows researchers to identify effects of testing (Figure 4.21).

FIGURE 4.21   A Solomon four-group design comparing two treatments

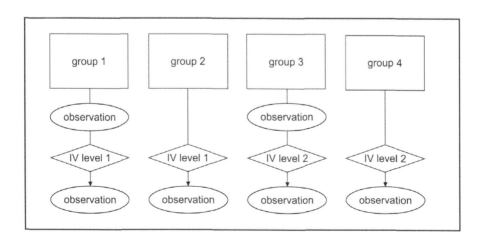

An example of this design would be if researchers wished to test the effect of conditioning on young children's liking for a given food. One experimental and one control group would be tested for their liking for the food, and then the experimental groups would go through an intervention whereby the researchers tried to condition the children to associate eating the food with pleasant experiences; during this phase the control groups would eat the food under neutral conditions. Subsequently, all groups would be given a post-test to measure their liking for the food.

This design is particularly expensive, as far as the number of participants used is concerned, because it involves double the number of participants as in design 2.1b or design 4.3a, for the same comparisons.

Design 4.5: a replicated, interrupted time series

This design is a modification of the interrupted time series given previously. The modification involves an additional comparison group, which can either be a control group or a group in which the intervention occurs at a different point from where it does in the original group (Figure 4.22). Once again, the study could be of training designed to help sufferers from Alzheimer's disease.

This design should be even better than the interrupted time series at detecting changes due to maturation or history as these should show up in both groups, whereas the effects of an intervention should appear as a discontinuity at the relevant point only.

FIGURE 4.22   A replicated, interrupted time series

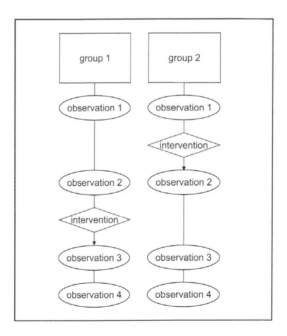

Within-subjects designs

Design 4.6: multi-way, within-subjects design

If the example of speed of recognition required every participant to be presented with familiar and unfamiliar faces, which were presented either upside down or the normal way up, this would be a two-way, within-subjects design (Figure 4.23).

FIGURE 4.23   A two-way, within-subjects design

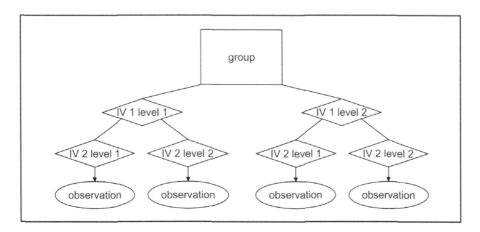

For more details on designs see Cochran and Cox (1957), Cook and Campbell (1979), Myers, Well, and Lorch (2010) or Winer, Brown, and Michels (1991).

Summary

Designs can be classified according to the number of IVs and DVs that they contain and the aims of the research. They can involve the same participants in more than one condition or they can employ different participants in different conditions. Designs also differ in the degree to which they measure participants at different stages in a process. Although it is possible to maximise the internal validity of a design in laboratory experiments, much research is conducted outside the laboratory. In this case, researchers have to choose the most internally valid design which is available to them in the circumstances. No design is perfect but some are more appropriate than others to answer a particular research question. Where possible it is best to allocate participants to the different conditions on a random basis.

The details for using an experimental method are contained in the first four chapters of this book. Other quantitative methods need further explanation. The next three chapters describe the conduct of research using different methods: those involving asking questions and observational methods.

PART 3

Methods

5

Asking questions I
Interviews and surveys

Introduction

This chapter describes the topics which can be covered in questions and the formats for the questions, ranging from informal to formal. It then concentrates on more formal questioning formats and discusses the different settings in which interviews and surveys can take place. It considers the wording and order of questions and the layout of a questionnaire. Finally, it emphasises the particular importance of conducting a pilot study when designing a questionnaire.

Topics for questions

The sorts of questions which can be asked fall under three general headings: demographic, behaviour and what can variously be termed opinions or beliefs or attitudes. In addition, questions can be asked about a person's state of health.

Demographic questions

These are to elicit descriptions of people, such as their age, gender, income and where they live.

Behaviour questions

Questions about behaviour could include whether, and how much, people smoke or drink.

Questions about opinions, beliefs and attitudes

These could include questions about what respondents think is the case, such as whether all politicians are corrupt. Alternatively, they could ask about what respondents think should be the case, such as whether politicians should be allowed to have a second job. The next chapter concentrates on how to devise measures of opinions, beliefs and attitudes.

Health status questions

These might include how much pain a person with a given condition was feeling or how nauseous a person felt after a given treatment.

The formats for asking questions

There are at least three formats for asking questions, ranging from the formal to the informal. When the person asking the questions is to be present, then it is possible to work with just one participant at a time or with a group such as in a focus group.

Structured interviews/questionnaires

The most formal format is a questionnaire. The exact wording of each question is selected beforehand and each participant is asked the same questions in the same order. For this particular format the participant and researcher do not have to be involved in an interview.

Semi-structured interviews

Less formal than the questionnaire is the semi-structured interview. Here the questioner has an agenda: a specific topic to ask about and a set of questions which he or she wants answered. However, the exact wording of the questions is not considered critical and the order in which the questions are asked is not fixed. This allows the interview to flow more like a conversation. Nonetheless, the interviewer may have to steer the conversation back to the given topic and check that the original questions have been answered.

Free or unstructured interviews

Free interviews, as their name implies, need have no agenda and no prearranged questions. The conversation can be allowed to take whatever path the participants find most interesting. In the context of research, however, the researcher is likely to have some preliminary ideas which will guide at least the initial questions. Nonetheless, he or she is not going to constrain the conversation.

Choosing between the formats

The choice of format will depend on three factors. Firstly, the aims of the particular stage in the research will guide your choice. If the area you are studying is already well researched or you have a clear idea of the questions you wish to ask, then you are likely to want to use either a structured or a semi-structured interview. However, if you are exploring a relatively unresearched area and you do not want to predetermine the direction of the interview, then you are more likely to use a free interview.

Secondly, the choice between the structured and semi-structured formats will depend on how worried you are about interviewer effects. If you use a structured format, then you will minimise the dangers of different participants responding differently because questions were phrased differently and asked in a different order. A third factor which will determine your choice of format will be the setting in which the questioning will take place; a free interview is likely to be highly constrained when respondents are not present or responding via computer, and even talking on the phone constrains you.

The settings for asking questions

Face-to-face interviews

Face-to-face interviews involve the interviewer and participant being present together or, in the case of video link, able to see and hear each other in real time. The interviewer asks the questions and notes down the responses. Such interviews can occur in a number of places. They can be conducted: on the interviewer's territory, when participants visit the researcher's place of work; on the participant's territory, when the interviewer visits the participant's home or place of work; or with each on his or her own territory via video link. Finally, they can be conducted on neutral territory such as outside a shop. When conducted on the participant's territory you obviously need to take the usual precautions as you would when entering a strange area and more particularly a stranger's home. It would be worth letting some-one know where you are going and when to expect you back; many organisations have what is termed a *lone worker procedure* to cover such situations.

Self-completed surveys

Self-completed questionnaires are read by the participant, who then records his or her own responses. They can take a number of forms and occur in a number of places.

Interviewer present

Like the face-to-face interview, the researcher can be present. This has the advantage that if a partici-pant wants to ask a question it can be answered quickly. As with face-to-face interviews, these can be conducted on the researcher's territory, the participant's territory or in a neutral place. The arrangement could entail each participant being dealt with individually. Alternatively, the interviewer could intro-duce the questionnaire to a group of participants and then each participant could complete his or her copy of the questionnaire.

Postal surveys

Participants are given the questionnaire to complete on their own. They then have to return it to the researchers.

Internet and email surveys

With the Internet, a questionnaire can be posted on a website and responses sent to the researcher or logged and later imported to a database. Via email, particular user groups can be sent a questionnaire again for returning to the researcher (see Birnbaum, 2004; Hewson, 2003).

Telephone surveys

The questioner asks the questions and notes down the participant's responses.

The relative merits of the different settings

The nature of the sample

If it is important that the sample in a survey is representative of a particular population, then how the participants are chosen is important. See Chapter 11 for details of how to select a sample.

Response rate

An additional problem for attempts to obtain a representative sample is the proportion of people for whom questionnaires are not successfully completed. The people who have not taken part may share some characteristic which undermines the original basis for sampling. For example, the sample may lack many people from a particular socio-economic group because they have chosen not to take part.

The response rate for a postal survey is generally the poorest of the methods, although it is possi-ble to remind the sample, for example, by post or even telephone, which can improve the response rate. In a survey about student accommodation at Staffordshire University the initial response rate was 50% but with a poster campaign reminding people to return their questionnaires this was improved to 70%.

Telephone surveys can produce a better response rate as the survey can be completed, there and then, rather than left and forgotten. The response rate can be improved if you send a letter beforehand introducing yourself and possibly including a copy of the questionnaire. In this way, the respondents have some warning, as some people react badly to 'cold-calling'. However, we found (McGowan, Pitts, & Clark-Carter, 1999), when trying to survey general practitioners, that a heavily surveyed group may be quite resistant, even to telephone surveys and even when they have received a copy of the questionnaire. Although many may not refuse outright, they may put the researcher off to a future occasion.

Face-to-face surveys produce the best response rate but you can still meet resistance. I found when trying to survey visually impaired people in their own homes that one person was suspicious, despite my assurances, that I might pass the information to the Inland Revenue. If you are going to other people's houses you also have the obvious problem that the person may not be in when you call. In the case of both telephone and face-to-face interviews, it is worth setting yourself a target that you will not make more than a certain number of attempts to survey a given person.

You should send an introductory letter, beforehand, possibly mentioning a time when you would like to call. Also include a stamped, addressed postcard, and/or an email address which allows respondents to say that the time you suggest is inconvenient and to suggest an alternative. This serves the dual purpose of being polite and lessening the likelihood that the person will be out. Always carry some official means of identification as people are often encouraged not to let strangers into their houses. Do not assume that because you have sent a letter beforehand that respondents will remember any of the details, so be prepared to explain once again.

Motivation of respondents

If you want people to be honest and, more particularly, if you want them to disclose sensitive details about themselves, then there can be an advantage in being able to establish a rapport with them. This is obviously not easily achieved in a postal survey, or even in other situations where participants complete a questionnaire themselves, though a carefully worded letter can help. It is more possible to establish rapport over the phone and more so still with face-to-face interviews.

The anonymity of respondents

You may be more likely to get honest responses to sensitive questions if the respondents remain anonymous, but, because you have not managed to establish any relationship with them, they have less personal investment in the survey.

Interviewer effects

While establishing rapport has certain advantages, as with any research, there can be a danger that the researcher has an unintended effect upon participants' behaviour. In the case of interviewers, many aspects of the researcher may affect responses, and affect them differently for different respondents. In face-to-face interviews, the way researchers dress, their accent, their gender, the particular intonation they use when asking a question and other aspects of non-verbal communication can all have an effect on respondents. This can lead to answers which are felt by the respondent to be acceptable to the researcher. You can try to minimise the effects by dressing as neutrally as possible. However, what you consider neutral may be very formal to one person or overly casual to someone else.

If your sample is of a particular subgroup, then it would be reasonable to modify your dress to a certain extent. I do not mean by this that when interviewing punks you should wear their type of clothes unless you yourself are a punk; the attempt to dress appropriately may jar with other aspects of your behaviour and make your attempts seem comic or condescending. For this group simply dress more casually than you might have for visiting a sample of elderly people. Some of these factors, such as accent, intonation and gender, are present during a telephone conversation and none, bar possibly the gender of the researcher, are present in a postal, email or Internet-based survey.

As an interviewer you want to create a professional impression, so make sure that you are thoroughly familiar with the questionnaire. In this way, you should avoid stumbling over the wording and be aware of the particular routes through the questionnaire. That is, you will know what questions are appropriate for each respondent.

To avoid affecting a respondent's answers it is important that the interviewer use the exact wording which has been chosen for each question. Changing the wording can produce a different meaning and therefore a different response. Sometimes it may be necessary to use what are described as 'probes' to elicit an appropriate response: for example, when the answer which is required to a given question is either yes or no, but the interviewee says 'I'm not sure'. The important thing to remember about probes is that they should not lead in a particular direction; they should be neutral. Silence and a quizzical look may be enough to produce an appropriate response. If this does not work, then you could draw the interviewee's attention to the nature of the permissible responses, or with other questions you could say, 'Is there anything else?'

Beware of rephrasing what respondents say, particularly when they are answering open-ended questions. During the analysis stage of the research you will be looking for patterns of responses and common themes. These may be hidden if the answers have not been recorded exactly.

Maximum length of interview

Another advantage of being able to establish rapport can be that respondents will be more motivated to continue with a longer interview. If your questionnaire takes a long time to complete, then a postal survey is ill-advised. The length of telephone interviews and face-to-face interviews will depend on how busy the person is, how useful they perceive your survey as being and, possibly, how lonely they are. With face-to-face interviews in the person's own house, an interview can extend across a number of visits.

Cost

The question of cost will depend on the aims of the survey and who is conducting it. If the sample is to be representative and the population from which it is drawn is geographically widespread, then face-to-face interviewing will be the most expensive. Telephoning will be expensive if researchers cannot take advantage of cheap-rate calls. Postal surveys will be cheaper, though a follow-up, designed to improve response rate, will add to the costs. The cheapest can be email or Internet surveys unless you are having to pay someone to create the web pages. If the quality of the sample is less important, then a face-to-face interview can be relatively cheap. Interviewers can stand in particularly popular places and attempt to interview passers-by – an opportunity sample. However, if the interviewers have to be employed by the researchers, then this can add to the cost.

Whether interviewers can be supervised

When employing others to administer a questionnaire it is important to supervise them in some way. Firstly, you should give them some training. You may be sampling participants from a special population and using terminology which you and your potential respondents may know but which you could not assume that your questioners would know. For example, you may be surveying blind people and be using technical terms related to the causes of their visual impairment. You may also want to give the questioners an idea of how to interact with a particular group. This could involve role play. You also want to reassure yourself that their manner will be appropriate for someone interviewing other people.

The second point is that there may be advantages in your being available to deal with questions from interviewers during the interview. If the interviews are being conducted in a central place, either face-to-face or over the phone, then it is possible to be available to answer questions. When the interviewers phone or use video links from their own homes or visit respondents' territory you do not have this facility.

A third point is that you may wish to check the honesty of your interviewers. One way to do this is to contact a random subsample of the people they claim to have interviewed to see that the interview did take place and that it took the predicted length of time.

The ability to check responses

A badly completed questionnaire can render that participant's data unusable. Obviously, clear instructions and simple questions can help but with a paper version of a self-completed questionnaire you have no check that the person has filled in all the relevant questions; sometimes they may even have turned over two pages and left a whole page of questions uncompleted. A well-laid-out questionnaire will allow interviewers, either face-to-face or over the telephone, to guide the person through the questionnaire.

The questionnaire can be computerised and this could guide the interviewer or respondent through the questions and record the responses at the same time. In addition, there could be checks at specific points, such as after completion of a section of the questionnaire, after which the respondent is told if particular items haven't been completed. Computers can be used for self-administered questionnaires. The respondent could come to a central point or use the Internet with his or her own computer and link. A portable computer could be used by a questioner in the respondent's home.

The speed with which the survey can be conducted

If the responses for the whole sample are needed quickly, then the telephone can be the quickest method. For example, political opinion pollsters often use telephone surveys when they want to gauge the response to a given pronouncement from a politician. However, if the nature of the sample is not critical, then other quick methods can be to stand in a public place and ask passers-by, or use the Internet or email.

Aspects of the respondents which may affect the sample

If you go to people's homes during the day you will miss those who go out to work; you will also not sample the homeless. You can go in the evening but if you need to be accompanied by a translator or sign language user, their availability may be a problem.

If you use the telephone you will have difficulty with those who are deaf or do not speak your language, and you will miss those who do not have a phone. In addition, if you sample using the phone book you will miss those who do not use a landline, those who are ex-directory and those who have just moved into the area and not been put in the phone book. You could get around these latter two problems by dialling random numbers which are plausible for the area you wish to sample. You may get some business numbers but if they were not required in your sample you could stop the interview once you were aware that they were businesses. Finally, because people are phoned, both on landlines and mobile phones, by those wishing to sell them things or defraud them they are more cautious about answering the phone. They are helped to filter calls by call recognition which shows the number of the caller and allows them to avoid calls from numbers they don't recognise.

If you use a postal survey you will miss those who cannot read print – people who are visually impaired, dyslexic, illiterate or unable to read the language in which you have printed the questionnaire. At greater expense you could send a cassette version or even a video/DVD version but this also depends on people having the correct equipment. You could also translate the questionnaire into another language or into Braille. However, in the latter case, only a small proportion of visually impaired people would be able to read it. You obviously need to do preliminary research to familiarise yourself with the problems which your sample may present.

Surveys using the Internet can be useful for dealing with relatively rare conditions or people who aren't accessible by other means; for example, Murray, Macdonald, and Fox (2008) surveyed people who had self-harmed. They recruited their sample via self-harm Internet groups and discussion groups. However, as Murray et al. note, there is a danger of having a biased sample as those using such groups may be different from those who self-harm but don't use the groups. Bethlehem (2010) warns about self-selection in completing online surveys and how this can also bias results. See Birnbaum (2004) for a review of research using the Internet.

Degree of control over the order in which questions are answered

For some questionnaires, the order in which the questions are asked can have an effect on the responses which are given. For example, it is generally advisable to put more sensitive questions later in the questionnaire so that respondents are not put off straight away, but meet such questions once they have invested some time and have become more motivated to complete the questionnaire. A self-administered, paper-and-pencil questionnaire allows respondents to look ahead and realise the overall context of the questions. In addition, they can check that they have not contradicted themselves by looking back at their previous responses and thus create a false impression of consistency.

Group size

When you want a discussion to take place among a group of participants, such as a focus group, then there can be an optimal number of people. If you include too few people this may not provide a sufficient range of ideas to generate a useful discussion, while having too many people is likely to inhibit discussion. Morgan (1998) says that a group size of six to 10 people is usual. However, he notes that when you are dealing with a complex topic, you are sampling experts or want more detail from each person you may be better choosing even fewer than six, while when the members of your sample have low personal involvement in the topic or you want a wide range of opinion, then you might go for more than 10.

The choice of setting

If speed is important, the questionnaire is not too long, cost is a consideration and a relatively good response rate is required, then use a telephone survey or the Internet/email.

If neither cost nor time nor the danger of interviewer bias are problems, if the questionnaire is long, if a very high response rate is required and if the sample may be so varied or is of a special group where language may be a problem, then use a face-to-face technique.

If cost or anonymity are overriding considerations, if the response rate is not critical and the questionnaire is short, then use a postal survey or the Internet.

The choice of participants

The population

The population will be defined by the aims of the research, which in turn will be guided partly by the aspect of the topic that you are interested in and partly by whether you wish to generalise to a clearly defined population. Your research topic may define your population. For example, you may be interested in female students who smoke. Alternatively, your population might be less well specified, such as all potential voters in a given election.

The sample

How you select your sample will depend on three considerations. Firstly, it will depend on whether you wish to make estimates about the nature of your population from what you have found within your sample: for example, if you wanted to be able to estimate how many females in the student population smoked. A second consideration will be the setting you are adopting for the research. This in turn will interact with the third set of considerations, which will be practicalities such as the distance apart of participants and the costs of sampling.

See Chapter 11 for a description of the methods of sampling and for details of the statistical methods which can be used in sampling, including decisions about how many participants to include in the sample.

A census

A census means a survey which has attempted to include all the members of the population. In Britain, every 10 years there is a national census; a questionnaire is sent to every household, and householders are legally obliged to fill in the questionnaire.

What questions to include

Before any question is included ask yourself why you want to include that particular one. It is often tempting to include a question because it seemed interesting at the time but when you come to analysing the data you fail to do anything with it; think about what you are going to do with the information. You may have an idea of how people are going to respond to a given question but also consider what additional information you would want if they responded in a way which was possible but unexpected. Not to include such a follow-up question may lose useful information and even force the need for a follow-up questionnaire to find the answer.

Types of questions

Open-ended questions

Open-ended questions are those where respondents are not constrained to a pre-specified set of responses: for example, 'What brand of cigarettes do you smoke?'

Closed questions

Closed questions constrain the way the respondent can answer a fixed set of alternatives. Thus they could be of the form 'Do you smoke?' or 'Mark which age group you are in: 20–29, 30–39, 40–49 or 50–59'. A closed version of the question about the brands of cigarettes smoked would list the alternatives. One way to allow a certain flexibility in a closed question is to include the alternative *other* which allows unexpected alternatives to be given by the respondent, but remember to ask them to specify what that other is. Another form of closed question would be to give alternatives and ask respondents to rate them on some dimension. For example, you could give respondents a set of pictures of people and ask for a rating of how attractive the people portrayed are, on a scale from 'very attractive' to 'very unattractive'. Alternatively, the photos could be ranked on attractiveness, that is, placed in an order based on their perceived attractiveness. In addition to the preceding, there are standard forms of closed questions which are used for attitude questions; see Chapter 6 for a description of these.

Closed questions have certain advantages in that they give respondents a context for their replies and they can help jog their memories. In addition, they can increase the likelihood that a questionnaire will be completed because they are easier for self-administration and quicker to complete. Finally, they are easier to score for the analysis phase. However, they can overly constrain the possible answers. It is a good idea to include more open-ended questions in the original version of a questionnaire. During the pilot study respondents will provide a number of alternative responses which can be used to produce a closed version of the question.

A popular format for questions about health status, such as the amount of pain being experienced, is the *visual analogue scale* (VAS). Typically this involves a horizontal line, frequently 10 cm long, with a word or phrase at each end of the scale. The participant is asked to mark a point on the line which they feel reflects their experience.

No pain _____**The worst pain I have ever experienced**

The score would then be the number of millimetres, from the left end of the line, where the person has marked.

There are various alternative visual analogue scales, including a line of cartoon faces (or emojis) which represent degrees of pain from ☺ through ☺ to ☹ or in the form of a thermometer like the ones sometimes outside churches which show how the appeal fund is progressing.

Filter questions

Your sample may include people who will respond in some fundamentally different ways and you may wish to explore those differences further. In this case, rather than ask inappropriate questions of some people you can include filter questions which guide people to the section which is appropriate for them. For example, 'If you smoke, go to question 7; otherwise go to question 31'.

Badly worded questions

There are many ways in which you can create bad questions. They should be avoided as they can create an impression that the questionnaire has been created sloppily and can confuse participants as to what the question means. Alternatively, they can suggest what response is expected or desired. The outcome can be that the answers will be less valid and the participants may be less motivated to fill in the questionnaire. Why should they invest time if you do not appear to have done so? In addition, you may not know the meaning of the responses. Many of the following points pertain to bad writing in general.

Questions which contain technical language or jargon

There is not much point in asking a question if your respondents do not know the terms you are using: for example, 'Do you suffer from dyspnoea?' It is generally possible to express yourself in simpler words (for example, 'Do you suffer from breathlessness?') but this can be at the cost of a longer question which in itself can be difficult to understand. The advantage of a phone or face-to-face interview is that you can find out whether respondents understand the terms and explain them, if necessary. Nonetheless, keep technical terminology to a minimum and do not use unnecessary abbreviations for the same reason.

Ambiguous questions

An example of an ambiguous question would be, 'Do you remember where you were when Kennedy was assassinated?' Even if the person was aware that you were talking about members of the famous American family, both John and Robert Kennedy were assassinated so it is unclear which one you mean.

Vague questions

Vague questions are those which, like ambiguous questions, could be interpreted by different people in different ways because you have failed to give sufficient guidance. For example, the answer to 'Do you drink much alcohol?' depends on what you mean by *much*. I might drink a glass of wine every day and consider that to be moderate, while another person might see me as a near alcoholic and a third person might see me as a near teetotaller, depending on their own habits, and each would see themselves as moderate drinkers. Better to give a range of possible amounts of alcohol from which they can indicate their consumption.

Leading questions

A leading question is one which indicates to the participant the response which is expected. For example, 'Do you believe in the myth that big boys don't cry?' suggests that the participant should not agree with the statement.

Questions with poor range indicators

If you give alternatives and you only want respondents to choose one, then they must be mutually exclusive; in other words, it should not be possible to fulfil more than one alternative. Imagine the difficulty for a 30-year-old when asked, 'Indicate which age group you are in: 20–30, 30–40, 40–50, 50–60'.

Questions with built-in assumptions

Some questions are inappropriate for some respondents and yet imply that everyone can answer them. An example would be 'What word-processing package do you use?' without giving the option *none*. A more common occurrence can be a question of the form: 'Does your mother smoke?' There are a number of reasons why this might not be appropriate – the person never knew his or her mother, or the mother is now dead.

Double-barrelled questions

Some questions involve two or more elements but only allow the respondent to answer one of them. Often they can be an extension of the question with a built-in assumption. For example, 'When you have a shower do you use a shower gel?' If you only have baths you have difficulty answering this question, for if you reply *no*, then this might suggest that you do have showers but only use a bar of soap to wash.

The use of double negatives

Double negatives are difficult to understand. For example, 'Do you agree with the statement: lawyers are paid a not inconsiderable amount?' If the questioner wants to know whether people think that lawyers are paid a large amount, then it would be better to say so directly.

Sensitive questions

Sensitive questions can range from demographic ones about age and income to questions about illegal behaviour or behaviour which transgresses social norms. Sensitive questions about demographic details can be made more acceptable by giving ranges rather than requiring exact information. Sometimes the sensitivity may simply apply to saying a person's age out loud, in which case you could ask for dates of birth and work out ages afterwards.

Behaviour questions can be more problematic. Assurances of anonymity can help but it may be necessary to word the question in such a way that it defuses the sensitivity of the question to a certain extent. For example, if asking about drug taking you may lead up to the question in a roundabout way, by having preliminary comments which suggest that you are aware that many people take drugs and possibly asking whether the participant's friends take drugs, and then asking the participant whether he or she does.

The layout of the questionnaire

The layout of a questionnaire can make it more readable and help to create a more professional air for the research, which in turn will make participants more motivated to complete it. This not only applies to self-completed questionnaires but can also help the interview run more smoothly whether it is administered face-to-face or over the telephone.

Break down the questionnaire into sections. For example, in a questionnaire on smoking you might have a section for demographic questions, a section on smoking behaviour, a section on attitudes to smoking, a section on knowledge about health and a section on the influence of others. This gives the questionnaire coherence and a context for the questions in a given section. Include filter questions where necessary. This may increase the complexity of administering the questionnaire but it will mean that participants are not asked inappropriate questions.

Provide instructions and explanatory notes for the entire questionnaire and for each section.

The use of space

Use only one side of the paper as this will lessen the likelihood that a page of questions will be missed. Follow the usual guidance for the layout of text by giving a good ratio of 'white space' to text (Wright, 1983). This will not only make it more readable but will also allow the person scoring the sheets reasonable space to make comments and make coding easier. Use reasonably sized margins, particularly side margins. When giving alternatives in a closed question, list them vertically rather than horizontally. For example:

How do you travel to work?
  on foot
  by bicycle
  by bus
  by train
  by another person's car
  by own car
  other (please specify).

Leave enough space for people to respond as much as they want to open-ended questions but not so much space that they feel daunted by it.

Order of questions

You want to motivate respondents, not put them off. Accordingly, put interesting but simple questions first, closed rather than open-ended first for ease of completion, and put the more sensitive questions last. Vary the question format, if possible, to maintain interest and to prevent participants from responding automatically without considering the question properly. You may wish to control the order of the sections so that when participants answer one section, they are not fully aware of other questions which you are going to ask. For example, you may ask behaviour questions before asking attitude questions.

If you are concerned that the specific order of questions or the wording of given questions can affect the responses, then you can adopt a *split-ballot* approach. This simply means that you create two versions of the questionnaire with the different orders/wording and give half your sample one version and half the other. You can then compare responses to see whether the participants who received the different versions responded differently. If you do have such concerns, then try them out at the pilot stage.

The pilot study

The pilot study is critical for a questionnaire for which you have created the questions or when you are trying an existing questionnaire on a new population. As usual it should be conducted on people who are from your target population. It is worth using a larger number of people in a pilot study where you are devising the measure than you would when using an existing measure such as in an experiment.

The pilot study can perform two roles. Firstly, it can help you refine your questionnaire. It can provide you with a range of responses to your open-ended questions and you can turn them into closed ones by including the alternatives which you have been given. Secondly, it can tell you the usefulness of a question. If everyone answers the question in the same way, then it can be dropped as it is redundant. If a question is badly worded, then this should become clear during the pilot study and you can rephrase it.

Summary

Researchers who wish to ask questions of their participants have to choose the topics of the questions – demographic, behavioural and attitude/opinion/belief or, where required, aspects of health status. They have to choose the format of the questioning – structured, semi-structured or free. In addition, they have to choose the settings for the questioning – face-to-face, self-completed by participants or over the telephone. Once these choices have been made it is necessary to refine the wording of the questions and choose the order in which they are asked and the layout of the questionnaire. Before the final study is carried out it is essential that a pilot study be conducted. This is particularly important when the researchers have devised the questionnaire.

The next chapter deals with the design and conduct of attitude questionnaires.

6 Asking questions II
Measuring attitudes and meaning

Introduction

There are many situations in which researchers want to measure people's attitudes. They may wish to explore a particular area to find out the variety of attitudes which exist – for example, people's views on animal welfare. Alternatively, they may want to find out how people feel about a specific thing – for example, whether the government is doing a good job. Yet again, they may wish to relate attitudes to aspects of behaviour – for example, to find out how people's attitudes to various forms of contraception relate to their use of such methods.

One way to find out people's attitudes is to ask them. A number of techniques have been devised to do this. This chapter describes three attitude scales which you are likely to meet when reading research into attitudes: the Thurstone, Guttman and Likert scales. It explains why the Likert scale has become the most frequently employed measure of attitudes. In addition, it describes four other methods which have been used to explore what certain entities mean to people: the semantic differential, Q-methodology, repertory grids and facet theory.

Reliability of measures

If we wanted to find out a person's attitude to something, such as his or her political attitude, we might be tempted to ask a single question, for example:

Do you like the policies of Conservative politicians? (Yes/No)

If you are trying to predict voting behaviour this may be a reasonable question. However, the question would fail to identify the subtleties of political attitude, as it assumes that there is a simple dichotomy between those who do and those who do not like such policies. Frequently, when confronted with such a question people will say that it depends on which policy is being considered. Thus, if a particular policy with which they disagreed was being given prominence in the media they might answer *No*, whereas if a policy with which they agreed was more prominent, they are likely to answer *Yes*. Yet, if attitudes are relatively constant we would want a measure which reflected this constancy. In other words, we want a reliable measure. A single question is generally an unreliable measure of attitudes.

To avoid the unreliability of single questions, researchers have devised multi-item scales. The answer to a single question may change from occasion to occasion, but the responses to a set of questions will provide a score which should remain relatively constant. A multi-item scale has the additional advantage that a given person's attitude can be placed on a dimension from having a positive attitude towards something to having a negative attitude towards it. In this way, the relative attitudes of different people can be compared in a more precise way.

Dimensions

The use of multi-item scales also allows researchers to explore the subtleties of attitudes to see whether a single dimension exists or whether there is more than one dimension. For example, in political attitudes it might be felt that there exists a single dimension from left-wing to right-wing. However, other dimensions also exist, such as libertarian–authoritarian. Thus, there are right-wing libertarians and left-wing libertarians, just as there are right-wing authoritarians and left-wing authoritarians. Therefore, if researchers wished to explore the domain of political attitude they would want some questions which identified where a person was on the left–right dimension and some questions which identified where he or she was on the libertarian–authoritarian dimension.

The three scales described next deal with the issue of dimensions in different ways. The Thurstone scale ignores the problem and treats attitudes as though they were on a single dimension. The Guttman scale recognises the problem and tries to produce a scale which is unidimensional (having one dimension) by removing questions which refer to other dimensions. The Likert scale explores the range of attitudes and can contain sub-scales which address different dimensions. The creation of any of these three scales involves producing a set of questions or statements and then selecting the most appropriate among them on the basis of how a sample of people have responded to them. As you will see, the criteria for what constitutes an appropriate statement depend on the particular scale.

However, the criteria of all three types of scale share certain features. As with all questionnaires, try to avoid badly worded questions or statements; refer to the previous chapter for a description of the common mistakes. Once you have produced an initial set of statements, as with any research, carry out a small pilot study to check that the wording of the statements, despite your best efforts, is not faulty. Then, once you have satisfied yourself on this point, you are ready to carry out the fuller study to explore your attitude scale.

Attitude scales

Thurstone scale

A Thurstone scale (Thurstone, 1931; Thurstone & Chave, 1929) is designed to have a set of questions which have different values from each other on a dimension. Respondents identify the statements with which they agree. For example, in a scale designed to measure attitudes about animal welfare, the statements might range from

Humans have a perfect right to hunt animals for pleasure.

to

No animal should be killed for the benefit of humans.

The designer of the scale gets judges to rate each statement as to where it lies on the dimension – for example, from totally unconcerned about animal welfare to highly concerned about animal welfare. On the basis of the ratings, a set of statements is chosen, such that the statements have ratings which are as equally spaced as possible across the range of possible values. Once the final set of statements has been chosen, it can be used in research. A participant's score on the scale is the mean value of the ratings of the statements with which he or she has agreed.

Choosing the statements

Compile a set of approximately 60 statements which are relevant to the attitude you wish to measure. Word the statements in such a way that they represent the complete range of possible attitudes. Place the statements in a random order rather than one based on their assumed position on the dimension.

Exploring the scale

Ask at least 100 judges to rate each statement on an 11-point scale. For example, a judge might be asked to rate the statements given previously as to where they lie on the dimension ranging from totally unconcerned about animal welfare (which would get a rating of 1) to highly concerned about animal welfare (which would get a rating of 11). They are not being asked to give their own attitudes to animals but their opinions about where each statement lies on the dimension.

Item analysis

The average (the mean) rating for each statement is calculated, as is a measure of how well judges agreed about each statement's rating (the standard deviation). The calculation of these two statistics is dealt with in Chapter 9.

Put the statements in order, based on the size of the mean rating for each statement, and identify statements which are given, approximately, mean ratings for each half-point on the scale. Thus, there should be statements with a rating of 1, others with a rating of 1.5 and so on up to a rating of 11. It is likely that you will have statements with similar ratings. Choose, for each interval on the scale, the question over which there was the most agreement, that is, with the smallest standard deviation. Discard the other statements. Place the selected statements in random order and add the possible response (agree/disagree) to each statement.

Criticisms of the Thurstone scale

The first criticism was mentioned earlier. Thurstone scales assume that the attitude being measured is on a single dimension but do not check whether this is the case. Secondly, two people achieving the same score on the scale, particularly in the mid-range of scores, could have achieved their scores from different patterns of responses. Thus, a given score does not denote a single attitude and so is not distinguishing clearly between people. A third criticism is that a large number of statements have to be created, to begin with, in order to stand a chance of ending with a set of equally spaced questions across the assumed dimension. Finally, a lot of people have to act as judges.

A Guttman scale deals with all but the last of these problems.

Guttman scale

The creation of a Guttman scale (Guttman, 1944) also involves statements with which respondents agree or disagree. Once again, a set of statements is designed to sample the range of possible attitudes. They are given to a sample of people and the pattern of responses is examined. The structure of a Guttman scale is such that the statements are forced to be on a single dimension. The statements are phrased in such a way that a person with an attitude at one end of the scale would agree with none of the items while a person with an attitude at the other end of the dimension would agree with all of the statements. Thus, a measure of attitudes to animal welfare might have statements ranging from:

It is acceptable to experiment on animals for medical purposes.

through

It is acceptable to experiment on animals for cosmetic purposes.

to

It is acceptable to experiment on animals for any reason.

If these items formed a Guttman scale, then a person agreeing with the final item should also agree with the previous ones and a person disagreeing with the first item should disagree with all the other items. Statements which do not fit into this pattern would be discarded. In this way, a person's score is based on how far along the dimension he or she is willing to agree with statements. Thus, if these statements formed a 3-point scale, agreeing with the first one would score 1, agreeing with the second one would score 2 and agreeing with the last one would score 3. Accordingly, two people with the same score can be said to lie at the same point on the dimension.

Bogardus social distance scale

The Bogardus social distance scale (Bogardus, 1925) can be seen as a version of the Guttman scale, in that it produces a scale which is unidimensional. In this case, the dimension is to do with how much contact a person would be willing to have with people who have certain characteristics, such as race or a disability. The items on the scale could range from asking about the respondent's willingness to allow people of a given race to visit his or her country to willingness to let them marry a member of the respondent's family.

Criticism of the Guttman scale

The very strength of dealing strictly with a single dimension means that, unless sub-scales are created to look at different, related dimensions, a Guttman scale misses the subtleties of attitudes about a given topic. For example, a Guttman scale looking at attitudes to race issues would probably require different scales for different races.

A Likert scale explores the dimensions within attitudes to a given topic and can contain sub-scales. It has become the most popular scaling technique.

Likert scale

Each item in a Likert scale (Likert, 1932) is a statement with which respondents can indicate their level of agreement on a dimension of possible responses. An example of the type of statement could again be:

No animal should be killed for the benefit of humans.

Typically the range of possible responses will be of the following form:

Strongly agree	*Agree*	*Undecided*	*Disagree*	*Strongly disagree*

I recommend that a 5- or a 7-point scale be used. Fewer points on the scale will miss the range of attitudes, while more points will require an artificial level of precision, as people will often not be able to provide such a subtle response. In addition, an odd number of possible responses can include a neutral position; not having such a possible response forces people to make a decision in a particular direction, when they may be undecided, and this can produce an unreliable measure.

Choosing the statements

I think you need at least 20 statements which are designed to evaluate a person's attitude to the topic you have chosen, because some are likely to be found not to be useful when you analyse people's responses. Remember that you want to distinguish between people's attitudes, so don't include items that everyone will agree with or that everyone will disagree with, for they will be redundant.

Wording of statements

In accordance with the previous point, don't make the statements too extreme; let the respondent indicate his or her level of agreement by the response chosen.

Phrase roughly half of the statements in the opposite direction to the rest. For example, if your scale was to do with attitudes to smoking, then half the statements should require people who were positively disposed towards smoking to reply *Agree* or *Strongly agree*, while the other half of the statements should require them to reply *Disagree* or *Strongly disagree*. In this way, you force respondents to read the statements and you may avoid what is termed a *response bias* – that is, a tendency by a given person to use one side of the range of responses. This does not mean that you simply take an existing, positively worded statement and produce a negative version of the same statement to add to the scale.

Part of the reason for the last point is that you are trying to explore the range of attitudes which exist and so you do not want redundant statements which add nothing to what is already covered by other questions. However, it may not always be possible to identify what will be a redundant question in advance of conducting the study.

Sample size

Chapter 13 contains an explanation for the choice of sample size for a given study. For the moment I will give the rule of thumb that sampling at least 68 people will mean that you are giving your questions a reasonable chance of showing themselves as useful in the analysis that you will conduct. To use fewer people would increase the likelihood that you would reject a question as not useful when it is measuring an aspect of the attitude under consideration.

Analysing the scale

There are two aspects to the analysis which can be conducted of the responses which you have been given by those in your sample. The first looks to see whether the attitude scale is measuring one or more dimensions; this will also identify statements which do not appear to be sufficiently related to the other statements in the scale. This can be done by exploratory factor analysis or by item analysis. The second aspect of analysis checks whether a given statement is receiving a sufficient range of responses – the discriminative power of the statement; remember that if everyone gives the same or very similar responses to a statement, even though their attitudes differ, then there is no point in including it as it does not tell you how people differ.

Chapters 9 and 19 cover the material on the statistical techniques used in the two analyses. Following is given a description of what item and discriminative analyses entail. For a fuller description of the process see Appendix XIV and for a description of exploratory factor analysis see Chapter 24 and Appendix XV.

Scoring the responses

Using a 5-point scale as an example, choose to score the negative side of the scale as 1 and the positive end as 5. For example, if your scale was about attitudes to animals, then a response which implied an extremely unfavourable attitude to animals would be scored 1, while a response which implied an extremely favourable attitude to animals would be scored 5. Thus, you will need to reverse the scoring of those statements which are worded so that agreement suggested a negative attitude to animals. For example, if the statement was of the form *Fox hunting is a good thing*, then extreme agreement would be scored 1, while extreme disagreement would be scored 5. This can be done in a straightforward manner and you can get the computer to do the reversing for you. Entering the data onto the computer in their original form is less prone to error than trying to reverse the scores before putting them into the computer. Appendix XIV describes how to reverse scores once they are entered into the computer.

Once the responses have been scored, and those items which need it have been reversed, find the total score for each respondent by simply adding together all that person's responses for each statement.

Conducting an item analysis

Statements which are part of a single dimension should correlate well with each other and with the total score; for two statements to correlate (in this context), people who give a high score to one statement will tend to give a high score to the other and those who give a low score to one will tend to give a low score to the other. Those statements which form a separate dimension will not correlate well with the total score but will correlate with each other. For example, in a study on attitudes to the British royal family, a group of students found that, in addition to the main dimension, there was a dimension which related to the way the royal family was portrayed in the newspapers.

If a statement does not correlate reasonably well with the total score or with other statements, then it should be discarded. It would be worth examining such statements to see what you could identify about them that might have produced this result. They may still be badly worded, despite having been tested in the pilot study. It could be that people differed little in the way they responded to a given item; for if there was not a range of scores for that statement, then it would not correlate with the total. Alternatively, although you included the statement because you thought that it was relevant to the attitude, this result may demonstrate that it is not relevant after all.

Analysing discriminatory power

Discard the items which failed the item analysis and conduct a separate analysis of discriminatory power for each dimension (or sub-scale) that you have identified. For each dimension find a new total score for each respondent. Find out which respondents were giving the top 25% of total scores and which were giving the bottom 25% of total scores.[3] You can then take each statement which is relevant to that dimension and see whether these two groups differ in the way they responded to it. If a statement fails to distinguish between those who give high scores and those who give low scores on the total scale, then that statement has poor discriminative power and can be dropped.

Kline (2000) recommends, where feasible, the use of exploratory factor analysis. An advantage of factor analysis is that it is designed to identify whether there is more than one scale being measured by a set of questions. A disadvantage is that it needs a larger sample than item analysis; for example, with two sub-scales and his recommended minimum of 20 items per sub-scale you would need a minimum of 120 people and preferably more than 200. Kline notes that where a single scale is being created and when the sample is relatively small, then item analysis can be used. However, even in these

---

3 Other proportions can be used, such as the top and bottom thirds.

circumstances, he recommends following it with factor analysis to check that only one scale is involved. See Chapter 24 for further advice on sample size in factor analysis.

Whichever analysis you employ, once you have refined the scale it is usual to find a measure of the scale's reliability. A common measure used with questionnaires based on a Likert scale is Cronbach's alpha. This is described and discussed in Chapter 19.

Criticism of Likert scales

Like Thurstone scales, two people with the same score on a Likert scale may have different patterns of responding. Accordingly, we cannot treat a given score as having a unique meaning about a person's attitude.

 Techniques to measure meaning

Q-methodology

Q-methodology is an approach to research which was devised by Stephenson (1953). It requires participants or judges to rate statements or other elements on a given dimension or on a given basis. One technique which Q-methodology employs is getting participants to perform Q-sorts. Typically a Q-sort involves participants being presented with a set of statements, each on an individual card, and being asked to place those statements on a dimension, such as from *very important to me* to *not important to me*. (Kerlinger, 1973, recommends that, for a Q-sort to be reliable, the number of statements should normally be no fewer than 60 but no more than 90.) The ratings can then be used in at least three ways. Firstly, similarities between people in the way they rate the elements can be sought. For example, researchers could ask potential voters to rank a set of statements in order of importance. The statements might include *inflation should be kept low, pensions should be increased, the current funding of health care should be maintained* and *we should maintain our present expenditure on defence*. The rankings could then be explored to see whether there is a consensus among voters as to what issues are seen to be the most important.

A second, and more interesting, use of Q-methodology can be to explore different subgroups of people who would produce similar rankings but would differ from other subgroups. Thus, in the previous example you might find that some people ranked pensions and the funding of health care as the most important, while others put higher priorities on defence and inflation, and a third group might see environmental issues as paramount.

A third use of Q-methodology can be to examine the degree of agreement which an individual has when rating different objects on the same scale. I could explore the degree to which a person views his or her parents as being similar by getting that person to rank a set of statements on the basis of how well they describe one parent and then to repeat the ranking of the statements for the second parent. Once again, I could get a number of people to do these rankings for each of their parents and then look to see whether there is a group of people who rank both their parents in a similar fashion and another group of people who rank each parent differently.

Rogers (1951, 1961) has used Q-sorts in the context of counselling. For example, a person attending counselling could be asked to rate statements on an 11-point scale on the basis of how typical the statements are of him- or herself. This Q-sort could be compared with another done on the basis of how typical the statements are of how the person would like to be (his or her ideal self). At various points during the period when the person is receiving counselling, the Q-sorts would be repeated. The aim of counselling would be to bring these two Q-sorts into greater agreement, either by improving a person's self-image or by making his or her ideal self more realistic. In addition, Rogers has used

Q-methodology to investigate how closely counsellors and their clients agree over certain issues. In this case, the counsellor and his or her client are given statements and asked to rank them in order of importance. According to Rogers, the degree of agreement between the two orderings can be a good predictor of the outcome of counselling.

Q-methodology can be used to explore theories. For example, rankings or sortings could be used to explore the different meanings which a concept has. Stenner and Marshall (1995) used this technique to investigate the different meanings which people have for *rebelliousness*. It is this latest use of the method which has produced a resurgence of interest, with other areas being investigated including *maturity* (Stenner & Marshall, 1999), *jealousy* (Stenner & Stainton Rogers, 1998), the beliefs of music teachers (Hewitt, 2006) and attitudes to help-seeking behaviour in men with depression (House, Marasli, Lister, & Brown, 2018).

Criticisms of Q-methodology

Often the people doing the sorting are forced to sort the statements according to a certain pattern. For example, they may be told how many statements can be given the score 1, how many 2 and so on throughout the scale. A typical pattern would be so that the piles of statements formed a 'normal distribution' (see Chapter 9 for an explanation of this term). A second criticism is over the statistical techniques which are applied to Q-methodology. As you will see in the relevant chapters on data analysis, certain techniques, such as analysis of variance (see Chapter 16) or factor analysis (see Chapter 24), are looking at the pattern of data across a number of people. However, some users of Q-methodology use such statistical techniques on data derived from a single person or to find clusters of people with similar sortings rather than clusters of statements which are similar.

Taking these criticisms into consideration, it would be best to use Q-methodology for exploratory purposes rather than to place too much faith in the statistical techniques which have been applied to it; in fact, that is how Stainton Rogers and his co-workers have been using it (see Stainton Rogers, 1995).

The semantic differential

Osgood, Suci, and Tannenbaum (1957) devised the semantic differential as a means of exploring a person's way of thinking about some entity or, as they put it, of measuring meaning quantitatively. An example they give is investigating how people view politicians. They suggested that there is a semantic space with many dimensions, in which a person's meaning for a given entity (e.g. a politician) will lie. They contrasted their method with other contemporary ones in that theirs was explicitly multi-dimensional, while others involved only one dimension.

Participants are given a list of bipolar adjective pairs such as *good–bad, fast–slow, active–passive, dry–wet, sharp–dull* and *hard–soft* and are asked to rate the entities (the politicians), one at a time, on a 7-point scale – 1 for *good* and 7 for *bad* – for each of the adjective pairs. They recommend the following layout:

Margaret Thatcher

fair							X	unfair
fast	X							slow
active	X							passive

The person making the ratings puts a cross in the open-topped box that seems most appropriate for that entity for each adjective pair.

Semantic differentiation is the process of placing a concept within the semantic space by rating it on each of the bipolar adjective pairs. The difference in meaning between two concepts can be seen by where they are placed in the semantic space. The responses for a given person or a group of people are analysed to see whether they form any patterns (factors). A common pattern is for the ratings to form three dimensions: *evaluation*, e.g. *clean–dirty*; *potency*, e.g. *strong–weak*; and *activity*, e.g. *fast–slow*.

The particular set of bipolar adjective pairs which are useful will depend on the particular study. Osgood et al. (1957) note that *beautiful–ugly* may be irrelevant when rating a presidential candidate but *fair–unfair* may be relevant, while for rating paintings the reverse is likely to be true. They provide a list of 50 adjective pairs.

The semantic differential can be used for a number of purposes: to explore an individual's attitudes, say, to a political party; to compare individuals to see what differences existed between people in the meanings which entities had for them; or to evaluate change after a therapy or after an experimental manipulation.

The results of the ratings gleaned from using the semantic differential can be analysed via multi-dimensional scaling (MDS; see Chapter 25). Osgood and Luria (1954) applied the method to a famous case of a patient who had been diagnosed with multiple personality. They looked at sortings from the three 'personalities' taken at two times separated by a period of 2 months to see how they differed and how they changed over time.

Repertory grids

Kelly (1955) developed a number of techniques which allow investigators or therapists to explore an individual's meanings and associations. For example, they could be used to explore how a smoker views smoking, by looking at how he or she views smokers and non-smokers and people who are not identified as either. The techniques stem from Kelly's personal construct theory, in which he views individuals as thinking in similar ways to scientists in that they build up a mental model of the world in which *elements* (for example, people) are categorised according to the presence or absence of certain *constructs* (for example, likableness).

A repertory grid typically involves asking an individual to think of two people (for example, the person's parents) and to think of one way in which they are similar. That similarity then forms the first construct in the grid. The nature of the constructs which people provide says something about them, as this shows what is salient to them, what bases they use to classify aspects of their world – in this case, people. They could use psychological constructs such as *nice*, or purely physical ones such as *old*. After providing the first construct, the person will be asked to consider a third person (say, a sibling) and think of a way in which this third person differs from the previous two. If this entails a new construct, then this is added to the grid. This process is continued until a set of elements is created and each is evaluated on each construct. The way the elements are perceived in terms of the constructs is analysed to look for patterns using techniques such as cluster analysis (see Chapter 25).

Repertory grids can be used in a therapeutic setting to see how a patient views the world and how that view changes during therapy. Alternatively, they could be used for research purposes to see how a particular group is viewed, such as how blind people are thought of by those who do not have a visual impairment. For an account of the use of repertory grids and other aspects of personal construct theory, as used in clinical psychology, see Winter (1992), Walker and Winter (2007).

Facet theory

Another approach which had early origins but which has shown a relatively recent resurgence of interest is facet theory. It was developed by Guttman in the 1950s but has been taken up by others wishing to explore the meanings and ways of structuring the elements in such diverse domains as intelligence, fairness, colour or even criminal behaviour. The Guttman scale, described earlier, can be seen as the simplest way in which people conceptualise a domain – i.e. on a single dimension. More complex conceptions take into account the multi-dimensional nature of much of what we think about. Thus, intelligence could be thought of as ranging from low intelligence to high intelligence, while more complex conceptions would include the type of task – numerical, spatial, verbal or social. Greater complexity still would be taken into account if types of tasks were separated into those where a rule is being identified, those where one is being recalled and those where one is being applied. A final layer of complexity would come if we allowed for the 'mode of expression' such as whether the task was performed by the manipulation of objects or by pencil and paper tests. Although the two-dimensional structures can be analysed using standard statistical software, such as Multiple Dimensional Scaling in SPSS (see Chapter 25), more complex structures involve specialist software (see Shye, Elizur, & Hoffman, 1994).

Summary

Multi-item scales are preferred for assessing people's attitudes because they are more reliable than single questions which are designed to assess the same attitude. Such scales require the creation of a large number of items which have to be evaluated on a reasonable sample of people before they are used in research. You should never devise a set of questions to measure an attitude and use it without having conducted an analysis of the items to see whether they do form a scale. The most popular scale at present is the Likert scale. Psychologists also use a number of other means to assess what people think of aspects of their lives – in particular, what such things mean to people.

The next chapter deals with observing people's behaviour.

7   Observation and content analysis

Introduction

The present chapter describes two methods which, on the surface, may not appear the same but in fact entail similar problems and similar solutions. Observation tends to be thought of in the context of noting the behaviour of people, while content analysis is usually associated with analysing text. However, given that one can observe behaviour which has been videoed and that content analysis has been applied to television adverts, the distinctions between the two methods can become blurred. In fact, as was pointed out in Chapter 2, all psychological research can be seen as being based on the observation and measurement of behaviour – whether it involves overt movement, language or physiological states – for we cannot directly observe thought. Nonetheless, I will restrict the meaning of observation, in this chapter, to the observation of some form of movement or speech.

Both observation and content analysis can be conducted qualitatively or quantitatively. I am going to concentrate on the quantitative approach, but many of the methodological points made in this chapter should guide someone conducting qualitative research. Because of the overlap between the two methods I will start by describing observation and then look at aspects of research which are common to the two methods. I will describe a form of structured observation and, finally, look at content analysis, including the use of diaries and logs as sources of data.

Observation

When applicable

There are a number of situations in which we might want to conduct an observation. Usually, it will be when there is no accurate verbal report available. One such occasion would be when the people being studied have little or no language, such as young children. Alternatively, we might wish to observe behaviour which occurs without the person producing it being aware of what he or she is doing, as in much non-verbal communication, such as making eye contact. Another area worth exploring is where researchers are interested in problem-solving. Experts, such as doctors attempting to diagnose diseases, often do not follow the path of reasoning that they were taught, yet when asked to describe the procedure they use will, nonetheless, report using the method they were originally taught. Observation would help to clarify the stages such diagnosis takes.

A fourth situation in which it would be appropriate to use observation would be when participants may wish to present themselves in a favourable light, such as people who are prejudiced against an ethnic minority and might not admit how they would behave towards members of that minority group. However, even if accurate verbal reports are available it would be worth conducting observation to complement such reports.

Types of observation

There are numerous ways in which observations can be classified. One way is based on the degree to which the observer is part of the behaviour being observed. This can range from the *complete participant*, whose role as an observer might be hidden from the other participants, to the *complete observer*, who does not participate at all and whose role is also kept from the people who are being observed. An example of the first could be a researcher who covertly joins an organisation to observe it from within. The second could involve watching people in a shopping centre to see how they utilise the space. Between these two extremes are a number of gradations. One is the *participant-as-observer*, which, as the name suggests, involves researchers taking part in the activity to be observed but revealing that they are researchers. The complete participant and the participant-as-observer are sometimes described as doing ethnographic research.

Next in distance from direct participation is the *marginal participant*: researchers might have taken steps, such as wearing particular clothing, in order to be unobtrusive. Next comes the *observer-as-participant*: researchers would reveal the fact that they were observing but not participating directly in the action being observed. Such a classification makes the important point that the presence of researchers can have an effect on others' behaviour and so, at some level, most observers are participating.

Another way in which types of observation are classified relates to the level at which the behaviour is being observed and recorded. *Molar* behaviour refers to larger-scale behaviour such as greeting a person who enters the room; this level of observation can involve interpretation by the observer as to the nature of the behaviour. On the other hand, *molecular* behaviour refers to the components which make up molar behaviour, and is less likely to involve interpretation. For example, a molecular description of the behaviour described earlier as greeting a person who enters the room might be stated thus: 'extends hand to newcomer; grips newcomer's hand and shakes it; turns corners of mouth up and makes eye contact, briefly; lets go of newcomer's hand'.

A further way of classifying observation depends on the degree to which the nature of the observation is predetermined. This can range from what is termed *informal* or *casual* observation to *formal* or *systematic* observation. In informal observation the researchers might note what strikes them as being of interest at the time; this approach may often be a precursor to systematic observation and will be used to get a feel for the range of possible behaviours. In systematic observation, researchers may be looking for specific aspects of behaviour with the view to testing hypotheses.

A final way to view types of observation is according to the theoretical perspectives of the researchers. *Ethology* – the study of animals and humans in their natural setting – is likely to entail observation of more molecular behaviour and use little interpretation. *Structured* observation may use more interpretation and observe more molar behaviour. *Ethnography* may entail more casual observation and interpretation, as well as introspection on the part of the observer. Those employing *ecological* observation will be interested in the context and setting in which the behaviour occurred and will be interested in inferring the meanings and intentions of the participants.

The use of words such as *may* and *likely* in the previous paragraph comes from my belief that none of these ways of classifying observation is describing mutually exclusive ways of conducting observation. Different ways are complementary and may be used by the same researchers, in a form of triangulation. Alternatively, different approaches may form different stages in a single piece of research, as suggested earlier.

Gaining access

If you are going to observe a situation which does not have public access – for example, a school, a prison, a mental institution or a company – you have an initial hurdle to overcome: gaining access to the people carrying out their daily tasks. If you are going to be totally covert, then you will probably have to join the institution by the same means that the other members have joined it. Before choosing to be totally covert you should consider the ethical issues involved (see Chapter 1). On the other hand, you can gain access without revealing to everyone what your intentions are if you take someone in the organisation into your confidence. However, even if you are going to be completely open about your role as a researcher you are going to need someone who will help introduce you and give your task some legitimacy.

Beware of becoming too identified with that person; people may not like that person or may worry about what you might reveal to that person, and this may colour their behaviour towards you.

You will need to reassure people about your aims. This may involve modifying what you say so that they are not put unnecessarily on their guard or even made hostile. Think whether you need to tell schoolteachers that, as a psychologist, you are trying to compare teachers' approaches to teaching mathematics with the recommendations of theorists. It might be better to say that you are interested in the way teachers teach this particular subject and in their opinions. I am not advocating deceit; what you are saying is true, but if you present your full brief the teachers may behave and talk to you in a way that conforms to what they think you ought to hear rather than reflecting what they really do. It is worth stressing the value, to them, of any research you are doing; guarantee confidentiality so that individuals will not be identified and show your willingness to share your findings with them; do keep such promises.

Methods of recording

The ideal method of recording what is observed is one which is both unobtrusive and preserves as much of the original behaviour as possible. An unobtrusive measure will minimise the effect of the observer on the participants, for there is little point in having a perfect record of behaviour which lacks ecological validity because the participants have altered their behaviour as a consequence of being observed. Equally, there is little point in observing behaviour which is thoroughly ecologically valid if you cannot record what you want. In the right circumstances, video cameras linked to a good sound recording system can provide the best of these two worlds.

It is possible to have a purpose-built room with cameras and microphones which can be controlled from a separate room. Movements of the camera such as changes in focus and angle need to be as silent as possible, and with modern cameras this can be achieved. Video provides the visual record which can be useful, even if the research is concentrating on language, because it can put the language in context. Having the cameras as near the ceiling as possible minimises their salience but means that a good-sized room is required so that more is recorded than just a view of people's heads.

A single camera can mean that, unless the people being observed have been highly constrained as to where they can place themselves, what is observed may be only part of the action. A combination of two or three cameras can minimise the number of blind spots in a room. It is possible to record the images from more than one camera directly onto a single video stream. This allows researchers to see the faces of two people conversing face-to-face, or to observe a single individual both in close-up and from a distance.

Apart from the advantages just given, video allows researchers to view the same piece of behaviour many times. In this way, the same behaviour can be observed at a number of different levels and it allows researchers to concentrate, on different occasions, on different aspects of the behaviour. It also allows a measure of elapsed time to be recorded along with the image, which helps in sampling and in noting the duration of certain behaviours. A further advantage is that the video can be played at different speeds so that behaviours which occur for a very short duration can be detected. Video also allows the reliability of measures to be checked more easily.

There are many reasons why you may not be able to use the purpose-built laboratory. However, even with field research you can use a hand-held camera or a camera on a tripod. Fortunately, people tend to habituate to the presence of a camera or an audio recorder if it is not too obtrusive. If people are hesitant about allowing themselves to be recorded, allow them to say when they want the recording device switched off and reassure them about the use to which the recordings will be put. Nonetheless, there will be situations in which you cannot guarantee taking recordings in the field, such as when you are observing covertly or when you have been denied permission to record. Under these circumstances you have a problem of selectivity and of when to note down what has happened or, if you are using a camera covertly, say, in a bag, there is the danger that it won't be pointing in the right direction.

If you are trying to achieve a more impressionistic observation, then you may need to take comparatively frequent breaks during which to write down your observations; you obviously have problems over relying on your memory and over being able to check on reliability. Even if you have taken notes, you need time to expand on them as soon as possible after the event. If you want a more formal observation, it would be advisable to create a checklist of behaviour in the most convenient form for noting down the occurrence and, if required, the duration of relevant behaviour. Under the latter circumstances you may be able to check the reliability of that particular set of observations by having a second observer using the checklist at the same time. Alternatively, you should at least check the general reliability of the checklist by having two or more observers use it while they are observing some relevant behaviour. More information can be noted by using multiple observers so that each concentrates on different aspects of behaviour or monitors different people.

Issues shared between observation and content analysis

As has been emphasised in earlier chapters, we need to be confident that our measures are both reliable and valid. In observation and content analysis these issues can be particularly problematic as we may start to employ more subjective measures. For example, in both methods we may wish to classify speech or text as being humorous or sarcastic. In order that others can use our classificatory system we will need to operationalise how we define these concepts. However, in so doing we have to be careful that we do not produce a reliable measure which lacks validity.

The categories in the classificatory system need to be mutually exclusive – that is, a piece of behaviour cannot be placed in more than one category.

Once you have devised a classificatory system, it should be written down, with examples, and another researcher should be trained in its use. Then, using a new episode of behaviour or piece of text, you will need to check the interrater reliability – that is, the degree to which raters, working separately, agree over their classification of behaviour or text. If the agreement is poor, then the classificatory system will need to be refined and differences between raters negotiated. See Chapter 19 for ways to quantify reliability and for what constitutes an acceptable level of agreement.

There is always a problem of observer or rater bias, where the rater allows his or her knowledge to affect the judgements. This can be lessened if they are blind to any hypotheses which the researchers may have, and also to the particular condition being observed. For example, if researchers were comparing participants given alcohol with those given a placebo they should not tell the raters which condition a given participant was in, or even what the possible conditions were. In addition, raters need to be blind to the judgements of other raters.

Another problem can be *observer drift* where, possibly through boredom, reliability worsens over time. Raters are likely to remain more vigilant and reliable if they think that a random sample of their ratings will be checked.

Transcribing

A disadvantage of video, and to a lesser extent of audio recordings, is the vast amount of information to be sifted through. This can be very time-consuming. It can be tempting to hand the recordings over to someone else to transcribe into descriptions or more particularly the words spoken. While this may save time for the researchers and can help to provide a record which may be more convenient to peruse, it is a good idea to view and listen to the original recordings, at least initially. Having the context in which behaviour and speech occurred and the intonation of the original speech is very useful. A compromise would be to have a transcription which you then annotate from your observations of the original recording.

Types of data

Firstly, you will probably draw up a list of categories and subcategories of relevant behaviour. Then you need to decide whether you are going to record the frequency with which a particular behaviour occurs, its duration or a combination of the two. In addition, you might be interested in particular sequences of events in order to look for patterns in the ways certain behaviours follow others. Even if you are simply interested in the frequency with which certain behaviour occurs, it can be worth putting this into different time frames to see whether there is a change over time. Also, with more subjective judgements you may want to get ratings of aspects such as degree of emotion.

Sampling

Sampling can be done on the basis of time or place as well as people. *Continuous real-time* sampling would be observing an entire duration. This can be very time-consuming and so there exist ways to select shorter durations from the complete duration. *Time point* sampling involves deciding on specific times and noting whether target behaviours are occurring then. This could be done on a regular basis or on a random basis. Alternatively, *time interval* sampling would be choosing periods of a fixed duration at selected stages in the overall duration and noting the frequency of target behaviours during the fixed durations.

You need to think about the different periods and settings which you might want to sample. Thus, if studying student behaviour at university, researchers would probably want to observe lectures, tutorials, seminars, libraries, refectories and living accommodation. In addition, they would want to observe during freshers' week, at various times during each of the years, including during examination periods, and at graduation.

An example of systematic sampling for a content analysis of television adverts could be to get adverts which represented the output from the different periods during the day, such as breakfast television, daytime television, late afternoon and early evening programmes when mainly children will be watching, peak-time viewing and late at night. The random approach could involve picking a certain number of issues from the previous year of a magazine, randomly, on the basis of their issue number. See Chapter 11 for a discussion of random selection.

Structured observation

A widely used form of structured observation is interaction process analysis (IPA), which was devised by Bales (1950).

Bales's interaction process analysis

This can be used to look at the dynamics in a small group in order to identify the different styles of interaction which are adopted by the members of the group. For example, different types of leader may emerge – those who are predominantly focused on the task and those who are concentrating on group cohesiveness. In addition, the period of the interaction can be subdivided so that changes in behaviour over time can be sought. A checklist of behaviours is used for noting down particular classes of behaviour, who made them and to whom they were addressed, including whether they were to the whole group. The behaviours fall into four general categories: positive, negative, asking questions and providing answers. If being conducted live, ideally there would be as many observers as participants, while more observers still would allow some check on interrater reliability.

Content analysis

Content analysis can be seen as a non-intrusive form of observation, in that the observer is not present when the actions are being performed but is analysing the traces left by the actions. It usually involves analysing text such as newspaper articles, blogs, interactions on Internet groups or the transcript of a speech or conversation. However, it can be conducted on some other medium such as television adverts or even the amount of wear suffered by particular books in a library or areas of carpet in an art gallery. It can be conducted on recent material or on more historical material such as early textbooks on a subject or personal diaries.

A typical content analysis might involve looking at the ways people represent themselves and the people they are seeking through adverts in lonely-hearts columns of a magazine. The analyst could be investigating whether males and females differ in the approaches they adopt and the words they use. For example, do males concentrate on their own wealth and possessions but refer to the physical attributes of the hoped-for partner? Do males and females make different uses of humour? The categories being sought could be derived from a theory of how males and females are likely to behave or from a preliminary look at a sample of adverts to see what the salient dimensions are. Once the categories have been defined, such an analysis could involve counting the number of males and females who deploy particular styles in their adverts.

Another example of a content analysis was conducted by Manstead and McCulloch (1981). They analysed advertisements which had been shown on British television to see whether males and females were being represented differently. To begin with they identified, where possible, the key male and female characters. Then they classified the adverts according to the nature of the product being sold and the roles in the adverts played by males and females – whether as imparters or receivers of information. C. O'Connor (2017) noted the occurrences of appeals to nature in the debate around a referendum about same sex marriage in Ireland in 2015. She looked at newspapers and Twitter.

Diaries and logs

An important source of material for a content analysis can be diaries or logs. These can range from diaries written spontaneously, either for the writer's own interest or for publication, to a log kept according to a researcher's specification. In the latter case they are sometimes indistinguishable from a questionnaire which is completed on more than one occasion. The frequency with which entries are made can also range widely, from more than once a day at regular intervals, through being triggered by a particular event such as a conversation, to being sampled randomly, possibly on receipt of a signal generated by a researcher. The duration of the period studied can range from one week to many years.

Diaries and logs can be used in many contexts. They can be used to generate theory such as by Reason and Lucas (1984, cited in Baddeley, 1990), who looked at slips of memory, such as getting out the keys for a door at work when approaching a door at home, while Young, Hay, and Ellis (1985) looked at errors in recognising people. The technique can be used to investigate people's dreams, to find the baseline of a type of behaviour, such as obsessional hand washing or the amount of exercise taken by people, to look at social behaviour in couples or groups and to look at consumer behaviour such as types of purchases made or television viewing.

It has certain advantages over laboratory-based methods in that it can be more ecologically valid and can allow researchers to study behaviour across a range of settings and under circumstances which it would be either difficult or ethically questionable to create, such as subjecting participants to stress. It doesn't have to rely on a person's memory as much as would a method where a person was interviewed at intervals. In this way, less salient events will be recorded rather than being masked by more salient ones and the order of events will be more accurately noted. It is particularly useful for plotting change over time, such as in degrees of pain suffered by a client, and there won't be a tendency for the average to be reported across a range of experiences.

Disadvantages include, among others, the fact that participants are likely to be highly self-selected, that because it may be onerous people may drop out, that they may forget to complete it on occasions and that the person may be more sensitised to the entity being recorded, such as their experience of pain. Finally there is the cost.

Ways have been found to lessen a number of the drawbacks and what is appropriate will depend on the nature of the task and the duration of the study. These include the following: interviewing potential participants to establish a rapport and so reduce self-selection; explaining the nature of the task thoroughly; giving small, regular rewards, such as a lottery ticket; keeping in touch by sending a birthday card; counteracting forgetting by phoning to remind, supplying a pager and paging the person, or even having a preprogrammed device which sends out a signal, such as a sound or vibration when the data are due to be recorded; making the task as easy as possible by supplying a printed booklet and even a pen or a computer tablet; making contact with the researchers as easy as possible by supplying contact numbers and email addresses; and making submission of the data as straightforward as possible such as by supplying stamped, addressed envelopes, collecting the material, receiving it via email or telephoning for it. It is important not to try to counter the cost by trying to squeeze too much out of the research; by making the task more onerous the likelihood of self-selection and dropout is increased.

Summary

Observation and content analysis are two non-experimental methods which look at behaviour. In the case of observation the observer is usually present when the action occurs and the degree to which participants are aware of the observer's presence and intentions can vary. On the other hand, content analysis is conducted on the product of the action, including data from diaries or logs, with the analyst not being present when the action is performed. Both can involve the analyst in devising a system for classifying the material being analysed. Therefore, both need to have the validity and reliability of such classificatory systems examined.

The next section, Chapters 8–27, deals with the data collected in research and how they can be analysed.

PART 4

Data and analysis

8 Scales of measurement

Introduction

Chapter 2 discussed the different forms of measurement which are used by psychologists. In addition, it emphasised the need to check that the measures are valid and reliable. The present chapter shows how all the measures which psychologists make can be classified under four different scales. It contrasts this with the way that statisticians refer to scales. The consequences of using a particular scale of measurement are discussed.

Examples of measures

The following questions produce answers which differ in the type of measurement which they involve. Before moving on to the next section look at the questions and see whether you can find differences in the type and precision of information which each answer provides.

1   Gender: female or male?
2   What is your mother's occupation?
3   How tall are you? (in centimetres)
4   How old are you? (in years)

   10–19 20–29 30–39 40–49 50–59

5   What is your favourite colour?
6   What daily newspaper do you read?
7   How many brothers have you?
8   What is your favourite non-alcoholic drink?
9   Do you eat meat?
10   How many hours do you like to sleep per night?
11   What colour are your eyes?
12   How many units of alcohol do you drink per week? (1 unit = half a pint of beer, a measure of spirit or a glass of wine)
13   Is your memory:

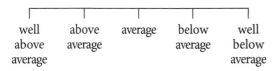

| well above average | above average | average | below average | well below average |

14   How old is your father?
15   At what room temperature (in degrees Celsius) do you feel comfortable?
16   What is your current yearly income?

Scales of measurement

There are four scales which are often used to describe the measures which we can take. Read the descriptions of the four scales below and then try to classify the 16 preceding questions into the four scales. The answers are given at the end of the next section.

Nominal

The nominal scale of measurement is used to describe data comprising simply names or categories (hence another name for this level of measurement: *categorical*). Thus, the answer to the question *Do you live in university accommodation?* is a form of nominal data; there are two categories: those who do live in university accommodation and those who don't. Nominal data are not only binary (or dichotomous) data, that is, data where there are only two possible answers. The answer to the question *How do you travel to the university?* is also nominal data.

Ordinal

The ordinal scale, as its name implies, refers to data which can be placed in an order. For example, the classifications of university degrees into 1st, 2(i), 2(ii) and 3rd form an ordinal scale.

Interval

The interval scale includes data which tell you more than simply an order; they tell you the degree of difference between two scores. For example, if you are told the temperature, in degrees Fahrenheit, of two different rooms, you know not only that one is warmer than the other but by how much.

Ratio

The ratio scale, like the interval scale, gives you information about the magnitude of differences between the things you are measuring. However, it has the additional property that the data should have a true zero; in other words, zero means the property being measured has no quantity. For example, weight in kilograms is on a ratio scale. This can be confusing as, when asked for their weight, people cannot sensibly reply that it is zero kilograms. Zero kilograms would mean that there was no weight. The reason why temperature in Fahrenheit is on an interval and not a ratio scale is because zero degrees Fahrenheit is a measurable temperature. Hence, with a ratio scale, because there is a fixed starting point for the measure, we can talk about the ratio of two entities measured on that scale. For example, if we are comparing two people's height – one of 100 cm and another of 200 cm – we can say that the first person is half the height of the second. With temperature, as there is no fixed starting point for the scale, it is not true to say that 40 degrees Celsius is half 80 degrees Celsius.

The point can be made by converting the scale into a different form of units to see whether the ratio between two points remains the same. If the height example is changed to inches, where every inch is the equivalent of 2.54 cm and zero cm is the same as zero inches, the shorter person is 39.37 inches tall and the taller person is 78.74 inches tall. The conversion has not changed the ratio between the two people; the first person is half the height of the second person. However, if we convert the temperatures from Celsius to Fahrenheit, we get 104 degrees and 176 degrees respectively. Notice that the first temperature is now clearly not half the second one. Fortunately for any reader who may still not understand the distinction between interval and ratio scales, the statistics covered in this book treat ratio and interval data in the same way.

The relevance of the four scales

As you move from nominal towards ratio data you gain more information about what is being measured. For example, if you ask,

Do you smoke? (Yes/No)

you will get nominal data. If you ask,

Do you smoke:
    not at all?
    between one and 10 cigarettes a day?
    more than 10 cigarettes a day?

you will get ordinal data which help you to distinguish, among those who do smoke, between heavier and lighter smokers.
    Finally, if you ask,

How many cigarettes do you smoke per day?

you will receive ratio data which tell you more precisely about how much people smoke.
    The important difference between these three versions of the question is that you can apply different statistical techniques depending on whether you have interval/ratio data, ordinal data or nominal data. The more information you can provide, the more informative will be the statistics which you can derive from it.
    Accordingly, if you are provided with a measure which is on a ratio scale you will be throwing information away if you treat it as ordinal or nominal.
    The following questions provide you with nominal data:

1   Gender: female or male?
2   What is your mother's occupation?
5   What is your favourite colour?
6   What daily newspaper do you read?
8   What is your favourite non-alcoholic drink?
9   Do you eat meat?
11   What colour are your eyes?

    The following questions yield ordinal data:

4   How old are you?

        10–19 20–29 30–39 40–49 50–59

13   Is your memory:

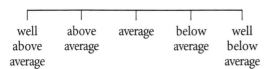

This last example can confuse people as they point out that the possible alternatives are simply names or categories, but you have to note that they form an order; a person who claims to have an above-average memory is claiming that his or her memory is better than someone with an average memory, someone with a below-average memory or someone with a well-below-average memory.

The following question is one of the few physical measures which give interval but not ratio data:

15 At what room temperature (in degrees Celsius) do you feel comfortable?

The following questions would give you ratio data:

3 How tall are you? (in centimetres)
7 How many brothers have you?
10 How many hours do you like to sleep per night?
12 How many units of alcohol do you drink per week?

   (1 unit = half a pint of beer, a measure of spirit or a glass of wine)

14 How old is your father?
16 What is your current yearly income?

Indicators

An additional consideration over the level of a particular measurement is how it is to be used: what it is indicating. It has already been pointed out that psychologists rarely have direct measures of that which they wish to observe. This can be particularly so if they are dealing with something, such as socio-economic status, which they may be attempting to define. Measures such as years in education or income are at the ratio level, but when used to indicate socio-economic status they may be merely ordinal because the same-sized difference in income will mean different things at different points on the scale. Thus, a person earning £20,000 per year is much better off than someone who is earning £10,000, whereas a person earning £260,000 a year is not that much better paid than a person earning £250,000. The previous example showed that an absolute increase will have different meanings at different points on the scale. However, even the same ratio increase can have different meanings at different points on the scale. A 10% increase for people on £10,000 is likely to be more important to them – and may lead them to be classified in a different socio-economic group – than a 10% increase will be for a person on £250,000. Another example of how a scale's level of measurement depends on what it is being used to indicate is mother's occupation. If you wanted to put the occupations in an order on the basis, say, of status, then you would have converted the data into an ordinal scale. However, if you did not have an order, then they remain on a nominal scale.

Pedhazur and Schmelkin (1991) point out that few measures that psychologists use are truly on a ratio scale even though they appear to have a true zero. As an example of this, if we create a test of mathematical ability and a person scores zero on it we cannot conclude that they have no knowledge of mathematics. Therefore, we cannot talk meaningfully about the ratio of maths ability of two people on the basis of this test.

Statisticians and scales

Statisticians tend to classify numerical scales into three types: continuous, discrete and dichotomous. The distinction between continuous and discrete can be illustrated by two types of clock. An analogue clock – one with hands which go round to indicate the time – gives time on a continuous scale because it is capable of indicating every possible time. The digital clock, however, chops time up into equal units and when one unit has passed it indicates the next unit but does not indicate the time in between the units; it gives time on a discrete scale. The distinction between a continuous and a discrete scale can become blurred. The clock examples can be used to illustrate this point. Unless the analogue clock is particularly large, it will be difficult to make very fine measurements; it may only be usable to give time in multiples of seconds, whereas a digital clock may give very precise measurement so that it can be used to record time in milliseconds.

Dichotomous refers to a variable which can have only two values, such as yes or no. Another term for dichotomous is *binary*. Sometimes you will also see reference to *polychotomous*, meaning categorical but having more than two values.

Return to the 16 questions given at the beginning of the chapter and try to identify those which could be classified as continuous, discrete or dichotomous.

The following questions yield answers which are measured on a continuous scale (as long as they are interpreted as allowing that level of precision):

3   How tall are you? (in centimetres)
10   How many hours do you like to sleep per night?
12   How many units of alcohol do you drink per week?

   (1 unit = half a pint of beer, a measure of spirit or a glass of wine)

14   How old is your father?
15   At what room temperature (in degrees Celsius) do you feel comfortable?
16   What is your current yearly income?

The following questions yield answers which are on a discrete scale:

2   What is your mother's occupation?
4   How old are you? (in years)

   10–19 20–29 30–39 40–49 50–59

5   What is your favourite colour?
6   What daily newspaper do you read?
7   How many brothers have you?
8   What is your favourite non-alcoholic drink?
11   What colour are your eyes?
13   Is your memory:

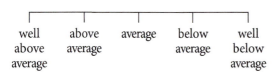

| well above average | above average | average | below average | well below average |

The following questions yield answers which are on a dichotomous scale:

1   Gender: female or male?
9   Do you eat meat?

Psychologists fall into at least two camps – those who apply the nominal, ordinal or interval/ratio classification of measures to decide what statistics to employ, and those who prefer to follow the statisticians' classificatory system. However, both systems need to be taken into account. As you will see in Chapter 14, there are other important criteria which indicate which version of a statistical procedure to employ. My feeling is that both ways of classifying the scales are valid and we can follow the statisticians' advice as far as choice of statistical test is concerned, but we must be aware of what the measures mean – what they indicate – and therefore what we can meaningfully conclude from the results of statistical analysis. In addition, as will be seen in the next chapter, when we wish to summarise the data which we have collected, the scale that they are on determines what are sensible ways of presenting the information.

The debate about what can be measured continues as can be seen in recent articles: Guyon, Kop, Juhel, and Falissard (2018), Michell (2012) and Sijtsma (2012).

Summary

There are two approaches to the classification of scales of measurement. Psychologists tend to describe four scales: nominal, ordinal, interval and ratio. Each provides a certain level of information, with nominal providing the least and ratio the most. For the purposes of the statistical techniques described in this book, interval and ratio scales of measurement can be treated as the same. Statisticians prefer to talk of continuous, discrete and dichotomous scales. Both classificatory systems need to be considered. A further consideration which determines how a measure should be classified is what it is being used to indicate. The scale of a measure has an effect on the type of statistics which can be employed on that measure.

The next chapter introduces the ways in which data can be described, both numerically and graphically.

9

Summarising and describing data

 ## Introduction

The first phase of data analysis is the production of a summary of the data. This way of describing the data can be done numerically or graphically. It is particularly useful because it can show whether the results of research are in line with the researcher's hypotheses. Statisticians see an increasing importance for this stage and have described it as exploratory data analysis (EDA; see Tukey, 1977). Psychologists have tended to underuse EDA as a stage in their analysis. EDA and other techniques allow researchers to do what is described as *data screening*. However, because many methods of data screening require techniques which will be dealt with in later chapters I am going to postpone a fuller discussion of it until Chapter 23.

Numerical methods

Ratio, interval or ordinal data

Measures of central tendency

When you have collected data about participants you will want to produce a summary which will give an impression of the results for the participants you have studied. Imagine that you have given a group of 15 adults a list of 100 words and you have asked each person to recall as many of the words as he or she can. The recall scores are as follows:

3, 7, 5, 9, 4, 6, 5, 7, 8, 11, 10, 7, 4, 6, 8

This is a list of what is termed the raw data. As it stands, it provides little information about the phenomenon being studied. The reader could scan the raw data and try to get a feel for what it is like but it is more useful to use some form of summary statistic or graphical display to present the data. This is even truer when there are even more data points.

The most common type of summary statistic is one which tries to present some sort of central value for the data. This is often termed an average. However, there is more than one average; the three most common are given next.

Mean

The mean is what people often think of when they use the term 'average'. It is found by adding the scores together and dividing the answer by the number of scores. To find the mean recall of the group of 15 participants, you would add the 15 recall scores, giving a total of 100, and then divide the result by 15, which gives a mean of 6.667. Statisticians use lower-case letters from the English alphabet to symbolise statistics which have been calculated from a sample. The most common symbol for the mean of a sample is $\bar{x}$. However, the APA (American Psychological Association, 2010) recommends using M to symbolise the mean in the reports of research.

Median

The median is the value which is in the middle of all the values. Thus, to find the median recall of the group of 15 participants, put the recall scores in order.

Now count up to the person with the 8th best recall (the person who has as many people with recall that is poorer than or as good as his or hers as there are people with recall which is as good or better). That person's recall is the median recall for the group. In this case, the median recall is 7. If there is an even number of people, then there will be no one person in the middle of the group. In such a case, the median will lie between the half with the lowest recall and the half with the highest recall. Take the mean of the person with the best recall of the lower half of the group and the person who has the poorest recall of the upper half of the group. That value is the median for the group. If a person with a score of below 7 was added to the 15 scores shown in Table 9.1, then the median would be between the current 7th and 8th ranks at 6.5. However, if a person with a score of 7 or more was added to the 15, then the median would be between the current 8th and 9th ranks at 7.

Mode

The mode is the most frequently occurring value among your participants. In Table 9.1 the most frequently occurring recall score was 7. As with the median, the mode can best be identified by putting the scores in order of magnitude.

TABLE 9.1   The number of words recalled by participants, in rank order

Order	Recall	
1	3	
2	4	
3	4	
4	5	
5	5	
6	6	
7	6	
8	7	← Median
9	7	
10	7	
11	8	
12	8	
13	9	
14	10	
15	11	

The relative merits of the measures of central tendency

The mean is the most common measure of central tendency used by psychologists. This is probably for three reasons. Its calculation takes into account all the values of the data. It is used in many statistical tests, as you will see in future chapters. It can be used in conjunction with other measures to give an impression of what range of scores most people will have obtained.

Nonetheless, the mean has at least two disadvantages. Firstly, far from representing the whole group it may represent no one in the group. The point can be made most clearly when the mean produces a value which is not possible: for example, when you are told that the average family has 2.4 children. Thus, we have to accept that the central point as represented by a mean is *mathematically* central. A value has been produced which is on a continuous scale when the original measure – number of children – was on a discrete scale.

A second, more serious problem with the mean is that it can be affected by one score which is very different from the rest. For example, if the mean recall for a group of 15 people is 6.667 words and another person, whose recall is 100 words, is also sampled, then the mean for the new group will now be 12.5. This is higher than all but one of the group and therefore does not provide a useful summary statistic.

Ways have been devised to deal with such an effect. Firstly, the trimmed mean can be calculated whereby the more extreme scores have been left out of the calculation. Different versions of the trimmed mean exist. The simplest involves removing the highest and lowest scores. However, often the top and bottom 10% of scores are removed. This version can be symbolised as $\bar{x}_{10}$. Alternatively, such an unusual person may be identified as an *outlier* or an extreme score and removed. Identifying possible outliers can be done by using a box plot (see the following) or by other techniques given in Chapter 12.

The median, like the mean, may be a value which represents no one when there is an even number of participants involved. If the median recall for the group had been 7.5 words this would be a score which no member of the group had achieved. However, the median is not affected by extreme values. If the person who has recalled 100 words joins the group, the median will stay at 7, whereas the mean rises by over 5.5 words. Another way to deal with the effect of outliers on central tendency is to report the median rather than, or as well as, the mean.

The mode is rarely used by psychologists. It has at least three disadvantages, the first two of which refer to the fact that a single mode may not even exist. Firstly, if no two values are the same, then there is no mode: for example, if all 15 people had different recall scores. Secondly, if there are two values which tie for having the most number of people, then again there is no single mode: for example, if in the sample of people, two had recalled five words and two seven words. You may come across the terms *bi-modal*, which means having two modes, or *multi-modal*, which means having more than one mode. The third problem with the mode is that it can be severely unrepresentative when all but a very few values are different. For example, if in a sample of 100 people, with scores ranging from 1 to 100, all but two had different recall scores, but those two both recalled 99 words, then the mode would be 99, which could hardly be seen as a central value. If there is no mode, then one strategy is to place the scores in ranges, e.g. 1 to 10, etc., and then find the range which has the highest number of scores: the modal range.

A measure of central tendency alone gives insufficient detail about the sample you are describing because the same value can be produced from very different sets of figures. For example, you can have two samples, each of which has a mean recall of 7, yet one could comprise people all of whose recall was 7, while the other sample may include a person with a recall of 3 and another with a recall of 11. Accordingly, it is useful to report some measure of this spread or dispersion of scores, to put the measure of central tendency in context.

Measures of spread or dispersion

Maxima and minima

If you report the largest value (the maximum) and the smallest value (the minimum) in the sample this can give an impression of the spread of that sample. Thus, if everyone in the sample recalled 7 words, then the maximum and minimum would both be 7, while the wider-spread sample would have a maximum of 11 and a minimum of 3.

Range

An alternative way of expressing the maxima and minima is to subtract the minimum from the maximum to give the range of values. This figure allows for the fact that different samples can have similar ranges even though their maxima and minima differ. For example, one sample may have a maximum recall of 9 and a minimum recall of 1, whereas a second sample may have a maximum recall of 11 and a minimum recall of 3. By reporting their range you can make clear that they both have the same spread of 8 words.

Both range and maxima and minima still fail to summarise the group sufficiently, because they only deal with the extreme values. They fail to take account of how common those extremes are. Thus, one sample of 15 people could have one person with a recall of 3, one person with a recall of 11 and the remaining people all with the same recall of 7. This group would have the same maximum and minimum (and therefore, range) as another group in which the recall scores were more evenly distributed between 3 and 11.

The interquartile range

This is calculated by finding the score which is at the 25th percentile (in other words, the value of the score which is the largest of the bottom 25% of scores) and the score which is at the 75th percentile (the value of the score which is the largest of the bottom 75% of scores) and noting their difference. Referring to Table 9.1 we see that the 25th percentile is 5 and the 75th percentile is 8. Therefore the interquartile range is 8 − 5 = 3. The interquartile range has the advantage that it is less affected by extreme scores than the range, which is calculated from the maximum and minimum.

Variance

The variance takes into account the degree to which the value for each person differs from the mean for the group. It is calculated by noting how much each score differs (or deviates) from the mean. I am going to use, as an example, the recall scores of a sample of five people:

Words recalled
1
2
3
4
5

The mean has to be calculated: $\bar{x} = 3$ words. Next we find the deviation of each score from the mean, by subtracting the mean from each score:

Words recalled	Deviation from the mean
1	−2
2	−1
3	0
4	1
5	2

Now we want to summarise the deviations. However, if we were to add the deviations we would get zero and this will always be true for any set of numbers. A way to get around this is to square the deviations before adding them, because this gets rid of the negative signs:

Words recalled	Deviation from the mean	Squared deviation
1	−2	4
2	−1	1
3	0	0
4	1	1
5	2	4

Now when we add the squared deviations we get 10. To get the variance we now divide the sum of the squared deviations by the number of scores (5) and get a variance of 2.

A more evenly spread group will have a higher variance, because there will be more people whose recall differs from the mean. If 2 out of 15 participants have recall scores of 3 and 11 words while the rest all recall 7 words, then the variance is 2.134. On the other hand, the more evenly distributed sample, shown in Table 9.1, has a variance of 4.889. The variance, like the mean, is used in many statistical techniques.

To confuse the issue, statisticians have noted that if they are trying to estimate, from the data they have collected, the variance for the population from which the participants came, then a more accurate estimate is given by dividing the sum of squared deviations by one fewer than the number in the sample. This version of the variance is the one usually given by computer programs and the one which is used in statistical tests. This version of the variance for the more evenly spread set of scores is thus 5.238.

Standard deviation

The standard deviation (s or SD) is directly linked to the variance because it is the square root of the variance; for this reason the variance of a sample is often represented as s^2. The usual standard deviation which is given by computer programs is derived from the variance, which entailed dividing the sum of the squared deviations by one fewer than the number of scores, as it is also the best estimate of the population's standard deviation.

There are three reasons why the standard deviation is preferred over all the other measures of spread when summarising data. Firstly, like the variance, it is a measure of spread which relates to the mean. Thus, when reporting the mean it is appropriate to report the standard deviation. Secondly, the units in which the standard deviation is expressed are the same as the original measure. In other words, one can talk about the standard deviation of recall being 2.289 words for the more evenly spread set of scores. Thirdly, in certain circumstances, the standard deviation can be used to give an indication of the proportion of people in a population who fall within a given range of values. See Chapter 12 for a fuller explanation of this point.

Semi-interquartile range

When quoting a median the appropriate measure of spread is the semi-interquartile range (sometimes referred to as the 'quartile deviation'). This is the interquartile range divided by 2. In the example of the 15 recall scores the semi-interquartile range is 3/2 = 1.5.

Nominal data

When dealing with variables which have levels in the form of categories, the numbers are frequencies, that is, the number of people who are in a particular category. For example, when we have found out how many people in a group are smokers, it makes little sense to use the preceding techniques to summarise the data. We can use a number of presentation methods which are based on the number of people who were in a given category. For example, we can simply report the number of smokers – say, 10 – and the number of non-smokers – say, 15. Alternatively, we can express these figures as fractions, proportions or percentages.

Fractions

To find a fraction we find the total number of people – 25 – and express the number of smokers as a fraction of this total. Thus, 10 out of 25, or $\frac{10}{25}$, of the sample were smokers, and 15 out of 25, or $\frac{15}{25}$, were non-smokers. We can further simplify this, because 10, 15 and 25 are all divisible by 5. Accordingly, we can say that $\frac{2}{5}$ were smokers and $\frac{3}{5}$ were non-smokers.

Proportions

We can find proportions from fractions by converting the fractions to decimals. Thus, dividing 10 by 25 (or 2 divided by 5) tells us that .4 of the sample were smokers, while 15 divided by 25 (or 3 divided by 5) tells us that .6 of the sample were non-smokers. Notice that the proportions for all the subgroups should add up to 1: .4 + .6 = 1; this can be a check that the calculations are correct.

Percentages

To find a percentage multiply a proportion by 100. Thus, 40% of the sample were smokers and 60% were non-smokers. The percentages for all the subgroups should add up to 100.

Frequency distributions

If we have asked a sample of 120 people what their age group is, we can represent it as a simple table (Table 9.2):

TABLE 9.2   The frequency distribution of participants' ages

Age (in years)	20–29	30–39	40–49	50–59	60–69
Number of people	15	45	30	20	10

From this table the reader can see what the distribution of ages is within our sample.

Note that if we were presented with the data in this form and we wanted to calculate the mean or median we could not do so exactly, as we only know the range of possible ages in which a person lies. The people in the 20–29 age group might all be 20 years old, 29 years old or evenly distributed within that age range. Techniques for calculating means and medians in such a situation are given in Appendix I.

Contingency tables

When the levels of the variables are nominal (or ordinal as in the last example) but two variables are being considered, the data can be presented as a contingency table (Table 9.3). Imagine that we have asked 80 people – 50 males and 30 females – whether they smoke.

TABLE 9.3   The distribution of smokers and non-smokers among males and females

	Smokers	Non-smokers
Males	20	30
Females	12	18

However, sometimes it is more appropriate, particularly for comparison across groups with unequal samples, to report proportions or percentages. Reporting the raw data that 20 males and 12 females were smokers makes comparison between the genders difficult. However, 20 out of 50 becomes $\frac{20}{50} = .4$ or 4 in 10. Twelve out of 30 becomes $\frac{12}{30} = .4$ or 4 in 10, as well. Expressed this way the reader can see that, despite the different sample sizes, there are equivalent proportions of smokers among the male and female samples (Table 9.4).

TABLE 9.4   The percentage of smokers and non-smokers among males and females

	Smokers	Non-smokers	Total
Males	40%	60%	100%
Females	40%	60%	100%

An additional advantage of reporting proportions or percentages is that the reader can quickly calculate the proportions or percentages of people who do not fall into a category. Thus .6 or 60% of males and 60% of females in the sample did not smoke. When reporting percentages or proportions it is a good idea to report the original numbers, from which they were derived, as well.

There is a danger when using computers to analyse nominal data. It is usually necessary to code the data numerically; for example, smokers may be coded as 1 and non-smokers as 2. I have seen a number of people learning to analyse data who get the computer to provide means and standard deviations of these numbers. Thus, in the preceding example, they would find that the mean score of males was 1.6. Remember that these numbers are totally arbitrary ways to tell the computer which category a person was in – smokers could have been coded as 25 and non-smokers as 7 – so it doesn't make sense to treat them as you would ordinal, interval or ratio data.

Graphical methods

There are many ways in which data can be summarised graphically. The advantage of a graphical summary is that it can convey aspects of the data, such as relative size, more immediately to the reader than the equivalent table. There are, however, at least two disadvantages. Firstly, it is sometimes difficult to obtain the exact values from a graph. Secondly, the person who produces them often is unaware that some readers may not be used to the conventions that are involved in graphs. This can be less of a problem when they are in an article because the reader can spend time working out what is being represented. The main danger arises when they are used to illustrate a talk and listeners are given insufficient time to view them and insufficient explanation of the particular conventions being used. The first problem can be solved by providing both tables and graphs, but some journals discourage this practice.

The majority of graphical displays of data use two dimensions, or axes, one for the values of the independent variable (IV) and one for the dependent variable (DV). There is a convention that the vertical axis represents the DV, while the horizontal axis represents the IV. Often there may be no obvious IV or DV, in which case, place the variables on the axes in the way which makes most sense in the light of the convention. Thus, if I were creating a graph with age and IQ, although I might not think of age as affecting IQ, putting age on the horizontal axis would be more consistent with the convention than placing it on the vertical axis and by so doing possibly implying that age could be affected by IQ.

Plots of totals and subtotals

Bar charts

A bar chart can be used when the levels of the variable are categorical, as in the example of male and female smokers (Figure 9.1).

FIGURE 9.1   The number of smokers and non-smokers among males and females

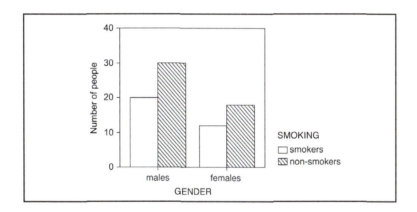

Alternatively, with unequal sample sizes, a preferable method is to show the numbers of smokers and non-smokers in the same bar (Figure 9.2).

FIGURE 9.2   The number of smokers and non-smokers among males and females

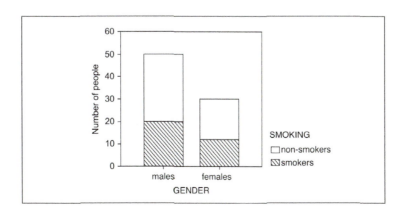

Histograms

Histograms are similar to bar charts but the latter are for more discrete measures such as gender (Figure 9.3), while the former are for more continuous measures such as age. Nonetheless, histograms can be used when the variable is discrete, as in the example shown in Table 9.2 where age groups have been formed.

FIGURE 9.3   Number of people in each age group

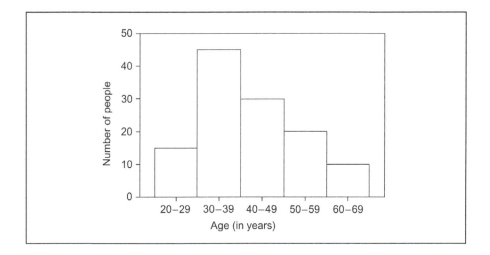

Pie charts

The pie chart differs from most of the graphs in that it does not use axes but represents the subtotals as areas of a pie (Figure 9.4). See Appendix I for a description of how to calculate the amount of the pie for each category.

FIGURE 9.4   Number of people in each age group

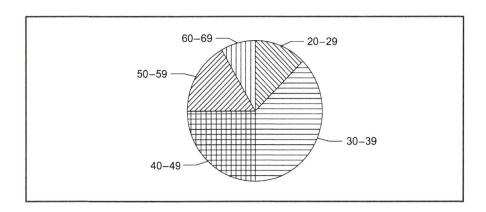

Alternatively the areas could be expressed as percentages (Figure 9.5).

FIGURE 9.5 Percentage of people in each age group

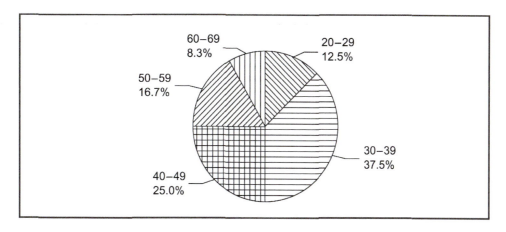

It is possible to emphasise one or more subtotals by lifting them out of the pie (Figure 9.6).

FIGURE 9.6 Percentage of people in each age group

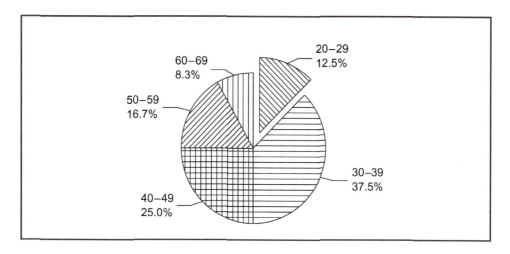

It is also possible to show more than one set of data in separate pie charts so that readers can compare them (Figure 9.7).

FIGURE 9.7 Percentage of smokers and non-smokers among males and females

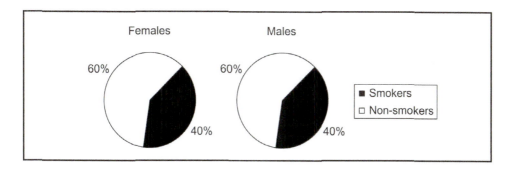

An added visual aid can come from representing the different numbers of participants in each pie by having a larger pie for a larger sample (Figure 9.8). One way to do this is to have the areas of the two pie charts in the same ratio as the two sample sizes (Appendix I shows how to calculate the appropriate relative area for a second pie chart).

FIGURE 9.8 Percentage of smokers and non-smokers among males and females

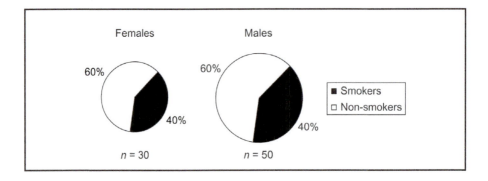

Frequency distributions

A frequency distribution can be shown as a histogram which presents a picture of the number of participants who gave a particular score or a range of scores. The width of the bars can be chosen to give the level of precision required. Figure 9.9 shows the recall scores from Table 9.1, with the width of a bar being such that each bar represents those who recalled a particular number of words, while the height of a bar shows how many people recalled that number of words.

From Figure 9.9 we can see at a glance that 7 is the mode, with three people recalling that number of words, that the mode is roughly in the middle of the spread of scores and that the minimum was 3 and the maximum 11. Figure 9.3 is a frequency distribution of age but the bars have widths of 10 years.

FIGURE 9.9 Frequency distribution of number of words recalled

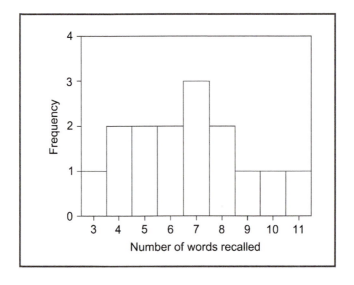

Stem-and-leaf plots

Stem-and-leaf plots are a variant of the histogram. Normally they are presented with the values of the variable (the stem) on the vertical axis and the frequencies (the leaves) on the horizontal axis. The recall scores for the 15 participants are plotted in Figure 9.10.

FIGURE 9.10   Stem-and-leaf plot of number of words recalled

2	0
4	0000
6	00000
8	000
10	00

The values on the stem give the first number in the range of scores contained in the leaf. In this version of a stem-and-leaf plot the 0s in the leaves simply denote the number of scores which fell in a particular range. Thus the 2 denotes that scores in the range 2 to 3 are contained on that leaf and the single 0 on the leaf shows that there was only one score in that range.

The nature of the stem can change depending on the distribution of scores. The plot when a 16th score of 25 and a 17th score of 15 are added is given in Figure 9.11.

FIGURE 9.11   Stem-and-leaf plot of number of words recalled (with two additional scores)

0	344
0	5566777889
1	01
1	7
2	
2	5

In this example, the distribution has been split into ranges of five figures: 0 to 4, 5 to 9 and so on. The plot assumes that all the numbers have two digits in them and so treats 3 as 03. The stem shows the first digit for each number. Accordingly, we can see that there are three scores in the range 0 to 4 and 10 in the range 5 to 9. Also we can see that there were no scores in the range 20 to 24. The advantage of this version of the stem-and-leaf plot over the histogram is that we can read the actual scores from the stem-and-leaf plot, even when each stem is based on a broad range of scores, as in the last example. Note that, even when a part of the stem has no corresponding leaf, that part of the stem should still be shown (see Figure 9.11). SPSS adopts a slightly different convention, whereby it treats scores which are more than one-and-a-half times the interquartile range above and below the interquartile range as *extreme* scores and doesn't display them as was done in Figure 9.11. See Figure 9.12.

From this we can see that one data point is equal to or greater than 25 and is classified as extreme.

FIGURE 9.12   Stem-and-leaf plot from SPSS of the data displayed in Figure 9.11

Frequency	Stem and leaf
3.00	0 . 344
10.00	0 . 5566777889
2.00	1 . 01
2.00	Extremes ($\geq$15)

Stem width: 10.00
Each leaf: 1 case (s)

Plots of bivariate scores

Scattergrams

A scattergram (or scatterplot) is a useful way to present the data for two variables which have been provided by each participant. This would be the case if, in the memory example, we had also tested the time it took for each participant to say the original list out loud (the articulation speed) (Table 9.5).

TABLE 9.5   Number of words recalled and articulation speed, ranked according to number of words recalled

recall	articulation speed
3	30
4	25
4	28
5	30
5	25
6	23
6	24
7	23
7	21
7	23
8	23
8	18
9	19
10	20
11	19

The position of each score on the graph is given by finding its value on the articulation speed axis and drawing an imaginary vertical line through that point, and then finding its value on the recall axis and drawing an imaginary horizontal line through this point. The circle is drawn where the two imaginary lines cross. Try this with the first pair of data points: 30 and 3.

The advantage of the scattergram is that the reader can see any trends at a glance. In this case it suggests that faster articulation is accompanied by better recall.

In the example, two participants recalled the same number of words and had the same articulation rate. The scattergram in Figure 9.13 has not shown this. However, there are ways of representing situations where scores coincide.

FIGURE 9.13   Scattergram of articulation time and number of words recalled

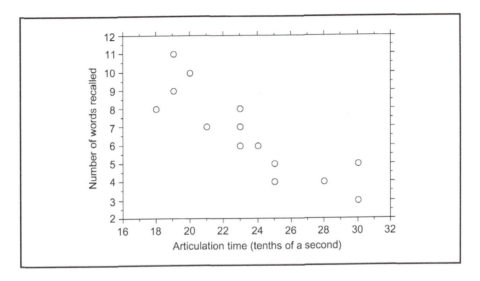

Ways of representing scores which are the same (ties)

There are a number of ways of showing that more than one data point is the same. One method is to use numbers as the symbols and to represent the number of data points which coincide by the value of the number (Figure 9.14).

FIGURE 9.14   Scattergram of articulation time and number of words recalled (with ties shown by numbers)

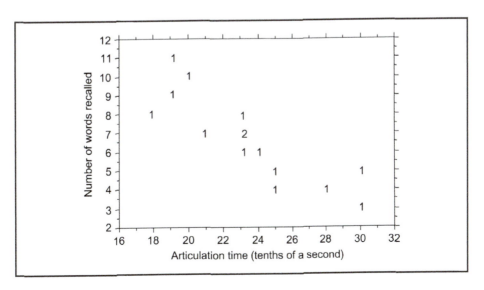

Another method is to make the size of the symbol denote the number of coinciding data points. The term *point binning* is sometimes used to describe using a symbol to denote that more than one data point coincides, or even that data points are close to each other, when there are a large number of data points in the graph. SPSS gives the option of denoting the number of points in a bin by size of circle (Figure 9.15) or by intensity of colour (not shown here).

FIGURE 9.15   Scattergram of articulation time and number of words recalled (showing ties as larger points)

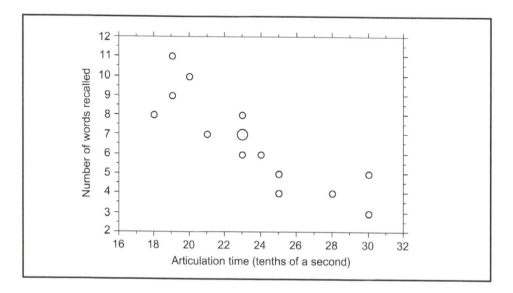

A further technique is to use what is called a *sunflower*. Here the number of data points which coincide is represented by the number of petals on the flower (Figure 9.16). This option has been dropped by SPSS.

FIGURE 9.16   Scattergram of articulation time and number of words recalled (showing ties as sunflower petals)

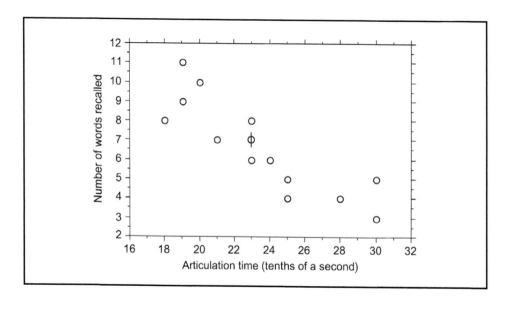

Plots of means

One IV

Line charts

Imagine for this example that researchers wish to explore the effectiveness of two different mnemonic techniques. The first technique involves participants in relating the items in a list of words to a set of pre-learned items which form a rhyme: one-bun, two-shoe and so on. For example, the list to be learned might begin with the words *horse* and *duck*. Participants are encouraged to form an image of a horse eating a bun and a duck wearing a shoe. This mnemonic technique is called *pegwords*. The second technique involves participants imagining that they are walking a route with which they are familiar and that they are placing each item from a list of words on the route, so that when they wish to recall the items they imagine themselves walking the route again (known as the *method of loci*). The researchers also include a control condition in which participants are not given any training.

The means and standard deviations for the three conditions are shown in Table 9.6 and in Figure 9.17.

TABLE 9.6   The mean and standard deviations of words recalled under three memory conditions

	control	*pegword*	*method of loci*
M	7.2	8.9	9.6
SD	1.62	1.91	1.58

FIGURE 9.17   Mean number of words recalled for three mnemonic strategies

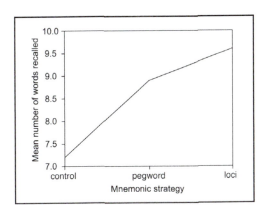

This suggests that using mnemonics improved recall and that the method of loci was the better of the two mnemonic techniques. However, it is important to be wary of how the information is displayed. Note that the range of possible memory scores shown on the vertical axis only runs between 7 and 10. Such truncation of the range of values can suggest a greater difference between groups than actually exists. Figure 9.18 shows the same means but with the vertical axis not truncated. Notice that the difference between the means does not seem so marked in this graph.

FIGURE 9.18   The mean word recall for three different memory groups (vertical axis not truncated)

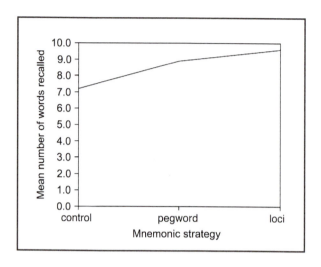

Bar charts

Means can also be shown using bar charts (Figure 9.19). In fact, given that the measure on the horizontal axis is discrete (and nominal in this case), bar charts could be considered more appropriate as they do not have lines connecting the means, which might imply a continuity between the levels of the IV which were used in the research.

FIGURE 9.19   Mean word recall under three mnemonic conditions

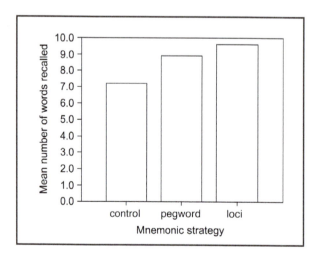

Two IVs

Line charts

When you have more than one IV it is usual to place the levels of one of them on the horizontal axis and the other as separate lines within the graph. An example of this would be if the previous design was enlarged to incorporate a second IV – the degree to which the words in the list were conceptually linked – with two levels, linked and unlinked, the linked list including items which are found in a kitchen. The means are shown in Table 9.7 and Figure 9.20.

From this the reader can see that recall was generally better from linked lists but this produced the greatest improvement, over unlinked lists, when participants were in the control condition where they were not using any mnemonics.

TABLE 9.7 The mean word recall of groups given linked and unlinked lists of words to remember using different mnemonic techniques

	control	pegword	loci
linked	11.0	10.6	10.6
unlinked	6.4	8.4	8.8

FIGURE 9.20 Mean number of words recalled for three mnemonic strategies when words in lists are linked or unlinked

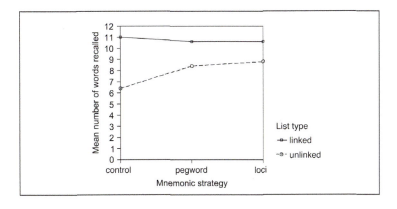

Bar charts

It is also possible to present the means of two IVs with a bar chart.

FIGURE 9.21 Mean number of words recalled for three mnemonic strategies when words in lists are linked or unlinked

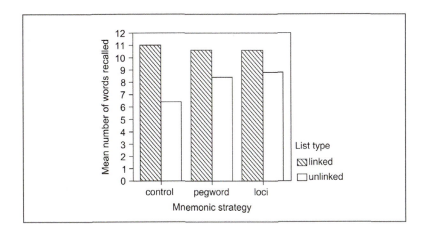

Plots of means and spread

As was pointed out under the discussion of numerical methods of describing data, means on their own do not tell the full story about the data. It can be useful to show the spread also in a graph because it gives an idea about how much overlap there is between the scores for the different levels of the IV. This can be done using a line chart, a bar chart or a box plot.

Error bar graphs

If we plot means and standard deviations for the three recall conditions we get the graph in Figure 9.22.

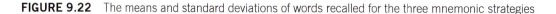

FIGURE 9.22   The means and standard deviations of words recalled for the three mnemonic strategies

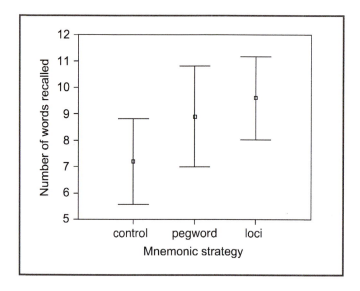

The vertical lines show one standard deviation above and below the mean. This shows that the difference between the three conditions is not as clear as was suggested by the graph, which just included the means. Here we can see that the three methods had a large degree of overlap. Chapter 12 shows other measures of spread which can be put on a line chart.

When more than one IV is involved in the study it is best not to show the standard deviation also on a line chart, because it will make reading the graph more difficult, as the standard deviation bars may lie on top of each other. However, if the lines are sufficiently well separated so that error bars do not overlap, then do include them.

Bar charts

With a bar chart, particularly if the bars are to be shaded, it is best to show just one standard deviation *above* the mean if the shading obscures the *SD* below the mean (see Figure 9.23).

FIGURE 9.23   The means and standard deviations of words recalled for the three mnemonic strategies

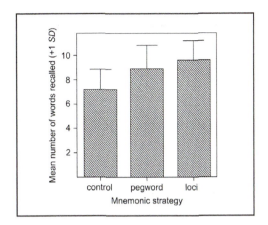

Figures 9.24 to 9.26 show two variables as in Figure 9.21 but with 1 *SD* error bars; above and below the mean because both are clearly visible. Each emphasises a different aspect of the display.

FIGURE 9.24   Mean and 1 *SD* error bars of number of words recalled for three mnemonic strategies when words in lists are linked or unlinked: emphasis on mnemonic strategy and clustered according to list type

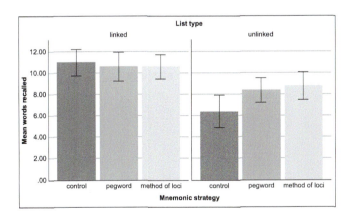

FIGURE 9.25   Mean and 1 *SD* error bars of number of words recalled for three mnemonic strategies when words in lists are linked or unlinked: emphasis on list type and clustered according to list type

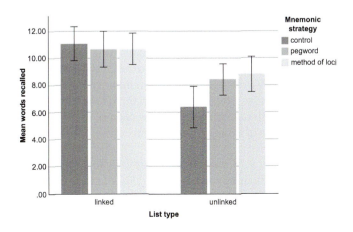

FIGURE 9.26   Mean and 1 *SD* error bars of number of words recalled for three mnemonic strategies when words in lists are linked or unlinked: emphasis on mnemonic strategy and clustered according to mnemonic strategy

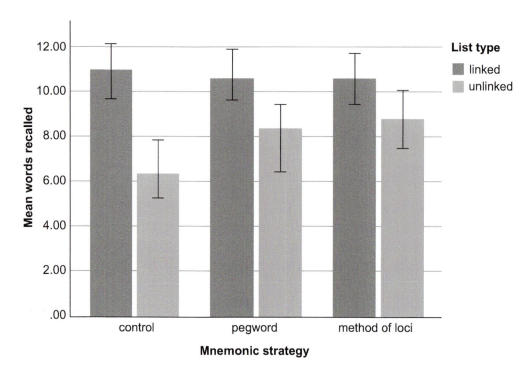

Box plots

A box plot provides the reader with a large amount of useful information. In this example I have illustrated the data for 17 people who were given a list to recall as represented in Figure 9.12.

The box represents the middle 50% of scores and the horizontal line in the box is the median. The upper and lower edges of the box are known as the *upper* and *lower hinges* and the range of scores within the box is known as the *H-range*, which is the same as the interquartile range given earlier in this chapter. The vertical lines above and below the box are known as *whiskers* – hence the box plot is sometimes called the *box-and-whisker plot*. The whiskers extend across what are known as the *upper* and *lower inner fences*. Figures 9.27 and 9.28 were created using SPSS, which has represented the upper and lower fences as extending as far as the highest and lowest data points which aren't considered to be outliers. It treats outliers as data points which are more than one-and-a-half times the box length above or below the box and they are symbolised by a circle and the 'case number' of the participant who provided that score. It treats as an extreme score one which is more than three times the box length above and below the box and it is denoted by an asterisk. An alternative version of the box plot is given by Cleveland (1985). Appendix I contains details of a more common convention for the position of the whiskers and how to calculate their length.

Looking at Figures 9.27 and 9.28, we have good grounds for treating participant 16, who has a score of 25, and possibly participant 17, who scored 15, as outliers which we may wish to drop

FIGURE 9.27 A box plot of number of words recalled

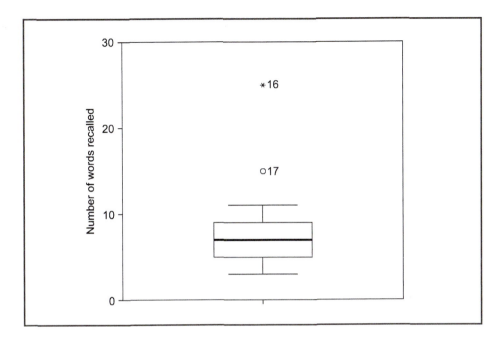

FIGURE 9.28 A box plot of words recalled, with elements of the box plot labelled

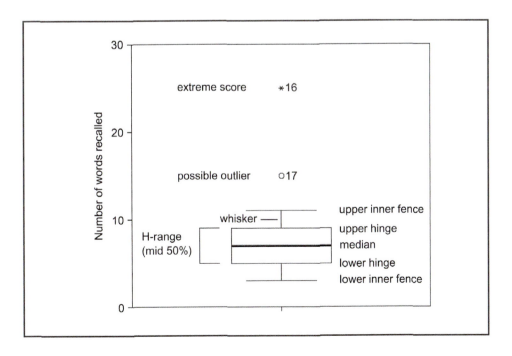

from further analysis. Nonetheless, we should be interested in how someone achieves such scores. I would recommend exploring why these data points are so discrepant from the rest, by checking that they have not been entered incorrectly into the computer or, possibly, by interviewing the people involved. Debriefing participants can help with identifying reasons for outlying scores. Chapter 12 gives another version of the box plot and another way of identifying what could be outlying scores.

The distribution of data

One reason for producing a histogram or stem-and-leaf plot is to see how the data are distributed. This can be important, as a number of statistical tests should only be applied to a set of data if the population from which the sample came conforms to a particular distribution – the *normal distribution*. In the remainder of this chapter histograms are going to be used to examine the distribution of data. However, in Chapter 12, I will introduce the normal quantile–quantile plot, which can be another useful way to examine distributions.

The normal distribution

When a variable is normally distributed, the mean, the median and the mode are all the same. In addition, the histogram shows that it has a symmetrical distribution either side of the mean (median and mode). For example, if an IQ test has a mean of 100 and a standard deviation of 15, then, if enough people are given the test, the distribution of their scores will be normally distributed as shown in Figure 9.29, where 16,000 people were in the sample.

FIGURE 9.29   The distribution of IQ scores in a sample of 16,000 people

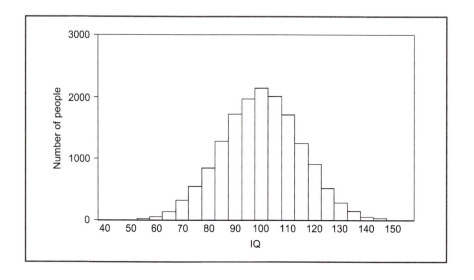

Notice that as the IQ being plotted on the graph moves further from the mean, fewer people have that IQ. Thus, fewer people have an IQ of 90 than have an IQ of 100. Because of its shape it is

sometimes referred to as the bell-shaped curve. Yet another name is the *Gaussian* curve after one of the mathematicians – Gauss – who identified it.

In fact, the normal distribution is a *theoretical* distribution, that is, one which does not ever truly exist. Data are considered to be normally distributed when they closely resemble the theoretical distribution. The normal distribution is continuous and, therefore, it forms a smooth curve, as shown in Figure 9.30.

FIGURE 9.30   The normal distribution curve

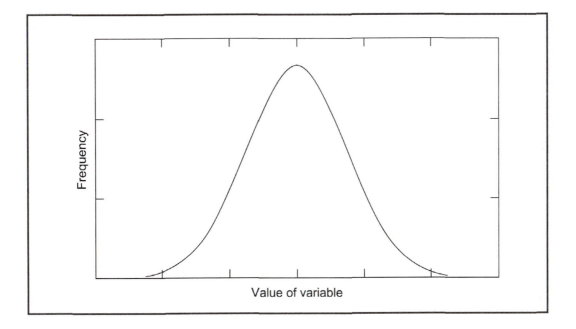

Skew

A distribution is said to be skewed when it is not symmetrical around the mean (median and mode). Skew can be positive or negative.

Positive skew

For example, we might test the recall of a sample of people and find that some people had particularly good memories. Note that the *tail* of the distribution is longer on the side where the recall scores are larger.

The mean of the distribution in Figure 9.31 is 9.69 words, the median is 8 words and the mode is 4 words. Notice that the measures of central tendency, when placed in alphabetical order, are decreasing.

FIGURE 9.31 A positively skewed frequency distribution of word recall

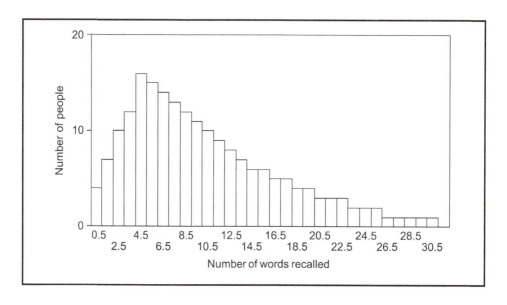

Negative skew

Our sample of people might include a large proportion who have been practising mnemonic techniques. Now the tail of the distribution is longer where the recall scores are smallest (Figure 9.32).

FIGURE 9.32 A negatively skewed distribution of words recalled

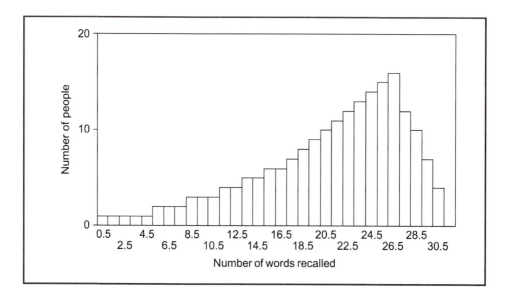

The mean of this distribution is 20.31 words, the median 22 words and the mode 26 words. Notice that this time the measures of central tendency, when placed in alphabetical order, are increasing.

Kurtosis

Kurtosis is a term used to describe how thin or broad the distribution is. When the distribution is relatively flat it is described as *platykurtic* (Figure 9.33), when it is relatively tall and thin it is described as *leptokurtic* (Figure 9.34) and the normal distribution is *mesokurtic*.

FIGURE 9.33 A platykurtic frequency distribution

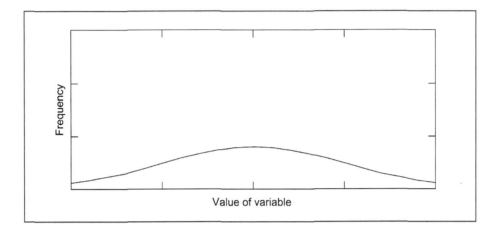

FIGURE 9.34 A leptokurtic frequency distribution

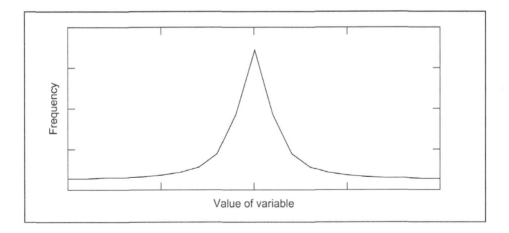

Skew and kurtosis can affect how data should be analysed and interpreted. Statistics packages give indexes of skew and kurtosis. However, as you will see when we look at statistical tests, the presence of skew in data is often more problematic than the presence of kurtosis. The effects of non-normal distributions are discussed in the appropriate chapters on analysis. Interpretation of the indexes is discussed in Appendix I.

Summary

The first stage of data analysis should always involve some form of summary of the data. This can be done numerically and/or graphically. This process can give a preliminary idea of whether the results of the research are in line with the researcher's hypotheses. In addition, they will be useful for helping to identify unusual scores and, when reporting the results, as a way of describing the data.

A frequent use of graphs is to identify the distribution of data. The normal distribution is a particularly important pattern for data to possess as, if present, certain statistical techniques can be applied to the data. The distribution of data can vary from normal by being skewed – non-symmetrical – or having kurtosis – forming a flat or a tall and thin shape.

The next chapter describes the process which researchers use to help them decide whether the results of their research have supported their hypotheses.

10 Going beyond description

Introduction

This chapter explains how the results of research are used to test hypotheses. It introduces the notion of probability and shows how the decision as to whether to reject or accept a hypothesis is dependent on how likely the results were to have occurred if the Null Hypothesis were true. An alternative approach – Bayesian statistics – is introduced in Chapter 27.

Hypothesis testing

The formal expression of a research hypothesis is always in terms of two related hypotheses. One hypothesis is the experimental, alternative or research hypothesis (often shown as H_A or H_1). It is a statement of what the researchers predict will be the outcome of the research. For example, in Chapter 9 we looked at a study which investigated the relationship between the speed with which people could speak a list of words (articulation speed) and memory for those words. In this case, the research hypothesis could have been: *There is a positive relationship between articulation speed and short-term memory.* The second hypothesis is the Null Hypothesis (H_0). It is, generally, a statement that there is no effect of an independent variable on a dependent variable or that there is no relationship between variables. For example, *there is no relationship between articulation speed and short-term memory.*

Only one H_A is ever set up for each H_0, even if more than one hypothesis is being tested in the research. In other words, each H_A should have a matching H_0. You will find that psychologists, when reporting their research, rarely mention their research hypotheses explicitly and even more rarely do they mention their Null Hypotheses. I recommend that during the stage when you are learning about research and hypothesis testing, you do make both research and Null Hypotheses explicit. In this way you will understand better the results of your hypothesis testing.

Probability

As was discussed in Chapter 1, it is never possible to prove that a hypothesis is true. The best we can do is evaluate the evidence to see whether H_0 is unlikely to be true. We can only do this on the basis of the probability of the result we have obtained having occurred, *if H_0 were true*. If it is unlikely that our result occurred if H_0 were true, then we can reject H_0 and accept H_A. On the other hand, if it *is* likely that our result occurred if H_0 were true, then we cannot reject H_0.

To discuss the meaning of probability I am going to use a simple example where the likelihood of a given chance outcome can be calculated straightforwardly. This is designed to demonstrate the point that different outcomes from the same chance event can have different likelihoods of occurring.

If we take a single coin which is not in any way biased and we toss it in the air and let it fall, then there are only two, equally possible, outcomes: it could fall as a head or it could fall as a tail. In other words, the probability that it will fall as a head is 1 out of 2 or 1/2. Similarly, the probability that it will fall as a tail is 1/2. We have listed the probabilities of each of the possible outcomes and in this case they are mutually exclusive;

in other words, only one of them can occur on a given occasion. Note that when we add the two probabilities the result is 1. This last point is always true: However many possible mutually exclusive outcomes there are in a given situation, if we calculate the probability of each of them and add those probabilities they will sum to 1. This simply means that the probability is 1 that at least one of the outcomes from such a set will occur. In the current example, the probability of the outcome being either a head or a tail is 1. Probabilities are usually expressed as proportions out of 1. Accordingly, the probability of a head is .5 and the probability of a tail is also .5. Probabilities are also sometimes expressed as percentages. Thus, there is a 50% chance that a single coin will fall as a head and there is a 100% chance that the coin will fall as a head or a tail.

Imagine that a friend says that she can affect the outcome of the fall of coins by making them fall as heads. Let us turn this into a study to test her claim. We would set up our hypotheses.

H_A: Our friend can make coins fall as heads.
H_0:   Our friend cannot affect the fall of coins.

We know that the likelihood of a coin falling as a head by chance is .5. Thus, if we tossed a single coin and it fell as a head we would know that it was highly likely to have been a chance event and we would not have sufficient evidence for rejecting the Null Hypothesis. In fact this is not a fair test of our hypothesis, for no outcome, in this particular study, is sufficiently unlikely by chance to act as evidence against the Null Hypothesis.

To give our hypothesis a fair chance we would need to have a situation where some possible outcomes were unlikely to happen by chance. If we make the situation slightly more complicated we can see that different outcomes can have different probabilities.

If we toss five coins at a time and note how they fall we have increased the number of possible outcomes. The possibilities range from all being heads through some being heads and some tails to all being tails. There are in fact six possible outcomes: five heads, four heads, three heads, two heads, one head or no heads.

However, some of the outcomes could have happened in more than one way, while others could only have been achieved in one way. For example, there are five ways in which we could have got four heads. Coin 1 could have been a tail while all the others were heads, coin 2 could have been a tail while all the others were heads, coin 3 could have been a tail while all the others were heads, coin 4 could have been a tail while all the others were heads, and finally coin 5 could have been a tail while all the others were heads. On the other hand, there is only one way in which we would have got five heads: all five coins fell as heads. Table 10.1 shows all the possible ways in which the five coins could have landed.

Note that there are 32 different ways in which the coins could have landed. We can produce a frequency distribution from these possible results; see Figure 10.1.

FIGURE 10.1   The distribution of heads from tosses of five coins

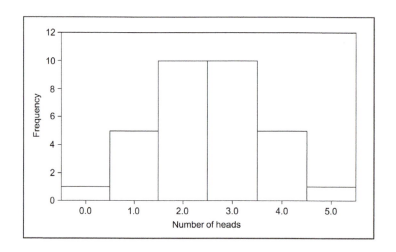

TABLE 10.1   The possible ways in which five coins could land

Outcome	Coin 1	Coin 2	Coin 3	Coin 4	Coin 5	Number of heads
1	T	T	T	T	T	0
2	H	T	T	T	T	1
3	T	H	T	T	T	1
4	T	T	H	T	T	1
5	T	T	T	H	T	1
6	T	T	T	T	H	1
7	H	H	T	T	T	2
8	H	T	H	T	T	2
9	H	T	T	H	T	2
10	H	T	T	T	H	2
11	T	H	H	T	T	2
12	T	H	T	H	T	2
13	T	H	T	T	H	2
14	T	T	H	H	T	2
15	T	T	H	T	H	2
16	T	T	T	H	H	2
17	H	H	H	T	T	3
18	H	H	T	H	T	3
19	H	H	T	T	H	3
20	H	T	H	H	T	3
21	H	T	H	T	H	3
22	H	T	T	H	H	3
23	T	H	H	H	T	3
24	T	H	H	T	H	3
25	T	H	T	H	H	3
26	T	T	H	H	H	3
27	H	H	H	H	T	4
28	H	H	H	T	H	4
29	H	H	T	H	H	4
30	H	T	H	H	H	4
31	T	H	H	H	H	4
32	H	H	H	H	H	5

From Table 10.1 we can calculate the probability of each outcome by taking the number of ways in which a particular outcome could have been achieved and dividing that by 32 – the total number of different ways in which the coins could have fallen (Table 10.2).

Thus, the least likely outcomes are either all heads or all tails, each with a probability of 1/32, or .031, of having occurred by chance. Remember that this can also be expressed as a 3.1% chance of

TABLE 10.2   The probabilities of different outcomes when five coins are tossed

Number of heads	Number of ways achieved	Probability
5	1	.031
4	5	.156
3	10	.313
2	10	.313
1	5	.156
0	1	.031

getting five heads. Put another way, if we tossed the five coins and noted the number of heads and the number of tails, and continued to do this until we had tossed the five coins 100 times, we would expect by chance to have got five heads on only approximately three occasions.

The most likely outcomes are that there will be three heads and two tails or that there will be two heads and three tails, each with the probability of 10/32, or .313, of occurring by chance. In other words, if we tossed the five coins 100 times we would expect to get exactly three heads approximately 31 times.

Now imagine that we have conducted the study to test whether our friend can affect the fall of coins such that they land as heads. We toss the five coins and they all land as heads. We know that this result *could* have occurred by chance but the question is, is it sufficiently unlikely to have been by chance for us to risk saying that we think that the Null Hypothesis can be rejected and our research hypothesis supported?

Before testing a hypothesis researchers set a critical probability level, such that the outcome of their research must have a probability which is equal to or less than the critical level before they will reject the Null Hypothesis that the outcome occurred by chance. They say that the range of outcomes which are as likely as or less likely than the critical probability are in the *rejection region*; in other words, such outcomes are sufficiently unlikely to occur when the Null Hypothesis is true that we can reject the Null Hypothesis.

Statistical significance

If the outcome of the research is in the rejection region the outcome is said to be statistically significant. If its probability is outside the rejection region, then the outcome is not statistically significant. By convention, generally attributed to Fisher (1925), in research the critical probability is frequently set at .05. The symbol α (the Greek letter *alpha*) is usually used to denote the critical probability. Thus, $\alpha = .05$ in much research. This level may seem rather high as it is another way of saying a 1-in-20 chance, but it has been chosen as a compromise between two types of error which researchers could commit when deciding whether they can reject the Null Hypothesis. If the probability of our outcome having occurred if the Null Hypothesis is true is the same as or less than α it is *statistically significant* and we can reject H_0. However, if the probability is greater than α it is not statistically significant and we cannot reject H_0.

As the probability (p) of getting five heads by chance is .031 (usually expressed as $p = .031$) and as p is less than .05 (our critical level of probability, α), then we would reject the Null Hypothesis and accept our research hypothesis. Thus, we conclude that our friend can affect the fall of coins to produce heads.

A further convention covers the writing about statistical significance. Often the word *statistical* is dropped and a result is simply described as being significant. In some ways this is unfortunate because it makes less explicit the fact that the significance is according to certain statistical criteria. However, it becomes cumbersome to describe a result as *statistically significantly different* and so I will follow the convention and avoid such expressions.

Error types

Any result *could* have been a chance event, even if it is very unlikely, but we have to decide whether we are willing to risk rejecting the Null Hypothesis despite this possibility. Given that we cannot know for sure that our hypothesis is correct, there are four possible outcomes of our decision process and these are based on which decision we make and the nature of reality (which we cannot know; Table 10.3).

TABLE 10.3   The possible errors which can be made in hypothesis testing

		Reality	
		H_0 false	H_0 true
Our decision	Reject H_0	Correct	Type I error
	Do not reject H_0	Type II error	Correct

Thus, there are two ways in which we can be correct and two types of error we could commit. When we make a decision we cannot know whether it is correct so we always risk making one type of error. A Type I error occurs when we choose to reject the Null Hypothesis even though it is true. A Type II error occurs when we reject our research hypothesis (H_A) even though *it* is true. The probability that we are willing to risk committing a Type I error is α. If we set α very small, although we lessen the danger of making a Type I error, we increase the likelihood that we will make a Type II error. Hence the convention that α is set at .05.

However, the actual level of α which we set for a given piece of research will depend on the relative importance of making a Type I or a Type II error. If it is more important to avoid a Type I error than to avoid a Type II error, then we can set α as smaller than .05. For example, if we were testing a drug which had unpleasant side effects to see whether it cured an illness which was not life-threatening, then it would be important not to commit a Type I error. However, if we were testing a drug which had few side effects but might save lives, then we would be more concerned about committing a Type II error, and we could set the α level to be larger than .05.

You may feel that this seems like making the statistics say whatever you want them to. While that is not true, unless there is good reason for setting α at a different level, psychologists often play safe and use an α level of .05. Thus, if you are uncomfortable with varying α, you could stick to .05 and not be seen as unusual by most other psychologists.

Calculating the probability of the outcome of research

Often in psychological research we do not make an exact prediction in our research hypotheses. Rather than say that our friend can make exactly five coins fall as heads, we say that she can affect the fall of coins so that they land as heads. Imagine that we reran the experiment but that now, instead of getting five heads, we get four heads. Remember that our friend did not say that she could make four out of five coins land as heads. If she had, the probability of this outcome would be 5/32 or .156 (see Table 10.2). Now, it may be the case that she *can* affect the coins but was having a slight off-day. We have to say that the probability of this result having occurred by chance is the probability of the actual outcome plus the probabilities of all the other possible outcomes which are more extreme than the one achieved but are in line with the research hypothesis; because if we only take account of the exact probability of the outcome, even though this was not the prediction made, we are unfairly advantaging the research hypothesis. The probability we are now using is that of getting four heads or more than four heads, that is, .156 + .031 = .187. Thus, if we only got four heads we would not be justified in rejecting the Null Hypothesis, as the probability is greater than .05. We therefore would conclude that there is insufficient evidence to support the hypothesis that our friend can affect the fall of coins to make them land as heads.

In the case of five coins we could only reject the Null Hypothesis if all the coins fell as heads. However, there are situations in which our prediction may not be totally fulfilled and yet we can still reject the Null Hypothesis.

To demonstrate this point, let us look at the situation where we throw 10 coins. Table 10.4 shows that in this case there are 11 possible results ranging from no heads to 10 heads, but now there are 1024 ways in which they could be achieved.

Imagine that to test our research hypothesis we toss the 10 coins but only nine fall as heads. The probability of this result (or ones more extreme and in the direction of our research hypothesis) would be the probability of getting nine heads plus the probability of getting 10 heads: .00976 + .00098 = .01074. In this case, we would be justified in rejecting the Null Hypothesis. Thus, the outcome does not have to be totally in line with our research hypothesis before we can treat it as supported.

Fortunately, it is very unlikely that you will ever find it necessary to calculate the probability for the outcome of your research yourself. The next chapter will demonstrate that you can use standard statistical tests to evaluate your research and that statisticians have already calculated the probabilities for you.

TABLE 10.4   The possible outcomes and their probabilities when 10 coins are tossed

Number of heads	Number of possible ways achieved	Probability
0	1	.00098
1	10	.00976
2	45	.04395
3	120	.11719
4	210	.20508
5	252	.24609
6	210	.20508
7	120	.11719
8	45	.04395
9	10	.00976
10	1	.00098

One- and two-tailed tests

So far we have considered the situation in which our friend tells us that she can cause coins to fall as *heads*. She has predicted the direction in which the outcome will occur. Imagine now instead that she has kept us guessing and has simply said that she can affect the fall of the coins such that there will be a majority of one type of side but she has not said whether we will get a majority of heads or a majority of tails.

We will again toss five coins and the hypotheses will be:

H_A: Our friend can cause the coins to fall such that a majority of them fall on the same side.
H_0: (*as before*) Our friend cannot affect the fall of coins.

When we made our original hypothesis, that the coins will fall as heads, we were saying that the result will be in the right-hand side of the distribution of Figure 10.1 (or the right-hand *tail* of the distribution). That is described as a *directional* or *unidirectional* hypothesis.

However, the new research hypothesis is *non-directional* or *bidirectional*, as we are not predicting the direction of the outcome; we are not saying in which tail of the distribution we expect the result to be. We can calculate the probability for this situation but now we have to take into account both tails of the distribution. If the coins now fall as five heads, the probability that the coins will all fall on the same side is the probability that they are all heads plus the probability that they are all tails; in other words, .031 + .031 = .062. Thus, in this new version of the experiment we would not reject the Null Hypothesis, because this outcome or more extreme ones, in the direction of our hypothesis, are too likely to have occurred when the Null Hypothesis is true (i.e. p is greater than .05, usually written as $p > .05$).

When the hypothesis states the direction of the outcome, we apply what is described as a one-tailed test of the hypothesis because the probability is only calculated in one 'tail' (or end) of the distribution. However, when the hypothesis is not directional the test is described as a two-tailed test because the probability is calculated for both tails (or ends) of the distribution.

With a one-tailed test the rejection region is in one tail of the distribution and so we are willing to accept a result as statistically significant as long as its probability is .05 or less, on the predicted side of the distribution. In other words, 5% of possible occurrences are within the rejection region (see Figure 10.2).

FIGURE 10.2   The rejection region for a one-tailed test with $\alpha = .05$

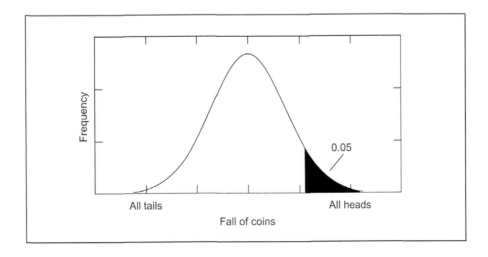

FIGURE 10.3   The rejection regions for a two-tailed test with $\alpha = .05$

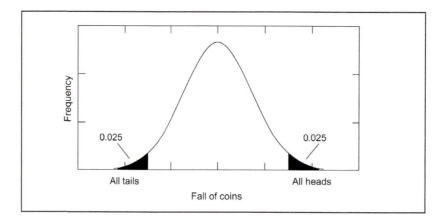

With a two-tailed test we usually split the probability of .05 into .025 on one side of the distribution and .025 in the other tail. In other words, 2.5% of possible occurrences are in one rejection region and 2.5% of them are in the other rejection region (see Figure 10.3).

If you compare Figures 10.2 and 10.3 you will see that for an outcome to be in the rejection region when we apply a one-tailed test, it can have fewer heads, and still be statistically significant, than it would have needed in order to be statistically significant had we applied a two-tailed test.

Summary

Researchers can never accept their hypotheses unequivocally. They have to evaluate how likely the results they achieved were to have occurred if the Null Hypothesis were true. On this basis they can choose whether or not to reject the Null Hypothesis. There is a convention that if the result has a probability of occurring, if the Null Hypothesis were true, of .05 or less then the result is described as statistically significant and the Null Hypothesis can be rejected. This probability level has been chosen as the best value for avoiding both a Type I error – rejecting the Null Hypothesis when it is true – and a Type II error – failing to reject the Null Hypothesis when it is false.

This chapter has only dealt with the way in which researchers take into account the danger of making a Type I error. Chapter 13 will show how they can also try to minimise the probability of committing a Type II error. In addition, it will show other ways to present our results which are less reliant on significance testing.

The next chapter explains how researchers can use summary statistics to draw conclusions about the population from which their sample came. It also discusses issues of how to select a sample from a population.

11 Samples and populations

Introduction

This chapter introduces the notion of population parameters and describes two basic approaches to choosing a sample from a population: random and non-random sampling. It explains the notion of a confidence interval and shows how proportions in a population may be estimated from the proportions found in a sample.

Statistics

The summary statistics, such as mean ($\bar{x}$ or M), variance (s^2) and standard deviation (s or SD), which were referred to in Chapter 9, describe the sample which was measured. Each statistic has an equivalent which describes the population from which the sample came; these are known as *parameters*.

Parameters

Each parameter is often symbolised by a lower-case letter from the Greek alphabet. The equivalent of the sample mean is the population mean and is denoted by μ (the Greek letter *mu*, pronounced 'mew'). The equivalent of the variance for the sample is the variance for the population, which is shown as σ^2 (the square of the Greek letter *sigma*). The equivalent of the standard deviation for the sample is the standard deviation for the population denoted by σ. There is a rationale for the choice of Greek letter in each case: μ is the equivalent of m in our alphabet, while σ is the equivalent of our s.

When a research hypothesis is proposed, the researcher is usually not only interested in the particular sample of participants which is involved in the research. Rather, the hypothesis will make a more general statement about the population from which the sample came. For example, the hypothesis *males do fewer domestic chores than their female partners* may be tested on a particular sample but the assumption is being made that the finding is generalisable to the wider population of males and females.

Parameters are often estimated from surveys which have been conducted to identify voting patterns or particular characteristics in a population, such as the proportion of people who take recommended amounts of daily exercise.

In addition, many statistical tests involve estimations of the parameters for the population, in order to assess the probability that the results of the particular study were likely to occur if the Null Hypothesis were true.

Choosing a sample

Often when experiments are conducted there is an implicit assumption, unless particular groups are being studied such as young children, that any sample of people will be representative of their population – people in general. This can lead to mistaken conclusions when the sample is limited to a group whose members come from a subpopulation, such as students. What may be true of students' performance on a task may not be true of non-students.

However, when researchers conduct a survey they frequently wish to be able to generalise explicitly from what they have found in their sample to the population from which the sample came. To do this they try to ensure that they have a sample which is representative of the wider population.

Before a sample can be chosen researchers have to be clear about what constitutes their population. In doing this they must decide what their unit of analysis is: that is, what constitutes a *population element*. Often the unit of analysis will be people. However, many of the principles of sampling also apply when the population elements are places, times, pieces of behaviour or even television programmes. For simplicity, the discussion will be based on the assumption that people are the population elements which are to be sampled.

The next decision about the population is what are the limiting factors – that is, what constraints are to be put on what constitutes a population element, such as people who are eligible to vote or people in full-time education. Sudman (1976) recommends that you operationalise the definition of a population element more precisely, at the risk of excluding some people. He gives the example of defining a precise age range rather than using the term 'of child-bearing age'. He does, however, note that it is possible to make the definition too rigid and in so doing to increase the costs of the survey by forcing the researchers to have to screen many people before the sample is identified.

The aims of the research will help to define the population and, to a large extent, the constitution of the sample. For example, if a comparison is desired between members of subpopulations, such as across the genders or across age groups, then researchers may try to achieve equal representation of the subgroups in the sample.

There are two general methods of sampling which are employed for surveys: random (or probability) sampling and non-random (or non-probability) sampling. Which one you choose will depend on the aims of your study and such considerations as accuracy, time and money.

Random samples

Random samples are those in which each population element has an equal probability, or a quantifiable probability, of being selected. The principle of random sampling can be most readily understood from a description of the process of simple random sampling.

Simple random sampling

Once the population has been chosen, the first stage is to choose the sample size. This will depend on the degree of accuracy which the researchers wish to have over their generalisations to the population. Clearly, the larger the sample, the more accurate are the generalisations which can be made about the population from which the sample came. (Details are given in Appendix II on how to calculate the appropriate sample size.) Secondly, each population element is identified. Thirdly, if it does not already possess one, each element is given a unique identifying code: for example, a number. Fourthly, codes are selected randomly until all the elements in the potential sample are identified.

Random selection can be done by using a computer program or a table of random numbers, or by putting all the numbers on separate pieces of paper and drawing them out of a hat. (Appendix XIX contains tables of random numbers.)

Problems in identifying the population elements

There can be a difficulty in using published lists of people because there may be systematic reasons why certain people are missing. For example, in the UK a tax was imposed in the 1990s which necessitated that the tax collectors knew where each person lived. Accordingly, many people tried to keep their names off lists which could be used to identify them, particularly lists of voters. If such a list had been used to identify people for a survey, people who were either too poor or were politically opposed to the tax would have been excluded, thus producing a biased sample.

Another example comes from the field of visual impairment. Local authorities in England and Wales keep a register of visually impaired people. However, for a person to have been registered they must have been recommended by an ophthalmologist. It is likely that many elderly people have simply accepted their visual impairment and have not visited an ophthalmologist, in which case the register will be under-represented by elderly people.

It may be that in order to identify population elements a wider survey has to be conducted. In the case of the visually impaired, it may be necessary to sample people in general to estimate what proportion of the population has a visual impairment and to estimate their characteristics.

Telephone surveys

When conducting a telephone survey it can be tempting to use a telephone directory. However, at least five groups will be excluded by this method: those who do not have a telephone; those who have call recognition and only answer calls from numbers they recognise; those who only have a mobile phone; those who have moved so recently to the area that they are not in the book; and those who have chosen to be ex-directory. In each case, missing such people may produce a biased sample.

One way around the last two problems is to select telephone numbers randomly from all possible permissible combinations for the given area(s) being sampled.

Alternative methods of random sampling

Simple random sampling is only one of many techniques. There are at least three other forms of random sampling, which can be simpler to administer but can make parameter estimation more complicated: systematic, stratified and cluster sampling.

Systematic sampling

Systematic sampling involves deciding on a sample size and then dividing the population size by the sample size. This will give a figure (rounded to the nearest whole number) which can be used as the basis for sampling. For example, if a sample of 100 people was required from a population of 2500, then the figure is 2500/100 = 25. Randomly choose a starting number among the population: let us say 70. The first person in the sample is the 70th person, the next is the 70 + 25 = 95th person, the next is the 95 + 25 = 120th person, and so on until we have a sample of 100. Note, however, that the 97th person we select for the sample will be the 2495th person in the population, and if we carry on adding 25 we will get 2520, which is 20 larger than the size of the population. To get around this, we can subtract 2500 from 2520 and say that we will continue by picking the 20th person followed by the 20 + 25 = 45th person.

One danger of systematic sampling could be if the cycle fits in with some naturally occurring cycle in the population. For example, if a sample was taken from people who lived on a particular road and the sampling basis used an even number, then only people who lived on one side of the road might be included. This could be particularly important if one side of the road was in one local authority and the other side in another authority.

Stratified sampling

A stratified sample involves breaking the population into mutually exclusive subgroups or strata. A typical example might be to break the sample down, on the basis of gender, into male and female strata.

Once the strata have been chosen, simple random sampling or systematic sampling can then be carried out within each stratum to choose the sample. An advantage of stratified sampling can be that there is a guarantee that the sample will contain sufficient representatives from each of the strata. A danger of both simple random and systematic sampling is that you cannot guarantee how well represented members of particular subgroups will be. There are two ways in which stratified sampling can be conducted: proportionately or disproportionately.

A case-control design can be seen as an example of a stratified sample where the strata are based on whether a potential participant has a condition, such as anxiety; see Chapter 4.

Proportionate sampling

Proportionate sampling would be involved if sampling from the strata reflected the proportions in the population. For example, a colleague wanted to interview people who were visiting a clinic for sexually transmitted diseases. She was aware that approximately one-seventh of the visitors to the clinic were female. Accordingly, if she wanted a proportionate stratified sample she would have sampled in such a way as to obtain six-sevenths males and one-seventh females.

Disproportionate sampling

If the researchers do not require their sample to have the proportions of the population they can choose to have the sampling be disproportionate. My colleague may have wanted her sample to have 50% males and 50% females. Clearly, it would not be reasonable simply to combine the subsamples from a disproportionate sample and try to extrapolate any results to the population. Such extrapolation would involve more sophisticated analysis (see Sudman, 1976).

Cluster sampling

Cluster sampling involves initially sampling on the basis of a larger unit than the population element. This can be done in two ways: in a single stage or in more stages (multi-stage).

Single-stage cluster sampling

An example would be if researchers wished to survey students studying psychology in Great Britain but instead of identifying all the psychology students in Great Britain they identified all the places where psychology courses were being run. They could randomly select a number of courses and then survey all the students on those courses.

Multi-stage cluster sampling

A multi-stage cluster sample could be used if researchers wished to survey children at secondary school. They could start by identifying all the education authorities in Great Britain and selecting randomly from them. Then, within the selected authorities they would identify all the schools and randomly select from those schools. They could then survey all the children in the selected schools or take random samples from each school which had been selected.

Cluster sampling has the advantage that if the population elements are widely spread geographically, then the sample is clustered in a limited number of locations. Thus, if the research necessitates the researchers meeting the participants, then fewer places would need to be visited. Similarly, if the research was to be conducted by trained interviewers, then these interviewers could be concentrated in a limited number of places.

Dealing with non-responders

Whatever random sampling technique you use, how you deal with non-responders can have an important effect on the random nature of your sampling. There will be occasions when a person selected is not available. You should make more than one attempt to include this person. If you still cannot sample this person, then do not go to the next population element, from the original list of the whole population, in order to complete your sample. By so doing you will have undermined the randomness of the sample because that population element will already have been rejected by the sampling procedure. When identifying the initial potential sample, it is better to include more people than are required. Then if someone cannot be sampled, move to the next person in the potential sample.

Non-random samples

Accidental/opportunity/convenience sampling

As the name implies this involves sampling those people one happens to meet. For example, researchers could stand outside a supermarket and approach as many people as are required. It is advisable, unless you are only interested in people who shop at a particular branch of a particular supermarket chain, to vary your location. I would recommend noting the refusal rate and some indication of who is refusing. In this way you can get an indication of any biases in your sample.

Quota sampling

A quota sample is an opportunity sample but with quotas set for the numbers of people from subsamples to be included. For example, researchers might want an equal number of males and females. Once they have achieved their quota for one gender they will only approach members of the other gender until they have sufficient people.

Sometimes the quota might be based on something, such as age group or socio-economic status, where it may be necessary to approach everyone and ask them a filter question to see whether they are in one of the subgroups to be sampled.

If quotas are being set on a number of dimensions, then the term *dimensional sampling* is sometimes used – for example, if researchers wanted to sample people with different levels of visual impairment, from different age groups and from different ages of onset for the visual condition. Such research could involve trying to find people who fulfilled quite precise specifications.

Purposive sampling

Purposive sampling is used when researchers wish to study a clearly defined sample. One example that is often given is where the researchers have a notion of what constitutes a typical example of what they are interested in. This could be a region where the voting pattern in elections has usually reflected the national pattern. The danger of this approach is that the region may no longer be typical.

Another use of purposive sampling is where participants with particular characteristics are being sought, such as people from each echelon in an organisation.

Snowball sampling

Snowball sampling involves using initial contacts to identify other potential participants. For example, in research into the way writers with a severe visual impairment compose, a colleague and I used our existing contacts to identify such writers and then asked those writers of others whom they knew.

The advantages of a random sample

If a random sample has been employed, then it is possible to generalise the results obtained from the sample to the population with a certain degree of accuracy. If a non-random sample has been used it is not possible to generalise to the population with any accuracy. The generalisation from a random sample can be achieved by calculating a *confidence interval* for any statistic obtained from the sample.

Confidence intervals

As with any estimate, we can never be totally certain that our estimate of a parameter is exact. However, what we can do is find a range of values within which we can have a certain level of confidence that the parameter may lie. This range is called a confidence interval. The level of confidence which we can have that the parameter will be within the range is generally expressed in terms of a percentage. A common level of confidence chosen is 95%. Not surprisingly, the higher the percentage of confidence which we require, the larger is the size of the interval in which the parameter may lie, in order that we can be more confident that we have included the parameter in the interval.

Appendix II contains an explanation of how confidence intervals are obtained and details of the calculations which would be necessary for each of the following examples. It also describes how you can decide on a sample size if you require a given amount of accuracy in your estimates.

For example, in the run-up to an election, a market research company runs an opinion poll to predict which party will win the election. It uses a random sample of 2500 voters and finds that 36% of the sample say that they will vote for a right-wing party – the Right Way – while 42% say that they will vote for a left-wing party – the Workers' Party. The pollsters calculate the appropriate confidence intervals. They find that they can be 95% confident that the percentage in the population who would vote for the Right Way is between 34.1% and 37.9%, and that the percentage who would vote for the Workers' Party is between 40.1% and 43.9%. Because the two confidence intervals do not overlap we can predict that if an election were held more people would vote for the Workers' Party than for the Right Way.

You may have noticed that polling organisations sometimes report what they call the *margin of error* for their results. In this case, the margin of error would be approximately 2%, for the predicted voting for either party is in a range which is between approximately 2% below and 2% above the figures found in the sample. The margin of error is half the confidence interval.

At least three factors affect the size of the confidence interval for the same degree of confidence: the proportion of the sample for which the confidence interval is being computed, the size of the sample and the relative sizes of the sample and the population.

The effect of the proportion on the confidence interval

The further the proportion, for which the confidence interval is being estimated, is from .5 (or 50%), the smaller is the size of the confidence interval. For example, imagine that the pollsters also found that .05 (or 5%) of their sample would vote for the far left party – the Very Very Left-Wing Party. When the confidence interval is calculated, it is estimated that the percentage in the population who would vote for the Very Very Left-Wing Party would be between 4.15% and 5.85%. Notice that the range for this confidence interval is only 1.7%, whereas with the same sample size the range of the confidence interval for those voting for the Workers' Party is just under 4%.

Table 11.1 gives examples of how the confidence interval of a subsample is affected by the size of the proportion which a subsample forms.

TABLE 11.1 The 95% confidence interval for a subsample depending on the proportion which the subsample forms of the sample of 2500

	Subsample as a proportion of entire sample					
	.05 or .95	.10 or .90	.20 or .80	.30 or .70	.40 or .60	.50
Confidence interval	1.7%	2.4%	3.1%	3.6%	3.8%	3.9%

The effect of sample size on the confidence interval

The degree of accuracy which can be obtained depends less on the relative size of the sample to the population than on the absolute size of the sample. This is true as long as the sample is less than approximately 5% (one-twentieth) of the size of the population. The larger the sample size, the smaller is the range of the confidence interval for the same level of confidence – that is, the more accurately we can pinpoint the population parameter.

To demonstrate that sample size affects the confidence interval, imagine that a second polling company samples only 100 people to find out how they will vote. Coincidentally, they get the same results as the first company. However, when they calculate the confidence interval, with 95% confidence for the percentage in the population who would vote for the Workers' Party, they find that it is between 32.33% and 51.67%, a range of 19.34%, or a margin of error of nearly 10%.

The larger the sample size, the greater is the increase in sample size that would be required to reduce the confidence interval by an equivalent amount. Note that the confidence interval shrank from 19.34% to 3.86%, a reduction of 15.48%, when an extra 2400 participants were sampled. If a further 2400 participants were added to make the sample 4900, the confidence interval would become 2.76%, which is only a reduction of a further 1.1%. In fact, you would need a sample of nearly 10 000 before you would get the confidence interval down to 2%. Table 11.2 shows the effect that sample size has on the width of the confidence interval for a subsample.

TABLE 11.2 The 95% confidence interval for a subsample, depending on the sample size, when the subsample forms half of the sample

Size of sample	Confidence interval
50	27.7%
100	19.6%
200	13.9%
300	11.3%
400	9.8%
500	8.8%
1000	6.2%
2000	4.4%
2500	3.9%
5000	2.8%
10 000	2.0%

You obviously have to think carefully before you invest the extra time and effort to sample 10 000 people as opposed to 2500 when you are only going to gain 1% in the margin of error.

The effect of sample size as a proportion of the population

The larger the sample is as a proportion of the population, the more accurate is the confidence interval (see Table 11.3).

Obviously, if you have taken a census of your population – that is, everyone in the population – then there is no confidence interval, for the statistics you calculate *are* the population parameters.

The final factor which affects the size of the confidence interval is the degree of confidence that you require about the size of the confidence interval.

The effect of degree of confidence on the size of a confidence interval

The figures which have been quoted previously have been for a 95% confidence interval, that is, a confidence interval when we wish to have 95% confidence that it contains the parameter we are estimating, which is the one usually calculated. However, it is possible to have other levels of confidence. The more confident you wish to be about where the parameter lies, the larger is the margin of error and therefore the larger the confidence interval. If we wished to be 99% confident about the proportion of supporters of the Right Way in the population, the margin of error would rise to 2.5% and the confidence interval would be between .335 and .385, or 33.5% to 38.5%. Table 11.4 shows the effects of varying confidence level on the width of the confidence interval when the subsample is .5 (50%) of the sample.

The preceding figures are only true for a simple random sample. The reader wishing to calculate confidence intervals or the sample size for other forms of random sample should consult a more advanced text, such as Sudman (1976). It must be borne in mind that this degree of accuracy is based on the assumption that the sample is in no way biased.

TABLE 11.3   The effect on the 95% confidence interval of varying the sample as a proportion of the population (for a subsample of 500 from a sample of 1000)

	Sample as percentage of population								
	10	20	30	40	50	60	70	80	90
Confidence interval	5.9%	5.5%	5.2%	4.8%	4.4%	3.9%	3.4%	2.8%	2.0%

TABLE 11.4   The effect of varying confidence level on confidence interval (for a subsample of 500 from a sample of 1000)

	Confidence level				
	80%	85%	90%	95%	99%
Confidence interval	4.0%	4.6%	5.2%	6.2%	8.1%

Summary

Researchers can choose the sample they wish to study either by random sampling or by non-random sampling. If they employ a random sample they can estimate from the figures they have obtained with their sample, with a certain degree of accuracy, the equivalent parameters for the population. The degree of accuracy of such estimates will depend on the sample size and the proportion of the population that they have sampled.

The next chapter describes how researchers can decide how likely it is that a sample has the same mean as a particular population.

12 Analysis of differences between a single sample and a population

Introduction

Sometimes researchers, having obtained a score for a person or a sample, wish to know how common such a score is within a population. In addition, researchers want to know whether a measure they have taken from a person, or a sample of people, is statistically different from the equivalent measure from a population. This chapter introduces a family of statistical tests – z-tests – which allow both these sorts of questions to be answered. In addition, it introduces a related family of tests – t-tests – which can be applied in some circumstances when there is insufficient information to use a z-test. The principles are explained through comparing a single score with a population mean and then a sample mean with a population mean. Confidence intervals for means are then introduced. The use of z-tests is then extended to the situation where a proportion in a sample is compared with a proportion in a population.

The chapter also includes additional versions of graphs and another way to identify outliers.

z-Tests

z-Tests allow researchers to compare a given statistic with the population mean for that statistic to see how common that statistic is within the population. In addition, they allow us to find out how likely the person, or sample of people, is to have come from a population which has a particular mean and standard deviation. A z-test can be used to test the statistical significance of a wide range of summary statistics, including the size of a single score, the size of a mean or the size of the difference between two means. In this chapter I will keep the examples to looking at a total for an individual participant or a mean which has come from one sample or a proportion which has come from one sample.

All z-tests are based on the same principle. They assess the distance which the particular statistic being evaluated is from the population's mean in terms of population standard deviations. For example, the statistic could be an individual's score on an IQ test, the population mean would be the mean IQ score for a given population and the standard deviation would be the standard deviation for the IQs of those in the population. The population parameters (or *norms*) will have been ascertained by the people who devised the test and will be reported in the manual which explains the appropriate use of the test.

The equation for a z-test which compares a single participant's score with that for the population is of the form:

$$z = \frac{\text{single score} - \text{population mean for the measure}}{\text{population standard deviation for the measure}} \tag{12.1}$$

At an intuitive level we can say that the z-test is looking at how large the difference is between the sample statistic and the population mean (the parameter) for the statistic. Therefore, the bigger the difference, the bigger z will be. However, z also takes into account the amount of spread which that statistic has in the population, expressed in terms of the standard deviation. Thus, the bigger the spread, the smaller z will be. Therefore, for z to be large, the difference between the statistic and the population mean for the statistic must be sufficiently large to counteract the effect of the size of the spread.

This stage in the explanation is critical because I am now introducing the general principle for most inferential statistics. So far when talking about a normal distribution (see Chapter 9) I have referred to a concrete entity such as an IQ score. Figure 12.1 shows the distribution of IQ scores for 7185 people, on a test which has a population mean of 100 IQ points and a standard deviation of 15 IQ points. Remember that in a normal distribution the mean value is also the most frequent value – the mode.

Imagine, now, that we select a person from the preceding sample. We put the IQ for that person into the equation for z and calculate z, and then we plot that z-value on a frequency graph. We repeat this for the entire sample; we select each person, one at a time, test his or her IQ, calculate the new z-value, and then plot it on the graph. Under these conditions, the most likely value of z would be zero because the most frequent IQ score will be the mean for the population:

$$z = \frac{100 - 100}{15}$$
$$= 0$$

FIGURE 12.1   The distribution of IQ scores in a sample of 7185 people, for a test with mean = 100 and $SD = 15$

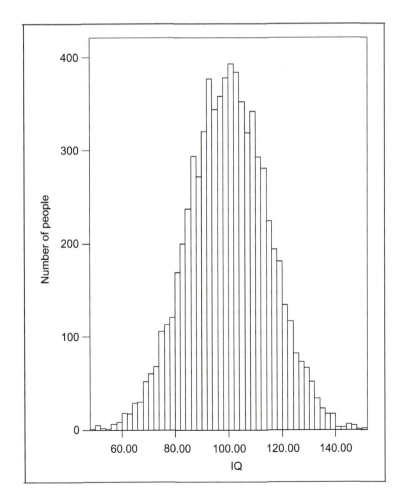

The larger the difference between the IQ score we are testing and the mean IQ for the population, the less frequently it will occur. Thus the distribution of the z-scores from the sample looks like the graph in Figure 12.2.

The theoretical distribution of z (the *standardised normal distribution*) is shown in Figure 12.3.

FIGURE 12.2   The distribution for 7185 z-scores calculated from the data in Figure 12.1

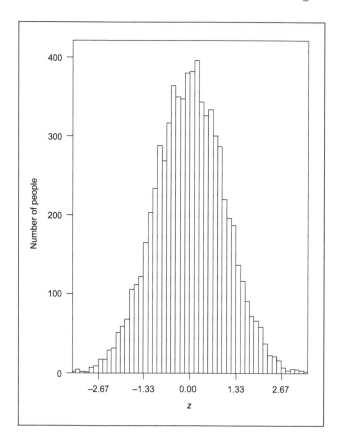

FIGURE 12.3   The standardised normal distribution

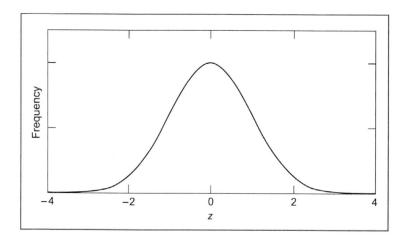

We can see that, as with all normal distributions, the distribution is symmetrical around the mean (and mode and median). However, the mean for z is 0. The standard deviation for z has the value 1.

Using the z-distribution, statisticians have calculated the proportion of a population which will have a particular score on a normally distributed measure.

Thus, if we have any measure which we know to be normally distributed in the population, we can work out how likely a given value for that measure is by applying a z-test. For example, if we know that a given IQ test has a mean of 100 and a standard deviation of 15, we can test a particular person's IQ and see how many people have an IQ which is as high (or low) as this person. Imagine that the person scores 120 on the IQ test. Using the equation for z we can see how many standard deviations this is above the mean:

$$z = \frac{120 - 100}{15}$$
$$= 1.333$$

We can now find out what proportion of people has a z-score which is at least this large by referring to z-tables.

Reading z-tables

Appendix XVII contains the table of z-values which can be used to find their significance. Table 12.1 shows a portion of Table A17.1 from Appendix XVII. To find the proportion for a z of 1.333, look in the first column until you find the row that indicates the first decimal place: 1.3. Now, because the figure (1.333) has more than one decimal place, look along the columns until you find the value of the second decimal place (3). Now look at the entry in the table where the row 1.3 meets the column 3 and this will give us the proportion of the population which would produce a z-score of 1.33 (or larger); we cannot look up a more precise z-score than one which has two decimal places in this table. The cell gives the figure .0918. This is the proportion of people who will have a score which is high enough to yield a z of *at least* 1.33, in other words, in this example, the proportion of people who have an IQ of 120 or more.

Converting the proportion to a percentage (by multiplying it by 100) tells us that the person whose IQ we have measured has an IQ which is in the top 9.18%. By subtracting this figure from 100% we can say that 90.82% of the population have a lower IQ than this person.

If a z-score is negative, then, because the z-distribution is symmetrical, we can still use Table 12.1 but now the proportions should be read as those below the z-score. Thus, if $z = -1.333$ (for a person with an IQ of 80), then 9.18% of people in the population have a score as low as or lower than this.

TABLE 12.1   An extract of the z-tables from Appendix XVII

z	0	1	2	3	4	5	6	7	8	9
1	0.1587	0.1562	0.1539	0.1515	0.1492	0.1469	0.1446	0.1423	0.1401	0.1379
1.1	0.1357	0.1335	0.1314	0.1292	0.1271	0.1251	0.1230	0.1210	0.1190	0.1170
1.2	0.1151	0.1131	0.1112	0.1093	0.1075	0.1056	0.1038	0.1020	0.1003	0.0985
1.3	0.0968	0.0951	0.0934	0.0918	0.0901	0.0885	0.0869	0.0853	0.0838	0.0823
1.4	0.0808	0.0793	0.0778	0.0764	0.0749	0.0735	0.0721	0.0708	0.0694	0.0681
1.5	0.0668	0.0655	0.0643	0.0630	0.0618	0.0606	0.0594	0.0582	0.0571	0.0559
1.6	0.0548	0.0537	0.0526	0.0516	0.0505	0.0495	0.0485	0.0475	0.0465	0.0455
1.7	0.0446	0.0436	0.0427	0.0418	0.0409	0.0401	0.0392	0.0384	0.0375	0.0367
1.8	0.0359	0.0351	0.0344	0.0336	0.0329	0.0322	0.0314	0.0307	0.0301	0.0294
1.9	0.0287	0.0281	0.0274	0.0268	0.0262	0.0256	0.0250	0.0244	0.0239	0.0233
2	0.0228	0.0222	0.0217	0.0212	0.0207	0.0202	0.0197	0.0192	0.0188	0.0183

2nd decimal place

Using z-scores in this way can show that a standard deviation can be a particularly useful summary statistic. If we know the mean and the standard deviation for a population (which is normally distributed), then if someone has a score which is one standard deviation higher than the mean, the z for that person will be 1.

For example, we know that the standard deviation for the IQ test is 15. If a person has an IQ one standard deviation higher than the mean, his or her IQ will be 115. Therefore,

$$z = \frac{115 - 100}{15}$$
$$= 1$$

If we look up, in Table 12.1, the proportion for $z = 1$ we use the column of Table 12.1 which is headed by 0, as a z of 1 is the same as a z of 1.00 – to two decimal places. The table shows the value .1587. In other words, 15.87% of the population have an IQ as large as or larger than one standard deviation above the mean. Similarly, if a person has an IQ which is one standard deviation below the mean (i.e. $100 - 15 = 85$), then the z of the score will equal -1. In other words, 15.87% of the population have an IQ which is one or more standard deviations below the population mean.

Using these two bits of information we can see that 15.87% + 15.87% = 31.74% of the population have an IQ which is either one or more standard deviations above or one or more standard deviations below the population mean. Therefore, the remainder of the population, approximately 68%, have an IQ which is within one standard deviation of the mean. That is, approximately 68% of the population will have an IQ in the range 85 to 115. Hence, if we assume that a given statistic is normally distributed we know that 68% of the population will lie within one standard deviation of the mean for that population.

Testing the significance of a single score when the population mean and standard deviation are known

Another way of looking at the z-test is to treat the z-distribution as telling us how likely a given score, or a more extreme score, is to occur in a given population. Thus, in the earlier example we can say that there is a probability of .0918 of someone who is picked randomly from the population achieving an IQ score as high as 120, or higher. In this way, we can test hypotheses about whether a given score is likely to have come from a population of scores with a particular mean and standard deviation.

For example, if an educational psychologist tests the IQ of a person, he or she can perform a z-test on that person's IQ to see whether it is significantly different from that which would be expected if the client came from the given population.

Let us say, again, that the mean for the IQ test is 100 and its standard deviation is 15. The educational psychologist could test the hypothesis:

H_A: The client has an IQ which is too low to be from the given population.

For this the Null Hypothesis would be:

H_0:   The client has an IQ which is from the given population.

The educational psychologist tests the client's IQ and it is 70. In order to evaluate the alternative hypothesis the psychologist applies a z-test to the data.

$$z = \frac{70 - 100}{15}$$
$$= -2$$

In other words, the client's IQ is two standard deviations below the population mean.

Finding out the statistical significance of a z-score

Computer programs will usually report the statistical significance of a z-score which they have calculated. However, sometimes you will need to refer to statistical tables to find out its significance.

To find out the probability that this person came from the population with a mean IQ of 100 and an SD of 15 we again read the z-tables. We take the negative sign as indicating a score below the population mean but for the purposes of reading the z-tables we ignore the sign, as the distribution is symmetrical.

The body of Table 12.1 (and Table A17.1) gives one-tailed probabilities for z's. In other words, it is testing a directional hypothesis. As the psychologist is assessing whether the person's IQ is lower than the mean IQ for the population, he or she has a directional hypothesis.

Looking at Table 12.1, we can see that with $z = 2$, $p = .0228$. This is the probability that a person with an IQ as low as (or lower than) 70 has come from the population on which the IQ test was standardised. As .0228 is smaller than .05, the educational psychologist can say that the client's IQ is significantly lower than the population mean and can reject the Null Hypothesis that this client comes from the given population.

Testing a non-directional hypothesis

If the educational psychologist had not had a directional hypothesis he or she would conduct a two-tailed test. To find a two-tailed probability, find the one-tailed probability (in this case .0228) and multiply it by two ($.0228 \times 2 = .0456$). We can do this because we need to look in both tails of the distribution: for a positive z-value *and* a negative z-value. In addition, as the distribution is symmetrical, the negative z will have the same probability as the positive z.

Examining the difference between a sample mean and a population mean

For the following discussion, imagine that researchers believe that children who have been brought up in a particular institution have been deprived of intellectual stimulation and that this will have detrimentally affected the children's IQs. They wish to test their hypothesis:

H_A: Children brought up in the institution have lower IQs than the general population.

The Null Hypothesis will be:

H_0: Children brought up in the institution have normal IQs.

Under these conditions we can employ a new version of the z-test: one to test a sample mean. However, in order to be able to apply a z-test to a given statistic we need to know how that statistic is distributed. Thus, in this case, we need to know what the distribution of means is.

The distribution of means

Instead of taking all the single scores from a population and looking at their distribution, we would need to take a random sample of a given size from the population and calculate the mean for the sample, and then repeat the exercise for another sample of the same size from the same population. If we did this often enough we would produce a distribution for the means, which would have its own mean and its own standard deviation.

Statisticians have calculated how means are distributed. They have found that the mean of such a distribution is the same as the population mean. However, the standard deviation of means depends on the sample size, such that the population of such means has a standard deviation which is $\dfrac{\sigma}{\sqrt{n}}$: that is, the standard deviation for the original scores divided by the square root of the sample size. The standard deviation of means is sometimes called the *standard error of the mean*.

Thus, if we know the mean and the standard deviation for the original population of scores, we can use a z-test to calculate the significance of the difference between a mean of a sample and the mean of the population, using the following equation:

$$z = \frac{\text{mean of sample} - \text{population mean}}{\left(\dfrac{\text{population standard deviation}}{\sqrt{\text{sample size}}} \right)} \tag{12.2}$$

In this way we can calculate how likely a mean from a given sample is to have come from a particular population.

Let us assume that 20 children from the institution are tested and that their mean IQ is 90, using a test which has a mean of 100 and a standard deviation of 15. We can calculate a z-score using the appropriate equation and this shows that $z = -2.98$. Referring to the table of probabilities for z-scores in Appendix XVII tells us that the one-tailed probability of such a z-score is .0014. As this is below .05, we can reject the Null Hypothesis and conclude that the institutionalised children have a significantly lower IQ than the normal population.

A z-test can be used when we know the necessary parameters for the population. However, when not all the parameters are known, alternative tests will be necessary. One such test is the *t*-test.

One-group *t*-tests

Evaluating a single sample mean when the population mean is known but the population standard deviation is not known

When we know, or are assuming that we know, the mean of a population but do not know the standard deviation for the population, the best we can do is to use an approximation of that standard deviation based on the standard deviation for the sample. Statisticians have worked out that it is not possible to produce such an approximation which is sufficiently close to the standard deviation of the population to be usable in a z-test. Instead they have devised a different type of distribution, which can be used to test the significance of the difference between the sample mean and the population mean, the *t*-distribution. You will sometimes see it described as Student's *t*. This is because William Gossett, who first published work describing it, worked for the brewer Guinness and chose this name as a pseudonym.

Using *t*-tests to test the significance of a single mean

The equation to calculate this version of *t* is similar to the equation for *z* when we are comparing a sample mean with a population mean, but in this case the sample standard deviation is used instead of the population standard deviation:

$$t = \frac{\text{mean of sample} - \text{population mean}}{\left(\dfrac{\text{sample standard deviation}}{\sqrt{\text{sample size}}} \right)} \tag{12.3}$$

The distribution of *t* is also similar to the distribution of *z*. It is bell-shaped with the mean at zero. However, it has the added complication that its distribution is partly dependent on the size of the sample, or rather the degrees of freedom (df). The latter are explained in the next section; for the present version of the *t*-test the df are one fewer than the sample size. Figure 12.4 shows the *t*-distribution when df is 1 and when df is 50.

FIGURE 12.4   *t*-Distributions with 1 and 50 degrees of freedom (df)

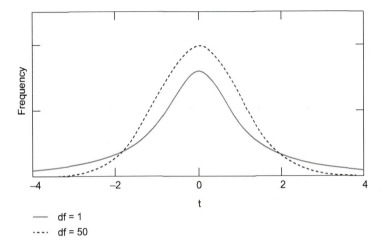

As the df increase so the distribution begins to look more like a normal distribution. Because the shape of the distribution depends on the df, instead of being able to produce a single distribution for *t*, there is a different distribution of *t* for each sized sample.

The significance of a number of different statistics, not just single means, can be tested using *t*-tests. Unlike *z*-tables, the probabilities shown in *t*-tables are dependent on the sample size and on the version of the *t*-test which is used. Statisticians have worked out that the distribution of *t* is dependent on a factor other than just the simple sample size: the degrees of freedom involved in the particular version of *t*. Instead of creating a different set of probability tables for each version of the *t*-test, the same table can be used if we know the degrees of freedom involved in the particular version of the *t*-test which we are using.

Degrees of freedom

The degrees of freedom for many statistical tests are partly dependent on the sample size and partly on the number of entities which are fixed in the equation for that test, in order that parameters can be estimated. In the case of a *t*-test, based on a single mean, only one entity is fixed – the mean – as it is being used to estimate the standard deviation for the population.

To demonstrate the meaning of degrees of freedom, imagine that we have given five people a maths exam. Their scores out of 10 were as follows:

Participant	Maths score
1	7
2	8
3	6
4	5
5	9

The mean score is 7; I can alter one number and, as long as I alter one or more of the other numbers to compensate, they will still have a mean of 7. In fact, I have the freedom to alter four of the numbers to whatever values I like but this will mean that the value of the fifth number will be fixed. For example, if I add 1 to each of the first four numbers, then the last number will have to be 5 for the mean to remain at 7. Hence, I have four degrees of freedom. Therefore, to obtain the degrees of freedom for this equation, we have to subtract 1 from the sample size.

The method of calculating the degrees of freedom for each version of the *t*-test will be given as each version is introduced. However, most computer programs will report the degrees of freedom for the *t*-test.

(Incidentally, as the sample gets larger, the sample standard deviation produces a better approximation of the population standard deviation. Hence, when the degrees of freedom for the *t*-test are over about 200 the probability for a given *t*-value is almost the same as for the same *z*-value.)

As an example of the use of this version of the *t*-test, known as the *one-group t*-test, let us stay with the scores on the maths exam. Imagine that researchers had devised a training method for improving maths performance in children. Ten 6-year-olds are given the training and then they are tested on the maths test, which produces an AA (arithmetic age) score.

The research hypothesis was directional:

H$_A$: The maths score of those given the training is better than that of the general population of 6-year-olds.

The Null Hypothesis was:

H$_0$: The maths score of those given training is not different from that of the population of 6-year-olds.

The mean for the sample was 7 and the *SD* was 1.247. The mean is consistent with the research hypothesis, in that the performance is better than for the population (which would be 6, their chronological age), but we want to know whether it is significantly so. Therefore the results were entered into the equation for a one-group *t*-test, with the result:

$$t_{(9)} = \frac{7-6}{\left(\dfrac{1.247}{\sqrt{10}}\right)}$$
$$= 2.536$$

where the 9 in parentheses shows the degrees of freedom.

Finding the significance of *t*

To find out the likelihood of achieving this size of *t*-value if the Null Hypothesis were true we need to look up the *t*-tables. A full version is given in Appendix XVII. Table 12.2 gives an extract of that table. Note that the *t*-tables are laid out differently from the *z*-tables. Here, probability levels are given at the top of the table, the degrees of freedom are given in the first column and the *t*-values are given in the body of the table. Note also that the one- and two-tailed probabilities are given.

To read the table find the degrees of freedom – in this case, 9. Read along that row until you come to a *t*-value which is just smaller than the result from your research (*t* = 2.536). Note that 2.262 is smaller than 2.536, while 2.821 is larger than it. Therefore, look to the top of the column which contains 2.262. As the research hypothesis is directional we want the one-tailed probability. We are told that had the *t*-value been 2.262, then the probability would have been .025. Our *t*-value is larger still and so we know that the probability is less than .025. This can be written *p* < .025, where the symbol < means *less*

TABLE 12.2 An extract of the *t*-table (from Appendix XVII)

Critical values for the t-test

	\multicolumn{9}{c}{One-tailed probabilities}								
	0.4	0.3	0.2	0.1	0.05	0.025	0.01	0.005	0.001	0.0005
	\multicolumn{9}{c}{Two-tailed probabilities}								
df	0.8	0.6	0.4	0.2	0.1	0.05	0.02	0.01	0.002	0.001
8	0.262	0.546	0.889	1.397	1.860	2.306	2.896	3.355	4.501	5.041
9	0.261	0.543	0.883	1.383	1.833	2.262	2.821	3.250	4.297	4.781
10	0.260	0.542	0.879	1.372	1.812	2.228	2.764	3.169	4.144	4.587

than. As .025 is smaller than the critical value of .05, the researchers can reject the Null Hypothesis and accept their hypothesis that the group who received maths training had better performance than the general population.

Reporting the results of a *t*-test

The column for the one-tailed $p = .01$ level in Table 12.2 shows that the *t*-value would have to be 2.821 to be significant at this level. As the *t*-value obtained in the research was larger than 2.262 but smaller than 2.821, we know that the probability level lies between .025 and .01. This can be represented as:

$$.01 < p < .025$$

There are many suggestions as to how to report probability levels. If you have been given the more exact probability level by a computer program, then report that more exact level; in this case it is $p = .016$. However, if you have to obtain the level from *t*-tables, I recommend the format that shows the range in which the p level lies, as this is the most informative way of presenting the information. If you simply write $p < .025$, the reader does not know whether p is less than or more than .001. The APA states that you shouldn't use a zero before the decimal point if the value of the number couldn't be greater than 1, as when reporting a probability. Personally, I don't like this convention but I will stick to it when showing how to report results formally. Another recommendation is that, unless you need greater precision, you should round decimals to two places. Accordingly, if the third decimal place is 5 or greater, then round up the second decimal place: in other words, increase it by 1. Therefore, 2.536 becomes 2.54. If the third decimal place is 4 or smaller, then leave the second decimal place as it is.

To report the results of the *t*-test use the following format:

$$t_{(9)} = 2.54, .01 < p < .025, \text{ one-tailed test}$$

Dealing with unexpected results

Sometimes researchers make a directional hypothesis but the result goes in the opposite way to that predicted. Clearly the result is outside the original rejection region (within which the Null Hypothesis could be rejected), because it is in the wrong tail of the distribution. However, it is possible, rather than simply to reject the research hypothesis, to ask whether the result would have been statistically significant had the hypothesis been non-directional. Abelson (1995) suggests that, if this happens, you look to see whether the result is statistically significant in the other tail of the distribution, but set the new α-level at .005 for a one-tailed test. In this way the overall α-level for the two assessments is the equivalent of a two-tailed probability of .05 + .005 = .055, which is only just over the conventional α-level. He calls this the *lopsided test*, because the regions in the two tails of the distribution are not the same, as they are in a conventional two-tailed test. As this is an unusual procedure, I recommend that if you use it, you explain thoroughly what you have done.

Another approach is to set up three hypotheses: a Null Hypothesis (H_0) – for example, that the means of two groups do not differ – and two directional hypotheses, one suggesting that group A has a larger mean than group B (H_1) and one suggesting that group B has a larger mean than group A (H_2) (in other words, two directional hypotheses). The results of our statistical test can lead to one of three decisions: fail to reject H_0, reject H_0 and favour H_1 or reject H_0 and favour H_2. See Dracup (2000), Harris (1997), Jones and Tukey (2000) and Leventhal and Huynh (1996) for more on this approach.

Confidence intervals for means

Confidence intervals (CIs) were introduced in Chapter 11 where the example used concerned proportions. Remember that a CI is a range of possible values within which a population parameter is likely to lie and that it is estimated from the statistic which has been found for a sample. You now have the necessary information to allow the CIs of a mean to be described. There are two ways in which the CI for the population mean can be calculated. The first is based on the z-test and would be used when the sample is as large as 30. The second is based on the t-test and is used when the sample is smaller than 30.

Appendix III gives worked examples of both methods of calculating the CI for a mean. The CI for the mean performance on the maths exam tells us where the mean is likely to lie if we gave the population of children the enhanced maths training. The 95% CI is 0.892 above and below the sample mean. The sample mean was 7 so the CI is between $7 - 0.892 = 6.108$ and $7 + 0.892 = 7.892$. Note that the interval does not include 6, which was the mean on the maths exam for the general population. This supports the conclusion that the enhanced maths training does produce better performance than would be expected from the general population.

z-Test comparing a sample proportion with a population proportion

Often researchers wish to test whether a proportion which they have found in a sample is different from either a known proportion in a population or a hypothetical proportion in the population. Thus, researchers might have found that a given proportion in the population smoked prior to a ban on smoking in public places. To test possible consequences of the ban, they wish to test whether the proportion of smokers they have found in a sample taken after the ban is different from the previous population proportion.

As long as the sample size multiplied by the proportion in the population and the sample size multiplied by (1 – the proportion in the population) are both greater than 5, the following equation is considered to be an accurate test. The further the proportion in the population is from .5, the larger the sample will need to be to achieve this requirement.

$$z = \frac{p - \pi}{\sqrt{\dfrac{\pi \times (1 - \pi)}{n}}} \qquad (12.4)$$

where p is the proportion in the sample, π is the proportion in the population and n is the sample size.

Returning to the smoking example, imagine that prior to a ban on smoking in public places 50% of people in the population smoked and that after the ban 45% of a sample of 1000 people were smokers. The researchers assume that there will be a reduction in the number of smokers after the ban. Then,

$$z = \frac{0.45 - 0.5}{\sqrt{\dfrac{0.5 \times (1 - 0.5)}{1000}}} = \frac{0.05}{\sqrt{\dfrac{0.25}{1000}}} = 3.16$$

Referring to the z-tables (A17.1 in Appendix XVII) we see that the one-tailed probability of this result is .00079. Thus, as long as the sample was a random one from the population for which the original figures had been derived, the researchers could conclude that there was a significant reduction in smoking after the ban.

Further graphical displays

We can now introduce three new versions of graphs which were originally discussed in Chapter 9: line charts of means with standard error of the mean; line charts with means and CIs; and notched box plots. In addition, we can introduce another graph which explores whether a set of data is normally distributed: the normal quantile–quantile plot.

Line charts with means and standard error of the mean

Some researchers, including those working in psychophysics, prefer to present the standard error of the mean as the measure of spread on a line chart. A line chart of means with standard deviations as the measure of spread (as shown in Figure 9.22) presents the range of scores which approximately 68% of the population would have if the measure was normally distributed. A line chart with the standard error of the mean as the measure of spread is presenting the range of scores which approximately 68% of *means* would have if the study were repeated with the same sample size.

Figure 12.5 presents the mean recall for the mnemonic strategies referred to in Chapter 9, but with the standard error of the mean as the measure of spread.

FIGURE 12.5 The mean recall and standard error of the mean for the three mnemonic strategies

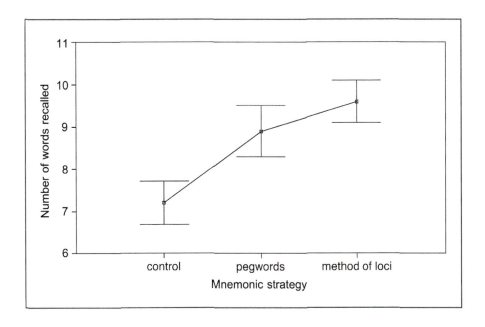

Line charts with means and CIs

An alternative measure which can be presented on a line chart is the CI. This allows comparison across groups to see whether the CIs overlap. If they do, as in Figure 12.6, this suggests that even if the result from the sample showed a significant difference between the means, the means for the three populations may not in fact differ.

FIGURE 12.6   The mean word recall and 95% confidence interval for the three mnemonic strategies

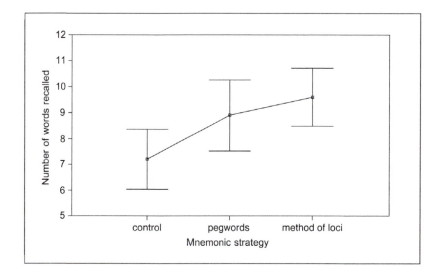

Notched box plots

Figure 12.7 shows the notched version of the box plot for the data given in Table 9.1 of participants' recall of words. This variant of the box plot allows the CI for the median to be presented in the notch. The way to calculate this CI is shown in Appendix III.

FIGURE 12.7   A notched box plot of number of words recalled

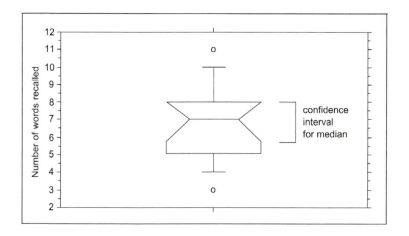

Normal quantile–quantile plots

Another form of graph, the normal quantile–quantile (normal Q–Q) plot, can help evaluate whether a distribution is normal. Quantiles are points on a distribution which split it into equal-sized proportions; for example, the median would be Q(.5), the lower quartile Q(.25) and the upper quartile Q(.75). Together these quartiles split the distribution into four equal parts. This graph is like a scattergram but it plots, on the horizontal axis, the quantiles against, on the vertical axis, what the quantiles would have been had the data been normally distributed. To find the *normal expected value* for an observed value, initially the quantile for the observed data point is calculated. The z-score which would have such a quantile in a normal distribution is then found. This is then converted back, based on the mean and *SD* of the original distribution, into the value which the data would have had had the distribution been normal. (An example of how this is calculated is given in Appendix III.) If the original data were normally distributed, then the points should form a straight line on the normal Q–Q plot. However, if the distribution was non-normal, then the points will not lie on a straight line. Figure 12.8 shows the normal Q–Q plot of the positively skewed data shown in Figure 9.28.

FIGURE 12.8 A normal Q–Q plot of data which are positively skewed

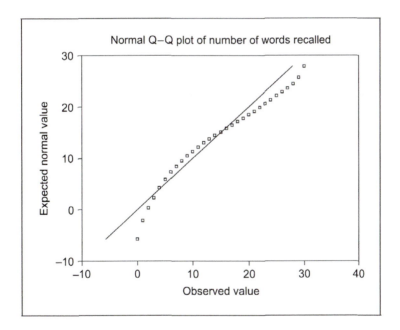

Identifying outliers with standardised scores

In addition to using box plots or stem-and-leaf plots to identify outliers, it is possible to standardise a set of numbers using a variant of the z-score and see how extreme any of the numbers are. To standardise the scores the following equation is used:

$$\text{standardised score} = \frac{\text{score} - \text{sample mean}}{\text{sample } SD}$$

Chapter 9 gave an example of the recall scores for a 16th person being added to the original group of 15 people. The 16th person had a score of 25, which was much higher than the rest. The mean for the

TABLE 12.3   The original and standardised scores for the word recall of sixteen participants

Original store	Standardised store
3	−.946
4	−.749
4	−.749
5	−.553
5	−.553
6	−.356
6	−.356
7	−.160
7	−.160
7	−.160
8	.037
8	.037
9	.233
10	.430
11	.626
25	3.378

enlarged sample is 7.8125 and the sample *SD* is 5.088. Table 12.3 shows the original and the standardised recall scores.

A standardised score of greater than 3 or less than −3 should be investigated further as a potential outlier. Note that the score of 25 produced a standardised score of 3.378.

Summary

When researchers know the population mean and standard deviation for a given summary statistic they can compare a value for the statistic which has been obtained from one person or a sample of people with the population mean for that statistic, using a z-test. In this way, they can see how common the value they have obtained is among the population and thus how likely the person or group is to have come from a population with that mean and standard deviation. When only the population mean is known for the statistic a t-test has to be employed rather than a z-test.

The present chapter has largely concentrated on statistical significance as a way of deciding between a research hypothesis and a Null Hypothesis. In other words, it has only addressed the probability of making a Type I error (rejecting the Null Hypothesis when it is true). The next chapter explains how researchers can attempt to avoid a Type II error and introduces additional summary statistics which can help researchers in their decisions.

13 Effect size and power

Introduction

There has been a tendency for psychologists and other behavioural scientists to concentrate on whether a result is statistically significant, to the exclusion of any other statistical consideration (Clark-Carter, 1997; Cohen, 1962; Sedlmeier & Gigerenzer, 1989). Early descriptions of the method of hypothesis testing (e.g. Fisher, 1935) only involved the Null Hypothesis. This chapter deals with the consequences of this approach and describes additional techniques, which come from the ideas of Neyman and Pearson (1933), which can enable researchers to make more informed decisions.

Limitations of statistical significance testing

Concentration on statistical significance misses an important aspect of inferential statistics – statistical significance is affected by sample size. This has two consequences. Firstly, statistical probability cannot be used as a measure of the magnitude of a result; two studies may produce very different results, in terms of statistical significance, simply because they have employed different sample sizes. Therefore, if only statistical significance is reported, then results cannot be sensibly compared. Secondly, two studies conducted in the same way in every respect except sample size may lead to different conclusions. The one with the larger sample size may achieve a statistically significant result while the other one does not. Thus, the researchers in the first study will reject the Null Hypothesis of no effect while the researchers in the smaller study will reject their research hypothesis. Accordingly, the smaller the sample size, the more likely we are to commit a Type II error – rejecting the research hypothesis when in fact it is correct.

Two new concepts will provide solutions to the two problems. *Effect size* gives a measure of magnitude of a result which is independent of sample size. Calculating the *power* of a statistical test helps researchers decide on the likelihood that a Type II error will be avoided.

Effect size

To allow the results of studies to be compared we need a measure which is independent of sample size. Effect sizes provide such a measure. In future chapters appropriate measures of effect size will be introduced for each research design. In this chapter I will deal with the designs described in the previous chapter, where a mean of a set of scores is being compared with a population mean, or a proportion from a sample is compared with a proportion in a population. A number of different versions exist for some effect size measures. In general I am going to use the measures suggested by Cohen (1988).

Comparing two means

In the case of the difference between two means we can use Cohen's *d* as the measure of effect size:

$$d = \frac{\mu_2 - \mu_1}{\sigma}$$

where μ_1 is the mean for one population, μ_2 is the mean for the other population and σ is the standard deviation for the population (explained next).

To make this less abstract, recall the example, used in the last chapter, in which the IQs of children brought up in an institution are compared with the IQs of children not reared in an institution. Then, μ_1 is the mean IQ of the population of children reared in institutions, μ_2 is the mean for the population of children not reared in institutions and σ is the standard deviation of IQ scores, which is assumed to be the same for both groups. This assumption will be explained in the next chapter but need not concern us here. Usually, we do not know the values of all the parameters which are needed to calculate an effect size and so we use the equivalent sample statistics.

Accordingly, *d* is a measure of how many standard deviations apart the two means are. Note that although this is similar to the equations for calculating *z*, given in the last chapter, *d* fulfils our requirement for a measure which is independent of the sample size.[1]

In the previous chapter we were told that, as usual, the mean for the 'normal' population's IQ is 100; the standard deviation for the particular test was 15 and the mean IQ for the institutionalised children was 90. Therefore,

$$d = \frac{90 - 100}{15}$$
$$= -0.67$$

After surveying published research, Cohen has defined, for each effect size measure, what constitutes a small effect, a medium effect and a large effect. In the case of *d*, a *d* of 0.2 (meaning that the mean IQs of the groups are just under ¼ of an *SD* apart) represents a small effect size, a *d* of 0.5 (½ an *SD*) constitutes a medium effect size and a *d* of 0.8 (just over ¾ of an *SD*) would be a large effect size (when evaluating the magnitude of an effect size, ignore the negative sign). Thus, in this study we can say that being reared in an institution has between a medium and a large effect on the IQs of children.

An additional use of effect size is that it allows the results of a number of related studies to be combined to see whether they produce a consistent effect. This technique – meta-analysis – will be dealt with in Chapter 26.

Comparing a proportion from a sample with a population proportion of .5

Cohen (1988) gives the effect size *g* for this situation, where $g = p - \pi$ (where *p* is the proportion in the sample and π is the proportion in the population). He defines a *g* of 0.05 as a small effect, a *g* of 0.15 as a medium effect and a *g* of 0.25 as a large effect.

The importance of an effect size

As Rosnow and Rosenthal (1989) have pointed out, the importance of an effect size will depend on the nature of the research being conducted. If a study into the effectiveness of a drug at saving lives found

---

1 The equation used to calculate effect size is independent of sample size. However, as with any statistic calculated from a sample, the larger the sample, the more accurate the statistic will be as an estimate of the value in the population (the parameter).

only a small effect size, even though the lives of only a small proportion of participants were being saved, this would be an important effect. However, if the study was into something trivial such as a technique for enhancing performance on a computer game, then even a large effect might not be considered to be important. Thus, Cohen's guidelines for what constitute large, medium and small effects can be useful to put a result in perspective, particularly in a new area of research, but they should not be used slavishly without thought to the context of the study from which an effect size has been derived.

Statistical power

Statistical power is defined as the probability of *avoiding* a Type II error. The probability of making a Type II error is usually symbolised by β (the Greek letter beta). Therefore, the power of a test is $1 - \beta$.

Figure 13.1 represents the situation where two means are being compared: for example, the mean IQ for the population on which a test has been standardised (μ_1) and the mean for the population of people given special training to enhance their IQs (μ_2). Formally stated, H_0 is $\mu_2 = \mu_1$, while the research hypothesis (H_A) is $\mu_2 > \mu_1$. As usual an α-level is set (say, $\alpha = .05$). This determines the critical mean, which is the mean IQ, for a given sample size, which would be just large enough to allow us to reject H_0. It determines β, which will be the area (in the distribution which is centred on μ_2) to the left of the critical mean. It also then determines the power ($1 - \beta$), which is the area (in the distribution which is centred on μ_2) lying to the right of the critical mean.

The power we require for a given piece of research will depend on the aims of the research. Thus, if it is particularly important that we avoid making a Type II error we will aim for a level of power which is as near 1 as possible. For example, if we were testing the effectiveness of a drug which could save lives we would not want wrongly to reject the research hypothesis that the drug was effective. However, as you will see, achieving such a level of power may involve an impractically large sample size. Therefore, Cohen and others recommend, as a rule of thumb, that a reasonable minimum level of power to aim for, under normal circumstances, is .8. In other words, the probability of making a Type II error (β) is $1 - $ power $= .2$. With an α-level set at .05 this will give us a ratio of the probabilities of committing a Type I and a Type II error of 1:4. However, as was stated in Chapter 10, it is possible to set a different level of α.

Statistical power depends on many factors, including the type of test being employed, the effect size, the design – whether it is a between-subjects or a within-subjects design – the α-level set, whether the test is one- or two-tailed and, in the case of between-subjects designs, the relative size of the samples.

FIGURE 13.1 A graphical representation of the links between statistical power, β and α

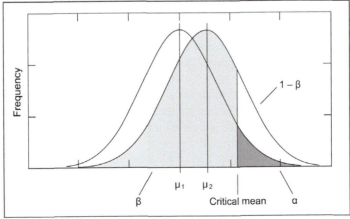

Power analysis can be used in two ways. It can be used prospectively during the design stage to decide on the sample size required to achieve a given level of power. It can also be used retrospectively, once the data have been collected, to ascertain what power the test had. The more useful approach is prospective power analysis. Once the design, α-level and tail of test have been decided, researchers can calculate the sample size they require. However, they still have the problem of arriving at an indication of the effect size before they can do the power calculations. But as the study has yet to be conducted this is unknown.

Choosing the effect size prior to conducting a study

There are at least four ways in which effect size can be chosen before a study is conducted. Firstly, researchers can look at previous research in the area to get an impression of the size of effects which have been found. This would be helped if researchers routinely reported the effect sizes they have found. The APA's publication manual (American Psychological Association, 2010) recommends the inclusion of effect sizes in the report of research. Nonetheless, if the appropriate descriptive statistics have been reported (such as means and SDs), then an effect size can be calculated. Secondly, in the absence of such information, researchers can calculate an effect size from the results of their pilot studies. However, as noted earlier, the accuracy of the estimate of the effect size will be affected by the sample size; the larger the sample in the pilot study, the more accurate the estimate of the population value will be. Thirdly, particularly in cases of intervention studies, the researchers could set a minimum effect size which would be useful. Thus, clinical psychologists might want to reduce scores on a depression measure by at least a certain amount, or health psychologists might want to increase exercise by at least a given amount. A final way around the problem is to decide beforehand what size of effect they wish to detect based on Cohen's classification of effects into small, medium and large. Researchers can decide that even a small effect is important in the context of their particular study. Alternatively, they can aim for the necessary power for detecting a medium or even a large effect if this is appropriate for their research. It should be emphasised that they are not saying that they know what effect size *will* be found but only that this is the effect size that they would be willing to put the effort in to detect as statistically significant.

I would only recommend this last approach if there is no other indication of what effect size your research is likely to entail. Nonetheless, this approach does at least allow you to do power calculations in the absence of any other information on the likely effect size.

To aid the reader with this approach I have provided power tables in Appendix XVIII for each statistical test and as each test is introduced I will explain the use of the appropriate table.

The power of a one-group z-test to compare a sample mean and population mean

Power analysis for this test is probably the simplest and for the interested reader I have provided, in Appendix IV, a description of how to calculate the exact power for the test and how to calculate the sample size needed for a given level of power. Here I will describe how to use power tables to decide sample size.

Table 13.1 shows part of the power table for a one-group z-test, from Appendix XVIII. The top row of the table shows effect sizes (d). The first column shows the sample size. The figures in the body of the table are the statistical power which will be achieved for a given effect size if a given sample size is used.

The table shows that for a one-group z-test with a medium effect size ($d = 0.5$), a one-tailed test and an α-level of .05, to achieve power of .80, 25 participants are required.

The following examples show the effect which altering one of these variables at a time has on power. Although these examples are for the one-group z-test, the power of all statistical tests will be

TABLE 13.1 An extract of the power tables for a one-group z-test, one-tailed probability, $\alpha = 0.05$ (*denotes that the power is over 0.995)

Effect size (d)

n	0.1	0.2	0.3	0.4	0.5	0.6	0.7	0.8	0.9	1.0	1.1	1.2	1.3	1.4
15	0.10	0.19	0.31	0.46	0.61	0.75	0.86	0.93	0.97	0.99	*	*	*	*
16	0.11	0.20	0.33	0.48	0.64	0.77	0.88	0.94	0.97	0.99	*	*	*	*
17	0.11	0.21	0.34	0.50	0.66	0.80	0.89	0.95	0.98	0.99	*	*	*	*
18	0.11	0.21	0.35	0.52	0.68	0.82	0.91	0.96	0.99	*	*	*	*	*
19	0.11	0.22	0.37	0.54	0.70	0.83	0.92	0.97	0.99	*	*	*	*	*
20	0.12	0.23	0.38	0.56	0.72	0.85	0.93	0.97	0.99	*	*	*	*	*
25	0.13	0.26	0.44	0.64	0.80	0.91	0.97	0.99	*	*	*	*	*	*
30	0.14	0.29	0.50	0.71	0.86	0.95	0.99	*	*	*	*	*	*	*
35	0.15	0.32	0.55	0.76	0.91	0.97	0.99	*	*	*	*	*	*	*
40	0.16	0.35	0.60	0.81	0.94	0.98	*	*	*	*	*	*	*	*

similarly affected by changes in sample size, effect size, the α-level and, where a one-tailed test is possible for the given statistical test, the nature of the research hypothesis.

Sample size and power

Increased sample size produces greater power. If everything else is held constant in the preceding example but we use 40 participants, then power rises to .94.

Effect size and power

The larger the effect size the greater the power. With an effect size of 0.7, power rises to .97 for 25 participants with a one-tailed α-level of .05.

Research hypothesis and power

A one-tailed test is more powerful than a two-tailed test. A two-tailed test using 25 people for an effect size of $d = 0.5$ would have given power of .71 (see Appendix XVIII), whereas the one-tailed version gave power of .8.

α-level and power

The smaller the α-level, the lower is the power. In other words, if everything else is held constant, then reducing the likelihood of making a Type I error increases the likelihood of making a Type II error. Setting α at .01 reduces power from .8 to .57. On the other hand, setting α at .1 increases power to nearly .99. These effects can be seen in Figure 13.1; as α gets smaller (the critical mean moves to the right), $1 - \beta$ gets smaller, and as α gets larger (the critical mean moves to the left), $1 - \beta$ gets larger.

The power of a one-group t-test

To assess the power of a one-group t-test or to decide on the sample size necessary to achieve a desired level of power, use the table provided in Appendix XVIII, part of which is reproduced in Table 13.2. The tables for a one-group t-test can be read in the same way as those for the one-group z-test. For example, imagine that researchers wished to detect a small effect size ($d = 0.2$) and have power of .8. They would

TABLE 13.2   An extract of a power table for one-group *t*-tests, one-tailed probability, α = 0.05 (* denotes that the power is over 0.995)

n	Effect size (d)													
	0.1	0.2	0.3	0.4	0.5	0.6	0.7	0.8	0.9	1	1.1	1.2	1.3	1.4
140	0.32	0.76	0.97	*	*	*	*	*	*	*	*	*	*	*
150	0.33	0.79	0.98	*	*	*	*	*	*	*	*	*	*	*
160	0.35	0.81	0.98	*	*	*	*	*	*	*	*	*	*	*
170	0.36	0.83	0.99	*	*	*	*	*	*	*	*	*	*	*
180	0.38	0.85	0.99	*	*	*	*	*	*	*	*	*	*	*
190	0.39	0.86	0.99	*	*	*	*	*	*	*	*	*	*	*
200	0.41	0.88	0.99	*	*	*	*	*	*	*	*	*	*	*
300	0.53	0.96	*	*	*	*	*	*	*	*	*	*	*	*
400	0.64	0.99	*	*	*	*	*	*	*	*	*	*	*	*
500	0.72	*	*	*	*	*	*	*	*	*	*	*	*	*
600	0.79	*	*	*	*	*	*	*	*	*	*	*	*	*
700	0.84	*	*	*	*	*	*	*	*	*	*	*	*	*
800	0.88	*	*	*	*	*	*	*	*	*	*	*	*	*

need to have between 150 and 160 participants in their study. Therefore, as .80 lies midway between .79 and .81, we can say that the sample would need to be 155 (midway between 150 and 160).

The power of the z-test to compare a proportion from a sample with a proportion of .5 in the population

In Chapter 12 an example was given of researchers wishing to compare the proportion of smokers in a sample taken after a ban on smoking in public places (.45) with the proportion in the population who smoked prior to the ban (.5). Using the effect size *g* (the difference between the two proportions) of .05, we can use Table A18.2 in Appendix XVIII, and find that if the researchers had a directional hypothesis and hence were using a one-tailed test, with an α-level of .05, then they would need over 600 participants to give their test power of .8.

Prospective power analysis after a study

If a study fails to support the research hypothesis, there are two possible explanations. The one that is usually assumed is that the hypothesis was in some way incorrect. However, an alternative explanation is that the test had insufficient power to achieve statistical significance. If statistical significance is not achieved I recommend that researchers calculate the sample size which would be necessary, for the effect size they have found in their study, to achieve power of .8.

Sometimes researchers, particularly students, state that had they used more participants they might have achieved a statistically significant result. This is not a very useful statement, as it will almost always be true if a big enough sample is employed, however small the effect size. For example, if a one-group *t*-test was being used, with α = .05 and the effect size was as small as *d* = 0.03, a sample size of approximately 10,000 would give power of .8 for a one-tailed test. This effect size is achieved if the sample mean is only one-thirtieth of a standard deviation from the population mean – a difference of half an IQ point if the sample *SD* is 15 IQ points.

It is far more useful to specify the number of participants which would be required to achieve power of .8. This would put the results in perspective. If the effect size is particularly small and the sample size required is vast, then it questions the value of trying to replicate the study as it stands, whereas if the sample size were reasonable, then it could be worth replicating the study.

As a demonstration, imagine that researchers conducted a study with 50 participants. They analysed their data using a one-group t-test, with a one-tailed probability and α-level of .05. The probability of their result having occurred if the Null Hypothesis was true was greater than .05 and so they had insufficient evidence to reject the Null Hypothesis. When they calculated the effect size, it was found to be $d = 0.1$. They then went on to calculate the power of the test and found that it was .17. In other words, the probability of committing a Type II error was $1 − .17 = .83$. Therefore, there was an 83% chance that they would reject their research hypothesis when it was true. They were hardly giving it a fair chance. Referring to Table 13.2 again, we can see that over 600 participants would be needed to give the test power of .8. The need for such a large sample should make researchers think twice before attempting a replication of the study. If they wished to test the same hypothesis, they might examine the efficiency of their design to see whether they could reduce the overall variability of the data and, in so doing, increase the effect size.

As a second example, imagine that researchers used 25 participants in a study but found after analysis of the data that the one-tailed, one-group t-test was not statistically significant at the .05 level. The effect size was found to be $d = 0.4$. The test, therefore, only had power of .61. In order to achieve the desired power of .8, 40 participants would have to be used. In this example the effect size is between a small and a medium one and as a sample size of 40 is not unreasonable, it would be worth replicating the study with the enlarged sample.

Summary

Effect size is a measure of the degree to which an independent variable is seen to affect a dependent variable or the degree to which two or more variables are related. As it is independent of the sample size it is useful for comparisons between studies.

The more powerful a statistical test, the more likely it is that a Type II error will be avoided. A major contributor to a test's power is the sample size. During the design stage researchers should conduct some form of power analysis to decide on the optimum sample size for the study. If they fail to achieve statistical significance, then they should calculate what sample size would be required to achieve a reasonable level of statistical power for the effect size they have found in their study.

This chapter has shown how to find statistical power using tables. However, computer programs exist for power analysis. These include G*Power, which is available via the Internet (see Faul, Erdfelder, Lang, & Buchner, 2007; Faul, Erdfelder, Buchner, & Lang, 2009).

The next chapter discusses the distinction between two types of statistical tests: parametric and non-parametric tests.

14 Parametric and non-parametric tests

Introduction

One way in which statistical tests are classified is into two types: parametric tests, such as the *t*-test, and non-parametric tests (sometimes known as distribution-free tests), such as the Kolmogorov–Smirnov test referred to in the following. The distinction is based on certain assumptions about the population parameters which exist and the type of data which can be analysed.

The χ^2 (pronounced *kie-squared* or *chi-squared*) goodness-of-fit test is introduced for analysing data from one group when the level of measurement is nominal.

Parametric tests

Parametric tests have two characteristics which can be seen as giving them their name. Firstly, they make assumptions about the nature of certain parameters for the measures which have been taken. Secondly, their calculation usually involves the estimation, from the sampled data, of population parameters.

The assumptions of parametric tests

Parametric tests frequently require that the population of scores, from which the sample came, be normally distributed. Additional criteria exist for certain parametric tests, and these will be outlined as each test is introduced. In the case of the one-group *t*-test the assumption is made that the data are independent of each other. This means that no person should contribute more than one score. In addition, there should be no influence from one person to another. In Chapter 12 an example was given where a group of people received enhanced maths training. The participants were then given a maths test. For the scores to be independent there should be no opportunity for the participants to confer over the answers to the questions in the test.

A common instance where data are unlikely to be independent is in social psychology research where data are provided by people who were tested in groups. An example would be if participants were in groups to discuss their opinions about a painting, with the dependent variable being each person's rating of his or her liking of the picture. Clearly, people in a group may be affected by the opinions of others in the group. One way to achieve independence of scores in this situation is to take group means as the dependent variable rather than individual scores. To do this, and maintain a reasonable level of statistical power, would mean having a larger number of participants than would be required if the individuals' ratings could be used. An alternative analysis which takes into account the lack of independence – multi-level modelling – is described in Chapter 25.

An additional criterion which psychologists often set for a parametric test is that the data must be interval or ratio. As has already been pointed out in Chapter 8, statisticians are less concerned with this criterion. Adhering to it can set constraints on what analyses are possible with the data. The following guidelines allow a less strict adherence to the rule. In the case of nominal data with more than two levels it makes no sense to apply parametric tests because there is no inherent order in the levels – for example, if the variable is political party, with the levels conservative, liberal and radical. However, if the variable is ordinal but is considered to be linked to an underlying continuous measure then, as long as the other parametric requirements are fulfilled, it is considered legitimate to conduct parametric tests on the data (e.g. Tabachnick & Fidell, 2013). An example of such a scale could be if, instead of using a visual analogue scale as in Chapter 5 to measure the degree of pain a person was in we were to use a Likert scale; we would still consider pain to be more continuous. Tabachnick and Fidell suggest that the scale must have sufficient levels, say, 7 or more as in a Likert scale. However, it is common to treat a 5-point Likert scale in the same way. Zimmerman and Zumbo (1993) point out that many non-parametric tests produce the same probability as converting the original data into ranks (and therefore ordinal level of measurement) and performing the equivalent parametric test on the ranked data. Accordingly, the restriction of parametric tests to interval or ratio data ignores the derivation of some non-parametric tests.

If the criteria for a given parametric test are not fulfilled, then it is inappropriate to use that parametric test. However, another misunderstanding among researchers is the belief that non-parametric statistics are free of any assumptions about the distribution of the data. Therefore, even when the assumptions of a parametric test are not fulfilled, the use of a non-parametric equivalent may not be recommended. Some variants of parametric tests have been developed for use even when some of the assumptions have been violated. Examples of these will be given when we meet the tests to which they are related. In addition, other methods have been developed to find accurate probabilities when assumptions about the distributions of data are not fulfilled; see *bootstrapping* in Chapter 23.

A further disadvantage of a non-parametric test is that it may have less power than its parametric equivalent. In other words, we may be more likely to commit a Type II error when using a non-parametric test. However, this is only usually true when the data fulfil the requirements of a parametric test and yet we still use a non-parametric test. *When those requirements are not fulfilled a non-parametric test can be the more powerful.*

Robustness

Despite the criteria which have been stated, statisticians have found that parametric tests are quite accurate even when some of their assumptions are violated; they are robust. However, this notion has to be treated with care. If more than one assumption underlying a particular parametric test is not fulfilled by the data, it would be better to use a parametric test which relaxes some of the assumptions or a non-parametric equivalent, as the probability levels given by standard tables or by computer may not reflect the true probabilities. The advent of computers has meant that researchers have been able to evaluate the effects of violations of assumptions on both parametric and non-parametric statistics. These studies have shown that, under certain conditions, both types of tests can be badly affected by such violations, in such a way that the probabilities which they report can be misleading; we may have very low power under some circumstances and under others the probability of making a Type I error may be markedly higher than the tables or computer program tell us.

Tests have been devised to tell whether an assumption of a parametric test has been violated. The trouble with these is that they rely on the same hypothesis testing procedure as the inferential test. Therefore they are going to suffer the same problems over statistical power. Accordingly, if the sample is small the assumptions of the test could be violated quite badly but they would suggest that there is not a problem. Alternatively, if a large sample is used, then a small and unimportant degree of violation could be shown to be significant. Therefore I do not recommend using such tests. Fortunately, there are rules of thumb as to how far away from the ideal conditions our data can be before we should do something to counteract the problem, and these will be given as each test is introduced.

One factor which can help to solve problems over assumptions of tests is that in psychology we are often interested in a summary statistic rather than the original scores which provided the statistic. Thus, we are usually interested in how the mean for a sample differs from the population or from another sample, rather than how the score for an individual differs from the population.

There is a rather convenient phenomenon – described by the *central limit theorem* – which is that if we take a summary statistic such as the mean, it has a normal distribution, even if the original population of scores from which it came do not. To understand the distribution of the mean, imagine that we take a sample of a given size from a population and work out the mean for that sample. We then take another sample of the same size from the same population and work out its mean. We continue to do this until we have found the means of a large number of samples from the population. If we produce a frequency distribution of those means it will be normally distributed. However, there is a caveat, that the sample size must be sufficiently large. Most authors seem to agree that a sample of 40 or more is sufficiently large, even if the original distribution of individual scores is quite skewed.

Often we do not know the distribution of scores in the population. I have said that the *population* usually has to be normally distributed. We may only have the data for our sample. Nonetheless, we can get an impression of the population's distribution from our sample. For example, I sampled 20 people's IQs from a normally distributed population, and it resulted in the distribution shown in Figure 14.1.

By creating a frequency distribution of the data from our sample we can see whether it is markedly skewed. If it is not, then we could continue with a parametric test. If it is skewed and the sample is smaller than about 40, then we could *transform* the data.

Data transformation

It is possible to apply a mathematical formula to each item of data and produce a data set which is more normally distributed. For example, if the data form a negatively skewed distribution, then squaring each score could reduce the skew and then it would be permissible to employ a parametric test on the data. If you are using a statistical test which looks for differences between the means of different levels of an independent variable, then you must use the same transformation on all the data. Data transformation is a perfectly legitimate procedure as long as you do not try out a number of transformations in order to find one which produces a statistically significant result. Nonetheless, many students are suspicious of this procedure. For those wishing to pursue the topic further, possible transformations for different distributions are given in Appendix V, along with illustrations of the effect of some transformations.

For most of the parametric tests described in this book skew is a greater problem than kurtosis. Therefore, a parametric test conducted on data which are not normally distributed but are symmetrical will have less of an effect on the accuracy of the probability given.

FIGURE 14.1   The distribution of IQs of 20 people selected from a normally distributed population

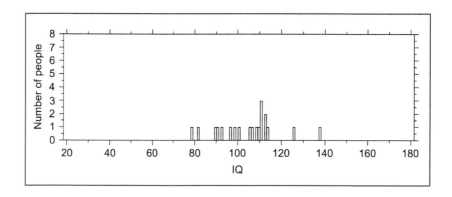

Finding statistical significance for non-parametric tests

There are two routes to finding the statistical significance of a test: one is to work out the exact probability; the other is to work out, from the non-parametric statistic, a value for a statistic which does have a known distribution, such as a z-score, often called a *z-approximation*. The latter approach produces a probability which is reasonably close to the exact probability but only if the sample size is large enough; the term *asymptotic* is used to signal that the probability is only accurate with a sufficiently large sample. However, what constitutes a large enough sample depends on the non-parametric statistic being used.

Exact probabilities involve what are sometimes called *permutation tests*. These entail finding a value for a statistic from the data which have been collected. Every possible alternative permutation of the data is then produced and the value of the statistic is calculated for each permutation. The proportion of the permutations which are as extreme as the value which came from the way the data actually fell, or more extreme and in line with the research hypothesis, is then calculated and that proportion is the probability of the test. The example of tossing coins, given in Chapter 10, is a version of this form of test. Here the number of heads is the statistic. We then worked out every possible fall of the coins and noted what proportion would have as many, or more heads, as those we actually got when the coins were tossed.

Clearly, where possible, we want to know the exact probability. Unfortunately, the number of permutations will sometimes be very large, particularly when a large sample is involved. However, powerful desktop computer programs can now handle samples up to a certain size, and statistical packages, such as SPSS, include an option, which may have to be bought as an addition to the basic package, that will calculate some exact probabilities. When even these programs cannot cope with the number of permutations they can use what is sometimes called a *Monte Carlo method*, which takes a pre-specified number of samples of the data and calculates the statistic for each sample. Again the proportion of statistics which are as big, or bigger and in line with the research hypothesis, is the probability for the test.

I recommend the following procedure for finding the probability of non-parametric tests. If you are analysing the data using a program which can calculate exact statistics *and* can cope with the sample size you have employed, then find the exact statistic. Otherwise, you have to find out, for the test you are using, whether the sample you are using is small enough that tables of exact probabilities exist. Finally, if the sample is bigger than the appropriate table allows for, then you will have to use the approximation test which has been found for that statistic. Be careful when using statistical packages where you don't have access to exact probabilities as they sometimes provide the approximation and its probability regardless of how small the sample is.

Non-parametric tests for one-group designs

At least ordinal data

When the data are on an ordinal scale it is possible to use the Kolmogorov– Smirnov one-sample test. However, this is an infrequently used test and the test used for nominal data – the one-sample χ^2 test – is often used in its place. Accordingly, the Kolmogorov–Smirnov one-sample test is only described in Appendix V.

Nominal data

One-sample χ^2 test

Sometimes we may wish to see whether a pattern of results from a sample differs from what could have been expected according to some assumption about what that pattern might have been. An example

TABLE 14.1   The number of children approaching a particular painting first and the expected number according to the Null Hypothesis

Painter	Approached first	Expected by H_0
Klee	11	5
Picasso	5	5
Modigliani	3	5
Cézanne	4	5
Rubens	2	5

would be where we are studying children's initial preferences for particular paintings in an art gallery. We observe 25 children as they enter a room which has five paintings in it and we note, in each child's case, which painting he or she approaches first. Our research hypothesis could be that the children will approach one painting first more than the other paintings. The Null Hypothesis would be that the number of children approaching each painting first will be the same for all the paintings. Thus, according to the Null Hypothesis we would expect each painting to be approached first by $\frac{25}{5}$ = 5 children.

The data can be seen in Table 14.1. The χ^2 test compares the actual, or observed, numbers with the expected numbers (according to the Null Hypothesis) to see whether they differ significantly. This example produces χ^2 = 10. The way in which a one-group χ^2 is calculated is shown in Appendix V.

Finding the statistical significance of χ^2

If you conducted the χ^2 test using a computer, it would tell you that the probability of the result was p = .0404 (SPSS provides, as an option, an exact probability for this test, which is p = .042). Both the exact probability and the probabilities from chi-square tables would be considered statistically significant and we could reject the Null Hypothesis. The probability for a χ^2 test given by computers, and in statistical tables, is always for a non-directional hypothesis. The notion of a one- or two-tailed test is not applicable here as there are many ways in which the data could have fallen; any one of the paintings could have been preferred.

If we do not know the exact probability of a χ^2, we can use a table which gives the probabilities for what is called the *chi-squared distribution*. As this table can be used for finding out the probabilities of statistical tests other than just the χ^2 tests, I am going to follow the practice of some authors and refer to *chi-squared* when I am talking about the table and χ^2 for the test.

In order to look up the probability of the results of a χ^2 test, you need to know the degrees of freedom (df). In the one-group version of the χ^2 test, they are based on the number of categories, which in this case was five (i.e. the number of paintings). The df is calculated by subtracting 1 from the number of categories. This is because the total number of participants is the fixed element in this test. In this case, as the total number of participants was 25, the number of participants who were in four of the categories could be changed but the number in the fifth category would have to be such that the total was 25. Therefore there are four df.

The probability table for the chi-squared distribution is given in Appendix XVII. Table 14.2 shows an extract of that table.

When there are four df, the critical level for χ^2 at p = .05 is 9.49; for p = .02, it is 11.67. Therefore, as our χ^2 was 10 and this is larger than 9.49, the probability that this result occurred by chance is less than .05. However, as 10 is smaller than 11.67, the probability is greater than .02. In this case, we would report the probability as .02 < p < .05. The complete way to report the result of a χ^2 test, when you do not know the more exact probability, is: $\chi^2_{(4)}$ = 10, .02 < p < .05, N = 25.

TABLE 14.2   An extract of the probability table for the chi-squared distribution

						Probability							
df	0.99	0.95	0.90	0.80	0.70	0.50	0.30	0.20	0.10	0.05	0.02	0.01	0.001
1	0.00	0.00	0.02	0.06	0.15	0.45	1.07	1.64	2.71	3.84	5.41	6.63	10.83
2	0.02	0.10	0.21	0.45	0.71	1.39	2.41	3.22	4.61	5.99	7.82	9.21	13.82
3	0.11	0.35	0.58	1.01	1.42	2.37	3.66	4.64	6.25	7.81	9.84	11.34	16.27
4	0.30	0.71	1.06	1.65	2.19	3.36	4.88	5.99	7.78	9.49	11.67	13.28	18.47
5	0.55	1.15	1.61	2.34	3.00	4.35	6.06	7.29	9.24	11.07	13.39	15.09	20.51

Notice that you should report N (the sample size) as, with this test, the df are not based on the sample size.

The effect size of χ^2

Cohen (1988) uses w as his effect size measure for χ^2, where

$$w = \sqrt{\frac{\chi^2}{N}} \tag{14.1}$$

and N is the sample size. Therefore, in the present case:

$$w = \sqrt{\frac{10}{25}}$$
$$= \sqrt{0.4}$$
$$= .632$$

Cohen defines a w of .1 as a small effect size, a w of .3 as a medium effect size and a w of .5 as a large effect size. Therefore, in this example, we can say that the effect size was large. The maximum possible value of w, in this goodness-of-fit test when the df are more than 1, is infinity.

An alternative in this situation is Pearson's coefficient of contingency (C):

$$C = \sqrt{\frac{\chi^2}{\chi^2 + N}} \tag{14.2}$$

where N is the total sample size.

C has the disadvantage that it can never equal exactly 1, even when the relationship is perfect. However, for the purposes of giving an impression of the size of effect in a psychological study this is not going to be a common problem; remember that Cohen (1988) considered a large effect to have been found when similar measures, r or w, equal .5.

The power of the χ^2 test

The tables in Appendix XVIII give the power of the χ^2 test. Table 14.3 gives an extract of the power tables when df = 4. From the table we can see that, when w is approximately .6, with α = .05, df = 4 and N = 25, the power of the test lies between .66 (for w = .6) and .82 (for w = .7). In fact, the power, when w = .632 is .72. That is, there is approximately a 72% probability of avoiding a Type II error. Appendix XVIII explains how to find power levels for samples or effect sizes which are not presented in the tables.

TABLE 14.3   An extract of the power tables for *w* when df = 4 and α = 0.05

	effect size (*w*)								
n	0.1	0.2	0.3	0.4	0.5	0.6	0.7	0.8	0.9
20	0.06	0.09	0.15	0.25	0.39	0.55	0.71	0.84	0.93
21	0.06	0.09	0.16	0.26	0.41	0.57	0.73	0.86	0.94
22	0.06	0.10	0.17	0.28	0.42	0.59	0.76	0.88	0.95
23	0.06	0.10	0.17	0.29	0.44	0.62	0.78	0.89	0.96
24	0.06	0.10	0.18	0.30	0.46	0.64	0.80	0.91	0.97
25	0.06	0.10	0.18	0.31	0.48	0.66	0.82	0.92	0.97
26	0.06	0.11	0.19	0.32	0.50	0.68	0.84	0.93	0.98

The assumptions of the χ^2 test

The first assumption is that all the observations are independent. In other words, in this case, each child should only be counted once – for 25 scores there should be 25 children. The second assumption is that the *expected* frequencies (if the Null Hypothesis is correct) will be at least a certain size. In the case where there is only one df – for example, only two paintings – all expected frequencies should be at least 5. When the df are greater than 1, then no more than 20% of the expected frequencies may be under 5. In the case of five categories, it would mean that only one of the expected frequencies could be less than 5. As the expected frequencies are partly governed by the sample size, in order to try to avoid the problem of small expected frequencies, it is advisable to have at least five participants per category. Therefore, the minimum sample size for this research would have been 25.

If too many categories have expected frequencies below 5, then it is possible to combine categories. For example, if the sample had had only 20 participants in it, as shown in Table 14.4, then we could combine the numbers for different paintings.

We could compare the numbers approaching the Klee or the Picasso with those approaching the other paintings, as in Table 14.5. We can only do this if it makes sense in terms of our research hypothesis. Thus we could only do this if our hypothesis was that different paintings would be approached by more children than would other paintings. We should not choose the combination, once we have seen the data, which we think would be most likely to give significance or try out different combinations in an attempt to find significance. Both procedures would make the probability from the test totally inaccurate and lead to a greater likelihood of committing a Type I error.

TABLE 14.4   The number of children approaching a particular painting first and the expected number according to the Null Hypothesis

Painter	Approached first	Expected by H_o
Klee	9	4
Picasso	4	4
Modigliani	2	4
Cézanne	3	4
Rubens	2	4

TABLE 14.5   The number of children approaching a particular painting first and the expected number according to the Null Hypothesis

Painting	Approached first	Expected by H_o
Klee or Picasso	13	8
Other paintings	7	12

Note that the expected frequencies for the paintings in a given row in Table 14.5 is the sum (or total) of the expected frequencies for each of the paintings in that row. The result of a χ^2 carried out on these data is $\chi^2_{(1)} = 5.21$, $p = .022$, $N = 20$, which is also statistically significant.

This last example demonstrates that the expected frequencies do not have to be the same as each other. The original example was testing whether the pictures had an equal likelihood of being approached first. However, another way to view the one-group χ^2 test is as a *goodness-of-fit* test. There may be situations in which we think that a set of data is distributed in a particular way and we wish to test whether this assumption is correct. For example, imagine that we are told that the population contains 20% smokers and 80% non-smokers. We have a sample of 100 participants whose smoking status we have noted and we wish to check that the sample is representative of the population. The data are shown in Table 14.6.

TABLE 14.6   The number of smokers and non-smokers in a sample and the expected numbers as predicted from the population

Smoking status	Observed	Expected
Smoker	25	20
Non-smoker	75	80

Unlike the usual inferential statistic where we are seeking a statistically significant result, in this case we are looking for a result that suggests that the difference between the expected and observed frequencies is not statistically significant. The analysis produces the following result: $\chi^2_{(1)} = 1.56$, $p = .21$, $N = 100$. We would conclude that the sample was not significantly unrepresentative with respect to smoking status.

However, this use of inferential tests is problematic because it is reversing the usual process, as our prediction is that there will be no difference. Therefore we are attempting to confirm an H_0 that assumes that the distribution does not differ from what would be expected if the sample had been selected randomly from the population. We have the problem that the lower the power of the test, the more likely this assumption is to be supported.

To take an extreme example, imagine that we were unwise enough to have a sample of only 25 people in this survey. If we found that 8 of those were smokers (that is, 32% rather than the 20% we are told is in the population), then the analysis produces the following result: $\chi^2_{(1)} = 2.25$, $p = .13$, $N = 25$, despite the fact that the effect size would be $w = .3$, which is a medium effect size. The power of the test would be .32. In other words, β – the probability of making a Type II error (that is, missing an effect when it was present) – would be .68 or 68%.

Cohen (1988) has suggested that one way round the problem is to select a sample size which would set the power of the test at .95. This would mean that β would be .05 and therefore the same as α. We would have to set the effect size which we were seeking as particularly small, say, a w of less than .1. The consequence of this would mean that with df = 1 we would need around 800 participants to have the required power for the test.

Summary

Parametric tests such as the *t*-test make certain assumptions about the measure being analysed. Many require that the data being analysed be independent of each other and have a normal distribution in the population. If the assumptions are not met, then modified versions of the parametric tests or non-parametric tests should be employed.

The next chapter describes statistical tests which allow us to compare the data from two levels of an independent variable to see whether they are significantly different.

15 Analysis of differences between two levels of an independent variable

Introduction

The present chapter deals with designs which involve one independent variable with only two levels. Parametric and non-parametric tests are introduced which analyse between- and within-subjects designs. Confidence intervals are described for parametric tests. The use of z-tests to evaluate larger samples in non-parametric tests is explained. The power and effect size of the two-sample t-test and its non-parametric equivalents are discussed. An additional measure of effect size for certain designs with nominal data – the odds ratio – is presented. Finally, analysis of the difference between two proportions is described in terms of a z-test, effect size and confidence interval.

Parametric tests

The distribution of the difference between two means

Because we are now looking at the difference between two sample means rather than a sample mean and a population mean, statisticians have had to identify how this new statistic is distributed – what its mean and standard error are – so that an inferential statistic can be used to evaluate it. In fact, there are different versions of the test, depending on whether the design is between- or within-subjects. The complete equations for the tests are shown in Appendix VI, where worked examples are given. All the versions of the test use the t-distribution and so the same probability table can be used as for the one-group t-test.

t-Tests to evaluate the difference between two sample means

Between-subjects designs

An additional assumption of the between-subjects t-test

In Chapter 14 it was pointed out that certain criteria have to be met before it is appropriate to use a parametric test such as the t-test. The level of measurement should be at least interval or, if ordinal, should be considered to have an underlying continuous scale as discussed in Chapter 14. The scores contributing to a given mean should be independent. The population of scores should be normally distributed, or at least the summary statistic being evaluated should be normally distributed, which in the case of the t-test of means is likely to be true if the sample has at least 40 participants in it.

In addition to the preceding, the t-test for comparison between two independent sample means requires what is called *homogeneity of variance*. This term means that the variances of the populations of the two sets of scores are the same. Usually researchers will be dealing with data from samples rather than from populations, and so it is unlikely that the two samples will have exactly the same variance, even if the populations from which they come do.

Fortunately, the *t*-test has been shown to be sufficiently robust that the variances can be different to a certain degree and yet the test will not be badly affected. As a rule of thumb, if the larger variance of the two samples is no more than four times the smaller variance, then it is still legitimate to use the *t*-test. However, if the population of scores is markedly non-normal *and* the variances differ, even by less than four times, the test becomes less robust. In addition, this rule of thumb should only be used when the sample sizes, in the two groups, are equal.

For this example researchers wish to evaluate the effectiveness of a therapeutic technique designed to rid people of arachnophobia (extreme aversion to spiders). They intend to have two groups of arachnophobics. One group is to act as the experimental (or intervention) group and receive therapy, and the other is the control group which does not receive therapy. The researchers measure anxiety using a self-report checklist which yields a score between 20 and 100 and is known to be normally distributed among the population; a high score means that the person is more anxious. The independent variable is therefore experience of therapy, with two levels: *experience* and *no experience*. The dependent variable is *anxiety level*. The research hypothesis is:

H$_A$: Those receiving therapy have lower anxiety levels than those not receiving it.

With the Null Hypothesis:

H$_0$: There is no difference in mean anxiety level between those receiving therapy and those not receiving therapy.

Put formally, the Null Hypothesis is that the mean anxiety level for the population of people who receive the therapy (μ_t) is the same as that for the population of those who do not receive the therapy (μ_c): that is, $\mu_t = \mu_c$ or ($\mu_t - \mu_c$) = 0. The research hypothesis is $\mu_t < \mu_c$ or ($\mu_t - \mu_c$) < 0.

In order to decide on a sample size the researchers conduct a power analysis.

Power analysis

The hypothesis is directional and so a one-tailed test will be appropriate. Alpha will be set to .05. The researchers are expecting that the therapy will produce a large effect size (*d* = 0.8). They are seeking power of .8. They look in the appropriate power tables (see Appendix XVIII), which show that they need 20 people in each group. They find 40 arachnophobics and randomly assign them to the two groups.

The results of the study are shown in Table 15.1 and Figure 15.1.

Effect size

In a case like the present study, where the effect we are looking at is the change between a control condition and an experimental condition, it makes sense to calculate *d* using the following equation, where the *SD* used is that for the control group:

$$d = \frac{\text{mean}_{\text{(for experimental group)}} - \text{mean}_{\text{(for control group)}}}{SD_{\text{(for control group)}}} \tag{15.1}$$

TABLE 15.1   The means and *SD*s of anxiety level in the therapy and control groups

	Therapy	Control
Mean	71.5	79.5
SD	6.56	7.64

FIGURE 15.1   Means and *SD*s of anxiety levels of therapy and control groups

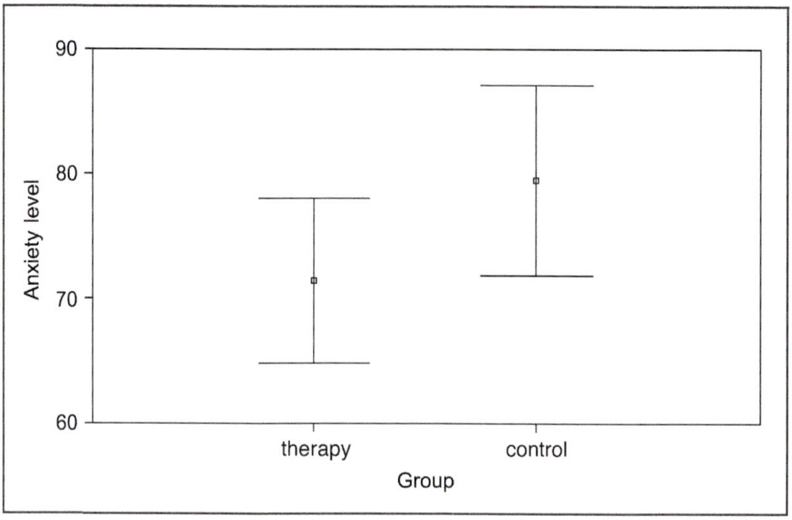

In this example:

$$d = \frac{71.5 - 79.5}{7.64}$$
$$= -1.047$$

This tells us that the therapy reduced anxiety by over 1 *SD*, which in Cohen's terms can be considered to be a large effect size.

If the research had involved comparing the means of two experimental groups, it would be more legitimate to use an *SD* which combines the information from both groups (the pooled *SD*) in the preceding equation rather than the *SD* of one group. (See Appendix VI for the equation for a pooled *SD*.)

We have seen that the result has gone in the hypothesised direction; now we wish to find out whether the result is statistically significant. But first it is necessary to check whether the data fulfil the requirements of a *t*-test. An additional requirement of the between-subjects *t*-test is that the data for the two conditions should be independent. This has been guaranteed by the researchers. However, they need to check whether there is homogeneity of variance between the two sets of data. Squaring the standard deviations gives the variances. The variance for the therapy group is 43.03 and for the control group it is 58.37. As the variance for the control group (the larger variance) is not more than four times that of the therapy group, and the anxiety scale is a ratio measure which is normally distributed in the population, the researchers decide that it is legitimate to use a *t*-test.

This version of the *t*-test is formed by:

$$\frac{\text{difference between the means} - \text{difference between the means if } H_0 \text{ is correct}}{\text{standard error of the difference between means}}$$

The difference between the means, if H_0 is true, is 0, in which case the equation can be rewritten:

$$\text{between-subjects } t = \frac{\text{difference between the means}}{\text{standard error of the difference between means}}$$

In the present case, this becomes:

$$t = \frac{71.5 - 79.5}{2.25131}$$
$$= -3.553$$

Finding the statistical significance of a between-subjects t-test

The same table can be used for this version of the *t*-test as for all other versions (see Appendix XVII). However, before the probability of this value can be evaluated we need to know the appropriate degrees of freedom (df) for this version of the *t*-test.

Degrees of freedom for a between-subjects *t*-test

This version of the *t*-test is based on the means of two groups and so has 2 df fewer than the sample size. Therefore, in this case, the df are 40 − 2 = 38.

Table 15.2 shows part of the *t*-tables from Appendix XVII.

Looking along the row for df = 38, we see that the *t*-value of 3.553 (remember to ignore the negative sign if the calculated *t*-value is negative) is between 3.319 and 3.566. Therefore, the one-tailed probability of the *t*-value is less than .001 but greater than .0005; we can say that $.0005 < p < .001$. In fact, the computer gives the *p* value as .00052. It is clear that the *p* value is less than the α-level of .05 and so the researchers can reject the Null Hypothesis and conclude that their therapeutic technique reduces the anxiety of arachnophobes. We would report the result as follows: *Participants in the therapeutic group had significantly lower anxiety levels than those in the control group* ($t_{(38)}$ = 3.55, p < .001, one-tailed test, d = −1.05).

If the exact df are not shown on tables it is often not a problem. The *t*-value will usually either be clearly statistically significant when the df are smaller than the exact value (for example, when df = 45 and *t* = 1.69), in which case the result will also be significant with the exact level, or, alternatively, the result will not be significant even with the next higher df for which the table has an entry (for example, when df = 45 and *t* = 1.67), in which case it would not be statistically significant with the exact df. A problem arises, if you are dependent on tables, when the *t*-value is not clearly in one of these two positions: for example, if it had been 1.682 with df = 43. (Appendix XVII shows how a more exact critical *t*-value can be found using *interpolation*.)

TABLE 15.2   An extract of the *t*-tables (from Appendix XVII)

	One-tailed probabilities									
	0.4	0.3	0.2	0.1	0.05	0.025	0.01	0.005	0.001	0.0005
	Two-tailed probabilities									
df	0.8	0.6	0.4	0.2	0.1	0.05	0.02	0.01	0.002	0.001
35	0.255	0.529	0.852	1.306	1.690	2.030	2.438	2.724	3.340	3.591
36	0.255	0.529	0.852	1.306	1.688	2.028	2.434	2.719	3.333	3.582
37	0.255	0.529	0.851	1.305	1.687	2.026	2.431	2.715	3.326	3.574
38	0.255	0.529	0.851	1.304	1.686	2.024	2.429	2.712	3.319	3.566
39	0.255	0.529	0.851	1.304	1.685	2.023	2.426	2.708	3.313	3.558
40	0.255	0.529	0.851	1.303	1.684	2.021	2.423	2.704	3.307	3.551
50	0.255	0.528	0.849	1.299	1.676	2.009	2.403	2.678	3.261	3.496

The effect on power of unequal sample sizes

In a between-subjects *t*-test, the power of the test is reduced by having unequal sample sizes. For example, if in the preceding example the researchers had used a control group of 10 and an experimental group of

30, although the overall sample size would be the same, the power for a large effect size of $d = 0.8$ would be reduced to .69, a drop of .11. Thus, when designing the research try to have equal-sized samples. Appendix XVIII shows how to calculate the sample size which is appropriate for reading power tables for a between-subjects t-test, when the sample sizes for the two groups are different.

Heterogeneity of variance

If the variances for the two samples differ by more than four times (and the samples have equal numbers of participants), then you are advised to use a modified version of the t-test. When the samples' sizes are unequal, then use the modified t-test if the variances differ by more than two times. In the version of the t-test given previously, the variances for the two conditions have been pooled, or summarised in a single measure. When the two variances are different it is more appropriate to estimate the standard error for the difference between the means without pooling the two variances.

This new version of the t-test, sometimes known as Welch's t-test, is not distributed in exactly the same way as the other versions. However, the standard tables can be used if an adjustment is made to the df. The calculations of this version of the t-test and of the df are shown in Appendix VI. Some computer programs report this version, along with the more usual t-value. In SPSS it is shown as the version of the t-test for which *equal variances are not assumed*. If the variances pass the rule of thumb for being considered sufficiently homogeneous, then quote the more usual t-value, with its df and p. However, if the variances are heterogeneous, then quote the modified version. If you are reporting the latter version, explain that you are doing so.

Within-subjects or matched designs

Racing cyclists have many ideas about what helps their performance; for example, many males don't shave their faces on the day of the race but they do shave their legs. In this example, sports psychologists are interested in whether such rituals really affect the performance of racing cyclists. They focus on one of these behaviours to see whether it actually affects performance, as measured by time taken to complete a standard route. They decide to compare the performance when male cyclists have shaved their faces with performance when they haven't shaved. Therefore, the independent variable is presence of facial hair, with two levels: *clean shaven* and *designer stubble*. The dependent variable is *time to complete the route*. To control for order effects they randomly assign participants to the order clean shaven and then designer stubble or the opposite order. Their research hypothesis is:

H_A: Cyclists take less time to complete a route when they don't shave their faces than when they do shave their faces.

And the Null Hypothesis is:

H_0: Cyclists take the same time to complete a route when they shave their faces as when they don't.

Formally stated, the Null Hypothesis is that the mean of the differences (μ_d), for each cyclist, between the times taken on the two occasions, is zero: that is, $\mu_d = 0$. The research hypothesis is $\mu_d > 0$.

In order to choose an appropriate sample size the researchers conduct a power analysis.

Power analysis

The nature of the hypothesis means that a one-tailed test is appropriate. Alpha is set at .05. The psychologists are only interested in detecting a large effect ($d = 0.8$) and they want power of .8. They look in the power tables for the within-subjects t-test (see Appendix XVIII) and decide that 11 cyclists are needed to take part in the study. As each participant in a within-subjects design provides a score for each level of the independent variable, fewer participants will be required than in a between-subjects design, for the same level of power. In addition, within-subjects designs are more powerful than between-subject designs, as there should be less variability in the overall set of scores, because the same person is providing two scores, and so they will need even fewer participants to achieve the same level of power. As will be seen later, this way of assessing power is very approximate and should only be used when no other guidelines about the effect size are available.

Degrees of freedom for a within-subjects or matched-pairs *t*-test

In this case the *t*-value is calculated on the basis of the differences between each pair of scores from each participant and so the df are one fewer than the number of pairs of scores (or one fewer than the number of participants). Therefore, in this example df = 11 − 1 = 10.

The results of the experiment are shown in Figure 15.2 and Table 15.3. (I have given the means to four decimal places in order that the calculations shown below produce consistent results. I do not recommend that you report results with such levels of accuracy.)

From the summary statistics we can see that there is a slight improvement in the mean time in the designer stubble condition but that there is a large overlap between the spreads of the two conditions.

FIGURE 15.2   The means and *SD*s of time taken to complete route by cyclists with and without shaving

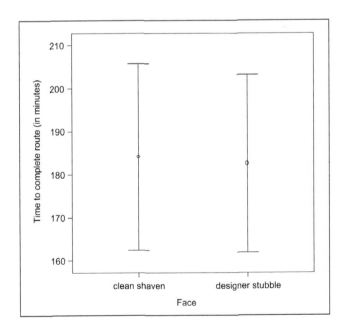

TABLE 15.3   The means and *SD*s of time taken (in minutes) to complete route by cyclists with and without shaving

	Face	
	Clean shaven	Designer stubble
Mean	184.0909	182.5455
SD	21.66	20.68

Effect size

The calculation of d and the guidelines which Cohen (1988) has proposed for what constitute small, medium and large effect sizes are all based on between-subjects designs. This means that when we have a within-subjects design there are two ways in which d can be calculated: one for the purposes of judging the magnitude of the effect relative to a between-subjects design and one for the purposes of reading the power tables. In order to be consistent with the way that effect size is calculated for a between-subjects design and because the designer stubble condition is the usual condition and can be treated as a control condition, we can use the following equation:

$$d = \frac{\text{mean for clean shaven} - \text{mean for designer stubble}}{SD \text{ for designer stubble}}$$

If neither condition could be treated as a control we would have found the pooled SD as in the between-subjects design.

In the present case:

$$d = \frac{184.0909 - 182.5455}{20.68}$$
$$= 0.07$$

which, according to Cohen (1988), is below a small effect size.

This version of the t-test is formed by:

$$\text{within-subjects } t = \frac{\text{mean difference-mean difference if H}_0 \text{ correct}}{\text{standard error of differences}}$$

The mean difference if H_0 is correct is 0. Therefore the equation can be rewritten as:

$$\text{within-subjects } t = \frac{\text{mean difference}}{\text{standard error of differences}}$$

In the present case:

$$t = \frac{184.091 - 182.546}{1.021} = 1.513$$

(NB: The mean of difference scores is the same as the difference between the means.)

Referring to the appropriate part of the t-tables from Appendix XVII, the researchers find that with df = 10, p lies between .1 and .05, for a one-tailed test; the computer shows the probability as .08. Accordingly, the psychologists cannot reject the Null Hypothesis and are forced to conclude that the ritual of wearing designer stubble does not improve performance. The result would be reported as: *Cyclists showed no significant difference in time taken to complete the route whether clean shaven or having designer stubble ($t_{(10)}$ = 1.51, p = .08, one-tailed test, d = 0.07).*

Retrospective power analysis

Because the result was not statistically significant, in order to guide future research, the psychologists wish to know what sample size would be necessary to replicate the study. There is a slight complication with within-subjects designs. The effect size measure allows comparison with between-subjects designs but will underestimate the power of the test because the t-value for a within-subjects design utilises the standard deviation of the differences between the scores for each participant (s_{diff}) and therefore, if we have this information, the effect size (d'), which we can use to calculate the power, is found from:

$$d' = \frac{\bar{x}_1 - \bar{x}_2}{s_{diff}} \tag{15.2}$$

As $s_{diff} = 3.387$,

$$d' = \frac{184.0909 - 182.5455}{3.387}$$
$$= 0.456$$

When the within-subjects t-value is known, d' can be calculated from:

$$d' = \frac{t}{\sqrt{n}} \tag{15.3}$$

Thus,

$$d' = \frac{1.513}{\sqrt{11}} = 0.456$$

The researchers note that, with such an effect size ($d = 0.456$), in order to achieve power of .8 they would have needed to use between 30 and 40 participants, or approximately 35 cyclists. Thus they can conclude that this study may be worth repeating with the larger sample size. (The discrepancy between the two values – for d and d' – which have been calculated for this study is explained in Appendix XVIII.)

Confidence intervals for the difference between two means

If a confidence interval (CI) for a difference between means contains 0, then this suggests that there is no real difference in the population. The 95% CI for the difference between the mean anxiety levels in the control and therapy groups in the earlier between-subjects design is −12.56 to −3.44, which doesn't contain 0. The 95% CI for the difference between time taken by the cyclists to complete the route clean shaven or with designer stubble is −0.73 to 3.82, which does contain 0. (Appendix VI shows how these figures were obtained.)

Non-parametric tests

Tests to evaluate the difference between two levels of an independent variable: at least ordinal scale

Between-subjects designs: the Mann–Whitney U test

The Mann–Whitney U test assumes that the distributions, in the population, of the two groups to be compared are the same. Thus, it is not as restrictive as the t-test and so can be used when the distributions are not normal. However, it does assume homogeneity of variance. This latter restriction may be less of a problem because the test entails placing the data in order rather than noting the size of any differences between scores and therefore the effect of extreme scores will be reduced. Nonetheless, if the original scores have heterogeneous variances, then it would be worth converting the data into ranks, with both samples being ranked together, and then checking that the variance of the ranks of one group is no greater than four times the variance of the other group. If the variances still remain heterogeneous, then Zimmerman and Zumbo (1993) recommend conducting a t-test for separate variances, Welch's t-test, mentioned earlier in the chapter, on the ranked data. As with the between-subjects t-test, the Mann–Whitney U test assumes that the scores are independent of each other.

Researchers wished to compare the attitudes of two groups of students – those studying physics and those studying sociology – about the hunting of animals. Each student was asked to rate his or her agreement with the statement 'hunting wild animals is cruel'. The ratings were made on a 5-point scale, ranging from disagree strongly to agree strongly, with a high score denoting an anti-hunting attitude.

The research hypothesis is:

H_A: Sociology students are more anti-hunting than physics students.

And the Null Hypothesis is:

H_0: There is no difference between sociology and physics students in their attitude to hunting.

Expressed formally, the Null Hypothesis is that the medians of the two groups do not differ.

Deciding on sample size

Effect size

There is no straightforward way to present effect sizes for non-parametric tests which involve small samples. However, as we will see, we can make certain assumptions based on the equivalent parametric test when we wish to do prospective power analysis. In addition, when we have a sufficiently large sample size (for many non-parametric tests this is around 20 to 25 participants, for within-subjects designs or pairs of participants, in a between-subjects design), then it is possible to calculate an effect size. This method will be shown later in the chapter.

Power

The power of non-parametric tests tends to be reported in terms of how they compare with their parametric equivalents, when the assumptions of the parametric test are fulfilled. The term *power efficiency* is used, meaning the relative number of participants which would be needed to achieve the same level of power as for the parametric test. As was noted in Chapter 14, when the assumptions of the parametric test are not fulfilled, the non-parametric test may have more power than its parametric equivalent. However, calculating the power under these circumstances is not straightforward, as it depends on the way in which the parametric assumptions have been violated. Accordingly, the procedure I will adopt is, where possible, to utilise the tables which are given for the equivalent parametric test, but suggest adjustments which can be made to the sample size to compensate for the relative power efficiency of the non-parametric test.

In the case of the Mann–Whitney U test, if we multiply the sample size suggested for the t-test by 1.05, then we will have, at least, the power suggested for the t-test. Thus, if the researchers wanted to detect a large effect size of $d = 0.8$, they would be told that they needed 20 participants per group to get power of .8 for a one-tailed between-subjects t-test, with $\alpha = .05$. Accordingly, they needed $20 \times 1.05 = 21$ participants per group for the Mann–Whitney U test.

The researchers collect the data and create Table 15.4.

TABLE 15.4 The mean, median and *SD*s of attitudes of sociology and physics students towards a question about hunting wild animals.

	Sociology	Physics
Mean	4.14	2.67
Median	4	3
SD	*0.91*	*1.24*

Statistical significance of the Mann–Whitney *U* test

The Mann–Whitney *U* test involves placing all the data in numerical order and then calculating how many data points are not in the hypothesised order. In the present case a data point which was out of order would be a physics student who was more anti-hunting than any sociology student.

The original data and calculations for the test are shown in Appendix VI. The analysis was performed and gave a *U* of 79.5. As was explained in Chapter 14, there are three possible ways of finding the probability for this result. The most appropriate one depends on whether you are using a statistical package which provides exact probabilities; if you are not, then it depends on the sample size. SPSS reports the exact probability as $p = .00009$. If we hadn't had this information, as the sample size in both groups is greater than 20, then it would have been necessary to use a version of a *z*-test to calculate the probability (see Appendix VI). In the present example, with 21 participants in each group, $z = -3.5469$, $p = .0002$, one-tailed test. Had both samples been 20 or smaller, then we could have found the probability from tables in Appendix XVII.

Correction for ties

It is likely that your computer program will also offer you an alternative value of *z*, which has taken into account the number of scores which had the same value (tied scores). The calculation for this is also shown in Appendix VI. The version allowing for ties gives $z = -3.6389$, $p = .00015$, one-tailed test. The correction for the ties is the more accurate version so only report that result, when it is given, and the sample size is large enough to make the *z*-test appropriate. SPSS only provides the version corrected for ties. The two versions produce the same result when there are no ties.

Reporting the results of a Mann–Whitney *U* test

Here I would say, *sociology students were significantly more opposed to hunting than were physics students (U = 79.5, p < .001, N = 42, one-tailed test).* If the probability was an exact one found from a statistical package, then add something along the lines of: *The probability is exact and was found using SPSS, version 25.* Report the value for *U* even if you had to use a *z*-test to find the probability but in that case also report the *z*-score.

Effect size revisited

Now that we have a *z*-score for the result we can convert this into an effect size (*r*), using the equation shown in Appendix VI. Putting the *z*-score corrected for ties (−3.64) into the equation gives an effect size of $r = -.56$, which in Cohen's (1988) terms would be considered a large effect size. (This measure of effect size is discussed more fully in Chapter 19.)

Within-subjects designs: the Wilcoxon signed rank test for matched pairs

When comparing two levels of an independent variable, in a within-subjects design with at least ordinal data which do not conform to the assumptions of a within-subjects *t*-test, it may be appropriate to use the Wilcoxon signed rank test for matched pairs. The test assumes that the distribution of the difference scores between the two conditions forms a symmetrical distribution in the population. Thus, it is less restrictive than the *t*-test. As with the within-subjects *t*-test it assumes that the scores in a given condition are independent of each other.

This test could be appropriate if researchers were comparing people's views of psychology as a science before and after hearing a talk on the nature of psychology. Their views were found from their responses to the statement: *Psychology is a science.* They used a 5-point rating scale ranging from

TABLE 15.5   The mean, median and *SD*s of ratings given by participants of psychology before and after a talk on the subject

	Before	After
Mean	2.667	3.883
Median	2.5	4.0
SD	*1.23*	*0.94*

agree strongly to disagree strongly, with a higher score denoting a belief that psychology is a science (Table 15.5).

Power

The researchers assumed a large effect size, set α to .05 and because they were making the directional hypothesis – *People rate psychology more clearly as a science after they have heard a talk on it* – they would use a one-tailed probability. They wanted to have power of .8. The Wilcoxon test has the same power efficiency as the Mann–Whitney *U* test. Accordingly, we can look for the sample size for a within-subjects *t*-test with an effect size of *d* = 0.8 and power of .8 and multiply the sample size by 1.05. Using the tables in Appendix XVIII we find that the sample size for the equivalent *t*-test would need to be 11. Therefore the sample size required for a Wilcoxon test is 11 × 1.05 = 11.55. We round this up to the nearest whole number, giving a sample size of 12 participants.

The Wilcoxon test looks at the size of differences between the two levels of the IV. It ranks the differences according to their size and gives each difference either a positive or a negative sign, depending on whether the second level is bigger or smaller than the first level. The ranks of the sign which occurs least frequently are then added together and the result forms the statistic *T*. In this case, a Wilcoxon test was conducted with the result that *T* = 0 (because there were no people for whom the second result was smaller than the first); the original data and workings are shown in Appendix VI.

Tied scores

The Wilcoxon test has two types of tied score – those where a participant gave the same score for each condition and those where the difference scores for different participants were the same.

This test discards those cases where there is no difference between the two levels of the IV and the *effective* sample size includes only those who did show a difference. Thus, in the present example, as four people did not change their ratings between the two occasions, the effective sample size is considered to be 12 – 4 = 8. If the range of possible scores is limited, there could be a high proportion of such ties and this could reduce the power of the test dramatically by reducing the effective sample size.

Statistical significance

SPSS reported the exact probability as *p* = .004. When you are not using a computer which calculates exact probabilities and the sample size is 25, or smaller, then use the table in Appendix XVII. With the revised sample size of eight we learn that *p* < .005, for a one-tailed test. Alternatively, when the sample size is greater than 25, then you could use a *z*-test to calculate the probability that *T* could have occurred by chance. If more than one person had the same size difference between the two levels of the IV, then a *z*-value which allows for such tied values is usually calculated by computer programs. As with the Mann–Whitney *U* test, the *z* corrected for ties is the more accurate. Workings for the *z*-test are given in Appendix VI.

Reporting the result of a Wilcoxon signed rank test for matched pairs

As with the Mann–Whitney U test, always report the original statistic from the test, in this case the T-value, and then, if appropriate, the z-value. If you are reporting the exact statistics, say so and give the statistical program you have used and the version: e.g. SPSS, Version 25. In this case I would say, *psychology was given a significantly higher rating as a science after a talk than before the talk ($T = 0$, $p = .004$, one-tailed test, $N = 8$).* You could also mention that four participants showed no change.

Tests to evaluate the difference between two levels of an independent variable: nominal scale

Between-subjects designs: the χ^2 test of contingencies

The χ^2 test of contingencies is appropriate if you have two variables measured at the nominal (or categorical) level and you wish to see whether different levels of one variable differ over the pattern which they form on the other variable. However, it is important that no person is counted more than once; the entries in the table must be independent.

For example, researchers had heard that there appeared to be a large number of female students who smoked. They wanted to see whether there were different proportions of males and females who smoked.

Effect size

The effect size for this version of the χ^2 test is the same as for the one-group χ^2 goodness-of-fit test. The measure of effect size given by Cohen (1988) is w, with .1, .3 and .5 being the values of w which he suggests constitute small, medium and large effect sizes.

Power

The researchers wish to detect, at least, a medium effect size ($w = .3$) and so they look in the tables in Appendix XVIII for a medium effect size, with $\alpha = .05$ and $df = 1$ (to be explained later). They find that, for power of .8, the recommended sample size is 85. They decide that they would like an equal number of males and females, to make comparison of proportions simpler, and they finally sample 44 males and 44 females.

The researchers asked the participants in their study whether they smoked and put the results into a table (Table 15.6).

TABLE 15.6   The numbers of male and female smokers and non-smokers in a sample

Observed frequency table

	Male	Female	Totals
Smoker	17	21	38
Non-smoker	27	23	50
Totals	44	44	88

This version of the χ^2 test tests the Null Hypothesis that smoking status and gender are not related (are independent). It does this by noting the proportions of males and females in the sample (44 out of 88 or .5 for each) and the proportions of smokers and non-smokers (38 out of 88, or approximately .43 for smokers, and 50 out of 88 or .57 for non-smokers). If the two variables – gender and smoking – are not related, then there should be the same proportion of smokers among the males as among the females (that is, .43 or 43%). Thus, under the Null Hypothesis that the proportion of males and females who smoke is the same, the expected frequencies would produce Table 15.7.

TABLE 15.7   The expected frequencies of male and female smokers and non-smokers if smoking and gender are not linked

Expected values

	Male	Female	Totals
Smoker	19	19	38
Non-smoker	25	25	50
Totals	44	44	88

However, 17 of the males, or 38.64%, were smokers, while 21, or 47.73%, of the females were smokers (Table 15.8).

TABLE 15.8   The percentages of male and female smokers and non-smokers

Percentages of column totals

	Male	Female	Totals
Smoker	38.64%	47.73%	43.18%
Non-smoker	61.36%	52.27%	56.82%
Totals	100%	100%	100%

The χ^2 test compares the expected frequencies with those which actually occurred (the observed frequencies). Workings for this example are given in Appendix VI. The result is that $\chi^2 = 0.741$. SPSS gives an exact probability of $p = .519$, while the probability based on the chi-squared distribution as calculated by the computer is $p = .3893$. Looking in the table for the chi-squared distribution in Appendix XVII shows that the probability that this result, with df = 1, would occur if the Null Hypothesis were true is $.3 < p < .5$.

Degrees of freedom and χ^2

The fixed elements in the calculation of a χ^2 test on contingency tables are what are termed the *marginal totals* – the number of smokers and non-smokers and the numbers of males and females – because the expected frequencies are calculated from these totals. Thus, in a 2 × 2 table, as in the preceding, as soon as one frequency is placed in the table, all the others are fixed. For example, given that the sample size was 88, if we are told that 17 males smoked, then we know how many females smoked (38 − 17 = 21) and how many males did not smoke (44 − 17 = 27), and we also then know how many females did not smoke (44 − 21 = 23). Thus, we only had the freedom to alter one of the four frequencies, and so df = 1. This particular version of the χ^2 test is not only usable on a 2 × 2 table; we can have more levels of either variable. For example, smoking status could have had the levels *never smoked, ex-smoker* and *currently a smoker*. The rule for working out the df is to take 1 from the number of columns in the table and 1 from the number of rows in the table and multiply the results:

df = (columns − 1) × (rows − 1)

Thus, in a 2 × 2 table we had (2 − 1) × (2 − 1) = 1 × 1 = 1.

One- and two-tailed tests and χ^2

As was mentioned in Chapter 14, the probability given in chi-squared tables and by computer programs is for a non-directional hypothesis. With a contingency table which is larger than 2 × 2, the possible directions in which a significant result could have gone are more than two. For example, if we looked at a study of smoking that included three possible smoking statuses, then we would reject the Null Hypothesis of no difference between the genders if smokers, non-smokers or ex-smokers were particularly high (or low) in either gender. However, in the case of a 2 × 2 table there are only two directions that the result could have gone when there was a difference between the groups: either a higher proportion of males were smokers or a higher proportion of females were smokers. In such a situation, if the result did go in the direction predicted, then we can find the probability by dividing the usual probability for a non-directional hypothesis by 2. Imagine that the researcher had predicted that there would be a higher proportion of smokers among the females than among the males. The result, summarised in Table 15.6, did go in the predicted direction and so we can divide the originally reported probability by 2; as a result $p = .259$. In fact, SPSS will report what it describes as an *Exact Sig. (1-sided)* when you ask it to calculate exact probabilities. If you do calculate such a probability, it would be advisable to explain this process, as, although legitimate, it is not a common practice. To avoid the need for explanation, as the result remained non-significant even after being converted to a directional probability, I would simply report the non-directional probability.

Reporting the results of a χ^2 test

As usual, report what test was used, what conclusion you draw from the result and your evidence for the conclusion. Thus, I would say: *A 2 × 2 χ^2 test was conducted to compare the proportions of smokers and non-smokers among the males and females. There was no significant difference in the proportions of smokers between females and males ($\chi^2_{(1)} = 0.741$, df = 1, p = .52, N = 88).* If you leave the probability as the one given by a computer or from a table, then there is no need to report that it is a two-tailed probability. Alternatively, if you had a directional hypothesis and the result went in the direction you predicted, then you could halve the probability and report that, as long as you explained what you had done.

Effect size revisited

The effect size w can be calculated from equation 14.1. In the present example,

$$w = \sqrt{\frac{0.741}{88}}$$
$$= .0918$$

which, in Cohen's terms, is a small effect size. Given this effect size, power was less than .2. To achieve power of .8 for this effect size it would be necessary to have a sample size of 900 participants. Thus, it is unlikely that you would recommend replicating the study without, at least, some modification of the design to increase the effect size and so reduce the necessary sample size.

Correction for continuity

The probability that the result of the χ^2 test would have occurred if the Null Hypothesis were true is calculated with reference to a particular distribution – the chi-squared distribution. The chi-squared distribution is what is termed a 'continuous distribution'. This means that every possible value for chi-squared could exist. However, the majority of tests which produce a χ^2 value cannot produce a truly continuous range of possible values and this will be particularly true with small sample sizes and a small number of categories. Thus, below a certain sample size and number of categories it was suggested that the χ^2 statistic did not have a distribution which was accurately represented by the chi-squared distribution.

Yates (1934) devised a way of correcting for continuity for a 2 × 2 contingency table, which will often be quoted by computer packages. In the gender by smoking status example, the corrected version gives $\chi^2 = 0.417$, $p = .5185$. Forty years ago Yates' corrected version of χ^2 was still considered to be the appropriate one to report. However, since then there has been a dispute over its appropriateness. My advice would be that, if the corrected and non-corrected versions of the test agree over whether the result was statistically significant, as in the smoking example, then there is no problem – report the uncorrected version. However, if the two versions disagree report them both and draw attention to the discrepancy. The reader can then make his or her own judgement. If you are using exact probabilities, then the problem is solved and you can just accept that probability.

Small expected frequencies

Another way to try to avoid the problem of χ^2 not being reflected in the chi-squared distribution, under certain circumstances, is to have reasonably sized expected frequencies. The usual rule of thumb is that all the expected frequencies in a 2 × 2 table should be at least five. In the case of tables which are larger than 2 × 2, at least 80% of expected frequencies should be at least five. These restrictions mean that even if we were not using statistical power to guide sample size we would want a minimum of five participants per cell of the contingency table, which means that a study which will be analysed by a 2 × 2 table should have at least 20 participants in it. Chapter 16 shows ways of solving the problem of small expected frequencies in contingency tables which are larger than 2 × 2.

Fisher's exact probability test

Fisher devised a test to cope with 2 × 2 contingency tables with small samples. Unfortunately, it is only applicable when all the marginal totals are fixed (Neave & Worthington, 1988). A fixed marginal total is where the numbers in that total have been specified before the study is conducted. In the smoking example the totals for males and females were fixed at 44 each, whereas the totals for smokers and non-smokers were free, that is, they were not known until the data were collected. In fact, it would be unusual to have all the marginal totals fixed and would have made no sense in the smoking example as it would have meant specifying how many smokers and non-smokers to sample, as well as how many males and females. Nonetheless, the method for calculating Fisher's exact probability test is provided in Appendix VI and probability tables for it are in Appendix XVII.

2 × 2 Frequency table quick test

A preferable way to deal with small expected frequencies is a modified version of the χ^2 test using the following equation (provided here as it is not generally available on computer):

$$\text{modified } \chi^2 = \frac{(N-1)\times[(A\times D)-(B\times C)]^2}{(A+B)\times(C+D)\times(A+C)\times(B+D)}$$

(15.5)

(Where N is the sample size and A to D are explained in Table 15.9)

For example, imagine that researchers explore whether having a pet improves the life expectancy of elderly people. They choose 10 people who are aged over 75 years, who have no pets and who are living on their own. They randomly choose half of the people to look after a pet dog. After two years they note how many of the people with and without pets are still alive.

TABLE 15.9 The numbers of elderly people alive and dead by whether they were previously given a dog to look after

	Given a dog	Not given a dog	
Still alive	4(A)	1(B)	5
Died	1(C)	4(D)	5
	5	5	

$$\text{modified } \chi^2 = \frac{(10-1)\times[(4\times4)-(1\times1)]^2}{(4+1)\times(1+4)\times(4+1)\times(1+4)}$$

$$= \frac{9\times(16-1)^2}{5\times5\times5\times5}$$

$$= 3.24$$

As with the previous example of a χ^2 test on a 2 × 2 contingency table, df = 1. The probability, for a non-directional hypothesis of this result, is $.05 < p < .1$.

Odds ratios

An alternative way to describe the size of an effect in contingency tables is the odds ratio. This is a popular measure in medical research and is becoming increasingly used by psychologists, such as health psychologists and clinical psychologists, who do research alongside medical researchers. In order to explain what an odds ratio is, it is necessary to define some other measures first.

Probability

We can take the data for male smokers in Table 15.6 and express the number of male smokers as a proportion of all the males in the sample: 17 out of 44 or $\frac{17}{44}$. Converting this into a proportion, we have .38636. We can say that the probability, in this sample, of a male being a smoker is .38636.

Odds

Odds are the probability that an event will occur divided by the probability that it will not occur. Therefore, we need to know the probability that a male will not be a smoker. Because we only have two possibilities, we can find this probability by subtracting the probability that a male *is* a smoker from 1:

probability that a male is not a smoker = 1 − .38636 = .61364

Now we can find the odds that a male is a smoker:

$$\text{odds that a male is a smoker} = \frac{\text{probability that a male is a smoker}}{\text{probability that a male is not a smoker}}$$

$$= \frac{0.38636}{0.61364}$$

$$= 0.6296$$

This is just under 2/3 and so we can interpret these odds as telling us that, among males, for every two smokers there will be approximately three non-smokers, or that non-smokers are one-and-a-half times more likely than smokers.

Odds ratios

An odds ratio, as its name suggests, is the ratio between two odds. Therefore, if we wanted to know the odds ratio of male to female smokers we need the odds for female smokers, which is .9130 and shows a higher likelihood of females being smokers. It is still more likely that a female will be a non-smoker than a smoker, but only just. Now we can calculate the odds ratio of males and females being smokers:

$$\text{odds ratio of males and females being smokers} = \frac{\text{odds of males being smokers}}{\text{odds of females being smokers}}$$
$$= \frac{.6296}{.9130}$$
$$= .6896$$

We can conclude from this that males are only just over two-thirds as likely to be smokers as females. An odds ratio can range from 0 upwards, with an odds ratio of 1 meaning that there was no difference in the two odds. A ratio below 1 means that the first odds is less likely, as it is here, while a ratio which is above 1 shows that the first odds is more likely. The odds ratio can be converted so that it is couched in terms of the other group by dividing it into 1. Thus, the odds ratio can be expressed in terms of female smokers:

$$\text{Odds ratio of female to male smokers} = \frac{1}{\text{odds ratio of male to female smokers}}$$
$$= \frac{1}{0.6896}$$
$$= 1.4501$$

This confirms that females are more likely to be smokers – in fact nearly one and a half times as likely. This can also be expressed as a percentage: the odds of being smokers for the females are 45% higher than the odds of being smokers for the males. For topics related to odds and odds ratios, *risk* and *relative risk*, see Appendix VI.

Confidence intervals (CIs) for odds ratios

As with other statistics, it is useful to be able to put an odds ratio in context. It is possible to calculate a CI for an odds ratio. If the interval contains 1, then it could be that there is no real difference between the groups. The 95% CI for the odds ratio of male to female smokers is 0.295 to 1.609. (The calculations are contained in Appendix VI.) This tells us that although the odds ratio suggests that males are less likely than females to be smokers in this sample, if we were to repeat the study with another sample we might very well find no difference, as there may be no difference in the population.

Within-subjects designs

If we have within-subjects data for two levels of an independent variable with nominal levels of measurement, then the data breach the requirements of the χ^2 test because the data points are not independent. McNemar's test of change allows us to analyse such data when they can be formed into a 2 × 2 contingency table; for example, if we were again studying people's attitudes to psychology as a science before and after a talk on the subject but this time we simply asked on each occasion whether or not they thought psychology was a science. The Stuart–Maxwell test can be used for larger tables; for example if we included an *unsure* response to the question about psychology being a science.

McNemar's test of change

Effect size and power

Although McNemar's test produces a χ^2 value, I know of no evidence that the effect size (w), which is used for the conventional χ^2 test, is applicable in this instance. To calculate power is also problematic unless we go via the power efficiency of the test relative to a within-subjects t-test. To be on the safe side, we should take the worst case, which is that the power efficiency can be as low as .63. Accordingly, we should find the sample size for the within-subjects t-test, with the required effect size and level of power, and multiply that by 1.6. For a one-tailed test, with α = .05, and a large effect size ($d = 0.8$), we would need a sample of 11 to have power of .8 with a within-subjects t-test. Thus, we should have a sample of 11 × 1.6 = 17.6 or 18 people with the McNemar's test of change. Vuolo, Uggen, and Lageson (2016) describe an alternative approach.

The data can be put into the form shown in Table 15.10.

TABLE 15.10   The numbers of people who agreed or disagreed that psychology is a science before and after hearing a talk

		After	
		Agree	Disagree
Before	Disagree	9(A)	3(B)
	Agree	6(C)	0(D)

This test is only interested in those people who have changed opinion. Accordingly, the Null Hypothesis which it tests is that the number of people changing in one direction will be the same as the numbers changing in the other direction. If we label the four cells as shown in Table 15.10, we can calculate McNemar's test by:

$$\chi^2 = \frac{(A - D)^2}{(A + D)} \tag{15.6}$$

$$= \frac{(9 - 0)^2}{(9 + 0)}$$

$$= \frac{81}{9}$$

$$= 9$$

The test has df = 1.

The statistical significance of McNemar's test of change

SPSS reports the exact probability as $p = .004$. It reports this as having come from the binomial distribution. Appendix VI explains this distribution and how it was used to find this probability. If we were dependent on the tables for the chi-squared distribution in Appendix XVII, then we would find that the likelihood of this result occurring by chance is $.001 < p < .01$. As with other tests which use the chi-squared distribution, this probability is for a non-directional hypothesis. If we had made a directional hypothesis that more people would change to agree that psychology was a science than would change to disagree that it was a science, then we could halve the probability. In which case, $.0005 < p < .005$, or $p = .002$ for the exact probability. Agresti (1996) notes that as long as the total number of participants who have changed from one category to another across the two measures is greater than 10, the probability from the chi-squared distribution is a good approximation of what would be found from using the binomial test. In the current case the number changing is only 9.

Stuart–Maxwell test

McNemar's test can be used when the variable of interest is dichotomous. The Stuart–Maxwell test can be used when there are more than two categories of a categorical variable (multinomial) in a within-subjects design. An example would be if the question about whether psychology was a science that was asked of participants before and after a talk on the subject had three options: no, unsure, yes. Table 15.11 shows that before the talk 20 people out of 60 thought that psychology was a science whereas after the talk the figure had risen to 38.

TABLE 15.11   The numbers of people who agreed or disagreed that psychology is a science before and after hearing a talk when they had a choice of three responses

| | | After | | | |
		Agree	Unsure	Disagree	Row total
Before	Agree	19	1	0	20
	Unsure	5	4	1	10
	Disagree	14	1	15	30
	Column total	38	6	16	60

Like McNemar's test the Stuart–Maxwell test only examines the cells where there has been change, for example those who have changed from disagree before the talk to agree afterwards (sometimes described as the *discordant* cells). The results from the Stuart–Maxwell test are $\chi^2 = 16.67$. The degrees of freedom $= (i \times (i-1))/2$, where i is the number of categories. As there are three categories, df = 3. The probability is $p = .0008$. Therefore, there has been a significant change in opinion. As we will find in the next chapter, because there are more than two categories, we cannot state that two particular categories differ significantly. Therefore, without further analysis we can't state that a significant number of people changed from disagreeing to agreeing. To do that we would have to run a McNemar's test on just the cells for agree and disagree. Appendix VI shows the calculations for the Stuart–Maxwell test.

Effect size and the Stuart–Maxwell test

We can convert the χ^2 to w as was shown earlier in the chapter. However, as discussed in Chapter 14, when df are greater than 1, w can be larger than 1, in which case we could use the coefficient of contingency (equation 14.2).

Sample size calculation

The Stuart–Maxwell test compares matched discordant cells. For example, those who disagreed before the talk but agreed afterwards and those who agreed before but disagreed afterwards. There are three such combinations in the preceding example. According to a method described by Vuolo et al. (2016), we need to set possible values for all three comparisons. In the example, the important comparison would be those who changed from agree to disagree and those who did the opposite. We could suggest a possible value for that comparison, possibly after a pilot study in which people were asked their opinion about whether psychology was a science. We would then need to set realistic values for the other two comparisons. Using the method in Vuolo et al. (2016) on the actual values derived from Table 15.11 shows that a minimum of 40 participants would be needed for power of 0.8 and alpha of 0.05. See Appendix VI for the calculations of sample size.

Differences between proportions

The χ^2 test applied to a contingency table is asking whether the two variables are independent of each other: For example, are gender and smoking status independent? At the same time it is answering the question: Do the proportions of smokers differ between males and females? This latter question can more obviously be seen to be being tested in an alternative way: we can directly compare the proportions who fall into a particular category for two different groups.

Between-subjects designs

A z-test exists for comparing proportions which have come from two independent samples:

$$z = \frac{p_1 - p_2}{\sqrt{\dfrac{p_1 \times (1 - p_1)}{n_1} + \dfrac{p_2 \times (1 - p_2)}{n_2}}} \tag{15.7}$$

where p_1 and p_2 are the proportions for the two groups and n_1 and n_2 are the samples sizes of the two groups.

We can reanalyse the data for smoking and gender using this test. Let females be group 1 and males group 2 and let the proportion we are interested in be the proportion of smokers. Then $p_1 = .4773$, $n_1 = 44$, $p_2 = .3864$, $n_2 = 44$. Therefore,

$$z = \frac{.4773 - .3864}{\sqrt{\dfrac{.4773 \times (.5227)}{44} + \dfrac{.3864 \times (.6136)}{44}}} = \frac{.0909}{\sqrt{.00567 + .005389}} = 0.864397$$

Table A17.1 in Appendix XVII shows that a two-tailed probability for a z-score of 0.86 is .3898. Note that if you square a z-score it should produce a statistic which is distributed like chi-squared with df = 1. Squaring 0.864397 produces 0.747182. Previously it was shown that the χ^2 test conducted on the same data produced $\chi^2 = 0.741$ with $p = .3893$.

Effect size for the difference between independent proportions

Cohen (1988) uses the effect size h for this situation. The reason he doesn't use g, which is appropriate when comparing a proportion in a sample with a population proportion of .5 (as shown in Chapter 13), is that power is affected by the actual values of the proportions in the sample and so the same value for g would have different levels of power. Using h is designed to get around this problem. However, a problem with h is that it involves a mathematical transformation, which I explain in Appendix VI. Here I will just describe a power analysis for the smoking example, where $h = 0.18$. According to Cohen an h of 0.2 is a small effect, 0.5 is medium and 0.8 is large. Thus the current effect size is just below a small one. Referring to Table A18.6 in Appendix XVIII shows that, with that effect size, a sample *in each group* of over 400 would be needed to achieve power of .8 with a two-tailed test and α = .05.

Confidence intervals for the difference between two independent proportions

If a CI for the difference between two proportions contains 0, then this suggests that there may be no difference between the proportions in the population. The 95% CI for the difference in the proportion of smokers among men and women is −.115 to .297, which does contain 0. (How these figures were obtained is explained in Appendix VI.)

Within-subjects designs

Following the previous reasoning that squaring a *z*-score produces a chi-squared value with df = 1, McNemar's test is the square of a *z*-test which can be used to test the difference between two proportions which aren't independent. Appendix VI shows the calculation of the *z*-test and how a confidence interval can be found for comparing the proportions in one category between the two occasions – for example, the proportions agreeing that psychology is a science before and after hearing the talk.

Summary

When two levels of an independent variable are being compared, the chart shown in Figure 15.3 can be used to decide which is the appropriate statistical test. However, remember that if homogeneity of variance is not present but the other requirements of a between-subjects *t*-test are fulfilled, then use Welch's *t*-test. In addition, *z*-tests exist for comparing two proportions.

FIGURE 15.3   Statistical tests for designs with one independent variable with two levels

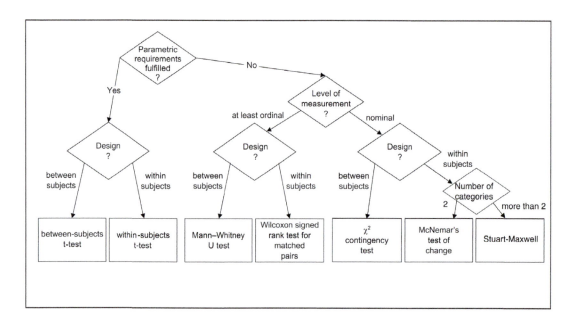

16 Preliminary analysis of designs with one independent variable with more than two levels

Introduction

So far you have been introduced to the analysis of designs which include a single independent variable (IV) that has a maximum of two levels. The present chapter describes how to carry out preliminary analysis of designs which have a single IV with more than two levels.

Parametric tests

For an example I will return to a study originally introduced in Chapter 9. Researchers wished to compare the recall of participants in three conditions: using the mnemonic system of pegwords, using the method of loci and not using any specific mnemonics (the control condition). In order not to have practice effects and introduce problems of having to match lists for difficulty, a between-subjects design was chosen.

The researchers now have a design which includes one IV – type of mnemonic – which has three levels (or conditions): pegword, method of loci and the control condition. They also have a single dependent variable (DV) – number of words recalled. When they come to analysing the results of their research, they could employ *t*-tests to compare pairs of levels. However, they will have to perform three *t*-tests: one between pegwords and method of loci, one between pegwords and the control group and one between method of loci and the control group. This approach would be possible, but there is a statistical problem which renders it inadvisable.

The rationale behind statistical significance testing is that when we decide to accept our hypothesis and reject the Null Hypothesis we are taking a risk – the risk of making a Type I error. Imagine that we have set $\alpha = .05$. We are saying that if the result which we found were really to be by chance, and we were to repeat the research a large number of times and analyse the data each time, we would expect that on about 5% of occasions the result would be as extreme or more extreme than this and therefore statistically significant. Therefore, if we perform the test more than once we are increasing the likelihood that we will find a significant result even when the Null Hypothesis is true.

It is possible to try to allow for the fact that a number of tests are being performed by making the α-level smaller and thus reducing the danger of making a Type I error. However, such techniques are rather inexact. It is considered better, at least initially, to perform a single test which takes into account all the data which have been collected in a piece of research. If this initial test demonstrates that there is a significant difference between the levels of the IV we are justified in exploring the data further to try to identify the specific contributions to that significant effect.

The test which is the most appropriate for analysing the memory experiment described previously is the analysis of variance (usually abbreviated to ANOVA). ANOVA can be seen as an extension of the *t*-test in that it compares the means for the different levels of the IV and, as with the *t*-test, the Null Hypothesis is that the means do not differ. In formal terms, the Null Hypothesis is that the three sets of data for the groups actually come from the same population and thus have the same mean. Also, as with the *t*-test, even if there is a difference between the means, if the variation in scores *within the groups* is large, then a significant difference will not be obtained. However, because we are now dealing with three rather than two means, the way to evaluate the difference between them is to see how much they vary.

To look at the nature of ANOVA entails reintroducing certain concepts and then expanding on your existing knowledge. This will help to read the summary table which comes from performing an ANOVA.

As was shown in Chapter 9, one way to ask how typical or atypical a particular score is, is to calculate how far away it is from the mean for its group, that is, its deviation from the group mean. If we want a measure of the spread within a group of scores we can square the deviation for each score and add them together; this is known as the *sum of squared deviations*, which is often shortened to *sum of squares*. If we divide the sum of squares by the appropriate degrees of freedom we arrive at the variance for the group of scores, usually described as a *mean square* (MS) in ANOVA. This is an estimate of the variance in the population. If the Null Hypothesis is correct, then all the scores come from the same population; the different levels of the IV do not produce differences in the DV. ANOVA relies on the fact that there is more than one way to estimate the population variance; in particular, it involves one estimate which is derived from the variance between the levels of the IV and another derived from the variance within the levels.

The estimate of the population variance which comes from within the levels of the IV is only going to be due to individual differences,[1] sometimes referred to as error. This is true regardless of whether the Null Hypothesis is true or false. The estimate of the population variance which comes from between the levels of the IV will contain only variance due to individual differences if the Null Hypothesis is correct. However, if the Null Hypothesis is false, it will also contain variance due to the differences between the treatments.

ANOVA has its own statistic – the *F*-test or *F*-ratio. It is called a ratio because it calculates the ratio between the variance which can be explained as being due to the differences between the groups and the error or unexplained variance. Thus,

$$F\text{-ratio} = \frac{\text{between} - \text{group estimate of population variance}}{\text{within} - \text{group estimate of population variance}}$$

In our example this would mean:

$$F\text{-ratio} = \frac{\text{variation between the recall conditions}}{\text{variation within the recall conditions}}$$

If the Null Hypothesis is true, then both estimates of the population variance should be roughly the same, in which case, the *F*-ratio should equal approximately 1.

However, if the Null Hypothesis is false the estimate of the population variance which comes from looking at the between-group variation should be larger, in which case, the *F*-ratio should be larger than 1.

In the process of making the estimates of variance due to different sources, the overall sum of squares for all the data, that is, the total variation in all the data, is split (or partitioned) into the different sources which are producing it. This has the consequence of identifying a specific amount of the overall variation as being linked to a particular IV and its related error variation. Hence, another way to view the *F*-ratio is to see it as:

$$F = \frac{\text{variation between the means}}{\text{unexplained (error) variation}}$$

---

1 Individuals treated in the same way will have different scores on most measures for at least two reasons: firstly, the participants have an inherent difference in ability; secondly, the measure which is being used is not 100% reliable and so is going to vary in the degree to which it manages to assess a person's 'true' score.

How the partitioning occurs depends on the research design and will be explained as each design is introduced.

Between-subjects designs

The simplest form of ANOVA to interpret (and to calculate) is a between-subjects design, as with the memory example. Figure 16.1 shows that the overall variation is split into two sources. There will only be one F-ratio which will be of the following form:

$$F = \frac{\text{between-groups variance}}{\text{within-groups variance}}$$

FIGURE 16.1   Partitioning of variance in a between-subjects ANOVA

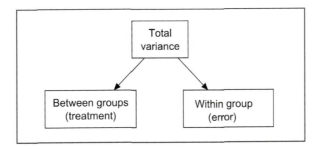

Imagine that the researchers randomly allocated 10 people to each group for the experiment. (I will leave power analysis until later in the chapter.) They gave the appropriate instructions to the members of each group and then presented them with 20 words. Twenty-four hours later the researchers asked them to recall as many words as they could, in any order. The research hypothesis is that the method of loci produces the best recall. Note, however, that ANOVA cannot test that hypothesis directly. At this stage the researchers can only ask whether the recall for the three groups differs significantly. Therefore their research hypothesis has another, preliminary, hypothesis which is tested first:

H_A: The mean recall of the three conditions is different.

This has the Null Hypothesis:

H_0:   The mean recall of the three conditions does not differ.

Formally, the Null Hypothesis is that the means for the populations for the different conditions are the same. In the case of three means, H_0 would be $\mu_1 = \mu_2 = \mu_3$.

If the preliminary hypothesis is not supported, then it is unlikely that the research hypothesis will be supported and it is usually not worth trying to test it. If, however, the preliminary hypothesis *is* supported, then it is worth conducting further analysis to see whether the research hypothesis is also supported.[2]

---

2   This account is true for most follow-up analysis which researchers currently conduct. However, situations are described in Chapter 18 which are exceptions to this rule.

Table 16.1 and Figure 16.2 summarise the results of the experiment.

We can see that the means are different. However, Figure 16.2 shows that there is some overlap between the three sets of scores. To test whether the differences between the means are statistically significant we need to carry out an ANOVA on the data. See Appendix VII for a worked example. Table 16.2 shows the results of the analysis; the term *one-way* is used to describe an ANOVA conducted on a design with a single IV.

TABLE 16.1   Means and *SD*s of word recall for the three memory conditions

	Control	*Pegword*	*Loci*
Mean	7.2	8.9	9.6
SD	1.62	1.91	1.58

FIGURE 16.2   Means and *SD*s of word recall for the three memory conditions

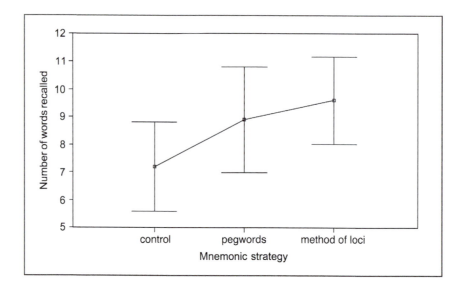

Interpreting a one-way between-subjects ANOVA

I will explain what the different elements of Table 16.2 mean. The first column (source) indicates what the figures in the other columns refer to and, in particular, to what the amounts of the variation in the data are attributable. In this case, you will see that some of the variation in scores is due to the difference

TABLE 16.2   A summary table for a one-way between-subjects ANOVA comparing recall under the three mnemonic conditions

Source	Sum of squares	df	Mean square	F-test	p
Between groups	30.467	2	15.233	5.213	.0122
Within groups	78.9	27	2.922		
Total	109.367	29			

between the groups; this is the variation we are interested in because it tells us about the differences between the mean recall for the three groups. Next we have the variation within the groups, that is, the error variation, which will be due to differences between people within the groups. Finally we have the total variation for the experiment.

The next column gives the sum of squares for each of the sources of variation in the data. Recall that a sum of squares is a descriptive statistic which describes amount of spread in data. The next column tells us about the degrees of freedom (df). Note that the df for groups is 2. This is simply one fewer than the number of groups because we are looking at the variation between the means for the groups. The df for the total is 29, which is one fewer than the number of participants used in the experiment. The df for within groups is 27, which is the difference between the total df and the df for between groups. The within group df can also be calculated by saying that there are three groups each with 9 df, that is, one fewer than the number in each group.

The next column gives the MS for each source of variation in the study. If you take the sum of squares for a given source of variation and divide it by its df you arrive at the appropriate MS; the MS is the estimate of variance. The next column provides the F-ratio, which in this case is found by dividing the MS for between groups by the MS for within groups (or error MS).

Tails of test

With the majority of the statistical tests which have been introduced thus far, we have wanted to know what tail of test we should employ. However, when there are more than two levels of an IV being tested in an ANOVA there is no choice – the test will be the equivalent of a two-tailed test. To find the reason for this we have to return to the nature of the Null Hypothesis for research designs which are analysed by ANOVA. The Null Hypothesis states that the means for the different conditions do not differ (because they come from the same population). The alternative hypothesis states that they do differ (because they come from different populations). The ANOVA as described so far is incapable of testing more precise hypotheses, such *as recall from the control group will be poorer than for the other two conditions*.

If you think about it, you will see that when there are three levels of an IV, such a precise hypothesis is only one of many possible directional alternative hypotheses which could have been stated, rather than the two which are possible when there are only two levels of an IV. If we wish to test a more precise, directional hypothesis, the convention is that we first check whether the non-directional hypothesis is supported. If it is we can explore further, using the techniques shown in Chapter 18. If it is not, then we have little evidence for a directional hypothesis.

Evaluating the statistical significance of an *F*-ratio

Usually, when you calculate an ANOVA by computer you will be told the significance of any resulting F-ratio. However, it is worth being able to read the significance tables for F-ratios. An F-ratio is evaluated in a slightly different way from other tests described so far. As it is the ratio between two variance estimates (MS), each with its own df, we need both df to evaluate the significance of an F-ratio. Table 16.3 is an extract from a table of the probabilities of F-ratios in Appendix XVII.

TABLE 16.3 An extract from the $\alpha = 0.05$ probability tables for an *F*-ratio

df_2	df_1											
	1	2	3	4	5	6	7	8	9	10	12	14
26	4.23	3.37	2.98	2.74	2.59	2.47	2.39	2.32	2.27	2.22	2.15	2.09
27	4.21	3.35	2.96	2.73	2.57	2.46	2.37	2.31	2.25	2.20	2.13	2.08
28	4.20	3.34	2.95	2.71	2.56	2.45	2.36	2.29	2.24	2.19	2.12	2.06

It is usual for significance tables for *F*-ratios to come in a set, with one table for each significance level. Frequently the tables are limited to $\alpha = .05$, $\alpha = .025$, $\alpha = .01$ and $\alpha = .001$, or an even smaller range, as in the present book, which only contains tables for $\alpha = .05$, $\alpha = .025$ and $\alpha = .01$. In this way, we can only tell that an *F*-ratio did or did not reach statistical significance and cannot be much more precise than that.

When reading Table 16.3 note that the df for the treatment are shown in the first row of the table (df_1), such that there is a column devoted to each different treatment df. The df for the error term are shown in the first column so that each row has a different df for the error term – in this case the *within-groups* source of variance – (df_2). Therefore, to find the critical value of *F* to be significant at $p = .05$, we look in the column for df = 2 and the row for df = 27. This shows us that the critical value is $F = 3.35$. As the *F*-value which we found from our analysis is larger than this we can say that our result is statistically significant at the $p < .05$ level. We could look further in the tables for lower significance levels, in which case we would learn that *p* lies between .025 and .05, that is, $.025 < p < .05$.

The researchers can therefore reject the Null Hypothesis and accept the preliminary research hypothesis that recall is different in the different recall conditions. Remember that they had a more specific hypothesis. Given that the preliminary research hypothesis has been supported, they are justified in conducting further analysis to evaluate their more specific hypothesis. I want to leave description of that analysis until the next but one chapter, by which time I will have introduced the various forms of ANOVA.

Reporting the results of an ANOVA

The minimum details which are needed are the following. *There was a significant difference in recall between the mnemonic strategies* ($F_{(2,27)} = 5.213$, $p = .012$). This entails reporting the source of the *F*-ratio, the appropriate df, the *F*-ratio and the probability level. In addition to this you should report the effect size, which is described later.

Within-subjects designs

These designs are also known as *repeated measures* designs. In a within-subjects design, with a single IV, the total variation in the data can be seen as being due to two main sources: differences between the participants (between-subjects variance) and differences within the participants (within-subjects variance), that is, how individuals varied across the different conditions. Within-subjects variance can be further divided into variance between the levels of the IV – the conditions (treatment variance) – and variance due to the way the different participants showed a different pattern of responses across the conditions (treatment by subjects, also known as error variance or residual variance) (Figure 16.3). An

FIGURE 16.3   Partitioning of variance in a within-subjects ANOVA

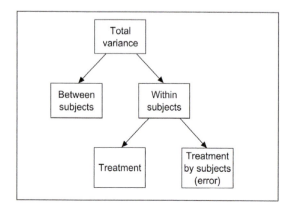

example of the latter would be if the previous study had been a within-subjects design and the first participant had recalled most words in the pegword condition, while the second participant had recalled most in the loci condition.

The *F*-ratio which addresses the hypothesis we are interested in is:

$$F = \frac{\text{treatment variation}}{\text{error variation}}$$

It will tell us whether the treatment conditions differed significantly. Although we are not usually interested in knowing whether the participants differed, the advantage of this design is that the variation in scores which can be seen as being due to the difference between participants can be removed from the analysis and so a smaller amount of variance which is not attributable to the differences between the treatments will remain. Hence this is a more efficient design which has more statistical power than a between-subjects design.

Note that there cannot be variance which is attributable to variation within participants in a between-subjects design because each participant only provides one data point and so we cannot ascertain how the same person varies across the levels of an IV.

For this example, imagine that a team of researchers is looking at the effects of the presence of others on judgements about the treatment of offenders. Participants are given a description of a crime and have to decide how much time the criminal should spend in prison. The experiment involves three conditions: in one, each participant is alone and is unaware of anyone else's judgement; in a second condition, each participant is alone but can see on a computer screen what others have 'decided'; in the third condition, each participant is in a group and is aware of what the others have 'decided'. The decisions which the participants learn that others have made are, in fact, pre-set by the experimenters but the participants are unaware of this. There are three different crimes, considered by a panel of judges to be of similar severity, so that the participants do not have to make their three judgements about the same crime. The confederates of the experimenters have been told to suggest a long sentence, even though the crimes are comparatively minor.

The experimental hypothesis is that participants will recommend longer sentences when they are aware of what others have recommended, and even longer sentences when they are in the presence of the confederates. However, remember that the initial ANOVA cannot test a directional hypothesis; it can only test the preliminary research hypothesis:

H$_A$: The mean length of sentence recommended by participants will differ between the three conditions.

The Null Hypothesis will be:

H$_0$: The mean length of sentence will not differ between the three conditions.

If the preliminary research hypothesis is supported, then analysis to evaluate the more specific research hypothesis is justified.

The experiment is run with 10 participants with the order in which each participant takes part in each condition being randomised. The DV, length of sentence in months, is noted for each decision. Again, power will be dealt with later. The results of the experiment are shown in Table 16.4 and Figure 16.4.

The results suggest that the sentences recommended do differ between the three different conditions. However, note that there is also quite a spread around the means and quite an overlap between the three different conditions. As usual, the descriptive statistics can only indicate which direction the results are going; they cannot tell us how likely the results are to have occurred if the Null Hypothesis

TABLE 16.4   The means and *SD*s of sentence length (in months) recommended by participants

	Alone	Computer	Group
Mean	14.7	18.2	20.0
SD	6.55	4.52	5.48

FIGURE 16.4   The means and *SD*s of sentence length (in months) recommended by participants

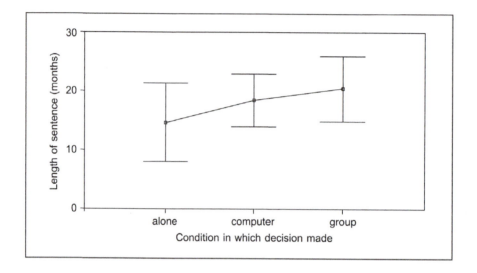

were true. Therefore, we cannot decide between the Null and experimental hypotheses until we have carried out an ANOVA on the data.

Table 16.5 shows the summary table for the ANOVA for this experiment.

TABLE 16.5   A summary table for a one-way within-subjects ANOVA comparing the sentences given to criminals when the decisions were made under three different conditions

Source	Sum of squares	df	Mean square	F-ratio	p
Between subjects	776.3	9			
Within subjects	208.667	20			
Treatments	145.267	2	72.633	20.621	.0001
Residual*	63.399	18	3.522		
Total	984.967	29			

*shown as treatment by subjects in Figure 16.3

Note that the summary table for the ANOVA of a within-subjects design looks more complicated than that for a between-subjects design. This is because we can identify more sources for the variation between all the scores.

The first column splits the sources of variance initially into two parts. There is the variance between subjects and the variance within subjects. The variance within subjects is then further divided into that which is due to the treatments (i.e. differences between the conditions) and the residual (i.e. the error or the variance which cannot be explained by the differences between subjects or by the differences between the conditions).

The second column tells us the size of the sum of squared deviations (sum of squares) for each of the sources of variance; see Appendix VII for a description of how these are obtained. The total sum of squares has been split into that which is attributable to between-subjects variation and that which can be attributed to within-subjects variation. The latter is then further subdivided into the variation due to the treatments and the variation due to error (the residual).

The third column informs us that the total df is 29; this is produced by noting how many scores we have – 3 for each of the 10 participants – and subtracting 1 from the result. The 29 df are initially split into 9 for the between-subjects variance – one fewer than the 10 participants – and 20 for the within-subjects variance – the difference between the total df and the between-subjects df. The within-subjects df can be further divided into 2 for the treatments – the number of treatments minus 1 – and 18 for the residual – 1 subtracted from the number of conditions multiplied by 1 subtracted from the number of participants: $(3-1) \times (10-1)$.

We are now in a position to calculate the estimates of the variance from the different sources (MS) by dividing the sum of squares by the appropriate df. These estimates are shown in the fourth column. Remember that under the Null Hypothesis each is an estimate of the same variance, that of the single population of scores from which the present sample of scores is considered to have come.

The summary table (Table 16.5) shows that we have two estimates for the population variance and from these an F-ratio is calculated to test the difference between the conditions. The MS for the residual contains the variation which is unexplained by either the overall variation between subjects or the overall variation between conditions.

If the conditions overall do not produce a difference in the length of recommended sentence, then the MS for treatments will only be an estimate of the general variance among scores (error). Therefore, the F-ratio for treatments is found by dividing the MS for treatments by the MS for residuals:

$$F_{(treatments)} = \frac{MS_{treatments}}{MS_{residuals}}$$

If the Null Hypothesis is correct, then $F_{(treatments)}$ will equal approximately 1, whereas, if the Null Hypothesis is false, then $F_{(treatments)}$ will tend to be greater than 1. Note, however, that it does not automatically follow that because an F-ratio is greater than 1 it is statistically significant; the critical level for F to be statistically significant depends on factors such as the sample size and the number of levels of the IV.

Interpreting a one-way within-subjects ANOVA

We are provided with the probability value for the difference between the conditions. If the computer does not provide probabilities, then the same F-tables described in the section on ANOVA for between-subjects designs (see Appendix XVII) can be used.

The experimental hypothesis is dealt with by the F-ratio for treatments. In this case the preliminary version of the experimental hypothesis is supported. Recommendations about the length of sentence for a crime *are* affected by knowledge of others' judgements. To test the directional hypothesis that length of sentence will be greater, the greater the proximity to other judges, we will have to wait until we know how to compare the individual conditions; this is shown in Chapter 18. What we do know is that it is worth conducting further analysis.

Reporting the results of a one-way within-subjects ANOVA

Report the relevant details for the F-ratio, including an explanation of the conclusions which you draw from it. The results would be reported in the following way:

> *There was a significant difference in the length of sentence recommended between the different conditions under which sentences were made ($F_{(2,18)} = 20.621$, p = .0001).*

Also include the effect size which is described later in the chapter.

The assumptions of ANOVA

You will recall that the use of a t-test requires certain assumptions to be fulfilled about the nature of the data. The use of ANOVA is also restricted to certain situations.

The form of ANOVA which I have described thus far is a parametric test. The restrictions on its use are related to the level of measurement, the nature of the distribution, the nature of the variance and the independence of the scores. However, as I will demonstrate, ANOVA can cope to a certain extent with cases in which some of these assumptions are contravened. In other words, ANOVA is a robust test.

Level of measurement

As with other parametric tests, psychologists agree that this version of ANOVA is appropriate when the DV is an interval or ratio measure. However, statisticians are less restrictive in their advice over its use for ordinal data. Nonetheless, one suggestion is that if you are using ordinal data, then they should be considered to have an underlying continuous scale; see Chapter 14.

Homogeneity of variance

As with the between-subjects t-test, the between-subjects ANOVA assumes that the variance for the population of scores for each of the conditions is the same.

Normal distribution

As with the between-subjects t-test, the between-subjects ANOVA assumes that the scores for each of the conditions come from a population which has a normal distribution.

Independence

ANOVA assumes that the scores for a given condition are independent of each other – in other words, that the scores of one person have not been affected by the scores of another participant. This would not be a problem for the experiment on recommendations of sentence length because we have not included in our analysis the recommendations of the confederates. However, if we had been looking at the judgements of participants after they had discussed the topic in groups and included all those judgements in our analysis, then each judgement in a given condition would not be independent of the others in a group.

The robustness of ANOVA

ANOVA can cope, to a certain extent, with contraventions of some of its assumptions and still be a valid test. However, if the assumptions are poorly met and if more than one is not met, then we increase the likelihood that we will make a Type I or a Type II error.

As long as the samples in a between-subjects design are roughly the same size, the recommendation is that ANOVA can cope with differences in variance between the groups, such that the largest variance can be as much as four times the smallest variance. Note that in the example given previously the variances of the different conditions do not differ by more than four times. If the variances do differ by more than four times, then it may be possible to transform the data in some way to reduce the variance (see Appendix V for ways to transform data). Alternatively, as with the t-test, there is a version of ANOVA (the Welch formula, F') which is designed for use with data which do not have homogeneity of variance. SPSS offers this statistic as an option. Appendix VII gives the Welch formula and an example of its use. If sample sizes are unequal, then treat the data as having *heterogeneous* variances if the largest variance is more than *two* times the smallest variance.

The assumption about normal distribution for the population of scores can also be contravened to a certain extent. Unfortunately, we often do not know what the distribution of the population of scores is as we only have the scores from our sample. I recommend that you produce a graph of the frequencies and if the distribution for any of the conditions differs markedly from normal, then again the data can be transformed to make it more normal. An alternative, which can save time when there are a number of groups, is to check the distribution of residuals – the difference between the actual values and the values predicted by the statistical test. They will be found when the statistical test is conducted. If they are normally distributed then it is safe to assume that the assumption of the test is fulfilled. If they aren't normally distributed then you need to explore the distributions of the individual conditions. Figure 16.5 shows the distribution of residuals from the recall data when there were three mnemonic conditions. Although it is not completely symmetrical it does not show evidence that the data come from a population which has a non-normal distribution.

FIGURE 16.5   The distribution of residuals for recall when there are three mnemonic conditions

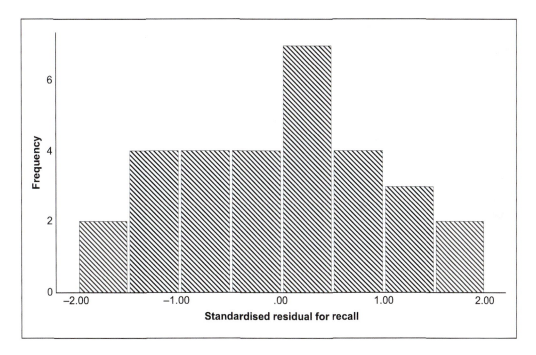

Following the reasoning of Zimmerman and Zumbo (1993), if you have both heterogeneity of variance and non-normal distributions, then convert the data into ranks and analyse the ranks using the Welch formula.

Assessing lack of independence

If there had been groups of participants in the pegword memory condition rather than just individuals, where the members of a group rehearsed the words together to try to improve recall, we could test whether there is a relationship between the group a person was in and recall. Imagine that there were

TABLE 16.6   The recall scores for people in three groups in the pegword condition

Group	Recall
1	12
1	11
1	10
2	10
2	9
2	8
3	9
3	7
3	7
3	6

three groups with the recall shown in Table 16.6. We can run a one-way between-subjects ANOVA with group as the IV and recall as the DV. This shows that there is a significant difference between the three groups ($F_{(2,7)} = 9.66$, $p = .01$). Therefore, there is likely to be a lack of independence in the scores.

In this context there is also a measure of the degree of agreement within groups, the intraclass correlation (ICC), where:

$$ICC = \frac{\text{variance between groups}}{\text{total variance}}$$

As with other coefficients of correlation, 0 would show no relationship and 1 would show a very high relationship. In this example ICC = .533 (the workings are shown in Appendix VII). A problem with ICC is that a low figure does not indicate that the results of an inferential test can be taken at face value. Cohen, Cohen, West, and Aiken (2003) report that an ICC as low as .01 can still mean that the true alpha-level is .11 instead of .05; in other words, the likelihood of committing a Type I error is more than doubled.

Dealing with lack of independence

If the data in a given condition are not independent, then we can render the scores independent. If the scores were taken after participants had discussed the recommendations about sentence length, then we could take the mean score for each discussion group and use the means as the dependent variable. The problem with this move is that we will reduce the number of scores that we are analysing and so we will make our test less powerful. In other words, we will increase the likelihood of making a Type II error. However, if we did not use the means we could be seriously violating the assumptions of the ANOVA and would thus be increasing the likelihood of making a Type I error. Alternative approaches to allow for the possible lack of independence are to include group as a factor in an ANOVA with more than one IV or to use multi-level (or hierarchical) modelling (described briefly in Chapter 25).

Within-subjects designs

Sphericity (or circularity)

Within-subjects ANOVA has another assumption which the data should fulfil – *sphericity*. If we were to find, for each participant, the difference between his or her score on two of the levels of an IV, such as that between the sentence given when alone and the sentence given when in a group, then we would have a set of difference scores. We could then calculate the variance of those difference scores. If we found the difference scores for each pair of levels of the IV and calculated the variance for each set of difference scores we would be in a position to check whether sphericity was present in the data. It would be present if the variances of the difference scores were homogeneous. When an IV only has two levels, and therefore df = 1, there is only one set of difference scores and so sphericity is not an issue.

When sphericity is not present, there are at least two possible ways around the problem. One is to use a different form of ANOVA, multivariate ANOVA or MANOVA. This technique is briefly described in Chapter 25, but its method of calculation is beyond the scope of this book. An alternative approach comes from the finding that even when sphericity is not present, the *F*-ratio calculated from a within-subjects ANOVA still conforms to the *F*-distribution. However, it is necessary to adjust the df to allow for the lack of sphericity. Computer programs such as SPSS report two such adjustments, so it is worth your while knowing about them; both are given the symbol ε (the Greek letter *epsilon*). The first is the Greenhouse–Geisser (G–G) epsilon, and the second is the Huynh–Feldt (H–F) epsilon. The first is more conservative – in other words, it is more likely to avoid a Type I error but increase the likelihood of a Type II error – and the second is more liberal.

Reworking the analysis for within-subjects ANOVA, the computer reported that the G–G epsilon was .913 and the H–F epsilon was 1.134. If the H–F epsilon is greater than 1, then it is treated as though it were 1, in which case the original df remain unaltered. To find the new df use the following equations:

adjusted treatment df = treatment df $\times$ ε
adjusted error df = error df $\times$ ε

Therefore in the present example, for G–G epsilon:

adjusted treatment df = 2 $\times$ .913 = 1.826
adjusted error df = 18 $\times$ .913 = 16.434

In fact, the probability of the result, reported by the computer as $p = .0001$, is little affected by the adjustment. If we had to rely on tables, then we would round the df to the nearest whole numbers, which in this case would be 2 and 16. Reading such tables would show that the results were statistically significant at the $p < .01$ level.

If you are using a computer program which reports the epsilon values, then check whether the three probability values which are given for each *F*-ratio agree over whether the result is statistically significant. As usual, if they agree, then there is no problem. If they disagree, then you have to report the different values and discuss the differences.

If the program does not compute the epsilon values, then the following can show whether they need to be calculated:

1   If the *F*-ratio is not statistically significant with unadjusted df, then it certainly will not be after adjustment, so there is no need to calculate either epsilon.
2   If the *F*-ratio is statistically significant with the unadjusted df and is still statistically significant even with df of 1 for the treatment and $n - 1$ (one fewer than the number of participants) for the error term, then there is no need to calculate epsilon as the result is clearly statistically significant.
3   If the *F*-ratio is statistically significant with the unadjusted df but is not so with df of 1 and $n - 1$, then you need to calculate the epsilons.

In the current example, as the result was statistically significant with the unadjusted df, we should check the probability of the *F*-ratio with df of 1 and 9 (as there were 10 participants). As the critical level of *F* for $p \leq .05$ is 5.12, the calculated level of F (20.621) is clearly statistically significant and so we would not have needed to calculate the epsilons had the computer not provided them.

The equations for the two forms of epsilon are given in Appendix VII.

Unequal sample sizes in between-subjects ANOVA

As was noted earlier, to minimise the effects of not having homogeneity of variance, in a between-subjects design it is best to try to have equal numbers of participants in each level of the IV (a balanced design). However, sometimes this will not be possible. When the samples are unequal, the computation of ANOVA is different from when the samples are equal. However, there are two possible ways in which the analysis can be conducted and these should depend on why the samples are unequal.

In some circumstances there may be good reason to have unequal samples: for example, if we were comparing people with normal memories with those with unusually good memories. In this case, there would be fewer of the latter group in the population. Under such circumstances, it makes sense to use what are described as weighted means, in other words, means which come from a larger sample are given more weight in the analysis. This is the analysis used by most computer programs when the samples are unequal.

However, there are situations in which the reason for the unequal samples is arbitrary. An example would be if some participants in a study, who were due to be included, were not available when required. As long as the reasons for their absence are not systematic, it makes more sense to use unweighted means. An example of systematic absence would be if we had originally selected our sample so that we could compare people from different socio-economic backgrounds but found that a disproportionate number of people from one type of background were subsequently unavailable to take part in the research.

The two methods for calculating ANOVAs when sample sizes are unequal are given in Appendix VII.

Effect size and ANOVA

There are a number of measures for the effect size of a treatment in ANOVA. The simplest to find is η^2 (eta-squared), which is the proportion of the overall sum of squares which can be attributed to the treatment and can be used to see the proportion (or percentage) of overall variance which is attributable to a given treatment. Thus,

$$\eta^2 = \frac{\text{sum of squares for treatments}}{\text{total sum of squares}}$$

Therefore, in the memory example:

$$\eta^2 = \frac{30.467}{109.367}$$
$$= .279$$

In this case, $.279 \times 100$ or 27.9% of the overall variance in scores can be explained as being due to the differences between the mnemonic strategies.

While in the sentencing example:

$$\eta^2 = \frac{145.267}{984.967}$$
$$= .147$$

Cohen (1988) uses a different measure of effect size (f) which can be derived from η^2; see Appendix VII. However, for consistency I have converted his recommendations for f into values for η^2. Accordingly, he states that an η^2 of .01 is a small effect size, η^2 of .059 is a medium effect size and η^2 of .138 is a large effect size. In this case, both studies produced large effect sizes.

Some computer packages, including SPSS, report what is described as *partial* eta-squared, the equation for which is shown in Appendix VII. I prefer the version of eta-squared described previously as it relates more clearly to the notion of proportion of variance accounted for than does partial eta-squared. For one thing, when there is more than one IV in the analysis, using partial eta-squared, the amount of variance accounted for by the different elements in the design may add up to more than 100%. In addition, the version I prefer is simpler to calculate and, as explained in Chapter 20, eta-squared is more straightforwardly analogous to the information provided by other ways of analysing the same data than is partial eta-squared. However, with a one-way between-subjects ANOVA, eta-squared and partial eta-squared produce the same result.

Calculating the power of a parametric one-way ANOVA

Appendix XVIII gives tables of the relationship between effect size, power and sample size for ANOVA. This shows that with 10 participants in each group and $\eta^2 = .279$, the power of the test for treatment df of 2 is between .77 and .87 (the exact figure is .83).

The power of within-subjects ANOVAs

The calculation of the power of within-subjects ANOVA is complicated by the fact that under certain circumstances, for the same number of data points, it will be more powerful than its equivalent between-subjects design, whereas, under other circumstances, the power will be reduced. To keep the process as simple as possible, I have followed other authors in only providing power tables for between-subjects ANOVA, where the values can be specified more precisely. These tables can be used for within-subjects designs to give approximate guidelines for sample size and power.

The relationship between t *and* F

If we are analysing an experimental design with one IV which only has two levels we can obviously use a *t*-test. However, we can also use an ANOVA on the same data. In fact, under these conditions, and only these conditions, they will give us the same answer as far as the probability is concerned. However, this is only true when we are using a two-tailed test for the *t*-test, because ANOVA only tests non-directional hypotheses. Under these circumstances the value for the *F*-ratio is the square of the value for *t*. In mathematical terms:

$$F = t^2$$

That is,

$$t = \sqrt{F}$$

Thus, if $F = 4$ with 1 and 15 df, then $t = 2$ with 15 df. To confirm this look at the critical values for *F* and *t* in their respective tables. You will see that when $\alpha = .05$ the critical value for *F* with 1 and 15 df is $F = 4.54$. The equivalent critical value for a two-tailed *t*-test with 15 df is 2.131 or $\sqrt{4.54}$.

Non-parametric equivalents of ANOVA

At least ordinal data

Between-subjects designs: Kruskal–Wallis one-way ANOVA by ranks

When the research design is between-subjects with more than two levels of the IV and the requirements of a parametric ANOVA are not fulfilled, then the analysis can be conducted using the Kruskal–Wallis one-way ANOVA, which is based on its parametric equivalent. This test does not assume that the distribution in the population is normal but that the distributions of the different conditions are the same. Therefore it is not as restrictive as the parametric, one-way between-subjects ANOVA. Nonetheless, it does assume that the individual scores are independent of each other.

In a study researchers wished to compare the grades given by lecturers to essays which were shown either to be by a male or a female, or the gender was not specified. The research hypothesis was that the grades given to the three different categories of author would be different. Formally, the Null Hypothesis would be that the medians for the three conditions do not differ.

Twenty-four college lecturers were each given an essay to mark and they were told that the writer of the essay was either a male student or a female student, or they were not given any indication of the student's gender. In fact, the same essay was given to all the lecturers. Each essay was given a grade between C– and A+, which was converted to a numerical grade ranging from 1 to 9. The summary statistics for the ratings of the essays of the three different 'authors' are shown in Table 16.7.

TABLE 16.7 The mean, median and *SD*s of grades given for the essay and the supposed gender of the author

	Gender of author		
	Female	*Neutral*	*Male*
Mean	3.25	4	4.25
Median	3	4	4
SD	*1.04*	*1.07*	*1.67*

A Kruskal–Wallis ANOVA was performed on the data; the workings are shown in Appendix VII. As with the Wilcoxon signed rank test for matched pairs, a rank is given to each grade and a statistic, H in this case, is calculated from these grades. In this example, $H = 2.086$. When some scores are the same, there is a version of the test which adjusts for ties. This is the more accurate version and the one which SPSS reports. In the present example, there were five places where the grades tied and the H corrected for ties was 2.231. SPSS gave the exact probability as .340. If you don't have access to programs which produce exact probabilities, then for an IV with three levels and sample size no greater than 8 in any of the groups, the critical values for H to produce significance at $p = .05$ and $p = .01$ are given in Appendix XVII (the critical values are also given for an IV with four levels with up to four participants in each and for an IV with five levels with up to three participants in each). Otherwise, H is distributed like chi-squared, with df of one fewer than the number of levels of the IV. The probability based on the chi-squared distribution is $p = .328$, and if we look in the table of the chi-squared distribution in Appendix XVII for df = 2 we will find that p lies between .5 and .3 (i.e. $.3 < p < .5$). This means that there is insufficient evidence to reject the Null Hypothesis.

Reporting the results of a Kruskal–Wallis ANOVA

The preceding result would be reported in the following way: *There was no significant difference in the median grades given to the three authors (H = 2.231, df = 2, p = .34, N = 24).* From this we could conclude that the lecturers did not differ in the grades they gave to essays on the basis of their knowledge of the author's gender. See below for details of a measure of effect size for Kruskal–Wallis ANOVA.

Power and the Kruskal–Wallis ANOVA

As with previous non-parametric tests, the power of the Kruskal–Wallis ANOVA is given in terms of power efficiency, that is, how statistically powerful it is relative to the parametric equivalent, when the assumptions of the parametric test are fulfilled. Accordingly, I advise finding the sample size which would be required for the one-way between-subjects parametric ANOVA and then adjusting the sample size according to the rule given below. If the researchers had been expecting a medium effect size, then they would have found, for α = .05, they needed a sample of 52 in each group in order to have power of .8 when running a parametric ANOVA. As they were using the Kruskal–Wallis test, they needed 52 × 1.05 = 54.6, in other words, 55 people in each group for the same level of power. As with other non-parametric tests, if the assumptions of the parametric ANOVA are not met, the Kruskal–Wallis test may well have greater power than its parametric equivalent.

Within-subjects designs: Friedman two-way ANOVA

When the design is within-subjects and the IV has more than two levels but the assumptions of the parametric ANOVA are not met, if the level of measurement is at least ordinal, then the Friedman two-way ANOVA is the appropriate test. The name of the test is somewhat confusing as it is used for one-way, within-subjects designs. As usual, the data in a given condition are assumed to be independent.

Researchers wished to see whether a group of seven students rated a particular course differently as they spent more time on the course. Each student was asked to rate the course on a 7-point scale ranging from *not enjoyable at all* to *very enjoyable*, on three occasions: after 1 week, after 5 weeks and after 10 weeks.

Friedman's ANOVA tests whether the medians of the levels of the IV are the same. The median ratings for weeks 1, 5 and 10 were 4, 4 and 5, respectively, suggesting a slight improvement in rating over time. However, to see whether this was likely by chance, Friedman's ANOVA was used to analyse the data; workings are given in Appendix VII. The test produces a statistic called χ_F^2 (sometimes given as χ_r^2). It also has a version corrected for ties which is the more accurate statistic and the one reported by SPSS. In this example, $\chi_F^2 = 4.071$ and χ_F^2 corrected for ties = 5.429. SPSS reported the exact probability as $p = .063$. When you do not have access to a program which provides the exact probability, for IVs with levels of 3, 4, 5 or 6, Table A17.10 in Appendix XVII gives critical values for χ_F^2 which are based on sample sizes of up to 20, and for IVs with three levels additional critical values are given for sample sizes of up to 50. When the number of levels and the sample size are both sufficiently large, the distribution of χ_F^2 is like chi-squared, with df which are one fewer than the number of levels of the IV. The probability based on the chi-squared distribution is $p = .066$.

Reporting the results of Friedman's test

Report the result in the following way: *There was not a significantly different rating given to the three different weeks* ($\chi_F^2 = 5.429$, $df = 2$, $p = .06$, $N = 7$). However, if the probability is given in Table A15.10, then report the result without the df: ($\chi_F^2 = 5.429$, $p > .05$, $N = 7$). See below for details of a measure of effect size for Friedman's two-way ANOVA.

Power and Friedman's test

The power efficiency of Friedman's test depends on the number of levels of the IV: the smaller the number of levels, the poorer is the power efficiency. It also depends on the distribution of the data in the population. Appendix VII gives guidelines on how to adjust the sample size, which is necessary for the within-subjects parametric ANOVA in order to get power of a particular size for Friedman's test; for example, when the IV has only three levels and the data are normally distributed, the sample size for Friedman's test would have to be nearly one-and-a-half times that of a parametric ANOVA.

Further analysis after an initial non-parametric ANOVA

If the results of a non-parametric ANOVA show a significant difference between the levels of the IV, then further analysis can be conducted which will help to pinpoint the source of the significance. Chapter 18 deals with such analysis.

Nominal data

Between-subjects designs: χ^2 contingency test

When a contingency table has variables with more than two levels, the analysis is basically the same as for one with variables which have only two levels. Thus, the appropriate test is the χ^2 contingency test (sometimes known as the test of independence), described in Chapter 15. For example, if one variable was type of smoker – with smoker, ex-smoker and non-smoker – and the other variable was gender we would have a 3 × 2 contingency table. As in this case, the terms 'IV' and 'DV' are often misnomers in the χ^2 test, as neither has been manipulated; the test is looking to see whether the pattern of one variable is different for different levels of another variable – for example, whether the proportions in each of the different smoking statuses differ between the males and the females – as this would suggest that smoking status and gender were not independent.

Remember that the frequencies should be independent – in the sense that each person should only appear under one category – and that not more than 20% of the *expected* frequencies should be smaller than 5; see Chapter 15 for a fuller explanation. If too many expected frequencies are below 5, then it is possible to combine categories for variables which have more than two levels. Thus, if the ex-smoker categories had expected frequencies which were too small, then a new category could be formed which combined ex-smoker and non-smoker. This would only make sense if the researchers were particularly interested in comparing those who smoke now with those who do not. If they were interested in comparing those who had smoked at some time with those who never had, then it would make more sense to combine ex-smokers with smokers.

Report the results in the same way as shown for a 2 × 2 contingency table. See below for an effect size for contingency tables which are larger than 2 × 2.

Within-subjects designs: Cochran's Q

If the measure taken is dichotomous – for example, yes or no – or can be converted into one or more dichotomies, then Cochran's Q can be used. An example would be if researchers wanted to compare students' choices of modules on *social psychology, research methods* and *historical issues* to see whether some modules were more popular than others. It is recommended that the test be conducted with at least 16 participants[3] and so the researchers asked this number of students what their module choices were. Twelve had chosen social psychology, eight research methods and six historical issues. Appendix VII shows the workings for Cochran's Q. In the example $Q = 4.668$. SPSS reports the exact probability as $p = .125$. However, if you do not have access to exact probabilities, then, with at least this sample size, Q

---

3   As with Wilcoxon's test described in the last chapter, only participants who show a difference across the levels of the IV contribute to the value of Cochran's Q.

is considered to be distributed like chi-squared with df equal to one fewer than the number of levels of the IV, 3 − 1 = 2. The probability based on the chi-squared distribution is $p = .097$. Accordingly, it was concluded that there was insufficient evidence to reject the Null Hypothesis that the numbers choosing the different modules are the same.

As with the within-subjects ANOVA, the accuracy of the probability, using the chi-squared distribution for Cochran's Q, is dependent on the data having sphericity (see Myers, DiCecco, White, & Borden, 1982, for a modified version of Q which is designed to cope with lack of sphericity).

Reporting the results of Cochran's Q

Report the result in the following way: *There was no significant difference in the proportion of students choosing the three modules* ($Q_{(2)} = 4.668$, $p = .13$ *(exact from SPSS version 25)*, N = 16). If you don't have access to the exact probability then give the figures as ($Q_{(2)} = 4.668$, $df = 2$, $p = .10$, N = 16). See below for details of a measure of effect size for Cochran's Q.

Converting nominal data with more than two levels into dichotomous data

In order to use Cochran's Q, it may be necessary to create dichotomous variables from non-dichotomous nominal (categorical) data. In this example, each student could choose more than one of the modules but for the analysis the response to each module was treated as a separate level of the IV, with *yes* (coded as *1*) being the score if a student did take that module and *no* (coded as *0*) if he or she did not.

Power analysis and Cochran's *Q*

Studies have been conducted to look at the power of Q relative to other statistics but none that I have found has produced a definitive method for calculating its power (see Myers et al., 1982; Wallenstein & Berger, 1981). However, see Vuolo et al. (2016) for a suggested approach; they also include approaches for estimating power and sample size in McNemar's test of change and the Stuart–Maxwell test, referred to in Chapter 15. All three tests can be described as coming under the family of the generalised *Cochran-Mantel-Haenszel* test.

Calculating an effect size for non-parametric tests

All the statistics from the Kruskal–Wallis ANOVA (*H*), Friedman's ANOVA (χ_F^2), χ^2 and Cochran's Q are treated as chi-squared values, but this is an approximation which is only accurate if the sample size is sufficiently large. We can use the equation to convert χ^2 into w given in Chapter 14. However, as discussed in Chapter 14, because they have more than 1 degree of freedom the value of w can be greater than 1. We could use the equation given in Chapter 14 for converting χ^2 to the coefficient of contingency.

For the difference between the grades given by the three authors, as tested by Kruskal–Wallis ANOVA, w = .30, C = .29; for the difference in ratings given to the three different weeks, as tested by Friedman's two-way ANOVA, w = .88, C = .66; and for the comparison of module choices, tested by Cochran's Q, w = .54, C = .48.

When the sample size is not sufficient for the chi-square probability to be accurate, then for *H*, χ_F^2 or Q a standard ANOVA could be run and an η^2 calculated in the way described previously.

Summary

When there are more than two levels of an IV it is not considered appropriate to use a series of tests of the difference between pairs of those conditions. Instead, as a preliminary stage, it is advisable to see whether there is an overall difference between the conditions. Such analysis can be conducted using the appropriate form of the ANOVA, or equivalent for nominal data; see Figure 16.6. However, remember that if homogeneity of variance is not present but the other requirements of a parametric between-subjects ANOVA are fulfilled, then use Welch's F-test. If there is an overall difference between the conditions, then its precise source can be sought using techniques given in Chapter 18.

The next chapter looks at the analysis of designs with more than one IV.

FIGURE 16.6   Statistical tests for designs with one independent variable with more than two levels

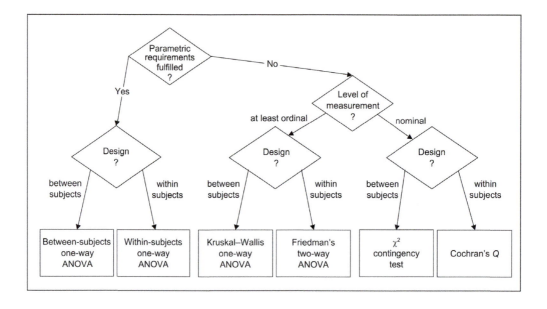

17 Analysis of designs with more than one independent variable

Introduction

In many psychological experiments we are not only interested in the effects of a single independent variable (IV) on the dependent variable (DV). Rather, we can be interested in the effects of two or more IVs. The main reason for wanting to do this is because we may hypothesise that the IVs work together in their effects, that is, that the IVs *interact* with each other. The present chapter gives full examples in which two IVs are involved and then describes how this can be extended to situations which entail more than two IVs.

How to evaluate effect size and conduct power analysis in such designs is also discussed. Worked examples of each of the stages are given in Appendix VIII.

Interactions between IVs

An interaction is where a pattern which is found across the levels of one IV differs according to the levels of another IV (Figure 17.1). Imagine that, in a study of face recognition, researchers have two IVs: familiarity, with two levels – familiar and unfamiliar (that is, familiar and unfamiliar prior to the experiment); and orientation of face, with two levels – correct and upside down. The DV is *time taken to recognise a face shown in a photograph*. An interaction between the two variables would exist if familiar faces were more quickly recognised than unfamiliar faces when they were presented in the correct orientation, while there was no difference in speed of recognition between the two levels of familiarity when

FIGURE 17.1 An example of an interaction between two independent variables

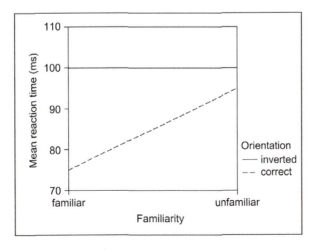

faces were presented upside down. Orientation could be described as a *moderator* variable because it moderates the relationship between degree of familiarity and reaction time. Similarly, familiarity could be seen as a moderator of the relationship between orientation and reaction time.

An interaction would also be present if familiar faces were recognised more slowly than unfamiliar ones when presented upside down but the pattern was reversed for correctly oriented faces (Figure 17.2).

FIGURE 17.2   A further example of an interaction between two independent variables

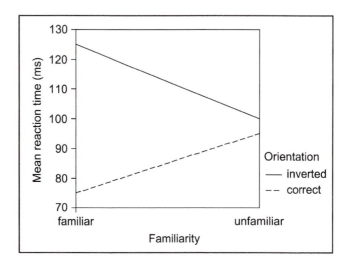

It is important to note that if the trend for familiar faces to be more quickly recognised were true to the same degree regardless of orientation, an interaction would not be present, even if correctly oriented faces were recognised more quickly than upside-down ones. In this last case orientation is not moderating the relationship between degree of familiarity and reaction time. When the lines representing the two levels of one of the IVs are roughly parallel, there is unlikely to be an interaction between the IVs (Figure 17.3).

FIGURE 17.3   An example of a lack of interaction between two independent variables

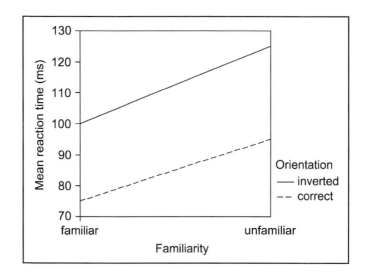

 Parametric tests

Two between-subjects IVs

The simplest version of ANOVA with two IVs to calculate and to interpret is where both IVs are between-subjects.

For the first example I am going to expand the between-subjects example from the previous chapter. This time imagine that the researchers want not only to look at the effect of mnemonic strategy on recall but also to investigate the effect of the nature of the list of words to be recalled. As before, one IV is *mnemonic strategy*, with groups either receiving no training (the control group), being trained to use pegwords or being trained to use the method of loci. A second IV is introduced, *the nature of the list*, with two levels: a list of words which are conceptually linked – all are things found in the kitchen – and words which are not conceptually linked. This design means that we have six different conditions; see Table 17.1.

TABLE 17.1   The conditions involved in a design for testing memory strategy and type of word list

List type	Control	Pegword	Loci
Linked	X	X	X
Unlinked	X	X	X

The design of this experiment is totally between-subjects. In other words, each participant is only in one condition. Therefore, there are six groups altogether. A totally between-subjects design is sometimes described as a *factorial* design.

It is possible to analyse the data from this type of design by using a version of ANOVA. In this case, it is a two-way ANOVA – two-way because there are two IVs: *nature of list* and *mnemonic strategy*.

A two-way ANOVA will test three hypotheses; the use of numbers helps to distinguish the hypotheses from each other. The first is as follows:

H_1: The means for the levels of the first IV are different.

With the Null Hypothesis:

H_{01}: The means for the levels of the first IV are not different.

The second is as follows:

H_2: The means for the levels of the second IV are different.

With the Null Hypothesis:

H_{02}: The means for the levels of the second IV are not different.

The third is as follows:

H_3: The pattern of the means for one IV differs between the levels of the other IV.

With the Null Hypothesis:

H_{03}: The pattern of means for one IV does not differ between the levels of the other IV.

The third hypothesis deals with an interaction between IVs.

The researchers conduct the experiment with five participants in each condition. They calculate the means (see Table 17.2) and plot them on a graph (see Figure 17.4). If we look at the column means in Table 17.2 we see the means for each mnemonic strategy, regardless of which list was presented. This suggests that there is a difference between the strategies, with the best recall produced by those using the method of loci (9.70 words), the next best by those using pegwords (9.50 words) and the worst by those using no strategy, the control group (8.70 words).

TABLE 17.2 The mean recall for participants showing effects of list type and mnemonic strategy

	Mnemonic strategy			
List	Control	Pegword	Loci	Row mean
Linked	11.00	10.60	10.60	10.73
Unlinked	6.40	8.40	8.80	7.87
Column mean	8.70	9.50	9.70	9.30

FIGURE 17.4 Mean recall of participants by list type and mnemonic strategy

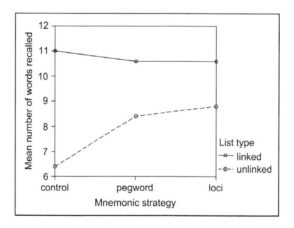

If we look at the row means for Table 17.2 we see the means for the two types of list, regardless of the mnemonic strategy employed. This suggests that those who were shown the list of linked words recalled more (10.73 words) than those who were shown the unlinked list (7.87 words).

Finally, if we look at the means for each of the six groups (sometimes called the cell means) in Table 17.2 and look at their relative position in Figure 17.4, this suggests that there is a different pattern between the two lists for the mnemonic strategies. It would appear that those in the control group have particularly poor recall compared with the other two mnemonic strategies when the list contained unlinked words. However, when the list contained linked words, the control group was no worse than those who used the two mnemonic strategies. This difference in the two patterns suggests that there is an interaction between the IVs; the relative performance of the participants in the three mnemonic conditions depends on the type of list used.

Partitioning the variance in a two-way between-subjects ANOVA

When there are two between-subjects variables, there are only between-subjects sources of variance. As with the one-way between-subjects ANOVA, the total variance can be split into between-groups and within-groups variance. Between-groups variance can be further divided into variance due to one IV, variance due to the other IV and variance due to the interaction between the two IVs. Within-groups variance is the residual (or error) term which will be needed to form F-ratios with each of the between-groups sources of variance. See Figure 17.5.

FIGURE 17.5   Partitioning of variance in two-way between-subjects ANOVA

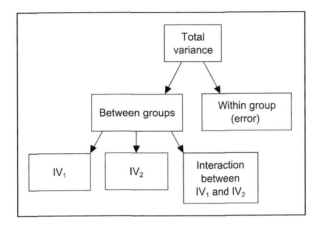

Returning to the example, as usual we want to know whether the impressions which are given by the summary statistics are supported by the inferential statistics. Therefore we will need to conduct a two-way, between-subjects ANOVA, the results of which are given in Table 17.3. Sometimes when describing multi-way ANOVAs (that is, having more than one IV) the number of levels of each IV is included in the description. Accordingly, the current analysis is a 2 × 3, two-way ANOVA.

TABLE 17.3   The summary table for a 2 × 3, two-way between-subjects ANOVA

Source	Sum of squares	df	Mean square	F	p
List	61.633	1	61.633	37.354	.0001
Mnemonic	5.600	2	2.800	1.697	.2045
List * Mnemonic	11.467	2	5.733	3.475	.0473
Error	39.600	24	1.650		
Total	118.300	29			

Interpreting the output from a two-way between-subjects ANOVA

Once again the first column shows the sources of variation in the data (the recall scores). We are shown that the total amount of variation can be split into four sources:

(i)   the variation which can be attributed to the differences between the two list types;
(ii)   the variation which can be attributed to the difference between mnemonic strategies;
(iii)   the variation which can be attributed to the interaction between list type and mnemonic strategy – in other words, the way in which the pattern of recall across the mnemonic strategies differs between the two lists; and
(iv)   the residual or variation which cannot be attributed to the actions of the IVs – the within-groups variation.

The second column shows the sum of squared deviations for each source of variance. The variation for the interaction needs further explanation. It measures the variation between the groups which remains once the variation due to differences between the list types and the variation due to differences between the mnemonic strategies have been subtracted from the overall variation between the groups.

The third column shows the df for each source of variation. The total df are one fewer than the number of scores: that is, $30 - 1 = 29$. The df for each of the IVs are simply one fewer than the number of levels in that IV: list df $= 2 - 1 = 1$; mnemonic strategy df $= 3 - 1 = 2$. The df for interaction is calculated by multiplying the df for each of the IVs: interaction df $= 1 \times 2 = 2$. The df for within groups (error) are the number of df which are left once all the df for the IVs have been removed from the total: error df $= 29 - 1 - 2 - 2 = 29 - 5 = 24$. Another way to look at the error df is that there are six groups, each of which has five participants in it. There is one fewer df in each group than the number of participants in that group: $5 - 1 = 4$. Therefore, error df $= 6 \times 4 = 24$.

The fourth column shows the mean squares (MSs) for each of the sources of variation. The MS is the estimate of the population variance. As usual, each MS is calculated by dividing the sum of squares by its df.

The fifth column shows the F-ratios for the analysis.

In this experiment we are interested in evaluating all three between-groups sources of variation. The last source, within-groups, is unwanted variation, as far as we are concerned. Therefore, there are three F-ratios which will need to be calculated to test our hypotheses: one for each of the IVs – list type and mnemonic strategy – and one for the interaction between them. In this particular design the within-groups source of variation is the appropriate error term for each of the three F-ratios. Thus:

$$F_{(list)} = \frac{\text{variance estimate from list type}}{\text{variance estimate from within groups}}$$

$$F_{(mnemonic)} = \frac{\text{variance estimate from mnemonic strategy}}{\text{variance estimate from within groups}}$$

$$F_{(interaction)} = \frac{\text{variance estimate from interaction}}{\text{variance estimate from within groups}}$$

As with one-way ANOVA, if a Null Hypothesis is correct, then the F-ratio for that hypothesis is the ratio between two estimates of the same variance, that is, the variance within a single population of scores which have not been affected by the experimental manipulations. Therefore the F-ratio will be close to 1. However, if the Null Hypothesis is incorrect, then the appropriate between-groups variance estimate will contain an additional amount of variance due to the effect of the given treatment or treatments. In this case, the F-ratio will tend to be greater than 1.

Note that the F-ratio for list type is well above 1, while the F-ratios for mnemonic strategy and for the interaction are closer to 1. As usual, we still need to know how likely each of these outcomes is to have occurred if the Null Hypothesis were true; that is, we cannot judge the significance based solely on the size of the F-ratio. We need to know the probability of each outcome, which will be dependent on the df for that F-ratio.

The sixth column shows the probability for each F-ratio. From this we can see that, overall: the lists produced significantly different recall; the mnemonic types did not produce significantly different recall; and the lists and mnemonic strategies interacted with each other to produce a significant effect.

Interpreting a two-way between-subjects ANOVA

A two-way design introduces the need to test the interaction between the two IVs, regardless of whether we had any hypothesis about an interaction. This introduces a complication because the effects of the IVs alone have to be evaluated in the context of an interaction.

When talking about a single IV, in an ANOVA which has more than one IV, we talk about the *main effect* of that IV. This is because there is more than one way to look at the effect of that IV. The main effect of the IV is when we ignore how it varies as a consequence of the other IV. Thus, in the present case, the overall pattern of the means for mnemonic strategy (the main effect) is not echoed in each case when only one type of word list is used. When linked words were presented, the control condition produced the best recall, whereas when unlinked words were presented, the control condition produced the worst recall.

We can say that there is a significant main effect of list type ($F_{(1,24)} = 37.354$, $p = .0001$, $\eta^2 = .521$). We can also say that there is no significant main effect of mnemonic strategy ($F_{(2,24)} = 1.697$, $p = .205$, $\eta^2 = .047$). However, these results are complicated by the presence of a significant interaction between list type and mnemonic strategy ($F_{(2,24)} = 3.475$, $p = .047$, $\eta^2 = .097$). Without further analysis we can only say that the interaction *appears* to be produced by the marked improvement in recall for the control group when they are given a list of linked words as opposed to one which contains unlinked words. The type of further analysis that is appropriate depends on our hypotheses and on the nature of these preliminary results. See the sections on *contrasts*, *simple effects* and *interaction contrasts* in the next chapter for details of how to analyse the results further.

Because there are only two levels of list type we could be more precise than just stating that there was a significant main effect of list type. We could note that significantly more words were recalled in the linked list condition. However, because the interaction between list type and mnemonic strategy is significant and more analysis is necessary the inclusion of the extra detail may not be useful; we may find that recall in linked lists is not significantly better than that for unlinked lists for every mnemonic strategy.

Unequal sample size

In the previous chapter it was stated that there are two basic ways to analyse a design which does not have the same sample size in each condition (an unbalanced design which is sometimes in this context also called a *non-orthogonal* design): by weighted means or by unweighted means. Whereas most computer programs use weighted means as the standard for one-way ANOVA, they do not for multi-way ANOVA.

There are at least three situations in which you might have an unbalanced design. One is if the samples are proportional and reflect an imbalance in the population from which the sample came. Thus, if we knew that two-thirds of psychology students were female and one-third male, we might have a sample of psychology students with a 2:1 ratio of females to males. For example, we might look at the way male and female psychology students differ in their exam performance after receiving two teaching techniques – seminars or lectures. The samples might be as shown in Table 17.4. With such proportional data it is legitimate to use the weighted means analysis.

A second possible reason for an unbalanced design is that participants were not available for particular treatments but there was no systematic reason for their unavailability; that is, there is no

TABLE 17.4 The numbers of male and female psychology students used in a study of gender and teaching technique

	Teaching technique	
Gender	Seminar	Lecture
Male	10	10
Female	20	20

connection between the treatment to which they were assigned and the lack of data for them. Under these circumstances it is legitimate to use the unweighted means method.

A third possible reason for an unbalanced design would be if there were a systematic link between the treatment group and the failure to have data for such participants; this is more likely in a quasi-experiment – for example, if research involved criminals who were allocated to different groups on the basis of the severity of their crimes. If the design lacked more of one type of criminal, even though the imbalance was not a reflection of the population, then, in such a case of self-selection by the participants, neither of the options can solve the problem.

Given the difficulties with unbalanced designs, unless you are dealing with proportional samples, some people recommend randomly removing data points from the treatments which have more than the others. Alternatively, it is possible to treat the participants who haven't been selected as though their data are missing and replace such missing data with the mean for the group, or even the overall mean. If you put in the group mean you may artificially enhance any differences between conditions, and if you use the overall mean you may obscure any genuine differences between groups. If either of these methods is used, then the total df (and, as a consequence, the error df) should be reduced by one for each data point estimated, which will have the consequence of reducing the power of the test.

My own preference would be to remove data, but I would only recommend this if you have a reasonable sample size, given the effect that removing data will have on the statistical power of the test. As an extra check you should do the analysis with and without the deleted cases to see whether this has an effect on the results. This is a form of *sensitivity analysis* and it helps to show how robust your results are.

Two within-subjects IVs

For the example of a two-way, within-subjects design I will expand the one-way design used in the previous chapter to evaluate how participants will differ in the length of sentence they recommend for a criminal, depending on the conditions under which they are making the decision. As before, the first IV – *the condition under which sentencing was decided* – has three levels: alone, communicating with others via computer and in the presence of others. A second IV is now introduced – *the nature of the defendant*. In this case, the defendants will be of two types: those with no previous record (novices) and habitual criminals (experienced).

We now have six possible conditions in this experiment (see Table 17.5) and because both IVs are within-subjects every participant provides a score for each of the six conditions. As with the between-subjects design, the ANOVA will test three hypotheses: two main effects and an interaction.

The experimenters collect the data from five participants and produce a table (see Table 17.6) and graph of the results (see Figure 17.6). It would appear that a novice defendant receives a shorter sentence than an experienced criminal but that both criminals will receive a heavier sentence if the judge is aware of the recommendations which have been made by others. The fact that the lines for the two defendant types are roughly parallel suggests that there is no interaction between defendant type and the context in which the sentencing occurred.

TABLE 17.5   The conditions involved in a two-way within-subjects design

Defendant	Context		
	Alone	Computer	Face-to-face
Novice	X	X	X
Experienced	X	X	X

TABLE 17.6 The mean sentence length, in months, recommended for defendants under different contexts

	Alone	Context computer	Face-to-face	Row mean
Novice	13.2	13.6	16.2	14.33
Experienced	16.0	17.6	20.6	18.07
Column mean	14.6	15.6	18.4	

FIGURE 17.6 The mean sentence length recommended for defendants under different contexts

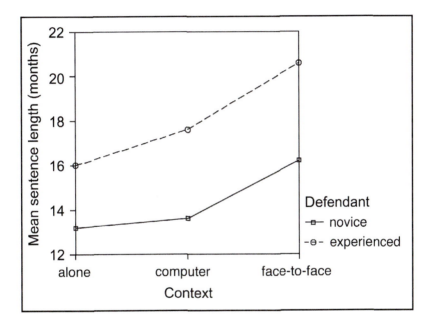

Partitioning the variance in a two-way within-subjects ANOVA

In designs with two within-subjects IVs, as with the one-way within-subjects design, there are two main sources of variance: between-subjects and within-subjects.

Within-subjects variance (Figure 17.7) can be further divided into:

(i)   variance due to the first IV;
(ii) variance due to the interaction between subjects and the first IV;
(iii) variance due to the second IV;
(iv) variance due to the interaction between the subjects and the second IV;
(v)   variance due to the interaction between the two IVs; and
(vi) variance due to the interaction between the two IVs and subjects.

Each of the interactions which involve subjects constitutes an error term for use in calculating an F-ratio.

FIGURE 17.7   Partitioning of variance in two-way within-subjects ANOVA

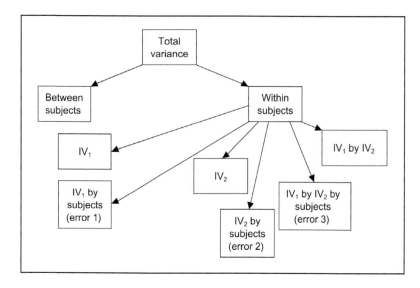

Before the researchers can evaluate their hypotheses properly they need to conduct a two-way, within-subjects ANOVA on their data, the results of which are shown in Table 17.7.

TABLE 17.7   The summary table for a 2 × 3, two-way within-subjects ANOVA

Source	S of S	df	MS	F	p	G–G	H–F
Subject	2.467	4	0.617				
Defendant	104.533	1	104.533	93.612	.0006	.0006	.0006
Defendant by subject	4.467	4	1.117				
Context	77.600	2	38.800	46.099	.0001	.0007	.0001
Context by subject	6.733	8	0.842				
Defendant by context	3.467	2	1.733	1.455	.2892	.2946	.2948
Defendant by context by subject	9.533	8	1.192				
Total	208.8	29					

Interpreting a two-way within-subjects ANOVA

The first column shows the sources of the variation in the experiment. The between-subjects variance is simply the main effect of subjects – the variation in sentencing between participants, regardless of conditions. In all there are seven identifiable sources of variation in the sentences: one between-subjects and six within-subjects.

The second column shows the sum of squared deviations for each of the sources of variation in the experiment, while the third column shows the df. The total df are one fewer than the number of scores: total df = 30 − 1 = 29. These can be split into the df for each of the other sources of variance. The df for between-subjects variance are one fewer than the number of participants; df = 5 − 1 = 4.

The df for within-subjects sources of variance can be split into:

defendant df = 2 − 1 = 1;
context df = 3 − 1 = 2;

interaction between defendant and context df = $1 \times 2 = 2$;
defendant by subject interaction df = $1 \times 4 = 4$;
context by subject interaction df = $2 \times 4 = 8$; and
defendant by context by subject interaction df = $1 \times 2 \times 4 = 8$.

The fourth column shows the MS for each of the sources of variation, created by dividing each sum of squares by its df.

The fifth column shows the F-ratios for each of the within-subjects sources of variation. The appropriate error term for each within-subjects source of variation is the interaction between subject and that source of variation. Thus:

$$F_{(interaction)} = \frac{MS_{defendant}}{MS_{defendant\ by\ subject}}$$

$$F_{(context)} = \frac{MS_{context}}{MS_{context\ by\ subject}}$$

$$F_{(defendant\ by\ context)} = \frac{MS_{defendant\ by\ context}}{MS_{defendant\ by\ context\ by\ subject}}$$

As usual, in each case the Null Hypothesis assumes that the variation is due solely to random differences within subjects, while, if the Null Hypothesis is incorrect, the treatment MS will have variation due to the treatment.

The sixth column tells us the probability of each treatment effect having occurred if the Null Hypothesis were true. From this we can see that there was a significant main effect of defendant type ($F_{(1,4)} = 93.612$, $p = .0006$, $\eta^2 = .501$), there was a significant main effect of context ($F_{(2,8)} = 46.099$, $p = .0001$, $\eta^2 = .372$), but there was no significant interaction between defendant type and context ($F_{(2,8)} = 1.455$, $p = .29$, $\eta^2 = .017$). I have added the effect sizes which have been calculated in the usual way of dividing the sum of squares for a given effect by the total sum of squares.

Those using SPSS to analyse the data will find that the results are laid out differently from how they are shown in Table 17.7. In the first place the between-subjects element will be in a separate table. Secondly, each error term, instead of being described as *by Subject*, as in *defendant by Subject*, is shown as *Error (defendant)*.

Sphericity

The term *sphericity* was introduced in the previous chapter. It refers to the need for within-subjects designs to have homogeneity of variance among difference scores. The columns headed G–G (for Greenhouse–Geisser) and H–F (for Huynh–Feldt) in Table 17.7 show where adjustments have been made, to compensate for possible lack of sphericity, to the df and the effects the adjustments have on the probability of a given F-ratio. As the probabilities shown for the adjustments are in line with the unadjusted probabilities, in that they agree over whether a result is significant, there is not a problem over sphericity. When df = 1, sphericity is not an issue and so no adjustment is made. In SPSS each method of adjusting for possible lack of sphericity is shown in a separate row, which includes the adjusted df. For context, G–G epsilon = 0.658, df = 1.317, 5.266; H–F epsilon = 0.854, df = 1.708, 6.831. For defendant by context, G–G epsilon = .524, df = 1.049, 4.195; H–F epsilon = .550, df = 1.099, 4.397.

The results from the experiment could be further analysed by comparing the means to identify the source of the significant main effect of context. Remember that a significant result in an ANOVA does not specify the precise contributions to that significance if there are more than two levels of the IV. In the case of defendant type, because there are only two means involved, we know that the significant difference is due to higher sentences being passed on habitual criminals. As the interaction between context and defendant type was not significant it is worth stating explicitly that experienced criminals were given significantly higher sentences than novice ones when reporting that main effect. The next chapter deals with ways to conduct the necessary further analysis.

Mixed (split-plot) designs

So far the designs which have been described have been straightforward in that they have either entailed IVs which are both between-subjects, in which case the design is between-subjects or factorial, or are both within-subjects, in which case the design is within-subjects or repeated measures. However, we now move to a design which contains both a between-subjects and a within-subjects IV. Such a design is described as *mixed, split-plot* or *repeated measures with one between-subjects factor*.

Imagine that experimenters want to compare the way that males and females rate their parents' IQs. In this design the IV *gender*, which has two levels – male and female – is a between-subjects variable. The IV *parent* which has two levels mother and father – is a within-subjects variable because each participant supplies data for each level of that variable.

The researchers hypothesise that males and females will differ in the way that they rate their parents' IQs, such that both may rate their fathers' IQs higher than they rate their mothers' IQs, but that males will show a larger difference between the ratings. Thus they are predicting an effect of parents' IQ estimate and an interaction between gender and parental IQ. They collect the estimates from five males and five females and the results are shown in Figure 17.8 and Table 17.8.

The results suggest that the males do estimate their fathers' IQs to be much higher than their mothers' IQs but females estimate their fathers' IQs to be only slightly higher than their mothers' IQs.

FIGURE 17.8   The mean IQ estimates by males and females of parental IQ

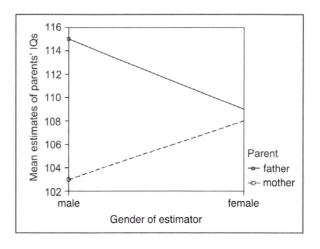

TABLE 17.8   The mean estimates of parental IQ by males and females

	Parent		
	Father	Mother	Row mean
Male	115	103	109.0
Female	109	108	108.5
Column mean	112.0	105.5	

Thus, there would appear to be a main effect of parental IQ, even though it is not totally in line with the hypothesis, while there would appear to be an interaction between gender and parental IQ which *is* in line with the hypothesis.

Partitioning of variance in a two-way mixed ANOVA

When a design combines between- and within-subjects IVs, it follows the rules described previously for the other types of design. Thus, the overall variance can be split into between-subjects and within-subjects sources of variance. The between-subjects variance pertains to the between-subjects variable and is split into variance due to the differences between the levels of the between-subjects variable (IV_1 or between-groups variance) and differences between subjects within the groups (subjects-within-groups variance). The latter forms the error term for the between-groups variance.

The within-subjects variance is split into:

(i) the variance due to differences between levels of the second (within-subjects) IV (IV_2);
(ii) the variance due to the interaction between the two IVs (IV_1 by IV_2); and
(iii) the variance due to the interaction between the second IV and the subjects within the groups for the first IV.

This last source of variance forms the error term for the other two within-subjects sources of variance.

FIGURE 17.9 Partitioning of variance in a two-way mixed ANOVA

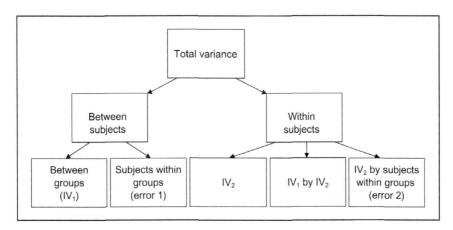

The next stage is to conduct a two-way mixed ANOVA on the data to see whether the effects are statistically significant (see Table 17.9).

TABLE 17.9 The summary table of a 2 × 2, two-way mixed ANOVA

	Source	S of S	df	MS	F	p	G–G	H–F
(a)	Gender	1.250	1	1.250	0.007	.9376		
(b)	Subject (group)	1530.000	8	191.250				
(c)	Parent	211.250	1	211.250	5.633	.0450	.0450	.0450
(d)	Parent by gender	151.250	1	151.250	4.033	.0795	.0795	.0795
(e)	Parent by subject (group)	300.000	8	37.500				
	Total	2193.75	19					

Reading the summary table of a two-way mixed ANOVA

The first column of Table 17.9 shows the sources for the variation in the study. Total variation can be split into between-subjects variation and within-subjects variation. These can be further divided. The between-subjects variation can be split into:

(a) variation between the genders, regardless of which parent they were making the estimate about; and
(b) the variation between subjects within the two genders (subject within groups).

The within-subjects variation can be split into:

(c) the differences in estimates for the two parents;
(d) the interaction between parent and gender; and
(e) the interaction between parent and subject within group.

The second column shows the sum of squares, while the third column shows the df. The total df is number of scores minus 1: $20 - 1 = 19$. This can be split into between-subjects sources and within-subjects sources:

Between-subjects

gender df $= 2 - 1 = 1$
subjects within group df: each group has df $= 5 - 1 = 4$, therefore the subjects within group df $= 2 \times 4 = 8$

Within-subjects

parent df $= 2 - 1 = 1$
interaction between parent and gender df $= 1 \times 1 = 1$
parent by subject within group df $= 1 \times 8 = 8$

The fourth column shows the MS for each of the sources of variance, while the fifth column shows the F-ratios, which are formed from the following equations:

$$F_{(gender)} = \frac{MS_{gender}}{MS_{subjects\ within\ gender}}$$

$$F_{(parent)} = \frac{MS_{parent}}{MS_{parent\ by\ subjects\ within\ groups}}$$

$$F_{(interaction)} = \frac{MS_{gender\ by\ parent}}{MS_{parent\ by\ subjects\ within\ groups}}$$

Interpreting a two-way mixed ANOVA

The summary table shows that there is no significant main effect of gender on ratings of IQ ($F_{(1,8)} = 0.007$, $p = .938$, $\eta^2 = .0006$). There is a significant main effect of parent on ratings of IQ with fathers being rated higher than mothers[1] ($F_{(1,8)}$ = 5.663, p = .045, η^2 = .096). There is no significant interaction between gender and parent on ratings of IQ ($F_{(1,8)}$ = 4.033, p = .0795, η^2 = .069).

Note that the table only reports adjusted probabilities for the F-ratios which entail a within-subjects element. As, in each case, df = 1, there is no adjustment as sphericity isn't an issue and so the probability remains the same.

Missing data

In designs with at least one within-subjects IV computers usually delete all the data for participants for whom there are missing values, although other options are sometimes available. Two possibilities mentioned earlier under unequal samples for between-subjects designs are also available here: to estimate (impute) the missing data by using the mean for the condition or the overall mean. As explained in Chapter 23, replacing missing data (imputing values) has to be done with caution as it can affect the likelihood of committing a Type I error.

Designs with more than two IVs

The principles which have been outlined for the previous designs can be extended to designs which have three or more IVs. The problem with such designs is that they will have more sources of variance which are due to interactions and they will have what are called *higher-order* interactions. Imagine that we extended the design in which we had participants recommend a sentence for a defendant so that we had gender of participant as one IV, nature of defendant as a second and context in which the judgement was made as a third. In addition to the three main effects, we would have the following interactions: defendant by context, defendant by gender, context by gender and defendant by context by gender. This makes interpretation of the results more difficult. In addition, it makes presentation of the results in graphical form more difficult, for we will need to represent the new dimension somehow. It is possible, if difficult to read, to represent a three-way design on a single graph or you can produce a separate two-way graph for each level of a third IV. For example, you could have a context by defendant graph for each level of gender. However, once you adopt a four-way design either approach ceases to be possible.

The account I have given of ANOVA has been simplified over such issues as whether the levels of the IV(s) can be viewed as fixed (chosen by the researchers) or random (randomly chosen); see Chapter 3. The analyses I have described have treated the levels of the IV(s) as fixed. This limits the conclusions which can be drawn from the results; we cannot safely generalise from the effects of the levels we have used to what effects other levels might have produced. If you have randomly selected the levels and wish to generalise I recommend that you read the account given in Winer et al. (1991).

Effect size and ANOVA

For each effect I have reported the η^2. I have calculated them in the same way that I did for the one-way ANOVA as shown in the previous chapter: the sum of squares for the effect is divided by the total sum of squares. SPSS reports partial η^2 but I think that this can be confusing and is different from η^2 even in the completely between-subjects design. Accordingly, I would calculate them myself for the reasons explained in the previous chapter.

Power and ANOVA

The power tables which were used for one-way ANOVAs (see Appendix XVIII) can be used to estimate the power and sample size required for a multi-way ANOVA. However, the power of each F-ratio can

---

1 Add this last part because there are only two levels of parent and the interaction is not significant.

be estimated separately. If you are trying to work out the necessary sample size to achieve a given level of power, you will need to include the largest sample size which your power analyses suggest.

'Interaction' terms in non-experimental designs

Pedhazur (1997) prefers the terms *multiplicative relations* or *joint relations* in such circumstances to alert the reader to the dangers of interpreting such an extra effect in the same way as for an interaction in an experimental design. He makes the point that there is a danger that the IVs could be correlated. Therefore, a joint relationship found in a multi-way ANOVA could be an artefact of the inherent relationship between the IVs.

Imagine that a study is conducted, in a country where a high proportion of the population go to university, of educational level, ethnic background and self-esteem. The self-esteem of four groups is measured: immigrants who have been to university, immigrants who haven't been to university, indigenous people who have been to university and indigenous people who haven't been to university. Imagine that the researchers find that those who have been to university have higher self-esteem than those who haven't. However, they also find that among those who haven't been to university the indigenous people and immigrants have equally low levels of self-esteem while among those who have been to university immigrants have higher self-esteem than do indigenous people. A simple interpretation might be that educational level moderates the relationship between ethnic background and self-esteem. However, it is likely that ethnic background is related to whether someone goes to university and so immigrants who go to university are unusual and may already have high self-esteem, whereas indigenous people who don't go to university are also unusual and may already have lower self-esteem.

Non-parametric tests

Standard tests for multi-way ANOVA with data which do not conform to the assumptions of parametric ANOVA are not generally available on computer. Nonetheless, bootstrapping, which is discussed in Chapter 23, can sometimes be used to deal with the nature of the data. Meddis (1984) describes two-way ANOVAs for data which are at least ordinal and for nominal data, while Neave and Worthington (1988) describe tests which can evaluate the interactions between two such variables. Sawilowsky (1990) also reviews a number of non-parametric tests of interactions. In addition, it is possible to use more advanced techniques on such data. Logistic regression, which can be used when the DV is categorical, is described in Chapter 21, but I recommend that you learn about linear regression in Chapter 20 before you tackle that subject. Log-linear modelling which can also be used when the DV is categorical is described briefly in Chapter 25, but its full use is beyond the scope of this book.

Summary

Multi-way ANOVA (for designs with more than one IV) allows the interaction between IVs to be evaluated, as well as the main effects of each IV. Beyond two-way ANOVA interpretation begins to be complicated and the results can be difficult to display graphically.

You have now been introduced to the preliminary analysis for one-way and two-way ANOVAs. The next chapter explains the types of analysis which can be conducted to follow up the findings from an ANOVA in order to test the more specific hypotheses which researchers often have.

18 Subsequent analysis after ANOVA or χ^2

 ## Introduction

The previous two chapters have introduced the first stage of analysis when a design has a single independent variable (IV) with more than two levels or more than one IV. As was pointed out, the preliminary analysis asks the limited question: Do the means for the different levels of one or more IVs appear to differ? If they do appear to differ, then the source of that difference may not be obvious. Therefore, in order to identify the source it is necessary to conduct further analysis. However, despite the title of this chapter, the methods described here can be used without having ascertained whether the F-ratios in an ANOVA are statistically significant.

This chapter describes four types of subsequent analysis – contrasts, trend tests, simple effects and interaction contrasts.

Contrasts

Parametric tests

Contrasts are comparisons between means in the case of parametric tests. To discuss them I am going to return to the word-recall experiment, described in Chapter 16, which involves a group using pegwords, a group using the method of loci and a control group. The mean recalls of participants in the three conditions were found to be significantly different. The types of contrast which you can perform are almost infinite. The main distinction is between *pairwise* contrasts, where you compare two means at a time, and other forms of contrast, such as a comparison of the control condition with the mean of the two other conditions. There are numerous tests of contrasts. Rather than describe all of them I will give a set of tests which cover most situations and an explanation of when each is appropriate.

The rationale behind all the tests of contrasts is an attempt to get round the problem I described when introducing ANOVA. If you have more than two means, then identifying which ones are significantly different involves more than one test; in the case of three means you would need to do three pairwise comparisons and in the case of four means you would need to do six pairwise comparisons. The probability given by the inferential statistics described in this book is the likelihood that an outcome would have occurred if the Null Hypothesis were correct. That probability is based on the observation that if the same test is conducted repeatedly on sets of data for which the Null Hypothesis is correct, then a result will be shown to be significant at the $p = .05$ level on approximately 5% of occasions. In other words, a Type I error will be committed on 5% of occasions. Therefore, whenever the same statistical test is repeated the likelihood of making a Type I error is increased.

The family of contrasts

A group of contrasts is sometimes described as a family of contrasts. Tests of contrasts adjust the probability level so that the probability is for the family of contrasts (the *error rate per family*, EF) rather than the individual contrast (*error rate per contrast*, EC). Thus, the probability for the family of contrasts is set at α = .05. How the adjustment is made depends on the nature and size of the family of contrasts. As a rule of thumb, treat the family of contrasts as those contrasts which are relevant to a single *F*-ratio from the original ANOVA. Thus, in a two-way ANOVA there will be three families of contrasts – one for each of the main effects and one for the interaction.

A test which makes too great an adjustment and thus overly decreases the likelihood of making a Type I error is described as being conservative. Remember that a conservative test will increase the likelihood of making a Type II error. It is important that you choose the correct contrast test, and therefore the correct adjustment, to avoid reducing the power of your test unnecessarily.

Planned and unplanned comparisons

An important distinction between comparisons is whether you decided which ones to do before looking at the data or afterwards. If you choose what comparisons you are going to conduct before looking at the data, they are described as *planned* or *a priori* comparisons. If you choose them after looking at the data, then they are described as *unplanned, post hoc* or *a posteriori* comparisons.

The distinction is not a trivial one because the test employed on unplanned comparisons will be more conservative than the one applied to planned comparisons. An example should make the reason clear. If I look at the means for the memory experiment and then decide to do a pairwise comparison of the mean for the control group and the mean for the method of loci group because these two means are the furthest apart, then it is as if I had conducted all three possible comparisons. Therefore, the family of contrasts, in this case, is all three contrasts and so the adjustment to the α-level will be made accordingly conservative. However, if, before looking at the data, I had planned to conduct a contrast between the means for controls and method of loci, then the family of contrasts contains only one and there will be no adjustment to the α-level.

When you are going to plan contrasts there is no advantage in planning to do all possible paired contrasts as that puts you in no different a position from doing unplanned contrasts as far as the need for adjustment to alpha is concerned. In fact, if you conducted all the possible paired contrasts but used the adjustment required for planned contrasts (Bonferroni's test, which is described on page 235) it would be unnecessarily conservative.

Before introducing the specific contrast tests I will deal with one last concept – orthogonality.

Orthogonality

You will recall that ANOVA takes the overall variation in scores in a study and attempts to identify the sources of that variation; in other words, it partitions the variance of the scores. Contrasts similarly partition the variance. The amount of variance which can be identified as being due to the treatments can be split into specific sources of variance, each based on a different contrast.

If you are going to split the overall variance into parts, such that each accounts for a different part of the variance, then the contrasts are described as orthogonal. Figure 18.1 is a schematic representation of the variance explained by a given IV, such as the mnemonic strategy – the rectangle denotes the overall variance for the treatments, while each segment represents the variance which has been accounted for by a particular contrast. The two contrasts are orthogonal because they are accounting for different parts of the overall variation in scores.

On the other hand, if the variance accounted for by one contrast includes some of the variance accounted for by another contrast, then the contrasts are non-orthogonal. Figure 18.2 shows the case where two contrasts are not orthogonal because they are trying to account for some of the same variance.

A consequence of limiting your contrasts to being orthogonal is that you can only conduct as many contrasts as there are degrees of freedom in the treatment. Thus, in the case of the memory

FIGURE 18.1   The variance accounted for by two orthogonal contrasts

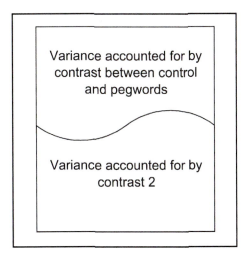

FIGURE 18.2   The variance accounted for by two non-orthogonal contrasts

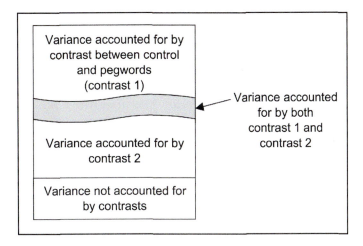

experiment, as the treatment (memory condition) has two degrees of freedom (df), only two contrasts could be conducted and remain orthogonal.

How one checks that a set of contrasts is orthogonal is difficult to understand without sufficient mathematical description. The check is given in Appendix IX. However, while statisticians used to see keeping contrasts orthogonal as important, this is no longer the case and all the tests of contrasts mentioned in this chapter can be legitimately conducted on non-orthogonal contrasts. Therefore, it should be possible to understand the rest of the chapter without having referred to Appendix IX. Nonetheless, it is important to be aware of the notion of orthogonality because some tests of contrasts are more conservative when the contrasts are not orthogonal.

The simplest, and most frequently used, contrast is the pairwise contrast where two means are compared. The description in this chapter, for contrasts following a one-way ANOVA, will therefore be restricted to pairwise contrasts. How to conduct more complex contrasts is described in Appendix IX.

All the pairwise contrasts described in this chapter are based on a t-value which is then compared with a critical value of t to see whether it is statistically significant. The method of calculation of t depends on whether the data are from a between- or a within-subjects design.

Contrasts on data from between-subjects designs

For between-subjects designs, use the following equation:

$$t = \frac{\text{mean}_1 - \text{mean}_2}{\sqrt{\left(\dfrac{1}{n_1} + \dfrac{1}{n_2}\right) \times MS_{error}}} \tag{18.1}$$

where mean_1 is the mean for one of the conditions (condition 1), mean_2 is the mean for the other condition (condition 2), n_1 is the sample size of the group producing mean_1, n_2 is the sample size of the group producing mean_2 and MS_{error} is the mean square (MS) for the appropriate error term in the original F-ratio.

When there are equal numbers in the groups this equation simplifies to:

$$t = \frac{\text{mean}_1 - \text{mean}_2}{\sqrt{\left(\dfrac{2}{n}\right) \times MS_{error}}} \tag{18.2}$$

where n is the sample size of the group producing one of the means.

Heterogeneous variances

If the groups for the ANOVA do not have similar variances, then the preceding equations are not appropriate. Following the rule of thumb given in Chapter 16, we can say that as long as the largest variance is no more than four times the smallest variance we have sufficient homogeneity of variance to use the preceding equations, *as long as the sample sizes are equal.* If we have a lack of homogeneity, then it would be advisable, for pairwise contrasts, to use the t-test for separate variances (Welch's t-test), which is discussed in Chapter 15 and Appendix VI. If the sample sizes are unequal, the largest variance should be no more than two times the smallest to be treated as homogeneous.

Contrasts on data from within-subjects designs

If the design is within-subjects and the data lack sphericity (see Chapter 16 for an explanation of this term), then once again neither of the preceding equations will be the correct one. To be on the safe side, therefore, for pairwise contrasts, the t for each contrast should be computed using the standard equation for a within-subjects design with two levels, given in Appendix VI and referred to in Chapter 15. Myers et al. (2010) note that most computer programs use this version of t for contrasts on within-subjects designs as the default. This option is not available for one of the tests – the Scheffé test, which is not recommended for pairwise contrasts, anyway, as it is considered too conservative to be used for such contrasts.

Conducting only one contrast

For data from either design, if you are only conducting one contrast, as you might with a planned contrast, then the probability of the t-value for that contrast can be checked using the standard t-tables. However, when more than one contrast is involved, you will need to use one of the procedures described next.

Table 18.1 gives the means and standard deviations for the memory experiment, and Table 18.2 provides the summary of the ANOVA conducted on those data.

TABLE 18.1   Means and *SD*s of word recall for the three memory conditions

	Control	Pegword	Loci
Mean	7.2	8.9	9.6
SD	1.62	1.91	1.58

TABLE 18.2   The summary table for the one-way between-subjects ANOVA on the recall data

Source	Sum of squares	df	Mean square	F	p
Between groups	30.467	2	15.233	5.213	.0122
Within groups	78.9	27	2.922		
Total	109.367	29			

Thus, if we wished to compare the method of loci condition with the control condition, we would have the following figures:

$$\text{mean}_1 = 9.6$$
$$\text{mean}_2 = 7.2$$
$$n = 10$$
$$\text{MS}_{\text{error}} = 2.922$$
$$\text{df}_{\text{error}} = 27$$

and we can use equation 18.2 because the design is between-subjects and the groups have the same sample size:

$$t_{(27)} = \frac{9.6 - 7.2}{\sqrt{\left(\frac{2}{10}\right) \times 2.922}}$$
$$= 3.139$$

Bonferroni's *t*

Bonferroni's *t* (sometimes known as the *Dunn multiple comparison test*) takes into consideration the actual number of contrasts which you are going to conduct. It is most appropriate when you have planned your comparisons and are keeping them to a minimum. It is conservative when the contrasts are not orthogonal. The adjustment it makes is based on an equation which, when the original α is set at .05 or lower, simplifies approximately to dividing α by the number of contrasts to be conducted. The α-level from the adjustment is for each contrast. However, it is more usual to express the α-level of the family. Table A17.11 in Appendix XVII gives the α-levels for the family of contrasts.

Choose the number of contrasts you are going to make. Look up the critical *t*-value in the tables of Bonferroni corrections for contrasts in Table A17.11 for that number of contrasts, using the appropriate df: from the appropriate MS$_{\text{error}}$ for the treatment you are investigating, in the case of a between-subjects design with homogeneity of variance; the df appropriate for a *t*-test with independent variances when there is heterogeneity of variance; or the df for the standard within-subjects *t*-test in the case of a within-subjects design. For the contrast to be statistically significant, the *t* computed for the contrast has to be as large as or larger than the critical *t*.

Table 18.3 gives a part of Table A17.11 from Appendix XVII.

TABLE 18.3   An extract from the Bonferroni tables for an error rate per family of $\alpha = 0.05$

df error	2	3	4	5	6	7	8	9	10	12	15
						Number of contrasts					
25	2.385	2.566	2.692	2.787	2.865	2.930	2.986	3.035	3.078	3.153	3.244
26	2.379	2.559	2.684	2.779	2.856	2.920	2.975	3.024	3.067	3.141	3.231
27	2.373	2.552	2.676	2.771	2.847	2.911	2.966	3.014	3.057	3.130	3.219
28	2.368	2.546	2.669	2.763	2.839	2.902	2.957	3.004	3.047	3.120	3.208
29	2.364	2.541	2.663	2.756	2.832	2.894	2.949	2.996	3.038	3.110	3.198
30	2.360	2.536	2.657	2.750	2.825	2.887	2.941	2.988	3.030	3.102	3.189

For illustration, imagine in the memory experiment that we have planned to conduct two paired contrasts – control vs method of loci and method of loci vs pegwords – then with df of 27 the critical t would be 2.373. The t computed for the contrast between control and the method of loci (3.139) shows us that they are significantly different at the $p < .05$ level.

The contrast t-value for method of loci vs pegwords is 0.916. Therefore, they are not significantly different at $\alpha = .05$, that is, $p > .05$. Using Bonferroni's t we can conclude that the method of loci produces significantly better recall than the control condition but not than the pegword method.

Dunnett's *t*

Dunnett's t (sometimes also known as d) is normally used when a particular mean (usually for a control group) is being contrasted with other means, one at a time. It is less conservative than Bonferroni's t because it does not assume that the contrasts are orthogonal.

Firstly, look up the critical value for t, with the error df (or df for Welch's t-test for between-subjects designs with heterogeneous variances, or df for the within-subjects t-test in within-subjects designs), in the table for Dunnett's t (A17.12) in Appendix XVII, and compare the computed t for the contrast with that critical value. If the computed t is as large as, or larger than, the critical value it is statistically significant.

Table 18.4 gives an extract of Table A17.12.

TABLE 18.4   An extract from the Dunnett's t tables for an error rate per family of $\alpha = 0.05$

df error	3	4	5	6	7	8	9	10	11	12	13	16	21
					Number of means (including the control)								
24	2.35	2.51	2.61	2.70	2.76	2.81	2.86	2.90	2.94	2.97	3.00	3.07	3.16
30	2.32	2.47	2.58	2.66	2.72	2.77	2.82	2.86	2.89	2.92	2.95	3.02	3.11

Assuming two contrasts are being conducted, each with 27 df, we have a critical value of t between 2.32 and 2.35, because Table 18.4 does not give values for df = 27. The contrast between method of loci and control conditions was statistically significant, while that between pegwords and control conditions (at $t = 2.224$) was not.

Scheffé's *t*

Scheffé's test is very conservative as it allows you to conduct any type of *post hoc* contrast. It is sufficiently conservative that there is no point in conducting it if the original F-ratio was not statistically significant. There are a confusing number of ways of calculating and expressing Scheffé's test: sometimes as a t-value and sometimes as an *F*-ratio. However, they will all give the same protection against making a Type I error. Here I give one version. Appendix IX gives three others because computer programs produce such versions.

Treated as a *t*-test we can take the calculated *t*-value and check it using standard *F*-tables (see Appendix XVII; yes, I do mean *F*-tables). To find the critical *t*-value, use the following equation:

$$\text{critical } t = \sqrt{df_{treatment} \times F(df_{treatment/}\ df_{error})}$$

In words, take the critical *F*-value which the *F*-tables give for the treatment df and error df (i.e. the original df for the *F*-ratio we are now trying to explain) and multiply it by the df for the treatment. The square root of the result is the critical value against which the calculated *t*-value has to be evaluated.

Table 18.5 shows the relevant part of the *F*-tables in Appendix XVII.

TABLE 18.5 An extract from the a = 0.05 probability tables for an *F*-ratio

	df_1											
df_2	1	2	3	4	5	6	7	8	9	10	12	14
26	4.23	3.37	2.98	2.74	2.59	2.47	2.39	2.32	2.27	2.22	2.15	2.09
27	4.21	3.35	2.96	2.73	2.57	2.46	2.37	2.31	2.25	2.20	2.13	2.08
28	4.20	3.34	2.95	2.71	2.56	2.45	2.36	2.29	2.24	2.19	2.12	2.06

The treatment and error df for the original *F*-ratio were 2 and 27, respectively. Looking in Table 18.5 we see that the critical *F*-ratio for these df is 3.35 for $p = .05$. Therefore:

$$\text{critical } t = \sqrt{2 \times 3.35}$$
$$= 2.588$$

This means that the only contrast which is statistically significant at $p < .05$ is the control group vs the method of loci group.

Scheffé's test is so conservative that it is not recommended for pairwise comparisons. Appendix IX shows its use with more appropriate comparisons.

Within-subjects designs

As was mentioned earlier, if the data in a within-subjects design lack sphericity, then it is not appropriate to use equation 18.1 or 18.2 to make contrasts. Given that Scheffé's test should not be used for pairwise contrasts, we do not have the option of computing a standard *t*-test (that is, one for comparing two means) for the more complex contrasts for which Scheffé's test is appropriate. Instead, if we wish to use Scheffé's test we have to check the sphericity of the data first. If the original ANOVA did not show the need to make an adjustment to the df, then the data have sphericity. If your computer program does not give such information, Appendix VII shows how the need for such an adjustment can be checked. If the data do have sphericity, then we can continue to conduct the Scheffé test as described previously.

Tukey's honestly significant difference (HSD)

This test is for use when the group sizes are the same. A variant – the Tukey–Kramer test – is for use when the groups are not the same size.

This method is less conservative than Scheffé's, as it assumes that not all possible types of comparison between the means are going to be made. However, it is more conservative than Dunnett's *t*.

Look up the critical t-value in the tables for Tukey's HSD in Appendix XVII for the number of means involved in the contrasts and the error df (or df for Welch's t-test for between-subjects designs with heterogeneous variances, or df for the standard within-subjects t-test, in within-subjects designs). Then compare the computed t-value for the contrast with the critical t. A comparison will only be significant when the value for computed t is as large as or greater than the critical t.

Table 18.6 shows part of the critical t-values for Tukey's HSD from Table A17.13 in Appendix XVII.

TABLE 18.6   An extract from the Tukey HSD t-tables for an error rate per family of $\alpha = 0.05$

df error	3	4	5	6	7	8	9	10	11	12	15
26	2.48	2.74	2.93	3.08	3.19	3.29	3.37	3.45	3.52	3.58	3.73
27	2.48	2.74	2.92	3.06	3.18	3.28	3.37	3.44	3.51	3.56	3.72
28	2.47	2.73	2.91	3.05	3.17	3.27	3.35	3.43	3.49	3.56	3.71

(Number of means to be contrasted)

With three means and error df of 27, the critical t-value is 2.48 for $p = .05$. In this case, only the contrast between method of loci and control conditions is statistically significant at $p < .05$ (Table 18.7).

TABLE 18.7   Summary of equations to be used to calculate t-values and df for critical t-values for pairwise contrasts

Design	Equation for t	df for critical t
Between-subjects		
Homogeneous variance	Equation 18.1 (or 18.2 if sample sizes are equal)	df for MS_{error} of original ANOVA
Heterogeneous variance	Welch's t-test (Chapter 15 and Appendix VI)	Adjusted df for Welch's t-test (Appendix VI)
Within-subjects	Standard t-test for within-subjects designs (Chapter 15 and Appendix VI)	$n - 1$ where n is the number of participants

Tukey–Kramer

This test is for between-subjects pairwise contrasts when the sample sizes for the two groups are not the same. It uses a variant of equation 18.1 for contrasts:

$$t = \frac{\text{mean}_1 - \text{mean}_2}{\sqrt{\frac{\left(\frac{MS_{error}}{n_2}\right) + \left(\frac{MS_{error}}{n_1}\right)}{2}}} \tag{18.3}$$

where n_1 and n_2 are the sizes of the two subsamples involved in the contrast. The critical t is found in exactly the same way as for the Tukey HSD method.

Other contrast tests

The tests of contrasts described thus far are sufficient for most situations. However, for completeness, further tests are described briefly in Appendix IX. You may find them in computer programs. In addition, as experienced researchers often have their favourite contrast tests, they may require you to use them.

One- and two-tailed tests and contrasts

The probabilities quoted in the extracts in this chapter from tables for the contrast tests are all two-tailed. Clearly, when using unplanned comparisons, the hypothesis, which underlies the test, is non-directional. However, when using a planned comparison, if it is testing a directional hypothesis, then it is legitimate to use a one-tailed probability. Accordingly, tables of one-tailed probabilities have been provided in Appendix XVII for Bonferroni's t and Dunnett's t for $\alpha = .05$.

Summary of contrast tests for parametric tests

You should be reassured by the fact that, of the recommended tests, all agreed over which contrasts were and were not statistically significant (Table 18.8). However, Dunnett's t, the least conservative, would have made the contrast between method of loci and the control condition statistically significant at $p < .01$ (even if all three contrasts had been conducted), while the others set the probability at $.01 < p < .05$. (Incidentally, for reasons of space, for Dunnett's t I have only included probability tables for $\alpha = .05$ in this book.)

TABLE 18.8   A summary of the tests of contrasts and when each is appropriate

Test	When to use
Bonferroni	A small number of planned or unplanned contrasts
Dunnett	Comparing one particular mean against others
Scheffé	Any post hoc contrast
Tukey's *HSD*	A set of post hoc pairwise contrasts, equal sample sizes
Tukey–Kramer	A set of post hoc pairwise contrasts, unequal sample sizes

Using a computer to conduct contrasts

Post hoc contrasts

For between-subjects designs, most of the procedures I have described can be made simpler if you have access to a computer program which will run them. However, you have to be careful about what probability it is reporting. Thus far I have described how you look in a table of critical values to find out what the t-value would have to be to achieve significance when the error rate per family of contrasts is being maintained at .05. In SPSS when a named *post hoc* contrast is conducted the probability which is reported is an adjusted version for the *individual* contrast which allows for the contrast test being employed and the size of the family of contrasts. To decide whether a contrast is statistically significant we compare the probability reported by the computer against an unadjusted alpha-level (usually .05). In SPSS you can run *Dunnett's* t and *Tukey's HSD* (which will also do *Tukey–Kramer* when the sample sizes are unequal). It is described as *Tukey* in SPSS (also included is a different test, called *Tukey-b*, which is *Tukey's WSD* and is described in Appendix IX). In addition, when the variances aren't homogeneous, by running *Games–Howell* you will be doing the equivalent of Tukey (or Tukey–Kramer) via Welch's t-test as described previously. Although *Bonferroni* is included among the *post hoc* tests, the probabilities will be adjusted by too much as it will assume that you are conducting all the possible pairwise contrasts.

Planned contrasts

SPSS will do the appropriate analysis under its *Contrasts* option when you tell it which particular pairs you are contrasting. In addition, you can set up more complex contrasts. However, it will make no adjustment to the probability, and so, if you are conducting more than one contrast, you will need to adjust alpha (using Bonferroni's adjustment) and compare the probability which SPSS reports against the adjusted alpha.

Non-parametric tests

At least ordinal data

One way to contrast two levels of an IV at a time, following Kruskal–Wallis one-way ANOVA or Friedman's two-way ANOVA, would be to conduct for each contrast the appropriate test for an IV with two levels. Thus, a Mann–Whitney U test would be used for contrasts on between-subjects designs, and a Wilcoxon signed rank test for matched pairs would be used for contrasts on within-subjects designs. However, it would be necessary to adjust the α-level, using a Bonferroni adjustment by dividing the α-level by the number of contrasts being made. Therefore, for four contrasts, the error rate per contrast (EC) becomes:

$$EC = \frac{.05}{4}$$
$$= .0125$$

There are also specific tests of contrasts for such data, as long as all the levels of the IV have five or more participants and the original statistical test was statistically significant. There are two types of such tests. One type is for use when all pairs of levels of the IV are being contrasted and the other is analogous to Dunnett's t in that it is for contrasting a control condition with another level of the IV. I include the former technique in Appendix IX. Those wishing to learn about the second technique can refer to Siegel and Castellan (1988).

Categorical data

When analysing a contingency table which is more than a 2×2 table there are a number of ways in which the result could be statistically significant: for example, if researchers are looking at the proportions of males and females who are smokers, non-smokers and ex-smokers. It is possible to conduct further analysis by *partitioning* the contingency table into a number of 2×2 subtables. Thus, the researchers could focus on smokers vs non-smokers and other, more specific, comparisons than are provided by the original analysis.

The analysis is also rather specialised and so is given in Appendix IX rather than here.

Trend tests

Trend tests are an extension of contrasts between means and use a very similar procedure. They are designed to test whether a group of means forms a single pattern, or trend. The most appropriate use for trend analysis is when the levels of the IV being tested are quantities rather than categories. For example, researchers hypothesise that reaction times will be slower as a result of the amount of alcohol consumed. They predict that the effect of the alcohol will be to increase reaction time by a regular amount – that is, that there is a *linear trend* for reaction time to increase with alcohol consumed.

In the example, 24 participants are placed into three equal-sized groups. Each group is given a different amount of alcohol: one, two or three units. Each participant is then given a task in which he or she has to detect the presence of an object on a computer screen.

There are a variety of possible trends which can be tested for but the number is dependent on the number of means involved and is the same as the df of the treatment being analysed. Thus, in the case of three means there are two types of possible trend – linear and quadratic. Figures 18.3 and 18.4 show the patterns which would constitute linear and quadratic trends.

FIGURE 18.3   An illustration of a linear trend

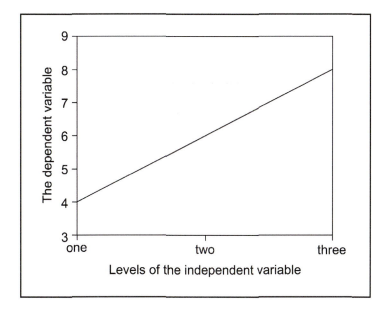

FIGURE 18.4   An illustration of a quadratic trend

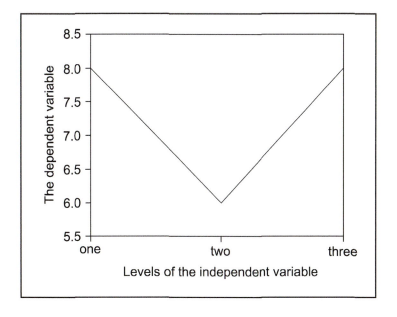

In the case of four means an additional possible trend is a cubic one (Figure 18.5).

FIGURE 18.5   An illustration of a cubic trend

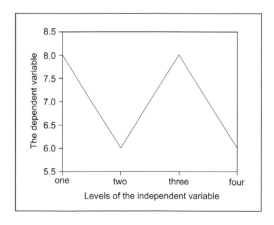

Table 18.9 and Figure 18.6 show the results of the experiment.

Notice that the means are going in the direction suggested but that they do not form a completely straight line. Before looking for any trend the convention is to conduct an initial ANOVA to find whether the treatment effect is statistically significant. In fact this is not essential as the trend test could

TABLE 18.9   The means and *SD*s of reaction times (in tenths of seconds) by number of units of alcohol consumed

	Units of alcohol consumed		
	one	two	three
Mean	151.25	163.38	168.75
SD	14.12	10.53	12.94

FIGURE 18.6   Mean reaction times with *SD*s, by number of units of alcohol consumed

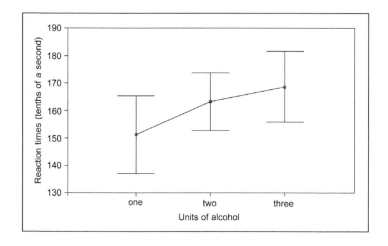

still be statistically significant even when the initial ANOVA is not. Table 18.10 shows the results of a between-subjects one-way ANOVA on the data.

TABLE 18.10   Summary table of the between-subjects ANOVA on the effects of alcohol on reaction times

Source	Sum of squares	df	Mean square	F	p
Between groups	1285.750	2	642.875	4.039	.0328
Within groups	3342.875	21	159.185		
Total	4628.625	23			

The fact that the means do not form a perfectly straight line suggests that the trend could be of a type other than linear.

For a trend analysis with three means with equal sample sizes you create a sum of squares (SS) for the trend you are testing according to the following equation:

$$SS_{trend} = \frac{n \times [(coef_1 \times \bar{x}_1) + (coef_2 \times \bar{x}_2) + (coef_3 \times \bar{x}_3)]^2}{coef_1^2 + coef_2^2 + coef_3^2}$$

where n is the number of participants in each group; $coef_1$, $coef_2$ and $coef_3$ are coefficients which are designed to test for a particular trend; and $\bar{x}_1$, $\bar{x}_2$ and $\bar{x}_3$ are the means for the three groups. Appendix IX gives the general equation for trend tests from which this has been derived. A table of the coefficients can be found in Appendix XIX. Table 18.11 shows the coefficients for trends involving three means.

TABLE 18.11   Coefficients for analysing trends with three means

Number of levels of IV					Level of IV							
	Type of trend	1	2	3	4	5	6	7	8	9	10	
3	Linear	−1	0	1								
	Quadratic	1	−2	1								

$$SS_{lin} = \frac{8 \times [(-1 \times 151.25) + (0 \times 163.38) + (1 \times 168.75)]^2}{(-1)^2 + (0)^2 + (1)^2}$$

$$= \frac{2450}{2}$$

$$= 1225$$

Each trend test always has 1 df. Therefore the MS_{trend} is also 1225.

The F-ratio for the MS_{trend} is found by dividing the MS_{trend} by the MS_{error}, which in this case is 159.185 (from Table 18.10). Thus,

$$F_{(1,21)} = 7.695$$

We can use standard F-tables to assess the statistical significance of this result. The critical F for this trend test is 4.32, in which case there is a significant linear trend in this study between quantity of alcohol consumed and reaction times.

The coefficients for trend tests have been chosen so that the trend tests partition the treatment sum of squares into separate sources of variation; they are orthogonal. In other words, if you add the sum of squares for all the permissible trend tests, the result will be the same as the treatment sum of squares.

We can therefore work out whether it is worth looking for other trends. Given that the overall sum of squares for alcohol consumption was 1285.75 (see Table 18.10) and the sum of squares for the linear trend was 1225, the sum of squares for any remaining trend (in this case quadratic) is:

$$1285.75 - 1225 = 60.75$$

As the df for any trend is 1, the MS for a quadratic trend will also be 60.75 and so the *F*-ratio for such a trend would be:

$$\frac{60.75}{159.185} = 0.382$$

which is not statistically significant. Accordingly, we can conclude that there is solely a significant linear trend.

Further exploration of an interaction

When there is an interaction between two or more IVs it is worth attempting to explore the nature of that interaction further. I am going to describe two approaches: *simple effects* and *interaction contrasts*. Simple effects are appropriate when you wish to explore the interaction fully without having planned particular contrasts between levels of the IVs. Interaction effects allow you to target very specific contrasts. They have more power if they are planned as when conducted post hoc the adjustment to alpha is very conservative as it relies on Scheffé's test.

▊ Simple effects

Let us return to the example, from Chapter 17, in which participants were shown a list of words and asked to recall as many words as they could. The two IVs were type of list (with words which were either linked or unlinked) and mnemonic strategy (method of loci, pegwords or a control condition). One method of analysing the interaction of the two IVs is to separate out the treatment effects of one IV for each of the levels of the other IV. In the example this would mean looking at the effects of mnemonic strategy on the recall of linked words and the effect of mnemonic strategy on recall of unlinked words. It could also mean looking at the effect of type of list on recall of those using method of loci, the effect of type of list on recall of those using pegwords and the effect of type of list on recall of the control group. Each of these analyses is described as a simple effect (sometimes referred to as a *simple main effect*).

Some books advise only looking for simple effects when there is a significant interaction. I disagree, because useful information can sometimes be found when the interaction is not significant, such as finding the pattern of a significant main effect only reproduced in some levels of the second IV. It is particularly worth testing simple effects when you have predicted that there will be an interaction. Remember that the interaction which has been tested deals with the variance remaining once the main effects have been tested and so a non-significant interaction can be followed by significant simple effects which show different patterns. Nonetheless, if the interaction is far from being statistically significant, then the simple effects are not worth conducting.

The method which is used to find the simple effects depends on whether the variable being considered is a within-subjects variable or a between-subjects variable. I am going to be more specific and say that you should use one technique when the design is totally between-subjects and one when it is either totally within-subjects or mixed (i.e. has some IVs which are within-subjects).

Between-subjects designs

The two-way ANOVA produced the summary table in Table 18.12.

TABLE 18.12   The summary table from the ANOVA of a 2 × 3, two-way, between-subjects ANOVA

Source	Sum of squares	df	Mean square	F	p
List	61.633	1	61.633	37.354	.0001
Mnemonic	5.600	2	2.800	1.697	.2045
List * Mnemonic	11.467	2	5.733	3.475	.0473
Error	39.600	24	1.650		
Total	118.300	29			

This tells us that there was a significant interaction between list type and mnemonic strategy.

A warning about heterogeneity of variance

The following procedure is only appropriate if the variances for all the conditions in the interaction are similar. Therefore, before you conduct a simple effects analysis on a between-subjects design, examine the variances. If they are different, then you should follow the procedure suggested for within-subjects and mixed designs shown next. In the example Table 18.13 shows the variances for the six conditions.

TABLE 18.13   The variances for the six memory conditions

| List | Mnemonic strategy | | |
	control	pegword	loci
Linked	1.50	1.86	1.30
Unlinked	2.30	1.30	1.70

If the largest variance is no more than two times the smallest variance, then we can continue with the procedure. In this case, 2.3, the largest variance, is less than two times 1.3, the smallest variance. Notice that the variances have to be closer together in this situation than they have to be to perform the initial ANOVA. See Myers and Well (1991) for a discussion of the problems of heterogeneity of variance when performing simple effects.

To analyse simple effects we need to form an F-ratio for each simple effect. When the design is completely between-subjects, and there is homogeneity of variance, the F-ratio for each level of one of the IVs is formed from the following equation:

$$F = \frac{MS_{\text{level of IV}}}{MS_{\text{error for interaction}}}$$

Thus, in the case of the preceding example, if we were looking at the simple effect of mnemonic strategy on unlinked words we would find the MS for unlinked words and divide it by the MS_{error} for the original interaction (i.e. MS_{residual}). The appropriate df for the F-ratio, as usual, would be the df from the MS for the level: in this case the df for the mnemonic strategies with unlinked words (2), and the df for the original interaction error term (24).

To simplify the process you can find the MS for each level by running a one-way ANOVA on just the data for the level in which you are interested. In this case, you would just include the data for participants who were shown unlinked words. Summary Table 18.14 is of a one-way, between-subjects ANOVA comparing the recall for the three mnemonic strategies on the unlinked lists.

TABLE 18.14   The one-way between-subjects ANOVA on mnemonic strategy for unlinked lists

Source	Sum of squares	df	Mean square	F	p
Mnemonic	16.533	2	8.267	4.679	.0315
Residual	21.200	12	1.767		

From this analysis we can see that the $MS_{mnemonic\ for\ unlinked}$ is 8.267 with df = 2. The error term for the simple effect is the same as the one used for the two-way ANOVA, that is, 1.650 with df = 24 (see Table 18.12). Therefore the simple effect for unlinked words is:

$$F_{(2,24)} = \frac{8.267}{1.650}$$
$$= 5.010$$

Referring to F-tables tells us that the critical F-ratio for $p = .05$ with df of 2 and 24 is 3.4. In this case, we can report that, for unlinked words, recall differed significantly between the three mnemonic strategies ($F_{(2,24)} = 5.010$, $p < .05$, $\eta^2 = .14$ as a proportion of the recall of the original data, and $\eta^2 = .438$ as a proportion of the recall of unlinked words). I am reporting both effect sizes as they inform future researchers about the effects for different aspects of the design.

The analysis could be repeated for linked words, as in Table 18.15.

TABLE 18.15   The one-way between-subjects ANOVA on mnemonic strategy for linked lists

Source	Sum of squares	df	Mean square	F	p
Mnemonic	0.533	2	0.267	0.174	.8425
Residual	18.400	12	1.533		

Here,

$$F_{linked} = \frac{MS_{linked}}{MS_{error}}$$
$$F_{(2,24)} = \frac{0.267}{1.650}$$
$$= 0.162$$

As this F-value is less than 1, it is definitely not statistically significant. We now have a clearer picture of what produced the significant interaction in the two-way ANOVA. Mnemonic strategy significantly affects recall when lists are unlinked but not when lists are linked.

To complete the analysis we would now perform comparisons on the means of the unlinked conditions to identify even more specifically the source of the significant effect. I leave that as an exercise for you to do.

Partitioning the sums of squares in simple effects

In analysing the simple effects you are taking the sum of squares for the interaction and for the IV, which will be tested in the simple effect, from the original two-way ANOVA and splitting this into separate parts for each simple effect. Looking at the original two-way ANOVA, the sum of squares for the interaction is 11.467 and for mnemonic is 5.600. Adding these together gives a sum of squares of 17.067. Notice that the sum of squares for the unlinked words is 16.533 and for linked words is 0.533. Adding these together gives 17.066 (which is only different from 17.067 because the figures have been rounded).

Interaction contrasts

I will continue with the study involving the IVs mnemonic strategy and list type. If we had a specific prediction about the relative size of recall for the different combinations of strategy and list type then this could lead to a single precise comparison of the means which included both IVs. As an example, we may predict that when participants do not use a mnemonic strategy (those in the control groups) then trying to recall a linked list will be of more benefit relative to trying to recall an unlinked list than when participants do use a mnemonic strategy.

Table 18.16 shows the different combinations of the mnemonic and list conditions (LC refers to Linked lists in the Control condition and the other abbreviations follow the same pattern).

TABLE 18.16   The six memory conditions

List	Mnemonic strategy		
	control	pegword	loci
Linked	LC	LP	LL
Unlinked	UC	UP	UL

The prediction just described would mean that the difference in recall between UC and LC would be greater than it would be for either UP and LP or UL and LL. An interaction contrast would allow us to compare the difference between UC and LC with the mean of the differences between UP and LP and UL and LL. The Null Hypothesis would be:

H_0:   UC – LC = mean of ((UP-LP) and (UL-LL))

The equation for the interaction contrast is following the same principle as for a trend test, described previously, where each mean is multiplied by a coefficient. However, this time the coefficients are calculated by combining information from the nature of the contrasts across each IV. To contrast linked and unlinked lists we can use the coefficients 1 and –1 so that they sum to 0. To contrast the control group with the mean of the two mnemonic groups we can use the coefficients 1, –.5 and –.5 so that again they sum to zero. To find the coefficient for a given cell mean we multiply the coefficient for the row that cell is in by the coefficient for the column that cell is in. Accordingly, the coefficient for LC is $1 \times 1 = 1$. Table 18.17 shows the coefficients for each cell.

TABLE 18.17   The coefficients for the six memory conditions

List	Mnemonic strategy		
	Control (1)	Pegword (-.5)	Loci (-.5)
Linked (1)	1	–.5	–.5
Unlinked (–1)	–1	.5	.5

As with simple effects and trend analysis we need to calculate a sum of squares for the interaction contrast. If the sample sizes are equal then we can use equation A9.3 from Appendix IX which is just a more formal and general way of presenting the equation shown previously for the sum of squares in trend tests. If the sample sizes are unequal then we need to use equation A9.2 (also from Appendix IX). This produces $SS_{contrast}$ = 11.267. As the contrast has df = 1, the $MS_{contrast}$ = 11.267. As usual an F-ratio is found by dividing the $MS_{contrast}$ by the appropriate MS_{error}. From Table 18.12 we find that MS_{error} = 1.65, with df = 24. Therefore the F-ratio for the interaction contrast = 6.83, with df of 1 and 24. Referring to the probability tables for the F-distribution, we find that $.01 < p < .05$.

Had the contrast been conducted on a post hoc basis then we would need to use Scheffé's test. To find the critical F-value we can use Method 2 in Appendix IX:

$$\text{critical } F = df_{treatment} \times F(df_{treatment}, df_{error})$$

Here the treatment is the interaction, where df = 2 and the critical value for $F_{(2,24)}$ for p = .05 is 3.4, so the critical F = 6.8. Therefore as the calculated F-value at 6.83 is larger than the critical F-value, the interaction contrast would still be statistically significant as a post hoc test at $p < .05$.

Designs with within-subjects variables

Totally within-subjects designs

Simple effects

To conduct simple effects on one IV, simply ignore the data for the other levels of that IV and conduct a one-way, within-subjects ANOVA on the remaining data. The F-ratio from that analysis is the appropriate F-ratio for the simple effect, with the df from that analysis.

Recall the study, described in Chapter 17, in which participants had to decide on a sentence for a crime. There were two IVs: the context in which the decision was made (alone, at a computer or face-to-face with other judges) and the nature of the defendant (experienced criminal or novice). The results did not show a significant interaction. However, for the purposes of illustration, I will analyse the simple effects for each level of the context.[1]

Tables 18.18–18.20 show the simple effects comparing defendant type for each of the three contexts. From these simple effects we can see that, whatever the context, the experienced defendant will be given a significantly more severe sentence than a novice defendant. As there were only two levels in each simple effect, we could have conducted the analysis using within-subjects t-tests.

TABLE 18.18   The one-way, within-subjects ANOVA of the effects of defendant type on suggested sentence length (for participants who made the decision alone)

Source	Sum of squares	df	Mean square	F	p
Subject	2.4	4	0.6		
Experience	19.6	1	19.6	12.25	.0249
Experience by subject	6.4	4	1.6		
Total	28.4	9			

---

1 The more appropriate analysis, when the interaction is not significant but a main effect with more than two levels is significant, is contrasts on the main effect, which is described later in the chapter.

TABLE 18.19 The one-way, within-subjects ANOVA of the effects of defendant type on suggested sentence length (for participants who made the decision while seeing other judges' decisions on computer)

Source	Sum of squares	df	Mean square	F	p
Subject	5.4	4	1.35		
Experience	40.0	1	40.00	160	.0002
Experience by subject	1.0	4	0.25		
Total	46.4	9			

TABLE 18.20 The one-way, within-subjects ANOVA of the effects of defendant type on suggested sentence length (for participants who made the decision in the presence of other judges)

Source	Sum of squares	df	Mean square	F	p
Subject	1.4	4	0.35		
Experience	48.4	1	48.40	29.333	.0056
Experience by subject	6.6	4	1.65		
Total	56.4	9			

Interaction contrasts

If all the combinations of the conditions are to be included in the contrast then the principles are the same as for a factorial design (Maxwell & Delaney, 2004, give details of the appropriate way to conduct interaction contrasts for within-subjects designs when not all the cells are to be analysed). I could have predicted that the difference in sentence between that given to a novice defendant and an experienced defendant is smaller when the decision is made by a participant on his or her own than when the participant sees other people's sentences, either by computer or when face-to-face with others.

If N and E refer to novice and experienced, while A, C and F refer to alone, computer and face-to-face, then the Null Hypothesis tested by the contrast would be:

H_0: EA – NA = mean of ((EC-NC) and (EF-NF))

Using equation 9.3, the sum of squares for the contrast (and therefore the MS as df = 1) is 3.267. To find the F-ratio for the contrast the $MS_{contrast}$ is divided by the MS_{error} (that for experience by condition by subject) which is 1.192 (from Table 17.7).
  This results in $F_{(1,8)}$ = 2.74.
  As the critical value of F at .05 with df of 1 and 8 is 5.32, $p > .05$.

Mixed designs

Simple effects

The example given in Chapter 17 of this design was of males and females giving ratings of their mothers' and fathers' IQ. When you are looking at the simple effects of the within-subjects variable (parent), conduct a one-way, between-subjects ANOVA on the between-subjects variable for each level of the within-subjects variable. Thus, you would conduct a one-way, between-subjects ANOVA on each level of parent. When looking at the simple effects of the between-subjects variable (gender), conduct a one-way, within-subjects ANOVA on each of the levels of the between-subjects variable. Thus, you would conduct a one-way, within-subjects ANOVA on each level of gender of participant. These recommendations are designed to simplify the analysis. Those of you who wish to pursue this further should read Howell's (2013) account for a more thorough way of conducting simple effects under these circumstances.

The original prediction of the researchers was that males and females would rate their parents differently. The graph of the means suggested that an interaction was present between gender and parent's IQ; see Figure 18.7. However, the F-ratio for interaction did not reach statistical significance ($p = .0795$; see Table 17.9).

FIGURE 18.7   The mean rating of parental IQ by males and females

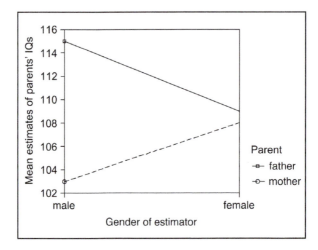

The simple effect of the IQ ratings made by females produced the result given in Table 18.21.
The simple effect of the IQ ratings made by males produced the result given in Table 18.22.
The researchers are forced to conclude that the simple effects for males and for females do not show a significant difference in their ratings of their mothers' and fathers' IQs. Nonetheless, it looks as though there is a possible effect which is worth further research.

TABLE 18.21   A one-way, within-subjects ANOVA of females' judgements of their parents' IQs

Source	Sum of squares	df	Mean square	F	p
Subject	315.00	4	78.75		
Parent	2.50	1	2.50	0.286	.6213
Parent by subject	35.00	4	8.75		

TABLE 18.22   A one-way, within-subjects ANOVA of males' judgements of their parents' IQs

Source	Sum of squares	df	Mean square	F	p
Subject	1215.00	4	303.75		
Parent	360.00	1	360.00	5.434	.0802
Parent by subject	265.00	4	66.25		

My advice would be to repeat the research with a larger sample size in order to give the test more power. Note that by analysing the simple effects we have based each ANOVA on five raters. The effect size (η^2) of parent being rated for the male raters is .196, which is a large effect size, according to Cohen's criteria. However, with the small sample size the test only had power of about .29. In order to achieve power of .8, with such an effect size, we need about 16 male raters. The effect size for female raters is .007, which is small.

Interaction contrasts

As with completely within-subjects designs the procedure depends on whether all the combination of cells are included in the contrast (see Maxwell & Delaney, 2004, for when they aren't). If I had predicted that female participants would rate the IQs of their parents as being more similar than would male participants then I could test this directly with an interaction contrast.

However, because there are only two levels in both of the two IVs, the F-ratio for the contrast would be the same as for the interaction in the original analysis and so there would be nothing gained by conducting the contrast.

A warning about Type I errors

We could be conducting a number of analyses for simple effects. If we continue to use an alpha-level of .05 we are increasing the danger of making a Type I error. Accordingly, we could use a Bonferroni adjustment. In the case of the three simple effects on sentencing patterns, the adjusted α-level for each simple effect would be:

$$\frac{.05}{3} = .0167$$

in order to leave the overall α-level at .05. It is best to keep the number of simple effects analyses to a minimum as the power of each test will be reduced by the adjustment to alpha.

Notice that, with this more stringent α-level, the simple effect for decisions made when the participants were on their own would not be statistically significant. When the probability for a given analysis reaches $p \leq .05$ but does not reach the adjusted level, I would suggest that it should not automatically be dismissed as not statistically significant but that it should be treated with more caution and the reader's attention should be drawn to the need to do more research on this particular aspect of the study. Thus three regions can be identified when alpha has been adjusted: $p > .05$, to be treated as not statistically significant; $.05 \geq p >$ adjusted alpha, the discussable region;[2] and $p \leq$ adjusted alpha, to be treated as statistically significant.

Interpreting main effects

When a two-way ANOVA does not reveal an interaction between the IVs, then it is possible to interpret the main effects more straightforwardly as they are not being complicated by the presence of an interaction. How we interpret the main effects depends on the number of levels which a significant main effect has. If there are only two levels, then we can refer directly to the means to see which group has the higher score. The means we will need to examine will be ones which are found by ignoring the presence of the other IV (the marginal means). In the two-way within-subjects design described earlier there was

---

2 I think another author proposed this idea first, but I cannot find the source.

a significant main effect of the type of defendant (novice or experienced) on the length of sentence recommended and a significant main effect of the context in which the recommendation was made (alone, via computer or in a face-to-face group). As type of defendant had only two levels we can find the mean length of sentence which was made for the novice and for the experienced defendant. These were 43 and 54.2 respectively. Therefore, we can conclude that a significantly longer sentence was recommended for an experienced defendant than for a novice.

To interpret the significant main effect of context we have to conduct further analysis as there are more than two levels. As with any such ANOVA, all the significant result has told us is that the conditions differ from each other but not how they differ.

For the follow-up analysis I am going to cover only paired contrasts as these are the most likely ones that people are going to want to conduct. Nonetheless, other tests could be applied, including trend tests, where appropriate. As with contrasts following a one-way ANOVA, we need to know two things: how to calculate the appropriate statistic and how to decide its significance. The reasoning is the same as for paired contrasts described earlier. The method of calculating the t-value for a contrast is dependent on whether the design was completely between-subjects, completely within-subjects or mixed and, if it was between-subjects, whether the groups had homogeneity of variance and whether the groups had equal-sized samples. To decide the significance of the t-value if we planned a set of contrasts before the analysis, we would use Bonferroni's test or Dunnett's test, if other groups were being compared with a control group. If the contrasts were unplanned, then we would use Tukey's test.

Between-subjects design

Throughout this explanation I am going to use the mnemonic by list example. However, remember that in that example the IV which has three levels (mnemonic) did not have a significant main effect and there was a significant interaction so we would not normally conduct such analysis on the data.

Homogeneity of variance present

We can use equation 18.1 or 18.2 as appropriate or, if we are using the Tukey– Kramer test, then equation 18.3. In each case the MS_{error} would be the MS_{error} from the original ANOVA (in the mnemonic by list example the MS_{error} was 1.650). To find the means for the contrast ignore the presence of the IV which you are not analysing in the contrast. In the mnemonic by list example if we are conducting contrasts comparing two mnemonic conditions, then we would calculate the means as though there hadn't been separate lists in the design. Table 17.2 shows that the means for the control, pegword and loci methods were 8.7, 9.5 and 9.7 respectively. The sample sizes to go in the equations come from the number of participants who contributed to the means involved in the contrast. In the mnemonic by list example, $n = 10$ for each of the mnemonic conditions. To find the critical value for t we would need to read the appropriate table using the df from the MS_{error}, which in the mnemonic by list example was 24.

Homogeneity of variance not present across the conditions of the two-way ANOVA

Although the full set of conditions in the two-way ANOVA may not have been homogeneous, if we ignore the presence of one variable we could find that we have sufficient homogeneity to conduct a standard one-way ANOVA which ignores the IV which will not be involved in the contrasts. In the mnemonic by list example the variances for the control, pegword and loci conditions are 7.57, 2.72 and 2.23 respectively. As the sample sizes are the same for the three groups these variances are sufficiently homogeneous to allow a standard one-way between-subjects ANOVA to be conducted, followed by contrasts based on equation 18.1, 18.2 or 18.3 as appropriate, but with the MS_{error} and df from the one-way ANOVA rather than from the original two-way ANOVA.

If variances for the levels of the IV which is to involve the contrast are not homogeneous even when the presence of the other IV has been ignored, then conduct the between-subjects t-tests for each contrast, just including the data for the two conditions being contrasted. When the pair of conditions have homogeneity of variance use the standard t-test, otherwise use Welch's t. The df used to find the critical value of t will then come from each t-test.

Within-subjects designs

For each level of the IV which will be involved in the contrasts find the mean across the levels of the IV which won't be in the contrasts. In the defendant by context example, we would find the mean for each participant for each context across the two defendant types. Run within-subjects t-tests for each contrast on the means. Table 18.23 shows the t-values and unadjusted p-values for each contrast; each has df = 4.

TABLE 18.23   The t- and unadjusted p-values of the paired contrasts from the main effect of context on sentence recommended

Contrast	t	p
Alone – computer	−1.907	.129
Alone – face-to-face	−14.905	.000
Computer – face-to-face	−6.893	.002

If we had planned only to do certain of the preceding contrasts rather than all of them, then we could divide .05 by the number of contrasts we planned (to form our adjusted alpha-level) and compare the probabilities for each contrast against them; we would be doing a Bonferroni correction. Alternatively, if we are using Tukey's test to conduct unplanned contrasts, then we would find the critical t for the contrasts, with df = 4, using the method described earlier in the chapter. This produces a critical t of 3.56. We would therefore judge that the alone and computer conditions did not produce significantly different lengths of recommended sentence, while sentences given when face-to-face with other members of a group were significantly higher than when the person recommending the sentence was alone and when the person thought he or she knew what the other members of the groups had recommended.

Mixed designs

The method of analysis depends on whether you are looking at a main effect for a between-subjects or for a within-subjects IV. If for a between-subjects IV, then find the mean for each participant across the levels of the within-subjects IV. If the variances of the levels of the between-subjects IV are homogeneous, then run a one-way, between-subjects ANOVA and the contrasts using equation 18.1, 18.2 or 18.3 as appropriate. If the variances are not homogeneous use the appropriate between-subjects t-test for each contrast.

For the within-subjects IV, ignore the presence of the between-subjects IV and run within-subjects t-tests for each contrast.

Beyond two-way ANOVA

Earlier in the chapter I described a hypothetical two-way within-subjects ANOVA which requires participants to sentence defendants who are either experienced or novices (IV$_1$) under the conditions of being alone, or seeing what sentences others suggest via a computer or being in the same room as other participants (IV_2). In Chapter 17, I described an extension of this design whereby the gender of the participant was a third IV. If the three-way interaction from this design was significant, then we could explore it further by analysing *simple interaction effects*. For example, we could take just the females and run a two-way ANOVA on the other IVs. Then we could do the same just for the males. If either of these interactions were significant (allowing for having adjusted alpha), then we would need to investigate that further via ordinary simple effects.

If the three-way interaction was not significant but one or more two-way interactions were significant, then we could investigate these interactions by interaction contrasts or by choosing to ignore the existence of one of the variables. The choice of variable to ignore would be most straightforward if one variable was not involved in any of the two-way interactions. Thus, if the only two-way interaction to be significant was type of defendant by condition under which sentence was given, then we could ignore gender and conduct two separate one-way ANOVAs comparing the three conditions under which the sentence was given: one for the sentence given to experienced defendants and one for inexperienced defendants.

Summary

After conducting an ANOVA, researchers often wish to explore the data further. Contrasts allow means to be compared to investigate more specific hypotheses than are tested by an ANOVA. Contrasts can be planned before the data have been examined, or be unplanned and conducted once the means have been calculated. A variant on contrasts – trend analysis – can be applied when levels of an IV are quantitative rather than qualitative. Trend analysis allows patterns across means to be explored to see whether there is a trend across the levels of the IV.

Simple effects analysis allows the nature of an interaction between two IVs to be explored further. It isolates one level of one IV at a time to see how the levels of the other IV vary. Simple effects can show differences in patterns even when the original interaction *F*-ratio is not significant. Interaction contrasts allow analysis of more complex contrasts which involve both variables in the interaction.

If there is a significant main effect and no interaction, then, if the main effect has only two levels, the direction in which the result went can be found by inspecting the marginal means for that IV. However, if the main effect has more than two levels, then contrasts need to be conducted to explore the source of the significant result further.

The analysis introduced in this and previous chapters has addressed the question of whether there are differences between levels of an IV, in means, medians or proportions. The next three chapters introduce techniques for analysing relationships between two or more variables. Once they have been introduced the following chapter will return to comparing levels of an IV but this time the comparison will be made after possible differences due to another variable have been allowed for.

19 Analysis of relationships I
Correlation

Introduction

Researchers are often interested in the relationship between two, or more, variables. For example, they may want to know how the variable *IQ* is related to the variable *earnings*.

The chapter starts by explaining the measures, including correlation, which are used to quantify the relationship between variables and how to interpret those measures. It discusses the basic forms of correlation for different types of data. It then introduces extensions of these techniques and the use of correlation for investigating the reliability and validity of measures.

Correlation

Two variables are said to be correlated when there is some predictability about the relationship between them. If people with low IQs had low incomes, people with medium IQs had medium incomes and people with high IQs had high incomes, then, if we knew an individual's IQ, we could predict, with a certain degree of accuracy, what his or her income was. This would be an example of a positive correlation: as one variable gets larger so does the other. If, on the other hand, we investigated the relationship between family size and income we might find that those with large families have low incomes, those with medium-sized families have medium incomes and those with small families have high incomes. We could now predict a person's income from his or her family size with a certain degree of accuracy. However, this example would be of a negative (or inverse) correlation: as one variable gets larger the other gets smaller.

One measure of the relationship between two variables is the *covariance* between them.

Covariance

Imagine that in the IQ and income example the information presented in Table 19.1 was found for a sample of five people.

Covariance, as its name suggests, is a measure of how the two variables vary together. To find the covariance we calculate how much each person's score on one variable deviates from the mean for that variable and multiply that by how much their score on the other variable deviates from its mean.

Thus, for the first person this would be:

$$(85 - 96) \times (12\,000 - 14\,800) = 30\,800$$

Repeat for each person and add the results together; this equals 131 000. In order to take account of the sample size, divide by one fewer than the number of people who have provided measures. In this case the covariance is:

$$\frac{131\,000}{5-1} = 32\,750$$

TABLE 19.1   The IQ and income of five people

Participant	IQ	Income
1	85	12 000
2	90	11 000
3	95	15 000
4	100	16 000
5	110	20 000
Mean	96	14 800
SD	9.618	3563.706

If the covariance is large and positive, then this is because people who were low on one variable tended to be low on the other, and people who were high on one tended to be high on the other, suggesting a positive relationship between the two variables. Similarly, a large negative covariance suggests a negative relationship. Covariance of zero shows no relationship between the two variables.

However, there is a problem with covariance being used as the measure of the relationship: it does not take the size of the variance of the variables into account. Hence, if in a study one or both of the variables had a large variance, then the covariance would be larger than in another study where the two variances were small, even if the degrees of relationship in the two studies were similar. Therefore, using covariance we would not be able to compare relationships to see whether one relationship was closer than another. For example, we might wish to see whether IQ and income were more closely related than IQ and family size.

Accordingly, we need a measure which takes the variances into account. The correlation coefficient is such a measure.

Correlation coefficients

The correlation coefficient (r), known as *Pearson's product moment correlation coefficient*, can be found by the following equation:

$$r = \frac{\text{covariance between two variables}}{SD_1 \times SD_2}$$

where SD_1 and SD_2 are the standard deviations of the two variables.

In this case, for the IQ and income example:

$$r = \frac{32\,750}{9.618 \times 3563.706}$$
$$= .9555$$

The effect of dividing by the standard deviations is to limit, mathematically, the range of r, such that the largest positive correlation which can be achieved is +1 and the largest negative correlation which can be achieved is −1. If r is 0, this means there is no relationship between the variables.

The statistical significance of a correlation coefficient

The Null Hypothesis against which r is usually tested is that there is no relationship between the two variables. More particularly, the Null Hypothesis is about the equivalent parameter to r – the correlation in the population, usually shown as ρ (the Greek letter *rho*). Formally stated, the Null Hypothesis is that the sample comes from a population in which the correlation between two variables is ρ = 0. Therefore, with a sufficiently large sample size, the frequency distribution of *r*, under this Null Hypothesis, has roughly the following shape, with 0 as the most frequently occurring value and with +1 and −1 as the least likely values to occur when there is no relationship, as shown in Figure 19.1.

FIGURE 19.1 The frequency distribution of *r*, when the samples are taken from a population in which there is no correlation

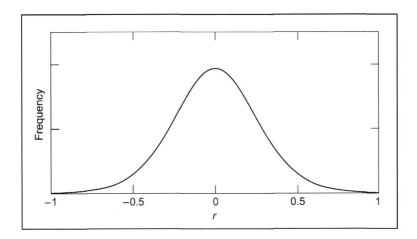

The exact shape of the distribution is dependent on the sample size, or more particularly on the degrees of freedom (df) of *r*, which are two fewer than the sample size because the significance of *r* is based on the significance of regression (which, as we will see in the next chapter, has to estimate two parameters when two variables are involved). The larger the sample size, the closer the distribution is to being normally distributed. Appendix XVII gives the probabilities for *r* (when the Null Hypothesis is that ρ = 0) and Table 19.2 is an extract from that table. (The way to find the probability of *r* when the Null Hypothesis is not ρ = 0 is explained later in this chapter.)

TABLE 19.2 An extract of the probability tables for *r* (when the Null Hypothesis is that ρ = 0)

	One-tailed probabilities									
	0.4	0.3	0.2	0.1	0.05	0.025	0.01	0.005	0.001	0.0005
	Two-tailed probabilities									
df = n-2	0.8	0.6	0.4	0.2	0.1	0.05	0.02	0.01	0.002	0.001
1	0.3090	0.5878	0.8090	0.9511	0.9877	0.9969	0.9995	0.9999	1.0000	1.0000
2	0.2000	0.4000	0.6000	0.8000	0.9000	0.9500	0.9800	0.9900	0.9980	0.9990
3	0.1577	0.3197	0.4919	0.6870	0.8054	0.8783	0.9343	0.9587	0.9859	0.9911
4	0.1341	0.2735	0.4257	0.6084	0.7293	0.8114	0.8822	0.9172	0.9633	0.9741

Note that Table 19.2 gives probabilities for both one- and two-tailed tests.

One-tailed probabilities for *r*

If the research hypothesis is directional, then a one-tailed probability is appropriate. An example would be if the research hypothesis was:

H$_A$: IQ and income are positively correlated.

For which the Null Hypothesis is:

H_0:   There is no relationship between IQ and income.

The Null Hypothesis is that there is no *linear* relationship between the two variables in the population. A *linear relationship* would exist if a scattergram were created between the two variables and the points on the scattergram formed a straight line.

As there were five participants, df = 3. In this case, the one-tailed probability provided by the computer is p = .0056. This result would be reported as: *There was a significant positive correlation between IQ and income (r = .956, df = 3, p = .0056, one-tailed test).* As with the reporting of other tests, the df can also be shown in the following way: $r_{(3)}$ = .956.

The prediction of a negative correlation between two variables would also be a directional hypothesis. An example would be if the research hypothesis was:

H_A: There is a negative correlation between family size and income.

For which the Null Hypothesis is:

H_0:   There is no relationship between family size and income.

To find the probability of a negative correlation ignore the negative sign and read the table as though the result had been a positive correlation; a correlation of r = −.9555 has the same probability as a correlation of r = .9555.

Two-tailed probabilities for *r*

If the research hypothesis is non-directional, then you would use a two-tailed probability. An example of a non-directional hypothesis would be if the research hypothesis was:

H_A: There is a relationship between IQ and income.

For which the Null Hypothesis as before is:

H_0:   There is no relationship between IQ and income.

Here we would use a two-tailed probability; with r = .9555 and df = 3, p = .0112.

The interpretation of r

Causality and correlation

A snare which people should avoid with correlation, but often fall into, is assuming that because two variables are correlated one is affecting or causing the other to vary. An example shows the dangers of this reasoning. Over the year the consumption of ice cream and the incidence of drownings are correlated. This does not suggest that consuming ice cream leads to drowning. Here the relationship is produced by the fact that each variable is linked to the weather; the hotter the weather, the more likely people are to consume ice cream and the more likely people are to go swimming and so put themselves in danger.

There are other situations in which two variables may correlate but there is no causal link between them. They may be part of a chain of causality. For example, amount of knowledge about healthy behaviour may be correlated with physical health. However, there may be one or more variables which are acting as *mediators* between them. Amount of knowledge about healthy behaviour may be related to the degree to which people feel in control of their own health, which in turn may be related to the type of behaviour that people display and this may be linked to their health.

Even when there is a causal link between two variables we may not know which is the cause and which the effect. If socio-economic status (SES) and incidence of mental illness were positively related we would not know whether people's SES affects the likelihood of their developing a mental illness or whether the development of mental illness affects their SES. As has been said in previous chapters, cause and effect are best identified through experiments, where the researchers manipulate the IV(s) and look for the effects of the manipulations on the DV(s).

The nature of the correlation

Whenever correlations are being investigated it is important that a scattergram be produced of the relationship between the two variables and aspects of the variables be considered. This is because in some situations a significant correlation may be produced when there is little or no relationship (a spurious correlation) while in other situations a relationship may exist which is not detected by *r*.

Figure 19.2 shows the pattern which can be expected when there is a high positive correlation between two variables.

FIGURE 19.2   A scattergram for a high positive correlation (*r* = .9555)

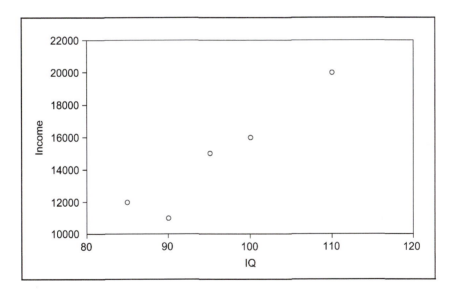

A line can be drawn on the diagram, which is sometimes called the *best-fit* line, to depict the relationship between the two variables. The best-fit line is the line which passes through the data points with the minimum distance between itself and all the points.[1] Note that in the case of a positive correlation the line runs from the bottom left-hand corner to the upper right-hand corner of the graph (Figure 19.3).

---

1 This is a simplification because the measure which is being kept to a minimum is the *square* of the distance between the data points and the line.

FIGURE 19.3   The best-fit line on a scattergram of a high positive correlation ($r = .9555$)

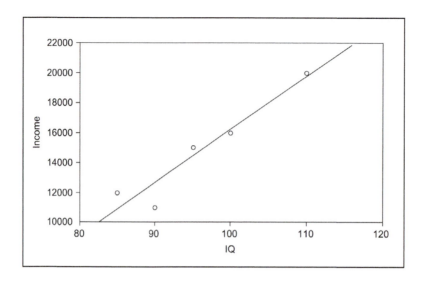

Figure 19.4 shows the scattergram which can be expected from a high negative correlation. Note that in the case of a negative correlation the line runs from the top left-hand corner to the bottom right-hand corner of the graph.

FIGURE 19.4   The scattergram for a high negative correlation ($r = -.877$)

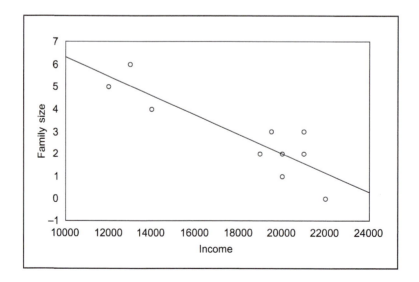

For a case where there is no relationship between two variables, imagine that we have looked at shoe size and income (Figure 19.5). In this example the correlation coefficient is $r = -.041$ (df = 8, $p = .9104$, two-tailed test). Note that although the computer has produced a best-fit line it does not represent the data satisfactorily.

FIGURE 19.5   The scattergram for a low correlation between two variables

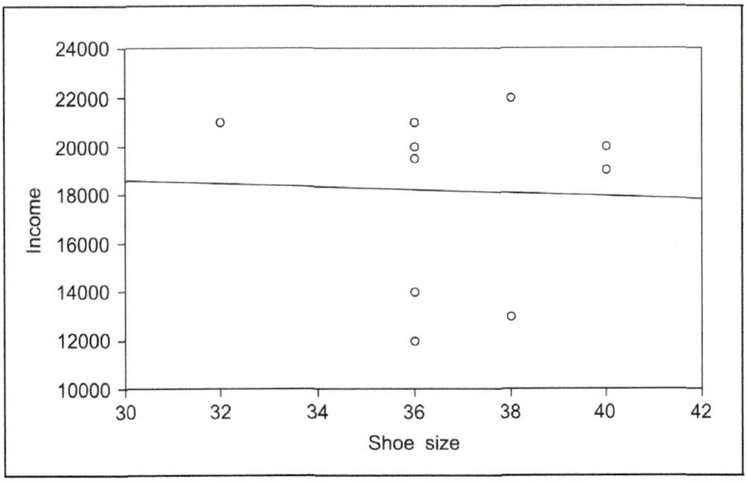

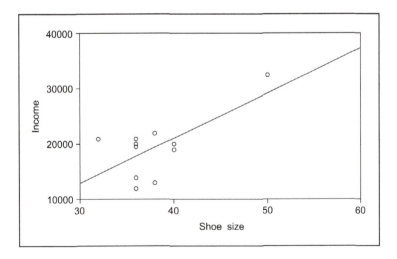

Situations in which a statistically significant r is spurious

Like the mean, *r* is highly affected by outliers. Thus, if a single person with a large shoe size and a large income were added to the previous sample we could get the result shown in Figure 19.6. Here the addition of one person has changed the correlation from a very low negative one to a large, statistically significant positive one ($r = .666$, df = 9, $p = .0252$, two-tailed test).

FIGURE 19.6   A scattergram which includes one outlier

Another situation which could produce a significant correlation would be if the sample included an unreasonably large range on one or both dimensions: for example, if we included children in the income by shoe size study. Here the correlation has become large, positive and significant ($r = .912$, df = 13, $p < .0001$, two-tailed test). The scattergram shows that we have really included samples from two populations, neither of which, on its own, would show the correlation (Figure 19.7).

FIGURE 19.7   A scattergram produced when samples from two populations are combined

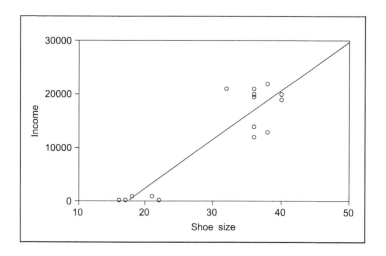

Situations in which *r* fails to detect a relationship

A non-linear relationship

In the example of family size and income we might have found the pattern shown in Figure 19.8.

FIGURE 19.8   The scattergram of a non-linear relationship

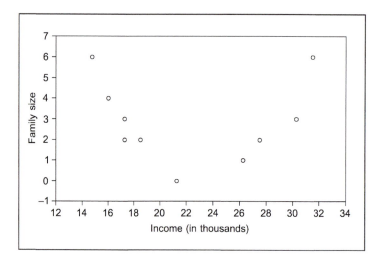

Here the correlation is given as $r = -.0243$ (df = 8, $p = .947$, two-tailed test). Note that the scattergram forms a U-shaped curve. Below an income of around £22 000 there is a negative relationship between family size and income. Above around £26 000 there is a positive relationship. There clearly is a relationship but it cannot be represented by a straight line. Pearson's *r* is a measure of linear, or straight line, relationships. The analysis of non-linear relationships is beyond the scope of this book. This non-linear form of relationship is described as *polynomial*. Under certain circumstances it is possible to transform one or both of the variables in a non-linear relationship so that the relationship becomes linear and then Pearson's *r* can be applied to the data. This is discussed in Appendix V.

Too restricted a range

The range of scores of one or both variables can be restricted in at least two ways. The first is a consequence of the very nature of correlation. Both variables have to have some variability, otherwise it is not possible to have a correlation.

If, in the IQ and income example, everyone in the sample had had an IQ of 100, then the correlation would be $r = 0$, because it makes no sense to ask whether income varies with IQ if IQ does not vary. (Recall the equation for r: as the covariance of IQ and income will be 0, so r must be 0.)

A second problem can be where only part of the range has been sampled. For example, if the incomes of only those with IQs in the 120–150 range were sampled there might be no relationship between income and IQ, whereas across the range 85–115 there might very well be a relationship.

To reiterate, when calculating the correlation between two variables, always create and view a scattergram of the variables to see whether the relationship is linear and not affected by outliers or separate clusters of scores. Also always think about the range you have sampled of each variable to check whether you have artificially restricted them and so hidden a possible relationship or extended the ranges too widely so that a relationship is artificially created.

Effect size (ES) and correlation

There is a useful measure of effect size (ES) in correlation which can be derived simply from the correlation coefficient.

$$ES = r^2 \times 100$$

Thus, in the case of IQ and income:

$$\begin{aligned} ES &= (.9555)^2 \times 100 \\ &= 91.298 \end{aligned}$$

The ES is a measure of the amount of the variance in one variable that can be explained by the variance in the other. In the example, we can therefore say that 91.298% of the variance in income can be explained by the variance in IQ. In other words, less than 9% of the variance in income is not explicable in terms of the variance in IQ.

Cohen (1988) prefers to use r itself as a measure of ES and I will keep to his convention for the power tables for r. Cohen judges that $r = .1$ constitutes a small ES, $r = .3$ is a medium ES and $r = .5$ is a large ES in psychological research. Converting these to percentage variance accounted for (by multiplying r^2 by 100) we have 1% is a small ES, 9% is a medium ES and 25% is a large ES.

Power and correlation

Appendix XVIII gives the power tables for r. Table 19.3 reproduces part of those tables. The extract shows the power which is achieved for a given effect and sample size. Thus, if we wished to achieve

TABLE 19.3 An extract from the power tables for r, when $\alpha = 0.05$ for a one-tailed test (* denotes that power is greater than 0.995)

	effect size (r)										
n	0.1	0.2	0.3	0.4	0.5	0.6	0.7	0.8	0.9	0.95	0.99
20	0.10	0.20	0.35	0.54	0.74	0.89	0.98	*	*	*	*
25	0.12	0.24	0.42	0.64	0.83	0.95	0.99	*	*	*	*
60	0.19	0.45	0.76	0.94	0.99	*	*	*	*	*	*
70	0.20	0.51	0.81	0.97	*	*	*	*	*	*	*
600	0.79	*	*	*	*	*	*	*	*	*	*
700	0.84	*	*	*	*	*	*	*	*	*	*

power of .8 at α = .05 with a directional hypothesis, we would need between 600 and 700 participants to detect a small ES, between 60 and 70 participants to detect a medium ES and between 20 and 25 to detect a large ES.

The assumptions of Pearson's r

The statistic which has been introduced thus far in this chapter is parametric and so, when used for inferential statistics, it makes certain assumptions about the level of measurement obtained and the nature of the populations from which the sample has come. The first assumption is that the scores in one variable will be independent, that is, they will not be influenced by other scores in that variable. The next assumption is that both variables are of interval or ratio level of measurement, or ordinal with the understanding that it is measuring an underlying more continuous variable (see Chapters 8 and 14). The third assumption is that the variables will be bivariately normal in the population. This means that not only will each variable be normally distributed in the population but also, for each value of one of the variables, the other variable will be normally distributed in the population; this is also sometimes referred to as *conditionally normal*. Figure 19.9 shows a bivariate normal distribution. In this graph the height tells us the proportion of people who had a particular combination of scores on two variables. If we were able to look down on the graph it would look like a scattergram with a net superimposed on it and we would see an oval shape characteristic of a correlation of r = .5. If we were able to take a vertical slice through the graph we would see a normal distribution.

FIGURE 19.9   A 3-D frequency plot showing a bivariate normal distribution when the correlation between the two variables is *r* = .5

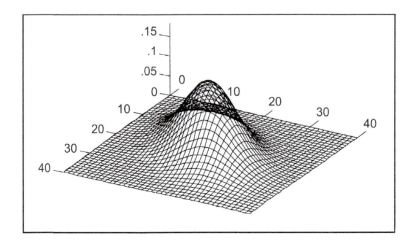

Once again we have the problem that we are usually dealing with samples and not populations and so we are unlikely to know what the population distributions are like. In fact, few researchers check for bivariate normal distribution for simple correlation, although it becomes important when using the multivariate statistics described in Chapter 25. Nonetheless, it is worth checking the distribution of each variable on its own. If one of the distributions is skewed or if the two distributions are skewed in opposite directions, this can limit the size of the correlation coefficient.

When the assumptions of Pearson's r are not fulfilled there are a number of alternative correlation coefficients which can be calculated. In addition, bootstrapping, which is dealt with in Chapter 23, may also be an option.

Point-biserial correlation

Sometimes one variable will be measured on a dichotomous scale: for example, male and female. There is a variant of Pearson's r, called the point-biserial correlation, which can be used in this situation. For example, researchers might be interested in the relationship, among smokers, between gender and number of cigarettes smoked. However, instead of comparing average number of cigarettes smoked by male and female smokers to see whether there is a difference (using between-subjects t-test or Mann–Whitney U test), they could look at the correlation between gender and smoking. The usual way to code the dichotomous variable is to call one level 0 and the other level 1. Which way round does not matter, except that it will affect whether the correlation is positive or negative. In Table 19.4 I have recoded the males as 0 and the females as 1. Figure 19.10 shows the scattergram for the recoded data.

The best-fit line crosses the levels of the IV at their means. Accordingly, it meets the males at 20.5 and the females at 13.2.

The correlation coefficient is $r = -.4478$, showing a medium-to-large relationship between gender and smoking. Had females been coded as 0 and males as 1, then the correlation would have been positive.

To find the probability of the point-biserial correlation you use the same method as for testing the probability of r. If the hypothesis had been that there would be a negative relationship between gender and smoking (which means, given the coding of males as 0, that males smoke more than females), then

TABLE 19.4   The number of cigarettes smoked daily by males and females

Gender	Coding	Smoking
Male	0	15
Male	0	15
Male	0	20
Male	0	30
Male	0	35
Male	0	10
Male	0	25
Male	0	20
Male	0	15
Male	0	20
Female	1	5
Female	1	7
Female	1	3
Female	1	20
Female	1	15
Female	1	20
Female	1	7
Female	1	10
Female	1	20
Female	1	25

FIGURE 19.10   The best-fit line for the relationship between gender and cigarette smoking (among smokers)

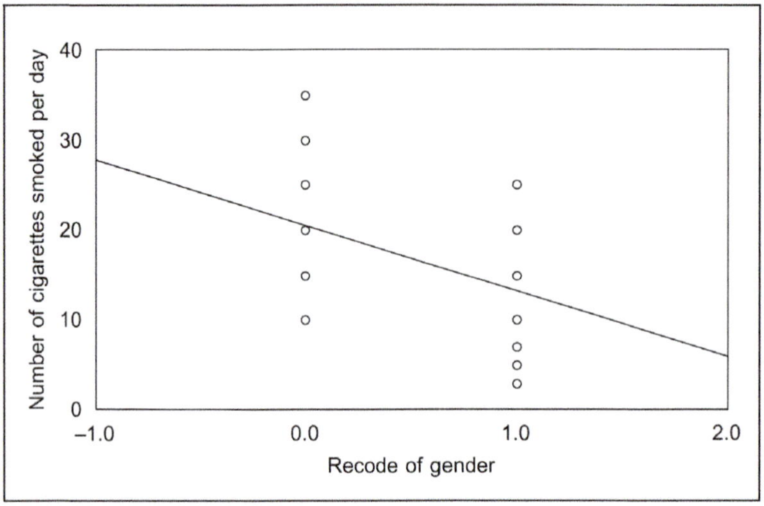

we can perform a one-tailed test. Thus with $r = -.4478$ and df $= 18$, the probability is $p = .0239$, one-tailed test.

The discussion of the point-biserial correlation shows that the distinction between tests which are designed to look for differences between groups and those which look for relationships between variables is a little artificial. I will return to this theme in the next chapter.

Biserial correlation

In the previous example, gender is genuinely dichotomous. However, sometimes the dichotomy has been imposed on a variable which really is not dichotomous: for example, if we put people into two groups – old and young. In such cases there is a variant of the point-biserial correlation called the biserial correlation. This method is rarely used, partly because it has certain problems entailed in its calculation and in its use when the distributions are not normal, and so interested readers are referred to Howell (1997); in his later editions (e.g. Howell, 2002), he decided not to include it. As an alternative, in such a situation it would be permissible to use phi or Cramér's phi, which are described later in this chapter, under *correlation and nominal data*. However, before producing such dichotomies from data see the section cautioning against the practice in the next chapter.

Non-parametric correlation

At least ordinal data

When the data are at least at the ordinal level of measurement we can use one of two measures of correlation: Spearman's rho (ρ) – sometimes known as the Spearman rank-order correlation coefficient – and Kendall's tau (τ) – sometimes known as the Kendall rank-order correlation coefficient. Spearman's rho has become more popular in statistical packages. I think this is partly due to the fact that before computers it was the easier to calculate. However, it has the drawback that it cannot be used simply for calculating *partial correlations*, whereas Kendall's tau can. Partial correlation, which is explained more fully later in the chapter, allows the possible effects of a third variable to be removed from the relationship between two variables.

As an example of non-parametric correlation, imagine that researchers wished to investigate the relationship between the length of time students have studied psychology and the degree to which they believe that psychology is a science. Eleven psychology students were asked how long they had studied psychology and were asked to rate, on a 5-point scale, ranging from 1 = *not at all* to 5 = *definitely a science*, their beliefs about whether psychology is a science. Table 19.5 shows the data from the study.

TABLE 19.5 The length of time students have studied psychology and their opinion of whether it is a science

Participant	Years studied psychology	Rating of psychology as a science
1	1	1
2	2	1
3	3	2
4	4	3
5	5	4
6	1	3
7	2	3
8	3	2
9	4	5
10	5	5
11	6	5

Both Spearman's rho and Kendall's tau can be calculated by converting the scores within a variable to ranks, though this conversion does not need to be used with Kendall's tau. As usual in such tests, scores which have the same value (ties) are given the mean rank. Thus, as two participants had been studying psychology for one year, they occupy the first two ranks and are each given the mean of those ranks: $\dfrac{1+2}{2}=1.5$. (Table 19.6) See the description of the Wilcoxon signed rank test for matched pairs in Appendix VI for a fuller explanation of ranking data.

TABLE 19.6 The years spent studying psychology and the opinion of whether psychology is a science plus rankings

Participant	Years spent studying psychology	Rating of psychology	Rank of years	Rank of rating
1	1	1	1.5	1.5
2	2	1	3.5	1.5
3	3	2	5.5	3.5
4	4	3	7.5	6
5	5	4	9.5	8
6	1	3	1.5	6
7	2	3	3.5	6
8	3	2	5.5	3.5
9	4	5	7.5	10
10	5	5	9.5	10
11	6	5	11	10

Spearman's rho

The calculation of Spearman's rho produces the same result as would be found if the scores in each variable were converted to ranks for that variable and Pearson's *r* was calculated. However, there is a version of rho which assumes that no scores are the same in a given variable and this is a value commonly given by computers. A worked example is given in Appendix X.

Using the simplified equation, rho = .77.

Tied observations

When there are no ties in the data, the two versions of Spearman's rho produce the same result. However, when two or more scores are the same in a given variable, the simplified equation is incorrect and then there is a version of rho which corrects for these 'ties', and produces the same result as would be obtained by applying Pearson's *r* procedure to the ranks. In the present example there is more than one student in each of the first 5 years and more than one person gave ratings of 1, 2, 3 or 5. Rho corrected for ties produces rho = .762, which is the version which SPSS calculates. The version of rho which corrects for ties is the one you should report.

The probability of Spearman's rho

Unlike for other non-parametric tests, SPSS does not offer the ability to find exact probabilities (at least this is true up to Version 25). With a sample of 100 or fewer participants, use the table of probabilities given in Appendix XVII. When the sample is over 100 there is an equation which converts rho to a *t*-value and allows you to use *t*-tables to check the probability.

Alternatively, when the sample size is greater than 100, there is a *z*-approximation which can be used to calculate the probability of rho, which, although less accurate than the conversion of rho to *t*, could be used if you have access to more finely detailed *z*-tables. (Appendix X gives the equations to convert rho to *t* and *z*.) The probability of this result, as a one-tailed test, found from Table A17.18, is $.0025 < p < .005$. The result should be reported as: *There was a significant positive correlation between the length of time students had spent studying psychology and their opinion that it is a science (rho = .762; .0025 < p < .005, one-tailed test, N = 11)*. If the sample size had been sufficiently large to justify using a *t*-test or a *z*-test to find the probability, then report the *t* or *z* value as well.

Kendall's tau

Kendall's tau differs from Spearman's rho. It places the original scores (or ranks) for one variable in numerical order and examines the order which has been created for the other variable; see Table 19.7.

Thus, if the two variables were perfectly positively related, then the order of the scores in the second variable should be from the lowest to the highest rating, and none would be out of order. In the preceding example, if we take the rating of psychology as a science we see that participant 6 had only been studying psychology for a year and yet gave it a rating of 3, while participants 2, 3 and 8 had been studying for longer but gave it a lower rating. Kendall's tau involves calculating how many scores are out of order relative to each person. If there are no scores out of order, tau = 1. If all the possible ranks are out of order, then tau = −1, which is the same pattern as given by other correlation coefficients; a perfect positive correlation is +1 and a perfect inverse correlation is −1.

If we reanalyse the data from the previous example using Kendall's tau, we get the result that tau = .564.

TABLE 19.7   The time spent studying psychology and the ratings of psychology, sorted in the numerical order of time spent studying psychology

Participant	Years spent studying psychology	Rating of psychology
6	1	3
1	1	1
2	2	1
7	2	3
3	3	2
8	3	2
9	4	5
4	4	3
10	5	5
5	5	4
11	6	5

Tied observations

As with Spearman's rho there is an adjustment for ties, which in this case gives tau = .639: the one provided by SPSS, which shows it as *Kendall's tau-b*. See Appendix X for a worked example.

The probability of tau

Again SPSS does not offer exact probabilities for this test. As with Spearman's rho there exists an approximation to the normal distribution for Kendall's tau. However, Kendall's tau has the advantage that this approximation is accurate for smaller sample sizes. Thus, if the sample is 10 or fewer, then use the appropriate table in Appendix XVII. Above this sample size use the z-approximation shown in Appendix X. The probability in the present example can be calculated via the z-test, as the sample size is over 10. This gives a z-value (adjusted for ties) of $z = 2.738$ with a one-tailed probability of $p = .0031$. The result should be reported using the same format as for Spearman's rho.

The relative merits of rho and tau

As has been explained, the two coefficients are based on different calculations, and will often yield different values. Therefore it makes no sense to compare the values derived from the two tests to see whether two relationships differ. With the advent of computers, the fact that Spearman's rho is easier to calculate, particularly for larger samples, is no longer a reason for preferring it. I prefer Kendall's tau because it has a straightforward means for finding a partial correlation. An additional reason for preferring Kendall's tau is, as Howell (2013) points out, that it provides a better estimation of the value which would have been obtained for the population from which the sample came than does Spearman's rho.

Power and ordinal measures of correlation

The power levels of tau and rho are given in terms of their power efficiency relative to their parametric equivalent, Pearson's r. In order to achieve the same level of power when using Spearman's rho or Kendall's tau, find the sample size necessary for the required effect size and power for Pearson's r and multiply the sample size by 1.1. For example, if we were seeking a medium effect size ($r = .3$), with a one-tailed test, an alpha-level of .05 and we wished to have power of .8, then we would need 68 participants. Therefore, if we were using Spearman's rho or Kendall's tau, then we would need $68 \times 1.1 = 74.8$ or 75 participants to achieve the same level of power.

Correlation and nominal data

In Chapter 15 the proportion of males and females in a sample who were smokers was compared with the proportion who were non-smokers, using a χ^2 test for contingency tables. We can reanalyse the data to ask whether there is a relationship between gender and smoking status (Table 19.8). The χ^2 value for this contingency table was 0.741.

TABLE 19.8   The number of smokers and non-smokers in a sample of males and females

Observed frequency table

	Male	Female	Totals
Smoker	17	21	38
Non-smoker	27	23	50
Totals	44	44	88

There are a number of measures of correlation which can be used with categorical data, all of which are based on χ^2: the Pearson's coefficient of contingency (C) also referred to as the contingency coefficient or coefficient of contingency (see Chapter 14), phi (φ) and Cramér's phi (φ_c).

$$phi = \sqrt{\frac{\chi^2}{N}}$$

Phi is limited to analysing 2 × 2 tables but there is an alternative version which is not – Cramér's phi (shown as Cramér's V in SPSS):

$$Cramér's\ phi = \sqrt{\frac{\chi^2}{N \times (k-1)}}$$

where k is the number of rows or the number of columns in the contingency table, whichever is smaller. With a 2 × 2 table Cramér's phi becomes the same as phi. In addition, with a 2 × 2 table, both give the same result as would Pearson's r, with each dichotomy being recoded into zeroes and ones.

In the present case:

$$contingency\ coefficient = \sqrt{\frac{0.741}{0.741 + 88}}$$
$$= \sqrt{0.00835}$$
$$= .091$$

$$phi = \sqrt{\frac{0.741}{88}}$$
$$= \sqrt{0.00842}$$
$$= .092$$

Finding the probability of correlations based on categorical data

As each of the measures described utilises χ^2 there is no need to find a separate source for the probability; we can use the probability for the χ^2 value.

Effect size (ES) and χ^2 revisited

In Chapter 15 the ES (w) for χ^2 was introduced. If you compare the equation for w and that for phi you will see that they are the same. Thus, for a 2 × 2 χ^2 the ES measure is the same as the recommended correlation measure for the same data. In addition, note that phi gives the same result as a product moment correlation (r) conducted on the same data and that the recommended values for small, medium and large ES for w are the same (0.1, 0.3 and 0.5, respectively) as those recommended for r. This equation only works when the number of rows or columns is 2. Beyond that the equation could produce a w greater than 1. Cramér's phi produces a more accurate estimate of w when the number of rows or columns is greater than 2; and when the number of rows or columns is 2, then Cramér's phi produces the same result as the one given for w. Alternatively, the contingency coefficient could be used for larger tables.

Summary of correlation methods

This summary is given in Table 19.9.

TABLE 19.9   A summary of the different forms of correlation introduced in this chapter

Coefficient	Symbol	When appropriate
Pearson's product moment	r	both variables at least ordinal
Point-biserial	r_{pb}	one variable at least ordinal, the other a true dichotomy
Biserial	r_b	one variable at least ordinal, the other an artificial dichotomy
Spearman's rho	ρ	both variables at least ordinal but not fulfilling criteria for Pearson's r (cannot be used, simply, for partial correlation)
Kendall's tau	τ	both variables at least ordinal but not fulfilling criteria for Pearson's r (can be used for partial correlation)
Contingency coefficient	C	both variables nominal (provides restricted range of values)
phi	φ	both variables nominal but with only 2 levels each
Cramer's phi	φ_c	both variables nominal

Other uses of correlation

This section shows how the possible influences of a third variable can be removed from the relationship between two variables, how two correlation coefficients can be compared, how a sample's correlation coefficient can be compared with a population's actual or hypothesised correlation coefficient and how confidence intervals can be obtained from r. It is followed by a section on how correlation and related measures can be used to check forms of consistency such as ratings made by judges and the reliability and validity of tests.

Partial and semi-partial correlation

Sometimes, as in the consumption of ice cream and drownings example, two variables may correlate but this is due to some third variable which correlates with both of the original variables. In such cases, if we know how each pair of variables correlate we can remove the effect of the third variable: we can *partial out* that effect using partial or semi-partial correlation.

Partial correlation with Pearson's *r*

In a study researchers wished to see whether mathematical ability and ability at English correlate among children but they were aware that age is likely to correlate with each of them and may explain any relationship they have. They gave a sample of 10 children, aged 12–14 years, tests of maths and English and they noted each child's age.

When a correlation coefficient has been calculated for every possible combination of pairs from a set of variables, the results are usually represented in what is called a *correlation matrix*. Table 19.10 gives the correlation matrix for the correlations between maths ability, English ability and age.

TABLE 19.10   The correlation matrix of mathematical ability, English ability and age

	Maths	English	Age
Maths	1		
English	.888	1	
Age	.748	.862	1

The figures in the correlation matrix are the correlation coefficients between pairs of variables. The correlation for a given pair of variables is given at the point where the column labelled with one variable's name meets the row which is labelled with the other variable's name. The first column shows correlations with maths and the second row shows correlations with English. This tells us that the correlation between maths and English abilities is $r = .888$, which with df $= 8$ is statistically significant at $p < .0005$ (one-tailed test).

Notice that the diagonal from the top left-hand to the bottom right-hand of the matrix contains the number 1 in each cell. This is because this is the correlation of each variable with itself. Notice also that the top right-hand part of the matrix is empty. This is because all the cells in this part of the matrix would represent correlations which are already shown in the matrix. Some computer programs give the full matrix, but the present format makes it easier to read.

The matrix tells us that there is a large correlation between ability at maths and English but there is also a large correlation between each of the abilities and age. The equation for calculating the correlation coefficient of maths and English ability with the effect of age partialled out is:

$$r_{me.a} = \frac{r_{me} - r_{ma} \times r_{ea}}{\sqrt{[1 - (r_{ma})^2] \times [1 - (r_{ea})^2]}}$$

where $r_{me.a}$ is the correlation between maths and English ability, with age partialled out, r_{me} is the correlation between maths and English ability, r_{ma} is the correlation between maths ability and age and r_{ea} is the correlation between English ability and age. Therefore:

$$r_{me.a} = \frac{.888 - .748 \times .862}{\sqrt{[1 - (.748)^2] \times [1 - (.862)^2]}}$$
$$= .723$$

To assess the statistical significance of a partial correlation read the standard *r*-tables but with df of three fewer than the sample size (when, as in this case, one variable has been partialled out). From the *r*-tables we learn that the correlation between mathematical and English abilities with age partialled out is still statistically significant ($.01 < p < .025$, df = 7, one-tailed test).

One way to view the original and the partial correlations between mathematical and English abilities is to note that the former suggests that the variance in English ability accounts for $(.888)^2 \times 100 = 78.85\%$ of the variance in mathematical ability. However, the variance in age accounts for $(.748)^2 \times 100 = 55.95\%$ of the variance in mathematics and $(.862)^2 \times 100 = 74.30\%$ of the variance in English ability. Partial correlation takes out the part of the variance in English ability which is accountable for in terms of the variance in age and the part of the variance in maths ability which can be accounted for by age, and looks at the amount of shared variance which is left, that is $(.723)^2 \times 100 = 52.27\%$.

It is possible to partial out the effects of more than one variable on a relationship. For example, we could partial out the effect of SES as well as age. This is dealt with in Appendix X. One way of referring to correlations uses the term *order* to show how many variables have been partialled out. Thus, a correlation with one variable partialled out would be called a first order correlation. This usage has led some writers to describe a bivariate correlation where no variables have been partialled out as a *zero-order* correlation.

Semi-partial correlation with Pearson's *r*

Sometimes, rather than look at the relationship between two variables with the effect of a third variable on each partialled out, researchers wish only to partial the effect of the third variable on one of them; this is termed *semi-partial correlation* (sometimes referred to as *part correlation*). I have never used semi-partial correlation in this context, but it becomes useful as part of multiple regression, as will be shown in the next chapter.

If researchers were particularly interested in finding how well English ability predicts mathematics ability when the degree to which age predicts English ability has been removed, then they can use semi-partial correlation, via the following equation:

$$r_{m(e.a)} = \frac{r_{me} - r_{ma} \times r_{ea}}{\sqrt{(1 - r_{ea}^2)}}$$

where $r_{m(e.a)}$ is the semi-partial correlation between maths and English ability with the relationship between English ability and age removed, r_{me} is the correlation between maths and English ability, r_{ma} is the correlation between maths ability and age and r_{ea} is the correlation between English ability and age.

In the example:

$$r_{m(e.a)} = \frac{.888 - .748 \times .862}{\sqrt{[1 - (.862)^2]}}$$

$$= .4798$$

Expressed as percentage of variance, $(.4798)^2 \times 100 = 23.02\%$, we can interpret this semi-partial correlation as showing that English ability explains an additional 23.02% of the variance in mathematical ability over and above the variance in mathematical ability which is explained by age.

Partial correlation using Kendall's tau

The equation for partial correlation using Kendall's tau is basically the same as that for partial correlation with Pearson's *r*. If the data for age, ability at mathematics and ability at English are re-analysed using Kendall's tau, we find that maths and English ability correlate, tau = .786. However, age correlates with maths (tau = .593) and English (tau = .723). Using the following equation, the effect of age can be partialled out of the relationship between maths and English:

$$\text{tau}_{me.a} = \frac{\tau_{me} - \tau_{ma} \times \tau_{ea}}{\sqrt{[1 - (\tau_{ma})^2] \times [1 - (\tau_{ea})^2]}}$$

where $\text{tau}_{me.a}$ is the correlation between maths and English with age partialled out, τ_{me} is the correlation between maths and English, τ_{ea} is the correlation between English and age and τ_{ma} is the correlation between maths and age.

Thus,

$$\text{tau}_{me.a} = \frac{.786 - .593 \times .723}{\sqrt{[1 - (.593)^2] \times [1 - (.723)^2]}}$$

$$= \frac{.357}{\sqrt{.309}}$$

$$= .6422$$

The probability of the partial correlation using Kendall's tau

To find the probability of Kendall's tau as a partial correlation use Table A17.20 in Appendix XVII. This shows that, with a sample size of 10, a tau of .6422 has a one-tailed probability of $.001 < p < .005$.

The difference between two correlations

Sometimes researchers want to compare two correlation coefficients to see whether they are significantly different. It is not sufficient to compare the significance levels of the two correlations and note that one is more statistically significant than the other. It is necessary to conduct a statistical test which compares the two correlations. As with other forms of analysis, different tests are used when the two correlations are from different groups of participants (independent groups), from the same or related groups of participants (non-independent groups) or from a sample and a population. I will discuss the tests first before dealing with effect sizes and power.

Comparing correlations from two independent groups

Researchers predicted that adults would have a more accurate idea of their memory ability (their meta-memory) than children would have. They devised a measure of meta-memory which they gave to a group of 30 adults and a group of 30 children. They also tested the actual memories of both groups.

They obtained the following results: the correlation for children's meta-memory and actual memory was $r = .5$; the correlation for adults' meta-memory and actual memory was $r = .8$. Before the equation for the test can be introduced it is necessary to deal with a complication.

As we are testing the difference between two correlation coefficients, rather than a correlation coefficient against the Null Hypothesis that the correlation is zero, the distribution can be skewed. Fisher devised a way of transforming r into r', which is more symmetrically distributed and allows the use of a z-test to compare the correlations. (Confusingly, this transformation is sometimes described as Fisher's Z_r. However, r' is preferable to prevent confusion with z-tests.)

Appendix XIX provides the equivalent r' for a range of r-values and the equation devised by Fisher for those wanting a more exact transformation when the r-value is not tabled.

The equation for comparing two independent correlation coefficients is:

$$z = \frac{r'_1 - r'_2}{\sqrt{\dfrac{1}{n_1 - 3} + \dfrac{1}{n_2 - 3}}}$$

where r'_1 is the Fisher's transformation of one correlation coefficient, r'_2 is the Fisher's transformation of the other correlation coefficient, n_1 is the sample size of one group and n_2 is the sample size of the other group.

Looking up the r to r' conversion tables shows that $r = .8$ becomes $r' = 1.099$ and $r = .5$ becomes $r' = 0.549$. Therefore, the z-test for comparison between the two correlation coefficients is:

$$z = \frac{1.099 - 0.549}{\sqrt{\dfrac{1}{30 - 3} + \dfrac{1}{30 - 3}}}$$
$$= 2.02$$

Looking up the one-tailed probability of this value in the z-tables (Appendix XVII), we find that $p = .0217$. The researchers therefore conclude that adults have more accurate meta-memories than children.

Comparing correlations from non-independent groups

The equations for the difference between non-independent correlation coefficients are different from the last one and are of such complexity that I have included their explanation in Appendix X.

Comparing a sample correlation with a population correlation (when H_0 is not $\rho = 0$)

As was noted earlier, r has an equivalent parameter for the population: ρ (not to be confused with Spearman's rho). Researchers sometimes wish to compare the correlation coefficient from a given study with that known, or assumed, to exist for a population. For example, researchers may know, from previous research, that the correlation between extroversion scores of monozygotic (identical) twins reared together is $r = .7$. They have a sample of 20 monozygotic twins reared apart whose extroversion scores correlate $r = .4$ and they want to see whether those reared apart have a significantly lower correlation than those reared together.

This form of comparison is similar to the one for two independent correlations and uses the equation:

$$z = \frac{r' - \rho'}{\sqrt{\dfrac{1}{n - 3}}}$$

where r' is the Fisher's transformation of the sample's correlation coefficient, ρ' is the Fisher's transformation of the population's correlation coefficient and n is the size of the sample (in this case, the number of pairs of twins).

A ρ of .7 converts to $\rho' = 0.867$ and an r of .4 converts to $r' = 0.424$. Therefore,

$$z = \frac{0.424 - 0.867}{\sqrt{\dfrac{1}{17}}}$$
$$= -1.83$$

The researchers hypothesised that the twins reared separately had a lower correlation (prior, of course, to collecting the data) and so were justified in using the one-tailed probabilities in the z-tables; remember to ignore the negative sign when reading the tables. The likelihood of this result (or one more extreme) having occurred if the monozygotic twins came from a population in which ρ had equalled .7 is given as $p = .0336$. Therefore, the researchers were justified in rejecting the Null Hypothesis that the correlations did not differ and in concluding that monozygotic twins reared apart show less similarity in extroversion score than do monozygotic twins who are reared together.

Effect size and power for the difference between two correlations

Cohen (1988) uses the effect size q:

$$q = r'_1 - r'_2$$

where r'_1 and r'_2 are the Fisher's transformations of the correlation coefficients of the two groups (described previously). Cohen (1988) saw $q = 0.1$ as a small ES, $q = 0.3$ as a medium ES and $q = 0.5$ as a large ES.

Power when the sample sizes are equal

According to Table A18.10, in order to have power of .8, for a medium ES of $q = 0.3$, with a one-tailed test and $\alpha = .05$, 140 people in each group would be required.

Power when the sample sizes are not equal

As with many other tests, the power of the test comparing two correlation coefficients is reduced if the sample sizes in the two groups are not the same and the loss of power is greater, the greater the disparity in the sample sizes. To illustrate the point, if, instead of the groups having equal samples of 140 each, one had 200 and the other 80, then the power of the test would only be the equivalent to that of a balanced design with a total sample of just under 228. Appendix XVIII shows how to read the power tables for q when the sample sizes are not equal.

Power when a sample correlation is compared with a population correlation (when H_0 is not $\rho = 0$)

When a sample correlation is compared with one from a population, then the test for the same ES is more powerful. While the measure of ES is the same, Cohen has adjusted what he considers to be small, medium and large ES for this test to be $q = 0.14, 0.42$ and 0.71. I have created power tables in Appendix XVIII for this version of the test and provided entries for each of these ES. If researchers were seeking a medium ES, then the sample size necessary to achieve power of .8 for a one-tailed test with $\alpha = .05$ would be between 35 and 40 (interpolation shows that the sample would need to be 38).

Confidence intervals and correlation

Correlation coefficients have a dual function. On the one hand, they are used as inferential statistics; researchers can test the likelihood of a correlation coefficient having arisen by chance. On the other hand, they are descriptive statistics describing the relationship between two variables. As with other sample descriptive statistics it is possible to use them to estimate the confidence interval for the equivalent parameter: the correlation within the population (ρ).

Appendix X gives a worked example of the calculation of the confidence interval for the population. Recall that the correlation between meta-memory and actual memory was found to be .8 with a sample of 30 adults. At the 95% level of confidence, ρ was found to lie within the interval .62 and .90. As the confidence interval does not contain zero this provides evidence that there is a positive correlation between meta-memory and actual memory in adults.

Measures of agreement between more than two people

Sometimes researchers wish to get independent judges to rate objects (or targets) in order to provide a scale which is not biased by their own views. For example, if researchers wished to look at the link between the physical attractiveness of a person and whether others would show altruistic behaviour towards that person, then they would need a measure of physical attractiveness. To avoid using their own judgements they could present the materials they wished to use in their study (e.g. photographs) to judges and ask them to rank the people in the photographs according to their physical attractiveness. Before they could use the judgements as the basis of their scale, it would be important to know how well the judges agreed. For, if there were lack of agreement, this would suggest that the measure was unreliable. Using *Kendall's coefficient of concordance* they can assess the degree of agreement among their judges.

Kendall's coefficient of concordance

This test yields a statistic W, which is a measure of how much a set of judges agree when asked to put a set of objects in rank order. The data are shown in Table 19.11. The equation for calculating W is given in Appendix X along with the workings for this example.

TABLE 19.11   The attractiveness rankings given by judges for five photographs

	Photograph				
Judge	A	B	C	D	E
One	1	2	3	4	5
Two	2	1	4	3	5
Three	3	2	1	5	4
Four	1	3	2	4	5

W was found to be .6875. SPSS shows the exact probability for this result as $p = .01$ and thus we can conclude that there is a significant degree of agreement among the judges about the attractiveness of the people represented in the photographs. The mean ratings for each photograph could then be used to provide the order of attractiveness of the five photographs. If you don't have access to exact probabilities, then Table A17.21 in Appendix XVII provides significance levels for W when the number of items to be rated is between three and seven. If the number of items is greater than seven, then Table A17.21 shows a chi-squared approximation which can be used to find the probability.

W cannot have negative values. It ranges between 0, which would be no agreement between the judges, and +1, which would denote perfect agreement between them.

Kendall's coefficient of concordance also allows for a judge to give two objects the same rank. In such a case, there is a modified equation for calculating W which adjusts for such ties. Appendix X provides the equation and a worked example. SPSS uses the version which corrects for ties; when there are no ties the two versions give the same answer.

The use of correlation to evaluate reliability and validity of measures

Reliability

A reliable measure was defined in Chapter 2 as a measure which will produce a consistent score from one occasion to another. The degree of consistency can be measured using a reliability coefficient.

Two forms of reliability will be dealt with. The first is what I will call *test* reliability, the reliability of a measure when taken from a number of people, such as a measure of depression or a test of ability. The second, *interrater* reliability, is the degree of agreement between two or more judges who are using a measure: for example, two researchers rating the type of interaction which is occurring between a mother and her child.

Test reliability

If a measure is not 100% reliable, then the score a person achieves on a given occasion can be seen as being made up of the true score (which they would have achieved if the test had been 100% reliable) and the error (the difference between the true score and the observed score). Formally, the reliability coefficient is the variance in true scores divided by the variance in measured scores. In other words, it tells us what proportion the variance of the true scores is of the variance in the measured scores. Therefore, the closer the proportion is to 1 the more reliable the measure is. We cannot know what a person's true score is. However, we can produce an estimate of the reliability coefficient from the data we have collected (see McDonald, 1999 or Pedhazur & Schmelkin, 1991 for more details).

There are three forms of test reliability which researchers might want to assess, depending on the use to be made of a measure: test–retest, alternative (or parallel or equivalent) form and internal consistency.

Test–retest reliability

If a test is designed to measure something which is considered to be relatively fixed, as some people believe IQ to be, then they will want a measure which will produce the same results from one occasion to the next. To check this, the designers of a test will give the test to a group of people on two occasions; Kline (2000) recommends that at least 100 people are tested and that the gap should be at least 3 months between occasions. Pearson's r can be used to correlate the results for the two occasions; see also intraclass correlation on page 280. Kline (2000) sees $r = .8$ as a minimum below which we would not want to go.

Alternative form reliability

There will be occasions when to give the same test on two occasions will not be practical, as taking the test once will affect how an individual performs on the test a second time. Under such circumstances, researchers prepare two versions of the test. Researchers may wish to measure a change over time: for example, in an ability before and after training. They will want to be sure that any differences in performance between the two occasions are not due to inherent differences in the two forms of the test, which could introduce the threat to internal validity known as *instrumentation*. Accordingly, when trying to establish the reliability of the two versions of the test, they will correlate the performance of their participants on the two versions of the test, which can be taken in the same session; once again Pearson's r can be used. (Kline, 2000, says that, ideally, r would be at least .9 but that this is achieved by few tests.)

Internal consistency reliability

In the absence of two forms of the test, it is possible to check that the test has items which are consistent with each other. There are a number of measures of internal consistency; the simplest is to correlate performance on two halves of the test – split-half reliability.

Split-half reliability

The test can be split into two parts in a number of ways. One would be to correlate the first and second halves. However, as many tests of performance increase the difficulty of items as the test progresses, this would not be ideal. An alternative is to treat all the even-numbered items as one half of the test and the odd-numbered items as the other. Once again Pearson's r could be used for this purpose. One criticism of this is that this measure of reliability is partly affected by the number of items in a test: the more items, the more reliable the test will appear. Spearman and Brown produced an adjustment which allowed for this (see Appendix X for the Spearman–Brown equation).

A further criticism of the simple split-half approach is that the allocation of items into the two halves is somewhat arbitrary. To avoid this a reliability coefficient has been devised which is the equivalent of having conducted all the possible split halves – Cronbach's alpha. Kline (2000) notes that alpha should ideally be around .9 and never be below .7. On the other hand, Pedhazur and Schmelkin (1991) point out that the user of the measure has to determine how reliable the test should be depending on the circumstances of the study. Nonetheless, it is worth pointing out that the .7 level is quoted so frequently that you would have to argue quite strongly to go below this level, particularly if you were hoping to get work based on the measure published. (Appendix X provides the equation for Cronbach's alpha.)

There are a number of criticisms of alpha as a measure of reliability and of how it is interpreted. Cortina (1993) and Grayson (2004) demonstrate that high levels of alpha can be obtained when the items actually contain more than one sub-scale and the sub-scales do not correlate with each other. This is an important reason for conducting a factor analysis on the set of items to see whether there is evidence of sub-scales or only a single scale. Chapter 24 deals with exploratory factor analysis. Cortina makes the point that the larger the number of items, for the same mean correlation between the items within a scale or sub-scale, the higher the value of alpha. Sijtsma (2009) shows that alpha is the lowest estimate of reliability among a set containing alternatives to it. He notes that Guttman's λ_2 will tend to be larger than alpha and closer to the true reliability score. He notes the problem that editors of journals are likely to expect alpha to be reported and suggests that Guttman's λ_2 be reported as well; Guttman's λ_2 is available in SPSS.

When calculating alpha, it is often possible to get a number of additional statistics. Among them are *corrected item-total correlation* and *Cronbach's Alpha if item deleted*. The former is the correlation between an item and the total of the other items. Thus it shows how an item correlates with the total that it hasn't contributed to and therefore how much it is related to a summary of the other items. This is useful as it can indicate that an item is only slightly related to the other items in the scale and therefore may not be a measure of the same underlying concept. Raykov (2007) criticises the use of Cronbach's alpha if item deleted as, although alpha might increase if that item were removed from the scale, the true reliability of the scale could be reduced markedly. Therefore I do not recommend using it.

An alternative to Cronbach's alpha – the Kuder–Richardson 20 (KR 20) – is available when the test involves questions which only have two possible responses – known as binary or dichotomous items – such as yes/no, correct/incorrect or true/false. (Appendix X provides the equation for KR 20.) When the data are dichotomous, analysing the data in SPSS as though for a Cronbach's alpha produces the appropriate answer.

Standard error of measurement

When a measure is not 100% reliable, the score which a person attains on one occasion will not necessarily be the same as on another occasion. *The standard error of measurement*, which is a statistic based on the reliability of the measure, can be used to find a confidence interval around the person's score, such that the range of scores in the interval is likely to contain the person's 'true' score. (Appendix X shows how the confidence interval can be found for a single score.)

Interrater reliability

Often researchers wish to check that a measure can be used consistently by different observers. The simplest checks could be to use the percentage of agreement between the two observers or a correlation coefficient. Percentage agreement fails to take into account the amount of agreement that could have been expected by chance. A large positive correlation coefficient does not necessarily show that two observers are agreeing, absolutely, rather that they are being consistent. Two lecturers could mark a set of essays and not give the same mark to any of them and yet the correlation between their marks could be perfect. This would occur if one lecturer gave each essay 10 marks more than the other lecturer; remember that correlation merely tells you about the direction in which the two measures move relative to each other. A measure which solves both these problems is Cohen's kappa (**K**). (Appendix X gives the equation and a worked example for Cohen's kappa.) It is worth pointing out that Pedhazur and Schmelkin (1991) would say that what I have been describing is more correctly called interrater *agreement*. See their account of what *they* term interrater reliability.

Another measure of interrater reliability is found from versions of the intraclass correlation.

Intraclass correlation

Intraclass correlations (shortened to ICCs but not to be confused with item characteristic curves which share the same acronym but are not dealt with in this book) can be used to examine the amount of similarity between two or more sets of data which are in some way related. That rather general introduction is because the sets of data could be various measures given by, for example, a pair of twins or they could be the ratings given by two or more judges to the pictures drawn by different children. I am going to concentrate on the second case where ICC is being used as a measure of interrater reliability. I am going to use the terms *judge* to refer to the person providing ratings and *target* to refer to the thing being rated.

Shrout and Fleiss (1979) distinguished between six different types of ICC. These have since been added to to produce 10 but many produce the same result and so there are still six distinct possible values (see McGraw & Wong, 1996). In each case the ICC can be seen as the proportion of variability in all the data which can be attributed to the differences between the targets. The higher the value of ICC the lower the contribution to variability of differences between judgements of the same target and so the more reliable the measure/judgements. There are at least three factors which need to be considered: Who supplied the ratings? Do we want the judges to agree absolutely with each other or just be consistent in the order of their judgements? How will the judgements be used?

Who supplied the ratings?

There are three possibilities. The first (situation 1) is that each rating was supplied by a randomly chosen judge, rather than each judge rating each of the targets. The second (situation 2) is that each judge was selected randomly but did rate all the targets. The third (situation 3) is that a set of judges has been chosen non-randomly and each rates all the targets. The ICCs which are calculated from the second and third situations will be the same. However, the conclusions we can draw from them are different. As with other situations where elements are chosen randomly, it is argued that we can generalise from them to the wider population; in this case the wider population of possible judges.

Absolute agreement or consistency?

If I rate five pictures, say, on a scale of how expressive they are (7, 3, 4, 6, 9) and another judge rates them (6, 2, 3, 5, 8) then we do not have absolute agreement. In fact we haven't agreed about any of them. However, because the other judge has supplied ratings which are, in every case, one lower than the rating I gave, we are being 100% consistent in the order we rate the five drawings. Therefore, you have to decide whether you need judges to agree completely or just be consistent in their ratings. Shrout and Fleiss (1979) originally stated that the equation they supplied for situation 2 (described previously) would provide a measure of absolute agreement between judges, while the equation for situation 3 would measure consistency between judges. Now one equation is used for both situations 2 and 3 when the measure is of consistency and another for both situations when the measure is of absolute agreement.

How will the judgements be used?

You could use the ratings supplied by a single judge; perhaps the original judgements were part of a stage in the research where you were checking the reliability of the measure before going on to apply it to the full set of data. Alternatively, you might continue to use multiple judges and take the mean of their judgements and use these as the scores you put into a subsequent analysis.

Table 19.12 summarises the different types of ICC and shows the values from data where the judges are not 100% consistent. I have modified the example I gave previously of two judges rating pictures. Now judge 1 gives ratings (7, 3, 4, 5, 9) and judge 2 gives ratings (6, 2, 3, 7, 8); the judges disagree over the where picture 4 would be if the ratings were put in order of rating. Appendix X shows how the different ICCs and their 95% confidence intervals are calculated.

The ICC from the average of fixed judges, with consistent agreement is the same as Cronbach's alpha. The absolute versions could also be used for intrarater and test–retest reliability.

Table 19.12 confirms that each of the values for the two-way random design is the same as its two-way mixed equivalent and that, therefore, there are only six unique types of ICC under this system. Notice that, for every type of ICC, the average version is larger than its one set equivalent. The 95% CIs are very wide. This is a consequence of the small number of targets.

TABLE 19.12   The different types of ICC used to assess interrater reliability, with values of ICC and 95% CI for two judges

Ratings made by	Description	Level of agreement	Ratings used	ICC	95% CI
Randomly chosen judge for each rating of each target	One-way random	absolute	one set	.871	.325, .985
			average	.931	.490, .993
Randomly chosen judges, each rates all targets	Two-way random	consistent	one set	.856	.146, .984
			average	.922	.255, .992
		absolute	one set	.870	.257, .985
			average	.930	.409, .993
Fixed judges, each rates all targets	Two-way mixed	consistent	One set	.856	.146, .984
			average	.922	.255, .992
		absolute	one set	.870	.257, .985
			average	.930	.409, .993

ICCs are often treated like correlation coefficients. However, Lahey, Downey, and Saal (1983) demonstrate that in every type of ICC the limits of possible values are not the same as for correlations (i.e. they are not −1 to +1). See Appendix X for the limits if each version of ICC.

Lahey et al. (1983) identify three factors which can limit the size of an ICC: some negative correlations between judges; lack of variability in the targets or at least in the ratings given to them by a judge; and disagreement between pairs of judges in their ratings leading to very low to zero correlations. A matrix of how the judges' ratings correlate can help to identify the first and last issue. Standard deviations or a frequency histogram of each judge's ratings might help to identify the second issue. See Lahey et al for statistical tests to assess these issues.

Statistical Significance of ICC

For those who want to know the statistical significance of an ICC, there is an F-test for the one-way random design and another for the remainder of the designs (see Appendix X). For the data I have been analysing, they are $F_{(4,5)}$ = 14.5, p = .006 and $F_{(4,4)}$ = 12.89, p = .015, respectively.

Criteria

Cicchetti (1994) and others have suggested that ICC below .4 is poor, between .4 and .59 is fair, between .6 and .74 is good and between .75 and 1 is excellent.

Recommendations for sample size of targets

Baumgartner and Chung (2001) note that a minimum of 30 targets is recommended for measuring interrater reliability. However if the criterion being used is a reasonably narrow confidence interval to estimate the population value then they recommend a minimum of 50 targets.

Indicators and reliability

Bollen and Lennox (1991) make the point that we should not slavishly follow guidelines about reliability and in particular internal consistency in our measures, without first thinking about the nature of the elements which make up our measure. They draw attention to a distinction between *effect* indicators and *causal* indicators. Effect indicators can be seen as being affected by the phenomenon we are trying to measure. Thus, if we believed that personality is a relatively fixed thing we would expect an individual's personality to affect their responses to items in a personality test and we would want internal consistency in a test of personality. On the other hand, causal indicators are seen as ones which affect the phenomenon we are assessing. We may be trying to measure SES by asking about education level and salary. In this case, changes in these elements will affect SES. Accordingly, internal consistency between the elements of this measure is not necessarily something we would expect.

Validity

Correlation can also be used to check aspects of the validity of a measure by assessing the degree of similarity between one measure of a concept and the measure being devised. An example would be if researchers correlated their measure of depression with the clinical judgements of psychiatrists. Alternatively, in the case of divergent construct validity, we could find the degree of correlation between our measure (e.g. reading ability) and one which is not designed to measure the same concept (e.g. IQ). If this correlation were to be too high, then we might suspect that our test was measuring aspects of IQ rather than being purely a measure of reading.

Standard error of estimate

Just as the standard error of measurement can be used to find a confidence interval around a person's score on a measure when the measure is not totally reliable, so the *standard error of estimate* is a statistic which can be used to find a confidence interval for a person's score when the validity of the measure is expressed as a correlation coefficient. (Appendix X shows how such a confidence interval can be found.)

Summary

A correlation coefficient describes the relationship between two variables. In addition, it can be used to find the statistical significance of a given relationship. It is necessary to produce a scattergram of the data for the two variables and to think about the nature of the sample being tested, otherwise there is a danger of missing a relationship because it is non-linear or suggesting a relationship which is actually an artefact of the sample.

The degree to which a test will produce the same score from one occasion to another – its reliability – and the degree to which judges agree in the way they use a scoring system – interrater reliability – can be ascertained using tests which are based on correlation. In addition, certain forms of validity of a measure can be checked by correlation.

The next chapter introduces an alternative, but related, way of investigating relationships – regression.

20 Analysis of relationships II
Linear regression

Introduction

Regression analysis is another way of describing and evaluating relationships between variables. However, unlike correlation there is an assumption that one variable is a variable to be predicted (a DV) and one or more variables (IVs) are used to predict the outcome of the DV. Strictly speaking, the terms 'DV' and 'IV' are more appropriate in experimental research: their equivalents in non-experimental research are *criterion* variable (CV) and *predictor* variable (PV) respectively. However, at the risk of annoying those who prefer the latter terms I am going to use DV and IV in this chapter. It allows me to use abbreviations without adding new ones in the form of CV and PV, which may introduce their own confusion. Although not one of the factors which affected my decision, it is also consistent with the descriptions used by SPSS. In addition, as we will see at the end of the chapter, techniques which analyse designs which look for differences between groups, such as ANOVA, and techniques which analyse designs which are looking for relationships among variables, such as regression, are in fact based on the same principles.

Regression analysis can be described as a form of modelling, for a mathematical model of the relationship between variables is more explicitly created than it has been for previous analyses covered so far in the book. Regression allows specific predictions to be made from the IV(s) about the DV for individual participants. Simple regression involves a single IV. Multiple regression allows more than one IV to be used to predict the DV and so improve the accuracy of the prediction. The chapter will only deal with linear regression – in other words, where the relationship between variables when represented on a scattergram is best shown as a straight line. Non-linear regression is beyond the scope of this book.

I am assuming that you will do the necessary calculations on a computer. This chapter is written to help you understand what regression is and how to interpret the results. Some of the simpler aspects of the mathematics are given in Appendix XI.

Simple regression

Let us return to the example of mathematical ability, English ability and age, introduced in the previous chapter. Assume that researchers want, initially, to predict mathematical ability from English ability. In other words, they are treating English ability as an IV and mathematical ability as a DV. This does not mean that English ability is assumed to be affecting mathematical ability; it simply allows researchers to see how accurately they can make their predictions of a person's mathematical ability if his or her English ability is known. To do this they find the straight line which best summarises the relationship between the two variables (the best-fit line). Figure 20.1 shows the scattergram of mathematical and English ability with the best-fit line superimposed on it.

FIGURE 20.1   The relationship between mathematical and English ability

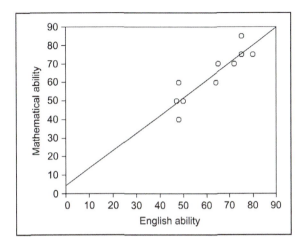

I have intentionally widened the range on both axes of the graph beyond those necessary to show the data, for reasons which will be made clear later. The best-fit line is the line which minimises the distance between itself and the data points on the graph.[1]

If you wished to find out what value would be predicted for mathematical ability for a child with a score of 30 on a test of English ability, first read along the horizontal axis (English ability) until you reach the value 30. Then draw a vertical line from that point to the best-fit line. Now draw a horizontal line from where you have met the best-fit line until you reach the vertical axis (mathematical ability). The point on the vertical axis will be the predicted value for mathematical ability.

FIGURE 20.2   Predicting mathematical ability from English ability using the best-fit line

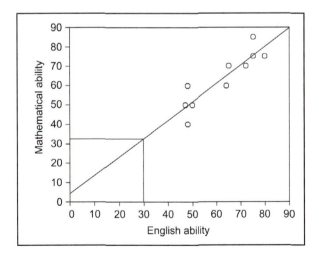

---

1   Once again this is a simplification. The best-fit line minimises the square of the distance between itself and the data points. Hence, you will sometimes see the term *least squares* used to describe the method of finding it.

This suggests that someone with a score of 30 for English would get a score of about 32 for maths. That illustration was just to demonstrate the links between the line of best-fit and the variables used to create it. A flaw in the illustration is that I have extrapolated beyond the data which were available; no one in the sample had scores on either variable which were that low.

Those of you who have done sufficient mathematics will know that any straight line on a graph can be described using a standard equation which will allow any point on the line to be specified. In this way we can get a more exact prediction than by trying to read the graph.

Often a convention is used of calling a value on the vertical axis Y and a value on the horizontal axis X. The equation for a straight line on a graph is always of the form:

$$\text{predicted } Y = a + (b \times X)$$

where a is the value of Y where the best-fit line cuts the Y-axis (the intercept) and b is a measure of the steepness of the best-fit line (the slope); a and b are usually referred to as *regression coefficients*. (Some versions of this equation will use different letters to represent the different elements in the equation, such as b_0 for the intercept, and may even change the order. However, they are, in fact, the same equation.)[2]

The larger the measure of the slope, the steeper is the slope. This makes intuitive sense because the larger the number you multiply the horizontal value by in order to get the vertical value, the quicker the vertical value will grow relative to the horizontal value.

Another way to view the equation for regression is:

$$\text{predicted DV} = a + (b \times \text{IV})$$

In this case, the regression coefficients have been calculated so that:[3]

$$\text{mathematical ability} = 4.28832 + (0.94891 \times \text{English ability})$$

The coefficient shown as b above can be interpreted as showing that the model predicts that for every increase of 1 in the IV (English ability) there will be an increase by the value of b (0.94891) in the DV (mathematical ability). The coefficient shown as a above is the value which the DV would have for someone whose score on the IV was 0. Thus, Figures 20.1 and 20.2 show that the best-fit line cuts the vertical axis where the mathematical ability is 4.28832.

The regression equation predicts that if a child scored 65 on the English test, then:

$$\text{mathematical ability} = 4.28832 + (0.94891 \times 65)$$
$$= 65.967$$

Figure 20.3 is an enlargement of the scattergram in the region where English ability is 65. In fact, the person who scored 65 on the English test scored 70 on the maths test. Therefore, the prediction is not perfect. This is no more than we should expect from the correlation coefficient between English and maths abilities of $r = .888$, as shown in Chapter 19, which meant that 78.85% of the variance in mathematical ability could be accounted for by the variance in English ability, thus leaving $100 - 78.85 = 21.15\%$ of the variance unexplained.

---

2   Those of you who have done some algebra may remember seeing the equation for a straight line written as $y = mx + c$. In that form m is the slope and c is the intercept.
3   Calculations can be found in Appendix XI.

FIGURE 20.3   Enlargement of area around scores of 65 for English ability

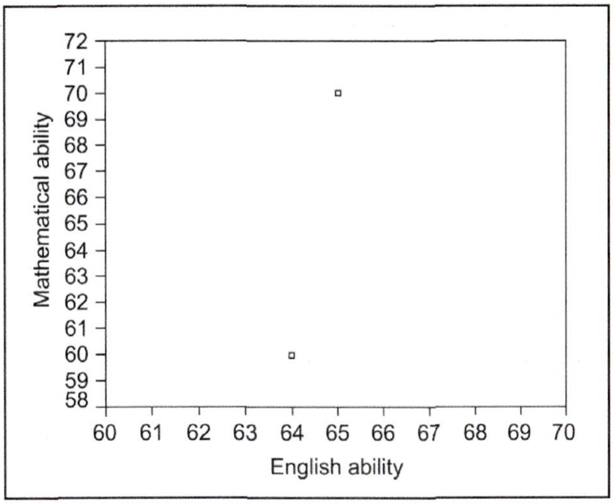

Testing the statistical significance of regression analysis

Regression analysis, like correlation, can be presented in terms of percentage of variance accounted for. This means that it could be subjected to ANOVA by splitting the variance in the DV into that which can be accounted for by the IV and that which remains unaccounted for (residual). The F-ratio is formed by:

$$F = \frac{\text{variance in DV explained by IV}}{\text{variance in DV not explained by IV}}$$

The summary table for the analysis is laid out in the same way as that given when a one-way between-subjects ANOVA is computed (see Table 20.1).

TABLE 20.1   Summary table of the analysis of variance in a simple regression with ability at English as the predictor and mathematical ability as the dependent variable

Source	Sum of squares	df	Mean square	F	p
Regression	1381.606	1	1381.606	29.801	.001
Residual	370.894	8	46.362		
Total	1752.500	9			

Reading the summary table for a simple regression

The sources of variance are clearly given as the regression, the residual and their sum – the total. Sums of squares are the sums of squared deviations from the mean. The total sum of squares is the sum of squares for the DV. The regression sum of squares is calculated by subtracting the mean for the DV from the predicted value of the DV for each person, squaring the result and adding these squared values together (see Appendix XI for a worked example). The residual sum of squares is the sum of the squared differences between the predicted value of the DV and the actual value for each person; it can also be found by subtracting the sum of squares for the regression from the total sum of squares.

The degrees of freedom (df) for the total is one fewer than the number of participants: $10 - 1 = 9$. The df for the regression is the number of IVs in the analysis, which in this case is 1. The residual df is found by subtracting the regression df from the total df: $9 - 1 = 8$.

Mean squares (MS) are formed, as usual, by dividing the sum of squares by its appropriate df. The F-ratio is calculated by dividing the regression MS by the residual MS. The p-value can be found from standard F-tables using the appropriate two values for the df: in this case 1 and 8. As usual with ANOVA, the p-value will be for the equivalent of a two-tailed test. Therefore, we can conclude that English ability predicts a significant proportion of the variance in mathematical ability.

Links between correlation and simple regression

If we divide the sum of squares due to the regression by the total sum of squares this tells us the proportion of the overall variance in the DV which is accounted for by the IV in the regression. Multiplying the result by 100 gives the percentage of variance accounted for by the regression.

$$\frac{1381.606}{1752.5} \times 100 = 78.84\%$$

This is the same figure (allowing for errors introduced by rounding up) as that found by squaring the correlation coefficient and multiplying the result by 100.

Other similarities between regression and correlation are explored in Appendix XI.

Given the close links between correlation and simple regression, much of the information which one of these analyses provides can be derived from the other. Therefore, unless you are interested in predicting the actual value of the DV from the IV, in psychology it is more usual to analyse the data solely by correlation when there is only one IV.

Multiple regression

Multiple regression can be seen as an extension of simple regression to situations where there is one DV and more than one IV (or predictor). (Incidentally, statisticians refer to regressing the DV onto the IVs.) In the mathematical ability example, we might measure a number of factors, such as IQ and socio-economic status (SES) as well as English ability and age. We could then see what combination of these variables best predicts mathematical ability. In this way we might be able to account for more of the variance in mathematical ability and thus have a better model which would allow us to predict it more accurately. Multiple regression is expressed both in terms of an equation which relates the DV and IVs and as a multiple correlation coefficient R.

Why is multiple regression necessary?

You might feel that it is enough simply to correlate a number of variables with mathematical ability and see which ones produce the highest correlation and retain them as measures you would wish to use to predict mathematical ability in the future. However, as the discussion of partial and semi-partial correlation in Chapter 19 demonstrated, there may be overlap among the IVs in the variance they explain in the DV. This means that without multiple regression we will not have a single mathematical model to predict mathematical ability. In addition, because of the possible overlap between IVs some may not add much, if anything, to our model; the variance they explain may already be explained by other variables. Knowing this would save taking an unnecessarily large number of measures from an individual when we want to predict his or her mathematical ability.

The equation for a multiple regression is an expansion of that for simple regression. If there were two IVs:

$$DV = a + b_1 \times IV_1 + b_2 \times IV_2$$

Thus, if we were going to look at the relationship between mathematical ability and English ability and age, the equation would be:

mathematical ability $= a + b_1 \times$ English ability $+ b_2 \times$ age

The regression analysis (with age in months) gives the following values:

mathematical ability $= 16.979 + 1.012 \times$ English ability $- 0.107 \times$ age

Now, if we knew that a child scored 65 on the English test and was 162 months old (13.5 years), the model would predict:

mathematical ability $= 16.979 + 1.012 \times 65 - 0.107 \times 162$
$= 65.425$

This is a little farther from the actual figure of 70 than was predicted by English ability alone. Below we find that 79% of the variance in mathematical ability is accounted for by the variance in English ability and age. It may seem odd that we now have a model which accounts for slightly more of the variance in the DV than previous models and yet makes a poorer prediction for a given individual. The point is that, although in this individual's case it is making a poorer prediction, over all the participants it is making a smaller error in prediction than the previous models. Let us look at the multiple correlation coefficient (R) and ANOVA (Table 20.2).

R is given as .889, which is only slightly larger than the correlation coefficient for English and maths ($r = .888$). R^2 is shown as .790; to four decimal places it is .7896. We can use R^2 to find the proportion of variance accounted for in the same way that we used r^2. Thus, the proportion of variance in mathematical ability which is accounted for by English ability and age together is $.7896 \times 100 = 78.96\%$. (As with simple regression, the percentage of variance accounted for can also be found by dividing the regression sum of squares by the total sum of squares: $\dfrac{1383.705}{1752.5} \times 100 = 78.96\%$.) This means that adding age into the equation has accounted for an additional $78.96 - 78.84 = 0.12\%$ of the variance

TABLE 20.2 The summary table from a multiple regression with mathematical ability as the dependent variable and English ability and age as the independent variables

R	R square	Adjusted R square
.889	.790	.729

Source	Sum of squares	df	Mean square	F	p
Regression	1383.705	2	691.852	13.132	.004
Residual	368.795	7	52.685		
Total	1752.500	9			

in mathematical ability. This value of 0.12% or .0012 (as a proportion of variance) is the square of the semi-partial correlation of mathematical ability and age with English ability partialled out of age. From this we can view regression as giving us:

$$R^2_{\text{m.ea}} = r^2_{\text{me}} + r^2_{\text{m(a.e)}}$$

where $R_{\text{m.ea}}$ is the multiple correlation coefficient of the IVs English ability and age with the DV mathematical ability, r_{me} is the simple correlation of mathematical ability and English ability, and $r_{\text{m(a.e)}}$ is the semi-partial correlation of mathematical ability and age with English ability partialled out of age (defined in Chapter 19).

If we added another IV – say, SES – to the model, then the additional variance would be the square of the semi-partial correlation of SES with mathematical ability when English ability and age have been partialled out of SES.

Adjusted R^2

The adjusted R^2 is an estimate of R^2 in the population and takes into account the sample size and the number of IVs; the smaller the sample and the larger the number of IVs, the larger is the adjustment. In my experience psychologists may report adjusted R^2 but they rarely go on to refer to it when interpreting their results. The equation for adjusted R^2 is given in Appendix XI.

Types of multiple regression

There are a number of ways of conducting multiple regression. They differ in the way the IVs are selected to be put into the model. I'm going to deal with two in this chapter and then cover the others, just for information, in Appendix XI.

Standard multiple regression

This involves simply putting all the IVs into the model in one stage. It is most useful when you are trying to explain as much of the variance in the DV as possible and are not concerned about wasting effort on measures which add only a small amount of information. In addition, it can be appropriate when you don't have any theory about the relative contributions of the different IVs and how they are related.

Sequential (or hierarchical) multiple regression

This involves the researcher placing the IVs into the model in a prearranged order, which will be determined by the model which the researcher has. In this way an explicit model can be tested and it is possible to see how much variance in the DV is accounted for by certain IVs when one or more other variables are already in the model. In fact, I have already demonstrated a sequential regression. I put English ability into the model first and then age in a second stage. However, it would be more usual to conduct the analysis the other way around. Thus, you are more likely to put demographic details into the model first – e.g. age and gender – and then ask how much extra variance English ability can explain. In this way you find out how much additional variance is explained by a variable which could be subject to being manipulated once variables which can't be manipulated have been accounted for. In addition, it tells us whether variables which involve people taking a test or answering a range of questions (such as an attitude scale) add much information above that already gained from simply knowing people's age and gender.

The following is an example of a sequential regression with mathematical ability as the DV and English ability, age, SES and IQ as possible IVs. As will be shown later, the sample size at 10 should have been much larger. Table 20.3 shows the correlations between each of the pairs of variables.

TABLE 20.3   The correlation matrix for mathematical ability, English ability, age, SES and IQ

Correlations

	Maths	*English*	*Age*	*SES*	*IQ*
Maths	1.000				
English	.888	1.000			
Age	.748	.862	1.000		
SES	.056	−.328	−.394	1.000	
IQ	.564	.700	.626	−.390	1.000

I'm interested in how much variance English ability explains in mathematical ability in addition to that explained by age, SES and IQ. Therefore, I will enter the variables into the model in two stages: in stage 1 I am entering age, SES and IQ into the regression; in stage 2 I am adding English ability.

Table 20.4 shows that IQ, SES and age together account for $.746 \times 100 = 74.6\%$ of the variance in mathematical ability. The standard error of the estimate for a regression is the square root of the mean square for the residuals (shown in Table 20.6). As the mean square is an estimate of the variance in the residuals, its square root is the *SD* of the residuals (defined later in the chapter); these are used to standardise the residuals (see Appendix XI). Table 20.5 shows that when English ability is added to IQ, SES and age, it adds a further $.181 \times 100 = 18.1\%$ and that that is a significant increase in variance explained ($p = .017$).

TABLE 20.4   The R, R^2, adjusted R^2 and standard error for a regression with IQ, SES and age used to predict mathematical ability

R	R square	Adjusted R square	Std. error of the estimate
.863	0.746	0.618	8.61972

TABLE 20.5   The R, R^2, adjusted R^2 and R^2 change for a regression with ability at English added to a regression used to predict mathematical ability which already has IQ, SES and age as IVs

Model	R	R square	Adjusted R square	Std. error of the estimate	*Change statistics*				
					R square change	F change	df 1	df 2	Sig. F change
2	.963	.927	.868	5.07448	.181	12.312	1	5	.017

Table 20.6 shows the ANOVAs for each stage in the regression.

TABLE 20.6 The *F*-tests for the two stages in a sequential regression predicting mathematical ability. Model 1: IQ, SES and age as IVs; Model 2 English ability added to the IVs in Model 1.

ANOVA

Model		Sum of squares	df	Mean square	F	p
1	Regression	1306.702	3	435.567	5.862	.032
	Residual	445.798	6	74.300		
	Total	1752.500	9			
2	Regression	1623.748	4	405.937	15.764	.005
	Residual	128.752	5	25.750		
	Total	1752.500	9			

From Table 20.6 we can see that both Model 1 and Model 2 explain a significant proportion of variance in mathematical ability.

Table 20.7 shows the details of the individual regression coefficients for each model.

TABLE 20.7 Regression coefficients for a sequential regression to predict mathematical ability

| Model | | *Coefficients* | | | | | | |
| | | *Unstandardized Coeffs* | | *Standardized Coeffs* | *t* | *Sig.* | *95.0% CI for B* | |
		B	Std. Error	Beta			Lower	Upper
1	(Constant)	−168.977	57.247		−2.952	0.026	−309.056	−28.899
	Age	1.191	0.421	0.763	2.826	0.03	0.16	2.222
	SES	5.652	2.81	0.46	2.011	0.091	−1.224	12.528
	IQ	0.327	0.333	0.265	0.982	0.364	−0.488	1.141
2	(Constant)	−35.751	50.768		−0.704	0.513	−166.254	94.751
	Age	0.165	0.383	0.105	0.429	0.686	−0.821	1.15
	SES	4.967	1.666	0.404	2.982	0.031	0.686	9.249
	IQ	0.01	0.216	0.008	0.045	0.966	−0.545	0.564
	English	0.988	0.281	0.924	3.509	0.017	0.264	1.711

Std Error is the standard error of the regression coefficient. The poorer the IV is as a predictor of the DV, the larger the standard error. In addition, the more correlated one IV is with the others in the model, the larger the standard error. The standard error of a regression coefficient can be used to find the statistical significance of the regression coefficient and a confidence interval for it (see Appendix XI for their calculation). The intercorrelation between IVs is discussed under multicollinearity later in the chapter. The *standardised coefficient* is explained later in the chapter.

From Table 20.7 we learn that the equation for mathematical ability is:

$$\text{mathematical ability} = -35.751 + (0.165 \times \text{age}) + (4.967 \times \text{SES}) + (0.010 \times \text{IQ})$$
$$+ (0.988 \times \text{English ability})$$

Accordingly, a person scoring 65 in the English test, aged 162 months, having an SES of 4 and an IQ of 100 will be predicted to have a score of 75.947 on the maths test. The person actually scored 70 on the maths test.

Interpreting a multiple regression

If you want to go beyond simply noting whether the regression accounts for a significant amount of the variance in the DV you can look at the size of the regression coefficients. Looking at the example of mathematical ability, taking English ability as the example, what they mean is that the predicted value of mathematical ability would be raised by 0.988 units for every increase by one unit of English ability, *if all other variables in the model were held constant*. This is a rather artificial idea because we know that IQ correlates significantly with English ability and thus may not remain constant with changes in English ability.

There is danger in simply comparing the magnitude of the unstandardised regression coefficients to see which IV is the best predictor of the DV. The regression coefficient for SES is much larger than that for English ability. However, this does not mean that SES explains more of the variance in mathematical ability than English ability explains. The reason is that the magnitude of the unstandardised regression coefficient is a function of the *SD* of that variable. A measure which solves this problem is the *standardised regression coefficient* (often denoted as β and called a *beta* coefficient; see Appendix XI for the calculation of β). When we look again at the summary table we see that the standardised coefficients tell a different story from the unstandardised regression coefficients and now English ability is seen to contribute the most to the model.

Each *t*-value is calculated from the *b* value and its standard error. They test the Null Hypothesis that the *b* is 0 in the population, that is, that the IV predicts no variance in the DV. However, the probability tells us whether the particular IV would add significantly to the model *if it were added to the model after all the other IVs* which have been included in the model have already been entered. Thus, we are told that SES adds significantly to the model ($p = .031$) even when age, IQ and English ability are already in the model; it is explaining a significant unique proportion of the variance in mathematical ability.

The probability from the ANOVA table and the probabilities from the individual IVs tell us different things. The ANOVA tells us whether the overall model predicts a significant proportion of the variance in the DV. The individual probabilities tell us whether a particular IV adds significantly to the model if it were added last. Thus, you can have an IV which is not considered significant but which is part of a model which *is* significant (for example, age or IQ). Also, because the individual probabilities tell us about what would happen if a given IV were added last, in a sequential or statistical model (described in Appendix XI) the *b* and probability will change from stage to stage in the analysis. We can also have the situation where a variable is significantly correlated with the dependent variable but is shown as not being significant in a particular multiple regression, as is the case with both age and IQ. This seeming anomaly is because, while significantly related to mathematical ability, neither explains significant *unique* variance over and above that explained by the other variables.

In a sequential regression, there is more information: the amount of additional variance a particular stage in the regression explains and whether that is significant. Thus, as shown in Table 20.5, English ability explains an additional 18.1% unique variance and that is significant ($p = .017$). This means that in a sequential regression it is possible to have four sources of probabilities which address related but different aspects of the relationship between the DV and the IV(s): Are the individual IVs significantly correlated with the DV? In other words, do any of them individually explain a significant proportion of variance in the DV? This is answered by examining the correlations. Do they together explain a significant proportion of variance in the DV? This is answered by examining the *F*-ratio which tests the overall model. Do one or more variables explain a significant amount of extra variance in a later stage of a sequential analysis? This is answered by examining the *F*-ratio which addresses the increase in R^2. Does each individual variable explain a significant proportion of unique variance? This is answered by examining the individual *t*-tests addressing the individual regression coefficients. Together, these sources of information may give seemingly different answers. It is our task to give an account which is consistent with those answers.

▍Recommended sample size

In multiple regression there is a requirement to use a reasonable sample size in order to maximise the reliability of the result. However, if statistical significance is to be a consideration then a preferable way to look at the necessary sample size is in terms of power (the likelihood of avoiding a Type II error). Cohen (1988) recommends power of at least .8. Nonetheless, you need to take into account the effect size that you wish to detect.

EFFECT SIZE AND REGRESSION

A convenient measure of effect size is R^2, which tells us the proportion of variance accounted for in the DV and is the same measure as η^2, used as the effect size for ANOVA. Cohen (1988) uses a different effect size from the one I have employed. However, following his guidelines produces R^2 of approximately 0.02 as a small effect size, 0.13 as a medium effect size and 0.26 as a large effect size. You may notice that these are different from the sizes recommended for ANOVA, where the effect size is also a measure of the proportion of variance which is explained. Remember that Cohen has identified these sizes from reviewing the research which utilises each technique. Also remember that these are only guidelines, and that if, for the purposes of choosing a sample size for a study, you have a better estimate of the effect, always use that estimate in preference to these guidelines.

POWER AND REGRESSION

The power of regression is dependent not only on the alpha-level set, the sample size and the effect size, but also on the number of IVs in the model. Power tables for multiple regression are provided in Appendix XVIII. There are at least three types of power analysis that can be conducted with multiple regression. Firstly, we can take account of the power for the whole model. In this case, all the IVs have been added to the analysis; this looks at the overall R^2. Secondly, we can take account of the power for a given variable: we could be interested in whether a particular IV accounts for a significant unique proportion of the variance; this looks at the equivalent of the t-test for the IV's regression coefficient. Thirdly, we could be interested in whether a set of IVs, which have been added after other variables, account for a significant unique proportion of the variance; this looks at the R^2-change.

Power analysis for the whole model

If you were holding alpha at .05, had one IV in the model and wanted power of .8, then for a medium effect size you would need approximately 55 participants. However, when you have 10 IVs, using power as the basis for choosing sample size, you would need around 120 participants in order to have the same power for a medium effect size. In addition, if a smaller effect size is involved, then the sample size would need to be increased further.

Power analysis for a single IV

Although we would be taking into account the significance of a single regression coefficient we can treat the effect size as R^2, or rather R^2-change: by how much would an IV, if added last to the model, increase R^2? In other words, what is the unique variance which the IV explains in the DV on top of that explained by the other variables in the model? To calculate the necessary sample size, we need all the usual information for a multiple regression: the alpha-level, the level of power, the effect size and the number of IVs in the model. However, we are going to deal with the last piece of information differently from when we are looking at the power for the whole model. We use the regression power tables for one predictor variable, as we are only adding one extra IV, but we need to adjust the required sample size to take into account the number of other predictor variables already in the model. As an example, researchers wish to test predictors of intention to quit smoking. For a sample of smokers they will have each participant's age, gender, number of cigarettes smoked per day, their intention to quit smoking and a measure of how much they think people close to them want them to quit smoking (referred to as *subjective norm* in the Theory of Planned Behaviour, see Conner & Sparks, 2015). They want a sample size which will give sufficient power to test the contribution of subjective norm to the model. They set alpha at .05 and require power of at least .8. They consider that, to be useful, subjective norm needs to explain at least 10% of the variance in intention to quit in addition to that explained by age, gender and number of cigarettes smoked. They look in Table A18.11a and find that with one predictor variable and an effect size of $R^2 = .10$ they would need a sample of 71. However, they need to adjust the sample size to allow for the three other predictor variables already in the model; they need an extra participant per extra predictor variable. In other words, they need $71 + 3 = 74$ participants. This sample size would also give sufficient power for the overall model with the effect size of at least $R^2 = .145$

Power analysis for an additional set of predictor variables

The procedure for this situation is similar to that for testing one additional predictor variable. We still need an alpha-level, a level of power and a value of R^2 that we consider to be the minimum worth testing for. The difference is that we would refer to the regression power table for the number of additional variables in the set. Thus, if we were testing the significance of the R^2-change for a set of four predictor variables, we would look in the table for four predictor variables. We would find the sample size necessary for the effect size and then add an extra participant for every predictor variable already in the model. As an example, I will expand the example given previously for intention to quit smoking. In this case the researchers are also measuring each participant's attitude to quitting smoking (attitude) and their perception of how in control they would feel if they attempted to quit smoking (perceived behavioural control, PBC). The researchers want to test the variance which subjective norm, attitude and PBC (three predictors) explain in intention to quit in addition to that explained by gender and number of cigarettes smoked (two predictors). They decide that the added variables need to explain at least 15% additional variance to be useful; in other words an R^2-change of .15. Consulting Table 18.11b they find that they would need 65 participants for power of .8 with an effect size of .15 and three predictor variables. They then need to increase the sample by one participant per variable already in the model. Therefore, the sample they require is $65 + 2 = 67$.

The examples I have given of power analysis when testing additional variance explained have not increased the sample size much above the sample required to test the overall model. However, as the number of predictor variables already in the model increases, we can see that the increase in sample size will be greater. As an illustration, imagine you wanted to have sufficient power to test the contribution of one out of 12 predictor variables the effect size for which is estimated as $R^2 = .1$. The sample necessary to have power of .8 to test that one variable would be 70 if it were the only variable. However, we need to add 11 to the sample size to adjust for the presence of the other 11 variables already in the model. Therefore, the sample required is 81. Without those extra 11 participants power would only be .73.

One practice I have seen used to try to limit the number of IVs in a regression which I do not recommend is to look at the correlations between the IVs and the DV and then remove the IVs which aren't significantly correlated with the DV. This is far too arbitrary a basis for selecting variables and ignores the possible interrelationships between the IVs which might yield results which aren't straightforwardly predictable from correlations with the DV.

Multicollinearity

Some authors prefer to use the term 'collinearity'. If some IVs intercorrelate too highly – say, at .8 or higher – then this can make the predicted values more unstable. This is because of the way in which the regression coefficients are calculated. An additional problem is that the analysis can give the wrong impression that a given variable is not a good predictor of the DV simply because most of the variance which it could explain has already been accounted for by other variables in the model. Identifying multicollinearity can be a problem as, even if no two variables correlate highly, multicollinearity can still be present because a combination of IVs might account for the variance in one of the IVs. To detect multicollinearity, a number of statistics are available. Two common ones, which are directly related, are tolerance and VIF (variance inflation factor).

Tolerance

This is the proportion of variance in an IV which is not predicted by the other IVs. To find tolerance a multiple regression is conducted with the IV of interest treated as the DV, which is then regressed on the other IVs. The R^2 from that regression is put into the following equation:

tolerance $= 1 - R^2$

High multicollinearity would be shown by a large R^2 and so a small tolerance value would suggest multicollinearity. A tolerance value of less than .1 is often given as the point when multicollinearity is likely to be a problem as this would mean that 90% (.9 × 100) of the variance in one IV can be explained by the other IVs.

VIF

This is found from the following equation:

$$\text{variance inflation factor} = \frac{1}{\text{tolerance}}$$

Therefore, a large VIF suggests multicollinearity. In keeping with the guidance for tolerance, a VIF which is larger than 10 is usually seen as problematic.

Table 20.8 shows the tolerance and VIF values for the regression when mathematical ability was regressed against English ability, age, SES and IQ. From Table 20.8 we can see that, according to the statistics provided there, there is not a problem of multicollinearity. Tolerance and VIF are produced by programs such as SPSS. As they are transformations of each other there is no need to quote both of them. A further check on multicollinearity is explained in Appendix XI.

TABLE 20.8 Multicollinearity statistics for the regression of mathematical ability on English ability, age, SES and IQ

| | Collinearity statistics | |
	Tolerance	VIF
English	.212	4.720
Age	.243	4.112
SES	.800	1.250
IQ	.481	2.078

Dealing with multicollinearity

There are a number of ways in which multicollinearity can be dealt with. The simplest is to remove one or more of the offending variables and rerun the multiple regression. It is also possible to create composite IVs by combining the problematic IVs either by adding them or by using principal components analysis (PCA). PCA can be used to produce a set of components which explain the same variance as the original variables but with the advantage that the components are completely uncorrelated with each other (see Chapter 24). A problem with using PCA in this way is that the components may not have an obvious meaning beyond a purely mathematical one. However, this is not an issue if the purpose of the regression is to explain variance in the outcome variable rather than contribute to a theoretical model.

Diagnostic checks

There are certain checks which it is advisable to do to see whether the assumptions of the regression are tenable. A number involve examining the residuals and thus are only obtained by running the regression.

Residuals

A residual is the difference between the predicted value for the DV and the actual value. Earlier it was shown that the predicted mathematical ability of an individual was 75.947 yet the actual score was 70. In this case, the residual would be 70 − 75.947 = − 5.947. Statistical packages offer versions of residuals which have been calculated and transformed in a number of ways; a number are described in Appendix XI. The one I recommend using is where they have been standardised by a transformation which gives them a mean of 0 and an *SD* of 1. This means that we can treat each residual in the same way that we use a *z*-value: namely to tell us how extreme such a value is. Accordingly, we can look at the standardised residuals to see whether any could be considered as outliers, which would need further investigation. Table 20.9 shows that none of the residuals, taken from the example analysis, are outside the range ±2.01 and are therefore within the normal range as they are not bigger than 3 *SD*s from the mean.

Although the residuals can be examined from this perspective, I wouldn't simply remove cases which have high standardised residuals. These are people that the model doesn't fit very well. Therefore,

TABLE 20.9 Maths ability, predicted maths ability (MA), residuals and standardised residuals from the regression of mathematical ability on English ability and SES

Maths ability	Predicted MA	Residual	Std residual
50	49.077	0.923	0.182
40	42.281	−2.281	−0.450
60	56.147	3.853	0.759
50	50.290	−0.290	−0.057
70	75.947	−5.947	−1.172
60	60.156	−0.156	−0.031
75	74.901	0.099	0.019
70	72.135	−2.135	−0.421
85	77.023	7.977	1.572
75	77.042	−2.042	−0.403

to remove them is to fit the people to the model. An additional problem, if using a standardised value of 3 as the criterion for an outlier, is that with a large sample you may easily have many people whose residuals are that high. One simple way to solve this would be to adjust the alpha-level for samples greater than 50 (by dividing .05 by the sample size) and then only treating as an outlier those standardised residuals which were equal to or greater than the z-score which would achieve that level of significance. Thus, if the sample size were 100, then the two-tailed, adjusted alpha-level would be .0005. Looking in Table A15.1 tells us that a z of 3.48 would be necessary to achieve that level of significance (for a two-tailed test) and thus we would only treat standardised residuals which were as big as or bigger than +3.48 or −3.48 as outliers.

A preferable check for outliers and possible influential data points is given later in the chapter. Nonetheless, residuals should be examined, via graphs, to check that they don't form a pattern.

Residual plots

There are two plots of residuals which we require. The first is to check that they are normally distributed (i.e. randomly distributed). We can do this either via a frequency histogram or via a normal quantile–quantile plot. The second type of check can be conducted by producing a scattergram between the predicted values of the DV and the standardised residuals. This should show no obvious pattern and would thus demonstrate that the residuals are randomly distributed relative to the predicted values of the DV. To produce Figure 20.4 I have also standardised the predicted values. This plot shows no obvious relationship between the two measures. There are ways in which the plot could have suggested that the assumptions of regression have been violated.

FIGURE 20.4   The plot of standardised predicted values and standardised residuals from the regression of mathematical ability on IQ, age SES and English ability

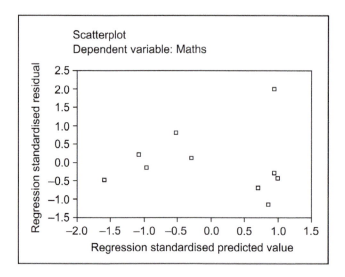

Heterogeneous variance

Figure 20.5 is an example where there is greater variance of errors for the higher predicted values, which suggests that the model will be better at prediction for the lower values of the DV. *Homoscedasticity* is the term used to denote that a set of residuals have homogeneous variance and *heteroscedasticity* denotes that the residuals have heterogeneous variance – i.e. that they are not randomly distributed.

FIGURE 20.5   An example of heterogeneous variance in the residuals from a regression analysis

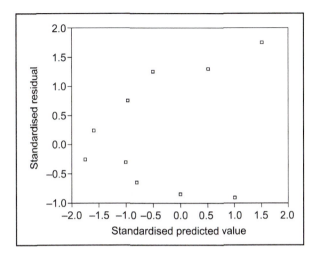

Curvilinearity

Figure 20.6 suggests that the model will underestimate the middle values of the DV and overestimate the more extreme values. Both forms of violation can be countered by adopting an appropriate transformation of the original data.

FIGURE 20.6   An example of curvilinear relationship between the residuals and the predicted values of the IV from a regression analysis

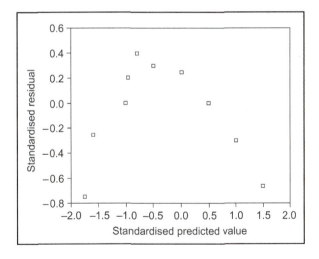

Leverage and influence

The outcome of regression analysis can be influenced by outliers among the IVs. One measure of whether an individual person's data contain outliers is *leverage* (also known as the *hat element*). It assesses whether a person's set of scores across the IVs is a *multivariate* outlier. Thus, a person might not be an outlier on any single IV, but the pattern of his or her scores across the IVs may be an outlier.

An additional measure which looks at how influential a given person's data are on the regression is Cook's distance. This is a measure of the degree to which outliers affect the regression and it takes into account a person's score on the DV as well as the IVs. Table 20.10 shows the Cook's distance and leverage scores for the regression.

TABLE 20.10   The leverage and Cook's distance statistics for the regression with maths as the DV and IQ, age, SES and ability at English as the IVs

Participant	Cook's distance	Leverage
1	.01937	.56191
2	.07710	.49208
3	.17189	.45039
4	.00120	.48569
5	1.98190	.69060
6	.00013	.32496
7	.00121	.77941
8	.07043	.49918
9	.39728	.34493
10	.03036	.37086

Many authors provide rules of thumb for Cook's distance and leverage as to what constitutes problematic cases, some of which are given in Appendix XI. A preferable method which other authors suggest is that problematic cases are better identified by plotting the leverage and Cook's distance scores against each other, as shown in Figure 20.7.

FIGURE 20.7   A scattergram of leverage and Cook's distance for the regression of mathematical ability on IQ, age, SES and English ability

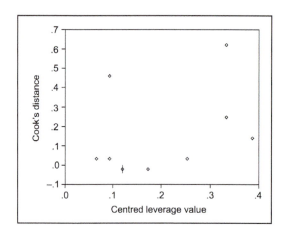

The scattergram shows that one person has a Cook's distance value which is markedly higher than the others. In addition, that person's leverage score is also on the high side relative to the others. In such a situation it is worth rerunning the analysis but with such high scorers removed to see whether their removal makes any difference (that is, doing sensitivity analysis). Table 20.11 shows some of the output from the regression with maths as the variable to be predicted and English ability and SES as the predictors but with the person with high Cook's distance and leverage removed.

TABLE 20.11 Regression with age, SES, IQ and English ability as predictors of mathematical ability with participant with high Cook's distance and leverage scores removed

R	R square	Adjusted R square	Std. error of the estimate
.996	0.992	0.983	1.89948

ANOVA

Source	Sum of squares	df	Mean square	F	p
Regression	1691.123	4	422.781	117.177	< .001
Residual	14.432	4	3.608		
Total	1705.556	8			

Coefficients

	Unstandardised coefficients		Standardised coefficients	t	p	95.0% Confidence interval for B	
	B	Std. error	Beta			Lower bound	Upper bound
(Constant)	−126.451	24.915		−5.075	0.007	−195.627	−57.276
Age	0.858	0.189	0.542	4.536	0.011	0.333	1.383
SES	8.921	0.939	0.611	9.499	0.001	6.313	11.529
IQ	−0.106	0.083	−0.086	−1.273	0.272	−0.337	0.125
English	0.794	0.111	0.751	7.162	0.002	0.486	1.102

Comparing the two models, we see that removing that person's scores has made a difference to the results. The amount of variance accounted for has risen by 6.5%, the model remains significant, and English and SES both remain significant. However, age is now significant. We could also have removed the person with a particularly high leverage value but low Cook's distance as the leverage score was well separated from the distribution of leverage scores. However, we need to be careful that changes of results to being non-significant are not as a consequence of loss of statistical power due to the reduced sample size, rather than to any fundamental change in the model. As removing such potentially influential scores has such a more marked effect on the results, then it is important to report the results with and without those scores. This can demonstrate how the model is relatively unstable and how it can be affected by the removal of only a few participants. On the other hand, if removal of such outliers had made little difference then it would be enough to state that, explaining that you mean that nothing has changed from being significant to becoming non-significant and vice versa. Other measures of leverage and influence exist and a number are offered by SPSS. These are described in Appendix XI.

The order of checks on the data and model

Some of the checks can be done before the analysis is conducted, while others are provided as part of the output from the multiple regression. If you are conducting sequential regression then don't do the checks at each stage but do them on the final model which contains all the IVs. The preliminary checks to conduct are the usual univariate and bivariate ones. Look at the distribution of the variables, in particular the DV. Next plot scattergrams between the DV and individual IVs and between pairs of IVs to check that they are not curvilinear. You should also calculate the bivariate correlations from which you can check for collinearity, remembering that this is not the only check for this problem. Then, as part of the regression save the leverage and Cook's distance values and create a scattergram between them. Identifying any problematic cases may solve later problems. Check for multicollinearity by using tolerance or VIF and the method described in Appendix XI. Finally, check the pattern of the residuals.

Where possible it is a good idea to check the validity of the model which you have found, otherwise there is always a possibility that what you have found is only true for the data you have collected.

Model validation

We obviously want to know how good the predictions are from the model – that is, can they be generalised to other data? I will mention two ways.

Data splitting

If you have a large enough sample you can perform the regression analysis on half the data and then see how well the predictions for that model account for the remaining data. Statistical programs, including SPSS, can be used to select a random subsample of your data for this purpose.

The PRESS statistic

Often you will not have enough data to carry out data splitting and so you can use another technique – PRESS (predicted residual sum of squares) – which repeats the regression by deleting one item and recalculating the predicted value for that item from the remaining data. From this it is possible to calculate a version of R^2 that is based on the PRESS statistic (R^2_{PRESS}), and that, if markedly different from the original R^2, would question the latter's reliability. This facility is no longer available in newer versions of SPSS. However, by a method described in Appendix XI it is possible to use information which is provided to create R^2_{PRESS}. In the case of the regression with mathematical ability as DV and English ability as IV, the original R^2 was .7884 while R^2_{PRESS} is .6523. This suggests that English is a strong predictor of mathematical ability but that the original analysis overestimated the amount of variance explained.

▉ Reporting a multiple regression

Start by reporting the correlation matrix of the DV and all the IVs, as shown in Table 20.3. Next give precise details of the type of multiple regression which you have conducted and, if you are using sequential analysis, the order in which you entered the variables into the model and the rationale for that order. Thus, if I were describing my sequential analysis I would say: *A sequential multiple regression was conducted in two stages with mathematical ability as the variable to be predicted. In the first stage IQ, SES and age were entered. In the second, English ability was entered.* Describe any problems that there were with the data, such as outliers or influential data points, non-linear relationships, multicollinearity and heterogeneity in the residuals, and explain what action you took to circumvent the problems. It is useful to conduct the analysis with and without the data from particular potentially problematic cases to see whether their inclusion affects the results.

The format for the rest of the results depends largely on the type of analysis you have conducted. Nonetheless, you should include details about the overall model and the individual IVs. For the overall model the necessary details are the R^2, adjusted R^2, F-ratio with degrees of freedom (for regression and residual) and probability. Thus I would write for the first stage: *With IQ, SES and age in the model a significant proportion of variance in mathematical ability was accounted for, $R^2 = .75$, adjusted $R^2 = .62$, $F_{(3,8)} = 5.86$, $p = .032$*. With a sequential analysis I would report how much variance was added (R^2-change) and whether it was significant and how much overall variance was accounted for, at each stage. *When English ability was added to the model there was a significant increase in R^2 of 0.18 ($F_{(1,5)} = 12.31$, $p = .017$) producing an overall model which was significant ($R^2 = .93$, adjusted $R^2 = .87$, $F_{(4,5)} = 5.86$, $p = .005$)*. The details for individual IVs should include the b, beta, t and probability. In addition, a confidence interval for b should be reported. If you are using sequential analysis, then you may want to include such detail for each stage, possibly in a table.

Mediation analysis

Sometimes the relationship between two variables may be explained via their relationships with a third variable. Baron and Kenny (1986) have devised a method for testing whether the third variable is acting as a mediator in the relationship. To illustrate this process I am going to use data I obtained from a sample of deaf schoolchildren. Although the children are described as deaf, they can hear some sound as long as it is amplified sufficiently. Each child's hearing is tested and the higher the score on the hearing test (the number of decibels at which the sound has to be transmitted for the child to be able to hear), the poorer is that child's hearing. I tested the children's ability to understand certain concepts and their knowledge of the labels for those concepts.

I tested 73 children aged between 11 years 9 months and 15 years 8 months. I found that there was a significant negative relationship between hearing and knowledge of concepts ($r_{(71)} = -.240$, $p = .041$, two-tailed test), indicating that the poorer the hearing ability, the poorer was the knowledge of the concepts. However, I also found significant relationships between knowledge of concepts and knowledge of words for the concepts ($r_{(71)} = .382$, $p = .001$, two-tailed test) and between knowledge of the words for the concepts and hearing level ($r_{(71)} = -.444$, $p < .001$, two-tailed test).

The conditions and method for assessing whether a mediating relationship exists are the following. I am going to test whether knowledge of words for concepts (labelling) can be seen as a mediator between knowledge of concepts (concepts) and hearing.

1   The first criterion is that the IV (hearing) and DV (concepts) should correlate significantly.
2   The second criterion is that the IV and mediator (labelling) should correlate significantly.
3   The third criterion is that the mediator and the DV should correlate significantly.

All three criteria are fulfilled so I move to the next phase.

I have run a multiple regression with concepts as the DV and both hearing and labelling as IVs (Figure 20.8). While the standardised regression coefficient for labelling (.343, $t = 2.790$, $p = .007$) remains significant, that for hearing ($-.087$, $t = -0.711$, $p = .479$) is not significant and is much smaller than its correlation with concepts. This fulfils the final criterion for treating labelling as a possible mediator, as the path between the IV and the DV is now not significant and the standardised regression coefficient has reduced markedly.

We can work out the indirect path between hearing and concepts via labelling by multiplying the correlation coefficient from hearing to labelling (which is the same as the standardised regression coefficient which would have been found had labelling been the DV and hearing the IV in a simple regression) by the regression coefficient from labelling to concepts: $-.444 \times .343 = -.15229$. If we add this indirect path to the direct one between hearing and concepts ($-.087$) we get $-.23929$, which, to two decimal places, is the same as the correlation between hearing and concepts. From this we can see

FIGURE 20.8 A path diagram from hearing and labelling to concepts

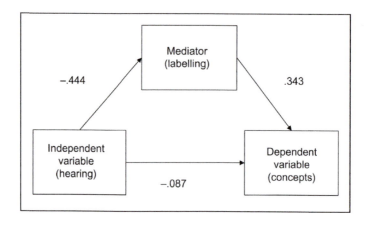

that the relationship between hearing and concepts can be mainly explained by the indirect route via labelling. Appendix XI shows how a z-test can be used to see whether an indirect path is significant. This shows that in this case it is significant ($z = -2.32$, $p = .02$, two-tailed test).

The similarity between ANOVA and multiple regression

Except for the discussions of χ^2 and point-biserial correlation, I have maintained the distinction between techniques which are designed to test for differences and techniques which test for relationships. This is a useful distinction to have when you are trying to learn the techniques; as we know, classification helps memory. However, psychologists are often criticised by statisticians for their ignorance of the fact that one technique underlies both approaches. I want to close this chapter with a demonstration which makes this point, by showing that ANOVA is a special case of multiple regression.

You will recall that regression looks at the *relationship* between one DV and one or more IVs. On the other hand, ANOVA looks at the *difference* between levels of one or more IVs. The levels are categories, such as male or female. However, statisticians have pointed out that these are no more than what they term *dummy variables* entered into a regression analysis.

In Chapter 16 an experiment was described in which three groups of participants were asked to recall a list of words. Each group was in a different mnemonic condition – pegwords, method of loci and a control group in which no strategy was used. The data were analysed using a one-way between-subjects ANOVA, the summary table for which is reproduced in Table 20.12.

TABLE 20.12 A summary table for a one-way between-subjects ANOVA comparing recall under the three mnemonic techniques

Source	Sum of squares	df	Mean square	F	p
Between groups	30.467	2	15.233	5.213	.0122
Within groups	78.9	27	2.922		
Total	109.367	29			

However, dummy variables can be used to distinguish the three groups (see Table 20.13).

TABLE 20.13   The data for the recall by mnemonic strategy with dummy variables used to identify the groups

Participant	Group	Recall	Dummy variable 1	Dummy variable 2
1	loci	10	1	0
2	loci	8	1	0
3	loci	11	1	0
4	loci	9	1	0
5	loci	12	1	0
6	loci	10	1	0
7	loci	7	1	0
8	loci	11	1	0
9	loci	8	1	0
10	loci	10	1	0
11	pegword	11	0	1
12	pegword	7	0	1
13	pegword	9	0	1
14	pegword	10	0	1
15	pegword	8	0	1
16	pegword	6	0	1
17	pegword	12	0	1
18	pegword	9	0	1
19	pegword	10	0	1
20	pegword	7	0	1
21	control	10	0	0
22	control	7	0	0
23	control	7	0	0
24	control	9	0	0
25	control	5	0	0
26	control	6	0	0
27	control	8	0	0
28	control	5	0	0
29	control	7	0	0
30	control	8	0	0

Dummy coding is achieved by coding the fact that someone had a given characteristic by a 1 and the lack of that characteristic by a 0. Thus, we can use dummy variable 1 to tell us who was in the method of loci condition, and so those in that group are coded as 1 while the others are coded as 0. Then dummy variable 2 tells us who was in the pegword condition. Notice that there is one fewer dummy variable than the number of levels of the IV. This is because with dummy variable 1 and dummy variable 2 we know who was in the final group – the control group. They are the people who were not in either of the other two groups. Thus, people in the method of loci condition are coded as 1 on the first variable and 0 on the other, people in the pegword group as 0 1 and the control group as 0 0. (Another method of coding categorical IVs – effect coding – is given in Appendix XI.)

By treating the dummy variables as IVs, the same design can be analysed as a multiple regression (see Table 20.14).

TABLE 20.14 Summary of the regression analysis of recall of words by three groups

R	R square	Adjusted R square	Std. error of the estimate
.528	.279	.225	1.71

ANOVA

	Sum of squares	df	Mean square	F	p
Regression	30.467	2	15.233	5.213	.012
Residual	78.900	27	2.922		
Total	109.367	29			

Note that the regression sum of squares is the same as the between-groups sum of squares from the one-way ANOVA and that the residual sum of squares is the same as the within-groups sum of squares. In addition, the value for η^2 in the ANOVA (.279) is the same as R^2 from the regression. Finally I can explain why I prefer η^2 to partial η^2 as a measure of effect size in ANOVA. The former is the same as the increase in R^2 which would be achieved by putting an additional IV into a multiple regression.

Thus we can see that ANOVA can be treated as an example of regression analysis. Both are models which are described by what is termed the *general linear model*, as is the technique described in the Chapter 22 – analysis of covariance (ANCOVA) – and at least two described in Chapter 25 – multivariate ANOVA (MANOVA) and multivariate ANCOVA (MANCOVA). Those wishing to read further will find good accounts in Howell (2013) and Tabachnick and Fidell (2013). The moral to be drawn from this point is that looking for differences, as per ANOVA, and looking for relationships, as per regression, are two ways of viewing the same thing. We can ask whether there is a difference in recall between the three mnemonic groups or we can ask whether there is a relationship between the type of mnemonic strategy employed and recall.

Given the similarities between ANOVA and multiple regression, it is important to point out that, as with ANOVA, interactions can be tested in multiple regression. However, as was noted in Chapter 17, with ANOVA we have to be careful how we interpret the interaction effect in non-experimental designs and that preferred terms might be *multiplicative relations* or *joint relations*. Thus, with the example where mathematical ability is being predicted by age and English ability we can ask whether the joint relation between age and English ability adds to the amount of variance of mathematical ability which can be explained. However, unlike with ANOVA, testing a joint relation between variables in multiple regression with some programs can be a relatively complex process and so I discuss it in Appendix XI.

Dichotomising continuous variables

Sometimes researchers produce dichotomous variables from continuous ones: for example, creating the groups *older* and *younger* from participants' ages. This is frequently done by splitting the sample in two, using what is termed a *median split*, which means putting those below the median in one group and those above the median in the other group. I think the reason is to make the data conform to the requirements of ANOVA or a *t*-test. However, as I've demonstrated in this chapter, ANOVA is in the same family of analysis as multiple regression. Therefore unless there is good reason for reducing a variable to one which is dichotomous, it would be better to leave it in its original form and conduct the analysis via regression.

There are at least two disadvantages with dichotomising data in this way. Firstly, a lot of information is being thrown away and so subtle relationships within the data are likely to be missed. Secondly, the use of a median split produces the split at a point which is totally dependent on the nature of the particular sample. Therefore two studies which are examining the same phenomenon might produce different results because the point at which the separation into the two groups occurred was different.

On the other hand, it could be legitimate to split a sample into groups if some external criterion was being used. Thus, a study might wish to compare people with and without depression and have used a test of depression which, although producing scores on a continuous scale, has a recognised score above which a person would be classified as having depression. In such a case, it could be legitimate to split the sample into those with and without depression. Nonetheless, given that the measure is unlikely to be 100% reliable, there will be people wrongly classified. Chen, Cohen, and Chen (2007), Cohen (1983), MacCallum, Zhang, Preacher, and Rucker (2002), Maxwell and Delaney (1993), Royston, Altman, and Sauerbrei (2005) and many others demonstrate the effects which dichotomising continuous data have on the results of statistical analysis.

Summary

Relationships between variables can be explored by regression analysis. Simple regression is used when only one IV is involved and multiple regression when more than one IV is included. Such analysis performs two functions. One function is to identify how much of the variance in the DV can be explained by variation in the IV(s). A second function is to build a model of how the DV is related to the IV(s) and so allow the DV to be predicted for specific values of the IV(s).

The form of regression which has been described in this chapter requires the outcome variable to be more continuous. The next chapter deals with a common situation where the outcome variable is categorical.

21 Analysis of relationships III
Logistic regression

Introduction

In Chapter 20 the point was made that several statistical tests, such as ANOVA and regression, are all examples of the general linear model (GLM). However, they have certain assumptions which make their use inappropriate when data do not conform to those assumptions, for example, when the outcome measure or dependent variable is on a categorical scale such as pass or fail on an aptitude test. To cope with a wider range of data than is covered by the GLM, statisticians have devised an extension of it, which is slightly confusingly called the *generalised* linear model (see Dobson & Barnett, 2018).

Logistic Regression is in the family of tests which conform to the generalised linear model and can be used to analyse data with a categorical outcome variable. Logistic Regression can be of two basic forms: *binary* (also described as *binomial*), where the outcome measure has only two possible outcomes, such as pass or fail, or *multinomial*, where the outcome measure has more than two possible outcomes, such as, if smoking status were to be classified as current smoker, current non-smoker, who has never smoked, and ex-smoker. I am going to restrict the description to an outcome measure which has only two possible outcomes: binary logistic regression. The popularity of this technique has meant that in software programs such as SPSS it can be selected more directly than just as a variant of the generalised linear model. For information on multinomial logistic regression see Hosmer, Lemeshow, and Sturdivant (2013).

A description of logistic regression can very quickly become quite mathematical. In order to minimise this, in this chapter I am going to describe how to conduct, interpret and report a binary logistic regression, restricting the account to what most psychologists would want to do; in Appendix XII I present more mathematical detail. Initially I will describe aspects of the generalised linear model and other concepts which will be needed to understand how logistic regression differs from other statistical methods covered so far in this book. I will then describe simple logistic regression, that is, where there is only one predictor variable. I will do this initially with a binary predictor and then with a more continuous predictor. I will then extend the example to multiple logistic regression where there is more than one predictor variable and finally cover an analysis where the predictor variables are added in stages: a sequential or hierarchical analysis.

The generalised linear model

Statistical tests which conform to the generalised linear model need additional information over those covered by the GLM. One of these is what is called the *link function*, the name given to a transformation that is needed to change the distribution of the DV so that its relation to the IV(s) is linear; more detail is given in Appendix XII. However, with the appropriate link function being provided, models which conform to the GLM can also be shown to be examples of the generalised linear model. The link function used with Logistic Regression is the *logit*. To find the logit initially the probability is calculated that a case will fall into the target value, for example will be a smoker. Then the odds for that case are calculated (see Appendix XII). The logit is the natural log of the odds.

Maximum likelihood estimation

Regression, as described in Chapter 20, is a statistical technique which uses what is called *ordinary least squares* (OLS). OLS in regression finds the smallest value for the squares of the distances of each data point from the best-fit line. The smaller the distance which the points have from the best-fit line, the more accurate that line is in describing the relationship between the predictor variable(s) and the outcome variable. An alternative form of statistical analysis is *maximum likelihood estimation* (known as MLE or, more usually, ML). ML finds a value for a parameter (an element in a mathematical model) which is the most likely to produce the data which are being analysed. ML involves *iteration*, whereby a computer program produces an initial solution and then uses that solution as a basis to rerun the analysis. The resultant solution of the new analysis is compared with the previous one. This process continues until the difference between solutions is below a certain predetermined size. Logistic Regression uses ML to find its solutions.

 ## Simple logistic regression

A single binary predictor variable

For this example I am going to analyse the data from Table 21.1, originally introduced in Chapter 15, in which gender is the predictor variable and smoking status (smoker or non-smoker) is the variable to be predicted. Forty-four males and 44 females are asked whether they are smokers.

TABLE 21.1   The numbers of male and female smokers and non-smokers in a sample

Observed frequency table

	Male	Female	Totals
Smoker	17	21	38
Non-smoker	27	23	50
Totals	44	44	88

The information provided by computer programs for logistic regression is similar to that provided for regression when the outcome measure is more continuous. Thus, there is a test of the overall model, tests of the individual predictor variables and measures of effect size. However, there are at least three tests of significance which have been devised: the Likelihood ratio test, the Wald test and the Score test. The Wald test is usually only applied to the individual predictor variables while the other two tests are usually given for the overall model, or a stage in a sequential regression. However, if there is only one predictor in the model, or only one predictor being added at a given stage then all three tests will be of that one predictor. Agresti (2002) and others note that in that situation the Likelihood ratio test is the more accurate for small or medium sample sizes.

Test of the overall model

In logistic regression a test of the overall model, as mentioned previously, is the Likelihood ratio test, which takes the chi-square distribution, with degrees of freedom equal to the number of predictor variables. In this case, with only one predictor, $\chi^2_{(1)} = 0.742$, $p = 0.389$. The test can be interpreted as telling us how much better the regression which includes the predictor variable is over one which doesn't include that predictor. Alternatively, there is the *Score test* (or *efficient score test*), which is also treated as a chi-square value. In this case the value is very similar to that from the Likelihood ratio test at $\chi^2_{(1)} = 0.741$, $p = 0.389$. It is the equivalent of a test the Null Hypothesis that the regression coefficient is 0.

Effect size for the whole model

There are several versions of R^2 in Logistic Regression. However, they should be treated with caution as they aren't completely equivalent to the R^2 which is provided from a linear regression, that is, when the outcome variable is more continuous. Cox and Snell's R^2, at 0.008, is, in this case, very similar to what would be produced from squaring the Pearson r calculated on the data or converting the chi-square to w and then squaring it. However, it is mathematically prevented from achieving a value of 1, even if the predictor variable perfectly predicted the values in the outcome variable. Nagelkerke's R^2 adjusts the Cox and Snell version to allow for a possible value of 1. In this case, Nagelkerke's R^2 is 0.011. There is another version of R^2, McFadden's.[1] In this example McFadden's $R^2 = 0.006$. Appendix XII explains how each of these versions of R^2 is calculated.

There is general agreement that these R^2 measures lack properties which their equivalent from multiple linear regression possesses. Mittlböck and Schemper (1996, 1999) note that none of them have an intuitive interpretation or would be numerically consistent with what would be produced by linear regression via the general linear model. Mittlböck and Schemper (1999) offer alternatives which do have the desired properties.[2] One of these is R^2_{SS} (based on sums of squares) which for the current example equals 0.008. (R^2_{SS} can be calculated relatively simply and I show how in Appendix XII.)

Individual predictors

The two questions usually asked are to do with whether a particular predictor is significant and how large an effect size it has. The Wald test is one of the most popular of the available tests of significance. It is often reported as the equivalent of a chi-square with df = 1. Here Wald = 0.739, $p = .390$. Notice that this is slightly different from the other two χ^2-value reported earlier. This is because logistic regression uses ML.

The effect size for the coefficient is in the form of an odds ratio (often shown as Exp(B) for reasons which are explained in Appendix XII). In this case, the odds ratio is 0.690, which tells us that the odds of being a smoker among the males are lower than the odds of being a smoker among the females. A confidence interval can also be found for the odds ratio; the 95% CI runs from 0.295 to 1.609. The fact that the interval includes 1 confirms the impression created by the non-significant result that there are no real differences in smoking status between males and females.

You might be reassured to see that many of these results were already presented (in Chapter 15) when the same data were analysed via the chi-square test for contingency tables. This confirms the point that when you only have one predictor variable, particularly when it is a binary measure, not much is added when regression is conducted as opposed to the chi-square test for contingency tables. Accordingly, I will leave a description of how to report the results of a logistic regression until a more realistic analysis has been conducted.

Classification

One way to evaluate the results of a logistic regression that might seem sensible is to see how accurately participants are predicted to fall into the outcome categories. As an example, we could ask how well

---

1 SPSS doesn't currently give McFadden's R^2 in binary logistic regression but you can get it via multinomial logistic regression – that is, when the outcome variable has more than two values – as it allows you to run that analysis even when the outcome is binary.

2 None of these are available in SPSS.

knowing a person's gender helps us to predict whether they will be a smoker. There is a problem with this approach as the classification will be affected by the original proportions falling into the different outcome categories. In the smoking example, the number of non-smokers is 50, while the number of smokers is 38 (56.82% and 43.18% respectively). Therefore, in the absence of any predictor the safest classification would be to classify everyone as a non-smoker and so be correct with 56.82% of the sample.

With gender as a predictor the classification is no more accurate and every participant is predicted to be a non-smoker. Therefore, the sensitivity of the model (the proportion or percentage of cases which fell into a given category (e.g. smoker) and which were correctly classified) is 0%. Specificity (the proportion or percentage of cases which didn't fall into that category and were successfully classified as not being in that category (e.g. non-smokers correctly identified as non-smokers)) was 100%.

Hosmer et al. (2013) demonstrate that it is possible to have an accurate model of the relationship between the predictors and the outcome variable in logistic regression which, nonetheless, produces poor classification. They note that classification should only act as additional information to other ways of assessing the model unless the actual aim of the study is classification. A further way to test how well the regression equation predicts the outcome is a goodness-of-fit test.

Testing Model fit (goodness of fit)

Hosmer et al. (2013) report a range of tests which were devised by the first two authors and which bear their name. However, in the case of a single binary categorical predictor the version I am going to present cannot be calculated because of the limited number of possible probabilities of being in one or the other outcome category. I will leave discussion of the test until I introduce an example for which it can be used.

A single continuous predictor variable

For the rest of the chapter I am going to analyse data which come from research by Michelle Meadows. Among other things, Michelle was looking at possible predictors of road traffic accidents. I have restricted the sample to people who had been driving for at least three years. The variable to be predicted is whether the motorists had an accident in the last three years. The sample I've taken had 332 people who had had an accident and 609 who hadn't. Among the possible predictors are age, gender, yearly mileage, experience at driving, unintentional mistakes while driving and intentional driving violations. I am going to start by looking at whether age is a useful predictor of accidents. Those who had had an accident were slightly younger (mean age 31.37 years, $SD = 11.05$) than those who hadn't (mean age = 34.66 years, $SD = 12.78$).

The logistic regression showed that the model which included age was a significantly better predictor of whether people had accidents than a model with no predictor variable ($\chi^2_{(1)} = 15.899, p < .001$). Cox and Snell $R^2 = 0.017$, Nagelkerke $R^2 = 0.023$, McFadden $R^2 = 0.013$ and $R^2_{ss} = 0.0016$. The odds ratio for age is 0.977 with a 95% CI of 0.966 to 0.989. This means for every extra year of age the odds of having an accident decreases to 97.7% of what it was. Thus, the odds of having an accident for a 40 year old are 97.7% the odds of having an accident for a 39 year old.

Hosmer and Lemeshow test of model fit

Hosmer and Lemeshow report two versions but I am going to describe the one which is implemented in SPSS. The predicted probabilities from the regression are put into groups of approximately equal size, with each consecutive group having a range of higher predicted probabilities; where possible, 10 groups will be created. A contingency table is then created of actual outcome by the 10 groups; see Table 21.2.

TABLE 21.2   The contingency table for the Hosmer & Lemeshow test, derived from the logistic regression with age as a predictor and having an accident in the last three years as the outcome

Probability range	Accident in last 3 years = .00		Accident in last 3 years = 1.00		Total
	Observed	Expected	Observed	Expected	
1	78	73.017	17	21.983	95
2	62	67.733	31	25.267	93
3	63	65.323	31	28.677	94
4	64	62.077	30	31.923	94
5	65	62.421	34	36.579	99
6	66	59.966	32	38.034	98
7	50	57.828	46	38.172	96
8	50	55.979	44	38.021	94
9	58	55.504	36	38.496	94
10	53	49.151	31	34.849	84

Expected frequencies are calculated using a method described in Appendix XII. A standard χ^2 is then calculated on the data, comparing observed and expected frequencies. However, this version of the test has df = number of groups – 2, rather than the (rows-1) × (columns-1) of the standard Pearson chi-square test. In the current example $\chi^2 = 10.799$, df = 8, p = .213. As the result is not statistically significant this is evidence that the model and the data are not a sufficiently poor fit to each other. However, other evidence shows that the model is not particularly accurate. All the participants are classified according to the model as not having had an accident, because the majority (64.7%) didn't have an accident, so sensitivity is 0%, as no one was classified as having an accident, and specificity is 100% as everyone who didn't have an accident is correctly classified. Further evidence of the usefulness of the model is given by the c-statistic.

C-statistic

The c-statistic or concordance index is another measure of how well the model classifies. It is derived from the receiver operator curve (ROC) which is a plot of sensitivity by 1-specificity (see Appendix XII for more details). A value of 0.5 is no better than chance. Hosmer et al. (2013) suggest that 0.7 to just under 0.8 is acceptable, 0.8 to just under 0.9 is excellent and 0.9 and above is outstanding. In the current case c = 0.572, which is not much better than chance.

Multiple logistic regression

For this example, I'm going to include age and sex as predictor variables of accidents. The overall model is statistically significant ($\chi^2_{(2)} = 26.44$, $p < .001$, Cox & Snell $R^2 = 0.028$, Nagelkerke $R^2 = 0.038$, McFadden $R^2 = 0.022$ and $R^2_{SS} = 0.027$). Both predictors were significant (see Table 21.3).

The Hosmer & Lemeshow test produced the following results: Chi-square = 11.783, df = 8, $p = 0.161$. The c-statistic = 0.596, which is still poor and the classification has not improved, with every case being classified as not having had an accident.

TABLE 21.3 Selected output for a multiple binary logistic regression with age and sex of drivers as predictors and presence or absence of car accidents as the outcome variable

	B	S.E.	Wald	df	p	Exp(B)	95% C.I. for Exp(B)	
							Lower	Upper
Age	−.021	.006	13.032	1	.000	.979	.968	.990
Sex	.472	.147	10.326	1	.001	1.603	1.202	2.137
Constant	−.207	.232	.799	1	.371	.813		

Interpretation and reporting

As with linear regression there are a number of sources of information and some of these may appear to conflict and so the interpretation needs to deal with the subtleties of the particular pattern of results. Prior to the regression we will look to see which variables are significantly related to the outcome variable. With three or more variables, as in this case, I would report the results in a correlation matrix. Note that as all the variables are either continuous or, where categorical, dichotomous, it is legitimate to produce correlations to examine their relationships. Had a variable been categorical but with more than two levels then the analysis you report at this stage depends on the other variable. If both variables were categorical then chi-square for a contingency table would tell whether they were significantly related and Cramér's phi would provide the effect size. When one is continuous and the other categorical then ANOVA could be used for significance and eta-squared for the effect size. Table 21.4 shows that both age and sex were significantly related to having an accident in the last three years; with increasing age the likelihood of having an accident decreases, as the coding of sex was male = 1 and female = 2, the negative relationship with accidents means that males are more likely to have had an accident. Both of these relationships are close to being small effect sizes. The relationship between age and sex is even smaller but is also significant because of the large sample size.

TABLE 21.4 The correlations between age, sex and whether the participant had an accident while driving in the last three years

	Accident in last 3 years	Age	Sex
Accident in last 3 years	1		
Age	−.128**	1	
Sex	−.116**	.089**	1

**p < .001

The results for the whole model with age and sex as predictors are reported above, including the range of R^2 calculations, the goodness-of-fit test and the c-statistic. Table 21.3 shows the results for the individual predictors. As there were only two, I would report them within the text. With more predictors I would report them in a table. Both age and sex were significant predictors: (age, B = −.021, $Wald_{(1)}$ = 13.032, p < .001, e^B = 0.979, 95% CI = 0.968, 0.990; sex, B = .472, $Wald_{(1)}$ = 10.326, p = .001, e^B = 1.603, 95% CI = 1.202, 2.137). Note that with age in the model the odds of having an accident as a female are higher than for males.

Sequential logistic regression

I am going to continue with the analysis of Michelle Meadows's data based on drivers. I will treat the first stage of the analysis as having age and gender entered into the model, as in the last analysis. The second and final stage will have two measures of driving behaviour added: how likely a driver is to commit (1) an unintentional mistake and (2) a driving violation such as driving through a junction when the lights are against you.

In Table 21.5 all the predictors correlate significantly with accidents. However the correlation involving mistakes is particularly small.

TABLE 21.5 The correlations between each of the variables to be included in the sequential logistic regression

	Age	Sex	Mistakes	Violations	Accident in last 3 years
Age	1				
Sex	.089	1			
Mistakes	−.020	.015	1		
Violations	−.318	−.275	.357	1	
Accident in last 3 years	−.128	−.116	.070	.153	1

The test of whether the stage adds significantly to the model shows that it does ($\chi^2_{(2)}$ = 9.486, p = .009) and the whole model remains significant ($\chi^2_{(4)}$ = 35.925, $p < .001$). The R^2 values have increased (Cox and Snell = .037, Nagelkerke = .052, McFadden = .029 and R^2_{SS} = .036). The Hosmer and Lemeshow test shows that the model fits the data ($\chi^2_{(8)}$ = 5.637, p = .688). Sensitivity has improved a little from previous models to 0.072 but specificity has become slightly poorer at 0.957. In fact the overall accuracy of classification has gone down slightly at 64.5% correct. The c-statistic is now 0.618, which according to Hosmer et al. (2013) is still below what could be considered acceptable. Table 21.6 shows that with the exception of mistakes all are significant predictors in the model.

TABLE 21.6 The results of the second stage of a sequential logistic regression in which forms of driving behaviour – mistakes and violations – were added to the model

	B	S.E.	Wald	df	p	Exp(B)	95% C.I. for Exp(B)	
							Lower	Upper
Age	−.017	.006	7.435	1	.006	.983	.971	.995
Sex	.388	.153	6.403	1	.011	1.474	1.091	1.992
Mistakes	.203	.178	1.300	1	.254	1.225	.864	1.734
Violations	.244	.111	4.814	1	.028	1.276	1.026	1.587
Constant	−1.103	.387	8.133	1	.004	.332		

 ## Assumptions

Logistic regression is relatively free of assumptions compared with linear regression. The predictor variables can be continuous, ordinal or categorical. In the latter case, as usual, it is important that the way in which the data have been coded numerically is not treated by the software as indicating an order and so it is necessary to indicate that the numbers denote categories. For example, if one variable were eye colour then coding them as brown = 1, blue = 2, green = 3, etc., should not be taken as meaning there is any order for the different colours. In the case of a dichotomous variable one level can be coded as 1 and the other as 0. Thus for gender if female was coded as 1 then male would be coded as 0. In the case where there are more than two levels, for example smoking status (current smoker, ex-smoker, never smoked), dummy variables need to be created. There will always be one fewer dummy variable than the number of levels in the original variable as that number is sufficient to classify every case. See Chapter 20 and Appendix XI for more detail on dummy variables. Some software, such as SPSS, will automatically create the necessary dummy variables when you indicate that a variable is categorical. The data must be independent; see Chapter 16 for more about this issue and possible solutions if it is not fulfilled.

The remainder of the assumptions are examined along with diagnostic checks.

Linearity of continuous predictor variables with the logit

In order to be able to make statements about the relationship between a predictor variable and the outcome variable, it is assumed that the rate of change of the logit across the range of the predictor variable is constant, otherwise the beta value is not valid for the entire range of the predictor variable. Once the analysis has been conducted it is possible to calculate the logit for each case and then plot this against each continuous predictor variable. Figure 21.1 shows a plot of age and the logit from the regression with age, sex, mistakes and violations as predictors of accidents. As there is no curvilinear relationship, we can be satisfied that there is no breach of this assumption.

FIGURE 21.1 A plot of age with the logit from the regression with age, sex, mistakes and violations as predictors of accidents

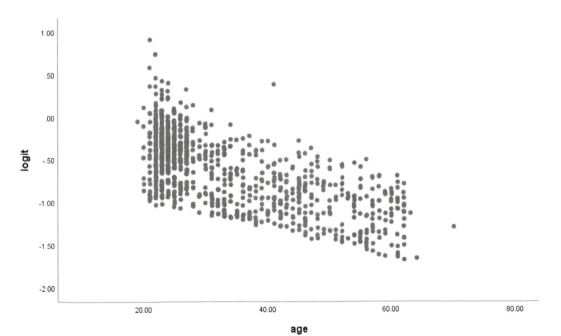

Data checks

An important issue, as with any statistical technique, is whether there are data points or combinations of data points which are unduly influencing the results. As usual for more continuous variables you would want to look for outliers. This could be done via standardised scores or plots such as box plots. I give my usual caution here that you should not just delete such cases without checking whether they are produced by some issue which means they do not contribute to a valid test of your hypotheses. See Chapter 23 for discussion of this issue. If you have no reason for believing that the data are in some way not legitimate then you should run the analysis with and without such cases to see how robust your results are to such cases. In other words, conduct sensitivity analysis. However, in the case of logistic regression I would note such cases but see whether they showed up when you conducted diagnostic checks which examine whether there are participants whose pattern of data may be influencing the results.

Zero frequencies

This refers to the situation where some categories have no cases in one or both outcome category. For example, if the outcome variable was smoking status and the predictor were gender but no males in the sample were smokers, then the frequency in the cell for male smokers would be zero. This will mean that a sensible model cannot be found; the analysis may not be able to find a solution and the estimates of standard errors and odds ratios may be meaningless. With small sample sizes, predictors with many categories or a large number of categorical predictors, it is more likely that there will be cells with zero frequency. In SPSS, and other statistical programs, you should get a warning about the presence of zero frequency in cells. However, you should have explored the data before conducting the analysis and so identified the problem.

Hosmer et al. (2013) suggest that if the predictor is categorical then categories could be collapsed to get rid of the empty cell. However, this should only be done if the newly created category makes sense (see Chapter 16 for a discussion about this solution). If the variable is ordinal they suggest that it could be treated as a continuous variable. They give other possible solutions.

Complete separation

If values on a predictor variable completely correctly predict the category for each participant then estimates of parameters cannot be calculated; the predictor variable is too perfect a predictor of the outcome variable and so estimates of standard error cannot be calculated. An example would be if age perfectly predicted whether a person would have a car accident, with all below 30 years having had an accident and no one aged 30 or over having had such an accident. The same problem can occur if there are few cases of overlap.

Collinearity and Multicollinearity

This issue is to do with how highly one predictor variable (collinearity) or more than one predictor variable (multicollinearity) explains the variance in one of the predictor variables. The issue is discussed in Chapter 20. If the software you are using does not include checks on multicollinearity for logistic regression but does for linear regression, then you can run a separate linear regression for each more continuous predictor variable, treating that predictor as an outcome variable and the other predictors as predictors and explore multicollinearity that way. Alternatively, you could run the regression as though it were a linear regression and explore multicollinearity that way. This latter method would be less labour intensive and is not affected by the choice of outcome variable as long as it does vary in values. Nonetheless, categorical predictor variables with more than two levels will be problematic; they will need to be converted to dummy variables and so the degree to which they are capable of being predicted by the other predictors cannot be calculated this way.

Fortunately, in the current example, none of the predictors is categorical with more than two levels. I treated a continuous variable which was also in the data set as an arbitrary outcome variable, ran a linear multiple regression with age, sex, mistakes and violations as predictors and asked for collinearity statistics. Table 21.7 shows that none of the variables is flagged as having an issue over multicollinearity, as all the tolerance values are well above .1; see Chapter 20 for an explanation of this criterion.

TABLE 21.7 The tolerance and VIF (variance inflation factor) of the predictors in the multiple logistic regression

	Tolerance	VIF
Age	.889	1.125
Sex	.910	1.099
Mistakes	.849	1.178
Violations	.712	1.405

Hosmer et al. (2013) make the general point that high beta values or standard errors can be a warning that something is wrong with the data. If either happens then you should explore further to find the source of the problem.

Diagnostic checks

There exists such a wide range of such checks and such a range of advice about which ones are the most useful that I am not going to go into all of them but just suggest a subset would be worth doing. For the wider range and further advice see Hosmer et al. (2013) and Agresti (2002).

Multivariate outliers

SPSS produces what is described as an analogue of Cook's distance. This allows you to produce a scatterplot of that analogue and leverage. As described in Chapter 20, rather than treat values above a certain criterion as potentially problematic, I recommend looking for values which are well separated from the rest. Figure 21.2 shows the plot for the data in the model with accidents as the outcome and age, gender, violations and mistakes as the predictors. From it we can see that no particular value is well separated from the others; after the initial cluster in the bottom left of the graph, the values gradually increase. With such a pattern I wouldn't treat any case as a possible outlier.

FIGURE 21.2   A plot of leverage and the analogue of Cook's distance from the multiple logistic regression

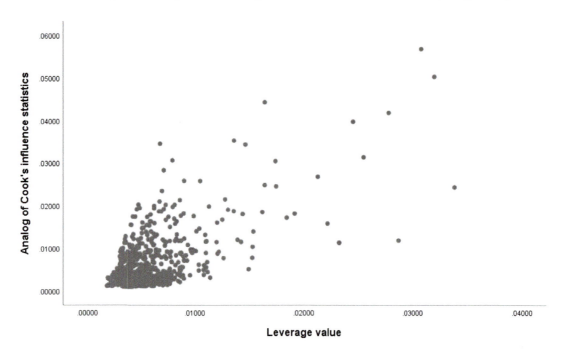

Sample size

At the time of writing, there appears to be no definitive way of calculating the sample size necessary to achieve a given level of power for a given effect size in multiple logistic regression. Hsieh (1989) has provided a method which is based on a single predictor variable and suggested an adjustment which can be made when there is more than one predictor; see Table A18.12. As an example I am going to take the target predictor as violations. If researchers wished to attempt to replicate the driving study and knew the results of the current study, they could utilise the details from the current study to conduct power calculations. In a simple logistic regression with violations as the only predictor and accidents in the last three years as the outcome variable, violations has the odds ratio of 1.548. The number of participants in the sample who had had an accident is 332 in a total sample of 941, so the proportion of those having an accident is .353. The equation which I used to create Table A18.12 shows that for power of 0.8, alpha of 0.05 and a two-tailed test, a sample of 216 would be needed. The adjustment to allow for a multiple logistic regression with age, sex and mistakes included raises the sample to 304; see Appendix XII for the calculations. Hosmer et al. (2013) describe the use of the adjustment as ad hoc. The adjustment takes into account the relationship between the target predictor variable and the other predictors. This adjustment makes sense, but it seems likely that there are other aspects of the situation that need to be taken into consideration to arrive at a more accurate estimate.

However, frequently we are trying to decide on the appropriate sample size without information from previous studies which would provide all the necessary details. In which case, we need to estimate what effect size we think is worth detecting. As an example, we could be comparing a new intervention to stop pregnant women smoking with those not taking part in the intervention. We know that without an intervention only 18% of pregnant women who smoke give up spontaneously. We want to increase the quit rate to at least 28%. Accordingly the odds of giving up without the intervention is 0.22 and the odds of giving up with our intervention would need to be 0.39 (see Chapter 15 for more on odds and odds ratios). Therefore the minimum odds ratio between our intervention and the control condition would be 1.77. If we are aiming for equal sample sizes in the intervention and the control conditions then the probability of quitting smoking for the whole sample would be .23. We can now use Table A18.12 to work out the required sample size.

Summary

This chapter has shown that when the outcome variable is categorical, logistic regression can be used to analyse a data set which contains one or more predictors. It has demonstrated the use of logistic regression when the outcome has two possible values. It has shown that there are a number of parallels with linear regression such as simple, multiple and sequential regression. However, there are also a number of differences including the use of odds ratios to measure the link between the outcome and a predictor variable.

One role of multiple regression is to analyse the relationship between an IV and the DV when the relationship of other variables and the DV are also taken into account. The next chapter introduces a way of doing this which is as an extension of ANOVA: analysis of covariance (ANCOVA).

22 Analysis of covariance (ANCOVA)

Introduction

Up to now when we have wished to test differences between different levels of an independent variable (IV) we have looked at using *t*-tests, when the IV has two levels, or ANOVA, when it has more than two. If we wanted to check for the influence of another IV we have used multi-way ANOVA to investigate interactions between IVs. However, we have been limited to including additional IVs which form categories such as mnemonic training technique or gender. This does not let us take into account other variables which are more continuous, such as age. We might test differences in recall between people taught the method of loci, people taught to use pegwords and a control group not taught any mnemonic method. However, there might be other variables which are affecting the link between mnemonic technique and recall, such as reasoning ability, which might also differ between the mnemonic conditions. When such variables are more continuous they are often described as covariates. In Chapter 20, I explained the problems with trying to force such variables into the appropriate form for an ANOVA by creating categories out of them. Analysis of covariance (ANCOVA) lets researchers who are investigating differences between levels of an IV allow for the possible effects of other more continuous variables (covariates) on the result.

An IV with two levels

Imagine that we have a test which is given to children to see whether they can sort a set of pictures into two groups according to a particular aspect of the pictures; for example, the relevant aspect might be shape and the two groups might be angular (such as squares and triangles) and round (such as circles and ovals). We present each child with 11 of these sorting problems and note how many that child sorts successfully. We might have devised a training technique which gives children experience with such sorting tasks with the training materials being different from those on which the children will be tested. We might then compare the sorting ability of children who have received such training with children who have not (the control group).

Eighty children were randomly assigned to the two conditions: training and control. After the training period the children were tested on their sorting ability. In the training condition the mean number of items correctly sorted was 7.68 items (*SD* = 2.36), while in the control condition the mean was 6.43 (*SD* = 2.86).

As there are only two levels of the IV we could use a between-subjects *t*-test to compare the sorting of the children in the two conditions. However, because I am going to build the analysis up in stages I am going to use a one-way between-subjects ANOVA.[1] Table 22.1 shows the output from the ANOVA.

---

1 Remember that the ANOVA will produce the same probability as a *t*-test with a two-tailed probability and in this case the researchers might make no prediction as they are unsure whether the training will improve ability or only work for the tasks on which the children were trained.

TABLE 22.1 The results from a one-way between-subjects ANOVA comparing the sorting abilities of children trained to sort with those of a control group

Source	Sum of squares	df	Mean square	F	p
Condition	31.250	1	31.250	4.543	.036
Error	536.550	78	6.879		
Total	567.800	79			

Based on this result, we might assume that the training produces improved sorting ability; the effect size for the treatment is $\eta^2 = .055$. However, given that our participants are children, the groups might differ in their ages and this could be producing the difference in sorting ability. By randomly assigning the children to the two conditions we might hope to have controlled for age, but there still might have been differences between the groups. The mean age (in months) was 156.18 ($SD = 37.32$) in the training condition and 142.73 ($SD = 41.61$) in the control group.

We can see that the children in the training condition are older. ANCOVA allows us to treat age as a covariate and so make allowance for the differences in ages to see whether the difference in sorting ability is maintained. Table 22.2 shows the output from the ANCOVA.

TABLE 22.2 The results from an ANCOVA in which the sorting ability of those trained to sort is compared with that of a control group but with age treated as a covariate

Source	Sum of squares	df	Mean square	F	p
Age	309.681	1	309.681	105.107	<.001
Condition	6.354	1	6.354	2.157	.146
Error	226.869	77	2.946		
Total	567.800	79			

The row for *age* shows that age explains a significant proportion of the variance in sorting ability. The row for *condition* shows that condition does not explain a significant proportion of the remaining variance. Thus, according to this analysis the training group and control groups do not differ significantly in sorting ability when an adjustment has been made for age; the effect size for the treatment has dropped to $\eta^2 = .011$.

ANCOVA adjusts the values of the DV in each group to allow for the differences in the covariate. The adjusted mean values are 7.336 for the group who were trained and 6.764 for the control group. This is more fully explained in Appendix XIII. However, at an intuitive level, the adjustment is the equivalent of calculating the mean sorting ability which each group would have had if they had had the same mean age. Figure 22.1 shows a scattergram for a selected range of age and sorting ability, with the regression lines of the training and control group. A vertical line is drawn to represent the mean of age (the covariate). For each group, a horizontal line is drawn from the point where the mean age line meets the regression line. The points where the horizontal lines meet the vertical axis are the adjusted means (for the DV) whose values are shown in italics.

Before describing how to report the results of an ANCOVA, I am going to deal with the assumptions of ANCOVA.

FIGURE 22.1   The adjustment of mean sorting ability as a result of the ANCOVA with age as the covariate

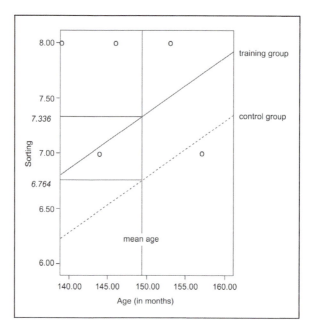

Assumptions of ANCOVA

In addition to the assumptions of ANOVA, the adjustments to the mean which are made by ANCOVA can only safely be made if what is called *homogeneity of regression slope* is present in the data. This means that the relationship between the covariate and the DV has the same slope in each group, in other words, the best-fit lines for the different levels of the IV are parallel.[2] One test of homogeneity of regression slope is to see whether there is an interaction between the IV and the covariate. As with tests of interactions in ANOVA, if the lines are not parallel, then this suggests an interaction, and in the case of ANCOVA the presence of such an interaction would mean the assumption of homogeneity of regression slope was not fulfilled. To test the interaction conduct an analysis which is the equivalent of an ANCOVA but in addition to the covariate and the IV the interaction between the covariate and the IV is included, with the latter added last. Table 22.3 shows the output for this 'augmented' ANCOVA.

TABLE 22.3   The results from an 'augmented' ANCOVA which compares the sorting abilities of those trained to sort and those in a control group, with age as a covariate and the interaction between the IV and covariate added

Source	Sum of squares	df	Mean square	F	p
Age	305.731	1	305.731	102.422	<.001
Condition	.519	1	0.519	0.174	.678
Condition* age	.007	1	0.007	0.002	.961
Error	226.862	76	2.985		
Total	567.800	79			

2   If for each level of the IV a regression was conducted with the covariate as the predictor variable and the DV as the variable to be predicted.

Here we can see that the interaction term is not statistically significant. As usual in such tests of assumptions, we do not want to be wholly dependent on statistical significance to make the judgement so it is a good idea to check the proportion of variance which the interaction explains. If this is particularly small, then we can be more confident that heterogeneity of regression slope is not present. In this case, $\eta^2 < .0001$ for the amount of additional variance explained by the interaction and so it confirms that the regression slopes are not heterogeneous.

Figure 22.2 shows the regression slopes of the two different groups. This is included just for illustration and isn't necessary in order to check for heterogeneity.

FIGURE 22.2   A scattergram of age (the covariate) and sorting ability (the DV) with the regression slopes of the training and control groups shown

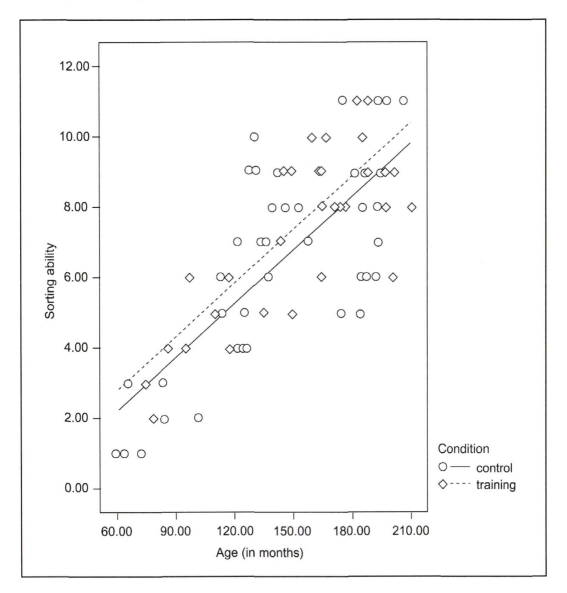

We have found that the slopes are approximately the same. This allows the adjustment in the group to be made to allow for the covariate as the same coefficient for the slope is used to calculate the adjusted means. This is illustrated in Appendix XIII. If the slopes are heterogeneous, then the adjustment in the means which is made by ANCOVA is inappropriate. Thus when there is heterogeneity of slope another method of analysis should be conducted, as the adjustments cannot be interpreted in the same way.

A number of alternative analyses are available if the slopes are heterogeneous. Maxwell and Delaney (2004) suggest that we can still decide whether there is an overall significant difference between the groups. To do this we would examine the F-ratio for the treatment from the analysis which was exploring heterogeneity of regression slope, shown in Table 22.3: what they term *ANCOHET*. Here we can see that $F(1, 76) = 0.174$, $p = .678$, which confirms that the groups do not differ significantly. Another analysis would be to run separate regressions for the different groups. Thus, we could treat sorting ability as the variable to be predicted and age as the predictor variable but analyse each group separately. A third possible analysis would be hierarchical linear modelling where the whole data set is used in one analysis but the regression slope is allowed to vary between groups; see Chapter 25 for more details about this method of analysis. Yet another possible analysis is that which looks at attribute–treatment–interaction (ATI), details of which can be found in Pedhazur (1997).

The relationship in each level of the IV between the DV and the covariate should be linear or, more confusingly but correctly, should not be non-linear. This can be tested by scattergrams of the covariate and the DV.

The DV should be normally distributed at each level of the covariate. Huitema (1980) notes that this assumption is less of a concern when the covariate is normally distributed and that this is particularly so when the design is balanced (i.e. the sample sizes in each group are the same). Therefore, you should test the distribution of the covariate for each level of the IV. I recommend checking the distribution of the residuals (i.e. the difference between predicted and actual values) and if these are sufficiently normally distributed then there is no need to investigate this assumption further. However, if they are clearly not normally distributed then investigate the distribution of the covariate for each level of the IV to identify the source of the problem. The variance of the DV for each level of the covariate should be the same across the levels of the IV and the variance of the DV should be the same for each level of the covariate. Huitema (1980) notes that this is also less of an issue when the covariate is normally distributed and the design balanced.

Huitema (1980) suggests that if the linearity or homogeneity assumptions are violated, then rank ANCOVA can be applied. Refer to Huitema for how to conduct such an analysis.

The assumption that participants have been allocated to conditions on a random basis is particularly important in ANCOVA. This is because the adjustment which it makes to the means is more justified in such designs. In a sense, what is being done is an attempt to counteract a problem which the randomisation process was designed to solve, namely, that the groups should have ended up with the same mean on the covariate. However, if the allocation to conditions isn't random or if the study is using pre-existing groups, then the adjustments made by ANCOVA may be inappropriate and be open to misinterpretation. For example, in studies of children with autism they are often matched with control children who do not have any form of autism, on the basis of verbal ability. A consequence of this is that the two groups are then going to be of different ages. It would make little sense then to use age as a covariate, as the adjusted means on the DV would be based on hypothetical children who either had autism but were younger than the population from which the original children with autism were drawn or were older than the population from which the control children were drawn.

The foregoing is not saying that ANCOVA is only appropriate when participants have been allocated randomly but rather that interpretation of the results has to be treated with greater caution when this hasn't happened.

The covariate should not be affected by the treatment and therefore it is safest to have measured the covariate prior to the treatment being applied. Imagine that in my study of sorting ability I am interested in whether linguistic ability might act as a covariate. If I test linguistic ability prior to the training phase, then once the training had been completed it would be legitimate to treat linguistic ability as a covariate in an ANCOVA comparing the sorting ability of the training and control groups. However, if I measure linguistic ability after the training and treat it as a covariate, then the basis of ANCOVA is being violated. It may be that my training has enhanced linguistic ability as well as sorting ability. An ANCOVA will treat the groups' linguistic abilities as the same and adjust the mean sorting abilities accordingly. Again it has extrapolated to hypothetical and non-existent groups: those given the training but having linguistic ability which has benefited only minimally from it and those given no training but have enhanced linguistic ability. Thus, a non-significant result from the ANCOVA could be misinterpreted as showing no benefit to sorting ability of the training.

Reporting an ANCOVA

Ideally, where space permitted, I would give as full information as possible of results before and after the covariate has been included and of the covariate itself. Accordingly, I would report means and *SD*s for the DV for each group before adjustment and after adjustment and the means and *SD*s of the covariate. Then, in reporting the inferential tests, I would report the results of an ANOVA or *t*-test before the covariate is included and then with the covariate included. I wouldn't bother with reporting an analysis just of the covariate; using the details you have given, the reader could calculate that if he or she wanted. I would report the results of the ANCOVA including each of the effect sizes. There is no need to provide the graph of the regression slopes for each group. However, you do need to reassure the reader that this has been tested and the slopes have been found not to be heterogeneous. Thus, I would report the result in the following way.

A one-way between-subjects ANOVA was conducted to compare the sorting ability of children given the training in sorting with that of the control group. The training group correctly sorted significantly more items (mean = 7.68 items, *SD* = 2.36) than the control group (mean = 6.43 items, *SD* = 2.86) ($F_{(1,78)}$ = 4.54, *p* = .036, η^2 = .055). Mean age (in months) was 156.18 (*SD* = 37.32) in the training condition and 142.73 (*SD* = 41.61) in the control group. An ANCOVA was then conducted, again comparing the training and control groups on their sorting ability but with age as a covariate. The groups did not differ significantly (adjusted means: training group = 7.336 items, control group = 6.764) ($F_{(1,77)}$ = 2.157, *p* = .146, η^2 = .011). Homogeneity of regression slope was checked via the interaction between age and condition. This was not significant and explained a very small proportion of additional variance ($F_{(1,76)}$ = 0.002, *p* = .961, η^2 < .0001).

Statistical power and ANCOVA

The effect of using ANCOVA instead of ANOVA should be to increase power as the inclusion of the covariate is reducing the amount of variance left to be explained. Thus as long as the size of the effect is not reduced once the adjustment for the covariate has been made, there will be less error variance and so the ratio of treatment variance to error variance will be greater. However, for each covariate included in the analysis the df for the error term will be reduced by 1 but this will only make an important difference for small samples. Cohen (1988) gives a rough estimate that as long as the number of conditions multiplied by *n* − 1 (the number in each group) is between 15 and 20, then the loss of 1 in the error df will not be important and standard power tables for ANOVA can be used for ANCOVA (see Appendix XVIII) and you should have at least the power shown in Table A18.7. For example, this would mean that for a design which has an IV with two levels and one covariate, having a sample of 11 in each group would be enough to allow the power tables for ANOVA to be sufficiently accurate for working out the power for ANCOVA. As this sample size would only give an adequate level of power of .8 if the effect size was very large (at least $\eta^2 = .28$), for most purposes a larger sample will be required and so the figures in Table A18.7 can safely be used for ANCOVA.

 ## Pre-treatment values as covariates

A second common use of ANCOVA is to allow for a pre-intervention score on the DV. For, once again, although we may have randomly assigned participants to conditions, there may still be pre-existing differences between the groups. If we consider the sorting task and we ignore pre-existing sorting ability and simply compare a control and training group after the intervention has taken place, then a number of possibilities exist, two of which could be misinterpreted. Firstly, we could find that those in the training group have better sorting ability but this could have nothing to do with the training and simply be because they were better anyway. Secondly, we could find no difference between the sorting ability of the groups after the intervention but this might be because although our intervention did produce an improvement, the control group started out being better at sorting and the improvement may not have been sufficient to overcome the initial deficit in the training group. By adjusting for the sorting ability prior to the intervention we should gain a clearer picture of the efficacy of the training method.

The example I am going to give is of the first situation where the control group starts at a disadvantage. The design is the same as before with participants assigned randomly to two conditions: control and training. In fact the data for sorting after the training phase are the same as in the previous example. The new element is that I have data for the participants' sorting ability prior to the intervention phase: training group mean = 7.08 ($SD = 2.25$); control group mean = 6.38 ($SD = 2.44$).

I run an ANCOVA with condition as the IV, post-intervention sorting ability as the DV and pre-intervention as the covariate. The output can be seen in Table 22.4.

TABLE 22.4   The results from an ANCOVA in which the sorting ability of a group trained to sort is compared with that of a control group but with pre-training sorting ability as a covariate

Source	Sum of squares	df	Mean square	F	p
Pre-sort	302.025	1	302.025	99.162	<.001
Condition	8.571	1	8.571	2.814	.098
Error	234.525	77	3.046		
Total	567.800	79			

The effect size for the treatment once the adjustment has been made for the covariate is $\eta^2 = .015$ and the adjusted means are 7.381 for the training group and 6.719 for the control group. The check on homogeneity of regression slope was $F_{(1,76)} < 0.001$, $p = .987$, $\eta^2 < .001$, showing no evidence of heterogeneity of regression slope.

 ## Alternatives to ANCOVA for pre–post designs

Given the same design – pre-treatment, post-treatment, with an intervention and a control group – at least two other analyses are possible: firstly, find the difference between pre- and post-stages and then compare control and training groups on those difference scores using a *t*-test; or, secondly, run a two-way mixed ANOVA with pre- and post-stage as the within-subjects variable and condition – control and training – as the between-subjects variable. If you are trying to find out whether an intervention is effective and you have used random assignment to the conditions, then ANCOVA can be preferable. It is more powerful than the use of difference scores as it reduces the variance which needs to be explained by the IV, as some has already been accounted for by the covariate; in other words, if the intervention is effective, then ANCOVA is more likely to demonstrate this.

The use of a mixed ANOVA is a rather circuitous route to answering the question and it still may fail to demonstrate that an effective treatment *is* effective. Initially, it will provide tests of three hypotheses, but none of these directly addresses the question we are interested in. The first test is of the main effect of stage. If the treatment is effective, then we would expect this to be significant because although the control condition will show little difference between pre- and post-, the training group should. However, this merely answers the question about whether there is a difference between the two stages and it could have occurred when both groups improved. Second is the main effect of group. If the treatment is effective, then the training group should have the higher mean and this main effect should be significant. However, this part of the test is taking both pre- and post-scores into account, so it still can't demonstrate that the intervention is effective; it is telling us that when the distinction between pre- and post- is ignored the two groups differ. Finally we have the interaction between the two IVs. If the treatment is effective, then the interaction should be significant as the control condition should show no change between the stages while the training condition should be better in the post-stage. We would need to follow up the analysis of the interaction with simple effects; for example, comparing pre- and post- just for the control group and then just for the training group. If the intervention was effective, then we should get a significant result for the training group and a non-significant one for the control group.

Regression discontinuity designs (RDD)

This design involves taking a measure of participants and then allocating them to different groups based on their scores on the measure. The groups are given different treatments and are then compared. This is another design usually included under the heading of quasi-experimental. I describe it in greater detail in Appendix XIII.

ANCOVA with more than two levels in an IV

So far I have presented two analyses where the IV has only two levels. In each case, had there been a significant difference, we needed only to look at the adjusted means to find which condition was producing the higher level of sorting. However, in ANCOVA, just as with ANOVA, where an IV has more than two levels, if we have a significant difference between the conditions, we will have to conduct further analysis to have a clearer idea of which specific groups differ.

Imagine an extension of the previous study on sorting ability which has a control group and two different training groups. There were 40 children in each condition. Table 22.5 shows the means and SDs for sorting ability after the treatment phase and for age.

TABLE 22.5 The means and SDs of sorting ability after the treatment phase and of age (in months)

Condition		Sorting	Age
Control	Mean	6.43	142.73
	SD	2.86	41.61
Training 1	Mean	7.68	156.18
	SD	2.36	37.32
Training 2	Mean	6.45	121.10
	SD	2.96	35.23

Table 22.6 shows the results of the ANOVA with sorting as the DV, from which we learn that the groups do not differ significantly.

TABLE 22.6   The results from an ANOVA comparing the sorting ability with of a control group and two training groups

Source	Sum of squares	df	Mean square	F	p
Condition	40.850	2	20.425	2.720	.070
Error	878.450	117	7.508		
Total	919.300	119			

Table 22.7 shows the results of an ANCOVA with age as the covariate and sorting as the DV. Here we see that once the possible influence of age on sorting ability has been allowed for, the groups do differ significantly in their sorting ability.

TABLE 22.7   The results from an ANCOVA comparing the sorting ability of a control group and two training groups with age as a covariate

Source	Sum of squares	df	Mean square	F	p
Age	472.173	1	472.173	134.815	<.001
Condition	25.697	2	12.849	3.669	.029
Error	406.277	116	3.502		
Total	919.300	119			

The check on heterogeneity of regression slope (the interaction between condition and age) was not statistically significant ($F_{(2, 114)} = 0.307$, $p = .736$, $\eta^2 = .002$). The adjusted means for the three groups were control = 6.281, training group 1 = 6.823 and training group 2 = 7.445. As the ANCOVA shows a significant effect of treatment we need to follow this up to explore the source of the significant result.

Follow-up analysis

Although many of the principles which apply to contrasts after an ANOVA also apply to contrasts after an ANCOVA, there are further considerations which have to be taken into account when deciding on the method to employ. The added aspects are (1) whether the design involved random assignment to the groups or a non-random basis including pre-existing groups, and (2) whether the covariate is a random or fixed variable – in other words, whether the particular values of the covariate were chosen by the researchers or were an artefact of the sample taken. In the current example age can be considered to be a random variable as the age of each child was not specified, only the range within which their ages would lie. To simplify the presentation I am going to restrict what I cover to the situations which researchers are most likely to meet. Thus, I am going to assume that the covariate is a random variable and I am only going to cover paired contrasts. For fixed covariates and non-paired contrasts see Huitema (1980). I am also going to assume that heterogeneity of regression slopes has not been found. In Appendix XIII a method for conducting contrasts when the slopes are heterogeneous is given.

With ANCOVA, just as with the contrasts following an ANOVA, we can have planned or unplanned contrasts and, as with ANOVA, this affects the degree to which alpha is adjusted. A further simplification in my description will be that I am restricting unplanned contrasts to those where all possible pairs are being contrasted.

All the types of contrasts following an ANCOVA require two different analyses to have been conducted: an ANOVA where the *covariate* is treated as the *DV* (i.e. the DV from the ANCOVA is not included in the analysis) and the full ANCOVA. The difference between the designs where the allocation to groups has been random and those where it hasn't is that in the latter there is a different calculation of the standard error for each contrast, whereas in the former the same standard error can be used for all contrasts.

Thus, we need two equations. For each I am going to use a version which will work whether the sample sizes are different or the same in each group. This is to limit the number of equations, for, as is usually the case, the equation for situations where the group sizes are the same can be simplified but the ones I am presenting will produce the same answer as the simplified version.

General terms in both equations

- $mean_{1 adjusted}$ is the adjusted mean of the DV for group 1 in the contrast.
- $mean_{2 adjusted}$ is the adjusted mean of the DV for group 2 in the contrast.
- $MS_{res\ w}$ is the mean square for the error from the ANCOVA.
- $MS_{bet\ x}$ is the mean square between the groups from the ANOVA with the covariate treated as the DV.
- $SS_{with\ x}$ is the sum of squares within the groups from the ANOVA with the covariate treated as the DV.
- n_1 is the sample size of group 1.
- n_2 is the sample size of group 2.

Randomised assignment

$$t = \frac{mean_{1\ adjusted} - mean_{2\ adjusted}}{\sqrt{MS_{res\ w} \times \left(1 + \frac{MS_{bet\ x}}{SS_{with\ x}}\right) \times \left(\frac{1}{n_1} + \frac{1}{n_2}\right)}} \tag{22.1}$$

Non-randomised assignment

$$t = \frac{mean_{1\ adjusted} - mean_{2\ adjusted}}{\sqrt{MS_{res\ w} \times \left\{\left[1 + \frac{(mean_1 - mean_2)^2}{SS_{with\ x}}\right] + \frac{1}{n_1} + \frac{1}{n_2}\right\}}} \tag{22.2}$$

where $mean_1$ is the mean of the *covariate* in group 1 and $mean_2$ is the mean of the *covariate* in group 2.

Planned contrasts

Randomised assignment

For this situation use equation 22.1 to find the observed *t*-value and use Bonferroni tables (Appendix XVII) to find the critical value of *t* in order to decide whether the result is statistically significant. Thus if we had planned to compare the first training group with the control group and the second training group with the first training group, then, as long as the assignment was random, the following would be appropriate.

Firstly we need to run an ANOVA comparing the three conditions with age (the covariate) as the DV. The results are shown in Table 22.8.

TABLE 22.8   The results of an ANOVA comparing the ages of the control and two training groups

Source	Sum of squares	df	Mean square	F	p
Condition	25050.65	2	12525.325	8.607	<.001
Error	170259.35	117	1455.208		
Total	195310.00	119			

From Table 22.5 we can find the means for sorting ability, from Table 22.8 we can find $MS_{bet\,x}$ and $SS_{within\,x}$ and from Table 22.7 we can find $MS_{res\,w}$. These are summarised in Table 22.9.

TABLE 22.9   The values needed to conduct contrasts following an ANCOVA which has involved random allocation to conditions

	Adjusted mean sorting
Control	6.281
Training 1	6.823
Training 2	7.445
$MS_{bet\,x}$	12525.325
$SS_{within\,x}$	170259.350
$MS_{res\,x}$	3.502

As an example I will compare the control and first treatment conditions.

$$t = \frac{6.823197 - 6.281497}{\sqrt{3.502389 \times \left(1 + \dfrac{12525.33}{170259.4}\right) \times \left(\dfrac{1}{40} + \dfrac{1}{40}\right)}} = \frac{0.5417}{0.433592} = 1.25$$

To find the critical level of t for the contrasts, we need to look in Table A17.11b for the error df from the ANCOVA (df = 116) and two contrasts, with alpha = .05. This shows that the critical value for t is between 2.271 (when df = 115) and 2.270 (when df = 120) or 2.27 to two decimal places. Accordingly, we can see that the sorting ability of those given the first training method is not significantly different from those in the control condition. Comparing the two training conditions $t_{(116)}$ = 1.43, which is also smaller than the critical t and so is also not significant.

Non-randomised assignment

Use equation 22.2 to find the t-value and use Bonferroni tables (A17.11) to decide whether the result is statistically significant. Rather than create a completely new example, I am going to illustrate the procedure on the previous study; however, now imagine that allocation to conditions was not random. Firstly we need to know the means for the covariate (mean age in months) for each group; these are contained in Table 22.5: control = 142.73, training group 1 = 156.18 and training group 2 = 121.10.

Comparing the control group with the first training group,

$$t = \frac{6.823197 - 6.281497}{\sqrt{3.502389 \times \left\{ \left[+ \frac{(156.18 - 142.73)^2}{170259.4} \right] + \frac{1}{40} + \frac{1}{40} \right\}}} = 1.28$$

We use the same critical value of t from the Bonferroni tables as in the previous example – 2.27, for alpha = .05 – and we conclude that the sorting ability in the first training group and that in the control group do not differ significantly. Comparing the two training groups $t_{(116)} = 1.39$, which is also smaller than the critical t value and so is also not significant.

Unplanned (pairwise) contrasts

To find the statistical significance of the observed t-value, we need to calculate an appropriate critical t-value for unplanned contrasts. The method we use is similar to that for Tukey's *HSD*, but we need a modification of the critical t-value, which is derived from Bryant and Paulson (1976).[3]

Randomised assignment

Use equation 22.1 to find the observed t-value. The observed t-values for the three contrasts are as follows: training group 1 vs control group = 1.25, training group 2 vs control group = 2.68 and training group 1 vs training group 2 = 1.43. The critical t-value for three means to be contrasted and only one covariate for alpha = .05 (for the family of contrasts) is between 2.39 for df = 110 and 2.38 for df = 120 (using Table A17.15). Bryant and Paulson (1976) say that interpolation should be harmonic to find critical values for intermediate df. Using the method shown in Appendix XVII we find that the critical t is the same as for df = 120, to two decimal places, and therefore the critical t is 2.38. Therefore, the only pair which shows a significant difference is between the second training group and the control group.

Non-randomised assignment

For the purpose of illustrating the technique, I'm going to treat the study as involving non-random allocation to conditions. Use equation 22.2 to find the observed t-value. The observed t-values for the three contrasts are as follows: training group 1 vs control group = 1.28, training group 2 vs control group = 2.71 and training group 1 vs training group 2 = 1.39.

The same critical value for t as for randomised groups is the appropriate one and we would come to the same conclusion as for the randomised design that the only groups which were significantly different were the second training group and the control group.

Effect sizes for contrasts

The effect size d can be used for the contrasts and can be calculated from the t-value using:

$$d = \sqrt{\frac{2}{n}} \times t$$

---

3 The method is usually described without calculating the critical t-value. Instead it relies on a modification of the equations and uses Q_p values (from Table A17.16) as the critical values. I've chosen to convert the calculated and critical values to t-values in order to produce a consistent account across all the contrasts.

where n is the sample in each of the two groups being contrasted when the sample sizes are equal or the harmonic mean sample size for the two groups when they are unequal (see Appendix XVIII for the method of finding the harmonic mean of two sample sizes). Therefore the effect sizes for the three contrasts are as follows: control group vs training group 1, $d = 0.29$; control group vs training group 2, $d = 0.61$; and the difference between the two training groups, $d = 0.31$.

Contrasts and confidence intervals (CIs)

We can calculate a CI for the difference between a pair of adjusted means. For a family of contrasts, using the tests contained in this chapter, we can produce what are called *simultaneous CIs* for the differences between the adjusted means. We will find a CI for each of the differences between the adjusted means in the set of contrasts that we are conducting and we will maintain the CI – say, 95% – for the family of contrasts. That is, we can be confident that on 95% of occasions the CIs will contain the values for the differences between the means which would be found in the population.

The CI can be found from:

$$\text{CI} = \text{difference between adjusted means} \pm (SE \times \text{critical } t)$$

where SE is the standard error for the difference between the means and critical t is the value of t which would give exactly the probability that we require. In the case of a 95% CI we want the critical t for a probability of .05.

Confidence intervals for unplanned contrasts and randomised allocation

From the preceding calculations for the contrasts we know that the difference between the adjusted means for the control and training group 1 was 0.5417, and the standard error for difference between the adjusted means was 0.433592. We found that the critical value of t for a probability of .05 was 2.39.

Therefore the CI is between $0.5417 - (0.433592 \times 2.39)$ and $0.5417 + (0.433592 \times 2.39)$; i.e. -0.495 and 1.578.

The CIs for the difference between the control group and training group 2 is 0.127 to 2.200, and the one for the difference between the two training groups is -0.414 to 1.658. As the CIs for the difference between the control group and training group 1 and between the two training groups both contain zero, this suggests that there may be no difference between those groups. The same equation can be used to calculate the CIs when the Bonferroni method has been used but the critical value for t would be found from the Bonferroni tables.

Reporting contrasts and CIs following an ANCOVA

Such reporting would be done after the details of the results of the original ANCOVA and could be presented in a number of ways. The main distinction would depend on the number of contrasts which have been conducted. If three or fewer, then I would report the details within the text, whereas for four or more contrasts I would tend to put the statistical evidence in a table. Whichever format you are using, the same details need to be included. As usual the reader needs to know what test you conducted and on what, what conclusions you draw and what the statistical evidence is for the conclusions. For contrasts following ANCOVA, the extra details compared with contrasts following ANOVA are to do with the equation employed, which, as we have seen, is based on the method of allocation of participants to groups and the nature of the covariate. I am going to use the example of unplanned contrasts where participants were allocated to groups randomly and the covariate is a random variable.

A set of three unplanned paired contrasts was conducted, using the Bryant and Paulson (1976) variation on Tukey's *HSD* for randomly allocated participants and a random covariate, to compare the sorting abilities of the groups. There was no significant difference between the control and first training groups ($t_{(116)} = 1.25, p > .05$, adjusted mean difference = 0.542, 95% CI = −0.495 to 1.578, $d = 0.29$). There was also no significant difference between the two training groups ($t_{(116)} = 1.43, p > .05$, adjusted mean difference = 0.622, 95% CI = −0.414 to 1.658, $d = 0.31$). However, the second training group sorted significantly more items correctly than the control group ($t_{(116)} = 2.68, p < .05$, mean difference = 1.164, 95% CI = 0.127 to 2.200, $d = 0.61$).

Using SPSS for contrasts after ANCOVA

At the time of writing, of the two preceding equations given, SPSS only conducts contrasts using equation 22.2, the one for non-randomised groups. In order to conduct planned or unplanned contrasts on such a design, the observed *t*-values can be found from Fisher's PLSD, described as LSD in SPSS. This makes no adjustment to the alpha-level. You will need to divide the mean difference by the standard error to find each *t*-value. You can then compare this with the critical *t* value derived from Bryant and Paulson (1976) (Table A17.15), for unplanned contrasts, or the Bonferroni tables, for planned contrasts. Using the Bonferroni contrasts which are provided by SPSS will give the wrong probability as it will adjust for all the possible paired contrasts, rather than just the ones required. The CIs which SPSS reports will also not be the equivalent of the simultaneous ones described previously for the same reasons that the adjustment will not be made in the LSD procedure and will be inappropriate in the case of the Bonferroni test.

Regression and ANCOVA

As was shown in Chapter 20, the results from an ANOVA can be obtained from an appropriately conducted regression (as long as IVs with more than two levels are coded as dummy variables). In the same way, multiple regression with the IV(s) and covariate treated as predictor variables could be used to produce the same results as ANCOVA. This is demonstrated in Appendix XIII.

Summary

Using ANCOVA allows levels of an IV to be compared after an adjustment has been made to allow for the differences between the levels of the IV which exist in a continuous variable (a covariate). The covariate could be a different variable from the DV or it could be pre-treatment values of the DV.

The results of an ANCOVA are interpreted most straightforwardly when the allocation to different levels of the IV has been made randomly. When allocation is not random, including in pre-existing groups, then greater caution has to be taken over use of ANCOVA. When there are more than two levels of the IV, tests of contrasts can be conducted after an ANCOVA but, in addition to the factors which have to be considered when following up an ANOVA, the method of calculating the contrast has to take into account whether the allocation to groups was random and whether the covariate was fixed or random.

The next chapter looks at the checks which data should be subject to before an analysis is conducted.

23 Screening data

Introduction

This chapter describes a range of different problems which can exist within a data set, how they can be identified and what can be done to solve them. They include values which aren't sensible ones for the variable being considered, missing data and values which might be affecting the results. The chapter introduces the notions of *intention to treat* and *bootstrapping* and suggests an order in which data checks should be conducted.

Checking for sensible values

It is easy to enter the wrong figure into an analysis: you can read a number wrongly or type it wrongly. Therefore it is essential to check your figures before starting any analysis. Some of the options in computer packages can help with checking. Maxima and minima will tell you whether any numbers are present which are beyond the possible range for a measure: for example, a 77 on a 7-point Likert scale. Tables or graphs of frequencies could reveal intermediate values which shouldn't be present: for example, a value of 0.5 on a scale which should only have 0 for male and 1 for female.

There will also be values which are perfectly legitimate for the scale but have still been entered incorrectly. If there aren't too many data points, then each one should be checked, preferably by one person reading out the figures which should have been entered and another person checking what has been entered. However, if there is a very large set of data, then a form of quality control could be conducted by taking a random sample of the data and checking that sample. If a perfect data set is required, then if any errors are found in the sample the full set of data needs to be checked. Alternatively, if a certain low level of error is felt not to be a problem, then, if some errors are found, the proportion of errors which are present in the sample could be calculated and the possible proportion in the whole data set could be found, by calculating a confidence interval. If the upper end of the confidence interval is within the acceptable level of error, then further checking could be stopped.

Missing data

There are numerous reasons why data might be missing: you failed to collect any data from some people you wanted to include but they weren't available, someone failed to complete a question or a whole section in a survey, a person dropped out of a longitudinal study or a person dropped out of one phase in a longitudinal study but reappeared later. Missing data are commonly seen to fall into three types, after a taxonomy which is usually attributed to Rubin (1976): missing completely at random (MCAR), missing at random (MAR) and missing not at random (MNAR, sometimes shown as NMAR).

Table 23.1 is an artificial illustration of the distinction between these three types of what is sometimes called *missingness*.

TABLE 23.1   An illustration of the different types of patterns of missing data

Age (in years)	Income complete	Income MCAR	Income MAR	Income MNAR
28.11	41418.75	41418.75	41418.75	
30.17	16984.33		16984.33	16984.33
38.93	11187.10		11187.10	11187.10
43.28	28325.65	28325.65	28325.65	28325.65
46.44	26387.07	26387.07	26387.07	26387.07
50.03	13925.85	13925.85	13925.85	13925.85
52.87	34606.20	34606.20	34606.20	
53.35	22189.38		22189.38	22189.38
58.34	18403.91	18403.91	18403.91	18403.91
58.78	38519.18	38519.18	38519.18	
66.94	30841.25	30841.25	30841.25	30841.25
67.20	24214.24	24214.24	24214.24	24214.24
71.45	32434.38		32434.38	
73.05	39226.88	39226.88	39226.88	
74.54	21634.16	21634.16		21634.16
75.55	7656.47			7656.47
75.90	18183.67	18183.67		18183.67
77.07	31905.17	31905.17		
85.65	19152.60	19152.60		19152.60
86.42	8562.17			8562.17

The first two columns show the complete data for age and income for a sample of people. In each example of missing data, the missing values are in income. In the column showing income MCAR the missing values are not linked to either income or age. There is no pattern in the missing data; they are randomly spread throughout the data set. In the column showing income MAR the missing values are not linked to income but they are linked to age. There is a pattern but it is not in the missing data: it is predictable from the data which are complete (the observed data). In the column showing income MNAR the missing values are linked to income. MNAR refers to missing data where the pattern is in the missing data; some writers say that to be classified as MNAR the pattern is in both the missing data and the observed data.

Checking for patterns in missing data: missing values analysis (MVA)

Some patterns of missing data will be discernible by exploring the question: Is there a difference in the means of other variables between those who do and those who don't have data on a given variable? Thus we could ask whether there is a difference in ages between those who have answered a question about income and those who haven't answered the question. The means of the two groups could be compared using a between-subjects *t*-test. Clearly, if there is a difference in ages, then the data are not MCAR. The problem is that, as Sinharay, Stern, and Russell (2001) note, it is difficult to distinguish between MAR and MNAR. In this example it may be that people with a certain income are choosing not to respond and they also happen to be older than those who have responded to the question about income.

To try to ascertain whether data are MNAR we need to know what range to expect in the population from which we are sampling. In this way we could look at the data we have collected and ask whether there are missing values from a part of the distribution which we might have expected; in the example we might find that there are fewer people who have said they have an income above a certain figure than would be expected.

Methods for dealing with missing data

There is no perfect solution for dealing with missing data which should be used in all situations. Leaving a participant out of an analysis because of missing data will reduce the sample size and hence the power of statistical tests; even with only a small percentage of data which are MCAR a large proportion of cases could be deleted if the missing data are spread across a number of variables. In addition, it may produce a biased sample if the pattern is MAR or MNAR. To solve these problems, a number of methods have been devised to preserve the fullest sample for analyses but none of them is wholly satisfactory, either. I'll describe methods for deleting participants and then describe the methods for keeping them in (imputation).

Deleting cases

There are two basic methods for removing participants because of missing data: *pairwise* deletion (*exclude cases pairwise* in SPSS) and *list-wise* deletion (*exclude cases list-wise* in SPSS). Pairwise deletion means deleting a participant if he or she has data missing from either variable from an analysis which only entails two measures from the same person. Thus, in a within-subjects *t*-test, if a person had missing data from one of the two levels of the IV, or, in a correlation, if a person had missing data from one of the variables, then that person would be deleted from the analysis. List-wise deletion means that if a person is missing data in any of the variables involved in an analysis, then all the data for that person are deleted.

A danger with pairwise deletion is that a false picture can be created within a set of analyses. An example would be if you were creating a correlation matrix to examine the interrelationship between a number of variables. Pairwise deletion in this instance could mean that the different correlation coefficients are based on slightly different people and slightly different sample sizes and so they are not really forming a coherent set. If they are a preliminary to a multiple regression, then the interpretation of relationships in the data will be further complicated by having correlation coefficients and regression coefficients for the same variables not being based on precisely the same set of people. If list-wise deletion were used when creating the correlation matrix, then all the correlations would be based on data from the same people.

Imputation

A range of solutions exist for trying to replace (or impute) missing values with a value which could be analysed. They form two basic approaches: single imputation, which involves replacing a missing value with a single value, and multiple imputation (MI), which involves creating more than one complete data set. In both cases, standard analysis can be conducted on the resulting data sets. However, in MI further analysis has to be conducted as well.

Single imputation

There is quite a range of single imputation methods which are available. I am going to describe three. Details of other methods can be found in Schafer and Graham (2002).

Mean imputation

The most basic form of single imputation is to replace a missing value with the mean value for the scores which are available for that variable on the grounds that the mean is the most likely value (when data are normally distributed).

Regression-based imputation

A regression model is calculated from the cases where there are complete data and this is used to predict values for the cases which have missing data.

Expectation maximisation (EM)

This is an iterative process which has a role beyond dealing with missing data (see Little & Rubin, 2002; Sinharay et al., 2001). Missing values are replaced with estimated values. Parameters are estimated from the data set and then the imputed values are re-estimated on the basis of the parameters. This process is repeated until the estimates settle down so that they don't change, beyond certain acceptable limits, from one iteration to the next.

Current thinking is that no form of single imputation is satisfactory because while single imputation might produce an accurate value for certain statistics such as measures of central tendency (as long as the pattern of missing data is MAR or MCAR), it will produce underestimates of measures of spread, such as standard errors. Given that we need standard errors to calculate inferential tests, it will mean that there is a danger of overestimating the size of the inferential statistic, such as a t-value, and so a greater danger of committing a Type I error. See Schafer and Graham (2002) for simulations which show the effects of different types of single imputation on different patterns of missing data.

Multiple imputation

As stated earlier, multiple imputation involves creating a number of complete data sets, sometimes as few as five. Each complete data set is then analysed by standard statistical methods. However, we now have a set of results for the same analysis and, from these, more accurate estimates of measures of variability can be obtained. In this way the likelihood of making a Type I error is lessened compared to the use of single imputation methods.

Advice on handling missing data

Always check for patterns in the missing data. MVA in SPSS allows you to do this. However, you need to look at the distribution of the observed data to check whether you are missing cases or data for cases which are in a range you should expect to have sampled given the population you have sampled from. Where the sample size is reasonably large and MI is available, use it. See Schafer and Graham (2002) for sources of MI.

If there is a small amount of missing data, there is no obvious pattern and they are not distributed in such a way that a large number of cases would be lost, then use list-wise deletion. If you are going to use single imputation, then EM or regression methods are preferable to mean substitution but be aware that they can also underestimate measures of spread and so affect inferential statistics and overestimate the size of statistics such as correlations. Most imputation methods assume that the data are at worst MAR. Schafer and Graham (2002) are reassuring in that they conclude that in many situations assuming MAR is reasonable.

Whatever method of imputation you use, it would be a good idea to conduct sensitivity analysis to see whether the results from analysis with and without imputation are different. It is particularly important to check whether effect sizes are different as probability changes may simply be a function of different sample sizes. Nonetheless, if you achieved significant results with the reduced data set and non-significant results with the fuller data set, then that would question the robustness of the first results. See also Graham (2009) for a discussion of types of missing data and possible ways to deal with them.

Intention to treat

In tests of the effectiveness of an intervention there can be particular difficulties with interpretation of the results when problematic cases are present. Such cases can include those who were allocated to a condition but were found subsequently to have been in the wrong condition, were found not to have followed the treatment for the condition to which they were allocated, were not given the intended treatment correctly or did not provide a complete set of data. If allocation to treatments is random and the interest is in the effectiveness of a treatment under real conditions, where all of the preceding problems could exist, then an *intention to treat* analysis can be appropriate. Hollis and Campbell (1999) make the point that the term 'intention to treat' is used to describe a wide range of practices. The main idea of intention to treat is that once participants have been allocated to groups, they should be included in the analysis as their removal could produce a false impression. Thus, if people who were in a treatment group were more likely to drop out if they found the treatment less effective, then removing them from the analysis could suggest that the treatment is more effective than it really is.

A frequent occurrence when collecting data from participants on more than one occasion is attrition: data is not available for everyone on later occasions. In the case where you are comparing groups which have been treated differently, it is good practice to collect baseline data: before the treatment phase. For example, you might be looking at desire to give up smoking in a treatment group and in a comparison group which have not received the treatment. Take a measure from those in each group before the treatment is applied. Imagine that you are looking at the long-term benefits of the treatment and so you try to take the same measure from all the participants 6 months after the treatment was administered. However, some people don't respond in the follow-up phase and so you have missing data for that phase. If you replace the missing data with those participants' baseline data you are able to include all your participants in the analysis. If you can still demonstrate that the treatment group is significantly better than the comparison group despite this pessimistic assumption that those with missing data have not improved then that shows that your result is robust. Whereas if you had only analysed the data from those for whom you had follow-up data there would be the danger that your result was biased.

Outliers and influential data

Elsewhere within this book I have described a number of methods which have been devised to look at values which could influence the statistics – for example, calculating standardised scores, creating box plots or creating stem-and-leaf plots to look at univariate outliers or plotting Cook's distance against leverage in multiple regression to look at multivariate outliers. The important thing to bear in mind is that as long as they are legitimate values, as far as your measures are concerned, there is no basic justification for removing them. By legitimate I mean that the value is within the range of the scale you are using. However, you could treat a value as not legitimate if you had good reason to believe that it came about because of a problem with the procedure or the inclusion of a participant who wasn't from the population to which you wished to extrapolate. Thus, if there was a distracting noise during a reaction time experiment or if you discovered that you had inadvertently included someone with senile dementia in a memory experiment, then such cases could be removed. Nonetheless, your sample may include extreme values which aren't very representative and are affecting your results. You should analyse the results with and without such cases to see how robust the results are to their presence or absence.

Distribution of data

For many parametric tests there is an assumption that the DV is normally distributed. Ways to check this are provided in Chapters 9 and 12, and some techniques which can be used to transform the data when they aren't normally distributed are given in Appendix V. For many tests the distribution which is important is described as a conditional distribution. For example, in a between-subjects ANOVA the distribution of data for each level of the IV should be normally distributed. In other words, the assumption is that the data are normally distributed conditional on it being from the same group. Similarly in correlation the assumption is that the data for one variable are normally distributed conditional on each value of the other variable (see Chapter 19 for an illustration of the resultant bivariate normal distribution). One preliminary method of screening for possible violations of normal distribution is to examine the distribution of the residuals. This usually involves running the statistical test and either saving the residuals and creating plots of them or asking for available plots of them (as in linear regression). If the residuals show no sign of skew or kurtosis then there is no need to investigate further. However, if the residuals are not normally distributed then it is necessary to investigate the individual variables to find the source of the problem.

Order of checks

Firstly, check for legitimate values. If values are not legitimate, then what you do will depend on the access you have to the original data. Where possible check whether the data point has been entered correctly. If it has been but the value was still not legitimate, for example, because a participant gave a non-legitimate response such as a rating of 9 on a 7-point scale, then treat it as a missing value. Secondly check for missing data and if they exist examine whether there are patterns. Next check whether the data fulfil the assumptions of the test(s) you are going to use. In the case of some statistical analyses you may need to conduct the test in order to check the assumptions. An example of this is examining the nature of residuals after a multiple regression.

A number of checks of assumptions have been devised which involve an inferential test themselves. Thus, Levene's tests of homogeneity of variance for between-subjects *t*-tests and ANOVA are designed to test the hypothesis that the variances are the same in the different groups. However, as with all inferential tests they are subject to the issue of statistical power and therefore can give misleading results. Zimmerman (2004) notes that statisticians tend not to recommend them and makes the point that applying such a preliminary inferential test prior to conducting the required test is affecting the Type I error rate. The rules of thumb for what constitute heterogeneity of variance for the *t*-test and ANOVA are given in Chapters 15 and 16 respectively. These are preferable to Levene's tests.

Similarly, Mauchly's *W* is designed to test for lack of sphericity in a within-subjects ANOVA. I think it is more important to look at whether the Greenhouse–Geisser and Huynh–Feldt adjustments for possible lack of sphericity have changed the decision you would have made. If the sphericity assumed and two adjusted versions all agree that a result is significant or all agree that it isn't significant, then there isn't a problem. However, if the unadjusted version shows a significant result and one or both of the adjusted versions show a non-significant result, then you need to report all three and draw the reader's attention to the discrepancy.

If data don't fulfil the assumptions of the statistical test you had originally chosen then alternatives are likely to exist. Some may be adjusted versions of the test you had chosen such as Welch's versions of the t-test and ANOVA which don't assume homogeneity of variance (see Chapters 15 and 16 and

Appendices VI and VII). Some may be non-parametric equivalents such as the Mann–Whitney U test instead of the between-subjects t-test (see Chapter 15). Some may be parametric tests but ones which come from the General*ised* Linear Model such as logistic regression (see Chapter 21). An alternative when we are not sure that the data fulfil the assumptions to do with distribution but are still not categorical is *bootstrapping*.

Bootstrap

The main thing that bootstrapping can do is to produce a confidence interval around the statistic that you wish to calculate, be that a descriptive statistic such as the mean or a measure such as a correlation coefficient. Parametric tests, such as the t-test, produce a value and then compare that with a distribution, such as the t-distribution, to see how likely the outcome would be if the Null Hypothesis were true. In a similar way, the confidence intervals linked to such tests involve the same form of probability distribution in their calculation. If the assumptions of the parametric test are not fulfilled then the probability distribution will be inappropriate, leading to probabilities and confidence intervals that are inaccurate. Bootstrapping uses the data from the sample to find a distribution from which a probability or a confidence interval can be calculated. The sampling used during the bootstrap process is called *sampling with replacement*. This means that after a data point has been sampled it is put back into the set. Therefore, the same data point can be sampled more than once. The advantage of bootstrap sampling is that the number of different samples can be very large. If sampling without replacement occurs then the number of different samples is more restricted. Permutation tests are described in Chapter 14. These find every possible permutation of the data in the sample and then calculate how likely the actual result found in the data is given the distribution provided by all the permutations (see Appendix VI). However, there is a finite number of permutations for a given set of numbers; for example, in a set of four numbers there are only 24 different permutations. Because bootstrapping uses sampling with replacement, the number of samples is greater; for example, in a set of four numbers there are 64 (or 4^4) unique samples. In addition, bootstrapping allows samples to be the same and so the number of samples can be as large as required and is only restricted by how long you are willing to wait for the computer to do the calculation. The general recommendation is to use at least 10 000 samples and Bias-Corrected and accelerated (BCa) confidence intervals.

Summary

There are a number of reasons why a data set needs to be checked prior to any statistical analysis being conducted. There could be values which are not part of the legitimate range for the measures used. There could be missing data. There could be participants whose data have a disproportionate influence on the results. The statistical test which seems appropriate to test a hypothesis may have specific assumptions about the data. A number of solutions are offered. However, often there is no perfect solution for dealing with such data and it is important to conduct sensitivity analysis to check whether the choice of solution has affected the results of the analysis.

The next chapter looks at ways to explore the possible dimensions in a set of data, such as to see whether a measure like an attitude questionnaire is dealing with a single concept or a set of related concepts.

24 Exploratory factor analysis (EFA)

Introduction

When describing the creation of scales to measure attitudes in Chapter 6, I mentioned that a useful preliminary check on responses would be to conduct factor analysis as this can help to show whether responses can be treated as being on a single scale or would be better treated as being on more than one dimension (or sub-scale). Factor analysis has been used more widely to look at how data and the assumed phenomenon underlying the data can be characterised. Examples are IQ or abilities such as in mathematics. Thus, mathematical ability could be found to have separate dimensions measuring abilities at abstraction, calculation and spatial reasoning. I am only going to present how to do factor analysis when you are creating a multi-item scale designed to measure a concept which has one or more related dimensions, such as personality. Nonetheless, many of the issues relate to other uses of factor analysis. Those wishing to read more widely on the subject can refer to books such as Gorsuch (1983), Comrey and Lee (1992), McDonald (1985) and Mulaik (2010).

I am going to avoid the full mathematics which underlies factor analysis. One complication is that it can be couched in terms of the algebra of matrixes and I don't want to go down the route of explaining how to do matrix algebra, not even in the appendix. Therefore, those who do know matrix algebra may feel dissatisfied with my explanations; they can look at the appropriate books (for example, Gorsuch, 1983 or Mulaik, 2010). I hope my explanations are sufficient to understand when to do factor analysis, how to do it using appropriate computer programs, how to interpret it and how to report it. However, one thing you need to brace yourself for is the number of new terms which we are going to meet in order to understand what factor analysis involves.

Why factor analysis is useful

When creating a multi-item scale it is good practice to check how many dimensions (or sub-scales) you are measuring. You should not just assume that you are measuring what you intended. Tests of reliability, such as Cronbach's alpha, do not always get around the problem; Grayson (2004) has demonstrated that two sub-scales which are totally uncorrelated themselves can be put into a single scale and produce a high reliability coefficient. The way to check how many dimensions there are in a set of items is to use factor analysis.

Types of factor analysis

There are two basic forms of factor analysis: Exploratory and Confirmatory. Exploratory factor analysis (EFA) is appropriate, as the name suggests, when you are exploring a set of variables to see whether there are underlying factors (latent variables) which could explain similarities between them. An example would be if you had devised a number of questions to measure aspects of a person's personality based on a new theory of what constitutes personality. You let the computer program look for patterns in the responses you have received from a sample of participants.

Confirmatory factor analysis (CFA) is used where you have a clearer idea about the structure of your theory. You set up a model in which you specify the number of factors and which variables are related to which factor. The computer program then checks how closely your model fits the data. An example would be if you were using an already existing personality questionnaire and you wanted to check that when using it with a new population it had the same factors as had been found previously. For the rest of the chapter I am only going to talk about exploratory methods. Those interested in conducting CFA can find chapters in Dugard, Todman, and Staines (2010), Mulaik (2010), Raykov and Marcoulides (2008) or Tabachnick and Fidell (2013).

There is some confusion about Principal Components Analysis (PCA) which is not helped by software which seems to imply that it is a form of EFA. The main distinction between PCA and EFA is that PCA tries to explain all the variance in the data set, whereas EFA tries to explain the variance which is determined by the factors it has identified. As evidence of the confusion between the two techniques, two papers I have recently been asked to review have stated that they used EFA when in fact they used PCA. PCA can be useful if you are trying to reduce a number of variables into a smaller number of components which explain a reasonable proportion of the variance in the original data. It can also be useful if you want a set of components which aren't correlated, such as when you have multicollinearity among predictor variables in a multiple regression. A problem could arise if you tried to explain what it was that linked the variables which were related to a given component. However, as we will see, this can be an issue with EFA as well.

It is only worth conducting factor analysis if you have a good reason for assuming that there are factors which underlie a set of variables. An example is where you have devised a set of questions to measure a particular concept, such as quality of life. You should not take a set of conceptually unrelated variables and run a factor analysis on it.

The data

I am going to use some data collected by Michelle Meadows. Michelle was exploring types of driving behaviour in the UK. She used a questionnaire which had a series of statements to which participants could respond using a 5-point scale ranging from *Never, Hardly ever, Occasionally, Quite often,* and *Frequently* to *Nearly all the time,* to the question: *How often do you do each of the following?* To simplify the explanation of factor analysis I have selected those items which relate to two sub-scales of the questionnaire.

The items can be found in Table 24.1.

TABLE 24.1   The items from a questionnaire about driving behaviour which will be explored through factor analysis

1   Attempt to overtake someone that you hadn't noticed to be signalling a right turn

2   Miss 'Give way' signs, and narrowly avoid traffic having right of way

3   Fail to notice that pedestrians are crossing when turning into a side street from the main road

4   Drive especially close to the car in front as a signal to its driver to go faster or get out of the way

5   Queuing to turn left onto a main road, you pay such close attention to the mainstream of traffic that you nearly hit the car in front

6   Cross a junction knowing that the traffic lights have already turned against you

7   On turning left nearly hit a cyclist who has come up on your inside

8   Disregard the speed limits late at night or very early in the morning

9   Fail to check your rearview mirror before pulling out, changing lanes, etc.

10   Have an aversion to a particular class of road user, and indicate your hostility by whatever means you can

11   Become impatient with a slow driver in the outer lane and overtake on the inside

TABLE 24.1   (Continued)

12	Underestimate the speed of an oncoming vehicle when overtaking
13	Brake too quickly on a slippery road, or steer the wrong way in a skid
14	Drive even though you realise that you may be over the legal blood-alcohol limit
15	Get involved in unofficial 'races' with other drivers
16	Angered by another driver's behaviour, you give chase with the intention of giving him/her a piece of your mind

Before running an EFA there are two checks which are usually conducted to see whether it is appropriate: Bartlett's test of sphericity and the Kaiser-Meyer-Olkin test of sampling adequacy (KMO). Both tests are looking at aspects of the correlation matrix of all the variables, in our case questionnaire items, which are to be included in the analysis (see Table 24.2).

TABLE 24.2   The lower triangle of the correlation matrix from 16 items in the driving questionnaire

	1	2	3	4	5	6	7	8	9	10	11	12	13	14	15	16
1	1															
2	.339	1														
3	.286	.300	1													
4	.162	.136	.156	1												
5	.265	.325	.331	.245	1											
6	.228	.268	.303	.399	.321	1										
7	.309	.299	.359	.127	.348	.281	1									
8	.144	.119	.202	.454	.235	.431	.187	1								
9	.236	.269	.309	.126	.255	.262	.236	.176	1							
10	.179	.130	.205	.403	.172	.306	.187	.320	.121	1						
11	.222	.174	.211	.487	.236	.402	.235	.444	.176	.400	1					
12	.365	.326	.370	.205	.317	.324	.295	.202	.285	.190	.265	1				
13	.245	.297	.293	.160	.333	.242	.290	.195	.242	.184	.225	.319	1			
14	.171	.180	.182	.276	.255	.332	.235	.301	.183	.230	.276	.198	.226	1		
15	.158	.110	.142	.486	.187	.300	.158	.460	.164	.414	.473	.207	.188	.313	1	
16	.128	.144	.183	.434	.210	.282	.206	.315	.149	.478	.441	.217	.214	.361	.601	1

Looking at the correlation matrix can give us an idea of why factor analysis can be useful. We can examine how particular items are related to others. For example we can see, if we use a medium effect size of .3 as a minimum to guide us as to which variables go together, that item 1 is related to item 2, item 7 and item 12; if we rounded to one decimal place then item 1 is also related to item 3 and item 5. However, we have 120 different correlations[1] to examine and so this could take a long time. It already gets to be unclear when we see that item 2 is related to item 3, item 5 and item 12 and possibly to item 6, item 7, item 9 and item 13.

Bartlett's test of sphericity

This tests the Null Hypothesis that all the correlations between the variables are zero. Thus, if it is significant then we can reject the Null Hypothesis. For two reasons, that doesn't automatically mean that

---

1   $i \times (i-1)/2$, where i is the number of items.

it would be worth conducting a factor analysis. Firstly, the correlations could be quite low and yet the result could be significant.[2] Secondly, factor analysis should be conducted with large sample sizes; see the later section on sample size. Bartlett's test, like most statistical tests, is affected by sample size; the larger the sample the more likely a significant result will be found.[3] Therefore some people argue that a stricter level of significance should be used for this test (for example $p \leq .001$) or that it should only be used when there are fewer than five cases per variable (Tabachnick & Fidell, 2013). One way to interpret the test is to say that if it fails to be significant then you definitely shouldn't try to factor analyse the variables. However, you shouldn't treat a significant result as indicating that factor analysis is appropriate. In the current data Bartlett's test = 5252.086, df = 120, $p < .001$ (see Appendix XV), but the ratio of participants to variables was 1239/16; i.e. over 77 per variable.

Kaiser-Meyer-Olkin test of sampling adequacy (KMO)

This is designed to test whether there is sufficient shared variance among the variables to make conducting a factor analysis worthwhile. There is an equivalent version for each variable (the Measure of Sampling Adequacy, MSA) and an overall figure for the correlation matrix. The value of KMO and each MSA is built around two calculations, for each variable: (1) the shared variance between that variable and each of the other variables (the square of their correlations) and (2) The unique variance shared by that variable and each of the other variables with the remaining variables partialled out (the square of the partial correlations). The squared correlations are added together, and the squared partial correlations are added together. The MSA for a variable is the sum of the squared correlations divided by the sum of the squared correlations plus the sum of the squared partial correlations (see Appendix XV). The higher the value of that calculation the better the sampling adequacy. The KMO is produced for the overall sampling adequacy of the set of variables by summing all the squared correlations and summing all the squared partial correlations and then making the same calculation:

$$KMO = \frac{sum\ of\ squared\ correlations}{sum\ of\ squared\ correlations + sum\ of\ squared\ partial\ correlations}$$

Kaiser and Rice (1974) give the following way of viewing the MSAs and the KMO:

.900 to .999 – marvellous
.800 to .899 – meritorious
.700 to .799 – middling
.600 to .699 – mediocre
.500 to .599 – miserable
Below .500 – unacceptable

Therefore, according to their criteria we would ideally want the MSAs and KMO to be at least 0.8. In the current data the overall Kaiser-Meyer-Olkin = .904 (see Appendix XV). SPSS reports the MSAs in the diagonal of the *anti-image* correlation matrix (See Appendix XV). The lowest value for an individual item is .843, which is for item 16.

The current data has passed the Bartlett and KMO tests and so we can proceed to conduct the EFA.

---

2 I created a correlation matrix of four variables in which all the correlations were only 0.1. With a sample of 239 participants Bartlett's test would be significant.

3 I created a second correlation matrix of four variables but this time only two variables correlated (at 0.1) and all the other correlations were zero. With a sample of 1257 the test would be significant.

Finding the number of factors

Eigenvalues

An eigenvalue is a mathematical entity which can be used to assess how much of the variance in a set of data is explained by a particular factor. Eigenvalues are usually given the symbol λ and a subscript to denote which eigenvalue is being referred to; thus, the first eigenvalue would be λ_1. I give a bit more explanation of eigenvalues later when I've introduced some additional concepts.

Although we will be using EFA, the size of the eigenvalues is calculated via Principal Components Analysis. It will find as many components as there are items, with the first component having the largest eigenvalue and each subsequent component having a smaller eigenvalue than the previous one; this will always be the case. See Table 24.3.

TABLE 24.3   The eigenvalues and percentage of variance which they account for

Component	Initial eigenvalues	% of variance	Cumulative %
1	5.022	31.387	31.387
2	1.940	12.127	43.515
3	.882	5.512	49.027
4	.854	5.335	54.362
5	.794	4.965	59.327
6	.761	4.756	64.083
7	.744	4.650	68.733
8	.685	4.283	73.016
9	.660	4.126	77.142
10	.641	4.006	81.148
11	.605	3.784	84.932
12	.580	3.622	88.554
13	.526	3.285	91.839
14	.485	3.034	94.873
15	.473	2.956	97.829
16	.347	2.171	100.000

One method for deciding the number of factors is to take just those with an eigenvalue equal to or greater than 1 (the Guttman-Kaiser rule). This is arbitrary as it would mean that a factor with an eigenvalue of 0.999 would be rejected. Also under certain circumstances it can lead to an overly large number of factors being identified.

The analysis has found that two components have eigenvalues which are at least 1. Note also that if we extracted as many components as there were variables then we would be able to explain all the variance in the data. However, we can see that components 5 onwards are each explaining less than 5% of the variance.

Scree plots

A scree plot is a graph where the sizes of the eigenvalues are plotted in order. As they will have been derived from PCA they will be in size order and so they can show visually how big the difference is between each pair of eigenvalues. It is suggested that the last factor to be extracted should be the one just before the scree plot forms a gradual slope.

FIGURE 24.1   The scree plot for the 16 eigenvalues from the driving questionnaire

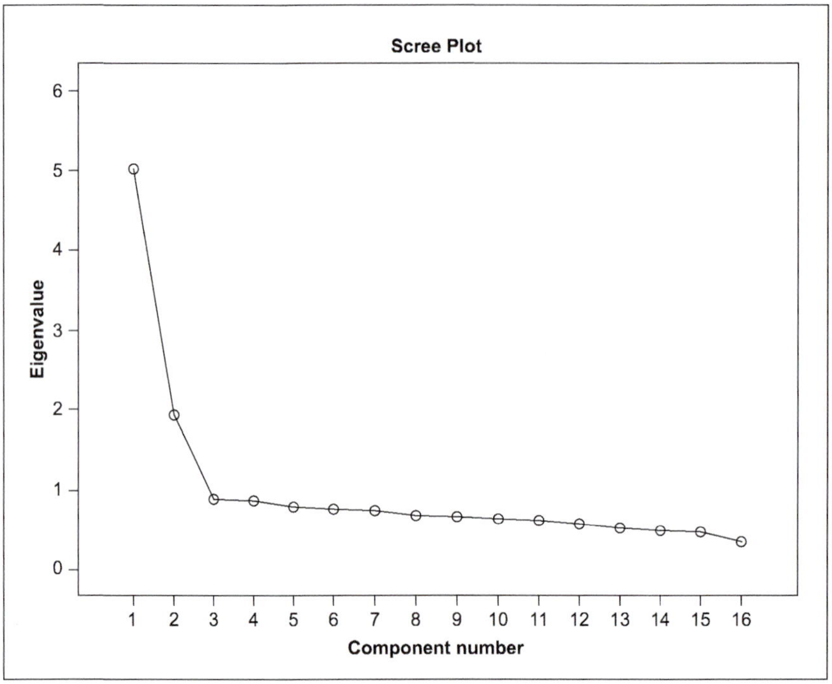

We can see from the scree plot in Figure 24.1 that there is a dramatic drop in the value of the eigenvalue between components 1 and 2 and again between components 2 and 3 but that after that there is a gradual diminution. Therefore it appears that the scree plot agrees that it is only worth extracting two factors.

The aim of a factor analysis is to produce what is called a simple solution. That is one in which each variable is clearly related to one factor and has little relationship to the other factor(s). Sometimes the scree plot does not give a neat answer as to how many factors should be extracted. When this is the case, rather than be governed by the Guttman-Kaiser rule, I recommend trying solutions with different numbers of factors based on the scree plot. Look at the different solutions to see which produces the result which is closest to the simple solution and makes theoretical sense.

In Appendix XV I briefly describe another method which is sometimes used to decide how many factors should be extracted: *Parallel Analysis*. This is so that if you come across a reference to it you are aware of what is involved. I think that, as with using the rule of only extracting components with eigenvalues greater than 1, it gives a false sense of objectivity which may produce a poor result. For other methods see Stellefson, Hanik, Chaney, and Chaney (2009) or Zwick and Velicer (1986).

I recommend using *Principal Axis Factoring* when trying to find whether there are sub-scales in a set of items in a questionnaire. See Comrey and Lee (1992), Gorsuch (1983) and Mulaik (2010) for details of other factor analytic techniques.

Initial solution

The initial solution from an EFA is a factor matrix which shows how each factor is related to each item. Table 24.4 shows the initial results from a principal axis factor analysis on the correlations in Table 24.2, where the analysis has been allowed to extract two factors.

TABLE 24.4   The factor matrix of two factors extracted from 16 items from the driving questionnaire

Item	Factor	
	1	2
1	.427	.303
2	.426	.374
3	.482	.340
4	.593	−.345
5	.508	.269
6	.607	.018
7	.470	.305
8	.566	−.235
9	.395	.256
10	.529	−.250
11	.633	−.242
12	.516	.301
13	.456	.248
14	.479	−.051
15	.617	−.422
16	.602	−.340

To read this table we can treat the values in the table (the loadings) as though they were correlations between an item and a factor. Therefore, we can see that factor 1 correlates with item 1 at .427 and with item 2 at .303. Before I go into further interpretation of the table I want to deal with another term: *communalities*.

Communalities

If we square a correlation that gives us the proportion of variance accounted for by one entity (here a factor) in another entity (here an item). Squaring .427 gives .182 and squaring .303 gives .092. That tells us that factor 1 explains more variance in item 1 than factor 2 does. Because this initial solution has intentionally found two factors which are uncorrelated (orthogonal), we can add the variance each explains to find out what proportion of the variance in the item is explained by the factors together (the communality): .274.

A principal axis factor analysis starts by replacing the diagonals in the correlation matrix with preliminary estimates of the communalities; the resultant matrix is sometimes called the *reduced* matrix. These are calculated by treating an item as the outcome variable of a multiple regression and the remaining items as the predictor variables. The R^2 value or overall amount of variance explained in the outcome variable is its preliminary communality for the purposes of the factor analysis (see Appendix XV).

Now that we've met loadings and the idea that they can be used to examine variance in the data, I want to provide another way of looking at eigenvalues. If instead of using factor analysis, I had looked at the components produced by Principal Components Analysis then I could have found how each component loaded on each item. If I square the loadings for a given component with each item and then add those squared loadings the result is the initial estimate of the eigenvalue for that component (see Appendix XV).

Returning to interpreting the table of loadings from the initial solution from the factor analysis, we can use the commonly applied criterion of .3 as a threshold to decide which item goes with which factor. From this initial solution we see that every item is related to factor 1. However, eight of them also relate to factor 2 and most of the remainder have quite high loadings with factor 2. In fact, there are only two items which give a clearer picture by being related to one factor and not the other: item 6 and item 14.

One way to view this initial solution is graphically as seen in Figure 24.2, where each loading is placed on the two dimensions representing the two factors.

FIGURE 24.2   The factor plot with factors as the dimensions from the preliminary principal axis factor analysis showing how each item from the driving questionnaire would be placed on the two dimensions

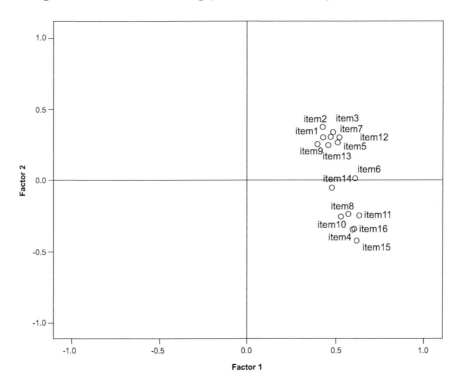

Making the picture clearer

One way to try to produce a result which is closer to the simple solution is to move the factors geometrically, which is the equivalent of rotating the axes in a graph. This can have the effect of making a variable have a higher loading on one factor while reducing its loading on other factors.

There are two main types of rotation: orthogonal – which is designed to keep the factors from correlating with each other – and oblique – which allows the factors to correlate. For investigation of a scale to see whether it contains sub-scales, I recommend using an oblique rotation as it is highly likely that the sub-scales will correlate and to force them not to would be an odd decision. If an oblique rotation shows the factors not to be correlated then it could be appropriate to use an orthogonal rotation to see whether a cleaner picture is produced as to which variable is linked to which factor. I recommend the oblique rotation method *direct oblimin*. See Figure 24.3. See Comrey and Lee (1992), Gorsuch (1983) and Mulaik (2010) for details of other methods of rotation.

FIGURE 24.3   A plot of the items and two factors after the oblique rotation direct oblimin

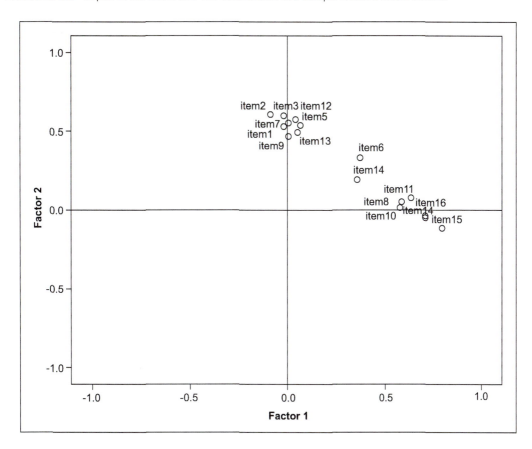

We can see from Figure 24.3 that items 1, 2, 3, 5, 7, 9, 12 and 13 have loadings which are close to zero on Factor 1 and relatively high loadings on factor 2, while items 4, 8, 10, 11, 15 and 16 have low loadings on factor 2 and relatively high loadings on factor 1. Item 14 and even more so item 6 have less clear loadings on one factor.

If an oblique solution is used then two matrixes are produced: one – the *structure* matrix – has loadings which are the correlations between the items and factors, and one – the *pattern* matrix – has loadings which are the equivalent of regression coefficients with an item treated as an outcome variable in a multiple regression and the factors treated as predictor variables (Tables 24.5 and 24.6).

Interpreting

Both matrixes are worth looking at. However, because the pattern matrix shows the unique variance which a factor explains in an item, while the structure matrix shows all the variance shared between factor and item, the pattern matrix may show a clearer picture.

We can see in the pattern matrix (Table 24.6) that the loadings look much closer to the simple solution with all but three items having loadings with the factor in which they have lower loadings which are smaller than .1 (items 6, 14 and 15). The only item which can be seen as problematic is item 6 which has loadings with both factors which are greater than .3. We can deal with this problem in a number of ways: drop the item as not clearly being linked to one factor; keep it in both factors; or wait

TABLE 24.5 The structure matrix for the oblique rotation of the two factors and their loadings on the 16 items from the driving questionnaire

	Factor	
Item	1	2
1	.246	.523
2	.212	.562
3	.278	.589
4	.685	.303
5	.333	.572
6	.534	.515
7	.283	.560
8	.611	.342
9	.238	.470
10	.586	.303
11	.675	.394
12	.326	.596
13	.296	.517
14	.451	.371
15	.740	.280
16	.690	.313

TABLE 24.6 The pattern matrix for the oblique rotation of the two factors and their loadings on the 16 items from the driving questionnaire

	Factor	
	1	2
1	−.018	.533
2	−.088	.605
3	−.019	.599
4	.708	−.048
5	.066	.539
6	.369	.332
7	.007	.557
8	.586	.051
9	.006	.467
10	.578	.016
11	.636	.078
12	.040	.576
13	.053	.491
14	.354	.195
15	.797	−.115
16	.709	−.038

until we have worked out what theoretical construct seems to embody each factor and see whether the errant item fits that structure. If it doesn't then we can remove it. We can also wait to see how it fairs when we do reliability and discriminant power analysis.

Correlation between the factors

When you use an oblique rotation it is worth checking how correlated the factors are. In this example $r = .496$.

Naming the factors

Items 4, 8, 10, 11, 14, 15 and 16 are clearly linked to factor 1. If we examine their wording, they are all to do with intentional acts. The remainder (leaving item 6 for the moment), apart possibly for item 7 (speaking personally as a cyclist who also drives), are all to do with making unintentional mistakes. Returning to item 6, that also is to do with intent and as it clearly is a common problem, I would argue that we retain it and associate it with factor 1. It is a good idea to check your naming of the factors with someone not involved in the study. For even greater objectivity, you could give people not involved with the study the wording of items which you have decided are linked to a particular factor and ask them to say what those items have in common.

Checking the solution

The reproduced matrix

The variance explained by the factors (the loadings) is used to recreate the correlations between the variables. See Table 24.7 and Appendix XV.

TABLE 24.7 The reproduced matrix of correlations which uses just the information from the two factors, with communalities in the diagonal

	1	2	3	4	5	6	7	8	9	10	11	12	13	14	15	16
1	.274															
2	.295	.321														
3	.309	.332	.348													
4	.149	.123	.168	.470												
5	.299	.317	.336	.209	.331											
6	.265	.265	.298	.354	.313	.368										
7	.293	.314	.330	.174	.321	.291	.314									
8	.171	.153	.193	.417	.225	.339	.195	.376								
9	.246	.264	.277	.146	.269	.244	.264	.164	.221							
10	.150	.132	.170	.400	.202	.317	.173	.359	.145	.343						
11	.197	.179	.223	.459	.257	.380	.224	.416	.188	.396	.460					
12	.312	.332	.351	.202	.343	.318	.334	.221	.281	.198	.254	.357				
13	.270	.287	.304	.185	.298	.281	.290	.200	.243	.179	.229	.310	.269			
14	.189	.185	.214	.302	.230	.290	.210	.283	.176	.267	.316	.232	.206	.232		
15	.136	.105	.154	.511	.200	.367	.161	.448	.136	.432	.493	.191	.177	.317	.558	
16	.154	.129	.174	.474	.215	.359	.179	.421	.151	.404	.463	.208	.190	.306	.514	.477

Residual matrix

The difference between the original correlation and the reproduced one is the *residual*, (see Table 24.8). This shows that 94% of the reproduced correlations were no more than .05 different from the original; those larger than .05 are shown in italics.

TABLE 24.8 The matrix of residuals: The difference between the original matrix of correlations and the reproduced matrix. Eight residuals (6%), shown in italics, are greater than .05

	1	2	3	4	5	6	7	8	9	10	11	12	13	14	15	16
1																
2	.044															
3	−.022	−.032														
4	.013	.013	−.013													
5	−.034	.008	−.005	.036												
6	−.037	.003	.005	.045	.008											
7	.015	−.015	.029	−.047	.027	−.010										
8	−.027	−.035	.009	.037	.010	*.092*	−.008									
9	−.010	.005	.032	−.020	−.014	.018	−.027	.012								
10	.028	−.001	.035	.002	−.030	−.010	.014	−.039	−.024							
11	.025	−.005	−.012	.028	−.021	.022	.011	.028	−.012	.004						
12	*.053*	−.006	.019	.003	−.026	.006	−.039	−.020	.004	−.008	.011					
13	−.025	.011	−.011	−.025	.035	−.039	.000	−.006	−.002	.004	−.004	.009				
14	−.019	−.005	−.031	−.026	.025	.042	.025	.018	.007	−.037	−.040	−.033	.020			
15	.022	.005	−.012	−.025	−.014	*−.067*	−.003	.012	.029	−.018	−.020	.016	.011	−.004		
16	−.026	.015	.009	−.040	−.004	*−.077*	.027	*−.105*	−.002	*.075*	−.022	.009	.024	*.055*	*.087*	

There is a danger, as with all statistical techniques, that the result is only true for the sample of participants. The structure should remain tentative until a replication with a different sample has been attempted. However, if a particularly large sample has been used then it could be split randomly into two equal subsamples and a factor analysis could be conducted on the data from each subsample separately to see whether the same pattern emerges.

Sample size

We have already seen that a large sample is required. This is to do with the reliability of the result and the likelihood that a solution will be found, rather than statistical power. MacCallum, Widaman, Zhang, and Hong (1999) conclude that the minimum sample size required is largely dependent on: (1) the size of the communalities – the larger the communalities the smaller the sample size needed – (2) the number of items per factor – the larger the ratio of items to factors the smaller the sample needed; however, don't overdo this as six or seven seems ideal – and (3) the number of factors – the smaller the number the smaller the sample size needed. As we won't know the communalities when designing the study, we are reliant on our hunches about the number of factors and the ratio of items to factors. To be on the safe side I recommend the following: if you have six or seven items per expected factor and a small number of expected factors (three or four) then you should have a sample of at least 100; if you have three or four items per factor and a small number of factors (again three or four) then you need at least 300 participants; if you have three or four items per factor but more factors then you need well over 500 participants. For each of these situations the results will be better the larger the sample size, so the general advice from MacCallum et al. (1999) is to have as large a sample as possible. If having collected the data you find that you have more factors than you expected and so your ratio of items to factors is smaller than intended, you have lower than ideal communalities (which would be all over .6 with a mean of at least .7) and the sample size is not large enough for these conditions then remove items which are not clear indicators of factors and factors which are not theoretically important.

Reporting

As with all statistical techniques you should report all the decisions you have made and why you made them. As we've seen, there are a lot of decisions to be made in factor analysis. The worst reports I have seen are those which say (with my queries in parentheses): we ran a factor analysis (which one?) and four factors were found (how was this decided?). They were (was a rotation used and if so which one? Who named them?) and they contained the following variables (what criteria were used and how clean was the picture?). When reporting matrices from the analysis, report complete ones rather than ones which just show loadings above a particular value. The fuller matrix, as in the pattern matrix (Table 24.6), shows the reader how high the loadings were on the factor to which it was decided an item wasn't linked and so doesn't create a falsely clean picture.

Summary

EFA can be used to check whether a set of items form one or more sub-scales or factors. There are many decisions which the analyst is required to make, such as the type of factor analysis, the number of factors to extract, whether to rotate the solution and if so which type of rotation, which items are linked to which factor and what the factors should be called. All these decisions should be reported explicitly and not hidden as though they were unproblematic and completely objective.

Apart from the current chapter, up to now analysis to test hypotheses has been described in which there is one dependent or outcome variable (univariate analysis) or where a relationship is explored between two variables (bivariate analysis). The next chapter briefly describes a range of statistical techniques which go beyond univariate and bivariate analysis to explore multivariate analysis.

25 Multivariate analysis

Introduction

The strict definition of multivariate analysis is that more than one dependent variable (DV) is involved in the analysis. However, I have included two techniques which do not fulfil this definition – log-linear modelling and survival analysis; in order to conduct them you will need to read more about them than there is space to devote to them here.

The techniques described in this chapter are less well understood by most psychologists than many of those covered in earlier chapters. This is partly because they are often not covered in an under-graduate research methods course, except possibly as an advanced option in the final year. Under-standing how they are calculated involves a level of mathematics which many undergraduates do not possess, and the majority of the techniques are not covered in many undergraduate texts. In addition, the results of these techniques are sometimes more difficult to interpret. These factors may contribute to the fact that such techniques are much less frequently used than the univariate and bivariate techniques described in earlier chapters.

However, another contributing factor is that a large number of participants should be used for the results of multivariate techniques to have any validity. For example, for every predictor variable included in a discriminant analysis there should be at least 20 participants.

The role of this chapter is to make the reader aware of the function of each of the techniques described and to warn about the constraints on their use. In this way you can judge when they will be useful to you. In addition, it will enable you to interpret and criticise other people's research which has used these techniques. This chapter is not designed to enable you to conduct the techniques. Those who wish to employ the techniques should read Raykov and Marcoulides (2008), Stevens (2009), Tabachnick and Fidell (2013), Dugard et al. (2010) or the more specific references given in this chapter.

Why use multivariate techniques?

Many multivariate techniques have univariate or bivariate counterparts. When we have more than one DV there are at least two advantages of using a multivariate technique rather than repeating a univar-iate equivalent for each DV. These advantages are the same as for preferring multi-way ANOVA over a series of one-way ANOVAs or even t-tests. Firstly, we do not conduct numerous analyses, which would increase the likelihood that we will achieve statistically significant results, even when the data we are analysing are not subject to any real effect. Secondly, we can see how different variables behave in com-bination, instead of looking at them in isolation.

I have classified the techniques according to whether they are used to seek differences between levels of independent variables (IVs) or to seek relationships between variables. As I demonstrated in Chapter 20, this separation is artificial. Nonetheless, it is a convenient fiction, as it does reflect the type of question we are likely to be asking when we choose a particular statistical technique to analyse our data.

Two terms which feature frequently in techniques which are described in this chapter are *maximum likelihood estimation* and *generalised linear modelling*. These are described more fully in Chapter 21 and Appendix XII.

Seeking a difference

Log-linear modelling for categorical data

Log-linear modelling can be seen as an extension of χ^2 analysis of contingency tables. Recall that χ^2 is used when you have categorical data in one or two dimensions.

There are occasions when a simple two-way classification is not enough and we may wish to look at a three-way or more than three-way analysis. For example, we may wish to see whether any differences in proportions of smokers have to do with gender, whether parents smoked, or both. Hence, log-linear modelling is sometimes referred to as *multi-way frequency analysis.*

Log-linear analysis allows us to compare a number of models to see which best fits the data. Given three variables there are a number of possible models from which we have to choose. In the smoking example there can be any combination of the single variables, interactions between pairs of the variables and the three-way interaction. Take my word for the fact that there are over 15 possible models. I am going to describe just one of the many ways of performing a log-linear analysis. The design is called hierarchical, in that it assumes that if there are interactions in the model, then the main effects will also be present. Thus, if there was an interaction between gender and parental smoking, the effects of gender and of smoking, singly, would also be in the model. Remember, however, from ANOVA that it is possible to have a statistically significant interaction without having a statistically significant main effect. The method the analysis employs is described as a backward solution where it starts with the full model, entailing all possible factors, and then selectively removes elements until the optimal solution is found. This can be seen as analogous to the backward solution to multiple regression.

The data to be analysed by log-linear modelling are given in Table 25.1.

The log-linear model which was found to fit the data best was one which included the interactions *gender by parents' smoking* and *participant's smoking by parents' smoking*. Left out were the three-way interaction and the interaction between *participant's smoking* and *gender*. The model was tested statistically, with the result that $\chi^2 = 0.225$, df $= 2$, $p = .894$. Note that in this case we are testing the fit of a model and not a Null Hypothesis. Thus, if it had been significant we would have had to reject the model. This result can be interpreted as showing that any link between gender and smoking is explicable in terms of the links between parental smoking and participant's smoking and between parental smoking and participant's gender. See Agresti (2006, 2002) or Wickens (1989) for details of how to conduct log-linear modelling.

TABLE 25.1   The numbers of males and females who smoke and whether their parents smoke

| Parental smoking | Gender of participant | | | | |
| | Male | | Female | |
	Smoker	Non-smoker	Smoker	Non-smoker
Yes	30	6	40	6
No	12	68	6	32

Hotelling's T^2

Hotelling's T^2 can be viewed as an extension of the *t*-test to situations where there are two levels of an IV but more than one DV. For example, I might be comparing the effects of two therapeutic techniques. However, instead of looking at only one outcome measure, I might look at how satisfied clients were with the treatment, how much they felt in control of their lives and how anxious they were.

Multivariate analysis of variance (MANOVA)

MANOVA is the extension of ANOVA to situations where there is more than one DV and either (a) one IV with more than two levels or (b) more than one IV. Thus, I might compare three or more therapeutic techniques on a number of outcomes. It can also be used to conduct within-subjects ANOVA as it avoids problems over lack of sphericity.

Controlling for covariates

When a difference is being sought between levels of IVs but it is suspected that another variable may be affecting the situation, it is possible to control for that variable and so minimise the influence which it is contributing to the variance in the data, as was seen in Chapter 22 on ANCOVA.

Multivariate analysis of covariance (MANCOVA)

MANCOVA is the multivariate extension of ANCOVA. For example, I might look at the reading ability and the mathematical ability of children in three school types – all-girls, all-boys and co-educational – while controlling for IQ.

Multi-level modelling (MLM)

MLM is also known by a number of other names, including 'hierarchical linear modelling' (HLM) and 'multi-level analysis'. It can be seen as an extension of multiple regression or ANOVA but one which allows us to take lack of independence of data into consideration. For example, imagine that we have devised a method of improving children's expressive drawing. We have allocated classes within a school to a control condition and a training condition, with teachers providing the training. After the intervention we test children in a school on a measure of their drawing ability. If we treated the data as though each child were independent of another we would be testing the wrong model. It is quite likely that children in the same class or taught by the same teacher will show some similarity. MLM allows us to include teacher as a factor in the model. Thus we have a multi-level analysis. At the lowest level is the child and each child is nested with the next level of class or teacher.

What makes this analysis also an extension of multiple regression is that instead of asking the simple question about the intercept and slope of the regression equation we can allow the regression equation to differ between teachers; for example, we could allow the intercept to vary, the slope to vary or both to vary. In this way we can ask the overall question – does the intervention work? But we can also ask whether it is more effective in some classes than others. The model could be extended to take a higher level still into account – for example, if the study were conducted across a number of schools.

Another use to which it is put is for longitudinal data. For example, we might look at how drawing ability develops in children over a period. Here the occasion the measurement was taken is the lowest level and the occasions are nested within the participants. This method of analysing within-subjects data can cope with missing data, as long as they are missing at random, and can analyse data where the times when measures are taken are not the same for each participant.

At the time of writing, SPSS does include a means of analysing some multi-level models by its *mixed* option. However, for more complex models or ones involving categorical outcome variables you need specialist software such as HLM6 or MLWin. For more on this set of techniques, see Hox, Moerbeek, and van de Schoot (2018), Raudenbush and Bryk (2002), Snijders and Bosker (2013) or the chapters in Maxwell and Delaney (2004) and Tabachnick and Fidell (2013).

Identifying the basis of difference

Discriminant analysis

Discriminant analysis can be seen as the obverse of Hotelling's T^2 and MANOVA. It is used in two situations: (a) when a difference is presumed in a categorical (or classificatory) variable and more than one predictor variable is used to identify the nature of that difference, or (b) when a set of predictor variables is being explored to see whether participants can be classified into categories on the basis of differences on the predictor variables. Huberty (1994) uses the term *descriptive discriminative analysis* (DDA) to describe the former, an example of which would be where two cultures are asked to rate a number of descriptions of people on the dimension of intelligence. Imagine that you were comparing British and Japanese people on the way they rated the intelligence of five hypothetical people whose descriptions you provided. Each hypothetical person had to be rated on the dimension, which ranged from *intelligent* to *unintelligent*. Thus, the classificatory variable was race and the predictor variables were the ratings supplied for each of the hypothetical people.

Discriminant analysis would allow you to see whether the profiles of ratings which the two races gave you differed significantly. If they did, then you can explore further to find out what was contributing to the difference.

Huberty (1994) describes the second approach as *predictive discriminative analysis* (PDA). An example of its use would be if an organisation wanted to distinguish those who would be more likely to succeed in learning a skill from those who would be unsuccessful on the basis of their profiles on a personality test. If the analysis achieved its aim, successful trainees would have similar profiles and would differ from the unsuccessful trainees. The ways in which the profiles of the two groups differed could then be used to screen applicants for training to decide who is likely to be successful.

Exploring relationships

When we look for relationships between variables there are two basic ways in which we can do this. Firstly, as with correlation and regression, we can seek any relationships between the measures which we have taken – our *observed* variables. This assumes that we have measured our variables directly and, implicitly, that the measures used were not subject to any error. Alternatively, we can see our measures as indicators of some higher-order variables – *latent* variables. Thus, more than one of our observed variables might be measuring the same latent variable. In factor analysis (see Chapter 24), each factor is a latent variable which usually is linked to more than one of the observed variables, such as items in a questionnaire.

Relationships among observed variables

Cluster analysis

Cluster analysis assumes that the elements, say, participants, can be classified into some form of hierarchy. Hierarchical cluster analysis starts by forming groups of participants which are the closest on some dimension (or combination of dimensions) and then forms combinations (or clusters) of those groups and continues to form higher-order combinations until all the elements are in one cluster. For example, I might be interested in classifying patients who had given me scores on a number of tests. The technique is sometimes used by those using repertory grids derived from Kelly's personal construct theory (see Chapter 6). It allows the researcher to see whether the elements (for example, people) which are being evaluated by a person form clusters based on the constructs attributed to them. In this way an analyst might find out the sort of people who are considered by the person to be similar to one of his or her parents. Whereas discriminant analysis starts with knowledge of group membership and looks for the combination of measures which distinguish the groups, cluster analysis looks for possible groups on the basis of the measures. In fact, discriminant analysis is sometimes used to explore further the nature of the groupings which have been identified by cluster analysis. See Everitt, Landau, and Leese (2011) for further details of cluster analysis.

Canonical correlation

Canonical correlation is an extension of bivariate correlation to situations where instead of two variables to be correlated there are two sets of variables. For example, I might look at the correlation between A-level results, locus of control, achievement motivation and various measures of intelligence as one set and the results for different courses which each student took at university as the other set. Because each set contains more than one variable, there is more than one possible relationship between the sets which might be identified.

Survival analysis

There are sometimes situations when you are interested in the degree to which certain variables predict how long it will take for an event to occur during a given period. As an example, suppose you had a sample of people who smoked cigarettes and you were interested in whether certain demographic and psychological measures predicted the length of time it would take for them to give up smoking. If at the end of your study some participants are still smoking then you could exclude them from the analysis. However, this would reduce the power of your test and lose useful information about people who continue to smoke. Survival analysis allows you to address your original research question while retaining those for whom the event hasn't yet occurred.

One form of survival analysis is Cox regression. The participants for whom the event hadn't occurred, in the example those who hadn't given up smoking, would be treated as *censored* but still included in the analysis. For more detail on survival analysis see Tabachnick and Fidell (2013) and Dugard et al. (2010).

Multivariate regression

This is an extension of univariate regression to situations where there is a set of dependent (or outcome) variables and a set of predictor variables. Using the example from canonical correlation above, I could ask how well A-level results, locus of control, achievement motivation and various measures of intelligence predict the results for different courses which each student took at university. Sometimes multiple regression is wrongly described as multivariate regression.

Path analysis

Path analysis is sometimes referred to as hierarchical multiple regression. It allows researchers to look at the relationships between variables both directly and indirectly. Whereas multiple regression looks at how well a set of IVs can be used to predict a single DV, path analysis can have the same variable

FIGURE 25.1 A path analysis of a model of the relationships between personality, IQ, previous employment and present employment

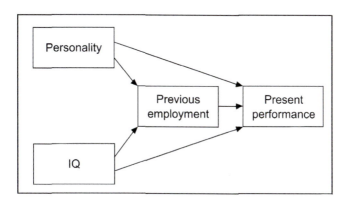

acting as a DV at one stage in the model and as an IV in another part of the model. In the simple model shown in Figure 25.1, personality and IQ are seen as predicting a person's previous employment record. In addition they predict a person's present employment performance both directly and indirectly, via previous employment. Thus, one regression analysis has previous employment as a DV and personality and IQ as IVs, while a second regression has present employment as a DV with personality, IQ and previous employment as the IVs.

It is usual to put what are termed *path coefficients* on each of the paths. These are usually standardised regression coefficients and so give an idea of the relative importance of given paths in the prediction process.

A danger of path analysis is that researchers will forget what they have been told about correlational techniques, namely, that we cannot use them to identify cause-and-effect relationships. There is a temptation to see the arrow in a path diagram as suggesting a direction of cause. As with regression, it is only telling you about the degree to which one variable can be used to predict another.

Path analysis can be conducted via a series of multiple regressions. However, a more informative analysis can be found by using specialist software such as AMOS, LISREL or EQS. These enable the fit of the whole model to be tested, in addition to exploring individual paths and more straightforwardly finding indirect paths such as the path from IQ to present performance via previous employment.

Seeking latent variables

There are two basic ways in which we can seek latent (unobserved) variables. Firstly, and at present more commonly, we hand the responsibility over to the computer and ask it to explore the variables to see whether it can identify any latent variables which could explain the relationships among our observed variables, as in factor analysis (described in Chapter 24). Alternatively we can test a theoretical model by asking the computer whether the latent variables which we assume to exist do a good job of explaining the relationships between our observed variables. The problem with the first – *exploratory* techniques – is that they can capitalise on chance and produce models which may only reflect relationships in the particular set of data. The second – *confirmatory* techniques – are preferable because they explicitly test a theory rather than rely on the computer to generate it. Nonetheless, as long as exploratory techniques are treated purely as exploratory and further data collection will follow to confirm the results of the exploration, they are perfectly legitimate.

Multi-dimensional scaling

Multi-dimensional scaling (MDS) is designed to investigate similarities between entities to try to see whether a set of entities can best be described as lying on two or more dimensions. For example, if I had 20 wines and I asked participants to compare them in pairs and rate how similar they were I would have 190 judgements for each participant. I could then run an MDS program on the data. The result might be that I had two dimensions, one of dryness/sweetness and the other ranging from white to red.

As an example with some real data, I have taken the mileage between 10 different cities in England and run an MDS program on the data. The result is shown in Figure 25.2.

FIGURE 25.2 The results of a multi-dimensional scaling of the distances between a number of English cities

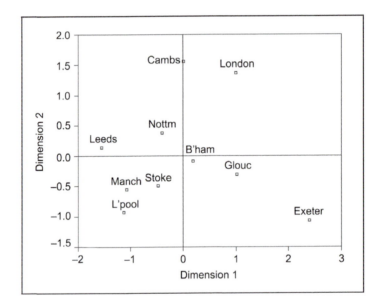

At first this seems to be wrong, in that Cambridge is shown as being north of Manchester. However, this is because the computer was asked to find the dimensions; it was not told about the concepts north and south. Turn the page through 90 degrees clockwise. Now you can see that Liverpool, Manchester and Stoke have been placed in the North-West, Gloucester and Exeter in the South-West, Leeds and Nottingham in the North-East, Cambridge and London in the South-East and Birmingham in the Midlands. The relationship between this model and the map of England is not perfect but then the original data were based on the road network, not on straight distances. This analysis may not seem very earth-shattering, but it does demonstrate that although I did not give the dimensions to the program, it discovered them.

Latent class analysis

While factor analysis assumes that the latent variable is continuous, latent class analysis (LCA) assumes that it is categorical. Thus factor analysis might treat a psychological concept such as addictive personality as forming a continuous variable from total abstinence to severe addiction, while LCA would treat addiction as falling into two or more categories. LCA can be seen as an alternative to some forms of cluster analysis, with each latent class being the equivalent of a cluster. Specialist software such as Mplus and Latent GOLD are needed to conduct LCA. For more information on LCA see Hagenaars and McCutcheon (2002).

Confirmatory Factor Analysis (CFA)

As an example of a CFA, if you were testing a theory of what abilities together made up mathematical ability, you might give a group of participants a battery of tests in mathematics ranging from tests of ability to perform simple calculations, through the ability to interpret graphs, to tests of algebra and calculus. CFA would allow you to test whether the data from your participants conformed with the model you had created based on your theory of mathematical ability. You may have assumed that certain items in your test related to ability to calculate, others involved more abstract concepts and others involved spatial reasoning.

Figure 25.3 shows the idealised results of a factor analysis conducted on a test which contained six mathematical questions. The model has three factors or latent variables (notice that the variables which were measured – the questions – are shown in rectangular boxes while the latent variables are in circles; this is a standard convention).

FIGURE 25.3 The model tested in a confirmatory factor analysis on three mathematical latent variables

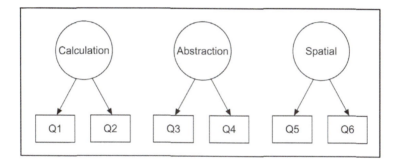

Structural Equation Modelling (SEM)

SEM allows researchers to perform confirmatory analysis – that is, explicitly to test a theoretical model. It allows them to do this for a number of the techniques described previously, individually or in combination. In addition, it allows you to assume that your observed measures could contain an element of error. It can also be used to combine a number of the other techniques in one model.

Figure 25.4 shows how the previous path analysis can be extended so that instead of involving only measured variables it now contains the latent variables which are believed to be related to the observed variables. This model combines path analysis (which, if you remember, can be the result of a series of regression analyses) and confirmatory factor analysis.

Specialist statistical packages are available for analysing CFA and SEM, such as AMOS, LISREL and EQS. They can also be used for path analysis.

As we've seen elsewhere where the fit of data to an assumed model is being evaluated (such as in the one group χ^2 goodness-of-fit test; see Chapter 14), if inferential statistics are employed this reverses our usual use of them for a good fit between data and model takes the role of the Null Hypothesis and the probability given will be the equivalent of: 'If the data come from a population in which this model is true then the likelihood of finding data which are as different from the model as these data is . . '.
In which case, if $p < .05$ and we reject the Null Hypothesis, we are concluding that the data are not a good fit to the model. Accordingly, the larger the sample we have for the same amount of discrepancy between the data and the model, the more likely we would be to reject the model as our statistic has greater power. This means we are caught in a bind: to improve the reliability of our findings we need a relatively large sample size but this means we are more likely to find even small differences between the

FIGURE 25.4   A structural equation model relating personality, IQ and previous and present employment

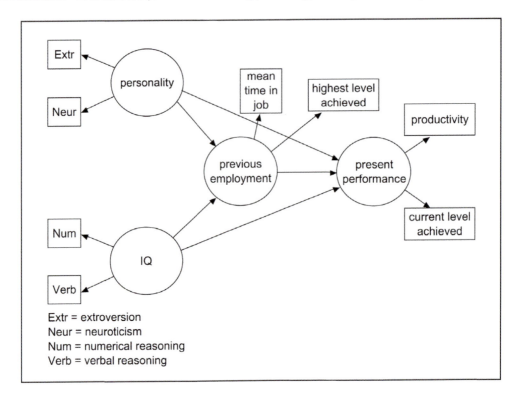

data and model to be significant. One way around this has been the development of what are called fit statistics, which instead of relying on probability have criteria as to what constitutes a good fit between data and model. There are a large number of these statistics, each devised to address specific issues, sometimes to solve problems identified with previous ones. To give you an impression of how large the number of these statistics which are available is, AMOS provides at least 26 and that is not an exhaustive set of those which exist.

For more information on SEM see Kline (2016), the chapter on the subject in Tabachnick and Fidell (2013), Raykov and Marcoulides (2008) or, if using AMOS, Byrne (2016).

Summary

There are a number of multivariate techniques (Tables 25.2 and 25.3) which extend the analytic methods given in the rest of the book to cover situations in which more than one DV is included or to other more complex data sets. They are more complicated to conduct and to interpret than the other techniques, and they involve more decisions about how the data will be treated. Such decisions can be made either by the researcher or by a computer program. They can be subject to inappropriate use or they may capitalise on chance and give a solution which is only applicable to the given data and not provide a reliable model. The particular decisions made, either by researcher or computer, should be fully reported, in order that the reader may put the results in the context of those decisions. They generally require a much larger sample size, both for power and to produce a reliable analysis, than their equivalent univariate technique.

TABLE 25.2 Summary of multivariate techniques used for exploring differences

DV	Predictor variables	Covariates	Test
>1	1 (2 levels)	–	Hotelling's T^2
>1	1 +	–	MANOVA
>1	1 +	yes	MANCOVA
1	>1	yes	Hierarchical linear modelling
1 (nominal)	>1 (nominal)	–	Log-linear modelling
1	1 +	–	Discriminant analysis

TABLE 25.3 Summary of multivariate techniques used to explore relationships between variables

DV	Predictor variables	Latent variables?	Test
1	≥ 1	–	Survival analysis
>1	–	–	Cluster analysis
>1	>1	–	Canonical correlation Multivariate regression Path analysis
>1	–	components	Principal components analysis
>1	–	yes	Exploratory and confirmatory factor analysis Multi-dimensional scaling Latent class analysis
>1	>1	yes	Structural equation modelling

The next chapter describes how to conduct a meta-analysis, which is a quantitative method for combining the results from related studies to produce a general measure of effect size and of probability.

26 Meta-analysis

Introduction

A meta-analysis is a quantitative equivalent of a narrative literature review. It has three major advantages over a narrative review. Firstly, it allows the reviewer to quantify the trends which are contained in the literature by combining the effect sizes and combining the probabilities which have been found in a number of studies. Secondly, by combining the results of a number of studies the power of the statistical test is increased. In this case, a number of non-significant findings which all show the same trend may, when combined, prove to be significant. Thirdly, the process of preparing the results of previous research for a meta-analysis forces the reviewer to read the studies more thoroughly than for a narrative review.

This chapter describes the various stages through which a meta-analysis is conducted. The necessary equations to conduct a meta-analysis are given in Appendix XVI, where a worked example of each stage is given. The example is based on a meta-analysis of chronic pelvic pain (McGowan, Clark-Carter, & Pitts, 1998). Many of the procedures I describe are the same as would be employed for a systematic review that was not a meta-analysis; a meta-analysis is only appropriate when there are sufficient similarities among studies that combining their information quantitatively makes sense. Thus, a researcher could be intending to conduct a meta-analysis but find that this is not appropriate; at that point the decision would be made to write the report as a systematic review. This would mean that the review had still benefited from the rigour which a meta-analysis demands and is more open to scrutiny than a more impressionistic narrative review.

Choosing the topic of the meta-analysis

As with any research you need to decide on the particular area on which you are going to concentrate. In addition, you will need a specific hypothesis which you are going to test with the meta-analysis. However, initially the exact nature of the hypothesis may be unspecified, only to be refined once you have seen the range of research.

Identifying the research

The next phase of a meta-analysis, as with a narrative review, is to identify the relevant research. This can be done by using the standard abstracting systems such as PsycINFO, or the Web of Science. See Chapter 2 for advice on searching such databases. The papers which are collected by these means can yield further papers from their reference lists. It is usual to identify particular journals which are likely to publish articles on the area of interest and to hand search or electronically search the abstracts across a range of years. Another source of material and of people with interests in the research field can be the Internet. In addition, the meta-analyst can write to authors who are known to work in the area to see whether they have any studies, as yet unpublished, the results of which they would be willing to share.

This process will help to show the complexity of the area. It will show the range of designs which have been employed, such as which groups have been used as control groups and what age ranges have been considered – whether children or adults have been employed. For example, in studies of the nature of pelvic pain, a variety of comparison groups have been employed. Comparisons have been made between women who have pelvic pain but no discernible cause and those with some identifiable physical cause. In addition, those with pelvic pain have been compared with those with other forms of chronic pain and with those who have no chronic pain.

The collection of papers will also show what measures have been taken, that is, what DVs have been used; for example, in the pelvic pain research measures have ranged from anxiety and depression to experience of childhood sexual abuse. This stage in the process is sometimes called a *scoping exercise*. Two important results of the exercise are: firstly you are going to find out whether there are sufficient studies to warrant the review and secondly whether anyone has produced a recent review and so made yours unnecessary.

Choosing the hypotheses to be tested

Once the range of designs and measures has been ascertained it is possible to identify the relevant hypothesis or hypotheses which will be tested in the meta-analysis. Frequently, more than one DV is employed in a single piece of research. The meta-analyst has the choice of conducting meta-analyses on each of the DVs or choosing some more global definition of the DV which will allow more studies to be included in each meta-analysis. For example, the experience of childhood sexual abuse and of adult sexual abuse could be combined under the heading of experience of sexual abuse at any age. Such decisions are legitimate as long as the analyst makes them explicit in the report of the analysis.

In each meta-analysis, there has to be a directional hypothesis which is being tested. Otherwise, if the direction of effect were ignored in each study, then results which pointed in one direction would be combined with results which pointed in the opposite direction and so suggest a more significant finding than is warranted. In fact, positive and negative effects should tend to cancel each other out. By direction of the finding I do not mean whether the results support the overall hypothesis being tested, by being statistically significant, but whether the results have gone in the direction of the hypothesis or in the opposite direction. Whether the original researchers had a directional hypothesis is irrelevant; it is the meta-analyst's hypothesis which determines the direction.

You should draw up criteria which will be used to decide whether a given study will be included in the meta-analysis (inclusion criteria). For example, in the case of chronic pelvic pain, the generally accepted definition requires that the sufferer has had the condition for at least 6 months. Therefore, papers which did not apply this way of classifying their participants were excluded from the meta-analysis.

Deciding which papers to obtain

Once you have conducted searches often you will have a vast number of titles or titles and abstracts. Often the titles and even the abstracts are sufficiently vague that you won't be able to tell whether a study will fulfil your inclusion criteria. You should read the titles and abstracts and decide which studies *could* fulfil your inclusion criteria. A colleague should do the same and you should compare notes and keep a record of your degree of agreement. At this stage it is better to err on the side of over-inclusion as a study can be removed if, once you have obtained the full details, you find it isn't appropriate for your review. Thus, if you and your colleague disagree and a convincing case cannot be made as to why a study should be excluded, then obtain the full description of that study.

Extracting the necessary information

For each measure the analyst wants to be able to identify the number of participants in each group, a significance level for the results, an effect size and a direction of the finding. Unfortunately, it will not always be possible, directly, to find all this information. In this case, further work will be entailed.

It is good practice to create a coding (or extraction) sheet on which you record, for each paper, the information which you have extracted from it. This should include details of design, sample size, and summary and inferential statistics. Give each study a reference number, which you should use whenever you refer to it so that you can keep track of the decisions you have made throughout the process. This will help you if you need to change aspects of the study such as revising the inclusion criteria or responding to comments made by reviewers of papers based on the meta-analysis.

Dealing with inadequately reported studies

There are a number of factors which render the report of a study inadequate for inclusion in a meta-analysis. Some can be got around by simple reanalysis of the results. Others will involve writing to the author(s) of the research for more details.

Often it is possible to calculate the required information from the detail which has been supplied in the original paper. Sometimes a specific hypothesis will not have been tested because the IV has more than two levels and the results are in the form of an ANOVA with more than one degree of freedom for the treatment effect. If means and standard deviations have been reported for the comparison groups, then both significance levels and effect sizes can be computed via a *t*-test. Similarly, if frequencies have been reported, then significance levels and effect sizes can be computed via χ^2.

However, sometimes even these details will not be available, particularly if the aspect of the study in which you are interested is only a part of the study and only passing reference has been made to it. In this case, you should write to the author(s) for the necessary information. This can have a useful side effect in that authors sometimes send you the results of their unpublished research or give you details of other researchers in the field. Another reason for writing to authors is when you have more than one paper from the same source and are unsure whether they are reports of different aspects of the same study; you do not want to include the same participants, more than once, in the same part of the meta-analysis because to do so would give that particular research undue influence over the outcome of the meta-analysis.

If the researchers do not reply, then you may be forced to quantify such vague reporting as 'the results were significant'. Ways of dealing with this are given in Appendix XVI.

The file-drawer problem

There is a bias on the part of both authors and journals towards publishing statistically significant results. This means that other research may have been conducted which did not yield significance and which has not been published. It is termed the file-drawer problem on the understanding that researchers' filing cabinets will contain their unpublished studies. This would mean that your meta-analysis is failing to take into account non-significant findings and in so doing gives a false impression of significance. There are standard ways of checking whether there is a file-drawer problem, which are given next. However, one way to try to minimise the bias is to include what is called *grey literature*.

Grey literature

Hopewell, Clarke, and Mallett (2005) define grey literature as work from government, academic institutions, business and industry which is in print or electronic form but which isn't published by commercial publishers. I think of it as work not published in peer-reviewed journals, as commercial publishers could publish journals which aren't subject to peer review and some organisations and learned bodies publish peer-reviewed journals. Whichever definition we use, the important point is that failure to include such sources could create a false impression. If grey literature is used, then it should also be subjected to the same quality rating system as all the other studies. Sensitivity analysis could then be used to see whether including or excluding studies below a certain quality threshold leads to different conclusions.

Classifying previous studies

Once you have collected the studies you can decide on the meta-analyses which you are going to conduct. This can be done on the basis of the comparison groups and DVs which have been employed. The larger the number of studies included in a given analysis, the better. Therefore, I would recommend using a broad categorisation process initially and then identifying relevant subcategories. For example, in the case of pelvic pain you could classify papers which have compared sufferers of pelvic pain with any other group, initially. You could then separate the papers into those which had sufferers from other forms of pain as a comparison group and those which had non-pain sufferers as a comparison group.

Each meta-analysis can involve two analyses: one of the combined probability for all the studies involved and one of their combined effect size. For each study you will need to convert each measure of probability to a standard measure and each effect size to a standard measure.

Some research papers will report the results from a number of subgroups. For example, in studies of gender differences in mathematical ability, papers may report the results from more than one school or even from more than one country. The meta-analyst has a choice over how to treat the results from such papers. On the one hand, the results for each subsample could be included as a separate element in the meta-analysis. However, it could be argued that this is giving undue weight to a given paper and its method. In this case, it would be better to create a single effect size and probability which summarised the subsamples in the paper. To be on the safe side, it would be best to conduct two meta-analyses: one with each substudy treated as a study in its own right and one where each paper only contributed once to the meta-analysis. If the two meta-analyses conflict, then this clearly questions the reliability of the findings.

Checking the reliability of coding

It is advisable to give a second person blank versions of your extraction sheets, details of your inclusion criteria and the papers which you have collected (or a sample of them if there are a large number of them). That person should code the studies and then you should check whether you agree over your decisions and the details which you have extracted.

As you go through each stage in deciding whether a study should be included, keep a record of the decisions and the number of studies excluded at a given stage. It can be useful to report a flow diagram which shows how many studies were excluded at each stage. Moher, Liberati, Tetzlaff, and Altman (2009) give guidelines for this, following PRISMA (Preferred Reporting Items for Systematic reviews and Meta-Analyses).

Weighting studies

Some texts on meta-analysis recommend that different studies should be given an appropriate weighting. In other words, rather than treat all studies as being of equivalent value, the quality of each, in terms of sample size or methodological soundness, should be taken into account. However, opinions differ over what constitutes an appropriate basis for weighting and even as to whether it is legitimate to apply any weighting. My own preference is simply to weight each study by the number of participants who were employed in that study. In this way, studies which used more participants would have greater influence on the results of the meta-analysis than studies which used smaller samples. This seems appropriate as the larger the sample size, the more accurate an estimate of the population value a study should produce.

Combining the results of studies

Effect size

Producing a standard measure of effect size

A useful standard measure of effect size is the correlation coefficient r. It is preferred to other measures because it is unaffected by differences in subsample size in between-subjects designs. This is only a problem when the meta-analyst does not have the necessary information about sample sizes to calculate effect sizes which do take account of unequal subsamples. Equations for converting various descriptive and comparative statistics into r are given in Appendix XVI. However, there is an unfortunate consequence of using r as the measure of effect size: it has to be converted itself into a Fisher's Z-transformation (for an explanation see Chapter 19). As there is a danger that this may be confused with the standard z used in the equation for combining probability, I will use the symbol r' to denote Fisher's Z. The equation for converting r to r' is given in Appendix XIX along with tables for converting r to r'.

Calculating a combined effect size

Once an r' has been calculated for each study they can be used to produce a combined r', which can be converted back to an r to give the combined effect size, either by using the appropriate equation given in Appendix XIX or by using the tables given there.

Probability

Producing a standard measure of probability

The standard measure for finding probability which I recommend is a z-score. Equations are given in Appendix XVI to convert various inferential statistics into a z-score.

Calculating a combined probability

Once you have a z-score for each study, a combined z-score can be calculated, which can then be treated as a conventional z-score would be and its probability can be found by consulting the standard z-table (see Appendix XVII).

Homogeneity

An important part of the process of meta-analysis is assessing whether the studies in a given meta-analysis are heterogeneous, in other words, whether they differ significantly from each other. This is a similar process to the one you would employ when finding a measure of spread for scores from a sample. If they do differ significantly, then you need to find which study or studies are contributing to the heterogeneity. You should then examine all the studies to try to ascertain what it is about the aberrant studies which might be contributing to the heterogeneity.

I recommend that you test the heterogeneity of studies on the basis of their effect size and take out the aberrant studies, one at a time, until you have a set of studies which are not significantly heterogeneous, leaving a homogeneous set. You can then report the results of the meta-analyses, with and without the aberrant studies. In the case of probability, remember that it is strongly dependent on sample size and therefore a study might produce a very different probability from others simply because its sample size was different, even when all the studies had similar effect sizes.

Testing the heterogeneity of effect sizes

The heterogeneity of the effect sizes can be found by using an equation which looks at the variation in the Fisher's transformed r-scores (r') of the studies to see whether they are significantly different (see Appendix XVI). If they are significantly different, then the effect sizes are heterogeneous. In that case, you should explore the reason for the heterogeneity (see *dealing with heterogeneity*). You could remove the study with the r' which contributes most to the variability. If the reduced set of studies is also heterogeneous, then continue to remove the study with the r' which contributes most to the heterogeneity until the resultant set is not significantly heterogeneous. You can now report the combined r for these remaining studies as being homogeneous.

Testing the heterogeneity of probabilities

Following the reasoning given previously, it is not necessary to test whether the probabilities of the studies are heterogeneous. For completeness the method is described in Appendix XVI. If you do test for such heterogeneity there is no point in continuing to test until you have a non-heterogeneous set of studies, with respect to their probabilities.

Confidence intervals

You need to calculate and report the confidence interval for the combined effect size. This takes into account the total number of participants who took part in all the studies in the particular meta-analysis. Remember that a confidence interval is an estimate, based on data from a sample, of where the population parameter is likely to lie. If the confidence interval for the effect size does not contain zero, then we can be more confident that there is a real effect being detected. For example, if a confidence interval showed that the effect size for the relationship between gender and smoking, for a number of studies, ranged between −0.1 and +0.4 (where a negative value denoted that a higher proportion of females smoked, while a positive value denoted that a higher proportion of males smoked), then, as this included the possibility that the effect size was zero, it would question whether there was a real difference between the genders in their smoking behaviours.

Checking the file-drawer problem

The fail-safe *N*

When a meta-analysis finds a statistically significant result, one method of assessing whether there is a file-drawer problem is to compute the number of non-significant studies which would have to be added to the meta-analysis to render it non-significant. This is known as the fail-safe *N*, and its calculation is dealt with in Appendix XVI. Rosenthal (1991) suggests that it is reasonable to assume that the number of unreported non-significant studies which exist is around $(5 \times k) + 10$, where k is the number of studies in the meta-analysis. For example, if the meta-analyst has found six studies, then we can reasonably assume that $(5 \times 6) + 10 = 40$ non-significant studies exist. If the fail-safe *N* is larger than this critical number of studies, then the meta-analysis can be considered to have yielded a result which is robust. In other words, it does not appear to suffer from the file-drawer problem. Becker (2005) discusses a number of versions of the fail-safe N and concludes that other methods for assessing whether publication bias exists are preferable. One such method is the funnel graph (or funnel plot).

Funnel graph

Although effect sizes are less affected by sample size than are tests of significance, it is still the case that the larger the sample, the closer the effect size calculated for that sample will be to the population effect size. Therefore, as sample sizes increase there should be less variability in the effect sizes. Accordingly, if we plot effect size against sample size (in this case using hypothetical data) we should get the pattern seen in Figure 26.1. This plot suggests that the true effect size is just over $r = 0.3$.

FIGURE 26.1   A funnel graph showing the pattern which can be expected when there is no publication bias

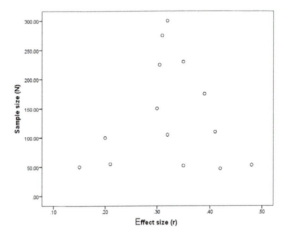

However, if there has been publication bias, then you are likely to get the pattern shown in Figure 26.2. Here the symmetrical funnel shape shown in Figure 26.1 is not present. The impression we can

FIGURE 26.2   A funnel graph showing the pattern which can be expected when publication bias is present

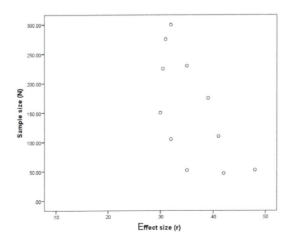

get from Figure 26.2 is that the true effect size is $r = 0.3$ but that some studies which employed smaller samples and have small effect sizes have not been published.

Funnel graphs are only really useful when there are a large number of studies in the meta-analysis, otherwise patterns are difficult to discern.

Dealing with heterogeneity

There are at least two ways to deal with heterogeneity, but both should lead to the same result. One is to conduct focused comparisons; the other is to treat the phenomenon you are trying to study as random.

Focused comparison

This involves looking for a consistent basis for the lack of homogeneity and testing it statistically. For example, in a meta-analysis on the relationship between gender and mathematical ability it might be found that studies give heterogeneous results. The meta-analyst might hypothesise that this is due to the type of mathematics being measured in each study. It would then be possible to classify the studies according to the type of mathematics tested to see whether they produced significantly different results. Other terms for focused comparison in the literature are tests of heterogeneity and contrasts. In Appendix XVI I demonstrate how to compare groups; for more on focused comparisons see Rosenthal (1991) and Hedges (1994).

Random model

You have met the word *random* in a number of contexts within this book and it is often contrasted with *fixed*. In this case, I interpret 'random' as meaning there is more than one population value for an effect size, while 'fixed' means there is one value. However, even if we adopt the assumption that the phenomenon is random, we still want to know what factors could explain the different effect sizes. In this case, if we find heterogeneity we should examine the studies to see whether we can identify such moderating factors. To demonstrate the effect of assuming a random model I have re-analysed the data reported in this chapter to see what effect they have on the interpretation. Workings are given in Appendix XVI.

Study quality

It is becoming increasingly common to rate studies on their quality. Thus, when appropriate, the highest level of quality could be studies which had a control group, randomly assigned participants to conditions, explained how the sample size was chosen, used standardised measures with good reliability, had those taking measures from participants blind to the condition a participant was in, contained clear reporting of attrition rates and so on. One problem can be that the phenomenon being studied may not lend itself to having such design features; for example, we cannot randomly allocate people to those with and without chronic pelvic pain. The solution is to look at a number of existing quality ratings and then use or adapt the most appropriate. Once you have decided on your quality ratings, then you and a colleague should grade the studies and, once again, compare notes and keep a record of your level of agreement (see Jüni, Altman, & Egger, 2001; Petticrew & Roberts, 2006; Wortman, 1994).

Reporting the results of a meta-analysis

Moher et al. (2009) give guidelines. However, at the time of writing, they are revising their guidelines. The abstracting systems which were searched to identify the studies, including the keywords used, the years covered and when they were last searched, should be reported. The titles and range of years of all journals which were hand or electronically searched should also be given. All decisions which have been made about how studies were classified and the bases for inclusion and exclusion of studies in a given meta-analysis should be made explicit in the report. Details of how reliability of coding was checked should be given, including how disagreements were resolved. All papers which have been consulted in the meta-analysis should be reported in an appendix to the paper, with an indication of which were included and which excluded. Given the vast number which may have been identified in the first stages of the analysis, I would only include this level of detail for those studies for which you obtained full copies of the reports. It is useful to use a symbol to indicate why each excluded study was rejected, with a key to what the symbols refer to.

Probably the best way to present the results of the meta-analyses is in a summary table which includes the following details:

- the DV;
- the nature of the experimental and control groups;
- the number of studies;
- the total number of participants in the meta-analysis;
- the combined effect size (r) and its confidence interval;
- the combined probability, as a z-value and as a probability; and
- checks for publication bias.

In the case of a significant result, we also need the number of non-significant studies which would have been needed to render the meta-analysis as not robust to the file-drawer problem (the fail-safe N) and the number of non-significant studies which are likely to exist. If the result was not statistically significant, then it cannot be subject to the file-drawer problem.

Table 26.1 shows the summary table for one meta-analysis based on the depression scores of sufferers of chronic pelvic pain and controls who do not have pelvic pain (the calculations for this meta-analysis are shown in Appendix XVI).

TABLE 26.1 The summary of a meta-analysis of studies which looked at depression in patients with chronic pelvic pain and controls

Groups compared: pelvic pain vs controls	Number of studies	Total number of participants	Combined effect size (r)	Confidence interval	Combined z	Combined p	Fail-safe N	Critical number for drawer
All studies	6	620	0.3418	0.2695–0.4104	8.789	<.0001	166	40
Homogeneous studies	5	510	0.3819	0.3042–0.4545	8.966	<.0001	144	35

Table 26.1 can be interpreted as showing that a meta-analysis was conducted into the relative depression experienced by those suffering chronic pelvic pain and controls who do not suffer pelvic pain. Initially, six studies were used in the meta-analysis, with a total of 620 participants. These studies produced a combined effect size of $r = 0.3418$, which Cohen (1988) considers to be above a medium effect size. However, the studies had significantly heterogeneous effect sizes. A non-heterogeneous set of five studies was identified. The combined effect size for the homogeneous set was $r = 0.3819$ (also above a medium effect size). The results are highly unlikely to have occurred if the Null Hypothesis of no difference between the groups had been true. It would have needed an additional 166 non-significant studies to render the full meta-analysis non-significant, and 144 for the homogeneous set, which means

that the file-drawer problem is unlikely to affect this study as only 40 or 35 additional non-significant studies, respectively, are likely to exist. Notice also that the lowest value in the confidence interval for the effect size of all the studies combined is just under 0.3 and for the homogeneous set it is over 0.3, suggesting that the effect in the population is at least a medium effect in Cohen's terms.

Some journals like to include a *Forest Plot*. In Figure 26.3 I have plotted each individual r-value and its 95% confidence interval (using equation A10.4). This shows whether the studies form a general trend and whether any have a CI which crosses 0 and so may not reflect a genuine effect. We can see that five of the studies have CIs which are clearly beyond 0 while one crosses into the negative range.

FIGURE 26.3   A Forest Plot of the r-values from the six studies included in the meta-analysis

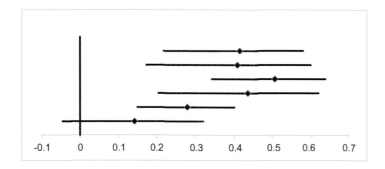

Summary

A meta-analysis involves identifying all the available studies which are relevant to the area being explored. These have to be classified according to their design and the DVs which they have employed. The decision has to be made as to how many meta-analyses will be necessary to describe the area fully. Each meta-analysis can have a combined effect size and a combined probability calculated for it. In addition, the heterogeneity of the effect sizes should be calculated. When heterogeneity of effect size is identified, either the analysis should follow that for a random model, a focused comparison of studies with different characteristics can be conducted or studies should be removed from the meta-analysis until a homogeneous set of studies has been identified. The combined probabilities for all the studies and for the homogeneous set should be reported, as should the combined effect size and confidence intervals for both the complete set of studies and the homogeneous set. All decisions about the inclusion and exclusion of studies should be made explicit in the report of the meta-analysis.

The next chapter describes a different approach to hypothesis testing to that covered up to now in the book: Bayesian statistics.

27 Bayesian statistics

Introduction

What follows is an explanation of certain ideas which come from an alternative view to the approach to hypothesis testing which is described in the rest of the book. This is designed to help you understand reports of other people's statistical analysis rather than to do the analysis yourself. As part of the explanation I cite works which could be useful if you did want to run the analysis yourself.

An alternative approach to probability and hypothesis testing

The probability provided when following the principles of Null Hypothesis Statistical Testing (NHST) is what is called a *conditional probability*: the probability of our result occurring *if* the Null Hypothesis is true; often shown as p(our result occuring|H_0 true). Hence the smaller that probability the more evidence we feel has been provided that the Null Hypothesis is unlikely to be true and we are willing to take the risk of rejecting the Null Hypothesis and accepting our Alternative Hypothesis. However, research has shown that the conditional probability is often misinterpreted (see Gigerenzer et al., 1989). Bayesian statistics[1] allows potentially more satisfactory probabilities to be derived from the evidence. For example, with sufficient information we could find a different conditional probability: how likely is the Null Hypothesis to be true if the particular result of our study occurs: p(H_0 true|our result occurred). The two approaches are often described as *frequentist* or classical (for NHST)[2] and *subjective* (for Bayesian). Those defending the latter approach argue that there are subjective elements in the way frequentist statistics are conducted (see Howson & Urbach, 1993).

Despite widespread dissatisfaction with NHST and suggestions of alternatives (Edwards, Lindman, & Savage, 1963; Phillips, 1973; Cohen, 1990; and even Clark-Carter, 1998), it has taken a long time for Bayesian statistics to become more widely accepted. This may be for a number of reasons. The first relates to the assumptions which have to be made about unknown elements. The original theorem upon which Bayesian statistics are based conform to the laws of probability and algebra; therefore, in cases where all the elements are known, the probabilities derived from applying Bayes's Theorem aren't open to dispute, as the following example shows.

In Table A13.2, I presented data relating to a test designed to measure depression in participants. The sensitivity of the test is a conditional probability: the probability of being given a positive diagnosis

---

1 Named after Thomas Bayes (1702–1761). The paper which contains the theorem attributed to him was published after his death (Bayes, 1763/1958).

2 It is essential for the theory of probability, that in the game of dice, as in all the other mass phenomena which we mentioned, the relative frequencies of certain attributes should become more and more stable as the number of observations is increased. We shall discuss this idea of the 'limiting value of the relative frequency' later on; meanwhile we shall regard it as the probability of the attribute in question, e.g. the probability of the result '12' in the game of dice (von Mises, 1928/1939, p. 16).

for depression if you have depression, p(positive|depressed), which for this test is 1. The specificity of the test is also a conditional probability: the probability of not being given a positive diagnosis with depression if you don't have depression, p(not positive|not depressed) = .88. Knowing just those two conditional probabilities and the prevalence of the condition (.25), rather than all the information in Table A13.2, it is possible to work out the probability of being diagnosed as having the condition: p(positive).[3] Bayes's theorem can then be used to calculate the conditional probability that a person will have the condition if the test identifies that person as having the condition (.7353).[4] This is the same figure as the PPV (Positive Predictive Value) of the test: the proportion of those who were diagnosed positively as depressed who were depressed (see Appendix XIII). That illustration involves discrete/binary conditions: the person either has depression or does not and is either diagnosed as having depression or is not. Nonetheless, Bayes's theorem extends to more continuous variables.

Unlike in my example, in much of psychological research we don't know the underlying probabilities and so we have to assume what they might be. This can lead to a second issue which may have delayed the adoption of Bayesian statistics: the difficulty or even impossibility of finding solutions to many of the equations which result from applying Bayesian methods through the use of what are described as analytic methods, such as calculus. The power of computers has reached a sufficient level that iterative methods can be applied (as described in Chapter 21) to produce the required solutions.[5] Further reasons for lack of wider adoption of Bayesian methods among psychologists may be inertia/fear of change, lack of awareness of the debate surrounding NHST, lack of availability of the tools within menu-based statistical software and accessible teaching materials.

The extent of the change in favour of Bayesian methods can be seen by some recent developments. The journal *Psychological Methods* published two special issues on Bayesian methods (Chow & Hoijtink, 2017; Hoijtink & Chow, 2017). IBM SPSS introduced, in version 25, some forms of Bayesian analysis. In

---

3 p(positive) = p(positive|depressed) × p(depressed) + p(positive|not depressed) × p(not depressed)

We can work out the missing elements:

$$p(\text{positive}|\text{not depressed}) = 1 - p(\text{not positive}|\text{not depressed})$$
$$= 1 - .88$$
$$= .12$$

And

$$p(\text{not depressed}) = 1 - p(\text{depressed})$$
$$= 1 - .25$$
$$= .75$$

Therefore,

$$p(\text{positive}) = 1 \times .25 + .12 \times .75$$
$$= .25 + .09$$
$$= .34$$

4 $$p(\text{depressed}|\text{positive}) = \frac{p(\text{positive}\,|\,\text{depressed}) \times p(\text{depressed})}{p(\text{positive})}$$

$$= \frac{1 \times .25}{.34}$$
$$= .7353$$

5 Methods such as *Markov chain Monte Carlo* (MCMC) are applied with variants, including the *Metropolis-Hastings* algorithm (MH) and *Gibbs sampling* for problems which are otherwise intractable. I include these terms so that when you meet them you have some idea about what is being referred to (for more details see Hoijtink, 2009; Lee, 2012; Gill, 2008; Jackman, 2009).

addition, the latest advice from the APA on reporting quantitative analysis notes that: 'Bayesian statistical analysis has become a more commonly used statistical procedure in behavioral research'. (Applebaum et al., 2018, p. 17) and gives guidance on reporting such analysis.

Although Bayesian methods can be used to find a p-value (called *a posterior predictive p-value*), analysts using such methods are usually more interested in producing a plausible distribution for a parameter of interest (such as a mean) and from this a range of the most plausible values for the parameter values can be derived. To illustrate these points I will use the example of correlation between ability in maths and in English (see Table 19.10). According to a frequentist approach, the correlation, $r = .888$, has a 95% confidence interval of .5860 to .9734 (following the procedure described in Appendix X). The confidence interval is wide because of the small sample size (n = 10) but as it doesn't include 0 we can conclude that there is good evidence for there being a positive correlation between the two variables.

Bayesian statistics starts with one or more prior distributions or probabilities (*priors*). It uses the priors, along with the likelihood to produce a posterior distribution or probability. In the example of the test of depression, the probability of being depressed, p(depressed), and the probability of being diagnosed as positive, p(positive), are the priors (they are given or assumed before the analysis is conducted), the probability of having a positive diagnosis if you are depressed, p(positive|depressed), is the likelihood and the probability of being depressed if you are diagnosed as positive, p(depressed|positive), is the posterior (the outcome after the analysis). Thus the posterior distribution or probability is found through combining the information from the priors, the likelihood and the data.

Estimation

In the correlation example, adopting a Bayesian approach, p(ρ) is the prior (where ρ is the value of r in the population), p(data|ρ) is the likelihood and p(ρ|data) is the posterior. However, instead of a single value for r, the posterior will be a probability density function[6] (pdf; named before Portable Document Format files existed) for the range of possible values for ρ, from which we can find some summary statistics. Leaving all the default values in SPSS produces a median (.876) and a mean (.801) for the value of ρ with a 95% credible interval (.560, .969).[7] Unlike a confidence interval a credible interval is found from the posterior distribution. The values of ρ, in this case, are plotted against their likelihood, as in Figure 27.1 and the range of values which include 95% of the area under the curve is the 95% credible interval; like confidence intervals, credible intervals can cover other percentages of the distribution, such as 90% or 99%.

FIGURE 27.1   The posterior distribution of the correlation coefficient for the relationship between English and mathematical ability

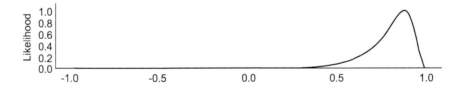

---

6   The normal distribution is an example of a graph created from a probability density function (see Figure 9.27).

7   Which is described as the 95% *highest probability density region* (HPD region or HDR) within the pdf. It is the interval encompassing 95% of the pdf which contains the values which have the most credibility.

As with the frequentist approach, because the lowest end of the credible interval is positive, and a large effect size, we could conclude that there is good evidence for there being a positive correlation between the two abilities.

Specifying the prior(s)

Possibly the main reason for describing Bayesian methods as subjective is that it is possible to set a prior which is based on the belief of the researcher. The belief could be well founded from previous research or other sources such as experts in a field of research. The nature of the posterior distribution and therefore everything which is concluded from it, such as the credible interval, can be affected by the choice of prior. There is a tension between, on the one hand, wishing to use information which is known or assumed about the prior and, on the other, not wanting to use a prior which will overly influence the nature of the posterior distribution despite the nature of the data. Using previous information can lead to what is called an *informative* prior. The alternative is to set a *non-informative* or *uninformative* prior. One example of a non-informative prior is where all possible values for the statistic of interest are treated as equally likely. This is called the *uniform* prior (see Figure 27.2).

FIGURE 27.2   A uniform prior: the likelihood is the same for every possible value of ρ

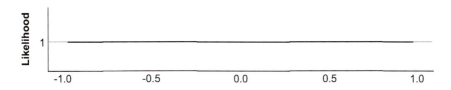

SPSS uses a uniform prior as the default value but offers the options of Jeffreys's prior, which is non-informative, or of choosing a prior. To do the latter, it is necessary to specify a value for c,[8] which affects the shape of the prior distribution. A uniform prior is the equivalent of setting c = 0 and, in the case of correlation, Jeffreys's prior sets c = −1.5 (see Figure 27.3).

FIGURE 27.3   The prior distribution for ρ using Jeffreys's prior (c = −1.5)

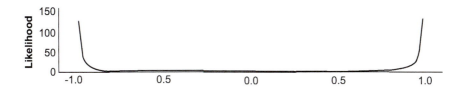

Jeffreys's priors follow his rule which is designed to lead to the same pdf for the prior regardless of transformations to the scale in which the variable is measured. Lee (2012) warns that there can be issues with following this rule for certain distributions and so it should only be used in the absence of better information about the nature of the prior. Negative values of c produce a concave distribution, as in Figure 27.3, while larger positive values of c produce an increasingly normal distribution (see Figure 27.4).

---

8 Where c is contained in the expression $(1-\rho^2)^c$, and the shape of the prior distribution is found by substituting values for ρ.

FIGURE 27.4   The prior distribution for ρ using c = 3

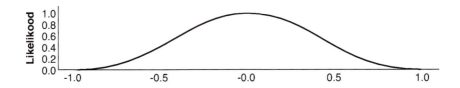

In the case of the correlation, the effect on the posterior distribution of changing the prior is to move the mode, with negative values of c moving it to a higher value of r and positive values of c moving r to a lower value. The mean remains the same and there is virtually no effect on the credible interval. B. P. O'Connor (2017) warns that evidence is emerging that non-informative priors can affect the posterior distribution.

Model comparison/hypothesis testing

Jackman (2009) states that under the Bayesian approach, for continuous parameters, point (sometimes called *sharp*) hypotheses such as ρ = 0 aren't tested but ones which are based on a range of values, such as ρ < .1 or −.1 < ρ < .1. However, some analysts do test point Null Hypotheses.

When comparing two hypotheses, such as the Null Hypothesis (H_0)[9] and an Alternative Hypothesis (H_A)[10] we can use an extension of Bayes's theorem:

Posterior odds of H_0 and H_A = ratio of their likelihoods × prior odds of H_0 and H_A (27.1)

Where the posterior odds are $\dfrac{p(H_0 \mid data}{p(H_A \mid data)}$

The ratio of their likelihoods is: $\dfrac{p(data \mid H_0)}{p(data \mid H_A)}$

And the prior odds are $\dfrac{p(H_0)}{P(H_A)}$

We can see that when the posterior odds are greater than 1 there is evidence in favour of H_0 rather than H_A. Similarly, when the prior odds are greater than 1 we are favouring H_0 over H_A.

Bayes Factor

One way to quantify the relative strength of belief in the two hypotheses is to use what is called the *Bayes Factor* (BF, sometimes shown just as B). This is the posterior odds of two hypotheses, such as the Null and Alternative Hypotheses, divided by the odds of their priors:

$$\text{BF} = \frac{p(H_0 \mid data)}{p(H_A \mid data)} \div \frac{p(H_0)}{p(H_A)}$$

---

9 e.g. there is no correlation between ability at mathematics and ability in English, i.e. ρ = 0.
10 e.g. there is a correlation between ability at mathematics and ability in English, i.e. ρ ≠ 0.

Which means that:

Posterior odds = BF × prior odds

If the probabilities of the two priors are equal, then their odds = 1 and the posterior odds = BF.

In such cases, therefore, when BF is 1 or more there is no support for the research hypothesis, whereas the smaller BF is the more evidence there is for the research hypothesis.[11]

Jeffreys (1961) suggested a set of rules of thumb for what constitutes evidence for either hypothesis. He identified 6 grades (0 to 5). Table 27.1 shows his grades, where there is evidence against H_0, and his evaluation of the strength of that evidence.[12] Also included in Table 27.1 are updated values in the light of more recent experience from Kass and Raftery (1995).[13]

TABLE 27.1 Jeffreys's and Kass & Raftery's grades for Bayes Factors when the ratio is presented as H_0/H_A. Their inverses are given in parentheses for when the ratio is presented as H_A/H_0

	Jeffreys's grades of Bayes Factor (BF)				
	1	2	3	4	5
Range of BF	>1, > .32 (1 to 3.125)	< .32, > .1 (3.125 to 10)	<.1, > .032 (10 to 31.25)	<.032, > .001 (31.25 to 1000)	< .001 (> 1000)
Evidence against H_0	not worth more than a bare mention	substantial	strong	very strong	decisive
	Kass & Raftery grades				
Range of BF	1 to .33 (1 to 3)	.33, to .05 (3 to 20)	.05 to .0067 (20 to 150)	< .0067 (> 150)	
Evidence against H_0	not worth more than a bare mention	positive	strong	very strong	

SPSS has options either to estimate the Bayes Factor or to suggest a Bayes Factor prior to the analysis. In the latter case, it is only possible to set the Factor to greater than 0 but less than 1.

With all defaults set the estimated BF for the correlation is .013, constituting very strong evidence against H_0, using Jeffreys's criteria, or strong evidence, using Kass and Raftery's criteria.

SPSS uses what it describes as JZS (Jeffreys-Zellner-Siow) as the default prior BF. This is based on priors which are sometimes described as *objective* to distinguish them from subjective ones which would be dependent on assumptions made by the analyst. Kruschke (2013) gives warnings about the use of Bayes Factors. He notes that the posterior BF can be very sensitive to the nature of the priors and that therefore unless there is good evidence to do otherwise it is safer to use 'relatively neutral priors'. He also notes that *Bayesian estimation, with its explicit parameter distribution, not only is more informative than Bayesian model comparison but is also more robust* (p. 600). Chow and Hoijtink (2017) argue for the importance of using sensitivity analysis to check the effects of assumptions such as priors on the outcome of the analysis.

---

11 Often you will see the criteria presented for when the ratio is presented as H_A/H_0, in which case, values over 1 are in favour of H_A.

12 What may seem to be unusual values arise because Jeffreys specified them as powers of 10; for example, $10^{-1/2} = .32$.

13 SPSS gives *thresholds to define significance of evidence* which differ from both Jeffreys's and Kass and Raftery's systems.

If the priors are equal and we have two competing hypotheses then we can use the BF to find the posterior probabilities for the two hypotheses.

$$p(H_0|\text{data}) = \frac{BF}{1+BF}$$

$$p(H_A|\text{data}) = \frac{1}{1+BF}$$

Substituting the BF for the correlation between maths and English abilities of 0.013 leads to the point probability of H_0, given the data, as .013 and for H_A given the data as .987 (which is the same as $1 - .013$). Accordingly, we have much stronger evidence for H_A than for H_0. In this example, the BF for the relationship appears to be the same as the probability for $p(H_0|\text{data})$ but that is only because of reporting to three decimal places; the difference can be seen when more decimal places are shown: they are .0134 and .0132, respectively.

Summary

Bayesian inference is different from Null Hypothesis Significance Testing. Its proponents argue that it is a more appropriate approach to examining data. The increasing capacity and speed of processing of computers has allowed problems which have previously been intractable, following a Bayesian approach, to be solved by iterative methods. As with all forms of statistics it needs to be used with care and, until it is more widely understood, its use will have to be reported with more detail than for currently conventional tests.

The next chapter explains how to report research.

PART 5

Sharing the results

28 Reporting research

Introduction

There are four points which you should communicate to a person reading or hearing an account of your research: what you did, how you did it, why you did it and what you found. A guiding principle is that you should express yourself in the clearest fashion possible for the medium you have chosen and for the audience which you can reasonably expect to be reading or hearing your account.

Accordingly, a report written for an academic journal will differ from a verbal presentation to the same audience. In the same way, a written report for an academic audience will differ from that written for a non-academic audience. In addition, you have to be aware of the conventions which exist, because your audience will have certain expectations about what level of detail they will be given and where in the account they will receive it.

Four different audiences can be identified, each of which needs a different approach. Firstly, there is the general public, for whom you have to make the most concessions, explaining and modifying terminology and even simplifying the sentence structure. Secondly, there is the educated layperson, who will still need terminology explained. Thirdly, there is the person from the same discipline as you who may only need aspects of your particular area explained. Finally, there is the researcher in your area for whom you need make the fewest concessions.

Non-sexist language

Many people no longer find it acceptable to treat pronouns such as *he* and *him* as though they were neutral and do not refer only to males. One way to avoid the necessity to give a person's gender explicitly is to use a plural. For example, *Researchers studied the effects of mnemonic strategy on recall; they selected three groups.* . . . In this way *they* is used rather than *he* or *she*. However, sometimes you do wish to refer to one person. Although some people use *they* as though it were a neutral, singular pronoun, this is not generally accepted and will jar with some readers. It is preferable, in this case, I think, to use the form *he or she*, rather than *s/he* or *he/she*. For example: *Each participant was trained to use one mnemonic strategy; he or she was then asked to remember as many words as possible.*

A written report

A written report can be of many types; for example, it can be for an academic journal, for a professional magazine, such as *The Psychologist*, for a newspaper or popular magazine, for a funding body or for a client. Students are generally required to adopt a style similar to an academic journal article when presenting their research. I am going to concentrate on reports written for an academic audience. I will start by describing the report of an experiment or quasi-experiment and then explain some variations on the theme.

Academic written reports of experiments or quasi-experiments

Such a report has a clearly defined set of sections. However, students often worry that they are repeating themselves throughout the report because they feel they need to say the same things in different sections. Each part of the academic report has a specific function and knowing that function should guide what you include in that part.

An academic written report of research differs from an essay in two crucial ways. Firstly, readers may choose not to read it in a linear fashion from the beginning to the end – they may jump about from section to section. Thus, each section needs to be as self-contained as possible. Secondly, you should assume your readers are trained in research practice. Accordingly, there is much that you do not need to explain. For example, if you are using a standard statistical technique you do not need to go into the principles which underlie that technique.

There are two aspects of a report of research, written for fellow academics, which should guide the level of detail you include. Firstly, you need to provide enough detail for someone to replicate your study, such that every essential element is reproduced. Secondly, readers should know precisely what the research entailed so that they can judge its merit.

A convention which is adopted for most academic written reports is that the third person passive voice is preferred over the first person active voice. In other words, write *a study was conducted* rather than *I conducted a study*. I do not see this as essential. However, if you are the sole author, then don't use the plural when referring to yourself; thus, it is better to write *I conducted a study* than *We conducted a study*.

The title

The wording of the title is critical, for this will often be all the reader sees, initially, of your report; it may be among a list of the contents of a journal or an entry in a list of publications. Thus, in the title you have to convey what your research was about to allow readers to decide whether they want to read on. It should be as short as possible, while clearly showing not only the area of research but giving more specific detail about the subarea. A title of the form *A report of an experiment in social psychology* is an extreme example of what not to do. It is true that this has informed the reader about the global area of the research but little else. Most of that title is redundant: readers know that it is a report, they can find out that it involves an experiment by reading the abstract and *social psychology* is a vast area. Generally readers have more specific interests and so will choose whether to read an article on the basis of the topic of the research. Thus, a better title would have the form: *The effects of the presence of others on altruistic behaviour.*

Another principle is that the title should accurately reflect the content of the report. This may seem obvious, but a sloppy use of terminology can mislead the reader. An ex-colleague was inundated with requests for copies of a paper which had the term *biofeedback* in its title when the paper was simply about *feedback*.

The abstract

The abstract is a very brief summary of the piece of research which you are reporting; a typical recommendation is that it should be between 100 and 200 words. However, don't feel that you need to add extra, unnecessary words just to get it to the upper limit. As the abstract is a summary it shouldn't contain details which are not presented elsewhere in the report. If a record of your research is held on a database, such as PsycINFO, the abstract may be the only information that readers have, apart from the title, about your research. Readers whose interest has been caught by the title will read the abstract and, on the basis of what you tell them there, they will choose whether they want to read more. The need for brevity in the abstract means that it should only include the essential details. It should tell readers what you did in your research, how you did it and what you found; why you did it is less important, here. I do not think that the reader needs to know your hypotheses at this stage. The abstract needs to be self-contained so don't refer to elements which cannot be understood without access to the rest of the report. For this reason, I also suggest avoiding references in the abstract, as the details of the reference will not be available to someone who only has the abstract and title. However, if the work referred to is sufficiently well known, then it seems reasonable to refer to it. For example, 'The experiment investigated Baddeley and Hitch's model of working memory'. The following is an example of how to write an abstract.

> Participants were left by an experimenter in a room in one of three situations: alone, with a stranger who was a stooge, or with a friend. The experimenter went into an adjoining room and, after a period, the impression was created that she had had an accident. The stooge implied by her behaviour that nothing was wrong. Significantly fewer of the participants who were with the stooge went to the experimenter's aid than in the other two situations; the other two conditions did not differ significantly.

Common mistakes made by students are that they give too much detail about the design, the number and nature of the participants (on occasions when such detail is not necessary), the procedure and the specific statistical tests used. On the other hand, they give too little detail, or even no detail at all, about the results; often the reader is simply told *the results were significant* or even that *the results are discussed*. Tell the reader in which direction the results went.

Some journals require authors to structure the abstract according to specific headings; for example, the *British Journal of Health Psychology* specifies use of the headings *Objectives, Design, Methods, Results* and *Conclusion* for empirical studies and *Purpose, Methods, Results* and *Conclusions* for reviews but they allow the abstract to be up to 250 words.

The Introduction and referring to others' work

The function of the Introduction is to put your research in the context of previous relevant research and explain why it was worth conducting your research. The level of detail needs to lie between two extremes: the first is to launch straight into the hypotheses without any explanation; the second is to be so all-encompassing as to explain what social psychology is. Summarise previous research and do not recount every minute detail.

When referring to an author, simply give his or her surname and the date of the publication, as you should in an essay. Do not inform the reader that 'Jean Piaget, a Swiss psychologist from Geneva, stated in 1963 that . . .' unless these details are critical to the argument you are presenting. Rather, write: 'Piaget (1963) stated that. . . .' When you refer to a work which you have already mentioned in the same paragraph, then do not include the date with the name. However, the first time the work is referred to in a new paragraph give the date again. If there are more than two authors (but fewer than six) the convention is that the first time you refer to them, give the full list of authors. Subsequently, refer to them in the form Piaget et al. (1977) rather than list all the authors (*et al.* simply means *and others*). However, if there are more than five authors, then even on the first reference to the work give the first author followed by et al. If you have more than one reference with the same list of authors and the same date, then use a lower-case letter as a suffix, starting with *a*. For example, Kennedy and Day (1998a) and Kennedy and Day (1998b). If the list of authors contains some of the same people and the same date, then, after the first time the work is referred to, give as many names as necessary to distinguish the two works. For example, if you were citing Page, Plant, Bonham, Jones, and Harper (1972) and Page, Plant, Jones, Bonham, and Harris (1972), then you would refer to the first as Page, Plant, Bonham et al. (1972) and the second as Page, Plant, Jones et al. (1972). If the first authors of two works have the same surname, then give the initials of the first author for each work. For example, D. Goldberg and Huxley (1985) and L. R. Goldberg (1971).

There are cases where two dates are given: firstly, when a work has been reprinted after a lapse of time and you have not read the original printing, e.g. Darwin (1859/1960); secondly, when you have read a work in translation, e.g. Ebbinghaus (1885/1913). In both cases, in the list of references at the end of the report only give the date of the version you read, e.g. Ebbinghaus (1913).

Sometimes you will want to cite a personal communication, such as from a conversation or an email, but because no one else can get access to it the APA (American Psychological Association, 2010) recommends that you only mention it in the text and not in the list of references. You should give the author's initials, name and as accurate a date as possible. For example, *G. D. Richards (personal communication, 16 July 2002)*.

When you know of a work which has been accepted by a journal or publisher for publication but hasn't yet been printed, then use the following form: *Burke, Hallas, Clark-Carter, and White (in press)*.

If one or more studies which you have read do not add to the argument but support previous relevant research which you have outlined, then it is enough to list the authors after a summary sentence of the form: *These results are supported by* Piaget (1963), Hartley (1977) and Cruikshank (1983). If you are referring to works in parentheses, then there are conventions for this as well. Separate the author(s) and the date by a comma. When there is more than one author, use & instead of *and*. When there is more than one work separate them by a semicolon. List them in alphabetical order of the first author's surname. To illustrate all these points: *A number of works have replicated this finding* (Hughes & Jarvis, 1985; Milligna, 1956; Wynn, 1990).

When you haven't read the original work (the primary source) but are referring to work which you found in a secondary source, then my own preference would be to give the name(s) and date of the original, in the place where you are referring to it. In the references you would then indicate where you read the reference to the work. However, many journals, including those of the British Psychological Society, require the use of the APA's conventions. In this method, when you refer to the work you also say where it was cited, e.g. *Miller's study (as cited in* Hebb, 1970). Then in the reference list you only give details of Hebb (1970). The disadvantage of this method is that if I want to follow up Miller's work I will have to find Hebb's first and look in the reference list of that work to find where to look for Miller's work.

If you are giving a direct quotation, then you need to give the page number of the reference, e.g. 'The value for which P = .05, or 1 in 20, is 1.96 or nearly 2 ; it is convenient to take this point as a limit in judging whether a deviation is to be considered significant or not' (Fisher, 1925, p. 47). If the quotation is relatively short (fewer than 40 words), then you can include it in the paragraph which introduced it, as I just did, but enclose it in single inverted commas. This allows you to use double inverted commas when the quotation itself contains a quotation or uses quotation marks. However, if it is longer, then it is better to separate it from the rest of the text as in the following example, complete with an indent on the left margin.

> When a graph is constructed, quantitative and categorical information is *encoded*, chiefly through position, size, symbols and color. When a person looks at a graph, the information is visually *decoded* by the person's visual system. A graphical method is successful only if the decoding process is effective.
>
> (Cleveland, 1985, p. 7; italics in the original)

Notice that I have indicated that the emphasis was not added by me. If I had changed any of the formatting, then I should indicate this, e.g. *italics added*. If you are quoting selectively, then use three full stops to denote that text has been omitted. However, if you are quoting selectively, then do not misrepresent the original. Thus, *this is not the best account I have ever read on the subject* should not become *this is . . . the best account I have ever read on the subject*.

The end of the Introduction should pave the way for the next section: The Method. This can be done by a lead-in sentence along the lines: *It was decided to conduct an experiment to see whether the presence of another person would have an effect on the altruistic behaviour of a participant.* Alternatively, you could formally state your research hypothesis. In a laboratory report it is probably wise to use the latter format – complete with the Null Hypothesis. However, few psychologists report their research in quite such terms when they have graduated, preferring to leave the hypotheses implied. The advantages of the formal approach are twofold. Firstly, as a student you can demonstrate to the person marking that you know what you are doing. Secondly, you are making clear what criteria will be applied when you carry out the statistics: for example, whether it is appropriate to use a one- or a two-tailed test.

The Method

The function of the Method section is to enable readers to replicate your study, if they want to. Accordingly, you need to decide whether you have given enough detail. However, at the same time you should not include irrelevant information, such as the make of word-processing package on which a questionnaire was prepared. The Method generally has the subheadings *Design, Participants, Materials/apparatus* and *Procedure*.

Design

The Design section should, not surprisingly, contain the details about the design which was used in the research. Where relevant, the reader should be told what the IVs and DVs were, and whether a between-, matched-, within- or mixed-subjects design was used. However, in the case of correlational studies it is not necessary to talk of IVs and DVs, unless you have manipulated one of the variables, or to talk of between- or within-subjects variables.

This section of the report should also include some justification for certain aspects of the design. For example, if, in an experiment on memory, you introduced a task between presentation and recall phases to prevent rehearsal, then explain why. In short, the Design section is used to explain why participants were required to do what they did, while the Procedure section explains what they were told and what they did.

If you have conducted pilot research, and I strongly recommend that you do, then I think it is clearer if you refer to this in the Design section and then create a subsection entitled *Pilot study*. In such a section you need to include the usual details about the participants (see next) and some brief reference to modifications which you made in the light of the pilot study. This is particularly important if your study has entailed the creation of a new measure, such as a questionnaire. You need to convince the reader that you have attempted to address the face validity of the measure, at the least.

Although the formal advice might be to state the alpha-level that you will apply to your statistical tests, this is very rarely done in practice.

Participants

In the past, participants have been referred to as *subjects* and before that even as *reagents*. There is a feeling that such terms imply that people are the objects of research, while *participants* suggests that they are more equal to the researchers. The APA recommends the use of *participants* or more specific terms, such as *university students*, in preference to *subjects* except when discussing statistics or when the people who took part in the study were not able to give consent.

Readers want to know about the representativeness of your sample, to have an idea about how far your findings can be safely generalised. You need to report the number of participants you used, including the numbers of males and females, the age range (preferably with means and standard deviations) and an indication of their occupations. Where you have participants in different groups, such as a control group and a treatment group, it is important to give details for each subgroup in order to reassure the reader that any differences which you find between the groups on some measure are not likely to be due to differences such as age or gender ratio. In addition, you should report the basis on which they were selected: if it was genuinely random, then say how this was done. If some people whom you selected to take part refused, then report how many refused and the basis of the refusal. It is important to know whether you have a sample which could be described as *self-selected* because they are the ones who did not refuse; you may have a biased sample which leads to your results being confounded by the nature of the sample. You need to explain the basis you used to decide on your sample size. This is true for both qualitative and quantitative studies. In the case of quantitative studies you should have a statistical justification for the sample size, such as power analysis.

Materials/apparatus

Once again, only include details which are relevant for a person trying to replicate your research. Thus, if the materials or apparatus you used had some distinct characteristics which were critical to the conduct of your study, then give full details of what you used. For example, if you were showing pictures of faces to your participants for a very precise duration, then it is worth reporting the make of the device used to present the faces. This is important information because the reader may wish to question the accuracy of the device you have used. Similarly, if you video-recorded behaviour in a room which was designed for the purpose, then you should describe the arrangement and the equipment. It is a good idea to include, here, an example of a stimulus or test item to help the reader understand. Thus, if you showed participants drawings of animals, put an example here and put the remainder of the items in an Appendix, and remember to refer the reader to the Appendix. If you are including an illustration, it is good practice to put it immediately after the reference to it. Placing it elsewhere means that the reader is less likely to look at it. If you are using a standard statistical technique to analyse your data, avoid reporting the statistical package you used. However, if the technique is not generally well known or if packages differ in the way they handle the data, then it is advisable to report the package and even the particular version of the package.

If no apparatus or materials were used in the research, then do not include this section.

Procedure

The Procedure should simply include what the participants were told, how they were told it and what they were required to do. Any explanation as to *why* participants were required to do things should have been given in the Design section. The reader wants to know: what story the participants were given; how much they were informed about the purpose of the study; whether they were informed in spoken or written form; whether they had practice trials, if this was appropriate; and whether, after they had completed their task, they were debriefed. Report the stages of the Procedure in chronological order.

Results

The Results section is only for summary statistics, supported graphically, and related inferential statistics, in that order. However, if you have more than one set of results, report them one set at a time. See Chapter 9 for the best way to present summary statistics and the appropriate chapter for presenting the particular inferential statistics you have used. If you want to include the raw data (that is, unanalysed or summarised for each participant), then put it in an appendix and refer the reader to it.

It can be worthwhile, particularly if you have conducted a number of analyses and sensitivity analysis to check the effects of possible outliers or ways of dealing with missing data on the results, to start with an analysis section. In this you would describe, briefly, the ways you had screened the data and any actions you had taken to deal with any problems which were identified.

How you present the statistics depends on how much there is. If there are only a few, then they can be contained within the text (usually in parentheses). However, this can be tedious to read when there is more information. In such a case, place the detail in a table and refer the reader to it. Thus, in the case of descriptive statistics you could write: *Recall was better in the method of loci group (M = 9.6, SD = 1.58; 95% CI: 8.6, 10.6) than in the pegword group (M = 8.9, SD = 1.91; 95% CI: 7.7, 10.1) and both recalled more than the control group (M = 7.2, SD = 1.62; 95% CI: 6.2, 8.2).* Where you are including detail in a table introduce it rather than just start the Results section with a table. You could write something of the form: *Table 1 shows the means, 95% confidence intervals and standard deviations of the words recalled by participants in each mnemonic group.*

I prefer summary statistics, such as means and standard deviations, to be presented in numerical as well as graphical representation, when the graph aids understanding, though some journals forbid the inclusion of both tables and graphs of the same information. The reason for my preference is that tables provide the exact figures, while graphs give a more immediate impression of the results.

Do report the effect size, where one exists, and state the particular version, for example Cohen's *d*, as more than one effect size measure may exist for the same type of data. The APA sees its omission as one of the 'defects in the . . . reporting of research' (American Psychological Association, 2001, p. 5). The latest edition of the APA Publication Manual (APA, 2010) and latest reporting standards from the APA (Applebaum et al., 2018) both emphasise the need to include effect sizes, and confidence intervals. Do not show equations directly in the text. Put them either in an appendix or in a footnote.

Give every table and figure a number and a title. There is a convention that everything that is not a table is referred to as a figure. Remember to show what units were used in your measures. For example, show that the table provides means and standard deviations of the number of words recalled. Try to make tables and graphs as self-contained as possible rather than force the reader to refer to the text to understand what the illustrations mean. Accordingly, generally avoid using descriptions such as *group 1* when you could put *immediate recall*. Nonetheless, if the description of the group is too complicated, then have a key, or, as a last resort, explicitly refer the reader to the text for an explanation.

There is no need to discuss the results in this section. In the case of descriptive statistics, all you need is a sentence which says something of the form: *The mean and standard deviations of words recalled for the immediate and delayed groups are shown in Table 1 and Figure 1.*

When you report inferential statistics I suggest you provide the information in three stages. Firstly, say what test was used and what was being analysed. For example: *A between-subjects t-test was used to compare the recall of those asked to recall immediately after presentation with the recall of those asked to recall after 10 minutes.* Secondly, say what the results showed, in words. For example: *Those given immediate recall remembered significantly more words than those recalling after 10 minutes.* Finally, give the evidence for your statement. For example: *($t_{(15)}$ = 2.48, p = .013, one-tailed test, d = 0.6).* Do report the version of the test which you conducted and, where appropriate, explain what the IVs and DVs were. It is not enough simply to say *a t-test was performed on the data.*

If the result was significant, then say so and where appropriate give the direction in which the result went. For example, if two conditions were being compared don't just say that the groups differed but say which one recalled more.

If you have used a statistical package which has provided the exact probability for your result, then report that probability. If, on the other hand, you have had to rely on statistical tables, then report the probability as accurately as you can. Thus, if the probability lies between two tabled levels, then give the range of possible values; e.g. *.01 < p < .05*. This tells readers more than $p < .05$, because it shows that *p* is bigger than .01.

The APA recommends that when reporting decimals only give a leading zero if the number could be larger than 1. Thus, for probabilities and correlation coefficients you would start with the decimal point – e.g. *p = .03* – whereas for *d* you would report *d = 0.6*. When your computer package tells you that the *p*-value is 0.000, replace the last zero with a 1 and report it as $p < .001$ as no probability is truly 0. Sometimes, for small or large numbers, computers and calculators report a figure in what is often called scientific notation, e.g. 2.15E-3. This example can be translated as 2.15×10^{-3}, which means 2.15 divided by $(10 \times 10 \times 10)$, or 2.15 divided by 1000 = 0.00215. The negative sign shows that you are dividing (which is the same as multiplying by a fraction, in this case $\frac{1}{1000}$) and the 3 that you are taking the cube of 10. Do not report results using scientific notation. Translate them into normal decimal format. In SPSS such numbers can be reformatted by asking for more decimal places in the output. Avoid reporting a result as *ns* (for *not significant*) as this doesn't tell the reader where between 1 and just greater than .05 the probability was.

If you conduct supplementary analyses, such as planned or *post hoc* comparisons after an ANOVA, then report these after the main analysis to which they relate.

Once again the formal advice may be that you should state whether you have chosen to accept or reject your research hypothesis, or some other form of words; this is rarely done in practice but may be advisable when you are learning the statistical techniques.

Unless the statistical techniques you have used are unusual do not explain them. However, if you have to perform preliminary exploration to decide whether or not a given test is appropriate, report the results of such an exploration: for example, if you checked for the homogeneity of variances before conducting a *t*-test. Similarly, if you transform the data, for example, using an arcsine transformation, then report this procedure; see Chapter 14 for a discussion of data transformation. When you have transformed data it is still better to report the descriptive statistics in the original units; the mean of arcsine of number of words doesn't tell people much. Also, if you are using a statistical procedure in which a number of decisions are available, then you should report the particular decisions you made. For example, in factor analysis you can choose how the factors are to be identified.

One of the conventions of report writing is that you are trying to present the impression of being an impartial scientist who is letting the figures decide whether your hypothesis is supported. Accordingly, do not undermine this impression with phrases such as *unfortunately, the result was not significant*. Apart from anything else, lack of significance can still be informative.

If you did find a non-significant result, then I recommend carrying out a power analysis. Work out the sample size which would be necessary to give power of .8 with the effect size you found in your study. This puts your result in context. If the effect size was below what Cohen (1988) would call small and you would need a very large sample to have power of .8, then ask yourself whether the study is worth attempting to replicate in an unmodified form. On the other hand, if the effect size was small, medium or even large and power was low, then it would seem reasonable to recommend replicating the study with the appropriate sample size. Don't conduct power analysis if the result was statistically significant as you won't have committed a Type II error.

Discussion and conclusion

Here you attempt to set your results in the context of the research which you referred to in the Introduction. In addition, you might mention other research for the first time which helps to explain your results but wasn't relevant when you were explaining why it was worth conducting the research in the first place. You can also suggest modifications or improvements to your research which would take the investigation further. Do not overdo the criticisms of your own research; some students seem to regard this as an opportunity for public self-humiliation and find fault where it does not exist.

I recommend the following order for a Discussion. Start with a very brief summary of the results. Do not go into the figures for the descriptive or inferential statistics, probability or effect size – just give the direction of the results and whether or not they were statistically significant. Follow this by placing the results in the context of previous research. If your results are in line with previous research, then point out that the results confirm the work of whoever you have referred to in the Introduction. There must be some reason why your research was worth conducting and so some new information is likely to be available and need explaining. If your results conflict with previous research, then try to explain this. At this point you may wish to criticise your research, particularly if you found a non-significant result but had a low level of statistical power. Avoid lame statements such as *if a larger sample had been used statistical significance might have been achieved*. As I demonstrated in Chapter 13, this is almost always going to be true, and so is pretty redundant information. Be more specific; recommend a particular sample size based on power calculations. This could show whether it is worth pursuing the same effect or whether the design needs modifying to increase effect size. If you are confident that your results reflect a well-designed and well-conducted piece of research, then say what the theoretical implications of those results are. Finally, recommend future, related research but do not go into the realms of fantasy here. Yes, you could look at all sorts of aspects of memory, if that is what your research was about, but try to stick to suggestions which would build on your findings.

If you are reporting more than one study – for example, a series of experiments – in the one report, it is usual to follow a single Introduction with a separate Method, Results and Discussion section devoted to each study. These are then followed by a general Discussion.

References

The important thing to bear in mind is that the reference list has two main purposes: to enable someone who doesn't know the particular work to be able to obtain it and to tell someone who does know the work which specific piece of work by a given author you are referring to. Accordingly, you need to give enough detail to enable someone to identify the work and, if they want to, to obtain it. Your own institution may have a preferred style of reporting references. However, the most popular style among psychology journals and books is that recommended by the APA (American Psychological Association, 2010). It differs slightly when referring to books, chapters in books and journal articles. There is also advice on how to report information you found on the Internet. I am including only the most common types of entry; for more details look at the *APA Publication Manual*, where you will find examples of 96 types of reference.

For books, chapters in books and journal articles, you start by reporting the author(s), in the order: surname, then initials, starting with the senior author and listing all the authors. Where there is more than one author use *&* in place of *and*. For example, *Smith, M., & Jones G. R.* According to the APA (2010) guidelines this format is used when the number of authors is seven or fewer. However, if there are more than seven authors give the details of the first six and then follow this with three dots followed by the last author's details (e.g. Flett, K., Grogan, S., Williams, A., Povey, R., Buckley, E., Cowap, L., . . . Clark-Carter, D.). Next, report the year, in parentheses, in which the reference was published, making sure, in the case of books, that you report the date of the edition you read, not the print run.

For journals, give the title of the article next, followed by the journal title (in italics), the volume number (in italics) and finally the page numbers of the article. For example:

Clark-Carter, D. (2007) Effect size and statistical power in psychological research. *The Irish Journal of Psychology*, *28*, 3–12.

Most journals have more than one issue (or part) per year. Notice that I haven't included the issue number in the preceding example. Only include the issue number (in parentheses after the volume number) if each issue starts at page 1.

Many publishers of journals display a unique digital object identifier (DOI) for each article. The current convention is to include the DOI, where it exists, after the other details. Thus the preceding article would be reported as:

Clark-Carter, D. (2007) Effect size and statistical power in psychological research. *The Irish Journal of Psychology, 28*, 3–12. doi: 10.1080/03033910.2007.10446244.

Increasingly, journal articles are being placed online before they are available in a complete part of the journal. In such cases, you are likely not to have the page numbers for the final version. Therefore, you need to state that the article is an advance online publication and give the DOI or, if that is not available, the web address (the uniform resource locator or URL).

Persson, S., Benn, Y., Dhingra, K., Clark-Carter, D., Owen, A. L. & Grogan, S. (2018), Appearance-based interventions to reduce UV exposure: A systematic review. *British Journal of Health Psychology*. Advance online publication. doi:10.1111/bjhp.12291

When you are close to submitting your work, check the latest details of such a reference. If it is now in a more conventional form including page numbers then update the details in the reference.

For books, report the title (in italics) with only the first letter of the title in capitals, except where there is a subtitle, in which case the first word of the subtitle also should start with a capital letter. Continue with the edition, if it is later than the first edition, then the place of publication and the publisher's name. For example:

Brown, A. (1975). *Choice reaction times made simple* (2nd ed.). London: University of Neasden Press.

If you are citing a whole book but one that is edited, in the sense that a number of authors have contributed identified chapters, then follow the name(s) of the editor(s) by (Ed. or Eds.). For example:

Jones, B. (Ed.). (1990). *Children's understanding of linear algebra*. Manchester: University of Stretford Press.

For chapters within an edited book, report the title of the chapter (not in italics or underlined) followed by the editor name(s), (Ed(s).), the title of the book (underlined or in italics), the page numbers of the chapter and then place of publication and publisher's name. For example:

Kropotkin, P. (1990). Who needs linear algebra, anyway? In B. Jones (Ed.), *Children's understanding of linear algebra* (pp. 51–73). Manchester: University of Stretford Press.

The use of *pp.* is an abbreviation for *pages*. Notice that the editor's initials are placed before the surname.

If you are citing a work which is not in English, then give the original title but provide an English translation of the title. For example:

Carpintero, H. (1994). *Historia de la psicología en España* [The history of psychology in Spain]. Madrid: Eudema.

When you are giving the details of a work which is *in press*, as described in the section on writing the Introduction to a report, then provide as much information as you can. In the case of a journal article you are unlikely to know the page numbers.

When you are referring to an Internet site give the URL. For example:

British Psychological Society (2014). *Code of human research ethics*. Retrieved from www.bps.org.uk/news-and-policy/bps-code-human-research-ethics-2nd-edition-2014

Check the details as close to the point when you last have a chance to update them – for example, when you check the proofs when the report is going to be published, or just before a verbal presentation is given. At one point someone changed my own web address and didn't tell me. If the address has changed, then update it, and if the pages can't be accessed any more, say so. Make sure that you get the details correct. One way to do this is to copy them directly from the web address line and paste them into your document, as I have done for the address above. I once reviewed a manuscript of a book and 50% of the web pages which were given were not accessible, either because they had changed or because the web address had been written incorrectly.

If the work is unpublished and isn't in press you need to give enough detail for the reader to be able to obtain it. Thus, it is no good writing:

Twobee, A. (2004). *Taking exercise on small wheels.* Unpublished manuscript.

As a minimum give details of the university or organisation for which the author works or worked when it was written.

Place the references in alphabetical order, based on the first author's surname. Notice that I have indented the second and subsequent lines of each reference. When the references are put together this makes finding a particular reference easier (see the Reference section of this book).

Appendices

The function of an appendix is to contain supporting evidence from your research which is of such a level of detail that it would affect the reader's flow if included in the main text. Therefore, if you have devised and used a measure which contains a number of items, put only a sufficient number of examples in the main text for the reader to understand the essential elements and refer the reader to an appendix. Similarly, if you wish to list a computer program which has been written or a description of a piece of apparatus, specially designed and used in the study, then place these in appendices. In addition, as mentioned previously, if you want to report unanalysed data or calculations/a worked example, then put it in an appendix.

It is useful, if you have more than one type of information to go into an appendix, to create an appendix for each rather than lump them together. Thus you could place a listing of a computer program in one appendix and raw data in another. It helps the reader, particularly if the report has a contents page, to locate the material more quickly.

An academic journal article

Each journal has its own style for layout, reporting of references and other conventions. Most journals contain details of these conventions in each copy of the journal or on the publisher's website; others, such as those for the APA, are contained in a book. Once you have chosen a journal to which you are going to submit your report, read the appropriate details on its conventions and read examples, in a copy of that journal, of studies which are similar to your own before preparing your article. In this way, you will learn such points as whether the first person active voice is preferred over the third person passive voice in that particular journal.

Some journals require you to supply a short list of keywords which describe the content of your report. This information can be used in databases such as Web of Science to help users search for articles on your area of research.

It is usual to submit an article to a journal in single-sided, double-spaced format. Illustrations and tables have to be of high definition and they are generally submitted on separate pages, with the place you want them put indicated in the text. Increasingly, journals require you to submit articles electronically. However, if they still want hard copies you are likely to be required to submit multiple copies of the manuscript. The majority of journals will pass your article on to one or more referees, who will generally remain anonymous to you. In order that they don't know who you are you should make the manuscript as anonymous as possible yourself. This usually requires you to have a title page which doesn't give your name and address; these details would be supplied on a separate page. Do follow the journal's advice to contributors carefully, as you are quite likely to have the manuscript returned by the journal's editor without its having been sent to referees if you haven't.

The referees will comment on the quality of the article, recommending whether it should be published and, if so, suggesting any alterations or additions which they think would improve it; they may make publication dependent on your carrying out some or all of their suggestions. You are obviously free to ignore their advice, but if you wanted that journal to publish your article you would need a very good case prepared, particularly if the same suggestions were made by different referees. I recommend listing each comment from each referee and saying how you have addressed that point. Some authors seem to think that if they just ignore a point which they don't agree with their revised manuscript will be accepted. Explain, if you disagree with the referee(s), why you disagree. Also remember that the referee is acting on behalf of the readers of the journal and so if you needed to explain something to the referee, then you probably need to alter the manuscript to explain the point to the reader.

Variations in presenting other research methods

A survey or questionnaire study

I will use as an example a survey of smoking behaviour. A survey is more complicated to report than an experiment for a number of reasons. Firstly, unless you are using a pre-existing questionnaire, you are creating a measure. Therefore, you have to check its validity via a pilot study and report this stage. Secondly, as you have not really manipulated any variables, the terms IV and DV are less clearly defined. Remember that when you are looking at the relationship between two variables, making one an IV and one a DV implies that the former is affecting the latter; in other words a causal relationship is suggested. Thirdly, a survey may not involve testing any specific hypotheses; it may be simply descriptions of the data and explorations of relationships within the data. The report can seem less obviously focused, as a result. Fourthly, it may feel even less focused because it involves a number of different comparisons between questions.

As a consequence of the preceding points, the Method, Results and Discussion sections of a report of a survey are going to be different from reports of other research. The Method will be longer because a questionnaire frequently is altered in the light of the pilot study. The best way to maintain the flow in the report is to put the initial and the final versions of the questionnaire in separate appendices to which the reader is referred.

The Results section is likely to be longer as the data may be reported at a number of levels. Firstly, summary statistics will be reported, accompanied by graphs, such as a bar chart of the ages in the sample. Secondly, two-way contingency tables may be formed, such as gender by smoking status, and inferential statistics may be performed on these. These in turn may be re-analysed on the basis of a third variable, such as the smoking status of parents. There is a danger of putting quite a strain on the reader's memory and of making the finding of subparts of the section difficult.

The best way to deal with the extra content in the Results section is to divide it into subsections into which you place analyses which share some theme. For example, you might have *Health* and *Social Influences* as two separate subsections. The Discussion section is likely to be longer, simply because you have reported more results.

A systematic review or meta-analysis

Chapter 26 deals with the reporting of the results of a meta-analysis. However, there is a major difference with the reports of other forms of research in the Introduction. In reports of other research you are reviewing the existing literature to explain why your research was worth doing. A systematic review or meta-analysis is itself a review and so the Introduction needs to *justify* the review and not *be* the review. Instead you need to explain why a systematic review or meta-analysis is needed. This will usually involve showing that the existing literature is inconsistent or that no recent review has been conducted.

In a systematic review or meta-analysis your data are derived from other people's research. The population, in one sense, contains all the papers on the topic of your analysis, while the sample contains all the papers included in the final version of the analysis. You need to explain how you identified your population, such as the databases you used and the search terms. Then you have to make explicit the criteria you used to select your sample: what constituted satisfactory and unsatisfactory studies. In addition, you have to explain the attempts you made to bring unsatisfactory studies into the sample: for example, by deriving inferential statistics from summary data; by using rules of thumb to quantify terms such as *significant*; or by writing to authors for further information.

Given that the aim of an academic report is to allow replication, it is accepted practice that you report all the studies which you considered at the stage of having obtained complete copies of the reports, in a summary table placed in an appendix or as supplementary material available on the journal's website, and identify all those which you used in the analysis. You also have to present tables of the statistics which you derived from the studies included in the analysis, complete with sample size and direction of results – i.e. whether or not they support a given hypothesis. Another expectation is that you will have a table which reports your assessment of the quality of the studies; on such criteria as whether they explain how they chose the sample and its size, whether they report attrition and how they dealt with it in their analysis.

You should report your statistical decisions explicitly, such as whether you used a random or fixed model, whether you weighted studies on the basis of sample size and the technique you used to convert results to a standard statistic. In addition, it is common for authors to cite specific works on meta-analysis as justification of their decisions. Moher et al. (2009) give guidelines, following PRISMA (Preferred Reporting Items for Systematic reviews and Meta-Analyses).

A verbal presentation

As with all other forms of presentation the style you adopt will depend on your audience. If for an academic audience, then many of the guiding principles for a journal article apply; whereas, if for non-academics, then a more journalistic style is appropriate. Nonetheless, remember that speech is a temporal medium; in other words, once you have said something, unless members of the audience have made complete enough notes they have to rely on memory to gain access to it. Therefore, give a pace of delivery which allows listeners to process what you are saying and do not overburden their memories. In addition, listeners cannot consult a dictionary. Accordingly, you should be more willing to explain the terms you use, including any abbreviations. Remember that your understanding of what an abbreviation means may be different from that of some of your audience. As an example, LSE can refer among many others to the London School of Economics, the London Stock Exchange, the Liverpool School of English and the current name of the school my department is in: Life Sciences and Education.

An obvious constraint is the length of time you have. When asking about this, find out whether time for questions has to be included and, if so, how much time.

Preparing your talk

Some people speak without notes; this is a rare skill. Others only prepare and use notes. Others still prepare a full version of their talk, which they read. I recommend that, unless you know you can do the first, you do none of these things. I suggest that you start by writing a complete version of the talk. This allows speakers to hone their arguments and to present a coherent story. In addition, it will give experienced speakers a good impression of whether it fits the time allowed and inexperienced speakers the chance to time their presentation.

I then suggest taking notes from the full version of the talk, which act as memory aids when giving the presentation. Keep the notes to a minimum but check that they are sufficient by reading them through again after a period. By putting the talk in note form the speaker is forced to compose the sentences afresh when speaking, and a greater air of naturalness is created. Space the notes well, indenting subpoints and placing lists in such a way that each item is on a new line. In this way, speakers can find their place more easily and not be too reliant on the notes for what they say. I also mark on my notes where an illustration, such as where the next slide, should be presented.

Some people use index cards for their notes; others use A4 paper. PowerPoint has the facility to include notes in a version which, in theory, only you can see. As with all computer-based systems, things can go wrong and your notes can be displayed to your audience, so be careful what you write. All this may seem like a lot of preparation. Nonetheless, the better prepared you are, the more natural your talk will appear. An additional advantage of preparing a complete version of your talk beforehand is that it is available if someone requests a copy of it.

If you are giving a paper at a conference you are usually required to provide an abstract for your talk. A pamphlet of titles and abstracts may be handed out at the conference to help those attending the conference choose which presentations to attend and to act as a fuller record of the conference. In addition, in order to get a paper accepted for a conference you are likely to be required to provide an expanded version of an abstract, which will then be vetted by a committee or by referees, in the same way that a journal article is.

Delivering your talk

You want your audience to understand what you are saying, despite the constraints of the situation. One way to do this is to give the same material more than once at different levels of detail – a bit like a news broadcast: the headlines, followed by greater depth and concluded with a summary of the main points. Another approach is sometimes characterised as *tell them what you are going to tell them, tell them and then tell them what you told them.*

One way to maximise the chance that the audience will understand is to maintain their interest. I have recommended using notes for your talk in order to create a more natural delivery which will help you establish a rapport with the audience. However, some people read the complete versions of their papers to the audience. The disadvantages of this form of delivery are many. Firstly, often the voice people use for reading aloud differs from the one they use in conversation; it is less animated. Secondly, readers spend more time looking down at their paper. This means that their voices are less well projected and that eye contact with the audience will be reduced.

If you are thinking of reading your paper in this way, ask yourself why. The only justification I can see for it is that every sentence you have written has to be delivered verbatim and any paraphrasing would ruin the meaning. This is very rarely the case. If your fear is that you will forget something critical, then go through all the preparation I have described previously, having the complete version available as a last resort. If, however, you do have to read the complete version, use print which is large enough, bold enough and sufficiently well spaced to enhance your ability to look up at the audience more frequently and not lose your place. Using a lectern can help. However short the talk, do not try to memorise it and reproduce it verbatim because this also usually lacks naturalness. In addition, as psychologists we know about state-specific learning: what you remember when you are in front of an audience may be less than what you were able to memorise in a different setting.

Part of maintaining the interest of your audience involves keeping their attention on what you are saying. Thus you have to be aware of your non-verbal behaviour. Give the audience eye contact but do not concentrate on just one person, as it will make them uncomfortable and exclude others. However, do not be surprised when even people you know in the audience have more passive faces than they would have in a conversation; theirs is a passive role. Do not stand like a statue, as you will appear uncomfortable and discomfort the audience. Instead, use a reasonable amount of gesture but not so much that it becomes distracting, and try not to fiddle with pens, keys or items of clothing. If you are nervous, then remember that a sheet of thin paper amplifies any shaking; this can be one advantage of using small index cards for your notes. Try to stay in a constrained area rather than stride around.

Illustrating your talk

Bear in mind the fact that you are talking and that therefore if you present your audience with anything else it may distract them and detract from what you are saying.

Handouts

If you give people a handout which contains prose, before or during your talk, they will read it. Similarly, if you give them pictures they will look at them. In both cases you have no control over the point at which they look at the handout. Think of the function of your handout. If it is to save people taking any notes, then tell them, before you start your talk, that a complete handout will be available at the end. If you want to give a structure to the talk to help note-taking, then give them a handout which merely has headings and subheadings on it. Make the handout well spaced so that they have room to make notes and do not have to spend time searching through it. You can include a list of references at the end of the handout.

If you are using a computer package such as PowerPoint, an overhead projector (OHP), or a slide projector and the facilities to copy into these formats, do not hand out pictures. Do not give copies of pictures for people to pass round; you will just add further chances for distraction. If you don't have such ways to project pictures, offer to pass them round at the end and leave sufficient time to do this.

Audio-visual aids

There used to be a rule for actors: avoid working with animals and children – they are unpredictable and may detract from your performance. The same could be said of supplementing a talk with some form of technology, be it a computer, an OHP, a 35 mm slide projector or a video player. There are two general rules for all such devices. Firstly, do not assume that they will be available for you; ask beforehand. Secondly, even if they can be supplied, do not make your talk so dependent on them that if something goes wrong your performance will be ruined; have contingency plans and do not get flustered by a failure.

Despite the danger of their failing, if used wisely, audio-visual aids, when they work, can be an asset. This is not only because a picture, particularly a moving one, is often more convincing and more easily understood than the equivalent time spent speaking, but also because in a longer talk they can introduce variety and thus maintain the attention of your audience. In addition, by giving information in more than one medium you can help the retention of details.

Computer projectors and OHP tablets

The image from a computer screen can be shown, via a computer projector or an OHP, on a large screen. You will obviously need to check that the software in which you have created your material is compatible with the machine you will be using during your presentation. Check also that the generation of the software is compatible. I attended a talk where a large number of mathematical symbols were involved but because the software in which the illustrations were created was different from the one on which they were presented the symbols were either missing or converted to different symbols from the ones intended. This left the speaker saying things such as, *This would have been a theta.*

If you are using colour and an OHP tablet, then you need to know that the tablet will be capable of reproducing it. At its best such a visual aid can be very useful. However, if the wrong projector is used with insufficient power or if the room lets in too much light in the wrong places, then the image can be so faint as to be virtually useless. As with all projectors, if the image is too small, then this too can make this visual aid worthless. Therefore, allow time to load the file onto the host computer or set up your own laptop and check such details when you arrive at the venue.

You could send a presentation in advance, either as an attachment to an email, on a USB stick, a CD-ROM or even on a floppy disc if there is space and the person receiving it can read it. This can have the advantage that it can be checked for compatibility and loaded onto the host computer before your talk is due. Too often a sizeable proportion of the time for a talk is spent fiddling with the hardware and software. Even if the program appears to run on the host computer you can find that if you have used unusual symbols they can be presented differently on the host computer from what you intended, such as a box shape instead of a letter of the Greek alphabet. One final point is to make sure that you know how to work the software. This may seem obvious, but I sat through one PowerPoint presentation where throughout the talk the speaker was unable to stop the program moving to the next slide – fascinating but distracting.

Such tools can be very useful. They allow you to give an outline of your talk, display lists of points, present longer quotations and show graphical displays, pictures, sounds and even video clips. However, do not overuse them. It is pointless to display all your talk on slides. It is also pointless just to read out what is on the slide unless it is a quotation (see the following). It is better to project a slide with a few short points on it and while it is being displayed to expand on the points.

Packages such as PowerPoint have a large number of options: for example, you can make text appear from one side of the screen and then bounce around before stopping; you can make it dissolve and disappear when it is no longer needed; and you can use an almost infinite variety of fonts and colours. Keep the gimmicks to a minimum as they are distracting, and think of what colour combinations of foreground and background work to make text legible and what should be the minimum font size.

The ideal layout of the area where you are standing will have a computer screen facing you so that you can face the audience and see what is being projected onto the larger screen. However, do check that the two screens are showing what you expect them to. This is the time when you want to check that the version with your notes is shown on the computer screen and not on the main screen. Do not stand in front of the main screen and do not turn your back on the audience to point to parts of the display projected on the screen for an extended period. If available, use a laser pointer which shows a red dot on the main screen to point at specific aspects of the display.

Do not put up a slide and then talk about something else; talk the audience through the contents of the slide, for otherwise it will have the same effect as a handout and the audience will have to choose between concentrating on what you are saying or on the content of the slide. If you are putting up a graphical display or a table, particularly if it is complex or you are using unusual conventions, explain the content, pointing to particular parts of the display as you do. Graphs and tables are forms of abstraction which, like any other means of presenting figures, impose the need for translation on the part of the reader. When putting up a quotation you could either stop and allow sufficient time for members of the audience to read it or, as I prefer, read out what it says yourself. That way you know that everyone has got to the end and you can continue.

During the question time, often questioners want to refer back to a slide; you and the questioner may remember the contents of the slide but you may lose the rest of the audience, while the pair of you discuss it, if it has not been projected again.

If there are aspects of the research which are relatively central to your argument but which you have had to summarise to such an extent that you might get questioned about the detail, then it can make sense to have extra slides ready, which can simplify your explanation of the details during questions. Speakers sometimes signal points during presentations by saying that they have not got time to deal with them during the talk but could return to them during questions.

Before you use any method to display aspects of your talk, think of whether it will really enhance your talk. Probably the best lecture I attended in 2017 was given by someone who presented no slides. If slides aren't really necessary then have the courage to go against expectations and don't use them.

For the occasions when you don't have access to a method for projecting a display from a computer I am including details of other visual aids which you might be using.

OHPs

Much of what I wrote about computer-based packages applies to OHP transparencies and 35 mm slides as well.

Preparing OHP transparencies

Leave wide margins on both sides and top and bottom of your acetates; not all projectors have the same-sized platen (the surface onto which you place the slide). Do not include too much detail, and do not make the size of the image too small or faint. If you are using pens to create the image, then I recommend you make a draft of each slide on a piece of paper, beforehand, and use permanent markers on the acetate, as the water-soluble ones can smudge, particularly in nervous hands. It is possible to photocopy directly onto them, even in colour. In addition, you can print from a laser or inkjet printer directly onto them. However, if you are going to photocopy or print onto them, you must use the correct type of acetate; the wrong type of transparency will melt in laser printers or smudge in inkjet printers. Prepare an introductory transparency which will allow you to check the nature of the display.

Showing OHP transparencies

If you can, allow time to put on your introductory transparency and check various aspects of the display: that it is lined up with the screen; that it is in focus; and by how much, if at all, the mirror obscures your display. You can only check the latter from the perspective of the audience. If the mirror does get in the way, make sure that you move the part of the image which you want the audience to see out of the way of the mirror, if possible. One technique which can be effective if you have a number of points on the same transparency is to cover the part which is not yet needed, otherwise people will read on. Another technique is to overlay related transparencies on each other: for example, if you are trying to build up a picture to make a point. If you are going to do this give each transparency a common reference mark that will allow you to align them.

Try to keep your transparencies in order after you have used them.

35 mm slides

My advice is, if possible, avoid using 35 mm slides, particularly if you are going to have to communicate with someone in a cubicle at the opposite end of the room to you who has control over the projector. You can put the content of slides onto computer slide packages such as PowerPoint. If they aren't available, you can do perfectly effective colour OHP transparencies and OHPs are far more commonly available than 35 mm slide projectors. In addition, I have lost count of the number of talks I have been to where the use of 35 mm slides fails, leaving the speaker illustration-less, or with the wrong illustration or one that is so badly out of focus that it is worse than useless. Another hazard with slides is that they can be put in the projector in a variety of orientations, including upside down and in mirror-image.

All these hazards take time from the talk while, often in vain, attempts are made to solve the problem. One solution to the orientation problem is to have a mark in the same corner of every slide as a reference point. However, unless you remember in which position the mark should be, you could end up with them all in the same but wrong orientation. As with OHP slides, if possible have an introductory slide which you can use to check the display before you start your talk. If you are lucky, the projector used for your talk may be compatible with one for which your institution has a spare carousel. In this case, you can check the orientation of the slides and bring them in the carousel with you. Unfortunately, there is no solution to the problems brought about by having someone else control the display of your slides.

A poster presentation

A poster presentation is a way of reporting research at a venue such as a conference. Like a verbal presentation it can be a way of presenting preliminary findings. It has a number of advantages over a verbal presentation and some disadvantages. Firstly, it does not have to compete with other presentations in those conferences where they have parallel sessions; if two presentations are on at the same time you can only attend one of them. Secondly, it cannot be placed at an inconvenient time in the programme which would limit its potential audience. Thirdly, it is not as transitory as a talk; readers can refer back to earlier parts of it and, as it may be in place for the duration of the conference, they can return to read it.

However, it will be competing for attention with other poster presentations and other aspects of the conference, such as the book displays which publishers put on or lunch. In addition, it will be allocated limited space. Thus, you will have to attract people's attention for them to look at your presentation in the first place and then maintain their attention for them to stay reading it.

The format you need to use for a poster presentation is more akin to that for a PowerPoint or OHP slide than for a written report. Thus, you should summarise as much as possible, only using large areas of print as a last resort. Give clear section headings, use a variety of font sizes to signal different levels of information and space material well; this will help readers find their way round the display. Similarly, you can use different fonts, in underlining, italic and bold, to attract the eye. However, as with all displays, avoid too much variety. Do not use a font just because your word-processing package can create it. Be selective and look at the overall effect. In the absence of a variety of font sizes mark the levels clearly by using Roman or Arabic numbers, and upper- or lower-case letters. Use tables and graphs in preference to prose but try to stick to common patterns of visual representation rather than devise your own. For, whereas in a talk you can explain such idiosyncrasies, a poster presentation usually has to stand alone. However, some conferences have specific times when authors can introduce their posters and there are likely to be other occasions when you can stand near your presentation and answer questions.

If you know the size allocated to the whole display, then it is possible to create a more durable version of the display – rather than a set of individual sheets. One way is to have the individual sheets or even the full display sealed in a plastic film. Another is to have the whole display reproduced on a colour printer. These two techniques should be available in art shops or firms who do work for surveyors or architects. You should also be able to buy tubes in which you can transport the full poster. If neither of these facilities is available to you, I would recommend having a second version of the poster available, in case you damage the first one when putting it up. It would be worth also taking along your own supply of drawing pins, or some other means of fastening your poster, just in case you are not provided with enough to do your display justice; try to find out what sort of fixing the organisers recommend, beforehand.

It is a good idea to have copies of a complete version of the report for interested people to take away. A better idea still is to offer to send those who are interested a copy; there is a tendency at conferences for people to pick up any handouts that are available and not necessarily to read them. Have a sheet of paper handy for people to write down their email or postal addresses and if you do make the offer, then do send the paper.

Trying the presentation out

Regardless of the medium in which a report of research is to be presented, it is difficult for an author to stand back and take a detached view of the content of a presentation. After you have finished your preparation on the content, ask someone less closely associated with the work to read it. Apart from telling him or her about the nature of the audience, give no other information. This is another advantage of preparing complete versions of a talk. In the case of a poster presentation, let your reader see the poster before he or she looks at a fuller version. In the case of a verbal presentation, particularly if you are inexperienced, give the presentation to a small audience. In all cases, your listener's or reader's comments are likely to be invaluable in improving the quality of your presentation.

Summary

There are a number of different ways in which a piece of research can be reported. Be aware of the conventions and limitations of the particular one you have chosen and of the likely audience of the report. A report of research written for an academic journal needs to have sufficient detail for the reader to be able to evaluate the worth of what you are reporting and to replicate the research in every relevant detail. On the other hand, a spoken presentation, particularly when time is available for questions, needs to have less detail in order to enhance understanding.

APPENDICES

This appendix illustrates the techniques introduced in Chapter 9.

Calculating the mean ($\bar{x}$)

The mean is sometimes referred to as the 'arithmetic mean' to distinguish it from other forms, some of which are described next. The equation for the arithmetic mean is:

$$\bar{x} = \frac{\Sigma x}{n}$$

where Σx means add all the scores and n is the number of scores.

In words, add all the scores and divide by the number of scores. Given the following data

3, 7, 5, 9, 4, 6, 5, 7, 8, 11, 10, 7, 4, 6, 8

$$\bar{x} = \frac{100}{15}$$
$$= 6.667$$

Calculating the variance (s^2)

The equation for the variance is:

$$s^2 = \frac{\Sigma\,(x - \bar{x})^2}{n - 1}$$

In words, this would be as follows. Find the deviation of each score from the mean and square it. Sum the squared deviations and divide the result by one fewer than the number of scores.

TABLE A1.1   Obtaining the total sum of the squared deviations from the mean

Recall	Deviation	Squared deviation
3	−3.667	13.447
7	0.333	0.111
5	−1.667	2.779
9	2.333	5.443
4	−2.667	7.113
6	−0.667	0.445
5	−1.667	2.779
7	0.333	0.111
8	1.333	1.777
11	4.333	18.775
10	3.333	11.109
7	0.333	0.111
4	−2.667	7.113
6	−0.667	0.445
8	1.333	1.777
Total sum of squared deviations		73.335

$$s^2 = \frac{73.335}{14}$$
$$= 5.238$$

Calculating the standard deviation (s)

$$s = \sqrt{s^2}$$

In words, take the square root of the variance.

$$s = \sqrt{5.238}$$
$$= 2.289$$

Calculating the mean and median from frequency distributions

Means

If we have asked a sample of 120 people what their age group is, we can represent it as a simple table (Table A1.2).

TABLE A1.2   The frequency distribution of participants' ages

Age (in years)	20–29	30–39	40–49	50–59	60–69
Number of people	15	45	30	20	10

As we cannot know the exact ages of the people in the groups, it is usual to take the mid-value for the range in each group. Thus, in the youngest group there are 15 people who will be treated as being aged $\frac{20+29}{2}$ = 24.5. The total of the ages for the group is found by multiplying the midpoint for the group by the group size. Accordingly, the total age for the first group is 24.5 × 15 = 367.5. It is then necessary to find the total age for all the groups and divide that total by the sample size (Table A1.3).

TABLE A1.3   Obtaining the total ages within a group

Group	Midpoint	Group size	Total age
1	24.5	15	367.5
2	34.5	45	1552.5
3	44.5	30	135.0
4	54.5	20	1090.0
5	64.5	10	645.0
Grand total		120	3790.0

$$\text{mean} = \frac{\text{total age}}{\text{sample size}}$$
$$= \frac{3790}{120}$$
$$= 31.583 \text{ years}$$

Medians

First find which group contains the median. As there are 120 people, the median point is between the 60th and 61st person. To find which group this is in, create what is called a *cumulative frequency*.

TABLE A1.4   Creating cumulative frequencies from grouped data (median between age groups)

Group	Age range (in years)	Group size	Cumulative frequency
1	20–29	15	15
2	30–39	45	60
3	40–49	30	90
4	50–59	20	110
5	60–69	10	120

In this case, the median lies between the second group and the third group. It can be calculated by taking the mean of the highest possible age in the second group and the lowest age in the third group:

$$\text{median} = \frac{39+40}{2}$$
$$= 39.5 \text{ years}$$

However, when the median point lies within a group the calculation is different. Table A1.5 contains data for which the median does lie within a group: the 40–49-year-olds.

TABLE A1.5   Creating cumulative frequencies from grouped data (median within an age group)

Group	Age range (in years)	Group size	Cumulative frequency
1	20–29	14	14
2	30–39	44	58
3	40–49	32	90
4	50–59	20	110
5	60–69	10	120

In this case, we find the median from the following equation:

$$\text{median} = L_m + \left[C_m \times \left(\frac{\left(\frac{1}{2}\times N\right) - F_{m-1}}{f_m} \right) \right]$$

where
L_m is the lowest value in the group which contains the median
C_m is the width of the group which contains the median
F_{m-1} is the cumulative frequency of the group below the one which contains the median
f_m is the frequency within the group which contains the median
N is the total sample size

Therefore in the present case:

$$\text{median} = 40 + \left[10 \times \left(\frac{\left(\frac{1}{2}\times 120\right) - 58}{32} \right) \right]$$
$$= 40 + \left[10 \times \left(\frac{60 - 58}{32} \right) \right]$$
$$= 40 + [10 \times 0.0625]$$
$$= 40.625$$

Winsorised mean

I mentioned in Chapter 9 that there are versions of the mean which have been designed to lessen the effects of outliers, such as the trimmed mean. Another method is described as *Winsorising*. This starts with the same idea as the trimmed mean in that the data are put in numerical order and then a certain number (or proportion) of the first and last scores are removed. However, in Winsorising they are replaced by the new lowest and highest scores and the mean is taken of the new set of values. As an example return to the recall data and place it in numerical order:

3, 4, 4, 5, 5, 6, 6, 7, 7, 7, 8, 8, 9, 10, 11

Now if we are Winsorising the data by just the two outer values, we need to replace 3 by 4 and 11 by 10. The new mean becomes 6.667. In other words the process has not changed the mean from what it was when it was calculated on the original data. This is no surprise as the data are relatively symmetrical. However, if the 15th person had remembered 25 words rather than 11, the normal way of calculating the mean would have produced a value of 7.6, while the Winsorised mean of the new data would have been 6.667 again. Thus, we can see that the effect of the possible outlier has been neutralised by the use of Winsorising.

Variants of the mean

Other versions of the mean include the *harmonic mean* and the *geometric mean*.

Harmonic mean

The harmonic mean is used in a number of equations when the sample sizes in different groups are not equal. As with many mathematical equations, the harmonic mean can be written in a number of ways, all of which will produce the same result. Elsewhere in the book I have given versions which simplify the calculations. However, here I will give the basic equation:

$$\text{harmonic mean} = \frac{1}{\left[\frac{\Sigma(\frac{1}{x})}{n}\right]}$$

where $\Sigma(\frac{1}{x})$ means divide each number into 1 and add the results together, and n is the number of numbers.

In words, you find the reciprocal of each number (that is, you divide each number into 1). You find the arithmetic mean of the reciprocals and then find the reciprocal of that arithmetic mean. The harmonic mean of the set of recall scores at the beginning of this appendix is 5.889.

Geometric mean

The geometric mean can be a more accurate value than the arithmetic mean when the numbers are part of a progression which is growing in a non-linear fashion. For example, if we knew the population in a country in 2006 and 2008, then the geometric mean would be a more accurate estimate of the population in 2007. The geometric mean is found from:

$$\text{geometric mean} = \sqrt[n]{\Pi x}$$

where Πx means multiply the numbers together (that is, find their product) and $\sqrt[n]{\ }$ means find the nth root (for example, if there were three numbers, then the nth root would be the cube root). The geometric mean of the set of recall scores at the beginning of this appendix is 6.283. Both the geometric mean and the harmonic mean are less affected by extreme scores than the arithmetic mean.

Creating a pie chart

An example given in Chapter 9 was of a group of 50 males being asked whether they smoked. Twenty were found to be smokers. We can express the figures in terms of proportions. Therefore, $\frac{20}{50} = .4$ of the sample were smokers and the remaining .6 of the sample were non-smokers.

As a circle has 360 degrees, we can find the number of degrees for smokers by multiplying 360 by the proportion of smokers:

$360 \times .4 = 144$ degrees

and for non-smokers

$360 \times .6 = 216$ degrees

This gives us the chart shown in Figure A1.1.

FIGURE A1.1   The degrees of a pie chart necessary to represent a given proportion of a sample

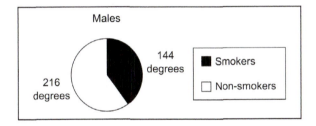

Representing relative sample size in a second pie chart

When pie charts are being created for two samples which have different sizes, Figure 9.8 (in Chapter 9) showed that the relative sample sizes can be represented through the area of the pie charts. Once the radius of one pie chart has been decided the radius of the other one can be found from the following equation:

$$r_2 = r_1 \times \sqrt{\frac{n_2}{n_1}}$$

where n_2 is the sample size of the second group, and n_1 and r_1 are the sample size and radius of the group for which the radius of the pie chart has already been decided.

Therefore, if the first sample was 30 and the second was 50 and we had decided to use a radius of 1 cm for the first pie chart, then the radius of the second pie chart would be:

$$1 \times \sqrt{\frac{50}{30}} = 1.291 \text{ cm}$$

Creating a box plot

Figure 9.28 (in Chapter 9) shows a labelled version of a box plot which was created in SPSS. Remember that SPSS uses slightly different conventions for the drawing of a box plot than those given here. Box plots are based on percentile points, including the median (50th percentile) and the 25th and 75th percentiles. Therefore the first stage is to put the scores in size order.

TABLE A1.6 The recall of 15 participants in order of number of words recalled

Order	Recall
1	3
2	4
3	4
4	5
5	5
6	6
7	6
8	7
9	7
10	7
11	8
12	8
13	9
14	10
15	11

The median

The median is located at the $\frac{n+1}{2}$-th score, where n is the number of scores. In this case it is at the 8th score. Therefore, the median is 7.

Hinge location

The hinges are located at the 25th and 75th percentiles. Their locations can be found using the equation:

$$\text{hinge location} = \frac{\text{median location} + 1}{2}$$

If the median location is not a whole number, then ignore the decimal part of the number. For example, if the median location had been 8.5 just put 8 in the above equation.

$$\text{hinge location} = \frac{9}{2} = 4.5$$

Thus, the lower hinge is between the 4th and 5th scores from the bottom and is therefore 5. The upper hinge is between the 4th and 5th scores from the top and is therefore 8.

The H-range

The H-range is the difference between the upper and lower hinges and is therefore $8 - 5 = 3$.

The inner fences

The inner fences are found from the equations:

> lower inner fence = lower hinge − (1.5 × H-range)
> upper inner fence = upper hinge + (1.5 × H-range)

Therefore:

> lower inner fence = 5 − (1.5 × 3)
> = 0.5

and

> upper inner fence = 8 + (1.5 × 3)
> = 12.5

Thus, we can see that all the scores are contained within the inner fences and we have no scores which could be considered outliers.

If the 15th score in Table A1.6 had been 25 it would have been worth calculating the outer fences. Note that because the number of scores remains the same, all the values calculated above for the box plot remain the same.

The outer fences

The outer fences are found from the equations:

> lower outer fence = lower hinge − (3 × H-range)
> upper outer fence = upper hinge + (3 × H-range)

Therefore:

> lower outer fence = 5 − (3 × 3)
> = −4.5 (which cannot exist in this example)

and

> upper outer fence = 8 + (3 × 3)
> = 17

Therefore a score of 25 (the 15th score) would lie outside the outer fence and could be treated as a possible outlier.

Indexes of skew and kurtosis

There are indexes of both measures of the shape of a distribution curve: skew – lack of symmetry – and kurtosis – sharpness or flatness in the peak of the distribution. For each there is a z-test which can be used, for samples below about 100, to decide whether the distribution is sufficiently non-normal that it needs transforming or that a non-parametric test would have to be used. With larger samples it would be better to rely on viewing a graph of the distribution, as the tests can be over-sensitive to minor variations from a normal distribution. For both indexes there are more complex variants of the index which are more suited for samples. However, I have decided to offer the simpler ones which are offered by computers, as I think they are adequate for the criteria which will be recommended for deciding about non-normality, even though they are, strictly speaking, for use with the distribution in a population.

Skew

There are a number of measures of skew, but the one which seems to be most commonly quoted by computers is the following:

$$\text{index of skew (IS)} = \frac{\Sigma (x - \bar{x})^3}{n \times s^3}$$

where n is the sample size and s is the standard deviation. In words, add together the cube of the deviation of each score from the mean. Divide the result by the sample size multiplied by the standard deviation cubed.

When the distribution is symmetrical, then IS = 0; when the distribution is negatively skewed, IS is negative; and when the distribution is positive, so is the IS.

A z-score can be obtained from the above result, which can indicate whether the distribution is significantly skewed:

$$z = \frac{\text{IS}}{\sqrt{\frac{6}{n}}}$$

It is recommended that you treat $p = .01$ as the α-level: in other words z would have to be at least 2.58 or −2.58 for you to treat the distribution as significantly skewed.

Kurtosis

The most common measure of kurtosis has two versions, a basic one and an adjusted one. The basic version is:

$$\text{index of kurtosis (IK)} = \frac{\Sigma (x - \bar{x})^4}{n \times s^4}$$

Notice that this is almost the same as the index of skew except that instead of cubing you now raise to the fourth power. The second version involves subtracting 3 from the first index of kurtosis (this is the version given by many statistical packages, including SPSS). This is because the original version is equal to 3 when the distribution is mesokurtic (i.e. like the normal distribution, it is neither markedly tall and thin nor flat and wide). When the adjusted index produces a negative value this suggests a platykurtic distribution, while a positive value suggests a leptokurtic distribution.

The z-test for kurtosis is:

$$z = \frac{\text{IK}}{\sqrt{\frac{24}{n}}}$$

where IK is the adjusted version of the index of kurtosis.

Sampling and confidence intervals for proportions

The illustrations in this appendix are linked to examples given in Chapter 11.

All the following statements and calculations are based on a survey which utilised a simple random (or probability) sample.

Finding the confidence interval of a proportion

The following account assumes that the sample which has been taken is smaller than 5% of the population. Refinements are given later in the appendix for situations where this is not the case. Imagine that a survey of voting patterns has been conducted. It uses a random sample of 2500 voters and finds that 900 (or 36%) of the sample say that they will vote for a right-wing party – the Right Way – while 1050 (or 42%) say that they will vote for a left-wing party – the Workers' Party. You wish to estimate what proportion of people, in the population from which the sample was taken, are likely to vote for each of the two parties. Note that the proportion in a sample is usually represented as p, while its equivalent parameter, the proportion in the population, is represented as π (the Greek letter *pi*). You can be confident at the 95% level that the proportion in the population (π) who will vote for the Right Way lies in the range:

$$p - 1.96 \times \sqrt{\frac{p \times (1-p)}{n}} \quad \text{to} \quad p + 1.96 \times \sqrt{\frac{p \times (1-p)}{n}}$$

where p is the proportion of the sample who said they would vote for the Right Way
$1 - p$ is the proportion of the sample who did not say they would vote for the Right Way
n is the sample size

$$\sqrt{\frac{p \times (1-p)}{n}} \text{ is the standard error of the distribution of proportions}$$

The figure of 1.96 is found from z-tables (see Appendix XVII). These show that 2.5% of a population will have 1.96 standard deviations or more above the mean for the population and 2.5% will have 1.96 or more standard deviations below the mean for the population. Therefore, the remaining 95% of the population will lie within 1.96 standard deviations from the mean. Accordingly, we can be confident at the 95% level that the confidence interval will contain the proportion in the population (π).[1]

Thus, if 900 people in a sample of 2500 say they will vote for the Right Way,

$$p = \frac{900}{2500}$$
$$= .36$$
$$1 - p = .64$$
$$n = 2500$$

and the confidence interval for the number of supporters for the Right Way in the population is:

$$\text{CI} = .36 - 1.96 \times \sqrt{\frac{.36 \times .64}{2500}}$$

to

$$.36 + 1.96 \times \sqrt{\frac{.36 \times .64}{2500}}$$
$$= .36 \pm 1.96 \times \sqrt{\frac{.23}{2500}}$$
$$= .36 \pm 1.96 \times \sqrt{.000092}$$
$$= .36 \pm 1.96 \times .0096$$
$$= .36 \pm .019$$
$$= .341 \text{ to } .379$$

Therefore, if the sample was taken from a population of 100 000, the number of supporters of the Right Way in the population is likely to lie between .341 × 100 000 and .379 × 100 000; i.e. 34 100 and 37 900.

Margin of error

We can express the standard error used in a confidence interval as a percentage error or margin of error.

$$\text{percentage error} = .019 \times 100$$
$$= 1.9\%$$

Note that the error is expressed as a percentage of the total sample and not of the subsample which supports a given political party.

---

1 Formally, the 95% confidence interval means that if we took samples of the same size and calculated a confidence interval, then on 95% of occasions the confidence interval would contain the parameter in the population: in this case the proportion who vote a particular way.

The relative size of the sample and the population

If the sample size is less than 5% of the population, then the preceding calculations produce a reasonable estimate of the percentage error. However, if the sample size represents a larger proportion of the population, then the following adjustment needs to be made:

$$\text{adjusted percentage error} = \text{original percentage error} \times \sqrt{1 - \frac{n}{N}}$$

where n is the number in the sample and N is the number in the population.

For example, if in the above situation the population was 25 000, then the sample would represent 10% of the population. Therefore:

$$\begin{aligned} \text{adjusted percentage error} &= 1.9 \times \sqrt{1 - \frac{2500}{25000}} \\ &= 1.9 \times \sqrt{1 - .1} \\ &= 1.9 \times \sqrt{.9} \\ &= 1.9 \times .949 \\ &= 1.803\% \end{aligned}$$

This demonstrates that the larger the sample relative to the population, the smaller will be the percentage error. This is not surprising as the larger the sample, the better the estimate of the population parameters you would expect. The logical endpoint of this trend is that there is no error if you conduct a census, that is, if you sample the entire population.

Estimating the required sample size

When no previous data are available as a guide

The nearer the proportion which you are attempting to estimate is to .5, the larger will be the percentage error. If we want to work out the sample size (n) that we will need in order to guarantee a particular margin of error for a proportion of .5, we can use the following equation:[2]

$$n = \frac{9604}{(\text{error})^2}$$

where error is the percentage margin of error which we are willing to accept.

For example, if we want a 2% margin of error,

---

2 Those of you who know algebra will be able to work out that the equations in this and the next section have been found from the original definition of a confidence interval given at the beginning of this appendix:

$$\text{error (for a 95\% CI)} = 1.96 \times \sqrt{\frac{p \times (1 - p)}{n}}$$

$$n = \frac{9604}{4}$$
$$= 2401$$

The larger the margin of error that you are willing to have, the smaller is the sample size you need.

If the proportion in the sample is smaller or larger than .5, then the margin of error will be smaller, for the same sample size. Therefore, the above equation will guarantee that the margin of error is no bigger than the one you require for the given sample size.

When previous data are available as a guide

Find the confidence interval, from the previous data, for the proportion in which you are interested. If this confidence interval includes .5, use the equation provided above for estimating the sample size. If the confidence interval does not include .5, take the value within the confidence interval which is nearest to .5 and put it into the following equation.

$$n = \frac{38416 \times p \times (1 - p)}{(\text{error})^2}$$

Accordingly, if you were using the data which were collected on voting for the Right Way, the confidence interval ranged from .341 to .379. Therefore the proportion (p) nearest to .5 would be .379 and the sample required for a 2% margin of error would be:

$$n = \frac{38416 \times .379 \times (1 - .379)}{4}$$
$$= \frac{38416 \times .379 \times .621}{4}$$
$$= \frac{9041.55}{4}$$
$$= 2261 \,(\text{rounded up to the nearest whole number of people})$$

When subsamples are of interest

The above calculations have all been based on situations where the proportions of the total sample are of interest. If you are interested in proportions within subsamples, then you need to calculate the size of the subsamples using the above equations. Thus, if you were interested in the proportion of males and the proportion of females in your sample who would vote for the Right Way and you were willing to accept a 2% margin of error, then you would need to include 2500 males and 2500 females in your sample. Alternatively, if you were using information from previous research to guide you, you could use the appropriate equation provided to find the number of participants required in each subsample.

The effect of increasing the degree of confidence on the margin of error

If we wish to have 99% confidence that our confidence interval will contain the parameter for the population, then we need to look up the z-tables again to find how many standard deviations above and below the mean will contain 99% of the population. The z-table in Appendix XVII tells us that the figure is 2.575 because .005 or 0.5% of a population will have a score which is 2.575 standard deviations or more above the population mean and 0.5% of a population will have a score which is 2.575 standard deviations or more below the population mean.

The confidence interval will therefore be:

$$p - 2.575 \times \sqrt{\frac{p \times (1-p)}{n}} \quad \text{to} \quad p + 2.575 \times \sqrt{\frac{p \times (1-p)}{n}}$$

$$\text{CI} = .36 - 2.575 \times \sqrt{\frac{.36 \times .64}{2500}} \quad \text{to} \quad .36 + 2.575 \times \sqrt{\frac{.36 \times .64}{2500}}$$

$$= .36 \pm 2.575 \times \sqrt{\frac{.23}{2500}}$$

$$= .36 \pm 2.575 \times \sqrt{.000092}$$

$$= .36 \pm 2.575 \times .0096$$

$$= .36 \pm .025$$

$$= .335 \text{ to } .385$$

or 33.5% to 38.5%

Comparing a sample with a population

This appendix illustrates the techniques introduced in Chapter 12.

A single score compared with a population mean (population *SD* known)

A *z*-test is used in this situation. The equation for a *z*-test which compares a single participant's score with the mean for a population is of the form:

$$z = \frac{\text{single score} - \text{population mean for the measure}}{\text{population standard deviation for the measure}}$$

In standard notation, this is usually shown as:

$$z = \frac{x - \mu}{\sigma}$$

For example, if we know that a person has scored 70 on an IQ test which has a mean of 100 and a standard deviation (*SD*) of 15, then, using the equation for *z*, we can see how many standard deviations this is below the mean:

$$z = \frac{70 - 100}{15}$$
$$= -2$$

A sample mean compared with a population mean

When the standard deviation for the population is known

We can use a z-test to calculate the significance of the difference between a mean of a sample and the mean of a population, using the following equation:

$$z = \frac{\text{mean of sample} - \text{population mean}}{\left(\dfrac{\text{population standard deviation}}{\sqrt{\text{sample size}}} \right)}$$

In standard notation, this is usually shown as:

$$z = \frac{\bar{x} - \mu}{\left(\dfrac{\sigma}{\sqrt{n}} \right)}$$

In this way we can calculate how likely a mean from a sample is to have come from a population with a given mean and *SD*.

Let us assume that the IQs of 20 children are tested and that their mean IQ is 90, using a test which has a population mean of 100 and a standard deviation of 15.

$$
\begin{aligned}
z &= \frac{90 - 100}{\left(\dfrac{15}{\sqrt{20}} \right)} \\[2ex]
&= \frac{-10}{3.354} \\[1ex]
&= -2.98
\end{aligned}
$$

When the standard deviation of the population is not known

We need to move from the z-test to a t-test for this situation. The equation to calculate this version of t is similar to the equation for the z when we are comparing a sample mean with a population mean; in this case the sample standard deviation is used instead of the population standard deviation:

$$t = \frac{\text{mean of sample} - \text{population mean}}{\left(\dfrac{\text{sample standard deviation}}{\sqrt{\text{sample size}}} \right)}$$

In standard notation, this is usually shown as:

$$t = \frac{\bar{x} - \mu}{\left(\dfrac{\sigma}{\sqrt{n}} \right)}$$

Imagine that ten 6-year-olds are given a maths test which provides an arithmetic age (AA) for the sample. We can treat the children's chronological age (6 years) as the expected mean for the t-test. The SD for the population is unknown. The mean for the sample was 7 and the SD was 1.247.

$$t = \frac{7-6}{\left(\dfrac{1.247}{\sqrt{10}}\right)}$$
$$= \frac{1}{0.3943}$$
$$= 2.536$$

Confidence intervals for means

The usual confidence level (CI) is 95%. There are two equations for finding the confidence interval for a mean: one when the sample size is at least 30 and the other when the sample is smaller than this.

Sample size is at least 30

This version is based on the z-test.

The general equation for this version of the confidence interval for the mean is:

$$CI = \text{sample mean} \pm z \times \left(\frac{\text{sample SD}}{\sqrt{n}}\right)$$

where the z-value depends on the confidence level we require and n is the sample size.

If we required the 95% confidence interval we would consult the z-tables to see what z-value has a two-tailed probability (p) of .05 or 5%. Then our confidence interval will be based on $1 - p = .95$ or 95%. Looking in the tables we find that $z = 1.96$; remember that the z-tables show the one-tailed probabilities and so to find z for a two-tailed probability of .05 we need to look up the z for a one-tailed probability of $\frac{0.05}{2} = .025$.

If we had data from a sample of 300 for word recall with a mean of 7 words and a standard deviation of 2, then:

$$CI\,(95\%) = 7 \pm 1.96 \times \frac{2}{\sqrt{300}}$$
$$= 7 \pm 1.96 \times 0.115$$
$$= 7 \pm 0.226$$

In other words, we are 95% confident that the mean word recall for the population from which this sample came lies between $7 - 0.226$ to $7 + 0.226$ or 6.774 to 7.226.

Sample size is fewer than 30

The general equation for this version of the confidence interval for the mean is very similar to the previous one:

$$CI = \text{sample mean} \pm t \times \left(\frac{\text{sample SD}}{\sqrt{n}} \right)$$

where the *t*-value depends on the confidence level we require and *n* is the sample size.

However, the *t*-value will vary depending on degrees of freedom (df), which are linked to the sample size (df = *n* – 1).

If we required the 95% confidence interval we would consult the *t*-tables to see what *t*-value has a two-tailed probability (*p*) of .05 or 5% for the df in question.

If 10 participants are given a maths test, then the df = 9. In this case, the *t*-tables show that the *t*-value required for a 95% confidence level is 2.262. If the mean for the sample is 7 and the *SD* is 1.247, then:

$$CI\,(95\%) = 7 \pm 2.262 \times \frac{1.247}{\sqrt{10}}$$
$$= 7 \pm 2.262 \times 0.3943$$
$$= 7 \pm 0.892$$

In other words, we are 95% confident that the mean mathematics score for the population from which this sample came lies between 7 – 0.892 to 7 + 0.892 or 6.108 to 7.892.

Confidence intervals for medians

The 95% confidence interval for the median, which can be used to create the notch in a notched box plot (see Figure 12.7 in Chapter 12), can be found from the following equation:

$$CI\,(\text{median}) = \text{median} \pm \frac{1.58 \times H\text{-range}}{\sqrt{n}}$$

where the H-range is the range of the mid-50% of values in the sample and *n* is the sample size.

Thus, in the example given in Chapter 9 and Appendix I in which a sample of 15 people had a median recall of 7 words and an H-range of 3,

$$CI\,(\text{median}) = 7 \pm \frac{1.58 \times 3}{\sqrt{15}}$$
$$= 7 \pm \frac{4.74}{3.873}$$
$$= 7 \pm 1.224$$

Therefore the confidence interval for the median lies between 5.776 and 8.224 words.

Quantiles and normal quantile–quantile plots

If a sample of data is put in ascending order a quantile is a point which divides the distribution such that a particular proportion is below that point. Thus, the .10 quantile – sometimes shown as Q(.10) – has 10% of the distribution below it (and therefore 90% above it). A quantile–quantile plot (a Q–Q plot) is a graph of a sample of data placed in ascending order plotted against what values the data points would have had if they conformed to a particular distribution. In Chapter 12, I gave the example of a normal Q–Q plot, in which the data were plotted against what the data points would have been had the distribution been normal. As an example of the process I have taken the data from Table 9.1, which showed the number of words recalled by a sample of 15 people.

Initially the data are placed in ascending order. Each score is then given a rank. The proportion of the data which lies at that rank or below it (the cumulative proportion) is calculated from the following equation:

$$\text{cumulative proportion} = \frac{(\text{rank} - 0.5)}{n}$$

where n is the sample size.

We can then calculate what z-score such a proportion would have if the distribution were normal. Looking at Table A17.1 we can see that if we wanted to find the z-score for the proportion .0333 (the first cumulative proportion in Table A3.1) of a sample, it would be somewhere between 1.83 and 1.84. However, as the proportion is in the bottom 50% of the distribution, the z-value will be negative and so it would be between −1.83 and −1.84 (see Chapter 12 and in particular Figure 12.2 if this seems puzzling). Table A3.1 shows that it is −1.8339. Once we have a z-score for each cumulative proportion we can then work out what expected normal value would have that z-score by putting the mean and standard deviation from the original data into the following equation:

$$\text{expected normal value} = (z\text{-score} \times SD) + \text{mean}$$

The mean for the recall data was 6.67 and the SD was 2.29. Table A3.1 shows each of these stages leading to the normalised values, and Figure A3.1 shows the plot of the original data against the expected normal values.

TABLE A3.1   The calculation of expected normal values for a normal quantile–quantile plot

Order	Recall	Rank	Cumulative proportion	z	Expected normal value
1	3	1	.0333	−1.8339	2.4694
2	4	2.5	.1333	−1.1108	4.1245
3	4	2.5	.1333	−1.1108	4.1245
4	5	4.5	.2667	−0.6229	5.2410
5	5	4.5	.2667	−0.6229	5.2410
6	6	6.5	.4000	−0.2533	6.0868
7	6	6.5	.4000	−0.2533	6.0868
8	7	9	.5667	0.1679	7.0509
9	7	9	.5667	0.1679	7.0509
10	7	9	.5667	0.1679	7.0509
11	8	11.5	.7333	0.6229	8.0923
12	8	11.5	.7333	0.6229	8.0923
13	9	13	.8333	0.9674	8.8808
14	10	14	.9000	1.2816	9.5997
15	11	15	.9667	1.8339	10.8639

FIGURE A3.1 A normal Q–Q plot of the recall data from Table A3.1

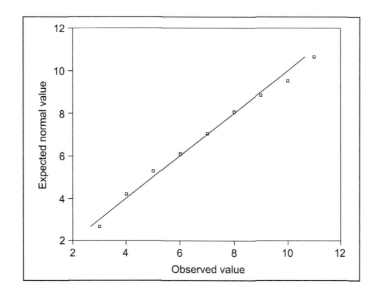

The power of a one-group z-test

The illustrations in this appendix are related to the material which was covered in Chapter 13.

Power analysis for a one-group z-test

Once a study has been conducted it is possible to work out the power of the statistical test which was conducted on the data: that is, the probability of rejecting a false Null Hypothesis and thus avoiding a Type II error.

For example, a sample of 20 children who have been brought up in an institution are given an enriched environment to try to enhance their IQs. The population mean IQ in the institution is 90 with an SD of 15. After a period in the enriched environment the IQs of the 20 children were tested and found to have a mean of 95.

To calculate the power of this test, we need to know whether the research hypothesis was directional and the α-level which was set. The research hypothesis was:

H_A: Children brought up in the enriched environment will have higher IQs than the mean for those in the institution.

As this is a directional hypothesis we will be employing a one-tailed test. The α-level is set at .05.

Stage 1: find the critical level of the mean IQ that would just have given us a significant result

To do this we need to know what z-value would have given us a one-tailed significance level of .05. Looking in z-tables in Appendix XVII we find that z is 1.645. The appropriate version of the z-test is:

$$z = \frac{\bar{x}_c - \text{population mean}}{\left(\dfrac{\text{population } SD}{\sqrt{n}}\right)}$$

where $\bar{x}_c$ (calculated below) is the critical mean for the sample which would give a z of 1.645 and n is the sample size.

Therefore:

$$1.645 = \frac{\bar{x}_c - 90}{\left(\dfrac{15}{\sqrt{20}}\right)}$$

Using algebra we can find out what $\bar{x}_c$ is:

$$1.645 \times \frac{15}{\sqrt{20}} = \bar{x}_c - 90$$

$$1.645 \times \frac{15}{\sqrt{20}} + 90 = \bar{x}_c$$

$$1.645 \times 3.354 + 90 = \bar{x}_c$$

$$95.517 = \bar{x}_c$$

Therefore, we would have achieved a statistically significant result if the mean IQ for the sample had been as high as 95.517.

Stage 2: find the β-level (the probability of making a type II error)

To do this we have to find the z-value which will give us the β-level; we treat the sample mean as an estimate of the mean which would be found in a population of children given the enrichment programme:

$$z = \frac{\bar{x}_c - \text{actual sample mean}}{\left(\dfrac{\text{population } SD}{\sqrt{n}}\right)}$$

$$= \frac{95.517 - 95}{\left(\dfrac{15}{\sqrt{20}}\right)}$$

$$= -0.1541$$

Looking up the one-tailed probability for this z-value we find that p is approximately .44. In other words, β = .44 and therefore the power of the test (1 − β) was approximately .56. As this is below the .8 recommended by Cohen (1988) we had a low probability of avoiding a Type II error.

Choosing the sample size

It is also possible to choose the sample size which we would require in order to achieve a particular level of power. To do this we would need to know the statistical test to be used, the α-level, whether the hypothesis was directional and the effect size.

Imagine that we wish to replicate the above study but we want a reasonable level of statistical power. Therefore, we want to know how many participants to use in order to get power of .8. We are testing the same hypothesis and so will be using a one-tailed hypothesis and the α-level will again be .05. We need to calculate the effect size (d):

$$d = \frac{\text{sample mean} - \text{population mean}}{\text{population } SD}$$

$$d = \frac{95 - 90}{15}$$

$$= 0.333$$

We can use the following equation:

$$n = \left(\frac{z_\beta + z_\alpha}{d} \right)^2$$

where z_β is the z-value which will give the probability of a Type II error (in this case, $\beta = .2$, so giving us power of .8, in which case z_β is approximately 0.84); z_α is the z-value which gives the α-level (in this case, a one-tailed probability of .05), which, as before, is 1.645; and d is the effect size we wish to detect.
Therefore,

$$n = \left(\frac{0.84 - 1.645}{0.333} \right)^2$$
$$= 55.69$$

which means that, rounded up to the nearest whole number, we need a sample of 56 people to give us power of .8, if the effect size is the same as that found in the previous study.

Appendix V

Data transformation and goodness-of-fit tests

This appendix illustrates the techniques introduced in Chapter 14.

Transforming data

When data are not normally distributed or when the variance of the DV for different levels of an IV is not homogeneous, then it is often inappropriate to use a parametric statistical test. However, it is sometimes possible to transform the data so that they are more normal or so that variances are closer to each other. In addition, when looking at the relationship between two variables (bivariate data), if there appears to be a relationship between them but it is one that is non-linear, then one of the variables can be transformed to produce a more linear relationship.

To transform data is to apply the same mathematical formula to each of the values in a set of data. You may think that this appears to be fiddling with the data to get the answer which you want. However, as long as you make the transformation in order to put the data into a form which would allow a parametric test or a linear test to be conducted, then it is perfectly legitimate. What is not legitimate is to try one transformation, run a statistical test on the data and then go on to try another transformation if you do not achieve statistical significance.

To demonstrate that we do use transformations, often without realising it, think of the measures we could take when we are interested in runners' performances. We could measure the time it takes them to complete a route, the distance they travelled in a given time or even their speed, which is the distance divided by the time taken. If we convert data from time to speed we have performed a transformation on the data.

Using a scientific calculator or a computer it should be possible to make all the suggested transformations.

Univariate data

Negatively skewed

If the distribution takes the form shown in Figure A5.1, one possibility is to raise the data points by a value (x^a) as long as a is greater than 1; for example, we could square all the data points. Alternatively, we could raise a number to the power of each data point, such as 10^x – that is, raise 10 to the power of each data point – or e^x, that is, raise the number e (approximately 2.718) to the power of each data point.

FIGURE A5.1   A negatively skewed distribution

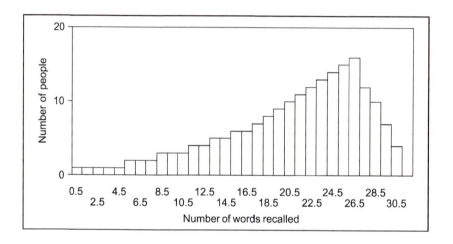

I squared each number of words recalled to produce the more symmetrical distribution shown in Figure A5.2.

FIGURE A5.2   A negatively skewed distribution after transformation

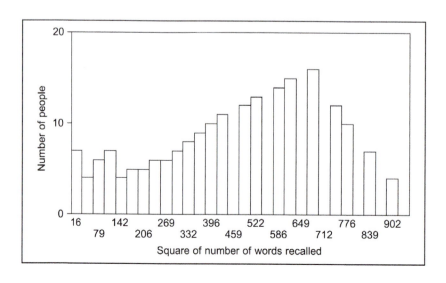

Positively skewed

When the distribution is positively skewed (Figure A5.3) there is a wide range of possible transformations which can be tried: reciprocals, logarithms, square roots or other fractional powers.

FIGURE A5.3   A positively skewed distribution

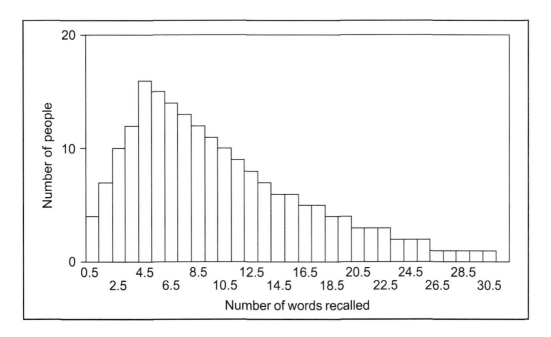

Reciprocals

Try $\dfrac{-1}{x^2}, \dfrac{-1}{x}$ or $\dfrac{-1}{\sqrt{x}}$. However, you cannot divide by zero, so you would need to use an initial transformation which made all the data points non-zero before you took a reciprocal: for example, adding 1 to each person's score.

Logarithms

Try $\log_{10}(x)$ (log to the base 10) or $\ln(x)$ (natural or Naperian logs: that is, log to the base e). If any of the data points are negative or zero, then add a fixed number to each data point to make them all greater than zero. Thus, if the biggest negative score in a set of data was −4, add 5 to all the scores and take the logarithm of the result.

Roots (fractional powers)

Try $\sqrt{x}$, or, particularly if the values are less than 10, $\sqrt{x + \frac{1}{2}}$ or $(\sqrt{x} + \sqrt{x+1})$. Square roots can also improve homogeneity of variance. If the square root does not do the trick, then try the cube root (i.e. $\sqrt[3]{x}$ or $x^{\frac{1}{3}}$). After trying a number of transformations, I found that $\sqrt{\text{recall} + 0.5}$ produced a more symmetrical distribution (Figure A5.4).

FIGURE A5.4   A positively skewed distribution after transformation

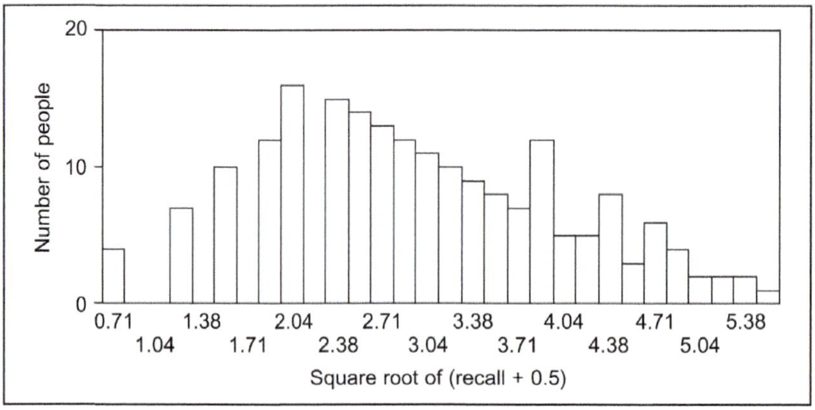

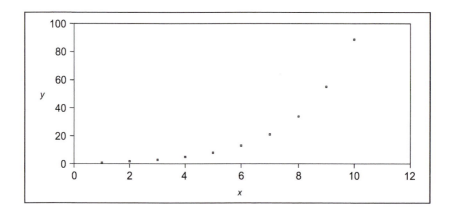

Kurtosis

When the data are proportions or percentages there may be a leptokurtic distribution (one with a tall, thin middle and long tails). In this case, try $2 \times \arcsine(\sqrt{x})$ (arcsine is sometimes shown as $\sin^{-1}$ on a calculator).

Bivariate data

When looking at the correlation between two variables, Pearson's product moment correlation assumes that the relationship is linear (that is, it forms a straight line). Thus, you may need to transform data if they have a pattern but one which is non-linear.

Curving upwards

When the curve of the line is upwards, as in Figure A5.5, then transform the values which are plotted on the vertical (y) axis. Try $\sqrt{y}$, $\ln(y)$, $\log_{10}(y)$ or $\dfrac{-1}{y}$.

FIGURE A5.5   An upwardly curving scattergram

I took the log of the *y*-values and produced the line shown in Figure A5.6.

FIGURE A5.6   The effect on an upwardly curving scattergram of transformation

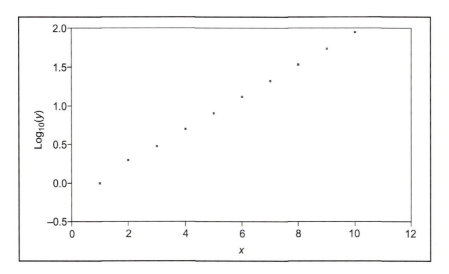

The correlation has changed from *r* = .868, for the non-linear relationship, to *r* = .999.

Curving downwards

When the curve is downwards, transform the values on the horizontal (*x*) axis. Try $\sqrt{x}$, $\ln(x)$, $\log_{10}(x)$ or $\dfrac{-1}{x}$.

Goodness-of-fit tests

Goodness-of-fit tests are used to compare the distribution in a set of data with a theoretical distribution. The theoretical distribution could be one derived from a Null Hypothesis that the data are evenly distributed throughout the range of scores or that the data conform to a distribution such as the normal distribution. The Kolmogorov–Smirnov one-sample test can be used when the data are at least ordinal, while the χ^2 goodness-of-fit test is for nominal data. However, the latter test is often used when the data are ordinal or even interval/ratio.

The Kolmogorov–Smirnov one-sample test

This test compares the cumulative frequency from the data with the cumulative frequency which would occur if the data conformed to a specified distribution. Taking the example where a sample of 120 people gave their age group, which was first presented in Chapter 9, we can see whether the distribution of ages is evenly spread across the age ranges (a *uniform* distribution). As there are five age groups, we would expect 15 = .2 of the people to be in each category, if they were evenly spread across the categories.

For each category you compare the observed cumulative frequency with the theoretical cumulative frequency ($F_o - F_t$), ignoring the sign if it is negative (Table A5.1).

TABLE A5.1   Obtaining the D_n statistic for The Kolmogorov–Smirnov One-Sample Test

Age group	Frequency	Frequency as a proportion	Observed cumulative frequency (F_o)	Theoretical cumulative proportion (F_t)	$F_o - F_t$
20–29	15	.125	.125	.2	.075
30–39	45	.375	.5	.4	.1
40–49	30	.25	.75	.6	.15
50–59	20	.167	.917	.8	.117
60–69	10	.083	1	1	

The statistic from this test is D_n, which is the largest value which $F_o - F_t$ reaches for the sample size n. In this case, $D_{120} = .15$.

Finding the statistical significance of D_n

Table A17.22 in Appendix XVII gives the critical values which D_n has to achieve or exceed to be statistically significant. Above a sample of 35 the critical level of D_n for $p = .05$ is $\dfrac{1.36}{\sqrt{n}}$. In this case,

$$\frac{1.36}{\sqrt{20}} = .124$$

Therefore, as .15 is greater than .124, we can say that the data differ significantly from a uniform distribution.

The χ^2 goodness-of-fit test

This test is appropriate, with nominal data, when comparing the frequencies found in a set of data with those which would occur under the Null Hypothesis. Alternatively, it could be used to compare the distribution in data with what would be predicted if the data had a particular theoretical distribution, such as the normal distribution. A statistically significant result in this test suggests that the data did not conform to the Null Hypothesis or to the theoretical distribution.

An example of the use of the test was given in Chapter 14, in which children's initial preferences for particular paintings in an art gallery were being studied (Table A5.2). Twenty-five children were observed as they entered a room which had five paintings in it and, in each child's case, which painting he or she approached first was noted. The research hypothesis was that the children would approach one painting first more than they would the other paintings. The Null Hypothesis was that the number of children approaching each painting first would be the same for all the paintings. Thus, according to the Null Hypothesis we would expect each painting to be approached by $\dfrac{25}{5} = 5$ children first.

TABLE A5.2   The number of children approaching a particular painting first and the expected number according to the Null Hypothesis

Painter	Approached first	Expected by H_0
Klee	11	5
Picasso	5	5
Modigliani	3	5
Cézanne	4	5
Rubens	2	5

The χ^2 test compares the actual, or observed, frequencies (f_o) with the expected frequencies (f_e) (according to the Null Hypothesis) to see whether they differ statistically significantly. It uses the following equation:

$$\chi^2 = \sum \frac{(f_o - f_e)^2}{f_e}$$

(A5.1)

In words, subtract each expected frequency from its observed frequency, square the result and divide that by the expected frequency. Repeat this for each category and add all the results. Therefore:

$$\chi^2 = \frac{(11-5)^2}{5} + \frac{(5-5)^2}{5} + \frac{(3-5)^2}{5} + \frac{(4-5)^2}{5} + \frac{(2-5)^2}{5}$$
$$= 7.2 + 0.0 + 0.8 + 0.2 + 1.8$$
$$= 10.0$$

This version of the χ^2 test has df which are one fewer than the number of categories. Therefore, in this case df = 5 − 1 = 4. The result can now be looked up in the table of the chi-squared distribution in Appendix XVII. With df = 4, the critical level of χ^2 for p = .05 is 9.49. As the calculated value of χ^2 exceeds this critical value, we can conclude that the different pictures were approached first by the children with significantly different frequencies.

Appendix VI

Seeking differences between two levels of an independent variable

This appendix illustrates the techniques introduced in Chapter 15.

Parametric tests

The t-test

There are different versions of the *t*-test, depending on whether the design is between- or within-subjects.

Between-subjects t-test

For this example researchers wish to evaluate the effectiveness of a therapeutic technique designed to rid people of arachnophobia. They have two groups of arachnophobics. One group acts as the experimental (or intervention) group and receives therapy; the other is the control group which does not receive therapy. The researchers measure anxiety on a self-report checklist.

TABLE A6.1   The anxiety scores of participants given therapy or acting as controls

Therapy	Control
85	80
65	88
70	86
70	85
65	64
75	82
83	89
60	81
62	83
70	67
65	65
79	70
76	84
72	88
74	85
69	82
76	79
71	75
68	77
75	80

TABLE A6.2   The means, variances and *SD*s of anxiety level in the therapy and control groups

	Therapy	Control
Mean	71.500	79.500
Variance	58.368	43.000
SD	7.640	6.557

The equation for the between-subjects *t*-test is:

$$t = \frac{\bar{x}_1 - \bar{x}_2}{\sqrt{\left[\frac{((n_1 - 1) \times s_1^2) + ((n_2 - 1) \times s_2^2)}{n_1 + n_2 - 2}\right] \times \left(\frac{1}{n_1} + \frac{1}{n_2}\right)}} \tag{A6.1}$$

where $\bar{x}_1$ and $\bar{x}_2$ are the means for the two groups
n_1 and n_2 are the sample sizes for the two groups
s_1^2 and s_2^2 are the variances for the two groups
$\left[\frac{((n_1 - 1) \times s_1^2) + ((n_2 - 1) \times s_2^2)}{(n_1 + n_2 - 2)}\right]$ is the *pooled variance*, that is, the mean
(weighted by sample size) of the variances for the two groups

When the sample sizes are the same this equation becomes simpler:

$$t = \frac{\bar{x}_1 - \bar{x}_2}{\sqrt{\left(\dfrac{s_1^2 + s_2^2}{n}\right)}} \tag{A6.2}$$

where n is the size of one sample.

Therefore, in the present case:

$$t = \frac{71.5 - 79.5}{\sqrt{\left(\dfrac{58.368 + 43.000}{20}\right)}} = \frac{-8}{2.2513} = -3.553$$

The degrees of freedom (df) for this version of the t-test are $(2 \times n) - 2$. Thus, in this case they would be $(2 \times 20) - 2 = 38$. When the sample sizes are unequal, df $= n_1 + n_2 - 2$.

The above version of the t-test assumes that the variances of the two groups are the same (homogeneous). If this is not the case, then an alternative version of the t-test should be applied.

Between-subjects t-test with heterogeneity of variance (independent variances – Welch's t-test)

When the sample variances for the two groups differ by more than four times, in the case where the sample sizes are the same (or when the sample variances differ by more than two times when the samples sizes are unequal), then a version of the t-test should be used which treats the variances as separate rather than producing a pooled variance estimate:

$$t = \frac{\bar{x}_1 - \bar{x}_2}{\sqrt{\left(\dfrac{s_1^2}{n_1} + \dfrac{s_2^2}{n_2}\right)}} \tag{A6.3}$$

When the sample sizes are the same for the two groups, this equation produces the same result as equation A6.2. However, it has its own method for calculating the df, which it may be necessary to know in order to test whether this result is statistically significant. Although, to save time, if you have not been given the df by a computer, then it is useful to check whether the result is likely to be statistically significant before working out the df. As the new version of the df will never be larger than the usual df for a between-subjects t-test, if the t-value is not statistically significant with the usual df, it will also not be with the modified version. Accordingly, if the t-value is not statistically significant at df $= n_1 + n_2 - 2$, then there is no need to calculate the modified df unless you want a more exact probability.

At the other end of the scale, the modified df will never be smaller than one fewer than the smaller of the two sample sizes. Accordingly, if the t-value is statistically significant when df $= n_{(smaller\ sample)} - 1$, then it will certainly be statistically significant for the modified version of the df. Again, there will then be no need to calculate the modified df unless you want a more exact probability.

If the t-value is not statistically significant with df of $n_{(smaller\ sample)} - 1$ but is statistically significant with df $= n_1 + n_2 - 2$, then you will need to calculate the modified (or *adjusted*) df.

The equation for adjusted df for a between-subjects t-test with separate variances is:

$$\text{adjusted } df = \frac{\left(\dfrac{s_1^2}{n_1} + \dfrac{s_2^2}{n_2}\right)^2}{\dfrac{\left(\dfrac{s_1^2}{n_1}\right)^2}{n_1 - 1} + \dfrac{\left(\dfrac{s_2^2}{n_2}\right)^2}{n_2 - 1}} - 2 \tag{A6.4}$$

As an example, imagine that the previous study had produced the results in Table A6.3.

TABLE A6.3 The means, variances and *SD*s of anxiety level for therapeutic and control groups (heterogeneous variance)

	Therapy	Control
Mean	71.5	79.5
Variance	112.053	24.053
SD	10.586	4.904

Notice that the variance for the group given therapy is more than four times the variance of the control group. Therefore, the *t*-test for groups with heterogeneous variances should be used:

$$t = \frac{71.5 - 79.5}{\sqrt{\left(\dfrac{112.053}{20} + \dfrac{24.053}{20}\right)}}$$

$$= -3.0667$$

The minimum df that this *t*-value could have are n − 1 = 19 (as both samples are the same size) and the maximum it could have are $n_1 + n_2 - 2 = 38$. As this value of *t* would be statistically significant at $p \le .05$ with df = 19, it clearly will be statistically significant for whatever the adjusted df. However, as an illustration, the adjusted df are calculated:

$$\text{adjusted } df = \frac{\left(\dfrac{112.053}{20} + \dfrac{24.053}{20}\right)^2}{\dfrac{\left(\dfrac{112.053}{20}\right)^2}{20 - 1} + \dfrac{\left(\dfrac{24.053}{20}\right)^2}{20 - 1}} - 2$$

$$= \frac{(6.8053)^2}{\left(\dfrac{31.389}{19} + \dfrac{1.446}{19}\right)} - 2$$

$$= \left(\frac{46.312}{1.728}\right) - 2$$

$$= 26.798 - 2$$

$$= 24.798$$

Within-subjects t-test

This version of the test is based on the difference, for each participant, in the score for the two conditions. In this example, a sports psychologist is testing whether a common ritual improves the performance of racing cyclists. He decides to compare performance, in terms of time taken to complete a route, when cyclists are clean shaven vs when they have designer stubble.

TABLE A6.4   The time taken (in minutes) by cyclists to complete a route clean shaven or with designer stubble, with the differences between the two times

Participant	Clean shaven	Designer stubble	Difference
1	195	195	0
2	200	190	10
3	180	182	−2
4	170	169	1
5	210	205	5
6	220	219	1
7	190	191	−1
8	185	183	2
9	150	148	2
10	160	160	0
11	165	166	−1
		Total	17
		Mean	1.545
		SD	3.387

The equation for this version of the t-test is:

$$\text{within-subjects } t = \frac{\text{mean of the differences}}{\left(\dfrac{SD \text{ of the differences}}{\sqrt{\text{sample size}}} \right)} \tag{A6.5}$$

Therefore, in this case:

$$t = \frac{1.545}{\left(\dfrac{3.387}{\sqrt{11}} \right)}$$
$$= 1.513$$

Calculating the effect size when two experimental groups are compared

The effect size for designs in which two sample means are compared is d and is found from:

$$d = \frac{\text{mean}_1 - \text{mean}_2}{SD}$$

If one of the groups is a control group, then the *SD* for that group can be used in the preceding equation. However, if the research had involved comparing the means of two experimental groups, it would be more legitimate to use an *SD* which combines the information from both groups (the pooled *SD*).

Remember that the *t*-test for a between-subjects design includes a calculation for the pooled variance (see earlier in this appendix). Remember also that the *SD* is the square root of the variance. Therefore:

$$\text{pooled } SD = \sqrt{\left[\frac{((n_1 - 1) \times s_1^2) + ((n_2 - 1) \times s_2^2)}{(n_1 + n_2 - 2)}\right]} \tag{A6.6}$$

However, when the sample sizes are equal this simplifies to:

$$\text{pooled } SD = \sqrt{\frac{s_1^2 + s_2^2}{2}} \tag{A6.7}$$

Non-parametric tests

The Mann–Whitney U test

When the design is between-subjects, has one independent variable (IV) with two levels and the requirements of a *t*-test are not fulfilled but the measurement is at least ordinal, then the Mann–Whitney *U* test can be used.

Researchers wished to compare the attitudes of two groups of students – those studying physics and those studying sociology – about the hunting of animals. Each student was asked to rate his or her agreement with the statement *hunting wild animals is cruel*. The ratings were made on a 5-point scale, ranging from *disagree strongly* to *agree strongly*, with a high score denoting an anti-hunting attitude.

TABLE A6.5   The responses of students to a statement regarding hunting

Sociology	Physics
5	1
4	2
3	3
3	4
5	5
4	2
2	1
5	3
5	4
4	2
4	1

(Continued)

TABLE A6.5 (Continued)

Sociology	Physics
3	3
3	2
5	3
4	3
4	5
4	4
5	3
5	2
5	1
5	2

All the scores are put in order of magnitude on a single scale, rather than separately for each level of the IV.

1	1	1	1	2	2	2	2	2	2	2	3	3	3	3	3	3	3	3	3	3
P	P	P	P	P	P	P	P	P	P	S	P	P	P	P	P	P	S	S	S	S

4	4	4	4	4	4	4	4	4	4	5	5	5	5	5	5	5	5	5	5	5
P	P	P	S	S	S	S	S	S	S	P	P	S	S	S	S	S	S	S	S	S

The statistic U is calculated by noting how many of one group are to the left of each member of the other group. As our prediction is that physicists will give low ratings, we count the number of sociologists who are to the left of each physicist, that is, counter to our prediction.

The four lowest ratings (of 1) were all made by physicists, so there are no sociologists to the left of them. Therefore, so far, $U = 0$. The next lowest rating (2) was made by seven students – six physicists and one sociologist. As the sociologist has the same rating as the six physicists, each physicist is counted as having 0.5 of a sociologist to his or her left (because they have the same rank as the sociologist). Therefore we now add $(6 \times 0.5) = 3$ to U. The next rating (3) has six physicists and four sociologists. Therefore, there is one sociologist (with the rating 2) to the left of each of the six physicists, so we add $(6 \times 1) = 6$ to U. In addition, the four sociologists with the rating 3 each count as 0.5; therefore each of the six physicists has $(4 \times 0.5) =$ two sociologists to his or her left, and so we add a further $(6 \times 2) = 12$ to U. This process continues until the relative position of each of the participants has been noted.

Rating	Contribution to U	U
1	0	0
2	(6×0.5)	3
3	$(6 \times 2) + (6 \times 1)$	18
4	$(3 \times 3.5) + (3 \times 4) + (3 \times 1)$	25.5
5	$(2 \times 4.5) + (2 \times 7) + (2 \times 4) + (2 \times 1)$	33
	Total U	79.5

If our prediction was a directional one that sociologists would give higher ratings than physicists, then we would seek the probability of this U-value. However, if we predicted that the physicists would give the higher ratings, then we would find the U for physicists.

Once the U for one group has been calculated, the other U can be found by the following equation:

$$U_2 = (n_1 \times n_2) - U_1$$

Therefore, U for physicists is:

$$U_2 = (21 \times 21) - 79.5$$
$$= 361.5$$

If the hypothesis is non-directional, then find U_1 and U_2 and the statistic used will be the smaller of the two; in this case U_1 would be the statistic.

The statistical significance of the Mann–Whitney U test

If you are not using a statistical package, such as later versions of SPSS, which provides exact probabilities, then if the sample size for both groups is 20 or fewer the probability of the result having occurred if the Null Hypothesis were true is given in Appendix XVII. However, if either group has more than 20 participants, then you will need to use a version of a z-test to calculate the probability:

$$z = \frac{u - \left(\frac{n_1 \times n_2}{2}\right)}{\sqrt{\frac{n_1 \times n_2 \times (n_1 + n_2 + 1)}{12}}} \qquad (A6.8)$$

$$z = \frac{79.5 - \left(\frac{21 \times 21}{2}\right)}{\sqrt{\frac{21 \times 21 \times (21 + 21 + 1)}{12}}}$$

$$= -3.5469$$

Correction for ties

It is likely that your computer program will also offer you an alternative value of z which has taken into account the number of scores which had the same value (tied scores). When the sample size is large enough to warrant using the z-test, then it is worth correcting for ties as this gives a more accurate value for z and therefore for p.

To correct for ties we need to know how many scores tied and how many were in each of the ties. There were four ties for the rating 1, seven with the rating 2 and so on. Form the following table:

Score	Number of ties (t)	Correction $= \frac{t^3 - t}{12}$
1	4	5
2	7	28

(*Continued*)

(Continued)

Score	Number of ties (t)	Correction $= \dfrac{t^3 - t}{12}$
3	10	82.5
4	10	82.5
5	11	110
	Total correction	308

We can now use the equation for z which is corrected for ties, but to simplify the equation let $N = n_1 + n_2$:

$$z \text{ (corrected for ties)} = \frac{u - \left(\dfrac{n_1 \times n_2}{2}\right)}{\sqrt{\dfrac{n_1 \times n_2}{[N \times (N-1)]} \times \left(\dfrac{N^3 - N}{12} - \text{total correction}\right)}} \qquad (A6.9)$$

Therefore, in this case:

$$z \text{ (corrected for ties)} = \frac{79.5 - \left(\dfrac{21 \times 21}{2}\right)}{\sqrt{\dfrac{21 \times 21}{(42 \times (42-1))} \times \left(\dfrac{(42)^3 - 42}{12} - 308\right)}}$$

$$= -3.6389$$

The Wilcoxon signed rank test for matched pairs

When the design is within-subjects, with one IV which has two levels and the requirements of a within-subjects t-test are not fulfilled but the measurement is at least ordinal, then the Wilcoxon signed rank test for matched pairs can be used. It looks at the size of differences between the two levels of the IV. It ranks the differences according to their size and gives each difference either a positive or a negative sign, depending on whether the score in the second level is bigger or smaller than that in the first level. The ranks of the sign which occurs fewest are then added together and the result forms the statistic T.

Researchers were comparing people's views of psychology as science before and after hearing a talk on the nature of psychology. Their views were found from their responses to the statement: *Psychology is a science.* They used a 5-point rating scale ranging from *agree strongly* to *disagree strongly*, with a higher score denoting a belief that psychology is a science.

When more than one score is the same (tied) the ranks are found by counting how many have the same rank, giving each the rank it would have had, had they not been tied, and then finding the mean rank for them. For example, there are three people who had a difference of −1 in rating between the two occasions. Therefore, had they not been tied they would have had the ranks: 1, 2 and 3. Their mean rank is:

$$\text{mean rank} = \frac{1 + 2 + 3}{3}$$

$$= 2$$

The next difference would be treated as though it had a rank of 4, if it was not tied.

TABLE A6.6   The ratings of participants of psychology before and after a talk on the subject

Before	After	Difference	Rank of difference	Positive	Negative
1	3	−3	7.5		7.5
1	4	−3	7.5		7.5
2	2	0			
2	4	−2	5		5
3	5	−2	5		5
2	4	−2	5		5
3	4	−1	2		2
4	4	0			
5	5	0			
4	5	−1	2		2
2	3	−1	2		2
3	3	0			
			Total (T)	0	36

We use the smaller of the two Ts, which in this case is the one for positive differences, $T = 0$.

Finding the probability of the Wilcoxon signed rank test

This test discards those cases where there is no difference between the two levels of the IV and the effective sample size is only those who did show a difference. Thus, in the present example, as four people did not change their ratings between the two occasions, the sample size is considered to be 12 − 4 = 8. If you are not using a statistical package which provides exact probabilities, then when the sample is 25 or fewer, use Table A17.6 in Appendix XVII. Therefore, in the present case, with a sample of eight, this is what we should do. When the sample is larger than 25 there is a z-test which we would have to use.

$$z = \frac{T - \dfrac{N \times (N+1)}{4}}{\sqrt{\dfrac{N \times (N+1) \times [(2 \times N) + 1]}{24}}} \tag{A6.10}$$

Although it is not appropriate to use the z-test in this example, I will use the result in order to illustrate the use of the z-test.

$$z = \frac{0 - \dfrac{8 \times (8+1)}{4}}{\sqrt{\dfrac{8 \times (8+1) \times ((2 \times 8) + 1)}{24}}}$$

$$z = \frac{-\dfrac{8 \times 9}{4}}{\sqrt{\dfrac{8 \times 9 \times 17}{24}}}$$

$$= \frac{-18}{\sqrt{51}}$$

$$= -2.521$$

Tied scores

To correct for ties we need to know how many scores tied and how many were in each of the ties. There were three ties for the rating 1, three with the rating 2 and so on. Form the following table:

Difference (regardless of sign)	Number of ties (t)	Correction $= \dfrac{t^3 - t}{2}$
1	3	12
2	3	12
3	2	3
	Total correction	27

We can now use the equation for z which is corrected for ties:

$$z \text{ (corrected for ties)} = \frac{T - \dfrac{N \times (N+1)}{4}}{\sqrt{\dfrac{N \times (N+1) \times [(2 \times N)+1]}{24} - \text{total correction}}} \qquad (A6.11)$$

Therefore, in the present case:

$$z \text{ (corrected for ties)} = \frac{0 - \dfrac{8 \times (8+1)}{4}}{\sqrt{\dfrac{8 \times (8+1) \times ((2 \times 8)+1)}{24} - 27}}$$

$$= \frac{-18}{\sqrt{51 - 27}}$$

$$= \frac{-18}{4.8989}$$

$$= -3.674$$

Calculating an effect size from a z-score for the Mann–Whitney U or Wilcoxon tests

Now that we have a z-score for the result we can convert this into an effect size (r), using the following equation

$$r = \frac{z}{\sqrt{N}}$$

where N is the total number of participants in the study.

Therefore, in the preceding example for the Mann–Whitney U test:

$$r = \frac{-3.6389}{\sqrt{42}}$$
$$= -0.56$$

This, in Cohen's (1988) terms, would be considered a large effect size. However, this conversion should only be used when the sample size is sufficiently large that the use of the z-test is appropriate because with small sample sizes you can get the anomaly of an r-value larger than +1 or −1. When the sample is below the recommended level to use a z-test, calculate Cohen's d from the means and SDs.

χ^2 test for analysis of a two-way contingency table

When the design is between-subjects and there are two variables (two-way) and the data are nominal, then the χ^2 test for contingencies can be used.

Researchers wanted to see whether there were different proportions of males and females who smoked. The expected frequency (f_e) for a given cell can be calculated by multiplying the total for the row in which the cell occurs by the total for the column in which that cell occurs and then dividing the result by the overall total.

TABLE A6.7 The numbers of males and females smokers and non-smokers

	Male	Female	Totals
	Observed frequency table		
Smoker	17	21	38
Non-smoker	27	23	50
Totals	44	44	88

Therefore, for the top left-hand cell the expected frequency is:

$$f_e = \frac{38 \times 44}{88} = 19$$

This is a simplified version of the full equation, which finds the marginal probabilities: the probability in the sample of being male is 44 out of 88; the probability of being a smoker is 38 out of 88. Therefore, if gender and smoking status are independent of each other:

$$\text{expected frequency of being a male smoker} = \frac{38}{88} \times \frac{44}{88} \times 88$$

As this involves multiplying by 88 and dividing by 88, these two operations cancel each other out and we get the simplified equation for expected frequency, as shown above. Table A6.8 shows the expected frequency for each cell.

TABLE A6.8   The frequencies which would be expected if smoking and gender were not linked

Expected values

	Male	Female	Totals
Smoker	19	19	38
Non-smoker	25	25	50
Totals	44	44	88

The χ^2 test compares the expected frequencies with those which actually occurred (the observed frequencies, f_o), using the same equation (A5.1) as for a one-group χ^2 test:

$$\chi^2 = \sum \frac{(f_o - f_e)^2}{f_e}$$

In words, subtract each expected frequency from its observed frequency, square the result and divide that by the expected frequency. Repeat this for each cell and add all the results.

$$\chi^2 = \frac{(17-19)^2}{19} + \frac{(21-19)^2}{19} + \frac{(27-25)^2}{25} + \frac{(23-25)^2}{25}$$
$$= 0.2105 + 0.2105 + 0.16 + 0.16$$
$$= 0.741$$

Correction for continuity

Yates (1934) devised a correction for the χ^2 test when it is being used for a 2 × 2 contingency table. As pointed out in Chapter 15, the rationale for this correction is that the probabilities given by the chi-squared distribution are calculated on the basis that the variables involved are continuous. It was felt that, as in a 2 × 2 table the measures are dichotomous, it was necessary to make the correction under these circumstances. However, the assumption is that the marginal totals are fixed.

This rarely happens in real research but an example would be asking a participant to sort 32 photographs of people into two equal piles on the basis of whether he or she thought that the photograph represented someone from the north or south of England. Thus the marginal totals for the sorting would be fixed at 16 each. The photographs would be of 16 people from the south and 16 from the north of England, thus fixing the other marginal totals.

TABLE A6.9   The way in which a participant sorted photographs of people from the north and south of England

Part of England person in photo comes from

Sorting	North	South	
North	10	6	16
South	6	10	16
	16	16	32

If, in a 2 × 2 contingency table, the assumption of fixed marginal totals is correct, then Yates's correction for χ^2 could be applied. Nonetheless, as computer programs often report the corrected version of χ^2, regardless of whether this restriction is fulfilled, it is worth being aware of the equation:

$$\text{corrected-}\chi^2 = \sum \frac{(|f_o - f_e| - 0.5)^2}{f_e} \tag{A6.12}$$

where $|f_o - f_e|$ means ignore the sign if the result is negative.
Therefore, in the photograph-sorting case:

$$\text{corrected-}\chi^2 = \frac{(|10-8|-0.5)^2}{8} + \frac{(|6-8|-0.5)^2}{8} + \frac{(|6-8|-0.5)^2}{8} + \frac{(|10-8|-0.5)^2}{8}$$

$$= \frac{(1.5)^2}{8} + \frac{(1.5)^2}{8} + \frac{(1.5)^2}{8} + \frac{(1.5)^2}{8}$$

$$= 1.125$$

(For the same table, the uncorrected-$\chi^2 = 2$.)
As usual with a χ^2 for a 2 × 2 contingency table, df = 1.

Odds ratios

Odds ratios are also called *cross-product ratios* because in a 2 × 2 table they can be found from the following equation:

$$\text{odds ratio} = \frac{n_{11} \times n_{22}}{n_{12} \times n_{21}} \tag{A6.13}$$

where the first subscript tells you what row the number came from and the second tells you what column it came from. Therefore n_{11} is the number from row 1 and column 1. Thus, in Table A6.7 n_{11} is 17. The odds ratio from Table A6.7 can be found from:

$$\text{odds ratio of males smokers to female smokers} = \frac{17 \times 23}{21 \times 27} = \frac{391}{567} = .6896$$

Confidence intervals for odds ratios

The confidence intervals (CI) for odds ratios are calculated in the following way. Because the distribution of odds ratios is skewed it is necessary to find the CI for the natural log of the odds ratio and then convert this back for an interval around the original ratio.
The data for Table A6.7 produced the following odds ratio:

odds ratio of males and females being smokers = .6896

Find the natural log of the odds ratio: $\ln(.6896) = -0.37164$.

Find the standard error (*SE*) for the natural log of the odds ratio (called the *asymptotic standard error*):

$$SE = \sqrt{\frac{1}{n_{11}} + \frac{1}{n_{12}} + \frac{1}{n_{21}} + \frac{1}{n_{22}}} \tag{A6.14}$$

where n_{11} to n_{22} are the samples in each of the cells of the 2 × 2 table.
Therefore,

$$SE = \sqrt{\frac{1}{17} + \frac{1}{21} + \frac{1}{27} + \frac{1}{23}} = 0.43239$$

The 95% CI of the natural log

$$= \ln(\text{odds ratio}) - (1.96 \times SE) \text{ to } \ln(\text{odds ratio}) + (1.96 \times SE)$$

which, in this case,

$$= -0.37164 - (1.96 \times 0.43239) \text{ to } -0.37164 + (1.96 \times 0.43239)$$
$$= -0.37164 - 0.84748 \text{ to } -0.37164 + 0.84748$$
$$= -1.21912 \text{ to } 0.47583$$

Convert these back to odds ratios by raising *e* by each of them, where *e* = 2.71828 approximately.

$$e^{-1.21912} = 0.295$$
$$e^{0.47583} = 1.609$$

Risk

In order to get SPSS to calculate an odds ratio and its CI you select *Risk*. Part of the output that is provided includes the risk values, as shown in Table A6.10.

TABLE A6.10   The risks, odds ratio and confidence intervals for the data in Table A6.7

Risk Estimate			
		95% Confidence Interval	
	Value	Lower	Upper
Odds Ratio for gender (female / male)	.690	.295	1.609
For cohort smoking = non-smoker	.852	.590	1.230
For cohort smoking = smoker	1.235	.761	2.004
N of Valid Cases	88		

relative risk (for females relative to males) of being a smoker =

$$\frac{\text{probability of being a smoker if female}}{\text{probability of being a smoker if male}}$$

where

$$\text{probability of being a smoker if female} = \frac{21}{44} = .477$$

and

$$\text{probability of being a smoker if male} = \frac{17}{44} = .386$$

Therefore the relative risk of being a smoker for males is $\frac{.477}{.386} = 1.235$.

Incidentally, odds ratios can be found from risks, using the equation:

$$\text{odds ratio} = \frac{\text{risk 1}}{\text{risk 2}}$$

Fisher's exact probability test

When there is a 2 × 2 contingency table and the *expected frequencies* of any of the cells are below 5, then the χ^2 test is not considered reliable. Fisher's exact probability test can be used, but it is only appropriate when the levels of both variables have fixed marginal totals. (In Chapter 15 it was pointed out that when the marginal totals are not fixed, but the expected frequencies are small, then an alternative test exists, the workings for which were given in the chapter.) Imagine that we repeated the example of giving a participant photographs of people to sort as to which region they came from but only used 10 photographs and told the participant that five were of people from the north and five of people from the south.

TABLE A6.11   The way in which a participant sorted 10 photographs of people from the north and south of England

	Part of England person in photo comes from		
Sorting	North	South	
North	4 (A)	1 (B)	5
South	1 (C)	4 (D)	5
	5	5	

As the marginal totals are fixed Fisher's exact probability test would be usable to analyse the data. The Null Hypothesis is that there is no link between participants' sorting and the place that the people photographed really came from, and so the expected frequencies for each of the cells is 2.5.

The equation for Fisher's test gives the exact probability of the outcome. Remember that usually we want the probability of that outcome plus the probabilities of more extreme probabilities which are in line with the hypothesis (see Chapter 10 for an explanation of this point). Therefore, we will want the probability of the outcome given in Table A6.11 and the probability of the more extreme outcome shown in Table A6.12.

TABLE A6.12   A more extreme outcome from the data shown in Table A6.11

	Part of England person in photo comes from		
Sorting	North	South	
North	5 (A)	0 (B)	5
South	0 (C)	5 (D)	5
	5	5	

Note that the marginal totals remain the same.
The probability from Fisher's exact probability test is found from:

$$p = \frac{(A+B)! \times (C+D)! \times (A+C)! \times (B+D)!}{N! \times A! \times B! \times C! \times D!} \tag{A6.15}$$

where 4! means the factorial of 4, which is 4 × 3 × 2 × 1 = 24. (Incidentally, 0! = 1.)
Therefore, in the present case, the probability of the outcome of Table A6.11 is:

$$p = \frac{(4+1)! \times (1+4)! \times (4+1)! \times (1+4)!}{10! \times 4! \times 1! \times 4! \times 1!}$$

$$= \frac{24 \times 24 \times 24 \times 24}{3628800 \times 24 \times 124 \times 1}$$

$$= .00015873$$

The probability for the more extreme outcome of Table A6.12 is:

$$p = .000031746$$

Therefore the probability that the results in this contingency table would have occurred if the Null Hypothesis were true is:

$$p = .00015873 + .000031746$$

$$= .000190476$$

To save calculating the probabilities in this way, tables of probabilities for this test are provided in Appendix XVII.

The binomial and sign tests

Two relatively simple tests which you may see referred to are the binomial test and a test which is based on it, the sign test.

The binomial test

The binomial test can be used when there are two possible types of event and we wish to calculate the likelihood of the outcomes we have found if the events had particular probabilities under the Null

Hypothesis. We could use it in the case mentioned in Chapter 10 where we were interested in whether a friend could cause coins to fall as heads. Here there are two possible events for each toss of the coin – a head or a tail – and each is equally likely to occur, if the Null Hypothesis is true, so for heads $p = .5$ and for tails $p = 1 - .5$, which is also .5.

The basic equation for a given outcome (or set of events), say, of getting all heads from five coins is:

$$p = {_n}C_r \times p^r \times (1 - p)^{(n-r)} \tag{A6.16}$$

where n is the number of trials (tosses of coins), r is the number of hits (occasions when the event we are looking for occurs) and ${_n}C_r$ is the number of ways in which the outcome we have achieved (e.g. five heads) could have occurred.

${_n}C_r$ is calculated from equation A6.17:

$$\frac{n!}{(n-r)! \times r!} \tag{A6.17}$$

where $n!$ means the factorial of n (as defined earlier).

We need one more mathematical convention to be able to work out the equation: any number raised to the power of $0 = 1$, e.g. $5^0 = 1$. Now we can work out the probability of five heads:

$$p = {_5}C_5 \times .5^5 \times (1-.5)^{(5-5)} = \frac{5!}{0! \times 5!} \times .5^5 \times (.5)^{(0)} = 1 \times .03125 \times 1 = .03125$$

Unfortunately that calculation has told us the probability of one particular outcome. Remember that the probability we are told by the computer is that of the outcome which occurred plus any other possible outcome which is more extreme and in line with the hypothesis. In this example the outcome was the most extreme and so this is the probability we would be interested in. If the outcome had been four heads and one tail, then we would need the probability of that outcome and we would have to add it to the probability for five heads to find the significance of the outcome.

The probability of exactly four heads out of five tosses is:

$$p = \frac{5!}{(5-4)! \times 4!} \times .5^4 \times (.5)^{(5-4)}$$

We need yet another mathematical convention to be able to work out this equation: any number raised to the power of 1 remains unchanged, e.g. $5^1 = 5$.

$$p = \frac{5!}{(1)! \times 4!} \times .5^4 \times (.5)^{(1)} = 5 \times .0625 \times .5 = 5 \times .03125 + .15625$$

Therefore the probability we need is:

the probability of 5 heads + the probability of 4 heads = .03125 + .15625

= .1875

Rather than calculate the probability of each possible outcome, it is useful to have tables which give the probabilities. Table A17.4 allows you to find the probability of an outcome when there are up to 25 trials, as long as the probabilities of the two events you are interested in are equal. If the probabilities are unequal, then you will need to use a computer or the preceding equations.

For larger sample sizes the probability can be found from a z-test.

z-Approximation for binomial test

For larger sample sizes, the following z-test can be used:[1]

$$z = \frac{\text{number of successes} - (n \times p)}{\sqrt{n \times p \times (1 - p)}} \tag{A6.18}$$

Although the sample size is small, as an illustration I will use the example where five coins are tossed and four land as a head, testing the research hypothesis that my friend can cause the coins to fall as heads.

$$z = \frac{4 - (5 \times .5)}{\sqrt{5 \times .5 \times .5}} = \frac{1.5}{1.118} = 1.34$$

Referring to the z-tables (Table A17.1 in Appendix XVII), we find that the one-tailed probability for this z-score is .0901. We can see that this underestimates the probability, which was shown previously to be .1875.

The sign test

The sign test can be used when we can convert our data into a format where, under the Null Hypothesis, there are two equally likely outcomes. As an example, we can reanalyse some data which were given in Chapter 15 (see Table 15.10). People were asked whether they agreed that psychology was a science, on two occasions: before they heard a talk on the subject and after the talk. We were interested in whether more people changed to have the view that psychology is a science than changed the other way. We can code those who changed from disagreeing with the statement to agreeing with as '+' and those who changed in the opposite direction as '−', with those who didn't change as 0; see Table A6.13.

TABLE A6.13   The opinions of participants, before and after a talk, on whether psychology is a science

Person	Opinion before	Opinion afterwards	Direction of change
1	disagree	agree	+
2	disagree	agree	+
3	disagree	agree	+
4	disagree	agree	+
5	disagree	agree	+
6	disagree	agree	+
7	disagree	agree	+
8	disagree	agree	+
9	disagree	agree	+
10	disagree	disagree	0

(Continued)

---

1 This is a different way of producing the same result as equation 12.4.

TABLE A6.13   (Continued)

Person	Opinion before	Opinion afterwards	Direction of change
11	disagree	disagree	0
12	disagree	disagree	0
13	agree	agree	0
14	agree	agree	0
15	agree	agree	0
16	agree	agree	0
17	agree	agree	0
18	agree	agree	0

In the example no one changed from agreeing to disagreeing, while nine people changed from disagreeing to agreeing. Thus, we can ask of those who changed, *did a significant number change from disagreeing to agreeing?* This can be calculated by the binomial test:

$$p = \frac{9!}{(9-9)! \times 0!} \times .5^9 \times (.5)^{(9-9)} = 1 \times .00195 \times 1 = .00195$$

which, when rounded to three decimal places, is .002, i.e. the one-tailed probability which was reported in Chapter 15 for these data.

The Stuart-Maxwell test

Table A6.14 is a copy of Table 15.11 from Chapter 15. It shows participants' responses, before and after a talk on the subject, about whether they thought that psychology was a science.

TABLE A6.14   The numbers of people who agreed or disagreed that psychology is a science before and after hearing a talk when they had a choice of three responses

		After			
		Agree	Unsure	Disagree	*Row total*
	Agree	19	1	0	20
Before	Unsure	5	4	1	10
	Disagree	14	1	15	30
	Column total	38	6	16	60

To simplify the description of the calculations I am going to use the same method to denote each cell as I did for the calculation of odds ratios, above. Using two numbers, the first for the row and the second for the column, we can describe the 19 participants who agreed on both occasions as n_{11}.

For each pair of discordant cells (e.g. n_{13} and n_{31}) we do the same calculation as for McNemar's test of change and then add those results together:

$$\frac{(n_{13} - n_{31})^2}{(n_{13} + n_{31})} + \frac{(n_{12} - n_{21})^2}{(n_{12} + n_{21})} + \frac{(n_{23} - n_{32})^2}{(n_{23} + n_{32})} \tag{A6.19}$$

$$= \frac{(0-14)^2}{(0+14)} + \frac{(1-5)^2}{(1+5)} + \frac{(1-1)^2}{(1+1)}$$

$$= 14 + 2.67 + 0 = 16.67$$

Sample size for the Stuart-Maxwell test

Start by calculating an equivalent of equation A6.19 but with the frequencies replaced by their probabilities. Table A6.15 shows the probabilities; for example, $p_{11} = n_{11}/N = 19/60 = .317$.

TABLE A6.15   The probabilities for each combination of categories for the cells in Table A6.14

		After			
		Agree	Unsure	Disagree	Row total
	Agree	0.317	0.017	0.000	0.333
Before	Unsure	0.083	0.067	0.017	0.167
	Disagree	0.233	0.017	0.250	0.500
	Column total	0.633	0.100	0.267	1

$$= \frac{(0-.233)^2}{(0+.233)} + \frac{(.017-.083)^2}{(.017+.083)} + \frac{(.017-.017)^2}{(.017+.017)}$$

$$= .233 + .044 + 0 = .277$$

Divide that number into what is called *the noncentral parameter for noncentral χ^2* (often shown as λ)[2] for alpha of 0.05 and power of 0.8 for the appropriate degrees of freedom, found from $(i \times (i-1))/2$, where i is the number of categories. As there are three categories, so df = 3. λ is 10.903 (Pearson & Hartley, 1972).

$$10.903/0.277 = 39.36$$

Therefore 40 participants would be needed to provide the required level of power. If you don't have access to a table of λ-values, an approximate value can be calculated using:

$$\lambda = w^2 \times N$$

where w is the effect size for χ^2 and N is the sample size which is needed to achieve power of 0.8 for that effect size (from the power tables for w in Appendix XVIII). For example, Table A18.5c shows that the sample size required to give power of .8 for w = .3 is 120; I chose w of .3 because that showed the sample size for power of .8 and so saved using interpolation.

Therefore,

$$\lambda = (.3)^2 \times 120 = 10.8$$

---

2   A noncentral distribution assumes that H_A is true, whereas the distributions, such as chi-square, that we usually consult to find a probability for a statistic assume that H_0 is true; they are called central distributions.

Using this value to calculate the sample size for the Stuart-Maxwell test,

$$N = 10.8/0.277 = 39.99$$

which, when rounded up to the next whole person, gives the same result as using the more exact figure for λ from Pearson and Hartley (1972).

z-test of changes in proportions

In Chapter 15 it was pointed out that McNemar's test of change can also be presented as being derived from a z-test. The example that was given for McNemar's test was of students' opinions of whether psychology was a science before and after hearing a talk on the subject as shown in Table A6.16.

TABLE A6.16 The numbers of people who agreed or disagreed that psychology is a science before and after hearing a talk

| | | After | | |
		Agree	Disagree	Total
	Disagree	9	3	12
Before	Agree	6	0	6
	Total	15	3	18

The z-test is found from:

$$z = \frac{\left[n_{11} - \dfrac{(n_{11}+n_{22})}{2}\right]}{\sqrt{\left[(n_{11}+n_{22})\times0.25\right]}}$$

(A6.20)

where n_{11} and n_{22} are the numbers changing in each direction. As a two-tailed test we can just treat n_{11} as the larger of the two numbers, whereas for a one-tailed test we would treat n_{11} as the number of people who had changed in the direction we assumed would be greatest. Thus, if in the current example we predicted that people would tend to change to agreeing with the statement that psychology is a science, then $n_{11} = 9$ and $n_{22} = 0$. Therefore,

$$z = \frac{\left[9 - \dfrac{(9+0)}{2}\right]}{\sqrt{\left[(9+0)\times0.25\right]}} = 3$$

Squaring z produces a chi-squared value with df = 1. In Chapter 15 McNemar's test on these was shown to be 9.

An alternative way to analyse the data in Table A6.16 is to compare the proportions agreeing with the statement *psychology is a science* before and after the talk. We can calculate this from the marginal totals. Before the talk 6 out of 18 people agreed, whereas after the talk 15 out of 18 agreed. Therefore the proportion agreeing before was .333, while after the talk it was .833. Therefore, the proportion has increased by .833–.333 = .5. A standard error can be calculated for this but it is only accurate for larger samples:

$$SE = \sqrt{\frac{(p_{11} + p_{22}) - (p_{11} - p_{22})^2}{N}}$$ (A6.21)

where p_{11} and p_{22} are the proportions of the whole sample who have changed between the two occasions and N is the overall sample size. Here 9 out of 18 people changed from disagreeing to agreeing (.5) while 0 out of 18 changed from agreeing to disagreeing (0).

In the current example the sample size is too small but for illustration:

$$z = \frac{.5}{\sqrt{\frac{(.5+0) - (.5-0)^2}{18}}} = 4.24264$$

Squaring this produces what is called a Wald statistic, which, like McNemar's test, is tested against the chi-squared distribution with df = 1. Here Wald = 18.

The calculation of a CI for the difference in proportions is shown later in this appendix.

Effect size for differences between independent proportions

Cohen (1988) uses the effect size h:

$$h = \left|2 \times \text{arcsine}(\sqrt{p_1})\right| - \left|2 \times \text{arcsine}(\sqrt{p_2})\right|$$ (A6.22)

where arcsine is the arcsine transformation (in radians), shown as *asin* in Excel and sin^{-1} on some calculators and *arsin* in SPSS, and p_1 and p_2 are the proportions in the two groups.

In the smoking and gender example given previously, let p_1 be the proportion of smokers in the female sample (.4773) and p_2 be the proportion of smokers in the male sample (.3864). Then,

$$h = [2 \times \text{arcsine}(\sqrt{.4773})] - [2 \times \text{arcsine}(\sqrt{.3864})] = 1.525381 - 1.341595 = 0.183786$$

Confidence intervals for differences between two sample statistics

To calculate CIs we need to know what is the appropriate standard error for the figure around which we are trying to find the CI and what is the critical value for the statistic test we are using to achieve the required level of confidence.

The general equation is:

CI = figure in sample ± (critical value of statistic × SE)

Between-subjects t-test

Here the standard error is the divisor in equation A6.1 (or, if the sample sizes are equal you could use equation A6.2). The critical value for the statistic depends on the df and the level of confidence which we want. If we want a 95% CI, then we need the t-value which gives exactly a two-tailed probability of .05. In the example of the anxiety levels for therapy and control conditions, the difference between the means is −8, and the SE is 2.2513. There were 40 participants and so the df = 38 for this test. The critical value we require is $t = 2.024$ (see Table A17.2 in Appendix XVII). Therefore,

CI = −8 ± (2.024 × 2.2513) = −12.557 to −3.443

Within-subjects *t*-test

In the cycling example the difference in time taken with and without shaving is 1.545 minutes and the SE (from equation A6.5) is 3.3166. Eleven cyclists took part in the study so the df for this test is 10. The critical t-value for a two-tailed test and $\alpha = .05$ is accordingly 2.228. Therefore,

CI = 1.545 ± (2.228 × 3.3166) = −0.73 to 3.82

z-Test comparing two independent sample proportions

In the comparison of proportions of males and females who smoke, the difference between the proportions is .0909, the SE (from equation 15.7) is .10516 and the critical value for z for a two-tailed test at $\alpha = .05$ is approximately 1.96. Therefore,

CI = .0909 ± (1.96 × .10516) = −.115 to .297

z-Test comparing two non-independent sample proportions

The difference between the proportions agreeing with the statement *psychology is a science* before and after a talk on the subject was shown above to be .5. The standard error for this difference is found from equation A6.20 and is .117851. Therefore the 95% CI is:

CI = .5 ± (1.96 × .117851) = .269 to .731

Seeking differences between more than two levels of an independent variable

This appendix illustrates the techniques introduced in Chapter 16.

The information provided in this appendix will allow you to calculate the statistics by hand or with a calculator, but the techniques shown are not always the conventional ones that you would find in most textbooks. They are provided more to enhance understanding and to allow the checking of computer printout. The workings will be given to five decimal places so that the results are consistent with the summary tables from the computer printout, once they have been rounded up or down; you do not normally need this level of precision.

Parametric tests

One-way between-subjects ANOVA

Researchers compared the effectiveness of two different mnemonic techniques – pegwords and method of loci – and a control condition.

TABLE A7.1   The number of words recalled under three memory conditions with mean and standard deviations

	Mnemonic strategy	
Control	Pegword	Loci
10	11	10
7	7	8
7	9	11
9	10	9
5	8	12
6	6	10
8	12	7
5	9	11
7	10	8
8	7	10

Mean	7.2	8.9	9.6
SD	1.61933	1.91195	1.57762

There are three sources of variation which we need to quantify: the overall variation in scores (total), which can be divided into the variation between the treatments (between groups) and the variation in scores within the groups (within groups).

The sum of squares is the sum of squared deviations from the mean, usually shown as:

$$\text{sum of squares} = \Sigma\ (x - \bar{x})^2 \tag{A7.1}$$

Total sum of squares

To obtain this it is necessary to find the overall mean for the scores. Then take the mean from each score to find each deviation. Next, square each deviation and add all the squared deviations.

In this case the overall mean is 8.56667 and the total sum of squares is 109.36654 (or 109.367 to three decimal places).

Between-groups sum of squares

The treatment or between-groups sum of squares is a comparison of the results for the three treatments; it takes into account the number of scores which were in each treatment. This can be obtained by finding the deviation of each treatment mean from the overall mean. Square each deviation and multiply it by the number of scores which provided that treatment mean, and then add all the results.

TABLE A7.2   Creating the treatments sum of squares for a one-way between-subjects ANOVA

Treatment	Mean	Deviation from overall mean (8.56667)	(Deviation)²	$n \times$ (Deviation)²
Control	7.2	1.36667	1.86779	18.6779
Pegwords	8.9	0.33333	0.11111	1.1111
Loci	9.6	1.03333	1.06777	10.6777
		Between-groups sum of squares		30.4667

Within-groups sum of squares

This can be obtained by finding the sum of squares within each group and adding them together. If we know the variance for a set of scores, then we can find out their sum of squares, because:

$$\text{variance} = \frac{\text{sum of squares}}{n-1}$$

Remember that:

$$\text{variance} = (SD)^2$$

TABLE A7.3   Creating the within-groups sum of squares for a one-way between-subjects ANOVA

Treatment	SD	Variance	Variance × (n − 1)
Control	1.61933	2.62223	23.60007
Pegwords	1.91195	3.65555	32.89995
Loci	1.57762	2.48888	22.39992
		Within-groups sum of squares	78.89994

The within-groups sum of squares (S of S) could also have been found from:

total S of S = between-groups S of S + within-groups S of S

which means that:

within-groups S of S = total S of S − between-groups S of S
= 109.36654 − 30.4667
= 78.89984

(which is the same, to three decimal places, as before)

We now have the necessary sums of squares to create the summary table for the ANOVA.

TABLE A7.4   A summary table for a one-way between-subjects ANOVA

Source	Sum of squares	df	Mean square	F	p
Between groups	30.467	2	15.233	5.213	.0122
Within groups	78.900	27	2.922		
Total	109.367	29			

See Chapter 16 for an explanation of how the degrees of freedom (df), mean squares and F-ratios are found.

Unequal sample sizes (unbalanced designs)

When the sample size is not the same for all the groups, then there are two possible ways to calculate the treatment sum of squares; the other sum of squares would be found as shown previously.

Weighted means

The preceding method gives what are described as the weighted means solution, which multiplies the sum of squared deviations of each mean by the sample size of the group providing that mean. In this way, larger samples are being given more weight. This is the method used by most computer programs.

Unweighted means

An alternative method is to multiply each sum of squared deviations by the harmonic mean of the sample size. The harmonic mean is found by:

$$n_h = \frac{k}{\dfrac{1}{n_1} + \dfrac{1}{n_2} \text{ up to } \dfrac{1}{n_k}} \tag{A7.2}$$

where k is the number of levels, n_1 is the sample size in the first group and n_k is the sample size for the last group.

Therefore, if in the preceding example, with three levels, the sample sizes had been 8, 10 and 7, the harmonic mean of the sample size would be:

$$n_h = \frac{3}{\left(\dfrac{1}{8} + \dfrac{1}{10} + \dfrac{1}{7}\right)}$$

$$= \frac{3}{(0.125 + 0.1 + 0.14286)}$$

$$= \frac{3}{0.36786}$$

$$= 8.155$$

Heterogeneity of variance (Welch's F')

There is a version of between-subjects ANOVA (the Welch formula, F') which allows for lack of homogeneity of variance between the levels of the independent variable (IV).

$$F' = \frac{\left[\dfrac{\sum\{w_j \times (\bar{x}_j - \bar{x})^2\}}{k-1}\right]}{1 + \left[\dfrac{2 \times (k-2)}{k^2 - 1}\right] \times \sum\left[\left(\dfrac{1}{n_j - 1}\right) \times \left(1 - \dfrac{w_j}{\sum w_j}\right)^2\right]} \tag{A7.3}$$

where $w_j = \dfrac{n_j}{s_j^2}$

n_j is the sample in level j

s_j^2 is the variance in level j

$\bar{x}_j$ is the mean of level j

$\bar{x} = \dfrac{\sum(w_j \times \bar{x}_j)}{\sum w_j}$

k is the number of levels in the IV

F' has the same df for treatment as a standard F-ratio ($k - 1$) but a modified error df compared with the standard F-ratio:

$$df_2' = \frac{k^2 - 1}{3 \times \sum \left[\left(\dfrac{1}{n_j - 1} \right) \times \left(1 - \dfrac{w_j}{\sum w_j} \right)^2 \right]} \qquad (A7.4)$$

Although the data in Table A7.1 have homogeneity of variance, the following is a reanalysis according to the Welch equation:

| | Mnemonic strategy | | |
	Control	Pegword	Loci
$\bar{x}_j$	7.2	8.9	9.6
SD_j	1.61933	1.91195	1.57762
Variance (s_j^2)	2.6222	3.6556	2.4889
w_j	3.8135	2.7356	4.0179
$w_j \times \bar{x}_j$	27.4572	24.3468	38.5718

$\sum w_j = 10.567$

$\bar{x} = 8.5526$

| | Mnemonic strategy | | |
	Control	Pegword	Loci
$\bar{x}_j - \bar{x}$	−1.3526	0.3474	1.0474
$(\bar{x}_j - \bar{x})^2$	1.8295	0.1207	1.0970
$w_j \times (\bar{x}_j - \bar{x})^2$	6.9768	0.3302	4.4076

$n = 10$ for each group

$k = 3$

$$F' = \frac{5.8573}{1 + \left(\dfrac{2}{8} \times 0.1491\right)}$$

$$= 5.6468$$

$$df_2' = \frac{8}{3 \times 0.1491}$$

$$= 17.8851$$

Referring to the tables for the F-distribution, we are told that with 2 and 18 df, the probability of F' is .01 $< p <$ .05. (The more exact probability is .013, which is very close to the probability given for the original F-ratio in Table A7.4.)

One-way within-subjects ANOVA

Researchers investigated the effects of the presence of others on judgements about the treatment of offenders. Participants were given a description of a crime and had to decide how long the criminal should spend in prison. The experiment involved three conditions: in one, each participant was alone and unaware of anyone else's judgement; in a second condition, each participant was alone but could see on a computer screen what others had 'decided'; in the third condition, each participant was in a group and aware of what the others had 'decided' (Table A7.5). The decisions which the participants learned that others had made were, in fact, pre-set by the experimenters but the participants were unaware of this.

TABLE A7.5   The sentences given to criminals when participants were in one of three situations

Participant	Alone	Computer	Group	Mean for participant
1	24	24	24	24
2	18	24	24	22
3	12	15	15	14
4	3	12	12	9
5	24	24	30	26
6	18	18	24	20
7	12	15	18	15
8	15	20	20	18.33333
9	12	15	18	15
10	9	15	15	13
Mean	14.7	18.2	20	17.63333
SD	6.55	4.52	5.48	

The sources of variation in scores are the total variation, which can be split into the variation due to participants – between-subjects – and that due to a combination of the participants and the treatments – within-subjects. The within-subjects variation can be further divided into between-groups (or treatment) variation – that is, the effect of the IV – and the residual (or error) variation – that is, what cannot be accounted for by differences between the treatments.

Thus, the total sum of squared (S of S) deviations can be split into:

$$\underset{\text{between subjects}}{\overset{\nearrow}{\text{}}}\quad\underset{\text{within subjects}}{\overset{\nwarrow}{\text{}}}$$

Total S of S = [Subjects S of S] + [treatment S of S + residual S of S]

Total sum of squares

The total sum of squares is obtained in the same way as for a one-way between-subjects ANOVA by finding the overall mean for the scores, then subtracting the mean from each score to find each deviation, then squaring each deviation and adding all the squared deviations.

In this case the overall mean is 17.63333, and the total sum of squares is 984.96673 (or 984.967 to three decimal places).

Between-subjects sum of squares

This is the sum of squared deviations of each participant's mean from the overall mean, multiplied by the number of treatments (k) (Table A7.6).

TABLE A7.6   Obtaining the between-subjects sum of squares for a one-way within-subjects ANOVA

Participant	Mean	Deviation from overall mean (17.63333)	(Deviation)^2	$k \times$ (Deviation)^2 (k is number of treatments)
1	24	6.36667	40.53449	121.60347
2	22	4.36667	19.06781	57.20343
3	14	–3.63333	13.20109	39.60327
4	9	–8.63333	74.53439	223.60317
5	26	8.36667	70.00117	210.00351
6	20	2.36667	5.60113	16.80339
7	15	–2.63333	6.93443	20.80329
8	18.33333	0.7	0.49	1.47
9	15	–2.63333	6.93443	20.80329
10	13	–4.63333	21.46775	64.40325
		Between-subjects sum of squares		776.30007

Within-subjects sum of squares

This is the sum of the squared deviations of each participant's score from the mean for that participant (Table A7.7). Thus the second participant's sum of squared deviation is:

$$\begin{aligned} \text{S of S}_{(\text{participant 2})} &= (18 - 22)^2 + (24 - 22)^2 + (24 - 22)^2 \\ &= (-4)^2 + 2^2 + 2^2 \\ &= 16 + 4 + 4 \\ &= 24 \end{aligned}$$

TABLE A7.7 Obtaining the within-subjects sum of squares for a one-way within-subjects ANOVA

Participant	Alone	Computer	Group	Mean	Sum of squared deviations from own mean
1	24	24	24	24	0
2	18	24	24	22	24
3	12	15	15	14	6
4	3	12	12	9	54
5	24	24	30	26	24
6	18	18	24	20	24
7	12	15	18	15	18
8	15	20	20	18.33333	16.66667
9	12	15	18	15	18
10	9	15	15	13	24
			Within-subjects S of S		208.66667

Between-groups (treatment) sum of squares

As with the between-subjects ANOVA, this is the sum of squares of the three treatment means multiplied by the sample size (Table A7.8).

TABLE A7.8 Obtaining the between-groups sum of squares for a one-way within-subjects ANOVA

Treatment	Mean for treatment	Deviation from overall mean (17.63333)	(Deviation)^2	$n \times$ (Deviation)^2
Alone	14.7	−2.93333	8.60442	86.0442
Computer	18.2	0.56667	0.32111	3.2111
Group	20	2.36667	5.60113	56.0113
		Between-groups sum of squares		145.2666

Residual sum of squares

The residual sum of squares is the sum of squares within the groups, once the between-subjects effect has been removed. The residuals can be found by subtracting each person's overall mean from his or her score in each condition.

Thus the second participant's residual for the alone treatment is $18 - 22 = -4$. Once the residuals have been found, calculate the within group sum of squares for those residuals by finding how each residual differs from the mean residual for that treatment (Table A7.9).

TABLE A7.9   The residuals for each participant under each condition, used to find the residual sum of squares for a one-way within-subjects ANOVA

Participant	Alone	Computer	Group	
1	0	0	0	
2	–4	2	2	
3	–2	1	1	
4	–6	3	3	
5	–2	–2	4	
6	–2	–2	4	
7	–3	0	3	
8	–3.33333	1.66667	1.66667	
9	–3	0	3	
10	–4	2	2	
Mean residual	–2.93333	0.566667	2.36667	
SD	*1.60093*	*1.68545*	*1.28091*	
Variance	2.56296	2.84074	1.64074	Residual S of S
Column S of S	23.06664	25.56667	14.76667	63.39997

Once the total and between-subjects sums of squares have been found, the within-subjects sum of squares can be found from:

within-subjects S of S = total S of S – between-subjects S of S

Once the treatment sum of squares has been found, the residual sum of squares can be found from:

residual S of S = within S of S – treatments S of S

Now that we have obtained all the necessary sums of squares, the summary table for the ANOVA can be created (Table A7.10). See Chapter 16 for details of how the df, mean squares and *F*-ratios are calculated.

TABLE A7.10   A summary table for a one-way within-subjects ANOVA

Source	Sum of squares	df	Mean square	*F*	p
Between subjects	776.3	9			
Within subjects	208.667	20	10.433		
Treatments	145.267	2	72.633	20.621	.0001
Residual	63.399	18	3.522		
Total	984.967	29			

Assessing lack of independence of data

To test the independence of the data in three groups given the pegword method, a one-way between-subjects ANOVA was conducted. This produced the following result (Table A7.11).

TABLE A7.11   A one-way within-subjects ANOVA comparing the recall score of three groups using pegwords

	Sum of squares	df	Mean square	F	p
Between groups	24.150	2	12.075	9.660	.010
Within groups	8.750	7	1.250		
Total	32.900	9			

An intraclass correlation (ICC) can be calculated using these figures, where

$$ICC = \frac{\text{variance between groups}}{\text{total variance}}$$

Variance between groups is symbolised by some as τ^2, while total variance = τ^2 + error variance (σ^2). Therefore,

$$ICC = \frac{\tau^2}{\tau^2 + \sigma^2}$$

Now τ^2 is estimated by

$$\frac{\text{mean square}_{\text{between groups}} - \text{mean square}_{\text{within groups}}}{n}$$

where n is the sample size in each group or, as in this case when the sample sizes are different, it is:

$$\text{adjusted } n = \text{mean } n - \frac{\text{variance of } n}{k \times \text{mean } n}$$

where k is the number of groups. Thus

$$\text{adjusted } n = 3.3333 - \frac{0.3333}{3 \times 3.3333} = 3.3$$

and σ^2 is estimated by mean square$_{\text{within groups}}$. Therefore,

$$\tau^2 = 3.280303, \sigma^2 = 1.25 \text{ and } ICC = \frac{3.280303}{3.280303 + 1.25} = .532923$$

Sphericity

Within-subjects ANOVA has a particular assumption which the data should fulfil. The variances of the differences between different pairs of levels of the IV will be the same (known as *sphericity* or *circularity*). That is, the variance of the difference between the scores for the alone and the computer condition will be the same as the variance of the difference scores between computer and face-to-face and the variance of the difference scores between alone and face-to-face conditions (Table A7.12).

When sphericity is not present, one approach to compensate for this and produce a more accurate probability for the test is to adjust the df for the *F*-ratios. The two adjustments are the Greenhouse–Geisser (G–G) epsilon and the Huynh–Feldt (H–F) epsilon.

TABLE A7.12   Calculating the variances of the difference scores between conditions

Participant	Alone – computer	Differences alone – group	Computer – group
1	0.00	0.00	0.00
2	–6.00	–6.00	0.00
3	–3.00	–3.00	0.00
4	–9.00	–9.00	0.00
5	0.00	–6.00	–6.00
6	0.00	–6.00	–6.00
7	–3.00	–6.00	–3.00
8	–5.00	–5.00	0.00
9	–3.00	–6.00	–3.00
10	–6.00	–6.00	0.00
Variance	9.17	5.57	6.40

A concept which is often linked to sphericity, in discussions of the issue, is *compound symmetry*. Compound symmetry exists when the variances in the original scores are homogeneous and the covariances are homogeneous. (Covariance is a measure of how closely two measures are related and is defined in Chapter 19.) Thus, for compound symmetry to be present, the variances of alone, computer and group should be the same as each other, while the covariances of alone and computer, alone and group, and computer and group should be the same as each other. When compound symmetry exists, sphericity will be present. However, it is possible to have sphericity without compound symmetry.

A variance–covariance matrix contains the covariances between each of the levels of the IV and, in the diagonal of the matrix, the variances for each of the levels. In Table A7.13, 42.9 is the variance for the alone condition, while 20.2 is the variance for the computer condition.

TABLE A7.13   The variance–covariance matrix for the conditions under which participants sentenced criminals, including column means

	Alone	Computer	Group
Alone	42.9	27.06667	33.66667
Computer	27.06667	20.2	22
Group	33.66667	22	30
Mean	34.54456	23.15556	28.55556

To calculate the epsilons we need the following information, which can be derived from Table A7.13.

overall mean = 28.75189 (the mean of all the nine values)
mean variance = 31.1 (the mean of the three variances)
sum of squared column means (SS_{means}) = 2554.92659 (the sum of the square of each of the column means)
sum of squared variances and covariances (SS_{all}) = 7856.68645 (the sum of the square of each of the nine values)

(Note that SS_{means} and SS_{all} are literally sums of squares and not sums of squared deviations as in previous calculations.)

The Greenhouse–Geisser epsilon ($\hat{\varepsilon}$) is found from the following equation:

$$\hat{\varepsilon} = \frac{k^2 \times (\text{mean variance} - \text{overall mean})^2}{(k-1) \times [SS_{all} - (2 \times k \times SS_{means}) + (k \times \text{overall mean})^2]}$$

$$= \frac{3^2 \times (31.1 - 28.75189)^2}{(3-1) \times [7856.68645 - (2 \times 3 \times 2554.92659) + (3 \times 28.75189)^2]}$$

$$= \frac{9 \times 5.51362}{2 \times (7856.68645 - 15269.55955 + 7440.04061)}$$

$$= \frac{49.62258}{54.33502}$$

$$= .91327$$

The Huynh–Feldt epsilon ($\tilde{\varepsilon}$) is based on the Greenhouse–Geisser $\hat{\varepsilon}$:

$$\tilde{\varepsilon} = \frac{[n \times (k-1) \times \hat{\varepsilon}] - 2}{(k-1) \times \{n - 1 - [(k-1) \times \hat{\varepsilon}]\}}$$

$$= \frac{[10 \times (3-1) \times .91327] - 2}{(3-1) \times \{10 - 1 - [(3-1) \times .91327]\}}$$

$$= \frac{(10 \times 2 \times .91327) - 2}{2 \times [9 - (2 \times .91327)]}$$

$$= \frac{18.2654 - 2}{2 \times (9 - 1.82654)}$$

$$= \frac{16.2654}{14.34692}$$

$$= 1.13372$$

These epsilons can be used to adjust the df for a within-subjects ANOVA, using the equation:

adjusted df = (old df) × epsilon

However, when epsilon is greater than 1, no adjustment is made. Therefore the Greenhouse–Geisser $\hat{\varepsilon}$ is the only one which needs to be used in this example. In the within-subjects one-way ANOVA, the df were 2 and 18, which means that, using the Greenhouse–Geisser $\hat{\varepsilon}$, they would become:

adjusted df = 2 × .913 and 18 × .913
= 1.826 and 16.434

The effect size f

Cohen (1988) uses f as the effect size for analysis of variance, where:

$$f = \sqrt{\frac{n^2}{1 - n^2}}$$

Partial eta-squared

In Chapter 16 the point was made that some computer packages, including SPSS, report partial eta-squared rather than eta-squared. Partial eta-squared is calculated from the following equation:

$$\text{partial eta-squared} = \frac{\text{sum of squares for treatment}}{\text{sum of squares for treatment} + \text{sum of squares for error}}$$

Thus, eta-squared and partial eta-squared will be the same for a one-way between-subjects ANOVA, as the elements in the equation for partial eta-squared are the only ones in the analysis and so total sum of squares is the same as sum of squares for the treatment plus sum of squares for error. However, in all other analyses the two versions of eta-squared will usually differ, with partial eta-squared being larger and sometimes much larger. As an illustration, in the case of the within-subjects ANOVA, partial eta-squared is .696, while eta-squared is .147. The difference is due to the fact that partial eta-squared does not include the between-subjects sum of squares in the calculation.

Non-parametric tests

At least ordinal measurement

Between-subjects designs – Kruskal–Wallis ANOVA by ranks

When the research design is between-subjects with more than two levels of the IV and the requirements of a parametric ANOVA are not fulfilled, then the analysis can be conducted by using the Kruskal–Wallis one-way ANOVA, as long as the data are at least ordinal.

Researchers wished to compare the grades given by lecturers to essays which were shown to be by either a male or a female or the gender was not specified. Twenty-four college lecturers were each given an essay to mark and they were told that the writer of the essay was a male student, or was a female student, or they were not given any indication of the student's gender. In fact, the same essay was given to all the lecturers. Each essay was given a grade between A+ and C−, which was converted to a numerical grade ranging from 1 to 9.

A rank is given to each grade, with tied ranks being treated in the same way as for the Wilcoxon signed rank test for matched pairs, in that the mean rank is given to all scores which are the same (Table A7.14).

TABLE A7.14 The grades given by participants for an essay depending on the presumed gender of its author, with the grades given ranks

| 'Gender' of author | | | | | |
| Female | | Neutral | | Male | |
Grade	Rank	Grade	Rank	Grade	Rank
2	2	3	7.5	3	7.5
3	7.5	3	7.5	4	15
2	2	4	15	5	20
3	7.5	4	15	6	22.5
4	15	5	20	7	24

(Continued)

TABLE A7.14   (Continued)

		'Gender' of author			
Female		Neutral		Male	
Grade	Rank	Grade	Rank	Grade	Rank
4	15	6	22.5	2	2
3	7.5	4	15	3	7.5
5	20	3	7.5	4	15
Total (R)	76.5		110		113.5

The statistic used for this test is H:

$$H = \left[\left\{\frac{12}{N \times (N+1)}\right\} \times \Sigma\left(\frac{R^2}{n_i}\right)\right] - [3 \times (N+1)]$$

where N is the overall number of participants, which in this case is 8 + 8 + 8 = 24, and $\Sigma\left(\dfrac{R^2}{n_i}\right)$ is the sum of each of the total ranks squared, divided by the number of participants in the group. Therefore:

$$\Sigma\left(\frac{R^2}{n_i}\right) = \frac{(76.5)^2}{8} + \frac{(110)^2}{8} + \frac{(113.5)^2}{8}$$

$$= 3854.3125$$

Therefore,

$$H = \left\{\left[\frac{12}{24 \times (24+1)}\right] \times (3854.3125)\right\} - [3 \times (24+1)]$$

$$= \left[\left(\frac{12}{600}\right) \times 3854.3125\right] - 75$$

$$= 77.08625 - 75$$

$$= 2.08625$$

Correction for ties

When some scores are the same, there is a version of the test which adjusts for ties. In the present example, there were five places where the grades tied (Table A7.15).

TABLE A7.15   Calculating the correction for tied scores for the Kruskal–Wallis ANOVA

Grade	Number of ties (t)	Correction = $(t^3 - t)$
2	3	24
3	8	504
4	7	336
5	3	24
6	2	6
Total correction		894

$$\text{corrected } H = \frac{\text{original } H}{\left[1 - \left(\dfrac{\text{total correction}}{N^3 - N}\right)\right]}$$

$$= \frac{2.08625}{\left\{1 - \left[\dfrac{894}{(24)^3 - 24}\right]\right\}}$$

$$= \frac{2.08625}{\left[1 - \left(\dfrac{894}{13824 - 24}\right)\right]}$$

$$= \frac{2.08625}{1 - 0.06478}$$

$$= 2.23076$$

Within-subjects designs: Friedman two-way ANOVA

When the design is within-subjects and the IV has more than two levels but the assumptions of the parametric ANOVA are not met, if the level of measurement is at least ordinal, then the Friedman two-way ANOVA is the appropriate test.

Researchers wished to see whether a group of seven students rated a particular course differently as they spent more time on it. Each student was asked to rate the course on a 7-point scale ranging from *not enjoyable at all* to *very enjoyable*, on three occasions: after 1 week, after 5 weeks and after 10 weeks (Table A7.16).

TABLE A7.16   The ratings given by students on three occasions of a course

	Week of course		
Participant	1	5	10
1	3	4	5
2	4	4	4
3	5	6	6
4	2	3	4
5	6	5	5
6	1	3	5
7	5	6	6

To calculate Friedman's ANOVA (Table A7.17) it is first necessary to give ranks to the scores for each person. Notice that the ranking is only for each person. Nonetheless, ties are treated in the usual way, as described for the Wilcoxon signed rank test for matched pairs. However, unlike the Wilcoxon signed rank test, a participant who scores the same in all levels of the IV is not dropped from the analysis.

TABLE A7.17 The ranks for each participant for the ratings given to the course for a Friedman two-way ANOVA

	Week of course		
Participant	1	5	10
1	1	2	3
2	2	2	2
3	1	2.5	2.5
4	1	2	3
5	3	1.5	1.5
6	1	2	3
7	1	2.5	2.5
Total (R)	10	14.5	17.5

The test produces a statistic called χ^2_F (sometimes given as χ^2_r):

$$\chi^2_F = \left[\left[\frac{12}{N \times k \times (k+1)} \right] \times (\Sigma R^2) \right] - [3 \times N \times (k+1)]$$

where N is the sample size, in this case 7; k is the number of levels of the IV, in this case 3; and ΣR^2 is the sum of the ranks squared. Therefore:

$$\Sigma R^2 = (10)^2 + (14.5)^2 + (17.5)^2$$
$$= 100 + 210.25 + 306.25$$
$$= 616.5$$

Therefore:

$$\chi^2_F = \left[\left[\frac{12}{7 \times 3 \times (3+1)} \right] \times 616.5 \right] - [3 \times 7 \times (3+1)]$$
$$= \left[\left(\frac{12}{84} \right) \times 616.5 \right] - 84$$
$$= 88.07143 - 84$$
$$= 4.07143$$

Correction for ties

Unlike previous corrections for ties, the one used with Friedman's test counts occasions when there is no tie, but counts it as a tie of 1. The ties are counted for each person (Table A7.18).

TABLE A7.18 Calculating the number of tied ranks of each size for a Friedman two-way ANOVA

Participant	Week of course			Size of ties		
	1	5	10	1	2	3
1	1	2	3	3	0	0
2	2	2	2	0	0	1
3	1	2.5	2.5	1	1	0
4	1	2	3	3	0	0
5	3	1.5	1.5	1	1	0
6	1	2	3	3	0	0
7	1	2.5	2.5	1	1	0
			Total	12	3	1

Now we cube each instance of each size of tie and add the results, so for the 12 ties which had one in each tie, the sum is:

$$(1)^3 + (1)^3 + (1)^3 + (1)^3 + (1)^3 + (1)^3 + (1)^3 + (1)^3 + (1)^3 + (1)^3 + (1)^3 + (1)^3 = 12$$

For the three ties which had two in each tie, the sum is:

$$(2)^3 + (2)^3 + (2)^3 = 8 + 8 + 8 = 24$$

and for the one tie which had three in it, the sum is $(3)^3 = 27$. Therefore the sum of the ties cubed is $12 + 24 + 27 = 63$.

The equation for corrected χ_F^2 is:

$$\text{corrrcted } \chi_F^2 = \frac{\left(12 \times \sum R^2\right) - [3 \times N^2 \times k \times (k+1)^2]}{[N \times k \times (k+1)] + \left[\dfrac{N \times k - \text{sum of cubed ties}}{(k-1)}\right]}$$

Therefore:

$$\text{corrrcted } \chi_F^2 = \frac{\left(12 \times 616.5\right) - [3 \times (7)^2 \times 3 \times (3+1)^2]}{[7 \times 3 \times (3+1)] + \left[\dfrac{7 \times 3 - 63}{(3-1)}\right]}$$

$$= \frac{7398 - [3 \times 49 \times 3 \times (4)^2]}{(7 \times 3 \times 4) + \left(\dfrac{7 \times 3 - 63}{2}\right)}$$

$$= \frac{7398 - (3 \times 49 \times 3 \times 16)}{84 + \left(\dfrac{21 - 63}{2}\right)}$$

$$= \frac{7398 - (3 \times 49 \times 3 \times 16)}{84 + \left(\dfrac{21 - 63}{2}\right)}$$

$$= \frac{7398 - (3 \times 49 \times 3 \times 16)}{84 + \left(\frac{21 - 63}{2}\right)}$$

$$= \frac{7398 - 7056}{84 - \left(\frac{42}{2}\right)}$$

$$= \frac{342}{63}$$

$$= 5.42857$$

The power of the Friedman test

The power of the Friedman test is found in terms of its power efficiency relative to the parametric within-subjects one-way ANOVA and depends on the number of levels of the IV: the smaller the number of levels, the poorer is the power efficiency. To find the sample size for the Friedman test, find the sample size necessary for the parametric within-subjects one-way ANOVA, for the number of levels of the IV, the α-level and the power required, and then multiply the sample size by the appropriate figure from Table A7.19.

TABLE A7.19   The amount it is necessary to multiply the sample size suggested for a parametric ANOVA in order to achieve the same power for the Friedman test

Number of levels in IV	Multiply sample size by
3	1.40
4	1.31
5	1.26
6	1.22
7	1.20
8	1.18
9	1.16
10	1.15

The general rule is: multiply the sample size by $\left(1.047 \times \frac{k+1}{k}\right)$, where k is the number of levels.

Nominal data

Within-subjects designs: Cochran's Q

If the measure taken is dichotomous, for example, yes or no, then Cochran's Q can be used. However, it is possible to recode data to be dichotomous, as shown next. Researchers wanted to compare students' choices of modules on social psychology, research methods and historical issues to see whether some modules were more popular than others. It is recommended that the test be conducted with at least 16 participants. The researchers asked this number of students what their module choices were. Twelve had chosen social psychology, eight methods and six historical issues. As Cochran's Q requires dichotomous variables, the data had to be recoded, with 1 denoting that a student took the course and 0 that he or she did not (see Table A7.20).

TABLE A7.20   The modules chosen by 16 students, coded as dummy variables, with column and row totals

Participant	Social psychology	Research methods	Historical issues	Row total	Row total squared
1	1	0	0	1	1
2	1	1	0	2	4
3	0	1	0	1	1
4	1	1	1	3	9
5	0	1	1	2	4
6	1	0	0	1	1
7	1	1	1	3	9
8	0	1	1	2	4
9	1	0	0	1	1
10	1	0	0	1	1
11	0	0	0	0	0
12	1	0	0	1	1
13	1	1	0	2	4
14	1	0	0	1	1
15	1	0	1	2	4
16	1	1	1	3	9
Column total	12	8	6	26	54

Cochran's Q can be found from the following equation:

$$Q = \frac{k \times (k-1) \times \Sigma (B_i - \bar{B})^2}{k \times \Sigma L_j - \Sigma L_j^2}$$

where k is the number of levels of the IV, B_i is the sum of scores in level i of the IV, L_j is the sum of the scores for participant j and $\bar{B}$ is the mean B.

Therefore, in the current case where the mean B is 8.667:

$$Q = \frac{3 \times (3-1) \times 18.667}{3 \times 26 - 54}$$

$$= \frac{112.002}{24}$$

$$= 4.667$$

Cochran's Q can also be found by running a one-way within-subjects ANOVA on the data, as per the method shown earlier in this appendix (see Table A7.21). This provides the necessary detail from which to form Q:

$$Q = \frac{\text{treatments sum of squares}}{\text{within-subjects means square}}$$

$$Q = \frac{1.167}{0.25}$$

$$= 4.668$$

TABLE A7.21 The summary table from a one-way within-subjects ANOVA for calculating Cochran's Q

Source	Sum of squares	df	Mean square	F	p
Between subjects	3.917	15			
Within subjects	8	32	0.25		
Treatments	1.167	2	0.583	2.561	.094
Residual	6.833	30	0.228		
Total	11.917	47			

Appendix VIII

Analysis of designs with more than one independent variable

This appendix illustrates the techniques introduced in Chapter 17.

Two-way between-subjects ANOVA

Researchers looked at the effect of mnemonic strategy and the nature of the list of words to be recalled upon recall (Table A8.1).

TABLE A8.1 The number of words recalled by participants when given a mnemonic strategy and a list type

	List type					
Mnemonic	Control	Linkedpegword	Loci	Control	Unlinked pegword	Loci
	10	9	9	4	10	8
	10	10	11	6	7	8
	11	10	11	7	8	8
	11	12	10	7	8	9

(Continued)

TABLE A8.1   (Continued)

Mnemonic	Control	Linkedpegword	List type Loci	Control	Unlinked pegword	Loci
	13	12	12	8	9	11
Total	55	53	53	32	42	44
Mean	11	10.6	10.6	6.4	8.4	8.8
Variance	1.5	1.8	1.3	2.3	1.3	1.7
SD	1.22474	1.34164	1.14018	1.51658	1.14018	1.30384

the overall mean = 9.3
the overall variance = 4.07931
the overall SD = 2.01973

Total sum of squares

The total sum of squares is the sum of the squared deviations of each score from the overall mean. It can also be found from:

total sum of squares = overall variance $\times$ ($N - 1$)

where N is the total sample size. Therefore,

total sum of squares = $4.07931 \times (30 - 1)$
= 118.29999

The total sum of squares can be split into:

the sum of squares for the first independent variable (IV$_1$) (SS$_A$)
the sum of squares for the second independent variable (IV$_2$) (SS$_B$)
the sum of squares for the interaction between the two IVs (SS$_{AB}$)
the sum of squares within groups (residual or error, which is the error term for the other three sums of squares) (SS$_{error}$)

Between-groups sum of squares for IV$_1$

Find the mean for each of the levels of IV$_1$ (list), regardless of the levels of IV$_2$ (mnemonic). Thus:

$$\text{mean for linked lists} = \frac{55 + 53 + 53}{15}$$

$$= \frac{161}{15}$$
$$= 10.73333$$

TABLE A8.2   Obtaining the between-groups sum of squared deviations for the first independent variable (IV_1) in a 2 × 3 two-way between-subjects ANOVA

List	Mean	Deviation from overall mean (9.3)	(Deviation)^2	(Deviation)^2 × number of scores contributing to each mean (15)
Linked	10.73333	1.43333	2.05444	30.81667
Unlinked	7.86667	−1.43333	2.05444	30.81667
			Between-groups S of S for IV_1	61.63334

Notice that, not surprisingly, when you have only two values they each deviate by the same amount from their mean – one positively and one negatively (Table A8.2).

Between-groups sum of squares for IV_2

This is found by using the same technique as for the sum of squares for IV_1 (Table A8.3).

TABLE A8.3   Obtaining the sum of squared deviations for the second independent variable (IV_2) in a 2 × 3 two-way between-subjects ANOVA

Mnemonic	Mean	Deviation from overall mean (9.3)	(Deviation)^2	(Deviation)^2 × the number of scores contributing to each mean (10)
Control	8.7	−0.6	0.36	3.6
Pegwords	9.5	0.2	0.04	0.4
Loci	9.7	0.4	0.16	1.6
			Between-groups S of S for IV_2	5.6

Interaction sum of squares (SS_{AB})

This is obtained, initially, by finding the sum of squared deviations for the means which relate to the interaction (the between-cells sum of squares) (Table A8.4). In this case, the interaction involves the six means for the different groups. The interaction sum of squares is then found by subtracting the sums of squares for the main effects involved in the interaction from the between-cells sum of squares:

$$SS_{AB} = IV_1 \text{ by } IV_2 \text{ cell S of S} - (SS_A + SS_B)$$

TABLE A8.4   Obtaining the IV_1 by IV_2 cells sum of squares in a 2 × 3 two-way between-subjects ANOVA

List type	Mnemonic	Mean	Deviation from overall mean (9.3)	(Deviation)^2	(Deviation)^2 × the number of scores contributing to each mean (5)
Linked	Control	11	1.7	2.89	14.45
	Pegword	10.6	1.3	1.69	8.45
	Loci	10.6	1.3	1.69	8.45
Unlinked	Control	6.4	−2.9	8.41	42.05
	Pegword	8.4	−0.9	0,81	4.05
	Loci	8.8	−0.5	0.25	1.25
			IV_1 by IV_2 cells S of S		78.70

$$SS_{AB} = 78.7 - (61.63334 + 5.6)$$
$$= 78.7 - 67.23334$$
$$= 11.46667$$

Within-groups (residual) sum of squares

This is, as usual, obtained by finding the sum of the squared deviations for each group and adding them together. Remembering that sum of squares (SS) = variance $\times$ $(n - 1)$,

$$SS_{residual} = (1.5 \times 4) + (1.8 \times 4) + (1.3 \times 4) + (2.3 \times 4) + (1.3 \times 4) + (1.7 \times 4)$$
$$= 6 + 7.2 + 5.2 + 9.2 + 5.2 + 6.8$$
$$= 39.6$$

As usual also, the residual sum of squares could have been found by subtracting all the other sums of squares from the total sum of squares (SS_{total}):

$$SS_{residual} = SS_{total} - (SS_{interaction} + SS_{A} + SS_{B})$$
$$= 118.29999 - (11.46667 + 61.63334 + 5.6)$$
$$= 118.29999 - 78.70001$$
$$= 39.59998 \text{ (or 39.6 to one decimal place)}$$

Now that we have found the sums of squares for all the aspects of the design we can create the summary table for the ANOVA (Table A8.5); see Chapter 17 for the ways in which the degrees of freedom, mean squares and F-values (F-ratios) are calculated.

TABLE A8.5   The summary table for a 2 × 3 two-way between-subjects ANOVA

Source	Sum of squares	df	Mean square	F	p
List	61.633	1	61.633	37.354	.0001
Mnemonic	5.600	2	2.800	1.697	.2045
List * Mnemonic	11.467	2	5.733	3.475	.0473
Error	39.600	24	1.650		
Total	118.300	29			

Two-way within-subjects ANOVA

Participants recommended the length of sentence a criminal should serve, in one of three situations: alone, communicating with others via computer and in the presence of others. In addition, they had to sentence defendants of two types: those with no previous record (novices) and habitual criminals (experienced).

The total sum of squares can be divided into the between-subjects sum of squares and the within-subjects sum of squares. The within-subjects sum of squares itself can be divided into:

sum of squares for IV_1 (defendant) (SS_A)
sum of squares for IV_1 by subjects (the error term for SS_A) (SS_{AS})
sum of squares for IV_2 (situation) (SS_B)
sum of squares for IV_2 by subjects (the error term for SS_B) (SS_{BS})
sum of squares for interaction between IV_1 and IV_2 (SS_{AB})
sum of squares for IV_1 by IV_2 by subjects (the error term for SS_{AB}) (SS_{ABS})

TABLE A8.6   The sentences (in months) given to criminals, depending on their record and the conditions under which the decision was made

			Defendant				
Participant	Alone	Novice computer	Face-to-face	Alone	Experienced computer	Face-to-face	Mean for participant
1	12	14	16	16	18	20	16
2	14	14	15	14	18	22	16.16667
3	13	13	17	17	17	21	16.33333
4	14	13	17	16	16	19	15.83333
5	13	14	16	17	19	21	16.66667
Mean	13.2	13.6	16.2	16.0	17.6	20.6	16.2
Variance	0.7	0.3	0.7	1.5	1.3	1.3	
SD	0.83667	0.54772	0.83667	1.22474	1.14018	1.14018	

Total sum of squares

As usual, this is the sum of squared deviations of each score from the overall mean (16.2). In this case it is 208.8.

The between-subjects sum of squares

As usual, this is the sum of squared deviations of each participant's mean score from the overall mean, multiplied by the number of conditions contributing to the means, which, in this case, is 6 (Table A8.7).

TABLE A8.7   Obtaining the between-subjects sum of squares for a 2 × 3 two-way within-subjects ANOVA

Participant	Mean	Deviation from overall mean (16.2)	(Deviation)^2	(Deviation)^2 × number of scores contributing to each mean (6)
1	16	−0.2	0.04	0.24
2	16.16667	−0.03333	0.00111	0.00665
3	16.33333	0.13333	0.01778	0.10668
4	15.83333	−0.36667	0.13445	0.8067
5	16.66667	0.46667	0.21778	1.30668
		Between-subjects S of S		2.46671

IV$_1$ sum of squares (SS$_A$)

This is obtained by finding the mean (across participants and all levels of IV$_2$) for each level of IV$_1$ (defendant) and finding the sum of squared deviations of the means for the levels (Table A8.8).

As we know the means for each condition and we know that each condition has the same number of scores, we can find the mean for each level of IV$_1$ in the following way:

$$\text{novice mean} = \frac{13.2 + 13.6 + 16.2}{3}$$

$$= \frac{43}{3}$$

$$= 14.33333$$

$$\text{experienced mean} = \frac{16 + 17.6 + 20.6}{3}$$

$$= \frac{54.2}{3}$$

$$= 18.06667$$

TABLE A8.8   Obtaining the sum of squares for the first independent variable of a 2 × 3 within-subjects ANOVA

Defendant	Mean	Deviation from overall mean (16.2)	(Deviation)^2	(Deviation)^2 × number of scores contributing to each mean (15)
Novice	14.33333	−1.86667	3.48446	52.26685
Experienced	18.06667	1.86667	3.48446	52.26685
			S of S for IV$_1$	104.5337

IV_1 by subjects sum of squares (SS_{AS})

The initial stage to obtain this is to find the subjects by IV$_1$ cell means. Thus, the first participant's cell mean for novice defendants is:

$$\frac{12 + 14 + 16}{3} = 14$$

We can then find the sum of squares for the subjects by IV$_1$ cells (see Table A8.9).

TABLE A8.9   Obtaining the first independent variable (IV$_1$) by subjects cell sum of squares for a 2 × 3 two-way within-subjects ANOVA

Defendant	Participant	Cell mean	Deviation from overall mean (16.2)	(Deviation)^2	(Deviation)^2 × number of scores contributing to each mean (3)
Novice	1	14	−2.2	4.84	14.52
	2	14.33333	−1.86667	3.48444	10.45333
	3	14.33333	−1.86667	3.48444	10.45333
	4	14.66667	−1.53333	2.35111	7.05333
	5	14.33333	−1.86667	3.48444	10.45333
Experienced	1	18	1.8	3.24	9.72
	2	18	1.8	3.24	9.72
	3	18.33333	2.13333	4.55111	13.65333
	4	17	0.8	0.64	1.92
	5	19	2.8	7.84	23.52
				Cells S of S	111.46665

We can then find the IV_1 by subjects sum of squares (SS_{AS}) from:

$SS_{AS} = IV_1$ by subjects cell S of S – (SS_A + between-subjects S of S)

Therefore,

defendant by subjects S of S = 111.46665 – (104.5337 + 2.46671)
= 111.46665 – 107.00041
= 4.46624

IV_2 sum of squares (SS_B)

This is obtained from the sum of the squared deviations of the means for the levels of the second IV, across participants and levels of the first IV (Table A8.10).

The mean for the first level of IV_2 can be found from:

$$\frac{13.2+16}{2} = \frac{29.2}{2} = 14.6$$

TABLE A8.10   Obtaining the sum of squares for the second independent variable (IV_2) in a 2 × 3 two-way within-subjects ANOVA

Condition	Mean	Deviation from overall mean (16.2)	(Deviation)²	(Deviation)² × number of scores which contributed to each mean (10)
Alone	14.6	–1.6	2.56	25.6
Computer	15.6	–0.6	0.36	3.6
Group	18.4	2.2	4.84	48.4

IV_2 S of S   77.6

IV_2 by subjects sum of squares (SS_{BS})

Again we find the means for the IV_2 by subjects cells, and then the sum of squared deviations for the cells (Table A8.11).

We can then find the IV_2 by subjects sum of squares (SS_{BS}) from:

$SS_{BS} = IV_2$ by subjects cell S of S – (IV_2 S of S + between-subjects S of S)

Therefore,

condition by subjects S of S = 86.8 – (77.6 + 2.46671)
= 86.8 – 80.06671
= 6.73329

TABLE A8.11 Obtaining the second independent variable (IV$_2$) by subjects cells sum of squares for a 2 × 3 two-way within-subjects ANOVA

Condition	Participant	Cell mean	Deviation from overall mean (16.2)	(Deviation)^2	(Deviation)^2 × number of scores contributing to each cell mean (2)
Alone	1	14	−2.2	4.84	9.68
	2	14	−2.2	4.84	9.68
	3	15	−1.2	1.44	2.88
	4	15	−1.2	1.44	2.88
	5	15	−1.2	1.44	2.88
Computer	1	16	−0.2	0.04	0.08
	2	16	−0.2	0.04	0.08
	3	15	−1.2	1.44	2.88
	4	14.5	−1.7	2.89	5.78
	5	16.5	0.3	0.09	0.18
Group	1	18	1.8	3.24	6.48
	2	18.5	2.3	5.29	10.58
	3	19	2.8	7.84	15.68
	4	18	1.8	3.24	6.48
	5	18.5	2.3	5.29	10.58

Cell S of S   86.8

IV$_1$ by IV$_2$ interaction sum of squares (SS$_{AB}$)

This can be obtained by firstly finding the cell means for each of the conditions; they are already given in Table A8.6. Then the sum of squared deviations for those means is found (Table A8.12).

TABLE A8.12 Obtaining the IV$_1$ by IV$_2$ *cell* sum of squares for a 2 × 3 two-way within-subjects ANOVA

Defendant	Condition	Cell mean	Deviation from overall mean (16.2)	(Deviation)^2	(Deviation) × number of scores contributing to each cell mean (5)
Novice	Alone	13.2	−3	9	45
	Computer	13.6	−2.6	6.76	33.8
	Group	16.2	0	0	0
Experienced	Alone	16.0	−0.2	0.04	0.2
	Computer	17.6	1.4	1.96	9.8
	Group	20.6	4.4	19.36	96.8

IV$_1$ by IV$_2$ cell S of S   185.6

The IV$_1$ by IV$_2$ sum of squares (SS$_{AB}$) can be obtained from:

$$SS_{AB} = IV_1 \text{ by } IV_2 \text{ cell S of S} - (SS_A + SS_B)$$
$$= 185.6 - (104.5337 + 77.6)$$
$$= 185.6 - 182.1337$$
$$= 3.4663$$

IV_1 by IV_2 by subjects sum of squares (SS_{ABS})

This can be obtained by first finding the total sum of squares, which is the same as the IV_1 by IV_2 by subjects cell sum of squares. The IV_1 by IV_2 by subjects sum of squares (SS_{ABS}) can then be found from:

$$SS_{ABS} = SS_{Total} - (SS_A + SS_B + SS_{AB} + SS_{AS} + SS_{BS} + SS_S)$$

where A is IV_1, B is IV_2, AB is the interaction between IV_1 and IV_2, AS is the interaction between IV_1 and subjects, BS is the interaction between IV_2 and subjects and S is subjects.
Therefore,

$$SS_{ABS} = 208.8 - (104.5337 + 77.6 + 3.4663 + 4.46624 + 6.73329 + 2.46671)$$
$$= 9.53376$$

We are now in a position to create the summary table for the ANOVA (Table A8.13); see Chapter 17 for an explanation of how the degrees of freedom, mean squares and F-ratios are calculated and Appendix VII for an explanation of how Greenhouse–Geisser (G–G) and Huynh–Feldt (H–F) adjustments are made.

TABLE A8.13   Summary table of 2 × 3, two-way within-subjects ANOVA

Source	S of S	df	MS	F	p	G–G	H–F
Subject	2.467	4	.617				
Defendant	104.533	1	104.533	93.612	.0006	.0006	.0006
Defendant by subject	4.467	4	1.117				
Context	77.600	2	38.800	46.099	.0001	.0007	.0001
Context by subject	6.733	8	.842				
Defendant by context	3.467	2	1.733	1.455	.2892	.2946	.2948
Defendant by context by subject	9.533	8	1.192				
Total	208.8	29					

Two-way mixed ANOVA

Experimenters compared the way that males and females rate their parents' IQs (Table A8.14). The IV *gender*, which has two levels – male and female – is a between-subjects variable. The IV *parent*, which has two levels – mother and father – is a within-subjects variable because each participant supplies data for each level of that variable.

The total sum of squares can be divided into the between-subjects sum of squares and the within-subjects sum of squares. The between-subjects sum of squares can be further divided into:

the IV_1 (gender) sum of squares (SS_A)
the subjects within groups sum of squares (the error term for the IV_1 sum of squares) ($SS_{S(groups)}$)

The within-subjects sum of squares can be subdivided into:

the IV_2 (parent) sum of squares, (SS_B)
the IV_1 by IV_2 sum of squares (the interaction between the two IVs – gender by parent) (SS_{AB})
the IV_2 by subjects within-groups sum of squares (the error term for both SS_B and SS_{AB}) ($SS_{B\ by\ S(groups)}$)

TABLE A8.14   The estimates made by males and females of their parents' IQs

| | | Parent | | | |
Participant	Gender of participant	Father	Mother	Mean for gender	Participant's mean
1	Male	120	100		110
2	Male	110	90		100
3	Male	100	105		102.5
4	Male	105	100		102.5
5	Male	140	120		130
mean		115	103	109	
6	Female	110	110		110
7	Female	110	105		107.5
8	Female	105	110		107.5
9	Female	120	115		117.5
10	Female	100	100		100
mean		109	108	108.5	
Mean for parent		112	105.5		

the overall mean = 108.75
the overall SD = 10.74526
the overall variance = 115.46053

Total sum of squares (SS_{total})

As usual, this can be found from the overall variance:

SS_{total} = overall variance × $(N - 1)$ (where N is the number of scores)
    = 115.46053 × 19
    = 2193.75007

Between-subjects sum of squares

As usual, this is obtained by forming the mean score for each participant and then finding the sum of squared deviations for these means (Table A8.15).

TABLE A8.15   Obtaining the between-subjects sum of squares for a 2 × 2 two-way mixed ANOVA

Participant	Mean rating of IQ for own parents	Deviation from overall mean (108.75)	(Deviation)^2	(Deviation)^2 × number of scores contributing to each mean (2)
1	110	1.25	1.5625	3.125
2	100	−8.75	76.5625	153.125
3	102.5	−6.25	39.0625	78.125
4	102.5	−6.25	39.0625	78.125
5	130	21.25	451.5625	903.125
6	110	1.25	1.5625	3.125
7	107.5	−1.25	1.5625	3.125

(Continued)

TABLE A8.15   (Continued)

Participant	Mean rating of IQ for own parents	Deviation from overall mean (108.75)	(Deviation)²	(Deviation)² × number of scores contributing to each mean (2)
8	107.5	−1.25	1.5625	3.125
9	117.5	8.75	76.5625	153.125
10	100	−8.75	76.5625	153.125
			Between-subjects S of S	1531.25

IV$_1$ sum of squares (SS$_A$)

The sum of squares for the between-subjects IV (gender) is obtained by finding the mean IQ given by each gender of participant, regardless of the parent being rated. The sum of squared deviations of these means is then found (Table A8.16).

TABLE A8.16   Obtaining the sum of squares for the between-subjects IV for a 2 × 2 two-way mixed ANOVA

Gender of participant	Mean estimated IQ	Deviation from overall mean (108.75)	(Deviation)²	(Deviation)² × number of scores contributing to each mean (10)
Male	109	0.25	0.0625	0.625
Female	108.5	−0.25	0.0625	0.625
			SS$_A$	1.25

Subjects-within-groups sum of squares (SS$_{S(groups)}$)

This can be obtained from:

$$SS_{S(groups)} = \text{between-subjects S of S} - SS_A$$
$$= 15321.25 - 1.25$$
$$= 1530$$

IV$_2$ sum of squares (SS$_B$)

This is obtained in the usual way for a within-subjects IV, by firstly finding the mean IQs for the levels of the IV (parent), regardless of the gender of the participant who supplied them (Table A8.17).

TABLE A8.17   Obtaining the sum of squares for the within-subjects IV for a 2 × 2 two-way mixed ANOVA

Parent	Mean rating of IQ made by participants	Deviation from overall mean (108.75)	(Deviation)²	(Deviation)² × number of scores contributing to each mean (10)
Father	112	3.25	10.5625	105.625
Mother	105.5	−3.25	10.5625	105.625
			SS$_B$	211.25

IV_1 by IV_2 sum of squares (SS_{AB})

The first stage in obtaining this interaction sum of squares is to find the means for the gender by parent cells. The sum of squares of these cell means is then found (Table A8.18).

TABLE A8.18   Obtaining the sum of squares for the IV_1 by IV_2 cells for a 2 × 2 two-way mixed ANOVA

Gender of participants	Parent	Mean rating of IQ	Deviation from overall mean (108.75)	(Deviation)²	(Deviation)² × number of scores contributing to each mean (5)
Male	Father	115	6.25	39.0625	195.3125
	Mother	103	−5.75	33.0625	165.3125
Female	Father	109	0.25	0.0625	0.3125
	Mother	108	−0.75	0.5625	2.8125
				IV_1 by IV_2 cell S of S	363.75

Now the interaction sum of squares (SS_{AB}) can be obtained from:

$$SS_{AB} = IV_1 \text{ by } IV_2 \text{ cell S of S} - (SS_A + SS_B)$$
$$= 363.75 - (1.25 + 211.25)$$
$$= 151.25$$

IV_2 by subjects-within-groups sum of squares $(SS_{B \text{ by } S(groups)})$

This can be obtained from:

$$SS_{B \text{ by } S(groups)} = SS_{total} - (SS_A + SS_{S(groups)} + SS_B + SS_{AB})$$

where SS is the sum of squares, B is IV_2 (parent), S is subjects, S(groups) is subjects within groups, B by S(groups) is IV_2 by subjects within groups and AB is the interaction between IV_1 and IV_2 (gender by parent). Or, because $SS_S = SS_A + SS_{S(groups)}$

$$SS_{B \text{ by } S(groups)} = SS_{Total} - (SS_S + SS_B + SS_{AB})$$

Therefore,

$$SS_{B \text{ by } S(Groups)} = 2193.75007 - (1531.25 + 211.25 + 151.25)$$
$$= 300.00007$$

The total sum of squares has now been divided into its constituent parts and the summary table for the ANOVA can be formed (Table A8.19). See Chapter 17 for an explanation of how the degrees of freedom, mean squares and the F-values (F-ratios) are calculated, and Appendix VII for the interpretation of G–G and H–F adjustments.

TABLE A8.19 The summary table for a 2 × 2 two-way mixed ANOVA

Source	S of S	df	MS	F	p	G–G	H–F
Gender	1.250	1	1.250	0.007	.9376		
Subject (group)	1530.000	8	191.250				
Parent	211.250	1	211.250	5.633	.0450	.0450	.0450
Parent by gender	151.250	1	151.250	4.033	.0795	.0795	.0795
Parent by subject (group)	300.000	8	37.500				
Total	2193.75	19					

Subsequent analysis after ANOVA or χ^2

This appendix illustrates the techniques introduced in Chapter 18.

Whenever a statistical test is used more than once, the likelihood of achieving a statistically significant result is increased, even though the Null Hypothesis of no effect is correct. That is, there is an increased danger of making a Type I error. It is possible to adjust the α-level, which a given test would have to achieve before statistical significance was considered to have been reached, to allow for the number of times the same test was being conducted. A general method is described as the Bonferroni adjustment.

Bonferroni adjustment

A simplified version of the Bonferroni adjustment is to divide the original α-level by the number of times the test is to be repeated. Thus, if three *t*-tests were to be conducted and the original α-level was .05, then the new α-level, which each *t*-test would be evaluated against, would be:

$$\frac{.05}{3} = .0167$$

This approximation is adequate for α-levels of .05 or smaller and is the one used to find the *t*-values which are contained in Bonferroni *t*-tables, such as those in Appendix XVII.

The full equation is:

$$\text{adjusted } \alpha\text{-level} = 1 - (1-\alpha)^{\frac{1}{k}}$$

which can be written as $1 - \sqrt[k]{1-\alpha}$, , where k is the number of times that the test is being conducted. Therefore, if the test was being conducted three times:

$$\text{adjusted } \alpha\text{-level} = 1 - (1-.05)^{\frac{1}{3}}$$
$$= 1 - (.95)^{\frac{1}{3}}$$
$$= 1 - (.95)^{0.333}$$
$$= 1 - .98306$$
$$= .0169$$

which is very close to the previous approximation (.0167).

Contrasts

When an ANOVA has been conducted, it is frequently the case that researchers want to compare particular treatments to see whether they are statistically different.

Parametric tests

There is a standard equation which can be used for between-subjects designs to find a t-value, the probability of which can be tested. However, as was pointed out in Chapter 18, such contrasts can be conducted even without conducting an initial ANOVA.

General contrast equation

The most general version of the equation is:

$$t = \frac{\Sigma(w_j \times \bar{x}_j)}{\sqrt{MS_{error} \times \Sigma \dfrac{w_j^2}{n_j}}} \tag{A9.1}$$

where $\bar{x}_j$ is a mean for one of the treatments, w_j is the weighting for x_j and will depend on the nature of the contrast, MS_{error} is the appropriate mean square of the error term from the ANOVA and n_j is the number of scores which contributed to $\bar{x}_j$.

In words, $\Sigma(w_j \times \bar{x}_j)$ tells you to multiply each mean in the contrast by an appropriate weighting and add the results; $\Sigma \dfrac{w_j^2}{n_j}$ tells you to square each weighting and divide it by the number of participants in the group and then add the results.

Pairwise contrasts

In comparing only two treatments (a pairwise contrast) the equation simplifies to the equation originally given in Chapter 18:

$$t = \frac{mean_1 - mean_2}{\sqrt{\left(\dfrac{1}{n_1} + \dfrac{1}{n_2}\right) \times MS_{error}}} \tag{18.1}$$

where $mean_1$ is the mean for one of the conditions (condition 1), $mean_2$ is the mean for the other condition (condition 2), n_1 is the sample size of the group producing $mean_1$, n_2 is the sample size of the group producing $mean_2$ and MS_{error} is the mean square for the appropriate error term in the original F-ratio.

The simplification occurs because the contrast requires the weighting for $mean_1$ to be 1 and the weighting for $mean_2$ to be −1, with the weighting for any other mean of 0; try putting these weightings into the original equation and see the effect.

When a pairwise contrast is being made and there are equal numbers of participants in the two groups, the equation simplifies further to:

$$t = \frac{mean_1 - mean_2}{\sqrt{\left(\dfrac{2}{n}\right) \times MS_{error}}} \tag{18.2}$$

where n is the sample size of the group producing one of the means.

An illustration of a pairwise contrast is given in Chapter 18. I will illustrate a non-pairwise contrast, here. As an example I am using the memory experiment (introduced in Chapters 9 and 16) in which participants were given one of three conditions: a control condition under which they were given no training, a group in which they were trained to use pegwords as a mnemonic strategy and a group in which they were trained to use the method of loci (Tables A9.1 and A9.2). There were 10 participants in each group.

TABLE A9.1   Means and SDs of word recall for the three memory conditions

	Control	Pegword	Loci
Mean	7.2	8.9	9.6
SD	1.62	1.91	1.58

TABLE A9.2   The summary table for the one-way between-subjects ANOVA on the recall data

Source	Sum of squares	df	Mean square	F	p
Between groups	30.467	2	15.233	5.213	.0122
Within groups	78.9	27	2.922		
Total	109.367	29			

If we wished to compare the two mnemonic techniques with the control condition, we would have the following figures:

$mean_1$ (control) = 7.2
$mean_2$ (pegwords) = 8.9

$\text{mean}_3 \text{ (loci)} = 9.6$
$n_1 = n_2 = n_3 = 10$
$MS_{error} = 2.922$

Next we have to find the weightings, with the restriction that they must add up to zero. Thus, we could multiply mean_1 by 2, mean_2 by -1 and mean_3 by -1. This is the equivalent of contrasting the control group with the mean of the other two groups; the same result would have been found if we had used weightings of 1, $-\dfrac{1}{2}$ and $-\dfrac{1}{2}$.

Therefore:

$$\text{weight}_1 + \text{weight}_2 + \text{weight}_3 = 2 + (-1) + (-1)$$
$$= 0$$

The restriction that the sum of the weights equals zero (i.e. $\Sigma w_j = 0$, where w_j is the weighting for a particular mean) is only true when the sample sizes are the same for the different groups. When the sample sizes are not the same the restriction is that $\Sigma(n_j \times w_j) = 0$, where n_j is the size of each sample. See Appendix XIX for a description of how to calculate the coefficients when the sample sizes are unequal.

Using the first equation (A9.1),

$$t = \frac{\Sigma(w_j \times \bar{x}_j)}{\sqrt{MS_{error} \times \Sigma \dfrac{w_j^2}{n_j}}}$$

$$= \frac{(w_1 \times \bar{x}_1) + (w_2 \times \bar{x}_2) + (w_3 \times \bar{x}_3)}{\sqrt{MS_{error} \times \left(\dfrac{w_1^2}{n_1} + \dfrac{w_2^2}{n_2} + \dfrac{w_3^2}{n_3}\right)}}$$

$$= \frac{(2 \times 7.2) + (-1 \times 8.9) + (-1 \times 9.6)}{\sqrt{2.922 \times \left(\dfrac{2^2}{10} + \dfrac{(-1)^2}{10} + \dfrac{(-1)^2}{10}\right)}}$$

$$= \frac{14.4 - 8.9 - 9.6}{\sqrt{2.922 \times \left(\dfrac{4}{10} + \dfrac{1}{10} + \dfrac{1}{10}\right)}}$$

$$= \frac{-4.1}{\sqrt{2.922 \times 0.6}}$$

$$= \frac{-4.1}{\sqrt{1.7532}}$$

$$= \frac{-4.1}{1.32408}$$

$$= -3.096$$

How we test the significance of this result depends on whether the contrast was planned and whether it was the only contrast, one of only a few contrasts or one of many. If it was a planned contrast or only a few unplanned contrasts, then we can use Bonferroni's test (based on Bonferroni's adjustment). However, if it is one unplanned contrast of many we are conducting, we will need to use Scheffé's test. The latter is dealt with in the next section.

Alternative versions of Scheffé's test

Method 1

Scheffé's test is sometimes given as a t-value and sometimes as an F-ratio. However, all versions will give the same protection against a Type I error. I gave one version in Chapter 18. This entailed finding the critical F-ratio which would have made the original treatment F-ratio statistically significant. In the mnemonic example, the appropriate degrees of freedom (df), necessary to read the F-table in Appendix XVII, are 2 and 27. For statistical significance at $\alpha = .05$, F would need to be at least 3.35. To find the critical level which t would need to achieve, we use the following equation:

$$\text{critical t} = \sqrt{df_{treatment} \times F(df_{treatment}, df_{error})}$$
$$= \sqrt{2 \times 3.35}$$
$$= \sqrt{6.7}$$
$$= 2.588$$

As F-tables do not give negative values we can say that t has to be equal to or greater than ± 2.588 (plus or minus 2.588).

As the t-value we obtained is larger in absolute terms, at -3.096, than the critical value, we can conclude that the control condition produced significantly poorer recall than the two mnemonic conditions.

Method 2

This method is based very closely on the previous one. We can square the t-value which we calculated from the contrast and this is an F-ratio (remember that $(t_{27})^2 = F_{1,27}$), and we can find a critical F-ratio from:

$$\text{critical } F = df_{treatment} \times F(df_{treatment}, df_{error})$$

which, in this case, means that the F-ratio for the contrast is $(-3.096)^2 = 9.585$ and the critical F-ratio is 6.7. Once again the contrast produces a larger value for the statistic than the critical value.

Method 3

In this method the critical F-ratio is simply the critical F-ratio given for the original treatment F-ratio, which, with 2 and 27 df, for $\alpha = .05$ we have already found to be 3.35. However, because we have arrived at the critical F-ratio in a different way, we need to adjust the F-ratio which we calculated for the contrast. Those of you familiar with algebra will see why the adjustment is made:

$$\text{calculated } F = \frac{(t \text{ for contrast})^2}{df \text{ for treatment}}$$
$$= \frac{(3.096)^2}{2}$$
$$= \frac{9.585}{2}$$
$$= 4.793$$

Once again the calculated value is larger than the critical one.

Method 4

Following the same reasoning that took us from method 1 to method 2 (or rather the reverse of it), we can say that method 3 can have a version which involves a *t*-value rather than an *F*-value. Therefore the critical *t* would be the square root of the critical *F* for the treatment:

$$\text{critical } t = \sqrt{3.35}$$
$$= 1.83$$

We now need to take the square root of the calculated *F*-ratio from method 3. Therefore the calculated *t* is:

$$= \sqrt{\frac{(\text{original } t \text{ for contrast})^2}{\text{df for treatment}}}$$

which is the equivalent of:

$$= \frac{\text{original } t \text{ for contrast}}{\sqrt{\text{df for treatment}}}$$
$$= \frac{3.096}{\sqrt{2}}$$
$$= 2.189$$

which is, once again, larger than the critical value. Of the four methods, methods 1 and 2 seem the most straightforward and, as so many of the contrast tests are based on the same equation for the *t*-test, method 1 is the most consistent with other tests.

Pairwise contrast tests

As stated in Chapter 18, the equations for *t* for contrasts are only appropriate in between-subjects designs when the variances in the subgroups are homogeneous. If the largest variance is less than four times the smallest variance (and the subsamples are the same size), then we can treat the variances as sufficiently homogeneous. However, if the variances are more disparate than this, then the *t*-test for independent variances (Welch's *t*), given in Appendix VI, should be used. Within-subjects designs have a different problem, in that they should have sphericity (see Chapter 16 and Appendix VII). Therefore, to be on the safe side, and consistent with most computer programs, you are advised to use the equation for the standard within-subjects *t*-test as the equation for the contrast.

In both the heterogeneous variance case and the within-subjects case, when looking up the critical value of *t* for a contrast, use the df which is used for the version of *t*-test you have computed. In the case of the within-subjects design this will be one fewer than the number of participants. In the independent variances case it will necessitate using the equation for df given in Appendix VI.

Tukey's HSD

In Chapter 18, I found the critical t-value for Tukey's *HSD* by looking in the appropriate table in Appendix XVII (Table A17.13a). The figures in that table were derived from another table which is used to find the critical t-value for a number of contrasts, the studentised range statistic, which is also given in Appendix XVII (Table A17.14). Here I will demonstrate the use of q with Tukey's *HSD*. Look up the critical q for the number of means involved in the contrasts and the error df (or df for the t-test, in within-subjects designs and independent variance cases). Place the value found for q in the following equation:

$$\text{critical } t = \frac{q}{\sqrt{2}} \qquad\qquad\qquad (A9.2)$$

In Tukey's *HSD* this critical value is used to assess all the calculated t-values in the family of contrasts. With three means to be contrasted and df = 27, the critical q is 3.51. Therefore,

$$\begin{aligned}
\text{critical } t &= \frac{3.51}{\sqrt{2}} \\
&= \frac{3.51}{1.4142} \\
&= 2.482
\end{aligned}$$

Newman–Keuls test

This test follows a similar principle to Tukey's *HSD* test. In Tukey's *HSD* test the calculated t had to reach a critical value, which was based on the number of means which were to be involved in the set (or family) of contrasts.

In the Newman–Keuls test, the means are set out in order of size and the t-value depends on the number of means apart that are involved in the particular contrast – their range. For example, we would place the three means from the mnemonic experiment in the order:

Control	Pegword	Loci
7.2	8.9	9.6

The comparison between loci and control means ranges across three means (including the two means in the contrast) and so we would again look for q with three means in the table of the studentised range statistic in Appendix XVII. We would then put that figure into equation A9.2 to find the critical t-value. This would produce the same value as was found using Tukey's *HSD* (i.e. 2.482).

To use the Newman–Keuls test for the comparison of control mean with pegword mean, and pegword mean with loci mean, then, in both cases the means range across only two means. Therefore, we do not need to use q to find the critical value of t; we can use the standard t-tables, with df = 27. Here the critical value of t is 2.052.

Tukey's *HSD* can be seen as rather conservative and therefore lacking power in comparison with the Newman–Keuls test. On the other hand, the Newman–Keuls test can be too liberal and therefore liable to commit a Type I error if used to test contrasts among more than three means.

Tukey's wholly significant difference (WSD)

This test can be seen as a compromise between the Tukey's HSD and the Newman–Keuls test. To find the critical value for Tukey's *WSD*, take the mean of the critical *t* for Tukey's *HSD* and the critical *t* for Newman–Keuls. Thus, for the contrasts involving two means (control vs pegword and pegword vs loci), the critical *t* using Tukey's *WSD* is:

$$\text{critical } t = \frac{2.482 + 2.052}{2}$$
$$= 2.267$$

Fisher's protected least significant difference (PLSD)

This is probably the most liberal test of all and, for that reason, it is often not recommended. However, there is a restriction on this test in that it should not be conducted unless the relevant *F*-ratio from the ANOVA is statistically significant. Once this criterion has been passed, look up the critical *t* in standard *t*-tables, with the df for the error term, and compare each calculated *t* by the usual equation for pairwise contrasts. Therefore, in the present case, the critical *t* is 2.052. Thus, this test does not take into account the number of contrasts and so, despite its initial restriction, it is not advisable to use it with more than three contrasts.

Orthogonality

As stated above, in each contrast when the sample sizes are equal, the sum of the weightings must equal zero, i.e. $\Sigma w_j = 0$.

It has been suggested in the past by statisticians that the comparisons which are made should be independent of each other because we are trying to find out how much of the overall sum of squares for the treatment is accounted for by the contrasts. Each treatment sum of squares can be broken down into the same number of independent contrasts as there are df for the treatment. In the memory example there are 2 df for the treatment and therefore there are two independent contrasts which can be made. If the contrasts are independent, then they are described as being orthogonal.

If they are orthogonal (and the sample sizes are equal), then:

$$\Sigma(w_{ja} \times w_{jb}) = 0$$

where *j* refers to the mean for which the weighting is appropriate and *a* and *b* are two different contrasts. If the sample sizes are not equal, then:

$$\Sigma(n_j \times w_{ja} \times w_{jb}) = 0$$

where n_j is the sample size which produced mean *j*.

To explain the equation, when the sample sizes are the same, I will use an example (Table A9.3). The mnemonic treatment will only allow two orthogonal (independent) contrasts (there are three levels of the IV and therefore 2 df in the original *F*-ratio; accordingly, for the set of contrasts to be orthogonal, there can only be two of them in the set). The first contrast in the table would be comparing the mean for pegwords with the mean for loci. Notice that we could not do simple pairwise comparisons between all the means and maintain orthogonal weightings.

TABLE A9.3   The weightings for a set of orthogonal contrasts, when sample sizes are the same

Weighting	Treatment Control	Pegword	Loci	Sum
w_{j1}	$w_{11} = 0$	$w_{21} = 1$	$w_{31} = -1$	0
w_{j2}	$w_{12} = 2$	$w_{22} = -1$	$w_{32} = -1$	0
	$w_{11} \times w_{12} = 0$	$w_{21} \times w_{22} = -1$	$w_{31} \times w_{32} = 1$	0

Non-parametric tests

At least ordinal data

Between-subjects designs: following a Kruskal–Wallis ANOVA

In Chapter 16 and Appendix VII, an example was given in which 24 college lecturers were each given an essay to mark and they were told that the writer of the essay was a male student or was a female student, or they were not given any indication of the student's gender. In fact, the same essay was given to all the lecturers. Each lecturer gave the essay a grade between C– and A+, which was converted to a numerical grade ranging from 1 to 9. The test I am going to explain should only be used if the initial Kruskal–Wallis test is statistically significant and if at least five people were used in each group. However, although the result was not statistically significant I am going to use that example to illustrate the technique.

In calculating the Kruskal–Wallis test a rank is given to each grade. In Appendix VII it was shown that the three conditions had the total ranks shown in Table A9.4, from which the mean ranks (out of eight participants) have been derived.

TABLE A9.4   The total and mean ranks of the grades given by participants for an essay depending on the presumed gender of its author

	'Gender' of author		
	Female	*Neutral*	*Male*
Total rank (R)	76.5	110	113.5
Mean rank ($\bar{R}$)	9.5625	13.75	14.1875

The difference between two of the mean ranks can be tested by z-test:

$$z = \frac{\bar{R}_1 - \bar{R}_2}{\sqrt{\left[\frac{N \times (N+1)}{12}\right] \times \left(\frac{1}{n_1} + \frac{1}{n_2}\right)}}$$

where N is the total sample size and n_1 and n_2 are the sizes of the two subsamples in the contrast. Therefore, if we compare the male and female essay conditions,

$$z = \frac{14.1875 - 9.5625}{\sqrt{\left(\frac{24 \times 25}{12}\right) \times \left(\frac{1}{8} + \frac{1}{8}\right)}}$$

$$= \frac{4.625}{\sqrt{50 \times \frac{1}{4}}}$$

$$= \frac{4.625}{\sqrt{12.5}}$$

$$= \frac{4.625}{3.53553}$$

$$= 1.308$$

However, we need to adjust the α-level to take account of the number of conditions which are to be contrasted. The adjustment is:

$$\text{adjusted } \alpha = \frac{\alpha}{k \times (k-1)}$$

where k is the number of levels of the IV.

Thus, if we set α for the family of three contrasts at .05, then, to be statistically significant, each contrast will have to have a probability of:

$$\text{adjusted } \alpha = \frac{.05}{3 \times 2} = .0083$$

The probabilities shown in z-tables are for one-tailed tests. Therefore if we were looking for a z which produced a two-tailed probability of .05, we would usually look for the z which produced a one-tailed probability of .025 or $\frac{\alpha}{2}$. In the present case, we are making an adjustment which takes into account the number of pairwise contrasts which will be made. The number of pairwise contrasts which can be made from the k levels of an IV will always be $\frac{k \times (k-1)}{2}$. To make the adjustment we will divide the probability we desire for the family of contrasts by the number of possible contrasts. In other words, we divide $\frac{\alpha}{2}$ by $\frac{k \times (k-1)}{2}$. Via algebra this becomes $\frac{\alpha}{k \times (k-1)}$. Therefore, we can find the appropriate critical z-value which would produce this two-tailed probability by looking up a *one-tailed* z-value in the z-tables in Appendix XVII. This tells us that the critical z is 2.395, which is more than the calculated z and so the contrast is not significant.

Correction for ties

As with the Kruskal–Wallis test, when some scores are the same, there is a more accurate version of the test which adjusts for ties. In the present example, there were five places where the grades tied, and the working in Appendix VII showed that the total correction was 894.

$$
\begin{aligned}
z \text{ (corrected for ties)} &= \frac{\bar{R}_1 - \bar{R}_2}{\sqrt{\left[\left[\frac{N \times (N+1)}{12}\right] - \left[\frac{\text{total correction}}{12 \times (N-1)}\right]\right] \times \left\{\frac{1}{n_1} + \frac{1}{n_2}\right\}}} \\[2mm]
&= \frac{14.1875 - 9.5625}{\sqrt{\left[\left(\frac{24 \times 25}{12}\right) - \left(\frac{894}{12 \times 23}\right)\right] \times \left(\frac{1}{8} + \frac{1}{8}\right)}} \\[2mm]
&= \frac{4.625}{\sqrt{(50 - 3.23913) \times \frac{1}{4}}} \\[2mm]
&= \frac{4.625}{\sqrt{11.69022}} \\[2mm]
&= \frac{4.625}{3.41909} \\[2mm]
&= 1.353
\end{aligned}
$$

This value is still less than the critical value for z and so we cannot conclude that there is a difference in the way the lecturers rated the essay when they thought it was written by a male than when they thought it was written by a female.

Within-subjects designs: following a Friedman two-way ANOVA

An example was given in Chapter 16 and Appendix VII, in which researchers wished to see whether a group of seven students rated a particular course differently as they spent more time on it. Each student was asked to rate the course on a 7-point scale ranging from *not enjoyable at all* to *very enjoyable*, on three occasions: after 1 week, after 5 weeks and after 10 weeks (Table A9.5).

TABLE A9.5   The total and mean ranks for the ratings given to the course

	Week of the course		
	1	5	10
Total rank (R)	10	14.5	17.5
Mean rank ($\bar{R}$)	1.42857	2.07143	2.5

The test for the pairwise comparison of levels of the IV follows the same principles as for the between-subjects design, in that it should only be conducted if the initial ANOVA was statistically significant, and, as long as the sample size is at least 15, there is a z-test, the value of which can be compared with a critical z-value which adjusts the α-level to take account of the number of comparisons being conducted. The z-test is derived from:

$$z = \frac{\bar{R}_1 - \bar{R}_2}{\sqrt{\frac{k \times (k+1)}{n \times 6}}}$$

where k is the number of levels of the IV – in this case, 3; and $\bar{R}_1$ and $\bar{R}_2$ are the mean ranks for the two levels of the IV which are being compared. (There is a version of the test which is based on the total ranks rather than the mean ranks, but I am using the present version so as to be consistent with the between-subjects analysis given previously.)

In the present case:

$$z = \frac{2.5 - 1.42857}{\sqrt{\frac{3 \times 4}{7 \times 6}}}$$

$$= \frac{1.07143}{\sqrt{0.2857}}$$

$$= 2.005$$

Following the same principles for finding the critical z-value as given previously for between-subjects design, with three levels of the IV, the critical z is 2.395, which is more than the calculated z. Accordingly, we cannot conclude that the students' opinions of the course changed between its first and tenth week.

There does not appear to be a correction for ties with this test.

Categorical data

When analysing a contingency table which is more than a 2 × 2 table, it is possible to conduct further analysis by *partitioning* the contingency table into a number of 2 × 2 subtables. The example I am giving is of a 3 × 2 table. Those wishing to partition a larger table can find details of how to do this in Agresti (2002).

For example, imagine that researchers have looked at the occupations of 100 school leavers: 50 from school A and 50 from school B. They find the pattern shown in Table A9.6.

TABLE A9.6   The occupations of school leavers from two schools

	Full-time	Part-time	Unemployed	Total
School A	10	26	14	50
School B	22	18	10	50
Total	32	44	24	100

The appropriate initial test is a χ^2 contingency test as described in Chapter 15. The researchers conducted the test and found that $\chi^2_{(2)} = 6.621$, $p = .0365$. As this showed that the frequencies for the two schools differed significantly, they decided to find the source of the significance by partitioning the contingency table.

Partitioning of a 2 × k table (where k is the number of columns) involves forming 2 × 2 subtables. As each subtable has 1 df, there are as many subtables which can be made as there were df in the original contingency table. Thus, as in the present case, a 2 × 3 table has df = 2 and so there are two partitions which can be made of this table. Table A9.7 shows codes for each of the cells in Table A9.6, while Tables A9.8 and A9.10 show the two partitions of the table using those codes and Tables A9.9 and A9.11 show the resulting numbers. A χ^2 can be conducted on each partition. Further details of the version I am going to give are contained in Agresti (2002), which also shows how to partition a table which has more than two rows. (An alternative approach is given by Siegel and Castellan, 1988.)

TABLE A9.7   A coding of the cells from Table A9.6

	Full-time	Part-time	Unemployed
School A	a	b	c
School B	d	e	f

The first partition involves the data in the first two columns.

TABLE A9.8   The cells involved in the first partition of the data in Table A9.6

	Full-time	Part-time
School A	a	b
School B	d	e

TABLE A9.9   The first partition of the original contingency table

	Full-time	Part-time
School A	10	26
School B	22	18

From this we can calculate a χ^2 value by using the usual equation (A5.1). From this we find $\chi^2_{(1)}$ = 5.760, p = .016.

The second partition entails combining parts of the first partition and reintroducing the missing column from the original contingency table.

TABLE A9.10   The elements in the second partition of the data in Table A9.6

	Full-time or part-time	Unemployed
School A	a + b	c
School B	d + e	f

TABLE A9.11   The data for the second partition of Table A9.6

	Full-time or part-time	Unemployed
School A	36	14
School B	40	10

Applying equation A5.1 to these data we find $\chi^2_{(1)}$ = 0.877, p = .349.

From these two partitions we can see that schools A and B differed significantly in the proportions who were in full- and part-time employment, while the schools did not differ significantly in the proportions who were in some form of employment.

We can check that the different partitions are independent of each other and therefore form an appropriate set of partitions. However, this involves introducing a new version of χ^2: the likelihood-ratio χ^2 (sometimes shown as G^2).

Likelihood-ratio χ^2

$$\text{Likelihood-ration } \chi^2 = 2 \times \sum \left[\text{obs} \times \ln\left(\frac{\text{obs}}{\text{exp}} \right) \right]$$

where, as usual in such tests: obs is the observed frequency; exp is the expected frequency if the variables are unrelated; and ln refers to the natural (or Napierian) log.

Table A9.12 shows the expected frequencies for the data in Table A9.11 if school and nature of employment are not related.

TABLE A9.12   The expected frequencies for the second partition of Table A9.6

	Full-time or part-time	Unemployed
School A	38	12
School B	38	12

From the information in Tables A9.11 and A9.12, the likelihood-ratio χ^2 is:

$$2 \times \left[\left(36 \times \ln\left(\frac{36}{38} \right) \right) + \left(14 \times \ln\left(\frac{14}{12} \right) \right) + \left(40 \times \ln\left(\frac{40}{38} \right) \right) + \left(\times \ln\left(\frac{10}{12} \right) \right) \right]$$
$$= 2 \times [(-1.9464) + (2.1581) + (2.0517) + (-1.8232)]$$
$$= 0.8804$$

The advantage of referring to the likelihood-ratio χ^2 is that if it is calculated for each of the partitions of the original contingency table, then the sum of those values should equal the value for the original contingency table. Fortunately, you probably won't have to calculate the likelihood-ratio χ^2 by hand as it should be available in the statistical package you use; SPSS reports it automatically when you run the more usual χ^2.

The likelihood-ratio χ^2 for the data in Table A9.6 is 6.7443. For the first partition it is 5.8639; 5.8639 + 0.8804 = 6.7443. Therefore the partitions are independent of each other.

Trend tests

In Chapter 18 an example was given of participants drinking either one, two or three units of alcohol and then having their reaction times recorded; there were eight participants in each group.

TABLE A9.13 The means and *SD*s of reaction times by number of units of alcohol consumed

	Units of alcohol consumed		
	1	2	3
Mean	151.25	163.38	168.75
SD	14.12	10.53	12.94

FIGURE A9.1 Mean reaction times (in tenths of seconds), with *SD*s, by number of units of alcohol consumed

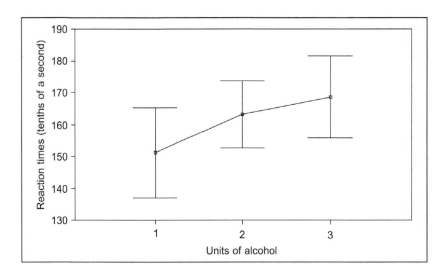

The means form a pattern such that the more alcohol consumed, the longer is the reaction time (Figure A9.1). However, they do not form a completely straight line. The summary table from the preliminary ANOVA for the data is Table A9.14.

TABLE A9.14 Summary table of the between-subjects ANOVA on the effects of alcohol on reaction times

Source	Sum of squares	df	Mean square	F	p
Between groups	1285.750	2	642.875	4.039	.0328
Within groups	3342.875	21	159.185		
Total	4628.625	23			

The general equation for a trend analysis

For trend analysis you create a sum of squares for the given trend you are testing according to the following equation:

$$SS_{trend} = \frac{\left[\sum\left(c_j \times \bar{x}_j\right)\right]^2}{\sum\left(\dfrac{c_j^2}{n_j}\right)} \tag{A9.2}$$

where $\bar{x}_j$ is a mean for one of the treatments, c_j is the coefficient for $\bar{x}_j$ and will depend on the nature of the contrast, and n_j is the number of scores which contributed to $\bar{x}_j$.

When the subsamples are the same size, the equation simplifies to:

$$SS_{trend} = \frac{n \times [\sum(c_j \times \bar{x}_j)]^2}{\sum(c_j^2)} \tag{A9.3}$$

where n is the number of participants in one group.

Each trend has its own set of coefficients and, because the idea is to split up the treatment sum of squares into its component parts, they should be orthogonal. Appendix XIX provides the coefficients for some trend tests.

Each trend test has 1 df. Therefore, as the mean square for the trend (MS_{trend}) is found from

$$MS_{trend} = \frac{SS_{trend}}{df_{trend}} = \frac{SS_{trend}}{1}$$

it is the same as the SS_{trend}.

An F-ratio for the trend is found from

$$\text{trend F - ratio} = \frac{MS_{trend}}{MS_{error}}$$

and the F-ratio has df = 1 for MS_{trend} and the df from the original error term in the ANOVA for the error. Thus, in the present example the df are 1 and 21. The probability of the F-ratio for the trend can then be found from standard F-tables.

A trend analysis is, in fact, an example of a contrast test. In keeping with convention, I have referred to *coefficients* when talking about trend analysis. They are performing the same role as the weightings which are referred to in the description of contrast testing. In this particular example, the test for the linear trend across the alcohol levels would be the same as a pairwise contrast between the one-unit and three-unit conditions, because the coefficient for two units is 0 in the trend test. However, the trend test will produce an F-ratio, while the contrast produces a t-value. Remember, though, that when, in an F-ratio, the treatment df = 1, then $t = \sqrt{F}$. In the present example, the F-ratio for the linear trend was 7.695, in which case $t = 2.774$. Try using equation 18.1 to check that the pairwise contrast between one unit and three units produces the same result.

Adjustment for unequal intervals

In the preceding example the levels of the IV (units of alcohol) went up by a regular amount (1 unit at a time). If the units do not go up by a regular amount – for example, if they were 1, 3, 7 and 15 units – then the coefficients need to be adjusted accordingly. Appendix XIX shows how to calculate coefficients when the intervals between the levels are unequal.

Appendix X

Correlation and reliability

This appendix illustrates the techniques introduced in Chapter 19.

Non-parametric correlation – at least ordinal data

The example was given in Chapter 19 of researchers wishing to investigate the relationship between the length of time students had studied psychology and the degree to which they believed that psychology is a science (Table A10.1). Eleven psychology students were asked how long they had studied psychology and were asked to rate, on a 5-point scale, ranging from 1 = *not at all* to 5 = *definitely a science*, their beliefs about whether psychology is a science.

TABLE A10.1   The length of time students have studied psychology and their opinion of whether it is a science

Participant	Years studied psychology	Rating of psychology as a science
1	1	1
2	2	1
3	3	2
4	4	3
5	5	4
6	1	3
7	2	3
8	3	2
9	4	5
10	5	5
11	6	5

Both Spearman's rho and Kendall's tau can be calculated by converting the scores, within a variable, to ranks, though this isn't essential for Kendall's tau (Table A10.2). As usual in such tests, scores which have the same value (ties) are given a mean rank; see the explanation for the Wilcoxon signed rank test for matched pairs in Appendix VI.

TABLE A10.2   The years spent studying psychology and the opinion over whether psychology is a science, plus rankings

Year	Rating	Rank of year	Rank of rating	Difference between rankings (d)	d^2
1	1	1.5	1.5	0	0
2	1	3.5	1.5	2	4
3	2	5.5	3.5	2	4
4	3	7.5	6	1.5	2.25
5	4	9.5	8	1.5	2.25
1	3	1.5	6	−4.5	20.25
2	3	3.5	6	−2.5	6.25
3	2	5.5	3.5	2	4
4	5	7.5	10	−2.5	6.25
5	5	9.5	10	−0.5	0.25
6	5	11	10	1	1
				Total	50.50

Spearman's rho

There are two versions of Spearman's rho. One is very straightforward but does not correct for tied ranks. The other corrects for tied ranks and is therefore more accurate when ties are present. The method for calculating the uncorrected version is shown here. The version which corrects for ties can be found by calculating Pearson's product moment correlation on the ranks of the data. It can also be found by a laborious modification of the uncorrected version. Therefore, in the absence of a computer I would only use the following technique when there are no ties. However, to illustrate its use I have calculated the uncorrected rho for the data in Table A10.1. The equation to use for rho when there are no ties is:

$$rho = 1 - \frac{6 \times (\text{sum of } d^2)}{n^3 - n}$$

where n is the sample size.
    Therefore:

$$rho = 1 - \frac{6 \times 50.5}{(11)^3 - 11}$$

$$rho = 1 - \frac{303}{1331 - 11}$$

$$= 1 - 0.22955$$

$$= .77$$

Testing the statistical significance of Spearman's rho

In Chapter 19 the value of rho, corrected for ties, of .762, was given for the correlation between the years students had spent studying psychology and their attitudes to psychology as a science.
    When the sample is not more than 100, the table for probabilities of rho given in Appendix XVII can be used. When the sample is above 100 there is an equation which converts rho to a t-value.

$$t = rho \times \sqrt{\frac{n-2}{1-(rho)^2}} \tag{A10.1}$$

The statistical significance of the result can be checked by standard t-tables with $n - 2$ degrees of freedom (df), where n is the sample size.
    Alternatively, although less accurate, if you have access to more exact values for z, use the z-approximation

$$z = rho \times \sqrt{(n-1)} \tag{A10.2}$$

and look up the probability in standard z-tables.

Kendall's tau

To reanalyse the data from the previous example using Kendall's tau, we do not, in fact, need to convert the scores to ranks; however, the same result is achieved whether ranks or the original scores are used.
    Kendall's tau can be calculated in a number of ways and some of them are quicker than the one I am going to show but they become complicated when there are ties on both variables. The method I am using is applicable to all situations.
    To calculate tau we first need to draw up a table which has the values from one variable, in numerical order, along the width of the table and the values of the other variable, also in numerical order, along the height of the table. The value of each pair of scores is then shown in the table by being placed in the

appropriate cell, with the number of pairs which have the same value shown: e.g. the two students who had studied for 3 years and given the course a rating of 2 (Table A10.3).

TABLE A10.3   The data from Table A10.1 recast into a table for initial analysis of Kendall's tau

			Rating given to course		
Years on course	1	2	3	4	5
1	1		1		
2	1		1		
3		2			
4			1		1
5				1	1
6					1

We now take each entry in the table, starting in the top left-hand corner, and note how many entries are below and to the right of that target cell, i.e. how many entries are in a position which is consistent with a positive correlation (Table A10.4).

TABLE A10.4   The data from Table A10.1 recast into a table for initial analysis of Kendall's tau, showing the area to the right and below the first cell in the table

			Rating given to course		
Years on course	1	2	3	4	5
1	1		1		
2	1		1		
3		2			
4			1		1
5				1	1
6					1

Add the numbers which are in the cells below and to the right of the cell; in the first case they are, taken row by row: 1, 2, 1, 1, 1, 1, 1 = 8. Then multiply this sum by the number in the target cell, which in this case is 1. We do this for each entry in the table and add the results together to find the number of entries in the correct order (S_+). Thus,

$$S_+ = (1 \times 8) + (1 \times 4) + (1 \times 7) + (1 \times 4) + (2 \times 5) + (1 \times 3) + (1 \times 1) = 37$$

Now we need to find the number of entries which are not in the correct order (S_-). To do this we take each entry in the table and count how many are below and to the left of that target entry and multiply the result by the number in the target entry. Thus,

$$S_- = (1 \times 3) + (1 \times 2) + (1 \times 1) = 6$$

We can now find tau from the following equation:

$$tau = \frac{2 \times [(S_+) - (S_-)]}{n \times (n-1)}$$

where n is the sample size.
Therefore:

$$tau = \frac{2 \times (37 - 6)}{11 \times 10}$$

$$= \frac{62}{110}$$

$$= .564$$

Tied observations

As with Spearman's rho there is an adjustment for ties. To calculate this it is necessary to find a correction factor to allow for the ties in each of the variables (Table A10.5).

TABLE A10.5   Obtaining the correction factors for Kendall's tau

	Years on course			Rating of course	
Rank	Number in tie (t)	$t \times (t - 1)$	Rank	Number in tie (t)	$t \times (t - 1)$
1.5	2	2	1.5	2	2
3.5	2	2	3.5	2	2
5.5	2	2	6	3	6
7.5	2	2	10	3	6
9.5	2	2			
	Total (correction for Var$_a$) 10			Total (correction for Var$_b$)	16

The equation for tau corrected for ties is:

$$tau = \frac{2 \times [(S_+) - (S_-)]}{\sqrt{[n \times (n-1)] - \text{correction for Var}_a} \times \sqrt{[n \times (n-1)] - \text{correction for Var}_b}}$$

$$= \frac{2 \times (37 - 6)}{\sqrt{(11 \times 10) - 10} \times \sqrt{(11 \times 10) - 16}}$$

$$= \frac{62}{\sqrt{100} \times \sqrt{94}}$$

$$= \frac{62}{10 \times 9.69536}$$

$$= .639$$

The probability of tau

As with Spearman's rho there is an approximation to the normal distribution for Kendall's tau. However, Kendall's tau has the advantage that this approximation is accurate for smaller sample sizes. Thus, if the sample is 10 or fewer, then use the appropriate table in Appendix XVII. Above this sample size use the z-approximation:

$$z = \frac{3 \times \text{tau} \times \sqrt{n \times (n-1)}}{\sqrt{2 \times [(2 \times n) + 5]}} \tag{A10.3}$$

where n is the size of the sample. The probability of this z-value can be found in standard z-tables. Therefore,

$$z = \frac{3 \times .639 \times \sqrt{110}}{\sqrt{2 \times (22 + 5)}}$$

$$= \frac{1.917 \times 10.48809}{\sqrt{54}}$$

$$= \frac{20.10567}{7.34847}$$

$$= 2.74$$

Partial correlation

As was pointed out in Chapter 19, partial correlation is the correlation between two variables with the possible influence of a third variable (or more variables) on the two original variables, taken out of the relationship. An example was given of the relationship between mathematical ability and ability at English with age taken out. This gave the partial correlation: $r_{\text{me.a}} = .723$.

Higher-order partial correlation

We can remove the possible influences of more than one variable on the relationship between two variables: for example, if we wished to remove the possible influences of age and socio-economic status (SES) from the relationship between mathematical ability and English ability.

$$r_{\text{me.as}} = \frac{r_{\text{me.a}} - (r_{\text{ms.a}} \times r_{\text{es.a}})}{\sqrt{(1 - r_{\text{ms.a}}^2) \times (1 - r_{\text{es.a}}^2)}}$$

where $r_{\text{me.a}}$ is the partial correlation between maths and English with age partialled out, $r_{\text{ms.a}}$ is the partial correlation of maths and SES with age partialled out and $r_{\text{es.a}}$ is the partial correlation between English and SES with age partialled out.

Method for calculating the probability of partial r

Appendix XVII gives the equation for calculating a t-value in order to find the probability of a Pearson's product moment correlation coefficient r (when the Null Hypothesis is that $\rho = 0$). The equation can be extended to encompass partial correlations, with the same Null Hypothesis:

$$t = \frac{r \times \sqrt{n - 2 - \text{order}}}{\sqrt{1 - r^2}}$$

where r is the correlation coefficient or partial correlation coefficient, n is the sample size and order is the order of the partial correlation. If we partial one variable out, then the order = 1; if we partial out two variables, as in the preceding example where age and SES are partialled out, then the order = 2; when it is a normal correlation, rather than a partial correlation, then the order = 0. (You will sometimes see reference made to a *zero-order correlation*. This means a bivariate correlation with no variables partialled out.) In each case, the df of the *t*-test are df = $(n - 2 - \text{order})$.

The difference between two correlation coefficients

Chapter 19 contained an explanation of how to compare two correlation coefficients to see whether they differ significantly from each other. However, the example given there was restricted to the situation where the two coefficients are from data from separate samples of people – independent groups. A more complex calculation is involved when the two correlation coefficients are from the same sample – non-independent samples. These procedures come from a paper by Steiger (1980) in which the merits of alternative procedures are discussed.

Non-independent groups

There are two different situations in which we might want to compare two correlations which come from the same people. One is where we have correlated one measure with a second measure and we have also correlated the first measure with a third measure (Table A10.6). For example, we might relate IQ to mathematical ability and IQ to musical ability and then compare the two correlations to see whether one of the abilities is more closely related to IQ than the other.

The second situation is where we have four measures and we wish to compare the correlations of pairs of them (Table A10.7). Imagine that we select a group of children and we ask each child to estimate how many words he or she will be able to remember from a list of 20 words. We then give each child a list of words to remember and then test his or her recall. We can correlate the two measures to find out whether there is a relationship between the estimate and the actual scores. We then train each child in a number of mnemonic techniques, such as grouping related words together. We then test the estimates and actual memories again, and correlate them. We could compare the two correlations to see whether there has been a change in the relationship between estimated and actual memory.

In both situations, as long as the sample size is greater than 20, we can compare the correlations.

In both of the preceding cases, because we are using the same participants we need to take account of the other intercorrelations between the variables. This makes the calculations appear daunting. In fact they are long-winded and require you to be very careful but they are not particularly complicated.

The first situation

TABLE A10.6   The correlation matrix for three variables

Variable	Variable 1	2	3
1	1		
2	r_{21}	1	
3	r_{31}	r_{32}	1

If we wished to compare the correlation between variables 1 and 2 (r_{21}) with that of variables 1 and 3 (r_{31}), then, firstly, we need to find what is called the *determinant* of this matrix; this is shown as $|R|$, where

$$|R| = [1 - (r_{21})^2 - (r_{31})^2 - (r_{32})^2] + (2 \times r_{21} \times r_{31} \times r_{32})$$

Next we need to find the mean of the two correlations which we are comparing:

$$\bar{r} = \frac{r_{21} + r_{31}}{2}$$

We can now find a *t*-value which has $n - 3$ df, where n is the sample size:

$$t_{(n-3)} = (r_{21} - r_{31}) \times \sqrt{\frac{(n-1) \times (1+r_{32})}{\left[2 \times \left(\frac{n-1}{n-3}\right) \times |R|\right] + \left[\bar{r}^2 \times (1-r_{32})^3\right]}}$$

The probability of this *t*-value can be looked up in the *t*-table in Appendix XVII.

The second situation

TABLE A10.7 The correlation matrix for four variables

		Variable		
Variable	1	2	3	4
1	1			
2	r_{21}	1		
3	r_{31}	r_{32}	1	
4	r_{41}	r_{42}	r_{43}	1

If we wished to compare the correlation between variables 1 and 2 (r_{21}) with the correlation between variables 3 and 4 (r_{43}), we first need to find the mean of the two correlations we are comparing ($\bar{r}$), where:

$$\bar{r} = \frac{r_{21} + r_{43}}{2}$$

We then need to find the covariance of r_{21} and r_{43}, which is denoted as $\psi_{12.34}$, where

$$\begin{aligned}
\psi_{12.34} = 0.5 \times \{&([(r_{31} - (\bar{r} \times r_{32})) \times (r_{42} - (r_{32} \times \bar{r}))] \\
&+ [(r_{41} - (r_{31} \times \bar{r})) \times (r_{32} - (\bar{r} \times r_{31}))] \\
&+ [(r_{31} - (r_{41} \times \bar{r})) \times (r_{42} - (\bar{r} \times r_{41}))] \\
&+ (r_{41} - (\bar{r} \times r_{42})) \times (r_{32} - (r_{42} \times \bar{r}))]\}
\end{aligned}$$

We also need to find the Fisher's transformation (r') for both of the correlation coefficients we wish to compare. I will denote them as r'_{21} and r'_{43} (see Appendix XIX for the transformation).

Using these results we find $\bar{s}_{12.34}$ from:

$$\bar{s}_{12.34} = \frac{\psi_{12.34}}{(1 - \bar{r}^2)^2}$$

From these calculations we can find a z-score from:

$$z = (r'_{21} - r'_{43}) \times \left(\frac{\sqrt{n-3}}{\sqrt{2 - (2 \times \bar{s}_{12.34})}} \right)$$

The probability of this z-value can be looked up in the standard z-table in Appendix XVII.

Now you know why computers were invented.

Confidence intervals for r

Having found a correlation coefficient for a sample it is useful to estimate the correlation in the population. One way to do this is to find the confidence interval (CI) for the coefficient: that is, the range of values within which the population parameter (ρ) is likely to lie. Chapter 19 provided an example in which the correlation, in a sample of 30 participants, between actual and estimated memory was $r = .8$.

To find the CI it is necessary to convert r to r', work out the CI for r' and then convert the limits shown back to r-values. The equation is:

$$CI = r' \pm z_{(prob)} \times \frac{1}{\sqrt{n-3}} \qquad (A10.4)$$

where r' is the Fisher's transformation for r, in this case 1.099, $z_{(prob)}$ is the z-value needed to give a particular CI; in the case of 95% confidence level we need to find the z which has one-tailed probability of $p = .025$, i.e. 1.96 (giving a two-tailed probability of $p = .05$), $\frac{1}{\sqrt{n-3}}$ is the standard deviation for r', n is the sample size.

Therefore,

$$CI = 1.099 \pm 1.96 \times \frac{1}{\sqrt{27}}$$
$$= 1.099 \pm 0.377$$

That is, ρ' lies between 0.722 and 1.476.

These limits have to be converted back to r-values by reading the r to r' conversion tables, or using the equation to convert r' to r given in Appendix XIX. An r' of 0.722 gives $r = .62$ and an r' of 1.476 gives $r = .90$. Therefore, the 95% CI for ρ is between .62 and .90.

Kendall's coefficient of concordance

This test yields a statistic W, which is a measure of how much a group of judges agree when asked to put a set of objects/targets in rank order. In Chapter 19 the example was given where four judges were asked to rank a set of five photographs on the attractiveness of the person portrayed.

TABLE A10.8   The attractiveness rankings given by judges for five photographs

	Photograph				
Judge	A	B	C	D	E
One	1	2	3	4	5
Two	2	1	4	3	5
Three	3	2	1	5	4
Four	1	3	2	4	5
Total ranking (R)	7	8	10	16	19
Mean R	1.75	2	2.5	4	4.75

$$\text{overall mean ranking} = \frac{\text{sum of mean rankings}}{k}$$

where k is the number of entities to be ranked. In the present example,

$$\text{overall mean ranking} = \frac{1.75 + 2 + 2.5 + 4 + 4.75}{5}$$
$$= 3$$

To find W, we can use the equation:

$$W = \frac{12 \times \sum (\text{mean R} - \text{overall mean R})^2}{k \times (k^2 - 1)}$$

where $\sum (\text{mean R} - \text{overall mean R})^2$ is the sum of squared deviations of each mean R from the overall mean R, and k is the number of photographs being judged (the equation always has the multiplier 12).

$$W = \frac{12 \times [(1.75 \times 3)^2 + (2-3)^2 + (2.5-3)^2 + (4-3)^2 + (4.75-3)^2]}{5 \times (5^2 - 1)}$$
$$= \frac{12 \times (1.5625 + 1 + 0.25 + 1 + 3.0625)}{5 \times 24}$$
$$= \frac{82.5}{120} = .6875$$

Once W has been found, the link between it and bivariate correlation can be seen as it is possible to find the mean Spearman's rho for the correlations between each of the pairs of judges (in this case $\frac{4 \times 3}{2} =$ 6 pairs) from:

$$\text{mean rho} = \frac{(n \times W) - 1}{n - 1}$$

where n is the number of judges.

The previous technique is for situations which contain no tied scores. As with other non-parametric correlation coefficients, there is a correction which should be used when ties exist. Below is how to calculate W when ties are present. The data in Table A10.9 have been modified from those in Table A10.8 in order to include tied scores.

TABLE A10.9   The attractiveness rankings given by judges of five photographs (including tied scores)

	Photograph				
Judge	A	B	C	D	E
One	1	2	3.5	3.5	5
Two	2	1	4	3	5
Three	2.5	2.5	1	5	4
Four	1	3	2	4	5
Total ranking (R)	6.5	8.5	10.5	15.5	19
Mean R	1.625	2.125	2.625	3.875	4.75

Correction for ties

This can be achieved by drawing up a table of the following form, such that the ties for each participant are noted (Table A10.10).

TABLE A10.10   Obtaining the correction for ties for a Kendall's coefficient of concordance W

Participant (judge)	Value of tied rank	Number in tied rank (t)	Correction ($t^3 - t$)
One	3.5	2	6
Three	2.5	2	6
		Total correction	12

W corrected for ties can be found from the equation:

$$W = \frac{12 \times \sum(\text{mean R} - \text{overall mean R})^2}{[k \times (k^2 - 1)] - \left(\dfrac{\text{total correction}}{n}\right)}$$

where the overall mean R is the mean of the mean Rs for each entity being

judged, which in this case is $\dfrac{1.625 + 2.125 + 2.625 + 3.875 + 4.75}{5} = 3$

Σ (mean R – overall mean R)^2 is the sum of squared deviations of each mean R from the overall mean R, which in this case is $(1.625 - 3)^2 + (2.125 - 3)^2 + (2.625 - 3)^2 + (3.875 - 3)^2 + (4.75 - 3)^2 = 6.625$

k is the number of photographs being judged

n is the number of judges

Therefore,

$$W = \frac{12 \times 6.625}{[5 \times (5^2 - 1)] - \left(\dfrac{12}{4}\right)}$$

$$= \frac{79.5}{(5 \times 24) - 3}$$

$$= \frac{79.5}{117}$$

$$= .6794$$

(whereas the version uncorrected for ties would be $W = .6625$). As noted in Chapter 19, SPSS reports the version corrected for ties.

Reliability

The following are the reliability coefficients, the appropriate uses of which were discussed in Chapter 19.

The Spearman–Brown equation for split-half reliability

This can be found from:

$$r_{kk} = \frac{2 \times r_{12}}{1 + r_{12}}$$

where r_{kk} is the reliability coefficient and r_{12} is the correlation between the participants' scores on the two halves of the test.

This equation can be extended to allow for the intercorrelation between all the items in the test, whence it becomes:

$$r_{kk} = \frac{k \times \text{mean}(r)}{1 + [(k - 1) \times \text{mean}(r)]}$$

where k is the number of items in the test and $\text{mean}(r)$ is the mean of the correlations between the items.

Cronbach's coefficient alpha

This is simpler to compute and produces the same result as would be found from the previous equation:

$$r_{kk} = \frac{k}{k - 1} \times \left[1 - \frac{\sum (s_i^2)}{s_t^2}\right]$$

where s_i^2 is the variance of item i, s_t^2 is the variance of the total scores and $\sum(s_i^2)$ means add the variances of each of the items together.

Kuder–Richardson 20 reliability coefficient

When each item has dichotomous (binary) responses, such as pass/fail or yes/no or agree/disagree, then Cronbach's alpha simplifies further to become the Kuder–Richardson 20 (KR 20) reliability coefficient:

$$\text{KR 20 } r_{kk} = \frac{k}{k-1} \times \left[1 - \frac{\sum (p \times q)}{s_t^2} \right]$$

where p is the proportion of people giving one type of response and $q = 1 - p$ (that is, the proportion of people giving the other type of response); $\Sigma(p \times q)$ means for each item in the test find the product $p \times q$ and then add each product.

Standard error of measurement (SEM)

The reliability of a measure can be used to produce a CI for a person's score on the measure. The CI is based on the SEM for the measure:

$$\text{SEM} = SD_t \times \sqrt{(1-r)}$$

where SD_t is standard deviation of the test and r is the reliability coefficient. The CI for a person's score can be found from:

$$\text{CI} = \text{score} \pm z_{\text{prob}} \times \text{SEM}$$

where z_{prob} is the z-value which gives the required level of confidence (e.g. $z = 1.96$ for 95% confidence).
For example, if an IQ test had an SD of 15 with a reliability coefficient of .9, then the SEM for the test would be:

$$\text{SEM} = 15 \times \sqrt{(1-.9)}$$
$$= 15 \times \sqrt{.1}$$
$$= 15 \times .316$$
$$= 4.74$$

If a boy scored 90 on the test, then the 95% CI for his IQ can be found from:

$$\text{CI} = 90 \pm 1.96 \times 4.74$$
$$= 90 \pm 9.2904$$

In other words, the boy's IQ is likely to lie between 80.71 and 99.29.

Interrater reliability – Cohen's kappa

In order to check that a measure can be used consistently by different observers we need a measure of the degree of agreement between two observers. As was noted in Chapter 19, percentage of agreement fails to take into account the amount of agreement that could have been expected by chance. On the other hand, a large positive correlation coefficient does not necessarily show that two observers are agreeing, as correlation merely tells you about the direction in which the two measures move relative to each other. A measure which solves both these problems is Cohen's kappa (K).

Although the following example involves an ordinal scale, Cohen's kappa would normally be calculated on nominal data.

Two lecturers read a set of essays and each gave a grade (on a 5-point scale) to each essay, without knowing what grades the other had awarded. These grades were then summarised in a table (Table A10.11).

TABLE A10.11   The grades given to 75 essays by two lecturers, working independently

Lecturer 2's grades		Lecturer 1's grades					
	1	2	3	4	5	Total
1	5	1				6
2	2	13	2			17
3		4	20	2		26
4			1	16	2	19
5				3	4	7
Total	7	18	23	21	6	75

The 5 in the top left-hand corner of the table tells us that there were five essays which both lecturer 1 and lecturer 2 graded as 1's. The 2 below that tells us that there were two essays which lecturer 1 graded as 1's but lecturer 2 graded as 2's. To check that you have entered the numbers in the table correctly, the numbers in the total row at the bottom of the table should show that lecturer 1 graded seven essays as 1's, eighteen as 2's, etc., up to six as 5's. The total column at the far right of the table should show that lecturer 2 graded six essays as 1's, seventeen as 2's, etc., up to seven as 5's.

We can see along the diagonal of the matrix those essays over which the two lecturers agreed: $\frac{58}{75}$ or 77.33%.

First we need to work out the expected frequencies by chance for each cell in the matrix where the lecturers agree. This is done in a similar way as for χ^2, in that:

$$\text{expected frequency } (f_e) = \frac{\text{row total} \times \text{column total}}{\text{overall total}}$$

Therefore the expected frequency for essays to which they both gave a grade of 1 is:

$$f_e = \frac{6 \times 7}{75}$$
$$= 0.56$$

and the other expected frequencies for the diagonal cells are 4.08, 7.973, 5.32 and 0.56, which means that the sum of the expected diagonal values (sum f_e) = 18.493.

Cohen's kappa is calculated from:

$$K = \frac{\text{sum } f_o - \text{sum } f_e}{N - \text{sum } f_e}$$

where sum f_o is the sum of the observed frequencies of the diagonal cells, which in this case is 58, and N is the total number of entities being classified by the raters – in this case 75 essays. Therefore:

$$K = \frac{58 - 18.493}{75 - 18.493}$$
$$= .699$$

or just under 70% agreement, once chance has been accounted for.

Robson (2002) reports that kappa in the range .4 to .6 is considered *fair*, that between .6 and .75 is *good*, and that above .75 is *excellent*.

Kappa can be calculated when there are more than two raters. To demonstrate the principle and show that when there are only two raters the result is the same as that shown above, I will use the data from Table A10.11. Initially, create a table which shows, for each entity being rated (in this case essays), how many raters gave that entity a particular rating (Table A10.12). Find p_i for each rating. To find each p_i, use the following formula:

$$p_i = \frac{1}{n \times (n-1)} \times \sum [n_{ij} \times (n_{ij} - 1)]$$

where n is the number of raters and n_{ij} is the number of raters who rated participant i as being in category j.

Thus, for the first participant $n = 2$, as there were two raters: $n_{11} = 2$, as both people rated the person as having a score of 1; and n_{12} to n_{15} all equal 0.

So p_i for that person is

$$p_i = \frac{1}{2 \times (2-1)} \times \{[2 \times (2-1)] + [0 \times (0-1)] + [0 \times (0-1)]$$
$$+ [0 \times (0-1)] + [0 \times (0-1)]\} = \tfrac{1}{2} \times (2 + 0 + 0 + 0 + 0) = 1$$

p_j is found by summing all the ratings which were given to participants in the jth category and then dividing that sum by $N \times n$, where N is the number of entities being rated and n is the number of raters.

TABLE A10.12   The data from Table A10.11 reconfigured into the layout necessary to produce Cohen's kappa for any number of raters

Essay	Rating					p_i
	1	2	3	4	5	
1	2					1
2	2					1
3	2					1
4	2					1
5	2					1
6	1	1				0
7	1	1				0
8	1	1				0
9		2				1
10		2				1

(Continued)

Essay	Rating 1	2	3	4	5	p_i
11		2				1
12		2				1
13		2				1
14		2				1
15		2				1
16		2				1
17		2				1
18		2				1
19		2				1
20		2				1
21		2				1
22		1	1			0
23		1	1			0
24		1	1			0
25		1	1			0
26		1	1			0
27		1	1			0
28			2			1
29			2			1
30			2			1
31			2			1
32			2			1
33			2			1
34			2			1
35			2			1
36			2			1
37			2			1
38			2			1
39			2			1
40			2			1
41			2			1
42			2			1
43			2			1
44			2			1
45			2			1
46			2			1
47			2			1
48			1	1		0
49			1	1		0
50			1	1		0

(*Continued*)

TABLE A10.12   (Continued)

Essay	Rating 1	2	3	4	5	p_i
			Rating			
51				2		1
52				2		1
53				2		1
54				2		1
55				2		1
56				2		1
57				2		1
58				2		1
59				2		1
60				2		1
61				2		1
62				2		1
63				2		1
64				2		1
65				2		1
66				2		1
67				1	1	0
68				1	1	0
69				1	1	0
70				1	1	0
71				1	1	0
72					2	1
73					2	1
74					2	1
75					2	1
Total	13	35	49	40	13	58
p_j	0.08667	0.23333	0.32667	0.26667	0.08667	
p_j^2	0.00751	0.05444	0.10671	0.07111	0.00751	

$$\text{kappa} = \frac{\text{mean } p_i - \text{sum of } p_j^2}{1 - \text{sum of } p_j^2}$$

$$= \frac{.77333 - .24728}{1 - .24728} = .69887, \text{ or } .699 \text{ to three decimal places}$$

Intraclass correlation for interrater reliability

I ran a one-way within-subjects ANOVA on the ratings made by two judges on five targets: judge 1 gave ratings (7, 3, 4, 5, 9) while judge 2 gave ratings (6, 2, 3, 7, 8), see Table A10.13. I am going to use Shrout and Fleiss's (1979) terminology but show the equivalent from McGraw and Wong (1996).

TABLE A10.13   The results of a one-way, within-subjects ANOVA on ratings made by two judges with acronyms from Shrout & Fleiss and McGraw & Wong for the mean squares

Source	Sum of squares	df	Mean Square	Shrout & Fleiss	McGraw & Wong
Between subjects	46.4	4	11.6	BMS	MS_R
Within subjects	4	5	0.8	WMS	MS_W
Judges	0.4	1	0.4	JMS	MS_C
Residual	3.6	4	0.9	EMS	MS_E

All the forms of ICC described in Chapter 19 can be calculated from the information contained in Table A10.13. Below is the equation for each type of ICC, its test of significance and its 95% confidence interval. I am not going to give a worked example of each as the principles are the same. In each equation the appropriate *mean square* is being referred to; for example, BMS is the mean square for between-subjects.

One-way random

One set of scores to be used, level of agreement between judges being measured is absolute

Shrout and Fleiss describe this as ICC(1,1), while McGraw and Wong refer to it as ICC(1). Lahey et al. (1983) show that the limits of possible values are $-1/(k-1)$, (where k is the number of judges) to +1. Therefore with two judges the lowest possible value is -1.

$$ICC(1,1) = \frac{BMS - WMS}{BMS + [(k-1) \times WMS]}$$

Where k is the number of judges

$$= \frac{11.6 - 0.8}{11.6 + (2-1) \times 0.8} = 0.871$$

Test of statistical significance

$$F = \frac{BMS}{WMS}$$

With the df taken from Table 10.13, where $df_1 = n-1$ and $df_2 = n \times (k-1)$; n is the number of targets, k is the number of judges.

$$F_{(4,5)} = \frac{11.6}{0.8} = 14.5$$

Shrout and Fleiss refer to this as F_o when calculating the 95% CI.

95% CI

Shrout and Fleiss produce intermediate calculations which then lead to the ends of the CI:

$$F_L = F_o/Fcrit_1 \tag{A10.4}$$

and

$$F_U = F_o \times Fcrit_2 \tag{A10.5}$$

Where $Fcrit_1$ is the value of F with df of n−1 and n×(k−1) which would give the probability = .025; $Fcrit_2$ is the value of F with df of n×(k−1) and n−1 for the same probability,[1] where n is the number of targets, k is the number of judges.

$Fcrit_{1(4,5)}$ for p = .025 is 7.39 and $Fcrit_{2(5,4)}$ for p = .025 is 9.36 and so F_L = 1.96 and F_U = 135.72

$$\text{The lower end of the CI is } \frac{F_L - 1}{F_L + (k-1)} \tag{A10.6}$$

$$\text{and the upper end is } \frac{F_U - 1}{F_U + (k-1)} \tag{A10.7}$$

This means that the 95% confidence interval is 0.325 to 0.985.

One-way random

The mean of judges' scores to be used and level of agreement between judges being measured is absolute

Shrout and Fleiss describe this as ICC(1,k), while McGraw and Wong refer to it as ICC(k). Lahey et al. (1983) show that the limits of possible values are − ∞ (i.e. minus infinity) to +1.

$$ICC(1,k) = \frac{BMS - WMS}{BMS}$$

Test of statistical significance

This is the same as for ICC(1,1)

95% CI

The 95% CI ranges from

---

1 If you wanted a different percentage CI then the probability sought would be:

$$\frac{1 - percentage\ CI}{2}$$

Thus, for 99% CI you would need the critical F-value for *p* = .005

$$1 - \frac{1}{F_L}$$ (A10.8)

to

$$1 - \frac{1}{F_U}$$ (A10.9)

Where F_L and F_U are the same as given by equation A10.4 and A10.5, respectively.

Two-way random

One set of scores to be used and the level of agreement between judges being measured is absolute

Shrout and Fleiss describe this as ICC(2,1), while McGraw and Wong refer to it as ICC(A1).[2] Lahey et al. (1983) show that the limits of possible values are $-\infty$ (i.e. minus infinity) to +1.

$$\text{ICC}(2,1) = \frac{BMS - EMS}{BMS + \left[(k-1) \times EMS\right] + \left[\frac{k}{n} \times (JMS - EMS)\right]}$$

where k is the number of judges and n the number of targets.

Test of statistical significance

$$F = \frac{BMS}{EMS}$$

With the df taken from Table A10.13, where $df_1 = n-1$ and $df_2 = (n-1) \times (k-1)$; n is the number of targets, k the number of judges.

$$F_{(4,4)} = \frac{11.6}{0.9} = 12.89$$

95% CI

The equation for the confidence interval involves finding an appropriate df (shown as v) to take account of the design. This involves so many terms that there are intermediary equations to arrive at the df and abbreviations to make equations shorter, as in using v instead of df.

---

2   The same calculations are used when the design is two-way mixed, one set of scores is to be used and the level of agreement is absolute.

$$\rho = \text{ICC}(2,1)$$

$$a = \frac{k \times \rho}{n \times (1-\rho)}, \ b = 1 + \frac{k \times \rho \times (n-1)}{n \times (1-\rho)}$$

$$\nu = \frac{\left[(a \times JMS) + (b \times EMS)\right]^2}{\left\{\left[\frac{(a \times JMS)^2}{k-1}\right] + \left[\frac{(b \times EMS)^2}{(n-1) \times (k-1)}\right]\right\}}$$

where n is the number of targets and k the number of judges.

I calculated v as 4.661681.

This value needs to be used to find an F-value (F_*) to use in the lower end of the CI and another F-value (F^*) to calculate the upper end of the CI.[3] As v isn't a whole number you will either need to find a program which gives you F-values for intermediate values for df or use harmonic interpolation between F-values which are based on df which are whole numbers. See Appendix XVII.

$$F_* = \text{Fcrit}_{3((n-1), \, \nu)}$$
$$F^* = \text{Fcrit}_{4(\nu, \, (n-1))}$$

where n is the number of targets.

I used harmonic interpolation for critical values with $p = .025$, between $F_{(4,4)}$ and $F_{(4,5)}$ for F_* and between $F_{(4,4)}$ and $F_{(5,4)}$ for F^*.

$$F_* = 7.99 \text{ and } F^* = 9.43$$

To find the lower end of the 95% CI calculate:

$$\frac{n \times \left[BMS - (F_* \times EMS)\right]}{F_* \times \left[k \times JMS + (k \times n - k - n) \times EMS\right] + (n \times BMS)}$$

To find the upper end of the 95% CI calculate:

$$\frac{n \times (F^* \times BMS) - EMS}{(k \times JMS) + (k \times n - k - n) \times EMS + (n \times F^* \times BMS)}$$

where n is the number of targets and k the number of judges.

---

3   I am showing McGraw and Wong's use of F_* and F^*, respectively, to denote the figures to use in the calculation of the lower and upper ends, respectively, of the CI as this makes more intuitive sense than Shrout and Fleiss's use.

Two-way random

The mean of the judges' ratings is to be used and the level of agreement between judges being measured is absolute

Shrout and Fleiss describe this as ICC(2,k), while McGraw and Wong refer to it as ICC(A,k).[4] Lahey et al. (1983) show that the limits of possible values are $-\infty$ (i.e. minus infinity) to $+\infty$.

$$\text{ICC}(2,k) = \frac{BMS - EMS}{BMS + \left(\dfrac{JMS - EMS}{n}\right)}$$

where n is the number of targets.

Test of statistical significance

This is the same as for the two-way random model shown above for ICC(2,1).

95% CI

Calculate $F_.$, F^* and v as shown for ICC(2,1) but with ρ = ICC(2,k) in the calculations of a and b. The lower end of the CI is:

$$\frac{n \times [BMS - (F_. \times EMS)]}{[F_. \times (JMS - EMS)] + (n \times BMS)}$$

And the upper end of the CI is:

$$\frac{n \times [(F^* \times BMS) - EMS]}{JMS - EMS + (n \times F^* \times BMS)}$$

Where n is the number of targets

Two-way mixed

One set of scores to be used and the level of agreement between judges being measured is consistency[5]

Shrout and Fleiss describe this as ICC(3,1), while McGraw and Wong refer to it as ICC(C,1). Lahey et al. (1983) show that the limits of possible values are $-1/(k-1)$ (where k is the number of judges) to $+1$.

---

4 The same calculations are used when the design is two-way mixed, the mean of the judges is to be used and the level of agreement is absolute.

5 The same calculations are used when the design is two-way random, one set of scores is to be used and the level of agreement is consistency.

$$ICC(3,1) = \frac{BMS - EMS}{BMS + (k-1) \times EMS}$$

where k is the number of judges.

Test of statistical significance

This is the same as for the two-way random model shown previously and is treated as F_o in later calculations.

95% CI

The critical F value used to calculate F_L which is then used to find the lower end of the CI is:

$$\text{Fcrit}_{5((n-1),\,(n-1)\times(k-1))}$$

The critical F used to calculate F_U which is then used to find the upper end of the CI is:

$$\text{Fcrit}_{6((n-1)\times(k-1),\,(n-1))}$$

F_L and F_U are found using equations A10.4 and A10.5, respectively, but using the appropriate F_o and Fcrit values from the current design.

The lower and upper ends of the CI are found using equations 10.8 and A10.9, respectively.

Two-way mixed

The mean of the judges' scores to be used and the level of agreement between judges being measured is consistency[6]

Shrout and Fleiss describe this as ICC(3,k), while McGraw and Wong refer to it as ICC(C,k). Lahey et al. (1983) show that the limits of possible values are $-\infty$ (i.e. minus infinity) to +1.

$$ICC(3,k) = \frac{BMS - EMS}{BMS}$$

Test of statistical significance

This is the same as for the two-way random model shown previously and is treated as F_o in later calculations.

95% CI

The critical F value used to calculate F_L which is then used to find the lower end of the CI is:

$$\text{Fcrit}_{7((n-1),\,(n-1)\times(k-1))}$$

---

6 The same calculations are used when the design is two-way random, the mean of judges' scores is to be used and the level of agreement is consistency.

The critical F value used to calculate F_U which is then used to find the upper end of the CI is:

$$\text{Fcrit}_{8((n-1)\times(k-1),\,(n-1))}$$

F_L and F_U are found using equations A10.4 and A10.5, respectively, but using the appropriate F_o and Fcrit values from the current design.

The lower and upper ends of the CI are found using equations 10.8 and A10.9, respectively.

Standard error of estimate

When the validity of a measure is expressed in terms of its correlation with another measure, then a CI for a person's score can be found, using the standard error of estimate for the measure:

$$SE_{est} = SD_x \times \sqrt{(1-r^2)}$$

where SD_x is the standard deviation of the criterion measure and r is the correlation between the criterion and the new measure.

A CI can then be formed from:

$$CI = \text{score} \pm z_{prob} \times SE_{est}$$

where z_{prob} is the z-value which gives the required level of confidence (e.g. $z = 1.96$ for 95% confidence).

If a new measure of extroversion had a standard deviation of 5 and correlated $r = .8$ with another measure of extroversion, then the standard error of estimate would be:

$$SE_{est} = 5 \times \sqrt{(1-(.8)^2)}$$
$$= 3$$

Therefore, if a girl scored 30 on the new measure, the 95% CI for her score would be:

$$CI = 30 \pm 1.96 \times 3$$
$$= 30 \pm 5.88$$

Therefore, her 'true' score is likely to lie between 24.12 and 35.88.

Linear regression

This appendix illustrates the techniques introduced in Chapter 20.

Simple linear regression

In Chapter 20 an example was given of attempts to predict mathematical ability from ability at English (Table A11.1).

TABLE A11.1 The scores on tests of mathematical ability and ability at English in a sample of 10 children

Participant	Mathematical ability	English ability
1	50	50
2	40	48
3	60	48
4	50	47
5	70	65
6	60	64
7	75	75
8	70	72
9	85	75
10	75	80
Mean	63.5	62.4
SD	13.95429	13.05713

It was pointed out that the equation for linear regression is the equation for the straight line which could be drawn through the data points on a scattergram such that the distance between the line and the points was at a minimum. This line is called the *best-fit line* and for simple linear regression (where there is one IV and one DV) is always of the form:

$$DV = a + (b \times IV)$$

or rather, when the prediction is not perfect:

$$predicted\ DV = a + (b \times IV)$$

(*a* and *b* are described as *regression coefficients*. If we were drawing the best-fit line on a graph, *a* would be the point where the line crosses the vertical axis. It is called the *intercept* and is the value which the predicted DV would have if the IV was 0. The *slope* of the line would be *b*: that is, the amount by which the DV would change for every change of one unit in the IV.)

To find *b*, we use the following equation:

$$b = \frac{[n \times total\ of\ (IV \times DV)] - (total\ for\ IV \times total\ for\ DV)}{[n \times total\ of\ (IV^2)] - (total\ for\ IV)^2}$$

where *n* is the sample size and *total of (IV × DV)* means multiply each person's score on the IV by the same person's score on the DV and add the results for each person together.

TABLE A11.2 Calculations leading to finding the slope of a best-fit line for a simple linear regression

Participant	Mathematical ability (MA)	English ability (EA)	(EA)²	MA × EA
1	50	50	2500	2500
2	40	48	2304	1920
3	60	48	2304	2880
4	50	47	2209	2350

(Continued)

TABLE A11.2 (Continued)

Participant	Mathematical ability (MA)	English ability (EA)	(EA)²	MA × EA
5	70	65	4225	4550
6	60	64	4096	3840
7	75	75	5625	5625
8	70	72	5184	5040
9	85	75	5625	6375
10	75	80	6400	6000
Total	635	624	40472	41080

Therefore, using the data from Table A11.2,

$$b = \frac{(10 \times 41080) - (635 \times 624)}{(10 \times 40472) - (624)^2}$$
$$= \frac{410800 - 396240}{404720 - 389376}$$
$$= .94890511$$

(I have had to go to this number of decimal places so that the answers are compatible with the ones provided by the computer.)

Having found b we can find a from the following equation:

$$a = \frac{\text{total for DV} - (b \times \text{total for IV})}{n}$$

or

$$a = \text{mean for DV} - (b \times \text{mean for IV})$$

which is often written as:

$$a = \bar{Y} - b\bar{X}$$

Therefore,

$$a = 63.5 - (.94890511 \times 62.4)$$
$$= 4.28832$$

Accordingly,

$$\text{predicted MA} = 4.28832 + (.94891 \times \text{EA})$$

Therefore, if a person scored 50 for English ability (EA), his or her mathematical ability (MA) would be predicted to be:

$$4.28832 + (.94891 \times 50) = 51.734$$

Finding the statistical significance of a regression analysis

To find the statistical significance of a regression, we perform an ANOVA on the data, in which the total sum of squares is separated into the sum of squares for the regression (the variance in the DV which has been successfully accounted for by the variance in the IV(s)) and the sum of squares for the residual (the variance in the DV not accounted for by the variance in the IV(s)).

Total sum of squares

The total sum of squares is the sum of squares for the DV. As usual, if we know the standard deviation we can square it to get the variance and multiply this by one fewer than the sample size ($n - 1$):

$$\text{total sum of squares} = (10 - 1) \times (13.95429)^2$$
$$= 9 \times 194.72221$$
$$= 1752.5$$

Regression sum of squares

The regression sum of squares is calculated by subtracting the mean for the DV from the predicted value of the DV for each person, squaring the result and adding these squared values together (Table A11.3).

TABLE A11.3   Obtaining the regression sum of squares for a simple linear regression. MA: maths ability

Participant	MA (Y)	Predicted MA ($\hat{Y}$)	Predicted MA – mean for actual MA (deviation) ($\hat{Y} - \bar{Y}$)	(Deviation)^2 ($\hat{Y} - \bar{Y}$)^2
1	50	51.734	−11.76642	138.44872
2	40	49.836	−13.66423	186.71128
3	60	49.836	−13.66423	186.71128
4	50	48.887	−14.61314	213.54382
5	70	65.967	2.46715	6.08685
6	60	65.018	1.51825	2.30508
7	75	75.456	11.9562	142.95082
8	70	72.609	9.10949	82.98279
9	85	75.456	11.9562	142.95082
10	75	80.201	16.70073	278.91438
			S of S for regression	1381.60600

The residual sum of squares

The residual sum of squares is the sum of the squared differences between the predicted value of the DV and the actual value for each person; it can also be found by subtracting the regression sum of squares from the total sum of squares (Table A11.4).

TABLE A11.4   Obtaining the residual sum of squares for a simple linear regression. MA: maths ability

Participant	MA (Y)	Predicted MA ($\hat{Y}$)	MA – predicted MA (residual), i.e. (Y – $\hat{Y}$)	(Residual)^2 i.e. (Y – $\hat{Y}$)^2
1	50	51.734	–1.73358	3.00529
2	40	49.836	–9.83577	96.74230
3	60	49.836	10.16423	103.31164
4	50	48.887	1.11314	1.23908
5	70	65.967	4.03285	16.26385
6	60	65.018	–5.01825	25.18281
7	75	75.456	–0.45620	0.20812
8	70	72.609	–2.60949	6.80943
9	85	75.456	9.54380	91.08403
10	75	80.201	–5.20073	27.04759
			S of S for residuals	370.89400

We now have sufficient detail to create the summary ANOVA for the regression analysis (Table A11.5). See Chapter 20 for an explanation of how the degrees of freedom (df), mean square and F-ratio are obtained.

TABLE A11.5   Summary table of the analysis of variance in a simple regression of the relationship between mathematical ability and ability at English

Source		Sum of squares	df	Mean square	F	p
	Regression	1381.606	1	1381.606	29.801	.001
	Residual	370.894	8	46.362		
	Total	1752.500	9			

If you know the R^2 value, the sample size and the number of predictors, the following equation can be used to find the F-value for a regression:

$$F_{(p, N-p-1)} = \frac{\left(\dfrac{R^2}{p}\right)}{\left(\dfrac{1-R^2}{N-p-1}\right)}$$

where N is the sample size and p is the number of predictors.

Significance of difference between two regressions

Two regressions can be compared to see whether they are significantly different when one is contained (or nested) in the other – that is, when one contains all the predictor variables of the other plus more predictor variables. Use the following equation:

$$F(p_1 - p_2, N - p_1 - 1) = \frac{(N - p_1 - 1) \times (R_1^2 - R_2^2)}{(p_1 - p_2) \times (1 - R_1^2)}$$

where p_1 is the number of predictors in the regression with more predictors, p_2 is the number of predictors in the regression with fewer predictors, N is the total sample size, R_1^2 is the squared multiple regression coefficient for the regression with more predictors and R_2^2 is the squared multiple regression coefficient for the regression with fewer predictors.

When the larger regression has only one more predictor variable than the smaller regression, then the result of this test will provide the same information as the t-test which is conducted on the extra predictor variable, and the t-value will be the square root of the F-value from the preceding equation. Thus, if we compared the regression with SES and English ability as predictors against that with just English ability, then the F-value would be the same as the square of the t-value for SES in the larger regression. However, when the larger regression is larger than the smaller one by more than one predictor variable, then this equation becomes more useful. It produces the same result as would be found from SPSS when the optional statistic R squared change has been chosen.

Additional links between correlation and simple linear regression

The covariance between two variables was defined in Chapter 19, where it was shown that the correlation coefficient (r) between two variables can be found from:

$$r = \frac{\text{covariance}}{SD_1 \times SD_2}$$

The covariance of mathematical ability and English ability is 161.77778.

As well as using the method described in the previous section for finding the regression coefficient b in a simple linear regression, it can be found from the equation:

$$b = \frac{\text{covariance}}{(SD \text{ for IV})^2}$$

which is the same as

$$b = \frac{\text{covariance}}{\text{variance for IV}}$$

Therefore,

$$b = \frac{161.77778}{170.48889}$$
$$= .948905$$

A standardised regression coefficient is calculated by the following equation:

$$\beta = \frac{b \times SD_x}{SD_y}$$

where b is the regression coefficient for an IV, SD_x is the standard deviation of the same IV, and SD_y is the standard deviation of the DV.

If, in simple linear regression, we convert b to a beta coefficient, we get:

$$\text{beta coefficient} = \frac{.94890511 \times 13.05713}{13.95429}$$
$$= .888$$

This is the same as the correlation coefficient (r) for the relationship between mathematical ability and English ability. The reason for this is that the standardised regression coefficient is the regression coefficient which would be found if we converted the values of the IV into standardised scores and did the same for the DV, and then did a regression analysis of the two standardised variables. Remember that standardising converts a distribution into one which has a mean of 0 and a standard deviation (and variance) of 1. The covariance of two standardised variables is the same as their correlation coefficient. In addition, the standardised regression coefficient a (the intercept or constant) becomes:

$$\text{standardised regression coefficient} = \text{mean for DV} - \text{beta} \times \text{mean for IV}$$
$$= 0 - .888 \times 0$$
$$= 0$$

Thus, in simple regression, the regression equation for the standardised variables is:

$$\text{standardised DV} = r \times \text{standardised IV}$$

Adjusted R^2

The adjusted R^2 is an estimate of R^2 in the population and takes into account the sample size and the number of IVs; the smaller the sample and the greater the number of IVs, the larger is the adjustment. The equation for adjusted R^2 is:

$$\text{adjusted } R^2 = 1 - \left[\frac{(1 - R^2) \times (n - 1)}{(n - p - 1)} \right]$$

where n is the sample size and p is the number of IVs in the model.

Thus, when in Chapter 20, R^2 was shown as .79, with two IVs (age and ability in English) and 10 participants,

$$\text{adjusted } R^2 = 1 - \left[\frac{(1 - .79) \times (10 - 1)}{(10 - 2 - 1)} \right]$$
$$= 1 - \left(\frac{.21 \times 9}{7} \right)$$
$$= .73$$

The standard error of a regression coefficient

The standard error (Std Err) of a regression coefficient is calculated from the following equation:

$$\text{Std Err of IV}_1 = \sqrt{\frac{\text{mean square}_\text{residual}}{\text{S of S of IV}_1 \times (1 - R^2_{1.2})}}$$

where mean square$_\text{residual}$ can be found from the ANOVA for the regression analysis; S of S of IV$_1$ is the sum of squared deviations (from the mean) of the IV for which the standard error is being calculated; and $R^2_{1.2}$ is the squared multiple correlation coefficient where IV$_1$ is being treated as a criterion variable and the other IVs are acting as predictor variables for it – when there are only two IVs it is the square of the correlation coefficient between the two IVs (i.e. r^2).

In the case of a simple regression (one with only one IV) the equation becomes:

$$\text{Std Err of IV} = \sqrt{\frac{\text{mean square}_\text{residual}}{\text{S of S of IV}}}$$

In Chapter 20 an example was given of a multiple regression with mathematical ability as the DV and ability at English, age, socio-economic status (SES) and IQ as IVs. Table A11.6 shows the original data entered into a sequential regression and Table A11.7 shows the ANOVA for the regression.

TABLE A11.6   The data entered into a sequential regression in which maths was the DV and the other variables the IVs

Participant	Maths	English	Age	SES	IQ
1	50	50	150	2	85
2	40	48	150	1	100
3	60	48	144	4	95
4	50	47	144	3	105
5	70	65	162	4	100
6	60	64	162	1	110
7	75	75	156	2	100
8	70	72	156	2	120
9	85	75	168	2	115
10	75	80	168	1	120

TABLE A11.7   The ANOVA table for a multiple regression with mathematical ability as the DV and age, IQ, SES and ability at English as IVs

Source	Sum of squares	df	Mean square	F	p
Regression	1623.748	4	405.937	15.764	.005
Residual	128.752	5	25.750		
Total	1752.500	9			

If ability at English is now treated as the DV and IQ, age and SES as the IVs, $R^2 = .7882$. The sum of squared deviations of English is 1534.4. Therefore:

$$\text{Std Err (for English)} = \sqrt{\frac{25.75}{1534.4 \times (1 - .7882)}}$$

$$= \sqrt{\frac{25.75}{1534.4 \times .2118}}$$

$$= \sqrt{\frac{25.75}{324.98592}}$$

$$= \sqrt{0.079234}$$

$$= 0.28149$$

$$= 0.281 \text{ (to 3 decimal places)}$$

Table A11.8 shows another part of the regression analysis when mathematical ability was the DV, while age, IQ, SES and ability at English were the IVs, including the standard errors of the regression coefficients.

TABLE A11.8 Statistics relating to the regression coefficients when mathematical ability was the DV and age, IQ, SES and ability at English were the IVs

Source					
	Unstandardised coefficients		Standardised coefficients		
	B	Std. error	Beta	t	p
(Constant)	−35.751	50.768		−.704	.513
Age	.165	.383	.105	.429	.686
SES	4.967	1.666	.404	2.982	.031
IQ	.010	.216	.008	.045	.966
English	.988	.281	.924	3.509	.017

Testing the statistical significance of a regression coefficient

A t-value can be formed, to test the statistical significance of a regression coefficient, using the following equation:

$$t_{(N-p-1)} = \frac{\text{regression coefficient}}{\text{standard error for regresssion coefficient}} \tag{A11.1}$$

where N is the sample size and p is the number of IVs in the regression.
Therefore, in the case of ability at English:

$$t_{(5)} = \frac{0.9876}{0.28149} = 3.509$$

(note: the regression coefficient had to be expanded to four decimal places to produce this result)

The probability of this t-value can be checked against the critical values given in the t-tables in Appendix XVII. Use the two-tailed probability. In this case, the t-value is statistically significant at the $p = .017$ level and so we would conclude that ability at English is a significant predictor of mathematical ability, even with age, IQ and SES already in the model.

In multiple regression, if we were to test the statistical significance of the regression coefficients, as this would involve more than one test some writers suggest that we ought to adjust the alpha-level to take account of the number of tests performed. This could be done using Bonferroni's adjustment. In the present case, as there are four IVs, the critical alpha-level would become $\frac{.05}{4} = .0125$.

Calculating a confidence interval for a regression coefficient

As with other confidence intervals (CIs), we need to know what the critical value for t would be for the df and for the confidence level. If we wish to have a 95% confidence level, then the critical t will be the t-value for a two-tailed probability for $\alpha = .05$, which, with df = 5, is 2.5705. Use the following equation to calculate the CI:

CI = regression coefficient $\pm$ ($t \times$ standard error of regression coefficient)

Therefore, in the case of ability at English:

CI = 0.988 $\pm$ (2.5705 $\times$ 0.2815)
   = 0.988 $\pm$ 0.7236

In other words, we can be confident, at the 95% level, that the value for the regression coefficient, in the population, lies between 0.264 and 1.711.

Suppressor variables

When looking at the correlations between the DV and the IVs it might be assumed that because a given IV has no correlation or a very small correlation with the DV that when it is added to a regression no more variance in the DV will be explained than before. However, this is not always the case. If the IV correlates with one or more of the other IVs its inclusion in the regression could lead to more variance being explained. Such a variable is sometimes described as a *suppressor* variable. Thus if we are trying to choose what variables to include in a regression and our aim is to explain as much variance as possible, then we shouldn't use the original correlations as our criterion for what variables to include. If you refer to Table 20.3 you will see that SES only correlated with mathematical ability at $r = .056$. However, in the regression it was found to be a significant predictor when age, IQ and English ability were also in the model (see Table 20.7). See Pedhazur (1997) for more on this topic.

Centring

One technique which is sometimes recommended to reduce multicollinearity is *centring*. This involves subtracting the mean of a variable from each of the scores, in the same way that we do in the first stage when a variable is being standardised. Prior to the use of computers it was felt that this would remove problems of rounding errors. However, this is no longer necessary when computers are being used and it does not change the correlations among the original variables. Nonetheless, it can still be a useful technique for removing multicollinearity when the analysis involves interaction terms or variables which are powers of other variables: for example, if we included age and the square of age in the same analysis in order to try to explain as much variance as possible.

Testing an interaction or joint relation

I mentioned, in Chapter 20, that an interaction (or joint relation) between variables can be tested by multiple regression. However, I pointed out that it can be less straightforward than testing an interaction in ANOVA. This is for at least two reasons. Firstly, statistical packages may not have a direct way to enter an interaction term into a multiple regression. Secondly, as mentioned in the previous section, a problem with multicollinearity can be created when interaction terms are entered in a regression. Fortunately, finding a variable which represents the interaction between two variables, which are themselves appropriate for entry into a multiple regression, is relatively simple: we can create a new variable by multiplying the two original variables. However, this will be highly correlated with each of the original variables and so we need to prevent this happening. One way is to centre the data as described previously. We could also standardise the original scores, as this is the equivalent of centring followed by dividing by the SD. As an example, I have saved the standardised scores for age and English ability. I have then created a variable by multiplying the values of standardised versions of age and English ability. In Table A11.9 are the results of a sequential multiple regression with mathematical ability as the variable to be predicted. Age and English were entered in the first stage and the joint relation between them in the second stage. In this way I can see how much extra variance in mathematical ability is accounted for by their joint relation and whether that amount is significant.

TABLE A11.9 Part of the output from a sequential multiple regression with mathematical ability regressed on age and ability at English, with an interaction term between the two IVs entered in the second stage

Model	R	R^2	Adjusted R^2	Std. error of the estimate
1	.889	.790	.729	7.25845
2	.899	.808	.711	7.49676

Coefficients

Model		Unstandardised coefficients B	Std. error	Standardised coefficients Beta	t	p
1	(Constant)	16.979	64.663		0.263	.800
	English	1.012	0.366	.947	2.768	.028
	Age	−0.107	0.534	−.068	−0.200	.847
2	(Constant)	17.931	66.799		0.268	.797
	English	1.062	0.384	.994	2.770	.032
	Age	−0.146	0.554	−.094	−0.264	.801
	Age by English	2.679	3.574	.137	0.750	.482

Table A11.9 shows that the joint relation between age and English ability only adds .018 (.808 − .790) to the R^2 value (i.e. it explains 1.8% more of the variance in mathematical ability). In addition, at $p = .482$, it does not add significantly to the model.

Diagnostic statistics

Residuals

In Chapter 20 residuals (unstandardised and standardised) were described. A residual is standardised by being divided by the *standard error of the estimate* (the *SD* of the residuals):

$$\text{standard error of the estimate} = \sqrt{\frac{\text{sum of squares of residuals}}{N - p - 1}}$$

where N is the sample size and p is the number of IVs.

In addition to the preceding versions there are also *deleted, studentised* and *studentised deleted* residuals. A deleted residual is found by running a regression but with that particular person's data excluded and then predicting the value for the DV for that person from the regression equation and calculating the difference between the new predicted value and the actual value. A studentised residual is similar to a standardised one except that instead of dividing each residual by the same standard error, the standard error is adjusted to take account of the individual's discrepancy from the rest of the scores on the IVs (using the leverage score for that person). A studentised deleted residual is a combination of the last two in that the residual is calculated from the regression equation which doesn't involve that person and the standard error is adjusted to take account of the person's leverage. Unfortunately, these terms don't appear to be consistently used. Nonetheless, the descriptions I've given do apply to the use made by SPSS of these terms.

Leverage and influence

Leverage is a measure of whether an individual's set of scores on the IVs makes that person an outlier, i.e. it checks whether that person is a multivariate outlier. Its description in multiple regression involves matrix algebra so I'll spare you the details. However, you can get an idea of what it is doing from *simple regression*, in which:

$$\text{leverage} = \frac{\text{squared deviation from mean on IV}}{\text{sum of squared deviations from mean on IV}} + \frac{1}{n}$$

where n is the sample size.

Therefore leverage is a measure of the proportion of the overall sum of squared deviations which is accounted for by that individual's score on the IV. Stevens (2009) recommends that if the leverage is greater than $3 \times (p + 1)/n$ (where p is the number of IVs in the model and n is the number of participants), then the data for that person need to be checked. Table 20.8 shows the leverage scores for each participant when IQ, age, SES and ability at English were IVs. As the critical level would be $3 \times (4 + 1)/10 = 1.5$ and the highest leverage value shown is less than .8, none of the participants has a particular problem of multivariate outliers, according to this criterion. Note that SPSS reports what it calls *centred* leverage values. To calculate these, $\frac{1}{n}$ is subtracted from the leverage value. Thus if you want to apply the criteria suggested above you will need to subtract $\frac{1}{n}$ from the critical level (or add $\frac{1}{n}$ to the values which SPSS reports). However, as I note in Chapter 20, to explore potential outliers it is better to plot leverage against Cook's distance and look for cases which are well separated from the rest of the distribution.

Mahalanobis's distance is a simple transformation of leverage and so they are looking at the same thing. Mahalanobis's distance can be found from:

$$\text{Mahalanobis's distance} = (n-1) \times \left[\text{leverage} - \frac{1}{n} \right]$$

where n is the sample size.

Therefore, as the version of leverage which SPSS reports (centred leverage) can be found by subtracting $\frac{1}{n}$ from leverage, Mahalanobis's distance is simply centred leverage multiplied by $n - 1$.

Cook's distance is a measure of how an individual's scores on the IVs *and* the DV are different from the other people's scores and it takes into account both the studentised residual and the leverage for the individual. Stevens (2009) notes that the data of a person whose Cook's distance is greater than 1 should be investigated further.

DfBeta is a measure of how much each regression coefficient (including the constant) would change if a given participant were removed. In addition, there is a standardised version of each DfBeta. *DfFit* is a measure of the change in the predicted DV if a case were removed and there is a standardised version of DfFit. By all means look at all the versions of residuals and fit but my own preference would be to use only standardised residuals, leverage and Cook's distance in the ways described in Chapter 20.

Multicollinearity

In addition to Tolerance and Variance inflation factor (VIF) which were described in Chapter 20, Belsley (1991) devised an approach to identifying possible multicollinearity. Table A11.10 contains the results of such analysis.

TABLE A11.10 The multicollinearity checks on the regression with age, SES, IQ and ability at English predicting mathematical ability

Collinearity diagnostics

	Eigenvalue	Condition index	(Constant)	Age	SES	IQ	English
					Variance proportions		
1	4.790	1.000	0.00	0.00	0.01	0.00	0.00
2	0.190	5.025	0.00	0.00	0.65	0.00	0.00
3	0.017	16.949	0.02	0.00	0.19	0.01	0.30
4	0.004	36.089	0.03	0.03	0.06	0.97	0.07
5	0.000	106.985	0.95	0.97	0.09	0.02	0.63

Eigenvalues are briefly described in Chapter 24 where it is noted that they summarise variance in a matrix. Each condition index is found from:

$$\text{Condition index} = \sqrt{\left(\frac{\text{Largest eigenvalue}}{\text{eigenvalue}} \right)}$$

Thus, the condition index for the second row is found by dividing 4.79 by 0.19 and taking the square root of the answer.

Condition indexes greater than 10 should be examined and those over 30 are likely to reveal a problem

Look in the row containing the highest condition index. If more than 1 variance proportion (for a variable) is > 0.5 then explore more fully. In the row containing the condition index of 106.895, both age and English have variance proportions greater than 0.5 and so they need exploring in the ways described in Chapter 20. It is worth noting that neither variable was shown to be problematic with Tolerance (and therefore VIF). The two other condition indexes which are greater than 10 do not show a problematic pattern.

For further information on checks on multicollinearity see Chatterjee and Hadi (1988), Chatterjee, Hadi, and Price (2000) and Lovie (1991).

PRESS statistic

The PRESS statistic is the sum of the squared deleted residuals. As with any sum of squared residuals the larger it is, the poorer the model is at estimating the values of the DV.

In SPSS one can save the deleted residuals. Summing the squares of these gives the PRESS statistic (see Table A11.11). R^2_{PRESS} can be calculated from

$$R^2_{PRESS} = 1 - \frac{PRESS}{total\ sum\ of\ squares}$$

Therefore, in the regression predicting mathematical ability from English ability,

$$R^2_{PRESS} = 1 - \frac{609.4142}{1752.5000} = .65226$$

TABLE A11.11 The deleted residuals and squared deleted residuals from the simple regression with mathematical ability as the DV and English ability as the IV

Participant	Deleted residual	Squared deleted residual
1	−2.16754	4.70
2	−12.85958	165.37
3	13.28903	176.60
4	1.49327	2.23
5	4.50298	20.28
6	−5.58619	31.21
7	−0.57274	0.33
8	−3.10677	9.65
9	11.98167	143.56
10	−7.44959	55.50
	PRESS	609.4142

Other forms of multiple regression

All subset multiple regression

This explores all possible combinations of IVs to see which combination is best. There are a number of criteria for assessing what constitutes the best combination. The technique is available on various computer packages but it is not generally recommended as a way of trying to produce a model. If we are using significance as our criterion for evaluating models, then we have the problem of multiple testing and the increased danger of making a Type I error.

Statistical multiple regression

Sometimes these are also referred to as sequential techniques. However, they involve the computer choosing the IVs to include in the model, according to some statistical criterion. They will attempt to find the solution which produces the combination of IVs which account for the maximum amount of variance in the DV and will leave out of the equation those IVs which do not contribute significantly to the model. Like any procedure which hands the responsibility for decisions to a computer, they are controversial and their use is only really appropriate when the researcher is exploring the data rather than testing a specific model.

There are three forms of statistical multiple regression: forward selection, backward deletion and stepwise.

Forward selection

Forward selection involves placing the variables one at a time into the model on the basis of which IV explains most of the variance in the DV. Once the first IV has been placed into the model the remaining variables are assessed to see which explains most of the remaining variance. This process continues until none of the remaining variables adds significantly to the model.

Backward deletion

Backward deletion puts all the variables into the model and then extracts the variable which contributes the least to the model to see whether there is a significant reduction in the variance explained. If removing that variable would not detract significantly from the model, then it is removed.

Stepwise regression

Stepwise regression is like forward selection in that the variables are placed in the model, one at a time. However, after each new one is added to the model the contribution of each variable already in the model is reassessed and if an earlier one does not contribute significantly it is removed.

Stepwise regression is considered the safest procedure of the three. Thus, I would recommend that if you are exploring the data for the solution which accounts for the maximum variance for a minimum of IVs, then use stepwise regression. On the other hand, if you are testing an explicit model use what I am calling *sequential multiple regression* (described earlier).

In stepwise regression it makes little sense to utilise the order in which an IV is entered into the model as a criterion for importance. As the description of the method should have made clear, the IV which is entered first could later be eliminated when other variables have been taken into consideration.

If you are using a statistical method (forward, backward or stepwise), then I don't think that it is useful to report all these details for each step.

Testing the statistical significance of an indirect regression path

In Chapter 20 it was shown that when an indirect route from an IV via a mediating variable to a DV is presented in terms of standardised regression coefficients, then the value of the indirect path can be calculated by multiplying the regression coefficients which make up the route. In the example, the standardised regression from the IV (hearing) to the mediator (labelling) was −.444 and the standardised regression from labelling to the DV (concepts) was .343. The product of these two values is −.15218. To work out the significance of this test we need a standard error for the statistic ($SE_{\beta_1\beta_2}$). According to MacKinnon, Lockwood, Hoffman, West, and Sheets (2002), the following version is used in specialist software which can be used to test indirect effects such as LISREL and EQS:

$$SE_{\beta_1\beta_2} = \sqrt{[\beta_2^2 \times (SE_{\beta_1})^2] + [\beta_1^2 \times (SE_{\beta_2})^2]}$$

The results of simple and multiple regression show us that β_2 = .343, β_2 = −.444, t_1 = 2.789634 and t_2 = −4.17548. Therefore, using equation A11.1 we can work out that SE_{β_1} = .122859 and SE_{β_2} = .106338. From these figures, $SE_{\beta_1\beta_2}$ = .066894.

We can now find a z-value:

$$z = \frac{\beta_1 \times \beta_2}{SE_{\beta_1\beta_2}} = \frac{-.15218}{.066894} = -2.31958$$

MacKinnon et al. (2002) compared this method of testing mediation with a number of others and found that it is not as powerful as some of the others. However, the alternatives which they find to be more powerful are less simply calculated and for some of them the testing of their statistical significance involves specialist tables.

Coding categorical variables

In Chapter 20 it was shown that the data which would normally be analysed by ANOVA can be analysed by multiple regression. However, it was necessary to recode categorical variables as dummy variables.

Dummy coding

When the IV to be coded has more than two levels, we will have more than one dummy variable. We have to be careful about how we interpret the individual IVs which are put into a regression as they can't be interpreted in the same way as variables such as age or SES. When we use dummy coding we can treat the level of the original IV which has been coded as 0 in all the dummy variables as a comparison level for paired contrasts, in the same way as Dunnett's *t* does. Thus in Chapter 20 the control condition was coded as 0 in both dummy variables, while method of loci was coded as 1 in the first variable and 0 in the second, and pegword was coded as 0 in the first and 1 in the second. Chapter 18 reported the paired contrasts which compared the control and method of loci conditions and the control and pegword conditions. The *t*-values were 3.139 and 0.916 respectively. The output from the regression analysis with mnemonic strategy coded as two dummy variables produced the result shown in Table A11.12.

TABLE A11.12   Output from a multiple regression with recall as the DV and mnemonic condition coded as two dummy variables as the IVs

	Unstandardised coefficients		Standardised coefficients		
	B	Std. error	Beta	t	p
(Constant)	9.600	0.541		17.759	<.001
Dummy variable 1	−2.400	0.764	−.593	−3.139	.004
Dummy variable 2	−0.700	0.764	−.173	−0.916	.368

Thus, we can see that the t-value for each dummy variable is the equivalent of one of those contrasts. Note that both are negative. This is because in the contrasts the control mean was subtracted from the other mean, whereas in the regression it is the equivalent of subtracting the other means from the control.

Other forms of coding exist. As with dummy coding, each involves producing a coded variable for each df in the IV. *Effect coding* is similar to dummy coding in that in each coded variable the target level of the IV is coded as 1. However, one level of the IV is always coded as −1 and the remainder are coded as 0. In the mnemonic example, in one effect variable method of loci would be coded as 1, pegword as 0 and the control condition as −1, while in the other effect variable method of loci would be 0, pegword would be 1 and control would again be −1. The unstandardised regression coefficient for the constant is the overall mean when effect coding is used. Effect coding is so called because the unstandardised regression coefficient for each effect variable is the difference between the mean for the group coded as 1 and the overall mean. Thus, that effect variable is showing the contribution which being in that group makes towards a person's predicted value of the DV. See Pedhazur (1997) for other forms of coding of categorical IVs.

Logistic regression

This appendix illustrates the techniques introduced in Chapter 21.

Generalised Linear Model

The generalised linear model is an extension of the general linear model (GLM, see Chapter 20). The GLM is the method used to conduct analyses such as ANOVA and regression, where the assumption is that there is a linear relationship between the DV or outcome variable and the IV(s) or predictor variable(s). The general*ised* linear model allows a wider range of data to be analysed than the GLM. One element of the generalised linear model is the link function.

Link function

The link function is the name given to a transformation that is needed to change the distribution of the dependent variable so that its relation to the independent variable(s) is linear. In Chapter 20 it was shown that for the case of linear regression, that is, where the dependent variable is on a more continuous scale, the relationship between the dependent variable y and the independent variable x could be shown by the equation.

$$y = b_0 + (b_1 \times x) \tag{A12.1}$$

where y is the value of the outcome variable, b_0 is the constant or intercept, b_1 is the regression coefficient for the predictor variable and x is the value of the predictor variable.

If this method of analysis were to be considered as part of the generalised linear model then the link function would simply be that after the transformation y should remain the same, i.e. not be transformed. This is known as the identity function: $y = y$.

However, in the case of a categorical dependent variable equation A12.1 isn't appropriate. Apart from anything else, it would allow values which did not exist in the categorical variable to be predicted. Thus, if the dependent variable was whether or not participants have passed a test with fail classified as 0 and pass classified as 1, then equation A12.1 could produce not only values of y which were between 0 and 1 but also less than 0 and more than 1.

A way around this problem is to transform the dependent variable and this is where the link function comes in. In the case of categorical variables the *logit* can be the link function.

Logit

The logit stands for the log of the odds. As shown in Chapter 15 the odds can be calculated from the probability of an outcome occurring. Using the example of gender and smoking status, it was found that for males, the probability of being a smoker, $p(y)$,[1] was 17 out of 44 or $17/44 = 0.38636$, which means that the probability for males of not being a smoker, $1 - p(y)$, is 0.61364. The odds of being a smoker for males is:

$$\text{Odds} = \frac{p(y)}{1 - p(y)}$$

The logit of y is therefore

$$\text{Logit}(y) = \ln\left(\frac{p(y)}{1 - p(y)}\right)$$

Where ln refers to the natural or Napierian log which is often shown as Ln on a calculator.

Using the logit allows an equation to be created which shows the relationship between gender and smoking status in the linear form which is similar to that for linear regression.

$$\text{Logit}(y) = b_0 + (b_1 \times x)$$

Now we can start to look at what the regression coefficients (b_0 and b_1) mean in the context of logistic regression.

---

1 In most accounts of logistic regression you will see what I am showing as p(y) shown as $\pi(x)$. This is shorthand for the probability that someone with a given value of the predictor variable x will have a given value for y. Put more formally still, this would be shown as $p(y = 1 | x = 0)$, that is, in the current example, the probability that someone is a smoker *if* they are male.

Regression coefficients

The constant b_0 is the value which Logit(y) has when the independent variable is 0. In the case of a categorical variable that would simply be what category had been coded as 0, whereas in the case of a more continuous variable then it would be a score of 0. Therefore, in the case of a categorical variable how you code the categories of the IV will have an effect on the constant. In SPSS if you haven't coded the categories with 0 for one category then, as long as you have made clear which variables are categorical, it will recode them and for multinomial variables (those having more than two categories) it will recode them into a set of binary (dummy) variables (see Chapter 20). Similarly it will recode the values for the dependent variable if you haven't coded one category as 0.

The coefficient b_1 can be interpreted as the amount by which the Logit(y) would change as the independent variable changes from the category coded as 0 to the one coded as 1, in the case of a categorical variable, and as the IV increases by 1 in a more continuous variable. In the gender and smoking example, non-smoker has been coded as 0 and smoker as 1, while female has been coded as 0 and male as 1.

The regression equation found is:

$$\text{Logit(y)} = 0.091 + (0.372 \times \text{gender})$$

Thus for females the predicted Logit(smoking status) is −0.091, while for males it is −0.091 − 0.372 × 1 = −0.463.

Before we can interpret this we need to transform these values into more meaningful variables. To reverse the process of taking the natural log of a number we raise e by the that log. Thus $e^{(\text{Logit})}$ gives us the odds, in which case:

Odds of being a smoker for females = $e^{-0.091}$ = 0.9130
Odds of being a smoker for males = $e^{-0.463}$ = 0.6296

From these the odds ratio can be calculated

$$\text{Odds ratio of being a smoker if male to being a smoker if female} = \frac{0.6296}{0.9130} = 0.6896$$

The output from some computer packages, for example SPSS, can be deceptive in that what is shown as Exp(B) isn't the odds in every case. For the constant what is shown as Exp(B) will be the regression coefficient for the constant used as a power for e. In which case, it is the *odds* for the category which is coded as 0. However, what is shown as Exp(B) for an IV will be the odds *ratio* for the category coded as 1 because:

$$\frac{e^{b_0+b_1 \times 1}}{e^{b_0}} \text{ (i.e. the odds ratio)}$$

$$= e^{b_1 \times 1} \left(\text{because} \frac{e^{b_0+b_1 \times 1}}{e^{b_0}} = e^{b_0+b_1 \times 1-b_0}\right)$$

$$= e^{b_1}$$

Continuous predictor

The interpretation is more complicated for a continuous predictor. The example in Chapter 21 is of predicting whether drivers were involved in accidents in the previous three years with age used as a predictor. Here, the regression coefficients were: 0.15039 for the constant and −0.02298 for age. In this case the constant is rather a mathematical fiction as it would be the Logit for accidents when age = 0. Given that the age of people in the sample is no lower than 20 years this isn't really interpretable. However, it contributes to the calculation of the odds for age. Of more use is the coefficient for age and the related odds ratio which can be derived from it.

$$e^{-0.02298} = 0.977$$

The odds ratio can be interpreted as being the change in the odds of having an accident for each extra year of age. As the odds ratio is less than one it suggests that the odds of having an accident decrease with age. A difficulty that can arise with continuous variables is the meaningfulness of a change of 1 unit or the usefulness of information related to it. For age this is not problematic. However, for other measures it could be. For example, if the measure of interest had a range below 1, such as if we had a rating scale for pain which went from 0 to .99, or if the scale were such that a change of one unit would be trivial, such as mileage driven per year. In such cases we need to transform the measure so that 1 unit becomes meaningful. For example, mileage could be changed to be expressed in terms of units of 1000 miles so that 12 500 miles becomes 12.5, then an increase of 1 unit in mileage would raise it to 13.5 or 13 500 miles.

Probabilities

As the odds is the ratio of the probability of being, in one previous example, a smoker divided by the probability of not being a smoker, we can find the probability when we are told the odds by using the following equation:

Probability = odds/(1 + odds)

Putting the appropriate figures into the equation shows us:

$$\text{Probability of being a smoker for females} = \frac{0.9130}{1.9130} = 0.47727$$

$$\text{Probability of being a smoker for males} = \frac{0.6296}{1.6296} = 0.38636$$

This leads us to the conclusion that if the equation to predict whether somebody will be a smoker only contains information about their gender it will not be accurate as it will predict that everyone is a non-smoker as the probabilities (of being a smoker in either gender) are both less than 0.5 and so all the participants will be classified in the category coded as 0, that is, as non-smokers.

The Wald statistic

One test of the significance of an individual regression coefficient can be expressed either as z-test or as a χ^2-value with df = 1. In the latter form it is called the Wald test. The two ways of presenting the result will give the same probability.

Treated as a z-test,

$$z = \frac{\text{regression coefficient}}{\text{standard error of regression coefficient}}$$

In the case of gender b = −0.3717

and its standard error is 0.4324
Therefore $z = -0.8596$.

There is a relationship between the z-test and χ^2:

$z^2 = \chi^2$ when df = 1.

Notice that if we take the square root of the critical values in Table A17.3 for χ^2 with df = 1 the results are the critical values for a two-tailed probability for z, shown in Table A17.1. As an example, the critical value for $p = .05$ for χ^2 with df = 1 is 3.84. The square root of 3.84 is 1.96, which is the critical value for two-tailed $p = .05$ for z.

Therefore, squaring the z value will give the Wald test which has a probability found from the chi-square distribution. In this example, Wald = 0.739 $p = 0.390$.

There is some agreement (see Agresti, 2002; Hosmer et al., 2013) that the Wald test provides a less accurate probability than the Likelihood ratio test.

The Likelihood ratio test

This is easier to demonstrate with an example where the predictor variable is binary. Accordingly, I'm going to use the smoking and gender example. The test is based on comparing two models. One model (the Null Model L_0) is where no predictor variables have been included, that is the Null Hypothesis that the predictor variable(s) are independent of the outcome variable; they do not explain any of the variation in the outcome variable. The second model (L_1) includes the predictor variable(s). The test is found by putting the two models into the equation

$$\chi^2 = -2 \times Ln(L_0 - L_1)$$

where Ln is the Natural or Napierian log.
The same result would be found from

$$\left[-2 \times Ln(L_0)\right] - \left[-2 \times Ln(L_1)\right]$$

A likelihood is calculated for the model where no predictor variable is involved. This combines the information from all the participants about their probabilities of being a smoker or a non-smoker. The probability of being a smoker is 38 out of 88 = 0.431818, while the probability of being a non-smoker is $1 - 0.431818 = 0.568182$, which is the same as 50 out of 88.
The combined probabilities for the whole sample is found from

$$\prod \left\{ \left[p(y)\right]^y \times \left[1 - p(y)\right]^{(1-y)} \right\}$$

where $p(y)$ is the probability that y is 1.
y is either 0 or 1 depending on the person.
$\prod$ means find the result in curly brackets for each person and then multiply all the answers together (i.e. find their product).

Thus we have 38 participants, that is those for whom y = 1, where the equation in the curly brackets is

$$\left\{ \left[0.431818 \right]^{1} \times \left[0.568182 \right]^{0} \right\}$$

which, because any number raised to the power 0 = 1 and any number raised to the power 1 remains unchanged, is the same as

0.431818

and we have 50 participants, that is those for whom y = 0, where the equation is:

$$\left\{ \left[0.431818 \right]^{0} \times \left[0.568182 \right]^{1} \right\}$$

which, following the same reasoning becomes:

0.568182

To find the product of the two sets of people, we have 0.431818 multiplied by itself 38 times multiplied by 0.568182 multiplied by itself 50 times, that is:

$$\left[0.431818 \right]^{38} \times \left[0.568182 \right]^{50}$$

The natural log of the result is found and the result of that is multiplied by –2.
This produces what is described as –2 Log likelihood or –2LL

In this case $-2LL_{0} = 120.3524$

where $-2LL_{0}$ denotes –2LL for the model where there is no predictor.
When gender is used as a predictor, there are four types of participants, from the combination of males and females and smokers and non-smokers.

17 males who smoke

$$\left\{ \left[0.38636364 \right]^{1} \times \left[0.61363636 \right]^{0} \right\}$$

27 males who don't smoke

$$\left\{ \left[0.38636364 \right]^{0} \times \left[0.61363636 \right]^{1} \right\}$$

21 female smokers

$$\left\{ \left[0.47727273 \right]^{1} \times \left[0.52272727 \right]^{0} \right\}$$

23 female non-smokers

$$\left\{ \left[0.47727273\right]^{0} \times \left[0.52272727\right]^{1} \right\}$$

in which case $-2LL_{1}$ ($-2LL$ for the model with 1 predictor in the model) =

$$-2 \times Ln \left\{ \left[0.38636364\right]^{17} \times \left[0.61363636\right]^{27} \times \left[0.47727273\right]^{21} \times \left[0.52272727\right]^{23} \right\}$$
$$= 119.6103$$

Now we can test the advantage of adding gender to the equation

$$(-2LL_{0}) - (-2LL_{1})$$
$$= 120.3524 - 119.6103$$
$$= 0.742$$

This can be treated as a χ^{2}. It has df = 1 as the difference between the two models is 1 predictor. The probability is $p = 0.389$.

▮ The Score test

When acting as a test of one predictor variable, the score test, like the Wald test, can be shown as a z-score or when squared as a χ^{2}-value. I will show the equation and workings for the χ^{2} square version.

$$Score = \frac{\left[\sum x_{i}\left(y_{i} - \bar{y}\right)\right]^{2}}{\left[\bar{y}\left(1 - \bar{y}\right)\sum\left(x_{i} - \bar{x}\right)^{2}\right]} \tag{A12.2}$$

Where, x_{i} is the value of participant i on the predictor variable
$\bar{x}$ is the mean value for the predictor variable
y_{i} is the value for participant i on the outcome variable
$\bar{y}$ is the mean value on the outcome variable,

In the smoking example, the mean score for the predictor variable, gender, is $\frac{44}{88} = 0.5$, because male is coded as 0 and female is coded as 1 and there are 44 females in the sample. The mean score for the outcome variable, smoking, is 0.431818, because smoking is coded as 1 and non-smoking as 0 and there are 38 smokers out of the 88 participants.

Therefore, to find the numerator of equation A12.2, only the females will contribute to the value as the males are coded as 0. There are 23 female non-smokers and 21 female smokers, so the numerator is:

$$\left[23 \times \left(0 - 0.431818\right) + 21 \times \left(1 - 0.431818\right)\right]^{2} = 4$$

To find the denominator of equation A12.2, we calculate:

$$0.431818 \times (1 - 0.431818) \times \left[44 \times (0 - 0.5)^2 + 44 \times (1 - 0.5)^2 \right]$$

$$= 0.245351 \times 22$$

$$= 5.397727$$

Therefore,

$$\text{Score} = \frac{4}{5.397727} = 0.741$$

Treating score as a χ^2-value with df = 1, $p = 0.389$.

Versions of analogues of R^2

Cox & Snell (R^2_{CS})

This is shown as R^2_{LR} by Mittlböck and Schemper (1999)

$$R^2_{CS} = 1 - \left(\frac{L_0}{L_1} \right)^{\left(\frac{2}{N} \right)}$$

where L_0 is the likelihood for the model without the predictor variable(s)
L_1 is the likelihood for the model which contains the predictor variable(s)
N is the total sample size.

As the workings earlier will have indicated L_0 and L_1 are extremely small numbers. Therefore, I am going to find L_0/L_1 by a different route. Division of one number by another can be found by converting both numbers to logs, then subtracting one from the other and then raising the base of the logarithm by the result of the subtraction.

We already know $(-2LL_0) - (-2LL_1) = 0.742$. If we divide that by -2 the result will be the same as $LL_0 - LL_1$:

$$\frac{0.742}{-2} = -0.37109$$

The base for the logarithm was e
Therefore,

$$\frac{L_0}{L_1} = e^{-0.37109} = 0.689983$$

Therefore,

$$R^2{}_{CS} = 1 - (0.689983)^{\left(\frac{2}{88}\right)} = 0.008398$$

(I'm reporting more than three decimal places because I want to show the differences between different versions of R^2.)

Nagelkerke $R^2{}_N$

This is shown as $R^2{}_{CU}$ by Mittlböck and Schemper (1996) after Cragg and Uhler (as cited in Mittlböck and Schemper, 1996) who also suggested the same adjustment.

$$R^2{}_N = \frac{1 - \left(\dfrac{L_0}{L_1}\right)^{\left(\frac{2}{N}\right)}}{1 - (L_0)^{\left(\frac{2}{N}\right)}}$$

In order to avoid the very small number that is L_0 I am going to introduce another mathematical way around the problem. The log of a number which has been raised to a power is the same as multiplying the log of the original number by the power. If the base of the logarithm is then raised by the resulting number, this produces the same value as the original number raised to the power.

Thus $e^{\left[\left(\frac{2}{N}\right) \times LN(L_0)\right]} = (L_0)^{\left(\frac{2}{N}\right)}$

Therefore,

$$(L_0)^{\left(\frac{2}{N}\right)} = 0.254707$$

Therefore,

$$R^2{}_N = \frac{0.008398}{1 - 0.254707} = 0.0112685$$

McFadden $R^2{}_M$

This is shown as $R^2{}_E$ by Mittlböck and Schemper (1996) as they refer to it as the entropy-based version.

$$R^2{}_M = 1 - \left|\frac{LL_1}{LL_0}\right|$$

where LL_1 is the log (to the base e) of the likelihood for the model with the predictor variable(s)
LL_0 is the log (to the base e) of the likelihood for the model without the predictor variable(s)
N is the total sample size.

By dividing $-2LL_0$ and $-2LL_1$ by -2 we find that:

$LL_0 = -60.1762$
$LL_1 = -59.8051$

Therefore,

$$R^2{}_M = 1 - \left(\frac{-59.8051}{-60.1762}\right) = 0.006167$$

Alternative versions of R^2

After evaluating the properties of a number of possible R^2 measures for logistic regression, Mittlböck and Schemper (1996, 1999) come to the conclusion that one measure which has all the desirable properties is what they refer to as Sum-of-squares R^2 ($R^2{}_{SS}$). Mittlböck and Schemper (1996, 1999) offer a number of versions of the equation for $R^2{}_{SS}$ of which the most straightforward is probably:

$$R^2{}_{SS} = 1 - \frac{\sum(y - \hat{p})^2}{N \times \bar{p} \times (1 - \bar{p})}$$

where y is the actual score of a participant on the outcome variable
$\hat{p}$ is the predicted probability that that same participant is in the target outcome category (for example, a smoker)
$\bar{p}$ is the mean outcome for the whole sample
N is the total sample size.

For smokers y = 1 and non-smokers y = 0
    For males, $\hat{p}$ is 0.38636, which means that $y - \hat{p} = 0.61364$ for male smokers and $y - \hat{p} = -0.38636$ for male non-smokers; squaring them they become 0.376554 and 0.149274, respectively.
    For females, $\hat{p} = 0.47727$, which means that $y - \hat{p} = 0.52273$ for female smokers and $y - \hat{p} = -0.47727$ for female non-smokers; squaring them they become 0.273247 and 0.227787, respectively.

$\bar{p} = 0.431818$

Therefore,

$$R^2{}_{SS} = 1 - \frac{17 \times 0.376554 + 27 \times 0.149274 + 21 \times 0.273247 + 23 \times 0.227787}{88 \times 0.431818 \times (1 - 0.431818)}$$

$$= 0.00842$$

Hosmer & Lemeshow test of model fit

$$HL = \sum \frac{\left[obs_i - \left(n_i \times \bar{p}_i\right)\right]^2}{n_i \times \bar{p}_i \times \left(1 - \bar{p}_i\right)} \tag{A12.3}$$

where obs_i is the number of participants in group i who have the target outcome,
e.g. at least one accident in the past three years
n_i is the sample size of group i
$\bar{p}_i$ is the mean predicted value for group i.

TABLE A12.1   The observed and expected frequencies of those who didn't (0) and did (1) have an accident in groups based on their predicted probability of having an accident with age as a predictor

	Accident in last 3 years = .00		Accident in last 3 years = 1.00		Total
Probability range	Observed	Expected	Observed	Expected	
1	78	73.017	17	21.983	95
2	62	67.733	31	25.267	93
3	63	65.323	31	28.677	94
4	64	62.077	30	31.923	94
5	65	62.421	34	36.579	99
6	66	59.966	32	38.034	98
7	50	57.828	46	38.172	96
8	50	55.979	44	38.021	94
9	58	55.504	36	38.496	94
10	53	49.151	31	34.849	84

TABLE A12.2   The calculations for the Hosmer and Lemeshow goodness-of-fit test

Group	n_i	obs_i	$\bar{p}_i$	Predicted$_i$ (Expected) $n_i \times \bar{p}_i$	diff$_i$	diff$_i^2$	prod$_i$	diff$_i^2$/prod$_i$
1	95	17	0.23140	21.983	−4.983	24.834	16.896	1.470
2	93	31	0.27169	25.267	5.733	32.869	18.402	1.786
3	94	31	0.30507	28.677	2.323	5.396	19.928	0.271
4	94	30	0.33960	31.923	−1.923	3.696	21.082	0.175
5	99	34	0.36948	36.579	−2.579	6.650	23.064	0.288
6	98	32	0.38811	38.034	−6.034	36.413	23.273	1.565
7	96	46	0.39762	38.172	7.828	61.279	22.994	2.665
8	94	44	0.40448	38.021	5.979	35.752	22.642	1.579
9	94	36	0.40953	38.496	−2.496	6.230	22.731	0.274
10	84	31	0.41487	34.849	−3.849	14.812	20.391	0.726
							χ^2	10.799

$$\text{diff}_i = obs_i - \bar{p}_i$$
$$\text{prod}_i = n_i \times \bar{p}_i \times (1 - predicted_i)$$

This version of the test sorts the participants in order of $p(y)$. It then divides the participants into 10 groups of roughly equal size based on their $p(y)$. For example, group 1 had 95 participants with $p(y)$ ranging from the lowest $p(y)$ which was .18848 up to .24713. The size of the groups varies slightly because of participants having the same $p(y)$ at the top end of the range for that group; in that first group three participants had that top $p(y)$. It then works out the mean $p(y)$ for each group. That mean multiplied by the sample size in the group gives the expected value. The expected value is subtracted from the observed value (i.e. the number having the target outcome, in this case an accident in the last three years) and that result is squared. The expected value is multiplied by 1 – mean $p(y)$. All the necessary elements for equation A12.3 are now present and can be seen in the last column in Table A12.2. Summing across the groups gives the χ^2 value with df = number of groups – 2.

ROC curve

The Receiver Operating Characteristic (ROC) curve is designed to evaluate the accuracy with which a signal would be detected. When used by someone designing a psychometric test or evaluating the predictive ability of a statistical model, the signal can be seen as the presence or absence of a condition, for example being a smoker.

In order to explain how to interpret the ROC curve I have created a model which nearly fits the smoking data perfectly; had it been a perfect fit then you wouldn't have seen any curve in the graph. If each participant is asked whether he or she believes that smoking kills and all but one non-smoker says that it does and all but one smoker says that it doesn't, then the pattern in Table A12.3 is produced.

TABLE A12.3   Smoking status by opinion over whether smoking kills

		Smoking kills		Total
		Yes	No	
Smoking status	Non-smoker	49	1	50
	Smoker	1	37	38
Total		50	38	88

If belief about whether smoking kills is used to predict smoking status then a logistic regression would produce the classification in Table A12.4. Table A12.4 and 12.3 look very similar except that A12.4 is looking at the predicted and actual smoking status.

TABLE A12.4   Near perfect fit of prediction and actual data

		Predicted		Total
		Non-smoker	Smoker	
Smoking status	Non-smoker	49	1	50
	Smoker	1	37	38
Total		50	38	88

From this we know that 37 out of 38 smokers are correctly identified by the model. Therefore the sensitivity of the model is 0.9737. We also know that 49 out of 50 non-smokers are correctly identified. Therefore the specificity of the model is 0.98. The predicted probability of being a smoker is 0.97368 for participants who said that smoking does not kill and 0.02 for people who said that it does. To create an ROC curve, the values of sensitivity and 1-specificity are calculated for each possible probability cut point from 0 to 1. The default value for the cut point is 0.5, meaning that if the probability for a given person is less than 0.5 that person is classified as a non-smoker, whereas if it is equal to or greater than 0.5 then the person is classified as a smoker.

From the data in Table A12.4 there are only three pairs of values for the sensitivity and 1-specificity as shown in Table A12.5.

TABLE A12.5   The sensitivity and 1-specificity for the different cut points when smoking status is predicted by belief in whether smoking kills

Cut point	Sensitivity	1-specificity
0.0000 to 0.0200	1.0000	1.0000
0.0201 to 0.9736	.9737	.0200
0.9737 to 1.0000	.0000	.0000

Figure A12.1 is a plot of sensitivity by 1-specificity.

FIGURE A12.1   The ROC curve for the data in Table A12.5

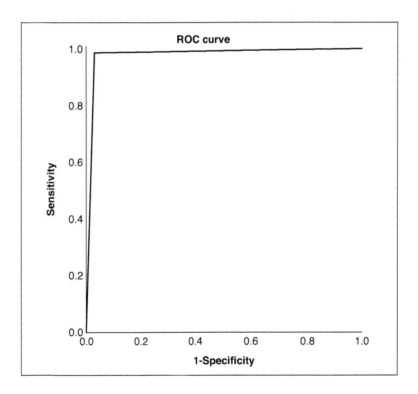

A measure of the accuracy of the model is the area under the curve, as a proportion of 1 which, in the context of logistic regression, is frequently described as the *c-statistic* or the *concordance index*. In this case the area is 0.977.

In the case of the data where smoking status was predicted from gender, using the default cut point of 0.5, sensitivity was 0, while specificity was 1; Table A12.6 shows the resulting classification.

TABLE A12.6 The classification of the sample into smokers or non-smokers based on the information supplied by gender about smoking status

		Predicted		Percentage correct
		Smoking status		
		Smoker	Non-smoker	
Smoking status	Smoker	0	38	0.0
	Non-smoker	0	50	100.0
Overall percentage				56.8

The resulting ROC curve is shown in Figure A12.2 and the area under the curve was 0.546.

FIGURE A12.2 The ROC curve when gender predicts smoking status

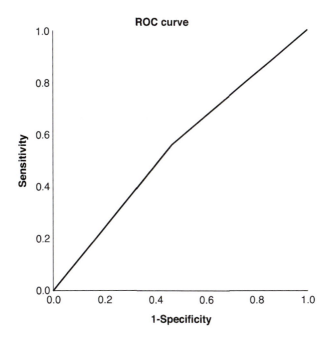

Continuous outcome variable

When car accidents in the last three years is the outcome variable and driver's age is the predictor variable, we have the same pattern of sensitivity being 0 and specificity being 1.

TABLE A12.7   The classification of drivers into whether they had an accident in the last three years based on the information supplied by their age

Observed		Predicted		Percentage correct
		Accident in last 3 years		
		No	Yes	
Accident in last 3 years	No	609	0	100.0
	Yes	332	0	0.0
Overall percentage				64.7

This produces the ROC curve shown in Figure A12.3; the area under the curve is 0.572.

FIGURE A12.3   ROC curve for age as a predictor of traffic accidents in the last 3 years

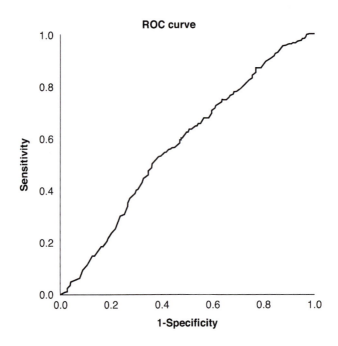

Sample size for multiple logistic regression

In Chapter 21 the sample size required for a simple logistic regression was calculated. The variable to be predicted was whether the driver had been involved in a car accident in the last three years. The degree to which participants committed driving violations was the predictor variable of interest. The sample size required to give power of .8 for alpha of .05 in a two-tailed test was 216. To allow for including participants' age, sex and degree of committing driving mistakes as well as violations as predictors, we can use an adjustment to the sample size (N) for multiple logistic regression suggested by Hsieh (1989):

$$\text{Adjusted N} = \frac{N}{1 - R^2}$$

Where R^2 is the proportion of variance in violations (as the outcome) which is accounted for by the other predictor variables in a multiple regression. I found that $R^2 = .288$. Therefore,

$$\text{Adjusted N} = \frac{216}{.712} = 303.37$$

which rounded up to the nearest whole number is 304.

This appendix illustrates the techniques introduced in Chapter 22.

ANCOVA as regression

In Chapter 22 the example was given of two groups of children – control and training condition – having their sorting ability tested. In addition, age was treated as a covariate. We can reanalyse the ANCOVA by multiple regression. In this case we have sorting ability as the variable to be predicted, with age and condition as predictor variables. Condition is a dummy variable with control coded as 0 and training coded as 1.

The results for the ANOVA table of the regression (see Table A13.1) are different from those of the ANCOVA (Table 22.2), as in the regression the whole model is summarised, whereas in the ANCOVA the contribution of each variable is presented.

TABLE A13.1 The test of the whole model from a regression with sorting ability as the DV and age and condition as IVs

	Sum of squares	df	Mean square	F	p
Regression	340.931	2	170.466	57.857	<.001
Residual	226.869	77	2.946		
Total	567.800	79			

However, the details about the regression coefficients are given separately for the covariate and the IV(s) and therefore it is the same information as for the ANCOVA; see Table A13.2. Remember that when the treatment df = 1, $t^2 = F$ and so in this case, as df = 1 for condition in the ANCOVA, the probabilities from the two ways of doing the analysis will be the same. (When the IV has more than two levels and there is therefore more than one dummy variable, to get the correct probability for the IV a sequential regression would have to be conducted with the dummy variables being added in one stage after the covariate had been added.)

TABLE A13.2   The regression coefficients for a multiple regression with sorting ability as the DV and age and condition as IVs

	Unstandardised coefficients		Standardised coefficients		
	B	Std. error	Beta	t	p
(Constant)	−0.77012	0.752		−1.023	.309
Age (in months)	0.05041	0.005	.749	10.252	<.001
Condition	0.57195	0.389	.107	1.469	.146

Calculation of adjusted means

ANCOVA adjusts the mean score on the DV for each group from the following equation:

adjusted mean = constant + (regression coefficient for covariate
× mean of covariate for the whole sample)
+ (regression coefficient for IV × code for dummy variable)

In the example this becomes:

adjusted mean = −0.77012 + (0.05041 × mean of age for the whole sample)
+ (0.57195 × code for dummy variable)

The mean age for the whole sample is 149.45 months. Thus, for the control condition which was coded as 0,

adjusted mean = −0.77012 + (0.05041 × 149.45) + (0.57195 × 0) = 6.764

while for the training condition (which was coded as 1) it is:

adjusted mean = −0.77012 + (0.05041 × 149.45) + (0.57195 × 1) = 7.336

Regression discontinuity designs (RDD)

These designs were described in Chapters 4 and 22. I can now explain why they get their name. A pre-test measure is taken and participants are allocated to conditions on the basis of how they score on the measure. For example, imagine that researchers wish to examine the effects of giving enhanced tuition to people who are good at mathematics. Participants are given a test of mathematical ability and if they score above a certain level (the cutting point), then they are placed in the group to receive extra tuition, while those below the cutting point are placed in the control group. The treatment is given and then all participants are retested on their mathematical ability. Figure A13.1 shows a version of the RDD.

FIGURE A13.1   The results from a regression discontinuity design

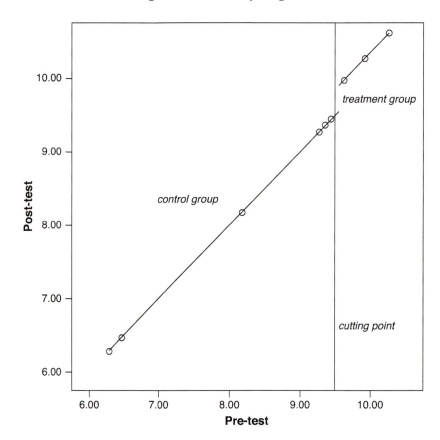

The cutting point was set at 9.5 on the pre-test and those above that level received the treatment. We can see the discontinuity in the regression line with those above the cutting point getting a higher score on the post-test than would have been predicted by the regression line for the control group.

This design can be analysed by using ANCOVA with the pre-test score as the covariate. Cook and Campbell (1979) and others argue that the post-test score should be adjusted by subtracting the value of the cutting point from it. The reason for the name of such designs is that if the treatment is effective, then if we plot a scattergram of the pre-test and post-test scores and try to impose a best-fit line on the data, there should be a discontinuity at the cutting point, with those given the enhanced training forming a different line from those not given the training. The effect of the ANCOVA will be to adjust the post-test means to allow for the pre-test scores.

Such designs have a number of qualities which make interpretation of the results more problematic than is the case for a design which used random allocation. As the allocation to groups is on the basis of the cutting point, there is no overlap between the groups in the covariate. This means that the adjustment made by ANCOVA, which assumes that the two groups have the same mean on the covariate, is more questionable. In addition, you need to examine the relationship between the pre-test and post-test values carefully to make sure that it is not curvilinear and that there isn't heterogeneity of regression slope, as the ANCOVA will attempt to fit straight and parallel regression lines to the data. The discontinuity might be created by curvilinearity and so falsely suggest that a treatment has been effective. In addition to these problems, there is one which is seen in many implementations of the design: the cutting point tends not to be set near the centre of the distribution of pre-test scores. In the mathematics example, the researchers are likely to be interested in those who are exceptionally good at maths rather than those who are just above average. This means that the effect of the treatment is being evaluated on a relatively small sample. Such an unbalanced design will additionally reduce statistical power. However, power is also markedly reduced compared with studies involving random allocation because, when the post-test scores show that the treatment and control groups differ in the direction that they did on the pre-test, the adjustment to the means has the effect of making them closer to each other. Therefore, even if the treatment is effective, the adjustment will reduce the effect size; an often-quoted figure is that you could need 2.75 times the sample size in a RDD to give the same level of power as a randomised design. See Cook and Campbell (1979) and Pedhazur and Schmelkin (1991) for further details about such designs.

Contrasts when regression slope is heterogeneous

Lisa Cowap and Rachel Povey studied two interventions to reduce unhealthy snacking in 320 children aged 7 to 11 years. They had three conditions: a group given a motivational workshop to change views of unhealthy snacks and reduce consumption of them (n = 108); a group given the same motivational workshop but coupled with *implementation intentions* where the children explicitly state what they would do to avoid snacking in given situations where they might have been tempted to eat unhealthy snacks (n = 113); and a control group (n = 99). I am going to concentrate on one of the measures – the children's attitude toward eating fewer unhealthy snacks.

The children's attitude was measured prior to the intervention groups taking part in their respective interventions (time 1). Their attitude was again measured 4 weeks after the intervention groups had received their interventions (time 2).

An analysis was conducted comparing the attitudes at time 2 of the three groups with attitude at time 1 as the covariate. The interaction between the IV and the covariate was included to test for heterogeneity of regression slope. There was significant heterogeneity of regression slope. There was also a significant difference between the three groups in attitude, see Table A13.3.

TABLE A13.3   The summary table from an analysis with attitude at time 2 as the DV, group as the IV and attitude at time 1 as the covariate, including the interaction between IV and covariate

Source	Sum of squares	df	Mean square	F	p
Group	1.461	2	0.730	4.104	0.017
Attitude at time 1	33.572	1	33.572	188.651	<0.001
Group by attitude at time1	1.170	2	0.585	3.287	0.039
Error	55.878	314	0.178		
Total	92.250	319			

As the effect of groups was significant we want to conduct contrasts between groups. However, because of heterogeneity of regression slope, we need information from a number of sources to conduct the contrasts (Maxwell & Delaney, 2004). We need to conduct an ANCOVA with groups as the IV, time 2 attitude as the DV and time 1 attitude as the covariate; this will provide the adjusted means that we are going to contrast.

Take the square root of the mean square for the error in Table A13.3; this will be referred to as S_{Het}. We need the mean and variance of the covariate for each group. Multiply each variance by one fewer than the sample size for that group; these will be referred to as SS_1, SS_2 and SS_3, for the three groups respectively. For each contrast we need to find an appropriate error term. I am going to use a paired contrast between group 1 and group 2 to see whether the two interventions differ to illustrate the calculations. Table A13.4 shows the elements we need to calculate the error term and then the contrast.

TABLE A13.4   The figures needed for a paired contrast between groups 1 and 2 when there is heterogeneity of regression slope

	Group	
	1	2
Adjusted DV mean(AdjMean)	2.752	2.783
Covariate mean (CovMean)	2.625	2.6755
Covariate variance	0.249	0.304
n	108	113
SS	26.674	34.047

Error term for contrasting groups 1 and 2 ($error_{12}$):

$$error_{12} = S_{Het} \times \sqrt{\frac{1}{n_1} + \frac{1}{n_2} + \left[\frac{(CovMean_1 - CovMean_2)}{(SS_1 + SS_2)} \right]^2}$$

$$= 0.056776$$

the t-value for the contrast with df of N−4 (where N is the overall sample size, including all the groups) is:

$$t_{(N-4)} = \frac{(AdjMean_1 - AdjMean_2)}{error_{12}}$$

Therefore:

$$t_{(316)} = 0.546$$

This is well below a critical value for t, even if we weren't adjusting alpha, and so the two interventions do not differ significantly.

Evaluation of measures: item and discriminative analysis, and accuracy of tests

This appendix illustrates the techniques introduced in Chapter 6. In addition, it examines a number of other ways of evaluating measures.

Conducting an item analysis

1   Score each person's response to each statement. Remember to keep the scoring consistent, given that approximately half the questions are worded in the opposite direction to the others, so that a 1 always means a negative attitude and a 5 a positive attitude. A computer can be used to reverse the scoring of those items which need it. To reverse a score you need to subtract the score from a figure, the size of which will depend on the minimum and maximum possible scores for the item. To find the figure add the minimum and maximum. For example, if you had a 5-point scale which ranged from 1 to 5, then the figure you need is $1 + 5 = 6$. If a person scored 1 on this item, then the reversed score would be $6 − 1 = 5$; 2 would become 4; and so on.

2   Calculate the total score for each participant.

3   Calculate a Pearson's product moment correlation (r) between each statement and the total score and between all the statements (see Chapter 19). In fact, each question is only on an ordinal scale, which has a limited number of possible values (5), in which case it would seem more appropriate to use Spearman's rho or Kendall's tau. However, the total score is likely to have a sufficient number of possible values to warrant using Pearson's r. The data are usually analysed by parametric tests. This is partly because there is a limit to the statistics that can be computed if we are restricted to non-parametric tests.

4   Find the critical value for r for a one-tailed test at $\alpha = .05$ (see Appendix XVII). It is a one-tailed test because you have chosen the questions on the expectation that they correlate positively with each other. In Chapter 6, I recommended that you use at least 68 participants. This was to give the test power of .8 for a medium effect size, which in this case would be $r = .3$. If you had used 68 participants, then the critical value of r, to be statistically significant at $p = .05$, would be .201.

   If you decided to analyse the data with Spearman's rho or Kendall's tau, then you should have at least 75 participants to have the same power. In the case of Spearman's rho the critical value would be rho $= .191$ for that number of participants. If you used Kendall's tau, then the critical value of tau would be .129 for 75 participants.

5   Check the correlation between each statement and the total scores. Any statement which has a correlation coefficient with the total which is the same size as, or larger than, the critical value can be said to have passed this stage of the item analysis and can remain, for the moment, in the scale.

6   Examine the statements which did not pass the previous stage of the item analysis to see whether they correlate with each other (at the same critical level as before). Any statements which not only do not correlate with the total but also do not correlate with any other statements should be rejected, unless they are addressing a specific aspect of what you are studying which is essential to your research. In this case, they would have to form a sub-scale on their own. Look at how they are worded to see why such statements might have failed.

A set of statements which do not correlate with the total but do correlate with each other may form a sub-scale of the attitude scale. Examine such statements to see what aspects, of the attitude you are measuring, they have in common. If there appears to be a coherent theme which relates them, then treat them as forming a sub-scale.

If you used the attitude scale at this stage to measure attitudes you would produce different total scores for the different sub-scales.

Analysing discriminative power

If the item analysis identified sub-scales, then the following should be conducted separately for each sub-scale.

1   For each participant form a new total score.
2   Identify the participants with the top 25% of total scores (the high scorers) and the participants with the bottom 25% of total scores (the low scorers) (other percentiles could be used, such as the top and bottom 30%).
3   For each question, compare the high and low scorers (on the basis of their total scores) using a one-tailed, between-subjects t-test. Alternatively, you could conduct a one-tailed Mann–Whitney U test, as it is the non-parametric equivalent of the between-subjects t-test.
4   Retain only statements which show a significant difference between high and low scorers. The others should be discarded as they are failing to discriminate sufficiently between high and low scorers and are therefore redundant.

Measures of accuracy of tests

When a test is used to classify people, they can fall into one of four categories (as shown in Table A14.1): those who have the condition and the test correctly identifies as having the condition (true positives), those who don't have the condition but are classified by the test as having the condition (false positives), those who do have the condition but are wrongly classified as not having it (false negatives) and those who do not have the condition and are correctly classified as not having it (true negatives).

TABLE A14.1   The possible ways in which people can be classified by a test and whether they have a condition or not

Test result	Has condition?	
	Yes	No
Positive	True positives	False positives
Negative	False negatives	True negatives

Sensitivity (sometimes known as *detection rate*) is the proportion of those who do have the condition and are shown by the test to have the condition. Thus,

$$\text{Sensitivity} = \frac{\text{true positives}}{\text{true positives} + \text{false negatives}}$$

Specificity is the proportion of those who do not have the condition and are correctly classified as not having the condition. Thus,

$$\text{Specificity} = \frac{\text{true negatives}}{\text{true negatives} + \text{false positives}}$$

Three more related terms are *accuracy rate, positive predictive value* (PPV or success ratio) and *negative predictive value* (NPV).

Accuracy rate is the proportion of the entire sample placed in the correct category. Thus,

$$\text{accuracy rate} = \frac{\text{true positives} + \text{true negatives}}{\text{whole sample}}$$

PPV is the proportion of those who were classified by the test as having the condition and who did have the condition. Thus,

$$\text{PPV} = \frac{\text{true positives}}{\text{false positives} + \text{true positives}}$$

NPV is the proportion of those who were classified by the test as not having the condition and who did not have the condition. Thus,

$$\text{NPV} = \frac{\text{true negatives}}{\text{false negatives} + \text{true negatives}}$$

Imagine that we have a test of depression which has been given to 3000 people. In addition, each person has only been included in the sample after being interviewed by two psychiatrists who have agreed as to whether that person is clinically depressed. The results are shown in Table A14.2.

TABLE A14.2   The classification and actual condition of people with and without depression

	Has condition?		
Test result	Yes	No	
Positive	750	270	1020
Negative	0	1980	1980
	750	2250	

$$\text{sensitivity} = \frac{750}{750 + 0} = 1.00 \text{ or } 100\%$$

$$\text{specificity} = \frac{1980}{1980 + 270} = .88 \text{ or } 88\%$$

$$\text{accuracy rate} = \frac{750 + 1980}{3000} = .91 \text{ or } 91\%$$

$$\text{PPV} = \frac{750}{750 + 270} = .74$$

$$\text{NPV} = \frac{1980}{1980 + 0} = 1.00$$

Exploratory factor analysis

This appendix illustrates the techniques introduced in Chapter 24.

Determinant

One way to view the determinant of a matrix is as the product of the eigenvalues of that matrix.

Bartlett's test of sphericity

Bartlett's test of sphericity utilises the fact that a correlation matrix in which none of the variables correlate will just have 1s in the diagonal and zeroes elsewhere. The product of the diagonal values will be a set of 1s multiplied together and so will be 1. Therefore, the determinant of such a matrix (an Identity Matrix) is 1. Thus the Null Hypothesis of Bartlett's test is that the determinant of the correlation matrix = 1.

$$\chi^2 = -(N-1) \times ((2 \times i) + 5)/6) \times LN(\text{determinant})$$

Where N is the sample size, (1239), i is the number of variables (16), LN is the natural logarithm (also known as Napierian logarithm or Log_e) and the determinant is that from the correlation matrix.

> The determinant of the correlation matrix from the data is 0.014071
> LN(determinant) = −4.26363
> Therefore $\chi^2 = 5252.086$

df

The degrees of freedom are the number of unique correlations in the matrix. The upper and lower triangles are duplicates of each other and the diagonals are 1s. We could find the number of unique correlations from the size of the matrix (which is the square of the number of variables: $16 \times 16 = 256$).

From which we need to subtract the number of items in the diagonal (which is the number of variables: 16; 256 − 16 = 240). We then half the result (240/2 = 120). Alternatively we could use the method to find the number of unique combinations of two items from a set: (i × (i−1))/2; in this case, (16 × 15)/2 = 120.

Sampling adequacy

Measure of sampling adequacy (MSA) for an individual item

$$MSA = \frac{sum\ of\ squared\ correlations}{sum\ of\ squared\ correlations + sum\ of\ squared\ partial\ correlations}$$

where the correlations are those between the item for which MSA is being calculated and each of the other items. Each partial correlation is between the item for which MSA is being calculated and another item with all the other items partialled out; for example, the partial correlation between item 1 and item 2 has item 3 to item 16 partialled out. If there are a large number of items per factor then the partial correlations should be small and so the sum of squared correlations should be relatively high and the MSA be high.

For item 1

TABLE A15.1   The correlations and partial correlations of item 1 with each of the other items, plus the squares of each r and partial-r to calculate the MSA of item 1

Item	r	Partial r	r-squared	Partial r squared
2	0.339	0.167	0.114755	0.027783
3	0.286	0.062	0.082014	0.003830
4	0.162	0.021	0.026342	0.000446
5	0.265	0.041	0.070178	0.001664
6	0.228	−0.006	0.051887	0.000032
7	0.309	0.123	0.095254	0.015249
8	0.144	−0.030	0.020792	0.000874
9	0.236	0.057	0.055595	0.003250
10	0.179	0.056	0.031906	0.003174
11	0.222	0.059	0.049457	0.003467
12	0.365	0.182	0.132965	0.033107
13	0.245	0.036	0.060123	0.001320
14	0.171	0.026	0.029182	0.000663
15	0.158	0.035	0.02483	0.001243
16	0.128	−0.075	0.016501	0.005623
		Sum	0.86178	0.101726

$$MSA = \frac{.86178}{.86178 + .101726}$$
$$= .894421$$

In SPSS the MSA values are shown in the diagonal of the anti-image correlation matrix (see below).

Kaiser-Meyer-Olkin test of sampling adequacy (KMO)

The KMO is a measure of the overall sampling adequacy of the original correlation matrix.

$$\text{KMO} = \frac{sum\ of\ squared\ correlations}{sum\ of\ squared\ correlations + sum\ of\ squared\ partial\ correlations}$$

Here, the correlations are for every pairing of items and the partial correlations are for every pairing of items.

$$= \frac{9.565}{9.565 + 0.46542}$$

$$= .954$$

Image

If you carried out a series of regressions such that in each one item was the outcome variable and the other items were the predictors, then the image would be the value predicted for a participant on an item.

Anti-image

The anti-image is the difference between the actual value for a participant and the predicted value (the residual, here used in its usual sense and different from that used when referring to the residual matrix). The anti-image correlation matrix contains the correlations between the residuals in each item. The anti-image correlations are also the same as the negative of the partial correlations. Thus, Table A15.1 shows that the partial correlation between item 1 and item 2 is .167, while the correlation between the residuals in item 1 and item 2 is −.167. SPSS puts the MSA in the diagonal. If there are a large number of items per factor then the partial correlations should be small; see Table A15.2.

Communalities

Initial

To create the reduced correlation matrix for principal axis factor analysis, the diagonal values in the matrix have the 1s replaced by an initial estimate of the communalities, the relationship between an item and the other items. The initial communality for an item is the proportion of variance explained in that item when it is treated as the outcome variable and the other items are treated as the predictors; in other words, the initial communality is the R^2 from the regression; see Table A15.3.

TABLE A15.2 The anti-image correlation matrix for the 16 items in the driving questionnaire with MSA values in the diagonal cells

	1	2	3	4	5	6	7	8	9	10	11	12	13	14	15	16
1	.894	-0.167	-0.062	-0.021	-0.041	0.006	-0.123	0.030	-0.057	-0.056	-0.059	-0.182	-0.036	-0.026	-0.035	0.075
2	-0.167	.904	-0.069	-0.006	-0.119	-0.081	-0.082	0.049	-0.093	0.010	-0.002	-0.096	-0.108	-0.020	0.029	-0.014
3	-0.062	-0.069	.909	0.023	-0.101	-0.075	-0.158	-0.040	-0.135	-0.066	0.001	-0.154	-0.074	0.012	0.046	-0.022
4	-0.021	-0.006	0.023	.907	-0.088	-0.144	0.084	-0.167	0.035	-0.124	-0.190	-0.008	0.031	-0.021	-0.157	-0.098
5	-0.041	-0.119	-0.101	-0.088	.923	-0.072	-0.144	-0.036	-0.055	0.029	0.004	-0.069	-0.138	-0.068	0.020	-0.017
6	0.006	-0.081	-0.075	-0.144	-0.072	.919	-0.059	-0.199	-0.080	-0.068	-0.115	-0.098	0.000	-0.129	0.033	0.027
7	-0.123	-0.082	-0.158	0.084	-0.144	-0.059	.911	-0.017	-0.032	-0.026	-0.056	-0.038	-0.078	-0.067	0.021	-0.049
8	0.030	0.049	-0.040	-0.167	-0.036	-0.199	-0.017	.892	-0.024	-0.044	-0.151	0.012	-0.027	-0.087	-0.224	0.085
9	-0.057	-0.093	-0.135	0.035	-0.055	-0.080	-0.032	-0.024	.927	0.027	-0.003	-0.083	-0.062	-0.035	-0.047	0.003
10	-0.056	0.010	-0.066	-0.124	0.029	-0.068	-0.026	-0.044	0.027	.917	-0.103	0.011	-0.025	0.018	-0.068	-0.248
11	-0.059	-0.002	0.001	-0.190	0.004	-0.115	-0.056	-0.151	-0.003	-0.103	.931	-0.049	-0.033	0.002	-0.126	-0.113
12	-0.182	-0.096	-0.154	-0.008	-0.069	-0.098	-0.038	0.012	-0.083	0.011	-0.049	.917	-0.112	0.007	-0.023	-0.032
13	-0.036	-0.108	-0.074	0.031	-0.138	0.000	-0.078	-0.027	-0.062	-0.025	-0.033	-0.112	.931	-0.060	-0.012	-0.037
14	-0.026	-0.020	0.012	-0.021	-0.068	-0.129	-0.067	-0.087	-0.035	0.018	0.002	0.007	-0.060	.931	-0.044	-0.173
15	-0.035	0.029	0.046	-0.157	0.020	0.033	0.021	-0.224	-0.047	-0.068	-0.126	-0.023	-0.012	-0.044	.860	-0.395
16	0.075	-0.014	-0.022	-0.098	-0.017	0.027	-0.049	0.085	0.003	-0.248	-0.113	-0.032	-0.037	-0.173	-0.395	.843

TABLE A15.3 The initial communalities prior to conducting factor analysis on the items

	Communalities
Item	Initial
1	.238
2	.249
3	.281
4	.405
5	.279
6	.360
7	.263
8	.369
9	.185
10	.317
11	.400
12	.296
13	.226
14	.228
15	.484
16	.472

After extraction

The first stage of a factor analysis produces a factor matrix which shows the loading of each factor on each item. These are used to find the post analysis communality for each item. Each loading can be treated as a correlation between the item and the factor. As the factors at this stage are intentionally uncorrelated (orthogonal) the square of each correlation is explaining a unique proportion of the variance in the item. Therefore, the sum of those squared correlations tells us what proportion of variance in the item is explained by the factors (the communality); see Table A15.4. Some of the communalities shown in Table A15.4 differ slightly from those shown in Table A15.5 due to rounding errors in the calculations.

TABLE A15.4 The loadings, their squares and the sum of the squares (communalities) for each item after the principal axis factor analysis

	Factor				
Item	1	2	1^2	2^2	Communality
1	0.427	0.303	0.182	0.092	0.274
2	0.426	0.374	0.181	0.140	0.321
3	0.482	0.340	0.232	0.116	0.348
4	0.593	−0.345	0.352	0.119	0.471

(*Continued*)

TABLE A15.4   (Continued)

Item	1	2	1^2	2^2	Communality
			Factor		
5	0.508	0.269	0.258	0.072	0.330
6	0.607	0.018	0.368	0.000	0.369
7	0.470	0.305	0.221	0.093	0.314
8	0.566	−0.235	0.320	0.055	0.376
9	0.395	0.256	0.156	0.066	0.222
10	0.529	−0.250	0.280	0.063	0.342
11	0.633	−0.242	0.401	0.059	0.459
12	0.516	0.301	0.266	0.091	0.357
13	0.456	0.248	0.208	0.062	0.269
14	0.479	−0.051	0.229	0.003	0.232
15	0.617	−0.422	0.381	0.178	0.559
16	0.602	−0.340	0.362	0.116	0.478

Reproduced correlation matrix

The Factor matrix is used to reproduce the correlations in a similar way to how the communalities are calculated. To reproduce the correlation between item 1 and item 2 (r_{12}) the following equation is used:

$$\text{Reproduced } r_{12} = \text{loading}_{11} \times \text{loading}_{21} + \text{loading}_{12} \times \text{loading}_{22}$$

Where loading_{11} is the loading for item 1 on Factor_1
loading_{21} is the loading for item 2 on Factor_1
loading_{12} is the loading for item 1 on Factor_2
loading_{22} is the loading for item 2 on Factor_2

$$\text{reproduced } r_{12} = .427 \times .426 + .303 \times .374 = .295$$

Once that has been done for each pair of items, the full matrix of reproduced correlations has been created.

TABLE A15.5   The reproduced correlation matrix, using just the information from the two factors, with communalities in the diagonal

	1	2	3	4	5	6	7	8	9	10	11	12	13	14	15	16
1	.274															
2	.295	.321														
3	.309	.332	.348													
4	.149	.123	.168	.470												
5	.299	.317	.336	.209	.331											

(Continued)

TABLE A15.5 (Continued)

	1	2	3	4	5	6	7	8	9	10	11	12	13	14	15	16
6	.265	.265	.298	.354	.313	.368										
7	.293	.314	.330	.174	.321	.291	.314									
8	.171	.153	.193	.417	.225	.339	.195	.376								
9	.246	.264	.277	.146	.269	.244	.264	.164	.221							
10	.150	.132	.170	.400	.202	.317	.173	.359	.145	.343						
11	.197	.179	.223	.459	.257	.380	.224	.416	.188	.396	.460					
12	.312	.332	.351	.202	.343	.318	.334	.221	.281	.198	.254	.357				
13	.270	.287	.304	.185	.298	.281	.290	.200	.243	.179	.229	.310	.269			
14	.189	.185	.214	.302	.230	.290	.210	.283	.176	.267	.316	.232	.206	.232		
15	.136	.105	.154	.511	.200	.367	.161	.448	.136	.432	.493	.191	.177	.317	.558	
16	.154	.129	.174	.474	.215	.359	.179	.421	.151	.404	.463	.208	.190	.306	.514	.477

Parallel analysis

Another way which has been devised to decide on the number of components and then factors which should be extracted is Parallel Analysis. A data set is created which contains randomly generated data with as many variables as the genuine data set and data in each variable for as many participants as in the original data set. The random data are put through a PCA and the size of each the 16 eigenvalues (in this example) is noted; remember that each eigenvalue will be smaller than the previous one, as seen in the factor analysis conducted in this book. This process is repeated as many times as required (for example, 100 times), each with a new randomly generated data set. The mean for each of the 16 eigenvalues across the random data sets is calculated. The result from the PCA on the genuine data set is then compared with the means from the randomly generated data sets. Starting with the first component, if its eigenvalue in the genuine data set is larger than the equivalent mean eigenvalue from the randomly generated sets then it is retained. This process continues until an eigenvalue in the genuine data set is not larger than its randomly generated equivalent, at which point the process stops. For example, if the first five eigenvalues passed the test and the sixth did not then only the first five factors would be extracted. Mulaik (2010) warns that with realistic simulated data sets it is possible for Parallel Analysis to identify the wrong number of components.

Appendix XVI

Meta-analysis

This appendix illustrates the techniques introduced in Chapter 26.

Introduction

This appendix takes you through a meta-analysis which compares scores for depression of women who suffer from chronic pelvic pain (who will be described as the experimental group) with control groups of women who do not. These data are taken from McGowan et al. (1998).

The studies

In all but one case the relevant details given in the papers are in the form of means and standard deviations rather than probability statistics (Table A16.1).

TABLE A16.1   Means, standard deviations and sample sizes for the papers to be included in the meta-analysis

Study	Experimental group			Control group			Probability statistic
	n	Mean	SD	n	Mean	SD	
1	41	1.26	0.89	41	0.61	0.50	t = 4.08
2	30	46.44	10.52	30	38.40	7.50	–
3	50	64.50	11.30	50	51.90	10.40	–
4	37	61.44	12.24	23	50.50	9.20	–
5	162	54.30	12.65	46	45.50	12.40	–
6	64	61.61	8.83	46	59.11	8.45	–

The next stage is to create a single probability statistic for each of the studies. Given the nature of the summary statistics which each of the present studies has provided, the most appropriate statistic is the between-subjects t-test.

However, if the level of reporting in a paper is so poor that you have no descriptive statistics and are simply told whether the result was statistically significant, then the best you can do is treat a non-significant result as having a z-value of 0 (which gives a probability of .5) and a statistically significant result as having a z-value of 1.645 (the critical one-tailed level for $p = .05$).

A new summary table can be produced (Table A16.2).

TABLE A16.2   The t-values for the studies in the meta-analysis

Study	Total N	t	Direction of effect
1	82	4.0771	+
2	60	3.4085	+
3	100	5.8015	+
4	60	3.6837	+
5	208	4.1818	+
6	110	1.4911	+

Computing a common effect size statistic

The following equations can be used for converting common statistics into r. In each case, if the original result showed a negative effect with respect to the hypothesis, that is, that the control group had a larger mean than the experimental group, then the r must be treated as negative.

To convert a t-*value to* r

$$r = \sqrt{\frac{t^2}{t^2 + df}}$$
(A16.1)

To convert an F-*ratio to* r

$$r = \sqrt{\frac{F_{1,\nu2}}{F_{1,\nu2} + df_{error}}}$$
(A16.2)

where $F_{1,\nu2}$ is an *F*-ratio with df = 1 for the treatment. (An *F*-ratio can only be used if the IV has two levels, that is, the df for the treatment = 1.)

To convert a χ^2 *to* r

$$r = \sqrt{\frac{\chi^2}{N}}$$
(A16.3)

where the χ^2 must have df = 1.

To convert a contingency coefficient (C) to r

$$r = \sqrt{\frac{C^2}{1 - C^2}}$$

where the χ^2 which was used to calculate C must have df = 1.

To convert a standard z-*value to* r

$$r = \frac{z}{\sqrt{N}}$$
(A16.4)

where *N* is the total number of participants in the study.

To convert a d-*value to* r

$$r = \frac{d}{\sqrt{d^2 + \frac{1}{(p \times q)}}}$$
(A16.5)

where *d* is the effect size, using Cohen's *d* (1988)
p   is the proportion of participants who were in the experimental group; thus if the total number of participants in the study was 100 and the number in the experimental group was 40, $p = \frac{40}{100} = .4$
q   is the proportion of participants in the control group

Alternatively, when the samples are the same size, to convert a d-value to r

$$r = \frac{d}{d^2 + 4} \qquad\qquad (A16.6)$$

To convert an odds ratio to a d-value

I don't know of a straight conversion from an odds ratio to r but Chinn (2000) has produced a method for converting from an odds ratio to d and then equation A16.5 or A16.6 could be used if the sample sizes are known. If the proportions are also known, then it would be better to calculate r directly. However, if they aren't known, then use:

$$d = \frac{Log_e \left(odds\,ratio\right)}{\left(\dfrac{\pi}{\sqrt{3}}\right)} \qquad\qquad (A16.7)$$

where log_e is the natural log (often shown as LN on a calculator).

We are now in a position to calculate the effect size for each study. I will use study 2 as an example:

$$r = \sqrt{\frac{t^2}{t^2 + df}}$$
$$= \sqrt{\frac{(3.4085)^2}{(3.4085)^2 + (60 - 2)}}$$
$$= \sqrt{\frac{11.6179}{11.6179 + 58}}$$
$$= \sqrt{0.1669}$$
$$= 0.4085$$

Using the same procedure all the t-values can now be converted into r-values (Table A16.3):

TABLE A16.3   The effect sizes (r) of the studies in the meta-analysis

Study	N	r	Direction of effect
1	82	0.4148	+
2	60	0.4085	+
3	100	0.5056	+
4	60	0.4354	+
5	208	0.2797	+
6	110	0.1420	+

Computing a common probability statistic

The following equations are for converting an inferential statistic or an effect size into a z-value. In each case, if the original finding showed a negative effect with respect to the hypothesis, that is, that the control group had a larger mean than the experimental group, then the z must be treated as negative.

To convert a t-*value to* z

$$z = \sqrt{df \times \log_e\left(1 + \frac{t^2}{df}\right)} \times \sqrt{\left(1 - \frac{1}{2 \times df}\right)} \qquad \text{(A16.8)}$$

where df $= N - 2$ for a between-subjects design and $N - 1$ for a within-subjects design, N is the total number of participants in the study and $\log_e$ is the natural log (often shown as LN on a calculator).

To convert an F-*ratio to* z

$$z = \sqrt{df_{error} \times \log_e\left(1 + \frac{F_{1,\nu2}}{df_{error}}\right)} \times \sqrt{\left(1 - \frac{1}{2 \times df_{error}}\right)} \qquad \text{(A16.9)}$$

where df_{error} are the degrees of freedom for the error term (the divisor) used to compute the F-ratio and $F_{1,\nu2}$ is an F-ratio with df $= 1$ for the treatment. (An F-ratio can only be used if the IV has two levels, that is, the df for the treatment $= 1$.)

To convert χ^2 *to* z

$$z = \sqrt{\chi^2} \qquad \text{(A16.10)}$$

where χ^2 must have df $= 1$.

To convert a d-*value to* z

$$z = \frac{d \times \sqrt{N}}{\sqrt{d^2 + \frac{1}{(p \times q)}}} \qquad \text{(A16.11)}$$

where d is the effect size, using Cohen's d (1988)
p is the proportion of participants who were in the experimental group; thus, if the total number of participants in the study was 100 and the number in the experimental group was 40, $p = \dfrac{40}{100} = .4$
q is the proportion of participants in the control group

Alternatively, when the samples are the same size, to convert a d-value to z:

$$z = \frac{d \times \sqrt{N}}{\sqrt{d^2 + 4}} \qquad \text{(A16.12)}$$

To convert an r *to* z

$$z = r \times \sqrt{N} \qquad \text{(A16.13)}$$

We are now in a position to compute a z for each study ready for computing a combined probability level. Given that each conversion (transformation) is likely to produce an approximation to the exact figure, it is better to do the conversion from the original statistic, where possible, rather than via a previous conversion. Thus, I would convert t to r and t to z rather than t to r and then r to z. Once again, I will use study 2 as an example.

$$z = \sqrt{df \times \log_e \left(1 + \frac{t^2}{df}\right)} \times \sqrt{\left(1 - \frac{1}{2 \times df}\right)}$$

$$= \sqrt{58 \times \log_e \left(1 + \frac{11.6179}{58}\right)} \times \sqrt{\left(1 - \frac{1}{2 \times 58}\right)}$$

$$= \sqrt{58 \times \log_e (1 + 0.2003)} \times \sqrt{(1 - 0.0086)}$$

$$= \sqrt{58 \times 0.18257} \times \sqrt{0.9914}$$

$$= \sqrt{10.5896} \times \sqrt{0.9914}$$

$$= 3.2541 \times 0.9957$$

$$= 3.2401$$

Following the same procedure a table of z-values can be created for the studies which can be used to produce a combined probability level (Table A16.4).

TABLE A16.4   The z-values for the studies in the meta-analysis

Study	N	z	Direction of effect
1	82	3.874095	+
2	60	3.240101	+
3	100	5.365210	+
4	60	3.476796	+
5	208	4.091938	+
6	110	1.480072	+

Combining effect size

Before the effect sizes can be combined we need to convert each r into a Fisher's transformation of r (r'); putting the effect size for Study 2, $r = 0.4085$, into the equation given in Appendix XIX produces $r' = 0.4338$.

Remember that if any of the studies had a negative direction of effect, the r for that study is negative when placed in the above equation and the resultant r' will be negative.

Now a table of r's can be created for all the studies (Table A16.5):

TABLE A16.5   The Fisher's transformed correlation coefficients (r') of the studies in the meta-analysis

Study	N	r'	Direction of effect
1	82	0.4414	+
2	60	0.4338	+
3	100	0.5568	+
4	60	0.4666	+
5	208	0.2874	+
6	110	0.1430	+

This information can be used to calculate to combine the effect sizes using the weighted mean r':

$$\text{Weighted Mean}(\bar{r}') = \frac{\sum\left(\left(N_j - 3\right) \times r'_j\right)}{\sum\left(N_j - 3\right)} \tag{A16.14}$$

where N_j is the number of participants in study j
r'_j is the r' for study j
$j = 1$ to k
k is the number of studies

$$\bar{r}' = \frac{\left(79 \times 0.4414 + 57 \times 0.4338 + 97 \times 0.5568 + 57 \times 0.4666 + 205 \times 0.2874 + 107 \times 0.1430\right)}{\left(79 + 57 + 97 + 57 + 205 + 107\right)}$$

$$= \frac{214.4166}{602}$$

$$= 0.3562$$

Remember that if any of the studies had a negative direction of effect, the r' for that study is negative when placed in the above equation.

We can use the weighted mean r' to find the combined effect size but we have to convert the weighted mean r' back to an r-value, using the equation given in Appendix XIX for transforming r' to r. This produces a combined effect size $(r) = 0.3418$, which, according to Cohen (1988), is a medium effect size.

The confidence interval

To find the confidence interval (CI) at the 95% level of confidence, we need to place the weighted mean effect size $(\bar{r}')$, prior to transforming to r, and the total number of participants in each study into the following equation; the example calculates the CI for all six studies:

$$\text{Confidence Interval for } \bar{r}'(CI) = \bar{r}' - \frac{1.96}{\sqrt{\sum(N_j - 3)}} \tag{A16.15}$$

$$\text{to } \bar{r}' + \frac{1.96}{\sqrt{\sum(Nj - 3)}}$$

where N_j is the total number of participants in study j, $j = 1$ to k, and k is the number of studies in the meta-analysis.

$$\text{CI for } \bar{r}' = 0.3562 - \frac{1.96}{\sqrt{79 + 57 + 97 + 57 + 205 + 107}}$$

to

$$= 0.3562 + \frac{1.96}{\sqrt{79 + 57 + 97 + 57 + 205 + 107}}$$

$$= 0.3562 - \frac{1.96}{\sqrt{602}} \quad \text{to} \quad 0.3562 + \frac{1.96}{\sqrt{602}}$$

$$= 0.3562 - 0.0799 \quad \text{to} \quad 0.3562 + 0.0799$$

$$= 0.2763 \text{ to } 0.4361$$

These then need to be converted into r's using the equation for transforming r' to r, given in Appendix XIX. The CI for r becomes:

CI for r = .2695 to .4104

Combining probability

Probability can be combined using the standard z-scores shown in Table A16.4 in the following equation:

$$\text{combined } z = \frac{\sum z_j}{\sqrt{k}}$$

(A16.16)

where z_j is the standard z-score for study j, $j = 1$ to k and k is the number of studies.

$$\text{combined } z = \frac{3.8741 + 3.2401 + 5.3652 + 3.4768 + 4.0919 + 1.4801}{\sqrt{6}}$$

$$= \frac{21.52821}{2.44949}$$

$$= 8.7888$$

Remember that if any of the studies had a negative direction of effect, the z for that study is negative when placed in the above equation.

Referring to the z-table in Appendix XVII shows that this combined z-value is significant at below the p = .00001 level. We can conclude that those suffering from chronic pelvic pain are significantly more depressed than the control groups used in the studies.

Heterogeneity

Heterogeneity for effect size

The heterogeneity of the effect size can be calculated, using the equation:

$$\chi^2_{(k-1)} = \sum \left(\left(N_j - 3 \right) \times \left(r'_j - \bar{r}' \right)^2 \right)$$

(A16.17)

where N_j is the number of participants in study j
r'_j is the r' for study j
$j = 1$ to k
k is the number of studies
$k - 1$ is the df for the χ^2
$\bar{r}'$ is the weighted mean r'

$$\chi^2_{(5)} = 79 \times \left(0.4414 - 0.3562 \right)^2 + 57 \times \left(0.4338 - 0.3562 \right)^2$$

$$+ 97 \times \left(0.5568 - 0.3562 \right)^2 + 57 \times \left(0.4666 - 0.3562 \right)^2$$

$$+ 205 \times \left(0.2874 - 0.3562 \right)^2 + 107 \times \left(0.1430 - 0.3562 \right)^2$$

$$= 0.5733 + 0.3437 + 3.9049 + 0.6948 + 0.96998 + 4.8626$$

$$= 11.3495$$

Remember that if any of the studies had a negative direction of effect, the r' for that study is negative when placed in the preceding equation.

Referring to the table of the chi-squared distribution in Appendix XVII we see that the probability of this χ^2 with 5 df lies between .05 and .02, in which case the effect sizes of the studies are significantly heterogeneous. Looking at the computation we can see that study 6 contributed the most to this outcome. If we remove that study and redo the calculations, including producing a new weighted mean r', we see that $\chi^2_{(4)} = 5.4356$. The probability of this new χ^2 lies between .3 and .2. In other words, the remaining five studies are not significantly heterogeneous with respect to effect size, in which case we do not need to remove any more studies from the meta-analysis.

Because we have found heterogeneity in the set of effect sizes and we have found the subset of studies which are homogeneous, we need to calculate a new CI for the new weighted mean r' and a new combined z of the homogeneous subset, convert the new weighted mean r' to a weighted mean r and convert the CI for the new weighted mean r' into a CI for the new weighted mean r, all using the methods shown previously.

Below I show how groups of studies can be compared (focused comparison) using the same principles as the check for heterogeneity of effect size.

Heterogeneity for probability

Heterogeneity for probability can be calculated by using the standard z-values for each study. As was pointed out in Chapter 26, this procedure is not necessary, as heterogeneity of probability can be produced by results which used different sample sizes even when the effect sizes are the same. However, for completeness I include it. We need to calculate the mean z-value ($\bar{z}$) using the usual procedure for finding means; all six studies are included in this analysis:

$$\bar{z} = \frac{\sum z_j}{k} \tag{A16.18}$$

where z_j is the z-value for study j, $j = 1$ to k and k is the number of studies.

$$\bar{z} = \frac{(3.8741 + 3.2401 + 5.3652 + 3.4768 + 4.0919 + 1.4801)}{6}$$
$$= 3.5880$$

Remember that if any of the studies had a negative direction of effect, the z for that study is negative when placed in the above equation.

The heterogeneity of the probability values can now be calculated by the following equation:

$$\chi^2_{(k-1)} = \sum \left(z_j - \bar{z}\right)^2 \tag{A16.19}$$

where $k - 1$ is the df for the χ^2.

$$\chi^2_{(5)} = (3.8741 - 3.588)^2 + (3.2401 - 3.588)^2$$
$$+ (5.3652 - 3.588)^2 + (3.4768 - 3.588)^2$$
$$+ (4.0919 - 3.588)^2 + (1.4801 - 3.588)^2$$
$$= 8.0710$$

Remember that if any of the studies had a negative direction of effect, the z for that study is negative when placed in the preceding equation.

Referring to the table of the chi-squared distribution in Appendix XVII we can see that the probability of this χ^2 with 5 df being a chance event lies between .2 and .1 and thus is not statistically significant. In this case we can conclude that the six studies are not significantly heterogeneous with respect to their probability levels.

Publication bias

Two methods for trying to identify whether the result of a meta-analysis is likely to be affected by publication bias are the funnel graph (described in Chapter 26) and checking fail-safe N against the likely number of unpublished studies.

The file-drawer problem

The fail-safe N

The fail-safe N is the number of unpublished, non-significant studies which would have to exist in researchers' filing cabinets in order to render the probability we have found for the meta-analysis non-significant. To find the fail-safe N, we use the following equation; the probability for the six studies is used as an example:

$$\text{Fail - safe } N = \frac{k \times (k \times \bar{z}^2 - 2.706)}{2.706} \tag{A16.20}$$

where k is the number of studies in the meta-analysis, and $\bar{z}$ is the mean z-value for the meta-analysis, calculated in the way shown under heterogeneity for probability, on the previous page.

Therefore,

$$\text{Fail - safe } N = \frac{6 \times (6 \times 3.5880^2 - 2.706)}{2.706}$$
$$= 165.2727$$

which, to the next highest whole number = 166.

Thus, there would have to exist at least 166 non-significant studies to render the meta-analysis non-significant. To interpret this figure we need to calculate the critical number of unpublished, non-significant studies which we could reasonably expect to be filed away.

The critical number of studies for the file-drawer problem

Rosenthal (1991) gives the following equation for the critical level of non-significant studies:

$$\text{critical number of studies} = (5 \times k) + 10 \tag{A16.21}$$

where k is the number of studies used in the meta-analysis

Therefore,

$$\text{critical number of studies} = (5 \times 6) + 10$$
$$= 40$$

The file-drawer issue is only a problem if the critical number of studies is equal to or more than the fail-safe N. In this case, as the critical number of studies is 40 and the fail-safe N is 166, the file-drawer issue is less likely to be a problem and we can be more confident about the combined effect size and combined probabilities which we have calculated.

Clearly, the fail-safe N and the critical number of studies only need to be calculated when the meta-analysis shows a significant result.

Focused comparison

We can test whether groups of effect sizes differ from each other. Using an equation based on A16.17, the variation that we found earlier when testing heterogeneity of effect sizes can be partitioned into that which can be attributed to differences between groups and that which can be attributed to differences within groups. For the sake of creating two groups, imagine that the six studies included in Table A16.1 involved different types of sufferer from chronic pelvic pain, with the first four made up of patients who had had no diagnosis for their pain while the patients in the remaining two studies had had a diagnosis. We can ask whether the patients in first set of studies suffer more depression compared to control samples than do patients in the second set of studies.

The process I am describing can be used to compare more than two groups, as well. However, as with an ANOVA with more than two groups/conditions, a significant difference between the groups would need to be followed up with more targeted comparisons between the groups, such as paired contrasts (see Hedges, 1994).

Find a weighted mean ($\bar{r}'$) for each group, using equation A16.14. For group 1 $\bar{r}'_1 = 0.48346$; for group 2 $\bar{r}'_2 = 0.23788$. Find the heterogeneity between groups (Q_{BET}) by using a variant of equation A16.17, where $N-3$ is replaced by the sum of $N-3$ for each study in a group and r' is replaced by the weighted mean r' for each group.

$$Q_{BET} = 209 \times (0.4835 - 0.3562)^2 + 312 \times (0.2379 - 0.3562)^2$$
$$= 9.0645$$

This can be compared with the chi-square distribution with df $= p-1$, where p is the number of groups being compared. In this case df $= 1$. Consulting Table A17.3 shows that $.01 > p > .001$ and so we can conclude that the patients in the first group of studies are suffering significantly higher levels of depression than those in the second group.

We can also test the heterogeneity within each group (Q_{Wi}, where i refers to the group) and sum these results to find the amount of variation that can be attributed to within the groups (Q_W). Again a variant of equation A16.17 is used. In this case the overall weighted mean is replaced by the weighted mean for the group.

$$Q_{W1} = \sum \left((N-3) \times (r' - 0.4835)^2 \right)$$
$$= 0.8183$$
$$Q_{W2} = \sum \left((N-3) \times (r' - 0.2379)^2 \right)$$
$$= 1.4659$$
$$Q_W = Q_{W1} + Q_{W2}$$
$$= 2.2842$$

This can be compared with the chi-square distribution with df $= k - p$, where k is the number of studies and p is the number of groups. With df $= 4$, the within group heterogeneity is not significant as $.7 > p > .5$.

As Q (for the overall heterogeneity) $= Q_{BET} + Q_W$, we could have found Q_W from:

$Q_W = Q - Q_{BET}$
$11.349 - 9.065 = 2.284.$

Fixed effects or random effects

The preceding description has been of a meta-analysis which would be described as a fixed effects model. It assumes that the true value for the effect size in the population is a single value (e.g. ρ) and that the true value is estimated by the sample value (e.g. r). Therefore,

$\rho = r +$ error due to the sample

A random effect model assumes that there are a number of values for the effect size in the population which vary due to some unknown factor. The mean ρ is still estimated by the sample (e.g. r). However,

mean $\rho = r +$ error due to sample + 'error' due to variability of ρ

We can't know which is the more appropriate model. However, if homogeneity of effect size is present we can use the assumption that the effect is random to calculate the mean effect size and CI for effect size to see whether this changes our view of the effect.

Stages when assuming random effects

1   Find c.

$$c = \sum(N-3) - \left[\frac{\sum(N-3)^2}{\sum(N-3)}\right]$$

where N is the total sample size in a given study. Therefore,

$$c = 602 - \frac{75622}{602}$$

2   Find variability due to random nature of ρ (between-studies variance: b-s var).

$$\text{b-s var} = \frac{[Q-(k-1)]}{c}$$

where k is the number of studies and Q is the test of heterogeneity of effect sizes from equation A16.17. Therefore,

$$\text{b-s var} = \frac{[11.3494-(6-1)]}{476.3821} = 0.013328$$

3   Calculate a new weighting (w^*) for each study.

$$w^* = \frac{N-3}{(N-3)\times(\text{b-s var})+1}$$

For example, for study 1

$$w^* = \frac{79}{(79 \times 0.013328) + 1} = 38.48136$$

4   Calculate a new weighted mean r' using w^*.

$$\text{weighted mean } r' = \frac{\sum(w^* \times r')}{\sum w^*}$$

where r' is the Fisher transformation of r for each study. Therefore,

$$\text{weighted mean } r' = \frac{91.79745}{244.5991} = 0.3753$$

5   Calculate the overall variance for the studies.

$$\text{overall variance} = \frac{1}{\sum w^*}$$

Therefore,

$$\text{overall variance} = \frac{1}{244.5991} = .004088$$

6   Calculate the overall standard error of measurement (*SEM*).

$$SEM = \sqrt{\text{overall variance}}$$

Therefore, *SEM* = .06394.

7   Find the upper and lower values for the 95% CI for r'.

upper end of CI = r' + 1.96 × *SEM*
lower end of CI = r' − 1.96 × *SEM*

where 1.96 is the z-value which would give you 95% of the population for a two-tailed test. Therefore,

CI for r' = 0.24998 to 0.50062

8   Convert all r' to r using the inverse of Fisher's transformation. This leads to a new weighted mean for r of 0.3586, a new CI of 0.2449 to 0.4626. We see that although the CI is larger when we assume that the effect is random, it still doesn't cross 0. And so we can still be confident that there is a real positive effect, that is, we can reject the Null Hypothesis that ρ = 0.

Appendix XVII

Probability tables

Most statistical computer packages will supply you with the necessary probability level for the results of your statistical tests, as will some spreadsheets such as Excel. However, there are occasions when you need to check the probability in a table. I have not included an exhaustive set of tables; instead, where a table is necessary for a single probability level, I have provided the critical levels of the statistic for $\alpha = .05$ on the grounds that this is the most frequently used alpha-level. However, where one-tailed probabilities are not available, or necessary, for a given statistic, I have also provided values for $\alpha = .01$. In the case of F-ratios, I have included tables for $\alpha = .025$ so that confidence intervals for intraclass correlations can be calculated. A wider range of tables can be found in books devoted to the subject, such as Neave (1978).

Finding the probability of a statistic for df which are not shown in the tables

I will use the *t*-test to illustrate the points but the principle will be true for other tests, including non-parametric tests where probabilities are shown for given sample sizes rather than degrees of freedom (df).

When the tables do not have probabilities for the exact df for the test you have conducted, then a quick initial check of the statistical significance is to note whether the *t*-value for the next lowest df is statistically significant. If it is, then it will also be significant with the correct df. For example, if df = 45, then a *t*-value of 1.7 would be statistically significant at α = .05 for a one-tailed test because the critical *t*-value for df = 40 is 1.684. On the other hand, if the *t*-value is not significant with the next highest df, then it will not be for the exact df. Accordingly, if df = 45 and the *t*-value was 1.6, then it would not be statistically significant at α = .05 for a one-tailed test because the critical *t*-value for df = 50 is 1.676. If using these approximate methods does not tell you whether the result is statistically significant, then use *linear interpolation* or in the case of Table A17.15 (the *t*-values for ANCOVA) and Table A17.16 (Bryant and Paulson's Q_p variant of the studentised range statistic) use *harmonic interpolation*.

Linear interpolation

When you are dependent on *t*-tables, and the df for your study are not shown in the table, you can use what is called *linear interpolation* to work out a more exact critical *t*-value for a given probability. For example, *t* = 1.682 with df = 43. To find what the critical *t*-value is for df = 43, with α = .05 and a one-tailed test, use the following equation:

$$\text{critical } t = t \text{ for upper df} + (t \text{ for lower df} - t \text{ for upper df}) \times \left(\frac{\text{upper df} - \text{calculated df}}{\text{upper df} - \text{lower df}} \right)$$

In the present case:

$$\text{critical } t_{(43)} = 1.676 + (1.684 - 1.676) \times \left(\frac{50 - 43}{50 - 40} \right)$$

$$= 1.682$$

As the calculated *t*-value is the same size as this critical value, it is statistically significant at α = .05.

Harmonic interpolation

Linear interpolation assumes that the relationship between the two variables we are interested in is a linear one. For example, we might assume that for every increase by 1 in df, the probability grows by the same amount. However, some variables are not related in such a linear fashion, and so if we try to find an intermediate value using linear interpolation, then we will arrive at a slightly inaccurate answer. Bryant and Paulson (1976) suggest that harmonic interpolation is a more accurate way to find intermediate values of critical Q_p in Table 17.16 and the critical *t*-values for ANCOVA in Table A17.15, which are derived from them. In Chapter 22, I gave the example where we needed to find the critical *t*-value for df = 116, for an ANCOVA with three levels of the IV and one covariate. Table A17.15 shows the critical *t* for df = 110 and df = 120. The first stage is to find the inverses (or reciprocals) of each of the df concerned in the calculation: the two ends of the interval that are in the table and the value we want, where the inverse is found by dividing 1 by the number whose inverse we want.

$$t_{(\text{intermediate df})} = t_1 + \left[\frac{\left(\dfrac{1}{df_{\text{intermediate}}} - \dfrac{1}{df_1} \right)}{\left(\dfrac{1}{df_2} - \dfrac{1}{df_1} \right)} \times (t_2 - t_1) \right]$$

In the example this becomes:

$$t_{(116)} = 2.39 + \left[\frac{\left(\frac{1}{116} - \frac{1}{110}\right)}{\left(\frac{1}{120} - \frac{1}{110}\right)} \times (2.38 - 2.39) \right]$$

$$= 2.39 + \left[\frac{(0.008621 - 0.009091)}{(0.008333 - 0.009091)} \times (-0.01) \right]$$

$$= 2.39 + \left[\frac{(-0.00047)}{(-0.00076)} \times (-0.01) \right]$$

$$= 2.39 + \left[0.62069 \times (-0.01) \right]$$

$$= 2.39 + \left[-0.00621 \right]$$

$$= 2.383793$$

which, rounded to two decimal places, is 2.38.

Table A17.1 The probabilities of z, the standardised normal distribution

One-tailed probabilities are in the body of Table A17.1. The first column shows z-values up to one decimal place, while the first row shows the second decimal place. To read the table, if you wish to find the probability of a z-score of 1.72, look, in the first column, for the row which begins with 1.7; the probability will be in that row. Now look in the first row for the column which is headed by 2; the probability will be in that column. Thus, the one-tailed probability of $z = 1.72$ is .0427. If you wish to look up the probability of a z-value which does not contain two decimal places, for example, 2.1, then the probability is contained in the first column of probabilities, the one headed 0, as 2.10 is 2.1 shown to two decimal places. Accordingly, the one-tailed probability of $z = 2.1$ is .0179.

Finding a z-value for a particular probability

To find the z-value which gives a one-tailed probability of .001, look in the body of the table until you find .001. Note the row and column which contain the probability; they are headed 3.0 and 8 respectively. Therefore the z-value is 3.08. Sometimes the exact probability you require is not shown on the table. This is true for $p = .05$. In this case, it is necessary to find out the probabilities just above and below the value you require: .0495 and .0505. The probability we require is half-way between the two and so the z-value will be half-way between the respective z-values, 1.64 and 1.65: i.e. $z = 1.645$.

Two-tailed probabilities

To find the two-tailed probability of a z-value, double the values shown in the body of the table. Thus the two-tailed probability of $z = 1.72$ is $.0427 \times 2 = .0854$. In order to find the z-value which has a particular two-tailed probability, find the z-value which would give a one-tailed probability which is half the two-tailed probability. For example, if you wished to find the z-value which has a two-tailed probability of .05, look in the body of the table for $p = \frac{.05}{2} = .025$. Proceed as before to find the z-value which gives this probability: $z = 1.96$.

Looking up negative z-values

The table only shows positive z-values. To look up a negative z-value, as the distribution of z is symmetrical, ignore the negative sign and use the table as described previously. For example, the one-tailed probability of a z-value of −1.25 is .1056.

TABLE A17.1   The probabilities of z, the standardised normal distribution

					2nd decimal place					
z	0	1	2	3	4	5	6	7	8	9
0.0	0.5000	0.4960	0.4920	0.4880	0.4840	0.4801	0.4761	0.4721	0.4681	0.4641
0.1	0.4602	0.4562	0.4522	0.4483	0.4443	0.4404	0.4364	0.4325	0.4286	0.4247
0.2	0.4207	0.4168	0.4129	0.4090	0.4052	0.4013	0.3974	0.3936	0.3897	0.3859
0.3	0.3821	0.3783	0.3745	0.3707	0.3669	0.3632	0.3594	0.3557	0.3520	0.3483
0.4	0.3446	0.3409	0.3372	0.3336	0.3300	0.3264	0.3228	0.3192	0.3156	0.3121
0.5	0.3085	0.3050	0.3015	0.2981	0.2946	0.2912	0.2877	0.2843	0.2810	0.2776
0.6	0.2743	0.2709	0.2676	0.2643	0.2611	0.2578	0.2546	0.2514	0.2483	0.2451
0.7	0.2420	0.2389	0.2358	0.2327	0.2296	0.2266	0.2236	0.2206	0.2177	0.2148
0.8	0.2119	0.2090	0.2061	0.2033	0.2005	0.1977	0.1949	0.1922	0.1894	0.1867
0.9	0.1841	0.1814	0.1788	0.1762	0.1736	0.1711	0.1685	0.1660	0.1635	0.1611
1.0	0.1587	0.1562	0.1539	0.1515	0.1492	0.1469	0.1446	0.1423	0.1401	0.1379
1.1	0.1357	0.1335	0.1314	0.1292	0.1271	0.1251	0.1230	0.1210	0.1190	0.1170
1.2	0.1151	0.1131	0.1112	0.1093	0.1075	0.1056	0.1038	0.1020	0.1003	0.0985
1.3	0.0968	0.0951	0.0934	0.0918	0.0901	0.0885	0.0869	0.0853	0.0838	0.0823
1.4	0.0808	0.0793	0.0778	0.0764	0.0749	0.0735	0.0721	0.0708	0.0694	0.0681
1.5	0.0668	0.0655	0.0643	0.0630	0.0618	0.0606	0.0594	0.0582	0.0571	0.0559
1.6	0.0548	0.0537	0.0526	0.0516	0.0505	0.0495	0.0485	0.0475	0.0465	0.0455
1.7	0.0446	0.0436	0.0427	0.0418	0.0409	0.0401	0.0392	0.0384	0.0375	0.0367
1.8	0.0359	0.0351	0.0344	0.0336	0.0329	0.0322	0.0314	0.0307	0.0301	0.0294
1.9	0.0287	0.0281	0.0274	0.0268	0.0262	0.0256	0.0250	0.0244	0.0239	0.0233
2.0	0.0228	0.0222	0.0217	0.0212	0.0207	0.0202	0.0197	0.0192	0.0188	0.0183
2.1	0.0179	0.0174	0.0170	0.0166	0.0162	0.0158	0.0154	0.0150	0.0146	0.0143
2.2	0.0139	0.0136	0.0132	0.0129	0.0125	0.0122	0.0119	0.0116	0.0113	0.0110
2.3	0.0107	0.0104	0.0102	0.0099	0.0096	0.0094	0.0091	0.0089	0.0087	0.0084
2.4	0.0082	0.0080	0.0078	0.0075	0.0073	0.0071	0.0069	0.0068	0.0066	0.0064
2.5	0.0062	0.0060	0.0059	0.0057	0.0055	0.0054	0.0052	0.0051	0.0049	0.0048
2.6	0.0047	0.0045	0.0044	0.0043	0.0041	0.0040	0.0039	0.0038	0.0037	0.0036
2.7	0.0035	0.0034	0.0033	0.0032	0.0031	0.0030	0.0029	0.0028	0.0027	0.0026
2.8	0.0026	0.0025	0.0024	0.0023	0.0023	0.0022	0.0021	0.0021	0.0020	0.0019
2.9	0.0019	0.0018	0.0018	0.0017	0.0016	0.0016	0.0015	0.0015	0.0014	0.0014
3.0	0.0013	0.0013	0.0013	0.0012	0.0012	0.0011	0.0011	0.0011	0.0010	0.0010
3.1	0.00097	0.00094	0.00090	0.00087	0.00084	0.00082	0.00079	0.00076	0.00074	0.00071
3.2	0.00069	0.00066	0.00064	0.00062	0.00060	0.00058	0.00056	0.00054	0.00052	0.00050
3.3	0.00048	0.00047	0.00045	0.00043	0.00042	0.00040	0.00039	0.00038	0.00036	0.00035
3.4	0.00034	0.00032	0.00031	0.00030	0.00029	0.00028	0.00027	0.00026	0.00025	0.00024
3.5	0.00023	0.00022	0.00022	0.00021	0.00020	0.00019	0.00019	0.00018	0.00017	0.00017
3.6	0.00016	0.00015	0.00015	0.00014	0.00014	0.00013	0.00013	0.00012	0.00012	0.00011
3.7	0.00011	0.00010	0.00010	0.00010	0.00009	0.00009	0.00008	0.00008	0.00008	0.00008
3.8	0.00007	0.00007	0.00007	0.00006	0.00006	0.00006	0.00006	0.00005	0.00005	0.00005
3.9	0.00005	0.00005	0.00004	0.00004	0.00004	0.00004	0.00004	0.00004	0.00003	0.00003
4.0	0.00003	0.00003	0.00003	0.00003	0.00003	0.00003	0.00002	0.00002	0.00002	0.00002

Table A17.2 The probabilities of *t*-distributions

Degrees of freedom

For a between-subjects *t*-test, df $= n_1 + n_2 - 2$, where n_1 and n_2 are the sizes of the two samples.

For a within-subjects *t*-test, df $= n - 1$, where n is the sample size.

For a test where you are comparing a sample mean with a population mean (a one-group *t*-test), df $= n - 1$.

The values for df of infinity (∞) are there to demonstrate that when the sample size is sufficiently large – that is, well above 120 – the *t*-distribution is the same as the *z*-distribution. Thus, the critical *t*-value for a one-tailed probability at $\alpha = .05$ is 1.645, when df equal infinity. The one-tailed probability for $z = 1.645$ is .05.

TABLE A17.2   The probabilities of *t*-distributions

a   Degrees of freedom from 1 to 20

	One-tailed probabilities									
	0.4	0.3	0.2	0.1	0.05	0.025	0.01	0.005	0.001	0.0005
	Two-tailed probabilities									
df	0.8	0.6	0.4	0.2	0.1	0.05	0.02	0.01	0.002	0.001
1	0.325	0.727	1.376	3.078	6.314	12.706	31.821	63.656	318.289	636.578
2	0.289	0.617	1.061	1.886	2.920	4.303	6.965	9.925	22.328	31.600
3	0.277	0.584	0.978	1.638	2.353	3.182	4.541	5.841	10.214	12.924
4	0.271	0.569	0.941	1.533	2.132	2.776	3.747	4.604	7.173	8.610
5	0.267	0.559	0.920	1.476	2.015	2.571	3.365	4.032	5.894	6.869
6	0.265	0.553	0.906	1.440	1.943	2.447	3.143	3.707	5.208	5.959
7	0.263	0.549	0.896	1.415	1.895	2.365	2.998	3.499	4.785	5.408
8	0.262	0.546	0.889	1.397	1.860	2.306	2.896	3.355	4.501	5.041
9	0.261	0.543	0.883	1.383	1.833	2.262	2.821	3.250	4.297	4.781
10	0.260	0.542	0.879	1.372	1.812	2.228	2.764	3.169	4.144	4.587
11	0.260	0.540	0.876	1.363	1.796	2.201	2.718	3.106	4.025	4.437
12	0.259	0.539	0.873	1.356	1.782	2.179	2.681	3.055	3.930	4.318
13	0.259	0.538	0.870	1.350	1.771	2.160	2.650	3.012	3.852	4.221
14	0.258	0.537	0.868	1.345	1.761	2.145	2.624	2.977	3.787	4.140
15	0.258	0.536	0.866	1.341	1.753	2.131	2.602	2.947	3.733	4.073
16	0.258	0.535	0.865	1.337	1.746	2.120	2.583	2.921	3.686	4.015
17	0.257	0.534	0.863	1.333	1.740	2.110	2.567	2.898	3.646	3.965
18	0.257	0.534	0.862	1.330	1.734	2.101	2.552	2.878	3.610	3.922
19	0.257	0.533	0.861	1.328	1.729	2.093	2.539	2.861	3.579	3.883
20	0.257	0.533	0.860	1.325	1.725	2.086	2.528	2.845	3.552	3.850

TABLE A17.2   The probabilities of *t*-distributions

b   Degrees of freedom from 21 to 120 and infinity

				One-tailed probabilities						
	0.4	0.3	0.2	0.1	0.05	0.025	0.01	0.005	0.001	0.0005
				Two-tailed probabilities						
df	0.8	0.6	0.4	0.2	0.1	0.05	0.02	0.01	0.002	0.001
21	0.257	0.532	0.859	1.323	1.721	2.080	2.518	2.831	3.527	3.819
22	0.256	0.532	0.858	1.321	1.717	2.074	2.508	2.819	3.505	3.792
23	0.256	0.532	0.858	1.319	1.714	2.069	2.500	2.807	3.485	3.768
24	0.256	0.531	0.857	1.318	1.711	2.064	2.492	2.797	3.467	3.745
25	0.256	0.531	0.856	1.316	1.708	2.060	2.485	2.787	3.450	3.725
26	0.256	0.531	0.856	1.315	1.706	2.056	2.479	2.779	3.435	3.707
27	0.256	0.531	0.855	1.314	1.703	2.052	2.473	2.771	3.421	3.689
28	0.256	0.530	0.855	1.313	1.701	2.048	2.467	2.763	3.408	3.674
29	0.256	0.530	0.854	1.311	1.699	2.045	2.462	2.756	3.396	3.660
30	0.256	0.530	0.854	1.310	1.697	2.042	2.457	2.750	3.385	3.646
31	0.256	0.530	0.853	1.309	1.696	2.040	2.453	2.744	3.375	3.633
32	0.255	0.530	0.853	1.309	1.694	2.037	2.449	2.738	3.365	3.622
33	0.255	0.530	0.853	1.308	1.692	2.035	2.445	2.733	3.356	3.611
34	0.255	0.529	0.852	1.307	1.691	2.032	2.441	2.728	3.348	3.601
35	0.255	0.529	0.852	1.306	1.690	2.030	2.438	2.724	3.340	3.591
36	0.255	0.529	0.852	1.306	1.688	2.028	2.434	2.719	3.333	3.582
37	0.255	0.529	0.851	1.305	1.687	2.026	2.431	2.715	3.326	3.574
38	0.255	0.529	0.851	1.304	1.686	2.024	2.429	2.712	3.319	3.566
39	0.255	0.529	0.851	1.304	1.685	2.023	2.426	2.708	3.313	3.558
40	0.255	0.529	0.851	1.303	1.684	2.021	2.423	2.704	3.307	3.551
50	0.255	0.528	0.849	1.299	1.676	2.009	2.403	2.678	3.261	3.496
60	0.254	0.527	0.848	1.296	1.671	2.000	2.390	2.660	3.232	3.460
70	0.254	0.527	0.847	1.294	1.667	1.994	2.381	2.648	3.211	3.435
80	0.254	0.526	0.846	1.292	1.664	1.990	2.374	2.639	3.195	3.416
90	0.254	0.526	0.846	1.291	1.662	1.987	2.368	2.632	3.183	3.402
100	0.254	0.526	0.845	1.290	1.660	1.984	2.364	2.626	3.174	3.390
110	0.254	0.526	0.845	1.289	1.659	1.982	2.361	2.621	3.166	3.381
120	0.254	0.526	0.845	1.289	1.658	1.980	2.358	2.617	3.160	3.373
∞	0.253	0.524	0.842	1.282	1.645	1.960	2.326	2.576	3.090	3.290

TABLE A17.3 The probabilities of chi-squared distributions

The shape of the chi-squared distribution becomes more symmetrical as the df increase.

The probabilities are shown along the first row of Table A17.3. These are for non-directional hypotheses. See Chapters 14 and 15 for discussion of how to obtain probabilities for a directional hypothesis. The body of the table contains the minimum size which a χ^2-value would need to be, for given df, to achieve statistical significance at a given probability level. Thus, with df = 1, χ^2 would have to be 3.84 or larger to be statistically significant at $\alpha = .05$.

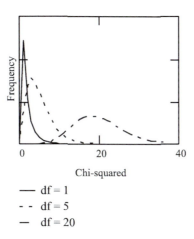

Chi-squared

— df = 1
- - df = 5
— df = 20

TABLE A17.3 The probabilities of chi-squared distributions

df	0.99	0.95	0.90	0.80	0.70	0.50	0.30	0.20	0.10	0.05	0.02	0.01	0.001
1	0.00	0.00	0.02	0.06	0.15	0.45	1.07	1.64	2.71	3.84	5.41	6.63	10.83
2	0.02	0.10	0.21	0.45	0.71	1.39	2.41	3.22	4.61	5.99	7.82	9.21	13.82
3	0.11	0.35	0.58	1.01	1.42	2.37	3.66	4.64	6.25	7.81	9.84	11.34	16.27
4	0.30	0.71	1.06	1.65	2.19	3.36	4.88	5.99	7.78	9.49	11.67	13.28	18.47
5	0.55	1.15	1.61	2.34	3.00	4.35	6.06	7.29	9.24	11.07	13.39	15.09	20.51
6	0.87	1.64	2.20	3.07	3.83	5.35	7.23	8.56	10.64	12.59	15.03	16.81	22.46
7	1.24	2.17	2.83	3.82	4.67	6.35	8.38	9.80	12.02	14.07	16.62	18.48	24.32
8	1.65	2.73	3.49	4.59	5.53	7.34	9.52	11.03	13.36	15.51	18.17	20.09	26.12
9	2.09	3.33	4.17	5.38	6.39	8.34	10.66	12.24	14.68	16.92	19.68	21.67	27.88
10	2.56	3.94	4.87	6.18	7.27	9.34	11.78	13.44	15.99	18.31	21.16	23.21	29.59
11	3.05	4.57	5.58	6.99	8.15	10.34	12.90	14.63	17.28	19.68	22.62	24.73	31.26
12	3.57	5.23	6.30	7.81	9.03	11.34	14.01	15.81	18.55	21.03	24.05	26.22	32.91
13	4.11	5.89	7.04	8.63	9.93	12.34	15.12	16.98	19.81	22.36	25.47	27.69	34.53
14	4.66	6.57	7.79	9.47	10.82	13.34	16.22	18.15	21.06	23.68	26.87	29.14	36.12
15	5.23	7.26	8.55	10.31	11.72	14.34	17.32	19.31	22.31	25.00	28.26	30.58	37.70
16	5.81	7.96	9.31	11.15	12.62	15.34	18.42	20.47	23.54	26.30	29.63	32.00	39.25
17	6.41	8.67	10.09	12.00	13.53	16.34	19.51	21.61	24.77	27.59	31.00	33.41	40.79
18	7.01	9.39	10.86	12.86	14.44	17.34	20.60	22.76	25.99	28.87	32.35	34.81	42.31
19	7.63	10.12	11.65	13.72	15.35	18.34	21.69	23.90	27.20	30.14	33.69	36.19	43.82
20	8.26	10.85	12.44	14.58	16.27	19.34	22.77	25.04	28.41	31.41	35.02	37.57	45.31
21	8.90	11.59	13.24	15.44	17.18	20.34	23.86	26.17	29.62	32.67	36.34	38.93	46.80
22	9.54	12.34	14.04	16.31	18.10	21.34	24.94	27.30	30.81	33.92	37.66	40.29	48.27
23	10.20	13.09	14.85	17.19	19.02	22.34	26.02	28.43	32.01	35.17	38.97	41.64	49.73
24	10.86	13.85	15.66	18.06	19.94	23.34	27.10	29.55	33.20	36.42	40.27	42.98	51.18
25	11.52	14.61	16.47	18.94	20.87	24.34	28.17	30.68	34.38	37.65	41.57	44.31	52.62
26	12.20	15.38	17.29	19.82	21.79	25.34	29.25	31.79	35.56	38.89	42.86	45.64	54.05
27	12.88	16.15	18.11	20.70	22.72	26.34	30.32	32.91	36.74	40.11	44.14	46.96	55.48
28	13.56	16.93	18.94	21.59	23.65	27.34	31.39	34.03	37.92	41.34	45.42	48.28	56.89
29	14.26	17.71	19.77	22.48	24.58	28.34	32.46	35.14	39.09	42.56	46.69	49.59	58.30
30	14.95	18.49	20.60	23.36	25.51	29.34	33.53	36.25	40.26	43.77	47.96	50.89	59.70
31	15.66	19.28	21.43	24.26	26.44	30.34	34.60	37.36	41.42	44.99	49.23	52.19	61.10

(*Continued*)

TABLE A17.3 (Continued)

df	0.99	0.95	0.90	0.80	0.70	0.50	0.30	0.20	0.10	0.05	0.02	0.01	0.001
32	16.36	20.07	22.27	25.15	27.37	31.34	35.66	38.47	42.58	46.19	50.49	53.49	62.49
33	17.07	20.87	23.11	26.04	28.31	32.34	36.73	39.57	43.75	47.40	51.74	54.78	63.87
34	17.79	21.66	23.95	26.94	29.24	33.34	37.80	40.68	44.90	48.60	53.00	56.06	65.25
35	18.51	22.47	24.80	27.84	30.18	34.34	38.86	41.78	46.06	49.80	54.24	57.34	66.62
36	19.23	23.27	25.64	28.73	31.12	35.34	39.92	42.88	47.21	51.00	55.49	58.62	67.98
37	19.96	24.07	26.49	29.64	32.05	36.34	40.98	43.98	48.36	52.19	56.73	59.89	69.35
38	20.69	24.88	27.34	30.54	32.99	37.34	42.05	45.08	49.51	53.38	57.97	61.16	70.70
39	21.43	25.70	28.20	31.44	33.93	38.34	43.11	46.17	50.66	54.57	59.20	62.43	72.06
40	22.16	26.51	29.05	32.34	34.87	39.34	44.16	47.27	51.81	55.76	60.44	63.69	73.40
50	29.71	34.76	37.69	41.45	44.31	49.33	54.72	58.16	63.17	67.50	72.61	76.15	86.66
60	37.48	43.19	46.46	50.64	53.81	59.33	65.23	68.97	74.40	79.08	84.58	88.38	99.61
70	45.44	51.74	55.33	59.90	63.35	69.33	75.69	79.71	85.53	90.53	96.39	100.43	112.32
80	53.54	60.39	64.28	69.21	72.92	79.33	86.12	90.41	96.58	101.88	108.07	112.33	124.84
90	61.75	69.13	73.29	78.56	82.51	89.33	96.52	101.05	107.57	113.15	119.65	124.12	137.21
100	70.06	77.93	82.36	87.95	92.13	99.33	106.91	111.67	118.50	124.34	131.14	135.81	149.45
110	78.46	86.79	91.47	97.36	101.77	109.33	117.27	122.25	129.39	135.48	142.56	147.41	161.58
120	86.92	95.70	100.62	106.81	111.42	119.33	127.62	132.81	140.23	146.57	153.92	158.95	173.62

Table A17.4 The cumulative probabilities from the binomial distribution when the probability of a success and the probability of a failure are both .5

The values in the table are for a one-tailed test. The result which would achieve statistical significance at α = .05 for a given number of trials for a one-tailed test has had its probability printed in italics *and* bold. To find a two-tailed probability double the probabilities in the table. In some cases the number of failures/successes necessary to achieve significance with a two-tailed test will be the same as for a one-tailed test. However, where the number of successes/failures necessary to achieve significance for a two-tailed test is different from those which are bold and italic, the probability is shown in italics only. Thus, if we had no failures out of six trials, the one-tailed probability would be .016 and the two-tailed probability would be .032. However, if we had one failure out of eight trials, the one-tailed probability would be considered significant at .035 but the two-tailed probability would not at .07. Accordingly, the probability for no failures is shown in italics, as even for a two-tailed probability this would be considered statistically significant at 2 × .004 = .008. Note that there is an exception to this system of signalling significance for a two-tailed test. When there are only five trials there is no outcome which would be significant at .05 for a two-tailed test, as was demonstrated in Chapter 10.

As an example of how to read the table, imagine that someone has taken a test with 20 questions in it, each of which is a simple multiple choice with only two alternatives. Under these circumstances if the person was responding purely by chance, then for each question they would have an equal probability of getting the answer right or wrong. We can treat the answering of questions as the trials and so we would look down the first column until we got to 20. We can then read across to find out

TABLE A17.4   The cumulative probabilities from the binomial distribution

Number of trials	0	1	2	3	4	5	6	7
				Number of failures or successes				
5	*0.031*	0.188	0.500	0.813	0.969	1.000		
6	*0.016*	0.109	0.344	0.656	0.891	0.984	1.000	
7	*0.008*	0.063	0.227	0.500	0.773	0.938	0.992	1.000
8	*0.004*	*0.035*	0.145	0.363	0.637	0.855	0.965	0.996
9	0.002	*0.020*	0.090	0.254	0.500	0.746	0.910	0.980
10	0.001	*0.011*	0.055	0.172	0.377	0.623	0.828	0.945
11	<0.001	0.006	*0.033*	0.113	0.274	0.500	0.726	0.887
12	<0.001	0.003	*0.019*	0.073	0.194	0.387	0.613	0.806
13	<0.001	0.002	*0.011*	*0.046*	0.133	0.291	0.500	0.709
14	<0.001	0.001	*0.006*	*0.029*	0.090	0.212	0.395	0.605
15	<0.001	<0.001	0.004	*0.018*	0.059	0.151	0.304	0.500
16	<0.001	<0.001	0.002	*0.011*	*0.038*	0.105	0.227	0.402
17	<0.001	<0.001	0.001	0.006	*0.025*	0.072	0.166	0.315
18	<0.001	<0.001	0.001	0.004	*0.015*	*0.048*	0.119	0.240
19	<0.001	<0.001	<0.001	0.002	*0.010*	*0.032*	0.084	0.180
20	<0.001	<0.001	<0.001	0.001	0.006	*0.021*	0.058	0.132
21	<0.001	<0.001	<0.001	0.001	0.004	*0.013*	*0.039*	0.095
22	<0.001	<0.001	<0.001	<0.001	0.002	0.008	*0.026*	0.067
23	<0.001	<0.001	<0.001	<0.001	0.001	0.005	*0.017*	*0.047*
24	<0.001	<0.001	<0.001	<0.001	0.001	0.003	*0.011*	*0.032*
25	<0.001	<0.001	<0.001	<0.001	<0.001	0.002	0.007	*0.022*

the probability of a given result (or one with fewer failures/successes). This tells us that if the person taking the exam got five or fewer wrong, then we can assume that they have produced a result which is significantly better than chance as the probability of this result is .021 and thus less than .05. However, if they got six or more wrong we could not assume that they were significantly better than chance. Similarly, if they got only five or fewer correct, then we could say that they were performing significantly worse than chance.

Table A17.5 The probabilities of the Mann–Whitney *U* test

If either sample has 20 or more participants it will be necessary to use the *z*-approximation equation A6.8 (or A6.9 when there are tied scores) in Appendix VI.

As an illustration, if the sample sizes were 5 and 8, then *U* would have to be 8 *or smaller* to be significant at $\alpha = .05$ for a one-tailed test.

a   The smaller sample size (n_1) = 2 to 7

one-tailed probabilities: 0.05 0.025 0.01 0.005
two-tailed probabilities: 0.10 0.05 0.02 0.01

n_1	n_2	0.10	0.05	0.02	0.01
2	5	0	-	-	-
	6	0	-	-	-
	7	0	-	-	-
	8	1	0	-	-
	9	1	0	-	-
	10	1	0	-	-
	11	1	0	-	-
	12	2	1	-	-
	13	2	1	0	-
	14	3	1	0	-
	15	3	1	0	-
	16	3	1	0	-
	17	3	2	0	-
	18	4	2	0	-
	19	4	2	1	0
	20	4	2	1	0
3	3	0	-	-	-
	4	0	-	-	-
	5	1	0	-	-
	6	2	1	-	-
	7	2	1	0	-
	8	3	2	0	-
	9	4	2	1	0
	10	4	3	1	0
	11	5	3	1	0
	12	5	4	2	1
	13	6	4	2	1
	14	7	5	2	1
	15	7	5	3	2
	16	8	6	3	2
	17	9	6	4	2
	18	9	7	4	2
	19	10	7	4	3
	20	11	8	5	3

one-tailed probabilities: 0.05 0.025 0.01 0.005
two-tailed probabilities: 0.10 0.05 0.02 0.01

n_1	n_2	0.10	0.05	0.02	0.01
4	4	1	0	-	-
	5	2	1	0	-
	6	3	2	1	0
	7	4	3	1	0
	8	5	4	2	1
	9	6	4	3	1
	10	7	5	3	2
	11	8	6	4	2
	12	9	7	5	3
	13	10	8	5	3
	14	11	9	6	4
	15	12	10	7	5
	16	14	11	7	5
	17	15	11	8	6
	18	16	12	9	6
	19	17	13	9	7
	20	18	14	10	8
5	5	4	2	1	0
	6	5	3	2	1
	7	6	5	3	1
	8	8	6	4	2
	9	9	7	5	3
	10	11	8	6	4
	11	12	9	7	5
	12	13	11	8	6
	13	15	12	9	7
	14	16	13	10	7
	15	18	14	11	8
	16	19	15	12	9
	17	20	17	13	10
	18	22	18	14	11
	19	23	19	15	12
	20	25	20	16	13

one-tailed probabilities: 0.05 0.025 0.01 0.005
two-tailed probabilities: 0.10 0.05 0.02 0.01

n_1	n_2	0.10	0.05	0.02	0.01
6	6	7	5	3	2
	7	8	6	4	3
	8	10	8	6	4
	9	12	10	7	5
	10	14	11	8	6
	11	16	13	9	7
	12	17	14	11	9
	13	19	16	12	10
	14	21	17	13	11
	15	23	19	15	12
	16	25	21	16	13
	17	26	22	18	15
	18	28	24	19	16
	19	30	25	20	17
	20	32	27	22	18
7	7	11	8	6	4
	8	13	10	7	6
	9	15	12	9	7
	10	17	14	11	9
	11	19	16	12	10
	12	21	18	14	12
	13	24	20	16	13
	14	26	22	17	15
	15	28	24	19	16
	16	30	26	21	18
	17	33	28	23	19
	18	35	30	24	21
	19	37	32	26	22
	20	39	34	28	24

(Adapted from Table G, p. 375, of Neave, H. R. and Worthington, P. L. (1988). *Distribution-Free Tests*. London: Routledge.)

b   The smaller sample size (n_1) = 8 to 20

		0.05	0.025	0.01	0.005			0.05	0.025	0.01	0.005			0.05	0.025	0.01	0.005
								one-tailed probabilities									
		0.10	0.05	0.02	0.01			0.10	0.05	0.02	0.01			0.10	0.05	0.02	0.01
								two-tailed probabilities									
n_1	n_2	0.10	0.05	0.02	0.01	n_1	n_2	0.10	0.05	0.02	0.01	n_1	n_2	0.10	0.05	0.02	0.01
8	8	15	13	9	7	11	11	34	30	25	21	14	14	61	55	47	42
	9	18	15	11	9		12	38	33	28	24		15	66	59	51	46
	10	20	17	13	11		13	42	37	31	27		16	71	64	56	50
	11	23	19	15	13		14	46	40	34	30		17	77	69	60	54
	12	26	22	17	15		15	50	44	37	33		18	82	74	65	58
	13	28	24	20	17		16	54	47	41	36		19	87	78	60	63
	14	31	26	22	18		17	57	51	44	39		20	92	83	73	67
	15	33	29	24	20		18	61	55	47	42						
	16	36	31	26	22		19	65	58	50	45	15	15	72	64	56	51
	17	39	34	28	24		20	69	62	53	48		16	77	70	61	55
	18	41	36	30	26								17	83	75	66	60
	19	44	38	32	28	12	12	42	37	31	27		18	88	80	70	64
	20	47	41	34	30		13	47	41	35	31		19	94	85	75	69
							14	51	45	38	34		20	100	90	80	73
9	9	21	17	14	11		15	55	49	42	37						
	10	24	20	16	13		16	60	53	46	41	16	16	83	75	66	60
	11	27	23	18	16		17	64	57	49	44		17	89	81	71	65
	12	30	26	21	18		18	68	61	53	47		18	95	86	76	70
	13	33	28	23	20		19	72	65	56	51		19	101	92	82	74
	14	36	31	26	22		20	77	69	60	54		20	107	98	87	79
	15	39	34	28	24												
	16	42	37	31	27	13	13	51	45	39	34	17	17	96	87	77	70
	17	45	39	33	29		14	56	50	43	38		18	102	92	82	75
	18	48	42	36	31		15	61	54	47	42		19	109	99	88	81
	19	51	45	38	33		16	65	59	51	45		20	115	105	93	86
	20	54	48	40	36		17	70	63	55	49						
							18	75	67	59	53	18	18	109	99	88	81
10	10	27	23	19	16		19	80	72	63	57		19	116	106	94	87
	11	31	26	22	18		20	84	76	67	60		20	123	112	100	92
	12	34	29	24	21												
	13	37	33	27	24							19	19	123	113	101	93
	14	41	36	30	26								20	130	119	107	99
	15	44	39	33	29												
	16	48	42	36	31							20	20	138	127	114	105
	17	51	45	38	34												
	18	55	48	41	37												
	19	58	52	44	39												
	20	62	55	47	42												

(Adapted from Table G, p. 376, of Neave, H. R. and Worthington, P. L. (1988). *Distribution-Free Tests*. London: Routledge.)

Table A17.6 The probabilities of *T* from Wilcoxon's signed rank test for matched pairs

If the sample has more than 25 participants, then use the *z*-approximation equation A6.10 (or A6.11 when there are tied scores) in Appendix VI. To be statistically significant *T* has to be as small or *smaller* than the value shown in the table.

	one-tailed probabilities			
	0.05	0.025	0.01	0.005
	two-tailed probabilities			
n	0.1	0.05	0.02	0.01
5	0			
6	2	0		
7	3	2	0	
8	5	3	1	0
9	8	5	3	1
10	10	8	5	3
11	13	10	7	5
12	17	13	9	7
13	21	17	12	9
14	25	21	15	12
15	30	25	19	15
16	35	29	23	19
17	41	34	27	23
18	47	40	32	27
19	53	46	37	32
20	60	52	43	37
21	67	58	49	42
22	75	65	55	48
23	83	73	62	54
24	91	81	69	61
25	100	89	76	68

(Adapted from Table D, p. 373, of Neave, H. R. and Worthington, P. L. (1988). *Distribution-Free Tests*. London: Routledge.)

Table A17.7 The probabilities of Fisher's exact probability test

To read these tables, note which is the smallest row or column total: this will be S_1. Then note the next smallest row or column total: this will be S_2; x will then be the number in the cell with which S_1 and S_2 intersect.

2	0	2
0	8	8
2	8	10

Thus, if a result was in line with a directional hypothesis, when the sample size (n) was 10, $S_1 = 2$, $S_2 = 2$ and $x = 2$, then the probability of this outcome is $p = .022$.

I have only included probabilities up to .1. For higher probabilities see Dixon and Massey (1983) or Siegel and Castellan (1988).

a $n = 5$ to 12

n	S_1	S_2	x	one-tailed	two-tailed
5	2	2	2	0.100	0.100
6	2	2	2	0.067	0.067
	3	3	0	0.050	0.100
			3	0.050	0.100
7	2	2	2	0.048	0.048
	3	3	3	0.029	0.029
8	2	2	2	0.036	0.036
	3	3	3	0.018	0.018
	3	4	0	0.071	0.143
			3	0.071	0.143
	4	4	0	0.014	0.029
			4	0.014	0.029
9	2	2	2	0.028	0.028
	2	3	2	0.083	0.083
	3	3	3	0.012	0.012
	3	4	3	0.048	0.048
	4	4	0	0.040	0.048
			4	0.008	0.008

n	S_1	S_2	x	one-tailed	two-tailed
10	1	1	1	0.100	0.100
	2	2	2	0.022	0.022
	2	3	2	0.067	0.067
	3	3	3	0.008	0.008
	3	4	3	0.033	0.033
	3	5	0	0.083	0.167
			3	0.083	0.167
	4	4	0	0.071	0.076
			4	0.005	0.005
	4	5	0	0.024	0.048
			4	0.024	0.048
	5	5	0	0.004	0.008
			5	0.004	0.008
11	1	1	1	0.091	0.091
	2	2	2	0.018	0.018
	2	3	2	0.055	0.055
	3	3	3	0.006	0.006
	3	4	3	0.024	0.024
	3	5	3	0.061	0.061
	4	4	3	0.088	0.088
			4	0.003	0.003
	4	5	0	0.045	0.061
			4	0.015	0.015
	5	5	0	0.013	0.015
			4	0.067	0.080
			5	0.002	0.002

n	S_1	S_2	x	one-tailed	two-tailed
12	1	1	1	0.083	0.083
	2	2	2	0.015	0.015
	2	3	2	0.045	0.045
	2	4	2	0.091	0.091
	3	3	3	0.005	0.005
	3	4	3	0.018	0.018
	3	5	3	0.045	0.045
	3	6	0	0.091	0.182
			3	0.091	0.182
	4	4	3	0.067	0.067
			4	0.002	0.002
	4	5	0	0.071	0.081
			4	0.010	0.010
	4	6	0	0.030	0.061
			4	0.030	0.061
	5	5	0	0.027	0.028
			4	0.045	0.072
			5	0.001	0.001
	5	6	0	0.008	0.015
			5	0.008	0.015
	6	6	0	0.001	0.002
			1	0.040	0.080
			5	0.040	0.080
			6	0.001	0.002

(Adapted from Dixon, W. J. and Massey, F. J. Jr. (1983). *Introduction to Statistical Analysis* (4th Edn.). New York: McGraw-Hill.)

b $n = 13$ to 15

n	S_1	S_2	x	one-tailed	two-tailed
13	1	1	1	0.077	0.077
	2	2	2	0.013	0.013
	2	3	2	0.038	0.038
	2	4	2	0.077	0.077
	3	3	3	0.003	0.003
	3	4	3	0.014	0.014
	3	5	3	0.035	0.035
	3	6	3	0.070	0.070
	4	4	3	0.052	0.052
			4	0.001	0.001
	4	5	0	0.098	0.105
			4	0.007	0.007
	4	6	0	0.049	0.070
			4	0.021	0.021
	5	5	0	0.044	0.075
			4	0.032	0.032
			5	0.001	0.001
	5	6	0	0.016	0.021
			4	0.086	0.103
			5	0.005	0.005
	6	6	0	0.004	0.005
			1	0.078	0.103
			5	0.025	0.029
			6	0.001	0.001

n	S_1	S_2	x	one-tailed	two-tailed
14	1	1	1	0.071	0.071
	2	2	2	0.011	0.011
	2	3	2	0.033	0.033
	2	4	2	0.066	0.066
	3	3	2	0.093	0.093
			3	0.003	0.003
	3	4	3	0.011	0.011
	3	5	3	0.027	0.027
	3	6	3	0.055	0.055
	3	7	0	0.096	0.192
			3	0.096	0.192
	4	4	3	0.041	0.041
			4	0.001	0.001
	4	5	3	0.095	0.095
			4	0.005	0.005
	4	6	0	0.070	0.085
			4	0.015	0.015
	4	7	0	0.035	0.070
			4	0.035	0.070
	5	5	0	0.063	0.086
			4	0.023	0.023
			5	0.0005	0.0005
	5	6	0	0.028	0.031
			4	0.063	0.091
			5	0.003	0.003
	5	7	0	0.010	0.021
			5	0.010	0.021
	6	6	0	0.009	0.010
			5	0.016	0.026
			6	0.0003	0.0003
	6	7	0	0.002	0.005
			1	0.051	0.103
			5	0.051	0.103
			6	0.002	0.005
	7	7	0	<0.0001	<0.0001
			1	0.015	0.029
			6	0.015	0.029
			7	<0.0001	<0.0001

n	S_1	S_2	x	one-tailed	two-tailed
15	1	1	1	0.067	0.067
	2	2	2	0.010	0.010
	2	3	2	0.029	0.029
	2	4	2	0.057	0.057
	2	5	2	0.095	0.095
	3	3	2	0.081	0.081
			3	0.002	0.002
	3	4	3	0.009	0.009
	3	5	3	0.022	0.022
	3	6	3	0.044	0.044
	3	7	3	0.077	0.077
	4	4	3	0.033	0.033
			4	0.001	0.001
	4	5	3	0.077	0.077
			4	0.004	0.004
	4	6	0	0.092	0.103
			4	0.011	0.011
	4	7	0	0.051	0.077
			4	0.026	0.026
	5	5	0	0.084	0.101
			4	0.017	0.017
			5	0.0003	0.0003
	5	6	0	0.042	0.089
			4	0.047	0.089
			5	0.002	0.002
	5	7	0	0.019	0.026
			4	0.100	0.119
			5	0.007	0.007
	6	6	0	0.017	0.028
			5	0.011	0.011
			6	0.0002	0.0002
	6	7	0	0.006	0.007
			1	0.084	0.119
			5	0.035	0.041
			6	0.001	0.001
	7	7	0	0.001	0.001
			1	0.032	0.041
			5	0.100	0.132
			6	0.009	0.010
			7	0.0002	0.0002

Table A17.8 The probabilities of *F*-distributions

The distribution of *F* depends on the df for the numerator (in ANOVA this is usually the treatment mean square) and the df for the divisor (in ANOVA this is usually the error, within-groups or residual mean square). The larger the df for the numerator, the less positively skewed is the distribution.

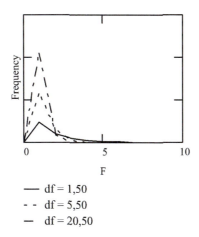

— df = 1,50
- - df = 5,50
— df = 20,50

To read the tables, the numerator df is shown in the first row of the table, while the divisor df is shown in the first column. Thus, with treatment df of 2 and error df of 20, the *F*-ratio would have to be 3.49 or larger to be statistically significant at $\alpha = .05$.

TABLE A17.8 Probabilities of the *F*-distribution

a $\alpha = .05$, $df_1 = 1$ to 14

						df_1						
df_2	1	2	3	4	5	6	7	8	9	10	12	14
1	161.45	199.50	215.71	224.58	230.16	233.99	236.77	238.88	240.54	241.88	243.90	245.36
2	18.51	19.00	19.16	19.25	19.30	19.33	19.35	19.37	19.38	19.40	19.41	19.42
3	10.13	9.55	9.28	9.12	9.01	8.94	8.89	8.85	8.81	8.79	8.74	8.71
4	7.71	6.94	6.59	6.39	6.26	6.16	6.09	6.04	6.00	5.96	5.91	5.87
5	6.61	5.79	5.41	5.19	5.05	4.95	4.88	4.82	4.77	4.74	4.68	4.64
6	5.99	5.14	4.76	4.53	4.39	4.28	4.21	4.15	4.10	4.06	4.00	3.96
7	5.59	4.74	4.35	4.12	3.97	3.87	3.79	3.73	3.68	3.64	3.57	3.53
8	5.32	4.46	4.07	3.84	3.69	3.58	3.50	3.44	3.39	3.35	3.28	3.24
9	5.12	4.26	3.86	3.63	3.48	3.37	3.29	3.23	3.18	3.14	3.07	3.03
10	4.96	4.10	3.71	3.48	3.33	3.22	3.14	3.07	3.02	2.98	2.91	2.86
11	4.84	3.98	3.59	3.36	3.20	3.09	3.01	2.95	2.90	2.85	2.79	2.74
12	4.75	3.89	3.49	3.26	3.11	3.00	2.91	2.85	2.80	2.75	2.69	2.64
13	4.67	3.81	3.41	3.18	3.03	2.92	2.83	2.77	2.71	2.67	2.60	2.55
14	4.60	3.74	3.34	3.11	2.96	2.85	2.76	2.70	2.65	2.60	2.53	2.48
15	4.54	3.68	3.29	3.06	2.90	2.79	2.71	2.64	2.59	2.54	2.48	2.42
16	4.49	3.63	3.24	3.01	2.85	2.74	2.66	2.59	2.54	2.49	2.42	2.37
17	4.45	3.59	3.20	2.96	2.81	2.70	2.61	2.55	2.49	2.45	2.38	2.33
18	4.41	3.55	3.16	2.93	2.77	2.66	2.58	2.51	2.46	2.41	2.34	2.29
19	4.38	3.52	3.13	2.90	2.74	2.63	2.54	2.48	2.42	2.38	2.31	2.26
20	4.35	3.49	3.10	2.87	2.71	2.60	2.51	2.45	2.39	2.35	2.28	2.22
21	4.32	3.47	3.07	2.84	2.68	2.57	2.49	2.42	2.37	2.32	2.25	2.20
22	4.30	3.44	3.05	2.82	2.66	2.55	2.46	2.40	2.34	2.30	2.23	2.17
23	4.28	3.42	3.03	2.80	2.64	2.53	2.44	2.37	2.32	2.27	2.20	2.15
24	4.26	3.40	3.01	2.78	2.62	2.51	2.42	2.36	2.30	2.25	2.18	2.13
25	4.24	3.39	2.99	2.76	2.60	2.49	2.40	2.34	2.28	2.24	2.16	2.11
26	4.23	3.37	2.98	2.74	2.59	2.47	2.39	2.32	2.27	2.22	2.15	2.09
27	4.21	3.35	2.96	2.73	2.57	2.46	2.37	2.31	2.25	2.20	2.13	2.08
28	4.20	3.34	2.95	2.71	2.56	2.45	2.36	2.29	2.24	2.19	2.12	2.06
29	4.18	3.33	2.93	2.70	2.55	2.43	2.35	2.28	2.22	2.18	2.10	2.05
30	4.17	3.32	2.92	2.69	2.53	2.42	2.33	2.27	2.21	2.16	2.09	2.04
35	4.12	3.27	2.87	2.64	2.49	2.37	2.29	2.22	2.16	2.11	2.04	1.99
40	4.08	3.23	2.84	2.61	2.45	2.34	2.25	2.18	2.12	2.08	2.00	1.95
45	4.06	3.20	2.81	2.58	2.42	2.31	2.22	2.15	2.10	2.05	1.97	1.92
50	4.03	3.18	2.79	2.56	2.40	2.29	2.20	2.13	2.07	2.03	1.95	1.89
55	4.02	3.16	2.77	2.54	2.38	2.27	2.18	2.11	2.06	2.01	1.93	1.88
60	4.00	3.15	2.76	2.53	2.37	2.25	2.17	2.10	2.04	1.99	1.92	1.86
65	3.99	3.14	2.75	2.51	2.36	2.24	2.15	2.08	2.03	1.98	1.90	1.85
70	3.98	3.13	2.74	2.50	2.35	2.23	2.14	2.07	2.02	1.97	1.89	1.84
75	3.97	3.12	2.73	2.49	2.34	2.22	2.13	2.06	2.01	1.96	1.88	1.83
80	3.96	3.11	2.72	2.49	2.33	2.21	2.13	2.06	2.00	1.95	1.88	1.82
85	3.95	3.10	2.71	2.48	2.32	2.21	2.12	2.05	1.99	1.94	1.87	1.81
90	3.95	3.10	2.71	2.47	2.32	2.20	2.11	2.04	1.99	1.94	1.86	1.80
95	3.94	3.09	2.70	2.47	2.31	2.20	2.11	2.04	1.98	1.93	1.86	1.80
100	3.94	3.09	2.70	2.46	2.31	2.19	2.10	2.03	1.97	1.93	1.85	1.79
110	3.93	3.08	2.69	2.45	2.30	2.18	2.09	2.02	1.97	1.92	1.84	1.78
120	3.92	3.07	2.68	2.45	2.29	2.18	2.09	2.02	1.96	1.91	1.83	1.78

TABLE A17.8 Probabilities of the *F*-distribution

b   α = .05, df$_1$ = 16 to 100

						df$_1$						
df$_2$	16	18	20	22	24	30	35	40	50	60	80	100
1	246.47	247.32	248.02	248.58	249.05	250.10	250.69	251.14	251.77	252.20	252.72	253.04
2	19.43	19.44	19.45	19.45	19.45	19.46	19.47	19.47	19.48	19.48	19.48	19.49
3	8.69	8.67	8.66	8.65	8.64	8.62	8.60	8.59	8.58	8.57	8.56	8.55
4	5.84	5.82	5.80	5.79	5.77	5.75	5.73	5.72	5.70	5.69	5.67	5.66
5	4.60	4.58	4.56	4.54	4.53	4.50	4.48	4.46	4.44	4.43	4.41	4.41
6	3.92	3.90	3.87	3.86	3.84	3.81	3.79	3.77	3.75	3.74	3.72	3.71
7	3.49	3.47	3.44	3.43	3.41	3.38	3.36	3.34	3.32	3.30	3.29	3.27
8	3.20	3.17	3.15	3.13	3.12	3.08	3.06	3.04	3.02	3.01	2.99	2.97
9	2.99	2.96	2.94	2.92	2.90	2.86	2.84	2.83	2.80	2.79	2.77	2.76
10	2.83	2.80	2.77	2.75	2.74	2.70	2.68	2.66	2.64	2.62	2.60	2.59
11	2.70	2.67	2.65	2.63	2.61	2.57	2.55	2.53	2.51	2.49	2.47	2.46
12	2.60	2.57	2.54	2.52	2.51	2.47	2.44	2.43	2.40	2.38	2.36	2.35
13	2.51	2.48	2.46	2.44	2.42	2.38	2.36	2.34	2.31	2.30	2.27	2.26
14	2.44	2.41	2.39	2.37	2.35	2.31	2.28	2.27	2.24	2.22	2.20	2.19
15	2.38	2.35	2.33	2.31	2.29	2.25	2.22	2.20	2.18	2.16	2.14	2.12
16	2.33	2.30	2.28	2.25	2.24	2.19	2.17	2.15	2.12	2.11	2.08	2.07
17	2.29	2.26	2.23	2.21	2.19	2.15	2.12	2.10	2.08	2.06	2.03	2.02
18	2.25	2.22	2.19	2.17	2.15	2.11	2.08	2.06	2.04	2.02	1.99	1.98
19	2.21	2.18	2.16	2.13	2.11	2.07	2.05	2.03	2.00	1.98	1.96	1.94
20	2.18	2.15	2.12	2.10	2.08	2.04	2.01	1.99	1.97	1.95	1.92	1.91
21	2.16	2.12	2.10	2.07	2.05	2.01	1.98	1.96	1.94	1.92	1.89	1.88
22	2.13	2.10	2.07	2.05	2.03	1.98	1.96	1.94	1.91	1.89	1.86	1.85
23	2.11	2.08	2.05	2.02	2.01	1.96	1.93	1.91	1.88	1.86	1.84	1.82
24	2.09	2.05	2.03	2.00	1.98	1.94	1.91	1.89	1.86	1.84	1.82	1.80
25	2.07	2.04	2.01	1.98	1.96	1.92	1.89	1.87	1.84	1.82	1.80	1.78
26	2.05	2.02	1.99	1.97	1.95	1.90	1.87	1.85	1.82	1.80	1.78	1.76
27	2.04	2.00	1.97	1.95	1.93	1.88	1.86	1.84	1.81	1.79	1.76	1.74
28	2.02	1.99	1.96	1.93	1.91	1.87	1.84	1.82	1.79	1.77	1.74	1.73
29	2.01	1.97	1.94	1.92	1.90	1.85	1.83	1.81	1.77	1.75	1.73	1.71
30	1.99	1.96	1.93	1.91	1.89	1.84	1.81	1.79	1.76	1.74	1.71	1.70
35	1.94	1.91	1.88	1.85	1.83	1.79	1.76	1.74	1.70	1.68	1.65	1.63
40	1.90	1.87	1.84	1.81	1.79	1.74	1.72	1.69	1.66	1.64	1.61	1.59
45	1.87	1.84	1.81	1.78	1.76	1.71	1.68	1.66	1.63	1.60	1.57	1.55
50	1.85	1.81	1.78	1.76	1.74	1.69	1.66	1.63	1.60	1.58	1.54	1.52
55	1.83	1.79	1.76	1.74	1.72	1.67	1.64	1.61	1.58	1.55	1.52	1.50
60	1.82	1.78	1.75	1.72	1.70	1.65	1.62	1.59	1.56	1.53	1.50	1.48
65	1.80	1.76	1.73	1.71	1.69	1.63	1.60	1.58	1.54	1.52	1.49	1.46
70	1.79	1.75	1.72	1.70	1.67	1.62	1.59	1.57	1.53	1.50	1.47	1.45
75	1.78	1.74	1.71	1.69	1.66	1.61	1.58	1.55	1.52	1.49	1.46	1.44
80	1.77	1.73	1.70	1.68	1.65	1.60	1.57	1.54	1.51	1.48	1.45	1.43
85	1.76	1.73	1.70	1.67	1.65	1.59	1.56	1.54	1.50	1.47	1.44	1.42
90	1.76	1.72	1.69	1.66	1.64	1.59	1.55	1.53	1.49	1.46	1.43	1.41
95	1.75	1.71	1.68	1.66	1.63	1.58	1.55	1.52	1.48	1.46	1.42	1.40
100	1.75	1.71	1.68	1.65	1.63	1.57	1.54	1.52	1.48	1.45	1.41	1.39
110	1.74	1.70	1.67	1.64	1.62	1.56	1.53	1.50	1.47	1.44	1.40	1.38
120	1.73	1.69	1.66	1.63	1.61	1.55	1.52	1.50	1.46	1.43	1.39	1.37

TABLE A17.8   Probabilities of the *F*-distribution

c $\alpha = .025$, $df_1 = 1$ to 24

df_2	1	2	3	4	5	6	7	8	9	10	12	24
1	647.79	799.50	864.16	899.58	921.85	937.11	948.22	956.66	963.28	968.63	976.71	997.25
2	38.51	39.00	39.17	39.25	39.30	39.33	39.36	39.37	39.39	39.40	39.41	39.46
3	17.44	16.04	15.44	15.10	14.88	14.73	14.62	14.54	14.47	14.42	14.34	14.12
4	12.22	10.65	9.98	9.60	9.36	9.20	9.07	8.98	8.90	8.84	8.75	8.51
5	10.01	8.43	7.76	7.39	7.15	6.98	6.85	6.76	6.68	6.62	6.52	6.28
6	8.81	7.26	6.60	6.23	5.99	5.82	5.70	5.60	5.52	5.46	5.37	5.12
7	8.07	6.54	5.89	5.52	5.29	5.12	4.99	4.90	4.82	4.76	4.67	4.41
8	7.57	6.06	5.42	5.05	4.82	4.65	4.53	4.43	4.36	4.30	4.20	3.95
9	7.21	5.71	5.08	4.72	4.48	4.32	4.20	4.10	4.03	3.96	3.87	3.61
10	6.94	5.46	4.83	4.47	4.24	4.07	3.95	3.85	3.78	3.72	3.62	3.37
11	6.72	5.26	4.63	4.28	4.04	3.88	3.76	3.66	3.59	3.53	3.43	3.17
12	6.55	5.10	4.47	4.12	3.89	3.73	3.61	3.51	3.44	3.37	3.28	3.02
13	6.41	4.97	4.35	4.00	3.77	3.60	3.48	3.39	3.31	3.25	3.15	2.89
14	6.30	4.86	4.24	3.89	3.66	3.50	3.38	3.29	3.21	3.15	3.05	2.79
15	6.20	4.77	4.15	3.80	3.58	3.41	3.29	3.20	3.12	3.06	2.96	2.70
16	6.12	4.69	4.08	3.73	3.50	3.34	3.22	3.12	3.05	2.99	2.89	2.63
17	6.04	4.62	4.01	3.66	3.44	3.28	3.16	3.06	2.98	2.92	2.82	2.56
18	5.98	4.56	3.95	3.61	3.38	3.22	3.10	3.01	2.93	2.87	2.77	2.50
19	5.92	4.51	3.90	3.56	3.33	3.17	3.05	2.96	2.88	2.82	2.72	2.45
20	5.87	4.46	3.86	3.51	3.29	3.13	3.01	2.91	2.84	2.77	2.68	2.41
21	5.83	4.42	3.82	3.48	3.25	3.09	2.97	2.87	2.80	2.73	2.64	2.37
22	5.79	4.38	3.78	3.44	3.22	3.05	2.93	2.84	2.76	2.70	2.60	2.33
23	5.75	4.35	3.75	3.41	3.18	3.02	2.90	2.81	2.73	2.67	2.57	2.30
24	5.72	4.32	3.72	3.38	3.15	2.99	2.87	2.78	2.70	2.64	2.54	2.27
25	5.69	4.29	3.69	3.35	3.13	2.97	2.85	2.75	2.68	2.61	2.51	2.24
26	5.66	4.27	3.67	3.33	3.10	2.94	2.82	2.73	2.65	2.59	2.49	2.22
27	5.63	4.24	3.65	3.31	3.08	2.92	2.80	2.71	2.63	2.57	2.47	2.19
28	5.61	4.22	3.63	3.29	3.06	2.90	2.78	2.69	2.61	2.55	2.45	2.17
29	5.59	4.20	3.61	3.27	3.04	2.88	2.76	2.67	2.59	2.53	2.43	2.15
30	5.57	4.18	3.59	3.25	3.03	2.87	2.75	2.65	2.57	2.51	2.41	2.14
35	5.48	4.11	3.52	3.18	2.96	2.80	2.68	2.58	2.50	2.44	2.34	2.06
40	5.42	4.05	3.46	3.13	2.90	2.74	2.62	2.53	2.45	2.39	2.29	2.01
45	5.38	4.01	3.42	3.09	2.86	2.70	2.58	2.49	2.41	2.35	2.25	1.96
50	5.34	3.97	3.39	3.05	2.83	2.67	2.55	2.46	2.38	2.32	2.22	1.93
55	5.31	3.95	3.36	3.03	2.81	2.65	2.53	2.43	2.36	2.29	2.19	1.90
60	5.29	3.93	3.34	3.01	2.79	2.63	2.51	2.41	2.33	2.27	2.17	1.88
65	5.26	3.91	3.32	2.99	2.77	2.61	2.49	2.39	2.32	2.25	2.15	1.86
70	5.25	3.89	3.31	2.97	2.75	2.59	2.47	2.38	2.30	2.24	2.14	1.85
75	5.23	3.88	3.30	2.96	2.74	2.58	2.46	2.37	2.29	2.22	2.12	1.83
80	5.22	3.86	3.28	2.95	2.73	2.57	2.45	2.35	2.28	2.21	2.11	1.82
85	5.21	3.85	3.27	2.94	2.72	2.56	2.44	2.35	2.27	2.20	2.10	1.81
90	5.20	3.84	3.26	2.93	2.71	2.55	2.43	2.34	2.26	2.19	2.09	1.80
95	5.19	3.84	3.26	2.92	2.70	2.54	2.42	2.33	2.25	2.19	2.08	1.79
100	5.18	3.83	3.25	2.92	2.70	2.54	2.42	2.32	2.24	2.18	2.08	1.78
110	5.16	3.82	3.24	2.90	2.68	2.53	2.40	2.31	2.23	2.17	2.07	1.77
120	5.15	3.80	3.23	2.89	2.67	2.52	2.39	2.30	2.22	2.16	2.05	1.76

TABLE A17.8   Probabilities of the *F*-distribution

d   α = .025, df$_1$ = 16 to 100

df$_1$

df$_2$	16	18	20	22	24	30	35	40	50	60	80	100
1	986.92	990.35	993.10	995.36	997.25	1001.41	1003.80	1005.60	1008.12	1009.80	1011.91	1013.17
2	39.44	39.44	39.45	39.45	39.46	39.46	39.47	39.47	39.48	39.48	39.49	39.49
3	14.23	14.20	14.17	14.14	14.12	14.08	14.06	14.04	14.01	13.99	13.97	13.96
4	8.63	8.59	8.56	8.53	8.51	8.46	8.43	8.41	8.38	8.36	8.33	8.32
5	6.40	6.36	6.33	6.30	6.28	6.23	6.20	6.18	6.14	6.12	6.10	6.08
6	5.24	5.20	5.17	5.14	5.12	5.07	5.04	5.01	4.98	4.96	4.93	4.92
7	4.54	4.50	4.47	4.44	4.41	4.36	4.33	4.31	4.28	4.25	4.23	4.21
8	4.08	4.03	4.00	3.97	3.95	3.89	3.86	3.84	3.81	3.78	3.76	3.74
9	3.74	3.70	3.67	3.64	3.61	3.56	3.53	3.51	3.47	3.45	3.42	3.40
10	3.50	3.45	3.42	3.39	3.37	3.31	3.28	3.26	3.22	3.20	3.17	3.15
11	3.30	3.26	3.23	3.20	3.17	3.12	3.09	3.06	3.03	3.00	2.97	2.96
12	3.15	3.11	3.07	3.04	3.02	2.96	2.93	2.91	2.87	2.85	2.82	2.80
13	3.03	2.98	2.95	2.92	2.89	2.84	2.80	2.78	2.74	2.72	2.69	2.67
14	2.92	2.88	2.84	2.81	2.79	2.73	2.70	2.67	2.64	2.61	2.58	2.56
15	2.84	2.79	2.76	2.73	2.70	2.64	2.61	2.59	2.55	2.52	2.49	2.47
16	2.76	2.72	2.68	2.65	2.63	2.57	2.53	2.51	2.47	2.45	2.42	2.40
17	2.70	2.65	2.62	2.59	2.56	2.50	2.47	2.44	2.41	2.38	2.35	2.33
18	2.64	2.60	2.56	2.53	2.50	2.44	2.41	2.38	2.35	2.32	2.29	2.27
19	2.59	2.55	2.51	2.48	2.45	2.39	2.36	2.33	2.30	2.27	2.24	2.22
20	2.55	2.50	2.46	2.43	2.41	2.35	2.31	2.29	2.25	2.22	2.19	2.17
21	2.51	2.46	2.42	2.39	2.37	2.31	2.27	2.25	2.21	2.18	2.15	2.13
22	2.47	2.43	2.39	2.36	2.33	2.27	2.24	2.21	2.17	2.14	2.11	2.09
23	2.44	2.39	2.36	2.33	2.30	2.24	2.20	2.18	2.14	2.11	2.08	2.06
24	2.41	2.36	2.33	2.30	2.27	2.21	2.17	2.15	2.11	2.08	2.05	2.02
25	2.38	2.34	2.30	2.27	2.24	2.18	2.15	2.12	2.08	2.05	2.02	2.00
26	2.36	2.31	2.28	2.24	2.22	2.16	2.12	2.09	2.05	2.03	1.99	1.97
27	2.34	2.29	2.25	2.22	2.19	2.13	2.10	2.07	2.03	2.00	1.97	1.94
28	2.32	2.27	2.23	2.20	2.17	2.11	2.08	2.05	2.01	1.98	1.94	1.92
29	2.30	2.25	2.21	2.18	2.15	2.09	2.06	2.03	1.99	1.96	1.92	1.90
30	2.28	2.23	2.20	2.16	2.14	2.07	2.04	2.01	1.97	1.94	1.90	1.88
35	2.21	2.16	2.12	2.09	2.06	2.00	1.96	1.93	1.89	1.86	1.82	1.80
40	2.15	2.11	2.07	2.03	2.01	1.94	1.90	1.88	1.83	1.80	1.76	1.74
45	2.11	2.07	2.03	1.99	1.96	1.90	1.86	1.83	1.79	1.76	1.72	1.69
50	2.08	2.03	1.99	1.96	1.93	1.87	1.83	1.80	1.75	1.72	1.68	1.66
55	2.05	2.01	1.97	1.93	1.90	1.84	1.80	1.77	1.72	1.69	1.65	1.62
60	2.03	1.98	1.94	1.91	1.88	1.82	1.78	1.74	1.70	1.67	1.63	1.60
65	2.01	1.97	1.93	1.89	1.86	1.80	1.76	1.72	1.68	1.65	1.60	1.58
70	2.00	1.95	1.91	1.88	1.85	1.78	1.74	1.71	1.66	1.63	1.59	1.56
75	1.99	1.94	1.90	1.86	1.83	1.76	1.72	1.69	1.65	1.61	1.57	1.54
80	1.97	1.92	1.88	1.85	1.82	1.75	1.71	1.68	1.63	1.60	1.55	1.53
85	1.96	1.91	1.87	1.84	1.81	1.74	1.70	1.67	1.62	1.59	1.54	1.51
90	1.95	1.91	1.86	1.83	1.80	1.73	1.69	1.66	1.61	1.58	1.53	1.50
95	1.95	1.90	1.86	1.82	1.79	1.72	1.68	1.65	1.60	1.57	1.52	1.49
100	1.94	1.89	1.85	1.81	1.78	1.71	1.67	1.64	1.59	1.56	1.51	1.48
110	1.93	1.88	1.84	1.80	1.77	1.70	1.66	1.63	1.58	1.54	1.50	1.47
120	1.92	1.87	1.82	1.79	1.76	1.69	1.65	1.61	1.56	1.53	1.48	1.45

TABLE A17.8   Probabilities of the *F*-distribution

e $\alpha = .01$, $df_1 = 1$ to 24

					df$_1$							
df$_2$	1	2	3	4	5	6	7	8	9	10	12	24
1	4052.18	4999.34	5403.53	5624.26	5763.96	5858.95	5928.33	5980.95	6022.40	6055.93	6106.68	6234.27
2	98.50	99.00	99.16	99.25	99.30	99.33	99.36	99.38	99.39	99.40	99.42	99.46
3	34.12	30.82	29.46	28.71	28.24	27.91	27.67	27.49	27.34	27.23	27.05	26.60
4	21.20	18.00	16.69	15.98	15.52	15.21	14.98	14.80	14.66	14.55	14.37	13.93
5	16.26	13.27	12.06	11.39	10.97	10.67	10.46	10.29	10.16	10.05	9.89	9.47
6	13.75	10.92	9.78	9.15	8.75	8.47	8.26	8.10	7.98	7.87	7.72	7.31
7	12.25	9.55	8.45	7.85	7.46	7.19	6.99	6.84	6.72	6.62	6.47	6.07
8	11.26	8.65	7.59	7.01	6.63	6.37	6.18	6.03	5.91	5.81	5.67	5.28
9	10.56	8.02	6.99	6.42	6.06	5.80	5.61	5.47	5.35	5.26	5.11	4.73
10	10.04	7.56	6.55	5.99	5.64	5.39	5.20	5.06	4.94	4.85	4.71	4.33
11	9.65	7.21	6.22	5.67	5.32	5.07	4.89	4.74	4.63	4.54	4.40	4.02
12	9.33	6.93	5.95	5.41	5.06	4.82	4.64	4.50	4.39	4.30	4.16	3.78
13	9.07	6.70	5.74	5.21	4.86	4.62	4.44	4.30	4.19	4.10	3.96	3.59
14	8.86	6.51	5.56	5.04	4.69	4.46	4.28	4.14	4.03	3.94	3.80	3.43
15	8.68	6.36	5.42	4.89	4.56	4.32	4.14	4.00	3.89	3.80	3.67	3.29
16	8.53	6.23	5.29	4.77	4.44	4.20	4.03	3.89	3.78	3.69	3.55	3.18
17	8.40	6.11	5.19	4.67	4.34	4.10	3.93	3.79	3.68	3.59	3.46	3.08
18	8.29	6.01	5.09	4.58	4.25	4.01	3.84	3.71	3.60	3.51	3.37	3.00
19	8.18	5.93	5.01	4.50	4.17	3.94	3.77	3.63	3.52	3.43	3.30	2.92
20	8.10	5.85	4.94	4.43	4.10	3.87	3.70	3.56	3.46	3.37	3.23	2.86
21	8.02	5.78	4.87	4.37	4.04	3.81	3.64	3.51	3.40	3.31	3.17	2.80
22	7.95	5.72	4.82	4.31	3.99	3.76	3.59	3.45	3.35	3.26	3.12	2.75
23	7.88	5.66	4.76	4.26	3.94	3.71	3.54	3.41	3.30	3.21	3.07	2.70
24	7.82	5.61	4.72	4.22	3.90	3.67	3.50	3.36	3.26	3.17	3.03	2.66
25	7.77	5.57	4.68	4.18	3.85	3.63	3.46	3.32	3.22	3.13	2.99	2.62
26	7.72	5.53	4.64	4.14	3.82	3.59	3.42	3.29	3.18	3.09	2.96	2.58
27	7.68	5.49	4.60	4.11	3.78	3.56	3.39	3.26	3.15	3.06	2.93	2.55
28	7.64	5.45	4.57	4.07	3.75	3.53	3.36	3.23	3.12	3.03	2.90	2.52
29	7.60	5.42	4.54	4.04	3.73	3.50	3.33	3.20	3.09	3.00	2.87	2.49
30	7.56	5.39	4.51	4.02	3.70	3.47	3.30	3.17	3.07	2.98	2.84	2.47
35	7.42	5.27	4.40	3.91	3.59	3.37	3.20	3.07	2.96	2.88	2.74	2.36
40	7.31	5.18	4.31	3.83	3.51	3.29	3.12	2.99	2.89	2.80	2.66	2.29
45	7.23	5.11	4.25	3.77	3.45	3.23	3.07	2.94	2.83	2.74	2.61	2.23
50	7.17	5.06	4.20	3.72	3.41	3.19	3.02	2.89	2.78	2.70	2.56	2.18
55	7.12	5.01	4.16	3.68	3.37	3.15	2.98	2.85	2.75	2.66	2.53	2.15
60	7.08	4.98	4.13	3.65	3.34	3.12	2.95	2.82	2.72	2.63	2.50	2.12
65	7.04	4.95	4.10	3.62	3.31	3.09	2.93	2.80	2.69	2.61	2.47	2.09
70	7.01	4.92	4.07	3.60	3.29	3.07	2.91	2.78	2.67	2.59	2.45	2.07
75	6.99	4.90	4.05	3.58	3.27	3.05	2.89	2.76	2.65	2.57	2.43	2.05
80	6.96	4.88	4.04	3.56	3.26	3.04	2.87	2.74	2.64	2.55	2.42	2.03
85	6.94	4.86	4.02	3.55	3.24	3.02	2.86	2.73	2.62	2.54	2.40	2.02
90	6.93	4.85	4.01	3.53	3.23	3.01	2.84	2.72	2.61	2.52	2.39	2.00
95	6.91	4.84	3.99	3.52	3.22	3.00	2.83	2.70	2.60	2.51	2.38	1.99
100	6.90	4.82	3.98	3.51	3.21	2.99	2.82	2.69	2.59	2.50	2.37	1.98
110	6.87	4.80	3.96	3.49	3.19	2.97	2.81	2.68	2.57	2.49	2.35	1.96
120	6.85	4.79	3.95	3.48	3.17	2.96	2.79	2.66	2.56	2.47	2.34	1.95

Table A17.9 The probabilities of H for the Kruskal–Wallis ANOVA

For samples not shown in this table use the probability values from the chi-squared distribution with df $= k - 1$.

k (number of levels) = 3 to 5

k = 3

sample sizes			probability 0.05	probability 0.01
2	2	2	-	-
3	2	1	-	-
3	2	2	4.714	-
3	3	1	5.143	-
3	3	2	5.361	-
3	3	3	5.600	7.200
4	2	1	-	-
4	2	2	5.333	-
4	3	1	5.208	-
4	3	2	5.444	6.444
4	3	3	5.791	6.745
4	4	1	4.967	6.667
4	4	2	5.455	7.036
4	4	3	5.598	7.144
4	4	4	5.692	7.654
5	2	1	5.000	-
5	2	2	5.160	6.533
5	3	1	4.960	-
5	3	2	5.251	6.909
5	3	3	5.648	7.079
5	4	1	4.985	6.955
5	4	2	5.273	7.205
5	4	3	5.656	7.445
5	4	4	5.657	7.760
5	5	1	5.127	7.309
5	5	2	5.338	7.338
5	5	3	5.705	7.578
5	5	4	5.666	7.823
5	5	5	5.780	8.000

k = 3

sample sizes			probability 0.05	probability 0.01
6	1	1	-	-
6	2	1	4.822	-
6	2	2	5.345	6.655
6	3	1	4.855	6.873
6	3	2	5.348	6.970
6	3	3	5.615	7.410
6	4	1	4.947	7.106
6	4	2	5.340	7.340
6	4	3	5.610	7.500
6	4	4	5.681	7.795
6	5	1	4.990	7.182
6	5	2	5.338	7.376
6	5	3	5.602	7.590
6	5	4	5.661	7.936
6	5	5	5.729	8.028
6	6	1	4.945	7.121
6	6	2	5.410	7.467
6	6	3	5.625	7.725
6	6	4	5.724	8.000
6	6	5	5.765	8.124
6	6	6	5.801	8.222
7	7	7	5.819	8.378
8	8	8	5.805	8.465

k = 4

sample sizes				probability 0.05	probability 0.01
2	2	1	1	-	-
2	2	2	1	5.679	-
2	2	2	2	6.167	6.667
3	1	1	1	-	-
3	2	1	1	-	-
3	2	2	1	5.833	-
3	2	2	2	6.333	7.133
3	3	1	1	6.333	-
3	3	2	1	6.244	7.200
3	3	2	2	6.527	7.636
3	3	3	1	6.600	7.400
3	3	3	2	6.727	8.015
3	3	3	3	7.000	8.538
4	1	1	1	-	-
4	2	1	1	5.833	-
4	2	2	1	6.133	7.000
4	2	2	2	6.545	7.391
4	3	1	1	6.178	7.067
4	3	2	1	6.309	7.455
4	3	2	2	6.621	7.871
4	3	3	1	6.545	7.758
4	3	3	2	6.795	8.333
4	3	3	3	6.984	8.659
4	4	1	1	5.945	7.909
4	4	2	1	6.386	7.909
4	4	2	2	6.731	8.346
4	4	3	1	6.635	8.231
4	4	3	2	6.874	8.621
4	4	3	3	7.038	8.876
4	4	4	1	6.725	8.588
4	4	4	2	6.957	8.871
4	4	4	3	7.142	9.075
4	4	4	4	7.235	9.287

k = 5

sample sizes					probability 0.05	probability 0.01
2	2	1	1	1	-	-
2	2	2	1	1	6.750	-
2	2	2	2	1	7.133	7.533
2	2	2	2	2	7.418	8.291
3	1	1	1	1	-	-
3	2	1	1	1	6.583	-
3	2	2	1	1	6.800	7.600
3	2	2	2	1	7.309	8.127
3	2	2	2	2	7.682	8.682
3	3	1	1	1	7.111	-
3	3	2	1	1	7.200	8.073
3	3	2	2	1	7.591	8.576
3	3	2	2	2	7.910	9.115
3	3	3	1	1	7.576	8.424
3	3	3	2	1	7.769	9.051
3	3	3	2	2	8.044	9.505
3	3	3	3	1	8.000	9.451
3	3	3	3	2	8.200	9.876
3	3	3	3	3	8.333	10.200

(Adapted from Table 4.2, p. 49, of Neave, H. R. (1978). *Statistics for Mathematicians, Engineers, Economists and the Behavioural and Management Sciences*. London: Routledge.)

Table A17.10 The probabilities of χ_F^2 (Friedman's non-parametric statistic for within-subjects ANOVA)

This table provides the critical values of χ_F^2 with k as the number of levels of the variable and n as the sample size.

For example, if, in a study which involved four participants ($n = 4$) and had three levels ($k = 3$), $\chi_F^2 = 6.5$, then χ_F^2 would be statistically significant with $\alpha = .05$. For larger samples or where variables have more levels use the table of chi-squared distribution with df $= k - 1$.

	k (number of levels of variable)							
	3		4		5		6	
significant at	0.05	0.01	0.05	0.01	0.05	0.01	0.05	0.01
n = 2	-	-	6.00	-	7.60	8.00	9.14	9.71
3	6.00	-	7.40	9.00	8.53	10.13	9.86	11.76
4	6.50	8.00	7.80	9.60	8.80	11.20	10.29	12.71
5	6.40	8.40	7.80	9.96	8.96	11.68	10.49	13.23
6	7.00	9.00	7.60	10.20	9.07	11.87	10.57	13.62
7	7.14	8.86	7.80	10.54	9.14	12.11	10.67	13.86
8	6.25	9.00	7.65	10.50	9.20	13.20	10.71	14.00
9	6.22	9.56	7.67	10.73	9.24	12.44	10.78	14.14
10	6.20	9.60	7.68	10.68	9.28	12.48	10.80	14.23
11	6.55	9.46	7.69	10.75	9.31	12.58	10.84	14.32
12	6.50	9.50	7.70	10.80	9.33	12.60	10.86	14.38
13	6.62	9.39	7.80	10.85	9.35	12.68	10.89	14.45
14	6.14	9.14	7.71	10.89	9.37	12.74	10.90	14.49
15	6.40	8.93	7.72	10.92	9.34	12.80	10.92	14.54
16	6.50	9.38	7.80	10.95	9.40	12.80	10.96	14.57
17	6.12	9.29	7.80	10.05	9.41	12.85	10.95	14.61
18	6.33	9.00	7.73	10.93	9.42	12.89	10.95	14.63
19	6.42	9.58	7.86	11.02	9.43	12.88	11.00	14.67
20	6.30	9.30	7.80	11.10	9.40	12.92	11.00	14.66
25	6.08	8.96						
30	6.20	9.27						
35	6.17	9.31						
40	6.05	9.15						
45	6.18	9.24						
50	6.04	9.16						

(Adapted from Table O, p. 395, of Neave, H. R. and Worthington, P. L. (1988). *Distribution-Free Tests*. London: Routledge and Table 4.3, p. 49, of Neave, H. R. (1978). *Statistics Tables for Mathematicians, Engineers, Economists and the Behavioural and Management Sciences*. London: Routledge.)

Table A17.11 Bonferroni corrections for contrasts

a   Error rate per family, α = .05, two-tailed probabilities (or α = .025, one-tailed probabilities), df for error = 1 to 20

Number of contrasts

df error	2	3	4	5	6	7	8	9	10	12	15
1	25.452	38.189	50.922	63.656	76.392	89.123	101.859	114.590	127.321	152.793	190.996
2	6.205	7.649	8.860	9.925	10.886	11.769	12.590	13.360	14.089	15.444	17.277
3	4.177	4.857	5.392	5.841	6.232	6.580	6.895	7.185	7.453	7.940	8.575
4	3.495	3.961	4.315	4.604	4.851	5.068	5.261	5.437	5.598	5.885	6.254
5	3.163	3.534	3.810	4.032	4.219	4.382	4.526	4.655	4.773	4.983	5.247
6	2.969	3.287	3.521	3.707	3.863	3.997	4.115	4.221	4.317	4.486	4.698
7	2.841	3.128	3.335	3.499	3.636	3.753	3.855	3.947	4.029	4.174	4.355
8	2.752	3.016	3.206	3.355	3.479	3.584	3.677	3.759	3.833	3.962	4.122
9	2.685	2.933	3.111	3.250	3.364	3.462	3.547	3.622	3.690	3.808	3.954
10	2.634	2.870	3.038	3.169	3.277	3.368	3.448	3.518	3.581	3.691	3.827
11	2.593	2.820	2.981	3.106	3.208	3.295	3.370	3.437	3.497	3.600	3.728
12	2.560	2.779	2.934	3.055	3.153	3.236	3.308	3.371	3.428	3.527	3.649
13	2.533	2.746	2.896	3.012	3.107	3.187	3.256	3.318	3.372	3.467	3.584
14	2.510	2.718	2.864	2.977	3.069	3.146	3.214	3.273	3.326	3.417	3.530
15	2.490	2.694	2.837	2.947	3.036	3.112	3.177	3.235	3.286	3.375	3.484
16	2.473	2.673	2.813	2.921	3.008	3.082	3.146	3.202	3.252	3.339	3.444
17	2.458	2.655	2.793	2.898	2.984	3.056	3.119	3.173	3.222	3.307	3.410
18	2.445	2.639	2.775	2.878	2.963	3.034	3.095	3.149	3.197	3.279	3.380
19	2.433	2.625	2.759	2.861	2.944	3.014	3.074	3.127	3.174	3.255	3.354
20	2.423	2.613	2.744	2.845	2.927	2.996	3.055	3.107	3.153	3.233	3.331

TABLE A17.11   Bonferroni corrections for contrasts

b   Error rate per family, $\alpha = .05$, two-tailed tests (or $\alpha = .025$, one-tailed tests), df for error = 21 to 120

Number of contrasts

df error	2	3	4	5	6	7	8	9	10	12	15
21	2.414	2.601	2.732	2.831	2.912	2.980	3.038	3.090	3.135	3.214	3.310
22	2.405	2.591	2.720	2.819	2.899	2.965	3.023	3.074	3.119	3.196	3.291
23	2.398	2.582	2.710	2.807	2.886	2.952	3.009	3.059	3.104	3.181	3.274
24	2.391	2.574	2.700	2.797	2.875	2.941	2.997	3.046	3.091	3.166	3.258
25	2.385	2.566	2.692	2.787	2.865	2.930	2.986	3.035	3.078	3.153	3.244
26	2.379	2.559	2.684	2.779	2.856	2.920	2.975	3.024	3.067	3.141	3.231
27	2.373	2.552	2.676	2.771	2.847	2.911	2.966	3.014	3.057	3.130	3.219
28	2.368	2.546	2.669	2.763	2.839	2.902	2.957	3.004	3.047	3.120	3.208
29	2.364	2.541	2.663	2.756	2.832	2.894	2.949	2.996	3.038	3.110	3.198
30	2.360	2.536	2.657	2.750	2.825	2.887	2.941	2.988	3.030	3.102	3.189
31	2.356	2.531	2.652	2.744	2.818	2.880	2.934	2.981	3.022	3.094	3.180
32	2.352	2.526	2.647	2.738	2.812	2.874	2.927	2.974	3.015	3.086	3.172
33	2.348	2.522	2.642	2.733	2.807	2.868	2.921	2.967	3.008	3.079	3.164
34	2.345	2.518	2.638	2.728	2.802	2.863	2.915	2.961	3.002	3.072	3.157
35	2.342	2.515	2.633	2.724	2.797	2.857	2.910	2.955	2.996	3.066	3.150
36	2.339	2.511	2.629	2.719	2.792	2.853	2.905	2.950	2.990	3.060	3.144
37	2.336	2.508	2.626	2.715	2.788	2.848	2.900	2.945	2.985	3.054	3.138
38	2.334	2.505	2.622	2.712	2.783	2.844	2.895	2.940	2.980	3.049	3.132
39	2.331	2.502	2.619	2.708	2.780	2.839	2.891	2.936	2.976	3.044	3.127
40	2.329	2.499	2.616	2.704	2.776	2.836	2.887	2.931	2.971	3.039	3.122
45	2.319	2.487	2.602	2.690	2.760	2.819	2.869	2.913	2.952	3.019	3.100
50	2.311	2.477	2.591	2.678	2.747	2.805	2.855	2.898	2.937	3.003	3.083
55	2.304	2.469	2.583	2.668	2.737	2.794	2.844	2.887	2.925	2.990	3.069
60	2.299	2.463	2.575	2.660	2.729	2.785	2.834	2.877	2.915	2.979	3.057
65	2.295	2.458	2.569	2.654	2.721	2.778	2.826	2.869	2.906	2.970	3.048
70	2.291	2.453	2.564	2.648	2.715	2.771	2.820	2.862	2.899	2.962	3.039
75	2.287	2.449	2.559	2.643	2.710	2.766	2.814	2.855	2.892	2.956	3.032
80	2.284	2.445	2.555	2.639	2.705	2.761	2.809	2.850	2.887	2.950	3.026
85	2.282	2.442	2.552	2.635	2.701	2.757	2.804	2.846	2.882	2.945	3.020
90	2.280	2.440	2.549	2.632	2.698	2.753	2.800	2.841	2.878	2.940	3.016
95	2.277	2.437	2.546	2.629	2.695	2.750	2.797	2.838	2.874	2.936	3.011
100	2.276	2.435	2.544	2.626	2.692	2.747	2.793	2.834	2.871	2.933	3.007
105	2.274	2.433	2.541	2.623	2.689	2.744	2.791	2.831	2.868	2.929	3.004
110	2.272	2.431	2.539	2.621	2.687	2.741	2.788	2.829	2.865	2.926	3.001
115	2.271	2.430	2.538	2.619	2.685	2.739	2.786	2.826	2.862	2.924	2.998
120	2.270	2.428	2.536	2.617	2.683	2.737	2.783	2.824	2.860	2.921	2.995

TABLE A17.11   Bonferroni corrections for contrasts

c   Error rate per family, α = .1, two-tailed tests (or α = .05, one-tailed tests), df for error = 1 to 30

Number of contrasts

df error	2	3	4	5	6	7	8	9	10	12	15
1	12.706	19.081	25.452	31.821	38.189	44.557	50.922	57.290	63.656	76.392	95.489
2	4.303	5.339	6.205	6.965	7.649	8.277	8.860	9.408	9.925	10.886	12.186
3	3.182	3.740	4.177	4.541	4.857	5.138	5.392	5.625	5.841	6.232	6.741
4	2.776	3.186	3.495	3.747	3.961	4.148	4.315	4.466	4.604	4.851	5.167
5	2.571	2.912	3.163	3.365	3.534	3.681	3.810	3.926	4.032	4.219	4.456
6	2.447	2.749	2.969	3.143	3.287	3.412	3.521	3.619	3.707	3.863	4.058
7	2.365	2.642	2.841	2.998	3.128	3.238	3.335	3.422	3.499	3.636	3.806
8	2.306	2.566	2.752	2.896	3.016	3.117	3.206	3.285	3.355	3.479	3.632
9	2.262	2.510	2.685	2.821	2.933	3.028	3.111	3.184	3.250	3.364	3.505
10	2.228	2.466	2.634	2.764	2.870	2.960	3.038	3.107	3.169	3.277	3.409
11	2.201	2.431	2.593	2.718	2.820	2.906	2.981	3.047	3.106	3.208	3.334
12	2.179	2.403	2.560	2.681	2.779	2.863	2.934	2.998	3.055	3.153	3.273
13	2.160	2.380	2.533	2.650	2.746	2.827	2.896	2.957	3.012	3.107	3.223
14	2.145	2.360	2.510	2.624	2.718	2.796	2.864	2.924	2.977	3.069	3.181
15	2.131	2.343	2.490	2.602	2.694	2.770	2.837	2.895	2.947	3.036	3.146
16	2.120	2.328	2.473	2.583	2.673	2.748	2.813	2.870	2.921	3.008	3.115
17	2.110	2.316	2.458	2.567	2.655	2.729	2.793	2.848	2.898	2.984	3.088
18	2.101	2.304	2.445	2.552	2.639	2.712	2.775	2.829	2.878	2.963	3.065
19	2.093	2.294	2.433	2.539	2.625	2.697	2.759	2.813	2.861	2.944	3.045
20	2.086	2.285	2.423	2.528	2.613	2.683	2.744	2.798	2.845	2.927	3.026
21	2.080	2.278	2.414	2.518	2.601	2.671	2.732	2.784	2.831	2.912	3.010
22	2.074	2.270	2.405	2.508	2.591	2.661	2.720	2.772	2.819	2.899	2.995
23	2.069	2.264	2.398	2.500	2.582	2.651	2.710	2.761	2.807	2.886	2.982
24	2.064	2.258	2.391	2.492	2.574	2.642	2.700	2.751	2.797	2.875	2.970
25	2.060	2.252	2.385	2.485	2.566	2.634	2.692	2.742	2.787	2.865	2.959
26	2.056	2.247	2.379	2.479	2.559	2.626	2.684	2.734	2.779	2.856	2.949
27	2.052	2.243	2.373	2.473	2.552	2.619	2.676	2.726	2.771	2.847	2.939
28	2.048	2.238	2.368	2.467	2.546	2.613	2.669	2.719	2.763	2.839	2.930
29	2.045	2.234	2.364	2.462	2.541	2.607	2.663	2.713	2.756	2.832	2.922
30	2.042	2.231	2.360	2.457	2.536	2.601	2.657	2.706	2.750	2.825	2.915

TABLE A17.11   Bonferroni corrections for contrasts

d   Error rate per family, α = .1, two-tailed tests (or α = .05, one-tailed tests), df for error = 31 to 120

Number of contrasts

df error	2	3	4	5	6	7	8	9	10	12	15
31	2.040	2.227	2.356	2.453	2.531	2.596	2.652	2.701	2.744	2.818	2.908
32	2.037	2.224	2.352	2.449	2.526	2.591	2.647	2.695	2.738	2.812	2.902
33	2.035	2.221	2.348	2.445	2.522	2.587	2.642	2.690	2.733	2.807	2.896
34	2.032	2.218	2.345	2.441	2.518	2.583	2.638	2.686	2.728	2.802	2.890
35	2.030	2.215	2.342	2.438	2.515	2.579	2.633	2.681	2.724	2.797	2.885
36	2.028	2.213	2.339	2.434	2.511	2.575	2.629	2.677	2.719	2.792	2.879
37	2.026	2.210	2.336	2.431	2.508	2.571	2.626	2.673	2.715	2.788	2.875
38	2.024	2.208	2.334	2.429	2.505	2.568	2.622	2.670	2.712	2.783	2.870
39	2.023	2.206	2.331	2.426	2.502	2.565	2.619	2.666	2.708	2.780	2.866
40	2.021	2.204	2.329	2.423	2.499	2.562	2.616	2.663	2.704	2.776	2.862
45	2.014	2.195	2.319	2.412	2.487	2.549	2.602	2.648	2.690	2.760	2.845
50	2.009	2.188	2.311	2.403	2.477	2.539	2.591	2.637	2.678	2.747	2.831
55	2.004	2.183	2.304	2.396	2.469	2.530	2.583	2.628	2.668	2.737	2.820
60	2.000	2.178	2.299	2.390	2.463	2.524	2.575	2.620	2.660	2.729	2.811
65	1.997	2.174	2.295	2.385	2.458	2.518	2.569	2.614	2.654	2.721	2.803
70	1.994	2.171	2.291	2.381	2.453	2.513	2.564	2.608	2.648	2.715	2.796
75	1.992	2.168	2.287	2.377	2.449	2.508	2.559	2.604	2.643	2.710	2.791
80	1.990	2.165	2.284	2.374	2.445	2.505	2.555	2.600	2.639	2.705	2.786
85	1.988	2.163	2.282	2.371	2.442	2.501	2.552	2.596	2.635	2.701	2.781
90	1.987	2.161	2.280	2.368	2.440	2.499	2.549	2.593	2.632	2.698	2.777
95	1.985	2.159	2.277	2.366	2.437	2.496	2.546	2.590	2.629	2.695	2.774
100	1.984	2.158	2.276	2.364	2.435	2.494	2.544	2.587	2.626	2.692	2.771
105	1.983	2.156	2.274	2.362	2.433	2.492	2.541	2.585	2.623	2.689	2.768
110	1.982	2.155	2.272	2.361	2.431	2.490	2.539	2.583	2.621	2.687	2.766
115	1.981	2.154	2.271	2.359	2.430	2.488	2.538	2.581	2.619	2.685	2.763
120	1.980	2.153	2.270	2.358	2.428	2.486	2.536	2.579	2.617	2.683	2.761

Table A17.12 Dunnett's *t*-test of contrasts

a   α = .05, two-tailed tests

number of means (including the control)

df error	3	4	5	6	7	8	9	10	11	12	13	16	21
5	3.03	3.29	3.48	3.62	3.73	3.82	3.90	3.97	4.03	4.09	4.14	4.26	4.42
6	2.86	3.10	3.26	3.39	3.49	3.57	3.64	3.71	3.76	3.81	3.86	3.97	4.11
7	2.75	2.97	3.12	3.24	3.33	3.41	3.47	3.53	3.58	3.63	3.67	3.78	3.91
8	2.67	2.88	3.02	3.13	3.22	3.29	3.35	3.41	3.46	3.50	3.54	3.64	3.76
9	2.61	2.81	2.95	3.05	3.14	3.20	3.26	3.32	3.36	3.40	3.44	3.53	3.65
10	2.57	2.76	2.89	2.99	3.07	3.14	3.19	3.24	3.29	3.33	3.36	3.45	3.57
11	2.53	2.72	2.84	2.94	3.02	3.08	3.14	3.19	3.23	3.27	3.30	3.39	3.50
12	2.50	2.68	2.81	2.90	2.98	3.04	3.09	3.14	3.18	3.22	3.25	3.34	3.45
13	2.48	2.65	2.78	2.87	2.94	3.00	3.06	3.10	3.14	3.18	3.21	3.29	3.40
14	2.46	2.63	2.75	2.84	2.91	2.97	3.02	3.07	3.11	3.14	3.18	3.26	3.36
15	2.44	2.61	2.73	2.82	2.89	2.95	3.00	3.04	3.08	3.12	3.15	3.23	3.33
16	2.42	2.59	2.71	2.80	2.87	2.92	2.97	3.02	3.06	3.09	3.12	3.20	3.30
17	2.41	2.58	2.69	2.78	2.85	2.90	2.95	3.00	3.03	3.07	3.10	3.18	3.27
18	2.40	2.56	2.68	2.76	2.83	2.89	2.94	2.98	3.01	3.05	3.08	3.16	3.25
19	2.39	2.55	2.66	2.75	2.81	2.87	2.92	2.96	3.00	3.03	3.06	3.14	3.23
20	2.38	2.54	2.65	2.73	2.80	2.86	2.90	2.95	2.98	3.02	3.05	3.12	3.22
24	2.35	2.51	2.61	2.70	2.76	2.81	2.86	2.90	2.94	2.97	3.00	3.07	3.16
30	2.32	2.47	2.58	2.66	2.72	2.77	2.82	2.86	2.89	2.92	2.95	3.02	3.11
40	2.29	2.44	2.54	2.62	2.68	2.73	2.77	2.81	2.85	2.87	2.90	2.97	3.06
60	2.27	2.41	2.51	2.58	2.64	2.69	2.73	2.77	2.80	2.83	2.86	2.92	3.00
120	2.24	2.38	2.47	2.55	2.60	2.65	2.69	2.73	2.76	2.79	2.81	2.87	2.95

TABLE A17.12   Dunnett's *t*-test of contrasts

b   α = .05, one-tailed tests

number of means (including the control)

df error	3	4	5	6	7	8	9	10
5	2.44	2.68	2.85	2.98	3.08	3.16	3.24	3.30
6	2.34	2.56	2.71	2.83	2.92	3.00	3.07	3.12
7	2.27	2.48	2.62	2.73	2.82	2.89	2.95	3.01
8	2.22	2.42	2.55	2.66	2.74	2.81	2.87	2.92
9	2.18	2.37	2.50	2.60	2.68	2.75	2.81	2.86
10	2.15	2.34	2.47	2.56	2.64	2.70	2.76	2.81
11	2.13	2.31	2.44	2.53	2.60	2.67	2.72	2.77
12	2.11	2.29	2.41	2.50	2.58	2.64	2.69	2.74
13	2.09	2.27	2.39	2.48	2.55	2.61	2.66	2.71
14	2.08	2.25	2.37	2.46	2.53	2.59	2.64	2.69
15	2.07	2.24	2.36	2.44	2.51	2.57	2.62	2.67
16	2.06	2.23	2.34	2.43	2.50	2.56	2.61	2.65
17	2.05	2.22	2.33	2.42	2.49	2.54	2.59	2.64
18	2.04	2.21	2.32	2.41	2.48	2.53	2.58	2.62
19	2.03	2.20	2.31	2.40	2.47	2.52	2.57	2.61
20	2.03	2.19	2.30	2.39	2.46	2.51	2.56	2.60
24	2.01	2.17	2.28	2.36	2.43	2.48	2.53	2.57
30	1.99	2.15	2.25	2.33	2.40	2.45	2.50	2.54
40	1.97	2.13	2.23	2.31	2.37	2.42	2.47	2.51
60	1.95	2.10	2.21	2.28	2.35	2.39	2.44	2.48
120	1.93	2.08	2.18	2.26	2.32	2.37	2.41	2.45

(Adapted from Table II of Dunnett, C. W. (1964). New tables for multiple comparisons with a control. *Biometrics*, *20*, 482–491.)

Table A17.13 The critical values of Tukey's *HSD*

a   Error rate per family α = .05, two-tailed tests

Number of means to be contrasted

df error	3	4	5	6	7	8	9	10	11	12	15
1	19.08	23.21	26.22	28.57	30.49	32.10	33.49	34.70	35.77	36.74	39.15
2	5.89	6.93	7.69	8.29	8.79	9.21	9.57	9.89	10.18	10.43	11.07
3	4.18	4.82	5.30	5.69	6.00	6.26	6.49	6.69	6.87	7.04	7.44
4	3.56	4.07	4.45	4.74	4.99	5.20	5.37	5.54	5.68	5.81	6.12
5	3.25	3.69	4.01	4.26	4.48	4.65	4.81	4.94	5.07	5.18	5.46
6	3.07	3.46	3.75	3.98	4.17	4.33	4.47	4.59	4.70	4.80	5.05
7	2.94	3.31	3.58	3.79	3.97	4.12	4.24	4.36	4.45	4.55	4.78
8	2.86	3.20	3.46	3.66	3.82	3.96	4.08	4.19	4.28	4.37	4.58
9	2.79	3.12	3.37	3.55	3.71	3.84	3.95	4.06	4.15	4.23	4.44
10	2.74	3.06	3.29	3.47	3.62	3.75	3.86	3.96	4.04	4.12	4.32
11	2.70	3.01	3.23	3.41	3.56	3.68	3.78	3.88	3.97	4.04	4.23
12	2.67	2.97	3.19	3.36	3.50	3.62	3.73	3.81	3.90	3.97	4.16
13	2.64	2.93	3.15	3.32	3.45	3.57	3.67	3.76	3.84	3.91	4.09
14	2.62	2.91	3.12	3.28	3.42	3.53	3.63	3.71	3.79	3.86	4.04
15	2.60	2.88	3.09	3.25	3.38	3.49	3.59	3.68	3.75	3.82	4.00
16	2.58	2.86	3.06	3.22	3.35	3.46	3.56	3.64	3.72	3.78	3.95
17	2.57	2.84	3.04	3.20	3.32	3.44	3.53	3.61	3.68	3.75	3.92
18	2.55	2.83	3.03	3.17	3.30	3.41	3.51	3.59	3.66	3.73	3.89
19	2.54	2.81	3.01	3.16	3.29	3.39	3.48	3.56	3.63	3.70	3.86
20	2.53	2.80	2.99	3.15	3.27	3.37	3.46	3.54	3.61	3.68	3.84
21	2.52	2.79	2.98	3.13	3.25	3.35	3.44	3.52	3.59	3.66	3.82
22	2.51	2.78	2.97	3.12	3.24	3.34	3.43	3.51	3.58	3.63	3.80
23	2.50	2.76	2.96	3.10	3.22	3.32	3.42	3.49	3.56	3.62	3.78
24	2.50	2.76	2.95	3.09	3.21	3.31	3.40	3.48	3.54	3.61	3.76
25	2.49	2.75	2.93	3.08	3.20	3.30	3.39	3.46	3.53	3.59	3.75
26	2.48	2.74	2.93	3.08	3.19	3.29	3.37	3.45	3.52	3.58	3.73
27	2.48	2.74	2.92	3.06	3.18	3.28	3.37	3.44	3.51	3.56	3.72
28	2.47	2.73	2.91	3.05	3.17	3.27	3.35	3.43	3.49	3.56	3.71
29	2.47	2.72	2.91	3.05	3.16	3.26	3.34	3.42	3.49	3.54	3.70
30	2.47	2.72	2.90	3.04	3.15	3.25	3.34	3.41	3.48	3.54	3.68
35	2.45	2.69	2.88	3.01	3.13	3.22	3.30	3.37	3.44	3.50	3.64
40	2.43	2.68	2.86	2.99	3.10	3.20	3.27	3.34	3.41	3.46	3.61
45	2.43	2.67	2.84	2.98	3.08	3.17	3.26	3.32	3.39	3.44	3.59
50	2.42	2.66	2.83	2.96	3.07	3.16	3.24	3.31	3.37	3.43	3.56
55	2.41	2.65	2.82	2.96	3.06	3.15	3.23	3.30	3.36	3.42	3.55
60	2.40	2.64	2.81	2.94	3.05	3.14	3.22	3.29	3.34	3.40	3.54
65	2.40	2.64	2.81	2.93	3.04	3.13	3.21	3.27	3.34	3.39	3.53
70	2.40	2.63	2.80	2.93	3.03	3.13	3.20	3.27	3.33	3.38	3.51
75	2.39	2.63	2.79	2.93	3.03	3.12	3.20	3.26	3.32	3.37	3.51
80	2.39	2.62	2.79	2.92	3.03	3.11	3.19	3.25	3.32	3.37	3.50
85	2.38	2.62	2.79	2.91	3.02	3.10	3.18	3.25	3.31	3.36	3.49
90	2.38	2.62	2.79	2.91	3.02	3.10	3.18	3.25	3.30	3.36	3.49
95	2.38	2.62	2.78	2.91	3.01	3.10	3.17	3.24	3.30	3.35	3.48
100	2.38	2.62	2.78	2.91	3.01	3.10	3.17	3.24	3.30	3.34	3.48
110	2.38	2.61	2.77	2.90	3.01	3.09	3.17	3.23	3.29	3.34	3.47
120	2.38	2.60	2.77	2.90	3.00	3.08	3.16	3.22	3.28	3.33	3.46
∞	2.34	2.57	2.73	2.85	2.95	3.03	3.10	3.16	3.22	3.27	3.39

TABLE A17.13   The critical values of Tukey's *HSD*

b   Error rate per family α = .01, two-tailed tests

Number of means to be contrasted

df error	3	4	5	6	7	8	9	10	11	12	15
1	95.50	116.15	131.22	142.98	152.57	160.63	167.56	173.63	179.01	183.85	195.90
2	13.45	15.76	17.48	18.83	19.94	20.88	21.69	22.41	23.04	23.62	25.05
3	7.51	8.61	9.42	10.07	10.61	11.06	11.46	11.80	12.11	12.40	13.10
4	5.74	6.48	7.04	7.48	7.85	8.16	8.44	8.67	8.89	9.08	9.57
5	4.94	5.52	5.95	6.30	6.59	6.84	7.05	7.24	7.41	7.57	7.95
6	4.48	4.97	5.35	5.64	5.88	6.09	6.27	6.43	6.58	6.70	7.04
7	4.19	4.62	4.95	5.21	5.43	5.61	5.78	5.92	6.05	6.16	6.45
8	3.99	4.38	4.68	4.92	5.12	5.28	5.43	5.56	5.68	5.78	6.05
9	3.84	4.21	4.49	4.71	4.89	5.04	5.18	5.30	5.41	5.50	5.75
10	3.73	4.08	4.34	4.55	4.72	4.86	4.99	5.10	5.20	5.30	5.52
11	3.64	3.97	4.22	4.42	4.58	4.72	4.84	4.94	5.04	5.13	5.35
12	3.57	3.89	4.13	4.31	4.47	4.60	4.72	4.82	4.91	4.99	5.20
13	3.51	3.82	4.05	4.23	4.38	4.50	4.62	4.72	4.80	4.88	5.08
14	3.46	3.76	3.98	4.16	4.30	4.43	4.53	4.62	4.71	4.79	4.99
15	3.42	3.71	3.93	4.10	4.24	4.36	4.46	4.55	4.63	4.71	4.90
16	3.39	3.67	3.88	4.04	4.19	4.30	4.40	4.49	4.57	4.64	4.82
17	3.35	3.63	3.84	4.00	4.14	4.25	4.35	4.43	4.51	4.58	4.76
18	3.32	3.60	3.80	3.96	4.09	4.20	4.30	4.38	4.46	4.53	4.70
19	3.30	3.57	3.77	3.92	4.05	4.16	4.26	4.34	4.42	4.48	4.65
20	3.28	3.55	3.74	3.90	4.02	4.13	4.22	4.31	4.38	4.44	4.61
21	3.26	3.53	3.72	3.87	4.00	4.09	4.19	4.27	4.34	4.41	4.57
22	3.25	3.51	3.69	3.84	3.97	4.07	4.16	4.24	4.31	4.38	4.54
23	3.23	3.49	3.68	3.82	3.94	4.04	4.13	4.21	4.28	4.34	4.50
24	3.22	3.47	3.66	3.80	3.92	4.02	4.11	4.19	4.26	4.32	4.48
25	3.20	3.46	3.63	3.78	3.90	4.00	4.09	4.16	4.23	4.29	4.45
26	3.19	3.44	3.62	3.76	3.88	3.98	4.07	4.14	4.21	4.27	4.43
27	3.17	3.43	3.61	3.75	3.86	3.96	4.04	4.12	4.19	4.25	4.40
28	3.17	3.42	3.59	3.73	3.85	3.95	4.03	4.10	4.17	4.23	4.38
29	3.16	3.40	3.58	3.72	3.83	3.93	4.01	4.09	4.15	4.21	4.36
30	3.15	3.39	3.57	3.71	3.82	3.92	4.00	4.07	4.14	4.19	4.34
35	3.11	3.35	3.52	3.66	3.76	3.85	3.94	4.01	4.07	4.13	4.27
40	3.09	3.32	3.49	3.61	3.72	3.81	3.89	3.96	4.02	4.07	4.21
45	3.07	3.30	3.46	3.59	3.69	3.78	3.85	3.92	3.98	4.04	4.17
50	3.05	3.27	3.44	3.56	3.67	3.75	3.83	3.90	3.95	4.01	4.14
55	3.04	3.26	3.42	3.54	3.65	3.73	3.80	3.87	3.93	3.98	4.12
60	3.03	3.25	3.41	3.53	3.63	3.71	3.79	3.85	3.91	3.96	4.09
65	3.02	3.24	3.39	3.51	3.61	3.70	3.77	3.83	3.89	3.95	4.07
70	3.01	3.23	3.39	3.51	3.61	3.68	3.75	3.82	3.87	3.93	4.06
75	3.01	3.22	3.37	3.49	3.59	3.68	3.75	3.81	3.87	3.92	4.04
80	3.00	3.22	3.37	3.49	3.59	3.66	3.73	3.80	3.85	3.90	4.03
85	2.99	3.21	3.36	3.48	3.58	3.66	3.73	3.79	3.85	3.90	4.02
90	2.99	3.20	3.35	3.47	3.57	3.65	3.72	3.78	3.84	3.88	4.01
95	2.98	3.20	3.35	3.46	3.56	3.64	3.71	3.78	3.83	3.87	4.00
100	2.98	3.20	3.34	3.46	3.56	3.63	3.71	3.77	3.82	3.87	4.00
110	2.98	3.19	3.34	3.45	3.55	3.63	3.70	3.75	3.81	3.86	3.98
120	2.97	3.18	3.33	3.44	3.54	3.62	3.68	3.75	3.80	3.85	3.97
∞	2.91	3.11	3.25	3.37	3.45	3.53	3.59	3.65	3.70	3.74	3.85

Table A17.14 The distribution of the studentised range statistic q

a   Error rate per family $\alpha = .05$, two-tailed tests

Number of means to be contrasted

df error	3	4	5	6	7	8	9	10	11	12	15
1	26.98	32.82	37.08	40.41	43.12	45.40	47.36	49.07	50.59	51.96	55.36
2	8.33	9.80	10.88	11.73	12.43	13.03	13.54	13.99	14.39	14.75	15.65
3	5.91	6.82	7.50	8.04	8.48	8.85	9.18	9.46	9.72	9.95	10.52
4	5.04	5.76	6.29	6.71	7.05	7.35	7.60	7.83	8.03	8.21	8.66
5	4.60	5.22	5.67	6.03	6.33	6.58	6.80	6.99	7.17	7.32	7.72
6	4.34	4.90	5.30	5.63	5.90	6.12	6.32	6.49	6.65	6.79	7.14
7	4.16	4.68	5.06	5.36	5.61	5.82	6.00	6.16	6.30	6.43	6.76
8	4.04	4.53	4.89	5.17	5.40	5.60	5.77	5.92	6.05	6.18	6.48
9	3.95	4.41	4.76	5.02	5.24	5.43	5.59	5.74	5.87	5.98	6.28
10	3.88	4.33	4.65	4.91	5.12	5.30	5.46	5.60	5.72	5.83	6.11
11	3.82	4.26	4.57	4.82	5.03	5.20	5.35	5.49	5.61	5.71	5.98
12	3.77	4.20	4.51	4.75	4.95	5.12	5.27	5.39	5.51	5.61	5.88
13	3.73	4.15	4.45	4.69	4.88	5.05	5.19	5.32	5.43	5.53	5.79
14	3.70	4.11	4.41	4.64	4.83	4.99	5.13	5.25	5.36	5.46	5.71
15	3.67	4.08	4.37	4.59	4.78	4.94	5.08	5.20	5.31	5.40	5.65
16	3.65	4.05	4.33	4.56	4.74	4.90	5.03	5.15	5.26	5.35	5.59
17	3.63	4.02	4.30	4.52	4.70	4.86	4.99	5.11	5.21	5.31	5.54
18	3.61	4.00	4.28	4.49	4.67	4.82	4.96	5.07	5.17	5.27	5.50
19	3.59	3.98	4.25	4.47	4.65	4.79	4.92	5.04	5.14	5.23	5.46
20	3.58	3.96	4.23	4.45	4.62	4.77	4.90	5.01	5.11	5.20	5.43
21	3.56	3.94	4.21	4.42	4.60	4.74	4.87	4.98	5.08	5.17	5.40
22	3.55	3.93	4.20	4.41	4.58	4.72	4.85	4.96	5.06	5.14	5.37
23	3.54	3.91	4.18	4.39	4.56	4.70	4.83	4.94	5.03	5.12	5.34
24	3.53	3.90	4.17	4.37	4.54	4.68	4.81	4.92	5.01	5.10	5.32
25	3.52	3.89	4.15	4.36	4.53	4.67	4.79	4.90	4.99	5.08	5.30
26	3.51	3.88	4.14	4.35	4.51	4.65	4.77	4.88	4.98	5.06	5.28
27	3.51	3.87	4.13	4.33	4.50	4.64	4.76	4.86	4.96	5.04	5.26
28	3.50	3.86	4.12	4.32	4.49	4.62	4.74	4.85	4.94	5.03	5.24
29	3.49	3.85	4.11	4.31	4.47	4.61	4.73	4.84	4.93	5.01	5.23
30	3.49	3.85	4.10	4.30	4.46	4.60	4.72	4.82	4.92	5.00	5.21
35	3.46	3.81	4.07	4.26	4.42	4.56	4.67	4.77	4.86	4.95	5.15
40	3.44	3.79	4.04	4.23	4.39	4.52	4.63	4.73	4.82	4.90	5.11
45	3.43	3.77	4.02	4.21	4.36	4.49	4.61	4.70	4.79	4.87	5.07
50	3.42	3.76	4.00	4.19	4.34	4.47	4.58	4.68	4.77	4.85	5.04
55	3.41	3.75	3.99	4.18	4.33	4.46	4.57	4.66	4.75	4.83	5.02
60	3.40	3.74	3.98	4.16	4.31	4.44	4.55	4.65	4.73	4.81	5.00
65	3.39	3.73	3.97	4.15	4.30	4.43	4.54	4.63	4.72	4.79	4.99
70	3.39	3.72	3.96	4.14	4.29	4.42	4.53	4.62	4.71	4.78	4.97
75	3.38	3.72	3.95	4.14	4.28	4.41	4.52	4.61	4.70	4.77	4.96
80	3.38	3.71	3.95	4.13	4.28	4.40	4.51	4.60	4.69	4.76	4.95
85	3.37	3.71	3.94	4.12	4.27	4.39	4.50	4.60	4.68	4.75	4.94
90	3.37	3.70	3.94	4.12	4.27	4.39	4.50	4.59	4.67	4.75	4.93
95	3.37	3.70	3.93	4.11	4.26	4.38	4.49	4.58	4.66	4.74	4.92
100	3.36	3.70	3.93	4.11	4.26	4.38	4.48	4.58	4.66	4.73	4.92
110	3.36	3.69	3.92	4.10	4.25	4.37	4.48	4.57	4.65	4.72	4.91
120	3.36	3.68	3.92	4.10	4.24	4.36	4.47	4.56	4.64	4.71	4.90
∞	3.31	3.63	3.86	4.03	4.17	4.29	4.39	4.47	4.55	4.62	4.80

TABLE A17.14　The distribution of the studentised range statistic q

b　　Error rate per family $\alpha = .01$, two-tailed tests

df error	Number of means to be contrasted										
	3	4	5	6	7	8	9	10	11	12	15
1	135.06	164.26	185.58	202.21	215.77	227.17	236.97	245.55	253.16	260.00	277.04
2	19.02	22.29	24.72	26.63	28.20	29.53	30.68	31.69	32.59	33.40	35.43
3	10.62	12.17	13.32	14.24	15.00	15.64	16.20	16.69	17.13	17.53	18.52
4	8.12	9.17	9.96	10.58	11.10	11.54	11.93	12.26	12.57	12.84	13.53
5	6.98	7.80	8.42	8.91	9.32	9.67	9.97	10.24	10.48	10.70	11.24
6	6.33	7.03	7.56	7.97	8.32	8.61	8.87	9.10	9.30	9.48	9.95
7	5.92	6.54	7.00	7.37	7.68	7.94	8.17	8.37	8.55	8.71	9.12
8	5.64	6.20	6.62	6.96	7.24	7.47	7.68	7.86	8.03	8.18	8.55
9	5.43	5.96	6.35	6.66	6.91	7.13	7.33	7.49	7.65	7.78	8.13
10	5.27	5.77	6.14	6.43	6.67	6.87	7.05	7.21	7.36	7.49	7.81
11	5.15	5.62	5.97	6.25	6.48	6.67	6.84	6.99	7.13	7.25	7.56
12	5.05	5.50	5.84	6.10	6.32	6.51	6.67	6.81	6.94	7.06	7.36
13	4.96	5.40	5.73	5.98	6.19	6.37	6.53	6.67	6.79	6.90	7.19
14	4.89	5.32	5.63	5.88	6.08	6.26	6.41	6.54	6.66	6.77	7.05
15	4.84	5.25	5.56	5.80	5.99	6.16	6.31	6.44	6.55	6.66	6.93
16	4.79	5.19	5.49	5.72	5.92	6.08	6.22	6.35	6.46	6.56	6.82
17	4.74	5.14	5.43	5.66	5.85	6.01	6.15	6.27	6.38	6.48	6.73
18	4.70	5.09	5.38	5.60	5.79	5.94	6.08	6.20	6.31	6.41	6.65
19	4.67	5.05	5.33	5.55	5.73	5.89	6.02	6.14	6.25	6.34	6.58
20	4.64	5.02	5.29	5.51	5.69	5.84	5.97	6.09	6.19	6.28	6.52
21	4.61	4.99	5.26	5.47	5.65	5.79	5.92	6.04	6.14	6.23	6.47
22	4.59	4.96	5.22	5.43	5.61	5.75	5.88	5.99	6.10	6.19	6.42
23	4.57	4.93	5.20	5.40	5.57	5.72	5.84	5.95	6.05	6.14	6.37
24	4.55	4.91	5.17	5.37	5.54	5.69	5.81	5.92	6.02	6.11	6.33
25	4.53	4.89	5.14	5.35	5.51	5.65	5.78	5.89	5.98	6.07	6.29
26	4.51	4.87	5.12	5.32	5.49	5.63	5.75	5.86	5.95	6.04	6.26
27	4.49	4.85	5.10	5.30	5.46	5.60	5.72	5.83	5.92	6.01	6.22
28	4.48	4.83	5.08	5.28	5.44	5.58	5.70	5.80	5.90	5.98	6.20
29	4.47	4.81	5.06	5.26	5.42	5.56	5.67	5.78	5.87	5.96	6.17
30	4.45	4.80	5.05	5.24	5.40	5.54	5.65	5.76	5.85	5.93	6.14
35	4.40	4.74	4.98	5.17	5.32	5.45	5.57	5.67	5.75	5.84	6.04
40	4.37	4.70	4.93	5.11	5.26	5.39	5.50	5.60	5.69	5.76	5.96
45	4.34	4.66	4.89	5.07	5.22	5.34	5.45	5.55	5.63	5.71	5.90
50	4.32	4.63	4.86	5.04	5.19	5.31	5.41	5.51	5.59	5.67	5.85
55	4.30	4.61	4.84	5.01	5.16	5.28	5.38	5.47	5.56	5.63	5.82
60	4.28	4.59	4.82	4.99	5.13	5.25	5.36	5.45	5.53	5.60	5.78
65	4.27	4.58	4.80	4.97	5.11	5.23	5.33	5.42	5.50	5.58	5.76
70	4.26	4.57	4.79	4.96	5.10	5.21	5.31	5.40	5.48	5.56	5.74
75	4.25	4.56	4.77	4.94	5.08	5.20	5.30	5.39	5.47	5.54	5.72
80	4.24	4.55	4.76	4.93	5.07	5.18	5.28	5.37	5.45	5.52	5.70
85	4.23	4.54	4.75	4.92	5.06	5.17	5.27	5.36	5.44	5.51	5.68
90	4.23	4.53	4.74	4.91	5.05	5.16	5.26	5.35	5.43	5.49	5.67
95	4.22	4.52	4.74	4.90	5.04	5.15	5.25	5.34	5.41	5.48	5.66
100	4.22	4.52	4.73	4.90	5.03	5.14	5.24	5.33	5.40	5.47	5.65
110	4.21	4.51	4.72	4.88	5.02	5.13	5.23	5.31	5.39	5.46	5.63
120	4.20	4.50	4.71	4.87	5.01	5.12	5.21	5.30	5.37	5.44	5.61
∞	4.12	4.4	4.6	4.76	4.88	4.99	5.08	5.16	5.23	5.29	5.45

Table A17.15 The critical values of Tukey's test derived from Bryant and Paulson, $\alpha = .05$

For use with ANCOVA with one covariate.

df error	2	3	4	5	6	7	8	9	10	11	12	15	16	20
2	5.63	7.78	9.19	10.22	11.04	11.71	12.28	12.73	13.19	13.55	13.92	14.74	15.01	15.84
3	3.83	5.08	5.88	6.48	6.96	7.35	7.68	7.95	8.22	8.43	8.64	9.13	9.29	9.78
4	3.19	4.13	4.73	5.18	5.53	5.82	6.07	6.27	6.47	6.63	6.80	7.16	7.28	7.65
5	2.87	3.66	4.16	4.53	4.82	5.06	5.27	5.44	5.61	5.74	5.87	6.18	6.28	6.59
6	2.68	3.38	3.82	4.14	4.41	4.62	4.79	4.94	5.09	5.21	5.32	5.59	5.69	5.96
7	2.56	3.20	3.60	3.90	4.13	4.32	4.48	4.62	4.75	4.86	4.97	5.21	5.30	5.54
8	2.47	3.07	3.44	3.72	3.94	4.12	4.26	4.39	4.52	4.62	4.72	4.94	5.02	5.25
9	2.40	2.97	3.33	3.59	3.80	3.96	4.11	4.22	4.34	4.43	4.53	4.74	4.82	5.03
10	2.35	2.90	3.24	3.49	3.68	3.84	3.98	4.09	4.20	4.29	4.38	4.58	4.65	4.86
11	2.31	2.84	3.17	3.41	3.60	3.75	3.88	3.99	4.10	4.18	4.27	4.46	4.53	4.73
12	2.28	2.79	3.11	3.34	3.52	3.67	3.80	3.90	4.01	4.09	4.17	4.36	4.43	4.62
13	2.25	2.75	3.07	3.29	3.46	3.61	3.73	3.83	3.94	4.02	4.10	4.28	4.34	4.53
14	2.23	2.72	3.03	3.25	3.42	3.56	3.68	3.78	3.87	3.95	4.03	4.21	4.26	4.45
15	2.21	2.69	2.99	3.21	3.37	3.51	3.63	3.73	3.82	3.90	3.97	4.15	4.20	4.38
16	2.19	2.67	2.96	3.17	3.34	3.47	3.59	3.68	3.78	3.85	3.92	4.09	4.15	4.33
17	2.18	2.65	2.94	3.14	3.30	3.44	3.55	3.64	3.73	3.81	3.88	4.05	4.11	4.28
18	2.16	2.63	2.91	3.12	3.27	3.41	3.52	3.61	3.70	3.77	3.85	4.01	4.07	4.23
19	2.15	2.61	2.89	3.10	3.25	3.38	3.49	3.58	3.67	3.74	3.81	3.97	4.03	4.19
20	2.14	2.60	2.88	3.08	3.23	3.36	3.46	3.55	3.64	3.71	3.78	3.94	4.00	4.16
21	2.13	2.58	2.86	3.06	3.21	3.34	3.44	3.53	3.62	3.69	3.76	3.91	3.97	4.13
22	2.12	2.57	2.85	3.04	3.19	3.32	3.42	3.51	3.60	3.66	3.73	3.89	3.94	4.10
23	2.11	2.56	2.83	3.03	3.18	3.30	3.40	3.49	3.58	3.64	3.71	3.87	3.92	4.07
24	2.11	2.55	2.82	3.01	3.16	3.29	3.39	3.47	3.56	3.62	3.69	3.84	3.90	4.05
25	2.10	2.54	2.81	3.00	3.15	3.27	3.37	3.46	3.54	3.61	3.67	3.83	3.88	4.03
26	2.10	2.54	2.80	2.99	3.14	3.26	3.36	3.44	3.52	3.59	3.66	3.81	3.86	4.01
27	2.09	2.53	2.79	2.98	3.13	3.24	3.35	3.43	3.51	3.57	3.64	3.79	3.84	3.99
28	2.09	2.52	2.78	2.97	3.12	3.23	3.34	3.42	3.50	3.56	3.63	3.78	3.83	3.98
29	2.08	2.52	2.77	2.96	3.11	3.22	3.33	3.40	3.48	3.55	3.61	3.76	3.81	3.96
30	2.08	2.51	2.76	2.96	3.10	3.21	3.32	3.39	3.47	3.54	3.60	3.75	3.80	3.95
35	2.06	2.49	2.74	2.92	3.06	3.17	3.27	3.35	3.43	3.49	3.55	3.69	3.74	3.89
40	2.04	2.47	2.72	2.89	3.03	3.15	3.24	3.32	3.39	3.45	3.51	3.65	3.70	3.84
45	2.03	2.45	2.70	2.87	3.01	3.12	3.21	3.29	3.37	3.43	3.49	3.62	3.67	3.81
50	2.03	2.44	2.69	2.86	3.00	3.10	3.20	3.27	3.35	3.41	3.46	3.60	3.64	3.78
55	2.02	2.43	2.67	2.85	2.98	3.09	3.18	3.26	3.33	3.39	3.44	3.58	3.62	3.76
60	2.02	2.43	2.67	2.84	2.97	3.08	3.17	3.24	3.32	3.37	3.43	3.56	3.61	3.74
65	2.01	2.42	2.66	2.83	2.96	3.07	3.16	3.23	3.30	3.36	3.42	3.55	3.59	3.73
70	2.01	2.41	2.65	2.82	2.95	3.06	3.15	3.22	3.29	3.35	3.41	3.54	3.58	3.71
75	2.00	2.41	2.65	2.81	2.94	3.05	3.14	3.21	3.29	3.34	3.40	3.53	3.57	3.70
80	2.00	2.40	2.64	2.81	2.94	3.04	3.13	3.20	3.28	3.33	3.39	3.52	3.56	3.69
85	2.00	2.40	2.64	2.80	2.93	3.04	3.13	3.20	3.27	3.33	3.38	3.51	3.55	3.68
90	2.00	2.40	2.63	2.80	2.93	3.03	3.12	3.19	3.26	3.32	3.37	3.50	3.54	3.67
95	1.99	2.39	2.63	2.79	2.92	3.03	3.12	3.19	3.26	3.31	3.37	3.50	3.54	3.67
100	1.99	2.39	2.63	2.79	2.92	3.03	3.11	3.18	3.25	3.31	3.36	3.49	3.53	3.66
110	1.99	2.39	2.62	2.78	2.91	3.02	3.10	3.17	3.25	3.30	3.35	3.48	3.52	3.65
120	1.99	2.38	2.62	2.78	2.91	3.01	3.10	3.17	3.24	3.29	3.34	3.47	3.51	3.64
∞	1.96	2.34	2.57	2.73	2.85	2.95	3.03	3.10	3.16	3.22	3.27	3.39	3.43	3.54

Table A17.16 The Bryant–Paulson variant Q_p of the studentised range statistic $\alpha = .05$

For use with ANCOVA with one covariate.

df error						Number of means to be contrasted								
	2	3	4	5	6	7	8	9	10	11	12	15	16	20
2	7.96	11.00	12.99	14.46	15.61	16.56	17.36	18.01	18.65	19.17	19.68	20.84	21.23	22.40
3	5.42	7.18	8.32	9.17	9.84	10.39	10.86	11.24	11.62	11.92	12.22	12.91	13.14	13.83
4	4.51	5.84	6.69	7.32	7.82	8.23	8.58	8.87	9.15	9.38	9.61	10.13	10.30	10.82
5	4.06	5.17	5.88	6.40	6.82	7.16	7.45	7.69	7.93	8.12	8.30	8.74	8.88	9.32
6	3.79	4.78	5.40	5.86	6.23	6.53	6.78	6.99	7.20	7.37	7.53	7.91	8.04	8.43
7	3.62	4.52	5.09	5.51	5.84	6.11	6.34	6.53	6.72	6.88	7.03	7.38	7.49	7.84
8	3.49	4.34	4.87	5.26	5.57	5.82	6.03	6.21	6.39	6.53	6.67	6.99	7.10	7.43
9	3.40	4.21	4.71	5.08	5.37	5.60	5.81	5.97	6.14	6.27	6.40	6.71	6.81	7.12
10	3.32	4.10	4.58	4.93	5.21	5.43	5.63	5.79	5.94	6.07	6.19	6.48	6.58	6.87
11	3.27	4.02	4.48	4.82	5.08	5.30	5.49	5.64	5.79	5.91	6.03	6.31	6.41	6.68
12	3.22	3.95	4.40	4.73	4.98	5.19	5.37	5.52	5.67	5.79	5.90	6.17	6.26	6.53
13	3.18	3.90	4.34	4.65	4.90	5.10	5.28	5.42	5.57	5.68	5.79	6.05	6.14	6.40
14	3.15	3.85	4.28	4.59	4.83	5.03	5.20	5.34	5.48	5.59	5.70	5.95	6.03	6.29
15	3.12	3.81	4.23	4.54	4.77	4.97	5.13	5.27	5.41	5.51	5.62	5.86	5.94	6.20
16	3.10	3.77	4.19	4.49	4.72	4.91	5.07	5.21	5.34	5.45	5.55	5.79	5.87	6.12
17	3.08	3.74	4.15	4.45	4.67	4.86	5.02	5.15	5.28	5.39	5.49	5.73	5.81	6.05
18	3.06	3.72	4.12	4.41	4.63	4.82	4.98	5.11	5.23	5.34	5.44	5.67	5.75	5.98
19	3.04	3.69	4.09	4.38	4.60	4.78	4.94	5.06	5.19	5.29	5.39	5.62	5.70	5.93
20	3.03	3.67	4.07	4.35	4.57	4.75	4.90	5.03	5.15	5.25	5.35	5.58	5.65	5.88
21	3.02	3.65	4.05	4.32	4.54	4.72	4.87	4.99	5.12	5.21	5.31	5.54	5.61	5.84
22	3.00	3.64	4.03	4.30	4.52	4.70	4.84	4.96	5.08	5.18	5.28	5.50	5.57	5.80
23	2.99	3.62	4.01	4.28	4.49	4.67	4.81	4.94	5.06	5.15	5.25	5.47	5.54	5.76
24	2.98	3.61	3.99	4.26	4.47	4.65	4.79	4.91	5.03	5.13	5.22	5.44	5.51	5.73
25	2.97	3.60	3.97	4.24	4.45	4.63	4.77	4.89	5.01	5.10	5.19	5.41	5.48	5.70
26	2.96	3.59	3.96	4.23	4.44	4.61	4.75	4.87	4.98	5.08	5.17	5.38	5.46	5.67
27	2.96	3.58	3.95	4.22	4.42	4.59	4.73	4.85	4.96	5.06	5.15	5.36	5.43	5.65
28	2.95	3.57	3.93	4.20	4.41	4.57	4.72	4.83	4.94	5.04	5.13	5.34	5.41	5.62
29	2.95	3.56	3.92	4.19	4.39	4.56	4.70	4.82	4.93	5.02	5.11	5.32	5.39	5.60
30	2.94	3.55	3.91	4.18	4.38	4.54	4.69	4.80	4.91	5.00	5.09	5.30	5.37	5.58
35	2.91	3.52	3.87	4.13	4.33	4.49	4.63	4.74	4.85	4.93	5.02	5.22	5.29	5.49
40	2.89	3.49	3.84	4.09	4.29	4.45	4.58	4.69	4.80	4.89	4.97	5.17	5.23	5.43
45	2.88	3.47	3.82	4.06	4.26	4.42	4.55	4.66	4.76	4.85	4.93	5.12	5.19	5.38
50	2.87	3.45	3.80	4.04	4.24	4.39	4.52	4.63	4.73	4.82	4.90	5.09	5.15	5.35
55	2.86	3.44	3.78	4.02	4.22	4.37	4.50	4.60	4.71	4.79	4.87	5.06	5.12	5.32
60	2.85	3.43	3.77	4.01	4.20	4.35	4.48	4.59	4.69	4.77	4.85	5.04	5.10	5.29
65	2.84	3.42	3.76	4.00	4.19	4.34	4.46	4.57	4.67	4.75	4.83	5.02	5.08	5.27
70	2.84	3.41	3.75	3.99	4.17	4.32	4.45	4.56	4.66	4.74	4.82	5.00	5.06	5.25
75	2.83	3.41	3.74	3.98	4.16	4.31	4.44	4.54	4.65	4.72	4.80	4.99	5.05	5.23
80	2.83	3.40	3.74	3.97	4.16	4.31	4.43	4.53	4.64	4.71	4.79	4.97	5.04	5.22
85	2.83	3.39	3.73	3.96	4.15	4.30	4.42	4.52	4.63	4.70	4.78	4.96	5.02	5.21
90	2.82	3.39	3.72	3.96	4.14	4.29	4.41	4.52	4.62	4.69	4.77	4.95	5.01	5.20
95	2.82	3.39	3.72	3.95	4.13	4.28	4.41	4.51	4.61	4.69	4.76	4.94	5.00	5.19
100	2.82	3.38	3.71	3.95	4.13	4.28	4.40	4.50	4.60	4.68	4.75	4.94	5.00	5.18
110	2.81	3.38	3.71	3.94	4.12	4.27	4.39	4.49	4.59	4.67	4.74	4.92	4.98	5.16
120	2.81	3.37	3.70	3.93	4.11	4.26	4.38	4.48	4.58	4.66	4.73	4.91	4.97	5.15
∞	2.77	3.31	3.63	3.86	4.03	4.17	4.29	4.39	4.47	4.55	4.62	4.80	4.85	5.01

(Adapted from Table 1(a) of Bryant, J. L. and Paulson, A. S. (1976). An extension of Tukey's method of multiple comparisons to experimental designs with random concomitant variables. *Biometrika, 63*, 631–638.)

Table A17.17 The probabilities of the distribution of r (Pearson's product moment correlation coefficient)

The probability of an r-value can also be found by converting r to a t-value and using the t-tables (Table A17.2).

To convert r to t use:

$$t = \frac{r \times \sqrt{n-2}}{1-r^2}$$

where n is the number of pairs of scores in the correlation.

TABLE A17.17 The probabilities of the distribution of r (Pearson's product moment correlation coefficient)

a   df = 1 to 20

					One-tailed probabilities						
	0.4	0.3	0.2	0.1	0.05	0.025	0.01	0.005	0.001	0.0005
					Two-tailed probabilities						
df = n-2	0.8	0.6	0.4	0.2	0.1	0.05	0.02	0.01	0.002	0.001
1	0.3090	0.5878	0.8090	0.9511	0.9877	0.9969	0.9995	0.9999	1.0000	1.0000
2	0.2000	0.4000	0.6000	0.8000	0.9000	0.9500	0.9800	0.9900	0.9980	0.9990
3	0.1577	0.3197	0.4919	0.6870	0.8054	0.8783	0.9343	0.9587	0.9859	0.9911
4	0.1341	0.2735	0.4257	0.6084	0.7293	0.8114	0.8822	0.9172	0.9633	0.9741
5	0.1186	0.2427	0.3803	0.5509	0.6694	0.7545	0.8329	0.8745	0.9350	0.9509
6	0.1075	0.2204	0.3468	0.5067	0.6215	0.7067	0.7887	0.8343	0.9049	0.9249
7	0.0990	0.2032	0.3208	0.4716	0.5822	0.6664	0.7498	0.7977	0.8751	0.8983
8	0.0922	0.1895	0.2998	0.4428	0.5494	0.6319	0.7155	0.7646	0.8467	0.8721
9	0.0867	0.1783	0.2825	0.4187	0.5214	0.6021	0.6851	0.7348	0.8199	0.8470
10	0.0820	0.1688	0.2678	0.3981	0.4973	0.5760	0.6581	0.7079	0.7950	0.8233
11	0.0780	0.1607	0.2552	0.3802	0.4762	0.5529	0.6339	0.6835	0.7717	0.8010
12	0.0746	0.1536	0.2443	0.3646	0.4575	0.5324	0.6120	0.6614	0.7501	0.7800
13	0.0715	0.1474	0.2346	0.3507	0.4409	0.5140	0.5923	0.6411	0.7301	0.7604
14	0.0688	0.1419	0.2260	0.3383	0.4259	0.4973	0.5742	0.6226	0.7114	0.7419
15	0.0664	0.1370	0.2183	0.3271	0.4124	0.4821	0.5577	0.6055	0.6940	0.7247
16	0.0643	0.1326	0.2113	0.3170	0.4000	0.4683	0.5425	0.5897	0.6777	0.7084
17	0.0623	0.1285	0.2049	0.3077	0.3887	0.4555	0.5285	0.5751	0.6624	0.6932
18	0.0605	0.1248	0.1991	0.2992	0.3783	0.4438	0.5155	0.5614	0.6481	0.6788
19	0.0588	0.1214	0.1938	0.2914	0.3687	0.4329	0.5034	0.5487	0.6346	0.6652
20	0.0573	0.1183	0.1888	0.2841	0.3598	0.4227	0.4921	0.5368	0.6219	0.6524

TABLE A17.17   The probabilities of the distribution of r (Pearson's product moment correlation coefficient)

b   df = 21 to 120

df = n-2	\multicolumn{10}{c}{One-tailed probabilities}
	0.4	0.3	0.2	0.1	0.05	0.025	0.01	0.005	0.001	0.0005
	\multicolumn{10}{c}{Two-tailed probabilities}
	0.8	0.6	0.4	0.2	0.1	0.05	0.02	0.01	0.002	0.001
21	0.0559	0.1154	0.1843	0.2774	0.3515	0.4132	0.4815	0.5256	0.6099	0.6402
22	0.0546	0.1127	0.1800	0.2711	0.3438	0.4044	0.4716	0.5151	0.5986	0.6287
23	0.0534	0.1102	0.1760	0.2653	0.3365	0.3961	0.4622	0.5052	0.5879	0.6178
24	0.0522	0.1078	0.1723	0.2598	0.3297	0.3882	0.4534	0.4958	0.5776	0.6074
25	0.0511	0.1056	0.1688	0.2546	0.3233	0.3809	0.4451	0.4869	0.5679	0.5974
26	0.0501	0.1036	0.1655	0.2497	0.3172	0.3739	0.4372	0.4785	0.5587	0.5880
27	0.0492	0.1016	0.1624	0.2451	0.3115	0.3673	0.4297	0.4705	0.5499	0.5789
28	0.0483	0.0997	0.1594	0.2407	0.3061	0.3610	0.4226	0.4629	0.5415	0.5703
29	0.0474	0.0980	0.1567	0.2366	0.3009	0.3550	0.4158	0.4556	0.5334	0.5621
30	0.0466	0.0963	0.1540	0.2327	0.2960	0.3494	0.4093	0.4487	0.5257	0.5541
31	0.0458	0.0947	0.1515	0.2289	0.2913	0.3440	0.4032	0.4421	0.5184	0.5465
32	0.0451	0.0932	0.1491	0.2254	0.2869	0.3388	0.3972	0.4357	0.5113	0.5392
33	0.0444	0.0918	0.1468	0.2220	0.2826	0.3338	0.3916	0.4296	0.5045	0.5322
34	0.0437	0.0904	0.1446	0.2187	0.2785	0.3291	0.3862	0.4238	0.4979	0.5254
35	0.0431	0.0891	0.1425	0.2156	0.2746	0.3246	0.3810	0.4182	0.4916	0.5189
36	0.0425	0.0878	0.1405	0.2126	0.2709	0.3202	0.3760	0.4128	0.4856	0.5126
37	0.0419	0.0866	0.1386	0.2097	0.2673	0.3160	0.3712	0.4076	0.4797	0.5066
38	0.0414	0.0855	0.1368	0.2070	0.2638	0.3120	0.3665	0.4026	0.4741	0.5007
39	0.0408	0.0844	0.1350	0.2043	0.2605	0.3081	0.3621	0.3978	0.4686	0.4950
40	0.0403	0.0833	0.1333	0.2018	0.2573	0.3044	0.3578	0.3932	0.4634	0.4896
50	0.0360	0.0744	0.1192	0.1806	0.2306	0.2732	0.3218	0.3542	0.4188	0.4432
60	0.0328	0.0679	0.1088	0.1650	0.2108	0.2500	0.2948	0.3248	0.3850	0.4079
70	0.0304	0.0628	0.1007	0.1528	0.1954	0.2319	0.2737	0.3017	0.3583	0.3798
80	0.0284	0.0588	0.0942	0.1430	0.1829	0.2172	0.2565	0.2830	0.3364	0.3568
90	0.0268	0.0554	0.0888	0.1348	0.1726	0.2050	0.2422	0.2673	0.3181	0.3375
100	0.0254	0.0525	0.0842	0.1279	0.1638	0.1946	0.2301	0.2540	0.3025	0.3211
110	0.0242	0.0501	0.0803	0.1220	0.1562	0.1857	0.2196	0.2425	0.2890	0.3068
120	0.0232	0.0479	0.0769	0.1168	0.1496	0.1779	0.2104	0.2324	0.2771	0.2943

Table A17.18 The critical values of Spearman's rho

When the sample size is greater than 100 use either the t-approximation (equation A10.1) or the z-approximation (equation A10.2) in Appendix X.

TABLE A17.18   The critical values of Spearman's rho

a $n = 4$ to 40

					one-tailed probabilities					
	0.25	0.10	0.05	0.025	0.01	0.005	0.0025	0.001	0.0005	
					two-tailed probabilities					
n	0.50	0.20	0.10	0.05	0.02	0.01	0.005	0.002	0.001
4	0.600	1.000	1.000						
5	0.500	0.800	0.900	1.000	1.000				
6	0.371	0.657	0.829	0.886	0.943	1.000	1.000		
7	0.321	0.571	0.714	0.786	0.893	0.929	0.964	1.000	1.000
8	0.310	0.524	0.643	0.738	0.833	0.881	0.905	0.952	0.976
9	0.267	0.483	0.600	0.700	0.783	0.833	0.867	0.917	0.933
10	0.248	0.455	0.564	0.648	0.745	0.794	0.830	0.879	0.903
11	0.236	0.427	0.536	0.618	0.709	0.755	0.800	0.845	0.873
12	0.224	0.406	0.503	0.587	0.671	0.727	0.776	0.825	0.860
13	0.209	0.385	0.484	0.560	0.648	0.703	0.747	0.802	0.835
14	0.200	0.367	0.464	0.538	0.622	0.675	0.723	0.776	0.811
15	0.189	0.354	0.443	0.521	0.604	0.654	0.700	0.754	0.786
16	0.182	0.341	0.429	0.503	0.582	0.635	0.679	0.732	0.765
17	0.176	0.328	0.414	0.485	0.566	0.615	0.662	0.713	0.748
18	0.170	0.317	0.401	0.472	0.550	0.600	0.643	0.695	0.728
19	0.165	0.309	0.391	0.460	0.535	0.584	0.628	0.677	0.712
20	0.161	0.299	0.380	0.447	0.520	0.570	0.612	0.662	0.696
21	0.156	0.292	0.370	0.435	0.508	0.556	0.599	0.648	0.681
22	0.152	0.284	0.361	0.425	0.496	0.544	0.586	0.634	0.667
23	0.148	0.278	0.353	0.415	0.486	0.532	0.573	0.622	0.654
24	0.144	0.271	0.344	0.406	0.476	0.521	0.562	0.610	0.642
25	0.142	0.265	0.337	0.398	0.466	0.511	0.551	0.598	0.630
26	0.138	0.259	0.331	0.390	0.457	0.501	0.541	0.587	0.619
27	0.136	0.255	0.324	0.382	0.448	0.491	0.531	0.577	0.608
28	0.133	0.250	0.317	0.375	0.440	0.483	0.522	0.567	0.598
29	0.130	0.245	0.312	0.368	0.433	0.475	0.513	0.558	0.589
30	0.128	0.240	0.306	0.362	0.425	0.467	0.504	0.549	0.580
31	0.126	0.236	0.301	0.356	0.418	0.459	0.496	0.541	0.571
32	0.124	0.232	0.296	0.350	0.412	0.452	0.489	0.533	0.563
33	0.121	0.229	0.291	0.345	0.405	0.446	0.482	0.525	0.554
34	0.120	0.225	0.287	0.340	0.399	0.439	0.475	0.517	0.547
35	0.118	0.222	0.283	0.335	0.394	0.433	0.468	0.510	0.539
36	0.116	0.219	0.279	0.330	0.388	0.427	0.462	0.504	0.533
37	0.114	0.216	0.275	0.325	0.383	0.421	0.456	0.497	0.526
38	0.113	0.212	0.271	0.321	0.378	0.415	0.450	0.491	0.519
39	0.111	0.210	0.267	0.317	0.373	0.410	0.444	0.485	0.513
40	0.110	0.207	0.264	0.313	0.368	0.405	0.439	0.479	0.507

(Adapted from Table I of Zar, J. H. (11972). Significance testing of the Spearman rank correlation coefficient. *Journal of the American Statistical Association*, 76, 578–580.)

TABLE A17.18   The critical values of Spearman's rho

b $n = 41$ to 100

	one-tailed probabilities								
	0.25	0.10	0.05	0.025	0.01	0.005	0.0025	0.001	0.0005
	two-tailed probabilities								
n	0.50	0.20	0.10	0.05	0.02	0.01	0.005	0.002	0.001
41	0.108	0.204	0.261	0.309	0.364	0.400	0.433	0.473	0.501
42	0.107	0.202	0.257	0.305	0.359	0.395	0.428	0.468	0.495
43	0.105	0.199	0.254	0.301	0.355	0.391	0.423	0.463	0.490
44	0.104	0.197	0.251	0.298	0.351	0.386	0.419	0.458	0.484
45	0.103	0.194	0.248	0.294	0.347	0.382	0.414	0.453	0.479
46	0.102	0.192	0.246	0.291	0.343	0.378	0.410	0.448	0.474
47	0.101	0.190	0.243	0.288	0.340	0.374	0.405	0.443	0.469
48	0.100	0.188	0.240	0.285	0.336	0.370	0.401	0.439	0.465
49	0.098	0.186	0.238	0.282	0.333	0.366	0.397	0.434	0.460
50	0.097	0.184	0.235	0.279	0.329	0.363	0.393	0.430	0.456
52	0.095	0.180	0.231	0.274	0.323	0.356	0.386	0.422	0.447
54	0.094	0.177	0.226	0.268	0.317	0.349	0.379	0.414	0.439
56	0.092	0.174	0.222	0.264	0.311	0.343	0.372	0.407	0.432
58	0.090	0.171	0.218	0.259	0.306	0.337	0.366	0.400	0.424
60	0.089	0.168	0.214	0.255	0.300	0.331	0.360	0.394	0.418
62	0.087	0.165	0.211	0.250	0.296	0.326	0.354	0.388	0.411
64	0.086	0.162	0.207	0.246	0.291	0.321	0.348	0.382	0.405
66	0.084	0.160	0.204	0.243	0.287	0.316	0.343	0.376	0.399
68	0.083	0.157	0.201	0.239	0.282	0.311	0.338	0.370	0.393
70	0.082	0.155	0.198	0.235	0.278	0.307	0.333	0.365	0.388
72	0.081	0.153	0.195	0.232	0.274	0.303	0.329	0.360	0.382
74	0.080	0.151	0.193	0.229	0.271	0.299	0.324	0.355	0.377
76	0.078	0.149	0.190	0.226	0.267	0.295	0.320	0.351	0.372
78	0.077	0.147	0.188	0.223	0.264	0.291	0.316	0.346	0.368
80	0.076	0.145	0.185	0.220	0.260	0.287	0.312	0.342	0.363
82	0.075	0.143	0.183	0.217	0.257	0.284	0.308	0.338	0.359
84	0.074	0.141	0.181	0.215	0.254	0.280	0.305	0.334	0.355
86	0.074	0.139	0.179	0.212	0.251	0.277	0.301	0.330	0.351
88	0.073	0.138	0.176	0.210	0.248	0.274	0.298	0.327	0.347
90	0.072	0.136	0.174	0.207	0.245	0.271	0.294	0.323	0.343
92	0.071	0.135	0.173	0.205	0.243	0.268	0.291	0.319	0.339
94	0.070	0.133	0.171	0.203	0.240	0.265	0.288	0.316	0.336
96	0.070	0.132	0.169	0.201	0.238	0.262	0.285	0.313	0.332
98	0.069	0.130	0.167	0.199	0.235	0.260	0.282	0.310	0.329
100	0.068	0.129	0.165	0.197	0.233	0.257	0.279	0.307	0.326

(Adapted from Table I of Zar, J. H. (11972). Significance testing of the Spearman rank correlation coefficient. *Journal of the American Statistical Association, 76*, 578–580.)

Table A17.19 The critical values of Kendall's tau

If the sample is greater than 10 use the z-approximation (equation A10.3) in Appendix X.

Critical values of α: one-tailed probabilities

n	0.1	0.05	0.025	0.01	0.005	0.001
4	1.0000	1.0000				
5	0.8000	0.8000	1.0000	1.0000		
6	0.6000	0.7333	0.8667	0.8667	1.0000	
7	0.5238	0.6190	0.7143	0.8095	0.9048	1.0000
8	0.4286	0.5714	0.6429	0.7143	0.7857	0.8571
9	0.3889	0.5000	0.5556	0.6667	0.7222	0.8333
10	0.3778	0.4667	0.5111	0.6000	0.6444	0.7778

Critical values of α: two-tailed probabilities

n	0.1	0.05	0.025	0.01	0.005	0.001
4	1.0000					
5	0.8000	1.0000	1.0000			
6	0.7333	0.8667	0.8667	1.0000	1.0000	
7	0.6190	0.7143	0.8095	0.9048	0.9048	1.0000
8	0.5714	0.6429	0.7143	0.7857	0.8571	0.9286
9	0.5000	0.5556	0.6111	0.7222	0.7778	0.8333
10	0.4667	0.5111	0.6000	0.6444	0.6889	0.7778

(Adapted from Kendall, M. G. (1970). *Rank Correlation Methods* (4th Edn.). London: Charles Griffin & Co. Ltd.)

Table A17.20 The probabilities of Kendall's tau as a partial correlation $\tau_{xy \cdot z}$.

The table shows the probabilities of tau for sample sizes up to 50. Maghsoodloo and Pallos (1981) note that beyond this sample size there is a normal approximation which can be used to find out the probability of Kendall's partial correlation coefficient:

$$z = \frac{\tau_{xy \cdot z}}{\sqrt{\left(-0.0008855 + \dfrac{0.5179}{n} + \dfrac{10.344}{n^3}\right)}}$$

where n is the sample size.

	0.2	0.1	two-tailed test 0.05	0.02	0.01	0.002
n	0.1	0.05	one-tailed test 0.025	0.01	0.005	0.001
4	0.707	0.707	1.000			
5	0.535	0.667	0.802	0.817	1.000	
6	0.473	0.600	0.667	0.764	0.866	1.000
7	0.421	0.527	0.617	0.712	0.761	0.901
8	0.382	0.484	0.565	0.648	0.713	0.807
9	0.347	0.443	0.515	0.602	0.660	0.757
10	0.325	0.413	0.480	0.562	0.614	0.718
11	0.305	0.387	0.453	0.530	0.581	0.677
12	0.288	0.465	0.430	0.505	0.548	0.643
13	0.273	0.347	0.410	0.481	0.527	0.616
14	0.260	0.331	0.391	0.458	0.503	0.590
15	0.251	0.319	0.377	0.442	0.485	0.570
16	0.240	0.305	0.361	0.423	0.466	0.549
17	0.231	0.294	0.348	0.410	0.450	0.532
18	0.222	0.284	0.336	0.395	0.434	0.514
19	0.215	0.275	0.326	0.382	0.421	0.498
20	0.210	0.268	0.318	0.374	0.412	0.488
25	0.185	0.236	0.279	0.329	0.363	0.430
30	0.167	0.213	0.253	0.298	0.329	0.390
35	0.153	0.196	0.232	0.274	0.303	0.361
40	0.142	0.182	0.216	0.255	0.282	0.335
45	0.133	0.171	0.203	0.240	0.265	0.316
50	0.126	0.161	0.192	0.225	0.250	0.298

(Adapted from Tables II and V of Maghsoodloo, S. (1975). Estimates of the quantiles of Kendall's partial rank correlation coefficient. *Journal of Statistical Computing and Simulation, 4*, 155–164, and Tables I and II of Maghsoodloo, S. and Pallos, L. L. (1981). Asymptotic behaviour of Kendall's partial rank correlation coefficient and additional quantile estimates. *Journal of Statistical Computing and Simulation, 13*, 41–48.)

Table A17.21 Kendall's coefficient of concordance (*W*)

k (number of items to be ranked) = 3 to 7, *n* (number of judges) = 3 to 20.

When *k* is more than 7 find the probability from the chi-squared distribution for:

$$\chi^2_{(k-1)} = n \times (k-1) \times W$$

	k = 3 probability	
n	0.05	0.01
8	0.3758	0.5219
9	0.3333	0.4685
10	0.3000	0.4255
12	0.2497	0.3594
14	0.2138	0.3110
15	0.1996	0.2911
16	0.1871	0.2738
18	0.1662	0.2448
20	0.1496	0.2213

	k = 4 probability		k = 5 probability		k = 6 probability		k = 7 probability	
n	0.05	0.01	0.05	0.01	0.05	0.01	0.05	0.01
3	-	-	0.7156	0.8400	0.6597	0.7797	0.6242	0.7365
4	0.6188	0.7675	0.5525	0.6831	0.5118	0.6293	0.4844	0.5915
5	0.5008	0.6440	0.4492	0.5712	0.4169	0.5243	0.3946	0.4911
6	0.4206	0.5528	0.3781	0.4892	0.3514	0.4483	0.3325	0.4192
8	0.3178	0.4294	0.2870	0.3792	0.2670	0.3467	0.2528	0.3236
10	0.2556	0.3506	0.2312	0.3091	0.2153	0.2823	0.2039	0.2632
15	0.1715	0.2398	0.1555	0.2112	0.1449	0.1926	0.1373	0.1793
20	0.1290	0.1821	0.1171	0.1603	0.1092	0.1460	0.1035	0.1359

(Adapted from Kendall, M. G. (1970). *Rank Correlation Methods* (4th Edn.). London: Charles Griffin & Co. Ltd.)

Table A17.22 The critical values of the Kolmogorov–Smirnov statistic (D_n)

To be statistically significant, D_n has to be as large as or larger than the critical value shown in the table. For example, with a sample size of 20, to be significant at $\alpha = .05$, D_n has to be at least 0.294.

n	0.20	0.15	0.10	0.05
1	0.900	0.925	0.950	0.975
2	0.684	0.726	0.776	0.842
3	0.565	0.597	0.642	0.708
4	0.494	0.525	0.564	0.624
5	0.446	0.474	0.510	0.565
6	0.410	0.436	0.470	0.521
7	0.381	0.405	0.438	0.486
8	0.358	0.381	0.411	0.457
9	0.339	0.360	0.388	0.432
10	0.322	0.342	0.368	0.410
11	0.307	0.326	0.352	0.391
12	0.295	0.313	0.338	0.375
13	0.284	0.302	0.325	0.361
14	0.274	0.292	0.314	0.349
15	0.266	0.283	0.304	0.338
16	0.258	0.274	0.295	0.328
17	0.250	0.266	0.286	0.318
18	0.244	0.259	0.278	0.309
19	0.237	0.252	0.272	0.301
20	0.231	0.246	0.264	0.294
25	0.210	0.220	0.240	0.270
30	0.190	0.200	0.220	0.240
35	0.180	0.190	0.210	0.230
over 35	$\dfrac{1.07}{\sqrt{n}}$	$\dfrac{1.14}{\sqrt{n}}$	$\dfrac{1.22}{\sqrt{n}}$	$\dfrac{1.36}{\sqrt{n}}$

(Adapted from Table I of Massey, F. J. (1951). The Kolmogorov–Smirnov test for goodness of fit. *Journal of the American Statistical Association, 46*, 68–78.)

Introduction

I have attempted to simplify the process of calculating power, while at the same time not overbalancing the book with power tables. This has involved a number of compromises. Firstly, I have only given tables for $\alpha = .05$. Secondly, for tests such as χ^2, ANOVA and linear regression I have given tables for a restricted set of degrees of freedom. Thirdly, in the case of ANOVA I have used η^2 as the measure of effect size. Fourthly, I have restricted the range of sample sizes for logistic regression as there are so many elements in the calculation of each table that I needed to put more than one table on a page so as not to have too many pages devoted to these. In addition to these points, some explanation is necessary for how to use the tables for within-subjects designs, for between-subjects designs with unequal sample sizes, for between-subjects ANOVA with more than one IV, for mixed designs, and for working out power for sample sizes and df which are not in the tables. Throughout the tables, an asterisk (*) denotes that the power of the test is over .995.

Adjusted sample size for power tables when using unequal samples

Between-subjects *t*-tests

When unequal sized samples are used in a between-subjects *t*-test, power is reduced relative to what it would be for a design with equal-sized samples. To read the standard power tables it is necessary to calculate an adjusted sample size n_h, which is the *harmonic mean* of the two samples sizes.

$$n_h = \frac{2 \times n_1 \times n_2}{n_1 \times n_2}$$

where n_1 is the size of one sample and n_2 is the size of the other sample.
    Thus, if $n_1 = 10$ and $n_2 = 30$:

$$n_h = \frac{2 \times 10 \times 30}{10 + 30}$$
$$= 15$$

In this case, the power of the test will be the same as that for a design with 15 people in each group, despite having 40 participants altogether.

Differences between two sample proportions

As with the between-subjects *t*-test, use the harmonic mean (n_h) to calculate the sample size which can be used to read the power tables.

Between-subjects ANOVA

In this case, use the arithmetic mean. Thus if there were three groups with 15, 20 and 30 in each, then the sample size per group should be treated as:

$$n = \frac{15 + 20 + 30}{3} = 21.67 \text{ or } 21 \text{ to the next lowest person}$$

Differences between two sample correlations

In this case use the following equation from Cohen (1988):

$$n = \frac{2 \times (n_1 - 3) \times (n_2 - 3)}{n_1 + n_2 - 6} + 3$$

where n_1 and n_2 are the sample sizes in the two groups. Therefore if one group had 18 participants and the other 70, then

$$n = \frac{2 \times (70 - 3) \times (18 - 3)}{70 + 18 - 6} + 3 = 27.51$$

Therefore, although the mean sample size is 44, the test would have less power than if the samples had been equal and each sample had had 28 participants.

Interpolation

Using the technique of linear interpolation, described in Appendix XVII for probability tables, approximate power values and sample sizes can be found where these are not contained in the tables given in the present appendix. Cohen (1988) gives a much wider range of tabled values.

Finding power for an intermediate sample size

Use the following equation:

$$\text{power} = \text{lower power} + (\text{upper power} - \text{lower power}) \times \left(\frac{\text{actual } n - \text{lower } n}{\text{upper } n - \text{lower } n} \right)$$

where upper and lower powers and sample sizes are those shown in the tables.

Imagine that we were conducting a one-tailed, between-subjects t-test with $\alpha = .05$, we had a sample of 22 people in each group and we found an effect size (d) of 0.5.

$$\text{power} = .46 + (.54 - .46) \times \left(\frac{22 - 20}{25 - 20} \right)$$

$$= .492$$

Finding power for an intermediate effect size (ES)

Use the following equation:

$$\text{power} = \text{lower power} + (\text{upper power} - \text{lower power})$$

$$\times \left(\frac{\text{actual ES} - \text{lower ES}}{\text{upper ES} - \text{lower ES}} \right)$$

If we conducted a one-tailed, between-subjects t-test on data which we had found had an effect size of 0.56, with a sample of 20 participants in each group, using $\alpha = .05$, then:

$$\text{power} = .46 + (.58 - .46) \times \left(\frac{0.56 - 0.5}{0.6 - 0.5} \right)$$

$$= .532$$

Finding a sample size for an intermediate level of power

Use the following equation:

$$n = \text{lower } n + (\text{upper } n - \text{lower } n) \times \left(\frac{\text{actual power} - \text{lower power}}{\text{upper power} - \text{lower power}} \right)$$

If we wished to have power of .8 for a one-tailed, between-subjects t-test with an effect size of 0.4, then the number of people we would need in each group would be:

$$n = 70 + (80 - 70) \times \left(\frac{.80 - .76}{.81 - .76} \right)$$

$$= 78$$

If this had not been a whole number, then I would have rounded up to the next whole number.

The effect size of a within-subjects t-test

In Chapter 15 it was pointed out that the effect size for comparing means in a within-subjects design with two levels of the IV can be calculated in two ways: one way produces d and allows comparison with between-subjects designs while the other way produces d' and allows calculation of statistical power. The example given showed $d = 0.07$ and $d' = 0.456$. The reason for the discrepancy is that d' is affected by the degree to which the participants' scores on the two levels of the IV are correlated. In the example given, the correlation was very high at $r = .9883$. The following equation can be used to convert d to d':

$$d' = \frac{d}{\sqrt{2 \times (1-r)}}$$

Thus,

$$d' = \frac{0.07}{\sqrt{2 \times (1-.9883)}}$$

$$= 0.458 \text{ (which, to two decimal places, agrees with the figure given above.)}$$

Explanation of the tables for ANOVA and linear regression

I have based the power tables for ANOVA on η^2 as the effect size, and for linear regression I have used R^2. In both cases this means that the tables are different from those provided by Cohen (1988). Nonetheless, I have provided tabled values for what he considers constitute small, medium and large effect sizes.

Effect size	η^2	R^2
Small	.01	.0196
Medium	.059	.13
Large	.138	.26

Logistic regression

I have based the tables on Hsieh (1989) equation (4). However, I have adjusted the equation to give power for a two-tailed test as tests such as the Wald test are the equivalent of two-tailed tests. The effect sizes (odds ratios) that I have used in each table have been chosen for a reason, even if it isn't obvious. As an odds ratio and its inverse will have the same power I have provided two rows of odds ratios with the second row being the inverse of the first row (and vice versa). Together the two rows provide odds ratios ranging from 0.33 to 3.00, with an attempt to produce roughly equal spaces between them. The sample sizes I have shown give power of 0.8 for each effect size (odds ratio), apart for odds of 1.1 (0.91) and 1.11 (.90). With these odds ratios the tabled power levels indicate just how low power will be with even large sample sizes. The equation isn't perfect and it produces some anomalies when the odds ratio is 3.00 and the proportion of the target event in the population is large. The tables are for simple logistic regression, that is for when there is only one predictor variable.

In Chapter 21 I gave the example of trying to predict which drivers will have had car accidents by looking at the number of driving violations they committed, the number of driving mistakes they made, their age and sex. I was treating violations as the predictor I was particularly interested in. I needed to know what proportion of the sample had had an accident (0.353) and what the odds ratio was for violations (1.548). I calculated, using the equation I had used to create the power tables, that the sample required for a simple regression with accidents as the outcome and violations as the sole predictor would be 216; the required sample could be found from the tables using linear interpolation.

When calculating the sample size for a multiple logistic regression, you need an estimate of how much of the variance in your most important predictor, in this case violations, can be explained by the other predictor variables (the R^2). To adjust the sample size to take account of this relationship, use the following equation:

$$\text{Adjusted N} = \frac{N}{1 - R^2}$$

Where N is the appropriate sample size shown in Table A18.12 for a simple logistic regression.

Taking the example where 216 participants were needed for a simple logistic regression, if the other predictors (age, sex and driving mistakes) account for $R^2 = 0.288$ in your main predictor, then,

$$\text{Adjusted N} = \frac{216}{.712} = 303.37$$

which rounded up to the nearest whole number is 304.

Therefore you will need 304 participants in the multiple logistic regression.

Multifactorial between-subjects ANOVA

Calculating power

When a between-subjects ANOVA has more than one IV it is necessary to adjust the sample size which is used to read the power tables. The adjusted sample size (n') is found using the following equation:

$$n' = \frac{\text{error df}}{\text{treatment df} + 1} + 1$$

The example given in Chapter 17 had the IVs mnemonic strategy (with three levels) and type of list (with two levels). Therefore, there were three possible effects: two main effects and the interaction between them. The main effect of mnemonic strategy had df = 2, the main effect of type of list had df = 1 and the interaction had df = 2. The error term was the same for each of the F-ratios and had df = 24. Therefore, in the case of mnemonic strategy (and the interaction),

$$n' = \frac{24}{2 + 1} + 1$$
$$= 9$$

For type of list, n' is 13.

The effect sizes (η^2) for the three effects were .57 for type of list, .05 for mnemonic strategy and .11 for the interaction. Table A18.7a shows that the power for the test with $\eta^2 = .57$, treatment df = 1 and $n' = 13$ was over .95. Table A18.7b shows that the power for the test with $\eta^2 = .05$, treatment df = 2 and $n' = 9$ was .16 and for $\eta^2 = .11$, treatment df = 2 and $n' = 9$ it was just over .29.

As the main effect of mnemonic strategy was not statistically significant it is worth finding what sample size would be necessary in order to achieve power of .8. The next section shows how to do this.

Choosing the sample size

I will use the example from the previous section in which the effect size (η^2) being sought is .05, treatment df = 2 and the design is a 2 × 3 ANOVA. Table A18.7b shows that n' would be between 60 and 70 to achieve power of .8. Using linear interpolation the figure is 62. The total sample size which is required can be found from:

total sample size = (treatment df + 1) × (n' − 1) + number of conditions

In the present case there are 3 × 2 conditions; therefore:

total sample size = 3 × (62 − 1) + 6
= 189

In order to have a balanced design the number of participants in each condition will be:

$$\frac{\text{total sample size}}{\text{number of conditions}}$$

which, in the present case, will be:

$$\frac{189}{6} = 31.5$$

In other words, 32 people will be needed in each condition to give power of at least .8 for the test of the main effect of mnemonic strategy.

If the effect sizes which are being sought for the different treatments differ, then the above analysis would be conducted using the treatment with the smallest expected effect size.

The power of within-subjects ANOVA

The power of a within-subjects ANOVA is affected by a number of factors. It is enhanced by the degree to which participants' scores correlate between the pairs of levels of the IV. However, it is lowered by lack of sphericity. In order to simplify the process, I recommend reading the tables in the same way as for a between-subjects ANOVA but treating the sample size suggested as the overall sample size. To illustrate the procedure I will use the example which entails participants recommending a sentence for a criminal under three different conditions. The analysis is by a one-way ANOVA with three levels of the IV. If the researchers wished to detect a large effect size (η^2 = .138), as defined by Cohen (1988), using power of .8, then they would find from Table A18.7b that the recommended sample size was between 20 and 25, giving power between .78 and .87. Using linear interpolation, this would show that the overall sample size required was 21.1. Therefore they require a sample of 22 people.

The power of mixed ANOVA

To simplify the process again I recommend the following procedure, using the example of the two-way ANOVA described in Chapter 17. The between-subjects IV was gender of rater, the within-subjects IV was the gender of the parent being rated and the DV was the IQ which was estimated for the parent. For the between-subjects variable – gender of rater – the power and necessary sample size can be found in the way shown above for multifactorial between-subjects designs. Accordingly, as the treatment df was 1 and the error df was 8, n' is 5. The effect size for the main effect of gender of rater was η^2 = .0006. From Table A18.7a we can see that even if the effect size had been η^2 = .01, the level of power with n of 5 would be as low as .06. For the within-subjects IV – parent being rated – ignore the fact that it is a mixed design, read the tables as though for a one-way between-subjects ANOVA and treat the n as the total sample required. Thus, if during the design stage a medium effect size was being considered, as the treatment df would be 1, the necessary sample size would be between 60 and 70, or 62 after interpolation.

Table A18.1 Power tables for a one-group z-test

a   One-tailed tests

Effect size (d)

n	0.1	0.2	0.3	0.4	0.5	0.6	0.7	0.8	0.9	1.0	1.1	1.2	1.3	1.4
4	0.07	0.11	0.15	0.20	0.26	0.33	0.40	0.48	0.56	0.64	0.71	0.77	0.83	0.88
5	0.08	0.12	0.17	0.23	0.30	0.38	0.47	0.56	0.64	0.72	0.79	0.85	0.90	0.93
6	0.08	0.12	0.18	0.25	0.34	0.43	0.53	0.62	0.71	0.79	0.85	0.90	0.94	0.96
7	0.08	0.13	0.20	0.28	0.37	0.48	0.58	0.68	0.77	0.84	0.90	0.94	0.96	0.98
8	0.09	0.14	0.21	0.30	0.41	0.52	0.63	0.73	0.82	0.88	0.93	0.96	0.98	0.99
9	0.09	0.15	0.23	0.33	0.44	0.56	0.68	0.77	0.85	0.91	0.95	0.97	0.99	0.99
10	0.09	0.16	0.24	0.35	0.47	0.60	0.72	0.81	0.89	0.94	0.97	0.98	0.99	*
11	0.09	0.16	0.26	0.38	0.51	0.63	0.75	0.84	0.91	0.95	0.98	0.99	*	*
12	0.10	0.17	0.27	0.40	0.53	0.67	0.78	0.87	0.93	0.97	0.98	0.99	*	*
13	0.10	0.18	0.29	0.42	0.56	0.70	0.81	0.89	0.95	0.98	0.99	*	*	*
14	0.10	0.18	0.30	0.44	0.59	0.73	0.84	0.91	0.96	0.98	0.99	*	*	*
15	0.10	0.19	0.31	0.46	0.61	0.75	0.86	0.93	0.97	0.99	*	*	*	*
16	0.11	0.20	0.33	0.48	0.64	0.77	0.88	0.94	0.97	0.99	*	*	*	*
17	0.11	0.21	0.34	0.50	0.66	0.80	0.89	0.95	0.98	0.99	*	*	*	*
18	0.11	0.21	0.35	0.52	0.68	0.82	0.91	0.96	0.99	*	*	*	*	*
19	0.11	0.22	0.37	0.54	0.70	0.83	0.92	0.97	0.99	*	*	*	*	*
20	0.12	0.23	0.38	0.56	0.72	0.85	0.93	0.97	0.99	*	*	*	*	*
25	0.13	0.26	0.44	0.64	0.80	0.91	0.97	0.99	*	*	*	*	*	*
30	0.14	0.29	0.50	0.71	0.86	0.95	0.99	*	*	*	*	*	*	*
35	0.15	0.32	0.55	0.76	0.91	0.97	0.99	*	*	*	*	*	*	*
40	0.16	0.35	0.60	0.81	0.94	0.98	*	*	*	*	*	*	*	*
45	0.17	0.38	0.64	0.85	0.96	0.99	*	*	*	*	*	*	*	*
50	0.17	0.41	0.68	0.88	0.97	*	*	*	*	*	*	*	*	*
60	0.19	0.46	0.75	0.93	0.99	*	*	*	*	*	*	*	*	*
70	0.21	0.51	0.81	0.96	0.99	*	*	*	*	*	*	*	*	*
80	0.23	0.56	0.85	0.97	*	*	*	*	*	*	*	*	*	*
90	0.24	0.60	0.89	0.98	*	*	*	*	*	*	*	*	*	*
100	0.26	0.64	0.91	0.99	*	*	*	*	*	*	*	*	*	*
120	0.29	0.71	0.95	*	*	*	*	*	*	*	*	*	*	*
140	0.32	0.76	0.97	*	*	*	*	*	*	*	*	*	*	*
160	0.35	0.81	0.98	*	*	*	*	*	*	*	*	*	*	*
180	0.38	0.85	0.99	*	*	*	*	*	*	*	*	*	*	*
200	0.41	0.88	*	*	*	*	*	*	*	*	*	*	*	*
300	0.53	0.97	*	*	*	*	*	*	*	*	*	*	*	*
400	0.64	0.99	*	*	*	*	*	*	*	*	*	*	*	*
500	0.72	*	*	*	*	*	*	*	*	*	*	*	*	*
600	0.79	*	*	*	*	*	*	*	*	*	*	*	*	*
700	0.84	*	*	*	*	*	*	*	*	*	*	*	*	*
800	0.88	*	*	*	*	*	*	*	*	*	*	*	*	*
900	0.91	*	*	*	*	*	*	*	*	*	*	*	*	*
1000	0.94	*	*	*	*	*	*	*	*	*	*	*	*	*

TABLE A18.1   Power tables for a one-group *z*-test

b   Two-tailed tests

Effect size (d)

n	0.1	0.2	0.3	0.4	0.5	0.6	0.7	0.8	0.9	1.0	1.1	1.2	1.3	1.4
4	0.04	0.06	0.09	0.12	0.17	0.22	0.29	0.36	0.44	0.52	0.59	0.67	0.74	0.80
5	0.04	0.07	0.10	0.14	0.20	0.27	0.35	0.43	0.52	0.61	0.69	0.77	0.83	0.88
6	0.04	0.07	0.11	0.16	0.23	0.31	0.40	0.50	0.60	0.69	0.77	0.84	0.89	0.93
7	0.05	0.08	0.12	0.18	0.26	0.35	0.46	0.56	0.66	0.75	0.83	0.89	0.93	0.96
8	0.05	0.08	0.13	0.20	0.29	0.40	0.51	0.62	0.72	0.81	0.88	0.92	0.96	0.98
9	0.05	0.09	0.14	0.22	0.32	0.44	0.56	0.67	0.77	0.85	0.91	0.95	0.97	0.99
10	0.05	0.09	0.16	0.24	0.35	0.48	0.60	0.72	0.81	0.89	0.94	0.97	0.98	0.99
11	0.05	0.10	0.17	0.26	0.38	0.51	0.64	0.76	0.85	0.91	0.95	0.98	0.99	*
12	0.05	0.10	0.18	0.28	0.41	0.55	0.68	0.79	0.88	0.93	0.97	0.99	0.99	*
13	0.05	0.11	0.19	0.30	0.44	0.58	0.71	0.82	0.90	0.95	0.98	0.99	*	*
14	0.06	0.11	0.20	0.32	0.46	0.61	0.75	0.85	0.92	0.96	0.98	0.99	*	*
15	0.06	0.12	0.21	0.34	0.49	0.64	0.77	0.87	0.94	0.97	0.99	*	*	*
16	0.06	0.12	0.22	0.36	0.52	0.67	0.80	0.89	0.95	0.98	0.99	*	*	*
17	0.06	0.13	0.23	0.38	0.54	0.70	0.82	0.91	0.96	0.98	0.99	*	*	*
18	0.06	0.13	0.25	0.40	0.56	0.72	0.84	0.92	0.97	0.99	*	*	*	*
19	0.06	0.14	0.26	0.41	0.59	0.74	0.86	0.94	0.98	0.99	*	*	*	*
20	0.07	0.14	0.27	0.43	0.61	0.77	0.88	0.95	0.98	0.99	*	*	*	*
25	0.07	0.17	0.32	0.52	0.71	0.85	0.94	0.98	0.99	*	*	*	*	*
30	0.08	0.19	0.38	0.59	0.78	0.91	0.97	0.99	*	*	*	*	*	*
35	0.09	0.22	0.43	0.66	0.84	0.94	0.99	*	*	*	*	*	*	*
40	0.09	0.24	0.48	0.72	0.89	0.97	0.99	*	*	*	*	*	*	*
45	0.10	0.27	0.52	0.77	0.92	0.98	*	*	*	*	*	*	*	*
50	0.11	0.29	0.56	0.81	0.94	0.99	*	*	*	*	*	*	*	*
60	0.12	0.34	0.64	0.87	0.97	*	*	*	*	*	*	*	*	*
70	0.13	0.39	0.71	0.92	0.99	*	*	*	*	*	*	*	*	*
80	0.14	0.43	0.77	0.95	0.99	*	*	*	*	*	*	*	*	*
90	0.16	0.48	0.81	0.97	*	*	*	*	*	*	*	*	*	*
100	0.17	0.52	0.85	0.98	*	*	*	*	*	*	*	*	*	*
120	0.19	0.59	0.91	0.99	*	*	*	*	*	*	*	*	*	*
140	0.22	0.66	0.94	*	*	*	*	*	*	*	*	*	*	*
160	0.24	0.72	0.97	*	*	*	*	*	*	*	*	*	*	*
180	0.27	0.77	0.98	*	*	*	*	*	*	*	*	*	*	*
200	0.29	0.81	0.99	*	*	*	*	*	*	*	*	*	*	*
300	0.41	0.93	*	*	*	*	*	*	*	*	*	*	*	*
400	0.52	0.98	*	*	*	*	*	*	*	*	*	*	*	*
500	0.61	0.99	*	*	*	*	*	*	*	*	*	*	*	*
600	0.69	*	*	*	*	*	*	*	*	*	*	*	*	*
700	0.75	*	*	*	*	*	*	*	*	*	*	*	*	*
800	0.81	*	*	*	*	*	*	*	*	*	*	*	*	*
900	0.85	*	*	*	*	*	*	*	*	*	*	*	*	*
1000	0.89	*	*	*	*	*	*	*	*	*	*	*	*	*

Table A18.2 Power of a comparison of a proportion in a sample with a proportion in the population of .5

a One-tailed test

				Effect size (g)				
n	0.05	0.10	0.15	0.20	0.25	0.30	0.35	0.40
11	0.09	0.16	0.26	0.39	0.54	0.69	0.82	0.92
12	0.10	0.17	0.28	0.41	0.57	0.72	0.85	0.94
13	0.10	0.18	0.29	0.44	0.60	0.75	0.88	0.96
14	0.10	0.19	0.31	0.46	0.62	0.78	0.90	0.97
15	0.10	0.19	0.32	0.48	0.65	0.80	0.91	0.97
16	0.11	0.20	0.34	0.50	0.67	0.82	0.93	0.98
17	0.11	0.21	0.35	0.52	0.70	0.84	0.94	0.99
18	0.11	0.21	0.36	0.54	0.72	0.86	0.95	0.99
19	0.11	0.22	0.38	0.56	0.74	0.88	0.96	0.99
20	0.12	0.23	0.39	0.58	0.76	0.89	0.97	0.99
25	0.13	0.26	0.45	0.66	0.83	0.94	0.99	*
30	0.14	0.29	0.51	0.73	0.89	0.97	*	*
35	0.15	0.33	0.56	0.79	0.93	0.98	*	*
40	0.16	0.36	0.61	0.83	0.95	0.99	*	*
45	0.17	0.38	0.66	0.87	0.97	*	*	*
50	0.17	0.41	0.69	0.90	0.98	*	*	*
60	0.19	0.47	0.76	0.94	0.99	*	*	*
70	0.21	0.52	0.82	0.96	*	*	*	*
80	0.23	0.56	0.86	0.98	*	*	*	*
90	0.24	0.60	0.89	0.99	*	*	*	*
100	0.26	0.64	0.92	0.99	*	*	*	*
110	0.28	0.68	0.94	*	*	*	*	*
120	0.29	0.71	0.95	*	*	*	*	*
130	0.31	0.74	0.97	*	*	*	*	*
140	0.32	0.77	0.98	*	*	*	*	*
150	0.34	0.79	0.98	*	*	*	*	*
160	0.35	0.82	0.99	*	*	*	*	*
170	0.37	0.84	0.99	*	*	*	*	*
180	0.38	0.85	0.99	*	*	*	*	*
190	0.40	0.87	0.99	*	*	*	*	*
200	0.41	0.89	*	*	*	*	*	*
250	0.48	0.94	*	*	*	*	*	*
300	0.54	0.97	*	*	*	*	*	*
350	0.59	0.98	*	*	*	*	*	*
400	0.64	0.99	*	*	*	*	*	*
450	0.68	*	*	*	*	*	*	*
500	0.72	*	*	*	*	*	*	*
600	0.79	*	*	*	*	*	*	*
700	0.84	*	*	*	*	*	*	*
800	0.88	*	*	*	*	*	*	*
900	0.91	*	*	*	*	*	*	*
1000	0.94	*	*	*	*	*	*	*

TABLE A18.2 Power of a comparison of a proportion in a sample with a proportion in the population of .5

b   Two-tailed test

				Effect size (g)				
n	0.05	0.10	0.15	0.20	0.25	0.30	0.35	0.40
11	0.05	0.10	0.17	0.28	0.41	0.57	0.73	0.87
12	0.05	0.10	0.18	0.30	0.44	0.61	0.77	0.89
13	0.05	0.11	0.19	0.32	0.47	0.64	0.80	0.92
14	0.06	0.11	0.21	0.34	0.50	0.67	0.83	0.93
15	0.06	0.12	0.22	0.36	0.53	0.70	0.85	0.95
16	0.06	0.12	0.23	0.38	0.55	0.73	0.87	0.96
17	0.06	0.13	0.24	0.40	0.58	0.76	0.89	0.97
18	0.06	0.13	0.25	0.42	0.60	0.78	0.91	0.98
19	0.06	0.14	0.26	0.43	0.63	0.80	0.92	0.98
20	0.07	0.14	0.28	0.45	0.65	0.82	0.93	0.99
25	0.07	0.17	0.33	0.54	0.74	0.90	0.97	*
30	0.08	0.20	0.39	0.62	0.82	0.94	0.99	*
35	0.09	0.22	0.44	0.68	0.87	0.97	*	*
40	0.09	0.25	0.49	0.74	0.91	0.98	*	*
45	0.10	0.27	0.53	0.79	0.94	0.99	*	*
50	0.11	0.30	0.58	0.83	0.96	*	*	*
60	0.12	0.34	0.66	0.89	0.98	*	*	*
70	0.13	0.39	0.72	0.93	0.99	*	*	*
80	0.14	0.44	0.78	0.96	*	*	*	*
90	0.16	0.48	0.82	0.97	*	*	*	*
100	0.17	0.52	0.86	0.98	*	*	*	*
110	0.18	0.56	0.89	0.99	*	*	*	*
120	0.19	0.60	0.92	0.99	*	*	*	*
130	0.21	0.63	0.93	*	*	*	*	*
140	0.22	0.66	0.95	*	*	*	*	*
150	0.23	0.69	0.96	*	*	*	*	*
160	0.24	0.72	0.97	*	*	*	*	*
170	0.26	0.75	0.98	*	*	*	*	*
180	0.27	0.77	0.98	*	*	*	*	*
190	0.28	0.79	0.99	*	*	*	*	*
200	0.29	0.81	0.99	*	*	*	*	*
250	0.35	0.89	*	*	*	*	*	*
300	0.41	0.94	*	*	*	*	*	*
350	0.47	0.96	*	*	*	*	*	*
400	0.52	0.98	*	*	*	*	*	*
450	0.57	0.99	*	*	*	*	*	*
500	0.61	0.99	*	*	*	*	*	*
600	0.69	*	*	*	*	*	*	*
700	0.75	*	*	*	*	*	*	*
800	0.81	*	*	*	*	*	*	*
900	0.85	*	*	*	*	*	*	*
1000	0.89	*	*	*	*	*	*	*

Table A18.3 Power of a between-subjects *t*-test

a   One-tailed tests (*n* is the number of people in each group; when the sample sizes are unequal *n* is the harmonic mean)

Effect size (d)

n	0.1	0.2	0.3	0.4	0.5	0.6	0.7	0.8	0.9	1.0	1.1	1.2	1.3	1.4
8	0.07	0.10	0.13	0.18	0.23	0.29	0.36	0.44	0.52	0.59	0.67	0.73	0.79	0.84
9	0.07	0.10	0.14	0.19	0.25	0.32	0.40	0.48	0.56	0.64	0.72	0.78	0.84	0.88
10	0.07	0.11	0.15	0.21	0.27	0.35	0.43	0.52	0.61	0.69	0.76	0.82	0.87	0.91
11	0.08	0.11	0.16	0.22	0.29	0.38	0.47	0.56	0.65	0.73	0.80	0.86	0.90	0.93
12	0.08	0.12	0.17	0.23	0.31	0.40	0.50	0.59	0.68	0.76	0.83	0.88	0.92	0.95
13	0.08	0.12	0.18	0.25	0.33	0.43	0.53	0.63	0.72	0.80	0.86	0.90	0.94	0.96
14	0.08	0.13	0.19	0.26	0.35	0.45	0.56	0.66	0.75	0.82	0.88	0.92	0.95	0.97
15	0.08	0.13	0.19	0.27	0.37	0.48	0.58	0.69	0.77	0.85	0.90	0.94	0.96	0.98
16	0.08	0.13	0.20	0.29	0.39	0.50	0.61	0.71	0.80	0.87	0.92	0.95	0.97	0.98
17	0.09	0.14	0.21	0.30	0.41	0.52	0.63	0.74	0.82	0.88	0.93	0.96	0.98	0.99
18	0.09	0.14	0.22	0.31	0.42	0.54	0.66	0.76	0.84	0.90	0.94	0.97	0.98	0.99
19	0.09	0.15	0.23	0.33	0.44	0.56	0.68	0.78	0.86	0.91	0.95	0.97	0.99	0.99
20	0.09	0.15	0.23	0.34	0.46	0.58	0.70	0.80	0.87	0.93	0.96	0.98	0.99	*
25	0.10	0.17	0.27	0.40	0.54	0.67	0.79	0.87	0.93	0.97	0.98	0.99	*	*
30	0.10	0.19	0.31	0.45	0.60	0.74	0.85	0.92	0.96	0.98	0.99	*	*	*
35	0.11	0.20	0.34	0.50	0.66	0.80	0.89	0.95	0.98	0.99	*	*	*	*
40	0.11	0.22	0.37	0.55	0.72	0.84	0.93	0.97	0.99	*	*	*	*	*
45	0.12	0.24	0.41	0.59	0.76	0.88	0.95	0.98	0.99	*	*	*	*	*
50	0.12	0.26	0.44	0.63	0.80	0.91	0.97	0.99	*	*	*	*	*	*
60	0.13	0.29	0.49	0.70	0.86	0.95	0.98	*	*	*	*	*	*	*
70	0.14	0.32	0.55	0.76	0.90	0.97	0.99	*	*	*	*	*	*	*
80	0.15	0.35	0.60	0.81	0.93	0.98	*	*	*	*	*	*	*	*
90	0.16	0.38	0.64	0.85	0.95	0.99	*	*	*	*	*	*	*	*
100	0.17	0.41	0.68	0.88	0.97	0.99	*	*	*	*	*	*	*	*
110	0.18	0.43	0.72	0.90	0.98	*	*	*	*	*	*	*	*	*
120	0.19	0.46	0.75	0.93	0.99	*	*	*	*	*	*	*	*	*
130	0.20	0.48	0.78	0.94	0.99	*	*	*	*	*	*	*	*	*
140	0.21	0.51	0.80	0.95	0.99	*	*	*	*	*	*	*	*	*
150	0.22	0.53	0.83	0.96	*	*	*	*	*	*	*	*	*	*
160	0.23	0.56	0.85	0.97	*	*	*	*	*	*	*	*	*	*
170	0.23	0.58	0.87	0.98	*	*	*	*	*	*	*	*	*	*
180	0.24	0.60	0.88	0.98	*	*	*	*	*	*	*	*	*	*
190	0.25	0.62	0.90	0.99	*	*	*	*	*	*	*	*	*	*
200	0.26	0.64	0.91	0.99	*	*	*	*	*	*	*	*	*	*
300	0.34	0.79	0.98	*	*	*	*	*	*	*	*	*	*	*
400	0.41	0.88	*	*	*	*	*	*	*	*	*	*	*	*
500	0.47	0.94	*	*	*	*	*	*	*	*	*	*	*	*
600	0.53	0.97	*	*	*	*	*	*	*	*	*	*	*	*
700	0.59	0.98	*	*	*	*	*	*	*	*	*	*	*	*
800	0.64	0.99	*	*	*	*	*	*	*	*	*	*	*	*
900	0.68	*	*	*	*	*	*	*	*	*	*	*	*	*
1000	0.72	*	*	*	*	*	*	*	*	*	*	*	*	*

TABLE A18.3   Power of a between-subjects *t*-test

b   Two-tailed tests (*n* is the sample in each group; when the sample sizes are unequal *n* is the harmonic mean)

Effect size (d)

n	0.1	0.2	0.3	0.4	0.5	0.6	0.7	0.8	0.9	1.0	1.1	1.2	1.3	1.4
8	0.04	0.05	0.07	0.10	0.14	0.18	0.23	0.30	0.37	0.44	0.52	0.60	0.67	0.74
9	0.04	0.05	0.08	0.11	0.15	0.20	0.27	0.34	0.42	0.50	0.58	0.66	0.73	0.80
10	0.04	0.06	0.08	0.12	0.17	0.23	0.30	0.38	0.47	0.55	0.64	0.72	0.78	0.84
11	0.04	0.06	0.09	0.13	0.19	0.25	0.33	0.42	0.51	0.60	0.69	0.76	0.83	0.88
12	0.04	0.06	0.10	0.14	0.20	0.28	0.36	0.46	0.55	0.64	0.73	0.80	0.86	0.91
13	0.04	0.07	0.10	0.15	0.22	0.30	0.39	0.49	0.59	0.68	0.77	0.84	0.89	0.93
14	0.04	0.07	0.11	0.16	0.24	0.32	0.42	0.52	0.63	0.72	0.80	0.86	0.91	0.94
15	0.04	0.07	0.12	0.17	0.25	0.34	0.45	0.56	0.66	0.75	0.83	0.89	0.93	0.96
16	0.04	0.08	0.12	0.18	0.27	0.37	0.48	0.59	0.69	0.78	0.85	0.91	0.94	0.97
17	0.05	0.08	0.13	0.20	0.28	0.39	0.50	0.62	0.72	0.81	0.87	0.92	0.96	0.98
18	0.05	0.08	0.13	0.21	0.30	0.41	0.53	0.64	0.75	0.83	0.89	0.94	0.96	0.98
19	0.05	0.08	0.14	0.22	0.31	0.43	0.55	0.67	0.77	0.85	0.91	0.95	0.97	0.99
20	0.05	0.09	0.14	0.23	0.33	0.45	0.57	0.69	0.79	0.87	0.92	0.96	0.98	0.99
25	0.05	0.10	0.17	0.28	0.40	0.54	0.68	0.79	0.88	0.93	0.97	0.98	0.99	*
30	0.06	0.11	0.20	0.33	0.47	0.63	0.76	0.86	0.93	0.97	0.99	0.99	*	*
35	0.06	0.13	0.23	0.37	0.54	0.70	0.82	0.91	0.96	0.98	0.99	*	*	*
40	0.06	0.14	0.26	0.42	0.60	0.75	0.87	0.94	0.98	0.99	*	*	*	*
45	0.07	0.15	0.29	0.46	0.65	0.80	0.91	0.96	0.99	*	*	*	*	*
50	0.07	0.16	0.31	0.51	0.70	0.84	0.93	0.98	0.99	*	*	*	*	*
60	0.08	0.19	0.37	0.58	0.78	0.90	0.97	0.99	*	*	*	*	*	*
70	0.08	0.21	0.42	0.65	0.84	0.94	0.98	*	*	*	*	*	*	*
80	0.09	0.24	0.47	0.71	0.88	0.96	0.99	*	*	*	*	*	*	*
90	0.10	0.26	0.52	0.76	0.92	0.98	*	*	*	*	*	*	*	*
100	0.10	0.29	0.56	0.80	0.94	0.99	*	*	*	*	*	*	*	*
110	0.11	0.31	0.60	0.84	0.96	0.99	*	*	*	*	*	*	*	*
120	0.12	0.34	0.64	0.87	0.97	*	*	*	*	*	*	*	*	*
130	0.12	0.36	0.67	0.89	0.98	*	*	*	*	*	*	*	*	*
140	0.13	0.38	0.71	0.92	0.99	*	*	*	*	*	*	*	*	*
150	0.14	0.41	0.74	0.93	0.99	*	*	*	*	*	*	*	*	*
160	0.14	0.43	0.76	0.95	0.99	*	*	*	*	*	*	*	*	*
170	0.15	0.45	0.79	0.96	*	*	*	*	*	*	*	*	*	*
180	0.15	0.47	0.81	0.97	*	*	*	*	*	*	*	*	*	*
190	0.16	0.49	0.83	0.97	*	*	*	*	*	*	*	*	*	*
200	0.17	0.51	0.85	0.98	*	*	*	*	*	*	*	*	*	*
300	0.23	0.69	0.96	*	*	*	*	*	*	*	*	*	*	*
400	0.29	0.81	0.99	*	*	*	*	*	*	*	*	*	*	*
500	0.35	0.88	*	*	*	*	*	*	*	*	*	*	*	*
600	0.41	0.93	*	*	*	*	*	*	*	*	*	*	*	*
700	0.46	0.96	*	*	*	*	*	*	*	*	*	*	*	*
800	0.52	0.98	*	*	*	*	*	*	*	*	*	*	*	*
900	0.56	0.99	*	*	*	*	*	*	*	*	*	*	*	*
1000	0.61	0.99	*	*	*	*	*	*	*	*	*	*	*	*

Table A18.4 Power of a within-subjects *t*-test or one-group *t*-test

a   One-tailed tests

Effect size (d)

n	0.1	0.2	0.3	0.4	0.5	0.6	0.7	0.8	0.9	1	1.1	1.2	1.3	1.4
5	0.06	0.08	0.11	0.14	0.18	0.24	0.30	0.37	0.46	0.54	0.62	0.69	0.76	0.81
6	0.07	0.09	0.13	0.17	0.23	0.30	0.39	0.48	0.57	0.66	0.74	0.80	0.85	0.89
7	0.07	0.10	0.15	0.21	0.28	0.37	0.47	0.57	0.66	0.75	0.81	0.87	0.91	0.94
8	0.08	0.11	0.17	0.24	0.32	0.42	0.53	0.64	0.73	0.81	0.87	0.91	0.94	0.96
9	0.08	0.12	0.18	0.26	0.36	0.48	0.59	0.70	0.79	0.86	0.91	0.94	0.96	0.98
10	0.08	0.13	0.20	0.29	0.40	0.52	0.64	0.75	0.83	0.89	0.93	0.96	0.98	0.99
11	0.08	0.14	0.22	0.32	0.44	0.57	0.69	0.79	0.87	0.92	0.95	0.97	0.98	0.99
12	0.09	0.15	0.23	0.34	0.48	0.61	0.73	0.82	0.89	0.94	0.97	0.98	0.99	0.99
13	0.09	0.15	0.25	0.37	0.49	0.65	0.76	0.85	0.92	0.95	0.98	0.99	0.99	*
14	0.09	0.16	0.26	0.39	0.54	0.68	0.79	0.88	0.93	0.96	0.98	0.99	*	*
15	0.10	0.17	0.28	0.42	0.57	0.71	0.82	0.90	0.95	0.97	0.99	0.99	*	*
16	0.10	0.18	0.29	0.44	0.60	0.74	0.84	0.92	0.96	0.98	0.99	*	*	*
17	0.10	0.19	0.31	0.46	0.62	0.76	0.86	0.93	0.97	0.98	0.99	*	*	*
18	0.10	0.19	0.32	0.48	0.65	0.78	0.88	0.94	0.97	0.99	*	*	*	*
19	0.11	0.20	0.34	0.50	0.67	0.81	0.90	0.95	0.98	0.99	*	*	*	*
20	0.11	0.21	0.35	0.52	0.69	0.82	0.91	0.96	0.98	0.99	*	*	*	*
25	0.12	0.24	0.42	0.61	0.78	0.90	0.96	0.98	0.99	*	*	*	*	*
30	0.13	0.28	0.48	0.69	0.85	0.94	0.98	0.99	*	*	*	*	*	*
35	0.14	0.31	0.53	0.75	0.89	0.96	0.99	*	*	*	*	*	*	*
40	0.15	0.34	0.58	0.80	0.93	0.98	*	*	*	*	*	*	*	*
45	0.16	0.37	0.63	0.84	0.95	0.99	*	*	*	*	*	*	*	*
50	0.17	0.40	0.67	0.87	0.97	0.99	*	*	*	*	*	*	*	*
60	0.19	0.45	0.74	0.92	0.98	*	*	*	*	*	*	*	*	*
70	0.20	0.50	0.80	0.95	0.99	*	*	*	*	*	*	*	*	*
80	0.22	0.55	0.84	0.97	*	*	*	*	*	*	*	*	*	*
90	0.24	0.59	0.88	0.98	*	*	*	*	*	*	*	*	*	*
100	0.26	0.63	0.91	0.99	*	*	*	*	*	*	*	*	*	*
110	0.27	0.67	0.93	0.99	*	*	*	*	*	*	*	*	*	*
120	0.29	0.70	0.95	*	*	*	*	*	*	*	*	*	*	*
130	0.30	0.73	0.96	*	*	*	*	*	*	*	*	*	*	*
140	0.32	0.76	0.97	*	*	*	*	*	*	*	*	*	*	*
150	0.33	0.79	0.98	*	*	*	*	*	*	*	*	*	*	*
160	0.35	0.81	0.98	*	*	*	*	*	*	*	*	*	*	*
170	0.36	0.83	0.99	*	*	*	*	*	*	*	*	*	*	*
180	0.38	0.85	0.99	*	*	*	*	*	*	*	*	*	*	*
190	0.39	0.86	0.99	*	*	*	*	*	*	*	*	*	*	*
200	0.41	0.88	0.99	*	*	*	*	*	*	*	*	*	*	*
300	0.53	0.96	*	*	*	*	*	*	*	*	*	*	*	*
400	0.64	0.99	*	*	*	*	*	*	*	*	*	*	*	*
500	0.72	*	*	*	*	*	*	*	*	*	*	*	*	*
600	0.79	*	*	*	*	*	*	*	*	*	*	*	*	*
700	0.84	*	*	*	*	*	*	*	*	*	*	*	*	*
800	0.88	*	*	*	*	*	*	*	*	*	*	*	*	*
900	0.91	*	*	*	*	*	*	*	*	*	*	*	*	*
1000	0.94	*	*	*	*	*	*	*	*	*	*	*	*	*

TABLE A18.4   Power of a within-subjects *t*-test or one-group *t*-test

b   Two-tailed tests

n	\multicolumn{14}{c}{Effect size (d)}

n	0.1	0.2	0.3	0.4	0.5	0.6	0.7	0.8	0.9	1	1.1	1.2	1.3	1.4
6	0.03	0.05	0.06	0.09	0.12	0.16	0.22	0.28	0.36	0.45	0.55	0.64	0.72	0.79
7	0.04	0.05	0.07	0.11	0.15	0.21	0.29	0.38	0.47	0.58	0.67	0.75	0.82	0.87
8	0.04	0.06	0.09	0.13	0.19	0.26	0.36	0.46	0.57	0.67	0.76	0.83	0.88	0.92
9	0.04	0.06	0.10	0.15	0.22	0.31	0.42	0.54	0.65	0.75	0.83	0.88	0.93	0.95
10	0.04	0.07	0.11	0.17	0.26	0.36	0.48	0.60	0.71	0.80	0.87	0.92	0.95	0.97
11	0.04	0.07	0.12	0.19	0.29	0.41	0.54	0.66	0.77	0.85	0.91	0.94	0.97	0.98
12	0.05	0.08	0.13	0.22	0.32	0.45	0.59	0.71	0.81	0.88	0.93	0.96	0.98	0.99
13	0.05	0.09	0.15	0.24	0.36	0.49	0.63	0.75	0.85	0.91	0.95	0.97	0.99	0.99
14	0.05	0.09	0.16	0.26	0.39	0.53	0.67	0.79	0.88	0.93	0.96	0.98	0.99	*
15	0.05	0.10	0.17	0.28	0.42	0.57	0.71	0.82	0.90	0.95	0.97	0.99	0.99	*
16	0.05	0.10	0.18	0.30	0.45	0.60	0.74	0.85	0.92	0.96	0.98	0.99	*	*
17	0.05	0.11	0.20	0.32	0.48	0.64	0.77	0.87	0.93	0.97	0.99	0.99	*	*
18	0.06	0.11	0.21	0.34	0.50	0.67	0.80	0.89	0.95	0.98	0.99	*	*	*
19	0.06	0.12	0.22	0.36	0.53	0.69	0.82	0.91	0.96	0.98	0.99	*	*	*
20	0.06	0.12	0.23	0.38	0.56	0.72	0.84	0.92	0.97	0.99	0.99	*	*	*
25	0.07	0.15	0.29	0.47	0.67	0.82	0.92	0.97	0.99	*	*	*	*	*
30	0.07	0.18	0.35	0.56	0.75	0.89	0.96	0.99	*	*	*	*	*	*
35	0.08	0.20	0.40	0.63	0.82	0.93	0.98	0.99	*	*	*	*	*	*
40	0.09	0.23	0.45	0.69	0.87	0.96	0.99	*	*	*	*	*	*	*
45	0.09	0.25	0.50	0.75	0.91	0.97	0.99	*	*	*	*	*	*	*
50	0.10	0.28	0.54	0.79	0.93	0.98	*	*	*	*	*	*	*	*
60	0.11	0.33	0.63	0.86	0.97	0.99	*	*	*	*	*	*	*	*
70	0.13	0.37	0.70	0.91	0.98	*	*	*	*	*	*	*	*	*
80	0.14	0.42	0.75	0.94	0.99	*	*	*	*	*	*	*	*	*
90	0.15	0.46	0.80	0.96	*	*	*	*	*	*	*	*	*	*
100	0.16	0.51	0.84	0.98	*	*	*	*	*	*	*	*	*	*
110	0.18	0.55	0.88	0.99	*	*	*	*	*	*	*	*	*	*
120	0.19	0.58	0.90	0.99	*	*	*	*	*	*	*	*	*	*
130	0.20	0.62	0.92	0.99	*	*	*	*	*	*	*	*	*	*
140	0.21	0.65	0.94	*	*	*	*	*	*	*	*	*	*	*
150	0.23	0.68	0.95	*	*	*	*	*	*	*	*	*	*	*
160	0.24	0.71	0.96	*	*	*	*	*	*	*	*	*	*	*
170	0.25	0.74	0.97	*	*	*	*	*	*	*	*	*	*	*
180	0.26	0.76	0.98	*	*	*	*	*	*	*	*	*	*	*
190	0.28	0.78	0.98	*	*	*	*	*	*	*	*	*	*	*
200	0.29	0.80	0.99	*	*	*	*	*	*	*	*	*	*	*
300	0.41	0.93	*	*	*	*	*	*	*	*	*	*	*	*
400	0.51	0.98	*	*	*	*	*	*	*	*	*	*	*	*
500	0.61	0.99	*	*	*	*	*	*	*	*	*	*	*	*
600	0.69	*	*	*	*	*	*	*	*	*	*	*	*	*
700	0.75	*	*	*	*	*	*	*	*	*	*	*	*	*
800	0.81	*	*	*	*	*	*	*	*	*	*	*	*	*
900	0.85	*	*	*	*	*	*	*	*	*	*	*	*	*
1000	0.88	*	*	*	*	*	*	*	*	*	*	*	*	*

Table A18.5 Power of a χ^2 test

a   df = 1

				effect size (w)					
n	0.1	0.2	0.3	0.4	0.5	0.6	0.7	0.8	0.9
20	0.07	0.14	0.25	0.42	0.61	0.78	0.90	0.96	0.99
21	0.07	0.14	0.26	0.44	0.63	0.80	0.91	0.97	0.99
22	0.07	0.14	0.27	0.45	0.65	0.82	0.93	0.98	0.99
23	0.07	0.15	0.28	0.47	0.67	0.84	0.94	0.98	*
24	0.07	0.15	0.29	0.49	0.69	0.85	0.95	0.99	*
25	0.07	0.16	0.31	0.51	0.71	0.87	0.96	0.99	*
26	0.08	0.16	0.32	0.52	0.73	0.88	0.96	0.99	*
27	0.08	0.17	0.33	0.54	0.75	0.90	0.97	0.99	*
28	0.08	0.17	0.34	0.56	0.76	0.91	0.97	0.99	*
29	0.08	0.18	0.35	0.57	0.78	0.92	0.98	*	*
30	0.08	0.18	0.36	0.59	0.80	0.93	0.98	*	*
31	0.08	0.19	0.37	0.60	0.81	0.94	0.99	*	*
32	0.08	0.19	0.38	0.62	0.82	0.94	0.99	*	*
33	0.08	0.19	0.39	0.63	0.84	0.95	0.99	*	*
34	0.08	0.20	0.40	0.65	0.85	0.96	0.99	*	*
35	0.09	0.20	0.41	0.66	0.86	0.96	0.99	*	*
36	0.09	0.21	0.42	0.67	0.87	0.97	0.99	*	*
37	0.09	0.21	0.43	0.69	0.88	0.97	*	*	*
38	0.09	0.22	0.44	0.70	0.89	0.97	*	*	*
39	0.09	0.22	0.45	0.71	0.90	0.98	*	*	*
40	0.09	0.23	0.46	0.72	0.90	0.98	*	*	*
41	0.09	0.23	0.47	0.73	0.91	0.98	*	*	*
42	0.09	0.24	0.48	0.75	0.92	0.98	*	*	*
43	0.09	0.24	0.49	0.76	0.93	0.99	*	*	*
44	0.09	0.25	0.50	0.77	0.93	0.99	*	*	*
45	0.10	0.25	0.51	0.78	0.94	0.99	*	*	*
46	0.10	0.26	0.52	0.79	0.94	0.99	*	*	*
47	0.10	0.26	0.53	0.80	0.95	0.99	*	*	*
48	0.10	0.27	0.54	0.81	0.95	0.99	*	*	*
49	0.10	0.27	0.55	0.81	0.96	0.99	*	*	*
50	0.10	0.28	0.56	0.82	0.96	*	*	*	*
55	0.11	0.30	0.60	0.86	0.97	*	*	*	*
60	0.11	0.32	0.64	0.89	0.98	*	*	*	*
65	0.12	0.35	0.68	0.92	0.99	*	*	*	*
70	0.12	0.37	0.72	0.94	0.99	*	*	*	*
75	0.13	0.39	0.75	0.95	*	*	*	*	*
80	0.14	0.42	0.78	0.96	*	*	*	*	*
85	0.14	0.44	0.80	0.97	*	*	*	*	*
90	0.15	0.46	0.83	0.98	*	*	*	*	*
95	0.15	0.48	0.85	0.99	*	*	*	*	*
100	0.16	0.51	0.87	0.99	*	*	*	*	*
110	0.17	0.55	0.90	0.99	*	*	*	*	*
120	0.18	0.59	0.93	*	*	*	*	*	*
130	0.19	0.62	0.95	*	*	*	*	*	*
140	0.20	0.66	0.96	*	*	*	*	*	*
150	0.22	0.69	0.97	*	*	*	*	*	*
160	0.23	0.72	0.98	*	*	*	*	*	*
170	0.24	0.75	0.99	*	*	*	*	*	*
180	0.25	0.78	0.99	*	*	*	*	*	*
190	0.26	0.80	0.99	*	*	*	*	*	*
200	0.28	0.82	*	*	*	*	*	*	*
250	0.34	0.90	*	*	*	*	*	*	*
300	0.39	0.95	*	*	*	*	*	*	*
350	0.45	0.98	*	*	*	*	*	*	*
400	0.51	0.99	*	*	*	*	*	*	*
450	0.56	*	*	*	*	*	*	*	*
500	0.61	*	*	*	*	*	*	*	*
600	0.69	*	*	*	*	*	*	*	*
700	0.76	*	*	*	*	*	*	*	*
800	0.82	*	*	*	*	*	*	*	*
900	0.87	*	*	*	*	*	*	*	*
1000	0.90	*	*	*	*	*	*	*	*

TABLE A18.5   Power of a χ^2 test

b   df = 2

<table>
<tr><th rowspan="2">n</th><th colspan="9">effect size (w)</th></tr>
<tr><th>0.1</th><th>0.2</th><th>0.3</th><th>0.4</th><th>0.5</th><th>0.6</th><th>0.7</th><th>0.8</th><th>0.9</th></tr>
<tr><td>20</td><td>0.06</td><td>0.11</td><td>0.20</td><td>0.33</td><td>0.49</td><td>0.67</td><td>0.82</td><td>0.92</td><td>0.97</td></tr>
<tr><td>21</td><td>0.06</td><td>0.11</td><td>0.21</td><td>0.34</td><td>0.52</td><td>0.69</td><td>0.84</td><td>0.93</td><td>0.98</td></tr>
<tr><td>22</td><td>0.06</td><td>0.12</td><td>0.21</td><td>0.36</td><td>0.54</td><td>0.72</td><td>0.86</td><td>0.94</td><td>0.98</td></tr>
<tr><td>23</td><td>0.07</td><td>0.12</td><td>0.22</td><td>0.37</td><td>0.56</td><td>0.74</td><td>0.87</td><td>0.95</td><td>0.99</td></tr>
<tr><td>24</td><td>0.07</td><td>0.12</td><td>0.23</td><td>0.39</td><td>0.58</td><td>0.76</td><td>0.89</td><td>0.96</td><td>0.99</td></tr>
<tr><td>25</td><td>0.07</td><td>0.13</td><td>0.24</td><td>0.40</td><td>0.60</td><td>0.78</td><td>0.90</td><td>0.97</td><td>0.99</td></tr>
<tr><td>26</td><td>0.07</td><td>0.13</td><td>0.25</td><td>0.42</td><td>0.62</td><td>0.80</td><td>0.92</td><td>0.97</td><td>0.99</td></tr>
<tr><td>27</td><td>0.07</td><td>0.13</td><td>0.26</td><td>0.43</td><td>0.64</td><td>0.81</td><td>0.93</td><td>0.98</td><td>*</td></tr>
<tr><td>28</td><td>0.07</td><td>0.14</td><td>0.26</td><td>0.45</td><td>0.65</td><td>0.83</td><td>0.94</td><td>0.98</td><td>*</td></tr>
<tr><td>29</td><td>0.07</td><td>0.14</td><td>0.27</td><td>0.46</td><td>0.67</td><td>0.84</td><td>0.95</td><td>0.99</td><td>*</td></tr>
<tr><td>30</td><td>0.07</td><td>0.14</td><td>0.28</td><td>0.48</td><td>0.69</td><td>0.86</td><td>0.95</td><td>0.99</td><td>*</td></tr>
<tr><td>31</td><td>0.07</td><td>0.15</td><td>0.29</td><td>0.49</td><td>0.70</td><td>0.87</td><td>0.96</td><td>0.99</td><td>*</td></tr>
<tr><td>32</td><td>0.07</td><td>0.15</td><td>0.30</td><td>0.50</td><td>0.72</td><td>0.88</td><td>0.97</td><td>0.99</td><td>*</td></tr>
<tr><td>33</td><td>0.07</td><td>0.15</td><td>0.31</td><td>0.52</td><td>0.74</td><td>0.89</td><td>0.97</td><td>0.99</td><td>*</td></tr>
<tr><td>34</td><td>0.07</td><td>0.16</td><td>0.31</td><td>0.53</td><td>0.75</td><td>0.90</td><td>0.97</td><td>*</td><td>*</td></tr>
<tr><td>35</td><td>0.07</td><td>0.16</td><td>0.32</td><td>0.54</td><td>0.76</td><td>0.91</td><td>0.98</td><td>*</td><td>*</td></tr>
<tr><td>36</td><td>0.08</td><td>0.17</td><td>0.33</td><td>0.56</td><td>0.78</td><td>0.92</td><td>0.98</td><td>*</td><td>*</td></tr>
<tr><td>37</td><td>0.08</td><td>0.17</td><td>0.34</td><td>0.57</td><td>0.79</td><td>0.93</td><td>0.98</td><td>*</td><td>*</td></tr>
<tr><td>38</td><td>0.08</td><td>0.17</td><td>0.35</td><td>0.58</td><td>0.80</td><td>0.94</td><td>0.99</td><td>*</td><td>*</td></tr>
<tr><td>39</td><td>0.08</td><td>0.18</td><td>0.36</td><td>0.60</td><td>0.81</td><td>0.94</td><td>0.99</td><td>*</td><td>*</td></tr>
<tr><td>40</td><td>0.08</td><td>0.18</td><td>0.37</td><td>0.61</td><td>0.83</td><td>0.95</td><td>0.99</td><td>*</td><td>*</td></tr>
<tr><td>41</td><td>0.08</td><td>0.18</td><td>0.37</td><td>0.62</td><td>0.84</td><td>0.95</td><td>0.99</td><td>*</td><td>*</td></tr>
<tr><td>42</td><td>0.08</td><td>0.19</td><td>0.38</td><td>0.63</td><td>0.85</td><td>0.96</td><td>0.99</td><td>*</td><td>*</td></tr>
<tr><td>43</td><td>0.08</td><td>0.19</td><td>0.39</td><td>0.65</td><td>0.86</td><td>0.96</td><td>0.99</td><td>*</td><td>*</td></tr>
<tr><td>44</td><td>0.08</td><td>0.19</td><td>0.40</td><td>0.66</td><td>0.87</td><td>0.97</td><td>*</td><td>*</td><td>*</td></tr>
<tr><td>45</td><td>0.08</td><td>0.20</td><td>0.41</td><td>0.67</td><td>0.87</td><td>0.97</td><td>*</td><td>*</td><td>*</td></tr>
<tr><td>46</td><td>0.08</td><td>0.20</td><td>0.42</td><td>0.68</td><td>0.88</td><td>0.97</td><td>*</td><td>*</td><td>*</td></tr>
<tr><td>47</td><td>0.08</td><td>0.20</td><td>0.42</td><td>0.69</td><td>0.89</td><td>0.98</td><td>*</td><td>*</td><td>*</td></tr>
<tr><td>48</td><td>0.08</td><td>0.21</td><td>0.43</td><td>0.70</td><td>0.90</td><td>0.98</td><td>*</td><td>*</td><td>*</td></tr>
<tr><td>49</td><td>0.09</td><td>0.21</td><td>0.44</td><td>0.71</td><td>0.90</td><td>0.98</td><td>*</td><td>*</td><td>*</td></tr>
<tr><td>50</td><td>0.09</td><td>0.22</td><td>0.45</td><td>0.72</td><td>0.91</td><td>0.98</td><td>*</td><td>*</td><td>*</td></tr>
<tr><td>55</td><td>0.09</td><td>0.23</td><td>0.49</td><td>0.77</td><td>0.94</td><td>0.99</td><td>*</td><td>*</td><td>*</td></tr>
<tr><td>60</td><td>0.09</td><td>0.25</td><td>0.53</td><td>0.81</td><td>0.96</td><td>*</td><td>*</td><td>*</td><td>*</td></tr>
<tr><td>65</td><td>0.10</td><td>0.27</td><td>0.57</td><td>0.84</td><td>0.97</td><td>*</td><td>*</td><td>*</td><td>*</td></tr>
<tr><td>70</td><td>0.10</td><td>0.29</td><td>0.60</td><td>0.87</td><td>0.98</td><td>*</td><td>*</td><td>*</td><td>*</td></tr>
<tr><td>75</td><td>0.11</td><td>0.31</td><td>0.64</td><td>0.90</td><td>0.99</td><td>*</td><td>*</td><td>*</td><td>*</td></tr>
<tr><td>80</td><td>0.11</td><td>0.33</td><td>0.67</td><td>0.92</td><td>0.99</td><td>*</td><td>*</td><td>*</td><td>*</td></tr>
<tr><td>85</td><td>0.11</td><td>0.35</td><td>0.70</td><td>0.93</td><td>0.99</td><td>*</td><td>*</td><td>*</td><td>*</td></tr>
<tr><td>90</td><td>0.12</td><td>0.37</td><td>0.73</td><td>0.95</td><td>*</td><td>*</td><td>*</td><td>*</td><td>*</td></tr>
<tr><td>95</td><td>0.12</td><td>0.38</td><td>0.75</td><td>0.96</td><td>*</td><td>*</td><td>*</td><td>*</td><td>*</td></tr>
<tr><td>100</td><td>0.13</td><td>0.40</td><td>0.78</td><td>0.97</td><td>*</td><td>*</td><td>*</td><td>*</td><td>*</td></tr>
<tr><td>110</td><td>0.14</td><td>0.44</td><td>0.82</td><td>0.98</td><td>*</td><td>*</td><td>*</td><td>*</td><td>*</td></tr>
<tr><td>120</td><td>0.14</td><td>0.48</td><td>0.86</td><td>0.99</td><td>*</td><td>*</td><td>*</td><td>*</td><td>*</td></tr>
<tr><td>130</td><td>0.15</td><td>0.51</td><td>0.89</td><td>0.99</td><td>*</td><td>*</td><td>*</td><td>*</td><td>*</td></tr>
<tr><td>140</td><td>0.16</td><td>0.54</td><td>0.91</td><td>*</td><td>*</td><td>*</td><td>*</td><td>*</td><td>*</td></tr>
<tr><td>150</td><td>0.17</td><td>0.58</td><td>0.93</td><td>*</td><td>*</td><td>*</td><td>*</td><td>*</td><td>*</td></tr>
<tr><td>160</td><td>0.18</td><td>0.61</td><td>0.95</td><td>*</td><td>*</td><td>*</td><td>*</td><td>*</td><td>*</td></tr>
<tr><td>170</td><td>0.19</td><td>0.64</td><td>0.96</td><td>*</td><td>*</td><td>*</td><td>*</td><td>*</td><td>*</td></tr>
<tr><td>180</td><td>0.20</td><td>0.67</td><td>0.97</td><td>*</td><td>*</td><td>*</td><td>*</td><td>*</td><td>*</td></tr>
<tr><td>190</td><td>0.21</td><td>0.70</td><td>0.98</td><td>*</td><td>*</td><td>*</td><td>*</td><td>*</td><td>*</td></tr>
<tr><td>200</td><td>0.22</td><td>0.72</td><td>0.98</td><td>*</td><td>*</td><td>*</td><td>*</td><td>*</td><td>*</td></tr>
<tr><td>250</td><td>0.26</td><td>0.83</td><td>*</td><td>*</td><td>*</td><td>*</td><td>*</td><td>*</td><td>*</td></tr>
<tr><td>300</td><td>0.31</td><td>0.90</td><td>*</td><td>*</td><td>*</td><td>*</td><td>*</td><td>*</td><td>*</td></tr>
<tr><td>350</td><td>0.36</td><td>0.94</td><td>*</td><td>*</td><td>*</td><td>*</td><td>*</td><td>*</td><td>*</td></tr>
<tr><td>400</td><td>0.40</td><td>0.97</td><td>*</td><td>*</td><td>*</td><td>*</td><td>*</td><td>*</td><td>*</td></tr>
<tr><td>450</td><td>0.45</td><td>0.98</td><td>*</td><td>*</td><td>*</td><td>*</td><td>*</td><td>*</td><td>*</td></tr>
<tr><td>500</td><td>0.49</td><td>0.99</td><td>*</td><td>*</td><td>*</td><td>*</td><td>*</td><td>*</td><td>*</td></tr>
<tr><td>600</td><td>0.58</td><td>*</td><td>*</td><td>*</td><td>*</td><td>*</td><td>*</td><td>*</td><td>*</td></tr>
<tr><td>700</td><td>0.65</td><td>*</td><td>*</td><td>*</td><td>*</td><td>*</td><td>*</td><td>*</td><td>*</td></tr>
<tr><td>800</td><td>0.72</td><td>*</td><td>*</td><td>*</td><td>*</td><td>*</td><td>*</td><td>*</td><td>*</td></tr>
<tr><td>900</td><td>0.78</td><td>*</td><td>*</td><td>*</td><td>*</td><td>*</td><td>*</td><td>*</td><td>*</td></tr>
<tr><td>1000</td><td>0.83</td><td>*</td><td>*</td><td>*</td><td>*</td><td>*</td><td>*</td><td>*</td><td>*</td></tr>
</table>

TABLE A18.5   Power of a χ^2 test

c   df = 3

n	\multicolumn{9}{c}{effect size (w)}
	0.1	0.2	0.3	0.4	0.5	0.6	0.7	0.8	0.9
20	0.06	0.10	0.17	0.28	0.43	0.60	0.76	0.88	0.95
21	0.06	0.10	0.18	0.30	0.45	0.62	0.78	0.89	0.96
22	0.06	0.10	0.18	0.31	0.47	0.65	0.80	0.91	0.97
23	0.06	0.11	0.19	0.32	0.49	0.67	0.82	0.92	0.97
24	0.06	0.11	0.20	0.33	0.51	0.69	0.84	0.93	0.98
25	0.06	0.11	0.21	0.35	0.53	0.71	0.86	0.95	0.98
26	0.06	0.12	0.21	0.36	0.55	0.73	0.87	0.95	0.99
27	0.07	0.12	0.22	0.37	0.57	0.75	0.89	0.96	0.99
28	0.07	0.12	0.23	0.39	0.58	0.77	0.90	0.97	0.99
29	0.07	0.12	0.23	0.40	0.60	0.79	0.91	0.97	0.99
30	0.07	0.13	0.24	0.41	0.62	0.80	0.92	0.98	*
31	0.07	0.13	0.25	0.43	0.64	0.82	0.93	0.98	*
32	0.07	0.13	0.26	0.44	0.65	0.83	0.94	0.99	*
33	0.07	0.14	0.26	0.45	0.67	0.84	0.95	0.99	*
34	0.07	0.14	0.27	0.47	0.68	0.86	0.95	0.99	*
35	0.07	0.14	0.28	0.48	0.70	0.87	0.96	0.99	*
36	0.07	0.14	0.29	0.49	0.71	0.88	0.97	0.99	*
37	0.07	0.15	0.29	0.50	0.73	0.89	0.97	0.99	*
38	0.07	0.15	0.30	0.52	0.74	0.90	0.97	*	*
39	0.07	0.15	0.31	0.53	0.75	0.91	0.98	*	*
40	0.07	0.16	0.31	0.54	0.77	0.92	0.98	*	*
41	0.07	0.16	0.32	0.55	0.78	0.92	0.98	*	*
42	0.07	0.16	0.33	0.56	0.79	0.93	0.99	*	*
43	0.07	0.16	0.34	0.58	0.80	0.94	0.99	*	*
44	0.08	0.17	0.34	0.59	0.81	0.94	0.99	*	*
45	0.08	0.17	0.35	0.60	0.82	0.95	0.99	*	*
46	0.08	0.17	0.36	0.61	0.83	0.95	0.99	*	*
47	0.08	0.18	0.37	0.62	0.84	0.96	0.99	*	*
48	0.08	0.18	0.37	0.63	0.85	0.96	0.99	*	*
49	0.08	0.18	0.38	0.64	0.86	0.97	*	*	*
50	0.08	0.19	0.39	0.65	0.87	0.97	*	*	*
55	0.08	0.20	0.43	0.70	0.90	0.98	*	*	*
60	0.09	0.22	0.46	0.74	0.93	0.99	*	*	*
65	0.09	0.23	0.50	0.78	0.95	0.99	*	*	*
70	0.09	0.25	0.53	0.82	0.96	*	*	*	*
75	0.10	0.27	0.57	0.85	0.97	*	*	*	*
80	0.10	0.28	0.60	0.88	0.98	*	*	*	*
85	0.10	0.30	0.63	0.90	0.99	*	*	*	*
90	0.11	0.31	0.66	0.92	0.99	*	*	*	*
95	0.11	0.33	0.69	0.93	0.99	*	*	*	*
100	0.11	0.35	0.71	0.95	*	*	*	*	*
110	0.12	0.38	0.76	0.96	*	*	*	*	*
120	0.13	0.41	0.80	0.98	*	*	*	*	*
130	0.13	0.45	0.84	0.99	*	*	*	*	*
140	0.14	0.48	0.87	0.99	*	*	*	*	*
150	0.15	0.51	0.89	*	*	*	*	*	*
160	0.16	0.54	0.92	*	*	*	*	*	*
170	0.16	0.57	0.93	*	*	*	*	*	*
180	0.17	0.60	0.95	*	*	*	*	*	*
190	0.18	0.63	0.96	*	*	*	*	*	*
200	0.19	0.65	0.97	*	*	*	*	*	*
250	0.23	0.77	0.99	*	*	*	*	*	*
300	0.27	0.85	*	*	*	*	*	*	*
350	0.31	0.91	*	*	*	*	*	*	*
400	0.35	0.95	*	*	*	*	*	*	*
450	0.39	0.97	*	*	*	*	*	*	*
500	0.43	0.98	*	*	*	*	*	*	*
600	0.51	*	*	*	*	*	*	*	*
700	0.58	*	*	*	*	*	*	*	*
800	0.65	*	*	*	*	*	*	*	*
900	0.71	*	*	*	*	*	*	*	*
1000	0.77	*	*	*	*	*	*	*	*
1100	0.81	*	*	*	*	*	*	*	*

TABLE A18.5   Power of a χ^2 test

d   df = 4

n	0.1	0.2	0.3	0.4	0.5	0.6	0.7	0.8	0.9
20	0.06	0.09	0.15	0.25	0.39	0.55	0.71	0.84	0.93
21	0.06	0.09	0.16	0.26	0.41	0.57	0.73	0.86	0.94
22	0.06	0.10	0.17	0.28	0.42	0.59	0.76	0.88	0.95
23	0.06	0.10	0.17	0.29	0.44	0.62	0.78	0.89	0.96
24	0.06	0.10	0.18	0.30	0.46	0.64	0.80	0.91	0.97
25	0.06	0.10	0.18	0.31	0.48	0.66	0.82	0.92	0.97
26	0.06	0.11	0.19	0.32	0.50	0.68	0.84	0.93	0.98
27	0.06	0.11	0.20	0.34	0.52	0.70	0.85	0.94	0.98
28	0.06	0.11	0.20	0.35	0.53	0.72	0.87	0.95	0.99
29	0.06	0.11	0.21	0.36	0.55	0.74	0.88	0.96	0.99
30	0.06	0.12	0.22	0.37	0.57	0.76	0.89	0.97	0.99
31	0.06	0.12	0.22	0.38	0.58	0.77	0.90	0.97	0.99
32	0.07	0.12	0.23	0.40	0.60	0.79	0.92	0.98	*
33	0.07	0.12	0.24	0.41	0.62	0.80	0.92	0.98	*
34	0.07	0.13	0.24	0.42	0.63	0.82	0.93	0.98	*
35	0.07	0.13	0.25	0.43	0.65	0.83	0.94	0.99	*
36	0.07	0.13	0.26	0.44	0.66	0.84	0.95	0.99	*
37	0.07	0.13	0.26	0.46	0.68	0.85	0.95	0.99	*
38	0.07	0.14	0.27	0.47	0.69	0.87	0.96	0.99	*
39	0.07	0.14	0.28	0.48	0.70	0.88	0.96	0.99	*
40	0.07	0.14	0.28	0.49	0.72	0.89	0.97	0.99	*
41	0.07	0.14	0.29	0.50	0.73	0.89	0.97	*	*
42	0.07	0.15	0.30	0.51	0.74	0.90	0.98	*	*
43	0.07	0.15	0.30	0.52	0.75	0.91	0.98	*	*
44	0.07	0.15	0.31	0.54	0.77	0.92	0.98	*	*
45	0.07	0.15	0.32	0.55	0.78	0.93	0.98	*	*
46	0.07	0.16	0.32	0.56	0.79	0.93	0.99	*	*
47	0.07	0.16	0.33	0.57	0.80	0.94	0.99	*	*
48	0.07	0.16	0.34	0.58	0.81	0.94	0.99	*	*
49	0.07	0.16	0.34	0.59	0.82	0.95	0.99	*	*
50	0.08	0.17	0.35	0.60	0.83	0.95	0.99	*	*
55	0.08	0.18	0.38	0.65	0.87	0.97	*	*	*
60	0.08	0.19	0.42	0.70	0.90	0.98	*	*	*
65	0.08	0.21	0.45	0.74	0.93	0.99	*	*	*
70	0.09	0.22	0.48	0.77	0.95	0.99	*	*	*
75	0.09	0.24	0.52	0.81	0.96	*	*	*	*
80	0.09	0.25	0.55	0.84	0.97	*	*	*	*
85	0.09	0.27	0.58	0.86	0.98	*	*	*	*
90	0.10	0.28	0.61	0.89	0.99	*	*	*	*
95	0.10	0.30	0.63	0.90	0.99	*	*	*	*
100	0.10	0.31	0.66	0.92	0.99	*	*	*	*
110	0.11	0.34	0.71	0.95	*	*	*	*	*
120	0.12	0.37	0.76	0.97	*	*	*	*	*
130	0.12	0.40	0.80	0.98	*	*	*	*	*
140	0.13	0.43	0.83	0.99	*	*	*	*	*
150	0.13	0.46	0.86	0.99	*	*	*	*	*
160	0.14	0.49	0.89	0.99	*	*	*	*	*
170	0.15	0.52	0.91	*	*	*	*	*	*
180	0.15	0.55	0.93	*	*	*	*	*	*
190	0.16	0.57	0.94	*	*	*	*	*	*
200	0.17	0.60	0.95	*	*	*	*	*	*
250	0.20	0.72	0.99	*	*	*	*	*	*
300	0.24	0.81	*	*	*	*	*	*	*
350	0.27	0.87	*	*	*	*	*	*	*
400	0.31	0.92	*	*	*	*	*	*	*
450	0.35	0.95	*	*	*	*	*	*	*
500	0.39	0.97	*	*	*	*	*	*	*
600	0.46	0.99	*	*	*	*	*	*	*
700	0.53	*	*	*	*	*	*	*	*
800	0.60	*	*	*	*	*	*	*	*
900	0.66	*	*	*	*	*	*	*	*
1000	0.72	*	*	*	*	*	*	*	*
1100	0.77	*	*	*	*	*	*	*	*
1200	0.81	*	*	*	*	*	*	*	*

TABLE A18.5 Power of a χ^2 test

e   df = 5

				effect size (*w*)					
n	0.1	0.2	0.3	0.4	0.5	0.6	0.7	0.8	0.9
20	0.06	0.09	0.14	0.23	0.36	0.51	0.66	0.80	0.90
21	0.06	0.09	0.15	0.24	0.37	0.53	0.69	0.83	0.92
22	0.06	0.09	0.15	0.25	0.39	0.55	0.72	0.85	0.93
23	0.06	0.09	0.16	0.26	0.41	0.58	0.74	0.87	0.94
24	0.06	0.10	0.16	0.27	0.43	0.60	0.76	0.88	0.95
25	0.06	0.10	0.17	0.29	0.44	0.62	0.78	0.90	0.96
26	0.06	0.10	0.18	0.30	0.46	0.64	0.80	0.91	0.97
27	0.06	0.10	0.18	0.31	0.48	0.66	0.82	0.92	0.98
28	0.06	0.10	0.19	0.32	0.49	0.68	0.84	0.93	0.98
29	0.06	0.11	0.19	0.33	0.51	0.70	0.85	0.94	0.98
30	0.06	0.11	0.20	0.34	0.53	0.72	0.87	0.95	0.99
31	0.06	0.11	0.20	0.35	0.54	0.73	0.88	0.96	0.99
32	0.06	0.11	0.21	0.36	0.56	0.75	0.89	0.96	0.99
33	0.06	0.11	0.22	0.37	0.57	0.77	0.90	0.97	0.99
34	0.06	0.12	0.22	0.39	0.59	0.78	0.91	0.97	*
35	0.06	0.12	0.23	0.40	0.60	0.80	0.92	0.98	*
36	0.07	0.12	0.23	0.41	0.62	0.81	0.93	0.98	*
37	0.07	0.12	0.24	0.42	0.63	0.82	0.94	0.98	*
38	0.07	0.13	0.25	0.43	0.65	0.83	0.94	0.99	*
39	0.07	0.13	0.25	0.44	0.66	0.85	0.95	0.99	*
40	0.07	0.13	0.26	0.45	0.68	0.86	0.96	0.99	*
41	0.07	0.13	0.26	0.46	0.69	0.87	0.96	0.99	*
42	0.07	0.14	0.27	0.47	0.70	0.88	0.97	0.99	*
43	0.07	0.14	0.28	0.49	0.71	0.89	0.97	0.99	*
44	0.07	0.14	0.28	0.50	0.73	0.89	0.97	*	*
45	0.07	0.14	0.29	0.51	0.74	0.90	0.98	*	*
46	0.07	0.14	0.29	0.52	0.75	0.91	0.98	*	*
47	0.07	0.15	0.30	0.53	0.76	0.92	0.98	*	*
48	0.07	0.15	0.31	0.54	0.77	0.92	0.98	*	*
49	0.07	0.15	0.31	0.55	0.78	0.93	0.99	*	*
50	0.07	0.15	0.32	0.56	0.79	0.94	0.99	*	*
55	0.07	0.17	0.35	0.61	0.84	0.96	0.99	*	*
60	0.08	0.18	0.38	0.65	0.87	0.97	*	*	*
65	0.08	0.19	0.41	0.70	0.90	0.98	*	*	*
70	0.08	0.20	0.45	0.74	0.93	0.99	*	*	*
75	0.08	0.22	0.48	0.77	0.95	0.99	*	*	*
80	0.09	0.23	0.51	0.80	0.96	*	*	*	*
85	0.09	0.24	0.54	0.83	0.97	*	*	*	*
90	0.09	0.26	0.56	0.86	0.98	*	*	*	*
95	0.09	0.27	0.59	0.88	0.99	*	*	*	*
100	0.10	0.29	0.62	0.90	0.99	*	*	*	*
110	0.10	0.31	0.67	0.93	0.99	*	*	*	*
120	0.11	0.34	0.72	0.95	*	*	*	*	*
130	0.11	0.37	0.76	0.97	*	*	*	*	*
140	0.12	0.40	0.80	0.98	*	*	*	*	*
150	0.12	0.43	0.83	0.99	*	*	*	*	*
160	0.13	0.45	0.86	0.99	*	*	*	*	*
170	0.14	0.48	0.88	0.99	*	*	*	*	*
180	0.14	0.51	0.90	*	*	*	*	*	*
190	0.15	0.53	0.92	*	*	*	*	*	*
200	0.15	0.56	0.94	*	*	*	*	*	*
250	0.19	0.68	0.98	*	*	*	*	*	*
300	0.22	0.77	0.99	*	*	*	*	*	*
350	0.25	0.84	*	*	*	*	*	*	*
400	0.29	0.90	*	*	*	*	*	*	*
450	0.32	0.94	*	*	*	*	*	*	*
500	0.36	0.96	*	*	*	*	*	*	*
600	0.43	0.99	*	*	*	*	*	*	*
700	0.49	*	*	*	*	*	*	*	*
800	0.56	*	*	*	*	*	*	*	*
900	0.62	*	*	*	*	*	*	*	*
1000	0.68	*	*	*	*	*	*	*	*
1100	0.73	*	*	*	*	*	*	*	*
1200	0.77	*	*	*	*	*	*	*	*
1300	0.81	*	*	*	*	*	*	*	*

TABLE A18.5   Power of a χ^2 test

f   df = 6

n	\multicolumn{9}{c}{effect size (w)}
	0.1	0.2	0.3	0.4	0.5	0.6	0.7	0.8	0.9
20	0.06	0.08	0.13	0.21	0.33	0.47	0.63	0.77	0.88
21	0.06	0.09	0.14	0.22	0.35	0.50	0.66	0.80	0.90
22	0.06	0.09	0.14	0.23	0.36	0.52	0.68	0.82	0.91
23	0.06	0.09	0.15	0.24	0.38	0.54	0.71	0.84	0.93
24	0.06	0.09	0.15	0.25	0.40	0.56	0.73	0.86	0.94
25	0.06	0.09	0.16	0.26	0.41	0.58	0.75	0.88	0.95
26	0.06	0.09	0.16	0.27	0.43	0.61	0.77	0.89	0.96
27	0.06	0.10	0.17	0.29	0.45	0.63	0.79	0.90	0.97
28	0.06	0.10	0.17	0.30	0.46	0.65	0.81	0.92	0.97
29	0.06	0.10	0.18	0.31	0.48	0.66	0.82	0.93	0.98
30	0.06	0.10	0.18	0.32	0.49	0.68	0.84	0.94	0.98
31	0.06	0.10	0.19	0.33	0.51	0.70	0.85	0.95	0.99
32	0.06	0.11	0.19	0.34	0.52	0.72	0.87	0.95	0.99
33	0.06	0.11	0.20	0.35	0.54	0.73	0.88	0.96	0.99
34	0.06	0.11	0.21	0.36	0.56	0.75	0.89	0.97	0.99
35	0.06	0.11	0.21	0.37	0.57	0.76	0.90	0.97	0.99
36	0.06	0.11	0.22	0.38	0.58	0.78	0.91	0.97	*
37	0.06	0.12	0.22	0.39	0.60	0.79	0.92	0.98	*
38	0.06	0.12	0.23	0.40	0.61	0.81	0.93	0.98	*
39	0.07	0.12	0.23	0.41	0.63	0.82	0.94	0.98	*
40	0.07	0.12	0.24	0.42	0.64	0.83	0.94	0.99	*
41	0.07	0.12	0.24	0.43	0.65	0.84	0.95	0.99	*
42	0.07	0.13	0.25	0.44	0.67	0.85	0.95	0.99	*
43	0.07	0.13	0.26	0.45	0.68	0.86	0.96	0.99	*
44	0.07	0.13	0.26	0.46	0.69	0.87	0.96	0.99	*
45	0.07	0.13	0.27	0.47	0.70	0.88	0.97	0.99	*
46	0.07	0.14	0.27	0.48	0.72	0.89	0.97	*	*
47	0.07	0.14	0.28	0.49	0.73	0.90	0.97	*	*
48	0.07	0.14	0.29	0.50	0.74	0.90	0.98	*	*
49	0.07	0.14	0.29	0.51	0.75	0.91	0.98	*	*
50	0.07	0.14	0.30	0.52	0.76	0.92	0.98	*	*
55	0.07	0.16	0.33	0.57	0.81	0.95	0.99	*	*
60	0.07	0.17	0.36	0.62	0.85	0.96	*	*	*
65	0.08	0.18	0.39	0.66	0.88	0.98	*	*	*
70	0.08	0.19	0.42	0.70	0.91	0.99	*	*	*
75	0.08	0.20	0.45	0.74	0.93	0.99	*	*	*
80	0.08	0.21	0.47	0.77	0.95	0.99	*	*	*
85	0.09	0.23	0.50	0.80	0.96	*	*	*	*
90	0.09	0.24	0.53	0.83	0.97	*	*	*	*
95	0.09	0.25	0.56	0.85	0.98	*	*	*	*
100	0.09	0.26	0.58	0.88	0.98	*	*	*	*
110	0.10	0.29	0.64	0.91	0.99	*	*	*	*
120	0.10	0.32	0.68	0.94	*	*	*	*	*
130	0.11	0.34	0.73	0.96	*	*	*	*	*
140	0.11	0.37	0.76	0.97	*	*	*	*	*
150	0.12	0.40	0.80	0.98	*	*	*	*	*
160	0.12	0.42	0.83	0.99	*	*	*	*	*
170	0.13	0.45	0.86	0.99	*	*	*	*	*
180	0.13	0.47	0.88	0.99	*	*	*	*	*
190	0.14	0.50	0.90	*	*	*	*	*	*
200	0.14	0.52	0.92	*	*	*	*	*	*
250	0.17	0.64	0.97	*	*	*	*	*	*
300	0.20	0.74	0.99	*	*	*	*	*	*
350	0.23	0.82	*	*	*	*	*	*	*
400	0.26	0.88	*	*	*	*	*	*	*
450	0.30	0.92	*	*	*	*	*	*	*
500	0.33	0.95	*	*	*	*	*	*	*
600	0.40	0.98	*	*	*	*	*	*	*
700	0.46	0.99	*	*	*	*	*	*	*
800	0.52	*	*	*	*	*	*	*	*
900	0.58	*	*	*	*	*	*	*	*
1000	0.64	*	*	*	*	*	*	*	*
1100	0.69	*	*	*	*	*	*	*	*
1200	0.74	*	*	*	*	*	*	*	*
1300	0.78	*	*	*	*	*	*	*	*
1400	0.82	*	*	*	*	*	*	*	*

TABLE A18.5   Power of a χ^2 test

g   df = 7

				effect size (w)					
n	0.1	0.2	0.3	0.4	0.5	0.6	0.7	0.8	0.9
20	0.06	0.08	0.13	0.20	0.31	0.45	0.60	0.74	0.86
21	0.06	0.08	0.13	0.21	0.32	0.47	0.63	0.77	0.88
22	0.06	0.08	0.14	0.22	0.34	0.49	0.65	0.79	0.90
23	0.06	0.09	0.14	0.23	0.36	0.51	0.68	0.82	0.91
24	0.06	0.09	0.14	0.24	0.37	0.53	0.70	0.84	0.93
25	0.06	0.09	0.15	0.25	0.39	0.55	0.72	0.85	0.94
26	0.06	0.09	0.15	0.26	0.40	0.58	0.74	0.87	0.95
27	0.06	0.09	0.16	0.27	0.42	0.60	0.76	0.89	0.96
28	0.06	0.09	0.16	0.28	0.43	0.61	0.78	0.90	0.96
29	0.06	0.10	0.17	0.29	0.45	0.63	0.80	0.91	0.97
30	0.06	0.10	0.17	0.30	0.47	0.65	0.81	0.92	0.98
31	0.06	0.10	0.18	0.31	0.48	0.67	0.83	0.93	0.98
32	0.06	0.10	0.18	0.32	0.50	0.69	0.84	0.94	0.98
33	0.06	0.10	0.19	0.33	0.51	0.70	0.86	0.95	0.99
34	0.06	0.11	0.19	0.34	0.53	0.72	0.87	0.96	0.99
35	0.06	0.11	0.20	0.35	0.54	0.74	0.88	0.96	0.99
36	0.06	0.11	0.20	0.36	0.55	0.75	0.89	0.97	0.99
37	0.06	0.11	0.21	0.37	0.57	0.77	0.90	0.97	0.99
38	0.06	0.11	0.21	0.38	0.58	0.78	0.91	0.98	*
39	0.06	0.11	0.22	0.39	0.60	0.79	0.92	0.98	*
40	0.06	0.12	0.22	0.40	0.61	0.80	0.93	0.98	*
41	0.06	0.12	0.23	0.41	0.62	0.82	0.94	0.98	*
42	0.07	0.12	0.23	0.42	0.64	0.83	0.94	0.99	*
43	0.07	0.12	0.24	0.43	0.65	0.84	0.95	0.99	*
44	0.07	0.12	0.25	0.44	0.66	0.85	0.95	0.99	*
45	0.07	0.13	0.25	0.45	0.67	0.86	0.96	0.99	*
46	0.07	0.13	0.26	0.46	0.69	0.87	0.96	0.99	*
47	0.07	0.13	0.26	0.47	0.70	0.88	0.97	0.99	*
48	0.07	0.13	0.27	0.48	0.71	0.89	0.97	*	*
49	0.07	0.13	0.27	0.49	0.72	0.89	0.97	*	*
50	0.07	0.14	0.28	0.50	0.73	0.90	0.98	*	*
55	0.07	0.15	0.31	0.54	0.78	0.93	0.99	*	*
60	0.07	0.16	0.33	0.59	0.82	0.95	0.99	*	*
65	0.07	0.17	0.36	0.63	0.86	0.97	*	*	*
70	0.08	0.18	0.39	0.67	0.89	0.98	*	*	*
75	0.08	0.19	0.42	0.71	0.92	0.99	*	*	*
80	0.08	0.20	0.45	0.74	0.93	0.99	*	*	*
85	0.08	0.21	0.47	0.78	0.95	*	*	*	*
90	0.08	0.22	0.50	0.80	0.96	*	*	*	*
95	0.09	0.24	0.53	0.83	0.97	*	*	*	*
100	0.09	0.25	0.55	0.85	0.98	*	*	*	*
110	0.09	0.27	0.61	0.89	0.99	*	*	*	*
120	0.10	0.30	0.65	0.92	0.99	*	*	*	*
130	0.10	0.32	0.70	0.95	*	*	*	*	*
140	0.11	0.35	0.74	0.96	*	*	*	*	*
150	0.11	0.37	0.77	0.97	*	*	*	*	*
160	0.12	0.40	0.80	0.98	*	*	*	*	*
170	0.12	0.42	0.83	0.99	*	*	*	*	*
180	0.13	0.45	0.86	0.99	*	*	*	*	*
190	0.13	0.47	0.88	*	*	*	*	*	*
200	0.14	0.50	0.90	*	*	*	*	*	*
250	0.16	0.61	0.96	*	*	*	*	*	*
300	0.19	0.71	0.99	*	*	*	*	*	*
350	0.22	0.79	*	*	*	*	*	*	*
400	0.25	0.85	*	*	*	*	*	*	*
450	0.28	0.90	*	*	*	*	*	*	*
500	0.31	0.93	*	*	*	*	*	*	*
600	0.37	0.97	*	*	*	*	*	*	*
700	0.43	0.99	*	*	*	*	*	*	*
800	0.50	*	*	*	*	*	*	*	*
900	0.55	*	*	*	*	*	*	*	*
1000	0.61	*	*	*	*	*	*	*	*
1100	0.66	*	*	*	*	*	*	*	*
1200	0.71	*	*	*	*	*	*	*	*
1300	0.75	*	*	*	*	*	*	*	*
1400	0.79	*	*	*	*	*	*	*	*
1500	0.82	*	*	*	*	*	*	*	*

TABLE A18.5   Power of a χ^2 test

h   df = 8

					effect size (w)				
n	0.1	0.2	0.3	0.4	0.5	0.6	0.7	0.8	0.9
20	0.06	0.08	0.12	0.19	0.29	0.42	0.57	0.72	0.84
21	0.06	0.08	0.12	0.20	0.31	0.45	0.60	0.74	0.86
22	0.06	0.08	0.13	0.21	0.32	0.47	0.62	0.77	0.88
23	0.06	0.08	0.13	0.22	0.34	0.49	0.65	0.79	0.90
24	0.06	0.08	0.14	0.23	0.35	0.51	0.67	0.81	0.91
25	0.06	0.09	0.14	0.23	0.37	0.53	0.69	0.83	0.93
26	0.06	0.09	0.15	0.24	0.38	0.55	0.72	0.85	0.94
27	0.06	0.09	0.15	0.25	0.40	0.57	0.74	0.87	0.95
28	0.06	0.09	0.16	0.26	0.41	0.59	0.76	0.88	0.96
29	0.06	0.09	0.16	0.27	0.43	0.61	0.77	0.90	0.96
30	0.06	0.09	0.16	0.28	0.44	0.63	0.79	0.91	0.97
31	0.06	0.10	0.17	0.29	0.46	0.64	0.81	0.92	0.97
32	0.06	0.10	0.17	0.30	0.47	0.66	0.82	0.93	0.98
33	0.06	0.10	0.18	0.31	0.49	0.68	0.84	0.94	0.98
34	0.06	0.10	0.18	0.32	0.50	0.69	0.85	0.95	0.99
35	0.06	0.10	0.19	0.33	0.51	0.71	0.86	0.95	0.99
36	0.06	0.10	0.19	0.34	0.53	0.73	0.88	0.96	0.99
37	0.06	0.11	0.20	0.35	0.54	0.74	0.89	0.96	0.99
38	0.06	0.11	0.20	0.36	0.56	0.75	0.90	0.97	0.99
39	0.06	0.11	0.21	0.37	0.57	0.77	0.91	0.97	0.99
40	0.06	0.11	0.21	0.38	0.58	0.78	0.92	0.98	*
41	0.06	0.11	0.22	0.39	0.60	0.79	0.92	0.98	*
42	0.06	0.11	0.22	0.39	0.61	0.81	0.93	0.98	*
43	0.06	0.12	0.23	0.40	0.62	0.82	0.94	0.99	*
44	0.06	0.12	0.23	0.41	0.64	0.83	0.94	0.99	*
45	0.06	0.12	0.24	0.42	0.65	0.84	0.95	0.99	*
46	0.07	0.12	0.24	0.43	0.66	0.85	0.95	0.99	*
47	0.07	0.12	0.25	0.44	0.67	0.86	0.96	0.99	*
48	0.07	0.13	0.25	0.45	0.68	0.87	0.96	0.99	*
49	0.07	0.13	0.26	0.46	0.69	0.88	0.97	0.99	*
50	0.07	0.13	0.26	0.47	0.71	0.88	0.97	*	*
55	0.07	0.14	0.29	0.52	0.76	0.92	0.98	*	*
60	0.07	0.15	0.32	0.56	0.80	0.94	0.99	*	*
65	0.07	0.16	0.34	0.60	0.84	0.96	*	*	*
70	0.07	0.17	0.37	0.65	0.87	0.97	*	*	*
75	0.08	0.18	0.40	0.68	0.90	0.98	*	*	*
80	0.08	0.19	0.42	0.72	0.92	0.99	*	*	*
85	0.08	0.20	0.45	0.75	0.94	0.99	*	*	*
90	0.08	0.21	0.48	0.78	0.95	*	*	*	*
95	0.08	0.22	0.50	0.81	0.96	*	*	*	*
100	0.09	0.23	0.53	0.83	0.97	*	*	*	*
110	0.09	0.26	0.58	0.88	0.99	*	*	*	*
120	0.09	0.28	0.63	0.91	0.99	*	*	*	*
130	0.10	0.30	0.67	0.93	*	*	*	*	*
140	0.10	0.33	0.71	0.95	*	*	*	*	*
150	0.11	0.35	0.75	0.97	*	*	*	*	*
160	0.11	0.38	0.78	0.98	*	*	*	*	*
170	0.12	0.40	0.81	0.98	*	*	*	*	*
180	0.12	0.42	0.84	0.99	*	*	*	*	*
190	0.13	0.45	0.86	0.99	*	*	*	*	*
200	0.13	0.47	0.88	*	*	*	*	*	*
250	0.15	0.58	0.95	*	*	*	*	*	*
300	0.18	0.68	0.98	*	*	*	*	*	*
350	0.21	0.77	0.99	*	*	*	*	*	*
400	0.23	0.83	*	*	*	*	*	*	*
450	0.26	0.88	*	*	*	*	*	*	*
500	0.29	0.92	*	*	*	*	*	*	*
600	0.35	0.97	*	*	*	*	*	*	*
700	0.41	0.99	*	*	*	*	*	*	*
800	0.47	*	*	*	*	*	*	*	*
900	0.53	*	*	*	*	*	*	*	*
1000	0.58	*	*	*	*	*	*	*	*
1100	0.64	*	*	*	*	*	*	*	*
1200	0.68	*	*	*	*	*	*	*	*
1300	0.73	*	*	*	*	*	*	*	*
1400	0.77	*	*	*	*	*	*	*	*
1500	0.80	*	*	*	*	*	*	*	*

TABLE A18.5   Power of a χ^2 test

i   df = 10

				effect size (w)					
n	0.1	0.2	0.3	0.4	0.5	0.6	0.7	0.8	0.9
20	0.06	0.07	0.11	0.17	0.26	0.39	0.53	0.67	0.80
21	0.06	0.08	0.12	0.18	0.28	0.41	0.55	0.70	0.82
22	0.06	0.08	0.12	0.19	0.29	0.43	0.58	0.73	0.85
23	0.06	0.08	0.12	0.20	0.31	0.45	0.60	0.75	0.87
24	0.06	0.08	0.13	0.20	0.32	0.47	0.63	0.77	0.88
25	0.06	0.08	0.13	0.21	0.33	0.49	0.65	0.79	0.90
26	0.06	0.08	0.13	0.22	0.35	0.50	0.67	0.81	0.91
27	0.06	0.08	0.14	0.23	0.36	0.52	0.69	0.83	0.93
28	0.06	0.09	0.14	0.24	0.37	0.54	0.71	0.85	0.94
29	0.06	0.09	0.15	0.25	0.39	0.56	0.73	0.86	0.95
30	0.06	0.09	0.15	0.25	0.40	0.58	0.75	0.88	0.95
31	0.06	0.09	0.15	0.26	0.42	0.60	0.77	0.89	0.96
32	0.06	0.09	0.16	0.27	0.43	0.61	0.78	0.90	0.97
33	0.06	0.09	0.16	0.28	0.44	0.63	0.80	0.91	0.97
34	0.06	0.09	0.17	0.29	0.46	0.65	0.81	0.92	0.98
35	0.06	0.10	0.17	0.30	0.47	0.66	0.83	0.93	0.98
36	0.06	0.10	0.18	0.31	0.49	0.68	0.84	0.94	0.98
37	0.06	0.10	0.18	0.31	0.50	0.70	0.85	0.95	0.99
38	0.06	0.10	0.18	0.32	0.51	0.71	0.87	0.95	0.99
39	0.06	0.10	0.19	0.33	0.53	0.72	0.88	0.96	0.99
40	0.06	0.10	0.19	0.34	0.54	0.74	0.89	0.97	0.99
41	0.06	0.11	0.20	0.35	0.55	0.75	0.90	0.97	0.99
42	0.06	0.11	0.20	0.36	0.56	0.76	0.91	0.97	*
43	0.06	0.11	0.21	0.37	0.58	0.78	0.91	0.98	*
44	0.06	0.11	0.21	0.38	0.59	0.79	0.92	0.98	*
45	0.06	0.11	0.22	0.39	0.60	0.80	0.93	0.98	*
46	0.06	0.11	0.22	0.39	0.61	0.81	0.94	0.99	*
47	0.06	0.11	0.22	0.40	0.63	0.82	0.94	0.99	*
48	0.06	0.12	0.23	0.41	0.64	0.83	0.95	0.99	*
49	0.06	0.12	0.23	0.42	0.65	0.84	0.95	0.99	*
50	0.06	0.12	0.24	0.43	0.66	0.85	0.96	0.99	*
55	0.07	0.13	0.26	0.47	0.71	0.89	0.97	*	*
60	0.07	0.14	0.29	0.52	0.76	0.92	0.99	*	*
65	0.07	0.15	0.31	0.56	0.80	0.95	0.99	*	*
70	0.07	0.15	0.34	0.60	0.84	0.96	*	*	*
75	0.07	0.16	0.36	0.64	0.87	0.97	*	*	*
80	0.07	0.17	0.39	0.67	0.90	0.98	*	*	*
85	0.08	0.18	0.41	0.71	0.92	0.99	*	*	*
90	0.08	0.19	0.44	0.74	0.93	0.99	*	*	*
95	0.08	0.20	0.46	0.77	0.95	*	*	*	*
100	0.08	0.21	0.49	0.79	0.96	*	*	*	*
110	0.09	0.23	0.53	0.84	0.98	*	*	*	*
120	0.09	0.25	0.58	0.88	0.99	*	*	*	*
130	0.09	0.28	0.62	0.91	0.99	*	*	*	*
140	0.10	0.30	0.66	0.93	*	*	*	*	*
150	0.10	0.32	0.70	0.95	*	*	*	*	*
160	0.10	0.34	0.74	0.97	*	*	*	*	*
170	0.11	0.36	0.77	0.98	*	*	*	*	*
180	0.11	0.39	0.80	0.98	*	*	*	*	*
190	0.12	0.41	0.83	0.99	*	*	*	*	*
200	0.12	0.43	0.85	0.99	*	*	*	*	*
250	0.14	0.54	0.93	*	*	*	*	*	*
300	0.16	0.64	0.97	*	*	*	*	*	*
350	0.19	0.72	0.99	*	*	*	*	*	*
400	0.21	0.79	*	*	*	*	*	*	*
450	0.24	0.85	*	*	*	*	*	*	*
500	0.26	0.90	*	*	*	*	*	*	*
600	0.32	0.95	*	*	*	*	*	*	*
700	0.37	0.98	*	*	*	*	*	*	*
800	0.43	0.99	*	*	*	*	*	*	*
900	0.49	*	*	*	*	*	*	*	*
1000	0.54	*	*	*	*	*	*	*	*
1100	0.59	*	*	*	*	*	*	*	*
1200	0.64	*	*	*	*	*	*	*	*
1300	0.68	*	*	*	*	*	*	*	*
1400	0.72	*	*	*	*	*	*	*	*
1500	0.76	*	*	*	*	*	*	*	*
1600	0.79	*	*	*	*	*	*	*	*
1700	0.82	*	*	*	*	*	*	*	*

Table A18.6 Power tables for comparing two sample proportions

a   One-tailed tests (n is the sample in each group; when the sample sizes are unequal n is the harmonic mean)

						Effect size (h)							
n	0.1	0.2	0.3	0.4	0.5	0.6	0.7	0.8	0.9	1	1.1	1.2	1.3	1.4
10	0.08	0.12	0.17	0.23	0.30	0.38	0.47	0.56	0.64	0.72	0.79	0.85	0.90	0.93
11	0.08	0.12	0.17	0.24	0.32	0.41	0.50	0.59	0.68	0.76	0.83	0.88	0.92	0.95
12	0.08	0.12	0.18	0.25	0.34	0.43	0.53	0.62	0.71	0.79	0.85	0.90	0.94	0.96
13	0.08	0.13	0.19	0.27	0.36	0.45	0.56	0.65	0.74	0.82	0.88	0.92	0.95	0.97
14	0.08	0.13	0.20	0.28	0.37	0.48	0.58	0.68	0.77	0.84	0.90	0.94	0.96	0.98
15	0.09	0.14	0.21	0.29	0.39	0.50	0.61	0.71	0.79	0.86	0.91	0.95	0.97	0.99
16	0.09	0.14	0.21	0.30	0.41	0.52	0.63	0.73	0.82	0.88	0.93	0.96	0.98	0.99
17	0.09	0.14	0.22	0.32	0.43	0.54	0.65	0.75	0.84	0.90	0.94	0.97	0.98	0.99
18	0.09	0.15	0.23	0.33	0.44	0.56	0.68	0.77	0.85	0.91	0.95	0.97	0.99	0.99
19	0.09	0.15	0.24	0.34	0.46	0.58	0.70	0.79	0.87	0.92	0.96	0.98	0.99	*
20	0.09	0.16	0.24	0.35	0.47	0.60	0.72	0.81	0.89	0.94	0.97	0.98	0.99	*
25	0.10	0.17	0.28	0.41	0.55	0.68	0.80	0.88	0.94	0.97	0.99	*	*	*
30	0.10	0.19	0.31	0.46	0.61	0.75	0.86	0.93	0.97	0.99	*	*	*	*
35	0.11	0.21	0.35	0.51	0.67	0.81	0.90	0.96	0.98	0.99	*	*	*	*
40	0.12	0.23	0.38	0.56	0.72	0.85	0.93	0.97	0.99	*	*	*	*	*
45	0.12	0.24	0.41	0.60	0.77	0.89	0.95	0.98	*	*	*	*	*	*
50	0.13	0.26	0.44	0.64	0.80	0.91	0.97	0.99	*	*	*	*	*	*
60	0.14	0.29	0.50	0.71	0.86	0.95	0.99	*	*	*	*	*	*	*
70	0.15	0.32	0.55	0.76	0.91	0.97	0.99	*	*	*	*	*	*	*
80	0.16	0.35	0.60	0.81	0.94	0.98	*	*	*	*	*	*	*	*
90	0.17	0.38	0.64	0.85	0.96	0.99	*	*	*	*	*	*	*	*
100	0.17	0.41	0.68	0.88	0.97	*	*	*	*	*	*	*	*	*
110	0.18	0.44	0.72	0.91	0.98	*	*	*	*	*	*	*	*	*
120	0.19	0.46	0.75	0.93	0.99	*	*	*	*	*	*	*	*	*
130	0.20	0.49	0.78	0.94	0.99	*	*	*	*	*	*	*	*	*
140	0.21	0.51	0.81	0.96	0.99	*	*	*	*	*	*	*	*	*
150	0.22	0.53	0.83	0.97	*	*	*	*	*	*	*	*	*	*
160	0.23	0.56	0.85	0.97	*	*	*	*	*	*	*	*	*	*
170	0.23	0.58	0.87	0.98	*	*	*	*	*	*	*	*	*	*
180	0.24	0.60	0.89	0.98	*	*	*	*	*	*	*	*	*	*
190	0.25	0.62	0.90	0.99	*	*	*	*	*	*	*	*	*	*
200	0.26	0.64	0.91	0.99	*	*	*	*	*	*	*	*	*	*
250	0.30	0.72	0.96	*	*	*	*	*	*	*	*	*	*	*
300	0.34	0.79	0.98	*	*	*	*	*	*	*	*	*	*	*
350	0.37	0.84	0.99	*	*	*	*	*	*	*	*	*	*	*
400	0.41	0.88	*	*	*	*	*	*	*	*	*	*	*	*
450	0.44	0.91	*	*	*	*	*	*	*	*	*	*	*	*
500	0.47	0.94	*	*	*	*	*	*	*	*	*	*	*	*
550	0.51	0.95	*	*	*	*	*	*	*	*	*	*	*	*
600	0.53	0.97	*	*	*	*	*	*	*	*	*	*	*	*
650	0.56	0.98	*	*	*	*	*	*	*	*	*	*	*	*
700	0.59	0.98	*	*	*	*	*	*	*	*	*	*	*	*
750	0.61	0.99	*	*	*	*	*	*	*	*	*	*	*	*
800	0.64	0.99	*	*	*	*	*	*	*	*	*	*	*	*
850	0.66	0.99	*	*	*	*	*	*	*	*	*	*	*	*
900	0.68	*	*	*	*	*	*	*	*	*	*	*	*	*
950	0.70	*	*	*	*	*	*	*	*	*	*	*	*	*
1000	0.72	*	*	*	*	*	*	*	*	*	*	*	*	*
1100	0.76	*	*	*	*	*	*	*	*	*	*	*	*	*
1200	0.79	*	*	*	*	*	*	*	*	*	*	*	*	*
1300	0.82	*	*	*	*	*	*	*	*	*	*	*	*	*

TABLE A18.6 Power tables for comparing two sample proportions

b Two-tailed tests (n is the sample in each group; when the sample sizes are unequal n is the harmonic mean)

	Effect size (h)													
n	0.1	0.2	0.3	0.4	0.5	0.6	0.7	0.8	0.9	1	1.1	1.2	1.3	1.4
10	0.04	0.07	0.10	0.14	0.20	0.27	0.35	0.43	0.52	0.61	0.69	0.77	0.83	0.88
11	0.04	0.07	0.10	0.15	0.22	0.29	0.38	0.47	0.56	0.65	0.73	0.80	0.86	0.91
12	0.04	0.07	0.11	0.16	0.23	0.31	0.40	0.50	0.60	0.69	0.77	0.84	0.89	0.93
13	0.04	0.07	0.12	0.17	0.25	0.33	0.43	0.53	0.63	0.72	0.80	0.86	0.91	0.95
14	0.05	0.08	0.12	0.18	0.26	0.35	0.46	0.56	0.66	0.75	0.83	0.89	0.93	0.96
15	0.05	0.08	0.13	0.19	0.28	0.38	0.48	0.59	0.69	0.78	0.85	0.91	0.95	0.97
16	0.05	0.08	0.13	0.20	0.29	0.40	0.51	0.62	0.72	0.81	0.88	0.92	0.96	0.98
17	0.05	0.08	0.14	0.21	0.31	0.42	0.53	0.65	0.75	0.83	0.89	0.94	0.97	0.98
18	0.05	0.09	0.14	0.22	0.32	0.44	0.56	0.67	0.77	0.85	0.91	0.95	0.97	0.99
19	0.05	0.09	0.15	0.23	0.34	0.46	0.58	0.69	0.79	0.87	0.92	0.96	0.98	0.99
20	0.05	0.09	0.16	0.24	0.35	0.48	0.60	0.72	0.81	0.89	0.94	0.97	0.98	0.99
25	0.05	0.11	0.18	0.29	0.42	0.56	0.70	0.81	0.89	0.94	0.97	0.99	*	*
30	0.06	0.12	0.21	0.34	0.49	0.64	0.77	0.87	0.94	0.97	0.99	*	*	*
35	0.06	0.13	0.24	0.39	0.55	0.71	0.83	0.92	0.96	0.99	*	*	*	*
40	0.07	0.14	0.27	0.43	0.61	0.77	0.88	0.95	0.98	0.99	*	*	*	*
45	0.07	0.16	0.30	0.48	0.66	0.81	0.91	0.97	0.99	*	*	*	*	*
50	0.07	0.17	0.32	0.52	0.71	0.85	0.94	0.98	0.99	*	*	*	*	*
60	0.08	0.19	0.38	0.59	0.78	0.91	0.97	0.99	*	*	*	*	*	*
70	0.09	0.22	0.43	0.66	0.84	0.94	0.99	*	*	*	*	*	*	*
80	0.09	0.24	0.48	0.72	0.89	0.97	0.99	*	*	*	*	*	*	*
90	0.10	0.27	0.52	0.77	0.92	0.98	*	*	*	*	*	*	*	*
100	0.11	0.29	0.56	0.81	0.94	0.99	*	*	*	*	*	*	*	*
110	0.11	0.32	0.60	0.84	0.96	0.99	*	*	*	*	*	*	*	*
120	0.12	0.34	0.64	0.87	0.97	*	*	*	*	*	*	*	*	*
130	0.12	0.36	0.68	0.90	0.98	*	*	*	*	*	*	*	*	*
140	0.13	0.39	0.71	0.92	0.99	*	*	*	*	*	*	*	*	*
150	0.14	0.41	0.74	0.93	0.99	*	*	*	*	*	*	*	*	*
160	0.14	0.43	0.77	0.95	0.99	*	*	*	*	*	*	*	*	*
170	0.15	0.45	0.79	0.96	*	*	*	*	*	*	*	*	*	*
180	0.16	0.48	0.81	0.97	*	*	*	*	*	*	*	*	*	*
190	0.16	0.50	0.83	0.97	*	*	*	*	*	*	*	*	*	*
200	0.17	0.52	0.85	0.98	*	*	*	*	*	*	*	*	*	*
250	0.20	0.61	0.92	0.99	*	*	*	*	*	*	*	*	*	*
300	0.23	0.69	0.96	*	*	*	*	*	*	*	*	*	*	*
350	0.26	0.75	0.98	*	*	*	*	*	*	*	*	*	*	*
400	0.29	0.81	0.99	*	*	*	*	*	*	*	*	*	*	*
450	0.32	0.85	0.99	*	*	*	*	*	*	*	*	*	*	*
500	0.35	0.89	*	*	*	*	*	*	*	*	*	*	*	*
550	0.38	0.91	*	*	*	*	*	*	*	*	*	*	*	*
600	0.41	0.93	*	*	*	*	*	*	*	*	*	*	*	*
650	0.44	0.95	*	*	*	*	*	*	*	*	*	*	*	*
700	0.46	0.96	*	*	*	*	*	*	*	*	*	*	*	*
750	0.49	0.97	*	*	*	*	*	*	*	*	*	*	*	*
800	0.52	0.98	*	*	*	*	*	*	*	*	*	*	*	*
850	0.54	0.98	*	*	*	*	*	*	*	*	*	*	*	*
900	0.56	0.99	*	*	*	*	*	*	*	*	*	*	*	*
950	0.59	0.99	*	*	*	*	*	*	*	*	*	*	*	*
1000	0.61	0.99	*	*	*	*	*	*	*	*	*	*	*	*
1100	0.65	*	*	*	*	*	*	*	*	*	*	*	*	*
1200	0.69	*	*	*	*	*	*	*	*	*	*	*	*	*
1300	0.72	*	*	*	*	*	*	*	*	*	*	*	*	*
1400	0.75	*	*	*	*	*	*	*	*	*	*	*	*	*
1500	0.78	*	*	*	*	*	*	*	*	*	*	*	*	*
1600	0.81	*	*	*	*	*	*	*	*	*	*	*	*	*

Table A18.7 Power of an *F*-ratio in analysis of variance

a   Treatment df = 1 (*n* is the number of people in each condition for a between-subjects design)

effect size (η^2)

n	0.01	0.05	0.059	0.10	0.138	0.15	0.20	0.25	0.30	0.35
3	0.06	0.08	0.08	0.11	0.13	0.13	0.17	0.20	0.24	0.29
4	0.06	0.09	0.09	0.13	0.16	0.17	0.23	0.28	0.35	0.42
5	0.06	0.10	0.11	0.15	0.20	0.22	0.29	0.37	0.45	0.54
6	0.06	0.11	0.12	0.18	0.24	0.26	0.35	0.45	0.54	0.64
7	0.06	0.12	0.14	0.21	0.28	0.31	0.41	0.52	0.62	0.72
8	0.06	0.13	0.15	0.24	0.32	0.35	0.47	0.58	0.69	0.79
9	0.06	0.15	0.17	0.27	0.36	0.39	0.52	0.64	0.75	0.84
10	0.06	0.16	0.18	0.30	0.40	0.44	0.57	0.69	0.80	0.88
11	0.07	0.17	0.20	0.32	0.44	0.47	0.62	0.74	0.84	0.91
12	0.07	0.19	0.22	0.35	0.47	0.51	0.66	0.78	0.87	0.93
13	0.07	0.20	0.23	0.38	0.51	0.55	0.70	0.81	0.90	0.95
14	0.07	0.21	0.25	0.40	0.54	0.58	0.73	0.84	0.92	0.96
15	0.07	0.23	0.26	0.43	0.57	0.61	0.76	0.87	0.94	0.97
16	0.08	0.24	0.28	0.46	0.60	0.64	0.79	0.89	0.95	0.98
17	0.08	0.26	0.30	0.48	0.63	0.67	0.82	0.91	0.96	0.99
18	0.08	0.27	0.31	0.50	0.66	0.70	0.84	0.92	0.97	0.99
19	0.08	0.28	0.33	0.53	0.68	0.72	0.86	0.94	0.98	0.99
20	0.09	0.30	0.34	0.55	0.70	0.75	0.88	0.95	0.98	*
25	0.10	0.36	0.42	0.65	0.80	0.84	0.94	0.98	*	*
30	0.11	0.42	0.49	0.73	0.87	0.90	0.97	0.99	*	*
35	0.12	0.48	0.55	0.79	0.92	0.94	0.99	*	*	*
40	0.14	0.54	0.61	0.85	0.95	0.96	0.99	*	*	*
45	0.15	0.59	0.66	0.89	0.97	0.98	*	*	*	*
50	0.16	0.63	0.71	0.92	0.98	0.99	*	*	*	*
60	0.19	0.71	0.79	0.96	0.99	*	*	*	*	*
70	0.22	0.78	0.85	0.98	*	*	*	*	*	*
80	0.24	0.83	0.89	0.99	*	*	*	*	*	*
90	0.27	0.87	0.92	0.99	*	*	*	*	*	*
100	0.30	0.90	0.95	*	*	*	*	*	*	*
120	0.35	0.95	0.97	*	*	*	*	*	*	*
140	0.40	0.97	0.99	*	*	*	*	*	*	*
160	0.44	0.98	0.99	*	*	*	*	*	*	*
180	0.49	0.99	*	*	*	*	*	*	*	*
200	0.53	*	*	*	*	*	*	*	*	*
300	0.70	*	*	*	*	*	*	*	*	*
400	0.82	*	*	*	*	*	*	*	*	*
500	0.89	*	*	*	*	*	*	*	*	*
600	0.94	*	*	*	*	*	*	*	*	*
700	0.97	*	*	*	*	*	*	*	*	*
800	0.98	*	*	*	*	*	*	*	*	*
900	0.99	*	*	*	*	*	*	*	*	*
1000	0.99	*	*	*	*	*	*	*	*	*

TABLE A18.7   Power of an *F*-ratio in analysis of variance

b   Treatment df = 2 (*n* is the number of people in each condition for a between-subjects design)

effect size (η^2)

n	0.01	0.05	0.059	0.10	0.138	0.15	0.20	0.25	0.30	0.35
3	0.06	0.08	0.08	0.11	0.13	0.14	0.17	0.21	0.26	0.32
4	0.06	0.09	0.09	0.13	0.17	0.18	0.24	0.31	0.39	0.47
5	0.06	0.10	0.11	0.16	0.22	0.23	0.32	0.41	0.51	0.61
6	0.06	0.11	0.13	0.19	0.26	0.29	0.39	0.50	0.61	0.72
7	0.06	0.13	0.14	0.23	0.31	0.34	0.46	0.58	0.70	0.80
8	0.06	0.14	0.16	0.26	0.36	0.39	0.53	0.66	0.77	0.86
9	0.06	0.16	0.18	0.29	0.40	0.44	0.59	0.72	0.83	0.91
10	0.07	0.17	0.20	0.32	0.45	0.49	0.64	0.77	0.87	0.94
11	0.07	0.19	0.22	0.36	0.49	0.53	0.69	0.82	0.91	0.96
12	0.07	0.20	0.23	0.39	0.53	0.58	0.74	0.85	0.93	0.97
13	0.07	0.22	0.25	0.42	0.57	0.62	0.77	0.89	0.95	0.98
14	0.08	0.23	0.27	0.45	0.61	0.65	0.81	0.91	0.96	0.99
15	0.08	0.25	0.29	0.48	0.64	0.69	0.84	0.93	0.97	0.99
16	0.08	0.26	0.31	0.51	0.68	0.72	0.86	0.95	0.98	*
17	0.08	0.28	0.33	0.54	0.71	0.75	0.89	0.96	0.99	*
18	0.09	0.30	0.35	0.57	0.73	0.78	0.90	0.97	0.99	*
19	0.09	0.31	0.36	0.59	0.76	0.80	0.92	0.98	0.99	*
20	0.09	0.33	0.38	0.62	0.78	0.82	0.93	0.98	*	*
25	0.10	0.40	0.47	0.72	0.87	0.90	0.98	*	*	*
30	0.12	0.48	0.55	0.81	0.93	0.95	0.99	*	*	*
35	0.13	0.54	0.62	0.87	0.96	0.98	*	*	*	*
40	0.15	0.60	0.69	0.91	0.98	0.99	*	*	*	*
45	0.16	0.66	0.74	0.94	0.99	0.99	*	*	*	*
50	0.18	0.71	0.79	0.96	0.99	*	*	*	*	*
60	0.21	0.79	0.86	0.98	*	*	*	*	*	*
70	0.24	0.85	0.91	0.99	*	*	*	*	*	*
80	0.27	0.90	0.94	*	*	*	*	*	*	*
90	0.30	0.93	0.97	*	*	*	*	*	*	*
100	0.33	0.95	0.98	*	*	*	*	*	*	*
120	0.39	0.98	0.99	*	*	*	*	*	*	*
140	0.44	0.99	*	*	*	*	*	*	*	*
160	0.50	*	*	*	*	*	*	*	*	*
180	0.55	*	*	*	*	*	*	*	*	*
200	0.60	*	*	*	*	*	*	*	*	*
300	0.78	*	*	*	*	*	*	*	*	*
400	0.89	*	*	*	*	*	*	*	*	*
500	0.95	*	*	*	*	*	*	*	*	*
600	0.98	*	*	*	*	*	*	*	*	*
700	0.99	*	*	*	*	*	*	*	*	*
800	*	*	*	*	*	*	*	*	*	*

TABLE A18.7   Power of an *F*-ratio in analysis of variance

c   Treatment df = 3 (*n* is the number of people in each condition for a between-subjects design)

effect size (η^2)

n	0.01	0.05	0.059	0.10	0.138	0.15	0.20	0.25	0.30	0.35
3	0.06	0.08	0.08	0.11	0.14	0.15	0.19	0.24	0.30	0.36
4	0.06	0.09	0.10	0.14	0.18	0.20	0.27	0.35	0.44	0.54
5	0.06	0.10	0.12	0.17	0.24	0.26	0.36	0.46	0.57	0.68
6	0.06	0.12	0.13	0.21	0.29	0.32	0.44	0.57	0.69	0.79
7	0.06	0.13	0.15	0.25	0.35	0.38	0.52	0.65	0.77	0.87
8	0.06	0.15	0.17	0.29	0.40	0.44	0.59	0.73	0.84	0.92
9	0.07	0.17	0.19	0.33	0.46	0.50	0.66	0.79	0.89	0.95
10	0.07	0.19	0.22	0.36	0.51	0.55	0.71	0.84	0.93	0.97
11	0.07	0.20	0.24	0.40	0.55	0.60	0.76	0.88	0.95	0.98
12	0.07	0.22	0.26	0.44	0.60	0.65	0.81	0.91	0.97	0.99
13	0.08	0.24	0.28	0.47	0.64	0.69	0.84	0.93	0.98	0.99
14	0.08	0.26	0.30	0.51	0.68	0.73	0.87	0.95	0.99	*
15	0.08	0.27	0.32	0.54	0.71	0.76	0.90	0.97	0.99	*
16	0.08	0.29	0.34	0.57	0.75	0.79	0.92	0.98	0.99	*
17	0.09	0.31	0.37	0.60	0.78	0.82	0.94	0.98	*	*
18	0.09	0.33	0.39	0.63	0.80	0.84	0.95	0.99	*	*
19	0.09	0.35	0.41	0.66	0.83	0.87	0.96	0.99	*	*
20	0.10	0.37	0.43	0.69	0.85	0.88	0.97	0.99	*	*
25	0.11	0.45	0.53	0.80	0.93	0.95	0.99	*	*	*
30	0.13	0.53	0.62	0.87	0.97	0.98	*	*	*	*
35	0.14	0.61	0.69	0.92	0.98	0.99	*	*	*	*
40	0.16	0.67	0.76	0.95	0.99	*	*	*	*	*
45	0.18	0.73	0.81	0.97	*	*	*	*	*	*
50	0.19	0.78	0.85	0.98	*	*	*	*	*	*
60	0.23	0.86	0.92	*	*	*	*	*	*	*
70	0.26	0.91	0.95	*	*	*	*	*	*	*
80	0.30	0.94	0.97	*	*	*	*	*	*	*
90	0.33	0.97	0.99	*	*	*	*	*	*	*
100	0.37	0.98	0.99	*	*	*	*	*	*	*
120	0.43	0.99	*	*	*	*	*	*	*	*
140	0.50	*	*	*	*	*	*	*	*	*
160	0.56	*	*	*	*	*	*	*	*	*
180	0.61	*	*	*	*	*	*	*	*	*
200	0.66	*	*	*	*	*	*	*	*	*
300	0.85	*	*	*	*	*	*	*	*	*
400	0.94	*	*	*	*	*	*	*	*	*
500	0.98	*	*	*	*	*	*	*	*	*
600	0.99	*	*	*	*	*	*	*	*	*
700	*	*	*	*	*	*	*	*	*	*

TABLE A18.7   Power of an *F*-ratio in analysis of variance

d   Treatment df = 4 (*n* is the number of people in each condition for a between-subjects design)

effect size (η^2)

n	0.01	0.05	0.059	0.10	0.138	0.15	0.20	0.25	0.30	0.35
3	0.06	0.08	0.09	0.11	0.14	0.16	0.20	0.26	0.33	0.41
4	0.06	0.09	0.10	0.15	0.20	0.22	0.30	0.39	0.50	0.60
5	0.06	0.11	0.12	0.19	0.26	0.29	0.40	0.52	0.64	0.75
6	0.06	0.13	0.14	0.23	0.32	0.36	0.49	0.63	0.75	0.85
7	0.06	0.14	0.16	0.27	0.39	0.42	0.58	0.72	0.83	0.91
8	0.07	0.16	0.19	0.32	0.45	0.49	0.65	0.79	0.89	0.95
9	0.07	0.18	0.21	0.36	0.51	0.55	0.72	0.85	0.93	0.97
10	0.07	0.20	0.23	0.40	0.56	0.61	0.78	0.89	0.96	0.99
11	0.07	0.22	0.26	0.45	0.61	0.66	0.82	0.92	0.97	0.99
12	0.08	0.24	0.28	0.49	0.66	0.71	0.86	0.95	0.98	*
13	0.08	0.26	0.31	0.53	0.70	0.75	0.89	0.96	0.99	*
14	0.08	0.28	0.33	0.56	0.74	0.79	0.92	0.98	0.99	*
15	0.08	0.30	0.36	0.60	0.78	0.82	0.94	0.98	*	*
16	0.09	0.32	0.38	0.63	0.81	0.85	0.95	0.99	*	*
17	0.09	0.34	0.41	0.66	0.83	0.87	0.96	0.99	*	*
18	0.09	0.36	0.43	0.69	0.86	0.89	0.97	*	*	*
19	0.10	0.38	0.45	0.72	0.88	0.91	0.98	*	*	*
20	0.10	0.40	0.48	0.75	0.90	0.93	0.99	*	*	*
25	0.12	0.50	0.58	0.85	0.96	0.97	*	*	*	*
30	0.13	0.59	0.68	0.92	0.98	0.99	*	*	*	*
35	0.15	0.67	0.75	0.95	0.99	*	*	*	*	*
40	0.17	0.73	0.81	0.98	*	*	*	*	*	*
45	0.19	0.79	0.86	0.99	*	*	*	*	*	*
50	0.21	0.84	0.90	0.99	*	*	*	*	*	*
60	0.25	0.90	0.95	*	*	*	*	*	*	*
70	0.29	0.95	0.98	*	*	*	*	*	*	*
80	0.33	0.97	0.99	*	*	*	*	*	*	*
90	0.37	0.98	0.99	*	*	*	*	*	*	*
100	0.40	0.99	*	*	*	*	*	*	*	*
120	0.48	*	*	*	*	*	*	*	*	*
140	0.55	*	*	*	*	*	*	*	*	*
160	0.61	*	*	*	*	*	*	*	*	*
180	0.67	*	*	*	*	*	*	*	*	*
200	0.72	*	*	*	*	*	*	*	*	*
300	0.90	*	*	*	*	*	*	*	*	*
400	0.97	*	*	*	*	*	*	*	*	*
500	0.99	*	*	*	*	*	*	*	*	*
600	*	*	*	*	*	*	*	*	*	*

TABLE A18.7   Power of an *F*-ratio in analysis of variance

e   Treatment df = 5 (*n* is the number of people in each condition for a between-subjects design)

effect size (η^2)

n	0.01	0.05	0.059	0.10	0.138	0.15	0.20	0.25	0.30	0.35
3	0.06	0.08	0.09	0.12	0.15	0.17	0.22	0.29	0.37	0.46
4	0.06	0.10	0.11	0.16	0.22	0.24	0.33	0.43	0.55	0.66
5	0.06	0.11	0.13	0.20	0.29	0.31	0.44	0.57	0.69	0.80
6	0.06	0.13	0.15	0.25	0.36	0.39	0.54	0.68	0.80	0.89
7	0.06	0.15	0.18	0.30	0.42	0.46	0.63	0.77	0.88	0.95
8	0.07	0.17	0.20	0.35	0.49	0.54	0.71	0.84	0.93	0.97
9	0.07	0.19	0.23	0.39	0.55	0.60	0.77	0.89	0.96	0.99
10	0.07	0.22	0.25	0.44	0.61	0.66	0.83	0.93	0.98	0.99
11	0.08	0.24	0.28	0.49	0.66	0.71	0.87	0.95	0.99	*
12	0.08	0.26	0.31	0.53	0.71	0.76	0.90	0.97	0.99	*
13	0.08	0.28	0.34	0.57	0.75	0.80	0.93	0.98	*	*
14	0.08	0.31	0.36	0.61	0.79	0.84	0.95	0.99	*	*
15	0.09	0.33	0.39	0.65	0.83	0.86	0.96	0.99	*	*
16	0.09	0.35	0.42	0.68	0.85	0.89	0.97	*	*	*
17	0.09	0.37	0.44	0.72	0.88	0.91	0.98	*	*	*
18	0.10	0.40	0.47	0.75	0.90	0.93	0.99	*	*	*
19	0.10	0.42	0.49	0.77	0.92	0.94	0.99	*	*	*
20	0.10	0.44	0.52	0.80	0.93	0.95	0.99	*	*	*
25	0.12	0.55	0.63	0.89	0.98	0.99	*	*	*	*
30	0.14	0.64	0.73	0.95	0.99	*	*	*	*	*
35	0.16	0.72	0.80	0.97	*	*	*	*	*	*
40	0.18	0.79	0.86	0.99	*	*	*	*	*	*
45	0.20	0.84	0.90	0.99	*	*	*	*	*	*
50	0.22	0.88	0.93	*	*	*	*	*	*	*
60	0.27	0.94	0.97	*	*	*	*	*	*	*
70	0.31	0.97	0.99	*	*	*	*	*	*	*
80	0.36	0.98	*	*	*	*	*	*	*	*
90	0.40	0.99	*	*	*	*	*	*	*	*
100	0.44	*	*	*	*	*	*	*	*	*
120	0.52	*	*	*	*	*	*	*	*	*
140	0.60	*	*	*	*	*	*	*	*	*
160	0.67	*	*	*	*	*	*	*	*	*
180	0.72	*	*	*	*	*	*	*	*	*
200	0.78	*	*	*	*	*	*	*	*	*
300	0.93	*	*	*	*	*	*	*	*	*
400	0.98	*	*	*	*	*	*	*	*	*
500	*	*	*	*	*	*	*	*	*	*

TABLE A18.7   Power of an F-ratio in analysis of variance

f   Treatment df = 6 (n is the number of people in each condition for a between-subjects design)

effect size (η^2)

n	0.01	0.05	0.059	0.10	0.138	0.15	0.20	0.25	0.30	0.35
3	0.06	0.08	0.09	0.13	0.16	0.18	0.24	0.32	0.40	0.50
4	0.06	0.10	0.11	0.17	0.23	0.26	0.36	0.47	0.59	0.71
5	0.06	0.12	0.13	0.22	0.31	0.34	0.48	0.62	0.74	0.85
6	0.06	0.14	0.16	0.27	0.39	0.42	0.58	0.73	0.85	0.93
7	0.06	0.16	0.19	0.32	0.46	0.50	0.68	0.82	0.91	0.97
8	0.07	0.18	0.21	0.37	0.53	0.58	0.76	0.88	0.95	0.99
9	0.07	0.21	0.24	0.43	0.60	0.65	0.82	0.92	0.98	0.99
10	0.07	0.23	0.27	0.48	0.66	0.71	0.87	0.95	0.99	*
11	0.08	0.26	0.30	0.53	0.71	0.76	0.90	0.97	0.99	*
12	0.08	0.28	0.33	0.57	0.76	0.80	0.93	0.98	*	*
13	0.08	0.31	0.36	0.62	0.80	0.84	0.95	0.99	*	*
14	0.09	0.33	0.39	0.66	0.83	0.87	0.97	0.99	*	*
15	0.09	0.36	0.42	0.70	0.86	0.90	0.98	*	*	*
16	0.09	0.38	0.45	0.73	0.89	0.92	0.98	*	*	*
17	0.10	0.41	0.48	0.76	0.91	0.94	0.99	*	*	*
18	0.10	0.43	0.51	0.79	0.93	0.95	0.99	*	*	*
19	0.11	0.45	0.53	0.82	0.94	0.96	*	*	*	*
20	0.11	0.48	0.56	0.84	0.95	0.97	*	*	*	*
25	0.13	0.59	0.68	0.92	0.99	0.99	*	*	*	*
30	0.15	0.69	0.77	0.97	*	*	*	*	*	*
35	0.17	0.76	0.84	0.99	*	*	*	*	*	*
40	0.19	0.83	0.90	0.99	*	*	*	*	*	*
45	0.22	0.88	0.93	*	*	*	*	*	*	*
50	0.24	0.91	0.96	*	*	*	*	*	*	*
60	0.29	0.96	0.98	*	*	*	*	*	*	*
70	0.34	0.98	0.99	*	*	*	*	*	*	*
80	0.38	0.99	*	*	*	*	*	*	*	*
90	0.43	*	*	*	*	*	*	*	*	*
100	0.48	*	*	*	*	*	*	*	*	*
120	0.56	*	*	*	*	*	*	*	*	*
140	0.64	*	*	*	*	*	*	*	*	*
160	0.71	*	*	*	*	*	*	*	*	*
180	0.77	*	*	*	*	*	*	*	*	*
200	0.82	*	*	*	*	*	*	*	*	*
300	0.95	*	*	*	*	*	*	*	*	*
400	0.99	*	*	*	*	*	*	*	*	*
500	*	*	*	*	*	*	*	*	*	*

TABLE A18.7 Power of an *F*-ratio in analysis of variance

g   Treatment df = 7 (*n* is the number of people in each condition for a between-subjects design)

effect size (η^2)

n	0.01	0.05	0.059	0.10	0.138	0.15	0.20	0.25	0.30	0.35
3	0.06	0.09	0.09	0.13	0.17	0.19	0.26	0.34	0.44	0.54
4	0.06	0.10	0.12	0.18	0.25	0.27	0.39	0.51	0.64	0.76
5	0.06	0.12	0.14	0.23	0.33	0.37	0.51	0.66	0.79	0.88
6	0.06	0.15	0.17	0.29	0.41	0.46	0.63	0.77	0.88	0.95
7	0.07	0.17	0.20	0.35	0.49	0.54	0.72	0.85	0.94	0.98
8	0.07	0.19	0.23	0.40	0.57	0.62	0.80	0.91	0.97	0.99
9	0.07	0.22	0.26	0.46	0.64	0.69	0.85	0.95	0.99	*
10	0.08	0.25	0.29	0.51	0.70	0.75	0.90	0.97	0.99	*
11	0.08	0.27	0.32	0.56	0.75	0.80	0.93	0.98	*	*
12	0.08	0.30	0.36	0.61	0.80	0.84	0.95	0.99	*	*
13	0.09	0.33	0.39	0.66	0.84	0.88	0.97	0.99	*	*
14	0.09	0.35	0.42	0.70	0.87	0.90	0.98	*	*	*
15	0.09	0.38	0.45	0.74	0.90	0.93	0.99	*	*	*
16	0.10	0.41	0.48	0.77	0.92	0.94	0.99	*	*	*
17	0.10	0.43	0.51	0.80	0.94	0.96	0.99	*	*	*
18	0.11	0.46	0.54	0.83	0.95	0.97	*	*	*	*
19	0.11	0.49	0.57	0.85	0.96	0.98	*	*	*	*
20	0.11	0.51	0.60	0.87	0.97	0.98	*	*	*	*
25	0.13	0.63	0.72	0.95	0.99	*	*	*	*	*
30	0.16	0.73	0.81	0.98	*	*	*	*	*	*
35	0.18	0.80	0.88	0.99	*	*	*	*	*	*
40	0.20	0.86	0.92	*	*	*	*	*	*	*
45	0.23	0.91	0.95	*	*	*	*	*	*	*
50	0.26	0.94	0.97	*	*	*	*	*	*	*
60	0.31	0.97	0.99	*	*	*	*	*	*	*
70	0.36	0.99	*	*	*	*	*	*	*	*
80	0.41	*	*	*	*	*	*	*	*	*
90	0.46	*	*	*	*	*	*	*	*	*
100	0.51	*	*	*	*	*	*	*	*	*
120	0.60	*	*	*	*	*	*	*	*	*
140	0.68	*	*	*	*	*	*	*	*	*
160	0.75	*	*	*	*	*	*	*	*	*
180	0.81	*	*	*	*	*	*	*	*	*
200	0.85	*	*	*	*	*	*	*	*	*
300	0.97	*	*	*	*	*	*	*	*	*
400	0.99	*	*	*	*	*	*	*	*	*
500	*	*	*	*	*	*	*	*	*	*

TABLE A18.7   Power of an *F*-ratio in analysis of variance

h   Treatment df = 8 (*n* is the number of people in each condition for a between-subjects design)

effect size (η^2)

n	0.01	0.05	0.059	0.10	0.138	0.15	0.20	0.25	0.30	0.35
3	0.06	0.09	0.10	0.14	0.18	0.20	0.28	0.37	0.47	0.58
4	0.06	0.11	0.12	0.19	0.27	0.29	0.42	0.55	0.68	0.79
5	0.06	0.13	0.15	0.25	0.35	0.39	0.55	0.70	0.82	0.91
6	0.06	0.15	0.18	0.31	0.44	0.49	0.66	0.81	0.91	0.97
7	0.07	0.18	0.21	0.37	0.53	0.58	0.76	0.88	0.96	0.99
8	0.07	0.20	0.24	0.43	0.60	0.66	0.83	0.93	0.98	*
9	0.07	0.23	0.28	0.49	0.67	0.73	0.88	0.96	0.99	*
10	0.08	0.26	0.31	0.55	0.74	0.78	0.92	0.98	*	*
11	0.08	0.29	0.34	0.60	0.79	0.83	0.95	0.99	*	*
12	0.08	0.32	0.38	0.65	0.83	0.87	0.97	0.99	*	*
13	0.09	0.35	0.41	0.69	0.87	0.90	0.98	*	*	*
14	0.09	0.38	0.45	0.74	0.90	0.93	0.99	*	*	*
15	0.10	0.41	0.48	0.77	0.92	0.95	0.99	*	*	*
16	0.10	0.43	0.51	0.81	0.94	0.96	*	*	*	*
17	0.10	0.46	0.55	0.83	0.95	0.97	*	*	*	*
18	0.11	0.49	0.58	0.86	0.97	0.98	*	*	*	*
19	0.11	0.52	0.61	0.88	0.97	0.99	*	*	*	*
20	0.12	0.54	0.63	0.90	0.98	0.99	*	*	*	*
25	0.14	0.66	0.75	0.96	*	*	*	*	*	*
30	0.16	0.76	0.84	0.99	*	*	*	*	*	*
35	0.19	0.84	0.90	*	*	*	*	*	*	*
40	0.22	0.89	0.94	*	*	*	*	*	*	*
45	0.24	0.93	0.97	*	*	*	*	*	*	*
50	0.27	0.95	0.98	*	*	*	*	*	*	*
60	0.33	0.98	0.99	*	*	*	*	*	*	*
70	0.38	0.99	*	*	*	*	*	*	*	*
80	0.44	*	*	*	*	*	*	*	*	*
90	0.49	*	*	*	*	*	*	*	*	*
100	0.54	*	*	*	*	*	*	*	*	*
120	0.64	*	*	*	*	*	*	*	*	*
140	0.72	*	*	*	*	*	*	*	*	*
160	0.78	*	*	*	*	*	*	*	*	*
180	0.84	*	*	*	*	*	*	*	*	*
200	0.88	*	*	*	*	*	*	*	*	*
300	0.98	*	*	*	*	*	*	*	*	*
400	*	*	*	*	*	*	*	*	*	*

TABLE A18.7   Power of an *F*-ratio in analysis of variance

i   Treatment df = 10 (*n* is the number of people in each condition for a between-subjects design)

effect size (η^2)

n	0.01	0.05	0.059	0.10	0.138	0.15	0.20	0.25	0.30	0.35
3	0.06	0.09	0.10	0.15	0.20	0.22	0.31	0.42	0.53	0.65
4	0.06	0.11	0.13	0.21	0.30	0.33	0.47	0.61	0.75	0.86
5	0.06	0.14	0.16	0.27	0.40	0.44	0.61	0.76	0.88	0.95
6	0.07	0.17	0.19	0.34	0.50	0.54	0.73	0.87	0.95	0.98
7	0.07	0.19	0.23	0.41	0.59	0.64	0.82	0.93	0.98	*
8	0.07	0.22	0.27	0.48	0.67	0.72	0.88	0.96	0.99	*
9	0.08	0.26	0.31	0.55	0.74	0.79	0.93	0.98	*	*
10	0.08	0.29	0.35	0.61	0.80	0.84	0.96	0.99	*	*
11	0.08	0.32	0.39	0.66	0.85	0.88	0.97	*	*	*
12	0.09	0.35	0.42	0.71	0.88	0.92	0.98	*	*	*
13	0.09	0.39	0.46	0.76	0.91	0.94	0.99	*	*	*
14	0.10	0.42	0.50	0.80	0.94	0.96	*	*	*	*
15	0.10	0.45	0.54	0.83	0.95	0.97	*	*	*	*
16	0.11	0.48	0.57	0.86	0.97	0.98	*	*	*	*
17	0.11	0.52	0.61	0.89	0.98	0.99	*	*	*	*
18	0.12	0.55	0.64	0.91	0.98	0.99	*	*	*	*
19	0.12	0.57	0.67	0.92	0.99	0.99	*	*	*	*
20	0.13	0.60	0.70	0.94	0.99	*	*	*	*	*
25	0.15	0.73	0.81	0.98	*	*	*	*	*	*
30	0.18	0.82	0.89	0.99	*	*	*	*	*	*
35	0.21	0.89	0.94	*	*	*	*	*	*	*
40	0.24	0.93	0.97	*	*	*	*	*	*	*
45	0.27	0.96	0.98	*	*	*	*	*	*	*
50	0.30	0.98	0.99	*	*	*	*	*	*	*
60	0.36	0.99	*	*	*	*	*	*	*	*
70	0.43	*	*	*	*	*	*	*	*	*
80	0.49	*	*	*	*	*	*	*	*	*
90	0.55	*	*	*	*	*	*	*	*	*
100	0.60	*	*	*	*	*	*	*	*	*
120	0.70	*	*	*	*	*	*	*	*	*
140	0.78	*	*	*	*	*	*	*	*	*
160	0.84	*	*	*	*	*	*	*	*	*
180	0.89	*	*	*	*	*	*	*	*	*
200	0.92	*	*	*	*	*	*	*	*	*
300	0.99	*	*	*	*	*	*	*	*	*
400	*	*	*	*	*	*	*	*	*	*

Table A18.8 Power of a Pearson's product moment correlation coefficient *r*

a   One-tailed tests

n	\multicolumn{12}{c}{effect size (r)}
	0.1	0.2	0.3	0.4	0.5	0.6	0.7	0.8	0.9	0.95	0.99
4	0.07	0.08	0.10	0.13	0.16	0.20	0.26	0.35	0.50	0.64	0.88
5	0.06	0.08	0.11	0.15	0.20	0.26	0.36	0.49	0.70	0.85	0.99
6	0.06	0.09	0.13	0.18	0.24	0.33	0.46	0.62	0.83	0.95	*
7	0.07	0.10	0.14	0.21	0.29	0.40	0.55	0.73	0.91	0.98	*
8	0.07	0.11	0.16	0.24	0.34	0.47	0.63	0.80	0.96	0.99	*
9	0.07	0.12	0.18	0.27	0.38	0.53	0.70	0.86	0.98	*	*
10	0.08	0.13	0.20	0.30	0.43	0.58	0.75	0.90	0.99	*	*
11	0.08	0.13	0.21	0.32	0.47	0.63	0.80	0.93	*	*	*
12	0.08	0.14	0.23	0.35	0.50	0.68	0.84	0.96	*	*	*
13	0.09	0.15	0.25	0.38	0.54	0.72	0.87	0.97	*	*	*
14	0.09	0.16	0.26	0.40	0.57	0.75	0.90	0.98	*	*	*
15	0.09	0.17	0.28	0.43	0.61	0.78	0.92	0.99	*	*	*
16	0.09	0.17	0.29	0.45	0.64	0.81	0.94	0.99	*	*	*
17	0.10	0.18	0.31	0.48	0.66	0.84	0.95	0.99	*	*	*
18	0.10	0.19	0.33	0.50	0.69	0.86	0.96	*	*	*	*
19	0.10	0.20	0.34	0.52	0.72	0.88	0.97	*	*	*	*
20	0.10	0.20	0.35	0.54	0.74	0.89	0.98	*	*	*	*
25	0.12	0.24	0.42	0.64	0.83	0.95	0.99	*	*	*	*
30	0.13	0.27	0.49	0.71	0.89	0.98	*	*	*	*	*
35	0.14	0.31	0.54	0.78	0.93	0.99	*	*	*	*	*
40	0.15	0.34	0.60	0.83	0.96	*	*	*	*	*	*
45	0.16	0.37	0.64	0.87	0.97	*	*	*	*	*	*
50	0.17	0.40	0.69	0.90	0.98	*	*	*	*	*	*
60	0.19	0.45	0.76	0.94	0.99	*	*	*	*	*	*
70	0.20	0.51	0.81	0.97	*	*	*	*	*	*	*
80	0.22	0.55	0.86	0.98	*	*	*	*	*	*	*
90	0.24	0.60	0.89	0.99	*	*	*	*	*	*	*
100	0.25	0.64	0.92	0.99	*	*	*	*	*	*	*
110	0.27	0.68	0.94	*	*	*	*	*	*	*	*
120	0.29	0.71	0.96	*	*	*	*	*	*	*	*
130	0.30	0.74	0.97	*	*	*	*	*	*	*	*
140	0.32	0.77	0.98	*	*	*	*	*	*	*	*
150	0.33	0.79	0.98	*	*	*	*	*	*	*	*
160	0.35	0.82	0.99	*	*	*	*	*	*	*	*
170	0.36	0.84	0.99	*	*	*	*	*	*	*	*
180	0.38	0.85	0.99	*	*	*	*	*	*	*	*
190	0.39	0.87	*	*	*	*	*	*	*	*	*
200	0.41	0.89	*	*	*	*	*	*	*	*	*
300	0.53	0.97	*	*	*	*	*	*	*	*	*
400	0.64	0.99	*	*	*	*	*	*	*	*	*
500	0.72	*	*	*	*	*	*	*	*	*	*
600	0.79	*	*	*	*	*	*	*	*	*	*
700	0.84	*	*	*	*	*	*	*	*	*	*
800	0.88	*	*	*	*	*	*	*	*	*	*
900	0.91	*	*	*	*	*	*	*	*	*	*
1000	0.94	*	*	*	*	*	*	*	*	*	*

TABLE A18.8   Power of a Pearson's product moment correlation coefficient *r*

b   Two-tailed tests

n	\multicolumn{11}{c}{effect size (r)}
	0.1	0.2	0.3	0.4	0.5	0.6	0.7	0.8	0.9	0.95	0.99
4	0.03	0.04	0.05	0.07	0.09	0.12	0.16	0.22	0.36	0.50	0.79
5	0.03	0.04	0.05	0.08	0.11	0.16	0.23	0.35	0.56	0.75	0.97
6	0.03	0.04	0.07	0.10	0.14	0.21	0.32	0.48	0.73	0.89	*
7	0.03	0.05	0.08	0.12	0.18	0.27	0.40	0.59	0.84	0.96	*
8	0.03	0.06	0.09	0.14	0.22	0.33	0.49	0.69	0.91	0.98	*
9	0.04	0.06	0.10	0.17	0.26	0.39	0.56	0.77	0.95	0.99	*
10	0.04	0.07	0.12	0.19	0.30	0.44	0.63	0.83	0.98	*	*
11	0.04	0.07	0.13	0.21	0.33	0.50	0.69	0.88	0.99	*	*
12	0.04	0.08	0.14	0.24	0.37	0.55	0.74	0.91	0.99	*	*
13	0.04	0.08	0.15	0.26	0.41	0.59	0.79	0.94	*	*	*
14	0.05	0.09	0.17	0.28	0.44	0.63	0.82	0.96	*	*	*
15	0.05	0.10	0.18	0.30	0.47	0.67	0.86	0.97	*	*	*
16	0.05	0.10	0.19	0.33	0.51	0.71	0.88	0.98	*	*	*
17	0.05	0.11	0.20	0.35	0.54	0.74	0.90	0.99	*	*	*
18	0.05	0.11	0.22	0.37	0.57	0.77	0.92	0.99	*	*	*
19	0.05	0.12	0.23	0.39	0.59	0.79	0.94	0.99	*	*	*
20	0.06	0.12	0.24	0.41	0.62	0.82	0.95	*	*	*	*
25	0.06	0.15	0.30	0.51	0.73	0.90	0.98	*	*	*	*
30	0.07	0.18	0.36	0.60	0.82	0.95	0.99	*	*	*	*
35	0.08	0.20	0.41	0.67	0.88	0.98	*	*	*	*	*
40	0.09	0.23	0.47	0.73	0.92	0.99	*	*	*	*	*
45	0.09	0.26	0.52	0.79	0.95	0.99	*	*	*	*	*
50	0.10	0.28	0.56	0.83	0.97	*	*	*	*	*	*
60	0.11	0.33	0.65	0.89	0.99	*	*	*	*	*	*
70	0.13	0.38	0.72	0.94	0.99	*	*	*	*	*	*
80	0.14	0.43	0.78	0.96	*	*	*	*	*	*	*
90	0.15	0.47	0.82	0.98	*	*	*	*	*	*	*
100	0.16	0.51	0.86	0.99	*	*	*	*	*	*	*
110	0.18	0.55	0.89	0.99	*	*	*	*	*	*	*
120	0.19	0.59	0.92	*	*	*	*	*	*	*	*
130	0.20	0.63	0.94	*	*	*	*	*	*	*	*
140	0.21	0.66	0.95	*	*	*	*	*	*	*	*
150	0.23	0.69	0.96	*	*	*	*	*	*	*	*
160	0.24	0.72	0.97	*	*	*	*	*	*	*	*
170	0.25	0.75	0.98	*	*	*	*	*	*	*	*
180	0.27	0.77	0.98	*	*	*	*	*	*	*	*
190	0.28	0.79	0.99	*	*	*	*	*	*	*	*
200	0.29	0.81	0.99	*	*	*	*	*	*	*	*
300	0.41	0.94	*	*	*	*	*	*	*	*	*
400	0.52	0.98	*	*	*	*	*	*	*	*	*
500	0.61	0.99	*	*	*	*	*	*	*	*	*
600	0.69	*	*	*	*	*	*	*	*	*	*
700	0.75	*	*	*	*	*	*	*	*	*	*
800	0.81	*	*	*	*	*	*	*	*	*	*
900	0.85	*	*	*	*	*	*	*	*	*	*
1000	0.89	*	*	*	*	*	*	*	*	*	*

Table A18.9 Power of Pearson's product moment correlation coefficient r when H_0 is not $\rho = 0$

a One-tailed tests

n	\multicolumn{18}{c}{Effect size (q)}
	0.1	0.14	0.2	0.3	0.4	0.42	0.5	0.6	0.7	0.71	0.8	0.9	1	1.1	1.2	1.3	1.4
8	0.08	0.09	0.12	0.17	0.23	0.24	0.30	0.38	0.47	0.48	0.56	0.64	0.72	0.79	0.85	0.90	0.93
9	0.08	0.10	0.12	0.18	0.25	0.27	0.34	0.43	0.53	0.54	0.62	0.71	0.79	0.85	0.90	0.94	0.96
10	0.08	0.10	0.13	0.20	0.28	0.30	0.37	0.48	0.58	0.59	0.68	0.77	0.84	0.90	0.94	0.96	0.98
11	0.09	0.11	0.14	0.21	0.30	0.32	0.41	0.52	0.63	0.64	0.73	0.82	0.88	0.93	0.96	0.98	0.99
12	0.09	0.11	0.15	0.23	0.33	0.35	0.44	0.56	0.68	0.69	0.77	0.85	0.91	0.95	0.97	0.99	0.99
13	0.09	0.11	0.16	0.24	0.35	0.38	0.47	0.60	0.72	0.73	0.81	0.89	0.94	0.97	0.98	0.99	*
14	0.09	0.12	0.16	0.26	0.38	0.40	0.51	0.63	0.75	0.76	0.84	0.91	0.95	0.98	0.99	*	*
15	0.10	0.12	0.17	0.27	0.40	0.42	0.53	0.67	0.78	0.79	0.87	0.93	0.97	0.98	0.99	*	*
16	0.10	0.13	0.18	0.29	0.42	0.45	0.56	0.70	0.81	0.82	0.89	0.95	0.98	0.99	*	*	*
17	0.10	0.13	0.18	0.30	0.44	0.47	0.59	0.73	0.84	0.84	0.91	0.96	0.98	0.99	*	*	*
18	0.10	0.14	0.19	0.31	0.46	0.49	0.61	0.75	0.86	0.87	0.93	0.97	0.99	*	*	*	*
19	0.11	0.14	0.20	0.33	0.48	0.51	0.64	0.77	0.88	0.88	0.94	0.97	0.99	*	*	*	*
20	0.11	0.14	0.21	0.34	0.50	0.53	0.66	0.80	0.89	0.90	0.95	0.98	0.99	*	*	*	*
25	0.12	0.16	0.24	0.41	0.59	0.63	0.76	0.88	0.95	0.95	0.98	*	*	*	*	*	*
30	0.13	0.18	0.27	0.47	0.67	0.70	0.83	0.93	0.98	0.98	0.99	*	*	*	*	*	*
35	0.14	0.20	0.30	0.52	0.73	0.77	0.88	0.96	0.99	0.99	*	*	*	*	*	*	*
40	0.15	0.21	0.33	0.57	0.78	0.82	0.92	0.98	*	*	*	*	*	*	*	*	*
45	0.16	0.23	0.36	0.62	0.83	0.86	0.94	0.99	*	*	*	*	*	*	*	*	*
50	0.17	0.25	0.39	0.66	0.86	0.89	0.96	0.99	*	*	*	*	*	*	*	*	*
60	0.19	0.28	0.45	0.73	0.92	0.94	0.98	*	*	*	*	*	*	*	*	*	*
70	0.20	0.31	0.50	0.79	0.95	0.96	0.99	*	*	*	*	*	*	*	*	*	*
80	0.22	0.34	0.54	0.84	0.97	0.98	*	*	*	*	*	*	*	*	*	*	*
90	0.24	0.37	0.59	0.88	0.98	0.99	*	*	*	*	*	*	*	*	*	*	*
100	0.25	0.40	0.63	0.90	0.99	0.99	*	*	*	*	*	*	*	*	*	*	*
110	0.27	0.42	0.66	0.93	0.99	*	*	*	*	*	*	*	*	*	*	*	*
120	0.29	0.45	0.70	0.95	*	*	*	*	*	*	*	*	*	*	*	*	*
130	0.30	0.47	0.73	0.96	*	*	*	*	*	*	*	*	*	*	*	*	*
140	0.32	0.50	0.76	0.97	*	*	*	*	*	*	*	*	*	*	*	*	*
150	0.33	0.52	0.78	0.98	*	*	*	*	*	*	*	*	*	*	*	*	*
160	0.35	0.54	0.81	0.98	*	*	*	*	*	*	*	*	*	*	*	*	*
170	0.36	0.57	0.83	0.99	*	*	*	*	*	*	*	*	*	*	*	*	*
180	0.38	0.59	0.85	0.99	*	*	*	*	*	*	*	*	*	*	*	*	*
190	0.39	0.61	0.86	0.99	*	*	*	*	*	*	*	*	*	*	*	*	*
200	0.40	0.63	0.88	0.99	*	*	*	*	*	*	*	*	*	*	*	*	*
250	0.47	0.71	0.93	*	*	*	*	*	*	*	*	*	*	*	*	*	*
300	0.53	0.78	0.96	*	*	*	*	*	*	*	*	*	*	*	*	*	*
350	0.59	0.83	0.98	*	*	*	*	*	*	*	*	*	*	*	*	*	*
400	0.64	0.87	0.99	*	*	*	*	*	*	*	*	*	*	*	*	*	*
450	0.68	0.91	*	*	*	*	*	*	*	*	*	*	*	*	*	*	*
500	0.72	0.93	*	*	*	*	*	*	*	*	*	*	*	*	*	*	*
550	0.76	0.95	*	*	*	*	*	*	*	*	*	*	*	*	*	*	*
600	0.79	0.96	*	*	*	*	*	*	*	*	*	*	*	*	*	*	*
650	0.82	0.97	*	*	*	*	*	*	*	*	*	*	*	*	*	*	*
700	0.84	0.98	*	*	*	*	*	*	*	*	*	*	*	*	*	*	*
750	0.86	0.99	*	*	*	*	*	*	*	*	*	*	*	*	*	*	*
800	0.88	0.99	*	*	*	*	*	*	*	*	*	*	*	*	*	*	*
850	0.90	0.99	*	*	*	*	*	*	*	*	*	*	*	*	*	*	*
900	0.91	0.99	*	*	*	*	*	*	*	*	*	*	*	*	*	*	*
950	0.92	*	*	*	*	*	*	*	*	*	*	*	*	*	*	*	*
1000	0.93	*	*	*	*	*	*	*	*	*	*	*	*	*	*	*	*

TABLE A18.9 Power of Pearson's product moment correlation coefficient *r* when H_0 is not $\rho = 0$

b Two-tailed tests

n	\multicolumn{17}{c}{Effect size (q)}
	0.1	0.14	0.2	0.3	0.4	0.42	0.5	0.6	0.7	0.71	0.8	0.9	1	1.1	1.2	1.3	1.4
8	0.04	0.05	0.07	0.10	0.14	0.15	0.20	0.27	0.35	0.35	0.43	0.52	0.61	0.69	0.77	0.83	0.88
9	0.04	0.05	0.07	0.11	0.16	0.18	0.23	0.31	0.40	0.41	0.50	0.60	0.69	0.77	0.84	0.89	0.93
10	0.05	0.06	0.08	0.12	0.18	0.20	0.26	0.35	0.46	0.47	0.56	0.66	0.75	0.83	0.89	0.93	0.96
11	0.05	0.06	0.08	0.13	0.20	0.22	0.29	0.40	0.51	0.52	0.62	0.72	0.81	0.88	0.92	0.96	0.98
12	0.05	0.06	0.09	0.14	0.22	0.24	0.32	0.44	0.56	0.57	0.67	0.77	0.85	0.91	0.95	0.97	0.99
13	0.05	0.06	0.09	0.16	0.24	0.26	0.35	0.48	0.60	0.61	0.72	0.81	0.89	0.94	0.97	0.98	0.99
14	0.05	0.07	0.10	0.17	0.26	0.29	0.38	0.51	0.64	0.65	0.76	0.85	0.91	0.95	0.98	0.99	*
15	0.05	0.07	0.10	0.18	0.28	0.31	0.41	0.55	0.68	0.69	0.79	0.88	0.93	0.97	0.99	0.99	*
16	0.05	0.07	0.11	0.19	0.30	0.33	0.44	0.58	0.71	0.73	0.82	0.90	0.95	0.98	0.99	*	*
17	0.06	0.08	0.11	0.20	0.32	0.35	0.46	0.61	0.75	0.76	0.85	0.92	0.96	0.98	0.99	*	*
18	0.06	0.08	0.12	0.21	0.34	0.37	0.49	0.64	0.77	0.79	0.87	0.94	0.97	0.99	*	*	*
19	0.06	0.08	0.12	0.22	0.36	0.39	0.52	0.67	0.80	0.81	0.89	0.95	0.98	0.99	*	*	*
20	0.06	0.08	0.13	0.23	0.38	0.41	0.54	0.70	0.82	0.83	0.91	0.96	0.98	0.99	*	*	*
25	0.07	0.10	0.15	0.29	0.47	0.50	0.65	0.80	0.91	0.91	0.96	0.99	*	*	*	*	*
30	0.07	0.11	0.18	0.34	0.55	0.59	0.74	0.88	0.95	0.96	0.99	*	*	*	*	*	*
35	0.08	0.12	0.20	0.40	0.62	0.66	0.81	0.92	0.98	0.98	0.99	*	*	*	*	*	*
40	0.09	0.13	0.23	0.45	0.68	0.72	0.86	0.95	0.99	0.99	*	*	*	*	*	*	*
45	0.09	0.15	0.25	0.49	0.74	0.78	0.90	0.97	*	*	*	*	*	*	*	*	*
50	0.10	0.16	0.28	0.54	0.78	0.82	0.93	0.98	*	*	*	*	*	*	*	*	*
60	0.11	0.18	0.33	0.62	0.86	0.89	0.97	0.99	*	*	*	*	*	*	*	*	*
70	0.13	0.21	0.37	0.69	0.91	0.93	0.98	*	*	*	*	*	*	*	*	*	*
80	0.14	0.23	0.42	0.75	0.94	0.96	0.99	*	*	*	*	*	*	*	*	*	*
90	0.15	0.26	0.46	0.80	0.96	0.97	*	*	*	*	*	*	*	*	*	*	*
100	0.16	0.28	0.50	0.84	0.98	0.99	*	*	*	*	*	*	*	*	*	*	*
110	0.18	0.30	0.54	0.87	0.99	0.99	*	*	*	*	*	*	*	*	*	*	*
120	0.19	0.33	0.58	0.90	0.99	*	*	*	*	*	*	*	*	*	*	*	*
130	0.20	0.35	0.62	0.92	0.99	*	*	*	*	*	*	*	*	*	*	*	*
140	0.21	0.37	0.65	0.94	*	*	*	*	*	*	*	*	*	*	*	*	*
150	0.23	0.40	0.68	0.95	*	*	*	*	*	*	*	*	*	*	*	*	*
160	0.24	0.42	0.71	0.96	*	*	*	*	*	*	*	*	*	*	*	*	*
170	0.25	0.44	0.73	0.97	*	*	*	*	*	*	*	*	*	*	*	*	*
180	0.26	0.46	0.76	0.98	*	*	*	*	*	*	*	*	*	*	*	*	*
190	0.28	0.48	0.78	0.98	*	*	*	*	*	*	*	*	*	*	*	*	*
200	0.29	0.50	0.80	0.99	*	*	*	*	*	*	*	*	*	*	*	*	*
250	0.35	0.59	0.88	*	*	*	*	*	*	*	*	*	*	*	*	*	*
300	0.41	0.67	0.93	*	*	*	*	*	*	*	*	*	*	*	*	*	*
350	0.46	0.74	0.96	*	*	*	*	*	*	*	*	*	*	*	*	*	*
400	0.51	0.80	0.98	*	*	*	*	*	*	*	*	*	*	*	*	*	*
450	0.56	0.84	0.99	*	*	*	*	*	*	*	*	*	*	*	*	*	*
500	0.61	0.88	0.99	*	*	*	*	*	*	*	*	*	*	*	*	*	*
550	0.65	0.91	*	*	*	*	*	*	*	*	*	*	*	*	*	*	*
600	0.69	0.93	*	*	*	*	*	*	*	*	*	*	*	*	*	*	*
650	0.72	0.95	*	*	*	*	*	*	*	*	*	*	*	*	*	*	*
700	0.75	0.96	*	*	*	*	*	*	*	*	*	*	*	*	*	*	*
750	0.78	0.97	*	*	*	*	*	*	*	*	*	*	*	*	*	*	*
800	0.81	0.98	*	*	*	*	*	*	*	*	*	*	*	*	*	*	*
850	0.83	0.98	*	*	*	*	*	*	*	*	*	*	*	*	*	*	*
900	0.85	0.99	*	*	*	*	*	*	*	*	*	*	*	*	*	*	*
950	0.87	0.99	*	*	*	*	*	*	*	*	*	*	*	*	*	*	*
1000	0.88	0.99	*	*	*	*	*	*	*	*	*	*	*	*	*	*	*

Table A18.10 Power of difference between two-sample Pearson's product moment correlation coefficient *r*

a   One-tailed tests (*n* is sample size in each group; for unequal sample sizes see method for reading table given earlier in this appendix)

n	\multicolumn{14}{c}{Effect size (q)}
	0.1	0.2	0.3	0.4	0.5	0.6	0.7	0.8	0.9	1	1.1	1.2	1.3	1.4
8	0.07	0.09	0.12	0.16	0.20	0.24	0.30	0.35	0.41	0.47	0.54	0.60	0.66	0.72
9	0.07	0.10	0.13	0.17	0.22	0.27	0.33	0.40	0.47	0.53	0.60	0.67	0.73	0.78
10	0.07	0.10	0.14	0.18	0.24	0.30	0.37	0.44	0.52	0.59	0.66	0.73	0.78	0.84
11	0.07	0.11	0.15	0.20	0.26	0.33	0.40	0.48	0.56	0.64	0.71	0.77	0.83	0.88
12	0.08	0.11	0.16	0.21	0.28	0.35	0.44	0.52	0.60	0.68	0.75	0.82	0.87	0.91
13	0.08	0.12	0.17	0.23	0.30	0.38	0.47	0.56	0.64	0.72	0.79	0.85	0.90	0.93
14	0.08	0.12	0.17	0.24	0.32	0.41	0.50	0.59	0.68	0.76	0.83	0.88	0.92	0.95
15	0.08	0.12	0.18	0.25	0.34	0.43	0.53	0.62	0.71	0.79	0.85	0.90	0.94	0.96
16	0.08	0.13	0.19	0.27	0.36	0.45	0.56	0.65	0.74	0.82	0.88	0.92	0.95	0.97
17	0.08	0.13	0.20	0.28	0.37	0.48	0.58	0.68	0.77	0.84	0.90	0.94	0.96	0.98
18	0.09	0.14	0.21	0.29	0.39	0.50	0.61	0.71	0.79	0.86	0.91	0.95	0.97	0.99
19	0.09	0.14	0.21	0.30	0.41	0.52	0.63	0.73	0.82	0.88	0.93	0.96	0.98	0.99
20	0.09	0.14	0.22	0.32	0.43	0.54	0.65	0.75	0.84	0.90	0.94	0.97	0.98	0.99
25	0.09	0.16	0.26	0.38	0.51	0.63	0.75	0.84	0.91	0.95	0.98	0.99	*	*
30	0.10	0.18	0.29	0.43	0.58	0.71	0.82	0.90	0.95	0.98	0.99	*	*	*
35	0.11	0.20	0.33	0.48	0.64	0.77	0.88	0.94	0.97	0.99	*	*	*	*
40	0.11	0.22	0.36	0.53	0.69	0.83	0.91	0.96	0.99	*	*	*	*	*
45	0.12	0.23	0.39	0.57	0.74	0.87	0.94	0.98	0.99	*	*	*	*	*
50	0.12	0.25	0.42	0.62	0.78	0.90	0.96	0.99	*	*	*	*	*	*
60	0.13	0.28	0.48	0.69	0.85	0.94	0.98	*	*	*	*	*	*	*
70	0.14	0.31	0.54	0.75	0.89	0.97	0.99	*	*	*	*	*	*	*
80	0.15	0.34	0.59	0.80	0.93	0.98	*	*	*	*	*	*	*	*
90	0.16	0.37	0.63	0.84	0.95	0.99	*	*	*	*	*	*	*	*
100	0.17	0.40	0.67	0.87	0.97	0.99	*	*	*	*	*	*	*	*
110	0.18	0.43	0.71	0.90	0.98	*	*	*	*	*	*	*	*	*
120	0.19	0.45	0.74	0.92	0.99	*	*	*	*	*	*	*	*	*
130	0.20	0.48	0.77	0.94	0.99	*	*	*	*	*	*	*	*	*
140	0.21	0.50	0.80	0.95	0.99	*	*	*	*	*	*	*	*	*
150	0.22	0.53	0.82	0.96	*	*	*	*	*	*	*	*	*	*
160	0.22	0.55	0.84	0.97	*	*	*	*	*	*	*	*	*	*
170	0.23	0.57	0.86	0.98	*	*	*	*	*	*	*	*	*	*
180	0.24	0.59	0.88	0.98	*	*	*	*	*	*	*	*	*	*
190	0.25	0.61	0.90	0.99	*	*	*	*	*	*	*	*	*	*
200	0.26	0.63	0.91	0.99	*	*	*	*	*	*	*	*	*	*
250	0.30	0.72	0.95	*	*	*	*	*	*	*	*	*	*	*
300	0.33	0.79	0.98	*	*	*	*	*	*	*	*	*	*	*
350	0.37	0.84	0.99	*	*	*	*	*	*	*	*	*	*	*
400	0.41	0.88	*	*	*	*	*	*	*	*	*	*	*	*
450	0.44	0.91	*	*	*	*	*	*	*	*	*	*	*	*
500	0.47	0.93	*	*	*	*	*	*	*	*	*	*	*	*
550	0.50	0.95	*	*	*	*	*	*	*	*	*	*	*	*
600	0.53	0.96	*	*	*	*	*	*	*	*	*	*	*	*
650	0.56	0.97	*	*	*	*	*	*	*	*	*	*	*	*
700	0.59	0.98	*	*	*	*	*	*	*	*	*	*	*	*
750	0.61	0.99	*	*	*	*	*	*	*	*	*	*	*	*
800	0.64	0.99	*	*	*	*	*	*	*	*	*	*	*	*
850	0.66	0.99	*	*	*	*	*	*	*	*	*	*	*	*
900	0.68	*	*	*	*	*	*	*	*	*	*	*	*	*
950	0.70	*	*	*	*	*	*	*	*	*	*	*	*	*
1000	0.72	*	*	*	*	*	*	*	*	*	*	*	*	*
1100	0.76	*	*	*	*	*	*	*	*	*	*	*	*	*
1200	0.79	*	*	*	*	*	*	*	*	*	*	*	*	*
1300	0.82	*	*	*	*	*	*	*	*	*	*	*	*	*

TABLE A18.10   Power of difference between two-sample Pearson's product moment correlation coefficient *r*

b   Two-tailed tests (*n* is sample size in each group; for unequal sample sizes see method for reading table given earlier in this appendix)

n	0.1	0.2	0.3	0.4	0.5	0.6	0.7	0.8	0.9	1	1.1	1.2	1.3	1.4
							Effect size (q)							
8	0.04	0.05	0.07	0.09	0.12	0.16	0.20	0.24	0.30	0.35	0.41	0.48	0.54	0.60
9	0.04	0.05	0.07	0.10	0.14	0.18	0.23	0.28	0.34	0.41	0.48	0.55	0.61	0.68
10	0.04	0.06	0.08	0.11	0.15	0.20	0.26	0.32	0.39	0.46	0.54	0.61	0.68	0.75
11	0.04	0.06	0.09	0.12	0.17	0.22	0.29	0.36	0.44	0.52	0.59	0.67	0.74	0.80
12	0.04	0.06	0.09	0.13	0.18	0.25	0.32	0.40	0.48	0.56	0.65	0.72	0.79	0.84
13	0.04	0.07	0.10	0.14	0.20	0.27	0.35	0.43	0.52	0.61	0.69	0.77	0.83	0.88
14	0.04	0.07	0.10	0.15	0.22	0.29	0.38	0.47	0.56	0.65	0.73	0.80	0.86	0.91
15	0.04	0.07	0.11	0.16	0.23	0.31	0.40	0.50	0.60	0.69	0.77	0.84	0.89	0.93
16	0.04	0.07	0.12	0.17	0.25	0.33	0.43	0.53	0.63	0.72	0.80	0.86	0.91	0.95
17	0.05	0.08	0.12	0.18	0.26	0.35	0.46	0.56	0.66	0.75	0.83	0.89	0.93	0.96
18	0.05	0.08	0.13	0.19	0.28	0.38	0.48	0.59	0.69	0.78	0.85	0.91	0.95	0.97
19	0.05	0.08	0.13	0.20	0.29	0.40	0.51	0.62	0.72	0.81	0.88	0.92	0.96	0.98
20	0.05	0.08	0.14	0.21	0.31	0.42	0.53	0.65	0.75	0.83	0.89	0.94	0.97	0.98
25	0.05	0.10	0.17	0.26	0.38	0.51	0.64	0.76	0.85	0.91	0.95	0.98	0.99	*
30	0.06	0.11	0.20	0.31	0.45	0.60	0.73	0.84	0.91	0.96	0.98	0.99	*	*
35	0.06	0.12	0.22	0.36	0.52	0.67	0.80	0.89	0.95	0.98	0.99	*	*	*
40	0.06	0.14	0.25	0.41	0.58	0.73	0.85	0.93	0.97	0.99	*	*	*	*
45	0.07	0.15	0.28	0.45	0.63	0.79	0.89	0.96	0.98	*	*	*	*	*
50	0.07	0.16	0.31	0.49	0.68	0.83	0.92	0.97	0.99	*	*	*	*	*
60	0.08	0.19	0.36	0.57	0.76	0.89	0.96	0.99	*	*	*	*	*	*
70	0.08	0.21	0.41	0.64	0.82	0.93	0.98	*	*	*	*	*	*	*
80	0.09	0.24	0.46	0.70	0.87	0.96	0.99	*	*	*	*	*	*	*
90	0.10	0.26	0.51	0.75	0.91	0.98	*	*	*	*	*	*	*	*
100	0.10	0.29	0.55	0.80	0.94	0.99	*	*	*	*	*	*	*	*
110	0.11	0.31	0.59	0.83	0.96	0.99	*	*	*	*	*	*	*	*
120	0.12	0.33	0.63	0.86	0.97	*	*	*	*	*	*	*	*	*
130	0.12	0.36	0.67	0.89	0.98	*	*	*	*	*	*	*	*	*
140	0.13	0.38	0.70	0.91	0.99	*	*	*	*	*	*	*	*	*
150	0.14	0.40	0.73	0.93	0.99	*	*	*	*	*	*	*	*	*
160	0.14	0.43	0.76	0.94	0.99	*	*	*	*	*	*	*	*	*
170	0.15	0.45	0.78	0.95	*	*	*	*	*	*	*	*	*	*
180	0.15	0.47	0.81	0.96	*	*	*	*	*	*	*	*	*	*
190	0.16	0.49	0.83	0.97	*	*	*	*	*	*	*	*	*	*
200	0.17	0.51	0.85	0.98	*	*	*	*	*	*	*	*	*	*
250	0.20	0.60	0.92	0.99	*	*	*	*	*	*	*	*	*	*
300	0.23	0.68	0.96	*	*	*	*	*	*	*	*	*	*	*
350	0.26	0.75	0.98	*	*	*	*	*	*	*	*	*	*	*
400	0.29	0.80	0.99	*	*	*	*	*	*	*	*	*	*	*
450	0.32	0.85	0.99	*	*	*	*	*	*	*	*	*	*	*
500	0.35	0.88	*	*	*	*	*	*	*	*	*	*	*	*
550	0.38	0.91	*	*	*	*	*	*	*	*	*	*	*	*
600	0.41	0.93	*	*	*	*	*	*	*	*	*	*	*	*
650	0.44	0.95	*	*	*	*	*	*	*	*	*	*	*	*
700	0.46	0.96	*	*	*	*	*	*	*	*	*	*	*	*
750	0.49	0.97	*	*	*	*	*	*	*	*	*	*	*	*
800	0.51	0.98	*	*	*	*	*	*	*	*	*	*	*	*
850	0.54	0.98	*	*	*	*	*	*	*	*	*	*	*	*
900	0.56	0.99	*	*	*	*	*	*	*	*	*	*	*	*
950	0.59	0.99	*	*	*	*	*	*	*	*	*	*	*	*
1000	0.61	0.99	*	*	*	*	*	*	*	*	*	*	*	*
1100	0.65	*	*	*	*	*	*	*	*	*	*	*	*	*
1200	0.69	*	*	*	*	*	*	*	*	*	*	*	*	*
1300	0.72	*	*	*	*	*	*	*	*	*	*	*	*	*
1400	0.75	*	*	*	*	*	*	*	*	*	*	*	*	*
1500	0.78	*	*	*	*	*	*	*	*	*	*	*	*	*
1600	0.81	*	*	*	*	*	*	*	*	*	*	*	*	*

Table A18.11 Power tables for linear regression

a   One or two predictor variables

One predictor variable

Effect size (R^2)

n	0.01	0.0196	0.05	0.10	0.13	0.15	0.20	0.25	0.26	0.30
10	0.06	0.07	0.10	0.15	0.19	0.22	0.29	0.37	0.38	0.45
15	0.06	0.07	0.13	0.22	0.29	0.33	0.44	0.55	0.57	0.66
20	0.06	0.08	0.16	0.30	0.38	0.44	0.57	0.69	0.72	0.80
30	0.07	0.11	0.23	0.43	0.54	0.61	0.76	0.87	0.89	0.94
40	0.09	0.13	0.30	0.55	0.67	0.75	0.88	0.95	0.96	0.98
50	0.10	0.16	0.36	0.65	0.77	0.84	0.94	0.98	0.99	*
60	0.11	0.19	0.42	0.73	0.85	0.90	0.97	0.99	*	*
80	0.14	0.24	0.54	0.85	0.93	0.96	0.99	*	*	*
100	0.16	0.29	0.63	0.92	0.97	0.99	*	*	*	*
120	0.19	0.34	0.71	0.96	0.99	*	*	*	*	*
150	0.23	0.41	0.81	0.98	*	*	*	*	*	*
200	0.30	0.52	0.90	*	*	*	*	*	*	*
250	0.36	0.62	0.95	*	*	*	*	*	*	*
500	0.62	0.89	*	*	*	*	*	*	*	*
750	0.79	0.97	*	*	*	*	*	*	*	*
1000	0.89	0.99	*	*	*	*	*	*	*	*

Two predictor variables

Effect size (R^2)

n	0.01	0.0196	0.05	0.10	0.13	0.15	0.20	0.25	0.26	0.30
10	0.06	0.06	0.08	0.11	0.14	0.15	0.19	0.25	0.26	0.30
15	0.06	0.07	0.10	0.16	0.20	0.23	0.32	0.41	0.43	0.51
20	0.06	0.07	0.12	0.21	0.28	0.32	0.44	0.56	0.58	0.67
30	0.07	0.09	0.17	0.32	0.42	0.49	0.64	0.77	0.80	0.87
40	0.07	0.11	0.22	0.43	0.55	0.63	0.79	0.89	0.91	0.96
50	0.08	0.12	0.27	0.53	0.66	0.74	0.88	0.95	0.96	0.99
60	0.09	0.14	0.33	0.62	0.75	0.82	0.93	0.98	0.99	*
80	0.11	0.18	0.43	0.75	0.87	0.92	0.98	*	*	*
100	0.13	0.22	0.52	0.85	0.94	0.97	*	*	*	*
120	0.15	0.26	0.60	0.91	0.97	0.99	*	*	*	*
150	0.18	0.32	0.71	0.96	0.99	*	*	*	*	*
200	0.23	0.42	0.84	0.99	*	*	*	*	*	*
250	0.28	0.51	0.91	*	*	*	*	*	*	*
500	0.51	0.82	*	*	*	*	*	*	*	*
750	0.70	0.95	*	*	*	*	*	*	*	*
1000	0.82	0.99	*	*	*	*	*	*	*	*

TABLE A18.11   Power tables for linear regression

b   Three or four predictor variables

three predictor variables
effect size (R^2)

n	0.01	0.0196	0.05	0.10	0.13	0.15	0.20	0.25	0.26	0.30
10	0.06	0.06	0.08	0.10	0.11	0.12	0.15	0.18	0.19	0.22
15	0.06	0.06	0.09	0.13	0.16	0.19	0.25	0.32	0.34	0.41
20	0.06	0.07	0.10	0.17	0.22	0.26	0.36	0.46	0.49	0.57
30	0.06	0.08	0.14	0.27	0.35	0.41	0.56	0.69	0.72	0.81
40	0.07	0.09	0.19	0.36	0.48	0.55	0.71	0.84	0.86	0.93
50	0.07	0.11	0.23	0.46	0.59	0.67	0.83	0.92	0.94	0.97
60	0.08	0.12	0.27	0.54	0.68	0.76	0.90	0.97	0.97	0.99
80	0.10	0.15	0.37	0.69	0.82	0.88	0.97	0.99	*	*
100	0.11	0.19	0.45	0.80	0.91	0.95	0.99	*	*	*
120	0.13	0.22	0.53	0.87	0.95	0.98	*	*	*	*
150	0.15	0.27	0.64	0.94	0.98	0.99	*	*	*	*
200	0.19	0.36	0.78	0.98	*	*	*	*	*	*
250	0.24	0.44	0.87	*	*	*	*	*	*	*
500	0.45	0.76	*	*	*	*	*	*	*	*
750	0.63	0.92	*	*	*	*	*	*	*	*
1000	0.77	0.97	*	*	*	*	*	*	*	*
1250	0.86	0.99	*	*	*	*	*	*	*	*

four predictor variables
effect size (R^2)

n	0.01	0.0196	0.05	0.10	0.13	0.15	0.20	0.25	0.26	0.30
15	0.06	0.06	0.08	0.11	0.14	0.16	0.20	0.26	0.28	0.33
20	0.06	0.07	0.09	0.15	0.19	0.22	0.30	0.39	0.41	0.50
30	0.06	0.07	0.13	0.23	0.30	0.36	0.49	0.63	0.65	0.75
40	0.07	0.09	0.16	0.32	0.42	0.49	0.65	0.79	0.82	0.89
50	0.07	0.10	0.20	0.40	0.53	0.61	0.78	0.89	0.91	0.96
60	0.08	0.11	0.24	0.49	0.62	0.71	0.86	0.95	0.96	0.98
80	0.09	0.14	0.32	0.63	0.78	0.85	0.95	0.99	0.99	*
100	0.10	0.17	0.40	0.75	0.87	0.93	0.99	*	*	*
120	0.11	0.20	0.48	0.83	0.93	0.97	*	*	*	*
150	0.13	0.24	0.59	0.92	0.98	0.99	*	*	*	*
200	0.17	0.32	0.73	0.98	*	*	*	*	*	*
250	0.21	0.40	0.84	0.99	*	*	*	*	*	*
500	0.40	0.72	0.99	*	*	*	*	*	*	*
750	0.58	0.89	*	*	*	*	*	*	*	*
1000	0.72	0.96	*	*	*	*	*	*	*	*
1250	0.83	0.99	*	*	*	*	*	*	*	*

TABLE A18.11   Power tables for linear regression

c   Six or eight predictor variables

six predictor variables
effect size (R^2)

n	0.01	0.0196	0.05	0.10	0.13	0.15	0.20	0.25	0.26	0.30
15	0.06	0.06	0.07	0.09	0.11	0.12	0.15	0.19	0.19	0.23
20	0.06	0.06	0.08	0.12	0.15	0.17	0.22	0.29	0.31	0.37
30	0.06	0.07	0.11	0.18	0.24	0.28	0.39	0.52	0.54	0.64
40	0.06	0.08	0.13	0.25	0.34	0.40	0.55	0.70	0.73	0.82
50	0.07	0.09	0.16	0.33	0.44	0.52	0.69	0.83	0.85	0.92
60	0.07	0.10	0.20	0.40	0.54	0.62	0.79	0.91	0.92	0.97
80	0.08	0.12	0.27	0.55	0.70	0.78	0.92	0.98	0.98	*
100	0.09	0.14	0.34	0.67	0.81	0.88	0.97	*	*	*
120	0.10	0.16	0.41	0.77	0.89	0.94	0.99	*	*	*
150	0.11	0.20	0.51	0.87	0.96	0.98	*	*	*	*
200	0.14	0.27	0.66	0.96	0.99	*	*	*	*	*
250	0.17	0.33	0.77	0.99	*	*	*	*	*	*
500	0.34	0.64	0.98	*	*	*	*	*	*	*
750	0.51	0.84	*	*	*	*	*	*	*	*
1000	0.65	0.94	*	*	*	*	*	*	*	*
1250	0.76	0.98	*	*	*	*	*	*	*	*
1500	0.85	0.99	*	*	*	*	*	*	*	*

eight predictor variables
effect size (R^2)

n	0.01	0.0196	0.05	0.10	0.13	0.15	0.20	0.25	0.26	0.30
15	0.06	0.06	0.07	0.09	0.09	0.10	0.12	0.14	0.15	0.17
20	0.06	0.06	0.08	0.10	0.12	0.14	0.18	0.23	0.24	0.29
30	0.06	0.07	0.09	0.15	0.20	0.23	0.32	0.43	0.45	0.55
40	0.06	0.07	0.12	0.21	0.28	0.34	0.48	0.62	0.65	0.75
50	0.06	0.08	0.14	0.28	0.38	0.44	0.61	0.76	0.79	0.88
60	0.07	0.09	0.17	0.35	0.47	0.55	0.73	0.86	0.88	0.94
80	0.07	0.10	0.23	0.48	0.63	0.72	0.88	0.96	0.97	*
100	0.08	0.12	0.29	0.60	0.76	0.84	0.95	*	*	*
120	0.09	0.14	0.36	0.71	0.85	0.91	*	*	*	*
150	0.10	0.17	0.45	0.82	0.93	0.97	*	*	*	*
200	0.13	0.23	0.60	0.93	*	*	*	*	*	*
250	0.15	0.29	0.72	0.98	*	*	*	*	*	*
500	0.30	0.59	0.97	*	*	*	*	*	*	*
750	0.46	0.80	*	*	*	*	*	*	*	*
1000	0.60	0.91	*	*	*	*	*	*	*	*
1250	0.71	0.97	*	*	*	*	*	*	*	*
1500	0.80	0.99	*	*	*	*	*	*	*	*

TABLE A18.11   Power tables for linear regression

d   Ten or twelve predictor variables

ten predictor variables
effect size (R^2)

n	0.01	0.0196	0.05	0.10	0.13	0.15	0.20	0.25	0.26	0.30
20	0.05	0.06	0.07	0.09	0.10	0.11	0.14	0.18	0.18	0.22
30	0.05	0.06	0.08	0.13	0.16	0.19	0.26	0.35	0.37	0.45
40	0.06	0.07	0.10	0.18	0.24	0.29	0.41	0.55	0.57	0.68
50	0.06	0.07	0.13	0.24	0.33	0.39	0.55	0.70	0.73	0.83
60	0.06	0.08	0.15	0.30	0.41	0.49	0.67	0.81	0.84	0.91
80	0.07	0.10	0.20	0.43	0.57	0.66	0.84	0.94	0.95	0.98
100	0.08	0.11	0.26	0.55	0.71	0.79	0.93	0.98	0.99	*
120	0.08	0.13	0.32	0.66	0.81	0.88	0.97	*	*	*
150	0.10	0.16	0.41	0.78	0.91	0.95	0.99	*	*	*
200	0.12	0.21	0.55	0.91	0.98	0.99	*	*	*	*
250	0.14	0.26	0.67	0.97	*	*	*	*	*	*
500	0.27	0.54	0.96	*	*	*	*	*	*	*
750	0.41	0.76	*	*	*	*	*	*	*	*
1000	0.55	0.89	*	*	*	*	*	*	*	*
1250	0.67	0.95	*	*	*	*	*	*	*	*
1500	0.77	0.98	*	*	*	*	*	*	*	*
1750	0.84	0.99	*	*	*	*	*	*	*	*

twelve predictor variables
effect size (R^2)

n	0.01	0.0196	0.05	0.10	0.13	0.15	0.20	0.25	0.26	0.30
20	0.05	0.06	0.07	0.09	0.09	0.10	0.12	0.14	0.15	0.17
30	0.05	0.06	0.08	0.11	0.14	0.16	0.22	0.29	0.30	0.37
40	0.06	0.07	0.10	0.16	0.21	0.25	0.36	0.48	0.51	0.61
50	0.06	0.07	0.12	0.21	0.29	0.34	0.49	0.64	0.67	0.78
60	0.06	0.08	0.13	0.27	0.37	0.44	0.61	0.77	0.79	0.88
80	0.07	0.09	0.18	0.39	0.53	0.61	0.80	0.92	0.93	0.97
100	0.07	0.10	0.23	0.51	0.66	0.75	0.91	0.97	0.98	*
120	0.08	0.12	0.29	0.61	0.77	0.85	0.96	0.99	*	*
150	0.09	0.14	0.37	0.74	0.88	0.94	0.99	*	*	*
200	0.11	0.19	0.51	0.89	0.97	0.99	*	*	*	*
250	0.13	0.24	0.63	0.96	0.99	*	*	*	*	*
500	0.25	0.50	0.95	*	*	*	*	*	*	*
750	0.38	0.72	*	*	*	*	*	*	*	*
1000	0.51	0.86	*	*	*	*	*	*	*	*
1250	0.63	0.94	*	*	*	*	*	*	*	*
1500	0.73	0.97	*	*	*	*	*	*	*	*
1750	0.81	0.99	*	*	*	*	*	*	*	*

Table A18.12 Power tables for logistic regression

a   predicted value as a proportion of the sample .01 or .02

event as a proportion of sample = .01

odds ratio

N	1.10 0.91	1.11 0.90	1.20 0.83	1.25 0.80	1.30 0.77	1.40 0.71	1.43 0.70	1.50 0.67	1.60 0.63	1.67 0.60	1.70 0.59	1.80 0.56	1.90 0.53	2.00 0.50	2.50 0.40	3.00 0.33
623	0.04	0.04	0.06	0.08	0.09	0.12	0.13	0.16	0.20	0.23	0.24	0.29	0.33	0.38	0.62	0.80
889	0.05	0.05	0.08	0.09	0.11	0.16	0.17	0.21	0.27	0.31	0.33	0.40	0.47	0.53	0.80	0.94
1585	0.06	0.06	0.11	0.14	0.17	0.26	0.28	0.35	0.45	0.52	0.55	0.65	0.73	0.80	0.97	*
1859	0.06	0.06	0.12	0.15	0.20	0.29	0.32	0.40	0.52	0.59	0.62	0.72	0.80	0.86	0.99	*
2230	0.06	0.07	0.13	0.18	0.23	0.34	0.38	0.47	0.60	0.67	0.71	0.80	0.87	0.92	*	*
2754	0.07	0.08	0.15	0.21	0.27	0.41	0.45	0.56	0.69	0.77	0.80	0.88	0.93	0.97	*	*
2954	0.07	0.08	0.16	0.22	0.29	0.44	0.48	0.59	0.72	0.80	0.83	0.90	0.95	0.97	*	*
3532	0.08	0.09	0.19	0.26	0.34	0.51	0.56	0.67	0.80	0.87	0.89	0.95	0.98	0.99	*	*
4775	0.09	0.11	0.24	0.33	0.43	0.64	0.69	0.80	0.91	0.95	0.96	0.99	*	*	*	*
6162	0.11	0.13	0.29	0.41	0.53	0.75	0.80	0.89	0.96	0.98	0.99	*	*	*	*	*
6975	0.12	0.14	0.32	0.45	0.58	0.80	0.85	0.93	0.98	0.99	*	*	*	*	*	*
11533	0.17	0.20	0.49	0.66	0.80	0.95	0.97	0.99	*	*	*	*	*	*	*	*
15980	0.22	0.26	0.63	0.80	0.91	0.99	*	*	*	*	*	*	*	*	*	*
23985	0.31	0.36	0.80	0.93	0.98	*	*	*	*	*	*	*	*	*	*	*

event as a proportion of sample = .02

odds ratio

N	1.10 0.91	1.11 0.90	1.20 0.83	1.25 0.80	1.30 0.77	1.40 0.71	1.43 0.70	1.50 0.67	1.60 0.63	1.67 0.60	1.70 0.59	1.80 0.56	1.90 0.53	2.00 0.50	2.50 0.40	3.00 0.33
346	0.04	0.05	0.07	0.08	0.10	0.13	0.14	0.17	0.21	0.24	0.26	0.31	0.36	0.41	0.64	0.80
474	0.05	0.05	0.08	0.10	0.12	0.16	0.18	0.22	0.28	0.32	0.34	0.41	0.48	0.54	0.80	0.92
822	0.06	0.06	0.11	0.14	0.17	0.26	0.29	0.36	0.46	0.52	0.56	0.65	0.73	0.80	0.97	*
961	0.06	0.07	0.12	0.16	0.20	0.30	0.33	0.41	0.52	0.59	0.63	0.72	0.80	0.86	0.99	*
1150	0.06	0.07	0.13	0.18	0.23	0.35	0.38	0.47	0.60	0.67	0.71	0.80	0.87	0.92	*	*
1416	0.07	0.08	0.15	0.21	0.27	0.41	0.46	0.56	0.69	0.77	0.80	0.88	0.93	0.96	*	*
1812	0.08	0.09	0.19	0.26	0.34	0.51	0.56	0.67	0.80	0.86	0.89	0.95	0.98	0.99	*	*
2446	0.10	0.11	0.24	0.33	0.43	0.64	0.69	0.80	0.91	0.95	0.96	0.99	*	*	*	*
3152	0.11	0.13	0.29	0.41	0.53	0.75	0.80	0.89	0.96	0.98	0.99	*	*	*	*	*
3567	0.12	0.14	0.32	0.45	0.58	0.80	0.85	0.93	0.98	0.99	0.99	*	*	*	*	*
5890	0.17	0.20	0.49	0.66	0.80	0.95	0.97	0.99	*	*	*	*	*	*	*	*
8157	0.22	0.26	0.63	0.80	0.91	0.99	0.99	*	*	*	*	*	*	*	*	*
12238	0.31	0.37	0.80	0.93	0.98	*	*	*	*	*	*	*	*	*	*	*

TABLE A18.12   Power tables for logistic regression

b   predicted value as a proportion of the sample .03 or .04

event as a proportion of sample = .03
odds ratio

N	1.10 / 0.91	1.11 / 0.90	1.20 / 0.83	1.25 / 0.80	1.30 / 0.77	1.40 / 0.71	1.43 / 0.70	1.50 / 0.67	1.60 / 0.63	1.67 / 0.60	1.70 / 0.59	1.80 / 0.56	1.90 / 0.53	2.00 / 0.50	2.50 / 0.40	3.00 / 0.33
254	0.04	0.05	0.07	0.08	0.10	0.14	0.15	0.18	0.23	0.26	0.28	0.33	0.38	0.43	0.66	0.80
335	0.05	0.05	0.08	0.10	0.12	0.17	0.19	0.23	0.29	0.33	0.35	0.42	0.49	0.55	0.80	0.91
568	0.06	0.06	0.11	0.14	0.18	0.26	0.29	0.36	0.46	0.53	0.56	0.65	0.73	0.80	0.97	0.99
662	0.06	0.07	0.12	0.16	0.20	0.30	0.33	0.41	0.52	0.60	0.63	0.72	0.80	0.86	0.98	*
790	0.07	0.07	0.13	0.18	0.23	0.35	0.39	0.48	0.60	0.68	0.71	0.80	0.87	0.92	*	*
970	0.07	0.08	0.16	0.21	0.27	0.42	0.46	0.56	0.69	0.77	0.80	0.88	0.93	0.96	*	*
1039	0.07	0.08	0.16	0.22	0.29	0.44	0.49	0.59	0.72	0.80	0.83	0.90	0.95	0.97	*	*
1239	0.08	0.09	0.19	0.26	0.34	0.51	0.56	0.67	0.80	0.86	0.89	0.94	0.97	0.99	*	*
1669	0.10	0.11	0.24	0.33	0.43	0.64	0.69	0.80	0.90	0.95	0.96	0.99	*	*	*	*
2149	0.11	0.13	0.29	0.41	0.53	0.75	0.80	0.89	0.96	0.98	0.99	*	*	*	*	*
2431	0.12	0.14	0.33	0.45	0.58	0.80	0.85	0.92	0.98	0.99	0.99	*	*	*	*	*
4009	0.17	0.20	0.49	0.66	0.80	0.95	0.97	0.99	*	*	*	*	*	*	*	*
5549	0.22	0.26	0.63	0.80	0.91	0.99	0.99	*	*	*	*	*	*	*	*	*
8322	0.31	0.37	0.80	0.93	0.98	*	*	*	*	*	*	*	*	*	*	*

event as a proportion of sample = .04
odds ratio

N	1.10 / 0.91	1.11 / 0.90	1.20 / 0.83	1.25 / 0.80	1.30 / 0.77	1.40 / 0.71	1.43 / 0.70	1.50 / 0.67	1.60 / 0.63	1.67 / 0.60	1.70 / 0.59	1.80 / 0.56	1.90 / 0.53	2.00 / 0.50	2.50 / 0.40	3.00 / 0.33
208	0.04	0.05	0.07	0.09	0.10	0.14	0.16	0.19	0.24	0.27	0.29	0.35	0.40	0.45	0.68	0.80
266	0.05	0.05	0.08	0.10	0.12	0.17	0.19	0.23	0.30	0.34	0.36	0.43	0.50	0.56	0.80	0.90
441	0.06	0.06	0.11	0.14	0.18	0.27	0.29	0.36	0.46	0.53	0.56	0.65	0.73	0.80	0.96	0.99
513	0.06	0.07	0.12	0.16	0.20	0.30	0.33	0.41	0.53	0.60	0.63	0.72	0.80	0.86	0.98	*
610	0.07	0.07	0.13	0.18	0.23	0.35	0.39	0.48	0.60	0.68	0.71	0.80	0.87	0.92	0.99	*
747	0.07	0.08	0.16	0.21	0.28	0.42	0.46	0.56	0.69	0.77	0.80	0.88	0.93	0.96	*	*
800	0.07	0.08	0.16	0.22	0.29	0.44	0.49	0.59	0.73	0.80	0.83	0.90	0.94	0.97	*	*
953	0.08	0.09	0.19	0.26	0.34	0.51	0.56	0.67	0.80	0.86	0.89	0.94	0.97	0.99	*	*
1281	0.10	0.11	0.24	0.33	0.44	0.64	0.69	0.80	0.90	0.95	0.96	0.99	*	*	*	*
1648	0.11	0.13	0.29	0.41	0.53	0.75	0.80	0.89	0.96	0.98	0.99	*	*	*	*	*
1863	0.12	0.14	0.33	0.46	0.59	0.80	0.84	0.92	0.98	0.99	0.99	*	*	*	*	*
3068	0.17	0.20	0.49	0.66	0.80	0.95	0.97	0.99	*	*	*	*	*	*	*	*
4245	0.22	0.26	0.63	0.80	0.91	0.99	0.99	*	*	*	*	*	*	*	*	*
6364	0.31	0.37	0.80	0.93	0.98	*	*	*	*	*	*	*	*	*	*	*

TABLE A18.12   Power tables for logistic regression

c   predicted value as a proportion of the sample .05 or .06

event as a proportion of sample = .05

odds ratio

N	1.10	1.11	1.20	1.25	1.30	1.40	1.43	1.50	1.60	1.67	1.70	1.80	1.90	2.00	2.50	3.00
	0.91	0.90	0.83	0.80	0.77	0.71	0.70	0.67	0.63	0.60	0.59	0.56	0.53	0.50	0.40	0.33
181	0.05	0.05	0.07	0.09	0.11	0.15	0.16	0.20	0.25	0.29	0.31	0.36	0.42	0.48	0.70	0.80
224	0.05	0.05	0.08	0.10	0.13	0.18	0.20	0.24	0.30	0.35	0.37	0.44	0.51	0.57	0.80	0.89
365	0.06	0.06	0.11	0.14	0.18	0.27	0.30	0.37	0.47	0.53	0.57	0.66	0.74	0.80	0.96	0.99
423	0.06	0.07	0.12	0.16	0.20	0.31	0.34	0.42	0.53	0.60	0.63	0.73	0.80	0.86	0.98	*
502	0.07	0.07	0.14	0.18	0.23	0.35	0.39	0.48	0.60	0.68	0.71	0.80	0.87	0.91	0.99	*
614	0.07	0.08	0.16	0.21	0.28	0.42	0.46	0.57	0.70	0.77	0.80	0.88	0.93	0.96	*	*
656	0.07	0.08	0.16	0.23	0.29	0.44	0.49	0.59	0.73	0.80	0.83	0.90	0.94	0.97	*	*
781	0.08	0.09	0.19	0.26	0.34	0.51	0.56	0.67	0.80	0.86	0.89	0.94	0.97	0.99	*	*
1048	0.10	0.11	0.24	0.33	0.44	0.64	0.69	0.80	0.90	0.95	0.96	0.98	0.99	*	*	*
1347	0.11	0.13	0.29	0.41	0.53	0.75	0.80	0.89	0.96	0.98	0.99	*	*	*	*	*
1522	0.12	0.14	0.33	0.46	0.59	0.80	0.84	0.92	0.98	0.99	0.99	*	*	*	*	*
2504	0.17	0.20	0.49	0.66	0.80	0.95	0.97	0.99	*	*	*	*	*	*	*	*
3463	0.22	0.26	0.63	0.80	0.91	0.99	0.99	*	*	*	*	*	*	*	*	*
5189	0.31	0.37	0.80	0.93	0.98	*	*	*	*	*	*	*	*	*	*	*

event as a proportion of sample = .06

odds ratio

N	1.10	1.11	1.20	1.25	1.30	1.40	1.43	1.50	1.60	1.67	1.70	1.80	1.90	2.00	2.50	3.00
	0.91	0.90	0.83	0.80	0.77	0.71	0.70	0.67	0.63	0.60	0.59	0.56	0.53	0.50	0.40	0.33
162	0.05	0.05	0.08	0.09	0.11	0.16	0.17	0.21	0.26	0.30	0.32	0.38	0.44	0.49	0.71	0.80
197	0.05	0.05	0.08	0.11	0.13	0.18	0.20	0.25	0.31	0.36	0.38	0.45	0.52	0.58	0.80	0.89
314	0.06	0.06	0.11	0.14	0.18	0.27	0.30	0.37	0.47	0.54	0.57	0.66	0.74	0.80	0.96	0.99
363	0.06	0.07	0.12	0.16	0.21	0.31	0.34	0.42	0.53	0.60	0.64	0.73	0.80	0.86	0.98	*
430	0.07	0.07	0.14	0.18	0.24	0.36	0.39	0.48	0.61	0.68	0.71	0.80	0.87	0.91	0.99	*
524	0.07	0.08	0.16	0.21	0.28	0.42	0.46	0.57	0.70	0.77	0.80	0.88	0.93	0.96	*	*
561	0.07	0.08	0.17	0.23	0.30	0.45	0.49	0.60	0.73	0.80	0.83	0.90	0.94	0.97	*	*
666	0.08	0.09	0.19	0.26	0.34	0.51	0.56	0.67	0.80	0.86	0.89	0.94	0.97	0.99	*	*
893	0.10	0.11	0.24	0.33	0.44	0.64	0.69	0.80	0.90	0.94	0.96	0.98	0.99	*	*	*
1146	0.11	0.13	0.29	0.41	0.53	0.75	0.80	0.89	0.96	0.98	0.99	*	*	*	*	*
1294	0.12	0.14	0.33	0.46	0.59	0.80	0.84	0.92	0.98	0.99	0.99	*	*	*	*	*
2128	0.17	0.20	0.49	0.66	0.80	0.95	0.97	0.99	*	*	*	*	*	*	*	*
2941	0.22	0.26	0.63	0.80	0.91	0.99	0.99	*	*	*	*	*	*	*	*	*
4406	0.31	0.37	0.80	0.93	0.98	*	*	*	*	*	*	*	*	*	*	*

TABLE A18.12   Power tables for logistic regression

d   predicted value as a proportion of the sample .07 or .08

event as a proportion of sample = .07

odds ratio

N	1.10 / 0.91	1.11 / 0.90	1.20 / 0.83	1.25 / 0.80	1.30 / 0.77	1.40 / 0.71	1.43 / 0.70	1.50 / 0.67	1.60 / 0.63	1.67 / 0.60	1.70 / 0.59	1.80 / 0.56	1.90 / 0.53	2.00 / 0.50	2.50 / 0.40	3.00 / 0.33
149	0.05	0.05	0.08	0.10	0.12	0.16	0.18	0.22	0.27	0.31	0.33	0.39	0.45	0.51	0.72	0.80
177	0.05	0.05	0.09	0.11	0.13	0.19	0.21	0.25	0.32	0.37	0.39	0.46	0.53	0.59	0.80	0.88
278	0.06	0.06	0.11	0.15	0.18	0.27	0.30	0.37	0.48	0.54	0.57	0.66	0.74	0.80	0.95	0.98
320	0.06	0.07	0.12	0.16	0.21	0.31	0.34	0.42	0.53	0.60	0.64	0.73	0.80	0.86	0.98	0.99
378	0.07	0.07	0.14	0.18	0.24	0.36	0.39	0.49	0.61	0.68	0.71	0.80	0.87	0.91	0.99	*
461	0.07	0.08	0.16	0.22	0.28	0.42	0.47	0.57	0.70	0.77	0.80	0.88	0.93	0.96	*	*
492	0.07	0.08	0.17	0.23	0.30	0.45	0.49	0.60	0.73	0.80	0.83	0.90	0.94	0.97	*	*
584	0.08	0.09	0.19	0.26	0.34	0.51	0.56	0.67	0.80	0.86	0.89	0.94	0.97	0.99	*	*
782	0.10	0.11	0.24	0.34	0.44	0.64	0.69	0.80	0.90	0.94	0.96	0.98	0.99	*	*	*
1003	0.11	0.13	0.30	0.41	0.54	0.75	0.80	0.89	0.96	0.98	0.99	*	*	*	*	*
1132	0.12	0.14	0.33	0.46	0.59	0.80	0.84	0.92	0.98	0.99	0.99	*	*	*	*	*
1859	0.17	0.20	0.49	0.66	0.80	0.95	0.97	0.99	*	*	*	*	*	*	*	*
2569	0.22	0.26	0.63	0.80	0.91	0.99	0.99	*	*	*	*	*	*	*	*	*
3847	0.31	0.37	0.80	0.93	0.98	*	*	*	*	*	*	*	*	*	*	*

event as a proportion of sample = .08

odds ratio

N	1.10 / 0.91	1.11 / 0.90	1.20 / 0.83	1.25 / 0.80	1.30 / 0.77	1.40 / 0.71	1.43 / 0.70	1.50 / 0.67	1.60 / 0.63	1.67 / 0.60	1.70 / 0.59	1.80 / 0.56	1.90 / 0.53	2.00 / 0.50	2.50 / 0.40	3.00 / 0.33
139	0.05	0.05	0.08	0.10	0.12	0.17	0.18	0.23	0.28	0.33	0.35	0.41	0.47	0.53	0.73	0.80
162	0.05	0.05	0.09	0.11	0.13	0.19	0.21	0.26	0.33	0.37	0.40	0.47	0.54	0.60	0.80	0.87
251	0.06	0.06	0.11	0.15	0.19	0.28	0.31	0.38	0.48	0.55	0.58	0.66	0.74	0.80	0.95	0.98
288	0.06	0.07	0.12	0.16	0.21	0.31	0.34	0.42	0.54	0.61	0.64	0.73	0.80	0.86	0.97	0.99
340	0.07	0.07	0.14	0.19	0.24	0.36	0.40	0.49	0.61	0.68	0.72	0.80	0.87	0.91	0.99	*
413	0.07	0.08	0.16	0.22	0.28	0.43	0.47	0.57	0.70	0.77	0.80	0.87	0.92	0.96	*	*
441	0.08	0.08	0.17	0.23	0.30	0.45	0.49	0.60	0.73	0.80	0.83	0.90	0.94	0.97	*	*
523	0.08	0.09	0.19	0.26	0.34	0.52	0.56	0.68	0.80	0.86	0.89	0.94	0.97	0.99	*	*
698	0.10	0.11	0.24	0.34	0.44	0.64	0.69	0.80	0.90	0.94	0.96	0.98	0.99	*	*	*
895	0.11	0.13	0.30	0.41	0.54	0.75	0.80	0.89	0.96	0.98	0.99	*	*	*	*	*
1010	0.12	0.14	0.33	0.46	0.59	0.80	0.84	0.92	0.98	0.99	0.99	*	*	*	*	*
1658	0.17	0.20	0.49	0.66	0.80	0.95	0.97	0.99	*	*	*	*	*	*	*	*
2290	0.22	0.26	0.63	0.80	0.91	0.99	0.99	*	*	*	*	*	*	*	*	*
3427	0.31	0.37	0.80	0.93	0.98	*	*	*	*	*	*	*	*	*	*	*

TABLE A18.12   Power tables for logistic regression

e   predicted value as a proportion of the sample .09 or .10

event as a proportion of sample = .09
odds ratio

N	1.10 / 0.91	1.11 / 0.90	1.20 / 0.83	1.25 / 0.80	1.30 / 0.77	1.40 / 0.71	1.43 / 0.70	1.50 / 0.67	1.60 / 0.63	1.67 / 0.60	1.70 / 0.59	1.80 / 0.56	1.90 / 0.53	2.00 / 0.50	2.50 / 0.40	3.00 / 0.33
132	0.05	0.05	0.08	0.10	0.12	0.18	0.19	0.23	0.30	0.34	0.36	0.42	0.49	0.54	0.74	0.80
150	0.05	0.05	0.09	0.11	0.14	0.20	0.21	0.26	0.33	0.38	0.40	0.48	0.54	0.60	0.80	0.86
230	0.06	0.06	0.11	0.15	0.19	0.28	0.31	0.38	0.48	0.55	0.58	0.67	0.74	0.80	0.95	0.98
263	0.06	0.07	0.12	0.16	0.21	0.31	0.35	0.43	0.54	0.61	0.64	0.73	0.80	0.86	0.97	0.99
310	0.07	0.07	0.14	0.19	0.24	0.36	0.40	0.49	0.61	0.68	0.72	0.80	0.86	0.91	0.99	*
376	0.07	0.08	0.16	0.22	0.28	0.43	0.47	0.57	0.70	0.77	0.80	0.87	0.92	0.96	*	*
401	0.08	0.08	0.17	0.23	0.30	0.45	0.49	0.60	0.73	0.80	0.83	0.90	0.94	0.97	*	*
475	0.08	0.09	0.19	0.26	0.35	0.52	0.56	0.68	0.80	0.86	0.89	0.94	0.97	0.99	*	*
634	0.10	0.11	0.24	0.34	0.44	0.64	0.69	0.80	0.90	0.94	0.96	0.98	0.99	*	*	*
811	0.11	0.13	0.30	0.41	0.54	0.75	0.80	0.89	0.96	0.98	0.99	*	*	*	*	*
916	0.12	0.14	0.33	0.46	0.59	0.80	0.84	0.92	0.98	0.99	0.99	*	*	*	*	*
1501	0.17	0.20	0.49	0.66	0.80	0.95	0.97	0.99	*	*	*	*	*	*	*	*
2072	0.22	0.26	0.63	0.80	0.91	0.99	0.99	*	*	*	*	*	*	*	*	*
3101	0.31	0.37	0.80	0.93	0.98	*	*	*	*	*	*	*	*	*	*	*

event as a proportion of sample = .10
odds ratio

N	1.10 / 0.91	1.11 / 0.90	1.20 / 0.83	1.25 / 0.80	1.30 / 0.77	1.40 / 0.71	1.43 / 0.70	1.50 / 0.67	1.60 / 0.63	1.67 / 0.60	1.70 / 0.59	1.80 / 0.56	1.90 / 0.53	2.00 / 0.50	2.50 / 0.40	3.00 / 0.33
125	0.05	0.05	0.08	0.10	0.13	0.18	0.20	0.24	0.30	0.35	0.37	0.43	0.50	0.55	0.74	0.80
141	0.05	0.05	0.09	0.11	0.14	0.20	0.22	0.27	0.34	0.39	0.41	0.48	0.55	0.61	0.80	0.86
213	0.06	0.06	0.11	0.15	0.19	0.28	0.31	0.38	0.49	0.55	0.58	0.67	0.74	0.80	0.94	0.97
243	0.06	0.07	0.12	0.17	0.21	0.32	0.35	0.43	0.54	0.61	0.64	0.73	0.80	0.85	0.97	0.99
286	0.07	0.07	0.14	0.19	0.24	0.36	0.40	0.49	0.61	0.68	0.72	0.80	0.86	0.91	0.99	*
346	0.07	0.08	0.16	0.22	0.28	0.43	0.47	0.57	0.70	0.77	0.80	0.87	0.92	0.95	*	*
369	0.08	0.08	0.17	0.23	0.30	0.45	0.50	0.60	0.73	0.80	0.83	0.89	0.94	0.97	*	*
437	0.08	0.09	0.19	0.26	0.35	0.52	0.57	0.68	0.80	0.86	0.89	0.94	0.97	0.98	*	*
582	0.10	0.11	0.24	0.34	0.44	0.64	0.69	0.80	0.90	0.94	0.96	0.98	0.99	*	*	*
745	0.11	0.13	0.30	0.42	0.54	0.75	0.80	0.89	0.96	0.98	0.99	*	*	*	*	*
840	0.12	0.14	0.33	0.46	0.59	0.80	0.84	0.92	0.98	0.99	0.99	*	*	*	*	*
1376	0.17	0.20	0.49	0.66	0.80	0.95	0.97	0.99	*	*	*	*	*	*	*	*
1898	0.22	0.26	0.63	0.80	0.91	0.99	0.99	*	*	*	*	*	*	*	*	*
2840	0.31	0.37	0.80	0.93	0.98	*	*	*	*	*	*	*	*	*	*	*

TABLE A18.12   Power tables for logistic regression

f   predicted value as a proportion of the sample .12 or .14

event as a proportion of sample = .12
odds ratio

N	1.10 0.91	1.11 0.90	1.20 0.83	1.25 0.80	1.30 0.77	1.40 0.71	1.43 0.70	1.50 0.67	1.60 0.63	1.67 0.60	1.70 0.59	1.80 0.56	1.90 0.53	2.00 0.50	2.50 0.40	3.00 0.33
116	0.05	0.05	0.09	0.11	0.13	0.19	0.21	0.26	0.32	0.37	0.39	0.46	0.52	0.58	0.76	0.80
127	0.05	0.06	0.09	0.12	0.14	0.21	0.23	0.28	0.35	0.40	0.42	0.50	0.56	0.62	0.80	0.84
187	0.06	0.06	0.12	0.15	0.19	0.29	0.31	0.39	0.49	0.56	0.59	0.67	0.74	0.80	0.94	0.96
214	0.06	0.07	0.13	0.17	0.21	0.32	0.35	0.44	0.55	0.62	0.65	0.73	0.80	0.85	0.97	0.98
250	0.07	0.07	0.14	0.19	0.24	0.37	0.40	0.50	0.62	0.69	0.72	0.80	0.86	0.91	0.98	0.99
302	0.07	0.08	0.16	0.22	0.29	0.43	0.47	0.58	0.70	0.77	0.80	0.87	0.92	0.95	*	*
321	0.08	0.08	0.17	0.23	0.30	0.45	0.50	0.60	0.73	0.80	0.83	0.89	0.94	0.96	*	*
379	0.08	0.09	0.19	0.27	0.35	0.52	0.57	0.68	0.80	0.86	0.89	0.94	0.97	0.98	*	*
504	0.10	0.11	0.24	0.34	0.44	0.64	0.69	0.80	0.90	0.94	0.96	0.98	0.99	*	*	*
644	0.11	0.13	0.30	0.42	0.54	0.75	0.80	0.89	0.96	0.98	0.99	*	*	*	*	*
726	0.12	0.14	0.33	0.46	0.59	0.80	0.84	0.92	0.98	0.99	0.99	*	*	*	*	*
1187	0.17	0.20	0.49	0.66	0.80	0.95	0.97	0.99	*	*	*	*	*	*	*	*
1638	0.22	0.26	0.63	0.80	0.91	0.99	0.99	*	*	*	*	*	*	*	*	*
2448	0.31	0.37	0.80	0.93	0.98	*	*	*	*	*	*	*	*	*	*	*

event as a proportion of sample = .14
odds ratio

N	1.10 0.91	1.11 0.90	1.20 0.83	1.25 0.80	1.30 0.77	1.40 0.71	1.43 0.70	1.50 0.67	1.60 0.63	1.67 0.60	1.70 0.59	1.80 0.56	1.90 0.53	2.00 0.50	2.50 0.40	3.00 0.33
110	0.05	0.05	0.09	0.11	0.14	0.20	0.22	0.27	0.34	0.39	0.41	0.48	0.54	0.60	0.77	0.80
117	0.05	0.06	0.09	0.12	0.15	0.21	0.23	0.28	0.36	0.41	0.44	0.51	0.57	0.63	0.80	0.83
169	0.06	0.07	0.12	0.15	0.20	0.29	0.32	0.39	0.50	0.56	0.59	0.67	0.74	0.80	0.93	0.95
192	0.06	0.07	0.13	0.17	0.22	0.32	0.36	0.44	0.55	0.62	0.65	0.73	0.80	0.85	0.96	0.98
224	0.07	0.07	0.14	0.19	0.25	0.37	0.41	0.50	0.62	0.69	0.72	0.80	0.86	0.90	0.98	0.99
270	0.07	0.08	0.16	0.22	0.29	0.43	0.48	0.58	0.70	0.77	0.80	0.87	0.92	0.95	0.99	*
287	0.08	0.08	0.17	0.23	0.30	0.46	0.50	0.60	0.73	0.80	0.83	0.89	0.94	0.96	*	*
338	0.08	0.09	0.19	0.27	0.35	0.52	0.57	0.68	0.80	0.86	0.88	0.94	0.97	0.98	*	*
449	0.10	0.11	0.24	0.34	0.44	0.64	0.69	0.80	0.90	0.94	0.96	0.98	0.99	*	*	*
573	0.11	0.13	0.30	0.42	0.54	0.75	0.80	0.89	0.96	0.98	0.99	*	*	*	*	*
645	0.12	0.14	0.33	0.46	0.59	0.80	0.84	0.92	0.97	0.99	0.99	*	*	*	*	*
1053	0.17	0.20	0.49	0.66	0.80	0.95	0.97	0.99	*	*	*	*	*	*	*	*
1451	0.22	0.26	0.63	0.80	0.91	0.99	0.99	*	*	*	*	*	*	*	*	*
2169	0.31	0.37	0.80	0.93	0.98	*	*	*	*	*	*	*	*	*	*	*

TABLE A18.12   Power tables for logistic regression

g   predicted value as a proportion of the sample .16 or .18

event as a proportion of sample = .16
odds ratio

N	1.10 / 0.91	1.11 / 0.90	1.20 / 0.83	1.25 / 0.80	1.30 / 0.77	1.40 / 0.71	1.43 / 0.70	1.50 / 0.67	1.60 / 0.63	1.67 / 0.60	1.70 / 0.59	1.80 / 0.56	1.90 / 0.53	2.00 / 0.50	2.50 / 0.40	3.00 / 0.33
105	0.05	0.06	0.09	0.12	0.15	0.21	0.23	0.28	0.36	0.41	0.43	0.50	0.56	0.62	0.78	0.80
110	0.05	0.06	0.10	0.12	0.15	0.22	0.24	0.29	0.37	0.42	0.45	0.52	0.58	0.64	0.80	0.83
156	0.06	0.07	0.12	0.16	0.20	0.29	0.32	0.40	0.50	0.57	0.60	0.68	0.75	0.80	0.93	0.95
176	0.06	0.07	0.13	0.17	0.22	0.33	0.36	0.44	0.55	0.62	0.65	0.73	0.80	0.85	0.96	0.97
205	0.07	0.07	0.14	0.19	0.25	0.37	0.41	0.50	0.62	0.69	0.72	0.80	0.86	0.90	0.98	0.99
246	0.07	0.08	0.16	0.22	0.29	0.44	0.48	0.58	0.70	0.77	0.80	0.87	0.92	0.95	0.99	*
262	0.08	0.09	0.17	0.24	0.31	0.46	0.50	0.61	0.73	0.80	0.83	0.89	0.93	0.96	*	*
308	0.08	0.09	0.20	0.27	0.35	0.52	0.57	0.68	0.80	0.86	0.88	0.94	0.97	0.98	*	*
407	0.10	0.11	0.24	0.34	0.44	0.64	0.69	0.80	0.90	0.94	0.95	0.98	0.99	*	*	*
522	0.11	0.13	0.30	0.42	0.54	0.75	0.80	0.89	0.96	0.98	0.99	*	*	*	*	*
584	0.12	0.14	0.33	0.46	0.59	0.80	0.84	0.92	0.97	0.99	0.99	*	*	*	*	*
952	0.17	0.20	0.50	0.66	0.80	0.95	0.97	0.99	*	*	*	*	*	*	*	*
1312	0.22	0.26	0.63	0.80	0.91	0.99	0.99	*	*	*	*	*	*	*	*	*
1959	0.31	0.37	0.80	0.93	0.98	*	*	*	*	*	*	*	*	*	*	*

event as a proportion of sample = .18
odds ratio

N	1.10 / 0.91	1.11 / 0.90	1.20 / 0.83	1.25 / 0.80	1.30 / 0.77	1.40 / 0.71	1.43 / 0.70	1.50 / 0.67	1.60 / 0.63	1.67 / 0.60	1.70 / 0.59	1.80 / 0.56	1.90 / 0.53	2.00 / 0.50	2.50 / 0.40	3.00 / 0.33
101	0.05	0.06	0.10	0.12	0.15	0.22	0.24	0.29	0.37	0.42	0.45	0.52	0.58	0.63	0.79	0.80
104	0.05	0.06	0.10	0.12	0.15	0.22	0.25	0.30	0.38	0.43	0.46	0.53	0.59	0.65	0.80	0.82
145	0.06	0.07	0.12	0.16	0.20	0.30	0.33	0.40	0.51	0.57	0.60	0.68	0.75	0.80	0.92	0.94
164	0.06	0.07	0.13	0.17	0.22	0.33	0.36	0.45	0.56	0.62	0.66	0.74	0.80	0.85	0.95	0.97
190	0.07	0.08	0.14	0.19	0.25	0.38	0.41	0.50	0.62	0.69	0.72	0.80	0.86	0.90	0.98	0.98
227	0.07	0.08	0.16	0.22	0.29	0.44	0.48	0.58	0.70	0.77	0.80	0.87	0.92	0.95	0.99	*
242	0.08	0.09	0.17	0.24	0.31	0.46	0.51	0.61	0.73	0.80	0.83	0.89	0.93	0.96	0.99	*
284	0.08	0.09	0.20	0.27	0.35	0.53	0.57	0.68	0.80	0.86	0.88	0.93	0.96	0.98	*	*
375	0.10	0.11	0.25	0.34	0.45	0.65	0.70	0.80	0.90	0.94	0.95	0.98	0.99	*	*	*
480	0.11	0.13	0.30	0.42	0.54	0.75	0.80	0.89	0.96	0.98	0.99	*	*	*	*	*
537	0.12	0.14	0.33	0.46	0.59	0.80	0.84	0.92	0.97	0.99	0.99	*	*	*	*	*
874	0.17	0.20	0.50	0.66	0.80	0.95	0.97	0.99	*	*	*	*	*	*	*	*
1203	0.22	0.26	0.63	0.80	0.91	0.99	0.99	*	*	*	*	*	*	*	*	*
1796	0.31	0.37	0.80	0.93	0.98	*	*	*	*	*	*	*	*	*	*	*

TABLE A18.12   Power tables for logistic regression

h   predicted value as a proportion of the sample .20 or .25

event as a proportion of sample = .20

odds ratio

N	1.10 / 0.91	1.11 / 0.90	1.20 / 0.83	1.25 / 0.80	1.30 / 0.77	1.40 / 0.71	1.43 / 0.70	1.50 / 0.67	1.60 / 0.63	1.67 / 0.60	1.70 / 0.59	1.80 / 0.56	1.90 / 0.53	2.00 / 0.50	2.50 / 0.40	3.00 / 0.33
98	0.05	0.06	0.10	0.13	0.16	0.23	0.25	0.30	0.38	0.43	0.46	0.53	0.59	0.65	0.80	0.80
100	0.05	0.06	0.10	0.13	0.16	0.23	0.25	0.31	0.39	0.44	0.47	0.54	0.60	0.66	0.80	0.81
136	0.06	0.07	0.12	0.16	0.20	0.30	0.33	0.40	0.51	0.57	0.60	0.68	0.75	0.80	0.92	0.93
154	0.06	0.07	0.13	0.18	0.22	0.33	0.37	0.45	0.56	0.63	0.66	0.74	0.80	0.85	0.95	0.96
178	0.07	0.08	0.15	0.20	0.25	0.38	0.42	0.51	0.63	0.69	0.72	0.80	0.86	0.90	0.97	0.98
212	0.07	0.08	0.17	0.23	0.29	0.44	0.48	0.58	0.70	0.77	0.80	0.87	0.92	0.95	0.99	0.99
226	0.08	0.09	0.17	0.24	0.31	0.46	0.51	0.61	0.73	0.80	0.83	0.89	0.93	0.96	0.99	*
265	0.08	0.09	0.20	0.27	0.35	0.53	0.57	0.68	0.80	0.86	0.88	0.93	0.96	0.98	*	*
349	0.10	0.11	0.25	0.34	0.45	0.65	0.70	0.80	0.90	0.94	0.95	0.98	0.99	*	*	*
446	0.11	0.13	0.30	0.42	0.54	0.75	0.80	0.89	0.96	0.98	0.98	*	*	*	*	*
499	0.12	0.14	0.33	0.46	0.59	0.80	0.84	0.92	0.97	0.99	0.99	*	*	*	*	*
811	0.17	0.20	0.50	0.66	0.80	0.95	0.97	0.99	*	*	*	*	*	*	*	*
1116	0.22	0.26	0.63	0.80	0.91	0.99	0.99	*	*	*	*	*	*	*	*	*
1665	0.31	0.37	0.80	0.93	0.98	*	*	*	*	*	*	*	*	*	*	*

event as a proportion of sample = .25

odds ratio

N	1.10 / 0.91	1.11 / 0.90	1.20 / 0.83	1.25 / 0.80	1.30 / 0.77	1.40 / 0.71	1.43 / 0.70	1.50 / 0.67	1.60 / 0.63	1.67 / 0.60	1.70 / 0.59	1.80 / 0.56	1.90 / 0.53	2.00 / 0.50	2.50 / 0.40	3.00 / 0.33
92	0.06	0.06	0.10	0.13	0.17	0.24	0.27	0.33	0.41	0.46	0.49	0.56	0.62	0.67	0.81	0.80
91	0.06	0.06	0.10	0.13	0.17	0.24	0.26	0.32	0.41	0.46	0.48	0.56	0.62	0.67	0.80	0.80
121	0.06	0.07	0.12	0.16	0.21	0.31	0.34	0.41	0.52	0.58	0.61	0.69	0.75	0.80	0.91	0.91
136	0.07	0.07	0.13	0.18	0.23	0.34	0.37	0.46	0.57	0.63	0.66	0.74	0.80	0.85	0.94	0.95
156	0.07	0.08	0.15	0.20	0.26	0.38	0.42	0.51	0.63	0.70	0.73	0.80	0.86	0.90	0.97	0.97
186	0.08	0.08	0.17	0.23	0.30	0.45	0.49	0.59	0.71	0.77	0.80	0.87	0.91	0.94	0.99	0.99
197	0.08	0.09	0.18	0.24	0.31	0.47	0.51	0.61	0.73	0.80	0.82	0.89	0.93	0.95	0.99	0.99
230	0.08	0.09	0.20	0.27	0.36	0.53	0.58	0.68	0.80	0.86	0.88	0.93	0.96	0.98	*	*
302	0.10	0.11	0.25	0.35	0.45	0.65	0.70	0.80	0.90	0.94	0.95	0.98	0.99	*	*	*
385	0.11	0.13	0.30	0.42	0.54	0.75	0.80	0.89	0.96	0.98	0.98	0.99	*	*	*	*
431	0.12	0.14	0.33	0.46	0.59	0.80	0.84	0.92	0.97	0.99	0.99	*	*	*	*	*
698	0.17	0.20	0.50	0.67	0.80	0.95	0.97	0.99	*	*	*	*	*	*	*	*
960	0.22	0.26	0.63	0.80	0.91	0.99	0.99	*	*	*	*	*	*	*	*	*
1430	0.31	0.37	0.80	0.93	0.98	*	*	*	*	*	*	*	*	*	*	*

TABLE A18.12   Power tables for logistic regression

i   predicted value as a proportion of the sample .30 or .35

event as a proportion of sample = .30

odds ratio

N	1.10	1.11	1.20	1.25	1.30	1.40	1.43	1.50	1.60	1.67	1.70	1.80	1.90	2.00	2.50	3.00
	0.91	0.90	0.83	0.80	0.77	0.71	0.70	0.67	0.63	0.60	0.59	0.56	0.53	0.50	0.40	0.33
89	0.06	0.06	0.11	0.14	0.18	0.26	0.29	0.35	0.44	0.49	0.52	0.59	0.65	0.70	0.82	0.80
86	0.06	0.06	0.11	0.14	0.17	0.25	0.28	0.34	0.42	0.48	0.50	0.57	0.63	0.68	0.80	0.79
111	0.06	0.07	0.13	0.17	0.21	0.31	0.35	0.42	0.52	0.59	0.62	0.69	0.75	0.80	0.90	0.90
124	0.07	0.07	0.14	0.18	0.23	0.35	0.38	0.46	0.57	0.64	0.67	0.74	0.80	0.85	0.94	0.93
142	0.07	0.08	0.15	0.20	0.26	0.39	0.43	0.52	0.63	0.70	0.73	0.80	0.86	0.89	0.96	0.96
168	0.08	0.08	0.17	0.23	0.30	0.45	0.49	0.59	0.71	0.77	0.80	0.87	0.91	0.94	0.98	0.99
178	0.08	0.09	0.18	0.24	0.32	0.47	0.51	0.62	0.74	0.80	0.82	0.89	0.93	0.95	0.99	0.99
207	0.09	0.10	0.20	0.28	0.36	0.53	0.58	0.68	0.80	0.86	0.88	0.93	0.96	0.98	*	*
271	0.10	0.11	0.25	0.35	0.45	0.65	0.70	0.80	0.90	0.94	0.95	0.98	0.99	0.99	*	*
345	0.12	0.13	0.31	0.42	0.55	0.75	0.80	0.89	0.95	0.98	0.98	0.99	*	*	*	*
386	0.12	0.14	0.34	0.47	0.59	0.80	0.84	0.92	0.97	0.99	0.99	*	*	*	*	*
623	0.18	0.20	0.50	0.67	0.80	0.95	0.97	0.99	*	*	*	*	*	*	*	*
855	0.22	0.26	0.63	0.80	0.91	0.99	0.99	*	*	*	*	*	*	*	*	*
1274	0.31	0.37	0.80	0.93	0.98	*	*	*	*	*	*	*	*	*	*	*

event as a proportion of sample = .35

odds ratio

N	1.10	1.11	1.20	1.25	1.30	1.40	1.43	1.50	1.60	1.67	1.70	1.80	1.90	2.00	2.50	3.00
	0.91	0.90	0.83	0.80	0.77	0.71	0.70	0.67	0.63	0.60	0.59	0.56	0.53	0.50	0.40	0.33
86	0.06	0.06	0.11	0.15	0.19	0.27	0.30	0.36	0.45	0.51	0.54	0.61	0.67	0.72	0.83	0.80
82	0.06	0.06	0.11	0.14	0.18	0.26	0.29	0.35	0.44	0.49	0.52	0.59	0.65	0.69	0.80	0.78
104	0.06	0.07	0.13	0.17	0.22	0.32	0.35	0.43	0.53	0.59	0.62	0.70	0.76	0.80	0.90	0.89
115	0.07	0.07	0.14	0.18	0.24	0.35	0.38	0.47	0.58	0.64	0.67	0.74	0.80	0.84	0.93	0.92
131	0.07	0.08	0.15	0.20	0.26	0.39	0.43	0.52	0.63	0.70	0.73	0.80	0.85	0.89	0.96	0.95
155	0.08	0.09	0.17	0.23	0.30	0.45	0.49	0.59	0.71	0.77	0.80	0.87	0.91	0.94	0.98	0.98
164	0.08	0.09	0.18	0.25	0.32	0.47	0.52	0.62	0.74	0.80	0.82	0.88	0.92	0.95	0.99	0.99
191	0.09	0.10	0.20	0.28	0.36	0.53	0.58	0.69	0.80	0.86	0.88	0.93	0.96	0.97	*	0.99
249	0.10	0.11	0.25	0.35	0.45	0.65	0.70	0.80	0.90	0.93	0.95	0.98	0.99	0.99	*	*
316	0.12	0.13	0.31	0.43	0.55	0.75	0.80	0.89	0.95	0.98	0.98	0.99	*	*	*	*
353	0.12	0.14	0.34	0.47	0.59	0.80	0.84	0.92	0.97	0.99	0.99	*	*	*	*	*
569	0.18	0.20	0.50	0.67	0.80	0.95	0.97	0.99	*	*	*	*	*	*	*	*
781	0.22	0.26	0.63	0.80	0.91	0.99	0.99	*	*	*	*	*	*	*	*	*
1162	0.31	0.37	0.80	0.93	0.98	*	*	*	*	*	*	*	*	*	*	*

TABLE A18.12   Power tables for logistic regression

j   predicted value as a proportion of the sample .40 or .45

event as a proportion of sample = .40

odds ratio

N	1.10	1.11	1.20	1.25	1.30	1.40	1.43	1.50	1.60	1.67	1.70	1.80	1.90	2.00	2.50	3.00
	0.91	0.90	0.83	0.80	0.77	0.71	0.70	0.67	0.63	0.60	0.59	0.56	0.53	0.50	0.40	0.33
84	0.06	0.07	0.12	0.15	0.19	0.28	0.31	0.38	0.47	0.53	0.55	0.63	0.68	0.73	0.83	0.80
79	0.06	0.06	0.11	0.15	0.18	0.27	0.30	0.36	0.45	0.50	0.53	0.60	0.66	0.70	0.80	0.77
98	0.06	0.07	0.13	0.17	0.22	0.32	0.36	0.43	0.54	0.60	0.62	0.70	0.76	0.80	0.89	0.87
109	0.07	0.07	0.14	0.19	0.24	0.36	0.39	0.47	0.58	0.65	0.67	0.75	0.80	0.84	0.92	0.91
124	0.07	0.08	0.15	0.21	0.27	0.40	0.44	0.53	0.64	0.70	0.73	0.80	0.85	0.89	0.95	0.95
146	0.08	0.09	0.17	0.24	0.31	0.46	0.50	0.60	0.71	0.78	0.80	0.87	0.91	0.94	0.98	0.98
154	0.08	0.09	0.18	0.25	0.32	0.48	0.52	0.62	0.74	0.80	0.82	0.88	0.92	0.95	0.98	0.98
179	0.09	0.10	0.20	0.28	0.37	0.54	0.58	0.69	0.80	0.86	0.88	0.93	0.96	0.97	0.99	0.99
233	0.10	0.11	0.25	0.35	0.46	0.65	0.70	0.80	0.90	0.93	0.95	0.97	0.99	0.99	*	*
295	0.12	0.13	0.31	0.43	0.55	0.76	0.80	0.89	0.95	0.98	0.98	0.99	*	*	*	*
329	0.13	0.14	0.34	0.47	0.60	0.80	0.84	0.92	0.97	0.99	0.99	*	*	*	*	*
529	0.18	0.21	0.50	0.67	0.80	0.95	0.97	0.99	*	*	*	*	*	*	*	*
725	0.23	0.26	0.63	0.80	0.91	0.99	0.99	*	*	*	*	*	*	*	*	*
1078	0.31	0.37	0.80	0.93	0.98	*	*	*	*	*	*	*	*	*	*	*

event as a proportion of sample = .45

odds ratio

N	1.10	1.11	1.20	1.25	1.30	1.40	1.43	1.50	1.60	1.67	1.70	1.80	1.90	2.00	2.50	3.00
	0.91	0.90	0.83	0.80	0.77	0.71	0.70	0.67	0.63	0.60	0.59	0.56	0.53	0.50	0.40	0.33
82	0.06	0.07	0.12	0.16	0.20	0.29	0.32	0.39	0.48	0.54	0.57	0.64	0.70	0.74	0.83	0.80
76	0.06	0.06	0.11	0.15	0.19	0.27	0.30	0.37	0.45	0.51	0.53	0.60	0.66	0.71	0.80	0.76
94	0.06	0.07	0.13	0.18	0.22	0.33	0.36	0.44	0.54	0.60	0.63	0.70	0.76	0.80	0.89	0.86
104	0.07	0.07	0.14	0.19	0.24	0.36	0.39	0.48	0.59	0.65	0.68	0.75	0.80	0.84	0.92	0.90
118	0.07	0.08	0.16	0.21	0.27	0.40	0.44	0.53	0.64	0.71	0.73	0.80	0.85	0.89	0.95	0.94
138	0.08	0.09	0.17	0.24	0.31	0.46	0.50	0.60	0.71	0.78	0.80	0.86	0.90	0.93	0.98	0.97
146	0.08	0.09	0.18	0.25	0.32	0.48	0.52	0.62	0.74	0.80	0.82	0.88	0.92	0.95	0.98	0.98
169	0.09	0.10	0.20	0.28	0.37	0.54	0.58	0.69	0.80	0.86	0.88	0.92	0.95	0.97	0.99	0.99
220	0.10	0.11	0.25	0.35	0.46	0.65	0.70	0.80	0.90	0.93	0.95	0.97	0.99	0.99	*	*
278	0.12	0.13	0.31	0.43	0.55	0.76	0.80	0.89	0.95	0.97	0.98	0.99	*	*	*	*
310	0.13	0.14	0.34	0.47	0.60	0.80	0.84	0.92	0.97	0.99	0.99	*	*	*	*	*
498	0.18	0.21	0.50	0.67	0.80	0.95	0.97	0.99	*	*	*	*	*	*	*	*
682	0.23	0.27	0.63	0.80	0.91	0.99	0.99	*	*	*	*	*	*	*	*	*
1013	0.31	0.37	0.80	0.93	0.98	*	*	*	*	*	*	*	*	*	*	*

TABLE A18.12   Power tables for logistic regression

k   predicted value as a proportion of the sample .50

event as a proportion of sample = .50
odds ratio

N	1.10	1.11	1.20	1.25	1.30	1.40	1.43	1.50	1.60	1.67	1.70	1.80	1.90	2.00	2.50	3.00
	0.91	0.90	0.83	0.80	0.77	0.71	0.70	0.67	0.63	0.60	0.59	0.56	0.53	0.50	0.40	0.33
81	0.06	0.07	0.12	0.16	0.21	0.30	0.33	0.40	0.50	0.56	0.58	0.65	0.71	0.75	0.84	0.80
74	0.06	0.07	0.12	0.15	0.19	0.28	0.31	0.37	0.46	0.52	0.54	0.61	0.67	0.71	0.80	0.76
91	0.07	0.07	0.13	0.18	0.23	0.33	0.37	0.45	0.55	0.61	0.64	0.71	0.76	0.80	0.88	0.85
100	0.07	0.08	0.14	0.19	0.25	0.36	0.40	0.48	0.59	0.65	0.68	0.75	0.80	0.84	0.91	0.89
113	0.07	0.08	0.16	0.21	0.27	0.40	0.44	0.53	0.64	0.71	0.73	0.80	0.85	0.89	0.95	0.93
132	0.08	0.09	0.18	0.24	0.31	0.46	0.50	0.60	0.71	0.78	0.80	0.86	0.90	0.93	0.97	0.97
140	0.08	0.09	0.18	0.25	0.33	0.48	0.53	0.63	0.74	0.80	0.82	0.88	0.92	0.94	0.98	0.97
162	0.09	0.10	0.21	0.28	0.37	0.54	0.59	0.69	0.80	0.86	0.88	0.92	0.95	0.97	0.99	0.99
209	0.10	0.11	0.25	0.35	0.46	0.65	0.70	0.80	0.89	0.93	0.95	0.97	0.99	0.99	*	*
264	0.12	0.13	0.31	0.43	0.55	0.76	0.80	0.89	0.95	0.97	0.98	0.99	*	*	*	*
295	0.13	0.14	0.34	0.47	0.60	0.80	0.84	0.92	0.97	0.98	0.99	*	*	*	*	*
473	0.18	0.21	0.50	0.67	0.80	0.95	0.97	0.99	*	*	*	*	*	*	*	*
647	0.23	0.27	0.63	0.80	0.91	0.99	0.99	*	*	*	*	*	*	*	*	*
960	0.31	0.37	0.80	0.93	0.98	*	*	*	*	*	*	*	*	*	*	*

Miscellaneous tables

Random numbers

To use Table A19.1 decide on a starting point by choosing a row and column, for example, row 7 and column 10. Then read off the numbers of the appropriate size. Thus, if the numbers to be chosen were between 0 and 99, then the first three numbers would be 66, 74 and 13. When looking for numbers in the range 0 to 9 treat 03 as 3, and so on.

TABLE A19.1 Random numbers

column

row	1	2	3	4	5	6	7	8	9	10	11	12	13	14	15	16	17	18	19	20	21	22	23	24	25	26	27	28	29	30
1	2	4	1	3	0	3	6	3	7	8	0	3	5	7	2	3	5	3	6	5	7	4	2	8	7	5	8	1	5	0
2	4	3	1	3	8	2	7	7	6	1	4	8	2	4	4	5	7	3	5	8	6	3	5	5	2	0	7	4	5	4
3	7	1	6	4	7	3	5	6	7	2	2	1	3	0	2	4	6	5	4	4	0	0	8	2	5	2	8	0	8	6
4	6	2	0	5	3	0	3	0	5	4	8	6	5	8	6	1	6	7	8	3	5	0	1	8	6	4	8	1	0	4
5	1	3	8	3	7	1	2	5	5	6	3	4	0	4	5	5	1	0	2	4	8	3	5	7	6	6	2	3	6	3
6	8	4	5	2	4	7	2	4	7	5	4	5	0	2	3	6	6	4	4	2	7	5	3	2	0	8	1	2	5	0
7	1	7	0	0	5	6	3	4	5	6	6	7	4	1	3	4	6	4	8	5	1	6	0	8	3	0	0	8	7	7
8	1	8	0	3	1	2	8	6	6	0	6	1	6	4	6	1	3	8	6	1	5	3	4	1	6	2	0	4	5	5
9	1	4	8	6	2	4	2	2	4	0	7	7	7	6	1	8	7	0	1	0	4	1	1	2	0	7	1	1	0	3
10	6	2	0	3	5	2	2	7	0	3	8	8	7	3	8	6	5	2	7	3	1	8	3	2	7	2	1	2	2	0
11	8	1	6	1	7	2	1	0	0	0	2	4	8	0	0	7	1	3	0	1	2	7	2	1	3	4	8	5	4	5
12	0	1	7	0	7	5	8	2	3	0	3	7	5	1	4	6	6	8	1	3	5	4	7	5	1	5	7	5	4	8
13	1	5	5	0	6	0	8	5	2	4	7	2	5	7	2	4	6	1	6	8	7	0	2	0	2	8	4	4	4	7
14	2	4	2	1	1	1	2	7	8	4	1	2	2	5	7	7	2	6	1	5	5	7	6	5	2	7	1	4	5	6
15	5	3	8	4	5	4	1	0	4	0	1	6	1	4	3	0	4	0	2	1	7	5	0	1	5	7	5	5	2	5
16	0	7	1	7	3	5	2	0	7	3	7	2	2	6	8	7	4	7	1	2	4	2	0	2	0	4	2	4	6	1
17	7	8	0	7	4	4	4	5	0	7	2	1	7	1	1	1	7	2	2	2	3	4	7	4	3	4	7	5	0	6
18	2	6	6	7	4	3	6	1	6	2	2	5	3	4	0	7	3	3	0	7	5	4	2	4	4	5	4	7	0	7
19	4	3	5	0	6	6	8	5	8	4	0	8	6	7	0	4	0	3	7	1	5	8	3	8	1	2	6	4	6	8
20	1	2	5	3	2	0	0	2	1	0	1	5	2	8	7	7	2	5	7	6	8	3	1	5	3	0	8	8	0	3
21	0	4	4	5	5	1	0	3	3	4	2	0	6	7	6	7	3	1	2	3	5	6	8	5	8	2	0	5	6	2
22	2	7	8	7	0	0	5	6	1	6	8	3	8	3	6	2	8	7	5	3	2	5	5	6	6	0	4	7	4	1
23	4	0	8	3	0	0	5	4	3	6	6	4	1	8	6	2	7	4	3	3	2	1	4	1	6	0	4	8	1	7
24	4	2	6	1	2	4	2	0	2	5	2	6	7	7	6	3	7	3	4	4	6	2	7	8	1	2	8	0	2	6
25	1	2	8	2	2	6	6	8	4	0	2	1	6	6	2	2	4	2	0	8	6	8	0	8	0	1	4	6	6	6
26	4	3	3	3	2	8	6	0	0	3	2	0	0	3	8	4	4	4	0	4	6	0	0	7	7	3	8	3	7	6
27	6	2	7	6	1	1	4	5	2	2	5	8	6	0	1	6	5	6	0	5	3	2	6	2	6	6	3	8	2	6
28	0	4	6	3	0	2	6	2	4	4	8	8	6	5	0	6	0	6	3	0	4	4	8	0	5	4	0	8	0	0
29	1	8	4	7	7	8	6	0	0	3	7	8	1	4	5	4	3	3	0	7	8	0	0	8	6	0	6	1	4	2
30	7	2	8	8	6	0	3	4	7	4	7	8	7	6	6	5	6	4	5	7	8	4	4	6	1	2	6	3	1	6
31	1	3	1	0	8	4	8	4	5	8	7	4	5	6	5	8	7	5	1	2	2	5	6	8	3	7	7	1	6	2
32	0	5	4	5	6	1	0	8	4	0	3	7	2	5	3	3	5	3	0	2	7	4	7	4	0	3	7	5	2	4
33	6	1	1	1	0	8	8	3	6	5	7	2	1	6	8	4	1	2	6	5	6	2	4	4	3	2	4	6	1	2
34	1	4	6	5	4	6	2	3	4	7	8	2	4	6	7	4	2	6	6	8	6	4	1	1	0	8	6	0	3	5
35	2	2	1	8	5	1	6	1	3	8	8	8	3	7	4	8	5	2	2	5	3	1	3	6	0	3	6	2	0	4
36	0	4	4	5	7	8	7	4	0	0	6	5	2	1	7	2	0	4	0	7	8	7	3	7	4	2	6	7	3	8
37	5	7	8	4	2	5	8	6	3	0	5	1	7	1	1	8	8	6	6	4	7	0	5	1	6	5	7	1	7	8
38	5	0	6	7	4	0	4	6	2	3	6	5	7	3	8	0	2	4	3	4	0	4	5	1	1	5	2	0	0	2
39	0	2	3	0	3	4	4	8	4	2	8	1	3	7	8	4	7	1	8	7	5	1	3	6	0	8	5	5	4	1
40	5	3	0	1	4	1	7	6	4	1	8	8	4	2	3	4	8	7	2	8	0	2	1	3	8	4	2	1	0	0

TABLE A19.1 Random numbers

row	1	2	3	4	5	6	7	8	9	10	11	12	13	14	15	16	17	18	19	20	21	22	23	24	25	26	27	28	29	30
41	0	6	7	1	5	6	3	3	1	8	0	6	1	1	6	7	5	0	7	5	3	3	3	3	1	2	8	5	4	2
42	6	1	8	6	1	5	6	7	2	5	3	6	4	3	0	2	4	4	5	8	2	3	5	8	2	1	2	3	0	3
43	0	4	1	8	7	6	2	7	3	5	6	8	1	1	5	6	4	4	3	7	3	0	1	7	7	3	8	5	7	1
44	0	1	1	7	6	7	5	2	1	7	3	6	8	3	0	0	5	3	4	4	6	3	2	6	5	4	3	2	6	2
45	2	2	0	4	7	1	5	6	7	4	7	5	1	8	6	7	3	5	2	0	0	7	1	7	3	0	6	8	6	6
46	8	2	7	5	2	5	2	6	4	1	5	4	0	0	3	4	4	4	8	5	2	4	1	2	1	8	5	3	4	2
47	2	0	4	1	4	8	4	5	3	8	6	2	7	3	2	2	3	8	1	2	3	7	1	1	2	6	5	0	2	4
48	2	0	7	8	3	5	0	6	8	2	4	4	5	8	0	6	5	8	8	0	7	2	8	8	1	6	2	3	0	3
49	0	7	5	5	7	7	8	0	1	3	2	8	0	8	0	3	6	6	5	5	3	3	4	8	2	8	4	0	1	1
50	1	7	4	7	3	6	8	3	0	5	6	2	8	6	8	1	4	3	7	0	5	2	2	6	8	1	8	2	5	5
51	7	1	3	3	4	2	1	8	0	5	4	3	2	2	3	3	7	6	1	0	8	3	1	1	5	0	8	8	0	6
52	5	4	7	6	6	6	4	0	2	4	4	2	2	0	6	8	1	1	6	3	4	2	0	2	1	7	6	0	4	2
53	7	4	6	8	8	0	7	4	5	0	1	6	7	3	8	1	1	0	1	3	2	4	1	8	2	2	6	6	4	3
54	3	0	7	2	3	8	6	4	6	4	1	8	0	6	4	3	0	6	2	6	5	4	3	7	2	2	5	0	1	4
55	0	1	0	2	0	7	1	6	5	3	2	0	1	4	4	5	8	5	7	0	4	8	4	7	5	5	6	4	8	7
56	8	3	6	4	7	2	8	6	1	8	5	7	6	8	0	2	6	7	6	7	5	7	6	2	7	7	0	3	4	7
57	2	8	7	0	4	6	3	8	8	3	2	5	2	5	3	6	3	2	7	7	2	8	8	3	6	1	3	2	8	8
58	6	5	0	4	6	0	7	4	8	6	6	3	2	1	7	1	0	2	0	1	0	7	6	8	7	4	2	1	3	6
59	3	7	2	3	4	3	3	6	5	5	0	8	1	2	1	5	3	5	2	2	3	3	7	3	7	4	2	8	5	2
60	8	5	6	7	3	5	3	4	3	4	6	3	0	6	2	3	1	0	8	3	1	6	2	2	0	2	0	3	0	4
61	7	1	8	4	7	6	0	8	1	1	1	5	2	6	6	7	7	8	4	1	0	1	8	3	1	5	2	1	7	0
62	0	5	4	3	3	3	4	7	1	6	7	5	2	8	7	1	8	3	1	0	2	1	6	6	5	7	7	5	5	7
63	5	2	5	0	3	1	8	5	6	5	5	7	1	3	7	6	4	5	0	8	5	8	6	8	8	8	0	0	2	8
64	4	2	2	2	0	1	3	0	3	6	1	0	0	7	5	8	2	6	1	1	4	8	1	1	1	2	4	4	4	4
65	5	5	2	3	8	3	0	1	6	5	8	8	0	5	4	5	7	6	1	3	7	2	6	6	4	6	4	8	6	2
66	6	3	1	8	3	1	7	2	2	3	7	5	8	7	1	4	6	8	3	2	6	1	1	5	3	8	4	5	2	3
67	7	2	2	7	2	4	7	2	7	5	7	8	4	5	5	0	2	6	6	6	8	6	5	8	1	7	6	5	0	4
68	3	1	1	6	3	4	7	1	1	5	0	5	6	6	0	5	3	8	0	6	5	5	6	5	5	4	2	2	8	6
69	1	2	3	5	6	0	1	6	1	3	3	8	7	6	6	6	7	5	0	2	0	5	0	4	1	7	6	4	8	8
70	7	0	2	3	6	3	4	7	4	2	4	8	1	4	0	8	7	8	5	2	1	0	7	7	7	0	4	1	7	3
71	1	3	2	1	8	1	5	6	6	2	5	5	4	3	1	0	8	3	0	7	4	2	7	5	5	2	8	0	5	2
72	5	6	1	6	2	2	7	0	0	3	8	1	3	3	1	0	0	2	4	1	2	6	7	4	8	3	4	3	7	5
73	6	0	5	1	1	3	6	1	7	0	5	7	3	3	8	6	6	1	8	6	4	3	6	1	7	8	1	2	0	2
74	8	7	6	0	0	8	5	4	0	3	2	6	7	5	1	6	4	5	8	8	1	2	4	8	4	2	4	1	8	1
75	1	3	7	2	2	0	1	3	2	7	5	1	8	5	3	6	6	1	7	3	4	6	4	2	6	4	4	8	2	1
76	8	6	7	3	8	1	3	7	0	4	8	7	3	3	8	7	3	0	5	0	8	6	3	4	6	6	2	3	0	2
77	0	4	6	8	1	2	8	6	2	8	0	1	8	3	3	8	5	8	6	4	2	1	5	2	8	5	1	4	7	3
78	6	8	8	7	4	3	5	8	4	2	8	4	4	6	2	4	7	0	2	0	5	4	4	7	2	0	0	0	1	0
79	6	3	4	5	4	4	6	3	8	8	0	0	5	6	8	7	6	0	0	7	0	3	3	5	6	5	5	7	8	1
80	3	0	1	3	2	2	8	1	0	6	1	5	7	8	8	3	1	6	0	8	7	4	5	2	1	8	5	4	4	3
81	7	1	4	6	4	1	3	2	0	0	7	4	2	0	5	2	8	6	4	2	5	6	6	3	0	2	6	4	5	7
82	8	3	8	4	8	3	6	0	5	8	1	5	5	3	8	3	8	4	8	4	0	5	1	3	0	8	5	4	4	6
83	6	3	6	7	2	5	1	3	6	7	8	7	5	8	6	6	5	6	6	2	0	8	8	7	8	7	5	5	7	5
84	6	8	5	5	2	3	4	1	5	6	5	3	3	6	8	1	0	2	6	5	3	8	5	5	3	6	8	7	0	8
85	2	7	3	4	4	0	2	6	5	4	4	4	1	5	8	3	6	2	4	6	2	2	2	5	4	8	1	1	1	0
86	1	8	7	1	3	4	1	7	5	5	0	2	8	2	8	6	8	4	0	7	2	2	6	2	1	7	2	2	5	6
87	3	0	8	1	1	5	1	1	5	8	6	7	1	1	7	5	3	3	8	4	1	6	8	7	6	8	3	4	8	7
88	2	5	5	4	4	2	1	8	0	2	1	6	4	4	2	7	7	1	2	5	2	0	3	2	5	0	4	0	1	6
89	7	3	7	4	4	5	2	1	2	1	2	1	8	2	7	0	7	5	2	6	8	4	5	4	1	3	4	6	3	6
90	0	5	0	0	1	7	3	6	7	2	8	3	7	8	7	4	3	0	2	4	5	1	5	3	0	7	5	1	5	6
91	1	6	4	2	7	2	6	1	7	8	6	3	4	0	6	6	0	4	3	8	4	2	6	5	5	0	2	5	0	4
92	7	4	6	4	5	7	3	5	4	7	0	0	3	7	1	0	1	8	1	4	0	2	5	0	1	4	0	4	2	1
93	8	6	6	1	7	1	3	8	0	7	5	1	3	4	5	1	3	8	3	6	6	4	0	6	5	8	2	6	5	1
94	3	3	7	7	2	4	8	3	1	1	2	6	7	7	7	7	1	1	5	2	4	3	3	1	7	4	3	5	1	4
95	5	8	6	8	3	3	0	5	0	6	3	8	5	5	0	8	5	3	4	8	8	4	4	2	1	6	8	2	4	1
96	1	3	3	1	8	7	8	8	3	3	0	6	8	6	5	3	4	7	2	8	6	4	1	6	3	4	2	6	1	7
97	7	7	6	2	4	4	3	1	7	5	1	1	5	4	1	6	0	3	8	0	6	3	4	5	8	3	8	0	7	4
98	3	6	4	5	1	7	6	1	6	1	5	3	8	4	7	6	3	5	3	5	5	0	8	2	1	8	6	0	3	4
99	0	8	3	5	6	1	4	1	8	7	2	6	2	3	5	2	4	0	8	3	7	5	6	6	8	8	0	4	8	3
100	4	3	6	4	4	8	1	8	0	8	2	5	2	2	3	4	4	6	8	3	4	8	4	0	5	2	2	1	1	3

Coefficients for trend tests

Table A19.2 provides the coefficients (c_j) which are appropriate for trend tests when the sample sizes in each level of the IV are the same and when the levels of the IV differ by a regular amount; an example of this would be if the IV was delay, in seconds, before participants were required to recall a list of words, with delays of 5, 10, 15 and 20 seconds. In addition, I have only provided coefficients for linear, quadratic and cubic trends (where applicable). See Myers and Well (2003) for the coefficients for other trends and details of how to calculate the coefficients for trends other than linear ones.

Calculating linear coefficients

With equal intervals and equal sample sizes

The two equations which we need for a linear coefficient, if the intervals between levels of the IV are equal and the sample sizes are the same, are as follows:

$$c_j = a + j \qquad\qquad (A19.1)$$

and

$$\sum(c_j) = 0 \qquad\qquad (A19.2)$$

where a is an algebraic value which will help us to find each c_j, j is the level of the IV and c_j is the coefficient for mean j.

Therefore, if we had three levels in the IV:

$c_1 = a + 1$
$c_2 = a + 2$
$c_3 = a + 3$

In this case, from equation A19.2:

$3a + 6 = 0$

Therefore:

$a = -2$

which means that:

$c_1 = -2 + 1 = -1$
$c_2 = -2 + 2 = 0$
$c_3 = -2 + 3 = 1$

With unequal intervals and unequal sample sizes

In this case, equation A19.1 becomes:

$$c_j = a + X_j \qquad\qquad (A19.3)$$

where X_j is the value of the jth level of the IV, and equation A19.2 becomes:

$$\Sigma(n_j \times c_j) = 0 \qquad\qquad (A19.4)$$

where n_j is the sample size in the jth level of the IV.

For example, imagine that we wanted the coefficients for a linear trend when there were three levels of an IV, we had samples of 10, 15 and 25 participants and the levels of the IV (years spent learning a skill) were 5, 12 and 20. Therefore, from equation A19.3:

$$c_1 = a + 5$$
$$c_2 = a + 12$$
$$c_3 = a + 20$$

and from equation A19.4:

$$10 \times (a + 5) + 15 \times (a + 12) + 25 \times (a + 20) = 0$$

Therefore,

$$50 \times a + 730 = 0$$

which means that:

$$a = \frac{-73}{5}$$

and, from equation A19.3:

$$c_1 = \frac{-48}{5}$$
$$c_2 = \frac{-13}{5}$$
$$c_3 = \frac{27}{5}$$

To simplify the calculations for the linear trend test, we can multiply each of the coefficients by 5 to make them into whole numbers.

With unequal intervals but equal sample sizes

In this case, we can use equation A19.3 and equation A19.2. Therefore, if in the previous example the sample sizes had been the same, from equation 19.3:

$$c_1 = a + 5$$
$$c_2 = a + 12$$
$$c_3 = a + 20$$

and from equation A19.2:

$$3 \times a + 37 = 0$$

in which case:

$$a = \frac{-37}{5}$$

Therefore, from equation A19.3:

$$c_1 = \frac{-22}{3}$$

$$c_2 = \frac{-1}{3}$$

$$c_3 = \frac{23}{3}$$

As with the last example we could simplify the coefficients – in this case, by multiplying each of them by 3.

With equal intervals but unequal sample sizes

In this case, we need equations A19.1 and A19.4. Therefore,

$$c_1 = a + 1$$
$$c_2 = a + 2$$
$$c_3 = a + 3$$

and if the samples had had 10, 15 and 25 participants in them:

$$10 \times (a + 1) + 15 \times (a + 2) + 25 \times (a + 3) = 0$$

which means that:

$$50 \times a + 115 = 0$$

Therefore,

$$a = \frac{-115}{50} \quad \text{or} \quad \frac{-23}{10}$$

In this case:

$$c_1 = \frac{-13}{10}$$

$$c_2 = \frac{-3}{10}$$

$$c_3 = \frac{7}{10}$$

We can multiply each coefficient by 10 to make the calculations for the trend test simpler.

Finding the weightings for a paired contrast with unequal sample sizes

We can use the same procedure as that shown above for finding the coefficients for a linear trend when the sample sizes are unequal but the intervals are the same. However, we are only looking for two coefficients. For example, if we had an IV with three levels, with samples of 5, 10 and 25 and we wished to contrast two conditions, then the equations we would use would be adaptations of equation A19.1 and equation A19.4, but with w_j substituted for c_j. Thus:

$$w_1 = a + 1$$
$$w_2 = a + 2$$

(in a pairwise contrast, always use 1 and 2 in these equations, regardless of the levels of the IV being contrasted)

and

$$\sum\left(n_j \times w_j\right) = 0 \qquad\qquad (A19.5)$$

Therefore, if we were contrasting the first and the third samples,

$$5 \times (a + 1) + 25 \times (a + 2) = 0$$

which means that:

$$30 \times a + 55 = 0$$

and

$$a = \frac{-55}{30} \quad \text{or} \quad \frac{-11}{6}$$

TABLE A19.2   Coefficients for trend tests

Number of levels of IV	Type of trend	Level of IV 1	2	3	4	5	6	7	8	9	10	$\Sigma(c_j)^2$
3	linear	−1	0	1								2
	quadratic	1	−2	1								6
4	linear	−3	−1	1	3							20
	quadratic	1	−1	−1	1							4
	cubic	−1	3	−3	1							20
5	linear	−2	−1	0	1	2						10
	quadratic	2	−1	−2	−1	2						14
	cubic	−1	2	0	−2	1						10
6	linear	−5	−3	−1	1	3	5					70
	quadratic	5	−1	−4	−4	−1	5					84
	cubic	−5	7	4	−4	−7	5					180
7	linear	−3	−2	−1	0	1	2	3				28
	quadratic	5	0	−3	−4	−3	0	5				84
	cubic	−1	1	1	0	−1	−1	1				6
8	linear	−7	−5	−3	−1	1	3	5	7			168
	quadratic	7	1	−3	−5	−5	−3	1	7			168
	cubic	−7	5	7	3	−3	−7	−5	7			264
9	linear	−4	−3	−2	−1	0	1	2	3	4		60
	quadratic	28	7	−8	−17	−20	−17	−8	7	28		2772
	cubic	−14	7	13	9	0	−9	−13	−7	14		990
10	linear	−9	−7	−5	−3	−1	1	3	5	7	9	330
	quadratic	6	2	−1	−3	−4	−4	−3	−1	2	6	132
	cubic	−42	14	35	31	12	−12	−31	−35	−14	42	8580

which means that:

$$w_1 = \frac{-5}{6}$$

$$w_2 = \frac{1}{6}$$

To simplify the calculations in the contrast, we can multiply the weightings by 6, to get −5 and 1.

Conversion of r to r' (Fisher's transformation)

Table A19.3 provides the conversion for a range of values of r. However, when you need to convert a value which is not shown in the table you can use the following equation:

$$r' = 0.5 \times \log_e \left(\frac{1+r}{1-r} \right)$$

This means find the value of $\left(\frac{1+r}{1-r} \right)$, calculate the logarithm to the base e of the result (the natural log, often shown as LN or ln on a calculator) and multiply the answer by 0.5.

For example, if $r = .7$, then:

$$r' = 0.5 \times \log_e \left(\frac{1+.7}{1-.7} \right)$$

$$= 0.5 \times \log_e \left(\frac{1.7}{0.3} \right)$$

$$= 0.5 \times \log_e 5.6667$$

$$= 0.5 \times 1.7346$$

$$= 0.8673$$

Conversion of r' to r

$$r = \frac{e^{(2 \times r')} - 1}{e^{(2 \times r')} + 1}$$

where e = 2.71828 (approximately). For example, if $r' = 0.8673$, then

$$r = \frac{e^{(2 \times 0.8673)} - 1}{e^{(2 \times 0.8673)} + 1}$$

$$= \frac{e^{(1.7346)} - 1}{e^{(1.7346)} + 1}$$

$$= \frac{5.6667 - 1}{5.6667 + 1}$$

$$= \frac{4.6667}{6.6667}$$

$$= .7$$

Fisher's transformation can be calculated by using the $\tanh^{-1}$ function: $r' = \tanh^{-1}(r)$; the conversion can be reversed by using tanh: $r = \tanh(r')$.

TABLE A19.3 Fisher's transformation

r	r'	r	r'	r	r'	r	r'	r	r'
0.000	0.000	0.200	0.203	0.400	0.424	0.600	0.693	0.800	1.099
0.005	0.005	0.205	0.208	0.405	0.430	0.605	0.701	0.805	1.113
0.010	0.010	0.210	0.213	0.410	0.436	0.610	0.709	0.810	1.127
0.015	0.015	0.215	0.218	0.415	0.442	0.615	0.717	0.815	1.142
0.020	0.020	0.220	0.224	0.420	0.448	0.620	0.725	0.820	1.157
0.025	0.025	0.225	0.229	0.425	0.454	0.625	0.733	0.825	1.172
0.030	0.030	0.230	0.234	0.430	0.460	0.630	0.741	0.830	1.188
0.035	0.035	0.235	0.239	0.435	0.466	0.635	0.750	0.835	1.204
0.040	0.040	0.240	0.245	0.440	0.472	0.640	0.758	0.840	1.221
0.045	0.045	0.245	0.250	0.445	0.478	0.645	0.767	0.845	1.238
0.050	0.050	0.250	0.255	0.450	0.485	0.650	0.775	0.850	1.256
0.055	0.055	0.255	0.261	0.455	0.491	0.655	0.784	0.855	1.274
0.060	0.060	0.260	0.266	0.460	0.497	0.660	0.793	0.860	1.293
0.065	0.065	0.265	0.271	0.465	0.504	0.665	0.802	0.865	1.313
0.070	0.070	0.270	0.277	0.470	0.510	0.670	0.811	0.870	1.333
0.075	0.075	0.275	0.282	0.475	0.517	0.675	0.820	0.875	1.354
0.080	0.080	0.280	0.288	0.480	0.523	0.680	0.829	0.880	1.376
0.085	0.085	0.285	0.293	0.485	0.530	0.685	0.838	0.885	1.398
0.090	0.090	0.290	0.299	0.490	0.536	0.690	0.848	0.890	1.422
0.095	0.095	0.295	0.304	0.495	0.543	0.695	0.858	0.895	1.447
0.100	0.100	0.300	0.310	0.500	0.549	0.700	0.867	0.900	1.472
0.105	0.105	0.305	0.315	0.505	0.556	0.705	0.877	0.905	1.499
0.110	0.110	0.310	0.321	0.510	0.563	0.710	0.887	0.910	1.528
0.115	0.116	0.315	0.326	0.515	0.570	0.715	0.897	0.915	1.557
0.120	0.121	0.320	0.332	0.520	0.576	0.720	0.908	0.920	1.589
0.125	0.126	0.325	0.337	0.525	0.583	0.725	0.918	0.925	1.623
0.130	0.131	0.330	0.343	0.530	0.590	0.730	0.929	0.930	1.658
0.135	0.136	0.335	0.348	0.535	0.597	0.735	0.940	0.935	1.697
0.140	0.141	0.340	0.354	0.540	0.604	0.740	0.950	0.940	1.738
0.145	0.146	0.345	0.360	0.545	0.611	0.745	0.962	0.945	1.783
0.150	0.151	0.350	0.365	0.550	0.618	0.750	0.973	0.950	1.832
0.155	0.156	0.355	0.371	0.555	0.626	0.755	0.984	0.955	1.886
0.160	0.161	0.360	0.377	0.560	0.633	0.760	0.996	0.960	1.946
0.165	0.167	0.365	0.383	0.565	0.640	0.765	1.008	0.965	2.014
0.170	0.172	0.370	0.388	0.570	0.648	0.770	1.020	0.970	2.092
0.175	0.177	0.375	0.394	0.575	0.655	0.775	1.033	0.975	2.185
0.180	0.182	0.380	0.400	0.580	0.662	0.780	1.045	0.980	2.298
0.185	0.187	0.385	0.406	0.585	0.670	0.785	1.058	0.985	2.443
0.190	0.192	0.390	0.412	0.590	0.678	0.790	1.071	0.990	2.647
0.195	0.198	0.395	0.418	0.595	0.685	0.795	1.085	0.995	2.994
								0.999	3.800

Abelson, R. P. (1995). *Statistics as principled argument*. Hillsdale, NJ: Lawrence Erlbaum Associates, Inc.

Agresti, A. (1996). *An introduction to categorical data analysis*. New York, NY: Wiley.

Agresti, A. (2002). *Categorical data analysis* (2nd ed.). New York, NY: Wiley.

Agresti, A. (2006). *An introduction to categorical data analysis* (2nd ed.). New York, NY: Wiley.

American Psychological Association (2001). *Publication manual of the American Psychological Association* (5th ed.). Washington, DC: Author.

American Psychological Association (2010). *Publication manual of the American Psychological Association* (6th ed.). Washington, DC: Author.

American Psychological Association (2017). *Ethical principles of psychologists and code of conduct*. Washington, DC: Author.

Anderson, C. J., Bahník, Š., Barnett-Cowan, M., Bosco, F. A., Chandler, J., Chartier, C. R., . . . Zuni, K. (2016). Response to comment on 'Estimating the reproducibility of psychological science'. *Science, 351*, 1037-c.

Anderson, S. F., & Maxwell, S. E. (2016). There's more than one way to conduct a replication study: Beyond statistical significance. *Psychological Methods, 21*, 1–12.

Applebaum, M., Cooper, H., Kline, R. B., Mayo-Wilson, E., Nezu, A. M., & Rao, S. M. (2018). Journal article standards for quantitative research in psychology: The APA publications and communications board task force report. *American Psychologist, 73*, 3–25.

Atkinson, R. C., & Shiffrin, R. M. (1971). The control of short-term memory. *Scientific American, 225*, 82–90.

Baddeley, A. (1990). *Human memory: Theory and practice*. Hove: Lawrence Erlbaum Associates Ltd, Inc.

Bales, R. F. (1950). A set of categories for analysis of small group interaction. *American Sociological Review, 15*, 257–263.

Banister, P., Bunn, G., Burman, E., Daniels, J., Duckett, P., Goodley, D., . . . Whelan, P. (2011). *Qualitative methods in psychology: A research guide* (2nd ed.). Maidenhead: McGraw-Hill/Open University Press.

Baron, R. M., & Kenny, D. A. (1986). The moderator-mediator variable distinction in social psychological research: Conceptual, strategic, and statistical considerations. *Journal of Personality and Social Psychology, 51*, 1173–1182.

Baumgartner, T. A., & Chung, H. (2001). Confidence limits for intraclass reliability coefficients. *Measurement in Physical Education and Exercise Science, 5*, 179–188.

Bayes, T. (1763/1958). An essay towards solving a problem in the doctrine of chances. *The Philosophical Transactions of the Royal Society, 53*, 370–418. Edited version with an introduction and biographical note by Bernard, G. A. (1958). Studies in the history of probability and statistics: IX. Thomas Bayes's essay towards solving a problem in the doctrine of chances. *Biometrika, 45*, 293–315.

Becker, B. J. (2005). Failsafe N of file-drawer number. In H. R. Rothstein, A. J. Sutton & M. Borenstein (Eds.), *Publication bias in meta-analysis: Prevention, assessment and adjustments* (pp. 111–125). Chichester, West Sussex: Wiley.

Belsley, D. A. (1991). *Conditioning diagnostics: Collinearity and weak data in regression*. New York, NY: Wiley.

Benjamin, D. J., Berger, J. O., Johannesson, M., Nosek, B. A., Wagenmakers, E.-J., Berk, R., . . . Johnson, V. E. (2018). Redefine statistical significance. *Nature Human Behavior, 2*, 6–10.

Bethlehem, J. (2010). Selection bias in web surveys. *International Statistical Review, 78*, 161–188.

Birnbaum, M. H. (2004). Human research and data collection via the Internet. *Annual Review of Psychology, 55*, 803–832.

Boden, M. A. (1987). *Artificial intelligence and natural man* (2nd rev. ed.). London: MIT Press.

Boden, M. A. (2016). *AI: Its nature and future*. Oxford: Oxford University Press.

Bogardus, E. S. (1925). Measuring social distances. *Journal of Applied Sociology, 9*, 299–308.

Bollen, K., & Lennox, R. (1991). Conventional wisdom on measurement: A structural equation perspective. *Psychological Bulletin, 110*, 305–314.

Bonge, D. R., Schuldt, W. J., & Harper, Y. Y. (1992). The experimenter-as-fixed-effect fallacy. *Journal of Psychology, 126*(5), 477–486.

Borckardt, J. J., Nash, M. R., Murphy, M. D., Moore, M., Shaw, D., & O'Neil, P. (2008). Clinical practice as natural laboratory for psychotherapy research. *American Psychologist, 63*, 77–95.

Bostrom, N. (2014). *Superintelligence: Paths, dangers, strategies*. Oxford: Oxford University Press.

Brattico, P. (2008). Shallow reductionism and the problem of complexity in psychology. *Theory and Psychology*, *18*, 483–504.

British Psychological Society. (2014). *Code of human research ethics*. Leicester: Author.

Bryant, J. L., & Paulson, A. S. (1976). An extension of Tukey's method of multiple comparisons to experimental designs with random concomitant variables. *Biometrika*, *63*, 631–638.

Buchanan, T., & Smith, J. L. (1999). Using the Internet for psychological research: Personality testing on the World Wide Web. *British Journal of Psychology*, *90*, 125–144.

Byrne, B. M. (2016). *Structural equation modeling with AMOS: Basic concepts, applications and programming* (3rd ed.). London: Routledge.

Chambless, D. L., & Ollendick, T. H. (2001). Empirically supported psychological interventions: Controversies and evidence. *Annual Review of Psychology*, *52*, 685–716.

Chatterjee, S., & Hadi, A. S. (1988). *Sensitivity analysis in linear regression*. New York, NY: Wiley.

Chatterjee, S., Hadi, A. S., & Price, B. (2000). *Regression analysis by example* (3rd ed.). New York, NY: Wiley.

Chen, H., Cohen, P., & Chen, S. (2007). Biased odds ratios from dichotomization of age. *Statistics in Medicine, 26*, 3487–3497.

Chinn, S. (2000). A simple method for converting an odds ratio to effect size for use in meta-analysis. *Statistics in Medicine, 19*, 3127–3131.

Chow, S.-M., & Hoijtink, H. (2017). Bayesian estimation and modeling: Editorial to the second special issue on Bayesian data analysis. *Psychological Methods, 22*, 609–615.

Cicchetti, D. V. (1994). Guidelines, criteria, and rules of thumb for evaluating normed and standardized assessment instruments in psychology. *Psychological Assessment, 6*, 284–290.

Clark-Carter, D. (1997). The account taken of statistical power in research published in the *British Journal of Psychology*. *British Journal of Psychology, 88*, 71–83.

Clark-Carter, D. (1998). Bayesian statistics and Psychology: An alternative to p < 0.05? Paper presented at the European Mathematical Psychology Group, Keele University, UK, 31st August 1998. *Journal of Mathematical Psychology, 42*, 505–506.

Cleveland, W. S. (1985). *The elements of graphing data*. Monterey, CA: Wadsworth.

Cochran, W. G., & Cox, G. M. (1957). *Experimental designs* (2nd ed.). London: Wiley.

Cohen, J. (1962). The statistical power of abnormal-social psychological research: A review. *Journal of Abnormal and Social Psychology, 65*, 145–153.

Cohen, J. (1983). The cost of dichotomization. *Applied Psychological Measurement, 7*, 249–253.

Cohen, J. (1988). *Statistical power analysis for the behavioral sciences* (2nd ed.). Hillsdale, NJ: Lawrence Erlbaum Associates, Inc.

Cohen, J. (1990). Things I have learned (so far). *American Psychologist, 45*, 1304–1312.

Cohen, J., Cohen, P., West, S. G., & Aiken, L. S. (2003). *Applied multiple regression/correlation analysis for the behavioral sciences* (3rd ed.). Mahwah, NJ: Lawrence Erlbaum Associates, Inc.

Comrey, A. L., & Lee, H. B. (1992). *A first course in factor analysis* (2nd ed.). Hillsdale, NJ: Lawrence Erlbaum Associates, Inc.

Conner, M., & Sparks, P. (2015). The theory of planned behavior and the reasoned action approach. In M. Conner & P. Norman (Eds.), *Predicting and changing health behaviour: Research and practice with social cognition models* (3rd ed., pp. 167–216). Maidenhead: Open University Press.

Conroy-Beam, D., & Buss, D. M. (2016). Do mate preferences influence actual mating decisions? Evidence from computer simulations and three studies of mated couples. *Journal of Personality and Social Psychology, 111*, 53–66.

Cook, T. D., & Campbell, D. T. (1979). *Quasi-experimentation: Design and analysis issues for field settings*. Boston, MA: Houghton Mifflin.

Cortina, J. M. (1993). What is coefficient alpha: An examination of theory and applications. *Journal of Applied Psychology, 78*, 98–104.

Danziger, K. (1990). *Constructing the subject*. Cambridge: Cambridge University Press.

Dixon, W. J., & Massey, F. J. Jr. (1983). *Introduction to statistical analysis* (4th ed.). London: McGraw-Hill.

Dobson, A. J., & Barnett, A. G. (2018). *An introduction to generalized linear models* (4th ed.). London: CRC Press.

Dracup, C. (2000). Hypothesis testing: Further misconceptions. *Psychology Teaching Review, 9*, 103–110.

Dugard, P., File, P., & Todman, J. B. (2011). *Single-case and small-n experimental designs: A practical guide to randomization tests* (2nd ed.). New York, NY: Routledge.

Dugard, P., Todman, J. B., & Staines, H. (2010). *Approaching multivariate analysis: A practical introduction* (2nd ed.). London: Routledge.

Duncan, D. (2001). Eighty years of human resource accountancy. *History and Philosophy of Psychology, 3*, 27–31.

Edwards, W., Lindman, H., & Savage, L. J. (1963). Bayesian statistical inference for psychological research. *Psychological Review, 70*, 193–242.

Ericsson, K. A., & Simon, H. A. (1980). Verbal reports as data. *Psychological Review, 87*, 215–251.

Estes, W. K. (1993). Mathematical models in psychology. In G. Keren & C. Lewis (Eds.), *A handbook for data analysis in the behavioural sciences: Methodological issues* (pp. 3–19). Hillsdale, NJ: Lawrence Erlbaum Associates, Inc.

Etz, A., & Vandekerckhove, J. (2016). A Bayesian perspective on the Reproducibility Project: Psychology. *PLoS ONE, 11*, e0149794.

Everitt, B. S., Landau, S., & Leese, M. (2011). *Cluster analysis* (5th ed.). London: Arnold.

Faul, F., Erdfelder, E., Buchner, A., & Lang, A.-G. (2009). Statistical power analyses using G*Power 3.1: Tests for correlation and regression analyses. *Behavior Research Methods, 41*, 1149–1160.

Faul, F., Erdfelder, E., Lang, A.-G., & Buchner, A. (2007). G*Power 3: A flexible statistical power analysis for the social, behavioral, and biomedical sciences. *Behavior Research Methods, 39*, 175–191.

Fisher, R. A. (1925). *Statistical methods for research workers*. Edinburgh: Oliver and Boyd.

Fisher, R. A. (1935). *The design of experiments*. Edinburgh: Oliver and Boyd.

Fodor, J. A. (2000). *The mind doesn't work that way: The scope and limits of computational psychology*. Cambridge, MA: MIT Press.

Friston, K. J. (2005). Models of brain function in neuroimaging. *Annual Review of Psychology, 56*, 57–87.

Gigerenzer, G., Swijtink, Z., Porter, T., Daston, L., Beatty, J., & Krüger, L. (1989). *The empire of chance: How probability changed science and everyday life*. Cambridge: Cambridge University Press.

Gilbert, D. T., King, G., Pettigrew, S., & Wilson, T. D. (2016). Comment on 'Estimating the reproducibility of psychological science'. *Science, 351*, 1037-b.

Gill, J. (2008). *Bayesian methods: A social and behavioural sciences approach* (2nd ed.). Boca Raton, FL: Chapman & Hall/CRC.

Goldberg, D., & Williams, P. (1991). *A user's guide to the General Health Questionnaire*. Windsor: NFER-Nelson.

Gorsuch, R. L. (1983). *Factor analysis*. Hillsdale, NJ: Lawrence Erlbaum Associates, Inc.

Graham, J. W. (2009). Missing data analysis: Making it work in the real world. *Annual Review of Psychology, 60*, 549–576.

Gray, C. D., & Kinnear, P. R. (2012). *IBM SPSS 19 made simple*. Hove: Psychology Press.

Grayson, D. (2004). Some myths and legends in quantitative psychology. *Understanding Statistics, 3*, 101–134.

Gregg, V. H. (1986). *Introduction to human memory*. London: Routledge.

Grice, J., Barrett, P., Cota, L., Felix, C., Taylor, Z., Garner, S., . . . Vest, A. (2017). Four bad habits of modern psychologists. *Behavioral Sciences, 7*, 53.

Guttman, L. (1944). A basis for scaling qualitative data. *American Sociological Review, 9*, 139–150.

Guyon, H., Kop, J.-L., Juhel, J., & Falissard, B. (2018). Measurement, ontology, and epistemology: Psychology needs pragmatism-realism. *Theory and Psychology, 28*, 149–171.

Hagenaars, J. A., & McCutcheon, A. L. (Eds.). (2002). *Applied latent class analysis*. Cambridge: Cambridge University Press.

Harris, R. J. (1997). Reforming significance testing via three-valued logic. In L. L. Harlow, S. A. Mulaik & J. H. Steiger (Eds.), *What if there were no significance tests?* (pp. 145–174). Mahwah, NJ: Lawrence Erlbaum Associates, Inc.

Hayes, N. (1997). *Doing qualitative analysis in psychology*. Hove: Psychology Press.

Hedges, L. V. (1994). Fixed effects models. In H. Cooper & L. V. Hedges (Eds.), *The handbook of research synthesis* (pp. 285–299). New York, NY: Russell Sage Foundation.

Hewitt, A. (2006). A Q study of music teachers' attitudes towards the significance of individual differences for teaching and learning music. *Psychology of Music, 34*, 63–80.

Hewson, C. (2003). Conducting research on the Internet. *The Psychologist, 16*, 290–293.

Hewstone, M., & Stroebe, W. (Eds.). (2001). *Introduction to social psychology: A European perspective* (3rd ed.). Oxford: Blackwell.

Hoijtink, H. (2009). Bayesian data analysis. In R. E. Millsap & A. Maydeu-Olivares (Eds.), *The Sage handbook of quantitative methods in psychology* (pp. 423–443). London: Sage.

Hoijtink, H., & Chow, S.-M. (2017). Bayesian hypothesis testing: Editorial to the special issue on Bayesian data analysis. *Psychological Methods, 22*, 211–216.

Hollis, S., & Campbell, F. (1999). What is meant by intention to treat analysis? Survey of published randomised controlled trails. *British Medical Journal, 319*, 670–674.

Hopewell, S., Clarke, M., & Mallett, S. (2005). Grey literature and systematic reviews. In H. R. Rothstein, A. J. Sutton & M. Borenstein (Eds.), *Publication bias in meta-analysis: Prevention, assessment and adjustments* (pp. 49–72). Chichester, West Sussex: Wiley.

Hosmer, D. W., Lemeshow, S., & Sturdivant, R. X. (2013). *Applied logistic regression* (3rd ed.). Hoboken, NJ: Wiley.

House, J., Marasli, P., Lister, M., & Brown, J. S. L. (2018). Male views on help-seeking for depression: A Q methodology study. *Psychology and Psychotherapy: Theory, Research and Practice, 91*, 117–140.

Howell, D. C. (1997). *Statistical methods for psychology* (4th ed.). Boston, MA: Duxbury.

Howell, D. C. (2002). *Statistical methods for psychology* (5th ed.). Boston, MA: Duxbury.

Howell, D. C. (2013). *Statistical methods for psychology* (8th ed.). Belmont, CA: Wadsworth.

Howson, C., & Urbach, P. (1993). *Scientific reasoning: The Bayesian approach* (2nd ed.). Peru, IL: Open Court.

Hox, J. J., Moerbeek, M., & van de Schoot, R. (2018). *Multilevel analysis: Techniques and applications* (3rd ed.). New York, NY: Routledge.

Hsieh, F. Y. (1989). Sample size tables for logistic regression. *Statistics in Medicine, 8*, 795–802.

Huberty, C. J. (1994). *Applied discriminant analysis.* New York, NY: Wiley.

Huitema, B. E. (1980). *The analysis of covariance and alternatives.* New York, NY: Wiley.

Humphreys, G., & Riddoch, J. M. (1987). *To see but not to be seen: A case study of visual agnosia.* Hove: Lawrence Erlbaum Associates, Inc.

Jackman, S. (2009). *Bayesian analysis for the social sciences.* New York, NY: Wiley.

Jeffreys, H. (1961). *The theory of probability* (3rd ed.). London: Oxford University Press.

Johnson, V. E., Payne, R. D., Wang, T., Asher, A., & Mandal, S. (2017). On the reproducibility of psychological science. *Journal of the American Statistical Association, 112*, 1–10.

Jones, L. V., & Tukey, J. W. (2000). A sensible formulation of the significance test. *Psychological Methods, 5*, 411–414.

Jüni, P., Altman, D. G., & Egger, M. (2001). Systematic reviews in health care: Assessing quality of controlled clinical trials. *British Medical Journal, 323*, 42–46.

Kabacoff, R. I. (2015). *R in action: Data analysis and graphics in R* (2nd ed.). Shelter Island, NY: Manning Publications Co.

Kaiser, H. F., & Rice, J. (1974). Little Jiffy Mark IV. *Educational and Psychological Measurement, 34*, 111–117.

Kass, R. E., & Raftery, A. E. (1995). Bayes factors. *Journal of the American Statistical Association, 90*, 773–795.

Kelly, G. (1955). *The psychology of personal constructs.* New York, NY: Norton.

Kerlinger, F. N. (1973). *Foundations of behavioral research* (2nd ed.). London: Holt, Rinehart & Winston.

Kline, P. (2000). *The handbook of psychological testing* (2nd ed.). London: Routledge.

Kline, R. B. (2016). *Principles and practice of structural equation modeling* (4th ed.). New York, NY: Guilford Press.

Kruschke, J. K. (2013). Bayesian estimation supersedes the t test. *Journal of Experimental Psychology: General, 142*, 573–603.

Lahey, M. A., Downey, R. G., & Saal, F. E. (1983). Intraclass correlations: There's more there than meets the eye. *Psychological Bulletin, 93*, 586–595.

Lee, P. M. (2012). *Bayesian statistics: An introduction* (4th ed.). West Sussex: Wiley.

Leventhal, L., & Huynh, C.-L. (1996). Directional decisions for two-tailed tests: Power, error rates and sample size. *Psychological Methods, 1*, 278–292.

Likert, R. (1932). A technique for the measurement of attitudes. *Archives of Psychology, 22*(140), 55.

Little, R. J. A., & Rubin, D. B. (2002). *Statistical analysis with missing data* (2nd ed.). New York, NY: Wiley.

Lovie, P. (1991). Regression diagnostics: A rough guide to safer regression. In P. Lovie & A. D. Lovie (Eds.), *New developments in statistics for psychology and the social sciences* (pp. 95–134). London: British Psychological Society and Routledge.

Luria, A. R. (1975a). *The mind of a mnemonist.* Harmondsworth: Penguin.

Luria, A. R. (1975b). *The man with a shattered world.* Harmondsworth: Penguin.

Lustgarten, S. D. (2015). Emerging ethical threats to client privacy in cloud communication and data storage. *Professional Psychology: Research and Practice, 46*, 154–160.

MacCallum, R. C., Widaman, K. F., Zhang, S., & Hong, S. (1999). Sample size in factor analysis. *Psychological Methods, 4*, 84–99.

MacCallum, R. C., Zhang, S., Preacher, K. J., & Rucker, D. D. (2002). On the practice of dichotomization of quantitative variables. *Psychological Methods, 7*, 19–40.

MacKinnon, D. P., Lockwood, C. M., Hoffman, J. M., West, S. G., & Sheets, V. (2002). A comparison of methods to test mediation and other intervening variable effects. *Psychological Methods, 7*, 83–104.

Maghsoodloo, S., & Pallos, L. L. (1981). Asymptotic behavior of Kendall's partial rank correlation coefficient and additional quantile estimates. *Journal of Statistical Computing and Simulation, 13*, 41–48.

Manstead, A. S. R., & McCulloch, C. (1981). Sex-role stereotyping in British television advertisements. *British Journal of Psychology, 20*, 171–180.

Maxwell, S. E., & Delaney, H. D. (1993). Bivariate median splits and spurious statistical significance. *Psychological Bulletin, 113*, 181–190.

Maxwell, S. E., & Delaney, H. D. (2004). *Designing experiments and analysing data: A model comparison perspective.* Mahwah, NJ: Lawrence Erlbaum Associates, Inc.

McCain, L. J., & McCleary, R. (1979). The statistical analysis of the simple interrupted time-series quasi-experiment. In T. D. Cook & D. T. Campbell (Eds.), *Quasi-experimentation: Design and analysis issues for field settings* (pp. 233–293). Boston, MA: Houghton Mifflin.

McDonald, R. P. (1985). *Factor analysis and related methods.* Hillsdale, NJ: Lawrence Erlbaum Associates, Inc.

McDonald, R. P. (1999). *Test theory: A unified treatment.* Mahwah, NJ: Lawrence Erlbaum Associates, Inc.

McGowan, L., Clark-Carter, D., & Pitts, M. (1998). Chronic pelvic pain: A meta-analytic review. *Psychology and Health*, *13*, 937–951.

McGowan, L., Pitts, M. K., & Clark-Carter, D. (1999). Chronic pelvic pain: The general practitioner's perspective. *Psychology, Health and Medicine*, *4*, 303–317.

McGraw, K. O., & Wong, S. P. (1996). Forming inferences about some intraclass correlation coefficients. *Psychological Methods*, *1*, 30–46.

Meddis, R. (1984). *Statistics using ranks: A unified approach*. Oxford: Blackwell.

Michell, J. (2012). 'The constantly recurring argument': Inferring quantity from order. *Theory and Psychology*, *22*, 255–271.

Milgram, S. (1974). *Obedience to authority*. London: Tavistock Publications.

Miller, G. A. (1985). Trends and debates in cognitive psychology. In A. M Aitkenhead & J. M. Slack (Eds.), *Issues in cognitive modelling* (pp. 3–11). Hove: Lawrence Erlbaum Associates, Inc.

Mittlböck, M., & Schemper, M. (1996). Explained variation for logistic regression. *Statistics in Medicine*, *15*, 1987–1991.

Mittlböck, M., & Schemper, M. (1999). Computing measures of explained variation for logistic regression models. *Computer Methods and Programs in Biomedicine*, *58*, 17–24.

Moher, D., Liberati, A., Tetzlaff, J., Altman, D. G., & The PRISMA Group. (2009). Preferred reporting items for systematic reviews and meta-analyses: The PRISMA statement. *British Medical Journal (BMJ)* Open Access, *339*, b2535.

Morgan, D. L. (1998). Planning focus groups. Vol. 2 of D. L. Morgan & R. A. Krueger, *The focus group kit*. London: Sage.

Mulaik, S. A. (2010). *Foundations of factor analysis* (2nd ed.). Boca Raton, FL: Chapman & Hall/CRC.

Munafò, M. F., Nosek, B. A., Bishop, D. V. M., Button, K. S., Chambers, C. D., du Sert, N. P., . . . Ioannidis, J. P. A. (2017). A manifesto for reproducible science. *Nature Human Behaviour*, *1*, 21.

Murray, C. D., Macdonald, S., & Fox, J. (2008). Body satisfaction, eating disorders and suicide ideation in an Internet sample of self-harmers reporting and not reporting childhood sexual abuse. *Psychology, Health and Medicine*, *13*, 29–42.

Myers, J. L., DiCecco, J. V., White, J. B., & Borden, V. M. (1982). Repeated measurements on dichotomous variables: Q and F tests. *Psychological Bulletin*, *92*, 517–525.

Myers, J. L., & Well, A. D. (1991). *Research design and statistical analysis*. New York, NY: HarperCollins.

Myers, J. L., & Well, A. D. (2003). *Research design and statistical analysis* (2nd ed.). Mahwah, NJ: Lawrence Erlbaum Associates, Inc.

Myers, J. L., Well, A. D., & Lorch, R. F. (2010). *Research design and statistical analysis* (3rd ed.). Hove: Routledge.

Neave, H. R. (1978). *Statistics tables: For mathematicians, engineers, economists and the behavioural and management sciences*. London: Unwin Hyman.

Neave, H. R., & Worthington, P. L. (1988). *Distribution-free tests*. London: Routledge.

Newell, A., & Simon, H. A. (1972). *Human problem solving*. Englewood Cliffs, NJ: Prentice-Hall.

Neyman, J., & Pearson, E. S. (1933). On the problem of the most efficient tests of statistical hypotheses. *Philosophical Transactions of the Royal Society (A)*, *231*, 289–337.

Nicholson, I. (2011). 'Torture at Yale': Experimental subjects, laboratory torment and the 'rehabilitation' of Milgram's 'Obedience to authority'. *Theory & Psychology*, *21*, 737–761.

Nisbett, R. E., & Wilson, T. D. (1977). Telling more than we can know: Verbal reports on mental processes. *Psychological Review*, *84*, 231–259.

O'Connor, B. P. (2017). A first steps guide to the transition from null hypothesis significance testing to more accurate and informative Bayesian analyses. *Canadian Journal of Behavioural Science/Revue Canadienne des Sciences du Comportement*, *49*, 166–182.

O'Connor, C. (2017). 'Appeals to nature' in marriage equality debates: A content analysis of newspaper and social media discourse. *British Journal of Social Psychology*, *56*, 493–514.

Open Science Collaboration. (2015). Estimating the reproducibility of psychological science. *Science*, *349*, aac4716.

Orne, M. T. (1962). On the social psychology of the psychological experiment: With particular reference to demand characteristics and their implications. *American Psychologist*, *17*, 776–783.

Osgood, C. E., & Luria, Z. (1954). A blind analysis of a case of multiple personality using the semantic differential. *Journal of Abnormal and Social Psychology*, *49*, 579–591. Reprinted in C. H. Thigpen & H. M. Cleckley (1957). *The three faces of Eve*. London: Secker and Warburg.

Osgood, C. E., Suci, G. J., & Tannenbaum, P. H. (1957). *The measurement of meaning*. Urbana, IL: University of Illinois Press.

Patel, S., Peacock, S. M., McKinley, R. K., Clark-Carter, D., & Watson, P. J. (2009). GPs' perceptions of the service needs of South Asian people with chronic pain a qualitative enquiry. *Journal of Health Psychology*, *14*, 909–918.

Pearson, E. S., & Hartley, H. O. (Eds.). (1972). *Biometrika tables for statisticians: Volume 2*. London: Cambridge University Press.

Pedhazur, E. J. (1997). *Multiple regression in behavioural research: Explanation and prediction* (3rd ed.). Orlando, FL: Holt, Rinehart & Winston.

Pedhazur, E. J., & Schmelkin, L. P. (1991). *Measurement, design, and analysis: An integrated approach*. Hillsdale, NJ: Lawrence Erlbaum Associates, Inc.

Petticrew, M., & Roberts, H. (2006). *Systematic reviews in the social sciences: A practical guide*. Oxford: Blackwell.

Pfungst, O. (1965). *Clever Hans: The horse of Mr von Osten* (C. L. Rahn, Trans.). New York, NY: Holt, Rinehart & Winston (original work published in 1911).

Phillips, L. D. (1973). *Bayesian statistics for social scientists*. London: Nelson.

Pitts, M., & Jackson, H. (1989). AIDS and the press: An analysis of the coverage of AIDS by Zimbabwe newspapers. *AIDS Care, 1*, 77–83.

Popper, K. R. (1972). *The logic of scientific discovery* (5th rev. ed.). London: Hutchinson.

Popper, K. R. (1974). *Conjectures and refutations: The growth of scientific knowledge* (5th ed.). London: Routledge.

Potter, J., & Wetherall, M. (1995). Discourse analysis. In J. A. Smith, R. Harré & L. Van Langenhove (Eds.), *Rethinking methods in psychology* (pp. 80–92). London: Sage.

Putnam, H. (1979). The 'corroboration' of theories. In T. Honderich & M. Burnyeat (Eds.), *Philosophy as it is* (pp. 353–380). Harmondsworth: Penguin.

Randall, W. L. (2007). From computer to compost: Rethinking our metaphors for memory. *Theory and Psychology, 17*, 611–633.

Raudenbush, S. W., & Bryk, A. S. (2002). *Hierarchical Linear Models: Applications and data analysis methods* (2nd ed.). New York, NY: Sage.

Raykov, T. (2007). Reliability if deleted, not 'alpha if deleted': Evaluation of scale reliability following component deletion. *British Journal of Mathematical and Statistical Psychology, 60*, 201–216.

Raykov, T., & Marcoulides, G. A. (2008). *An introduction to applied multivariate analysis*. New York, NY: Routledge.

Reason, J. T., & Lucas, D. A. (1984) Using cognitive diaries to investigate naturally-occurring memory blocks. In J. Harris & P. Morris (Eds.), *Everyday memory, actions and absent-mindedness*. (pp. 53–70). London: Academic Press.

Robson, C. (2002). *Real world research: A resource for social scientists and practitioner-researchers* (2nd ed.). Oxford: Blackwell.

Rogers, C. R. (1951). *Client-centred therapy*. London: Constable.

Rogers, C. R. (1961). *On becoming a person: A therapist's view of psychotherapy*. London: Constable.

Rosenthal, R. (1991). *Meta-analytic procedures for social research*. London: Sage.

Rosnow, R. L., & Rosenthal, R. (1989). Statistical procedures and the justification of knowledge in psychological science. *American Psychologist, 44*, 1276–1284.

Rovelli, C. (2017). *Reality is not what it seems: The journey to quantum gravity* (S. Carnell & E. Segre, Trans.). London: Penguin.

Royston, P., Altman, D. G., & Sauerbrei, W. (2005). Dichotomizing continuous predictors in multiple regression: A bad idea. *Statistics in Medicine, 25*, 127–141.

Rubin, D. B. (1976). Inference and missing data (with discussion by R. J. A. Little). *Biometrika, 63*, 581–592.

Saunders, B., Kitzinger, J., & Kitzinger, C. (2015). Anonymising interview data: Challenges and compromise in practice. *Qualitative Research, 15*, 616–632.

Sawilowsky, S. S. (1990). Nonparametric tests of interaction in experimental design. *Review of Educational Research, 60*, 91–126.

Schafer, J. L., & Graham, J. W. (2002). Missing data: Our view of the state of the art. *Psychological Methods, 7*, 147–177.

Sears, D. O. (1986). College sophomores in the laboratory: Influences of a narrow data base on psychology's view of human nature. *Journal of Personality and Social Psychology, 51*, 513–530.

Sedlmeier, P., & Gigerenzer, G. (1989). Do studies of statistical power have an effect on the power of studies? *Psychological Bulletin, 105*, 309–316.

Seitz, M. J., Templeton, A., Drury, J., Köster, G., & Philippedes, A. (2017). Parsimony versus reductionism: How can crowd psychology be introduced into computer simulation? *Review of General Psychology, 21*, 95–102.

Shadish, W. R., & Luellen, J. K. (2005). Quasi-experimental designs. In B. Everitt & D. C. Howell (Eds.), *Encyclopedia of behavioural statistics* (pp. 1641–1644). London: Wiley.

Shrout, P. E., & Fleiss, J. L. (1979). Intraclass correlations: Uses in assessing rater reliability. *Psychological Bulletin, 86*, 420–428.

Shrout, P. E., & Rodgers, J. L. (2018). Psychology, science, and knowledge construction: Broadening perspectives from the replication crisis. *Annual Review of Psychology, 69*, 487–510.

Shye, S., Elizur, D., & Hoffman, M. (1994). *Introduction to facet theory: Content design and intrinsic data analysis in behavioral research*. London: Sage.

Siegel, S., & Castellan, N. J. (1988). *Nonparametric statistics for the behavioral sciences* (2nd ed.). New York, NY: McGraw-Hill.

Sijtsma, K. (2009). On the use, the misuse, and the very limited usefulness of Cronbach's alpha. *Psychometrika, 74,* 107–120.

Sijtsma, K. (2012). Psychological measurement between physics and statistics. *Theory and Psychology, 22,* 786–809.

Sinharay, S., Stern, H. S., & Russell, D. (2001). The use of multiple imputation for the analysis of missing data. *Psychological Methods, 6,* 317–329.

Smith, J. (Ed.). (2015). *Qualitative psychology: A practical guide to research methods* (3rd ed.). London: Sage.

Smith, J., Flowers, P., & Larkin, M. (2009). *Interpretative phenomenological analysis: Theory, method and research.* London: Sage.

Snijders, T. A. B., & Bosker, R. J. (2013). *Multilevel analysis: An introduction to basic and advanced multilevel modelling* (2nd ed.). London: Sage.

Stainton Rogers, R. (1995). Q Methodology. In J. A. Smith, R. Harré & L. Van Langenhove (Eds.), *Rethinking methods in psychology* (pp. 178–207). London: Sage.

Steiger, J. H. (1980). Tests for comparing elements of a correlation matrix. *Psychological Bulletin, 87,* 245–251.

Stellefson, M. L., Hanik, B. W., Chaney, B. H., & Chaney, J. D. (2009). Factor retention in EFA: Strategies for health behavior researchers. *American Journal of Health Behavior, 33,* 587–599.

Stenner, P., & Marshall, H. (1995). A Q methodological study of rebelliousness. *European Journal of Social Psychology, 25,* 621–636.

Stenner, P., & Marshall, H. (1999). On developmentality: Researching the varied meanings of 'independence' and 'maturity' extant amongst a sample of young people in East London. *Journal of Youth Studies, 2,* 297–315.

Stenner, P., & Stainton Rogers, R. (1998). Jealousy as a manifold of divergent understandings: A Q methodological investigation. *European Journal of Social Psychology, 28,* 71–94.

Stephenson, W. (1953). *The study of behavior: Q-Technique and its methodology.* Chicago, IL: University of Chicago Press.

Stevens, J. (2009). *Applied multivariate statistics for the social sciences* (5th ed.). Hove: Lawrence Routledge.

Sudman, S. (1976). *Applied sampling.* London: Academic Press.

Suedfeld, P. (1980). *Restricted environmental stimulation: Research and clinical applications.* New York, NY: Wiley.

Tabachnick, B. G., & Fidell, L. S. (2013). *Using multivariate statistics* (6th ed.). Boston, MA: Pearson.

Thurstone, L. L. (1931). The measurement of social attitudes. *Journal of Abnormal and Social Psychology, 26,* 249–269.

Thurstone, L. L., & Chave, E. J. (1929). *The measurement of attitude: A psychophysical method and some experiments with a scale for measuring attitude toward the Church.* Chicago, IL: University of Chicago Press.

Tileagă, C., & Stokoe, E. (Eds.). (2016). *Discursive psychology: Classic and contemporary issues.* London: Routledge.

Tukey, J. W. (1977). *Exploratory data analysis.* Reading, MA: Addison-Wesley.

Valentine, E. R. (1992). *Conceptual issues in psychology* (2nd ed.). London: Routledge.

von Mises, R. (1939). *Probability, statistics and truth* (J. Neyman, D Scholl & E. Rabinowitsch, Trans.). London: Willam Hodge & Co.

Vuolo, M., Uggen, C., & Lageson, S. (2016). Statistical power in experimental audit studies: Cautions and calculations for matched tests with nominal outcomes. *Sociological Methods & Research, 45,* 260–303.

Walker, B. M., & Winter, D. A. (2007). The elaboration of personal construct psychology. *Annual Review of Psychology, 58,* 453–477.

Wallenstein, S., & Berger, A. (1981). On the asymptotic power of tests for comparing K correlated proportions. *Journal of the American Statistical Association, 76,* 114–118.

Weiss, N. S., & Koepsell, T. D. (2014). *Epidemiological methods: Studying the occurrence of illness.* New York, NY: Oxford University Press.

Wickens, T. D. (1989). *Multiway contingency table analysis for the social sciences.* Hillsdale, NJ: Lawrence Erlbaum Associates, Inc.

Willig, C. (2013). *Introducing qualitative research in psychology* (3rd ed.). Buckingham: McGraw-Hill/Open University Press.

Winer, B. J., Brown, D. R., & Michels, K. M. (1991). *Statistical principles in experimental design* (3rd ed.). London: McGraw-Hill.

Winter, D. A. (1992). *Personal construct psychology in clinical practice: Theory, research and applications.* London: Routledge.

Wortman, P. M. (1994). Judging research quality. In H. Cooper & L. V. Hedges (Eds.), *The handbook of research synthesis* (pp. 97–109). New York, NY: Russell Sage Foundation.

Wright, P. (1983). Writing and reading technical information. In J. Nicholson & B. Foss (Eds.), *Psychology survey no 4* (pp. 323–354). Leicester: British Psychological Society.

Yates, F. (1934). Contingency tables involving small numbers and the χ^2 test. *Supplement to the Journal of the Royal Statistical Society, 1,* 217–235.

Young, A. W., Hay, D. C., & Ellis, A. W. (1985). The faces that launched a thousand slips: Everyday difficulties and errors in recognizing people. *British Journal of Psychology, 76,* 495–523.

Zimmerman, D. W. (2004). A note on preliminary test of equality of variances. *British Journal of Mathematical and Statistical Psychology, 57,* 173–181.

Zimmerman, D. W., & Zumbo, B. D. (1993). The relative power of parametric and non-parametric statistics. In G. Keren & C. Lewis (Eds.), *A handbook for data analysis in the behavioral Sciences: Methodological issues* (pp. 481–517). Hillsdale, NJ: Lawrence Erlbaum Associates, Inc.

Zwick, W. R., & Velicer, W. F. (1986). Comparison of five rules for determining the number of components to retain. *Psychological Bulletin, 99,* 452–442.

Glossary of symbols

Using the English alphabet

d	an effect size for designs measuring the difference in means between two levels of an independent variable (IV)
F	a statistic used in parametric ANOVA, when comparing more than two levels of an IV or more than one IV
g	an effect size for the difference between a proportion in a sample and a proportion in the population
h	an effect size for the difference between two sample proportions
M	the mean of a variable in a sample
n_h	the harmonic mean sample size
Q_p	The Bryant–Paulson variant of the studentised range statistic for use with ANCOVA
q	an effect size for the difference between two Pearson's product moment correlation coefficients or the studentised range statistic
r	Pearson's product moment correlation coefficient in a sample
r'	Fisher's transformation of r
r^2	an effect size measure in correlation (the proportion of variance in one variable which can be explained by the variance in a second variable with which it is correlated)
R	the multiple correlation coefficient from multiple regression
R^2	an effect size in regression analysis (the proportion of variance in a variable which can be explained by the variance in a set of predictor variables)
s	the standard deviation of a variable in a sample
s^2	the variance of a variable in a sample
t	a parametric statistic used for designs comparing two levels of an IV
w	an effect size for nominal data
$\bar{x}$	the mean of a variable in a sample

Using the Greek alphabet

α	alpha	the probability of committing a Type I error or an estimate of reliability of a measure, proposed by Cronbach
β	beta	the probability of committing a Type II error or a standardised regression coefficient
η^2	eta-squared	an effect size in ANOVA
χ^2	chi-squared	a statistic for nominal data
λ	lambda	an estimate of reliability of a measure, proposed by Guttman, or an eigenvalue, for example, in factor analysis
μ	mu	the mean of a variable in the population
π	pi	the proportion in the population (e.g. the proportion of smokers)
ρ	rho	the correlation coefficient for a relationship in the population
σ	sigma	the standard deviation of a variable in the population
σ^2	sigma-squared	the variance of a variable in the population

Author index

Subject index